CLYMER®

HARLEY-DAVIDSON

XL SPORTSTER • 2004-2011

The world's finest publisher of mechanical how-to manuals

CLYMER®

P.O. Box 12901, Overland Park, Kansas 66282-2901

FIRST EDITION
First Printing March, 2006
Second Printing June, 2008

SECOND EDITION
First Printing August, 2009

THIRD EDITION
First Printing July, 2011

Printed in U.S.A.

CLYMER and colophon are registered trademarks of Penton Business Media, Inc.

ISBN-10: 1-59969-389-5

ISBN-13: 978-1-59969-389-7

Library of Congress: 2011927469

MEMBER MOTORCYCLE INDUSTRY COUNCIL, INC.

AUTHOR: Mike Morlan.

TECHNICAL PHOTOGRAPHY: Mike Morlan. Special thanks to Marc Linman and Steve Wright for their assistance with this project.

TECHNICAL ILLUSTRATIONS: Errol McCarthy.

WIRING DIAGRAMS: Bob Meyer.

EDITORS: James Grooms and Steven Thomas.

PRODUCTION: Susan Hartington.

TOOLS AND EQUIPMENT: K&L Supply Co. at www.klsupply.com, JIMS Tools at www.jimsusa.com and Park Tool USA at www.parktool.com.

COVER: Mark Clifford Photography at www.markclifford.com.

CLYMER®

Publisher Ron Rogers

EDITORIAL

Editorial Director
James Grooms

Editor
Steven Thomas

Associate Editor
Rick Arens

Authors
Michael Morlan
George Parise
Ed Scott
Ron Wright

Technical Illustrators
Steve Amos
Errol McCarthy
Mitzi McCarthy
Bob Meyer

SALES

Sales Manager–Marine
Jay Lipton

Sales Manager–Powersport/I&T
Matt Tusken

CUSTOMER SERVICE

Customer Service Manager
Terri Cannon

Customer Service Representatives
Karen Barker
Dinah Bunnell
Suzanne Johnson
April LeBlond
Sherry Rudkin

PRODUCTION

Director of Production
Dylan Goodwin

Production Manager
Greg Araujo

Senior Production Editor
Darin Watson

Production Editor
Adriane Roberts

Associate Production Editor
Ashley Bally

PENTON

P.O. Box 12901, Overland Park, KS 66282-2901 • 800-262-1954 • 913-967-1719

CLYMER® CLYMER® PROSERIES I&T SHOP SERVICE

More information available at *clymer.com*

CONTENTS

QUICK REFERENCE DATA

MODEL:______________________________ YEAR:______________________________

VIN NUMBER:______________________________

ENGINE SERIAL NUMBER:______________________________

CARBURETOR SERIAL NUMBER:______________________________

TIRE INFLATION PRESSURE (COLD)*

	PSI	kPa
Front wheel		
Rider only	30	207
Rider and passenger	30	207
Rear wheel		
Rider only	36	248
Rider and passenger	40	276

*Tire pressure for original equipment tires. Aftermarket tires may require different inflation pressure.

ENGINE OIL SPECIFICTIONS

Type	HD rating	Viscosity	Ambient operating temperature
HD Multi-grade	HD360	SAE 10W/40	Below 40° F (4.4° C)
HD Multi-grade	HD360	SAE 20W/50	Above 40° F (4.4° C)
HD Regular heavy	HD360	SAE 50	Above 60° F (15.5° C)
HD Extra heavy	HD360	SAE 60	Above 80° F (26.7° C)

RECOMMENDED LUBRICANTS AND FLUIDS

Brake	
2004-2006 models	DOT 5
2007-on models	DOT 4
Front fork oil	HD Type E or equivalent
Fuel	
Type*	Unleaded
Octane	
2004-2006 models	
XL883 models	Pump research octane of 87 or higher
XL1200 models	Pump research octane of 91 or higher
2007-on models	Pump research octane of 91 or higher
Transmission	
2004-2005 models	HD Sport Trans Fluid or equivalent
2006-on models	HD Formulat Lubricant or equivalent

*Refer to *Fuel Type* in Chapter Three.

ENGINE AND PRIMARY DRIVE/TRANSMISSION OIL CAPACITIES

Engine oil with filter replacement	
2004-2007	3.6 qt. (3.4 L)
2008-2011	2.8 qt. (2.65 L)
Transmission oil (includes primary chaincase)	32 oz (946 ml)

FRONT FORK OIL CAPACITY

Model	Capacity*	Oil level
2004-2006 models		
XL883L, XL1200L	12.3 oz. (364 ml)	4.80 in. (122 mm)
All other models	11.6 oz. (342 ml)	5.75 in. (146 mm)
2007, 2008 models		
XL883L, XL1200L, XL1200N	12.3 oz. (364 mL)	4.80 in. (122 mm)
All other models	11.6 oz. (343 mL)	5.75 in. (146 mm)
2009, 2010 models		
XL883L, XL883N, XL1200N	13.6 oz. (401 mL)	3.11 in. (79 mm)
XL1200L	12.3 oz. (364 mL)	4.80 in. (122 mm)
All other models	11.6 oz. (343 mL)	5.75 in. (146 mm)
2011 models		
XL883R	12.4 oz. (367 mL)	4.92 in. (125 mm)
XL883L, XL1200L	12.3 oz. (364 mL)	4.80 in. (122 mm)
XL883N, XL1200N	13.6 oz. (402 mL)	3.11 in. (79 mm)
XL1200C	12.4 oz. (367 mL)	4.72 in. (120 mm)
XL1200X	11.4 oz. (337 mL)	6.34 in. (161 mm)

*Each fork leg.

FUEL TANK CAPACITY

Model	Capacity*
2004-2007, 2009, 2010 models	
XL883C, XL1200C, XL1200L	4.5 gal. (17.0 L)
All other models	3.3 gal. (12.5 L)
2008 models	
XL883C, XL1200C, XL1200L, XL1200R	4.5 gal. (17.0 L)
All other models	3.3 gal. (12.5 L)
2011 models	
XL883L, XL1200C, XL1200L	4.5 gal. (17.0 L)
XL1200X	2.1 gal. (7.9 L)
All other models	3.3 gal. (12.5 L)
Low fuel warning light on	
2.1 gal. tank	0.65 gal. (2.5 L)
3.3 gal. tank	0.8 gal. (3.0 L)
4.5 gal. tank	1.5 gal. (3.8 L)

*Including reserve.

MAINTENANCE AND TUNE-UP SPECIFICATIONS

Item	Specification
Brake pad minimum thickness	0.04 in. (1.02 mm)
Clutch cable free play	1/16-1/8 in. (1.6-3.2 mm)
Drive belt deflection	
2004-2009 models	
XL883, XL883R, XL1200R	9/16-5/8 in. (14.3-15.9 mm)
All other models	1/4-5/16 in. (6.4-7.9 mm)
2010-2011 models	
XL883R	9/16-5/8 in. (14.3-15.9 mm)
All other models	1/4-5/16 in. (6.4-7.9 mm)

(continued)

MAINTENANCE AND TUNE-UP SPECIFICATIONS (continued)

Item	Specification
Engine compression	
XL883 models	
2004-2006	125-140 psi (862-966 kPa)
2007	125-140 psi (862-966 kPa)
2008-on	165-180 psi (1138-1242 kPa)
XL1200 models	200-225 psi (1380-1552 kPa)
Idle speed	950-1050 rpm
Ignition timing	Non-adjustable
Spark plug	HD-6R12*
Gap	0.038-0.043 in. (0.97-1.09 mm)

*The manufacturer does not recommend another spark plug type.

MAINTENANCE AND TUNE-UP TORQUE SPECIFICATIONS

Item	ft.-lb.	in.-lb.	N•m
Air filter cover screws	–	36-60	4.1-6.8
Air filter element retaining screws	–	40-60	4.5-6.8
Clutch inspection cover screws		90-120	10.2-13.6
Front fork cap	22-58	–	30-78
Front fork drain screw	–	13-17	1.5-2.0
Primary chain adjuster locknut	20-25	–	28-34
Primary chain inspection cover bolts	–	90-120	10.2-13.6
Rear axle nut*			
2004 models	60-65	–	81-88
2005-2007 models	72-78	–	98-106
2008-on models	95-105	–	129-142
Spark plug	12-18	–	17-24
Transmission drain plug	14-30	–	19-40

*Refer to procedure.

NOTE: Refer to the Supplement at the end of this manual for information unique to 2007-2011 models.

CHAPTER ONE

GENERAL INFORMATION

This detailed and comprehensive manual covers 2004-2011 Harley-Davidson XL Sportster models. Refer to the Supplement at the end of this manual for information *unique* to 2007-2011 models. The text provides complete information on maintenance, tune-up, repair and overhaul. Hundreds of photographs and illustrations created during the complete disassembly of the motorcycle guide the reader through every job. All procedures are in step-by-step format and designed for the reader who may be working on the motorcycle for the first time.

MANUAL ORGANIZATION

A shop manual is a tool and, as in all Clymer manuals, the chapters are thumb tabbed for easy reference. Main headings are listed in the table of contents and the index. Frequently used specifications and capacities from the tables at the end of each individual chapter are listed in the *Quick Reference Data* section at the front of the manual. Specifications and capacities are provided in U.S. standard and metric units of measure.

During some of the procedures there will be references to headings in other chapters or sections of the manual. When a specific heading is called out in a step it will be *italicized* as it appears in the manual. If a sub-heading is indicated as being "in this section" it is located within the same main heading. For example, the sub-heading *Handling Gasoline Safely* is located within the main heading *SAFETY.*

This chapter provides general information on shop safety, tools and their usage, service fundamentals and shop supplies.

Tables 1-10 are located at the end of this chapter.

Table 1 lists motorcycle dimensions.

Table 2 lists motorcycle weight.

Table 3 lists fuel tank capacity.

Table 4 lists general torque specifications.

Table 5 lists conversion formulas.

Table 6 lists technical abbreviations.

Table 7 lists U.S. tap and drill sizes.

Table 8 lists metric tap and drill sizes.

Table 9 lists fraction, decimal and metric equivalents.

Table 10 lists special tools.

Chapter Two provides methods for quick and accurate diagnosis of problems. Troubleshooting procedures present typical symptoms and logical methods to pinpoint and repair the problem.

Chapter Three explains all routine maintenance necessary to keep the motorcycle running well. Chapter Three also includes recommended tune-up procedures.

Subsequent chapters describe specific systems such as engine, transmission, clutch, drive system, fuel and exhaust systems, suspension and brakes.

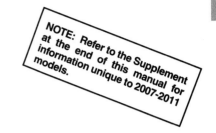

WARNINGS, CAUTIONS AND NOTES

The terms, WARNING, CAUTION and NOTE have specific meanings in this manual.

A WARNING emphasizes areas where injury or even death could result from negligence. Mechanical damage may also occur. WARNINGS *are to be taken seriously.*

A CAUTION emphasizes areas where equipment damage could result. Disregarding a CAUTION could cause permanent mechanical damage, though injury is unlikely.

A NOTE provides additional information to make a step or procedure easier or clearer. Disregarding a NOTE could cause inconvenience, but would not cause equipment damage or injury.

SAFETY

Professional mechanics can work for years and never sustain a serious injury or mishap. Follow these guidelines and practice common sense to safely service the motorcycle.

1. Do not operate the motorcycle in an enclosed area. The exhaust gasses contain carbon monoxide, an odorless, colorless, and tasteless poisonous gas. Carbon monoxide levels build quickly in small enclosed areas and can cause unconsciousness and death in a short time. Make sure to ventilate the work area properly or to operate the motorcycle outside.
2. *Never* use gasoline or any extremely flammable liquid to clean parts. Refer to *Handling Gasoline Safely* and *Cleaning Parts* in this secition.
3. *Never* smoke or use a torch in the vicinity of flammable liquids, such as gasoline or cleaning solvent.
4. If welding or brazing on the motorcycle, remove the fuel tank, carburetor and shocks to a safe distance at least 50 ft. (15 m) away.
5. Use the correct type and size of tools to avoid damaging fasteners.
6. Keep tools clean and in good condition. Replace or repair worn or damaged equipment.
7. When loosening a tight fastener, be guided by what would happen if the tool slips.
8. When replacing fasteners, make sure the new fasteners are the same size and strength as the original ones.
9. Keep the work area clean and organized.
10. Wear eye protection *anytime* the safety of the eyes is in question. This includes procedures involving drilling, grinding, hammering, compressed air and chemicals.
11. Wear the correct clothing for the job. Tie up or cover long hair so it can not get caught in moving equipment.
12. Do not carry sharp tools in clothing pockets.

13. Always have an approved fire extinguisher available. Make sure it is rated for gasoline (Class B) and electrical (Class C) fires.
14. Do not use compressed air to clean clothes, the motorcycle or the work area. Debris may be blown into the eyes or skin. *Never* direct compressed air at anyone. Do not allow children to use or play with any compressed air equipment.
15. When using compressed air to dry rotating parts, hold the part so it cannot rotate. Do not allow the force of the air to spin the part. The air jet is capable of rotating parts at extreme speed. The part may be damaged or disintegrate, causing serious injury.
16. Do not inhale the dust created by brake pad and clutch wear. These particles may contain asbestos. In addition, some types of insulating materials and gaskets may contain asbestos. Inhaling asbestos particles is hazardous to health.
17. Never work on the motorcycle while someone is working under it.
18. When placing the motorcycle on a stand, make sure it is secure before walking away.

Handling Gasoline Safely

Gasoline is a volatile flammable liquid and is one of the most dangerous items in the shop. Because gasoline is used so often, many people forget that it is hazardous. Only use gasoline as fuel for gasoline internal combustion engines. Keep in mind, when working on a motorcycle, gasoline is always present in the fuel tank, fuel line and carburetor. To avoid an accident when working around the fuel system, carefully observe the following precautions:

1. *Never* use gasoline to clean parts. See *Cleaning Parts* in this section.
2. When working on the fuel system, work outside or in a well-ventilated area.

3. Do not add fuel to the fuel tank or service the fuel system while the motorcycle is near open flames, sparks or where someone is smoking. Gasoline vapor is heavier than air. It collects in low areas and is more easily ignited than liquid gasoline.
4. Allow the engine to cool completely before working on any fuel system component.
5. When draining the carburetor, catch the fuel in a plastic container and then pour it into an approved gasoline storage devise.
6. Do not store gasoline in glass containers. If the glass breaks, an explosion or fire may occur.
7. Immediately wipe up spilled gasoline with rags. Store the rags in a metal container with a lid until they can be properly disposed of, or place them outside in a safe place for the fuel to evaporate.
8. Do not pour water onto a gasoline fire. Water spreads the fire and makes it more difficult to put out. Use a class B, BC or ABC fire extinguisher to extinguish the fire.
9. Always turn off the engine before refueling. Do not spill fuel onto the engine or exhaust system. Do not overfill the fuel tank. Leave an air space at the top of the tank to allow room for the fuel to expand due to temperature fluctuations.

Cleaning Parts

Cleaning parts is one of the more tedious and difficult service jobs performed in the home garage. There are many types of chemical cleaners and solvents available for shop use. Most are poisonous and extremely flammable. To prevent chemical exposure, vapor buildup, fire and injury, observe each product warning label and note the following:

1. Read and observe the entire product label before using any chemical. Always know what type of chemical is being used and whether it is poisonous and/or flammable.
2. Do not use more than one type of cleaning solvent at a time. If mixing chemicals is called for, measure the proper amounts according to the manufacturer.
3. Work in a well-ventilated area.
4. Wear chemical-resistant gloves.
5. Wear safety glasses.
6. Wear a vapor respirator if the instructions call for it.
7. Wash hands and arms thoroughly after cleaning parts.
8. Keep chemical products away from children and pets.
9. Thoroughly clean all oil, grease and cleaner residue from any part that must be heated.
10. Use a nylon brush when cleaning parts. Metal brushes may cause a spark.
11. When using a parts washer, only use the solvent recommended by the manufacturer. Make sure the parts washer is equipped with a metal lid that will lower in case of fire.

Warning Labels

Most manufacturers attach information and warning labels to the motorcycle. These labels contain instructions that are important to personal safety when operating, servicing, transporting and storing the motorcycle. Refer to the owner's manual for the description and location of labels. Order replacement labels from the manufacturer if they are missing or damaged.

SERIAL NUMBERS

Serial numbers are stamped on various locations on the frame, engine and carburetor. Record these numbers in the *Quick Reference Data* section in the front of the manual. Have these numbers available when ordering parts.

The VIN number is stamped on the right side of the steering head (A, **Figure 1**). The VIN number also appears on a label affixed to the right, front frame downtube (B, **Figure 1**).

The engine serial number is stamped on a pad at the left side surface of the crankcase between the cylinders (**Figure 2**). The engine serial number consists of digits used in the VIN number.

The carburetor serial number (**Figure 3**) is located adjacent to the accelerator pump linkage.

FASTENERS

WARNING
Do not install fasteners with a strength classification lower than what was originally in-

stalled by the manufacturer. Doing so may cause equipment failure and/or damage.

Proper fastener selection and installation is important to ensure that the motorcycle operates as designed and can be serviced efficiently. The choice of original equipment fasteners is not arrived at by chance. Make sure replacement fasteners meet all the same requirements as the originals.

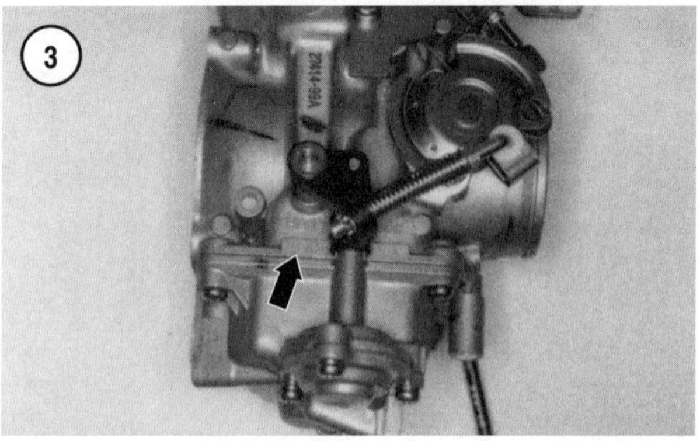

Threaded Fasteners

CAUTION
To ensure that the fastener threads are not mismatched or cross-threaded, start all fasteners by hand. If a fastener is hard to start or turn, determine the cause before tightening with a wrench.

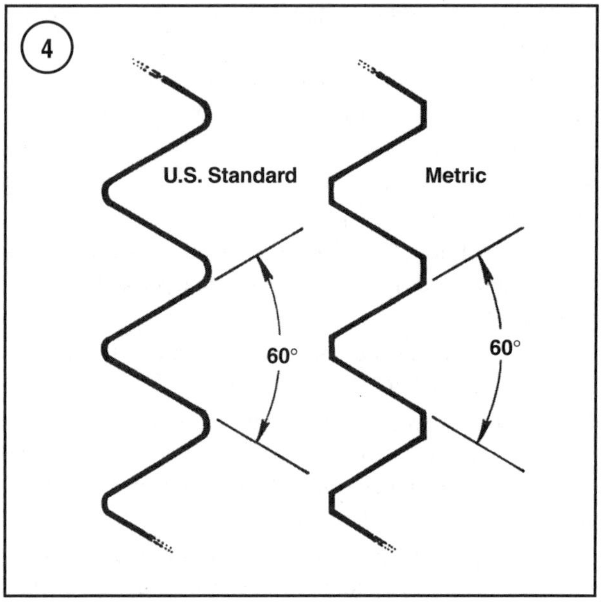

Threaded fasteners secure most of the components on the motorcycle. Most are tightened by turning them clockwise (right-hand threads). If the normal rotation of the component being tightened would loosen the fastener, it may have left-hand threads. If a left-hand threaded fastener is used, it is noted in the text.

Two dimensions are required to match the thread size of the fastener: the number of threads in a given distance and the outside diameter of the threads.

Two systems are currently used to specify threaded fastener dimensions: the U.S. Standard system and the metric system (**Figure 4**). Pay particular attention when working with unidentified fasteners; mismatching thread types can damage threads.

Match fasteners by their length (L, **Figure 5**), diameter (D) and distance between thread crests (pitch) (T). A typical metric bolt may be identified by the numbers, 8—1.25 × 130. This indicates the bolt has a diameter of 8 mm, the distance between thread crests is 1.25 mm and the length is 130 mm. Always measure bolt length as shown in L, **Figure 5** to avoid installing replacements of the wrong length.

The numbers located on the top of the fastener (A, **Figure 5**) indicate the strength grade of metric screws and bolts. The higher the number, the stronger the fastener is. Typically, unnumbered fasteners are the weakest.

Refer to **Table 4** for SAE fastener classification.

Many screws, bolts and studs are combined with nuts to secure particular components. To indicate the size of a nut, manufacturers specify the internal diameter and the thread pitch.

The measurement across two flats on a nut or bolt indicates the wrench size.

Torque Specifications

The materials used in the manufacture of the motorcycle may be subjected to uneven stresses if the fasteners of the various subassemblies are not installed and tightened correctly. Fasteners that are improperly installed or work loose can cause damage. It is essential to use an accurate torque wrench, described in this chapter, with the torque specifications in this manual.

Specifications for torque are provided in foot-pounds (ft.-lb.), inch-pounds (in.-lb.) and Newton-meters (N•m). Refer to **Table 4** for general torque specifications. To use **Table 4**, first determine the size of the fastener as described in this section. Torque specifications for specific components are at the end of the appropriate chapters. Torque wrenches are covered in the *Tools* section.

5

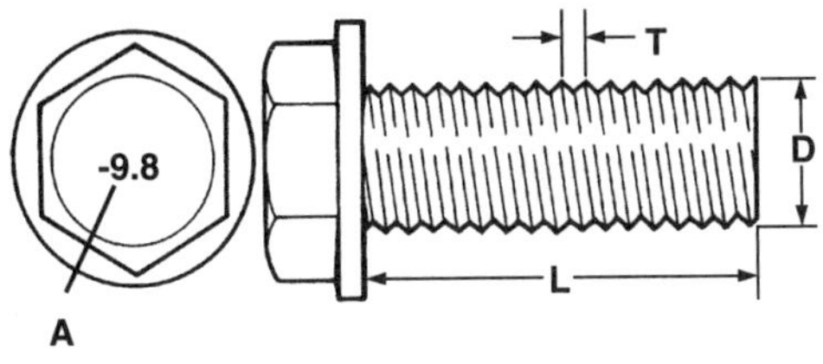

6

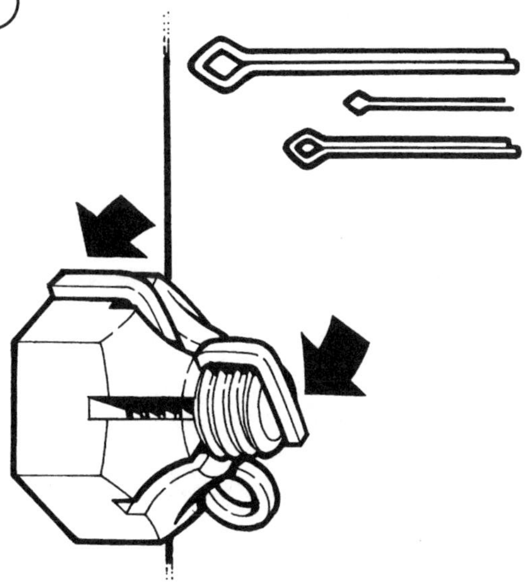

Self-Locking Fasteners

Several types of bolts, screws and nuts incorporate a system that creates interference between two fasteners. Interference is achieved in various ways. The most common type is the nylon insert nut and a dry adhesive coating on the threads of a bolt.

Self-locking fasteners offer greater holding strength than standard fasteners, which improves their resistance to vibration. Most self-locking fasteners should not be reused. The materials used to form the lock become distorted after the initial installation and removal. It is a good practice to discard and replace self-locking fasteners after their removal. Do not replace self-locking fasteners with standard fasteners.

Washers

There are two basic types of washers: flat washers and lockwashers. Flat washers are simple discs with a hole to fit a screw or bolt. Lockwashers are used to prevent a fastener from working loose. Washers can be used as spacers and seals, or to help distribute fastener load and to prevent the fastener from damaging the component.

As with fasteners, when replacing washers make sure the replacement washers are of the same design and quality.

Cotter Pins

A cotter pin is a split metal pin inserted into a hole or slot to prevent a fastener from loosening. In certain applications, such as the rear axle on an ATV or motorcycle, the fastener must be secured in this way. For these applications, a cotter pin and castellated (slotted) nut are used.

To use a cotter pin, first make sure the diameter is correct for the hole in the fastener. After correctly tightening the fastener and aligning the holes, insert the cotter pin through the hole and bend the ends over the fastener (**Figure 6**). Unless instructed to do so, never loosen a tightened fastener to align the holes. If the holes do not align, tighten the fastener just enough to achieve alignment.

Cotter pins are available in various diameters and lengths (**Figure 6**). Measure length from the bottom of the head to the tip of the shortest pin.

Snap Rings and E-clips

Snap rings (**Figure 7**) are circular-shaped metal retaining clips. They are required to secure parts and gears in place on parts such as shafts, pins or rods. External type snap rings are used to retain items on shafts. Internal type snap rings secure parts within housing bores. In some applications, in addition to securing the component(s), snap rings of varying thickness also determine endplay. These are usually called selective snap rings.

Two basic types of snap rings are used: machined and stamped snap rings. Machined snap rings (**Figure 8**) can be installed in either direction, since both faces have sharp edges. Stamped snap rings (**Figure 9**) are manufactured with a sharp edge and a round edge. When installing a stamped snap ring in a thrust application, install the sharp edge facing away from the part producing the thrust.

E-clips are used when it is not practical to use a snap ring. Remove E-clips with a flat blade screwdriver by prying between the shaft and E-clip. To install an E-clip, center it over the shaft groove and push or tap it into place.

Observe the following when installing snap rings:

1. Remove and install snap rings with snap ring pliers. Refer to *Snap Ring Pliers* in this chapter.
2. In some applications, it may be necessary to replace snap rings after removing them.
3. Compress or expand snap rings only enough to install them. If overly expanded, they lose their retaining ability.
4. After installing a snap ring, make sure it seats completely.
5. Wear eye protection when removing and installing snap rings.

7

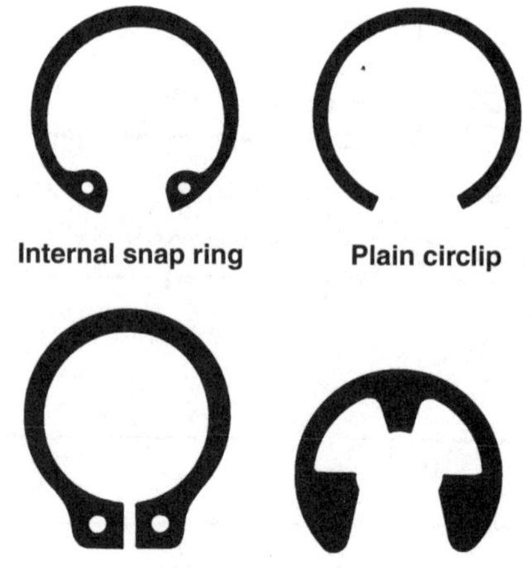

8

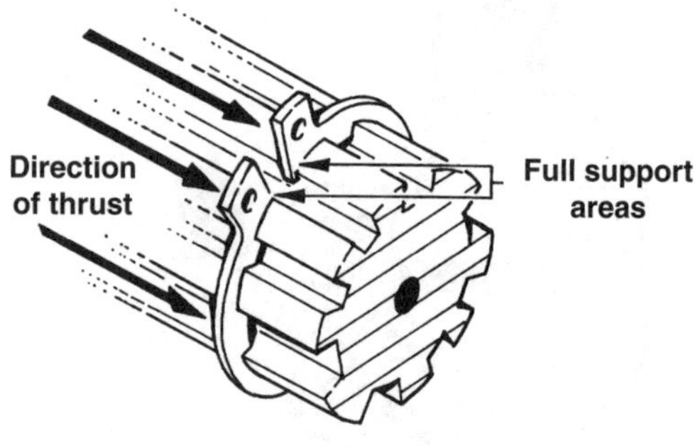

SHOP SUPPLIES

Lubricants and Fluids

Periodic lubrication helps ensure a long service life for any type of equipment. Use the correct type of lubricant when performing lubrication service. The following section describes the types of lubricants most often required. Make sure to follow the manufacturer's recommendations for lubricant types.

Engine oils

Engine oil is classified by two standards: the American Petroleum Institute (API) service classification and the Society of Automotive Engineers (SAE) viscosity rating. This information is on the oil container label. Two letters indicate the API service classification. The number or sequence of numbers and letter (10W-40 for example) is the oil's viscosity rating. The API service classification and the SAE viscosity index are not indications of oil quality.

The service classification indicates that the oil meets specific lubrication standards. The first letter in the classification *S* indicates that the oil is for gasoline engines. The second letter indicates the standard the oil satisfies.

Viscosity is an indication of the oil's thickness. Thin oils have a lower number while thick oils have a higher number. Engine oils fall into the 5- to 50-weight range for single-grade oils.

Most manufacturers recommend multi-grade oil. These oils perform efficiently across a wide range of operating conditions. Multi-grade oils are identified by a *W* after the first number, which indicates the low-temperature viscosity.

Engine oils are most commonly mineral (petroleum) based; however, synthetic and semi-synthetic types are used more frequently.

When selecting engine oil, follow the manufacturer's recommendation for type, classification and viscosity. Using a non-recommended oil can cause engine, clutch and/or transmission damage. Carefully consider if an oil designed for automobile applications is compatible with motorcycles.

Greases

Grease is lubricating oil with thickening agents added to it. The National Lubricating Grease Institute (NLGI) grades grease. Grades range from No. 000 to No. 6, with No. 6 being the thickest. Typical multipurpose grease is NLGI No. 2. For specific applications, manufacturers may recommend water-resistant type grease or one with an additive such as molybdenum disulfide (MoS_2).

Brake fluid

WARNING

Never put a mineral-based (petroleum) oil into the brake system. Mineral oil will cause

9

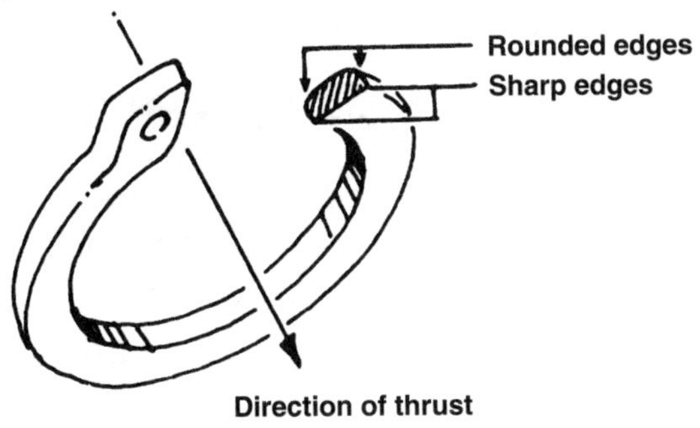

rubber parts in the system to swell and break apart, causing complete brake failure.

Brake fluid is the hydraulic fluid used to transmit hydraulic pressure (force) to the wheel brakes. Brake fluid is classified by the Department of Transportation (DOT). Current designations for brake fluid are DOT 3, DOT 4 and DOT 5. This classification appears on the fluid container.

Each type of brake fluid has its own definite characteristics. Do not intermix different types of brake fluid as this may cause brake system failure. DOT 5 brake fluid is silicone based and the type required for XL sportsters. Other types are not compatible with DOT 5 brake fluid. When adding brake fluid, *only* use the fluid recommended by the manufacturer (DOT 5).

Brake fluid will damage any plastic, painted or plated surface it contacts. Use extreme care when working with brake fluid and remove any spills immediately with soap and water.

Hydraulic brake systems require clean and moisture free brake fluid. Never reuse brake fluid. Keep containers and reservoirs properly sealed.

Cleaners, Degreasers and Solvents

Many chemicals are available to remove oil, grease and other residue from the motorcycle. Before using cleaning solvents, consider how they will be used and disposed of, particularly if they are not water-soluble. Local ordinances may require special procedures for the disposal of many types of cleaning chemicals. Refer to *Safety* and *Cleaning Parts* in this chapter for more information on their use.

Use brake parts cleaner to clean brake system components when contact with petroleum-based products will damage seals. Brake parts cleaner leaves no residue. Use electrical contact cleaner to clean electrical connections and components without leaving any residue. Carburetor cleaner is a powerful solvent used to remove fuel deposits and varnish from fuel system components. Use this cleaner carefully, as it may damage finishes.

Generally, degreasers are strong cleaners used to remove heavy accumulations of grease from engine and frame components.

Most solvents are designed to be used with a parts washing cabinet for individual component cleaning. For safety, use only nonflammable or high flash point solvents.

Gasket Sealant

Sealants are sometimes used in combination with a gasket or seal and occasionally alone. Follow the manufacturer's recommendation when using sealants. Use extreme care when choosing a sealant different from the type originally recommended. Choose sealants based on their resistance to heat, various fluids and their sealing capabilities.

One of the most common sealants is RTV, or room temperature vulcanizing sealant. This sealant cures at room temperature over a specific time period. This allows the repositioning of components without damaging gaskets.

Moisture in the air causes the RTV sealant to cure. Always install the tube cap as soon as possible after applying RTV sealant. RTV sealant has a limited shelf life and will not cure properly if the shelf life has expired. Keep partial tubes sealed and discard them if they have surpassed the expiration date.

Applying RTV sealant

Clean all old gasket residue from the mating surfaces. Remove all gasket material from blind threaded holes; it can cause inaccurate bolt torque. Spray the mating surfaces with aerosol parts cleaner and then wipe with a lint-free cloth. The area must be clean for the sealant to adhere.

Apply RTV sealant in a continuous bead 0.08-0.12 in. (2-3 mm) thick. Circle all the fastener holes unless otherwise specified. Do not allow any sealant to enter these holes. Assemble and tighten the fasteners to the specified torque within the time frame recommended by the RTV sealant manufacturer.

Gasket Remover

Aerosol gasket remover can help remove stubborn gaskets. This product can speed up the removal process and prevent damage to the mating surface that may be caused by using a scraping tool. Most of these types of products are very caustic. Follow the gasket remover manufacturer's instructions for use.

Threadlocking Compound

CAUTION
Threadlocking compounds are anaerobic and damage most plastic parts and surfaces. Use caution when using these products in areas where plastic components are located.

A threadlocking compound is a fluid applied to the threads of fasteners. After tightening the fastener, the fluid dries and becomes a solid filler between the threads. This makes it difficult for the fastener to work loose from vibration, or heat expansion and contraction. Some threadlocking compounds also provide a seal against fluid leaks.

Before applying threadlocking compound, remove any old compound from both thread areas and clean them with aerosol parts cleaner. Use the compound sparingly. Excess fluid can run into adjoining parts.

Threadlocking compounds are available in different strengths. Follow the particular manufacturer's recommendations regarding compound selection.

TOOLS

Most of the procedures in this manual can be carried out with familiar hand tools and test equipment. Always use the correct tools for the job at hand. Keep tools organized and clean. Store them in a tool chest with related tools organized together.

Quality tools are essential. The best are constructed of high-strength alloy steel. These tools are light, easy to use and resistant to wear. Their working surface is devoid of sharp edges and the tool is carefully polished. They have an easy-to-clean finish and are comfortable to use. Quality tools are a good investment.

When purchasing tools to perform the procedures covered in this manual, consider the tool's potential frequency of use. If a tool kit is just now being started, consider purchasing a basic tool set from a quality tool supplier. These sets are available in many tool combinations and offer substantial savings when compared to in-

10

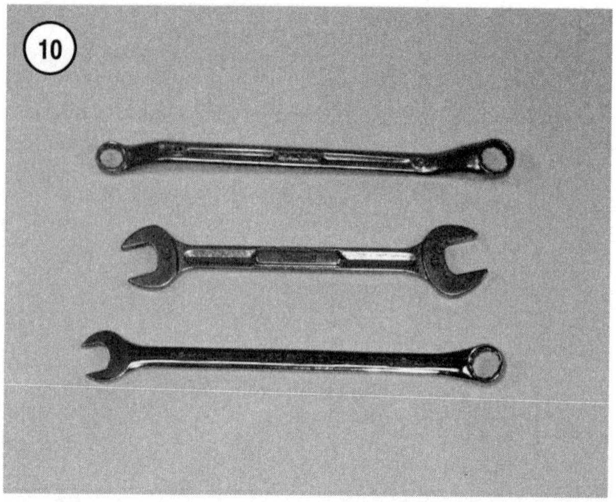

11

dividually purchased tools. As work experience grows and tasks become more complicated, specialized tools can be added.

Some of the procedures described in this manual require specialized tools and/or equipment. In most cases, the tool is described in use. In some cases a substitute tool may work. However, do not risk injury or damage to the equipment by using the incorrect tool. If the required tools are expensive it may be more cost effective to have the task performed by a dealership or qualified shop.

The manufacturer's part number is provided for many of the tools mentioned in this manual. These part numbers are correct at the time of original publication. The publisher cannot guarantee the part numbers or tools listed in this manual will be available in the future.

Screwdrivers

Screwdrivers of various lengths and types are mandatory for the simplest tool kit. The two basic types are the

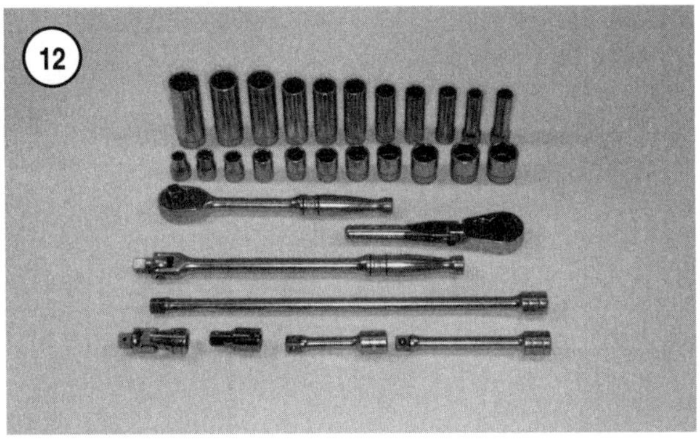

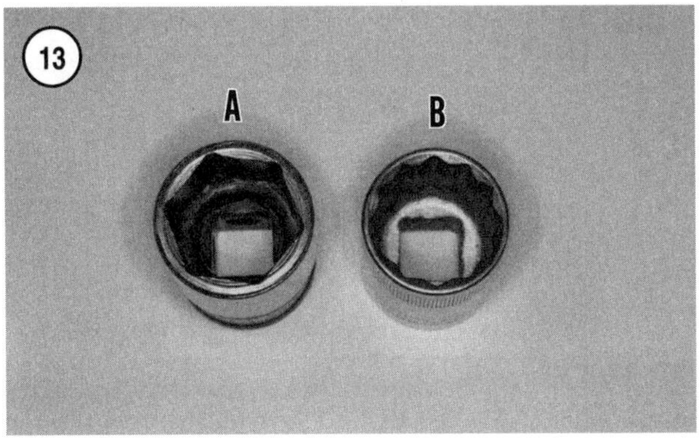

slotted tip (flat blade) and the Phillips tip. These are available in sets that often include an assortment of tip sizes and shaft lengths.

As with all tools, use a screwdriver designed for the job. Make sure the size of the tip conforms to the size and shape of the fastener. Use them only for driving screws. Never use a screwdriver for prying or chiseling metal. Repair or replace worn or damaged screwdrivers. A worn tip may damage the fastener, making it difficult to remove.

Wrenches

Open-end, box-end and combination wrenches (**Figure 10**) are available in a variety of types and sizes.

The number stamped on the wrench refers to the distance between the work areas. This size must match the size of the fastener head.

The box-end wrench is an excellent tool because it grips the fastener on all sides. This reduces the chance of the tool slipping. The box-end wrench is designed with either a 6- or 12-point opening. For stubborn or damaged fasteners, the 6-point provides superior holding ability by contacting the fastener across a wider area at all six edges. For general use, the 12-point works well. It allows the wrench to be removed and reinstalled without moving the handle over such a wide arc.

An open-end wrench is fast and works best in areas with limited overhead access. It contacts the fastener at only two points, and is subject to slipping under heavy force, or if the tool or fastener is worn. A box-end wrench is preferred in most instances, especially when breaking loose and applying the final tightness to a fastener.

The combination wrench has a box-end on one end, and an open-end on the other. This combination makes it a very convenient tool.

Adjustable Wrenches

An adjustable wrench or Crescent wrench (**Figure 11**) can fit nearly any nut or bolt head that has clear access around its entire perimeter. Adjustable wrenches are best used as a backup wrench to keep a large nut or bolt from turning while the other end is being loosened or tightened with a box-end or socket wrench.

Adjustable wrenches contact the fastener at only two points, which makes them more subject to slipping off the fastener. The fact that one jaw is adjustable and may loosen increases this possibility. Make certain the solid jaw is the one transmitting the force.

Socket Wrenches, Ratchets and Handles

Sockets that attach to a ratchet handle (**Figure 12**) are available with 6-point (A, **Figure 13**) or 12-point (B) openings and different drive sizes. The drive size indicates the size of the square hole that accepts the ratchet handle. The number stamped on the socket is the size of the work area and must match the fastener head.

As with wrenches, a 6-point socket provides superior-holding ability, while a 12-point socket needs to be moved only half as far to reposition it on the fastener.

WARNING

Do not use hand sockets with air or impact tools, as they may shatter and cause injury. Always wear eye protection when using impact or air tools.

Sockets are designated for either hand or impact use. Impact sockets are made of thicker material for more durability. Compare the size and wall thickness of a 19-mm hand socket (A, **Figure 14**) and the 19-mm impact socket (B). Use impact sockets when using an impact driver or air tools. Use hand sockets with hand-driven attachments.

Various handles are available for sockets. The speed handle is used for fast operation. Flexible ratchet heads in

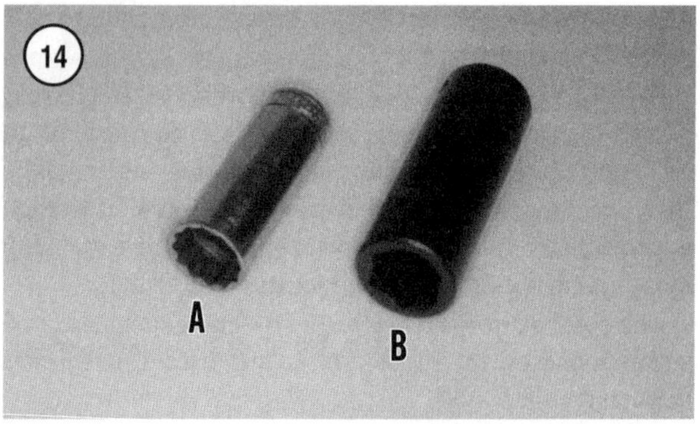

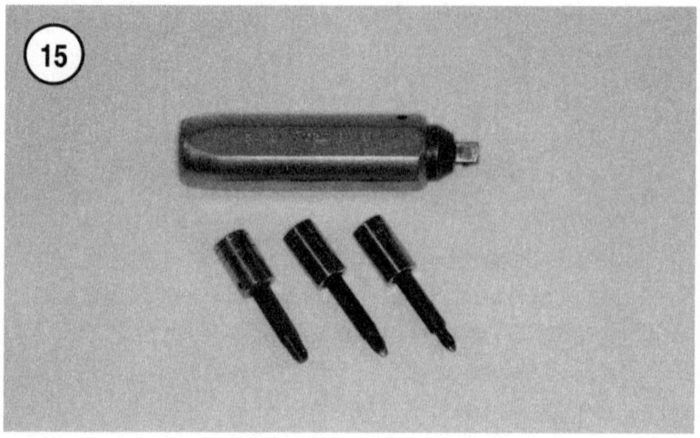

varying lengths allow the socket to be turned with varying force, and at odd angles. Extension bars allow the socket setup to reach difficult areas. The ratchet is the most versatile. It allows the user to install or remove the nut without removing the socket.

Sockets combined with any number of drivers make them undoubtedly the fastest, safest and most convenient tool for fastener removal and installation.

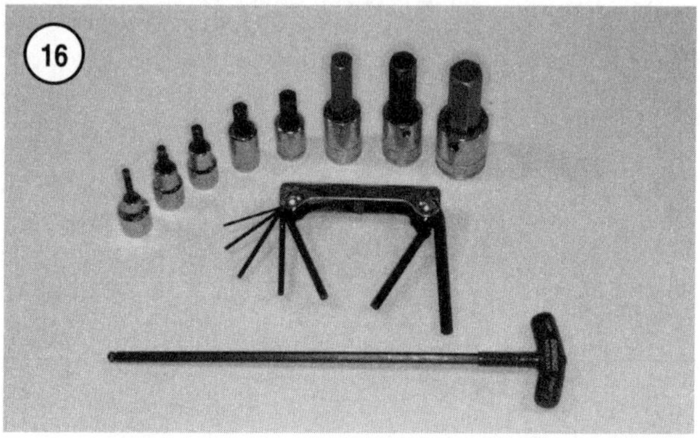

Impact Driver

WARNING
Do not use hand sockets with air or impact tools as they may shatter and cause injury. Always wear eye protection when using impact or air tools.

An impact driver provides extra force for removing fasteners, by converting the impact of a hammer into a turning motion. This makes it possible to remove stubborn fasteners without damaging them. Impact drivers and interchangeable bits (**Figure 15**) are available from most tool suppliers. When using a socket with an impact driver make sure the socket is designed for impact use. Refer to *Socket Wrenches, Ratchets and Handles* in this section.

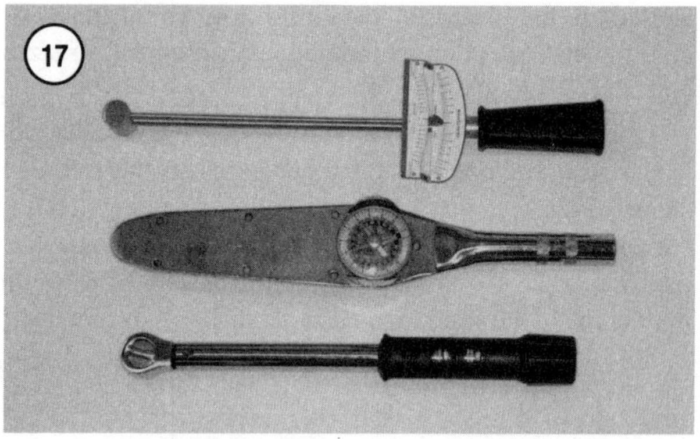

Allen Wrenches

Allen or setscrew wrenches (**Figure 16**) are used on fasteners with hexagonal recesses in the fastener head. These wrenches are available in L-shaped bar, socket and T-handle types. Allen bolts are sometimes called socket bolts.

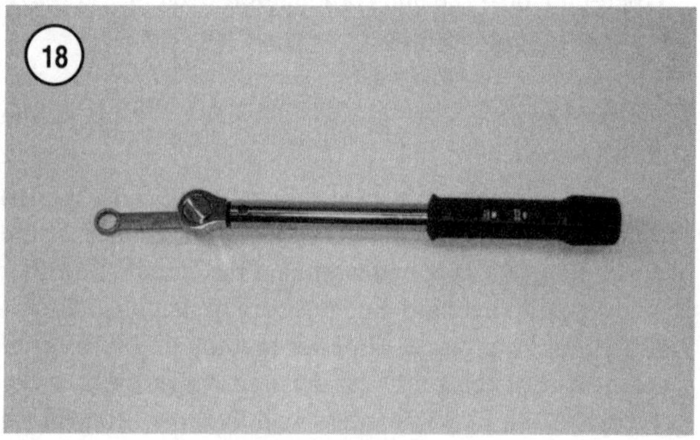

Torque Wrenches

A torque wrench is used with a socket, torque adapter or similar extension to tighten a fastener to a measured torque. Torque wrenches come in several drive sizes (1/4,

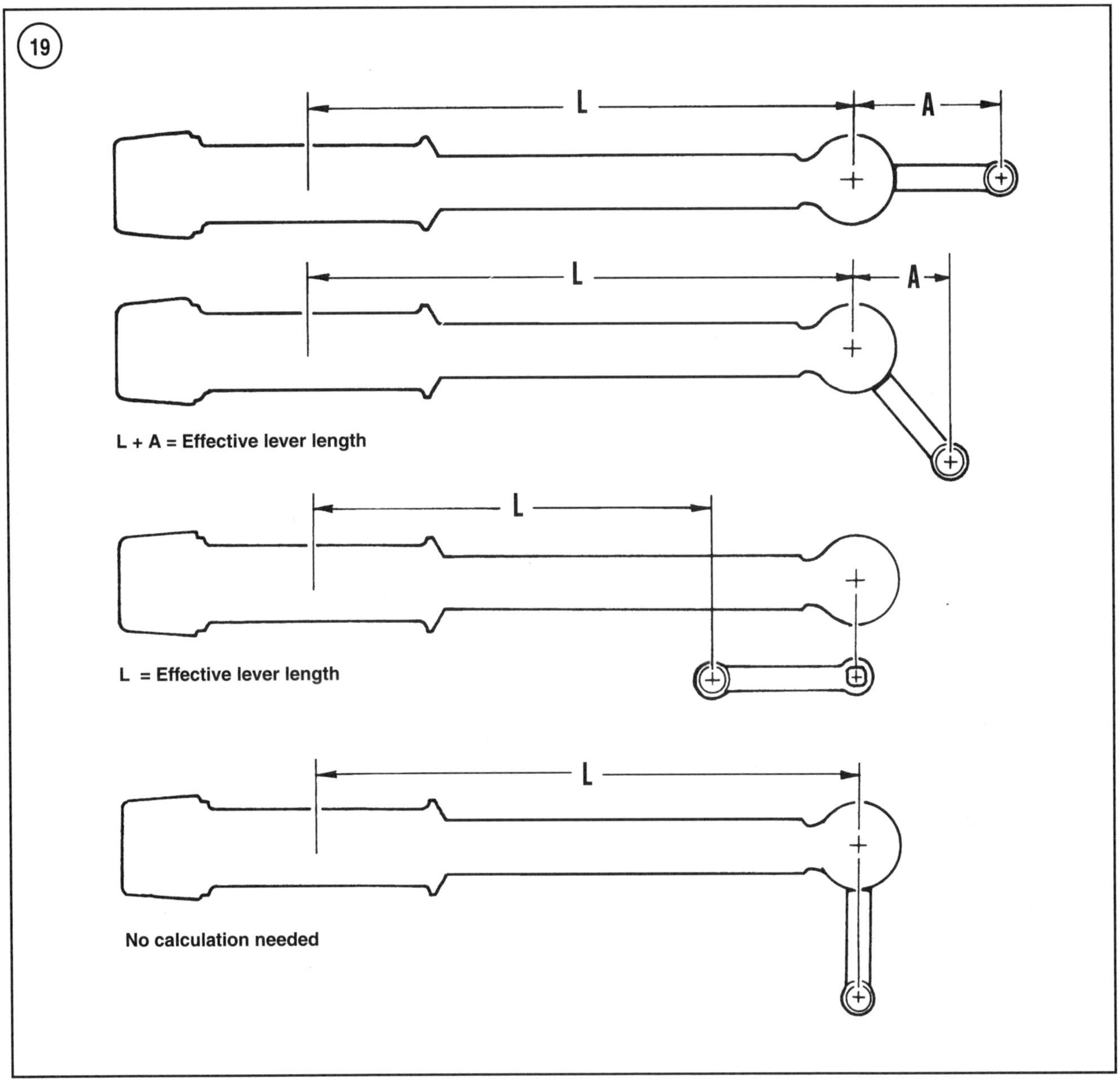

3/8, 1/2 and 3/4) and have various methods of reading the torque value. The drive size indicates the size of the square drive that accepts the socket, adapter or extension. Common methods of reading the torque value are the deflecting beam, the dial indicator and the audible click (**Figure 17**).

When choosing a torque wrench, consider the torque range, drive size and accuracy. The torque specifications in this manual provide an indication of the range required.

A torque wrench is a precision tool that must be properly cared for to remain accurate. Store torque wrenches in cases or separate padded drawers within a toolbox. Follow the manufacturer's instructions for their care and calibration.

Torque Adapters

Torque adapters or extensions extend or reduce the reach of a torque wrench. The torque adapter shown in **Figure 18** is used to tighten a fastener that cannot be reached due to the size of the torque wrench head, drive, and socket. If a torque adapter changes the effective lever length (**Figure 19**), the torque reading on the wrench will not equal the actual torque applied to the fastener. It is necessary to recalibrate the torque setting on the wrench to compensate for the change of lever length. When a torque adapter is used at a right angle to the drive head, calibration is not required, since the lever length has not changed.

To recalculate a torque reading when using a torque adapter, use the following formula, and refer to **Figure 19**.

$$TW = \frac{TA \times L}{L + A}$$

TW is the torque setting or dial reading on the wrench.

TA is the torque specification and the actual amount of torque that will be applied to the fastener.

A is the amount that the adapter increases (or in some cases reduces) the effective lever length as measured along the centerline of the torque wrench (**Figure 19**).

L is the lever length of the wrench as measured from the center of the drive to the center of the grip.

The effective lever length is the sum of L and A (**Figure 19**).

Example:

TA = 20 ft.-lb.

A = 3 in.

L = 14 in.

$$TW = \frac{20 \times 14}{14 + 3} = \frac{280}{17} = 16.5 \text{ ft. lb.}$$

In this example, the torque wrench would be set to the recalculated torque value (TW = 16.5 ft.-lb.) . When using a beam-type wrench, tighten the fastener until the pointer aligns with 16.5 ft.-lb. In this example, although the torque wrench is preset to 16.5 ft.-lb., the actual torque is 20 ft.-lb.

Pliers

Pliers come in a wide range of types and sizes. Pliers are useful for holding, cutting, bending, and crimping. Do not use them to turn fasteners. **Figure 20** and **Figure 21** show several types of useful pliers. Each design has a specialized function. Slip-joint pliers are general-purpose pliers used for gripping and bending. Diagonal cutting pliers are needed to cut wire and can be used to remove cotter pins. Needlenose pliers are used to hold or bend small objects. Locking pliers (**Figure 21**), sometimes called Vise-Grips, are used to hold objects very tightly. They have many uses ranging from holding two parts together, to gripping the end of a broken stud. Use caution when using locking pliers, as the sharp jaws will damage the objects they hold.

20

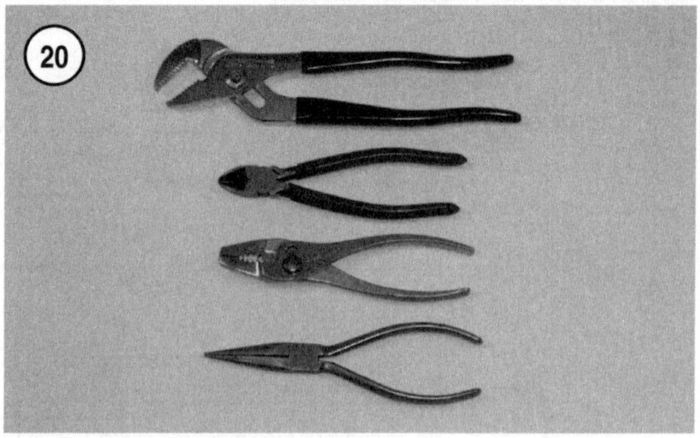

21

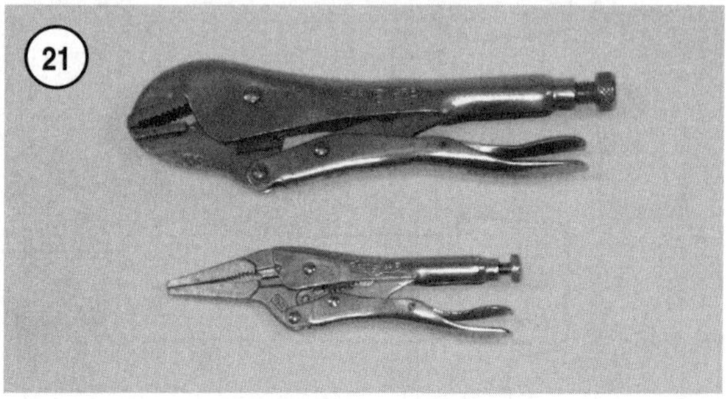

22

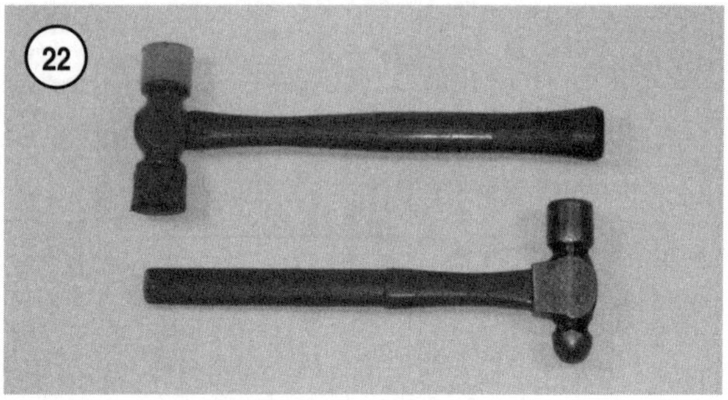

Snap Ring Pliers

WARNING
Snap rings can slip and fly off when removing and installing them. Also, the snap ring plier tips may break. Always wear eye protection when using snap ring pliers.

Snap ring pliers are specialized pliers with tips that fit into the ends of snap rings to remove and install them.

Snap ring pliers are available with a fixed action (either internal or external) or convertible (one tool works on both internal and external snap rings). They may have fixed tips or interchangeable ones of various sizes and angles. For general use, select a convertible type of pliers with interchangeable tips.

23

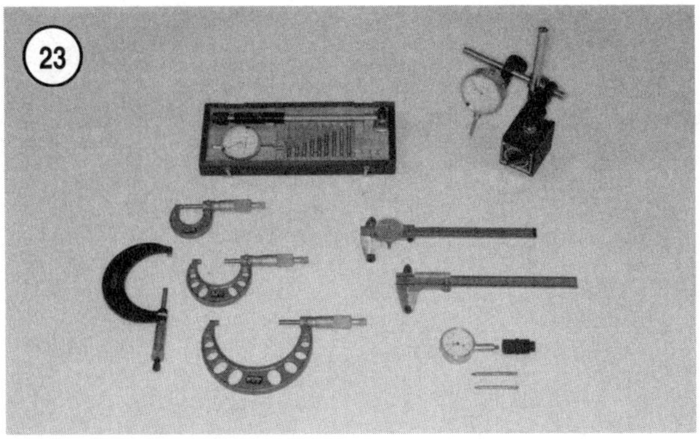

24

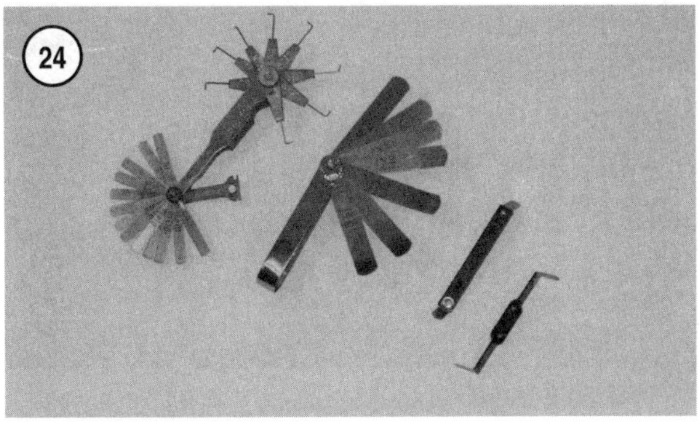

25

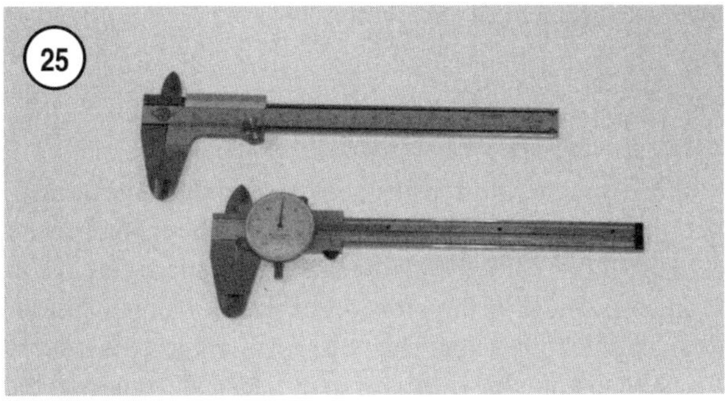

Hammers

WARNING
Wear eye protection when using hammers. Make sure the hammer face is in good condition and the handle is not cracked. Select the correct hammer for the job and make sure to strike the object squarely. Do not use the handle or the side of the hammer to strike an object.

Various types of hammers (**Figure 22**) are available to fit a number of applications. A ball-peen hammer is used to strike another tool, such as a punch or chisel. Soft-faced hammers are required when a metal object must be struck without damaging it. *Never* use a metal-faced hammer on engine and suspension components, as damage will occur in most cases.

MEASURING TOOLS

The ability to accurately measure components is essential to many of the procedures in this manual. Equipment is manufactured to close tolerances, and obtaining consistently accurate measurements is required to determine which components need replacement or further service.

Each type of measuring instrument is designed to measure a dimension with a certain degree of accuracy and within a certain range. When selecting the measuring tool, make sure it is applicable to the task. Refer to **Figure 23** for a comprehensive measuring set.

As with all tools, measuring tools provide the best results if cared for properly. Improper use can damage the tool and cause inaccurate results. If any measurement is questionable, verify the measurement using another tool. A standard gauge is usually provided with measuring tools to check accuracy and calibrate the tool if necessary.

Precision measurements can vary according to the experience of the person performing the procedure. Accurate results are only possible if the mechanic possesses a feel for using the tool. Heavy-handed use of measuring tools will produce less accurate results. Hold the tool gently by the fingertips so the point at which the tool contacts the object is easily felt. This feel for the equipment will produce more accurate measurements and reduce the risk of damaging the tool or component. Refer to the following sections for specific measuring tools.

Feeler Gauge

The feeler or thickness gauge (**Figure 24**) is used for measuring the distance between two surfaces.

A feeler gauge set consists of an assortment of steel strips of graduated thickness. Each blade is marked with its thickness. Blades can be of various lengths and angles for different procedures.

A common use for a feeler gauge is to measure valve clearance. Wire (round) type gauges are used to measure spark plug gap.

Calipers

Calipers (**Figure 25**) are used for obtaining inside, outside and depth measurements. Although not as precise as a micrometer, they typically allow measurement to within

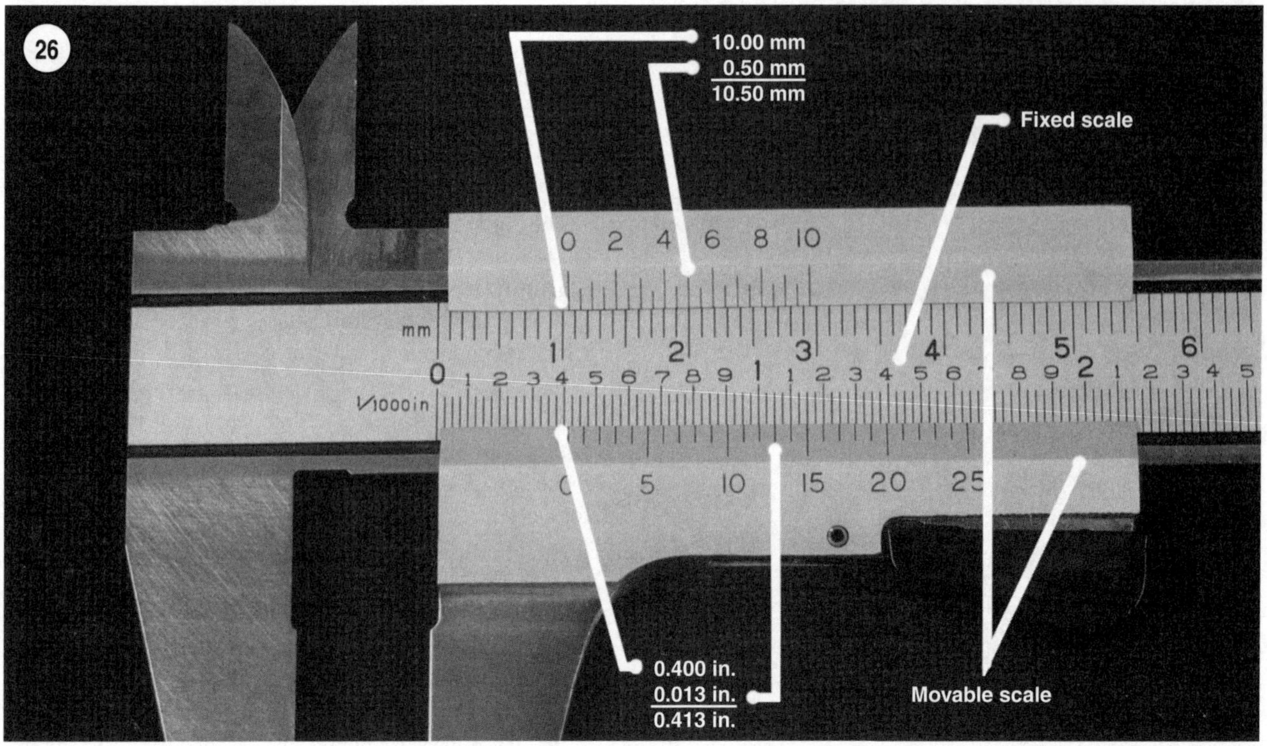

0.05 mm (0.001 in.). Most calipers have a range up to150 mm (6 in.).

Calipers are available in dial, vernier or digital versions. Dial calipers have a dial readout that provides convenient reading. Vernier calipers have marked scales that must be compared to determine the measurement. The digital caliper uses a LCD to show the measurement.

Properly maintain the measuring surfaces of the caliper. There must not be any dirt or burrs between the tool and the measured object. Never force the caliper closed around an object; close the caliper around the highest point so it can be removed with a slight drag. Some calipers require calibration. Always refer to the manufacturer's instructions when using a new or unfamiliar caliper.

To read a vernier caliper refer to **Figure 26**. The fixed scale is marked in 1 mm increments. Ten individual lines on the fixed scale equal 1 cm. The movable scale is marked in 0.05 mm (hundredth) increments. To obtain a reading, establish the first number by the location of the 0 line on the movable scale in relation to the first line to the left on the fixed scale. In this example, the number is 10 mm. To determine the next number, note which of the lines on the movable scale align with a mark on the fixed scale. A number of lines will seem close, but only one will align exactly. In this case, 0.50 mm is the reading to add to the first number. The result of adding 10 mm and 0.50 mm is a measurement of 10.50 mm.

Micrometers

A micrometer is an instrument designed for linear measurement using the decimal divisions of the inch or meter (**Figure 27**). While there are many types and styles of micrometers, most of the procedures in this manual call for an outside micrometer. The outside micrometer is used to measure the outside diameter of cylindrical forms and the thickness of materials.

A micrometer's size indicates the minimum and maximum size of a part that it can measure. The usual sizes (**Figure 28**) are 0-1 in. (0-25 mm), 1-2 in. (25-50 mm), 2-3 in. (50-75 mm) and 3-4 in. (75-100 mm).

Micrometers that cover a wider range of measurements are available. These use a large frame with interchangeable anvils of various lengths. This type of micrometer offers a cost savings; however, its overall size may make it less convenient.

Adjustment

Before using a micrometer, check its adjustment as follows.

(27)

DECIMAL PLACE VALUES*

0.1	Indicates 1/10 (one tenth of an inch or millimeter)
0.010	Indicates 1/100 (one one-hundreth of an inch or millimeter)
0.001	Indicates 1/1000 (one one-thousandth of an inch or millimeter)

*This chart represents the values of figures placed to the right of the decimal point. Use it when reading decimals from one-tenth to one one-thousandth of an inch or millimeter. It is not a conversion chart (for example: 0.001 in. is not equal to 0.001 mm).

(28)

1. Clean the anvil and spindle faces.

2A. To check a 0-1 in. or 0-25 mm micrometer:

a. Turn the thimble until the spindle contacts the anvil. If the micrometer has a ratchet stop, use it to ensure that the proper amount of pressure is applied.

b. If the adjustment is correct, the 0 mark on the thimble will align exactly with the 0 mark on the sleeve line. If the marks do not align, the micrometer is out of adjustment.

c. Follow the manufacturer's instructions to adjust the micrometer.

2B. To check a micrometer larger than 1 in. or 25 mm, use the standard gauge supplied by the manufacturer. A standard gauge is a steel block, disc or rod that is machined to an exact size.

a. Place the standard gauge between the spindle and anvil, and measure its outside diameter or length. If the micrometer has a ratchet stop, use it to ensure that the proper amount of pressure is applied.

b. If the adjustment is correct, the 0 mark on the thimble will align exactly with the 0 mark on the sleeve line. If the marks do not align, the micrometer is out of adjustment.

c. Follow the manufacturer's instructions to adjust the micrometer.

Care

Micrometers are precision instruments. They must be used and maintained with great care. Note the following:

1. Store micrometers in protective cases or separate padded drawers in a toolbox.
2. When in storage, make sure the spindle and anvil faces do not contact each other or another object. If they do, temperature changes and corrosion may damage the contact faces.
3. Do not clean a micrometer with compressed air. Dirt forced into the tool causes wear.
4. Lubricate micrometers to prevent corrosion.

Reading

When reading a micrometer, numbers are taken from different scales and added together. Make sure there is no dirt or burrs between the tool and the measured object. Never force the micrometer closed around an object. Close the micrometer around the highest point so it can be removed with a slight drag.

The standard inch micrometer (**Figure 29**) is accurate to one-thousandth of an inch or 0.001 in. The sleeve is marked in 0.025 in. increments. Every fourth sleeve mark is numbered 1, 2, 3, 4, 5, 6, 7, 8, 9. These numbers indicate 0.100, 0.200, 0.300, and so on.

The tapered end of the thimble has twenty-five lines marked around it. Each mark equals 0.001 in. One complete turn of the thimble will align its zero mark with the first mark on the sleeve or 0.025 in.

When reading a standard inch micrometer, perform the following steps while referring to **Figure 30**.

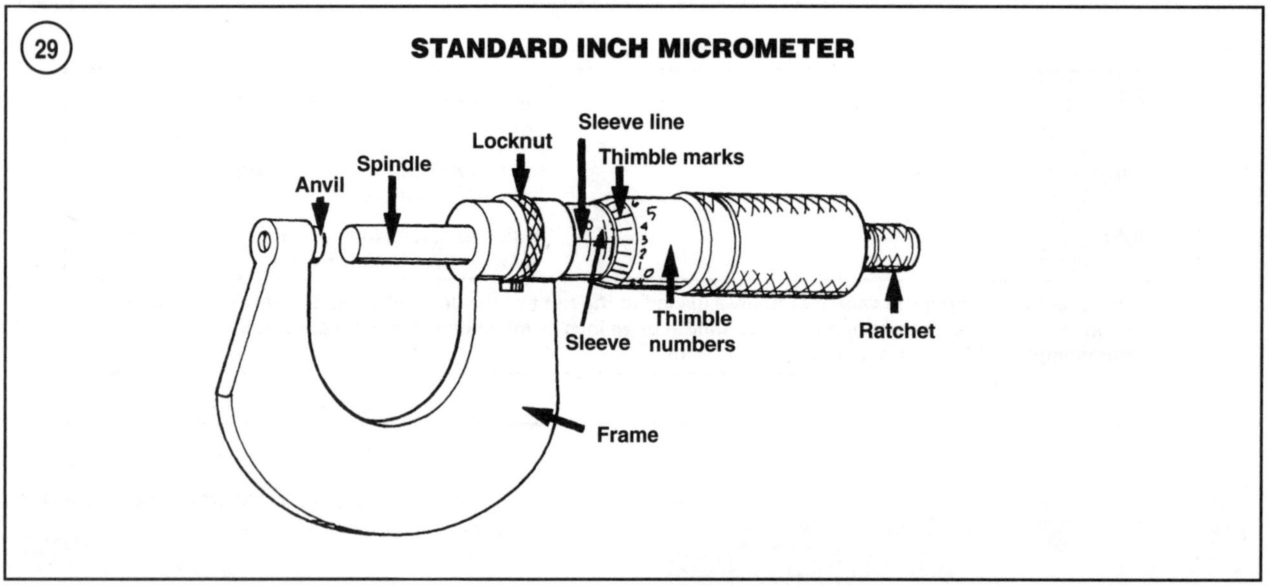

1. Read the sleeve and find the largest number visible. Each sleeve number equals 0.100 in.
2. Count the number of lines between the numbered sleeve mark and the edge of the thimble. Each sleeve mark equals 0.025 in.
3. Read the thimble mark that aligns with the sleeve line. Each thimble mark equals 0.001 in.

NOTE
If a thimble mark does not align exactly with the sleeve line, estimate the amount between the lines or use a vernier inch micrometer.

4. Add the readings from Steps 1-3.

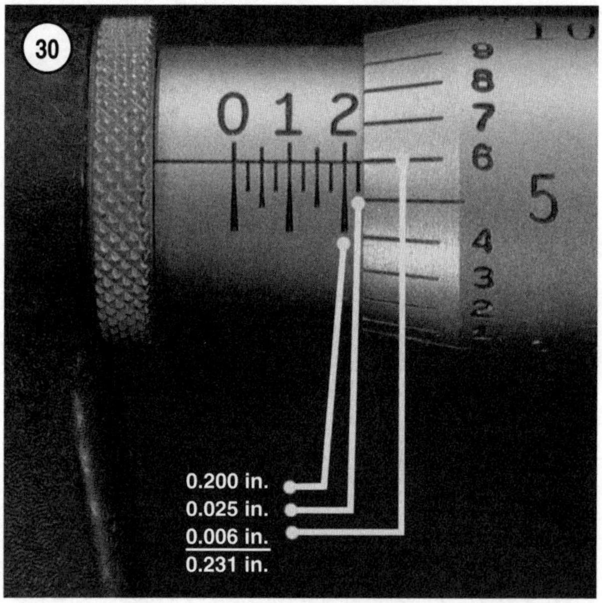

Telescoping and Small Hole Gauges

Use telescoping gauges (**Figure 31**) and small hole gauges (**Figure 32**) to measure bores. Neither gauge has a scale for direct readings. An outside micrometer must be used to determine the reading.

To use a telescoping gauge, select the correct size gauge for the bore. Compress the movable post and carefully insert the gauge into the bore. Carefully move the gauge in the bore to make sure it is centered. Tighten the knurled end of the gauge to hold the movable post in position. Remove the gauge and measure the length of the posts. Telescoping gauges are typically used to measure cylinder bores.

To use a small-hole gauge, select the correct size gauge for the bore. Carefully insert the gauge into the bore. Tighten the knurled end of the gauge to carefully expand the gauge fingers to the limit within the bore. Do not overtighten the gauge, as there is no built-in release. Excessive tightening can damage the bore surface and damage the tool. Remove the gauge and measure the outside dimension (**Figure 33**). Small hole gauges are typically used to measure valve guides.

Dial Indicator

A dial indicator (**Figure 34**) is a gauge with a dial face and needle used to measure variations in dimensions and

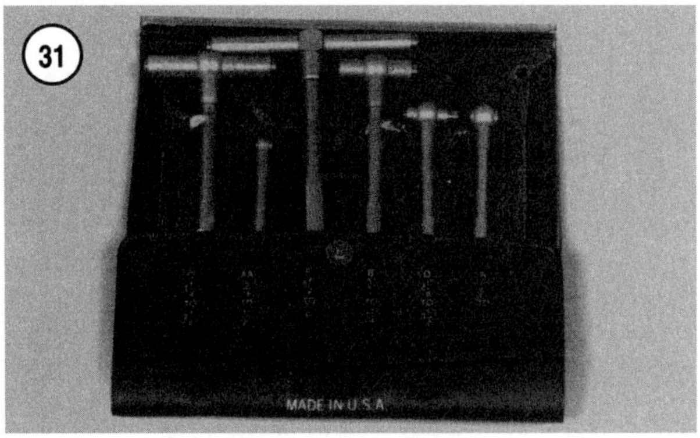

31

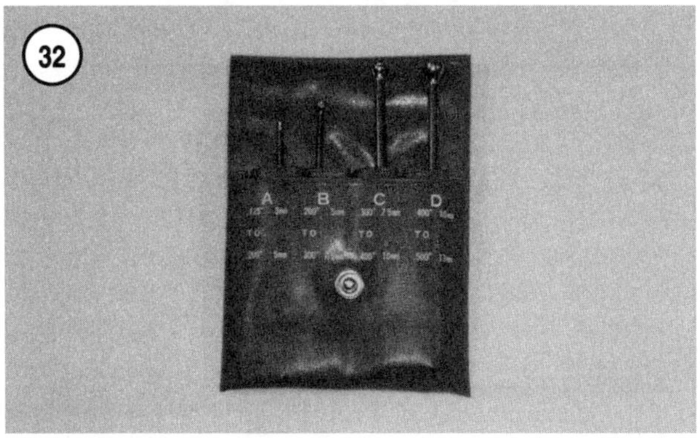

32

33

34

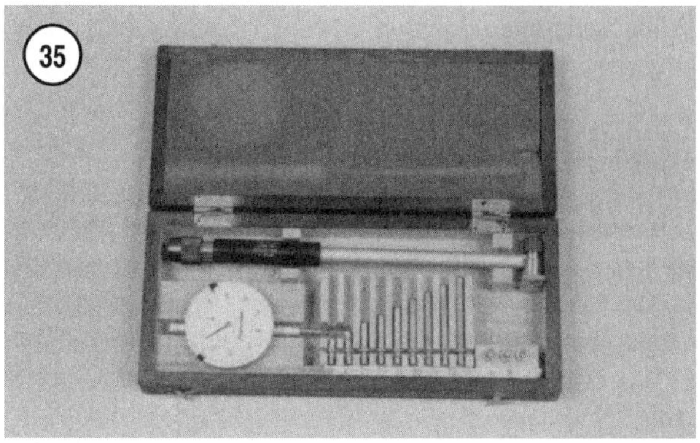
35

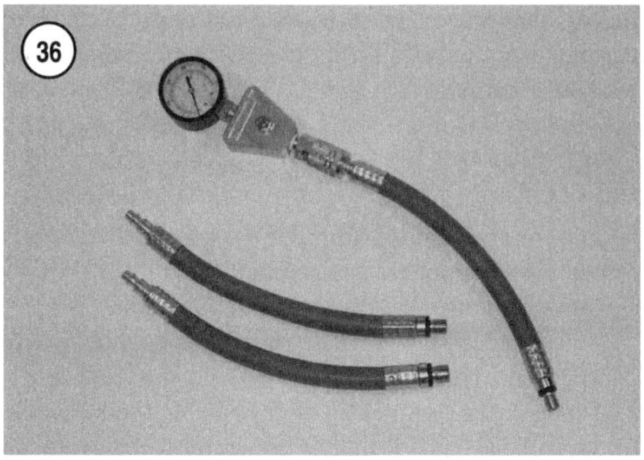
36

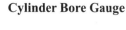

movements. Measuring brake rotor runout is a typical use for a dial indicator.

Dial indicators are available in various ranges and graduations and with three basic types of mounting bases: magnetic (**Figure 34**), clamp, or screw-in stud.

Cylinder Bore Gauge

A cylinder bore gauge is similar to a dial indicator. The gauge set shown in **Figure 35** consists of a dial indicator, handle, and different length adapters (anvils) to fit the gauge to various bore sizes. The bore gauge is used to measure bore size, taper and out-of-round. When using a bore gauge, follow the manufacturer's instructions.

Compression Gauge

A compression gauge (**Figure 36**) measures combustion chamber (cylinder) pressure, usually in psi or kg/cm^2. The gauge adapter is either inserted and held in place or screwed into the spark plug hole to obtain the reading. Disable the engine so it does not start and hold the throttle in the wide-open position when performing a compression test.

Multimeter

A multimeter (**Figure 37**) is an essential tool for electrical system diagnosis. The voltage function indicates the voltage applied or available to various electrical components. The ohmmeter function tests circuits for continuity, or lack of continuity, and measures the resistance of a circuit.

Some manufacturers' specifications for electrical components are based on results using a specific test meter. Results may vary if using a meter not recommended by the manufacturer is used. Such requirements are noted when applicable.

Ohmmeter (analog) calibration

Each time an analog ohmmeter is used or if the scale is changed, the ohmmeter must be calibrated.

Digital ohmmeters do not require calibration.

1. Make sure the meter battery is in good condition.
2. Make sure the meter probes are in good condition.
3. Touch the two probes together and observe the needle location on the ohms scale. The needle must align with the 0 mark to obtain accurate measurements.
4. If necessary, rotate the meter ohms adjust knob until the needle and 0 mark align.

ELECTRICAL SYSTEM FUNDAMENTALS

A thorough study of the many types of electrical systems used in today's motorcycles is beyond the scope of this manual. However, an understanding of electrical basics is necessary to perform simple diagnostic tests.

Voltage

Voltage is the electrical potential or pressure in an electrical circuit and is expressed in volts. The more pressure (voltage) in a circuit, the more work that can be performed.

Direct current (DC) voltage means the electricity flows in one direction. All circuits powered by a battery are DC circuits.

Alternating current (AC) means that the electricity flows in one direction momentarily then switches to the opposite direction. Alternator output is an example of AC voltage. This voltage must be changed or rectified to direct current to operate in a battery powered system.

37

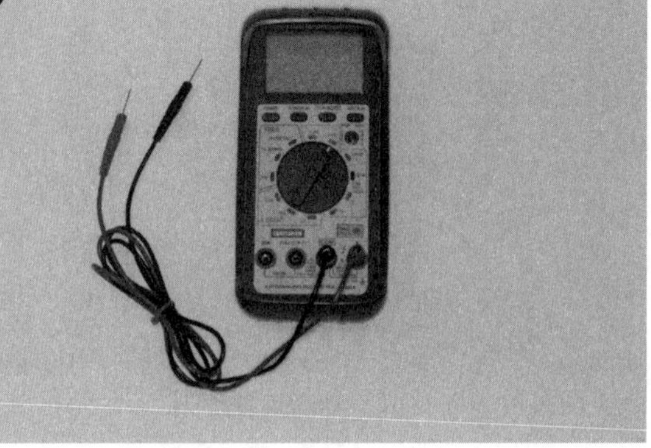

38

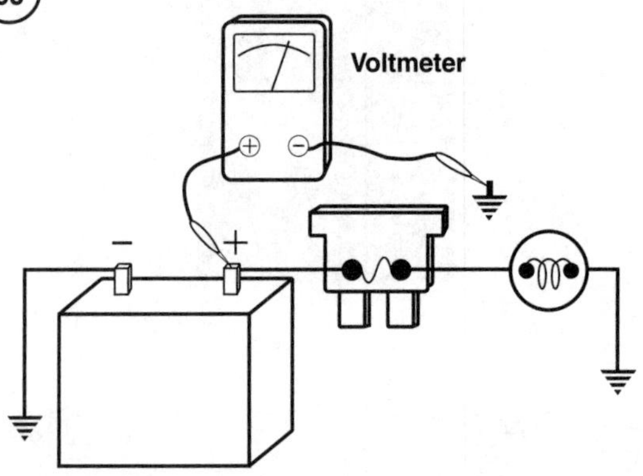

Measuring voltage

Unless otherwise specified, perform all voltage tests with the electrical connectors attached. When measuring voltage, select the meter range that is one scale higher than the expected voltage of the circuit to prevent damage to the meter. To determine the actual voltage in a circuit, use a voltmeter. To simply check if voltage is present, use a test light. When using a test light, either lead can be attached to ground.

1. Attach the negative meter test lead to a good ground (bare metal). Make sure the ground is not insulated with a rubber gasket or grommet.
2. Attach the positive meter test lead to the point being checked for voltage (**Figure 38**).
3. Turn on the ignition switch. The test light should light or the meter should display a reading. The reading should be within one volt of battery voltage. If the voltage is less, there is a problem in the circuit.

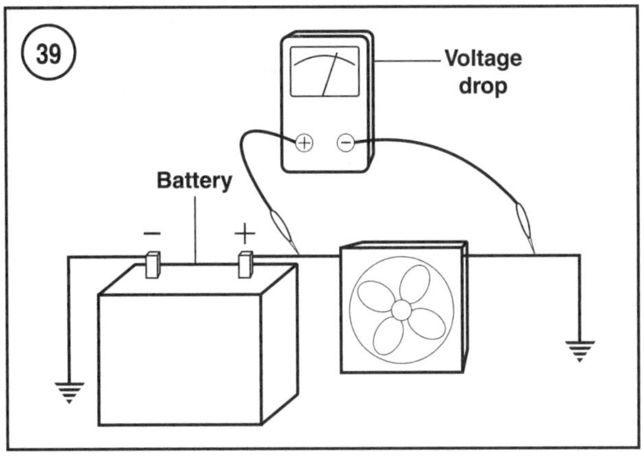

Voltage drop test

Resistance causes voltage to drop. This resistance can be measured in an active circuit by using a voltmeter to perform a voltage drop test. A voltage drop test compares the difference between the voltage available at the start of a circuit to the voltage at the end of the circuit while the circuit is operational. If the circuit has no resistance, there will be no voltage drop. The greater the resistance, the greater the voltage drop will be. A voltage drop of one volt or more indicates excessive circuit resistance.

1. Connect the positive meter test lead to the electrical source (where electricity is coming from).
2. Connect the negative meter test lead to the electrical load (where electricity is going). See **Figure 39**.
3. If necessary, activate the component(s) in the circuit.
4. A voltage reading of 1 volt or more indicates excessive resistance in the circuit. A reading equal to battery voltage indicates an open circuit.

Resistance

Resistance is the opposition to the flow of electricity within a circuit or component and is measured in ohms. Resistance causes a reduction in available current and voltage.

Resistance is measured in an *inactive* circuit with an ohmmeter. The ohmmeter sends a small amount of current into the circuit and measures how difficult it is to push the current through the circuit.

An ohmmeter, although useful, is not always a good indicator of a circuit's actual ability under operating conditions. This is due to the low voltage (6-9 volts) that the meter uses to test the circuit. The voltage in an ignition coil secondary winding can be several thousand volts. Such high voltage can cause the coil to malfunction, even though it tests acceptable during a resistance test.

Resistance generally increases with temperature. Perform all testing with the component or circuit at room temperature. Resistance tests performed at high temperatures may indicate high resistance readings and cause the unnecessary replacement of a component.

Measuring resistance and continuity testing

CAUTION
Only use an ohmmeter on a circuit that has no voltage present. The meter will be damaged if it is connected to a live circuit. An analog meter must be calibrated each time it is used or the scale is changed. Refer to ***Multimeter*** *in this chapter.*

A continuity test can determine if the circuit is complete. This type of test is performed with an ohmmeter or a self-powered test lamp.

1. Disconnect the negative battery cable.
2. Attach one test lead (ohmmeter or test light) to one end of the component or circuit.
3. Attach the other test lead to the opposite end of the component or circuit.
4. A self-powered test light will come on if the circuit has continuity or is complete. An ohmmeter will indicate either low or no resistance if the circuit has continuity. An open circuit is indicated if the meter displays infinite resistance.

Amperage

Amperage is the unit of measure for the amount of current within a circuit. Current is the actual flow of electricity. The higher the current, the more work that can be performed up to a given point. If the current flow exceeds the circuit or component capacity, the system will be damaged.

Measuring amps

An ammeter measures the current flow or amps of a circuit (**Figure 40**). Amperage measurement requires that the circuit be disconnected and the ammeter be connected in series to the circuit. Always use an ammeter that can read higher than the anticipated current flow to prevent damage to the meter. Connect the red test lead to the electrical source and the black test lead to the electrical load.

BASIC SERVICE METHODS

Many of the procedures in this manual are straightforward and can be performed by anyone reasonably competent with tools. However, consider previous experience carefully before attempting any operation involving complicated procedures.

1. Front, in this manual, refers to the front of the motorcycle. The front of any component is the end closest to the front of the motorcycle. The left and right sides refer to the position of the parts as viewed by the rider sitting on the seat facing forward.
2. Whenever servicing an engine, transmission or suspension component, secure the motorcycle in a safe manner.
3. Tag all similar parts for location and mark all mating parts for position. Record the number and thickness of any shims as they are removed. Identify parts by placing them in sealed and labeled plastic bags.
4. Tag disconnected wires and connectors with masking tape and a marking pen. Do not rely on memory alone.
5. Protect finished surfaces from physical damage or corrosion. Keep gasoline and other chemicals off painted surfaces.
6. Use penetrating oil on frozen or tight bolts. Avoid using heat where possible. Heat can warp, melt or affect the temper of parts. Heat also damages the finish of paint and plastics. If necessary, use a heat gun.
7. When a part is a press fit or requires a special tool for removal, the information or type of tool is identified in the text. Otherwise, if a part is difficult to remove or install, determine the cause before proceeding.
8. To prevent objects or debris from falling into the engine, cover all openings.
9. Read each procedure thoroughly and compare the figures to the actual components before starting the procedure. Perform the procedure in sequence.
10. Recommendations are occasionally made to refer service to a dealership or specialist. In these cases, the work can be performed more economically by the specialist, than by the home mechanic.
11. The term *replace* means to discard a defective part and replace it with a new part. *Overhaul* means to remove, disassemble, inspect, measure, repair and/or replace parts as required to recondition an assembly.
12. Some operations require using a hydraulic press. If a press is not available, have these operations performed by a shop equipped with the necessary equipment. Do not use makeshift equipment that may damage the motorcycle.
13. Repairs are much faster and easier if the motorcycle is clean before starting work than if the motorcycle is dirty. Degrease the motorcycle with a commercial degreaser; follow the directions on the container for the best results. Clean all parts with cleaning solvent as they are removed. Do not direct high-pressure water at steering bearings, carburetor hoses, wheel bearings, suspension and electrical components.

40

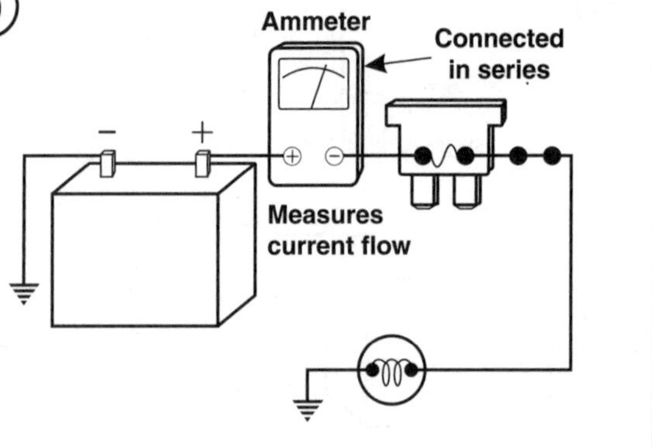

41

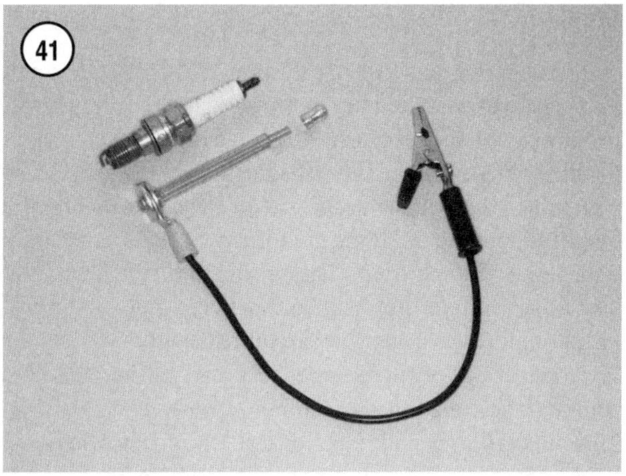

14. If special tools are required, have them available before starting the procedure. When special tools are required, they are described at the beginning of the procedure.
15. Make diagrams of similar-appearing parts. For instance, crankcase bolts are often not the same lengths. Do not rely on memory alone. Carefully laid out parts can become disturbed, making it difficult to reassemble the components correctly without a diagram.
16. Make sure all shims and washers are reinstalled in the same location and position.
17. Whenever rotating parts contact a stationary part, look for a shim or washer.
18. Use new gaskets if there is any doubt about the condition of old ones.

42

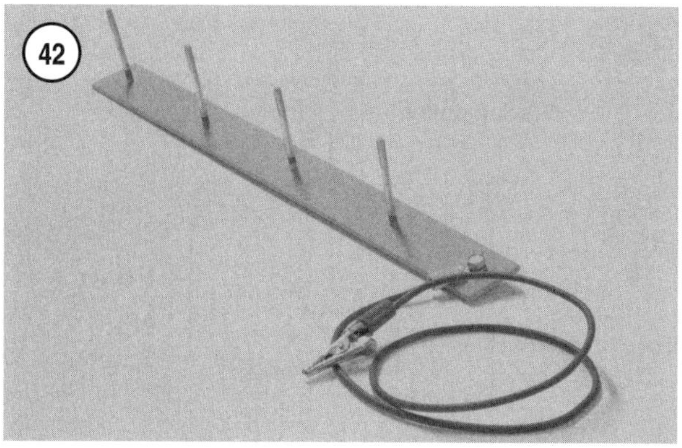

43

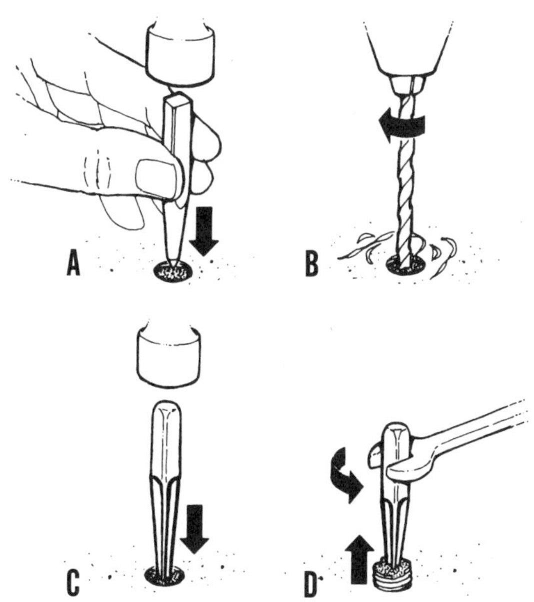

19. If using self-locking fasteners, replace them with new ones. Do not install standard fasteners in place of self-locking ones.
20. Use grease to hold small parts in place if they tend to fall out during assembly. Do not apply grease to electrical or brake components.

Ignition Grounding

The ignition system produces sufficient voltage to damage ignition components if the secondary voltage is not grounded during operation. During normal operation, grounding of the secondary circuit occurs at the spark plug. When performing some tests, such as compression testing, it may be necessary to disconnect the spark plug cap from the spark plug. It is a good practice to ground a disconnected spark plug cap to the engine if the ignition is on, and may be required by some manufacturers to protect the ignition system.

A grounding device may be fabricated to route secondary circuit voltage to the engine. **Figure 41** shows a tool that is useful when grounding a single spark plug cap, and **Figure 42** shows a grounding strap that allows the grounding of several spark plug caps. Both tools use a stud or bolt that fits the spark plug connector in the spark plug cap. An alligator clip permits electrical connection to suitable points on the engine. Do not ground the ignition voltage through alloy components and/or ones that are specially coated. Damage to the finish may occur.

Removing Frozen Fasteners

If a fastener cannot be removed, several methods may be used to loosen it. First, apply penetrating oil. Apply it liberally and let it penetrate for 10-15 minutes. Rap the fastener several times with a small hammer. Do not hit it hard enough to cause damage. Reapply the penetrating oil if necessary.

For frozen screws, apply penetrating oil as described, then insert a screwdriver in the slot and rap the top of the screwdriver with a hammer. This loosens the rust so the screw can be removed in the normal way. If the screw head is too damaged to use this method, grip the head with locking pliers and twist the screw out.

Avoid applying heat unless specifically instructed, as it may melt, warp or remove the temper from parts.

Removing Broken Fasteners

If the head breaks off a screw or bolt, several methods are available for removing the remaining portion. If a large portion of the remainder projects out, try gripping it with locking pliers. If the projecting portion is too small, file it to fit a wrench or cut a slot in it to fit a screwdriver.

If the head breaks off flush, use a screw extractor. To do this, centerpunch the exact center of the remaining portion of the screw or bolt (A, **Figure 43**) and then drill a small hole in the screw (B) and tap the extractor into the hole (C). Back the screw out with a wrench on the extractor (D, **Figure 43**).

44
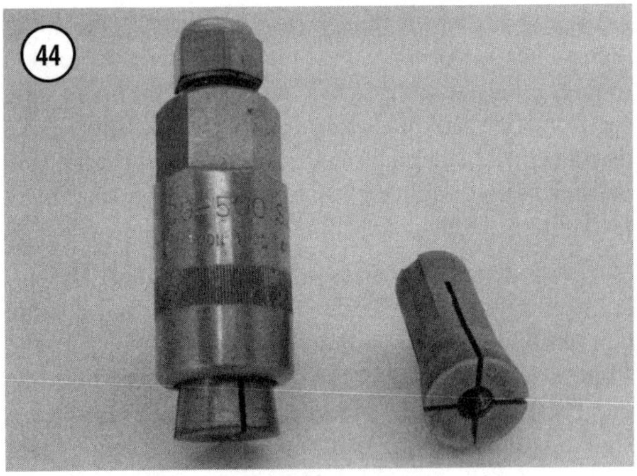

Repairing Damaged Threads

Occasionally, threads are stripped through carelessness or impact damage. Often the threads can be repaired by running a tap (for internal threads on nuts) or die (for external threads on bolts) through the threads. To clean or repair spark plug threads, use a spark plug tap.

If an internal thread is damaged, it may be necessary to install a Helicoil or some other type of thread insert. Follow the manufacturer's instructions when installing their insert.

If it is necessary to drill and tap a hole, refer to **Table 7** for U.S. tap and drill sizes or **Table 8** for metric tap and drill sizes.

Stud Removal/Installation

A stud removal tool (**Figure 44**) is available from most tool suppliers. This tool makes the removal and installation of studs easier. If one is not available, thread two nuts onto the stud and tighten them against each other. Remove the stud by turning the lower nut.

1. Measure the height of the stud above the surface.
2. Thread the stud removal tool onto the stud and tighten it, or thread two nuts onto the stud.
3. Remove the stud by turning the stud remover or the lower nut.
4. Remove any threadlocking compound from the threaded hole. Clean the threads with an aerosol parts cleaner.
5. Install the stud removal tool onto the new stud or thread two nuts onto the stud.
6. Apply threadlocking compound to the threads of the stud.
7. Install the stud and tighten with the stud removal tool or the top nut.

45
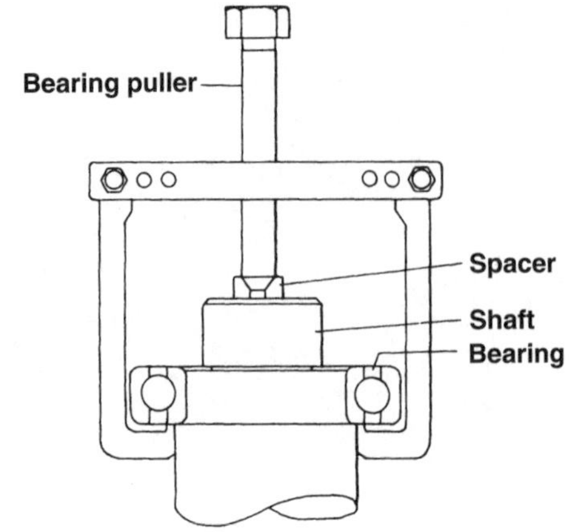

46
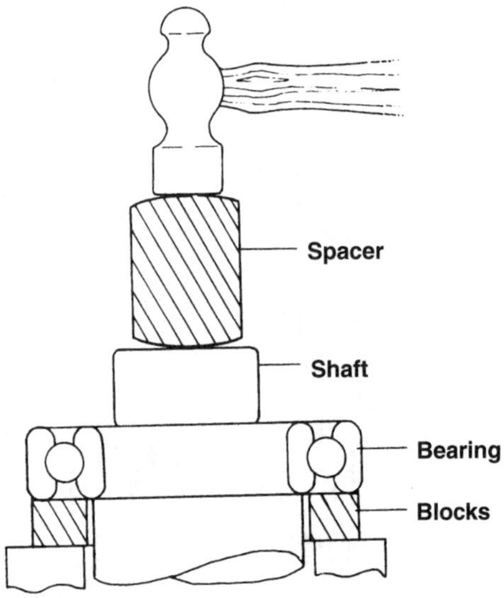

8. Install the stud to the height noted in Step 1 or to its torque specification.
9. Remove the stud removal tool or the two nuts.

Removing Hoses

When removing stubborn hoses, do not exert excessive force on the hose or fitting. Remove the hose clamp and carefully insert a small screwdriver or pick tool between the fitting and hose. Apply a spray lubricant under the hose and carefully twist the hose off the fitting. Clean the fitting of any corrosion or rubber hose material with a wire brush. Clean the inside of the hose thoroughly. Do

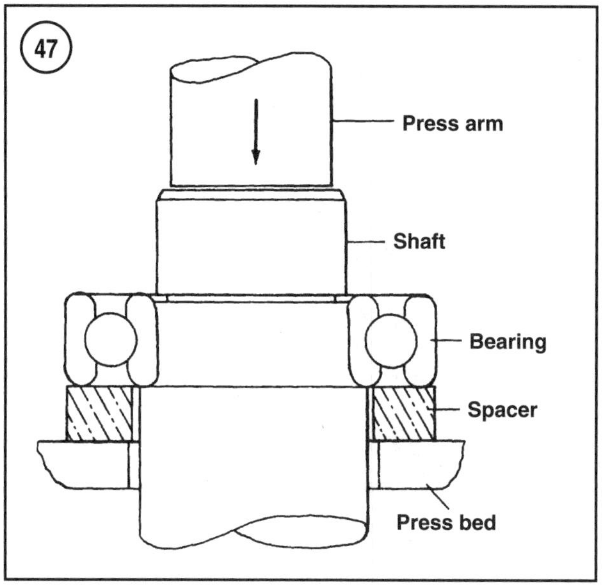

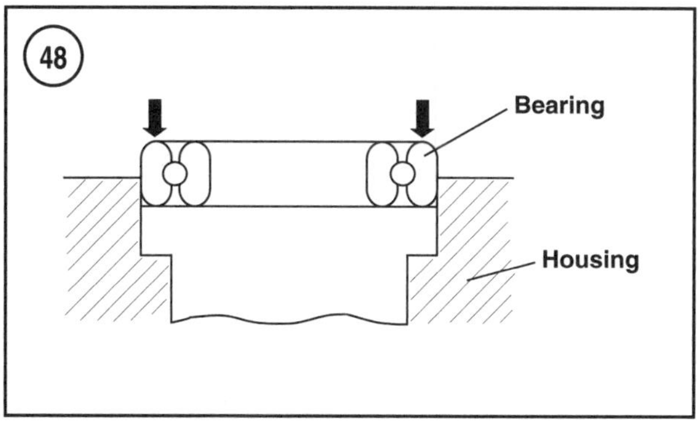

not use any lubricant when installing the hose (new or old). The lubricant may allow the hose to come off the fitting, even with the clamp secure.

Bearings

Bearings are precision parts and must be maintained with proper lubrication and maintenance. If a bearing is damaged, replace it immediately. When installing a new bearing, be careful not to damage it. Bearing replacement procedures are included in the individual chapters where applicable; however, use the following sections as a guideline.

NOTE
Unless otherwise specified, install bearings with the manufacturer's mark or number facing outward.

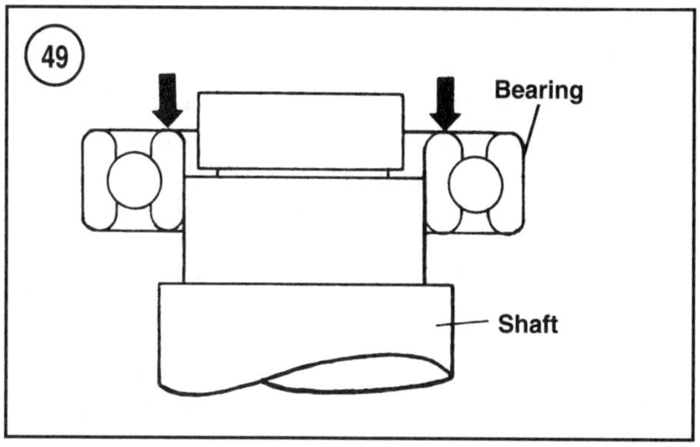

Removal

While bearings are normally removed only when damaged, there may be times when it is necessary to remove a bearing that is in good condition. However, improper bearing removal will damage the bearing and maybe the shaft or case half. Note the following when removing bearings.

1. When using a puller to remove a bearing from a shaft, make sure the shaft does not get damaged. Always place a piece of metal between the end of the shaft and the puller screw. In addition, place the puller arms next to the inner bearing race (**Figure 45**).
2. When using a hammer to remove a bearing from a shaft, do not strike the hammer directly against the shaft. Instead, use a brass or aluminum rod between the hammer and shaft (**Figure 46**) and make sure to support both bearing races with wooden blocks as shown.
3. The ideal method of bearing removal is with a hydraulic press. Note the following when using a press:
   a. Always support the inner and outer bearing races with a suitable size wooden or aluminum ring (**Figure 47**). If only the outer race is supported, pressure applied against the balls and/or the inner race will damage them.
   b. Always make sure the press arm (**Figure 47**) aligns with the center of the shaft. If the arm is not centered, it may damage the bearing and/or shaft.
   c. The moment the shaft is free of the bearing, it will drop to the floor. Secure or hold the shaft to prevent it from falling.

Installation

1. When installing a bearing in a housing, apply pressure to the *outer* bearing race (**Figure 48**). When installing a bearing on a shaft, apply pressure to the *inner* bearing race (**Figure 49**).

2. When installing a bearing as described in Step 1, some type of driver is required. Never strike the bearing directly with a hammer or the bearing will be damaged. When installing a bearing, use a piece of pipe or a driver with a diameter that matches the bearing inner race. **Figure 50** shows the correct way to use a driver and hammer to install a bearing.

3. Step 1 describes how to install a bearing in a housing or over a shaft. However, when installing a bearing over a shaft and into the housing at the same time, a tight fit is required for both outer and inner bearing races. In this situation, install a spacer underneath the driver tool so that pressure is applied evenly across both races (**Figure 51**). If the outer race is not supported as shown, the balls will push against the outer bearing race and damage it.

50

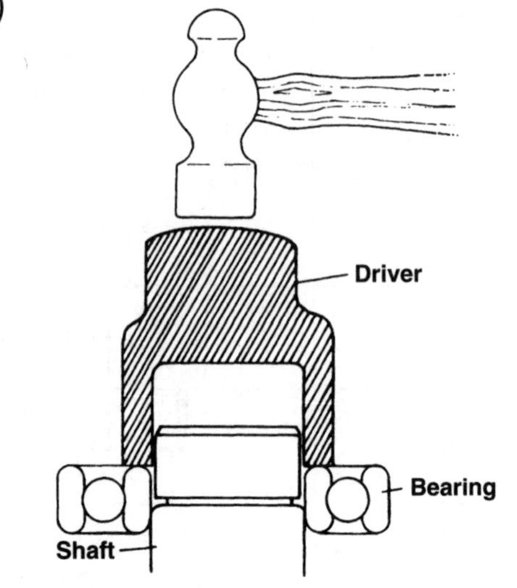

Interference fit

1. Follow this procedure when installing a bearing over a shaft. When a tight fit is required, the bearing inside diameter will be smaller than the shaft. In this case, driving the bearing on the shaft using normal methods may cause bearing damage. Instead, heat the bearing before installation. Note the following:
   a. Secure the shaft so it is ready for bearing installation.
   b. Clean all residues from the bearing surface of the shaft. Remove burrs with a file or sandpaper.
   c. Fill a suitable pot or beaker with clean mineral oil. Place a thermometer rated above 248° F (120° C) in the oil. Support the thermometer so it does not rest on the bottom or side of the pot.
   d. Remove the bearing from its wrapper and secure it with a piece of heavy wire bent to hold it in the pot. Hang the bearing in the pot so it does not touch the bottom or sides of the pot.
   e. Turn the heat on and monitor the thermometer. When the oil temperature rises to approximately 248° F (120° C), remove the bearing from the pot and quickly install it. If necessary, place a socket on the inner bearing race and tap the bearing into place. As the bearing chills, it will tighten on the shaft, so install it quickly. Make sure the bearing is installed completely.

2. Follow this step when installing a bearing in a housing. Bearings are generally installed in a housing with a slight interference fit. Driving the bearing into the housing using normal methods may damage the housing or bearing. Instead, heat the housing before installing the bearing. Note the following:

51

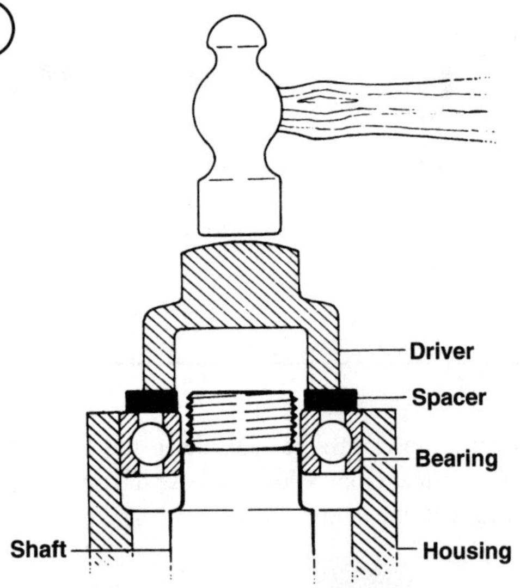

CAUTION

Before heating the housing in this procedure, wash the housing thoroughly with detergent and water. Rinse and rewash the housing as required to remove all traces of oil and other chemical deposits.

   a. Heat the housing to approximately 212° F (100° C) in an oven or on a hot plate. An easy way to check that it is the proper temperature is to place tiny drops of water on the housing; if they sizzle and evaporate immediately, the temperature is correct. Heat only one housing at a time.

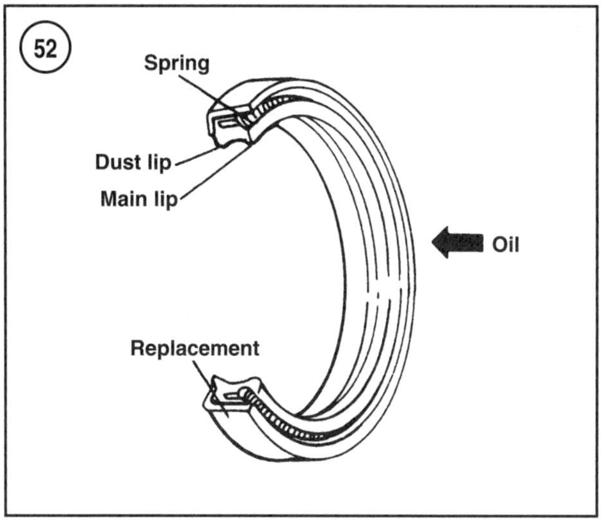

CAUTION

Do not heat the housing with a propane or acetylene torch. Never bring a flame into contact with the bearing or housing. The direct heat will destroy the case hardening of the bearing and will likely warp the housing.

b. Remove the housing from the oven or hot plate, and hold onto the housing with a kitchen potholder, heavy gloves or heavy shop cloth.

c. Hold the housing with the bearing side down and tap the bearing out. Repeat for all bearings in the housing. Remove and install the bearings with a suitable size socket and extension.

d. Before heating the bearing housing, place the new bearing(s) in a freezer if possible. Chilling a bearing slightly reduces its outside diameter while the heated bearing housing assembly is slightly larger due to heat expansion. This will make bearing installation easier.

NOTE

Unless noted otherwise, install bearings with the manufacturer's mark or number facing out.

e. While the housing is still hot, install the new bearing(s) into the housing. Install the bearings by hand, if possible. If necessary, lightly tap the bearing(s) into the housing with a socket placed on the outer bearing race (**Figure 48**). Do not install new bearings by driving on the inner-bearing race. Install the bearing(s) until it seats completely.

Seal Replacement

Seals (**Figure 52**) are used to contain oil, water, grease or combustion gasses in a housing or shaft. Improper removal of a seal can damage the housing or shaft. Improper installation of the seal can damage the seal. Note the following:

1. Prying is generally the easiest and most effective method of removing a seal from the housing. However, always place a rag underneath the pry tool (**Figure 53**) to prevent damage to the housing.
2. Pack waterproof grease in the seal lips before installing the seal.
3. In most cases, install seals with the manufacturer's numbers or marks face out.
4. Install seals with a socket placed on the outside of the seal as shown in **Figure 54**. Drive the seal squarely into the housing until it is flush. Never install a seal by hitting against the top of the seal with a hammer.

STORAGE

Several months of non-use can cause a general deterioration of the motorcycle. This is especially true in areas of extreme temperature variations. This deterioration can be minimized with careful preparation for storage. A properly stored motorcycle is much easier to return to service.

Storage Area Selection

When selecting a storage area, consider the following:

1. The storage area must be dry. A heated area is best, but not necessary. It should be insulated to minimize extreme temperature variations.
2. If the building has large window areas, mask them to keep sunlight off the motorcycle.
3. Avoid buildings in industrial areas where corrosive emissions may be present. Avoid areas close to saltwater.
4. Consider the area's risk of fire, theft or vandalism. Check with your insurer regarding motorcycle coverage while in storage.

Preparing the Motorcycle for Storage

The amount of motorcycle preparation before storage depends on the expected length of non-use, storage area conditions and personal preference. Consider the following list the minimum requirement:

1. Wash the motorcycle thoroughly. Make sure all dirt, mud and road debris are removed.
2. Start the engine and allow it to reach operating temperature. Drain the engine oil and transmission oil, regardless of the riding time since the last service. Fill the engine and transmission with the recommended type of oil.
3. Drain all fuel from the fuel tank. Run the engine until all the fuel is consumed from the lines and carburetor.
4. Drain the fuel from the carburetor as follows:
   a. Remove the fuel tank as described in Chapter Eight
   b. Open the drain screw and thoroughly drain the fuel from the float bowl into a suitable container.
   c. Move the choke knob to the full open position.
   d. Operate the start button and try to start the engine. This will draw out all remaining fuel from the jets.
5. Remove the spark plugs and pour a teaspoon of engine oil into the cylinders. Place a rag over the openings and slowly turn the engine over to distribute the oil. Reinstall the spark plugs.
6. Remove the battery. Store the battery in a cool and dry location.
7. Cover the exhaust and intake openings.
8. Apply a protective substance to the plastic and rubber components, including the tires. Make sure to follow the manufacturer's instructions for each type of product being used.
9. Place the motorcycle on a stand or wooden blocks, so the wheels are off the ground. If this is not possible, place a piece of plywood between the tires and the ground. Inflate the tires to the recommended pressure if the motorcycle cannot be elevated.
10. Cover the motorcycle with old bed sheets or something similar. Do not cover it with any plastic material that will trap moisture.

Returning the Motorcycle to Service

The amount of service required when returning a motorcycle to service after storage depends on the length of non-use and storage conditions. In addition to performing the reverse of the above procedure, make sure the brakes, clutch, throttle and engine stop switch work properly before operating the motorcycle. Refer to Chapter Three and evaluate the service intervals to determine which areas require service.

Table 1 MOTORCYCLE DIMENSIONS

Overall length	
XL883, XL883L, XL883R, XL1200R	**90.1 in. (2288 mm)**
XL883C, XL1200C, XL1200L	**90.3 in. (2294 mm)**
Overall width	
XL883, XL883C, XL883L, XL883R, XL1200C	**32.7 in. (831 mm)**
XL1200R	**36.7 in. (932 mm)**

(continued)

Table 1 MOTORCYCLE DIMENSIONS (continued)

Overall height	
XL883, XL883L, XL883R	44.8 in. (1138 mm)
XL883C, XL1200C	45.7 in. (1161 mm)
XL1200R	49.2 in. (1250 mm)
Wheelbase	
XL883, XL883L, XL883R, XL1200L, XL1200R	60.0 in. (1524 mm)
XL883C, XL1200C	60.4 in. (1534 mm)
Seat height	
XL883	27.3 in. (693 mm)
XL883C, XL1200C	26.5 in. (673 mm)
XL883L	26.0 in. (660 mm)
XL1200L	26.25 in. (667 mm)
XL883R, XL1200R	28.1 in. (714 mm)
Ground clearance	
XL883, XL883R, XL1200R	5.6 in. (142 mm)
XL883C, XL883L, XL1200C, XL1200L	4.4 in. (112 mm)

Table 2 MOTORCYCLE WEIGHT

Dry weight	
XL883, XL883L, XL1200R	553 lb. (250 kg)
XL883C, XL1200C	562 lb. (255 kg)
XL883R	560 lb. (254 kg)
XL1200L	554 lb. (251 kg)
Maximum load capacity	1000 lb. (453.6 kg)

Table 3 FUEL TANK CAPACITY

Total	
XL883, XL883L, XL883R, XL1200R	3.3 gal. (12.5 L)
XL883C, XL1200C, XL1200L	4.5 gal. (17.0 L)
Reserve	
XL883, XL883L, XL883R, XL1200R	0.8 gal. (3.0 L)
XL883C, XL1200C, XL1200L	1.0 gal. (3.8 L)

Table 4 GENERAL TORQUE SPECIFICATIONS (ft.-lb.)[1]

Size/Grade[2]	1/4	5/16	3/8	7/16	1/2	9/16	5/8	3/4	7/8	1
SAE 2	6	12	20	32	47	69	96	155	206	310
SAE 5	10	19	33	54	78	114	154	257	382	587

(continued)

Table 4 GENERAL TORQUE SPECIFICATIONS (ft.-lb.)[1] (continued)

Size/Grade[2]	1/4	5/16	3/8	7/16	1/2	9/16	5/8	3/4	7/8	1
SAE 7	13	25	44	71	110	154	215	360	570	840
SAE 8	14	29	47	78	119	169	230	380	600	700

1. Convert ft.-lb. specification to N•m by multiplying by 1.3558.
2. Fastener strength of SAE bolts can be determined by the bolt head grade markings. Unmarked bolt heads and cap screws are usually mild steel. More grade markings indicate higher fastener strength.

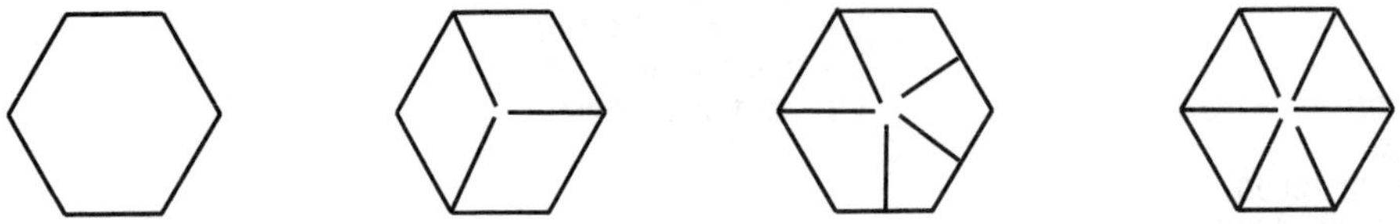
SAE 2 SAE 5 SAE 7 SAE 8

Table 5 CONVERSION FORMULAS

Multiply:	By:	To get the equivalent of:
Length		
Inches	25.4	Millimeter
Inches	2.54	Centimeter
Miles	1.609	Kilometer
Feet	0.3048	Meter
Millimeter	0.03937	Inches
Centimeter	0.3937	Inches
Kilometer	0.6214	Mile
Meter	3.281	Feet
Fluid volume		
U.S. quarts	0.9463	Liters
U.S. gallons	3.785	Liters
U.S. ounces	29.573529	Milliliters
Imperial gallons	4.54609	Liters
Imperial quarts	1.1365	Liters
Liters	0.2641721	U.S. gallons
Liters	1.0566882	U.S. quarts
Liters	33.814023	U.S. ounces
Liters	0.22	Imperial gallons
Liters	0.8799	Imperial quarts
Milliliters	1.0	Cubic centimeters
Milliliters	0.001	Liters
Milliliters	0.033814	U.S. ounces

(continued)

Table 5 CONVERSION FORMULAS (continued)

Multiply:	By:	To get the equivalent of:
Torque		
Foot-pounds	1.3558	Newton-meters
Foot-pounds	0.138255	Meters-kilograms
Inch-pounds	0.11299	Newton-meters
Newton-meters	0.7375622	Foot-pounds
Newton-meters	8.8507	Inch-pounds
Meters-kilograms	7.2330139	Foot-pounds
Volume		
Cubic inches	16.387064	Cubic centimeters
Cubic centimeters	0.0610237	Cubic inches
Temperature		
Fahrenheit	(°F – 32) × 0.556	Centigrade
Centigrade	(°C × 1.8) + 32	Fahrenheit
Weight		
Ounces	28.3495	Grams
Pounds	0.4535924	Kilograms
Grams	0.035274	Ounces
Kilograms	2.2046224	Pounds
Pressure		
Pounds per square inch	0.070307	Kilograms per square centimeter
Kilograms per square centimeter	14.223343	Pounds per square inch
Kilopascals	0.1450	Pounds per square inch
Pounds per square inch	6.895	Kilopascals
Speed		
Miles per hour	1.609344	Kilometers per hour
Kilometers per hour	0.6213712	Miles per hour

Table 6 TECHNICAL ABBREVIATIONS

A	Ampere
ABDC	After bottom dead center
AC	Alternating current
A•h	Ampere hour
ATDC	After top dead center
BAS	Bank angle sensor
BBDC	Before bottom dead center
BDC	Bottom dead center
BTDC	Before top dead center
C	Celsius
cc	Cubic centimeter
CDI	Capacitor discharge ignition
CKP	Crankshaft position sensor
cm	Centimeter

(continued)

Table 6 TECHNICAL ABBREVIATIONS (continued)

cu. in.	Cubic inch and cubic inches
cyl.	Cylinder
DTC	Diagnostic trouble code
DC	Direct current
F	Fahrenheit
fl. oz.	Fluid ounces
ft.	Foot
ft.-lb.	Foot pounds
gal.	Gallon and gallons
hp	Horsepower
Hz	Hertz
ICM	Ignition control module
in.	Inch and inches
in.-lb.	Inch-pounds
in. Hg	Inches of mercury
kg	Kilogram
kg/cm^2	Kilogram per square centimeter
kgm	Kilogram meter
km	Kilometer
km/h	Kilometer per hour
kPa	Kilopascals
kW	Kilowatt
L	Liter and liters
L/m	Liters per minute
lb.	Pound and pounds
m	Meter
mL	Milliliter
mm	Millimeter
MAP	Manifold absolute pressure sensor
MPa	Megapascal
N	Newton
N•m	Newton meter
oz.	Ounce and ounces
p	Pascal
psi	Pounds per square inch
pt.	Pint and pints
qt.	Quart and quarts
rpm	Revolution per minute
TSM/TSSM	Turn signal module/Turn signal security module
V	Volt
VAC	Alternating current voltage
VDC	Direct current voltage
W	Watt

*Add model/manual specific abbreviations as needed.

Table 7 U.S. TAP AND DRILL SIZES

Tap thread	Drill size	Tap thread	Drill size
#0-80	3/64	1/4-28	No. 3
#1-64	No. 53	5/16-18	F

(continued)

Table 7 U.S. TAP AND DRILL SIZES (continued)

Tap thread	Drill size	Tap thread	Drill size
#1-72	No. 53	5/16-24	I
#2-56	No. 51	3/8-16	5/16
#2-64	No. 50	3/8-24	Q
#3-48	5/64	7/16-14	U
#3-56	No. 46	7/16-20	W
#4-40	No. 43	1/2-13	27/64
#4-48	No. 42	1/2-20	29/64
#5-40	No. 39	9/16-12	31/64
#5-44	No. 37	9/16-18	33/64
#6-32	No. 36	5/8-11	17/32
#6-40	No. 33	5/18-18	37/64
#8-32	No. 29	3/4-10	21/32
#8-36	No. 29	3/4-16	11/16
#10-24	No. 25	7/8-9	49/64
#10-32	No. 21	7/8-14	13/16
#12-24	No. 17	1-8	7/8
#12-28	No. 15	1-14	15/16
1/4-20	No. 8		

Table 8 METRIC TAP AND DRILL SIZES

Metric size	Drill equivalent	Decimal fraction	Nearest fraction
3 × 0.50	No. 39	0.0995	3/32
3 × 0.60	3/32	0.0937	3/32
4 × 0.70	No. 30	0.1285	1/8
4 × 0.75	1/8	0.125	1/8
5 × 0.80	No. 19	0.166	11/64
5 × 0.90	No. 20	0.161	5/32
6 × 1.00	No. 9	0.196	13/64
7 × 1.00	16/64	0.234	15/64
8 × 1.00	J	0.277	9/32
8 × 1.25	17/64	0.265	17/64
9 × 1.00	5/16	0.3125	5/16
9 × 1.25	5/16	0.3125	5/16
10 × 1.25	11/32	0.3437	11/32
10 × 1.50	R	0.339	11/32
11 × 1.50	3/8	0.375	3/8
12 × 1.50	13/32	0.406	13/32
12 × 1.75	13/32	0.406	13/32

Table 9 FRACTIONAL, DECIMAL AND METRIC EQUIVALENTS

Fractions	Decimal in.	Metric mm	Fractions	Decimal in.	Metric mm
1/64	0.015625	0.39688	33/64	0.515625	13.09687
1/32	0.03125	0.79375	17/32	0.53125	13.49375
3/64	0.046875	1.19062	35/64	0.546875	13.89062
1/16	0.0625	1.58750	9/16	0.5625	14.28750
5/64	0.078125	1.98437	37/64	0.578125	14.68437
3/32	0.09375	2.38125	19/32	0.59375	15.08125
7/64	0.109375	2.77812	39/64	0.609375	15.47812
1/8	0.125	3.1750	5/8	0.625	15.87500
9/64	0.140625	3.57187	41/64	0.640625	16.27187
5/32	0.15625	3.96875	21/32	0.65625	16.66875
11/64	0.171875	4.36562	43/64	0.671875	17.06562
3/16	0.1875	4.76250	11/16	0.6875	17.46250
13/64	0.203125	5.15937	45/64	0.703125	17.85937
7/32	0.21875	5.55625	23/32	0.71875	18.25625
15/64	0.234375	5.95312	47/64	0.734375	18.65312
1/4	0.250	6.35000	3/4	0.750	19.05000
17/64	0.265625	6.74687	49/64	0.765625	19.44687
9/32	0.28125	7.14375	25/32	0.78125	19.84375
19/64	0.296875	7.54062	51/64	0.796875	20.24062
5/16	0.3125	7.93750	13/16	0.8125	20.63750
21/64	0.328125	8.33437	53/64	0.828125	21.03437
11/32	0.34375	8.73125	27/32	0.84375	21.43125
23/64	0.359375	9.12812	55/64	0.859375	22.82812
3/8	0.375	9.52500	7/8	0.875	22.22500
25/64	0.390625	9.92187	57/64	0.890625	22.62187
13/32	0.40625	10.31875	29/32	0.90625	23.01875
27/64	0.421875	10.71562	59/64	0.921875	23.41562
7/16	0.4375	11.11250	15/16	0.9375	23.81250
29/64	0.453125	11.50937	61/64	0.953125	24.20937
15/32	0.46875	11.90625	31/32	0.96875	24.60625
31/64	0.484375	12.30312	63/64	0.984375	25.00312
1/2	0.500	12.70000	1	1.00	25.40000

Table 10 SPECIAL TOOLS

Tool description	Part No.	Manufacturer
Belt tension gauge	HD-35381-A	H-D
Breakout box	HD-42682	H-D
Breakout box adapters	HD-46601	H-D
Bushing reamer tool	1726-2	JIMS
Clutch spring compression tool	HD-38515A	H-D
Connecting rod bushing hone	HD-42569	H-D
Connecting rod bushing tool	95970-32C	JIMS
Connecting rod clamp tool	1284	JIMS
Connector terminal pick	HD-39621-28	H-D
Connector terminal tool	HD-45928	H-D
Crankshaft locking tool	1665	JIMS
Crankshaft roller bearing pilot/driver	B-45655	H-D
Crankshaft roller bearing support tube	HD-42720-2	H-D
Fork seal driver	HD-36583	H-D
Fuel injector test lamp	HD-34730-2C	H-D
Hose clamp pliers	HD-97087-65B	H-D
Ignition coil circuit test adapter	HD-44687	H-D

(continued)

Table 10 SPECIAL TOOLS (continued)

Tool description	Part No.	Manufacturer
Main bearing removal/installation adapter	HD-46663	H-D
Main drive gear needle bearing installation tool		
2004-2005	HD-37842-A	H-D
2006-on	HD-47855	H-D
Main drive gear remover and installer		
2004-2005	HD-35316-B	H-D
2006-on	HD-35316-C	H-D
Main drive gear seal installer		
2004-2005	HD-41496	H-D
2006-on	HD-47856	H-D
Neway valve seat cutter set	HD-35758-B	H-D
Rocker arm bushing reamer	HD-94804-57	H-D
Speedometer tester	HD-41354	H-D
Sprocket holding tool	HD-46282	H-D
Sprocket locking link	HD-38362/HD-46283	H-D
Steering head bearing race installation tool	HD-39302	H-D
Transmission assembly fixture	HD-46285	H-D
Transmission cross plate	B-45847	H-D
Transmission detent lever tool	B-45520	H-D
Valve guide brush	HD-34751	H-D

NOTE: Refer to the Supplement at the end of this manual for information unique to 2007-2011 models.

CHAPTER TWO

TROUBLESHOOTING

Begin any troubleshooting procedure by defining the symptoms as precisely as possible. Gather as much information as possible to aid diagnosis. Never assume anything and do not overlook the obvious. Make sure there is fuel in the tank, and the fuel valve is in the on position. Make sure the engine stop switch is in the run position and the spark plug wires are attached to the spark plugs.

If a quick check does not reveal the problem, turn to the troubleshooting procedures described in this chapter. Identify the procedure that most closely describes the symptoms, and perform the indicated tests.

In most cases, expensive and complicated test equipment is not needed to determine whether repairs can be performed at home. A few simple checks could prevent an unnecessary repair charge. On the other hand, be realistic and do not attempt repairs beyond your capabilities. Many service departments will not take work that involves the assembly of damaged or abused equipment. If they do, expect the cost to be high.

Refer to **Tables 1-3**, at the end of this chapter, for electrical specifications and diagnostic trouble codes.

ENGINE OPERATING REQUIREMENTS

An engine needs three basics to run properly: correct air/fuel mixture, compression and a spark at the right time. If one basic requirement is missing, the engine will not run. Refer to **Figure 1** for four-stroke engine operating principles.

ENGINE STARTING

Engine Fails to Start (Spark Test)

Perform the following spark test to determine if the ignition system is operating properly:

CAUTION

Before removing the spark plugs in Step 1, clean all dirt and debris away from the plug base. Dirt that falls into the cylinder causes rapid engine wear.

1. Disconnect the spark plug wire and remove the spark plug as described in Chapter Three.

NOTE

A spark tester is a useful tool for testing spark output. ***Figure 2*** *shows the Motion Pro Ignition System Tester (part No. 08-0122). This tool is inserted in the spark plug cap and its base is grounded against the cylinder head. The tool's air gap is adjustable, and it allows the visual inspection*

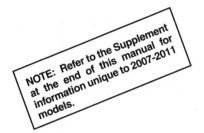

(1)

FOUR-STROKE ENGINE OPERATING PRINCIPLES

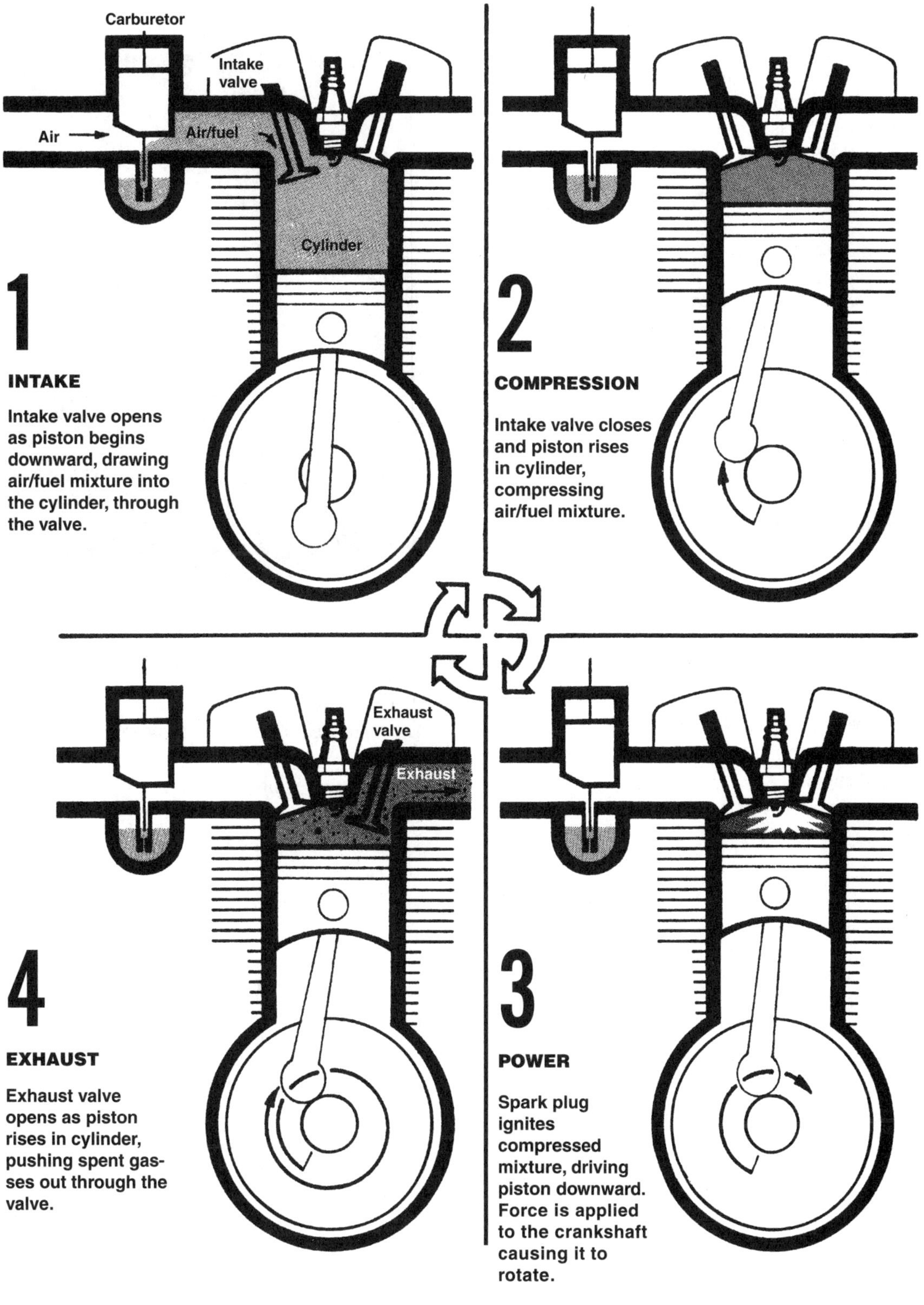

Carburetor
Intake valve
Air
Air/fuel
Cylinder
1
INTAKE
Intake valve opens as piston begins downward, drawing air/fuel mixture into the cylinder, through the valve.
2
COMPRESSION
Intake valve closes and piston rises in cylinder, compressing air/fuel mixture.
Exhaust valve
Exhaust
4
EXHAUST
Exhaust valve opens as piston rises in cylinder, pushing spent gasses out through the valve.
3
POWER
Spark plug ignites compressed mixture, driving piston downward. Force is applied to the crankshaft causing it to rotate.

of the spark. This tool is available at motorcycle repair shops.

2. Cover the spark plug hole with a clean shop cloth to reduce the chance of gasoline vapors being emitted from the hole.
3. Insert the spark plug (**Figure 3**), or spark tester (**Figure 4**), into its plug cap and ground the spark plug base against the cylinder head. Position the spark plug so the electrode is visible.

WARNING
Mount the spark plug, or tester, away from the spark plug hole in the cylinder so the spark plug or tester cannot ignite the gasoline vapors in the cylinder. If the engine is flooded, do not perform this test. The firing of the spark plug can ignite fuel that is ejected through the spark plug hole.

4. Turn the ignition switch on.

WARNING
Do not hold the spark plug, wire or connector, or a serious electrical shock may result.

5. Turn the engine over with the starter. A crisp blue spark should be evident across the spark plug electrode or spark tester terminals. If there is strong sunlight on the plug, shade the plug to better see the spark.
6. If the spark is good, check for one or more of the following possible malfunctions:
   a. Obstructed fuel line or fuel filter.
   b. Low compression or engine damage.
   c. Flooded engine.
   d. Incorrect ignition timing.

NOTE
If the engine backfires during starting, the ignition timing may be incorrect due to a defective ignition component.

7. If the spark is weak or if there is no spark, refer to *Engine is Difficult to Start* in this section.

Engine is Difficult to Start

Check for one or more of the following possible malfunctions:
1. Fouled spark plug(s).
2. Improperly adjusted enrichment valve.
3. Intake manifold air leak.
4. Plugged fuel tank filler cap.
5. Clogged fuel line.
6. Contaminated fuel system.

2

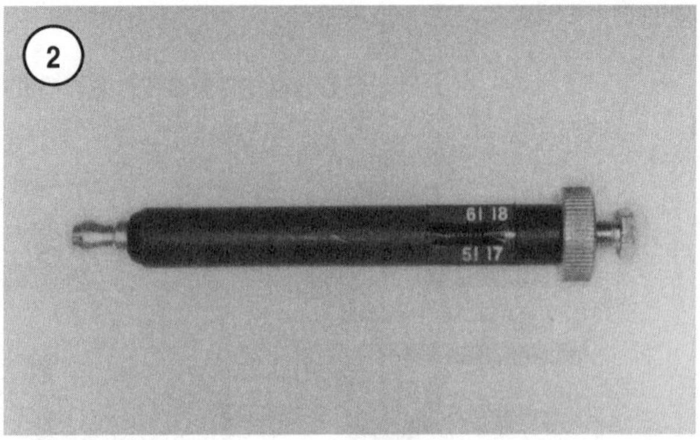

3

7. Improperly adjusted carburetor.
8. Defective ignition module.
9. Defective ignition coil.
10. Damaged ignition coil primary and/or secondary wires.
11. Incorrect ignition timing.
12. Low engine compression.
13. Discharged battery.
14. Defective starter.
15. Loose or corroded starter and/or battery cables.
16. Loose ignition sensor and module electrical connector.
17. Incorrect pushrod length (intake and exhaust valve pushrods interchanged).

Engine Does Not Crank

Check for one or more of the following possible malfunctions:
1. Ignition switch turned off.
2. Faulty ignition switch.
3. Engine run switch in off position.
4. Defective engine run switch.
5. Blown Maxi-fuse.

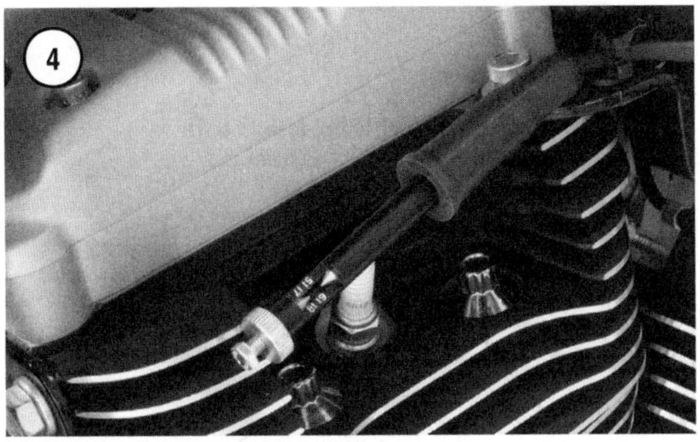

6. Loose or corroded starter and battery cables (solenoid chatters).
7. Discharged or defective battery.
8. Defective starter.
9. Defective starter solenoid.
10. Defective starter shaft pinion gear.
11. Slipping overrunning clutch assembly.
12. Seized piston(s).
13. Seized crankshaft bearings.
14. Broken connecting rod.

ENGINE PERFORMANCE

If the engine runs, but is not operating at peak performance, refer to the following as a starting point from which to isolate a performance malfunction.

Spark Plugs Fouled

1. Severely contaminated air filter element.
2. Incorrect spark plug heat range. Refer to Chapter Three.
3. Rich fuel mixture.
4. Worn or damaged piston rings.
5. Worn or damaged valve guide oil seals.
6. Excessive valve stem-to-guide clearance.
7. Incorrect carburetor float level.

Engine Misfire

1. Fouled or improper spark plug gap.
2. Damaged spark plug cables.
3. Incorrect ignition timing.
4. Defective ignition components.
5. Obstructed fuel line or fuel shutoff valve.
6. Obstructed fuel filter.
7. Clogged carburetor jets.
8. Loose battery connection.
9. Wiring or connector damage.
10. Water or other contaminates in the fuel.
11. Weak or damaged valve springs.
12. Incorrect camshaft/valve timing.
13. Damaged valve(s).
14. Dirty electrical connections.
15. Intake manifold or carburetor air leak.
16. Plugged carburetor vent hose.
17. Plugged fuel tank vent system.

Engine Overheating

1. Incorrect carburetor adjustment or jet selection.
2. Incorrect ignition timing or defective ignition system components.
3. Improper spark plug heat range. Refer to Chapter Three.
4. Damaged or blocked cooling fins.
5. Low oil level.
6. Oil not circulating properly.
7. Leaking valves.
8. Heavy combustion chamber carbon deposits.

Engine Runs Rough with Excessive Exhaust Smoke

1. Clogged air filter element.
2. Rich carburetor adjustment.
3. Choke not operating correctly.
4. Water or other fuel contaminants.
5. Clogged fuel line and/or filter.
6. Spark plug(s) fouled.
7. Defective ignition coil.
8. Defective ignition module or sensor(s).
9. Loose or defective ignition circuit wire.
10. Short circuits from damaged wire insulation.
11. Loose battery cable connections.
12. Incorrect camshaft/valve timing.
13. Intake manifold or air filter air leak.

Engine Lacks Power

1. Incorrect carburetor adjustment.
2. Clogged fuel line.
3. Incorrect ignition timing.
4. Dragging brake(s).
5. Engine overheating.
6. Incorrect ignition timing.
7. Incorrect spark plug gap.

Valve Train Noise

1. Bent pushrod(s).
2. Defective hydraulic lifter(s).
3. Bent valve(s).
4. Rocker arm seizure or damage (binding on shaft).
5. Worn or damaged camshaft gear bushing(s).
6. Worn or damaged camshaft gear(s).

STARTING SYSTEM

The starting system consists of the battery, starter, starter relay, solenoid, start button, and related wiring.

When the ignition switch is turned on and the start button is pushed in, current is transmitted from the battery to the starter relay. When the relay is activated, it activates the starter solenoid that mechanically engages the starter with the engine.

Starting system problems are most often related to a loose or corroded electrical connection.

Refer to **Figure 5** for starter and solenoid terminal identification.

Troubleshooting Preparation

Before troubleshooting the starting system, check for the following:

1. The battery is fully charged.
2. Battery cables are the proper size and length. Replace damaged or undersized cables.
3. All electrical connections are clean and tight. High resistance caused from dirty or loose connectors can affect voltage and current levels.
4. The wiring harness is in good condition, with no worn or frayed insulation or loose harness sockets.
5. The fuel tank is filled with an adequate supply of fresh gasoline.
6. The spark plugs are in good condition and properly gapped.
7. The ignition system is working correctly.

Voltage Drop Test

Prior to performing procedures in the *Starter Testing* section, perform a voltage drop test.

1. To check voltage drop in the solenoid circuit, connect the positive voltmeter lead to the positive battery terminal. Connect the negative voltmeter lead to the solenoid terminal (**Figure 6**).
2. Turn the ignition switch on and push the starter button while reading the voltmeter scale. Note the following:

5

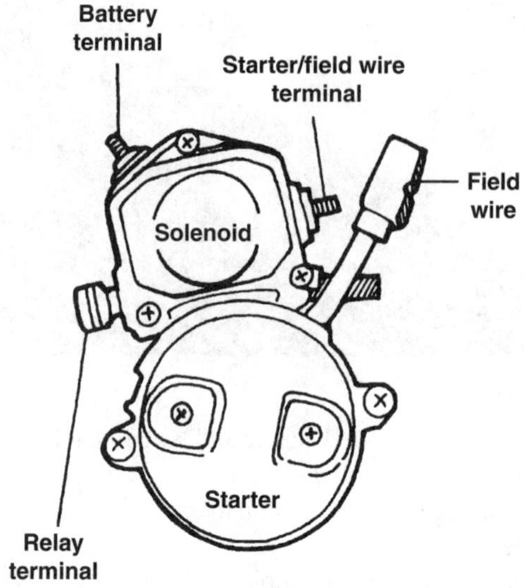

6

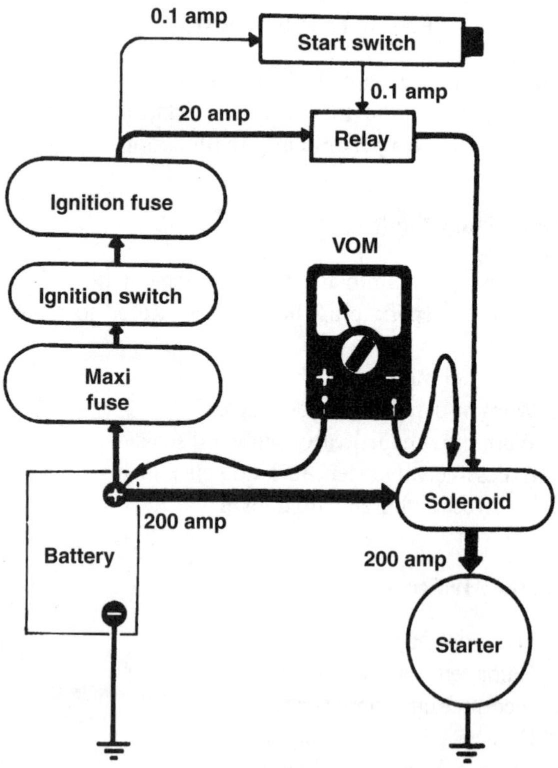

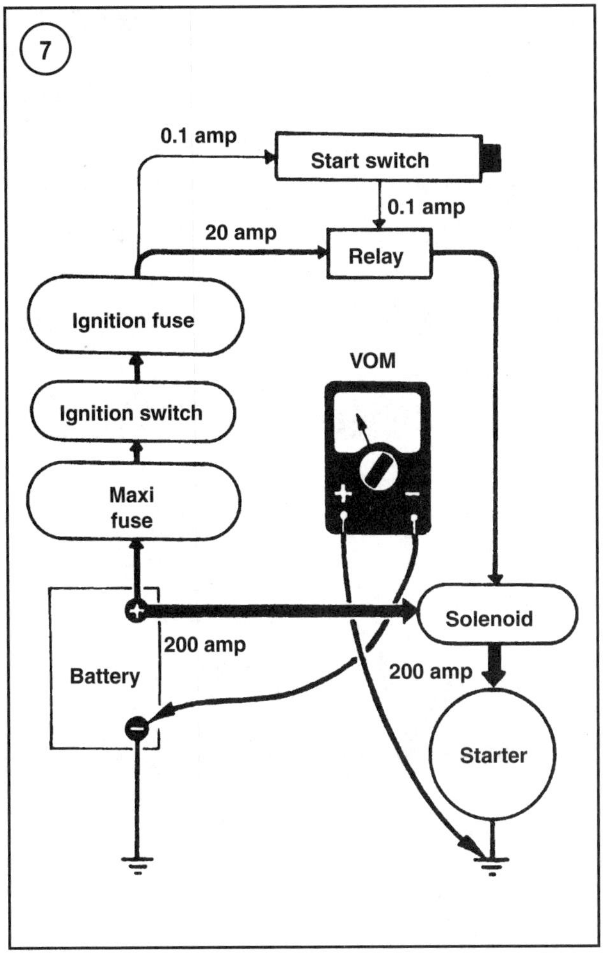

a. The circuit is operating correctly if the voltmeter reading is 1.0 volt or less. A voltmeter reading of 12 volts indicates an open circuit.

b. A voltage drop of more than 1.0 volt indicates a problem in the solenoid circuit.

c. If the voltage drop reading is correct, continue with Step 3.

3. To check the starter ground circuit, connect the negative voltmeter lead to the negative battery terminal. Connect the positive voltmeter lead to the starter housing (**Figure 7**).

4. Turn the ignition switch on and push the starter button while reading the voltmeter scale. The voltage drop must not exceed 0.2 volt. If it does, check the ground connections between the meter leads.

5. If the problem is not found, refer to the *Starter Testing* section.

NOTE
Step 3 and Step 4 check the voltage drop across the starter ground circuit. To check any ground circuit in the starting circuit, repeat this test and leave the negative voltmeter lead connected to the battery and connect the positive voltmeter lead to the ground in question.

Starter Testing

CAUTION
Never operate the starter for more than 30 seconds at a time. Allow the starter to cool before reusing it. Failing to allow the starter to cool after continual starting attempts can damage the starter.

The basic starter-related troubles are:

1. Starter does not spin.
2. Starter spins but does not engage.
3. The starter does not disengage after the start button is released.
4. Loud grinding noises when starter turns.
5. Starter stalls or spins too slowly.

Starter does not spin

1. Turn the ignition switch on and push the starter button while listening for a click at the starter relay. Turn the ignition switch off and note the following:

a. If the starter relay clicks, test the starter relay as described in this section. If the starter relay test readings are correct, continue with Step 2.

b. If the solenoid clicks, go to Step 3.

c. If there was no click, go to Step 5.

2. Check the wiring connectors between the starter relay and solenoid. Note the following:

a. Repair any dirty, loose-fitting or damaged connectors or wiring.

b. If the wiring is in good condition, remove the starter as described in Chapter Nine. Perform the solenoid and starter bench tests as described in this section.

3. Perform a voltage drop test between the battery and solenoid terminals as described in *Voltage Drop Test* in this section. The normal voltage drop is less than 1.0 volt. Note the following:

a. If the voltage drop is less than 1.0 volt, perform Step 4.

b. If the voltage drop is more than 1.0 volt, check the solenoid and battery wires and connections for dirty or loose fitting terminals; clean and repair as required.

4. Remove the starter as described in Chapter Nine. Momentarily connect a fully charged 12-volt battery to the

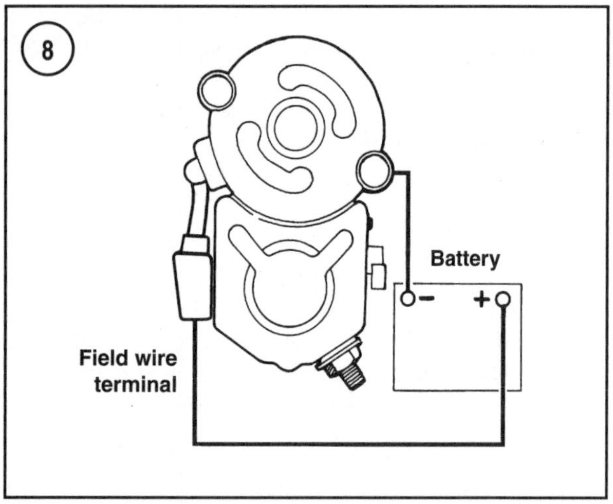

starter as shown in **Figure 8**. If the starter is operational, it will turn when connected to the battery. Disconnect the battery and note the following:

a. If the starter turns, perform the solenoid pull-in and hold-in tests as described in *Solenoid Testing (Bench Tests)* in this section.

b. If the starter does not turn, disassemble the starter as described in Chapter Nine, and check it for opens, shorts and grounds.

5. If there is no click when performing Step 1, measure voltage between the starter button and the starter relay. The voltmeter must read battery voltage. Note the following:

a. If there is battery voltage, continue with Step 6.

b. If there is no voltage, go to Step 6.

6. Check for voltage at the starter button. Note the following:

a. If there is voltage at the starter button, test the starter relay as described in this section.

b. If there is no voltage at the starter button, check continuity across the starter button. If there is voltage leading to the starter button, but no voltage leaving the starter button, replace the button switch and retest. If there is no voltage leading to the starter button, check the starter button wiring for dirty or loose-fitting terminals or damaged wiring; clean and/or repair as required.

Starter spins but does not engage

If the starter spins but the pinion gear does not engage the clutch shell ring gear, perform the following:

1. Remove the primary drive cover as described in Chapter Six.

2. Check the starter pinion gear (A, **Figure 9**). If the teeth are chipped or worn, inspect the clutch shell ring gear (B, **Figure 9**) for the same problems. Note the following:

a. If the starter pinion gear or clutch ring gear is damaged, service the parts.

b. If the starter pinion gear and clutch shell ring gear are not damaged, continue with Step 3.

c. Make sure the pinion does not run in overrunning direction.

3. Remove and disassemble the starter as described in Chapter Nine. Then check the overrunning clutch assembly (**Figure 10** and **Figure 11**) components for wear and/or damage:

a. Rollers (**Figure 12**).

b. Compression spring (A, **Figure 13**).

c. Pinion teeth.

d. Clutch shaft splines (B, **Figure 13**).

4. Replace worn or damaged parts as required.

11

12

13

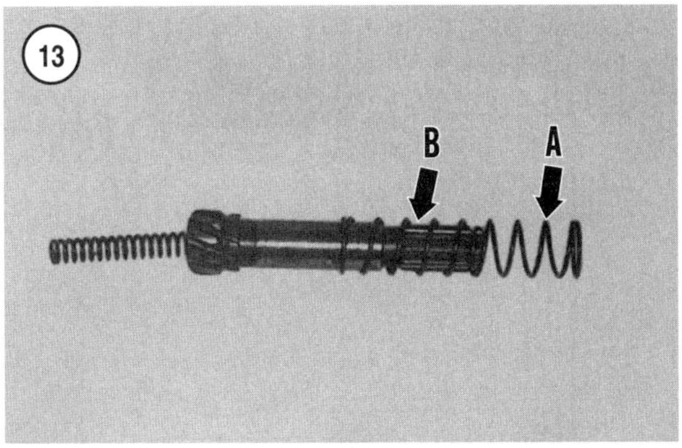

Starter does not disengage after releasing the start button

1. A sticking solenoid, caused by a worn solenoid compression spring (A, **Figure 13**), can cause this problem. Replace the solenoid if damaged.

2. On high-mileage motorcycles, the starter pinion gear (A, **Figure 9**) can jam on a worn clutch ring gear (B). Unable to return, the starter will continue to run. This condition usually requires ring gear replacement.

3. Check the start button switch and starter relay for internal damage. Test the start switch as described in Chapter Eight. Test the starter relay as described in this chapter.

Loud grinding noises when the starter turns

Incorrect starter pinion gear and clutch shell ring gear engagement (B, **Figure 9**) or a broken overrunning clutch mechanism (**Figure 11**) can cause this problem. Remove and inspect the starter as described in Chapter Nine.

Starter stalls or spins too slowly

1. Perform a voltage drop test between the battery and solenoid terminals as described under *Voltage Drop Test* in this section. The normal voltage drop is less than 1.0 volt. Note the following:
   a. If the voltage drop is less than 1.0 volt, continue with Step 2.
   b. If the voltage drop exceeds 1.0 volt, check the solenoid and battery wires and connections for dirty or loose-fitting terminals; clean and repair as required.
2. Perform a voltage drop test between the solenoid terminals and the starter. The normal voltage drop is less than 1.0 volt. Note the following:
   a. If the voltage drop is less than 1.0 volt, continue with Step 3.
   b. If the voltage drop exceeds 1.0 volt, check the solenoid and starter wires and connections for dirty or loose-fitting terminals; clean and repair as required.
3. Perform a voltage drop test between the battery ground wire and the starter as described under *Voltage Drop Test* in this section. The normal voltage drop is less than 0.2 volt. Note the following:
   a. If the voltage drop is less than 0.2 volt, continue with Step 4.
   b. If the voltage drop exceeds 0.2 volt, check the battery ground wire connections for dirty or loose-fitting terminals; clean and repair as required.
4. Refer to *Starter Current Draw Testing* in this section and perform the first test. Note the following:
   a. If the current draw is excessive, check for a damaged starter. Remove the starter as described in Chapter Nine and perform the second test.
   b. If the current draw reading is correct, continue with Step 5.
5. Remove the primary cover as described in Chapter Six. Check the starter pinion gear (A, **Figure 9**). If the teeth are chipped or worn, inspect the clutch ring gear (B, **Figure 9**) for the same problem.

a. If the starter pinion gear or clutch ring gear is damaged, service it.
b. If the starter pinion gear and clutch ring gear are not damaged, continue with Step 6.

6. Remove and disassemble the starter as described in Chapter Nine. Check the disassembled starter for opens, shorts and grounds.

Starter Current Draw Testing

A short circuit in the starter or a damaged pinion gear assembly can cause excessive current draw. If the current draw is low, suspect an undercharged battery or an open circuit in the starting circuit.

Refer to **Table 1** for current draw specifications.

Starter installed

This test requires a fully charged battery and an inductive ammeter.

1. Shift the transmission into neutral.
2. Disconnect the two spark plug caps from the spark plugs. Then ground the plug caps with two extra spark plugs. Do not remove the spark plugs from the cylinder heads.
3. Connect an inductive ammeter between the battery terminal and positive battery terminal (**Figure 14**). Connect a jumper cable from the negative battery terminal to ground.
4. Turn the ignition switch on and press the start button for approximately ten seconds. Note the ammeter reading.

NOTE
The current draw is high when the start button is first pressed, then it will drop and stabilize at a lower reading. Refer to the lower stabilized reading during this test.

5. If the current draw exceeds the specification in **Table 1**, check for a defective starter or starter drive mechanism. Remove and service these components as described in Chapter Nine.
6. Disconnect the ammeter and jumper cables.

14

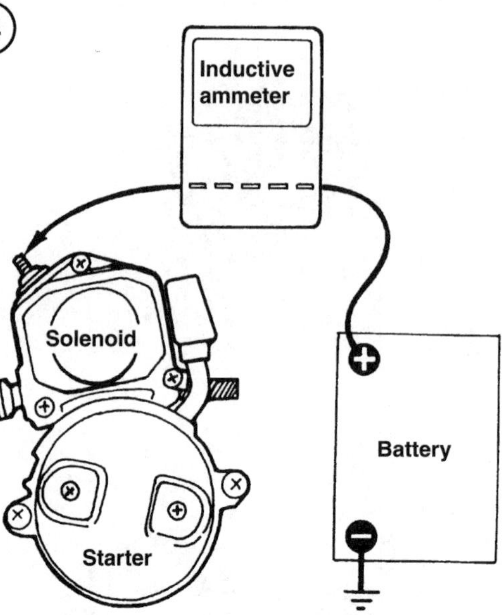

15

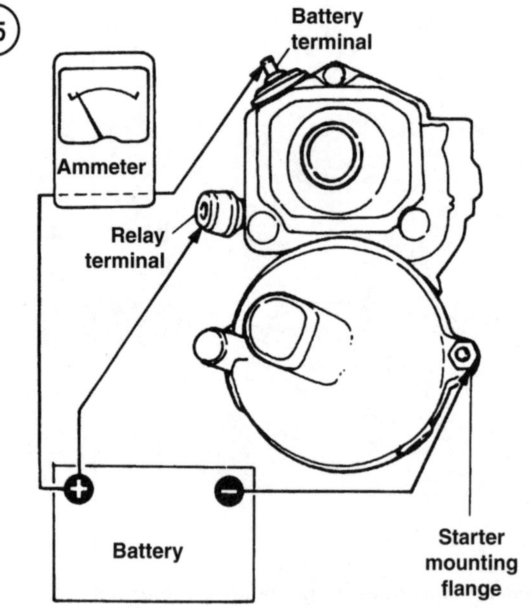

Starter removed

This test requires a fully charged 12-volt battery, an inductive ammeter, a jumper wire (14-gauge minimum) and three jumper cables (6-gauge minimum).

Refer to **Figure 15**.

1. Remove the starter as described in Chapter nine.

NOTE
The solenoid must be installed on the starter during the following tests.

2. Mount the starter in a vise with soft jaws.
3. Connect the 14-gauge jumper cable between the positive battery terminal and the solenoid relay terminal.

16

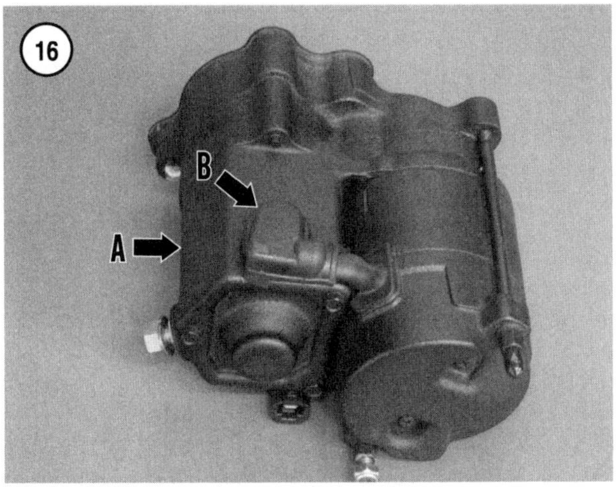

17

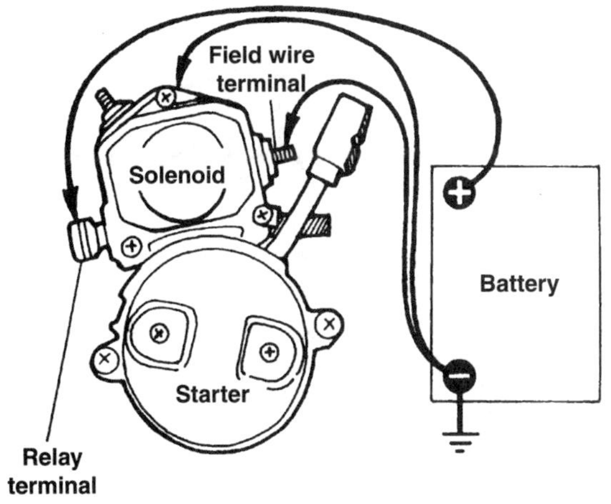

18

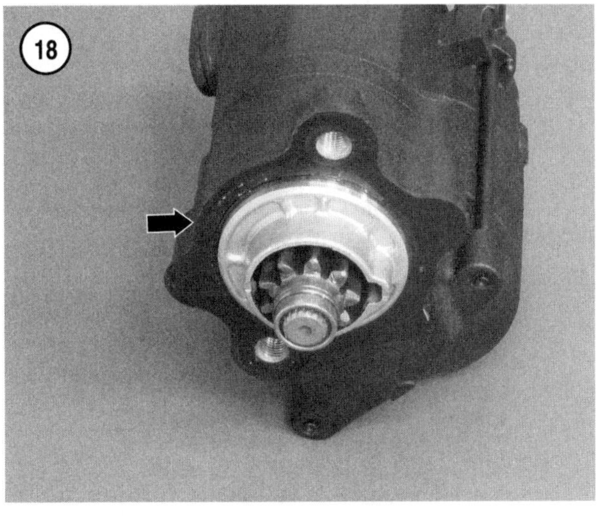

4. Connect a jumper cable (6-gauge minimum) between the positive battery terminal and the ammeter.

5. Connect the second jumper cable between the ammeter and the battery terminal on the starter solenoid.

6. Connect the third jumper cable between the battery ground terminal and the starter mounting flange.

7. Read the ammeter and refer to the maximum no-load current specification in **Table 1**. A damaged pinion gear assembly will cause an excessively high current draw reading. If the current draw reading is low, check for an undercharged battery, or an open field winding or armature in the starter.

Solenoid Testing (Bench Tests)

This test requires a fully charged 12-volt battery and three jumper wires.

1. Remove the starter as described in Chapter Nine.

NOTE
*The solenoid (A, **Figure 16**) must be installed on the starter during the following tests.*

2. Disconnect the field wire (B, **Figure 16**) from the solenoid before performing the following tests. Insulate the end of the wire terminal so it cannot short out on any of the test connectors.

CAUTION
Because battery voltage is being applied directly to the solenoid and starter in the following tests, do not leave the jumper cables connected to the solenoid for more than three-five seconds; otherwise, the voltage will damage the solenoid.

NOTE
Thoroughly read the following procedure to become familiar with and understand the procedures and test connections, then perform the tests in the order listed and without interruption.

3. Refer to **Figure 17** and perform the solenoid pull-in test as follows:

   a. Connect one jumper wire from the negative battery terminal to the field wire terminal on the solenoid.
   b. Connect one jumper wire from the negative battery terminal to the solenoid housing (ground).
   c. Touch a jumper wire from the positive battery terminal to the starter relay terminal. The pinion shaft (**Figure 18**) should pull into the housing.

d. Leave the jumper wires connected and continue with Step 4.

4. To perform the solenoid hold-in test, perform the following:

a. With the pinion shaft pulled in (Step 3), disconnect the field wire terminal jumper wire from the negative battery terminal and connect it to the positive battery terminal (**Figure 19**). The pinion shaft should remain in the housing. If the pinion shaft returns to its original position, replace the solenoid.

b. Leave the jumper wires connected and continue with Step 5.

5. To perform the solenoid return test, perform the following:

a. Disconnect the jumper wire from the starter relay terminal (**Figure 20**); the pinion shaft should return to its original position.

b. Disconnect all the jumper wires from the solenoid and battery.

6. Replace the solenoid if the starter shaft failed to operate as described in Steps 3-5. Refer to *Solenoid Replacement* in Chapter Nine.

Starter Relay Test

Check the starter relay operation with an ohmmeter, jumper wires and a fully charged 12-volt battery.

NOTE

*Relay terminals may be marked 30, 85, 86 and 87 or 1, 2, 3 and 5. Refer to terminal identification in **Figure 21**.*

1. Remove the starter relay as described in Chapter Nine.

CAUTION

The battery negative lead must be connected to the relay terminal No. 2 or 85 to avoid internal diode damage.

2. Connect an ohmmeter and 12-volt battery between the relay terminals as shown in **Figure 21**. This setup will energize the relay for testing.
3. Check for continuity through the relay contacts using an ohmmeter while the relay coil is energized. The correct reading is 0 ohm. If resistance is excessive or if there is no continuity, replace the relay.
4. If the starter relay passes this test, reinstall the relay.

CHARGING SYSTEM

The charging system consists of the battery, alternator and voltage regulator/rectifier.

19

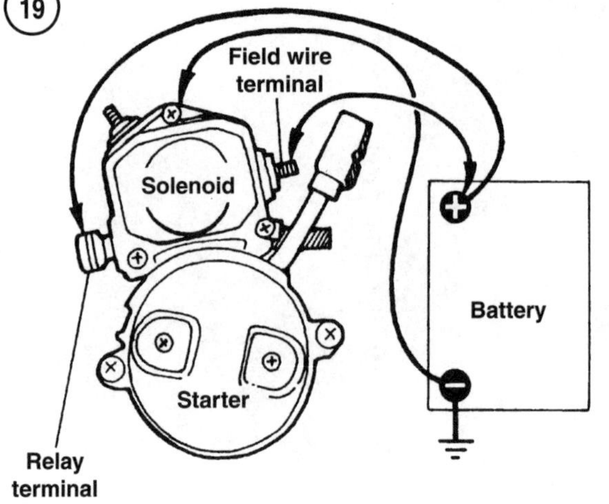

20

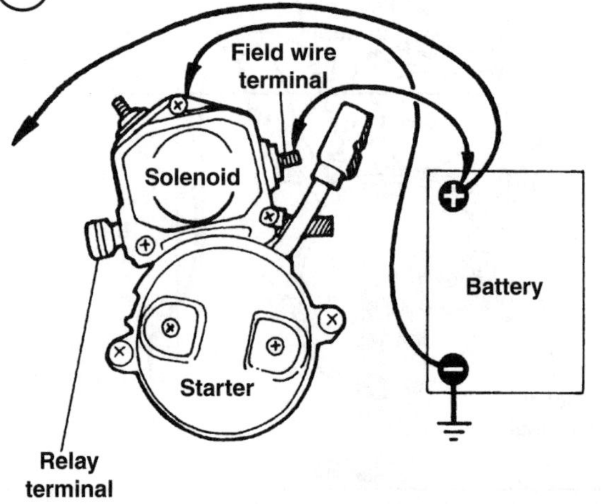

The alternator generates alternating current (AC) which the rectifier converts to direct current (DC). The regulator maintains the voltage to the battery and load (lights, ignition and accessories) at a constant voltage despite variations in engine speed and load.

A malfunction in the charging system generally causes the battery to remain undercharged.

Precautions

Before testing the charging system, observe the following precautions to prevent damage to the system:

1. Never reverse battery connections.
2. Do not short across any connection.

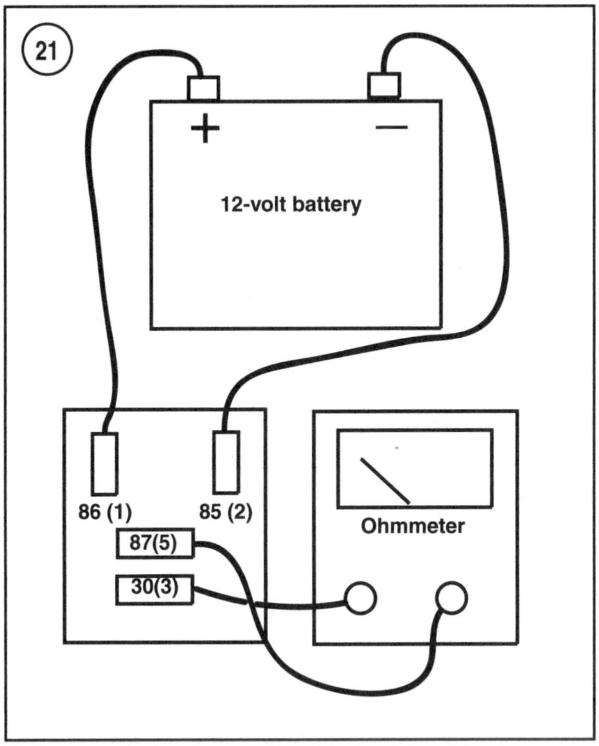

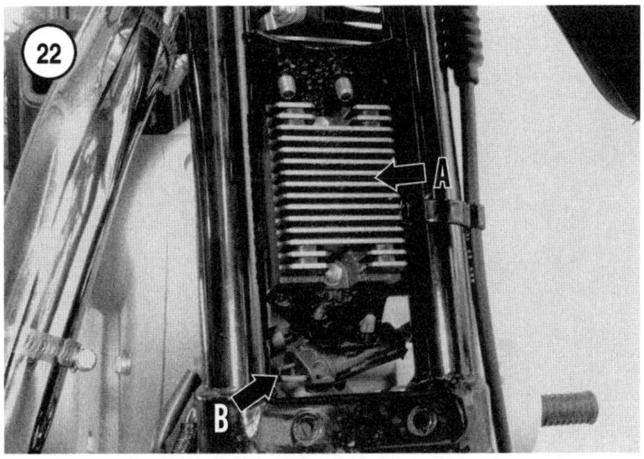

3. Never start the engine with the alternator disconnected from the voltage regulator/rectifier unless instructed to do so during testing.
4. Never start or run the engine with the battery disconnected.
5. Never use a high-output battery charger to help start the engine.
6. Before charging the battery, remove it from the motorcycle as described in Chapter Nine.
7. Never disconnect the voltage regulator/rectifier connector with the engine running. The voltage regulator/rectifier (A, **Figure 22**) is mounted on the front frame cross member.
8. Do not mount the voltage regulator/rectifier in another location.
9. Make sure the negative battery terminal is connected to the terminal on the engine.

Troubleshooting Sequence

If the battery is discharged, perform the following:
1. Test the battery as described in Chapter Nine. Charge the battery if necessary. If the battery does hold a charge while riding, perform the *Charging System Output Test.*
2. If the charging system output is within specification, determine the total amount of current demand by the electrical system and all accessories as described in *Electrical System Current Load Test.*
3. If the charging system output exceeds the current demand and the battery continues to not hold a charge, perform the *Battery Current Draw Test.*
4. If the charging system output is not within specification, test the stator and voltage regulator as described in Chapter Nine.

Charging System Output Test

CAUTION
When using a load tester, refer to the manufacturer's instructions. To prevent tester damage caused by overheating, do not leave the load switch on for more than 20 seconds at a time.

This test requires a load tester.
1. To perform this test, the battery must be fully charged.
2. Connect the load tester negative and positive leads to the battery terminals. Then place the load tester's induction pickup around the Maxi-fuse to voltage regulator red wire (B, **Figure 22**).
3. Start the engine and slowly bring the speed up to 3000 rpm while reading the load tester scale. With the engine running at 3000 rpm, operate the load tester switch until the voltage scale reads 13.0 volts. The tester should show a regulated (DC) current output reading of 19-23 amps.
4. With the engine still running at 3000 rpm, turn the load off and read the load tester voltage scale. Battery voltage should not exceed 15 volts. Turn the engine off and disconnect the load tester from the motorcycle.
5. Refer to *Alternator* in Chapter Nine and test the stator. If the stator tests acceptable, there is a defective voltage regulator/rectifier or a wiring short circuit. Make sure to eliminate the possibility of a poor connection or damaged wiring before replacing the voltage regulator/rectifier.

Electrical System Current Load Test

CAUTION

When using a load tester, refer to the manufacturer's instructions. To prevent tester damage caused by overheating, do not leave the load switch on for more than 20 seconds at a time.

This test, requiring a load tester, measures the total current load of the electrical system and any additional accessories while the engine is running. Perform this test if the battery is continually discharged, yet the charging system output is within specification.

If aftermarket electrical components have been added to the motorcycle, the increased current demand may exceed the charging system's capacity and cause a discharged battery.

1. Connect a load tester to the battery per the manufacturer's instructions.
2. Turn the ignition switch on, but do not start the engine. Then turn on all electrical accessories and switch the headlight beam to HIGH.
3. Read the ampere reading (current draw) on the load tester and compare it to the *Charging System Output Test*. The charging system output test results (current reading) must exceed the electrical system current load by 3.5 amps for the battery to remain sufficiently charged.
4. If aftermarket accessories have been added to the motorcycle, disconnect them and repeat Step 3. If the electrical system current load is now within the specification, the problem is with the additional accessories.
5. If no accessories have been added to the motorcycle, a short circuit may be causing the battery to discharge.

Battery Current Draw Test

This test measures the current draw on the battery when all electrical systems and accessories are off. Perform this test if the battery does not hold a charge when the motorcycle is not being used. A current draw that exceeds 3.5 mA will discharge the battery. The voltage regulator (0.5 mA), TSM (0.5 mA) and TSSM (2.5 mA) account for a 3.5 mA current draw. The battery must be fully charged to perform this test.

1. Disconnect the negative battery cable as described in Chapter Nine.
2. Connect an ammeter between the negative battery cable end and the ground stud on the engine crankcase as shown in **Figure 23**.
3. With the ignition switch, lights and all accessories turned off, read the ammeter. If the current exceeds 3.5 mA, continue with Step 4.

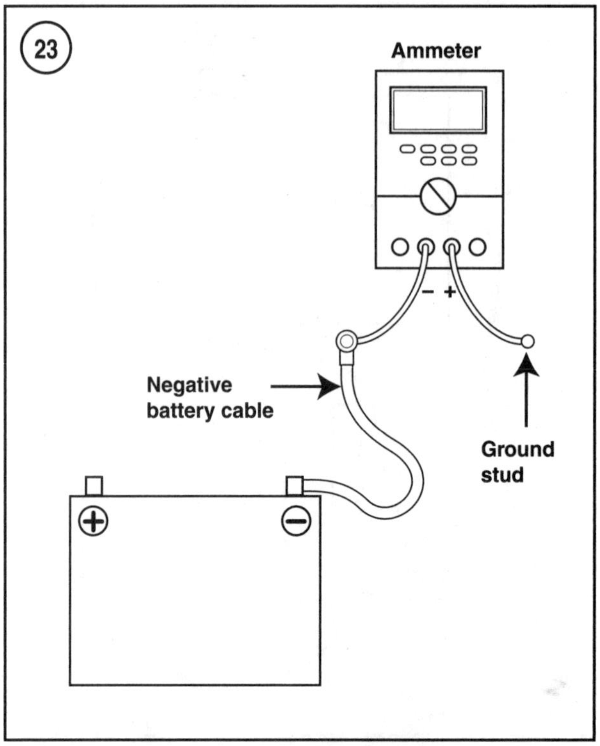

4. Refer to the appropriate wiring diagram at the end of this manual. Check the charging system wires and connectors for shorts or other damage.

5. Unplug each electrical connector separately and check for a reduction in the current draw. If the meter reading changes after a connector is disconnected, the source of the current draw has been found. Check the electrical connectors carefully before testing the individual component.

6. After completing the test, disconnect the ammeter and reconnect the negative battery cable.

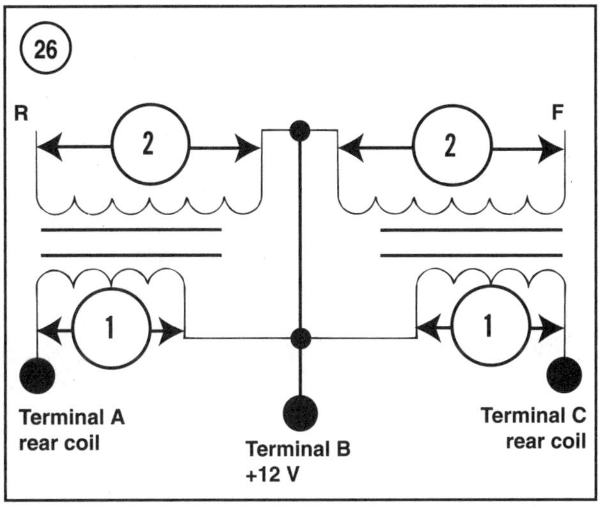

IGNITION SYSTEM

Precautions

Before testing the ignition system, observe the following precautions to prevent damage to the system.

1. Never disconnect any of the electrical connectors while the engine is running.
2. Apply dielectric grease to all electrical connectors prior to reconnecting them. This will help seal out moisture.
3. Make sure all electrical connectors are free of corrosion and are completely coupled to each other.
4. The ignition module (**Figure 24**) must always be mounted securely to the mounting bracket under the seat.

Troubleshooting Preparation

1. Refer to the wiring diagram at the end of this manual for the specific model.
2. Check the wiring harness for visible signs of damage.
3. Make sure all connectors are properly attached to each other and locked in place.

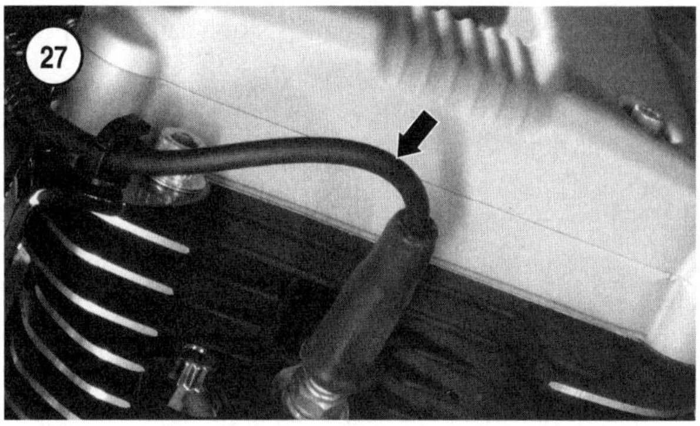

4. Check all electrical components for a good ground to the engine.
5. Check all wiring for short circuits or open circuits.
6. Remove the rear fender inner panel as described in Chapter Fourteen.
7. Remove the left side cover and check for a blown ignition circuit fuse (**Figure 25**).
8. Make sure the fuel tank has an adequate supply of fresh gasoline.
9. Check the spark plug cable routing and the connections at the spark plugs. If there is no spark or only a weak one, repeat the test with new spark plugs. If the condition remains the same with new spark plugs and if all external wiring connections are good, the problem is most likely in the ignition system. If a strong spark is present, the problem is probably not in the ignition system. Check the fuel system.

Ignition Coil Testing

Use an ohmmeter to check the ignition coil secondary and primary resistance. Test the coil twice: first when it is cold (room temperature), then at normal operating temperature. If the engine does not start, heat the coil with a hair dryer, then test with the ohmmeter.

1. Remove the ignition coil as described in Chapter Nine.
2. Measure the ignition coil primary resistance between the primary coil terminals. Refer to **Figure 26**. Compare the reading to the specification in **Table 2**. Replace the ignition coil if the reading is not within specification.
3. Measure the resistance between the secondary terminals. Refer to **Figure 26**. Compare the reading to the specification in **Table 2**. Replace the ignition coil if the reading is not within specification.

Spark Plug Cable and Cap Inspection

All models are equipped with resistor-type spark plug cables (**Figure 27**). These cables reduce radio interference. The cable's conductor consists of a carbon-impregnated fabric core material instead of solid wire.

Spark plug cable resistance will increase in a corroded, broken or otherwise damaged cable. Excessive cable resistance will cause engine misfire and other ignition or drivability problems.

When troubleshooting the ignition system, inspect the spark plug cables for:

1. Corroded or damaged connector ends.
2. Breaks in the cable insulation that could allow arcing.
3. Split or damaged plug caps that could allow arcing to the cylinder heads.
4. Replace damaged or questionable spark plug cables.

ELECTRONIC DIAGNOSTIC SYSTEM

All models are equipped with an electronic diagnostic system that monitors the operating condition of the speedometer, ignition control module (ICM), turn signal/security module (TSM/TSSM) and tachometer, if so equipped. A serial data bus connects the components. If a malfunction occurs, a diagnostic trouble code (DTC) may be generated.

The DTC identifies an anamoly detected by an electrical component. The trouble code is retained in the memory of the ICM, TSM/TSSM, speedometer and tachometer, if so equipped. A DTC is categorized as current or historic.

A current DTC identifies a problem that affects present motorcycle operation.

A historic DTC identifies a problem that has been resolved either through servicing or a changed condition. Historic DTCs are retained to provide information should an intermittent problem exist. A historic DTC is retained in memory until fifty start/run cycles have occurred, at which point the DTC is erased.

Not all malfunctions cause the generation of a DTC. Refer to *No-DTC Fault.*

Startup Check

The diagnostic system indicates a normal condition or an operating problem each time the ignition key is turned on (ignition).

1. During normal startup, the following occurs after the key is turned on:
   a. The *check engine* symbol (A, **Figure 28**) illuminates for four seconds, then goes out.
   b. The *security* symbol (B, **Figure 28**) illuminates for four seconds, then goes out.

28

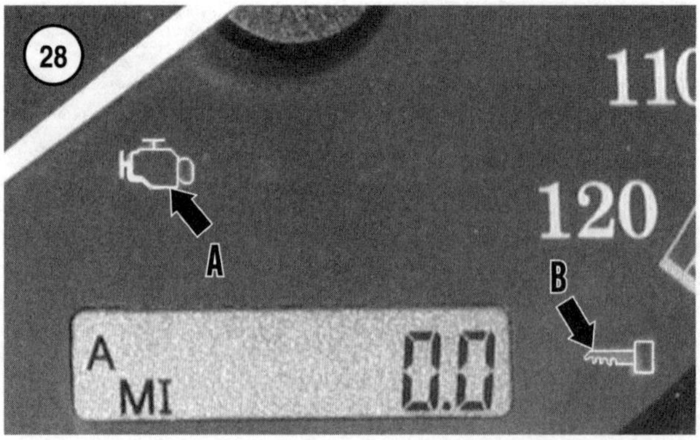

29

2. Note the following indications of potential problems during startup:
   a. If the check engine symbol or security symbol does not illuminate, an instrument may be faulty. Refer to *Initial Diagnostic Check.*
   b. If the check engine symbol or security symbol illuminates after 20 seconds, a serial data bus problem may exist. Check for a DTC.
   c. If the check engine symbol or security symbol stays on, an instrument may be faulty or a DTC exists. Refer to *Initial Diagnostic Check.*

DTC Retrieval

Trouble codes are configured in a five digit format consisting of a letter prefix followed by four numbers.

NOTE
*The message **BusEr** is a trouble code which may appear during diagnostic troubleshooting. **BusEr** indicates a problem in the serial bus data circuit.*

Two methods may be used to retrieve trouble codes, either through performing the retrieval sequence at the speedometer or using the H-D Digital Technician tool. The following

30

31

describes using the speedometer to retrieve DTCs. If necessary, take the motorcycle to a dealership equipped with the H-D Digital Technician.

Perform the following to read a DTC:

NOTE
Make sure the run/stop handlebar switch is in the run position.

1. Push and hold in the odometer reset button on the back of the speedometer.
2. Turn the ignition key on, then release the reset button. The following should occur:
   a. The speedometer backlighting comes on.
   b. The speedometer needle rotates to full deflection position (A, **Figure 29**).

NOTE
The security symbol may come on even though the motorcycle is not equipped with a security system.

   c. The check engine, battery and security symbols illuminate.
3. The message *diag* appears in the odometer window on the speedometer (B, **Figure 29**).
4. Press and release the odometer reset button. The letters *PSSPt* appear in the odometer window (**Figure 30**). The letter *P* will flash indicating that information concerning the ICM is obtainable. The letters *PSSPt* identify the following components:
   a. The letter *P* identifies the ICM.
   b. The letter *S* identifies the TSM/TSSM.
   c. The letters *SP* identify the speedometer.
   d. The letter *t* identifies the tachometer.
5. To cycle through the PSSPt letter identifiers, push and quickly release the odometer reset button. The selected component letter identifier will flash.
6. To obtain a DTC, select a component (identifier letter(s) flashes) then push and hold in the odometer reset button for at least 5 seconds. Release the button. The code will appear in the odometer window (**Figure 31**), or *none*. Record the DTC.

NOTE
When reading codes in Step 7 push in and release the reset button only long enough to retreive the next code. Holding in the reset button for more than 5 seconds will erase the codes.

7. Press and release the reset button as needed to read additional trouble codes until *end* appears.

NOTE
On models not equipped with a tachometer, ***No Rsp*** *will appear when the tachometer identifier is selected.*

8. If *none* appears, pushing and releasing the reset button will cause the display of the component part number. For instance, the display may read *Pn 32478-04* for the ICM.
9. Push and release the reset button to return to the PSSPt display.
10. Turn off the ignition key to exit the diagnostic program.

Diagnostic Tools

The troubleshooting steps in some of the flowcharts in this chapter require using H-D breakout box part No. HD-42682 (**Figure 32**) and adapters HD-46601.

The H-D computer program Digital Technician (part No. HD-44750) must be used to read historic DTCs, and to erase them. The Digital Technician is also necessary to reprogram a new ICM.

The H-D breakout box is separated into two panels (black and gray). The panel colors relate to the box connector colors: one pair black and one pair gray.

Refer to the following when connecting the breakout box:

1. Speedometer/tachometer—Refer to Chapter Nine and remove the back of the speedometer or tachometer. Disconnect the connector (**Figure 33**) and attach the adapters. Connect the black breakout box connectors to the adapters. Use the sockets on the black breakout box panel during testing.
2. TSM/TSSM—Refer to Chapter Nine and remove the TSM/TSSM. Connect the gray breakout box connectors to the TSM/TSSM and to the connector. Use the sockets on the gray breakout box panel during testing. Reinstall the battery.
3. ICM—Remove the seat. Disconnect the ICM connector (**Figure 34**). Connect the black breakout box connectors to the ICM and to the connector. Use the sockets on the black breakout box panel during testing.

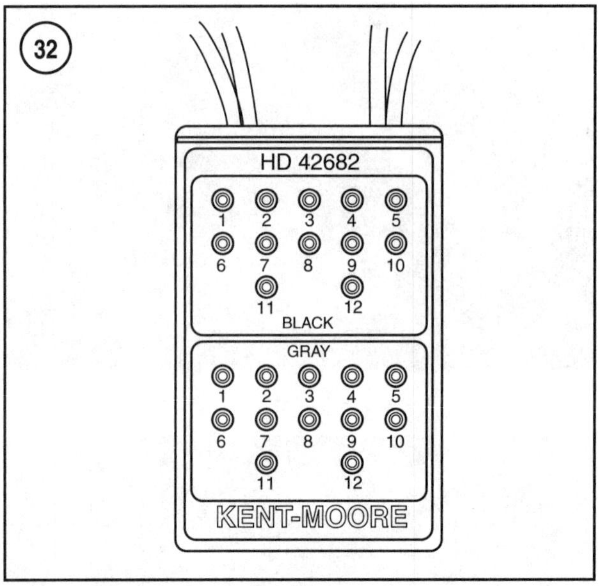

Data Link Connector

A data link connector provides access to the data bus and provides a testing terminal when troubleshooting. The connector is located behind the left side cover. Remove the connector cap (**Figure 35**) for access to the connector terminals.

DTC Troubleshooting

A list of DTCs is found in **Table 3** at the end of this chapter, which also identifies the possible problem and a troubleshooting flowchart. Refer to the applicable flowchart in **Figures 36-60**. Note the following before beginning troubleshooting:

1. Before retrieving DTCs, refer to *Initial Diagnostic Check* in this section.
2. Not all malfunctions will set a DTC. If this occurs, refer to Chapter Nine and the wiring diagrams at the end of this manual to assist in troubleshooting.
3. Check for obvious causes before undertaking what may be a complicated troubleshooting procedure. Look for loose or disconnected connectors, damaged wiring and other possible causes.
4. The DTCs are prioritized according to importance. If multiple DTCs occur, correct the DTC with the highest priority listed in **Table 3**. It is possible for one fault to trigger more than one DTC.
5. Refer to the wiring diagrams at the end of this manual to identify connectors. Each connector is noted with a corresponding number on the wiring diagram. This connector number is noted in the flow charts. Refer to the appropriate sections in this chapter and Chapter Nine for additional component testing.

No-DTC fault

Some malfunctions, such as fuel and starting system problems, do not trigger a DTC. In those cases, the troubleshooting guidelines found in this chapter will serve to locate the problem. However, there are faults that can be diagnosed using the procedures implemented when diagnosing a DTC. The following faults may not generate a DTC, but the specified flowchart will help identify the problem.

1. No spark or ICM power—**Figure 55**.
2. Tachometer faulty—**Figure 56**.
3. No security lamp—**Figure 57**.
4. Security lamp always on—**Figure 58**.
5. Key fob signal weak to TSSM—**Figure 59**.
6. Turn signal cancels improperly—**Figure 60**.

Initial diagnostic check

Because the speedometer provides the DTCs, it may be necessary to troubleshoot it before initiating a diagnostic sequence. Check speedometer operation as described, then refer to **Figure 36** and follow the *Initial Checks* flowchart.

1. During normal operation the speedometer should operate as follows when the ignition key is turned on (make sure the run/stop handlebar switch is in the run position):
   a. The speedometer backlighting comes on.

NOTE

The security symbol may come on even though the motorcycle is not equipped with a security system.

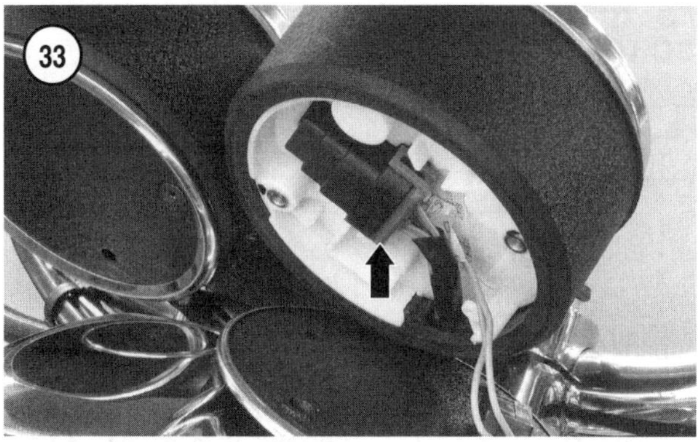
33

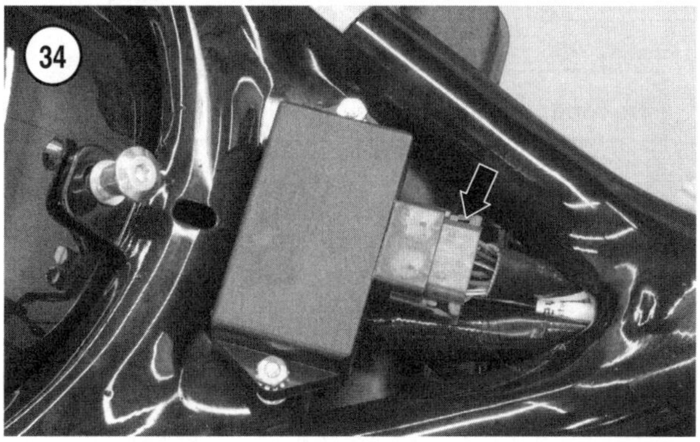
34

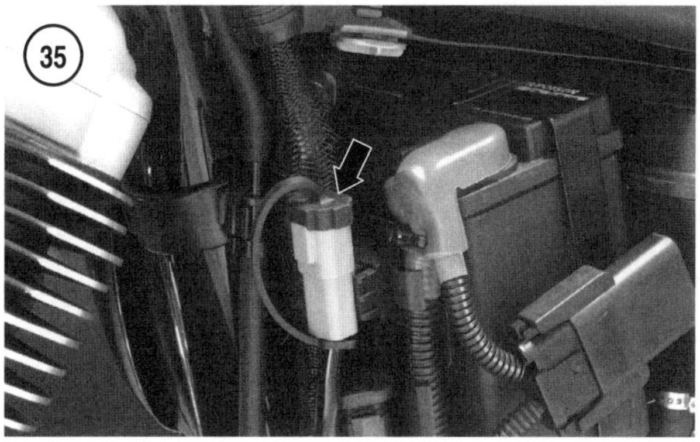
35

b. The check engine and security symbols illuminate.
c. The odometer display illuminates.

2. If the speedometer performs normally during startup, perform the following WOW test:

a. Push in the odometer reset button on the back of the speedometer.
b. Turn the ignition key on and release the odometer reset button.
c. The speedometer backlighting should come on.
d. The speedometer needle should rotate to the full deflection position (A, **Figure 29**).

NOTE
The security symbol may come on even though the motorcycle is not equipped with a security system.

e. The check engine, battery and security symbols should illuminate.
f. The message *diag* should appear in the odometer window on the speedometer (B, **Figure 29**).

3. If the speedometer operates abnormally, check the wiring for the battery, ground, ignition, odometer reset switch and accessories.

FUEL SYSTEM

WARNING
Gasoline is highly flammable. When servicing the fuel system, work in a well-ventilated area. Do not expose gasoline and gasoline vapors to sparks or other ignition sources.

Begin fuel system troubleshooting with the fuel tank and work through the system, reserving the carburetor as the final point. Most fuel system problems result from an empty fuel tank, a plugged fuel filter or fuel valve, old fuel, a dirty air filter or clogged carburetor jets. Do not assume the carburetor is the problem. Unnecessary carburetor adjustment can compound the problem.

Running Conditions

Refer to the following conditions to identify whether the engine is running lean or rich.

Rich

1. Fouled spark plugs.
2. Engine misfires and runs rough under load.
3. Excessive exhaust smoke as the throttle is increased.
4. An extreme rich condition causes a choked or dull sound from the exhaust and an inability to clear the exhaust with the throttle held wide open.

Lean

1. Blistered or very white spark plug electrodes.
2. Engine overheats.
3. Slow acceleration and engine power is reduced.
4. Flat spots on acceleration that are similar in feel to when the engine starts to run out of gas.
5. Engine speed fluctuates at full throttle.

36

INITIAL CHECKS

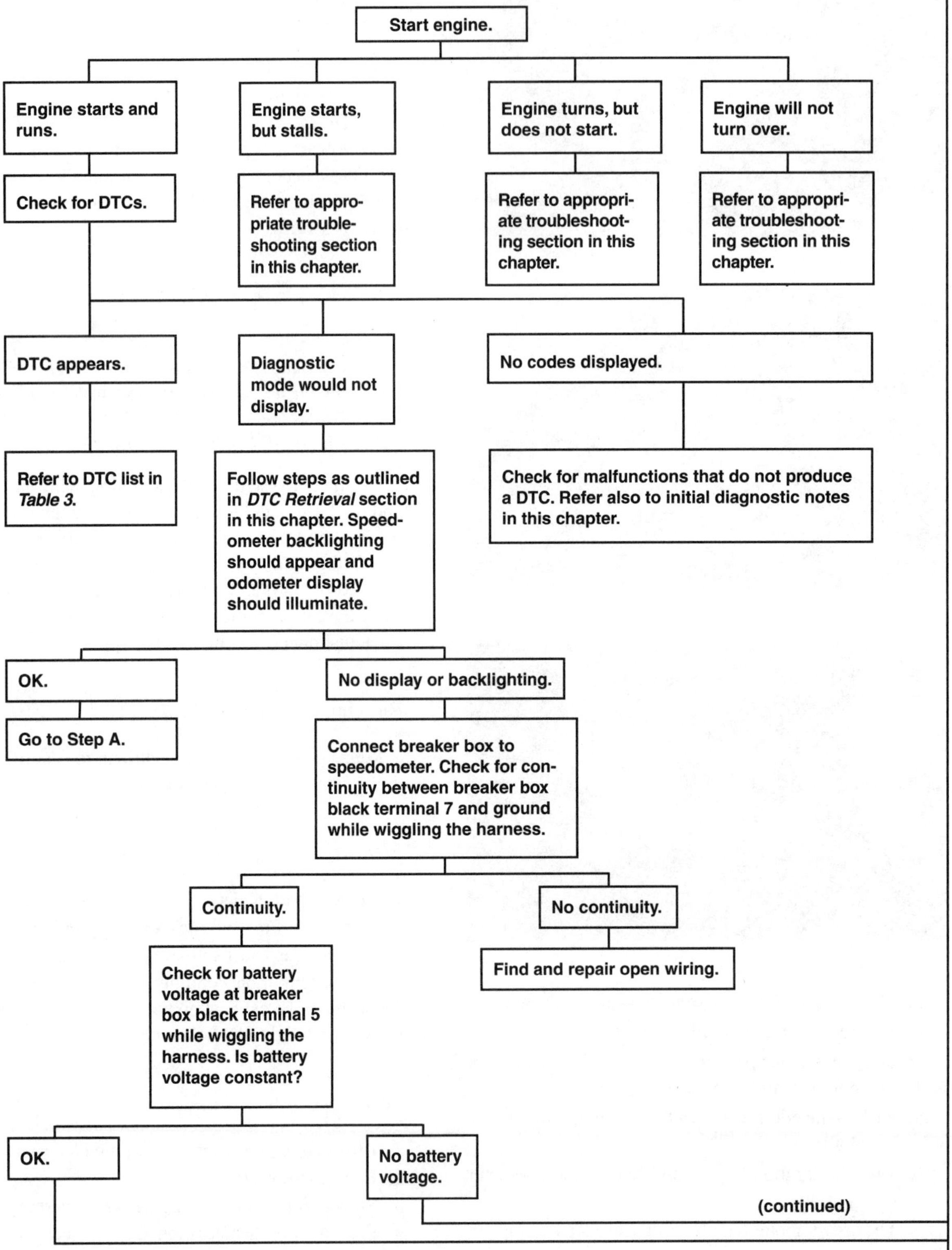

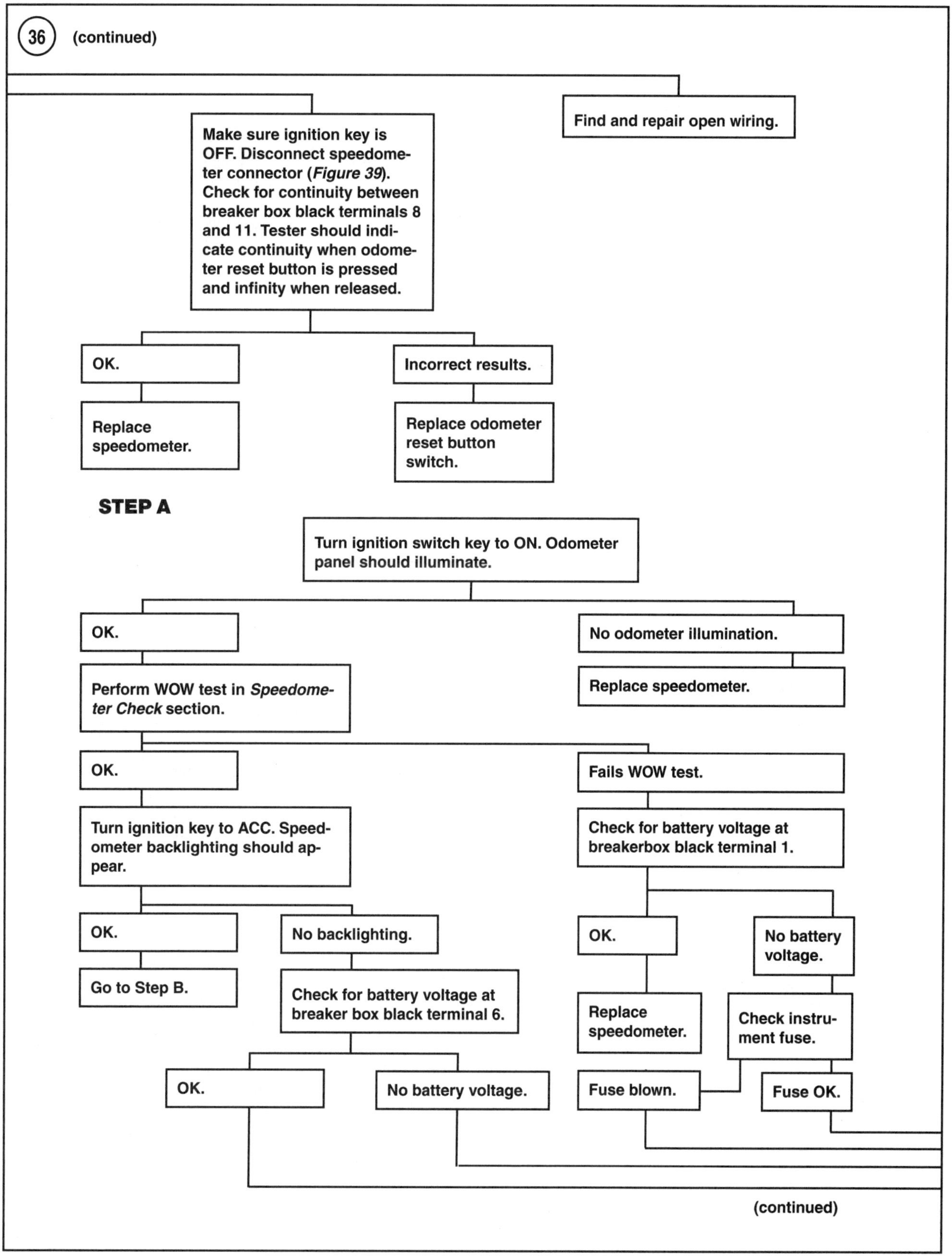
36 (continued)
Find and repair open wiring.
Make sure ignition key is OFF. Disconnect speedometer connector (*Figure 39*). Check for continuity between breaker box black terminals 8 and 11. Tester should indicate continuity when odometer reset button is pressed and infinity when released.
OK.
Replace speedometer.
Incorrect results.
Replace odometer reset button switch.
STEP A
Turn ignition switch key to ON. Odometer panel should illuminate.
OK.
Perform WOW test in *Speedometer Check* section.
No odometer illumination.
Replace speedometer.
OK.
Turn ignition key to ACC. Speedometer backlighting should appear.
Fails WOW test.
Check for battery voltage at breakerbox black terminal 1.
OK.
Go to Step B.
No backlighting.
Check for battery voltage at breaker box black terminal 6.
OK.
No battery voltage.
OK.
Replace speedometer.
No battery voltage.
Check instrument fuse.
Fuse blown.
Fuse OK.
(continued)

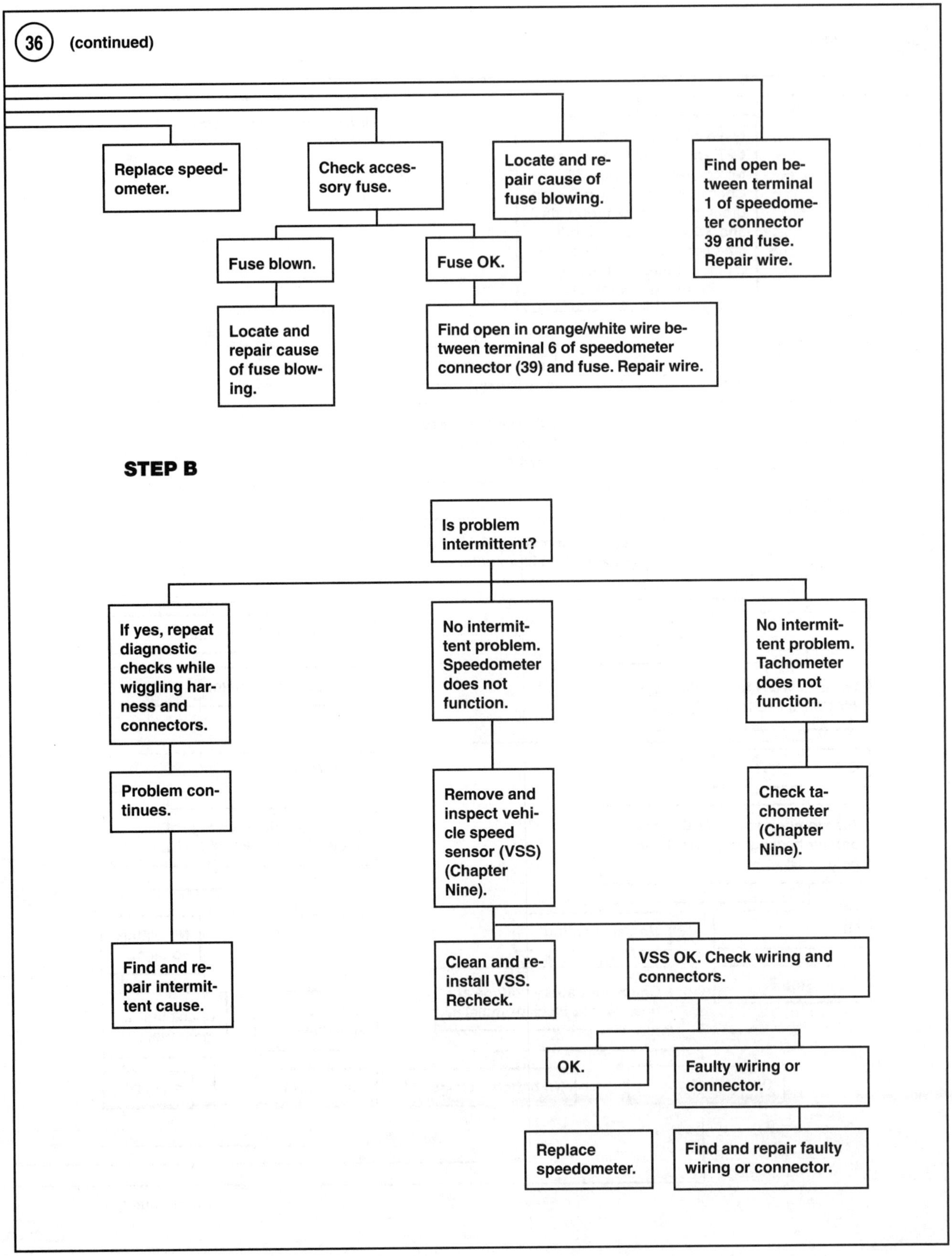
36 (continued)
Replace speedometer.
Check accessory fuse.
Locate and repair cause of fuse blowing.
Find open between terminal 1 of speedometer connector 39 and fuse. Repair wire.
Fuse blown.
Fuse OK.
Locate and repair cause of fuse blowing.
Find open in orange/white wire between terminal 6 of speedometer connector (39) and fuse. Repair wire.
STEP B
Is problem intermittent?
If yes, repeat diagnostic checks while wiggling harness and connectors.
No intermittent problem. Speedometer does not function.
No intermittent problem. Tachometer does not function.
Problem continues.
Remove and inspect vehicle speed sensor (VSS) (Chapter Nine).
Check tachometer (Chapter Nine).
Find and repair intermittent cause.
Clean and reinstall VSS. Recheck.
VSS OK. Check wiring and connectors.
OK.
Faulty wiring or connector.
Replace speedometer.
Find and repair faulty wiring or connector.

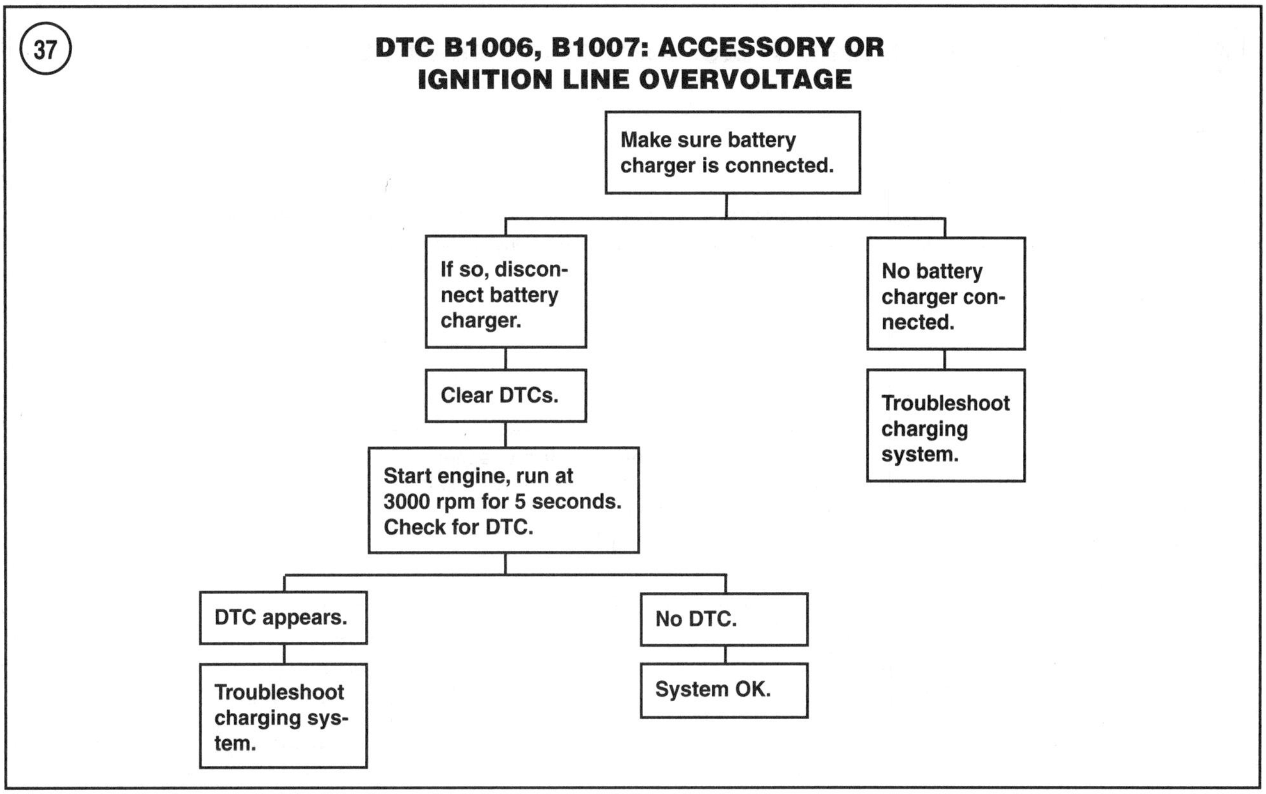

37

DTC B1006, B1007: ACCESSORY OR IGNITION LINE OVERVOLTAGE

Make sure battery charger is connected.

→ If so, disconnect battery charger. → Clear DTCs. → Start engine, run at 3000 rpm for 5 seconds. Check for DTC.
 - DTC appears. → Troubleshoot charging system.
 - No DTC. → System OK.

→ No battery charger connected. → Troubleshoot charging system.

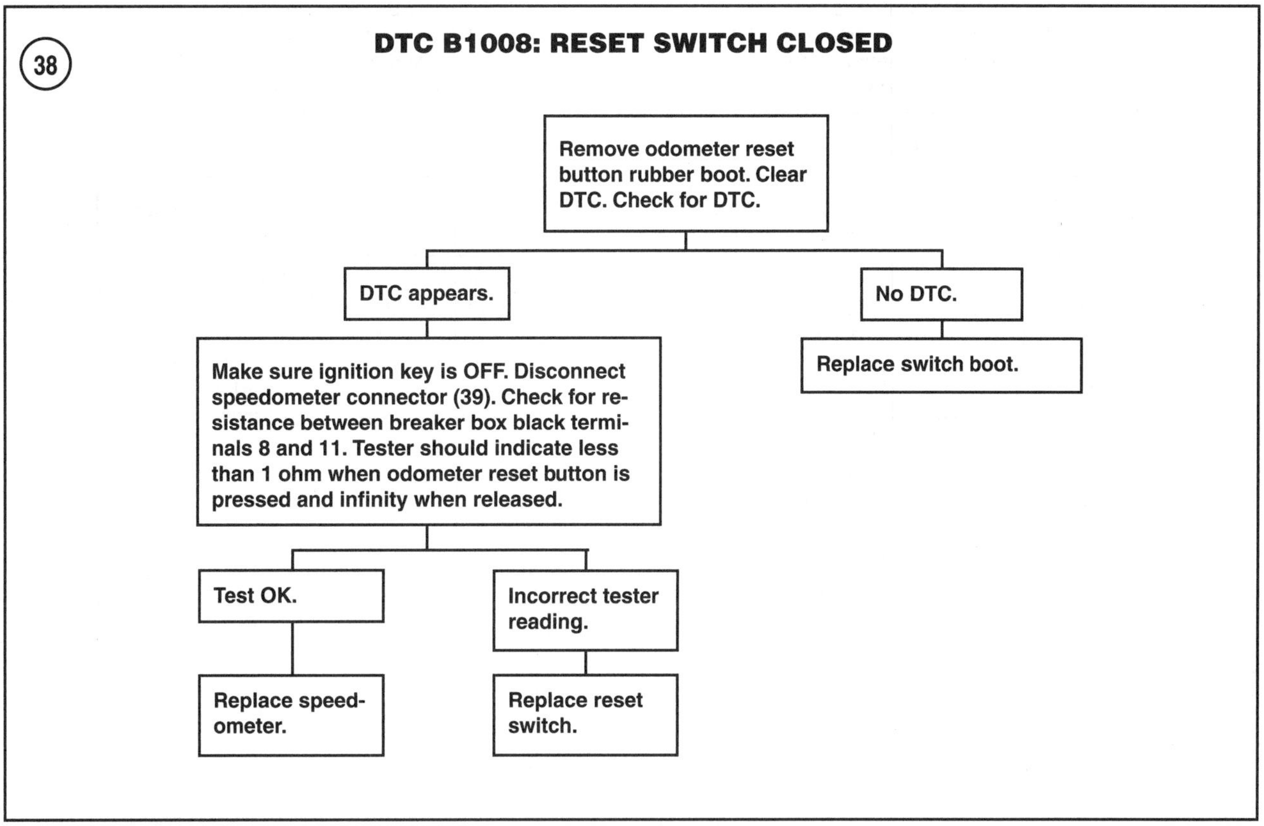

38

DTC B1008: RESET SWITCH CLOSED

Remove odometer reset button rubber boot. Clear DTC. Check for DTC.

- DTC appears. → Make sure ignition key is OFF. Disconnect speedometer connector (39). Check for resistance between breaker box black terminals 8 and 11. Tester should indicate less than 1 ohm when odometer reset button is pressed and infinity when released.
 - Test OK. → Replace speedometer.
 - Incorrect tester reading. → Replace reset switch.

- No DTC. → Replace switch boot.

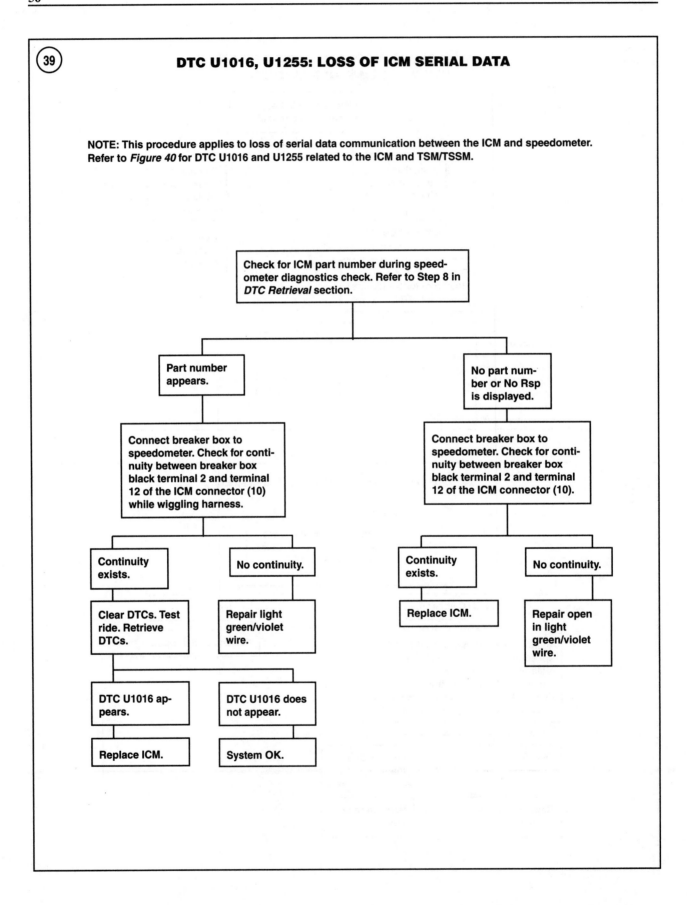

39

DTC U1016, U1255: LOSS OF ICM SERIAL DATA

NOTE: This procedure applies to loss of serial data communication between the ICM and speedometer. Refer to *Figure 40* for DTC U1016 and U1255 related to the ICM and TSM/TSSM.

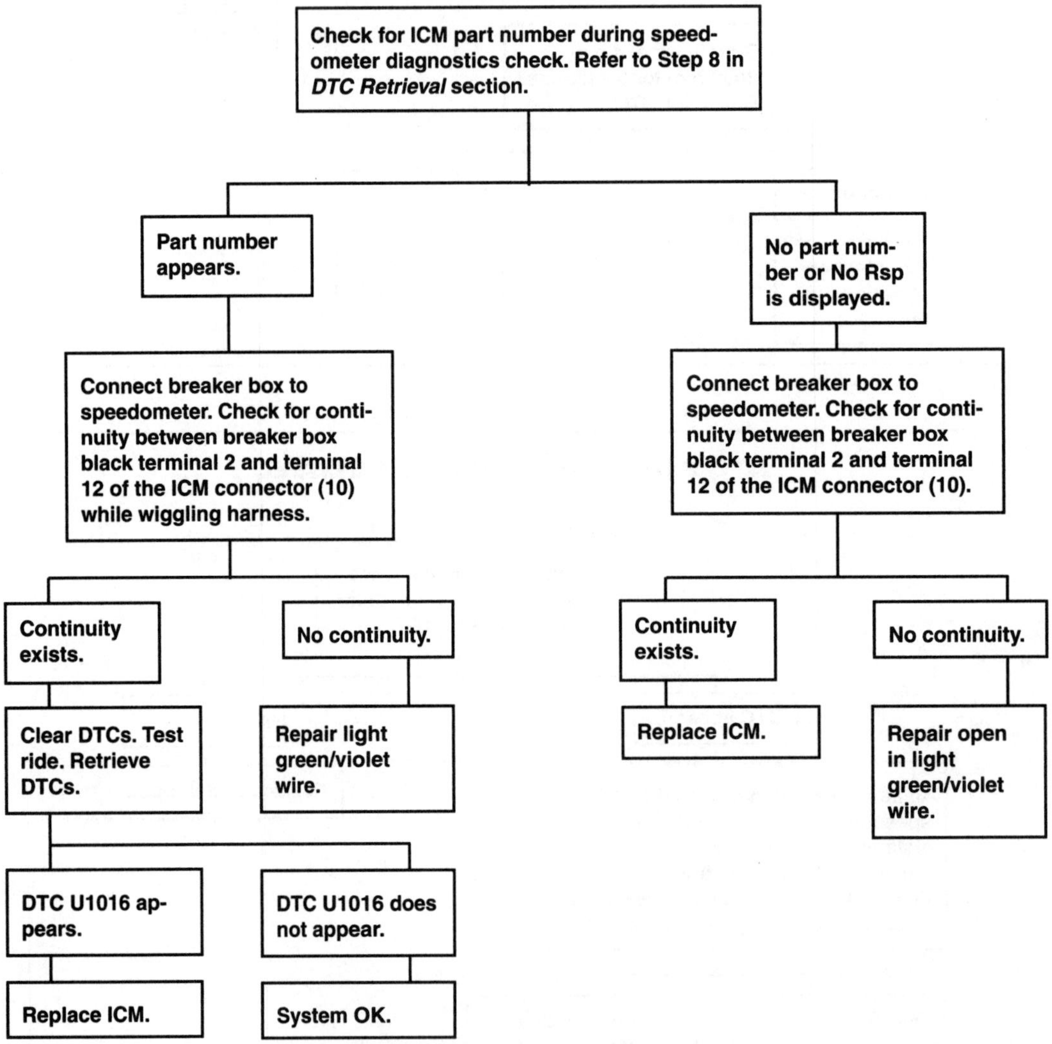
Check for ICM part number during speedometer diagnostics check. Refer to Step 8 in DTC Retrieval section.
Part number appears.
No part number or No Rsp is displayed.
Connect breaker box to speedometer. Check for continuity between breaker box black terminal 2 and terminal 12 of the ICM connector (10) while wiggling harness.
Connect breaker box to speedometer. Check for continuity between breaker box black terminal 2 and terminal 12 of the ICM connector (10).
Continuity exists.
No continuity.
Continuity exists.
No continuity.
Clear DTCs. Test ride. Retrieve DTCs.
Repair light green/violet wire.
Replace ICM.
Repair open in light green/violet wire.
DTC U1016 appears.
DTC U1016 does not appear.
Replace ICM.
System OK.

40

DTC U1016, U1255: LOSS OF ICM SERIAL DATA

NOTE: This procedure applies to loss of serial data communication between the ICM and TSM/TSSM. Refer to *Figure 39* for DTC U1016 and U1255 related to the ICM and speedometer.

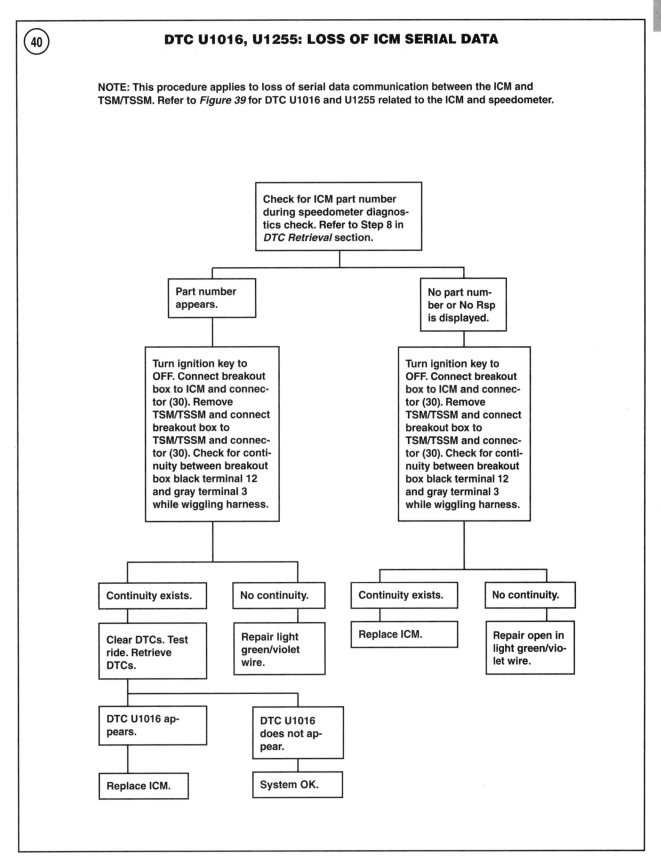

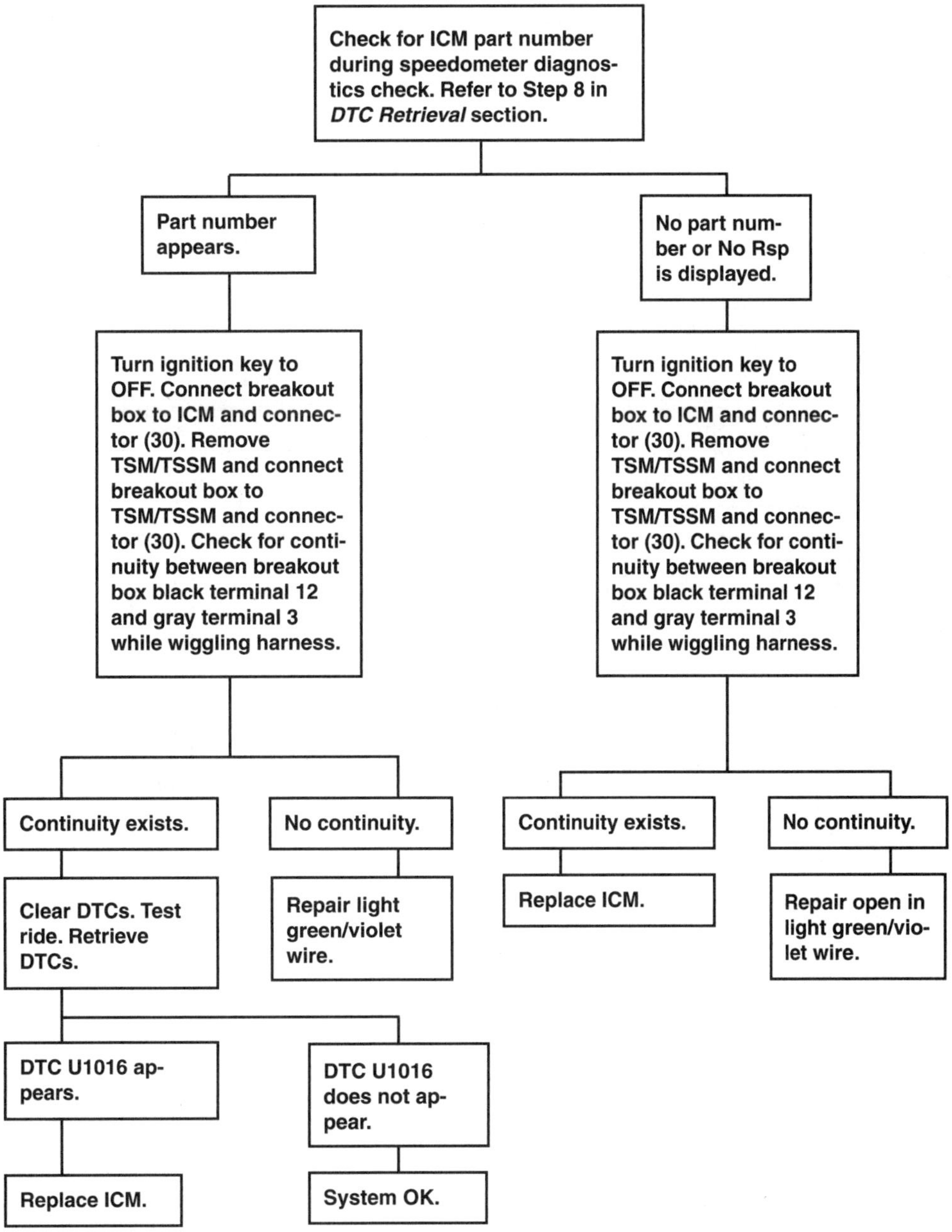
Check for ICM part number during speedometer diagnostics check. Refer to Step 8 in *DTC Retrieval* section.
Part number appears.
No part number or No Rsp is displayed.
Turn ignition key to OFF. Connect breakout box to ICM and connector (30). Remove TSM/TSSM and connect breakout box to TSM/TSSM and connector (30). Check for continuity between breakout box black terminal 12 and gray terminal 3 while wiggling harness.
Turn ignition key to OFF. Connect breakout box to ICM and connector (30). Remove TSM/TSSM and connect breakout box to TSM/TSSM and connector (30). Check for continuity between breakout box black terminal 12 and gray terminal 3 while wiggling harness.
Continuity exists.
No continuity.
Continuity exists.
No continuity.
Clear DTCs. Test ride. Retrieve DTCs.
Repair light green/violet wire.
Replace ICM.
Repair open in light green/violet wire.
DTC U1016 appears.
DTC U1016 does not appear.
Replace ICM.
System OK.

41

DTC U1064, U1255: LOSS OF TSM/TSSM SERIAL DATA

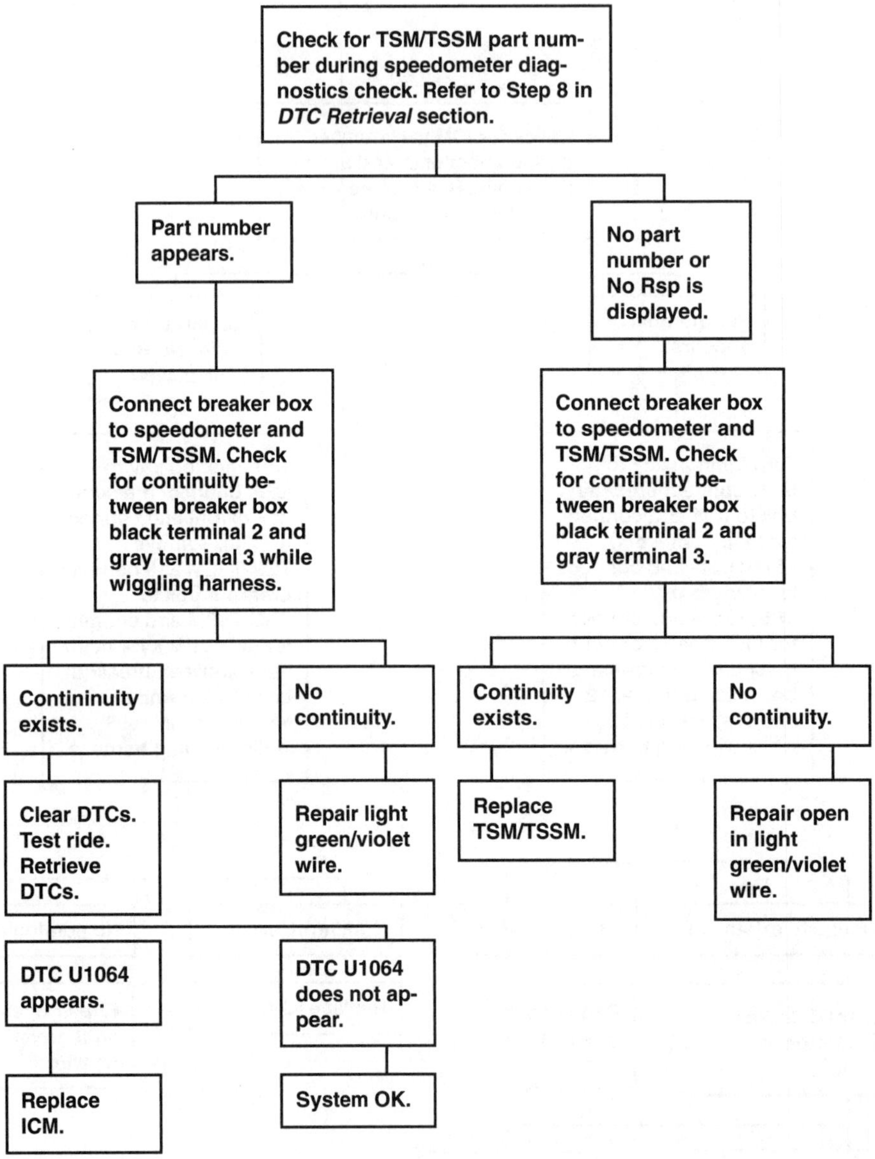
Check for TSM/TSSM part number during speedometer diagnostics check. Refer to Step 8 in *DTC Retrieval* section.
Part number appears.
No part number or No Rsp is displayed.
Connect breaker box to speedometer and TSM/TSSM. Check for continuity between breaker box black terminal 2 and gray terminal 3 while wiggling harness.
Connect breaker box to speedometer and TSM/TSSM. Check for continuity between breaker box black terminal 2 and gray terminal 3.
Contininuity exists.
No continuity.
Continuity exists.
No continuity.
Clear DTCs. Test ride. Retrieve DTCs.
Repair light green/violet wire.
Replace TSM/TSSM.
Repair open in light green/violet wire.
DTC U1064 appears.
DTC U1064 does not appear.
Replace ICM.
System OK.

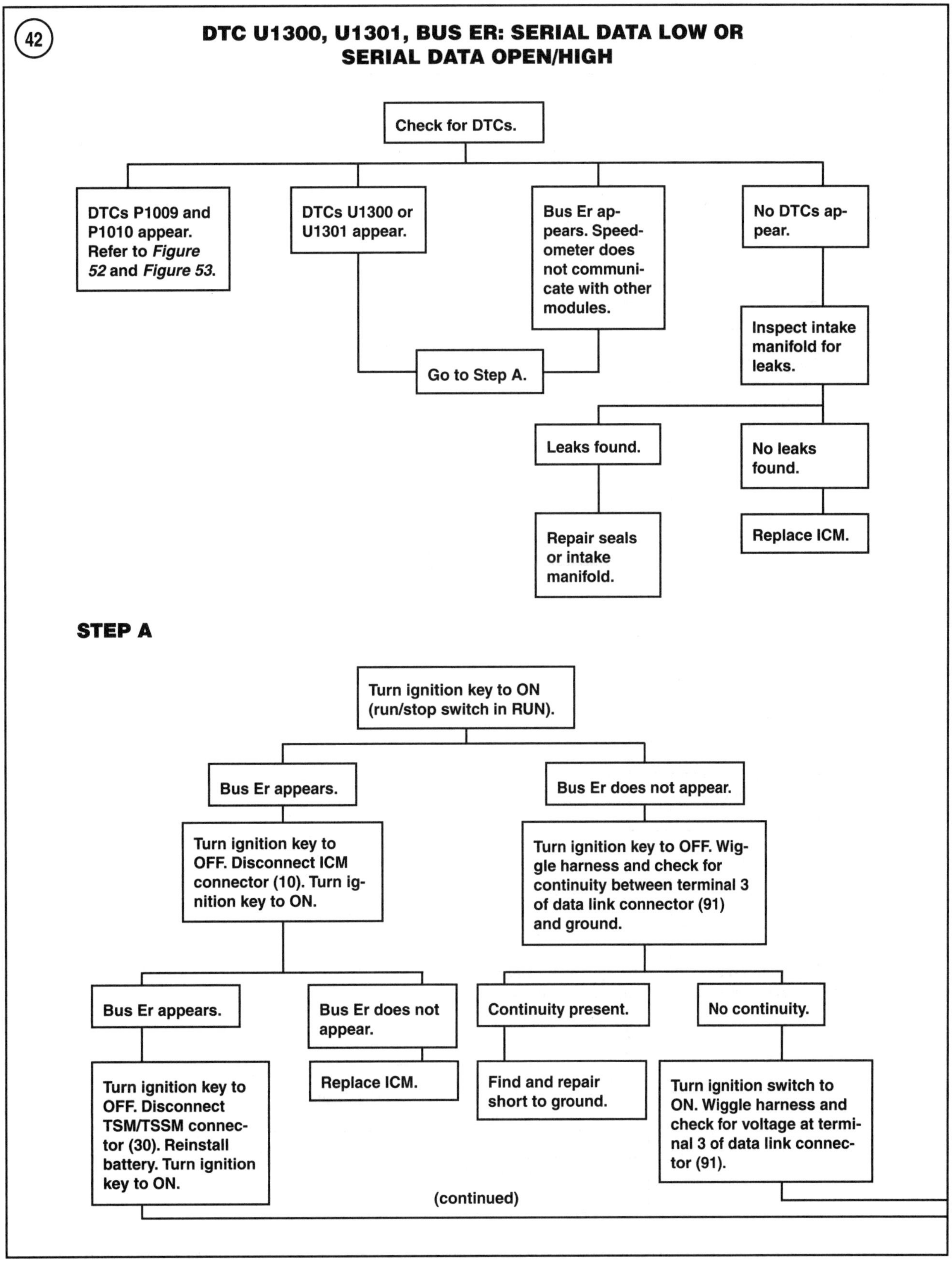
42
DTC U1300, U1301, BUS ER: SERIAL DATA LOW OR SERIAL DATA OPEN/HIGH
Check for DTCs.
DTCs P1009 and P1010 appear. Refer to Figure 52 and Figure 53.
DTCs U1300 or U1301 appear.
Bus Er appears. Speedometer does not communicate with other modules.
No DTCs appear.
Go to Step A.
Inspect intake manifold for leaks.
Leaks found.
No leaks found.
Repair seals or intake manifold.
Replace ICM.
STEP A
Turn ignition key to ON (run/stop switch in RUN).
Bus Er appears.
Bus Er does not appear.
Turn ignition key to OFF. Disconnect ICM connector (10). Turn ignition key to ON.
Turn ignition key to OFF. Wiggle harness and check for continuity between terminal 3 of data link connector (91) and ground.
Bus Er appears.
Bus Er does not appear.
Continuity present.
No continuity.
Replace ICM.
Find and repair short to ground.
Turn ignition key to OFF. Disconnect TSM/TSSM connector (30). Reinstall battery. Turn ignition key to ON.
Turn ignition switch to ON. Wiggle harness and check for voltage at terminal 3 of data link connector (91).
(continued)

42 (continued)

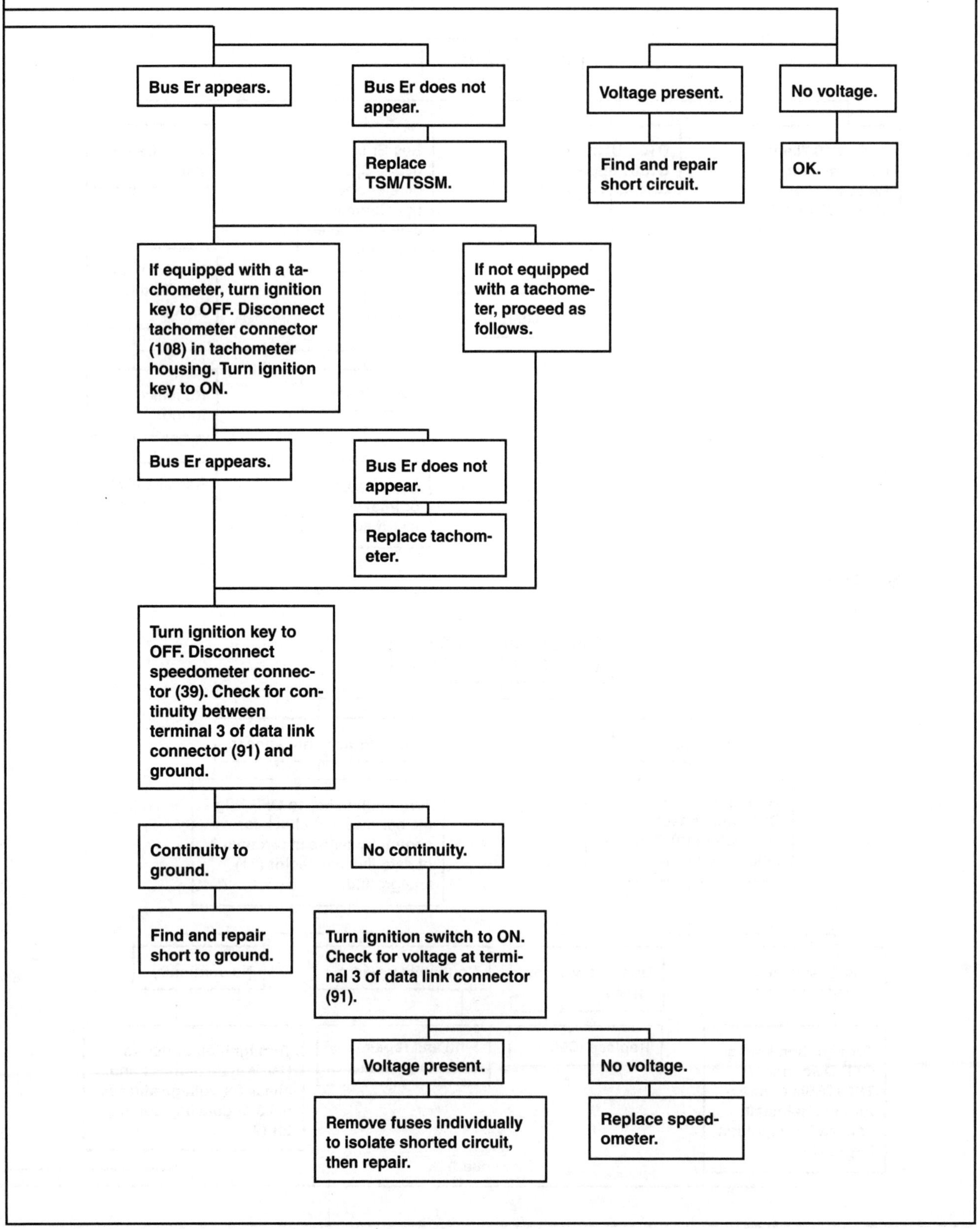

Bus Er appears.
Bus Er does not appear.
Replace TSM/TSSM.
Voltage present.
Find and repair short circuit.
No voltage.
OK.
If equipped with a tachometer, turn ignition key to OFF. Disconnect tachometer connector (108) in tachometer housing. Turn ignition key to ON.
If not equipped with a tachometer, proceed as follows.
Bus Er appears.
Bus Er does not appear.
Replace tachometer.
Turn ignition key to OFF. Disconnect speedometer connector (39). Check for continuity between terminal 3 of data link connector (91) and ground.
Continuity to ground.
Find and repair short to ground.
No continuity.
Turn ignition switch to ON. Check for voltage at terminal 3 of data link connector (91).
Voltage present.
Remove fuses individually to isolate shorted circuit, then repair.
No voltage.
Replace speedometer.

43

DTC U1300, U1301, BUS ER: ENGINE STARTS, THEN STALLS

NOTE: If problem is not resolved, refer also to *Figure 42*.

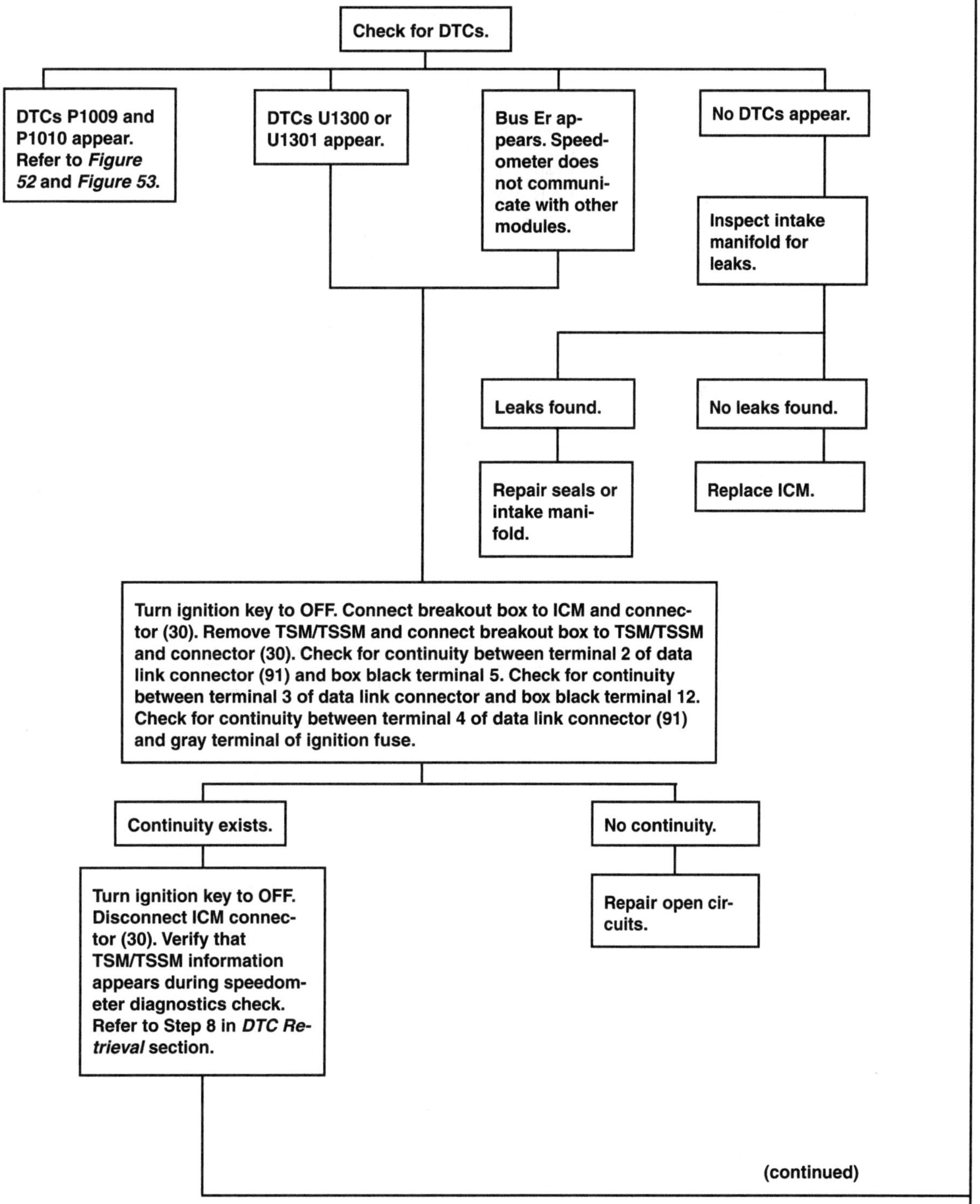

Check for DTCs.
DTCs P1009 and P1010 appear. Refer to Figure 52 and Figure 53.
DTCs U1300 or U1301 appear.
Bus Er appears. Speedometer does not communicate with other modules.
No DTCs appear.
Inspect intake manifold for leaks.
Leaks found.
No leaks found.
Repair seals or intake manifold.
Replace ICM.
Turn ignition key to OFF. Connect breakout box to ICM and connector (30). Remove TSM/TSSM and connect breakout box to TSM/TSSM and connector (30). Check for continuity between terminal 2 of data link connector (91) and box black terminal 5. Check for continuity between terminal 3 of data link connector and box black terminal 12. Check for continuity between terminal 4 of data link connector (91) and gray terminal of ignition fuse.
Continuity exists.
No continuity.
Turn ignition key to OFF. Disconnect ICM connector (30). Verify that TSM/TSSM information appears during speedometer diagnostics check. Refer to Step 8 in DTC Retrieval section.
Repair open circuits.
(continued)

43 (continued)

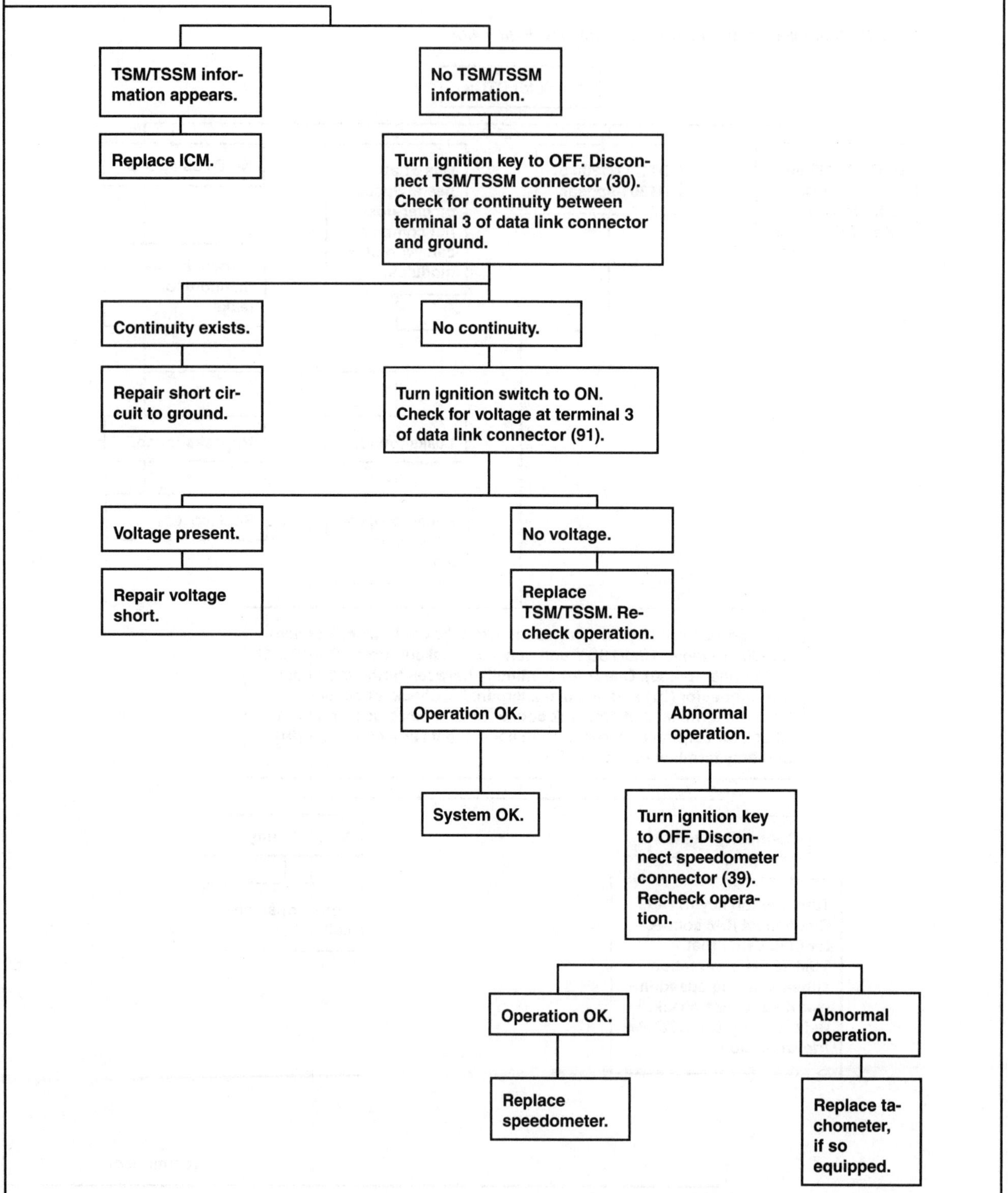
TSM/TSSM information appears.
Replace ICM.
No TSM/TSSM information.
Turn ignition key to OFF. Disconnect TSM/TSSM connector (30). Check for continuity between terminal 3 of data link connector and ground.
Continuity exists.
Repair short circuit to ground.
No continuity.
Turn ignition switch to ON. Check for voltage at terminal 3 of data link connector (91).
Voltage present.
Repair voltage short.
No voltage.
Replace TSM/TSSM. Recheck operation.
Operation OK.
System OK.
Abnormal operation.
Turn ignition key to OFF. Disconnect speedometer connector (39). Recheck operation.
Operation OK.
Replace speedometer.
Abnormal operation.
Replace tachometer, if so equipped.

(44)

DTC B1121, B1122, B1141: TURN SIGNALS WILL NOT FLASH; 4-WAY FLASHERS INOPERABLE

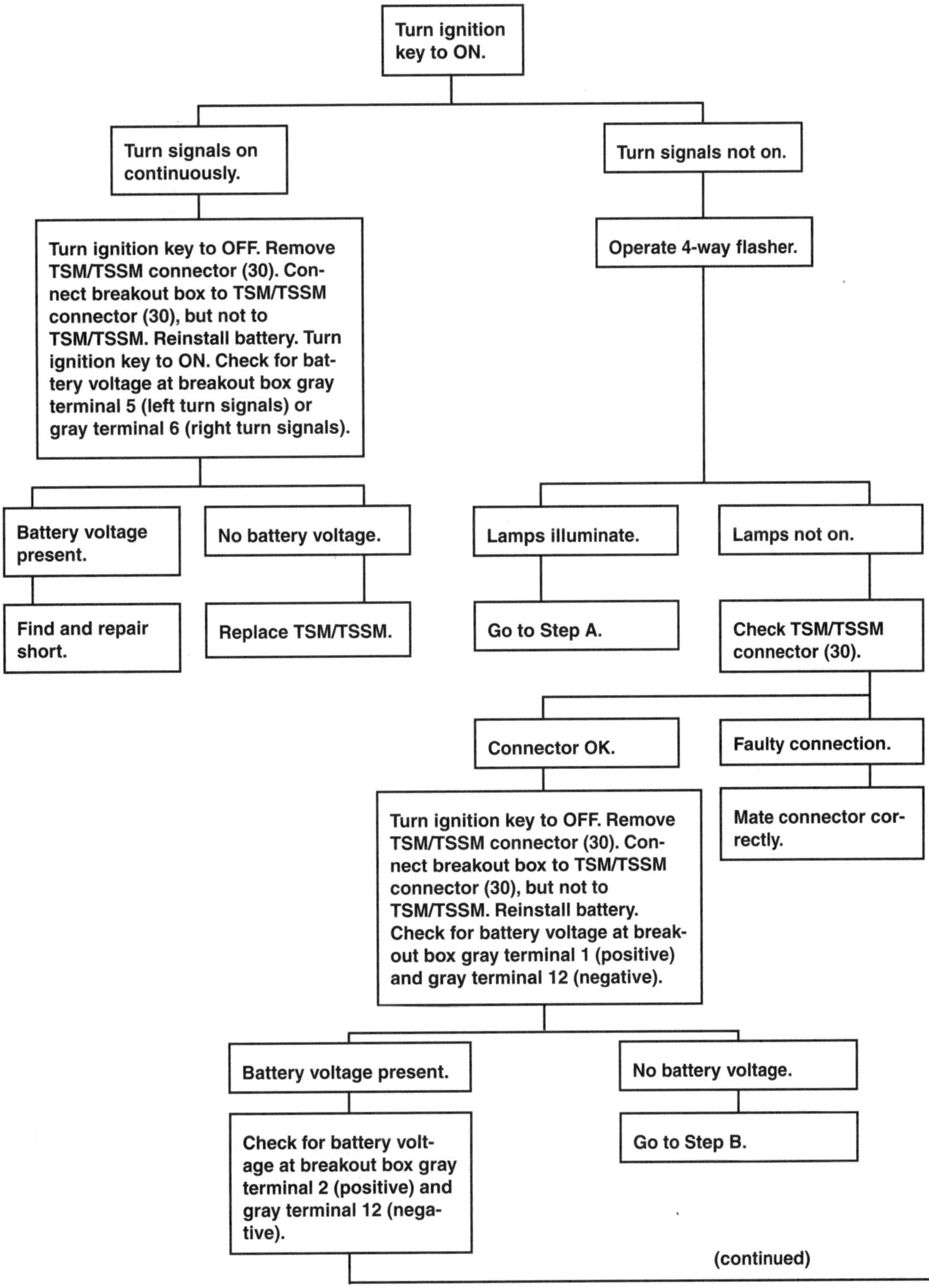
Turn ignition key to ON.
Turn signals on continuously.
Turn signals not on.
Turn ignition key to OFF. Remove TSM/TSSM connector (30). Connect breakout box to TSM/TSSM connector (30), but not to TSM/TSSM. Reinstall battery. Turn ignition key to ON. Check for battery voltage at breakout box gray terminal 5 (left turn signals) or gray terminal 6 (right turn signals).
Operate 4-way flasher.
Battery voltage present.
No battery voltage.
Lamps illuminate.
Lamps not on.
Find and repair short.
Replace TSM/TSSM.
Go to Step A.
Check TSM/TSSM connector (30).
Connector OK.
Faulty connection.
Mate connector correctly.
Turn ignition key to OFF. Remove TSM/TSSM connector (30). Connect breakout box to TSM/TSSM connector (30), but not to TSM/TSSM. Reinstall battery. Check for battery voltage at breakout box gray terminal 1 (positive) and gray terminal 12 (negative).
Battery voltage present.
No battery voltage.
Check for battery voltage at breakout box gray terminal 2 (positive) and gray terminal 12 (negative).
Go to Step B.

(continued)

44 (continued)

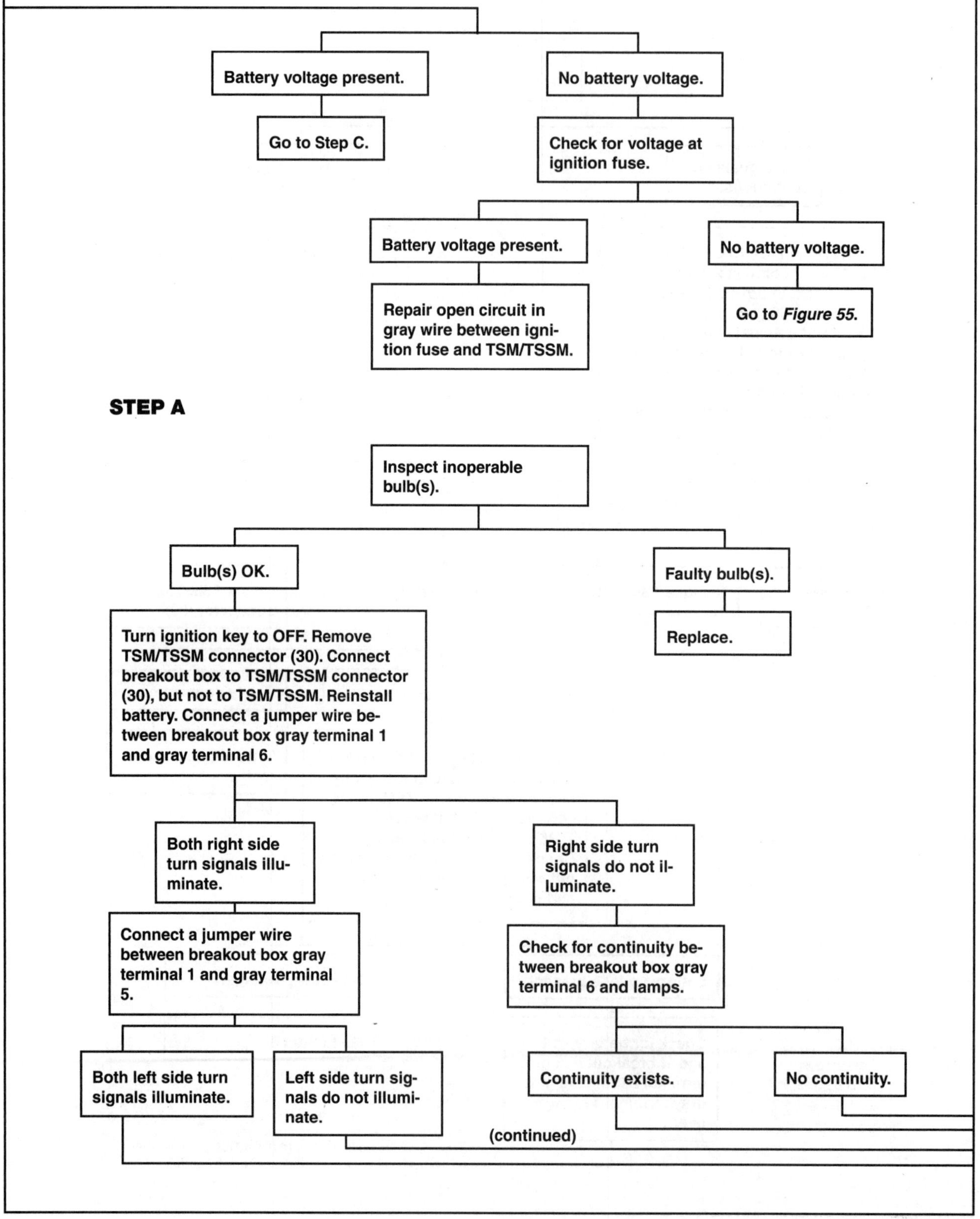
Battery voltage present.
Go to Step C.
No battery voltage.
Check for voltage at ignition fuse.
Battery voltage present.
Repair open circuit in gray wire between ignition fuse and TSM/TSSM.
No battery voltage.
Go to *Figure 55*.
STEP A
Inspect inoperable bulb(s).
Bulb(s) OK.
Turn ignition key to OFF. Remove TSM/TSSM connector (30). Connect breakout box to TSM/TSSM connector (30), but not to TSM/TSSM. Reinstall battery. Connect a jumper wire between breakout box gray terminal 1 and gray terminal 6.
Faulty bulb(s).
Replace.
Both right side turn signals illuminate.
Connect a jumper wire between breakout box gray terminal 1 and gray terminal 5.
Both left side turn signals illuminate.
Left side turn signals do not illuminate.
Right side turn signals do not illuminate.
Check for continuity between breakout box gray terminal 6 and lamps.
Continuity exists.
No continuity.
(continued)

44 (continued)

Go to Step D.

Check for continuity between breakout box gray terminal 5 and lamps.

- Continuity exists.
  - Repair open ground circuit.
- No continuity.
  - Repair open between TSM/TSSM connector (30) and lamps.

Repair open ground circuit.

Repair open between TSM/TSSM connector (30) and lamps.

STEP B

Turn ignition key to OFF. Disconnect the TSM/TSSM connector (30). Connect breakout box to TSM/TSSM connector (30), but not to TSM/TSSM. Reinstall battery. Check resistance between breakout box gray terminal 12 and ground.

- Resistance less than 1 ohm.
  - Check for battery voltage at both 15 amp battery fuse terminals.
    - Voltage present at both terminals.
      - Repair open in brown/gray wire between TSM/TSSM and battery fuse.
    - No voltage.
      - Voltage present at one terminal.
      - No voltage at either terminal.
- Resistance greater than 1 ohm.
  - Repair ground circuit.

(continued)

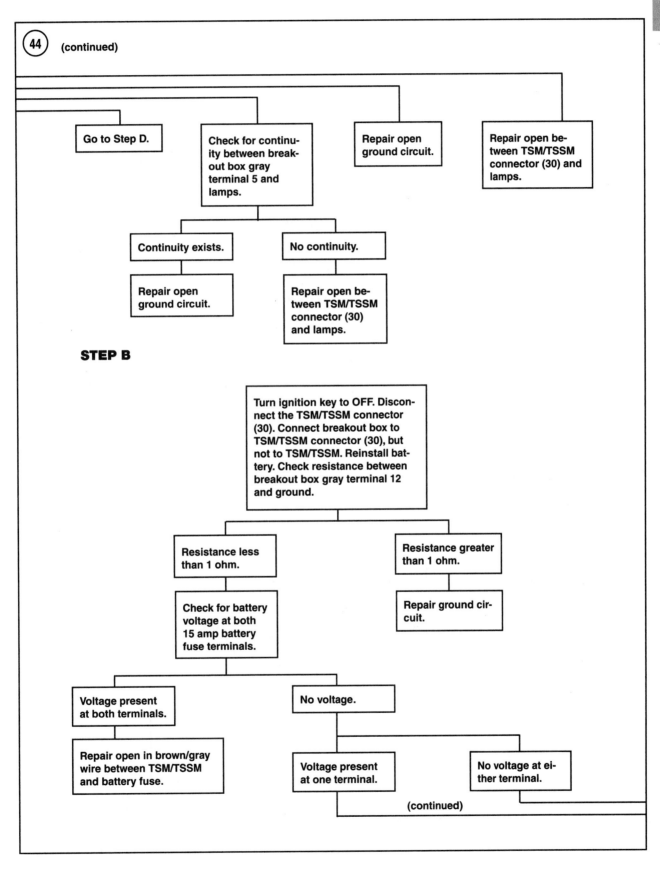

44 (continued)

Replace fuse.

Repair open circuit between fuse block and 30 amp Maxi-fuse.

STEP C

Turn ignition key to OFF. Disconnect TSM/TSSM connector (30). Connect breakout box to TSM/TSSM and connector (30). Reinstall battery. Turn ignition key to ON. Check for battery voltage at breakout box gray terminal 7 when right turn signal button is depressed.

Battery voltage present.

No voltage.

Check for battery voltage at breakout box gray terminal 8 when left turn signal button is depressed.

Remove fuel tank and connect breakout box and adapters between right handlebar switch connectors (22). Turn ignition switch to ON. Check voltage at breakout box black terminal 5 when right turn signal button is depressed.

Battery voltage present.

No voltage.

Battery voltage present.

No voltage.

Go to Step A.

Remove fuel tank and connect breakout box and adapters between left handlebar switch connectors (24). Turn ignition switch to ON. Check voltage at breakout box black terminal 5 when left turn signal button is depressed.

Repair open circuit between TSM/TSSM and right handlebar switch connector (22).

Turn ignition switch to OFF. Check for continuity between breakout box black terminal 5 and ground.

(continued)

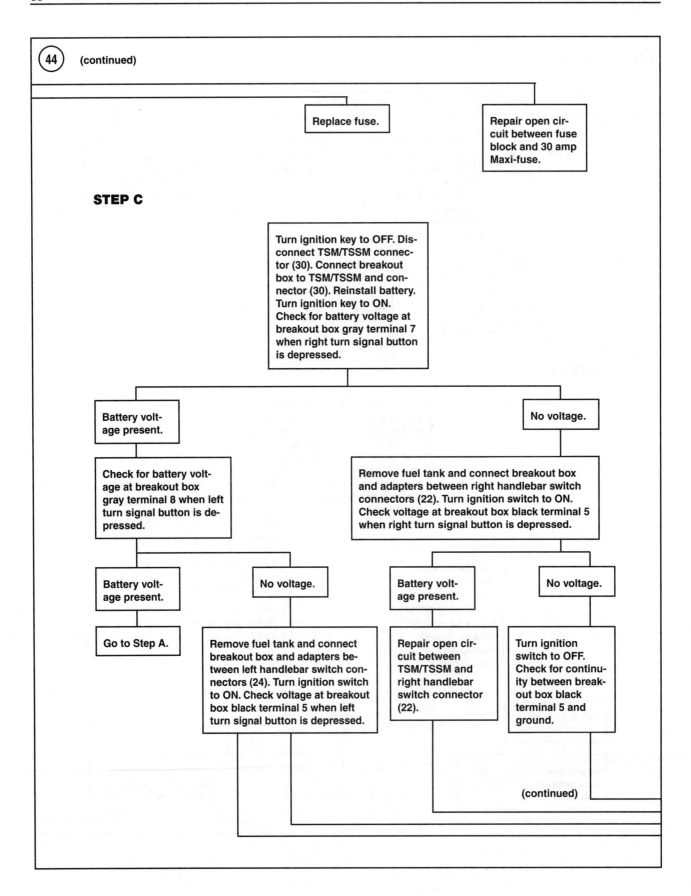

2

(44) (continued)

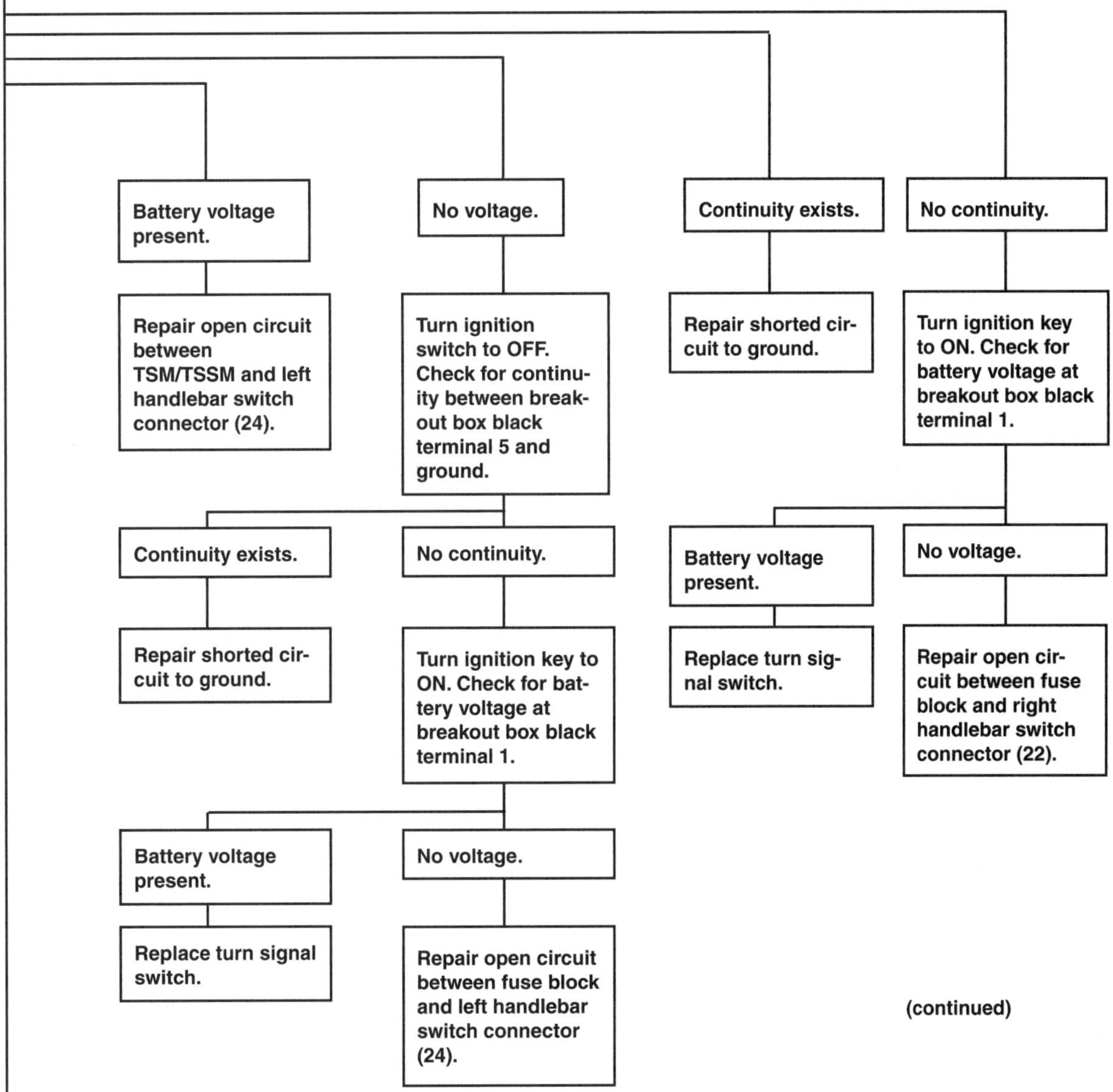
Battery voltage present.
Repair open circuit between TSM/TSSM and left handlebar switch connector (24).
No voltage.
Turn ignition switch to OFF. Check for continuity between breakout box black terminal 5 and ground.
Continuity exists.
Repair shorted circuit to ground.
No continuity.
Turn ignition key to ON. Check for battery voltage at breakout box black terminal 1.
Battery voltage present.
Replace turn signal switch.
No voltage.
Repair open circuit between fuse block and left handlebar switch connector (24).
Continuity exists.
Repair shorted circuit to ground.
No continuity.
Turn ignition key to ON. Check for battery voltage at breakout box black terminal 1.
Battery voltage present.
Replace turn signal switch.
No voltage.
Repair open circuit between fuse block and right handlebar switch connector (22).

(continued)

(44) (continued)

STEP D

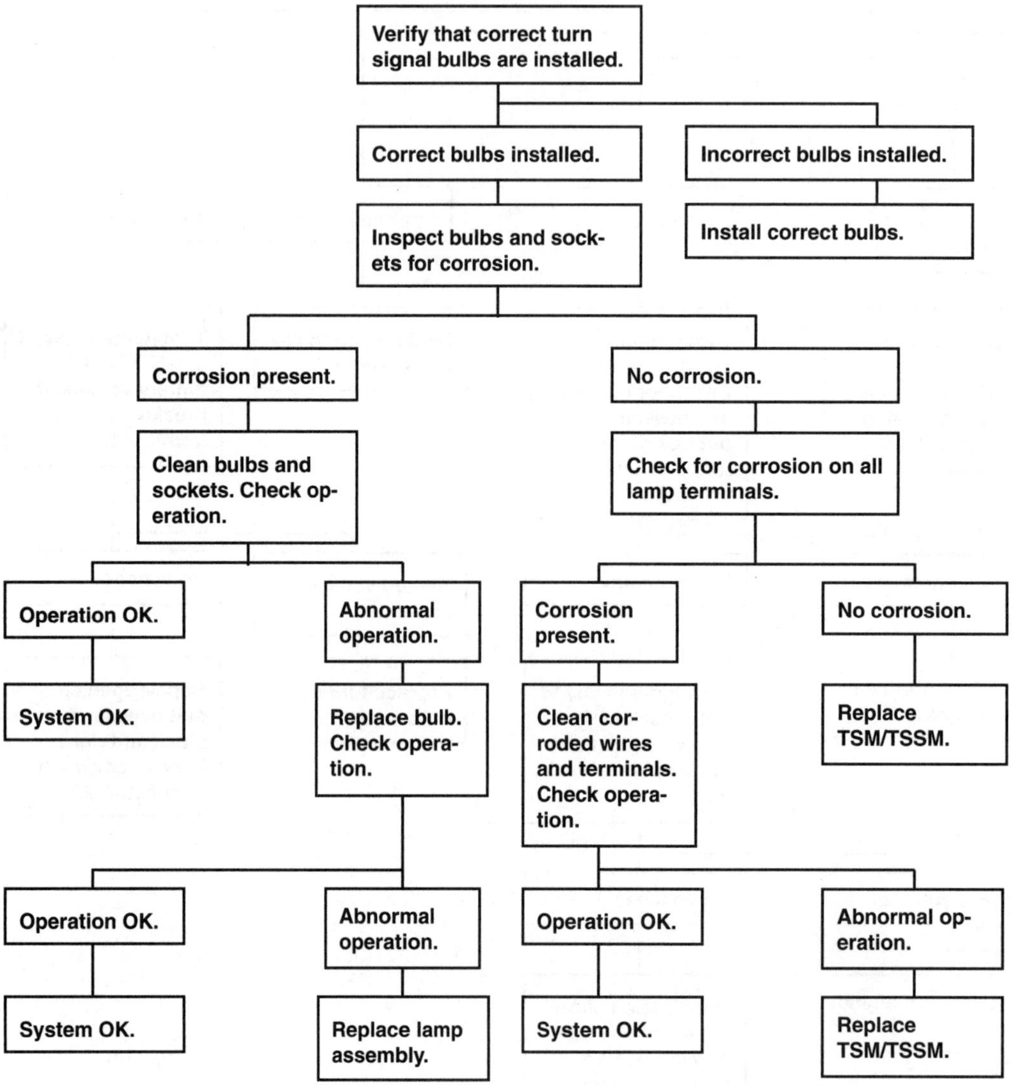

(45)

DTC B1131, B1132: ALARM OUTPUT

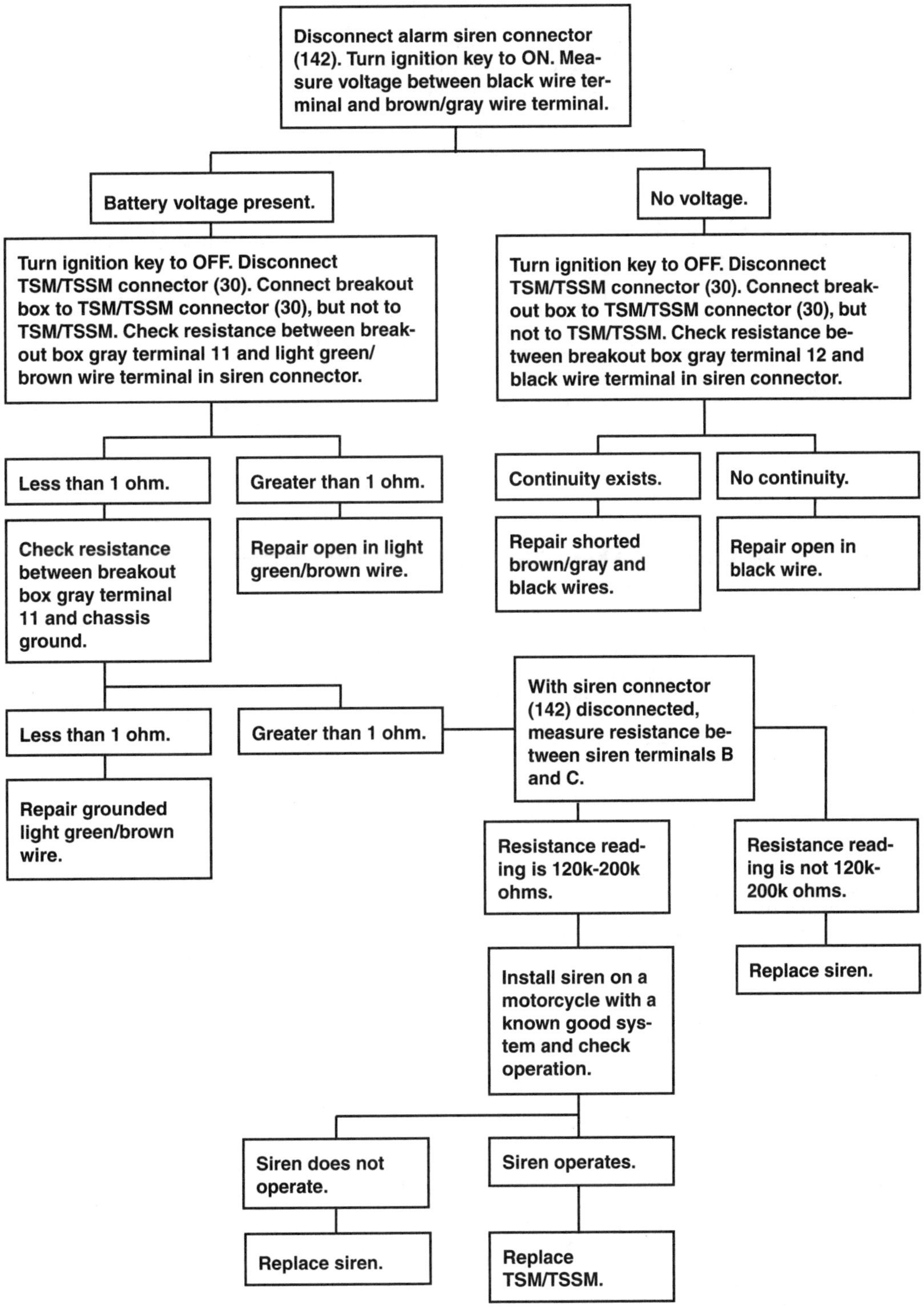

Disconnect alarm siren connector (142). Turn ignition key to ON. Measure voltage between black wire terminal and brown/gray wire terminal.
Battery voltage present.
No voltage.
Turn ignition key to OFF. Disconnect TSM/TSSM connector (30). Connect breakout box to TSM/TSSM connector (30), but not to TSM/TSSM. Check resistance between breakout box gray terminal 11 and light green/brown wire terminal in siren connector.
Turn ignition key to OFF. Disconnect TSM/TSSM connector (30). Connect breakout box to TSM/TSSM connector (30), but not to TSM/TSSM. Check resistance between breakout box gray terminal 12 and black wire terminal in siren connector.
Less than 1 ohm.
Greater than 1 ohm.
Continuity exists.
No continuity.
Check resistance between breakout box gray terminal 11 and chassis ground.
Repair open in light green/brown wire.
Repair shorted brown/gray and black wires.
Repair open in black wire.
Less than 1 ohm.
Greater than 1 ohm.
With siren connector (142) disconnected, measure resistance between siren terminals B and C.
Repair grounded light green/brown wire.
Resistance reading is 120k-200k ohms.
Resistance reading is not 120k-200k ohms.
Install siren on a motorcycle with a known good system and check operation.
Replace siren.
Siren does not operate.
Siren operates.
Replace siren.
Replace TSM/TSSM.

46

DTC B1134: STARTER OUTPUT HIGH

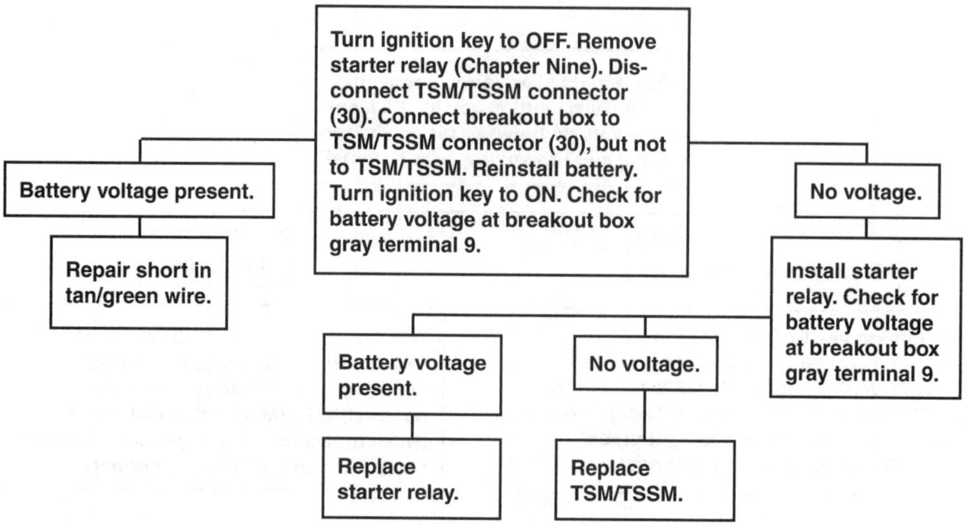

Turn ignition key to OFF. Remove starter relay (Chapter Nine). Disconnect TSM/TSSM connector (30). Connect breakout box to TSM/TSSM connector (30), but not to TSM/TSSM. Reinstall battery. Turn ignition key to ON. Check for battery voltage at breakout box gray terminal 9.
Battery voltage present.
Repair short in tan/green wire.
No voltage.
Install starter relay. Check for battery voltage at breakout box gray terminal 9.
Battery voltage present.
Replace starter relay.
No voltage.
Replace TSM/TSSM.

47

DTC U1097, U1255: LOSS OF SPEEDOMETER OR TSM/TSSM SERIAL DATA

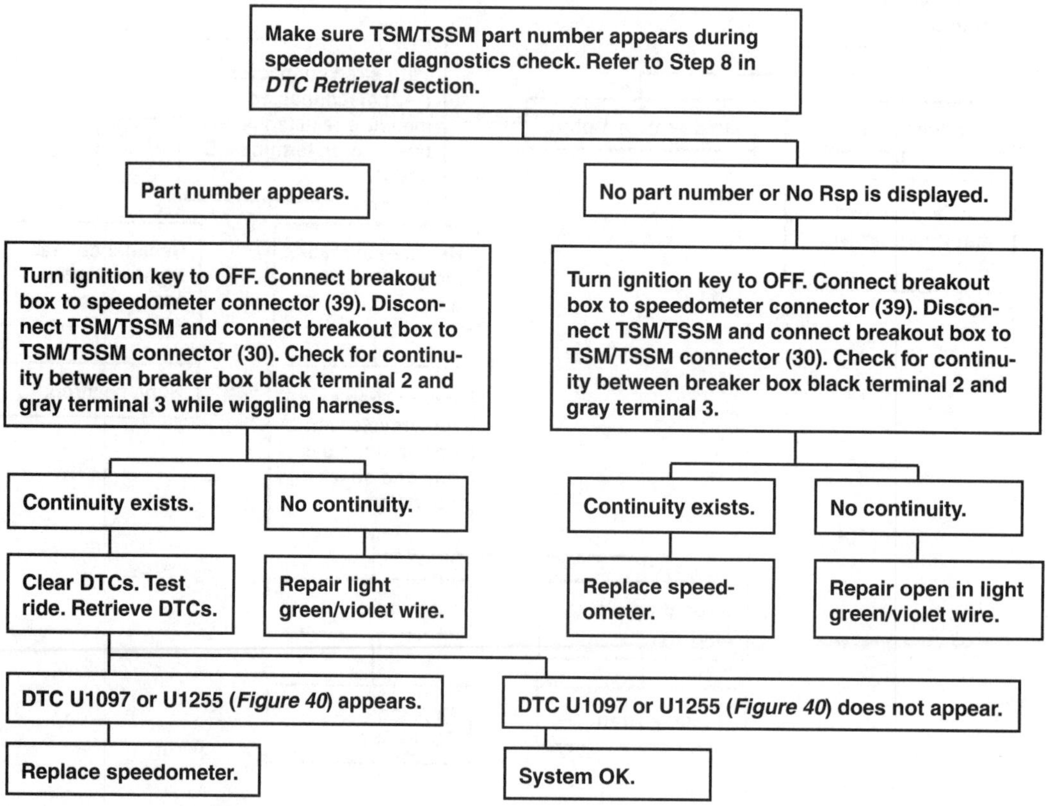

Make sure TSM/TSSM part number appears during speedometer diagnostics check. Refer to Step 8 in *DTC Retrieval* section.
Part number appears.
Turn ignition key to OFF. Connect breakout box to speedometer connector (39). Disconnect TSM/TSSM and connect breakout box to TSM/TSSM connector (30). Check for continuity between breaker box black terminal 2 and gray terminal 3 while wiggling harness.
Continuity exists.
Clear DTCs. Test ride. Retrieve DTCs.
DTC U1097 or U1255 (*Figure 40*) appears.
Replace speedometer.
DTC U1097 or U1255 (*Figure 40*) does not appear.
System OK.
No continuity.
Repair light green/violet wire.
No part number or No Rsp is displayed.
Turn ignition key to OFF. Connect breakout box to speedometer connector (39). Disconnect TSM/TSSM and connect breakout box to TSM/TSSM connector (30). Check for continuity between breaker box black terminal 2 and gray terminal 3.
Continuity exists.
Replace speedometer.
No continuity.
Repair open in light green/violet wire.

48

DTC P0106, P0107, P0108: MAP SENSOR

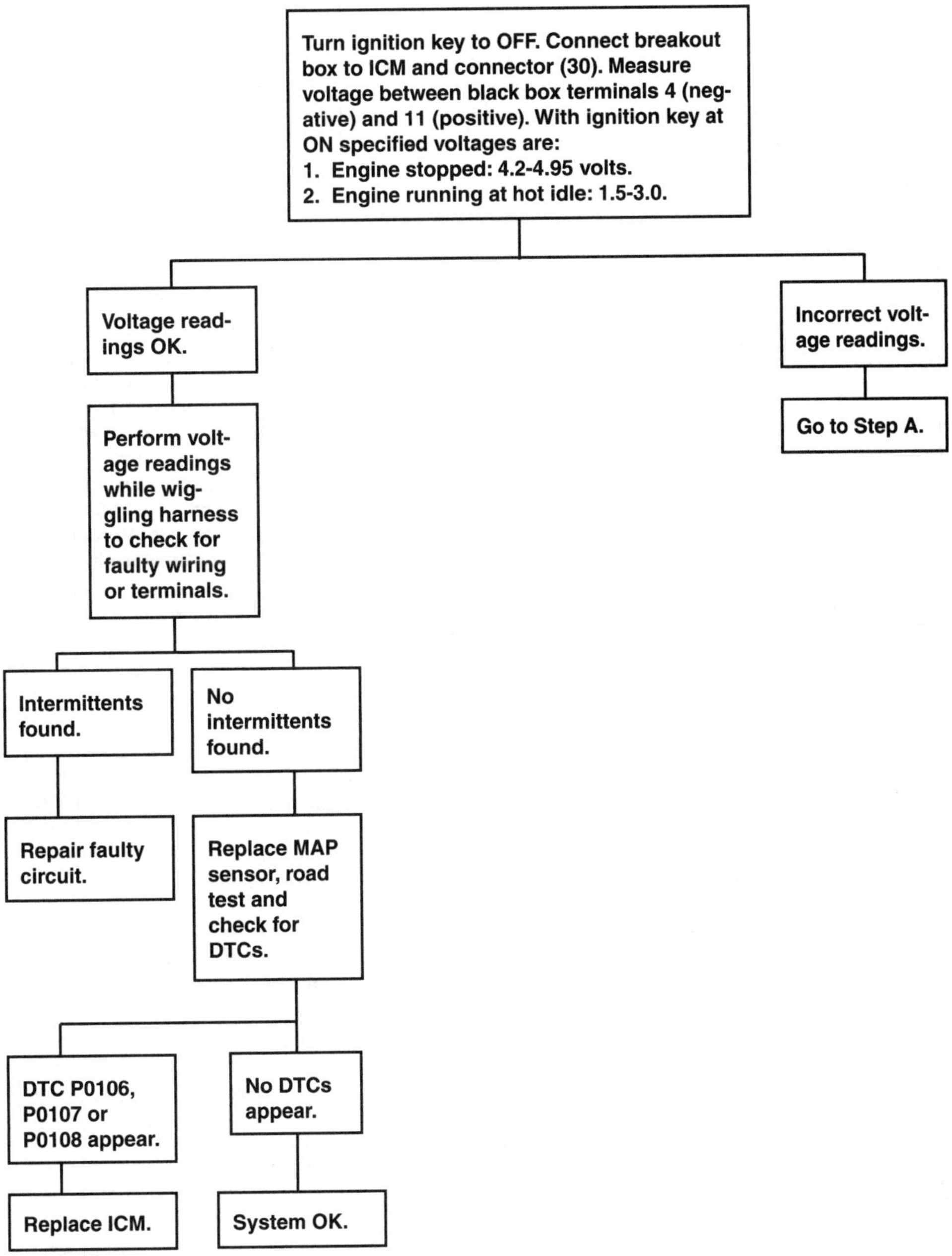
Turn ignition key to OFF. Connect breakout box to ICM and connector (30). Measure voltage between black box terminals 4 (negative) and 11 (positive). With ignition key at ON specified voltages are:
1. Engine stopped: 4.2-4.95 volts.
2. Engine running at hot idle: 1.5-3.0.
Voltage readings OK.
Incorrect voltage readings.
Go to Step A.
Perform voltage readings while wiggling harness to check for faulty wiring or terminals.
Intermittents found.
No intermittents found.
Repair faulty circuit.
Replace MAP sensor, road test and check for DTCs.
DTC P0106, P0107 or P0108 appear.
No DTCs appear.
Replace ICM.
System OK.

(continued)

48 (continued)

STEP A

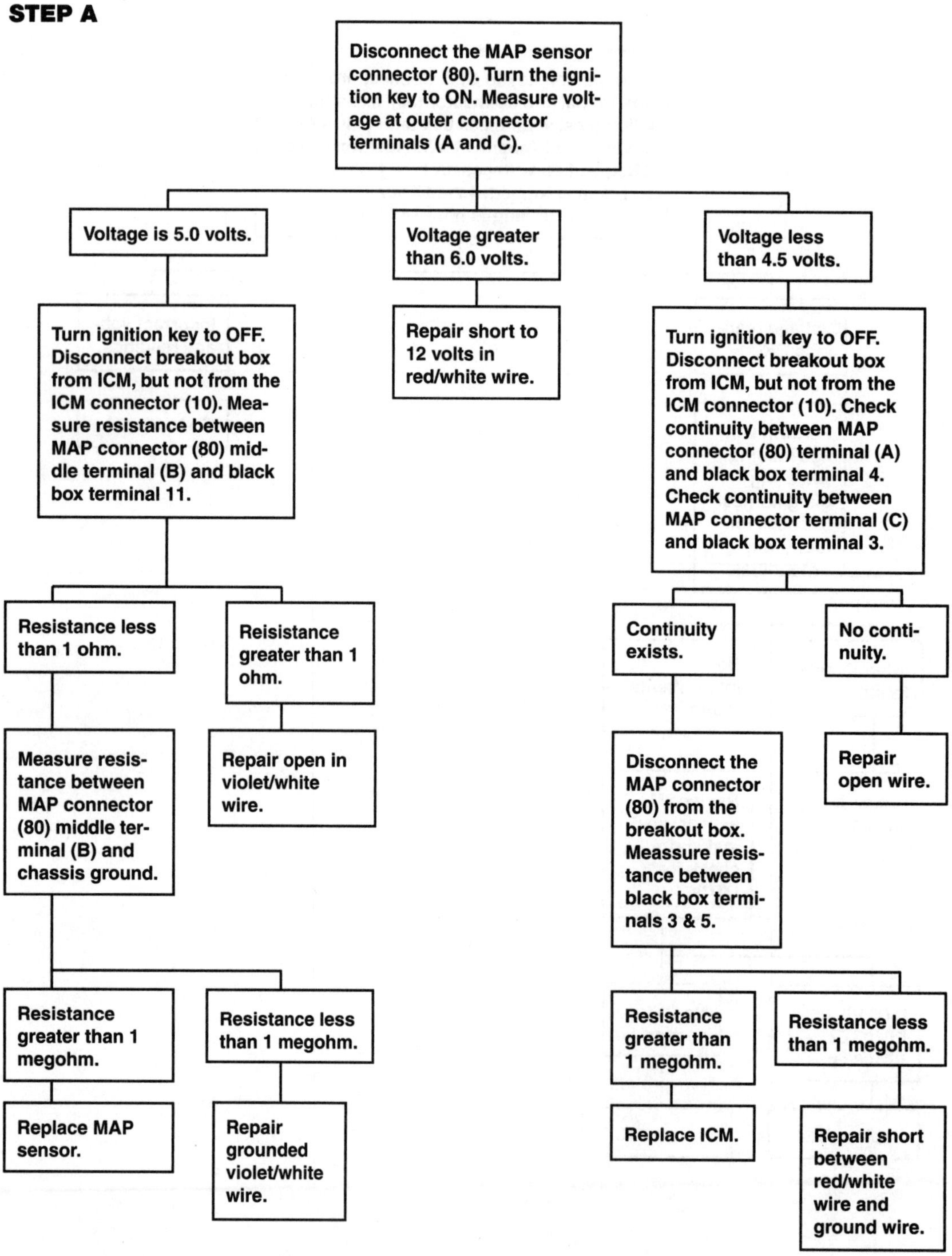
Disconnect the MAP sensor connector (80). Turn the ignition key to ON. Measure voltage at outer connector terminals (A and C).
Voltage is 5.0 volts.
Voltage greater than 6.0 volts.
Voltage less than 4.5 volts.
Turn ignition key to OFF. Disconnect breakout box from ICM, but not from the ICM connector (10). Measure resistance between MAP connector (80) middle terminal (B) and black box terminal 11.
Repair short to 12 volts in red/white wire.
Turn ignition key to OFF. Disconnect breakout box from ICM, but not from the ICM connector (10). Check continuity between MAP connector (80) terminal (A) and black box terminal 4. Check continuity between MAP connector terminal (C) and black box terminal 3.
Resistance less than 1 ohm.
Reisistance greater than 1 ohm.
Continuity exists.
No continuity.
Measure resistance between MAP connector (80) middle terminal (B) and chassis ground.
Repair open in violet/white wire.
Disconnect the MAP connector (80) from the breakout box. Meassure resistance between black box terminals 3 & 5.
Repair open wire.
Resistance greater than 1 megohm.
Resistance less than 1 megohm.
Resistance greater than 1 megohm.
Resistance less than 1 megohm.
Replace MAP sensor.
Repair grounded violet/white wire.
Replace ICM.
Repair short between red/white wire and ground wire.

(49)

DTC P0371, P0372, P0374: CRANK POSITION (CKP) SENSOR

Turn ignition key to OFF. Connect breakout box to ICM connector (10). Measure resistance between black box terminals 5 (negative) and 8 (positive). Measure resistance between black box terminals 5 (negative) and 9 (positive).

- Resistance is greater than 1 megohm.
  - Turn ignition key to ON. Measure voltage between black box terminals 5 and 8. Measure voltage between black box terminals 5 and 9.
    - Voltage present.
      - Disconnect CKP sensor connector (79). Measure voltage between black box terminals 5 and 8. Measure voltage between black box terminals 5 and 9.
        - Voltage present.
        - No voltage.
    - No voltage.
      - Check for faulty wiring, connections or loose CKP sensor bolt.
        - Faulty connection, wiring or loose CKP sensor bolt found.
        - No faults found.
- Resistance is less than 1 megohm.
  - Disconnected CKP sensor connector (79). Measure resistance bewtween black box terminals 5 and 8. Measure resistance between black box terminals 5 and 9.
    - Resistance is less than 1 megohm.
      - Repair grounded red or black wire.
    - Resistance is greater than 1 megohm.
      - Replace CKP sensor.

(continued)

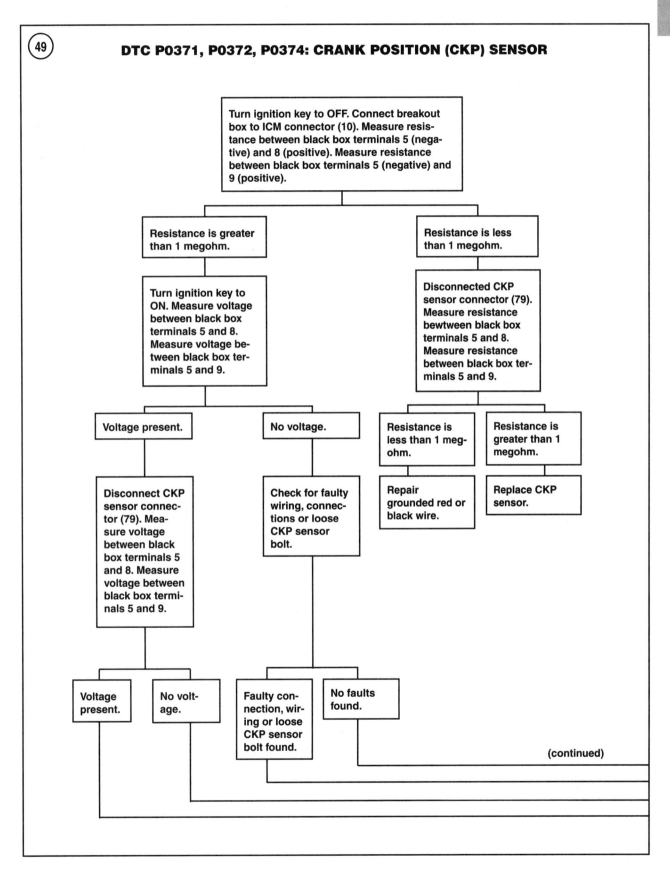

49 (continued)

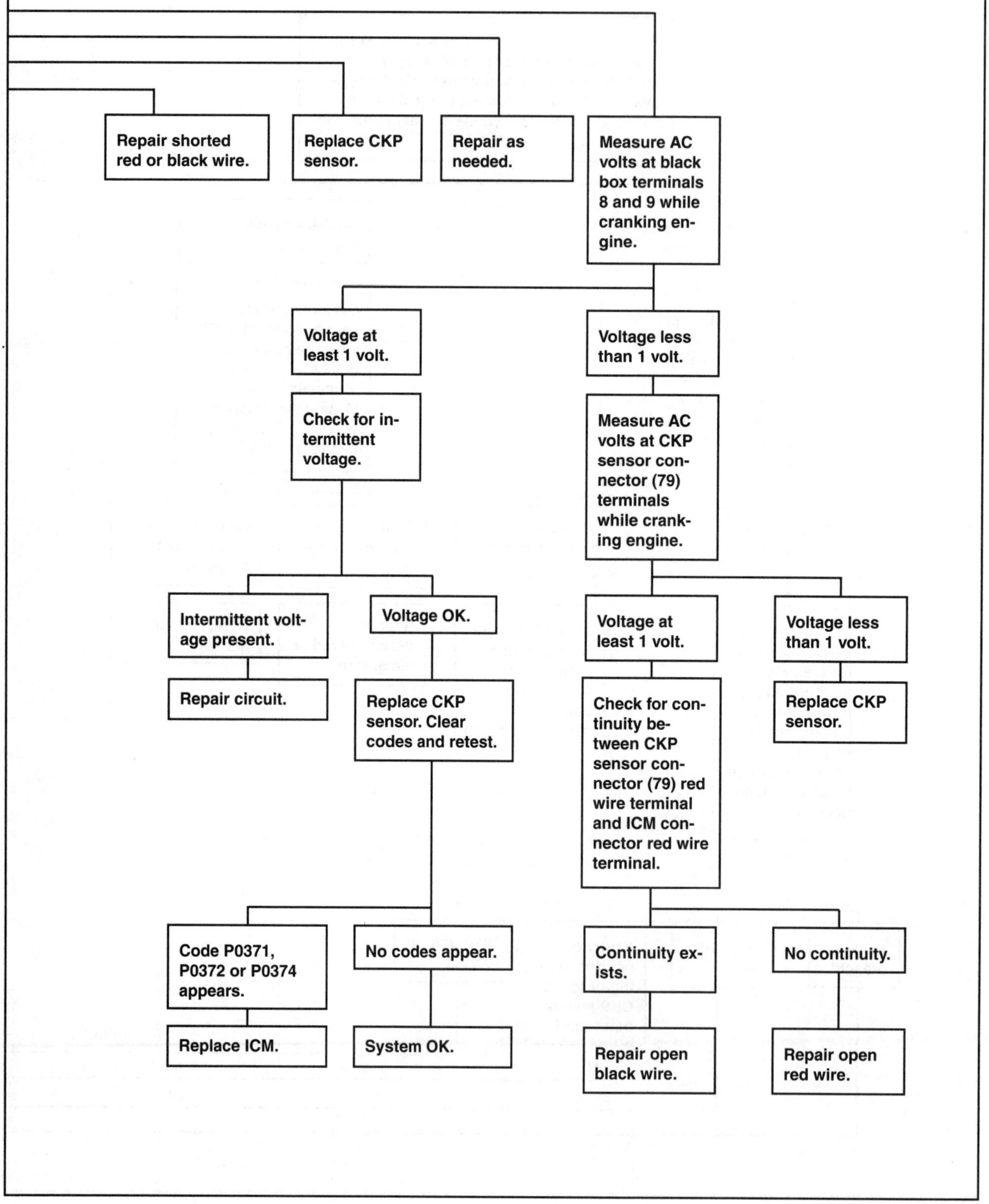

50

DTC P0501, P0502: VEHICLE SPEED SENSOR (VSS)

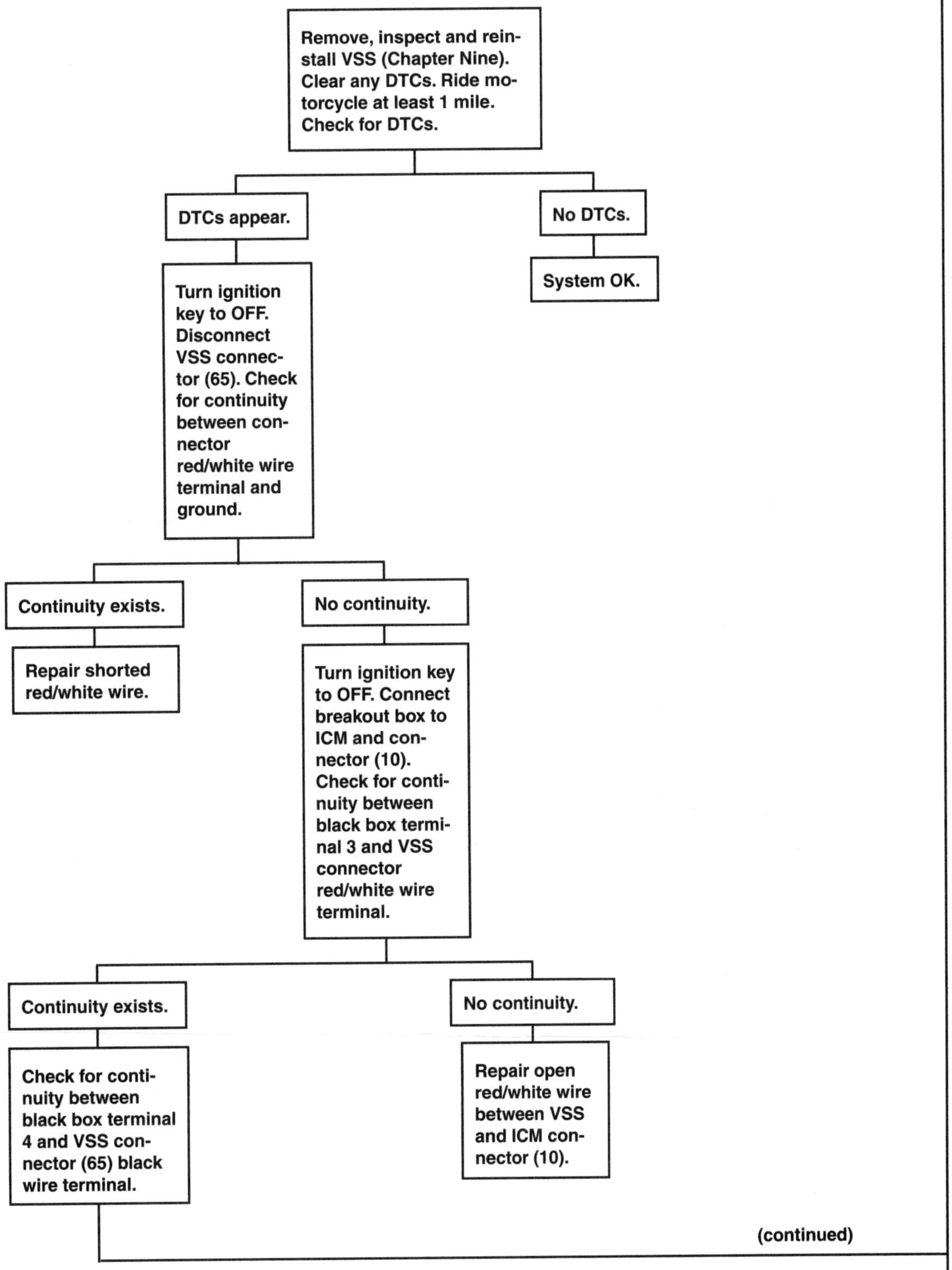

Remove, inspect and reinstall VSS (Chapter Nine). Clear any DTCs. Ride motorcycle at least 1 mile. Check for DTCs.
DTCs appear.
No DTCs.
System OK.
Turn ignition key to OFF. Disconnect VSS connector (65). Check for continuity between connector red/white wire terminal and ground.
Continuity exists.
Repair shorted red/white wire.
No continuity.
Turn ignition key to OFF. Connect breakout box to ICM and connector (10). Check for continuity between black box terminal 3 and VSS connector red/white wire terminal.
Continuity exists.
Check for continuity between black box terminal 4 and VSS connector (65) black wire terminal.
No continuity.
Repair open red/white wire between VSS and ICM connector (10).
(continued)

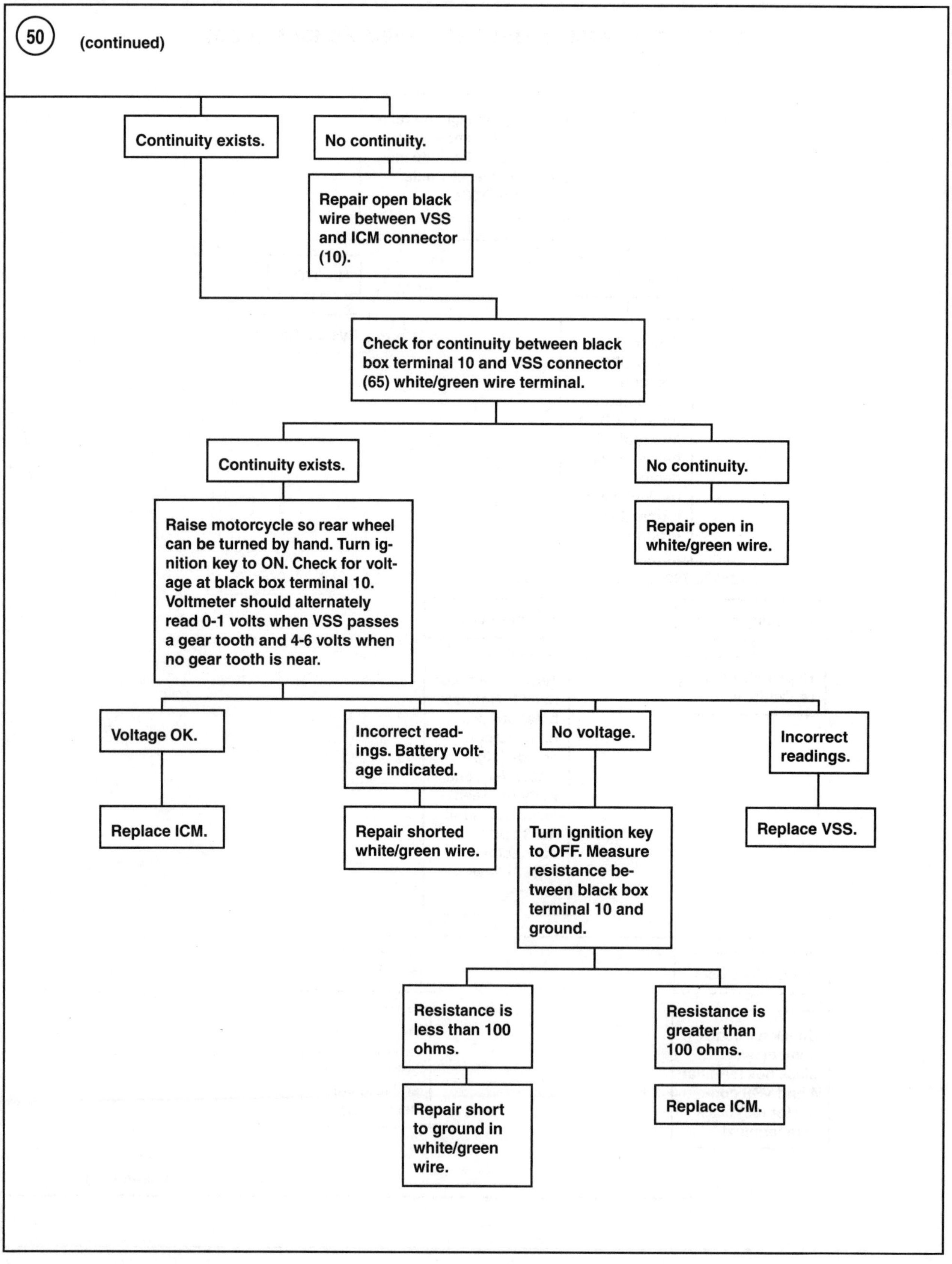
50
(continued)
Continuity exists.
No continuity.
Repair open black wire between VSS and ICM connector (10).
Check for continuity between black box terminal 10 and VSS connector (65) white/green wire terminal.
Continuity exists.
No continuity.
Raise motorcycle so rear wheel can be turned by hand. Turn ignition key to ON. Check for voltage at black box terminal 10. Voltmeter should alternately read 0-1 volts when VSS passes a gear tooth and 4-6 volts when no gear tooth is near.
Repair open in white/green wire.
Voltage OK.
Incorrect readings. Battery voltage indicated.
No voltage.
Incorrect readings.
Replace ICM.
Repair shorted white/green wire.
Turn ignition key to OFF. Measure resistance between black box terminal 10 and ground.
Replace VSS.
Resistance is less than 100 ohms.
Resistance is greater than 100 ohms.
Repair short to ground in white/green wire.
Replace ICM.

51

DTC P0562, P0563: SYSTEM VOLTAGE

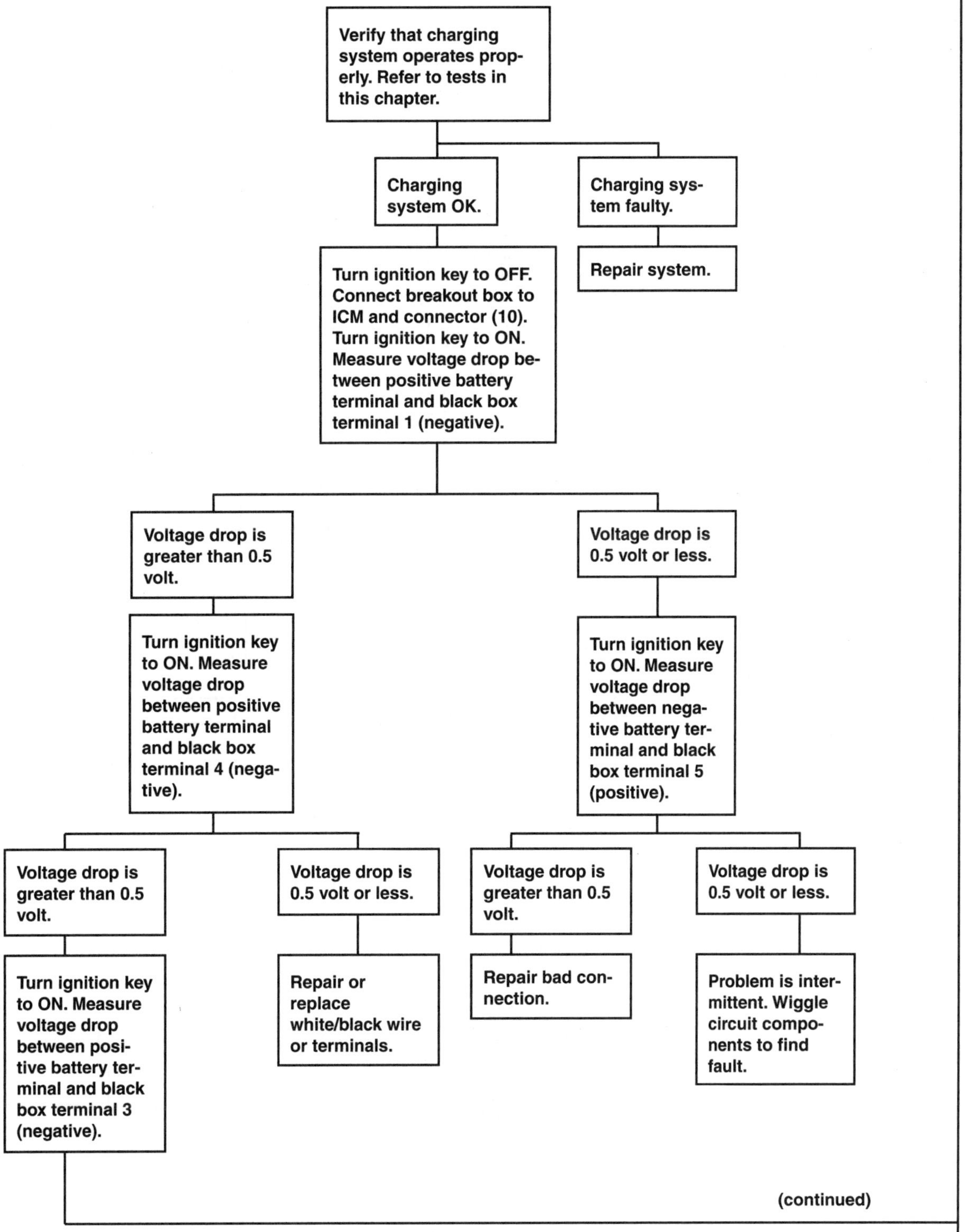

Verify that charging system operates properly. Refer to tests in this chapter.
Charging system OK.
Charging system faulty.
Repair system.
Turn ignition key to OFF. Connect breakout box to ICM and connector (10). Turn ignition key to ON. Measure voltage drop between positive battery terminal and black box terminal 1 (negative).
Voltage drop is greater than 0.5 volt.
Voltage drop is 0.5 volt or less.
Turn ignition key to ON. Measure voltage drop between positive battery terminal and black box terminal 4 (negative).
Turn ignition key to ON. Measure voltage drop between negative battery terminal and black box terminal 5 (positive).
Voltage drop is greater than 0.5 volt.
Voltage drop is 0.5 volt or less.
Voltage drop is greater than 0.5 volt.
Voltage drop is 0.5 volt or less.
Turn ignition key to ON. Measure voltage drop between positive battery terminal and black box terminal 3 (negative).
Repair or replace white/black wire or terminals.
Repair bad connection.
Problem is intermittent. Wiggle circuit components to find fault.

(continued)

51 (continued)

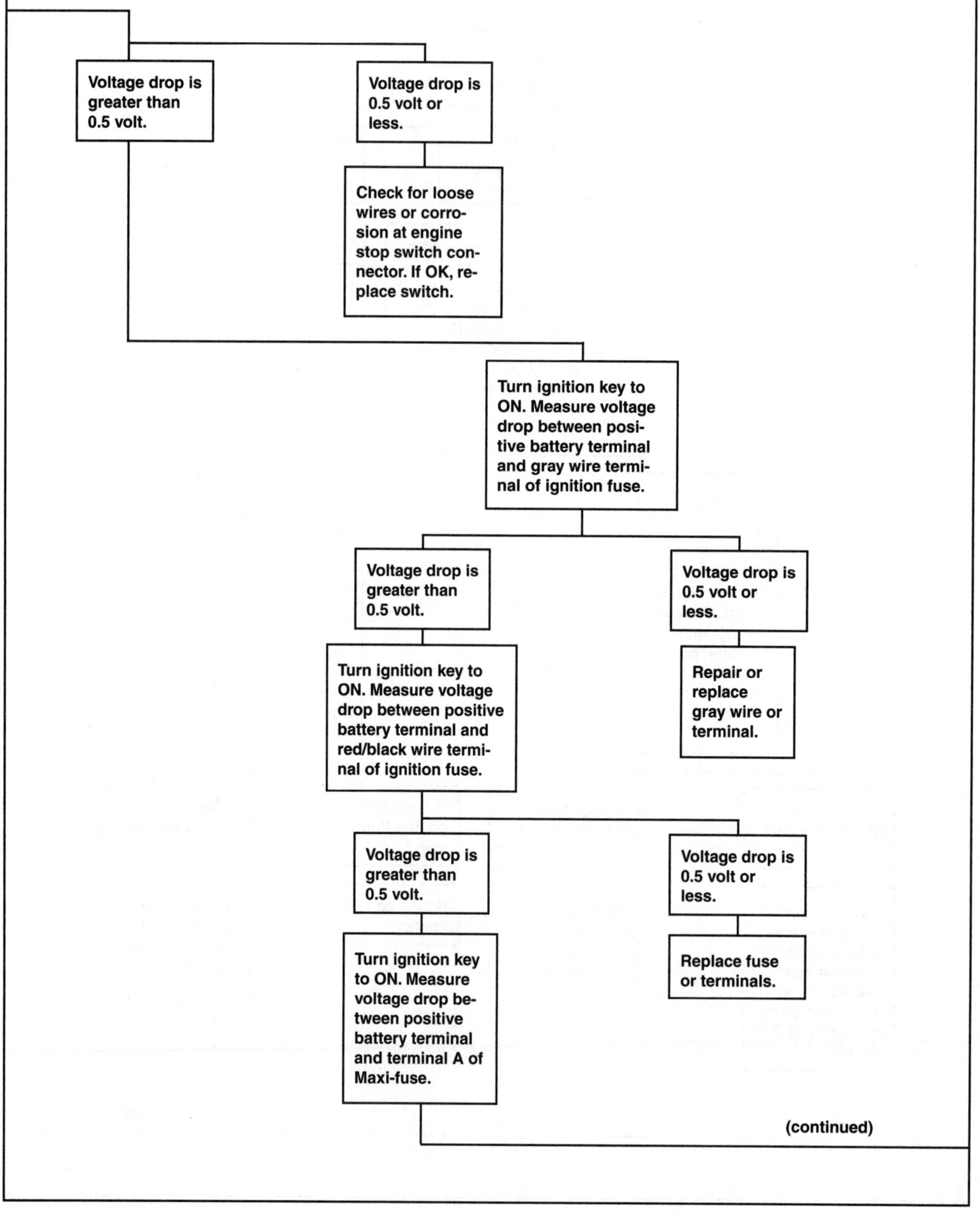
Voltage drop is greater than 0.5 volt.
Voltage drop is 0.5 volt or less.
Check for loose wires or corrosion at engine stop switch connector. If OK, replace switch.
Turn ignition key to ON. Measure voltage drop between positive battery terminal and gray wire terminal of ignition fuse.
Voltage drop is greater than 0.5 volt.
Voltage drop is 0.5 volt or less.
Turn ignition key to ON. Measure voltage drop between positive battery terminal and red/black wire terminal of ignition fuse.
Repair or replace gray wire or terminal.
Voltage drop is greater than 0.5 volt.
Voltage drop is 0.5 volt or less.
Turn ignition key to ON. Measure voltage drop between positive battery terminal and terminal A of Maxi-fuse.
Replace fuse or terminals.
(continued)

51 (continued)

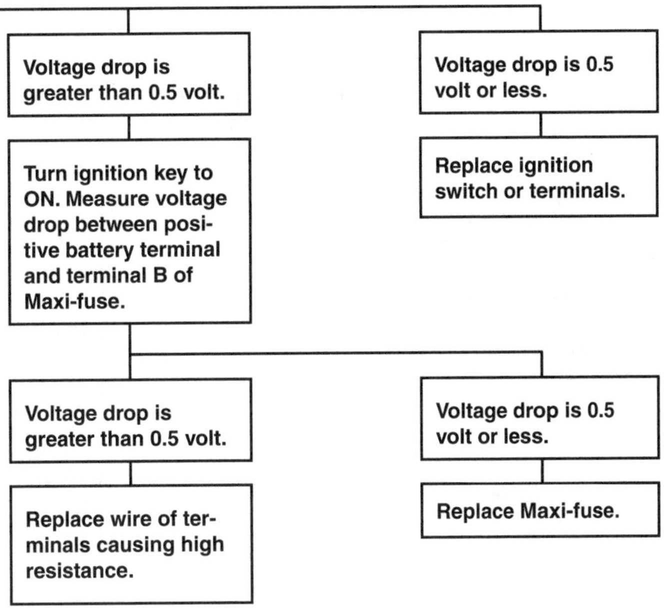
Voltage drop is greater than 0.5 volt.
Voltage drop is 0.5 volt or less.
Turn ignition key to ON. Measure voltage drop between positive battery terminal and terminal B of Maxi-fuse.
Replace ignition switch or terminals.
Voltage drop is greater than 0.5 volt.
Voltage drop is 0.5 volt or less.
Replace wire of terminals causing high resistance.
Replace Maxi-fuse.

52

DTC P1009: INCORRECT PASSWORD

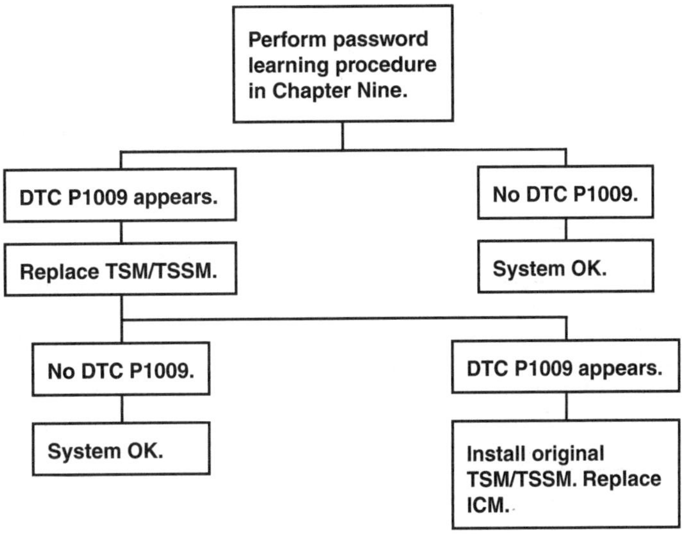
Perform password learning procedure in Chapter Nine.
DTC P1009 appears.
No DTC P1009.
Replace TSM/TSSM.
System OK.
No DTC P1009.
DTC P1009 appears.
System OK.
Install original TSM/TSSM. Replace ICM.

53

DTC P1010: MISSING PASSWORD

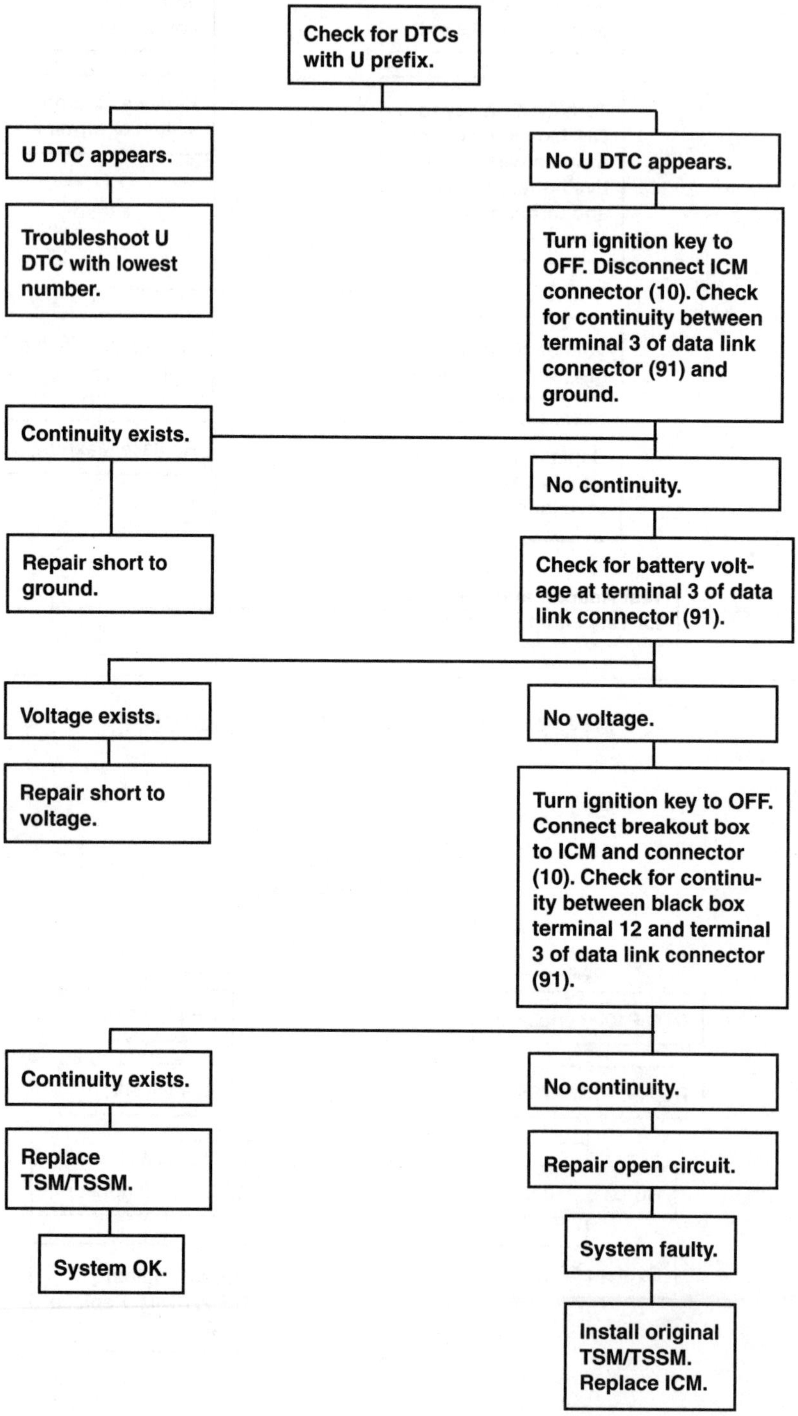
Check for DTCs with U prefix.
U DTC appears.
No U DTC appears.
Troubleshoot U DTC with lowest number.
Turn ignition key to OFF. Disconnect ICM connector (10). Check for continuity between terminal 3 of data link connector (91) and ground.
Continuity exists.
No continuity.
Repair short to ground.
Check for battery voltage at terminal 3 of data link connector (91).
Voltage exists.
No voltage.
Repair short to voltage.
Turn ignition key to OFF. Connect breakout box to ICM and connector (10). Check for continuity between black box terminal 12 and terminal 3 of data link connector (91).
Continuity exists.
No continuity.
Replace TSM/TSSM.
Repair open circuit.
System OK.
System faulty.
Install original TSM/TSSM. Replace ICM.

54

DTC P1351, P1352, P1354, P1355: IGNITION COIL

NOTE: This procedure uses H-D tools Ignition Coil Circuit Test Adapter (part No. HD-44687) and Fuel Injector Test Lamp (part No. HD-34730-2C).

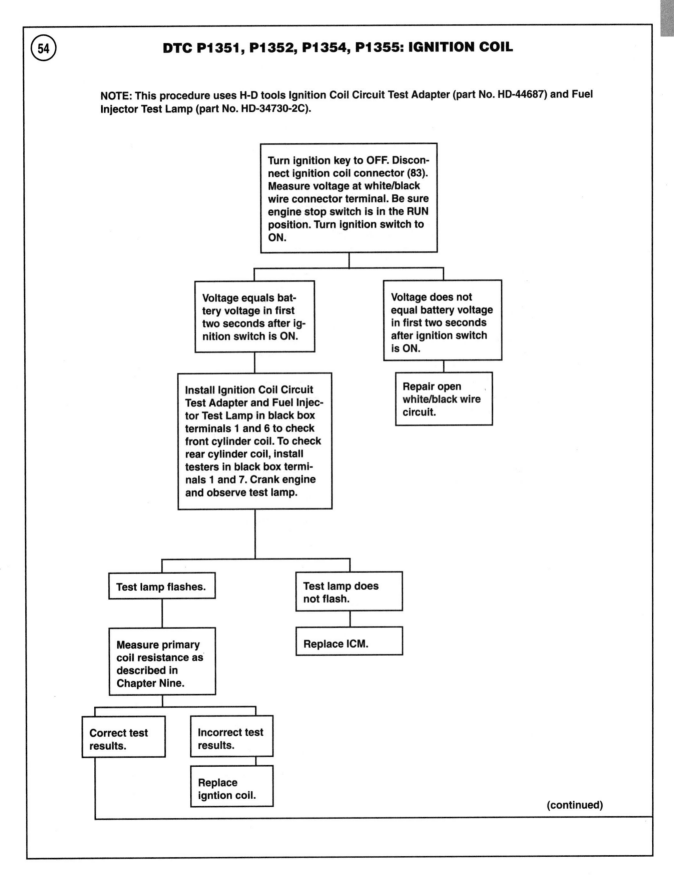

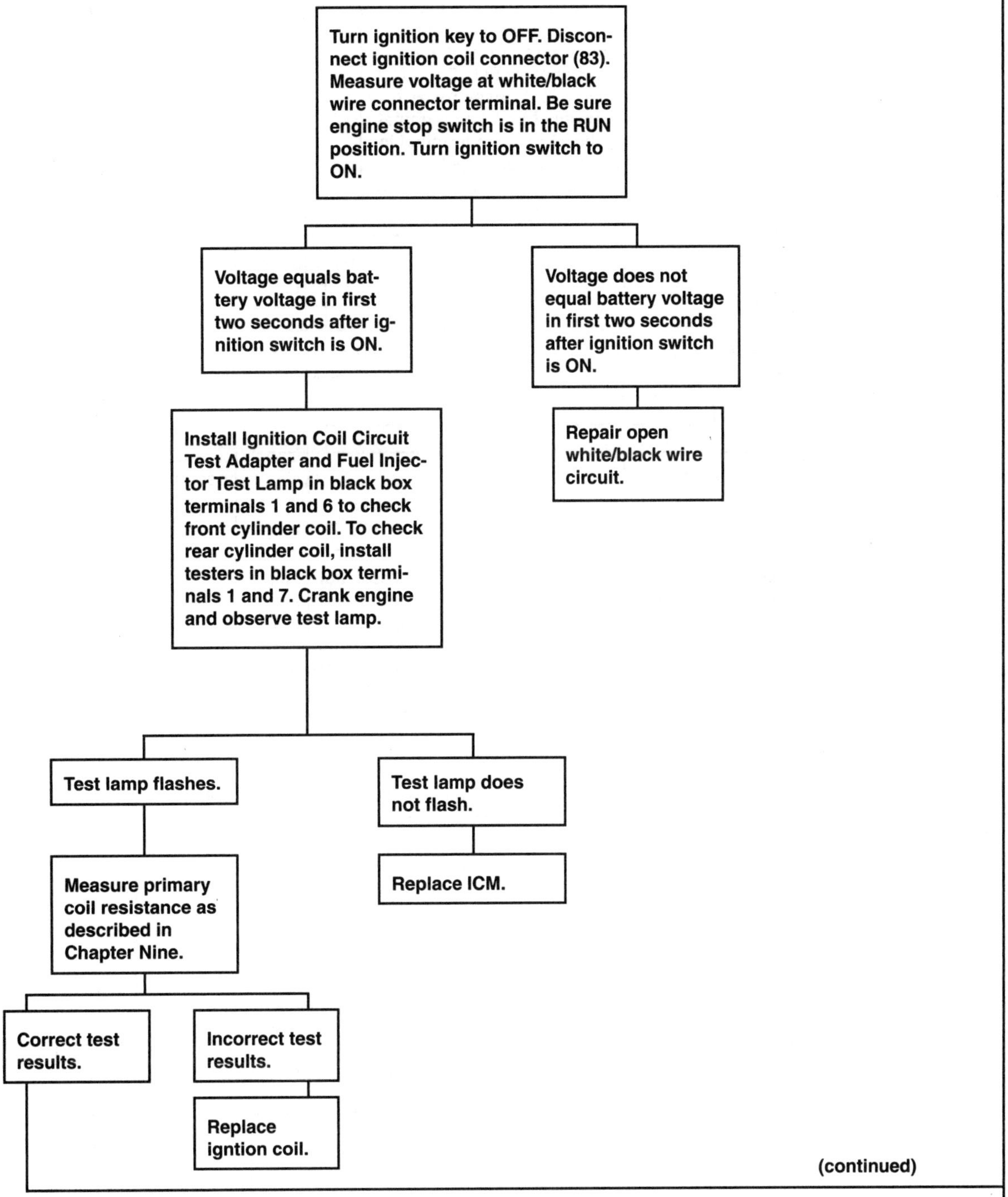

Turn ignition key to OFF. Disconnect ignition coil connector (83). Measure voltage at white/black wire connector terminal. Be sure engine stop switch is in the RUN position. Turn ignition switch to ON.
Voltage equals battery voltage in first two seconds after ignition switch is ON.
Voltage does not equal battery voltage in first two seconds after ignition switch is ON.
Repair open white/black wire circuit.
Install Ignition Coil Circuit Test Adapter and Fuel Injector Test Lamp in black box terminals 1 and 6 to check front cylinder coil. To check rear cylinder coil, install testers in black box terminals 1 and 7. Crank engine and observe test lamp.
Test lamp flashes.
Test lamp does not flash.
Replace ICM.
Measure primary coil resistance as described in Chapter Nine.
Correct test results.
Incorrect test results.
Replace igntion coil.

(continued)

54 (continued)

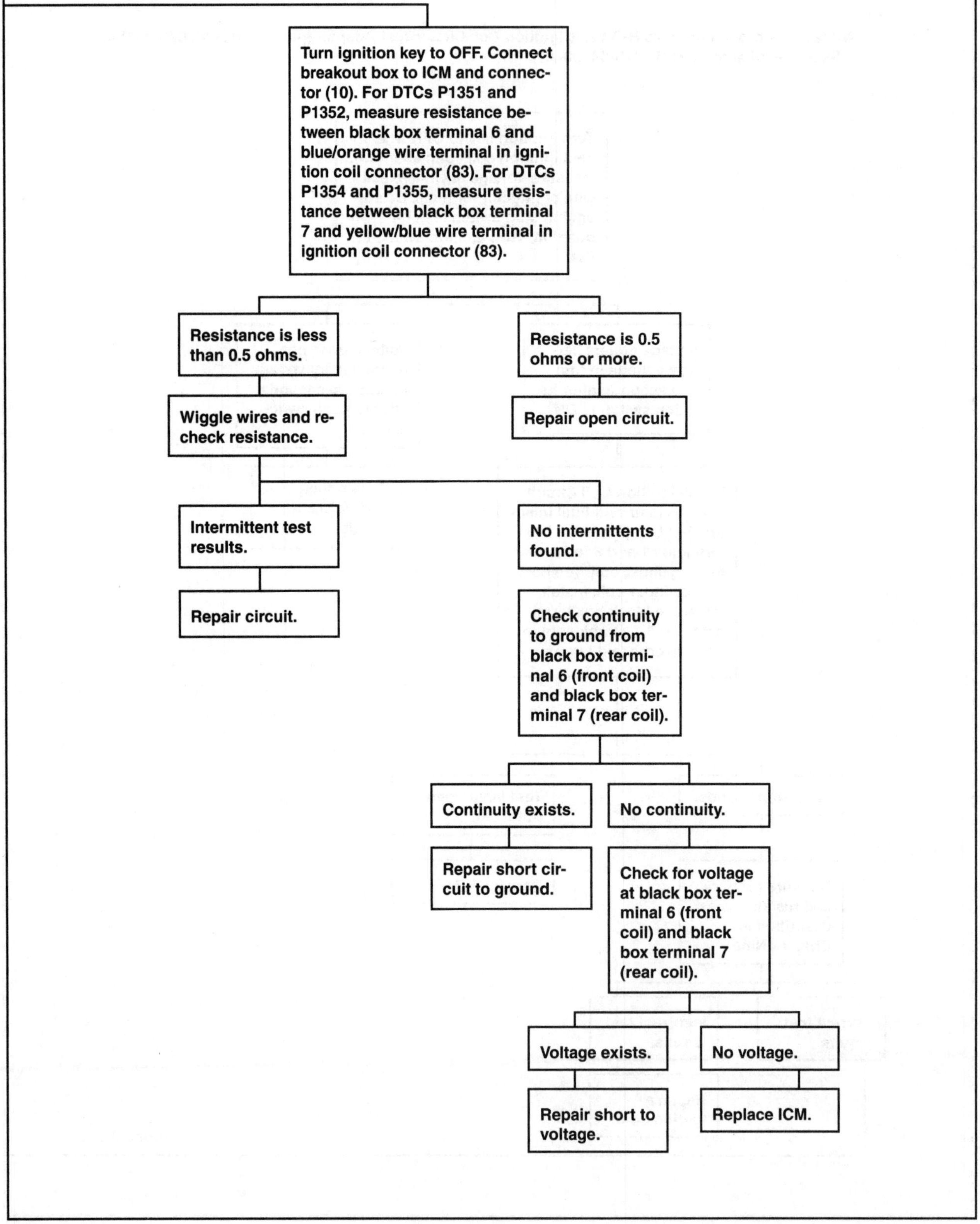

Turn ignition key to OFF. Connect breakout box to ICM and connector (10). For DTCs P1351 and P1352, measure resistance between black box terminal 6 and blue/orange wire terminal in ignition coil connector (83). For DTCs P1354 and P1355, measure resistance between black box terminal 7 and yellow/blue wire terminal in ignition coil connector (83).
Resistance is less than 0.5 ohms.
Resistance is 0.5 ohms or more.
Wiggle wires and recheck resistance.
Repair open circuit.
Intermittent test results.
No intermittents found.
Repair circuit.
Check continuity to ground from black box terminal 6 (front coil) and black box terminal 7 (rear coil).
Continuity exists.
No continuity.
Repair short circuit to ground.
Check for voltage at black box terminal 6 (front coil) and black box terminal 7 (rear coil).
Voltage exists.
No voltage.
Repair short to voltage.
Replace ICM.

55

NO SPARK OR ICM POWER

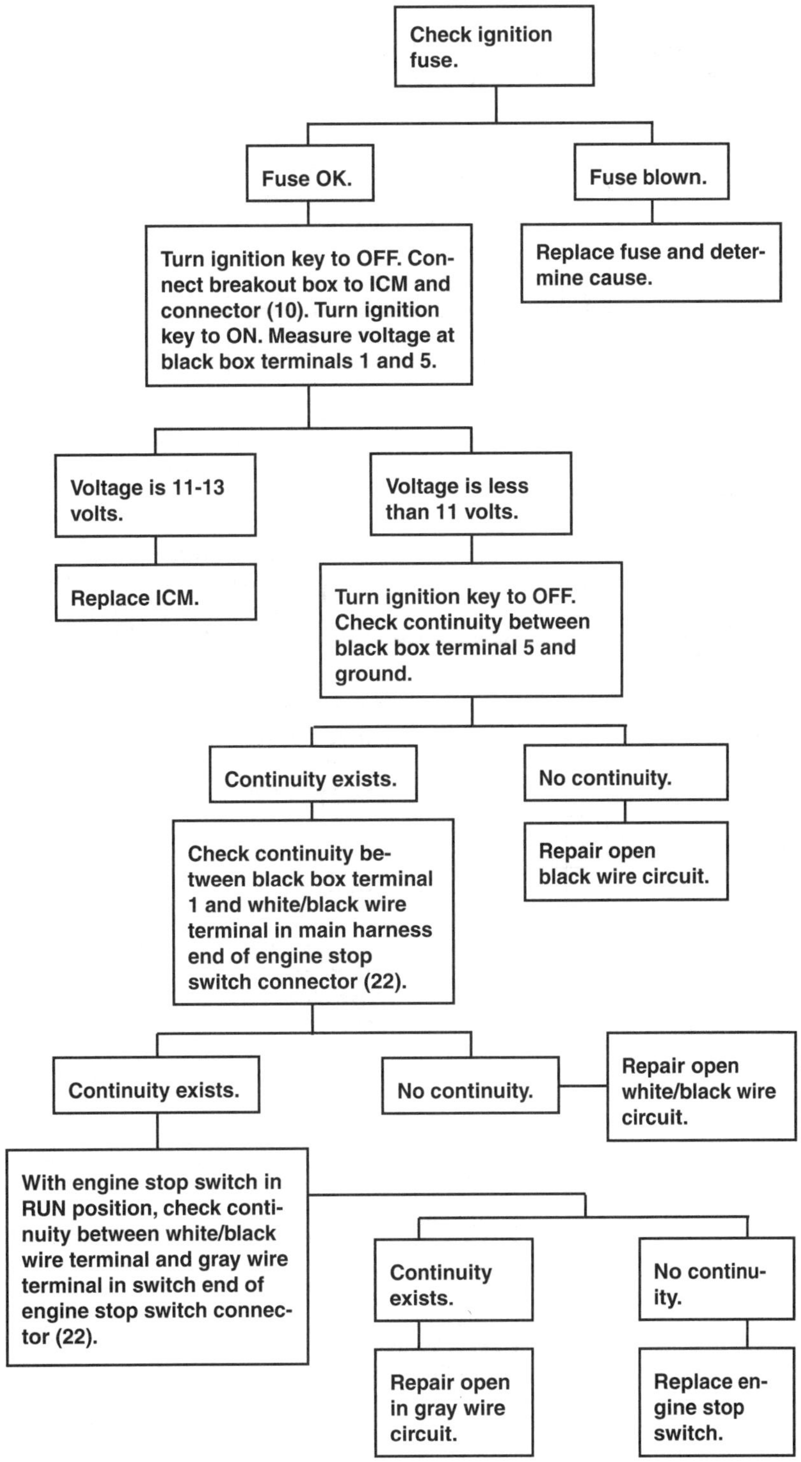

Check ignition fuse.
Fuse OK.
Fuse blown.
Replace fuse and determine cause.
Turn ignition key to OFF. Connect breakout box to ICM and connector (10). Turn ignition key to ON. Measure voltage at black box terminals 1 and 5.
Voltage is 11-13 volts.
Replace ICM.
Voltage is less than 11 volts.
Turn ignition key to OFF. Check continuity between black box terminal 5 and ground.
Continuity exists.
No continuity.
Repair open black wire circuit.
Check continuity between black box terminal 1 and white/black wire terminal in main harness end of engine stop switch connector (22).
Continuity exists.
No continuity.
Repair open white/black wire circuit.
With engine stop switch in RUN position, check continuity between white/black wire terminal and gray wire terminal in switch end of engine stop switch connector (22).
Continuity exists.
Repair open in gray wire circuit.
No continuity.
Replace engine stop switch.

56

TACHOMETER FAULTY

NOTE: The green and orange symbols in the initial test represent cruise (green) and pursuit (orange) functions on models other than Sportsters.

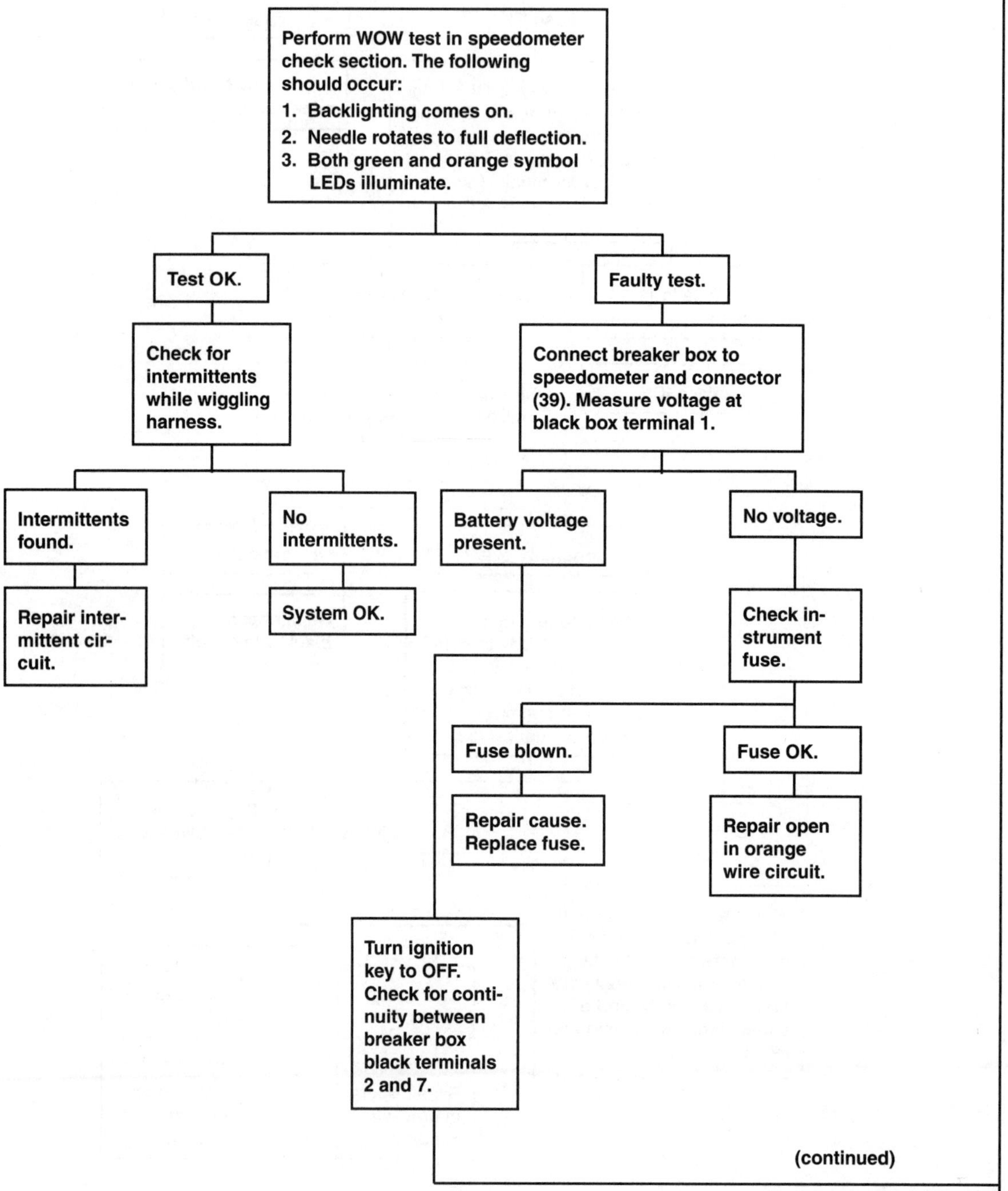

Perform WOW test in speedometer check section. The following should occur:
1. Backlighting comes on.
2. Needle rotates to full deflection.
3. Both green and orange symbol LEDs illuminate.
Test OK.
Faulty test.
Check for intermittents while wiggling harness.
Connect breaker box to speedometer and connector (39). Measure voltage at black box terminal 1.
Intermittents found.
No intermittents.
Battery voltage present.
No voltage.
Repair intermittent circuit.
System OK.
Check instrument fuse.
Fuse blown.
Fuse OK.
Repair cause. Replace fuse.
Repair open in orange wire circuit.
Turn ignition key to OFF. Check for continuity between breaker box black terminals 2 and 7.

(continued)

56 (continued)

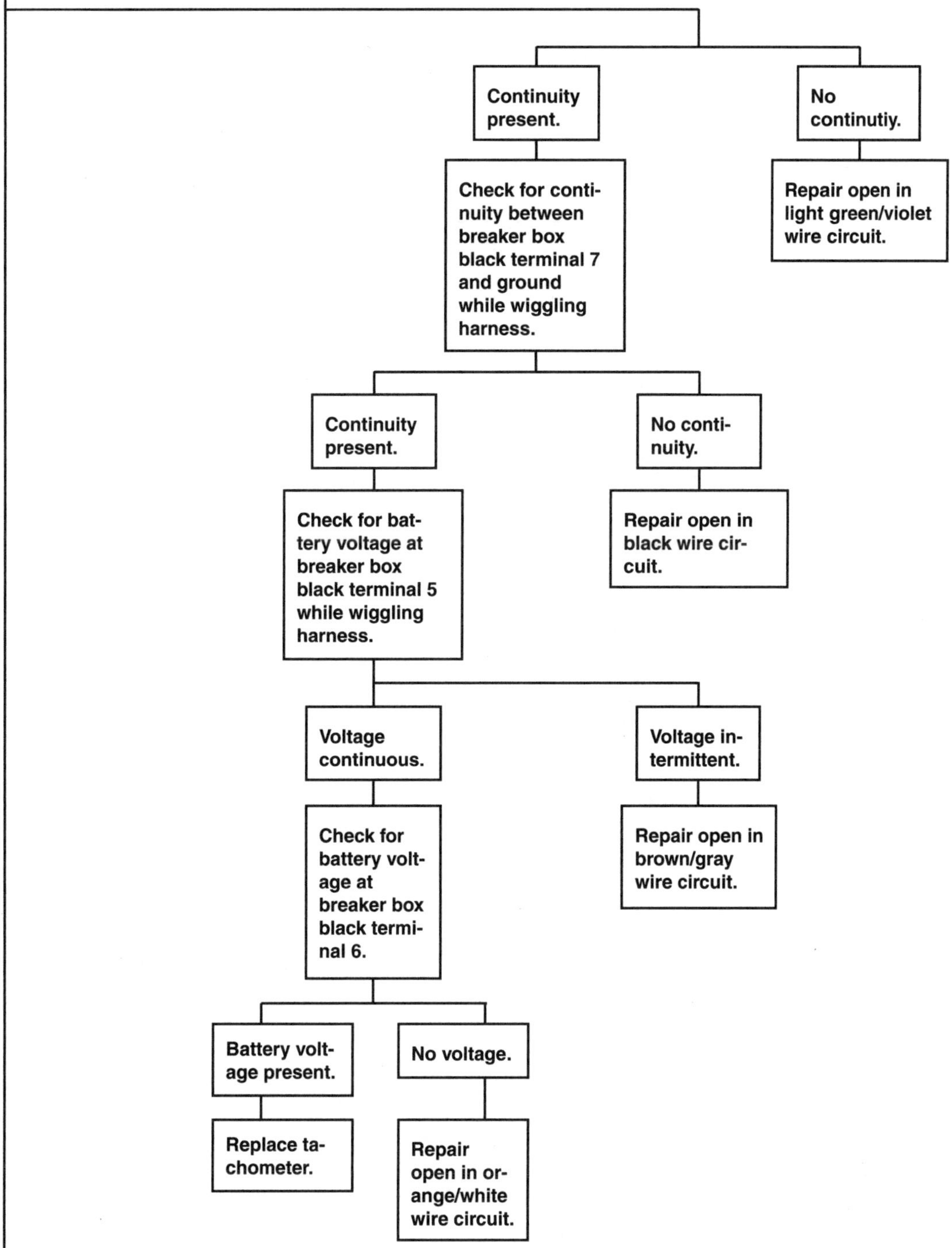
Continuity present.
No continutiy.
Check for continuity between breaker box black terminal 7 and ground while wiggling harness.
Repair open in light green/violet wire circuit.
Continuity present.
No continuity.
Check for battery voltage at breaker box black terminal 5 while wiggling harness.
Repair open in black wire circuit.
Voltage continuous.
Voltage intermittent.
Check for battery voltage at breaker box black terminal 6.
Repair open in brown/gray wire circuit.
Battery voltage present.
No voltage.
Replace tachometer.
Repair open in orange/white wire circuit.

57

SECURITY SYMBOL DOES NOT LIGHT WITH IGNITION KEY TURNED TO ON

NOTE: This chart applies to motorcycles equipped with the security system.

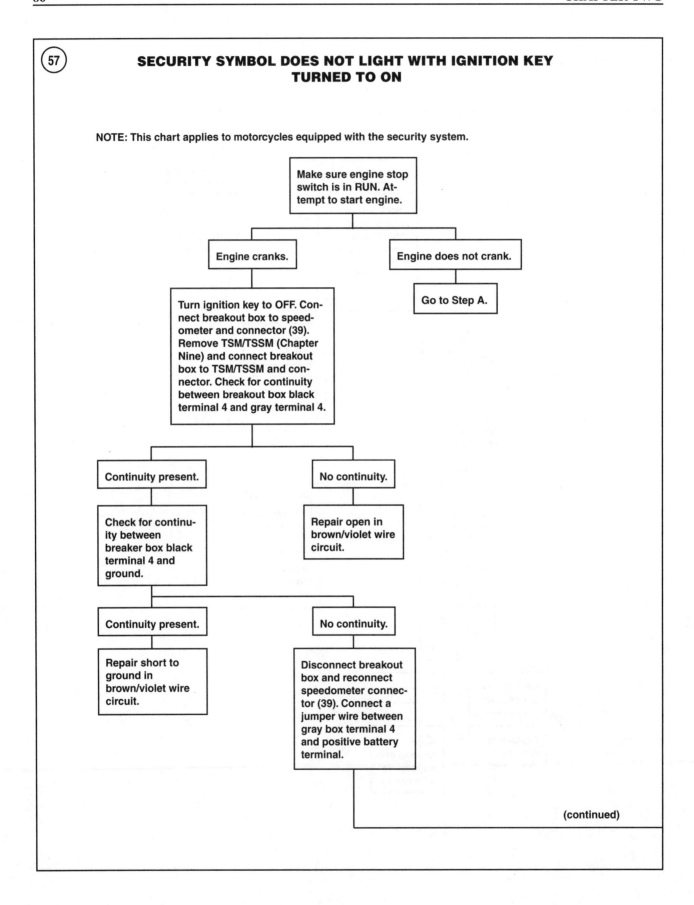

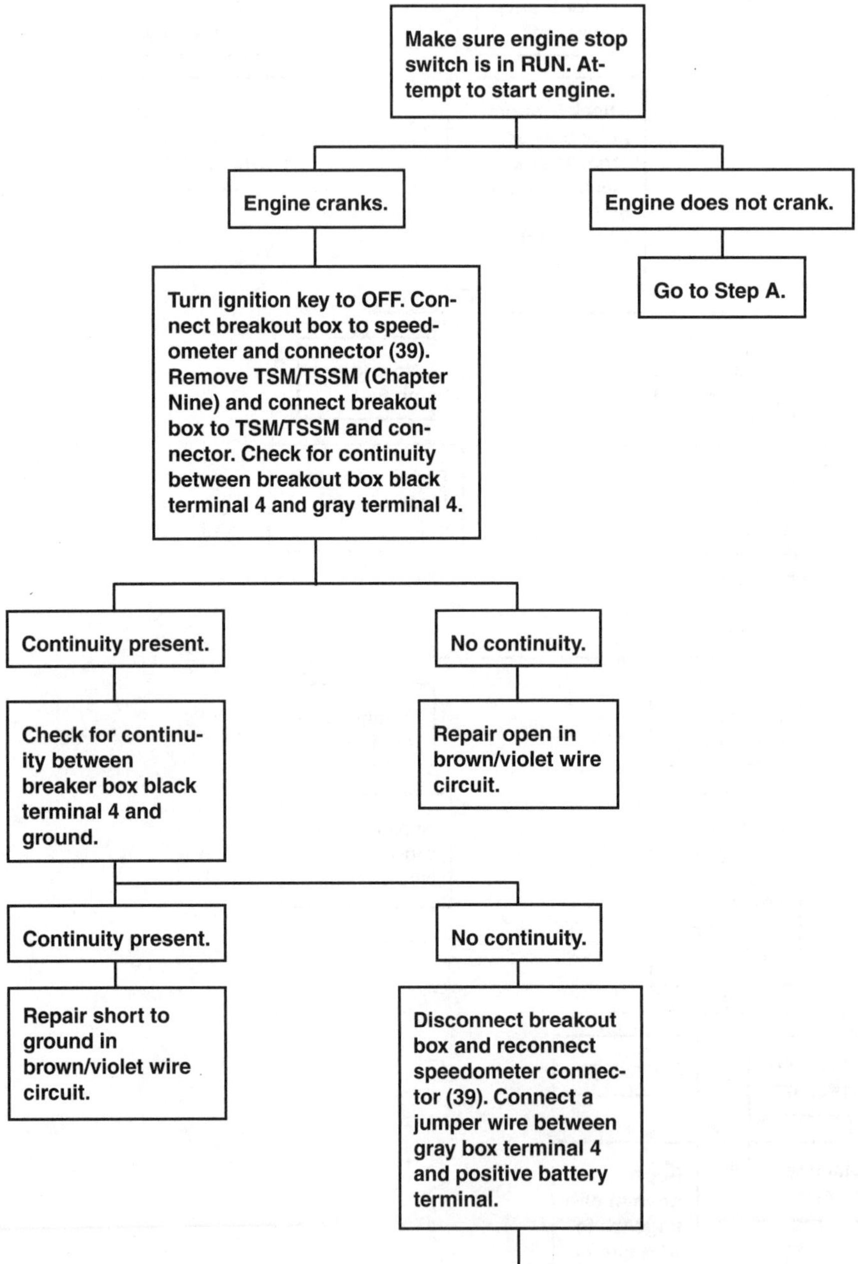
Make sure engine stop switch is in RUN. Attempt to start engine.
Engine cranks.
Engine does not crank.
Go to Step A.
Turn ignition key to OFF. Connect breakout box to speedometer and connector (39). Remove TSM/TSSM (Chapter Nine) and connect breakout box to TSM/TSSM and connector. Check for continuity between breakout box black terminal 4 and gray terminal 4.
Continuity present.
No continuity.
Repair open in brown/violet wire circuit.
Check for continuity between breaker box black terminal 4 and ground.
Continuity present.
No continuity.
Repair short to ground in brown/violet wire circuit.
Disconnect breakout box and reconnect speedometer connector (39). Connect a jumper wire between gray box terminal 4 and positive battery terminal.

(continued)

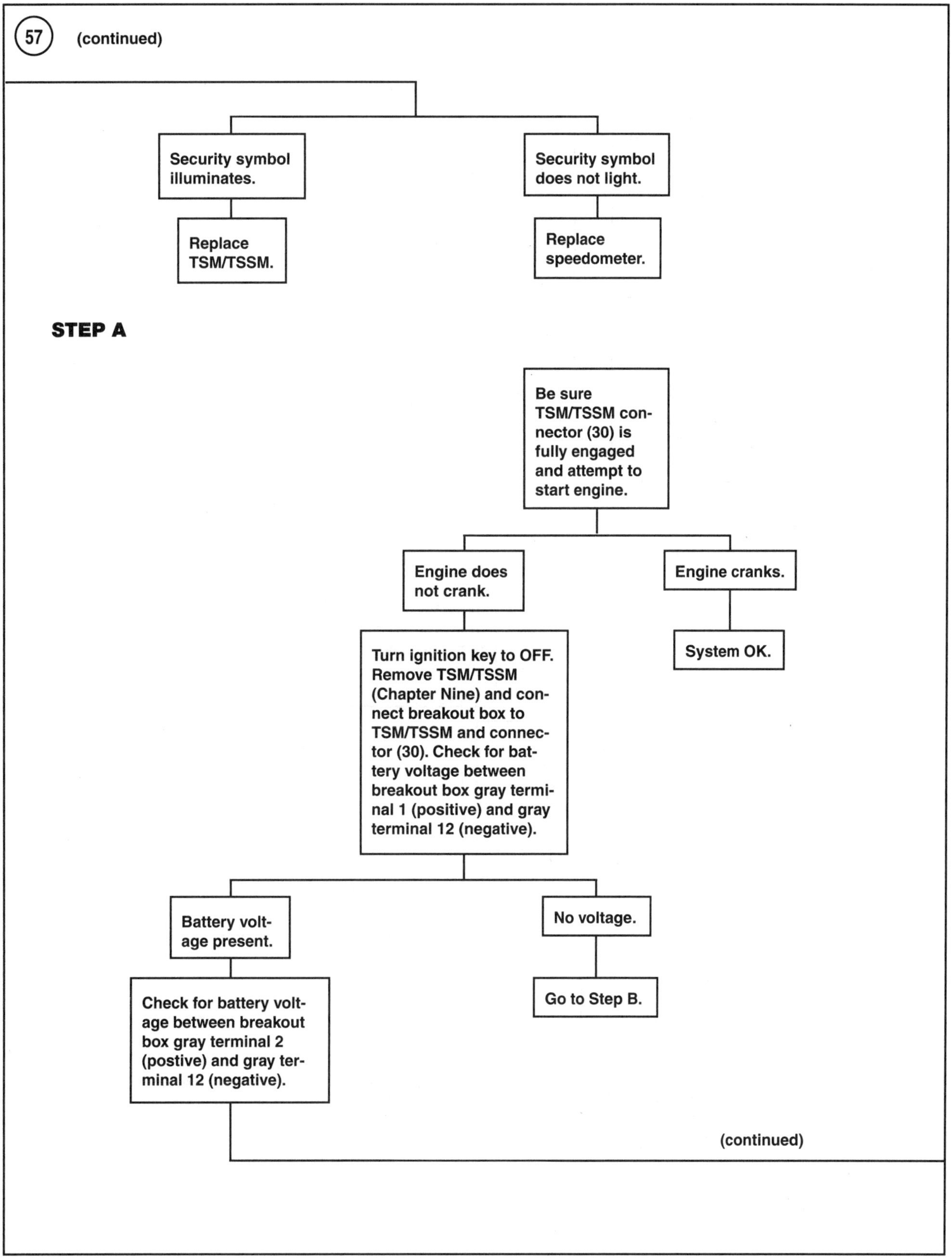
57
(continued)
Security symbol illuminates.
Replace TSM/TSSM.
Security symbol does not light.
Replace speedometer.
STEP A
Be sure TSM/TSSM connector (30) is fully engaged and attempt to start engine.
Engine does not crank.
Turn ignition key to OFF. Remove TSM/TSSM (Chapter Nine) and connect breakout box to TSM/TSSM and connector (30). Check for battery voltage between breakout box gray terminal 1 (positive) and gray terminal 12 (negative).
Battery voltage present.
Check for battery voltage between breakout box gray terminal 2 (postive) and gray terminal 12 (negative).
No voltage.
Go to Step B.
Engine cranks.
System OK.
(continued)

57 (continued)

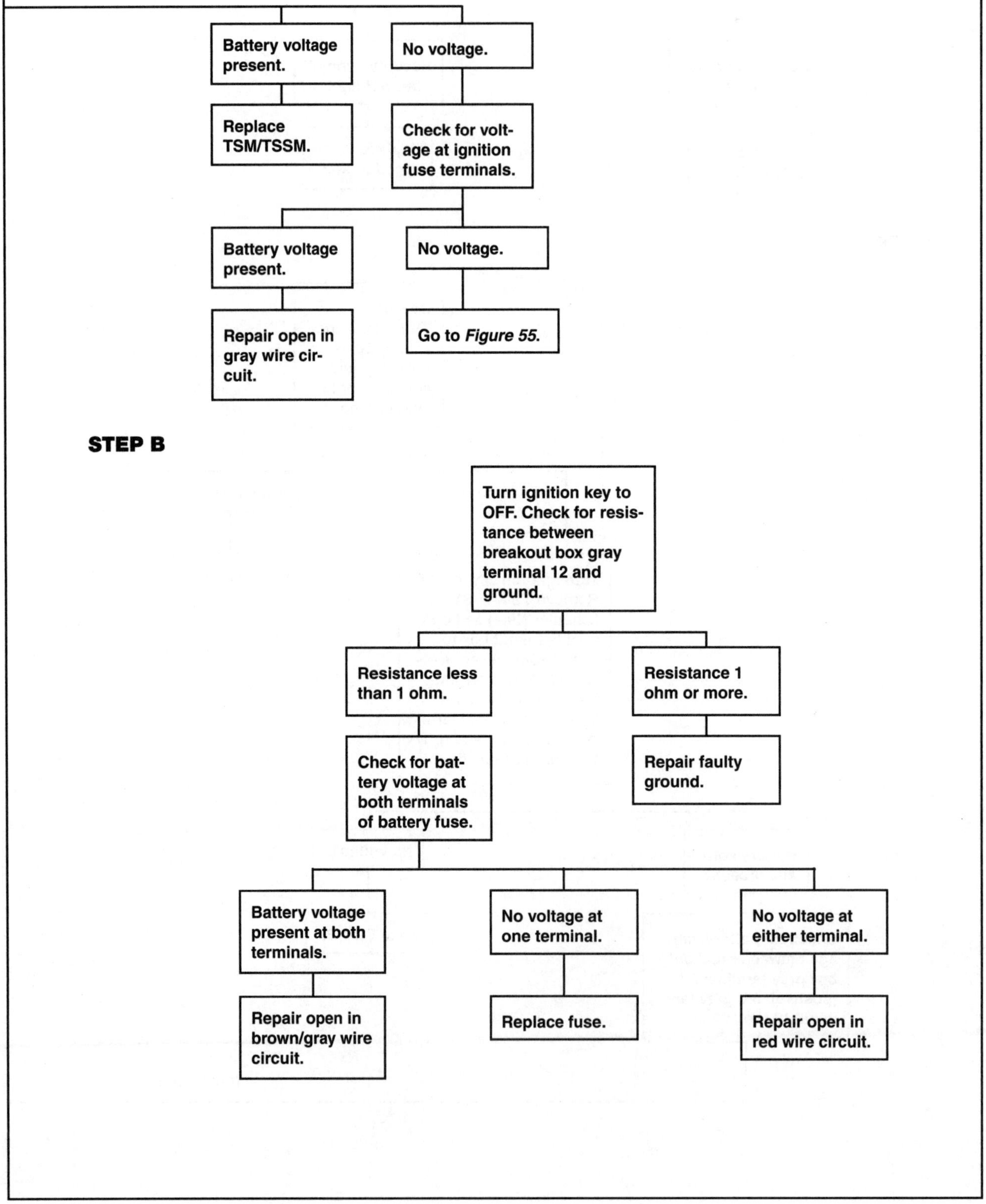
Battery voltage present.
Replace TSM/TSSM.
No voltage.
Check for voltage at ignition fuse terminals.
Battery voltage present.
Repair open in gray wire circuit.
No voltage.
Go to *Figure 55*.
STEP B
Turn ignition key to OFF. Check for resistance between breakout box gray terminal 12 and ground.
Resistance less than 1 ohm.
Check for battery voltage at both terminals of battery fuse.
Resistance 1 ohm or more.
Repair faulty ground.
Battery voltage present at both terminals.
Repair open in brown/gray wire circuit.
No voltage at one terminal.
Replace fuse.
No voltage at either terminal.
Repair open in red wire circuit.

2

58

SECURITY SYMBOL ON CONTINUOUSLY

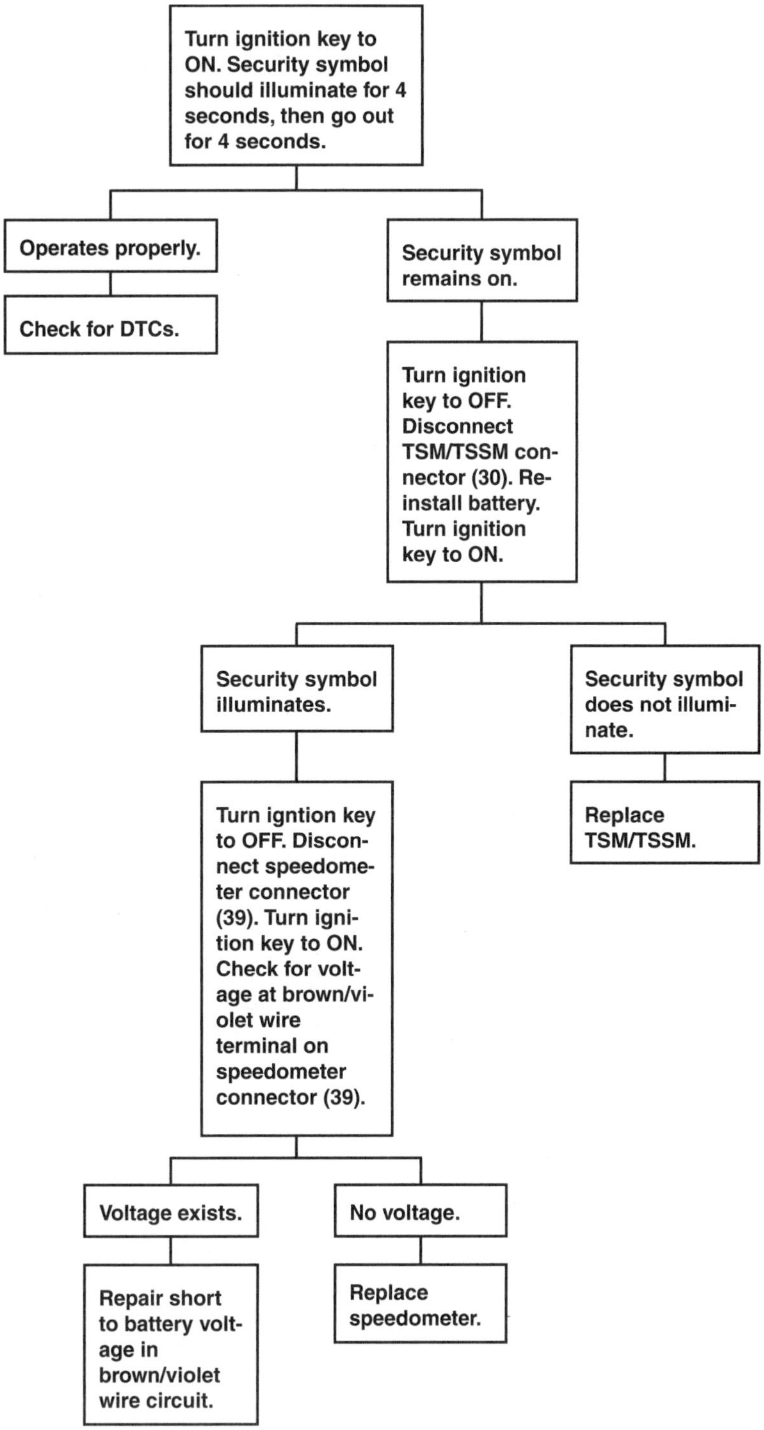

Turn ignition key to ON. Security symbol should illuminate for 4 seconds, then go out for 4 seconds.
Operates properly.
Check for DTCs.
Security symbol remains on.
Turn ignition key to OFF. Disconnect TSM/TSSM connector (30). Reinstall battery. Turn ignition key to ON.
Security symbol illuminates.
Turn igntion key to OFF. Disconnect speedometer connector (39). Turn ignition key to ON. Check for voltage at brown/violet wire terminal on speedometer connector (39).
Voltage exists.
Repair short to battery voltage in brown/violet wire circuit.
No voltage.
Replace speedometer.
Security symbol does not illuminate.
Replace TSM/TSSM.

59

WEAK OR NO KEY FOB SIGNAL TO TSSM

NOTE: At least two attempts are required for the TSSM to recognize the new fob.

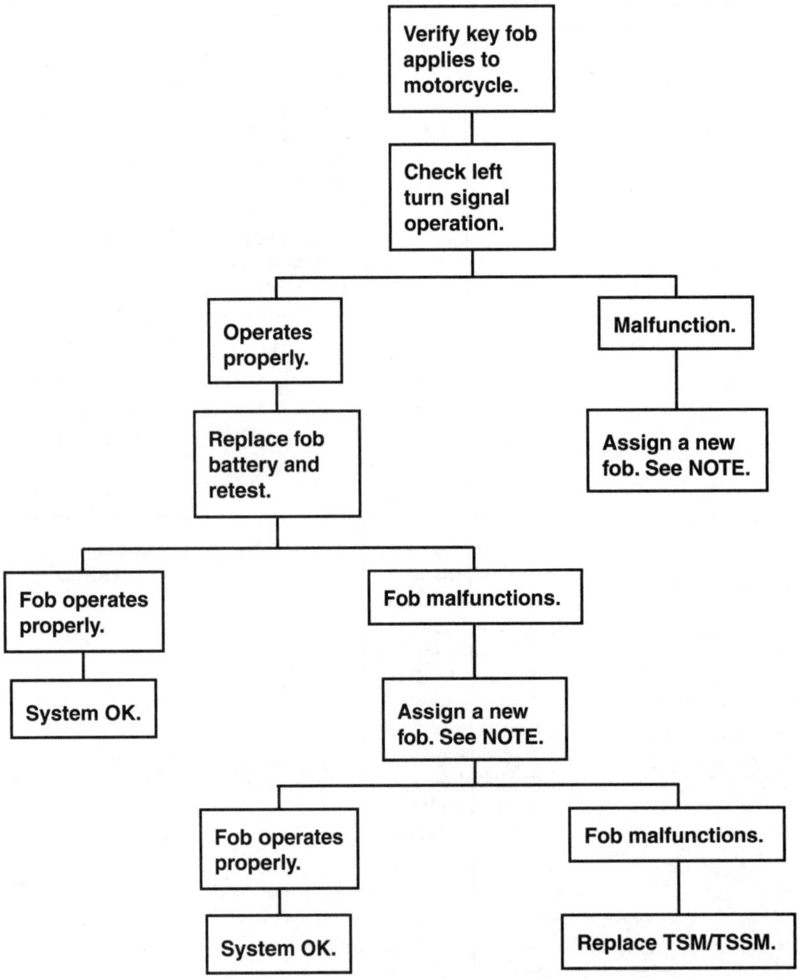
Verify key fob applies to motorcycle.
Check left turn signal operation.
Operates properly.
Malfunction.
Replace fob battery and retest.
Assign a new fob. See NOTE.
Fob operates properly.
Fob malfunctions.
System OK.
Assign a new fob. See NOTE.
Fob operates properly.
Fob malfunctions.
System OK.
Replace TSM/TSSM.

(60)

TURN SIGNAL CANCELS IMPROPERLY

NOTE: The following troubleshooting requires H-D Speedometer tester (part No. HD-41354).

Make sure TSM/TSSM is installed properly.

Make sure TSM/TSSM is configured for solo (not sidecar) operation.

Remove TSM/TSSM and reconnect connector (30). Reinstall battery. Activate 4-way flashers. Verify that 4-way flashers cancel when TSM/TSSM is tllted at least 45 degrees in both directions (as if mounted in bike).

- Operates properly.
  - Disconnect VSS connector (65). Connect speedometer tester to VSS and connector (65). Connect jumper wire between terminal B of tester and white/green wire terminal of VSS connector (65). Connect jumper wire between terminal C of tester and black wire terminal of VSS connector (65). Operate turn signals. Turn ignition key to ON (engine stop switch must be in the RUN position). Set tester so speedometer indicates greater than 20 mph. Key number 528 into tester. Turn signals should cancel after 20 flashes.
- Operates improperly.
  - Replace TSM/TSSM.

(continued)

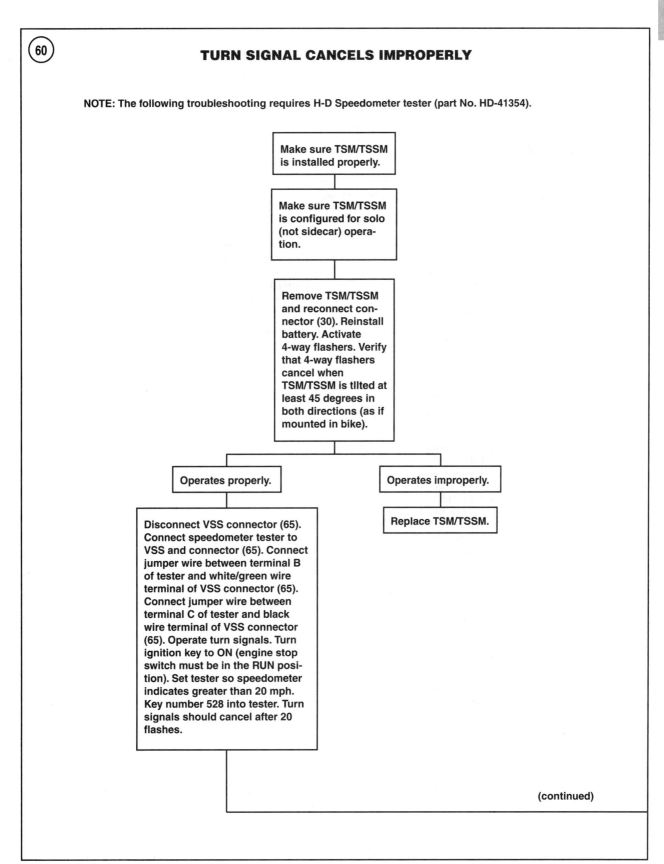

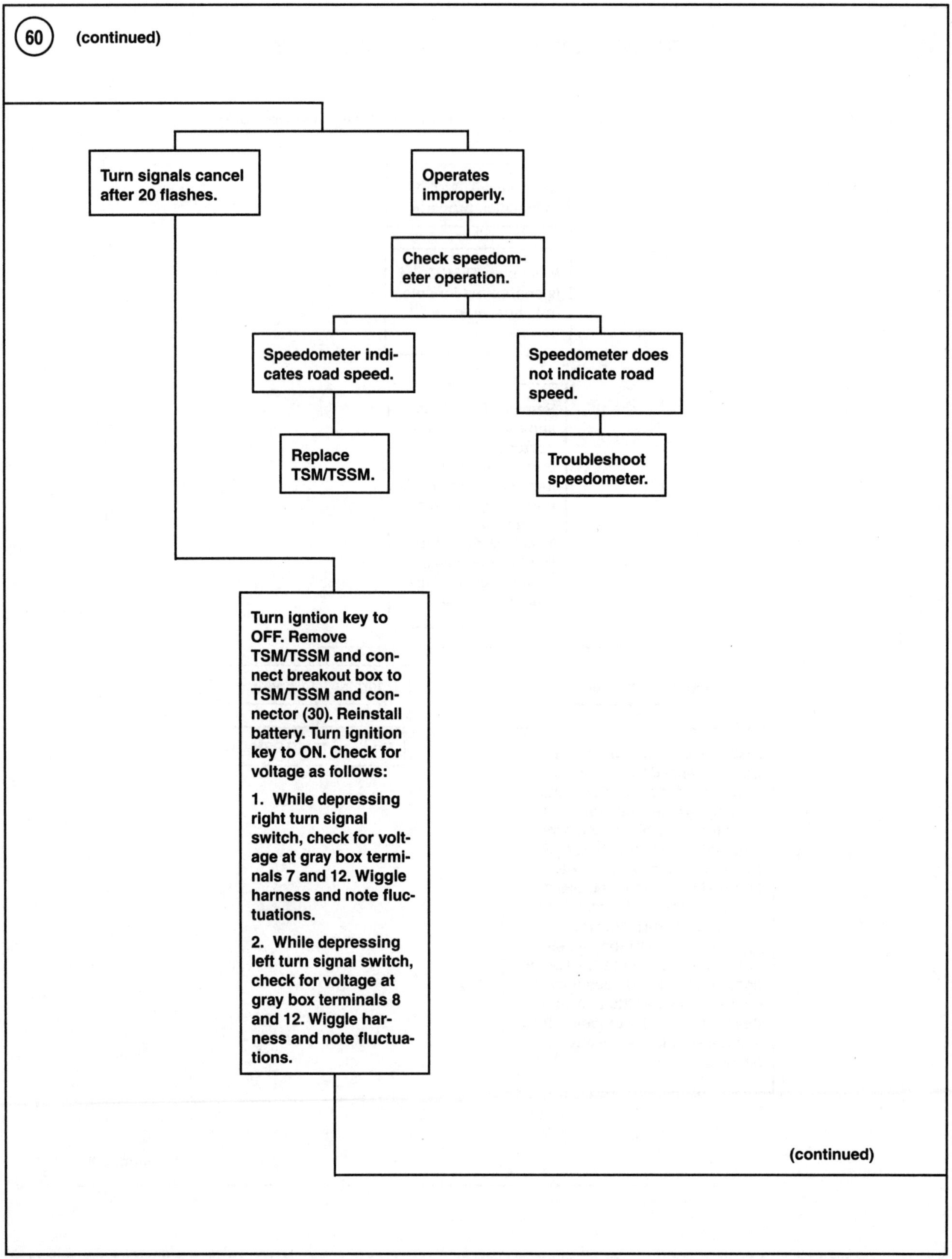
60 (continued)
Turn signals cancel after 20 flashes.
Operates improperly.
Check speedometer operation.
Speedometer indicates road speed.
Speedometer does not indicate road speed.
Replace TSM/TSSM.
Troubleshoot speedometer.
Turn igntion key to OFF. Remove TSM/TSSM and connect breakout box to TSM/TSSM and connector (30). Reinstall battery. Turn ignition key to ON. Check for voltage as follows:
1. While depressing right turn signal switch, check for voltage at gray box terminals 7 and 12. Wiggle harness and note fluctuations.
2. While depressing left turn signal switch, check for voltage at gray box terminals 8 and 12. Wiggle harness and note fluctuations.
(continued)

60 (continued)

- **Voltage fluctuates.**
  - Repair open in circuit.
- **No voltage fluctuations.**
  - Turn igntion key to ON. Check for voltage as follows:
    1. With right turn signal switch released, check for voltage at gray box terminals 7 and 12. Wiggle harness and note fluctuations.
    2. With left turn signal switch released, check for voltage at gray box terminals 8 and 12. Wiggle harness and note fluctuations.
    - **Voltage fluctuates.**
      - Repair short in circuit.
    - **No voltage fluctuations.**
      - Turn ignition key to OFF. Check for continuity as follows:
        1. While depressing right turn signal switch, check for continuity between gray box terminals 7 and 12. Wiggle harness and note fluctuations.
        2. While depressing left turn signal switch, check for continuity between gray box terminals 8 and 12. Wiggle harness and note fluctuations.
        - **Continuity exists.**
          - Repair short in circuit.
        - **No continuity.**
          - System OK.

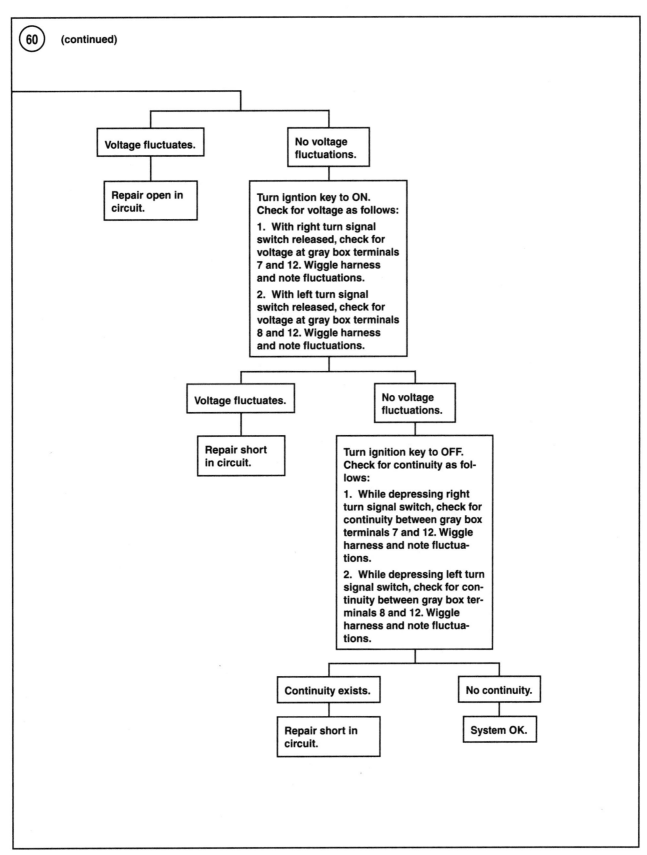

(61)

CARBURETOR TROUBLESHOOTING

Hard starting
- Fuel overflow from float assembly
- Enrichment system inoperative
- Plugged pilot jet and/or passage
- Fuel overflow

Fuel overflows
- Incorrect fuel level
- Damaged float assembly
- Worn float needle valve or dirty seat
- Incorrect float alignment
- Damaged float bowl O-ring or loose float bowl mounting screws
- Plugged vent in fuel tank cap
- Incorrect fuel tank cap installed

Poor idling
- Incorrect idle speed
- Plugged pilot jet system
- Loose pilot jet
- Air leak at carburetor mounting
- Enrichment valve nut loose or damaged

Poor acceleration
- Fuel level too low
- Clogged fuel passages
- Clogged jets
- Plugged vent in fuel tank cap
- Incorrect fuel tank cap installed (non-vent type)
- Enrichment valve nut loose or damaged
- Worn or damaged needle jet or needle
- Throttle cable misadjusted
- Air leak at carburetor mounting
- Damaged vacuum piston

Poor power at low engine speeds
- Incorrect idle speed adjustment
- Contaminated air filter element
- Damaged vacuum piston
- Worn or damaged needle jet or needle
- Clogged pilot jet system
- Plugged vent in fuel tank cap
- Enrichment valve nut loose or damaged
- Clogged fuel supply
- Air leak at carburetor mounting

(continued)

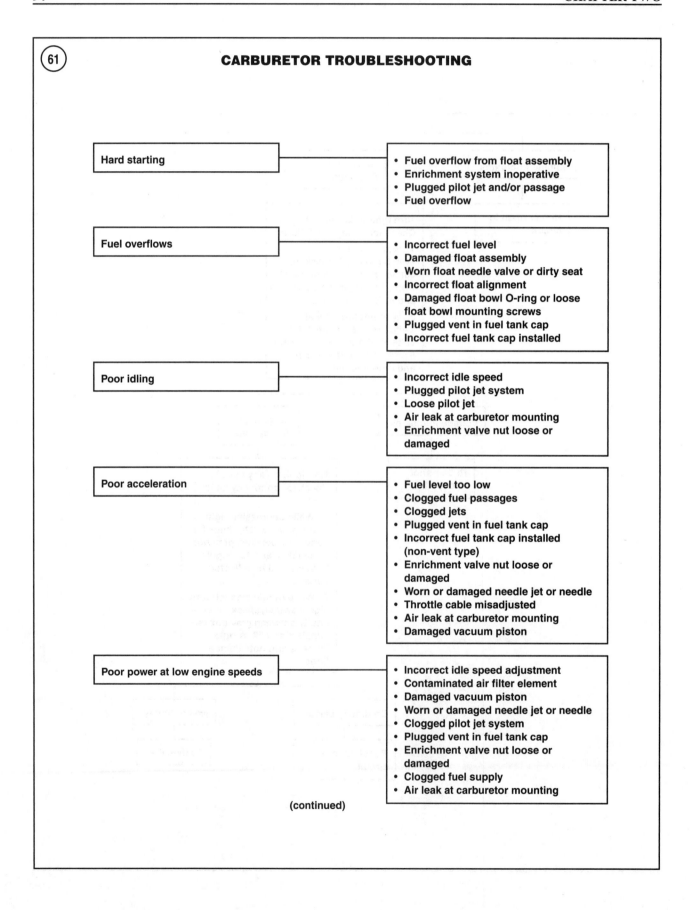

(61) (continued)

Poor power at high engine speeds

- Incorrect fuel level
- Loose or plugged main jet
- Contaminated air filter element
- Damaged vacuum piston
- Worn or damaged needle jet or needle
- Plugged float bowl vent or overflow
- Enrichment valve nut loose or damaged
- Plugged vent in fuel tank cap
- Clogged fuel supply
- Air leak at carburetor mounting

Poor fuel economy

- Incorrect enrichment use
- Damaged vacuum piston
- Contaminated air filter element
- Loose jets
- Fuel level too high
- Worn or damaged needle jet or needle
- Plugged float bowl vent
- Enrichment valve nut loose or damaged
- Incorrect carburetor adjustment

Vacuum piston does not rise in bore correctly

- Vacuum piston binds in bore
- Diaphragm torn or damaged
- Vacuum piston spring binding
- Diaphragm cap loose or damaged
- Piston vent clogged
- Diaphragm incorrectly installed (pinched at lip)

Vacuum piston does not close

- Broken spring
- Diaphragm torn or damaged
- Vacuum piston binds in bore

Troubleshooting

Isolate fuel system problems to the fuel tank, fuel shutoff valve and filter, fuel hoses, external fuel filter (if used) or carburetor. In the following procedures, it is assumed that the ignition system is working properly.

Refer to **Figure 61** for possible causes of fuel system problems.

Fuel level system

The fuel level system is shown in **Figure 62**. Proper carburetor operation depends on a constant and correct carburetor fuel level. As fuel is drawn from the float bowl during engine operation, the float level in the bowl drops. As the float drops, the fuel valve moves from its seat and allows fuel to flow through the seat into the float bowl. Fuel entering the float bowl causes the float to rise and push against the fuel valve. When the fuel level reaches a predetermined level, the fuel valve is pushed against the seat to prevent the float bowl from overfilling.

If the fuel valve fails to close, the engine will run too rich or flood with fuel. Symptoms of this problem are rough running, excessive black smoke and poor acceleration. This condition sometimes clears up when the engine is run at wide-open throttle and the fuel is being drawn

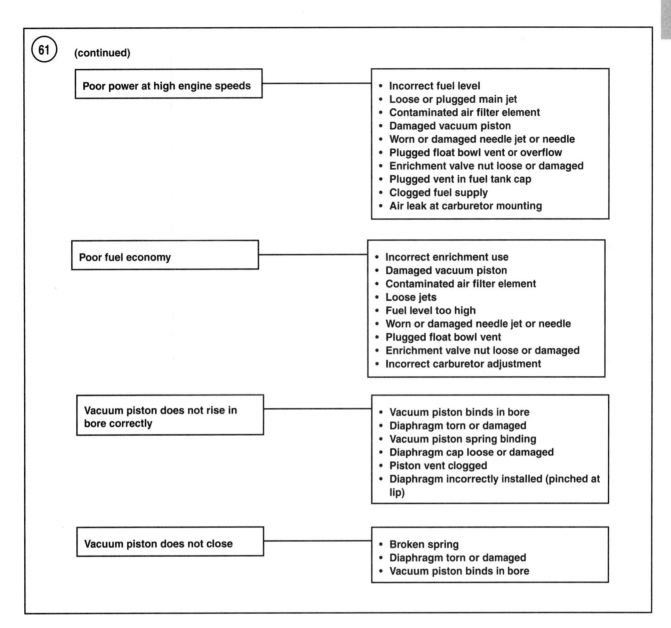

62

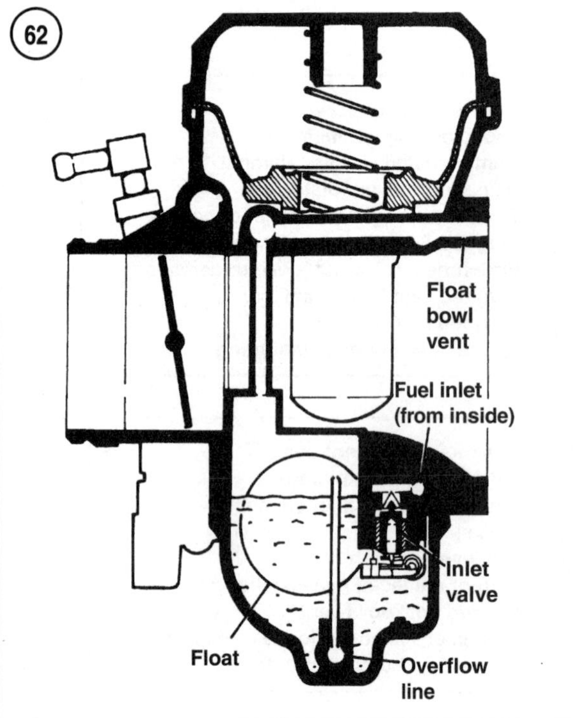

63

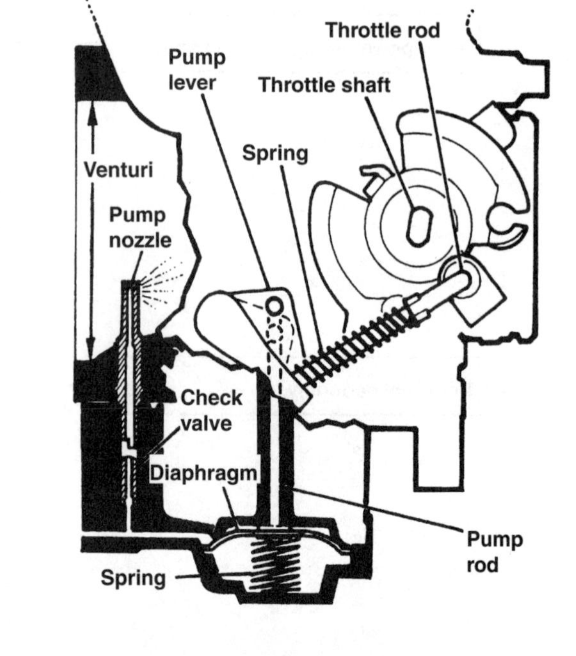

into the engine before the float bowl can overfill. However, as the engine speed is reduced, the rich running condition returns.

Several things can cause fuel overflow. In most instances, a small piece of dirt is trapped between the fuel valve and seat, or the float level is incorrect. If fuel is flowing out of the overflow tube connected to the bottom of the float bowl, the fuel valve inside the carburetor is being held open. First check the position of the fuel shutoff valve lever. Turn the fuel shutoff valve lever off. Then lightly tap on the carburetor float bowl and turn the fuel shutoff valve lever on. If fuel stops running out of the overflow tube, whatever was holding the fuel valve off of its seat has been dislodged. If fuel continues to flow from the overflow tube, remove and service the carburetor. See Chapter Eight.

NOTE
Fuel will not flow from the vacuum-operated fuel shutoff valve until the engine is running.

Starting enrichment (choke) system

A cold engine requires a rich mixture to start and run properly. On all models, a cable-actuated starter enrichment valve is used for cold starting.

If the engine is difficult to start when cold, check the starting enrichment (choke) cable adjustment as described in Chapter Three.

Accelerator pump system

During sudden acceleration, the diaphragm type accelerator pump system (**Figure 63**) provides additional fuel to the engine. Without this system, the carburetor would not be able to provide a sufficient amount of fuel.

The system consists of a spring-loaded neoprene diaphragm that is compressed by the pump lever during sudden acceleration. This causes the diaphragm to force fuel from the pump chamber, through a check valve and into the carburetor venturi. The diaphragm spring returns the diaphragm to the uncompressed position, which allows the chamber to refill with fuel.

If the engine hesitates during sudden acceleration, check the operation of the accelerator pump system. Carburetor service is covered in Chapter Eight.

Vacuum-operated fuel shutoff valve testing

All models are equipped with a vacuum-operated fuel shutoff valve. A vacuum hose is connected between the fuel shutoff valve diaphragm and the carburetor. When

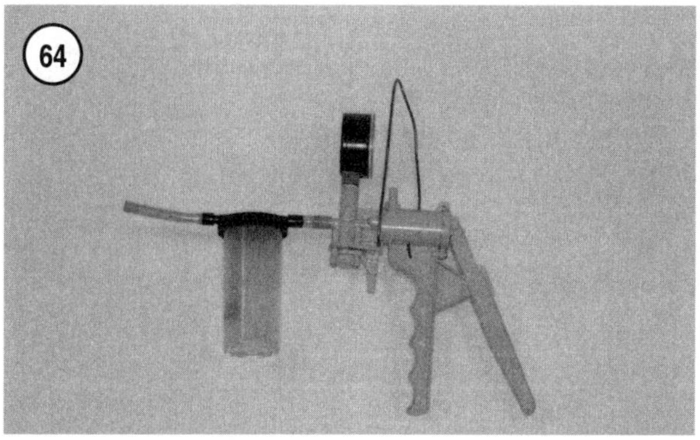

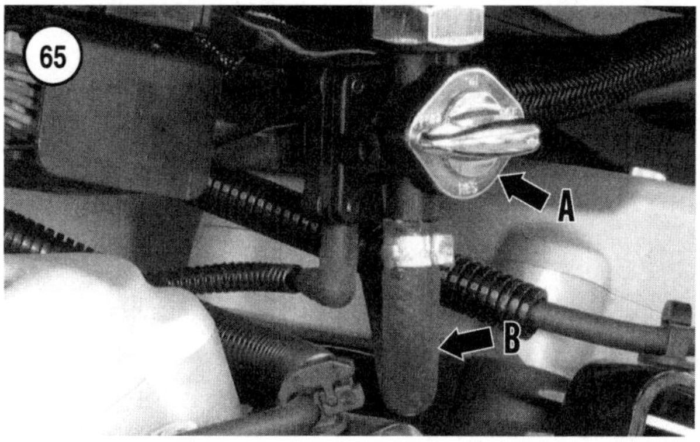

the engine is running, vacuum is applied to the fuel shutoff valve through this hose. For fuel to flow through the fuel valve, a vacuum must be present with the fuel shutoff valve handle in the on or reserve position. A Miti-Vac hand-operated vacuum pump (**Figure 64**), gas can, drain hose that is long enough to reach from the fuel valve to the gas can, and hose clamp are required for this test.

1. Disconnect the negative battery cable as described in Chapter Nine.

2. Visually check the amount of fuel in the tank. Add fuel if necessary.

3. Turn the fuel shutoff valve (A, **Figure 65**) off and disconnect the fuel hose (B) from the fuel shutoff valve. Plug the open end of the hose.

4. Connect the drain hose to the fuel shutoff valve and secure it with a hose clamp. Insert the end of the drain hose into a gas can.

5. Disconnect the vacuum hose from the fuel shutoff valve.

6. Connect a hand-operated vacuum pump to the fuel shutoff valve vacuum hose nozzle.

7. Turn the fuel shutoff valve on.

CAUTION

In Step 8, do not apply more than 25 in. (635 mm) Hg vacuum or the fuel shutoff valve diaphragm will be damaged.

8. Apply 25 in. (635 mm) Hg of vacuum to the valve. Fuel should flow through the fuel shutoff valve when the vacuum is applied.
9. With the vacuum still applied, turn the fuel shutoff valve lever to the reserve position. Fuel should continue to flow through the valve.
10. Release the vacuum and make sure the fuel flow stops.
11. Repeat Steps 8-10 five times. Fuel should flow with vacuum applied and stop flowing when the vacuum is released.
12. Turn the fuel shutoff valve off. Disconnect the vacuum pump and drain hoses.
13. Reconnect the fuel hose (B, **Figure 65**) to the fuel shutoff valve.
14. If the fuel valve failed this test, replace the fuel shutoff valve as described in Chapter Eight.

ENGINE NOISES

1. Knocking or pinging during acceleration can be caused by using a lower octane fuel than recommended or a poor grade of fuel. Incorrect carburetor jetting and an incorrect spark plug heat range (too hot) can cause pinging. Refer to *Spark Plugs* in Chapter Three. Also check for excessive carbon buildup in the combustion chamber or a defective ignition module.
2. Slapping or rattling noise at low speed or during acceleration can be caused by excessive piston-to-cylinder wall clearance. Also check for a bent connecting rod(s) or worn piston pin and/or piston pin hole in the piston(s).
3. Knocking or rapping during deceleration is usually caused by excessive rod bearing clearance.
4. Persistent knocking and vibration or other noises are usually caused by worn main bearings. If the main bearings are in good condition, consider the following:
   a. Loose engine mounts.
   b. Cracked frame.
   c. Leaking cylinder head gasket(s).
   d. Exhaust pipe leak at cylinder head(s).
   e. Stuck piston ring(s).
   f. Broken piston ring(s).
   g. Partial engine seizure.
   h. Excessive connecting rod bearing clearance.
   i. Excessive connecting rod side clearance.
   j. Excessive crankshaft runout.

5. Rapid on-off squeal indicates a compression leak around the cylinder head gasket or spark plug.
6. For valve train noise, check for the following:
   a. Bent pushrod(s).
   b. Defective lifter(s).
   c. Valve sticking in guide.
   d. Worn cam gears and/or cam.
   e. Damaged rocker arm or shaft. Rocker arm may be binding on shaft.

ENGINE LUBRICATION

Check weekly and, if necessary, fill the engine oil tank as described in Chapter Three.

Oil pump service is covered in Chapter Five.

Refer to Chapter Four for oil pressure specifications.

Oil Light

The oil light, mounted on the indicator light panel (**Figure 66**), will come on when the ignition switch is turned on before starting the engine. After starting the engine, the oil light should go off when the engine speed is above idle.

If the oil light does not come on when the ignition switch is turned on and the engine is not running, check for a burned out oil light bulb. If the bulb is good, check the oil pressure switch (**Figure 67**) as described in Chapter Nine.

If the oil light remains on when the engine speed is above idle, turn the engine off and check the oil level in the oil tank as described in Chapter Three. If the oil level is satisfactory, check the following:

1. Oil may not be returning to the tank from the return line. Check for a clogged or damaged return line or a damaged oil pump.
2. If operating the motorcycle in conditions where the ambient temperature is below freezing, ice and sludge may be blocking the oil feed pipe. This condition will prevent the oil from circulating properly.
3. If necessary, remove the pressure switch (Chapter Nine) and test the oil pressure with a gauge (H-D 96921-52B or equivalent).

Oil Consumption High or Engine Smokes Excessively

1. Worn valve guides.
2. Worn valve guide seals.
3. Worn or damaged piston rings.
4. Restricted oil tank return line.
5. Oil tank overfilled.
6. Oil filter restricted.
7. Leaking cylinder head surfaces.

66

Oil Fails to Return to Oil Tank

1. Oil lines or fittings restricted or damaged.
2. Oil pump damaged or operating incorrectly.
3. Oil tank empty.
4. Oil filter restricted.

Excessive Engine Oil Leaks

1. Clogged air filter breather hose.
2. Restricted or damaged oil return line to oil tank.
3. Loose engine parts.
4. Damaged gasket sealing surfaces.
5. Oil tank overfilled.

CLUTCH

All clutch troubles, except adjustments, require partial clutch disassembly to identify and repair the problem. Refer to Chapter Six for clutch service procedures.

Clutch Chatter or Noise

This problem is generally caused by worn or warped friction and steel plates. Also check for worn or damaged bearings.

Clutch Slip

1. Incorrect clutch adjustment.
2. Worn friction plates.
3. Weak or damaged diaphragm spring.
4. Damaged pressure plate.

Clutch Drag

1. Incorrect clutch adjustment.
2. Warped clutch plates.
3. Worn or damaged clutch shell or clutch hub.

TRANSMISSION

Transmission symptoms are sometimes hard to distinguish from clutch symptoms. Refer to Chapter Seven for transmission service procedures. Make sure the clutch is not causing the trouble before working on the transmission.

Jumping Out of Gear

1. Incorrect shifter pawl adjuster.
2. Worn or damaged shifter parts.
3. Bent shift forks.
4. Excessively worn or damaged gears.

Difficult Shifting

1. Worn or damaged shift forks.
2. Loose or damaged detent plate.
3. Worn or damaged shifter shaft assembly.
4. Worn or damaged detent arm.
5. Worn shift fork drum groove(s).
6. Loose, worn or damaged shifter fork pin(s).
7. Damaged shifter shaft splines.

Excessive Gear Noise

1. Worn or damaged bearings.
2. Worn or damaged gears.
3. Excessive gear backlash.

EXCESSIVE VIBRATION

Excessive vibration is usually caused by loose engine mounting hardware. High speed vibration may be due to a bent axle shaft or loose or faulty suspension components. Vibration can also be caused by the following conditions:

1. Broken frame.
2. Excessively worn primary chain.
3. Tight primary chain links.
4. Loose or damaged engine mounting bracket.
5. Improperly balanced wheel(s).
6. Defective or damaged wheel(s).
7. Defective or damaged tire(s).
8. Internal engine wear or damage.

SUSPENSION AND STEERING

Poor handling may be caused by improper pressure, a damaged or bent frame or front steering components, worn wheel bearings or dragging brakes. Possible causes for suspension and steering malfunctions are listed below.

Irregular or Wobbly Steering

1. Loose wheel axle nut(s).
2. Loose or worn steering head bearings.
3. Excessive wheel hub bearing play.
4. Damaged cast wheel.
5. Spoke wheel out of alignment.
6. Unbalanced wheel assembly.
7. Worn hub bearings.
8. Incorrect wheel alignment.
9. Bent or damaged steering stem or frame (at steering neck).
10. Tire incorrectly seated on rim.
11. Heavy front end loading from non-standard equipment.

Stiff Steering

1. Low front tire air pressure.
2. Bent or damaged steering stem or frame (at steering neck).
3. Loose or worn steering head bearings.

Stiff or Heavy Fork Operation

1. Incorrect fork springs.
2. Incorrect fork oil viscosity.
3. Excessive amount of fork oil.
4. Bent fork tubes.

Poor Fork Operation

1. Worn or damaged fork tubes.
2. Fork oil capacity low due to leaking fork seals.
3. Bent or damaged fork tubes.
4. Contaminated fork oil.
5. Incorrect fork springs.
6. Heavy front end loading from non-standard equipment.

Poor Rear Shock Absorber Operation

1. Weak or worn springs.
2. Damper unit leaking.
3. Shock shaft worn or bent.
4. Incorrect rear shock springs.
5. Rear shocks adjusted incorrectly.
6. Heavy rear end loading from non-standard equipment.
7. Incorrect loading.

BRAKES

All models are equipped with front and rear disc brakes. Brakes operation is vital to the safe operation of any vehicle. Perform the maintenance specified in Chapter Three to minimize brake system problems. Brake system service is covered in Chapter Thirteen. When refilling the front and rear master cylinders, use only DOT 5 silicone-based brake fluid.

Insufficient Braking Power

Worn brake pads or disc, air in the hydraulic system, glazed or contaminated pads, low brake fluid level, or a leaking brake line or hose can cause this problem. Visually check for leaks. Check for worn brake pads. Check also for a leaking or damaged primary cup seal in the master cylinder. Bleed and adjust the brakes. Rebuild a leaking master cylinder or brake caliper. Brake drag will cause excessive heat and brake fade. See *Brake Drag* in this section.

Spongy Brake Feel

This problem is generally caused by air in the hydraulic system. Bleed and adjust the brakes as described in Chapter Thirteen.

Brake Drag

Check brake adjustment, looking for insufficient brake pedal and/or hand lever free play. Also check for worn, loose or missing parts in the brake calipers. Check the brake disc for warpage or excessive runout.

Brakes Squeal or Chatter

Check brake pad thickness and disc condition. Make sure the pads are not loose; check that the anti-rattle springs are properly installed and in good condition. Clean off any dirt on the pads. Loose components can also cause this. Check for:

1. Warped brake disc.
2. Loose brake disc.
3. Loose caliper mounting bolts.
4. Loose front axle nut.
5. Worn wheel bearings.
6. Damaged hub.

Table 1 STARTER SPECIFICATIONS

Brush length (minimum)	0.443 in. (11.0 mm)
Commutator diameter (minimum)	1.141 in. (28.98 mm)
Commutator runout (maximum)	0.016 (0.41 mm)
Current draw	
Normal	160-200 amps
Maximum	250 amps
Maximum no-load speed at 11.5 volts	90 amps
Minimum no-load current at 11.5 volts	3000 rpm

Table 2 ELECTRICAL SPECIFICATIONS

Battery capacity	12 volt, 12 amp hr.
Ignition coil	
Primary resistance	0.5-0.7 ohms
Secondary resistance	5500-7500 ohms
Alternator	
Stator coil resistance	0.2-0.4 ohms
AC voltage output	19-26 Vac per 1000 rpm
Voltage regulator	
Voltage output	14.3-14.7 VDC at 75° F
Amps at 3600 rpm	22 amps

Table 3 DIAGNOSTIC TROUBLE CODES

DTC	Problem	Priority[1]	Troubleshooting chart
BusEr	Serial data bus fault	1	Figure 42 or 43
B0563[2]	Battery voltage high	12	
B1006	Accessory line overvoltage	7	Figure 37
B1007	Ignition line overvoltage	6	Figure 37
B1008	Reset switch closed	8	Figure 38
B1121	Left turn output fault	10	Figure 44
B1122	Right turn output fault	11	Figure 44
B1131	Alarm output low	13	Figure 45
B1132	Alarm output high	14	Figure 45
B1134	Starter output high	9	Figure 46
B1135[3]	Accelerometer fault	7	
B1141	Ignition switch open/low	15	Figure 44
B1151[4]			
B1152[4]			
B1153[4]			
P0106	MAP sensor rate-of-change error	16	Figure 48
P0107	MAP sensor failed open/low	17	Figure 48
P0108	MAP sensor failed high	18	Figure 48
P0371	CKP shorted low	13	Figure 49
P0372	CKP shorted high	14	Figure 49
P0374	CKP not detected/cannot synchronize	15	Figure 49
P0501	VSS failed low	23	Figure 50
P0502	VSS failed high/open	24	Figure 50
P0562	System voltage low	21	Figure 51
P0563	System voltage high	22	Figure 51
P0602[5]	Calibration memory error	1	
P0603[5]	EEProm memory error	2	
P0604[5]	RAM memory error	3	
P0605[5]	Program memory error	4	
P0607[5]	A to D error	5	
P1009	Incorrect password	11	Figure 52
P1010	Missing password	12	Figure 53
P1351	Ignition coil driver front low/open	19	Figure 54
P1352	Ignition coil driver front high/shorted	20	Figure 54
P1354	Ignition coil driver rear low/open	19	Figure 54
P1355	Ignition coil driver rear high/shorted	20	Figure 54
U1016	Loss of ICM serial data	4	Figure 39 or 40
U1064	Loss of TSM/TSSM serial data	9	Figure 41
U1097	Loss of speedometer serial data	10	Figure 47
U1255	Loss of ICM or TSM/TSSM serial data	6	Figure 39, 40, 41 or 47
U1300	Serial data low	7	Figure 42 or 43
U1301	Serial data open/high	8	Figure 42 or 43

1. Priority numbers are relative. There may be more than one DTC for a specific priority number due to differing systems, such as engine management and TSM/TSSM.
2. Follow the troubleshooting procedures for the charging system in this chapter.
3. Replace the TSM/TSSM due to an internal malfunction.
4. Not applicable to Sportster models. If DTC appears, reconfigure TSM/TSSM.
5. Replace the ICM due to an internal malfunction.

NOTE: Refer to the Supplement at the end of this manual for information unique to 2007-2011 models.

CHAPTER THREE

LUBRICATION, MAINTENANCE AND TUNE-UP

This chapter covers lubrication, maintenance and tune-up procedures. If a procedure requires more than minor disassembly, reference to the appropriate chapter is listed. Maintenance intervals, capacities, recommendations and specification are in **Tables 1-9** at the end of this chapter.

To maximize the service life of the motorcycle, and gain maximum safety and performance, it is necessary to perform periodic inspections and maintenance. Minor problems found during routine service can be corrected before they develop into major ones.

Consider the maintenance schedule a guide. Harder than normal use and exposure to mud, water or high humidity indicates the need for more frequent servicing of most maintenance items. Record all service and repairs in the maintenance log at the back of this manual. A running record makes it easier to evaluate future maintenance requirements and maintain the motorcycle in top condition.

FUEL TYPE

XL883 models require fuel with a pump octane number of 87 or higher. XL1200 models require fuel with a pump octane number of 91 or higher. Using fuel with a lower octane number can cause pinging or spark knock, and lead to engine damage.

When choosing gasoline and filling the fuel tank, note the following:

1. When filling the tank, do not overfill it. There should be no fuel in the filler neck located between the fuel cap and tank.
2. Use care to avoid spilled fuel.
3. Do not use gasoline containing methanol (methyl or wood alcohol).
4. Do not use gasoline containing more than 10% of ethanol (ethyl or grain alcohol).
5. Do not use gasoline containing more than 15% of MTBE (methyl tertiary butyl ether).

PRE-RIDE INSPECTION

1. Check wheel and tire condition. Check tire pressure. Refer to *Tires and Wheels* in this chapter.
2. Check engine, transmission and primary drive chaincase for oil leaks. If necessary, add oil as described in this chapter.
3. Check brake fluid level and condition. If necessary, add fluid as described in this chapter.
4. Check the operation of the front and rear brakes.
5. Check clutch operation. If necessary, adjust the clutch as described in this chapter.

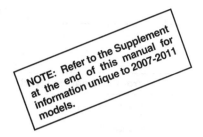

1

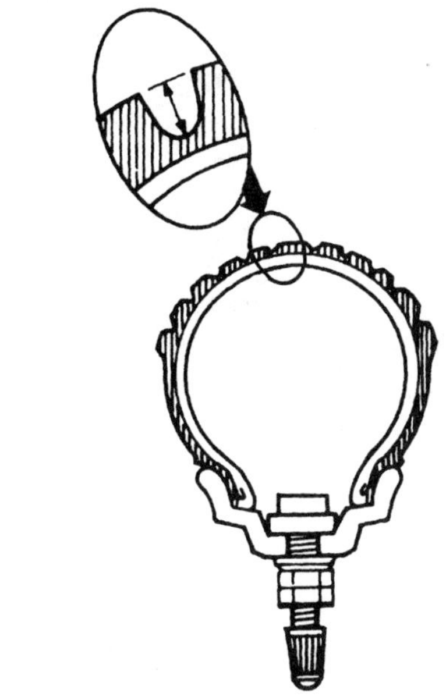

6. Check the throttle operation. The throttle should move smoothly and return quickly when released. If necessary, adjust throttle free play as described in this chapter.
7. Inspect the front and rear suspension. They should have a solid feel with no looseness.
8. Check the exhaust system for leaks or damage.
9. Inspect the fuel system for leaks.
10. Check the fuel level.
11. Check drive belt tension as described in this chapter.

CAUTION
When checking the tightness of the exposed fasteners, do not check the cylinder head bolts without following the procedure described in Chapter Four.

12. Turn the ignition switch on, and check the following:
   a. Pull the front brake lever and make sure the brake light works.
   b. Push the rear brake pedal down and check that the brake light comes on soon after depressing the pedal.
   c. Make sure the headlight (high and low) and taillight work.
   d. Make sure all four turn signal lights are working.
   e. Make sure all accessory lights work properly, if so equipped.
   f. Check the horn operation.

TIRES AND WHEELS

Tire Pressure

Check the tire pressure often to maintain tire profile, traction and handling, and to get the maximum life out of the tire. Carry a tire gauge in the motorcycle's tool kit. Refer to **Table 2** for the tire pressures for the original equipment tires.

Tire Inspection

Inspect the tires periodically for excessive wear, deep cuts and embedded objects such as stones or nails. If a nail or other object is found in a tire, mark its location with a light crayon prior to removing it. This helps locate the hole for repair.

Measure the tread depth (**Figure 1**) with a gauge or a small ruler. As a guideline, replace tires when the tread depth is 1/16 in. (1.6 mm.) or less. On original equipment tires, wear bars on the tire first appear flush with the surrounding rubber when wear depth reaches 1/32 in. (0.8 mm). Replace the tire before wear reaches the wear bars. Refer to Chapter Ten for tire changing and repair information.

Spoke Tension

On models with laced wheels, check for loose or damaged spokes. Refer to Chapter Ten for spoke service.

Wheel Inspection

Check the wheels rims for cracks and other damage. Refer to Chapter Ten for wheel service.

PERIODIC LUBRICATION

Oil Tank Inspection

Before inspecting the oil level, inspect the oil tank for cracks or other damage. If oil seepage is evident on or near the oil tank, locate and repair the problem. Check the oil tank mounting bolts for loose or missing fasteners; replace or tighten all fasteners. Check all oil line connections on the tank (**Figure 2** and **Figure 3**) and the engine crankcase (**Figure 4**). Each oil line is connected with a special connector assembly. Replace damaged oil lines as described in Chapter Four.

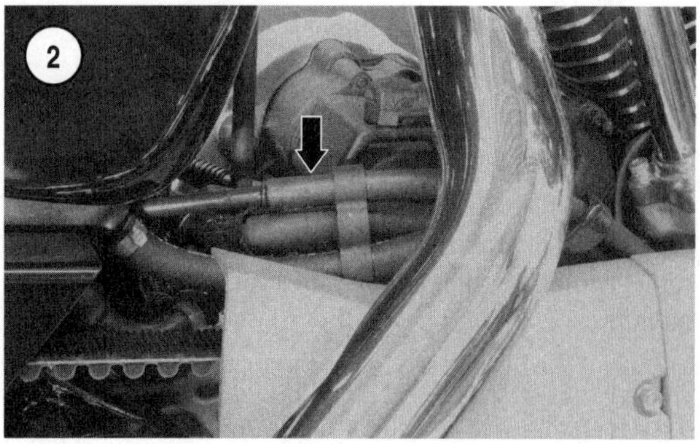

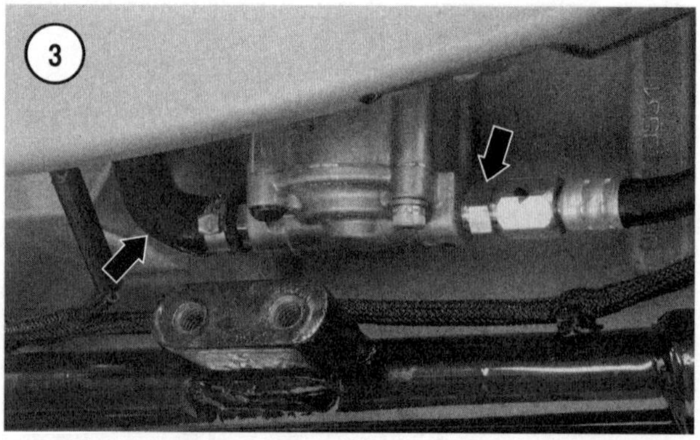

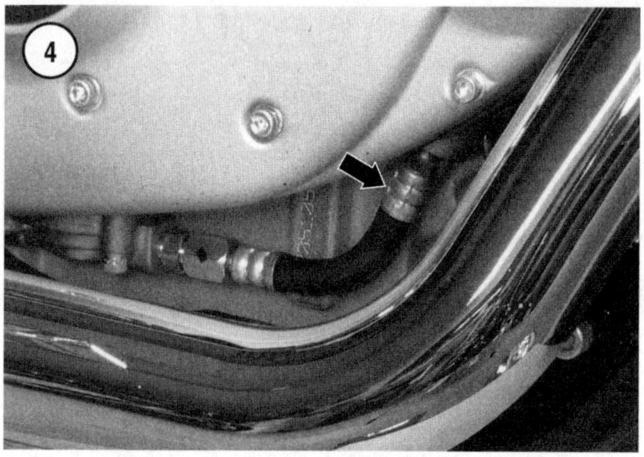

Engine Oil Level Inspection

Check the engine oil level using the dipstick/oil filler cap (**Figure 5**).

1. Start and run the engine for approximately ten minutes or until the engine has reached normal operating temperature. Then turn the engine off and allow the oil to settle in the oil tank.

CAUTION
Do not hold the motorcycle straight up when checking the oil level. Doing so causes an incorrect reading.

2. Place the motorcycle on a level surface and park it on the sidestand.
3. Wipe the area around the oil filler cap with a clean rag. Push down on the cap, then release it. The cap top should pop up so it can be grasped (**Figure 6**). Remove the cap by turning it counterclockwise while pulling up.

NOTE
The oil filler cap body has a wide slot and a narrow slot which allows cap installation in one direction only.

4. Wipe the dipstick with a clean rag, then reinstall the oil filler cap; but do not push down the cap. Unscrew and remove the oil filler cap.
5. Check the oil level on the dipstick (A, **Figure 7**). The oil level should be between the FULL and FILL marks on the dipstick. If the oil level is even with or below the FILL mark, continue with Step 6. If the oil level is correct, go to Step 7.

CAUTION
Do not overfill the oil tank. If the engine is cold, do not add oil so the oil level reaches the full mark. Oil may be forced into the air cleaner causing engine damage.

6. Add the recommended engine oil listed in **Table 3**.
7. Inspect the oil filler cap O-ring (B, **Figure 7**) for cracks or other damage. Replace the O-ring if necessary.
8. Reinstall the oil filler cap. Push down on the cap until it locks in the down position.

Engine Oil and Filter Change

Regular oil and filter changes contribute more to engine longevity than any other maintenance performed. Refer to **Table 1** for the recommended oil and filter change intervals for motorcycles operated in moderate climates. If the motorcycle is operated under dusty conditions, the oil becomes contaminated more quickly and should be changed more frequently than recommended.

Harley-Davidson recommends using Harley- Davidson oils. If Harley-Davidson oil is not available, Harley-Davidson recommends using oil certified for use in diesel engines. Acceptable certifications include: CF, CF-4, CG-4 and CH-4. Follow the viscosity recommendations applicable to Harley-Davidson oil.

Always use the same brand of oil at each change. Refer to **Table 3** for correct oil viscosity to use in anticipated

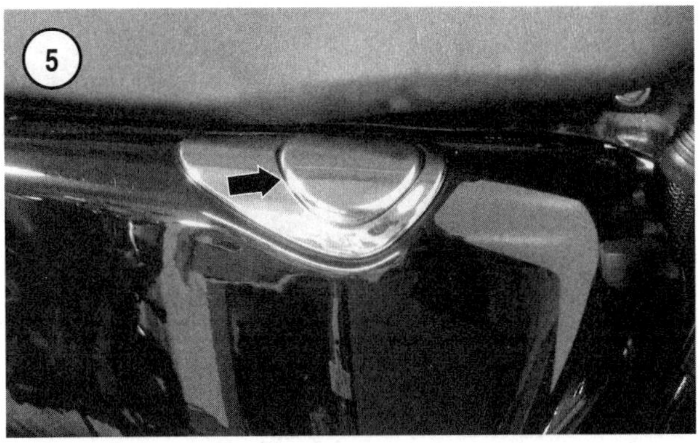

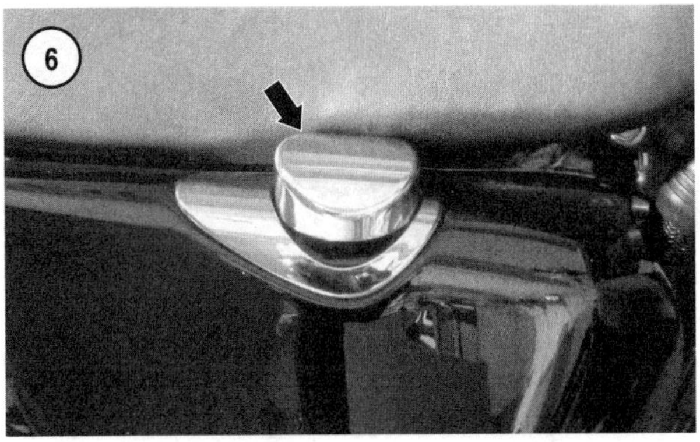

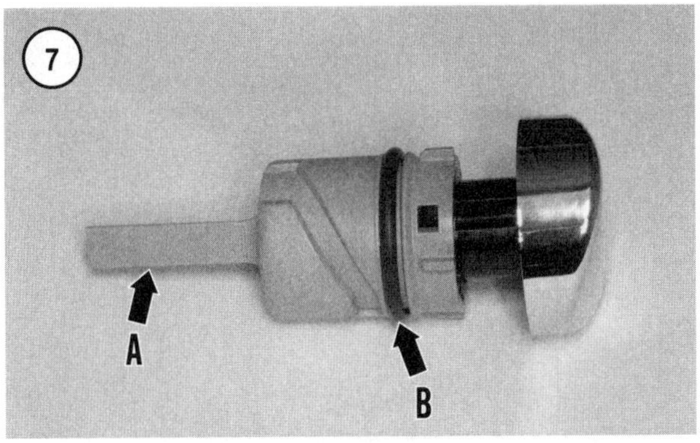

ambient temperatures, not engine oil temperature. Using oil additives is not recommended as they may cause clutch damage.

WARNING
Contact with oil may cause skin cancer. Wash oil from hands with soap and water as soon as possible after handling engine oil.

CAUTION
Do not use the current SH and SJ automotive oils in motorcycle engines. The SH and SJ oils contain friction modifiers that reduce frictional losses on engine components. Specifically designed for automotive engines, these oils can damage motorcycle engines and clutches.

NOTE
*Never dispose of engine oil in the trash, on the ground or down a storm drain. Many service stations and oil retailers accept used oil for recycling. Do not combine other fluids with engine oil to be recycled. To locate a recycler, contact the American Petroleum Institute (API) at **www.recycleoil.org**.*

1. Start and run the engine for approximately ten minutes or until the engine has reached normal operating temperature. Turn the engine off and allow the oil to settle in the oil tank. Support the motorcycle so the oil can drain completely.
2. Wipe the area around the oil filler cap (**Figure 5**) with a clean rag. Push down on the cap, then release it. The cap top should pop up so it can be grasped (**Figure 6**). Remove the cap by turning it counterclockwise while pulling up.

NOTE
The oil filler cap body has a wide slot and a narrow slot which allows cap installation in one direction only.

NOTE
*The oil tank is equipped with an oil drain line and hose that is connected to a fitting clip attached to the underside of the frame (A, **Figure 8**).*

3. Detach the fitting clip (A, **Figure 8**) from the frame tube by pulling the clip straight out.
4. Place a drain pan underneath the oil tank drain line.
5. Unscrew the screw clamp (B, **Figure 8**), then separate the drain hose (C) from the fitting on the clip body.
6. Allow the oil to drain completely.

7. Reconnect the oil drain hose to the fitting on the clip body. Tighten the screw clamp.
8. Attach the fitting clip to the frame tube (A, **Figure 8**). Make sure the clip and hose do not hang down from the frame.
9. To replace the oil filter (**Figure 9**), perform the following:
   a. Place a drain pan underneath the front portion of the crankcase and the oil filter.
   b. Install a suitable oil filter wrench (**Figure 10**) squarely onto the oil filter and loosen it counterclockwise. Quickly remove the oil filter as oil will begin to run out of it.
   c. Hold the filter over the drain pan and pour out the remaining oil. Place the filter in a plastic bag, seal the bag and dispose of it properly.
   d. Thoroughly wipe off all oil that drained onto the engine. Clean with a contact cleaner to eliminate all oil residue from the engine prior to installing the new oil filter.
   e. Coat the gasket on the new filter with clean oil.

CAUTION
Tighten the oil filter by hand. Do not overtighten.

   f. Screw the oil filter onto the mounting pad by hand and tighten it until the filter gasket touches the sealing surface, then tighten the filter by hand an additional 1/2 to 3/4 turn.

CAUTION
Do not overfill the oil tank. Oil may be forced into the air cleaner causing engine malfunction or damage.

NOTE
The oil filler cap body has a wide slot and a narrow slot which allows cap installation in one direction only.

10. Add the correct viscosity (**Table 3**) and quantity (**Table 4**) of oil to the oil tank. Reinstall the oil filler cap; but do not push down the cap. Unscrew and remove the oil filler cap.

CAUTION
*After oil has been added, the oil level will register above the upper groove dipstick mark (A, **Figure** 7) until the engine runs and the filter fills with oil. To obtain a correct reading after adding oil and installing a new oil filter, follow the procedure in Step 11.*

9

10

11

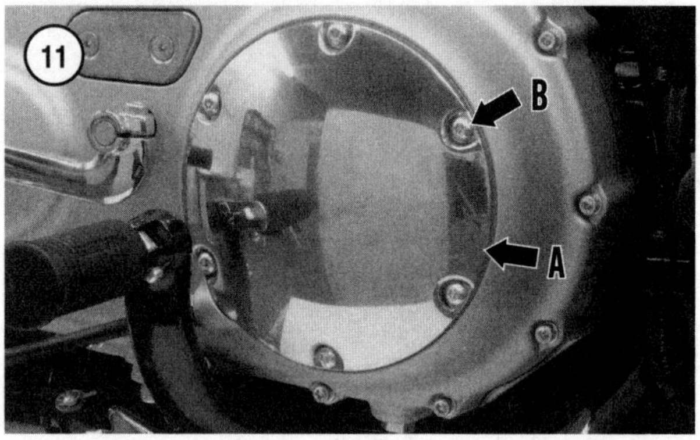

11. After changing the engine oil and filter, check the oil level as follows:
   a. Start and run the engine for one minute, then shut it off.
   b. Check the oil level on the dipstick as described in this chapter.
   c. If the oil level is correct, it will register in the dipstick's safe operating level range. If so, do not top off or add oil to bring it to the upper groove level on the dipstick.
12. Check the oil filter and drain plug for leaks.

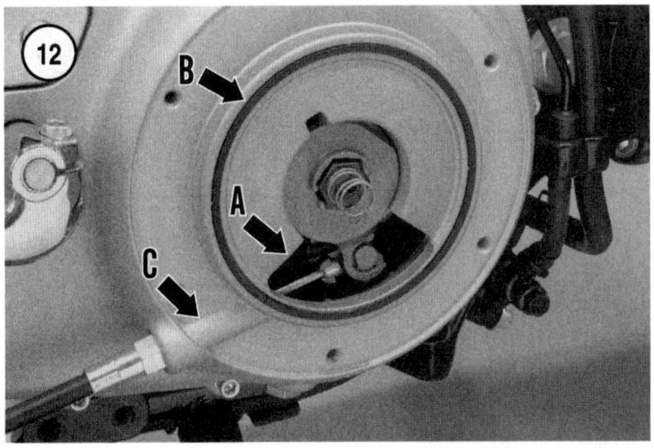

13. Dispose of the used oil properly.

Transmission Oil Level Inspection

The transmission oil also lubricates the clutch, primary drive chain and sprockets.

Periodically inspect the transmission oil level. When checking the transmission oil level, do not allow any debris to enter the transmission. The transmission oil level dipstick is on the forward portion of the clutch release cover.

WARNING
Contact with oil may cause skin cancer. Wash oil from hands with soap and water as soon as possible after handling engine oil.

CAUTION
Do not check the oil level with the motorcycle supported on the sidestand. Doing so causes an incorrect reading.

1. Ride the motorcycle for approximately ten minutes and shift through the gears so the transmission reaches normal operating temperature. Turn the engine off and allow the oil to settle in the case. Park the motorcycle on a level surface and have an assistant support it so it is standing straight up.
2. Clean the area around the clutch inspection cover (A, **Figure 11**).

NOTE
If a suitable tool is not available to remove the lower, left cover screw, remove the footrest as described in Chapter Fourteen.

3. Remove the clutch inspection cover retaining screws (B, **Figure 11**), then remove the cover.

NOTE
*The primary cover is removed in **Figure 13** for clarity. It is not necessary to remove the cover.*

4. Check the transmission oil level through the primary cover opening (A, **Figure 12**). It should be even with the bottom of the clutch diaphragm spring (**Figure 13**).

CAUTION
*Do not add engine oil. Add only the recommended transmission oil (**Table 5**). Overfilling may cause clutch malfunctioning.*

5. If the oil level is low, add the recommended type of transmission oil in **Table 5**. Do not overfill.
6. Make sure the quad ring is located in the primary cover groove (B, **Figure 12**).
7. Install the inspection cover so the notch in the cover (**Figure 14**) fits over the cable boss (C, **Figure 12**) on the primary cover. Tighten the retaining screws to 90-120 in.-lb. (10.2-13.6 N•m).

Transmission Oil Change

Table 1 lists the recommended transmission oil change intervals.

1. Ride the motorcycle for approximately ten minutes and shift through the gears until the transmission reaches normal operating temperature. Turn off the engine and allow the oil to settle in the case. Park the motorcycle on a level surface and have an assistant support it so it is standing straight up.

2. Place a drain pan underneath the primary drive cover and remove the drain plug (**Figure 15**).

3. Inspect the drain plug O-ring for damage and replace it if necessary.

4. The drain plug is equipped with a magnet (**Figure 16**). Check the plug for metal debris that may indicate transmission damage, then wipe the plug off. Replace the plug if it is damaged.

5. Install the drain plug and O-ring and tighten to 14-30 ft.-lb. (19-40 N•m).

6. Clean the area around the clutch inspection cover (A, **Figure 11**).

NOTE
If a suitable tool is not available to remove the lower, left cover screw, remove the footrest as described in Chapter Fourteen.

7. Remove the clutch inspection cover retaining screws (B, **Figure 11**), then remove the cover.

CAUTION
*Do not fill with engine oil. Only add the recommended transmission oil (**Table 5**). Overfilling may cause clutch malfunctioning.*

NOTE
*The primary cover is removed in **Figure 13** for clarity. It is not necessary to remove the cover.*

8. Refill the transmission through the cover opening in the primary cover with the recommended quantity (**Table 4**) and type (**Table 5**) of transmission oil. The transmission oil level should be even with the bottom of the clutch diaphragm spring (**Figure 13**).

9. Install the clutch inspection cover. Tighten the retaining screws to 90-120 in.-lb. (10.2-13.6 N•m).

10. Remove the oil drain pan and dispose the oil properly.

11. Ride the motorcycle until the transmission oil reaches normal operating temperature. Then shut the engine off.

12. Check the drain plug for leaks.

13. Check the transmission oil level as described in this section. Readjust the level if necessary.

Front Fork Oil Change

This procedure is for a routine fork oil change. If the fork has been disassembled for service, refer to Chapter Eleven for fork oil refilling and specifications.

Refer to **Table 1** for the recommended fork oil change intervals.

WARNING
Do not allow the fork oil to come in contact with the brake pads.

1. Place a drain pan beside one fork tube, then remove the drain screw (**Figure 17**) from the slider.

2. Straddle the motorcycle and apply the front brake lever. Push down on the fork and release. Repeat to force as much oil out of the fork tube and slider as possible.

3. Repeat Steps 1-2 for the opposite fork tube.

4. After the fork oil has thoroughly drained, install the drain screw (**Figure 17**) onto the fork slider. Tighten the drain screw to 13-17 in.-lb. (1.5-2.0 N•m).

5. Support the front of the motorcycle so the front wheel is off the ground.

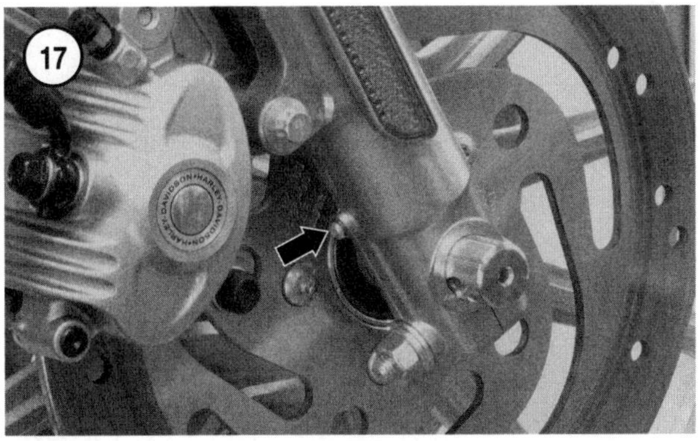

17

18

19

WARNING
Keep body parts away from the fork cap when removing it. The fork cap is under spring pressure and may fly off when loosening it. In addition, make sure the fork tube is fully extended from the slider.

CAUTION
Use a 6-point socket to loosen and tighten the fork tube cap to avoid cosmetic damage to the fork tube cap. Using a 12-point socket may round off the corners of the fork tube cap.

6. Remove the fork cap from the top of the fork tube (**Figure 18**).
7. Refill each fork leg with the correct viscosity (**Table 5**) and quantity of fork oil (**Table 6**).
8. Repeat Step 7 for the opposite fork tube.
9. Replace the fork cap O-ring (**Figure 19**) if leaking, excessively worn or damaged.

CAUTION
It takes considerable pressure to push the fork cap down against spring pressure while turning it. Attach a suitable socket to a speed wrench, then push down on the speed wrench to turn the fork cap. It may be necessary to move the handlebar and lower handlebar holder so the socket will fit properly on the fork cap. A fork spring compression kit is available from Motion Pro.

10. Install the fork cap (**Figure 18**) onto the top of the fork tube. Tighten the fork cap to 22-58 ft.-lb. (30-78 N•m).
11. Road test the motorcycle and check for leaks.

Control Cable Lubrication (Non-Nylon Lined Cables)

The major cause of cable breakage or cable stiffness is improper lubrication. Maintaining the cables will ensure long service life. Lubricate the control cables with a cable lubricant at the intervals in **Table 1**, or when they become stiff or sluggish. When lubricating the control cables, inspect each cable for fraying and cable sheath damage. Replace damaged cables.

CAUTION
If the original equipment cables have been replaced with nylon-lined cables, do not lubricate them as described in this procedure. Oil and most cable lubricant causes the cable liner to expand, pushing the liner against the cable sheath. Nylon-lined cables are normally used dry. When servicing nylon-lined and other aftermarket cables, follow the manufacturer's instructions.

CAUTION
Do not use chain lubricant to lubricate control cables.

CAUTION
The starting enrichment valve (choke) cable is designed to operate with a certain amount of cable resistance. Do not lubricate the enrichment cable or its conduit.

1A. Disconnect the clutch cable ends as described in *Clutch Cable Replacement* in Chapter Six.

1B. Disconnect both throttle cable ends as described in *Throttle and Idle Cables* in Chapter Eight.

2. Attach a lubricator tool (**Figure 20**) to the cable following the tool manufacturer's instructions. Place a shop cloth at the end of the cable to catch all excess lubricant.

3. Insert the lubricant nozzle tube into the lubricator, press the button on the can and hold it down until the lubricant begins to flow out of the other end of the cable. If the lubricant squirts out from around the lubricator, it is not clamped to the cable properly. Loosen and reposition the cable lubricator.

NOTE

If the lubricant does not flow out of the other end of the cable, check the cable for fraying, bending or other damage. Replace damaged cables.

4. Remove the lubricator tool and wipe off both ends of the cable.

5A. Reconnect the clutch cable ends as described in *Clutch Cable Replacement* in Chapter Six.

5B. Reconnect both throttle cable ends as described in *Throttle and Idle Cable Replacement* in Chapter Eight.

6. Adjust the cables as described in *Periodic Maintenance* in this chapter.

Throttle Control Grip Lubrication

Table 1 lists the recommended throttle control grip lubrication intervals. To remove and install the throttle grip, refer to the *Throttle and Idle Cable Replacement* in Chapter Eight. Lubricate the throttle control grip where it contacts the handlebar with graphite.

Front Brake Lever Pivot Pin Lubrication

Inspect the front brake lever pivot pin (**Figure 21**) for lubricant at the intervals in **Table 1**. If the pin is dry, lubricate it with a lightweight oil. To service the pivot pin, refer to the *Front Master Cylinder* in Chapter Thirteen.

Clutch Lever Pivot Pin Lubrication

Inspect the clutch lever pivot pin (**Figure 22**) at the intervals in **Table 1**. Lubricate the pin with a lightweight oil. To service the pivot pin, refer to *Clutch Cable Replacement* in Chapter Six.

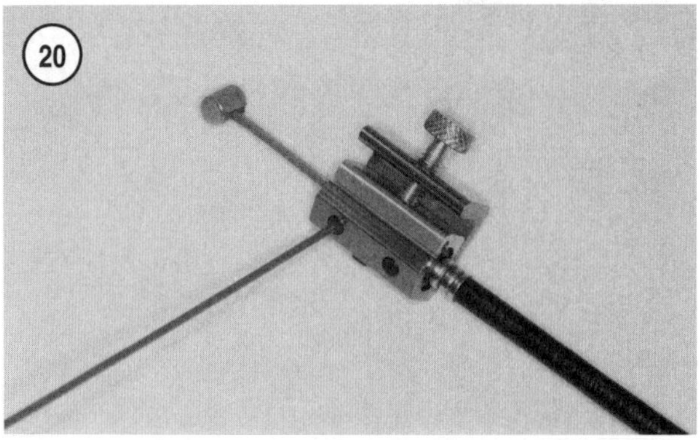
20

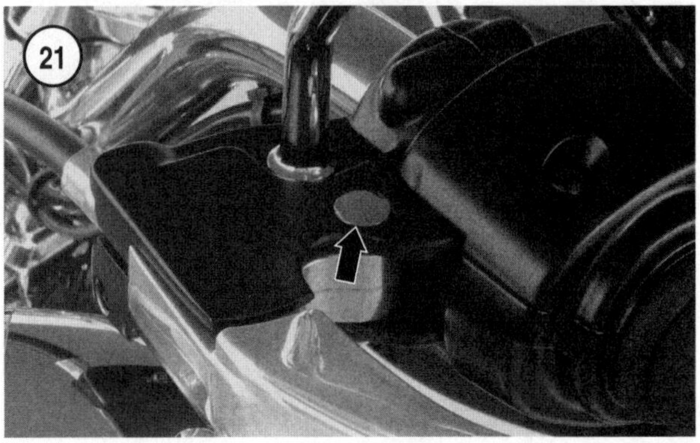
21

22

Sidestand Lubrication

Refer to **Table 1** for the specified lubrication interval for the sidestand. Refer to Chapter Fourteen and disassemble the sidestand. Lubricate the bushings with wheel bearing grease, then reassemble the sidestand.

Steering Head Lubrication

Refer to **Table 1** for the specified lubrication interval for the steering head bearings. Refer to Chapter Eleven

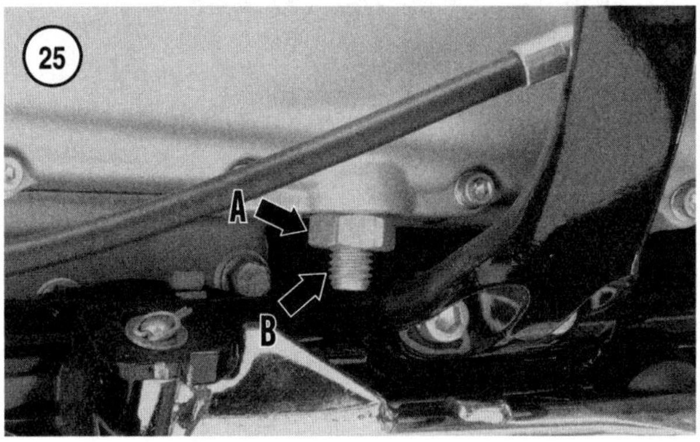

and disassemble the steering head as needed for access to the bearings. Lubricate the bearings with wheel bearing grease, then reassemble the steering head.

Brake Caliper Pin Lubrication

Refer to **Table 1** for the specified lubrication interval for the brake caliper pins. Refer to Chapter Thirteen and disassemble the brake caliper as needed for access to the brake pad pins. Lubricate the pins and boots with brake grease, then reassemble the brake caliper.

PERIODIC MAINTENANCE

Perform these periodic inspection, adjustment and replacement procedures at the intervals in **Table 1**, or earlier, if necessary.

Primary Chain Adjustment

As the primary chain stretches and wears, its free play movement increases. Excessive free play causes premature chain and sprocket wear and increases chain noise. If the free play is adjusted too tight, the chain wears prematurely.

NOTE

On models equipped with the TSSM security system, always disarm the system prior to disconnecting the battery or the siren will sound.

1. Disconnect the negative battery cable as described in Chapter Nine.
2. Support the motorcycle on a stand or floor jack with the rear wheel off the ground. Refer to *Motorcycle Stands* in Chapter Ten.
3. Remove the primary chain inspection cover and gasket (**Figure 23**).
4. Turn the primary chain to find the tightest point on the chain. Measure chain free play at this point.
5. Check primary chain free play at the upper chain run midway between the sprockets (**Figure 24**). Refer to **Table 8** for cold and hot specifications. If the primary chain free play is incorrect, continue with Step 6. If the free play is correct, go to Step 7.
6. To adjust the chain, perform the following:
   a. Loosen the primary chain adjuster locknut (A, **Figure 25**).
   b. Rotate the adjuster (B, **Figure 25**) to obtain the desired chain free play. Turning the adjuster clockwise decreases free play.
   c. Tighten the primary chain adjuster locknut (A, **Figure 25**) to 20-25 ft.-lb. (28-34 N•m), then recheck free play.

NOTE

If specified primary chain free play cannot be obtained using the adjuster, the primary chain or adjuster mechanism is worn. Refer to Chapter Six for removal and inspection.

7. Install the primary chain inspection cover (**Figure 23**) and a new gasket. Tighten the cover bolts to 84-120 in.-lb. (9.5-13.6 N•m).
8. Lower the motorcycle to the ground.

Final Drive Belt Inspection

CAUTION
Check the drive belt deflection when the belt is cold.

Inspect drive belt deflection at the intervals in **Table 1**. If the drive belt is excessively worn, or if it is wearing incorrectly, refer to Chapter Ten for inspection and replacement procedures.

1. Support the motorcycle on a stand or floor jack with the rear wheel off the ground. Refer to *Motorcycle Stands* in Chapter Ten.
2. Then turn the rear wheel and check the drive belt for its tightest point. After locating this point, turn the wheel so the belt's tight spot is on the lower belt run, midway between the front and rear sprockets.
3. Lower the motorcycle to the ground.
4. Position the motorcycle so both wheels are on the ground. When checking and adjusting drive belt deflection in the following steps, have an assistant sit on the seat facing forward.
5. Observe the belt position through the window in the debris deflector (**Figure 26**). Using chalk or another removeable marker, mark the position of the belt.

NOTE
*Use Harley-Davidson belt tension gauge part No. HD-35381-A (A, **Figure 27**) or equivalent to apply pressure against the drive belt in Step 6. A suitable equivalent is the Yamaha belt tension tool (B, **Figure 27**).*

NOTE
Make sure the belt tension gauge is positioned so it applies force squarely against the belt.

6. Apply a force of 10 lb. (4.5 kg) to the middle of the lower belt run and make another mark on the debris deflector to indicate the position of the deflected belt.
7. Note the number of graduations between the marks. Each graduation next to the window equals 1/8 in. (3.2 mm). Calculate the amount of belt deflection and refer to **Table 8** for the specification. If the deflection measurement is incorrect, adjust the drive belt as described in *Final Drive Belt Deflection Adjustment*.

Final Drive Belt Deflection Adjustment

2004 models

1. Install and measure the belt deflection as described in this section.

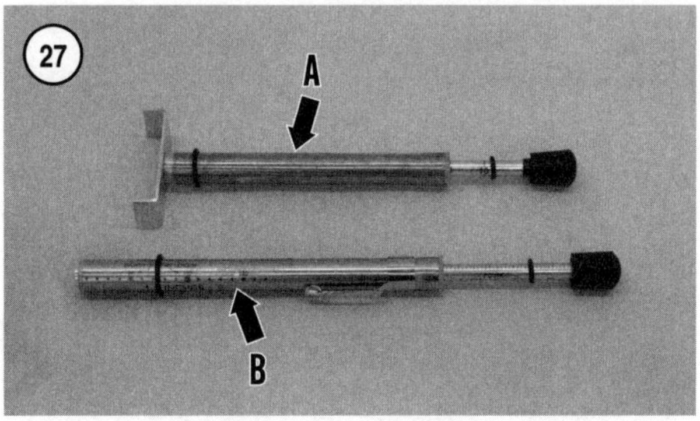

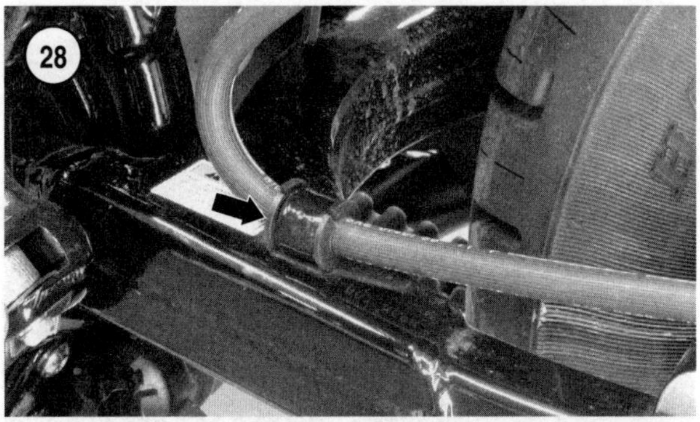

2. Remove the rear brake hose clamp (**Figure 28**) from the swing arm. This will provide additional slack in the rear brake hose.
3. On the left side, remove the spring pin (**Figure 29**) and loosen the rear axle nut.
4. Turn the adjuster locknut (**Figure 29**) on each side, in either direction, an equal number of turns to obtain the correct drive belt deflection.
5. Recheck the drive belt deflection. Tighten the locknuts securely.
6. Check that the rear axle is positioned correctly within the swing arm as described in *Rear Wheel Alignment Inspection* in this section.

29

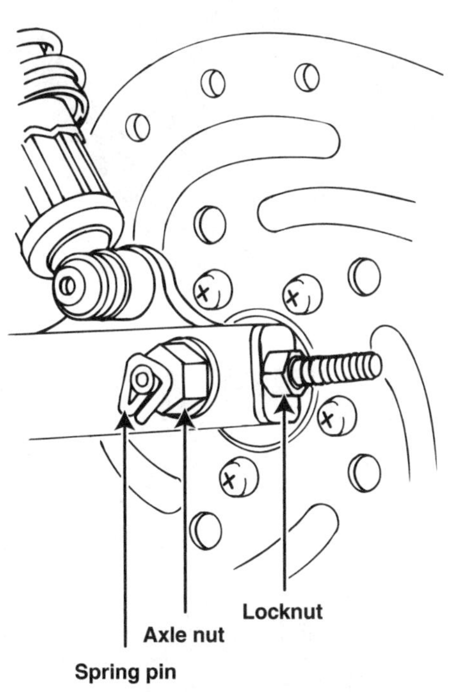

30

WARNING

Do not exceed 65 ft.-lb. (88 N•m) when tightening the rear axle nut. Overtightening the nut may cause bearing failure and possible loss of control during motorcycle operation.

7. Tighten the rear axle nut to 60-65 ft.-lb. (81-88 N•m) using the following procedure:
   a. Tighten the rear axle nut to 60 ft.-lb. (81 N•m).
   b. Check for alignment of a slot on the axle nut and the hole in the axle end. Install the spring pin (**Figure 29**) and snap it into place if the slot and hole are aligned.
   c. If the nut slot and axle hole are not aligned, continue to tighten the axle nut until alignment occurs, but do not exceed 65 ft.-lb. (88 N•m). Install the spring pin (**Figure 29**) and snap it into place.
   d. If nut slot and axle hole alignment do not occur before the torque reaches 65 ft.-lb. (88 N•m), loosen the axle nut and repeat the procedure.
8. Install the rear brake hose clamp.

2005-on models

1. Remove the rear brake hose clamp (**Figure 28**) from the swing arm. This will provide additional slack in the rear brake hose.
2. If so equipped, remove the cap (A, **Figure 30**) from each axle adjuster.
3. On the left side, remove the E-clip (B, **Figure 30**) and loosen the rear axle nut (C).
4. Turn the adjuster locknut (D, **Figure 30**) on each side, in either direction, an equal number of turns to obtain the correct drive belt deflection.
5. Recheck the drive belt deflection. Tighten the adjuster locknuts securely.
6. Check that the rear axle is positioned correctly within the swing arm as described in *Rear Wheel Alignment Inspection* in this section.

WARNING

Do not exceed 78 ft.-lb. (106 N•m) when tightening the rear axle nut. Overtightening the nut may cause bearing failure and possible loss of control during motorcycle operation.

7. When the drive belt deflection and axle alignment adjustments are correct, tighten the rear axle nut to 72-78 ft.-lb. (98-106 N•m).
8. Install the E-clip onto the rear axle (B, **Figure 30**).

Rear Wheel Alignment Inspection

The rear wheel must be properly aligned with the chassis so the drive belt runs true on the front and rear sprockets. A misaligned rear wheel causes uneven and rapid drive belt wear.

Verify that drive belt deflection is correct as described in *Final Drive Belt Deflection Adjustment*. If correct, check wheel alignment using the following procedure.

31

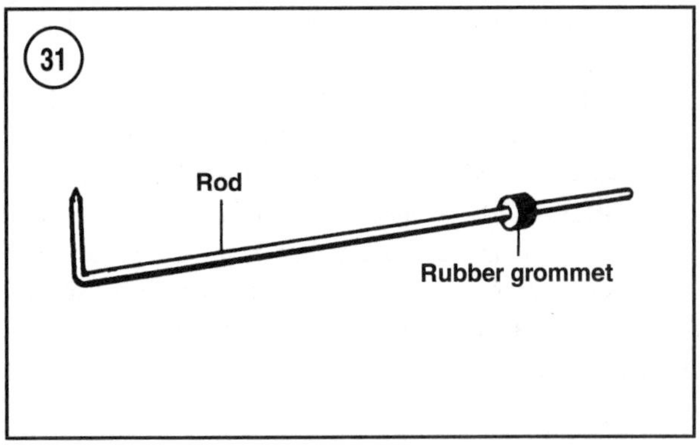

32

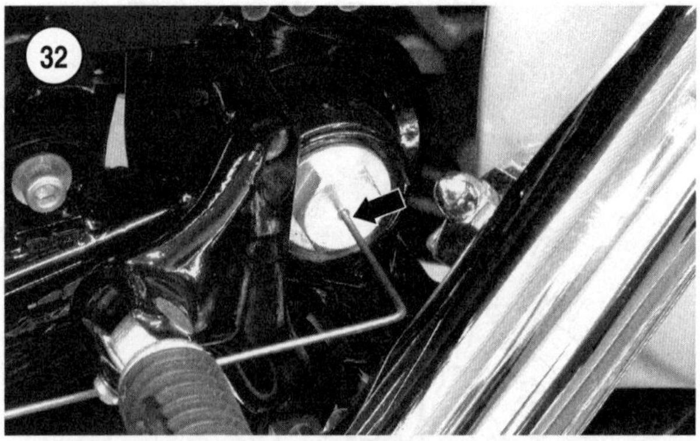

33

1. Using a suitable metal rod, fabricate the tool shown in **Figure 31**.

2. Insert the end of the tool into the index dimple in the swing arm mounting bolt as shown in **Figure 32**.

3. Slide the rubber grommet along the tool until it aligns with the center of the axle as shown in **Figure 33**.

4. Check the alignment on the opposite side, comparing the rubber grommet position with the center of the axle. The alignment on both sides of the axle must be the same. If necessary, adjust the axle with the axle adjusters, while at the same time maintaining correct drive belt deflection.

Brake Pad Inspection

1. Without removing the front or rear brake calipers, inspect the brake pads for damage.

2. Measure the thickness of each brake pad lining on the front caliper(s) (**Figure 34**) and rear caliper (**Figure 35**) with a ruler. Replace the brake pad if its minimum thickness (**Figure 36**) is worn to or less than the specification in **Table 8**. Replace the brake pads as described in Chapter Thirteen.

34

Front Brake Fluid Level Inspection

NOTE

The master cylinder sight glass (A, ***Figure 37****) only provides a quick means to determine if the brake fluid level is low, not whether the reservoir is full.*

1. Move the handlebar so the front master cylinder is level.

2. Clean the top of the master cylinder of all debris.

3. Remove the screws securing the cover (B, **Figure 37**). Remove the cover, diaphragm plate and diaphragm.

35

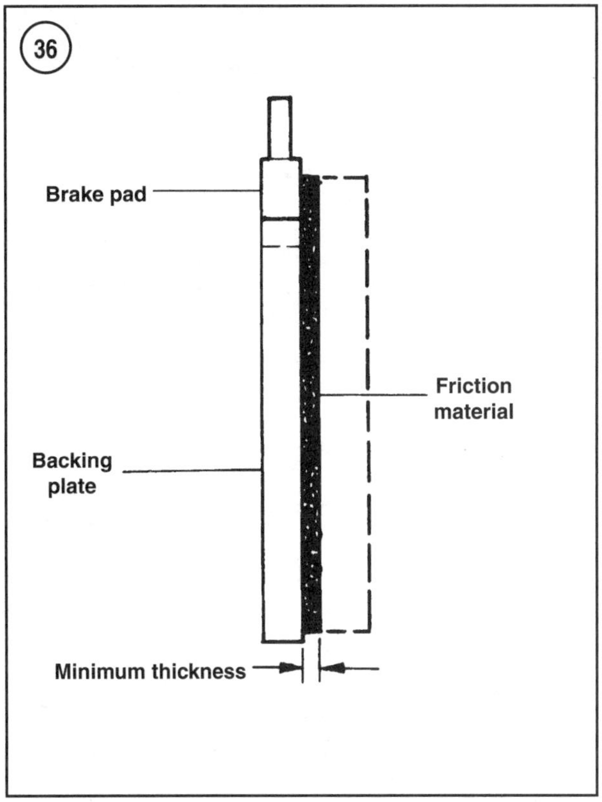

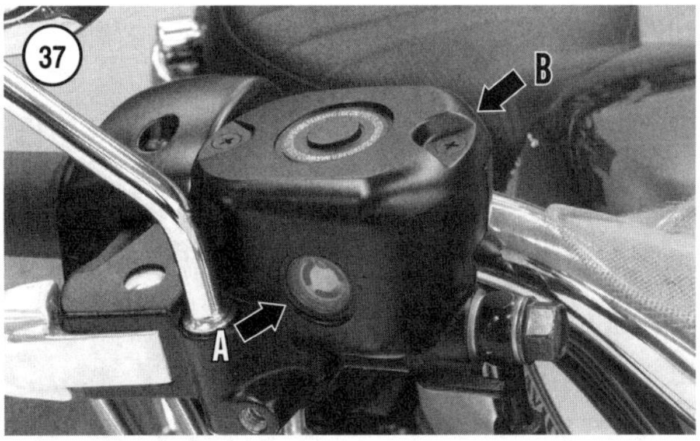

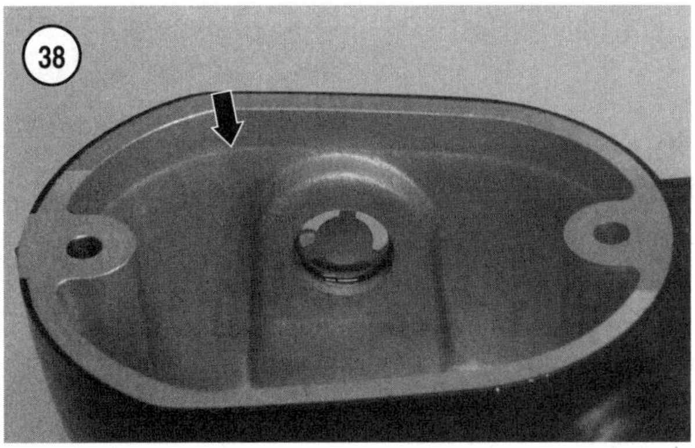

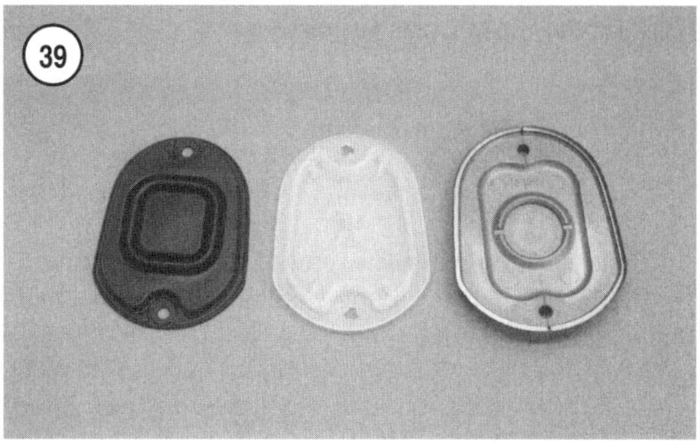

WARNING
If the reservoir is empty, air has probably entered the brake system. Bleed the front brakes as described in Chapter Thirteen.

4. The brake fluid level must be even with the casting ridge (**Figure 38**) on the reservoir housing. If the brake fluid level is below the casting ridge, continue with Step 5.

WARNING
Do not use brake fluid labeled DOT 5.1. This is a gylcol-based fluid that is not compatible with silicone-based DOT 5. DOT 5 brake fluid is purple while DOT 5.1 is amber/clear. Do not intermix these two different types of brake fluid as it can cause brake component damage and lead to brake system failure.

WARNING
Do not intermix DOT 3, DOT 4 or DOT 5.1 brake fluids as they are not silicone-based. Using non-silicone brake fluid in these models can cause brake failure.

5. Add new DOT 5 brake fluid to raise the brake fluid level.
6. Reinstall the diaphragm, diaphragm plate and cover (**Figure 39**). Install the screws and tighten securely.

NOTE
A low brake fluid level usually indicates brake pad wear. As the pads wear and become thinner, the brake caliper pistons automatically extend farther out of their bores. As the caliper pistons move outward, the brake fluid level drops in the system. However, if the brake fluid level is low and the brake pads are not worn excessively, check all the brake hoses for leaks.

Rear Brake Fluid Level Inspection

WARNING
Do not check the rear brake fluid level with the motorcycle resting on its sidestand. A false reading will result.

1. Park the motorcycle on level ground so the bike is upright.
2. The brake fluid level must be above the lower level line (**Figure 40**) on the reservoir cover. If the brake fluid level is at or below the lower level line, proceed to Step 3.

WARINING
If the reservoir is empty, air has probably entered the brake system. Bleed the rear brake as described in Chapter Thirteen.

NOTE
If the fluid level is difficult to see, remove the cover from the reservoir and use the markings on the reservoir.

3. Unscrew the reservoir cap, which may contain the diaphragm holder and diaphragm. If not, remove the diaphragm and holder from the reservoir.

WARNING
Do not use DOT 5.1 brake fluid. This is a gylcol-based fluid that is not compatible with silicone-based DOT 5. DOT 5 brake fluid is purple while DOT 5.1 is amber/clear. Do not intermix these two different types of brake fluid as it can cause brake component damage and lead to brake system failure.

WARNING
Do not intermix DOT 3, DOT 4 or DOT 5.1 brake fluids as they are not silicone-based. Using non-silicone brake fluid in these models can cause brake failure.

4. Add new DOT 5 brake fluid to fill the reservoir to the upper level mark on the reservoir housing.
5. Install the diaphragm, diaphragm holder and cap.
6. If the brake fluid level was low, check the brake pads for excessive wear as described in this section.

NOTE
A low brake fluid level usually indicates brake pad wear. As the pads wear and become thinner, the brake caliper pistons automatically extend farther out of their bores. As the caliper pistons move outward, the brake fluid level drops in the system. However, if the brake fluid level is low and the brake pads are not worn excessively, check all the brake hoses and lines for leaks.

40

41

42

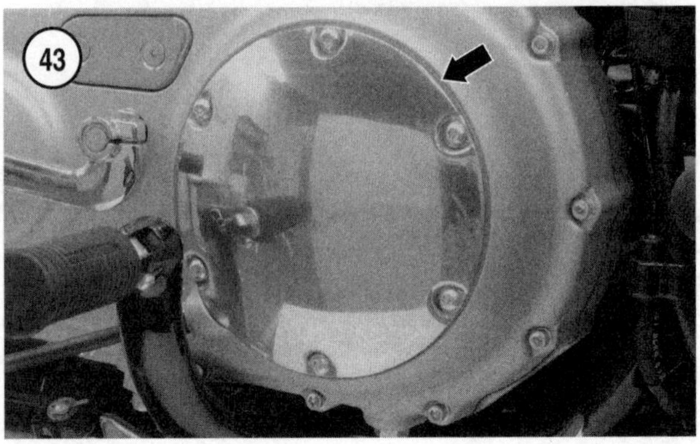
43

44

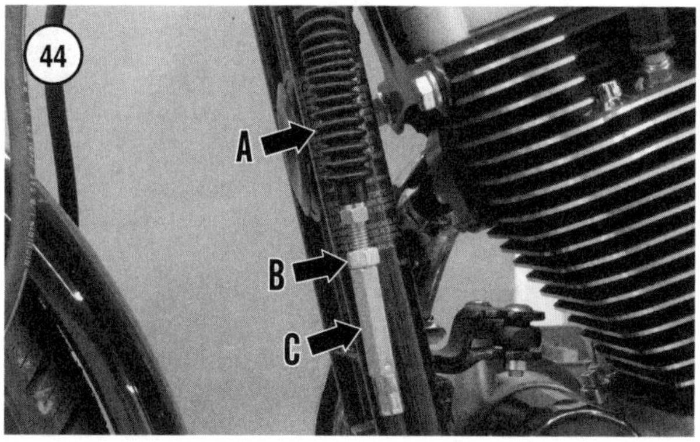

45

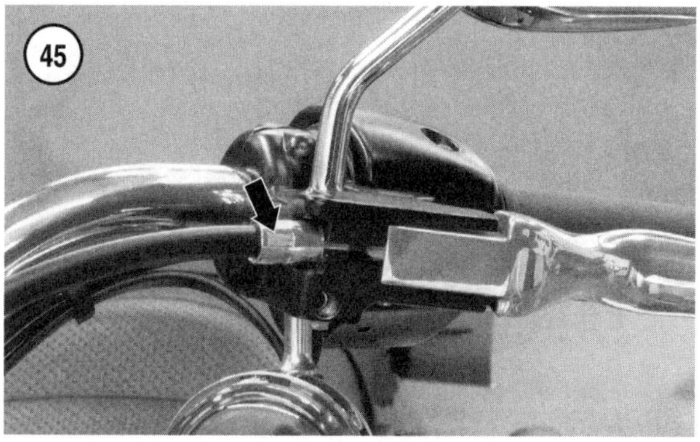

46

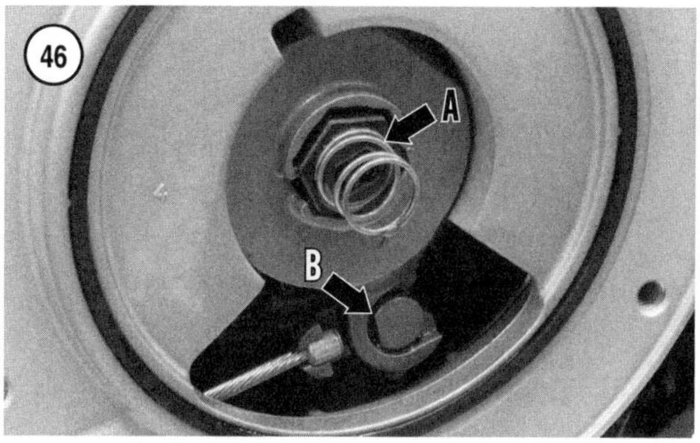

47

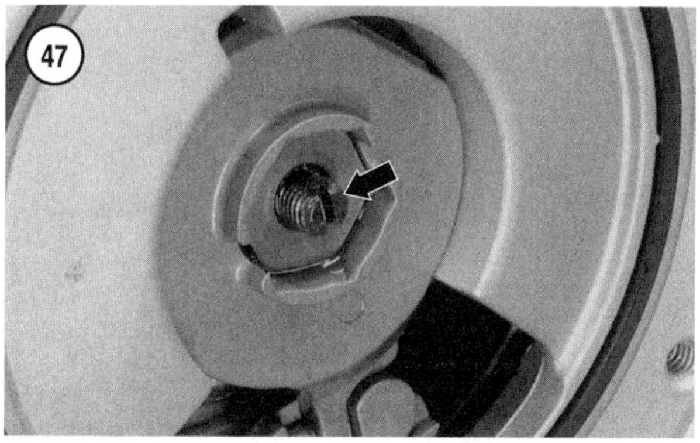

Front and Rear Brake Disc Inspection

Visually inspect the front and rear brake discs (**Figure 41**, typical) for scoring, cracks or other damage. Measure the brake disc thickness (**Figure 42**) and, if necessary, service the brake discs as described in Chapter Thirteen.

Brake Line and Seal Inspection

Check the brake lines between each master cylinder and each brake caliper. If there is any leakage, tighten the connections and bleed the brakes as described in Chapter Thirteen.

Brake Fluid Change

WARNING
Do not use DOT 5.1 brake fluid. This is a glycol-based fluid that is not compatible with silicone-based DOT 5. DOT 5 brake fluid is purple while DOT 5.1 is an amber/clear color. Do not intermix these different types of brake fluid as it can lead to brake component damage and possible brake failure.

Every time the reservoir cover is removed, moisture enters the brake fluid. The same thing happens if there is a leak or if any part of the hydraulic system is loosened or disconnected. Water in the fluid vaporizes at high temperatures, impairing the hydraulic action and reducing brake performance.

To change brake fluid, follow the brake bleeding procedure in Chapter Thirteen. Continue adding new fluid to the master cylinder until the fluid leaving the caliper is clean and free of contaminants and air bubbles.

Clutch Adjustment

1. On models with mid-mount footrests, remove the left footrest bracket as described in Chapter Fourteen.
2. Remove the clutch mechanism inspection cover (**Figure 43**) and quad ring.
3. Slide the rubber boot (A, **Figure 44**) upwards off the clutch in-line cable adjuster.
4. Loosen the adjuster locknut (B, **Figure 44**) and turn the adjuster (C) to provide maximum cable slack.
5. Make sure the clutch cable ferrule (**Figure 45**) seats squarely in the lever housing receptacle on the handlebar.
6. At the clutch mechanism, remove the spring and lockplate assembly (A, **Figure 46**).
7. Turn the adjusting screw (**Figure 47**) counterclockwise until it lightly seats.

8. Turn the adjusting screw 1/4 turn clockwise.
9. Reinstall the spring and lockplate assembly (A, **Figure 46**) so it fits inside the outer ramp recess (B). If necessary, turn the adjusting screw clockwise just until the flats on the lockplate fit into the flats in the outer ramp.
10. Make sure the quad ring is located in the primary cover groove (A, **Figure 48**).
11. Install the inspection cover so the notch in the cover (**Figure 49**) fits over the cable boss on the primary cover (B, **Figure 48**). Tighten the retaining screws to 90-120 in.-lb. (10.2-13.6 N•m).
12. Check the free play as follows:
   a. At the inline cable adjuster, turn the adjuster away from the locknut until free play is eliminated at the clutch hand lever.
   b. Pull the clutch cable end away from the clutch lever, then turn the clutch cable adjuster to obtain the free play (**Figure 50**) specified in **Table 8**.
   c. When the adjustment is correct, tighten the clutch inline cable jam nut and slide the rubber boot over the cable adjuster.
13. On models with mid-mount footrests, install the left footrest assembly as described in Chapter Fourteen.

48

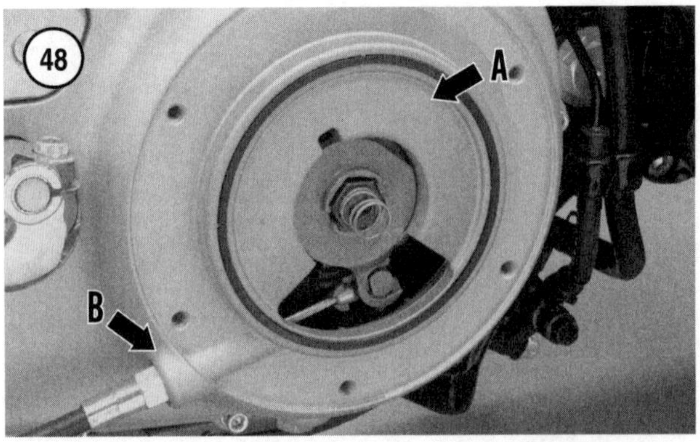

49

50

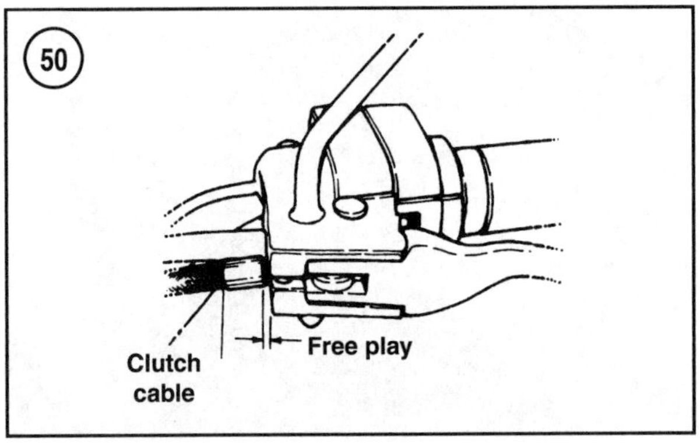

51

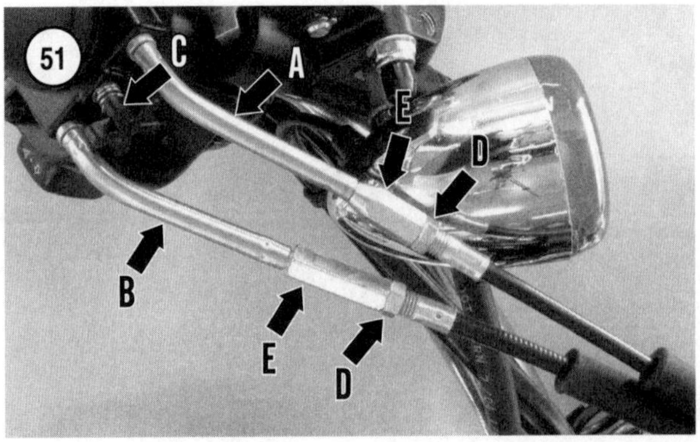

Throttle Cables

WARNING
Do not ride the motorcycle if the throttle cables are not properly adjusted. The cables must not catch or pull when the handlebar is turned from side to side. Improper cable routing and adjustment can cause the throttle to remain open. This could cause loss of control and a possible crash. Recheck all adjustments before riding the motorcycle.

Inspection

Inspect the throttle cables from the grip to the carburetor. Make sure they are not kinked or chafed. Replace them if necessary as described in Chapter Eight.

Make sure the throttle grip rotates smoothly from fully closed to fully open. Check with the handlebar at the center, full left and full right positions.

Adjustment

There are two different throttle cables. At the throttle grip, the front cable is the throttle cable (A, **Figure 51**) and the rear cable is the idle cable (B).

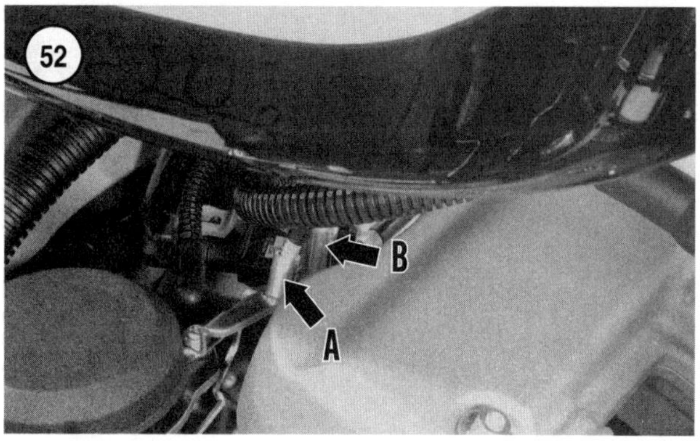

At the carburetor, the outboard cable is the throttle control cable (A, **Figure 52**) and the inboard cable is the idle cable (B).

1. Remove the air filter and backing plate as described in Chapter Eight.

2. Push back the rubber boots from the adjusters.

3. Loosen the throttle friction screw (C, **Figure 51**).

4. At the handlebar, loosen both control cable adjuster locknuts (D, **Figure 51**), then turn the cable adjusters (E) clockwise as far as possible to increase cable free play.

5. Turn the handlebars so the front wheel points straight ahead. Turn the throttle grip to open the throttle completely and hold it in this position.

NOTE
*The air cleaner backplate is shown removed in **Figure 53** to better illustrate the steps.*

6. At the handlebar, turn the front throttle cable adjuster (D, **Figure 51**) counterclockwise until the throttle cam (A, **Figure 53**) stop just touches the stop (B) on the carburetor body. Tighten the throttle cable adjuster locknut and release the throttle grip.
7. Turn the front wheel all the way to the full right lock position and hold it there.
8. At the handlebar, turn the idle cable adjuster (E, **Figure 51**) until the lower end of the idle cable (B, **Figure 52**) just contacts the spring in the carburetor cable guide. Tighten the idle cable locknut.
9. Install the backing plate and the air filter as described in Chapter Eight.
10. Shift the transmission into neutral and start the engine.
11. Increase engine speed several times. Release the throttle and make sure the engine speed returns to idle. If the engine speed does not return to idle, at the handlebar, loosen the idle cable adjuster jam nut and turn the cable adjuster clockwise as required. Tighten the idle cable adjuster locknut.
12. Allow the engine to idle in neutral, then turn the handlebar from side to side. Do not operate the throttle. If the engine speed increases when the handlebar assembly is turned, the throttle cables are routed incorrectly or damaged. Turn off the engine. Recheck cable routing and adjustment.
13. Push the rubber boots back onto the adjusters.

Starting Enrichment Valve (Choke) Cable Adjustment

The starting enrichment (choke) knob should move from the fully open to the fully closed position without any sign of binding. The knob should also stay in its fully closed or fully open position without creeping. If the knob does not stay in position, adjust tension on the cable by turning the plastic knurled nut behind the knob as follows:

CAUTION
The starting enrichment (choke) cable must have sufficient cable resistance to work properly. Do not lubricate the enrichment cable or its conduit.

1. Loosen the hex nut (**Figure 54**) behind the mounting bracket. Disengage the cable from the mounting bracket.

2. Hold the cable flats with a wrench (A, **Figure 55**) and turn the knurled plastic nut (B) counterclockwise to reduce cable resistance. Continue until the knob can slide inward freely.

3. Turn the knurled plastic nut (B, **Figure 55**) clockwise to increase cable resistance. Continue adjustment until the knob will remain stationary when it is pulled all the way out, but will move inward relatively easily. The knob must move without any roughness or binding.

4. Reinstall the cable into the mounting bracket slot with the star washer located between the bracket and hex nut. Tighten the hex nut securely.

5. Recheck the knob movement and readjust if necessary.

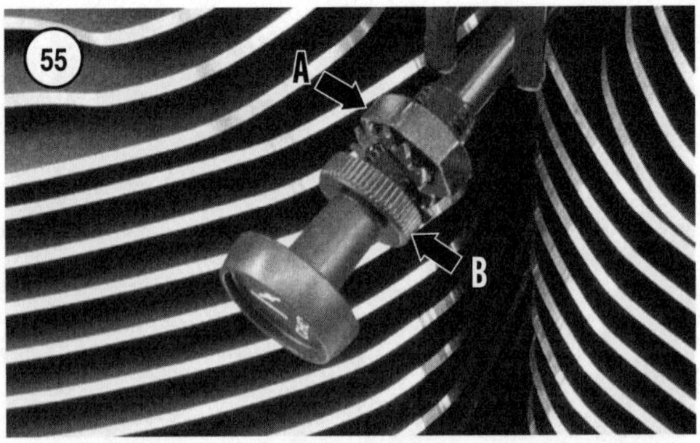

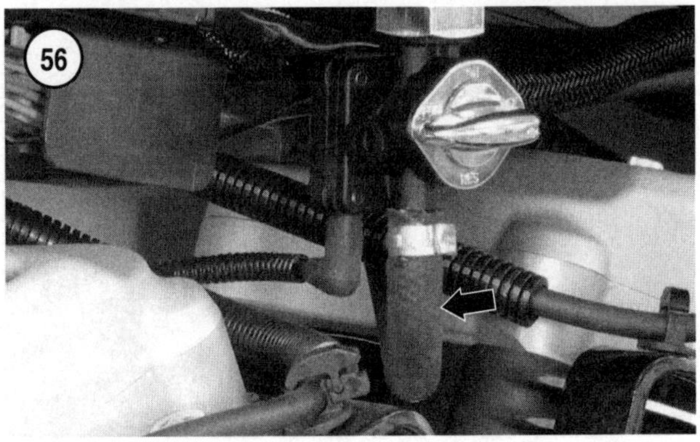

Fuel Line Inspection

WARNING
A damaged or deteriorated fuel line can cause a fire or explosion if fuel spills onto a hot engine or exhaust pipe.

Inspect the fuel line (**Figure 56**) from the fuel tank to the carburetor. Replace a leaking or damaged fuel line. Make sure the hose clamps are in place and holding securely. Check the hose fittings for looseness.

Exhaust System Inspection

Check all fittings for exhaust leaks, including the crossover pipe connections. Tighten all bolts and nuts. Replace gaskets as necessary. Refer to Chapter Eight for removal and installation procedures.

Steering Play Inspection

Check the steering head play (Chapter Eleven) at the intervals in **Table 1**.

Rear Swing Arm Inspection

Check the rear swing arm pivot bolt tightness (Chapter Twelve) at the intervals specified in **Table 1**.

Rear Shock Absorber Inspection

Check the rear shock absorbers for oil leaks or damaged bushings. Check the shock absorber mounting bolts and nuts for tightness. Refer to Chapter Twelve.

Fastener Inspection

CAUTION
*Special procedures must be used to tighten the cylinder head mounting bolts. To accurately check these bolts for tightness, refer to **Cylinder Head** in Chapter Four. Tightening these bolts incorrectly can damage the cylinder head.*

Vibration can loosen many fasteners on a motorcycle. Check the tightness of all fasteners, especially those on:

1. Engine mounting hardware.
2. Engine and primary covers.
3. Handlebar and front fork.
4. Gearshift lever.
5. Sprocket bolts and nuts.
6. Brake lever and pedal.
7. Exhaust system.
8. Lighting equipment.

Electrical Equipment Inspection

Check all electrical equipment and switches for proper operation. Rcfcr to Chapter Nine.

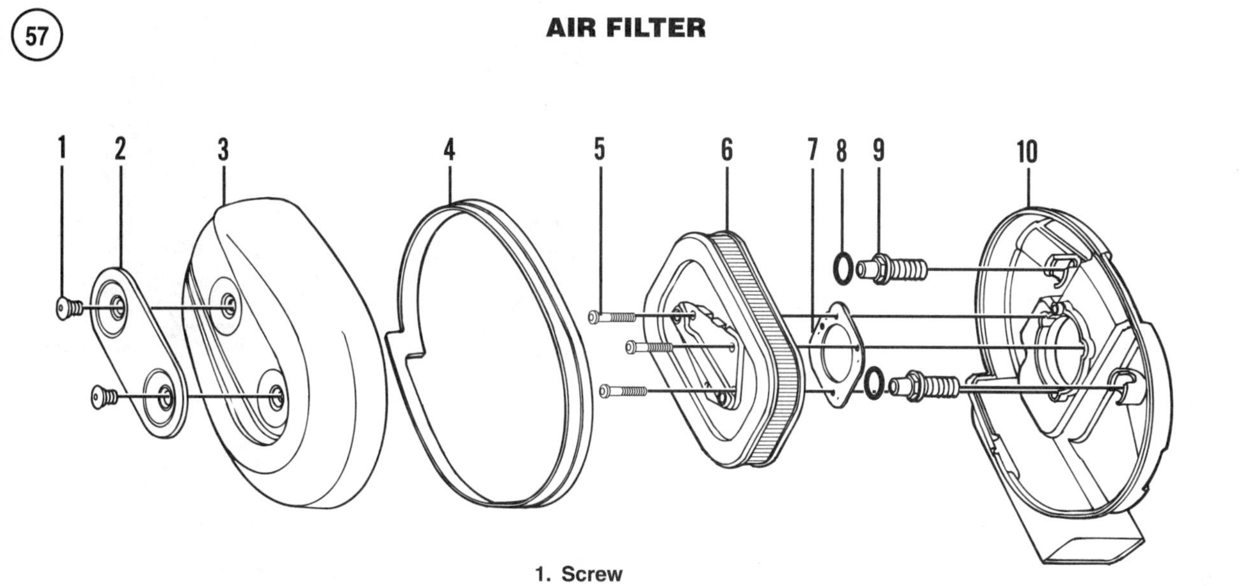

1. Screw
2. Trim panel
3. Cover
4. Seal ring
5. Retaining screw
6. Air filter element
7. Gasket
8. O-ring
9. Breather bolt
10. Backplate

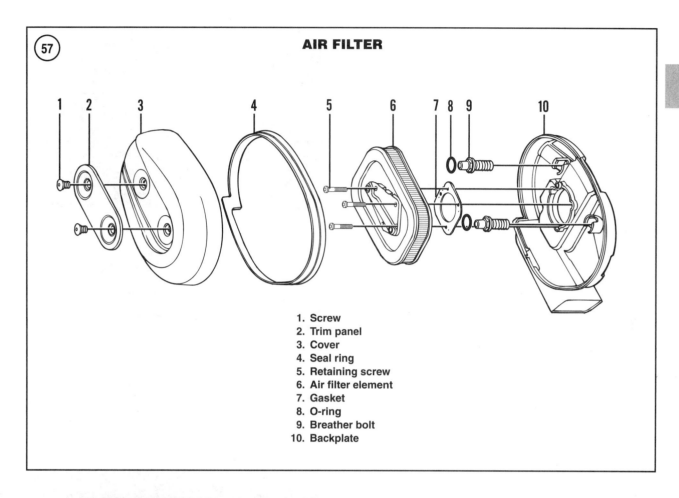

TUNE-UP

The following sections cover tune-up procedures. Perform the tasks at the intervals in **Table 1**. Perform a complete tune-up in the following order:

1. Clean or replace the air filter element.
2. Check engine compression.
3. Check or replace the spark plugs.
4. Adjust the idle speed.

AIR FILTER ELEMENT

Removal/Installation

Remove and inspect the air filter at the interval in **Table 1**. If necessary, clean the element. Replace the element if it is damaged or starting to deteriorate.

The air filter removes dust and debris from the air before it enters the carburetor and the engine. Without the air filter, abrasive particles will enter the engine and cause rapid engine wear. Particles also might clog small passages in the carburetor. Never run the motorcycle without the element installed.

Refer to **Figure 57**.

1. Remove the air filter cover screws (A, **Figure 58**) and remove the cover (B).
2. Remove the air filter element retaining screws (A, **Figure 59**) and remove the air filter element (B).
3. Clean the air filter as described in this section.
4. Inspect the gasket (**Figure 60**) for damage. Replace it if necessary.
5. Inspect the breather bolt O-rings (**Figure 61**) and replace if damaged.

6. If they were removed, install the breather bolt O-rings (**Figure 61**). Lubricate the O-rings with engine oil before installing the O-rings and the air filter element.
7. Install the gasket (**Figure 60**) onto the back of the air filter element. Make sure all holes are aligned.
8. Install the air filter element (B, **Figure 59**). Tighten the retaining screws to 40-60 in.-lb. (4.5-6.8 N•m).
9. Inspect the seal ring (**Figure 62**) on the air filter cover for hardness or deterioration. Replace it if necessary.
10. Install the air filter cover (B, **Figure 58**) and the screws (A). Make sure the seal ring fits properly inside the backplate. Tighten the screws to 36-60 in.-lb. (4.1-6.8 N•m).

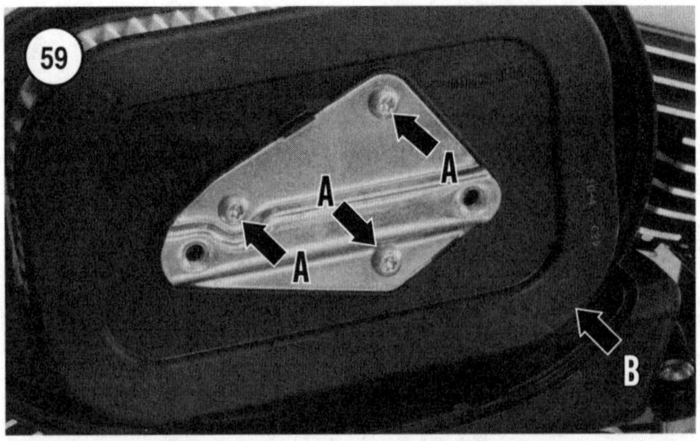

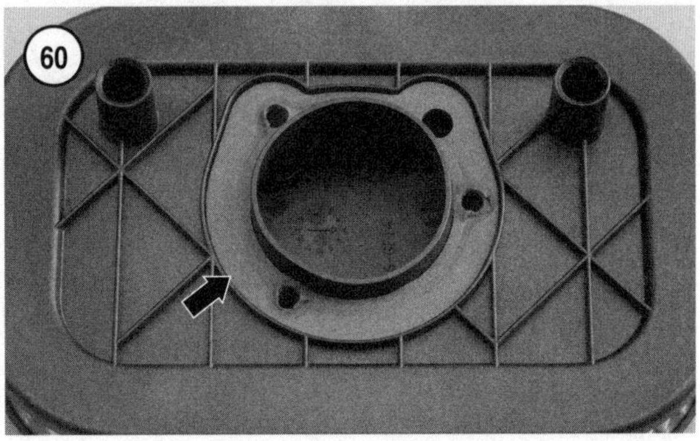

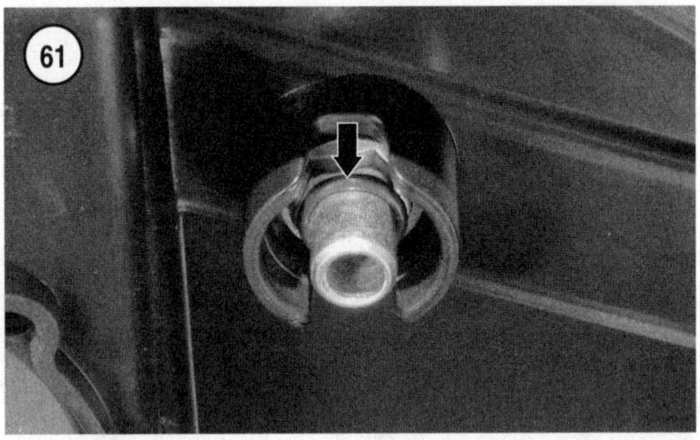

Cleaning

WARNING
Never clean the air filter element in gasoline or low flash point solvent. The residual solvent or vapors may cause a fire or explosion after the filter is reinstalled.

CAUTION
Do not tap or strike the air filter element on a hard surface to dislodge dirt. Doing so will damage the element.

The air filter element is a paper/wire type (**Figure 63**). If an aftermarket element is installed, refer to the manufacturer's cleaning instructions.

1. Remove the air filter element as described in this section.
2. Replace the air filter if damaged.
3. Place the air filter in a pan filled with lukewarm water and mild detergent. Move the air filter element back and forth to help dislodge trapped dirt. Thoroughly rinse it in clean water to remove all detergent residue.
4. Hold the air filter up to a strong light. Check the filter pores for dirt and oil. Repeat Step 3 until there is no dirt and oil in the filter pores. If the air filter cannot be cleaned, or if the filter is saturated with oil or other chemicals, replace it.

CAUTION
Do not use high air pressure to dry the filter, as this will damage it. Maximum air pressure should be 32 psi (220kPa).

CAUTION
In the next step, do not blow compressed air through the outer surface of the air filter element. Doing so can force dirt trapped on the outer filter surface deeper into the air filter element, restricting airflow and damaging the air filter element.

5. Gently apply compressed air through the inside surface of the air filter element to remove loosened dirt and dust trapped in the filter.
6. Inspect the air filter element. Replace it if it is torn or damaged. Do not ride the motorcycle with a damaged air filter element as it will allow dirt to enter the engine.
7. Wipe the inside of the cover and backplate with a clean, damp shop rag.

62

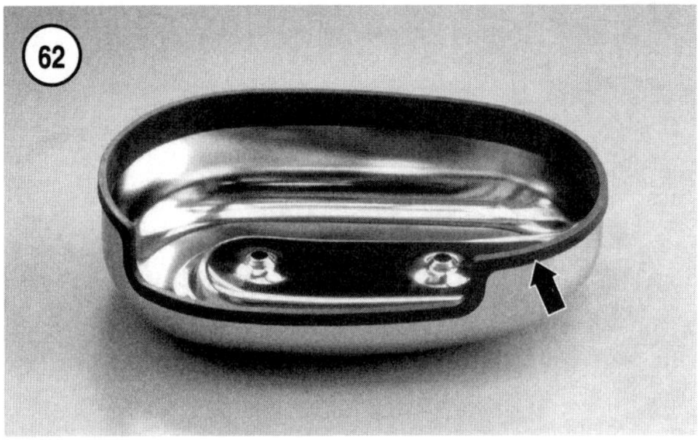

63

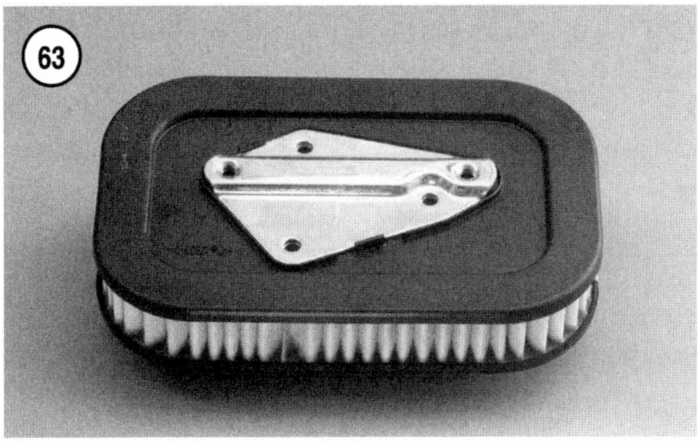

64

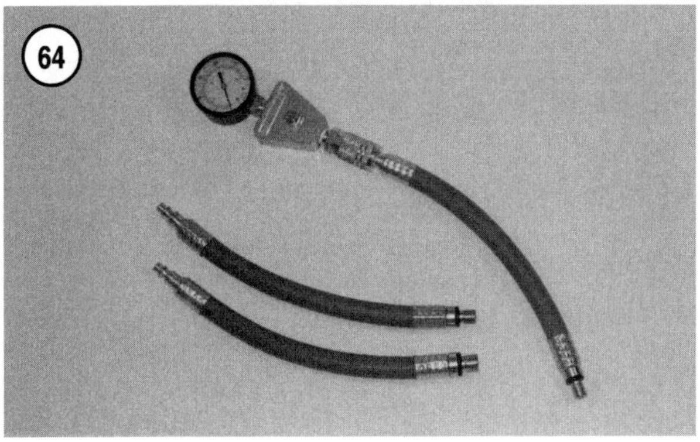

CAUTION
Air will not pass through a wet or damp filter. Make sure the filter is dry before installing it.

8. Allow the filter to dry completely, then reinstall it as described in this chapter.

ENGINE COMPRESSION TEST

An engine compression test is one of the quickest ways to check the internal condition of the engine (piston rings, pistons, head gasket, valves and cylinders). It is a good idea to check compression at each tune-up, record it in the maintenance log at the back of the manual, and compare it with subsequent readings.

Use a screw-in type compression gauge (**Figure 64**) with any necessary adapter (refer to Chapter One). Before using the gauge, make sure that the rubber gasket on the end of the gauge hose adapter is in good condition; this gasket seals the cylinder to ensure accurate compression readings.

1. Make sure the battery is fully charged to ensure proper engine cranking speed.
2. Run the engine until it reaches normal operating temperature, then turn it off.
3. Remove the spark plugs as described in this chapter.
4. Connect a grounding tool (refer to Chapter One) to the spark plug wires to prevent possible damage to the ignition system components.
5. Lubricate the threads of the compression gauge adapter with a small amount of antiseize compound and carefully thread the gauge into one of the spark plug holes.
6. Move the engine stop switch to run, then turn the ignition switch on. Open the throttle completely and using the starter, crank the engine over until there is no further rise in pressure. Maximum pressure is usually reached within 4-7 seconds of engine cranking. Record the reading and the cylinder location.
7. Repeat Step 5 and Step 6 for the other cylinder.
8. When interpreting the results, note the readings and the difference between the two cylinders, if any. Compression is considered normal if the indicated pressure is as specified in **Table 8**, and the compression readings do not differ by more than 10 percent. Low compression indicates worn or broken rings, leaky or sticky valves, blown head gasket or a combination of all three.
   a. If the compression reading does not differ between cylinders by more than 10 percent, the rings and valves are in good condition.
   b. If a low reading (10 percent or more) is obtained on one of the cylinders, it indicates valve or piston ring trouble. To determine which, pour about a teaspoon of engine oil into the spark plug hole. Turn the engine over once to distribute the oil, then take another compression test and record the reading. If the compression increases significantly, the valves are good but the rings are defective in that cylinder. If compression does not increase, the valves require servicing.
9. Install the spark plugs as described in this chapter.

SPARK PLUGS

Removal

When properly read, a spark plug can reveal the operating condition of its cylinder. While removing each spark plug, label it with its cylinder location.

NOTE

Make sure the socket used to remove the spark plugs is equipped with a rubber insert that holds the spark plug. This type of socket is necessary for both removal and installation because the spark plugs are recessed in the cylinder head.

1. Grasp the spark plug lead (**Figure 65**) by the cap portion, not by the wire. Pull the lead off the plug.
2. Clean the area around the spark plug using compressed air. Check for and remove all loose debris that could fall into the spark plug holes.
3. Install the spark plug socket onto the spark plug. Make sure it is correctly seated, then loosen and remove the spark plug. Identify the spark plug according to the cylinder from which it was removed.
4. Repeat Step 3 for the remaining spark plug.
5. Inspect the spark plugs carefully. Look for plugs with broken center porcelain, excessively eroded electrodes and excessive carbon or oil fouling. Replace defective plugs.
6. Inspect the spark plug cap and wire. Replace the spark plug wire if the receptacle or wire is damaged.

Gap

Carefully adjust the gap of new plugs to ensure a reliable, consistent spark. To do this, use a spark plug gapping tool with a wire gauge.

1. Insert a round feeler gauge between the center and the side electrode of the plug (**Figure 66**). The gap specification is in **Table 8**. If the gap is correct, a slight drag should be felt as the gauge is pulled through. If there is no drag, or if the gauge does not pass through, bend the side electrode with the gapping tool (**Figure 67**) to set the gap.
2. Repeat for the remaining spark plug.
3. Install the terminal nut (A, **Figure 68**).

Installation

1. Apply a *light* coat of antiseize compound onto the threads of the spark plug before installing it. Remove any compound that contacts the plug electrodes. Do not use engine oil on the plug threads.

65

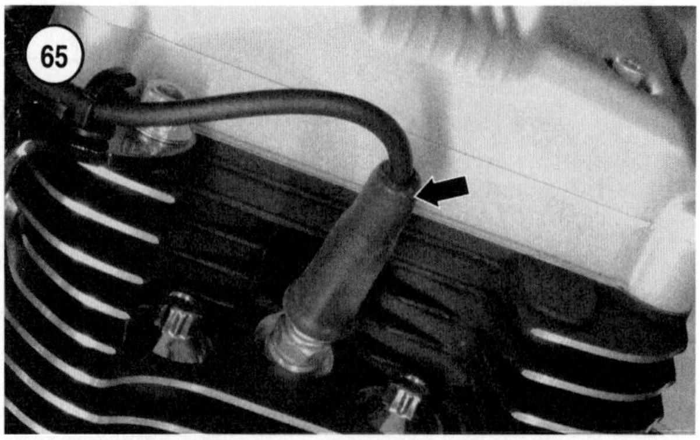

66

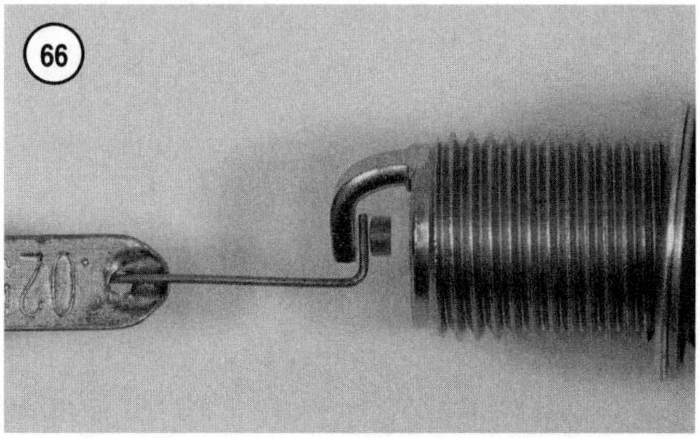

67

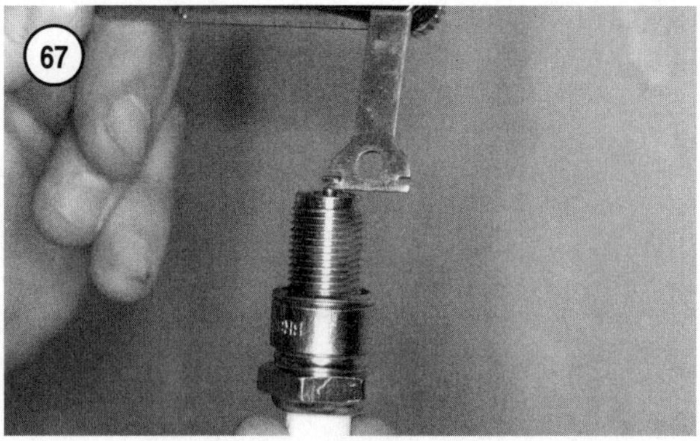

CAUTION

The cylinder head is aluminum. If the spark plug is cross-threaded into the cylinder head, the internal threads will be damaged.

2. Carefully screw the spark plug in by hand until it seats. Very little effort is required. If force is necessary, the plug may be cross-threaded. Unscrew it and try again.

CAUTION

Do not overtighten the spark plug. This will damage the gasket. Overtightening may also

(68)

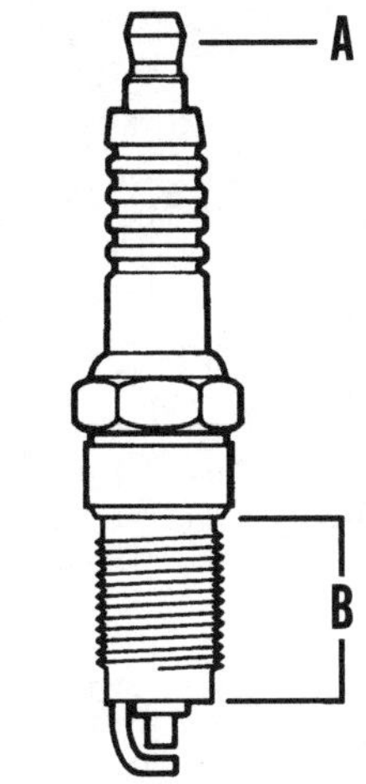

(69)

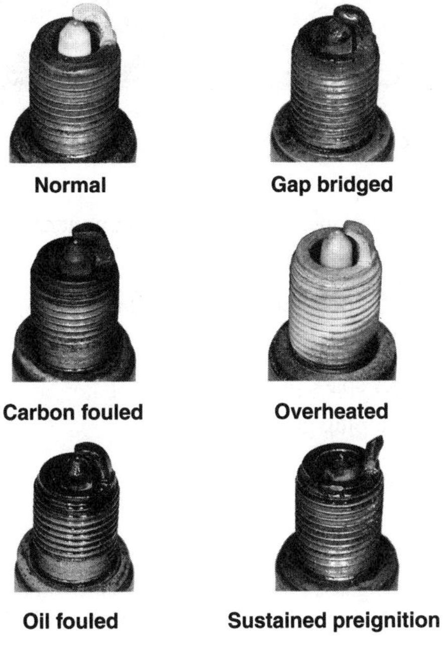

damage the spark plug threads in the cylinder head.

3. Tighten the spark plug to 12-18 ft.-lb. (17-24 N•m). If a torque wrench is not available, tighten it 1/4 turn after the gasket contacts the head.
4. Connect the spark plug leads and push them down until they are completely seated. Repeat for the remaining spark plug.

Heat Range

Spark plugs are available in various heat ranges, hotter or colder than the plugs originally installed by the manufacturer.

Select a plug with a heat range designed for the loads and conditions under which the motorcycle will be operated. A plug with an incorrect heat range can foul, overheat and cause piston damage.

In general, use a hot plug for low speeds and low temperatures. Use a cold plug for high speeds, high engine loads and high temperatures. The plug should operate hot enough to burn off unwanted deposits, but not so hot that it becomes damaged or causes preignition. To determine if plug heat range is correct, remove each spark plug and examine the insulator.

Do not change the spark plug heat range to compensate for adverse engine or air/fuel mixture conditions. Compare the insulator to those in **Figure 69** when reading plugs.

When replacing plugs, make sure the reach (B, **Figure 68**) is correct. A longer than standard plug could interfere with the piston, causing engine damage. Refer to **Table 8** for the recommended spark plug.

The manufacturer does not provide an alternative spark plug recommendation.

Inspection

Inspecting or reading the spark plugs can provide a significant amount of information regarding engine performance. Reading plugs that have been in use will give an indication of spark plug operation, air/fuel mixture composition and engine conditions (such as oil consumption or piston wear). Before checking new spark plugs, operate the motorcycle under a medium load for approximately 6 miles (10 km). Avoid prolonged idling before shutting off the engine. Remove the spark plugs as described in this section. Examine each plug and compare it to those in **Figure 69**.

Normal condition

If the plug has a light tan- or gray-colored deposit and no abnormal gap wear or erosion, good engine, fuel system and ignition conditions are indicated. The plug in use is of the proper heat range and may be serviced and returned to use.

Carbon fouled

Soft, dry, sooty deposits covering the entire firing end of the plug are evidence of incomplete combustion. Even though the firing end of the plug is dry, the plug's insulation decreases when in this condition. The carbon forms an electrical path that bypasses the spark plug electrodes, causing a misfire condition. One or more of the following can cause carbon fouling:

1. Rich fuel mixture.
2. Cold spark plug heat range.
3. Clogged air filter.
4. Improperly operating ignition component.
5. Ignition component failure.
6. Low engine compression.
7. Prolonged idling.

Oil fouled

The tip of an oil fouled plug has a black insulator tip, a damp oily film over the firing end and a carbon layer over the entire nose. The electrodes are not worn. Oil fouled spark plugs may be cleaned in an emergency, but it is better to replace them. It is important to correct the cause of the fouling before the engine is returned to service. Common causes for this condition are:

1. Incorrect air/fuel mixture.
2. Low idle speed or prolonged idling.
3. Ignition component failure.
4. Cold spark plug heat range.
5. Engine still being broken in.
6. Valve guides worn.
7. Piston rings worn or broken.

Gap bridging

Plugs with this condition exhibit gaps shorted out by combustion deposits between the electrodes. If this condition is encountered, check for excessive carbon or oil in the combustion chamber. Make sure to locate and correct the cause of this condition.

Overheating

Badly worn electrodes and premature gap wear are signs of overheating, along with a gray or white blistered porcelain insulator surface. The most common cause for this condition is using a spark plug of the wrong heat range (too hot). If the spark plug is in the correct heat range and is overheating, consider the following causes:

1. Lean air/fuel mixture.

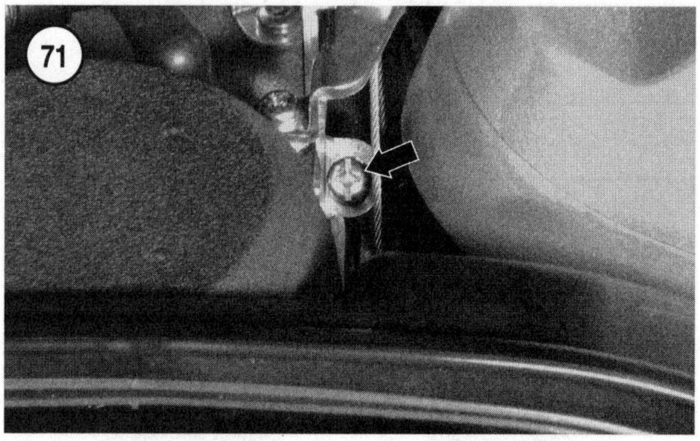

2. Improperly operating ignition component.
3. Cooling system malfunction.
4. Engine lubrication system malfunction.
5. Engine air leak.
6. Improper spark plug installation.
7. No spark plug gasket.

Worn out

Corrosive gasses formed by combustion and high voltage sparks have eroded the electrodes. A spark plug in this condition requires more voltage to fire under hard acceleration. Replace with a new spark plug.

Preignition

If the electrodes are melted, preignition is almost certainly the cause. Check for intake air leaks at the manifolds and carburetors, and advanced ignition timing. It is also possible that a plug of the wrong heat range (too hot) is being used. Find the cause of the preignition before returning the engine into service.

IDLE SPEED ADJUSTMENT

WARNING

With the engine running at idle speed, move the handlebars from side to side. If the idle speed increases during this movement, either the throttle cables need adjusting or they may be incorrectly routed through the frame. Correct this problem immediately. Do not attempt to adjust the idle speed or ride the motorcycle in this unsafe condition.

Prior to adjusting the idle speed, make sure the air filter element is clean and the engine is at normal operating temperature.

1. Make sure the throttle cable free play is adjusted correctly. Check and adjust as described in this chapter.
2. Start the engine. Run the engine until engine temperature reaches its normal operating temperature.
3. Make sure the starting enrichment (choke) knob (**Figure 70**) is pushed in all the way.
4. On models not equipped with a tachometer, connect a portable engine tachometer as described by the tachometer manufacturer.
5. On the carburetor, turn the idle speed screw (**Figure 71**) in or out to adjust the idle speed. Refer to **Table 8** for the idle speed specification.
6. Open and close the throttle a couple of times and check for variations in idle speed. Readjust if necessary.

3

Table 1 MAINTENANCE SCHEDULE[1]

Pre-ride inspection
Inspect tire condition and pressure
Inspect wheel condition
Inspect light and horn operation
Inspect engine oil level; add oil if necessary
Inspect brake fluid level and condition; add fluid if necessary
Inspect operation of the front and rear brakes
Inspect throttle operation
Inspect clutch lever operation
Inspect fuel level; top off if necessary
Inspect fuel system for leaks
Initial 1000 miles (1600 km)
Change engine oil and filter
Inspect battery condition; clean cable connections if necessary
Inspect brake fluid level and condition; add fluid if necessary
(continued)

Table 1 MAINTENANCE SCHEDULE[1] (continued)

Initial 1000 miles (1600 km) (continued)
- Inspect front and rear brake pads and discs for wear
- Inspect tire condition and pressure
- Inspect primary chain deflection; adjust if necessary
- Inspect drive belt deflection; adjust if necessary
- Change primary chaincase lubricant
- Change transmission lubricant
- Inspect clutch lever operation; adjust if necessary
- Inspect drive belt deflection and sprocket condition
- Inspect spark plugs
- Inspect air filter element
- Lubricate front brake and clutch lever pivot pin
- Lubricate clutch cable if necessary
- Inspect throttle cable operation
- Inspect enrichment cable (choke) operation
- Inspect engine idle speed; adjust if necessary
- Inspect fuel system for leaks
- Inspect electrical switches and equipment for proper operation
- Inspect oil and brake lines for leaks
- Inspect steering head bearing adjustment; adjust if necessary
- Inspect spoke nipple tightness; adjust if necessary (models so equipped)
- Lubricate sidestand
- Inspect shock absorbers
- Inspect all fasteners for tightness[2]
- Road test the motorcycle

After initial 5000 miles (8000 km), then every 5000 miles (8000 km) thereafter
- Change engine oil and filter
- Change transmission lubricant
- Inspect air filter element; clean or replace if necessary
- Inspect spark plugs
- Inspect engine idle speed; adjust if necessary
- Inspect battery condition; clean cable connections if necessary
- Inspect brake fluid level and condition; add fluid if necessary
- Inspect oil and brake lines for leaks
- Inspect front and rear brake pads and discs for wear
- Inspect brake caliper pins, boots and bushings
- Lubricate front brake and clutch lever pivot pin
- Lubricate clutch cable if necessary
- Inspect clutch lever operation; adjust If necessary
- Inspect throttle cable operation
- Inspect enrichment cable (choke) operation
- Inspect fuel system for leaks
- Inspect electrical switches and equipment for proper operation
- Inspect tire condition and pressure
- Inspect spoke nipple tightness; adjust if necessary (models so equipped)
- Inspect primary chain deflection; adjust if necessary
- Inspect drive belt deflection and sprocket condition
- Inspect shock absorbers
- Road test the motorcycle

Every 10,000 miles (16,000 km)
- Replace spark plugs
- Lubricate sidestand
- Inspect engine mounts for wear or damage; replace if necessary
- Inspect all fasteners for tightness, including the swing arm pivot bolt[2]

Every 20,000 miles (32,000 km)
- Change front fork oil
- Lubricate steering head bearings

(continued)

3

Table 1 MAINTENANCE SCHEDULE[1] (continued)

Every 25,000 miles (40,000 km)
Replace rubber components in brake calipers and master cylinders[3]
Clean and inspect fuel tank filter, replace if necessary
Every 30,000 miles (48,000 km)
Inspect swing arm bearings

1. Consider this maintenance schedule a guide to general maintenance and lubrication intervals. Harder than normal use and exposure to mud, water, high humidity indicates more frequent servicing to most of the maintenance items.
2. Except cylinder head bolts. Cylinder head bolts must be tightened following the procedure in Chapter Four. Improper tightening of the cylinder head bolts may cause cylinder gasket damage and/or cylinder head leaks.
3. Manufacturer's recommendation.

Table 2 TIRE INFLATION PRESSURE (COLD)*

	PSI	kPa
Front wheel		
Rider only	30	207
Rider and passenger	30	207
Rear wheel		
Rider only	36	248
Rider and passenger	40	276

*Tire pressure for original equipment tires. Aftermarket tires may require different inflation pressure.

Table 3 ENGINE OIL SPECIFICATION

Type	HD rating	Viscosity	Ambient operating temperature
HD Multi-grade	HD360	SAE 10W/40	Below 40° F
HD Multi-grade	HD360	SAE 20W/50	Above 40° F
HD Regular heavy	HD360	SAE 50	Above 60° F
HD Extra heavy	HD360	SAE 60	Above 80° F

Table 4 ENGINE AND PRIMARY DRIVE/TRANSMISSION OIL CAPACITY

Engine oil with filter replacement	3.6 qt. (3.4 L)
Transmission oil (includes primary chaincase)	32 oz. (946 ml)

Table 5 RECOMMENDED LUBRICANTS AND FLUIDS

Brake fluid	DOT 5
Engine oil	Refer to Table 3
Front fork oil	HD Type E or equivalent

(continued)

Table 5 RECOMMENDED LUBRICANTS AND FLUIDS (continued)

Fuel	
Type*	Unleaded
Octane	
XL883 models	Pump research octane of 87 or higher
XL1200 models	Pump research octane of 91 or higher
Transmission	
2004-2005	H-D Sport Trans Fluid or equivalent
2006-on	H-D Formulate Lubricant or equivalent

*Refer to *Fuel Type* in this chapter.

Table 6 FRONT FORK OIL CAPACITY

Model	Capacity
XL883L, XL1200L	12.3 oz. (364 ml)
All other models	11.6 oz. (342 ml)

*Each fork leg.

Table 7 FUEL TANK CAPACITY

Model	Capacity
XL883, XL883L, XL883R, XL1200R	3.3 gal. (12.5 L)
XL883C, XL1200C, XL1200L	4.5 gal. (17.0 L)

*Including reserve.

Table 8 MAINTENANCE AND TUNE-UP SPECIFICATIONS

Item	Specification
Brake pad minimum thickness	0.04 in. (1.02 mm)
Clutch cable free play	1/16-1/8 in. (1.6-3.2 mm)
Drive belt deflection	
XL883, XL883R, XL1200R	3/8-7/16 in. (9.5-11.1 mm)
XL883C, XL883L, XL1200C, XL1200L	1/4-5/16 in. (6.4-7.9 mm)
Engine compression	
XL883 models	125-140 psi (862-966 kPa)
XL1200 models	200-225 psi (1380-1552 kPa)
Idle speed	950-1050 rpm
Ignition timing	Non-adjustable
Primary chain free play	
Cold engine	3/8-1/2 in. (9.6-12.7 mm)
Hot engine	1/4-3/8 in. (6.4-9.6 mm)
Spark plug	HD-6R12*
Gap	0.038-0.043 in. (0.97-1.09 mm)

*The manufacturer does not recommend another spark plug type.

Table 9 MAINTENANCE AND TUNE-UP TORQUE SPECIFICATIONS

Item	ft.-lb.	in.-lb.	N•m
Air filter cover screws	–	36-60	4.1-6.8
Air filter element retaining screws	–	40-60	4.5-6.8
Clutch inspection cover screws	–	90-120	10.2-13.6

(continued)

Table 9 MAINTENANCE AND TUNE-UP TORQUE SPECIFICATIONS (continued)

Item	ft.-lb.	in.-lb.	N•m
Front fork cap	22-58	–	30-78
Front fork drain screw	–	13-17	1.5-2.0
Primary chain adjuster locknut	20-25	–	28-34
Primary chain inspection cover bolts	–	90-120	10.2-13.6
Rear axle nut*			
2004 models	60-65	–	81-88
2005-2006 models	72-78	–	98-106
Spark plugs	12-18	–	17-24
Transmission drain plug	14-30	–	19-40

*Refer to procedure.

NOTE: Refer to the Supplement at the end of this manual for information unique to 2007-2011 models.

CHAPTER FOUR

ENGINE TOP END

This chapter provides service and overhaul procedures for the engine top end components. The oil tank is also included in this chapter. Refer to Chapter Three for valve adjustment.

Specifications are in **Tables 1-4** at the end of this chapter.

OUTER ROCKER COVERS

The outer and inner rocker covers (**Figure 1**) can be removed from either cylinder with the engine installed in the frame. The outer rocker cover sits on top of the inner rocker cover, which contains the rocker arms and shafts.

Removal/Installation

1. Remove the fuel tank as described in Chapter Eight.
2. If removing the rocker cover on the front cylinder, remove the ignition coil as described in Chapter Nine.

NOTE
Each rocker cover bolt has a captive washer.

3. Remove the upper rocker cover bolts (A, **Figure 2**).
4. Remove the upper rocker cover (B, **Figure 2**).

NOTE
Breather valve removal is necessary to remove the outer cover gasket.

5. Remove the breather valve mounting screw (A, **Figure 3**), then remove the breather valve (B).
6. Remove and discard the outer and inner gaskets (A and B, **Figure 4**).
7. Remove and discard the fiber washers, which may remain in the cover bolt recesses on the top of the rocker cover.
8. Reverse the removal steps to install the outer rocker covers while noting the following:
   a. The front and rear cylinder breather valves are different. The front cylinder breather valve is black. The rear cylinder breather valve is brown.
   b. Install new fiber washers on the cover bolts (**Figure 5**).
   c. Tighten the breather valve retaining screw to 35-55 in.-lb. (4.0-6.2 N•m).
   d. Tighten the rocker cover retaining bolts to 120-168 in.-lb. (13.6-19.0 N•m).

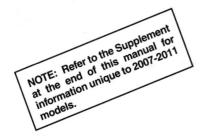

1

ROCKER COVERS

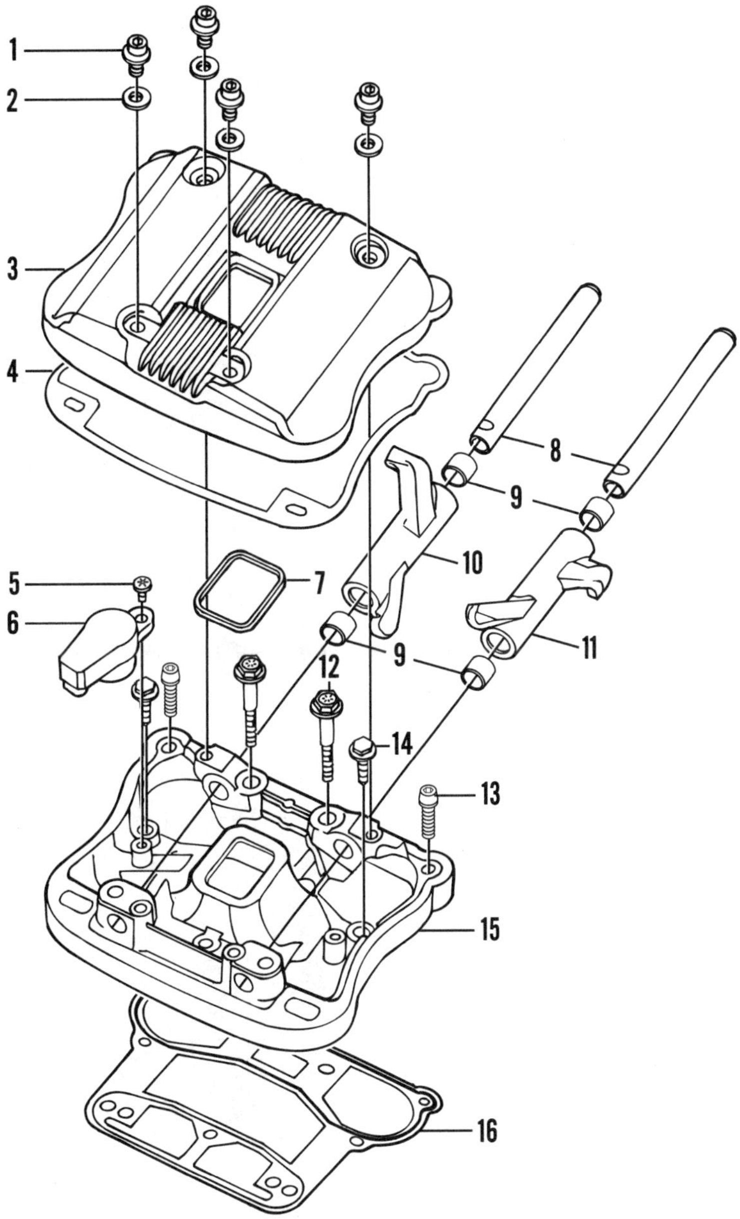

1. Bolt
2. Fiber seal
3. Outer rocker cover
4. Gasket
5. Screw
6. Breather valve
7. Gasket
8. Rocker shaft
9. Bushing
10. Rocker arm
11. Rocker arm
12. Bolt
13. Bolt
14. Bolt
15. Inner rocker cover
16. Gasket

INNER ROCKER COVERS

The outer and inner rocker covers (**Figure 1**) can be removed from either cylinder with the engine installed in the frame. The outer rocker cover sits on top of the inner rocker cover, which contains the rocker arms and shafts.

Cover Removal

1. Remove the air cleaner backplate as described in Chapter Eight.
2. Remove the outer rocker cover as described in this chapter.

NOTE

Steps 3A and 3B describe two methods for turning the engine over by hand. When performing Step 3A, the bike must be supported with the rear wheel off the ground.

3A. Shift the transmission into fifth gear. While watching the rocker arms, turn the rear wheel until both valves are closed on the cylinder being serviced.
3B. Remove the primary cover as described in Chapter Six. While watching the rocker arms, turn the engine sprocket nut (with a socket and ratchet) until both valves are closed on the cylinder being serviced.
4. Remove the socket head bolts and washers (A, **Figure 6**).
5. Remove the bolts and washer (B, **Figure 6**).
6. Remove the four rocker arm mounting bolts and washers (C, **Figure 6**) by unscrewing each bolt 1/4 turn in a crossing pattern.
7. Remove the lower rocker cover (A, **Figure 7**). Discard the gasket.

Cover Installation

1. Install a new gasket (A, **Figure 8**) with the sealer bead facing up.
2. Place the lower rocker cover into position (A, **Figure 7**), while at the same time inserting the pushrods (B, **Figure 8**) into the rocker arm sockets (B, **Figure 7**).

CAUTION

To ensure proper installation and tappet bleeding, the bolts must be tightened in a crisscross pattern as specified.

CAUTION

The rocker arm shafts have cutouts in them. The cutouts must align with the rocker cover bolt holes.

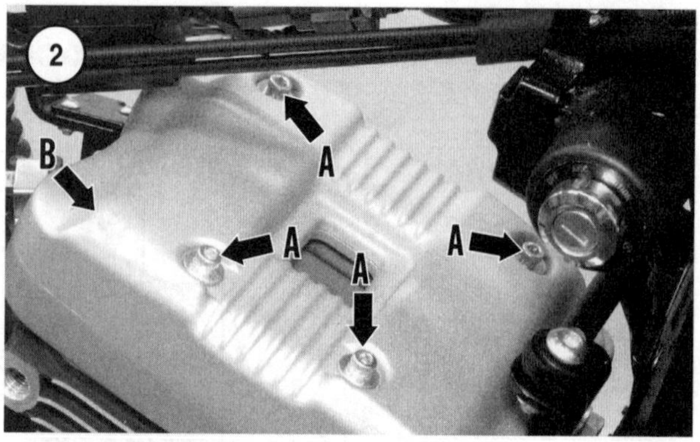

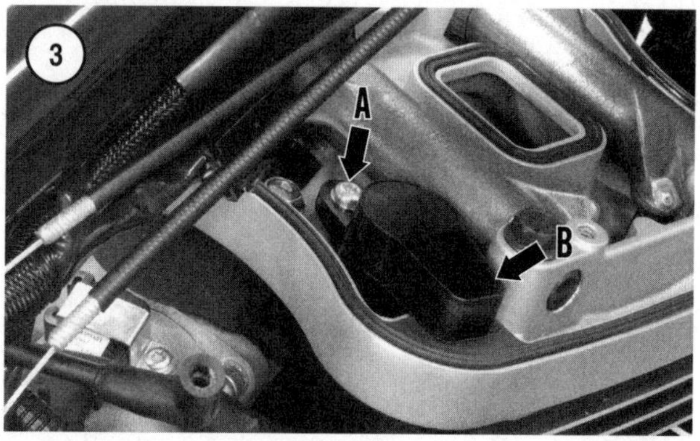

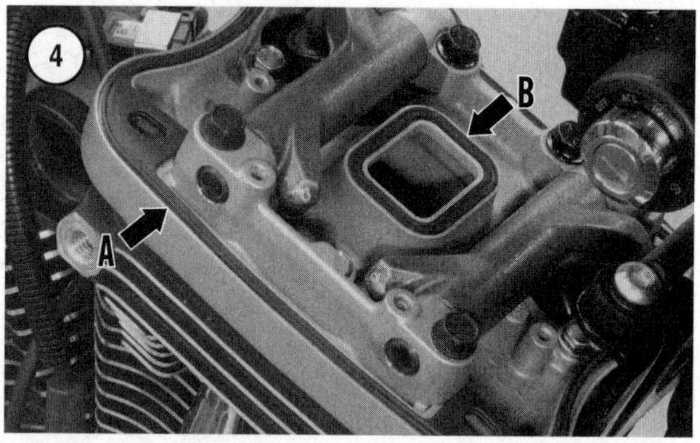

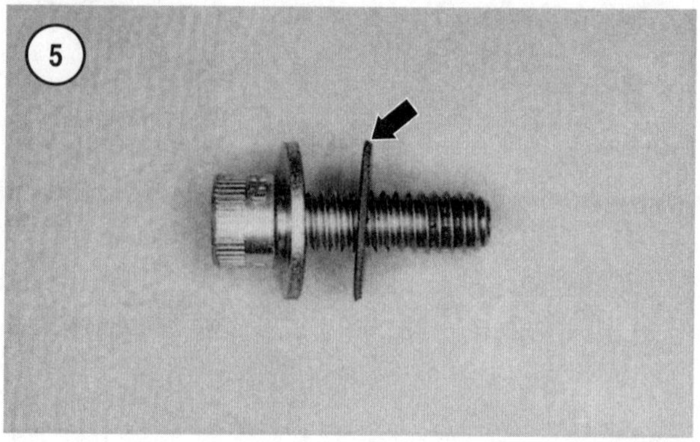

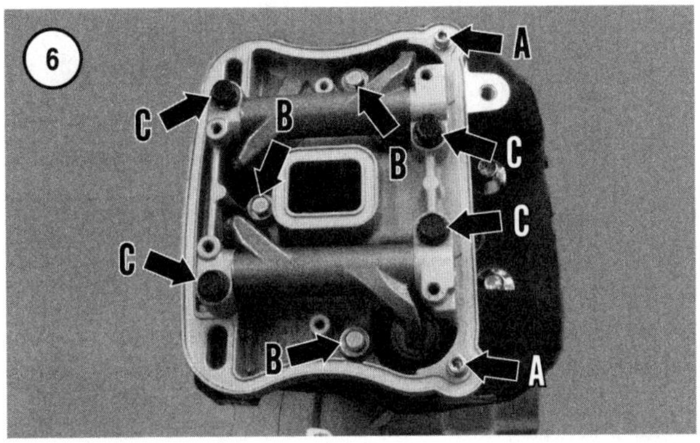

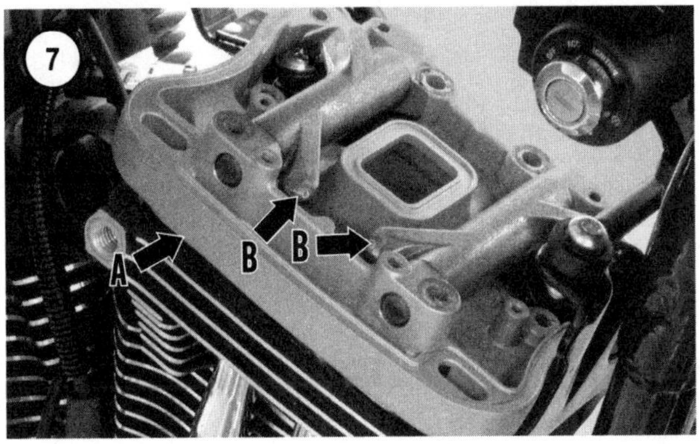

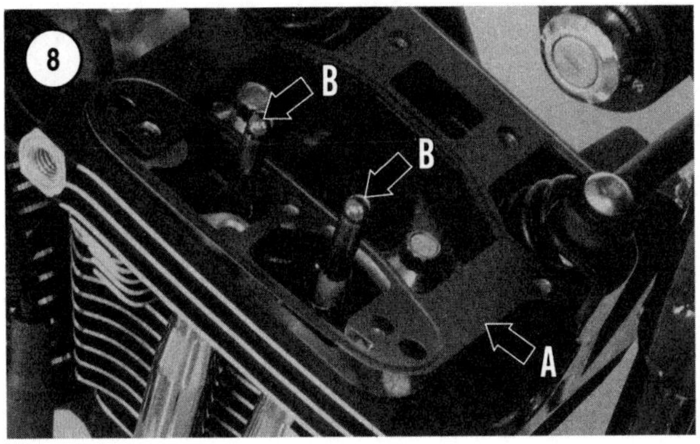

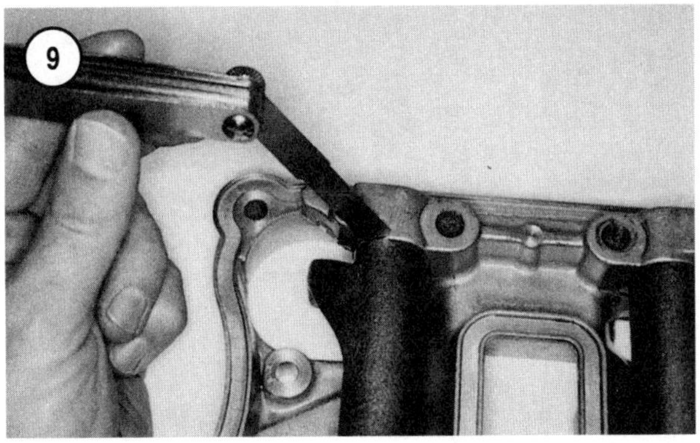

NOTE

When the lower rocker cover mounting bolts are tightened, the rocker arms will be pulled down at the same time. The rocker arms will in turn force the pushrods down, bleeding the lifters.

4

3. Install all the lower rocker cover bolts and washers in their respective bolt holes. Pull the cover into place evenly by tightening the bolts slowly in one turn increments. Then tighten the bolts to specification as follows:
   a. Tighten the rocker arm shaft bolts in a crossing pattern (C, **Figure 6**) to 18-22 ft.-lb. (25-30 N•m).
   b. Tighten the bolts (B, **Figure 6**) to 135-155 in.-lb. (15.3-17.5 N•m).
   c. Tighten the socket head bolts (A, **Figure 6**) to 135-155 in.-lb. (15.3-17.5 N•m).

CAUTION

Do not turn the engine over until all the pushrods can be turned by hand. Otherwise, damage may occur to the rocker arms or pushrods.

4. Check that each pushrod can be turned by hand.
5. Install the outer rocker cover as described in this chapter.
6. Install the air cleaner backplate as described in Chapter Eight.

Rocker Arm Removal/Inspection/Installation

Label all parts prior to disassembly in order to install them in their original positions.

1. Before removing the rocker arms, measure rocker arm end clearance as follows:
   a. Insert a feeler gauge between the rocker arm and the inside rocker arm cover boss as shown in **Figure 9**.
   b. Record the measurement.
   c. Repeat for each rocker arm.
   d. Replace the rocker arm and/or the lower rocker cover if the end clearance exceeds the service limit in **Table 2**.
2. Using a soft-faced punch, tap each rocker arm shaft out of the lower rocker arm cover.
3. Remove the rocker arms.
4. Clean the rocker covers, rocker arms and shafts (**Figure 10**) in solvent. Then clean with hot, soapy water and rinse with clear, cold water. Dry with compressed air.
5. Blow compressed air through all oil passages to make sure they are clear.
6. Examine the rocker arm pads (A, **Figure 11**). Each rocker arm pad should be shiny and convex (curving out-

ward). Replace the rocker arm if the pad shows signs of pitting, grooves or excessive wear.

7. Examine the rocker arm socket (B, **Figure 11**). The socket will show wear, but it should be smooth without any sign of a step or lip. Replace the rocker arm if the socket is excessivily worn, cracked or has a step or lip.

8. Examine the rocker arm shaft (**Figure 12**) for scoring, ridge wear or other damage. If these conditions are present, replace the rocker arm shaft. If the shaft does not show any visual wear or damage, perform Step 9.

9. Measure the rocker arm shaft outside diameter with a micrometer where it rides in the rocker arm and in the lower rocker arm cover (**Figure 13**). Record both measurements.

10. Measure the rocker arm bushing inside diameter (**Figure 14**) and the lower rocker arm cover bore diameter where the shaft rides (**Figure 15**). Record both measurements.

11. Subtract the measurements taken in Step 9 from those in Step 10 to obtain the following rocker arm shaft clearance measurements:

   a. Shaft fit in rocker cover.
   b. Shaft fit in rocker arm bushing.

12. Replace the rocker arm bushings or the lower rocker arm cover if the clearance exceeds the specifications in **Table 2**. Also, replace any parts which are worn beyond the service limit specification in **Table 2**. Rocker arm bushing replacement is described in this section.

13. Install the rocker arms into their original positions.

14. Align the notch (A, **Figure 16**) in the rocker arm shaft with the bolt hole (B) in the lower rocker arm cover and install the rocker arm shaft. Repeat for the opposite rocker arm shaft. See **Figure 17**.

Rocker Arm Bushing Replacement

Each rocker arm is equipped with two bushings (**Figure 14**). Replacement bushings must be reamed using the Harley-Davidson rocker arm bushing reamer (part No. HD-94804-57). If the correct size reamer is not available, refer service to a Harley-Davidson dealership. Remove only one bushing at a time. Use the opposite bushing as a guide when reaming the first bushing.

1. Press or drive one of the bushings from the rocker arm. Do not remove the second bushing. If the bushing is difficult to remove, perform the following:

   a. Thread a 9/16-18 in. tap into the bushing to be removed.
   b. Support the rocker arm in a press so the tap is at the bottom.
   c. Insert a mandrel through the top of the rocker arm and seat it on top of the tap.

10

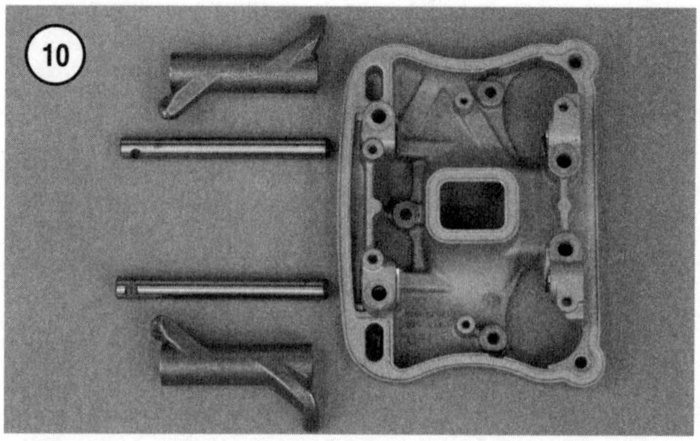

11

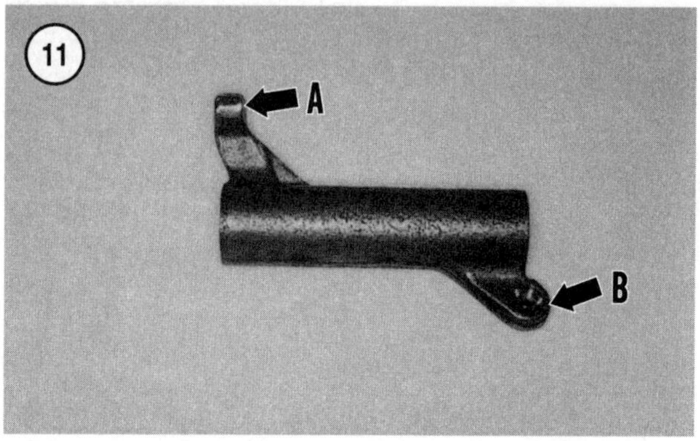

12

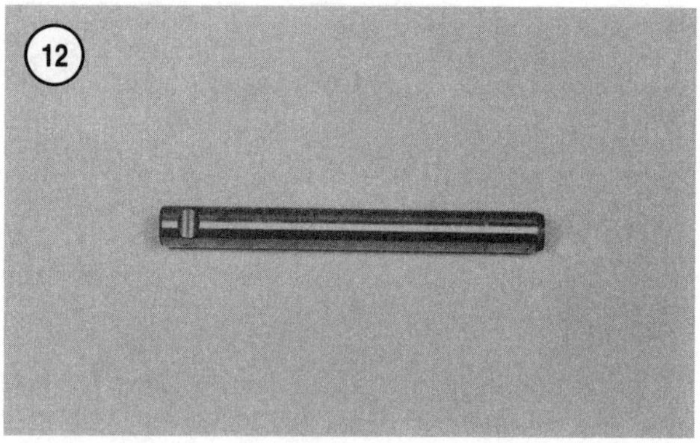

13

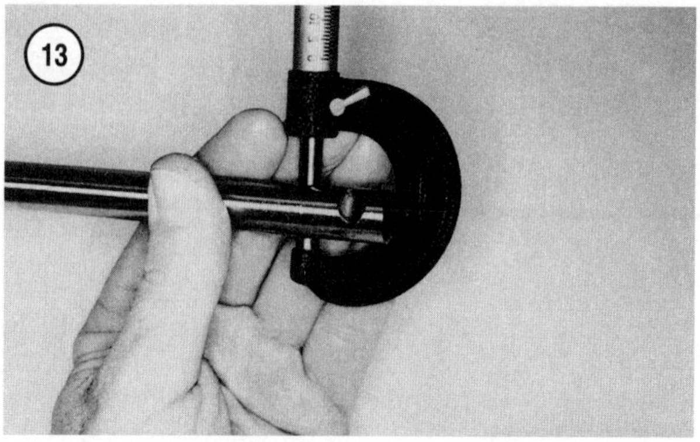

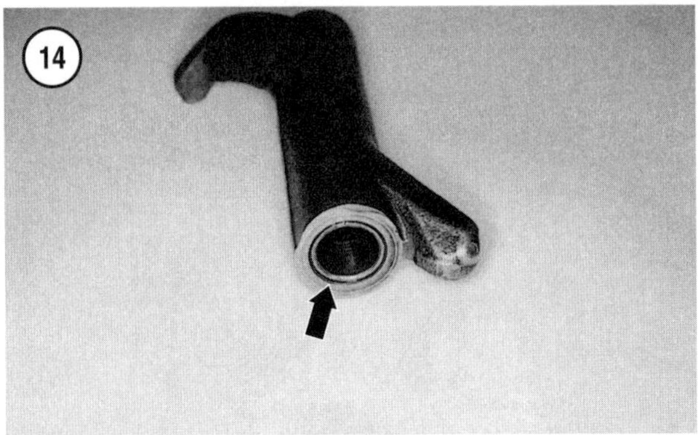

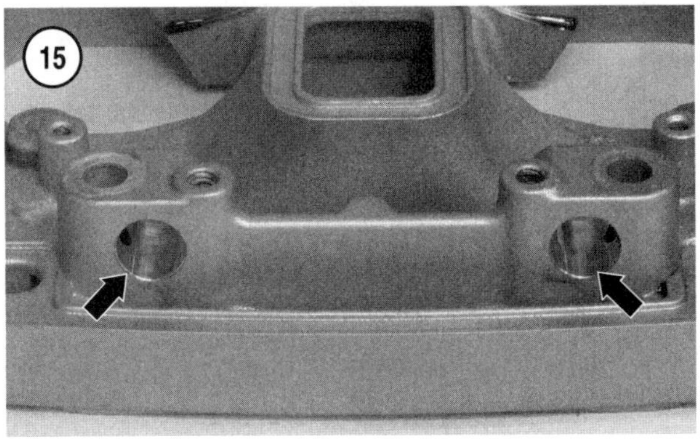

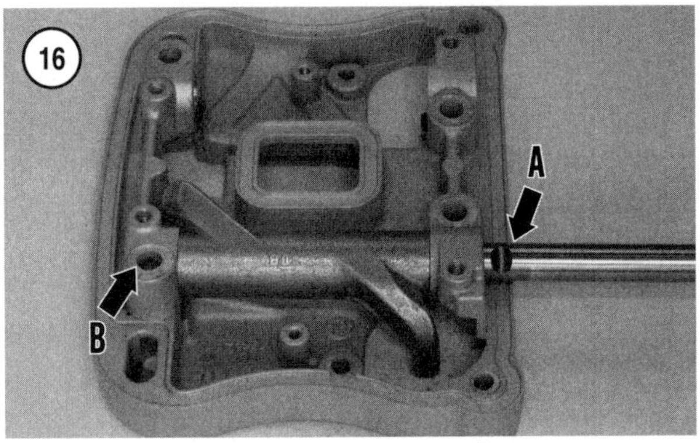

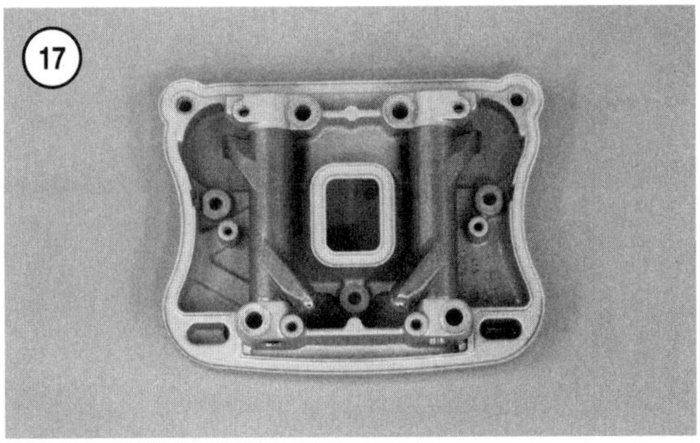

d. Press on the mandrel to force the bushing/tap out of the rocker arm. Do not let the tap fall to the floor where it can shatter.

e. Remove the tap from the bushing and discard the bushing.

2. Position a new bushing so the split portion faces the top of the rocker arm. Press in the new bushing until its outer surface is flush with the rocker arm bore inside surface (**Figure 14**).

3. Ream the new rocker arm bushing using the rocker arm bushing reamer as follows:

a. Mount the rocker arm in a vise with soft jaws so the new bushing is at the bottom.

CAUTION
Do not turn the reamer backwards (counterclockwise) or the reamer may be damaged.

b. Mount a tap handle on top of the reamer and insert the reamer into the bushing. Turn the reamer *clockwise* until it passes through the new bushing and remove it from the bottom side. The old bushing left in the rocker arm is used as a guide for the reamer.

4. Remove the rocker arm from the vise and repeat Steps 1-3 to replace the second bushing. The first bushing will now act as a guide for the reamer.

5. After replacing and reaming both bushings, clean the rocker arm and bushings in solvent. Clean with hot, soapy water and rinse with clear, cold water. Dry with compressed air.

6. Measure the inside diameter of each bushing with a snap gauge. When properly reamed, the bushings should provide the shaft clearance specified in **Table 2**.

CYLINDER HEAD

Removal

Refer to **Figure 18**.

1. Remove the fuel tank as described in Chapter Eight.
2. Remove the exhaust system as described in Chapter Eight.
3. Remove the air filter, carburetor and intake manifold as described in Chapter Eight.
4. On XL1200C models, remove the horn as described in Chapter Nine.
5. Disconnect the spark plug wires from the spark plugs.
6. Disconnect the spark plug wires (**Figure 19**) from the ignition coil .
7. Remove the cylinder head bracket mounting bolts (A, **Figure 20**), then remove the bracket (B) and wires.
8. Remove the inner rocker cover as described in this chapter.

(18)

CYLINDER HEAD

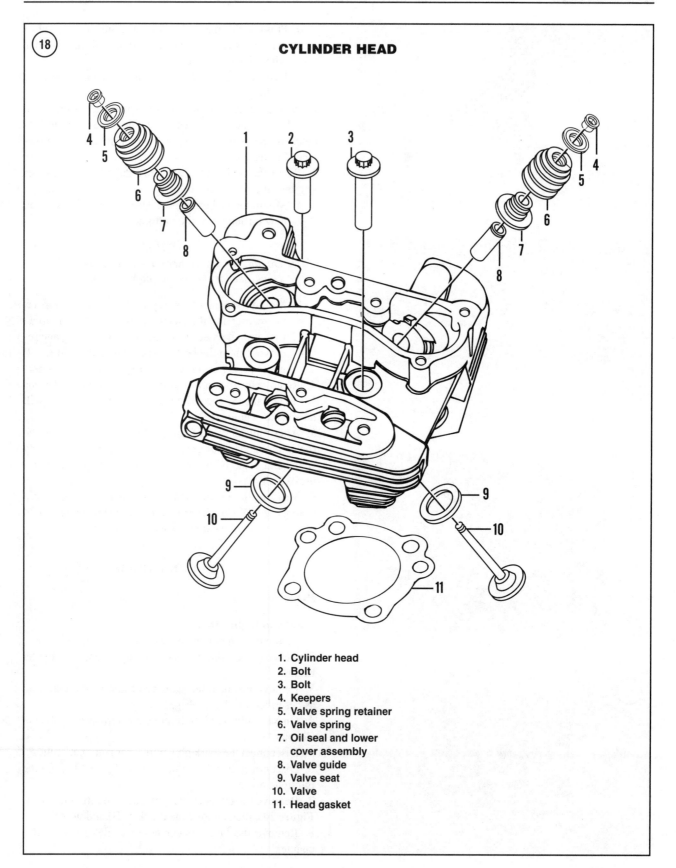

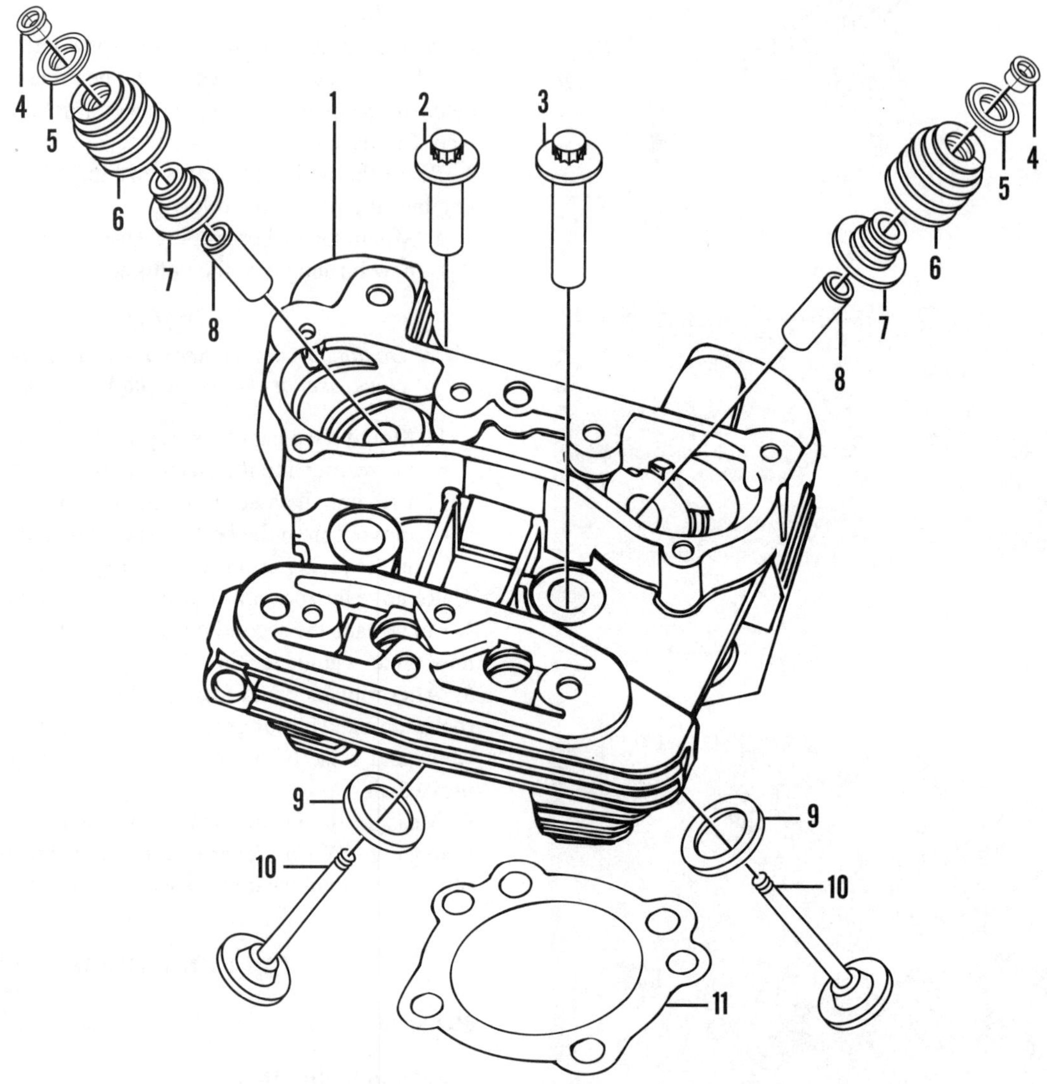

1. Cylinder head
2. Bolt
3. Bolt
4. Keepers
5. Valve spring retainer
6. Valve spring
7. Oil seal and lower cover assembly
8. Valve guide
9. Valve seat
10. Valve
11. Head gasket

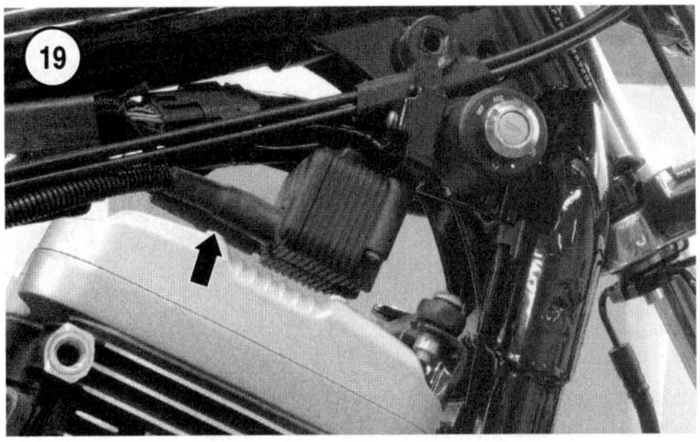

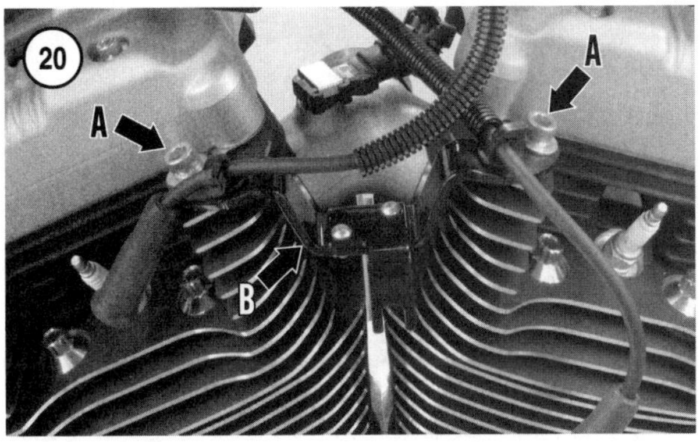

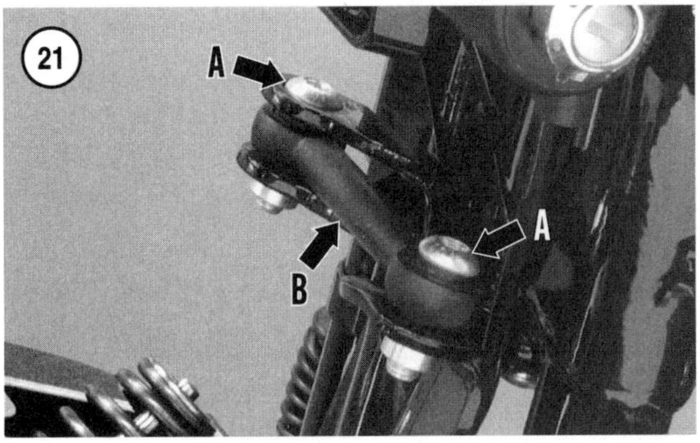

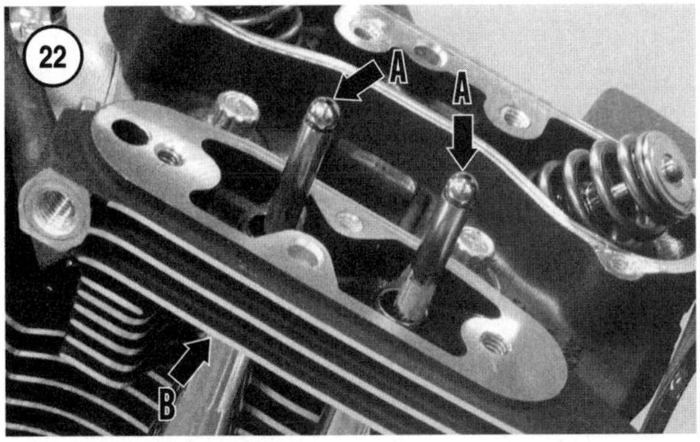

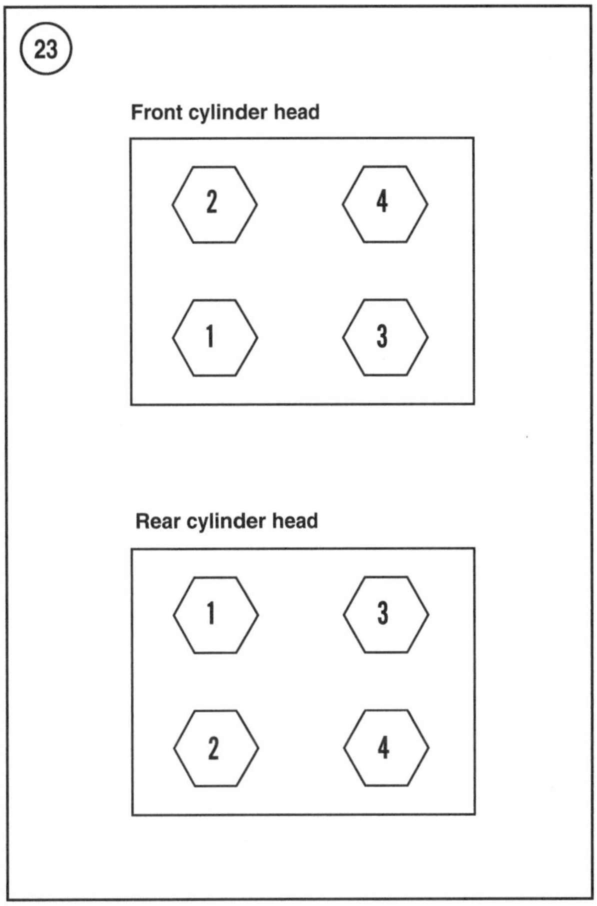

9. If removing the front cylinder head, perform the following:

   a. Remove the bolts in each end of the upper stabilizer link (A, **Figure 21**).

   b. Remove the stabilizer link (B, **Figure 21**).

NOTE
Identify and store the pushrods in a container in order to reinstall them in their original positions.

10. Label and then remove both pushrods (A, **Figure 22**).

CAUTION
Failure to loosen and remove the cylinder head mounting bolts properly can damage the cylinder head and cylinder studs.

11. Loosen the cylinder head mounting bolts 1/8 turn at a time in the reverse of the order shown in **Figure 23**. Continue loosening the bolts 1/8 turn at a time until they are all loose. Then remove the bolts and washers.

12. Lift the cylinder head (B, **Figure 22**) off the cylinder. If the head is tight, tap it with a soft-faced hammer, then remove it.

13. Remove and discard the cylinder head gasket.

14. Remove the O-rings around the cylinder dowel pins (**Figure 24**). Discard the O-rings.

15. If necessary, remove the pushrod covers (**Figure 25**) by pulling each cover out of the pushrod retainer.

16. To remove the valve tappets, refer to *Valve Tappets* in Chapter Five.

17. On the front cylinder head, remove the stabilizer bracket bolts (A, **Figure 26**) and remove the bracket (B).

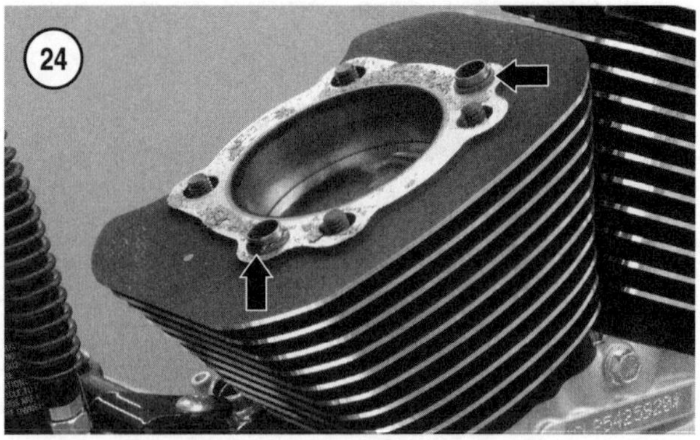

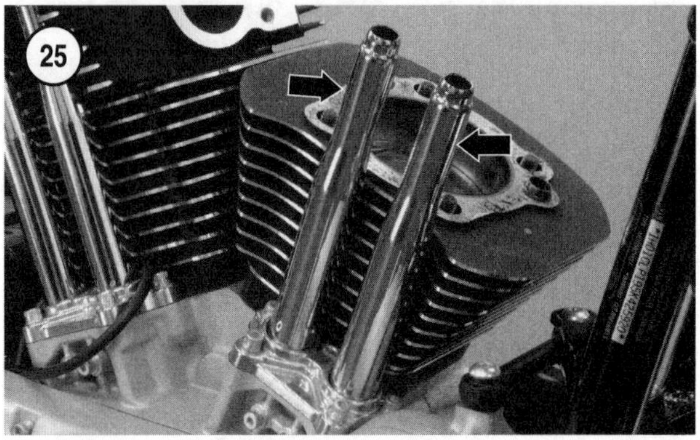

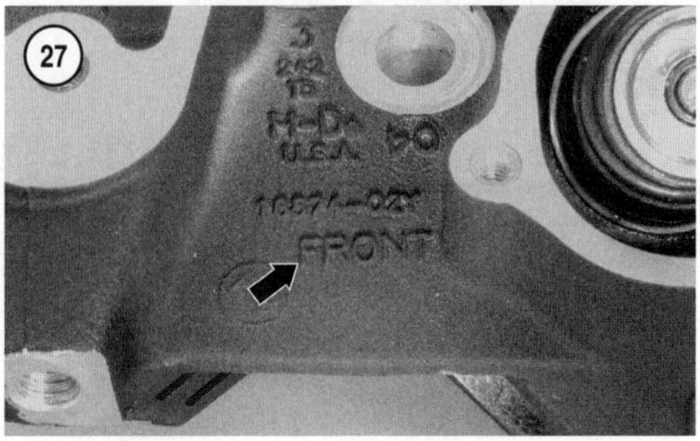

Inspection

CAUTION
If the combustion chambers are cleaned while the valves are removed, make sure to keep the scraper or wire brush away from the valve seats to prevent damaging the seat surfaces. A damaged or scratched valve seat causes poor valve seating.

NOTE
*The front and rear cylinder heads are identified by FRONT or REAR cast into the cylinder head (**Figure 27**).*

1. Remove the exhaust gasket (A, **Figure 28**) from the cylinder head.

2. Remove and inspect the valves and valve seals as described in *Valves and Valve Components* in this chapter. Fabricate a cardboard or wooden holder to store the valves as they are removed.

3. Clean the cylinder head as follows:

   a. First scrape the upper and lower gasket surfaces. Work slowly and carefully, making sure not to scratch or gouge these surfaces. Damage could cause the head to leak when it is returned to service.

CAUTION
Use only solvent or cleaners that are compatible with aluminum parts.

   b. Soak the head in a solvent tank. This helps to soften the carbon buildup in the combustion chambers and exhaust port and to remove oil and grease from the head surfaces. If a solvent tank is not available, spray the head with an aerosol cleaner, following the manufacturer's instructions. Then wash the head in hot, soapy water and rinse with clear, cold water. Dry with compressed air.

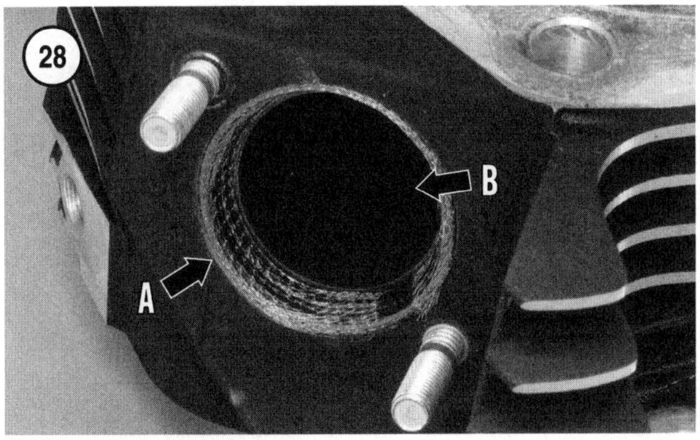

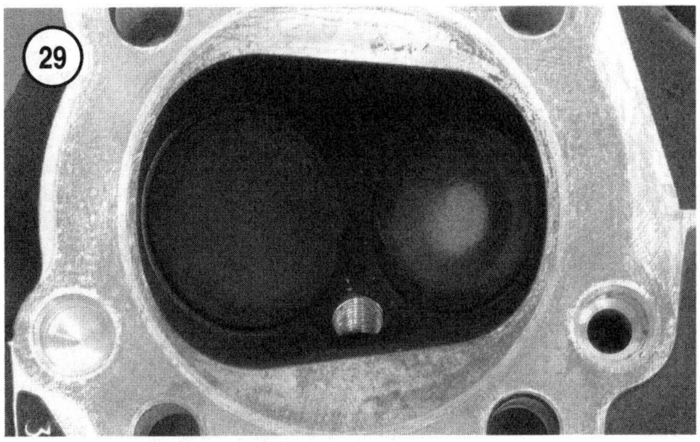

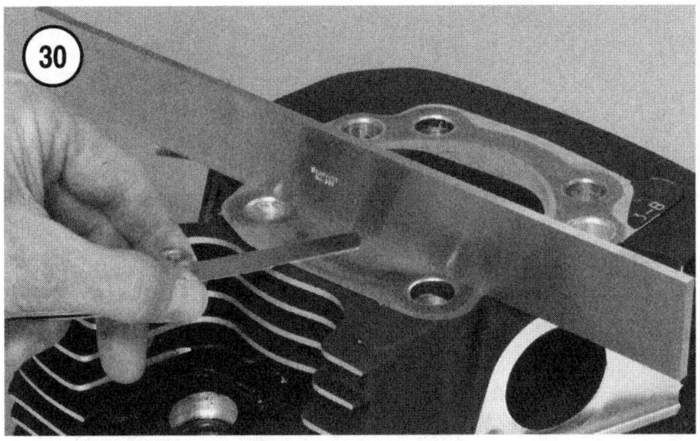

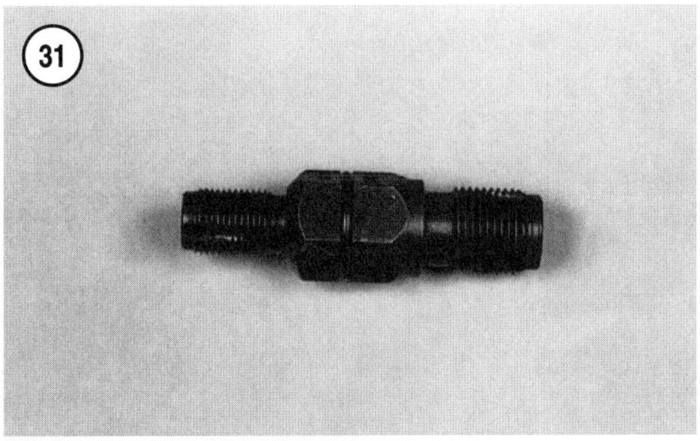

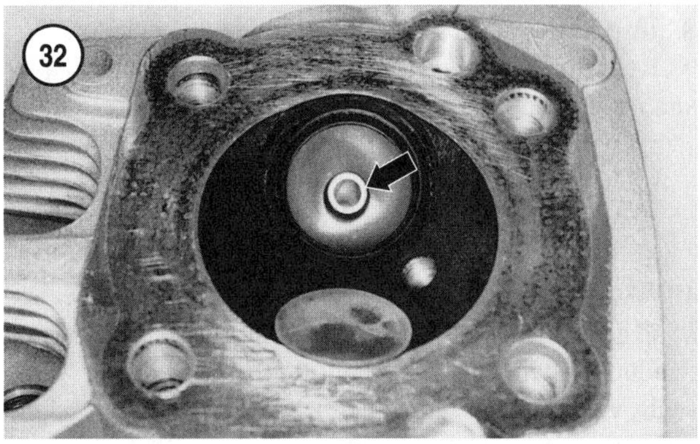

CAUTION

*Substep c describes cleaning the combustion chambers (**Figure 29**). Do not use a power-driven wire brush to clean the combustion chambers. The bristles may leave scratches that could become hot spots after returning the head to service. If bead-blasting a head, clean it thoroughly to remove all blasting residue. Initially wash and soak the head in a solvent tank, Then use hot, soapy water, rinse in cold water and dry with compressed air. Blasting residue that is not removed will enter the lubrication system and cause premature and rapid engine wear.*

c. Bead-blasting is the most efficient way of removing deposits from the combustion chamber. If scraping the combustion chambers, work carefully around the valve seats. A damaged or even slightly scratched valve seat will cause poor valve seat seating.

4. Place a straightedge across the gasket surface at several points (**Figure 30**). Measure warp by inserting a feeler gauge between the straightedge and cylinder head at each location. If the warp meets or exceeds the service limit in **Table 2**, take the head to a dealership for resurfacing or replace it.

5. Examine the spark plug threads in the cylinder head for damage. If damage is minor or if the threads are dirty or clogged with carbon, use a spark plug thread tap (**Figure 31**) to clean the threads following the manufacturer's instructions. If thread damage is excessive and cannot be repaired with the thread tap, install the correct size steel insert from a spark plug repair kit.

6. Check for cracks in the combustion chamber, exhaust port (B, **Figure 28**) and valve guide (**Figure 32**). If there is a crack, refer repair to a qualified service shop or replace the cylinder head.

7. Measure the rocker arm shaft bore diameter as described in this chapter.

8. Inspect the pushrods as described in this chapter.
9. Refer to *Valves and Valve Components* in this chapter and inspect the following:
   a. Valve guides.
   b. Valve springs.
   c. Valve seats.
   d. Valves.
10. After the cylinder head has been thoroughly cleaned of all carbon, valve grinding compound and bead-blasting residue, install new valve guides (if necessary), valve seals, valve springs and valves as described in *Valves and Valve Components* this chapter.

Installation

1. If removed, install the pushrod covers. Install a new O-ring in each recess in the retainer. Refer to *Pushrods and Covers* in this chapter.
2. Lubricate the cylinder studs and cylinder head bolts as follows:
   a. Clean the cylinder studs and cylinder bolts.
   b. Apply clean engine oil to the cylinder stud threads and to the flat shoulder surface on the cylinder head bolts (**Figure 33**).

CAUTION
Excessive oil on the cylinder studs can collect inside the top of cylinder head bolt, causing an oil lock and preventing the bolt from being tightened correctly.

   c. Remove excess oil from both parts with a lint-free cloth or compressed air. An oil film is all that is necessary on these surfaces.
3. If removed, install the cylinder dowel pins.
4. Install a new O-ring around each dowel pin (**Figure 34**).

CAUTION
Because the O-rings help to center the head gasket on the cylinder, make sure to install the O-rings before the head gasket.

5. Install a new cylinder head gasket (**Figure 35**). Make sure to install the correct gasket; an overhaul gasket set may include gaskets for both 883 cc and 1200 cc engines. The gasket part number is stamped into the head gasket. Identify the gasket as follows:
   a. On 883 cc engines, use part No. 16664-86B.
   b. On 1200 cc engines, use part No. 16770-84D.

CAUTION
Do not apply any sealer on the head gaskets. If using an aftermarket head gasket,

33
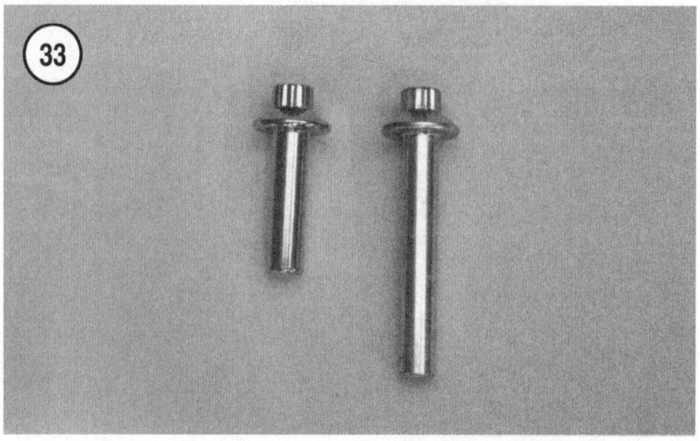

34

35
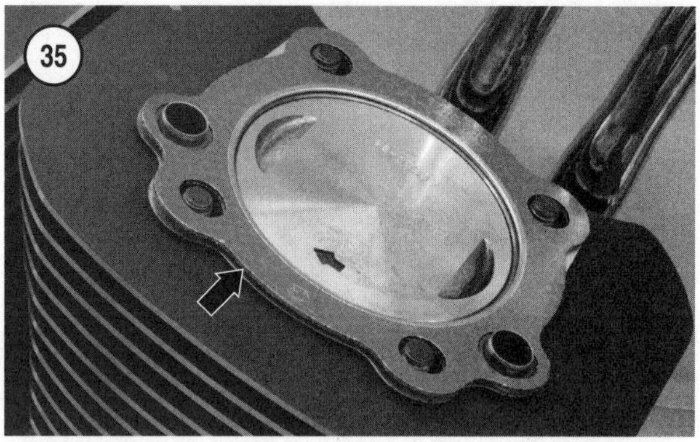

36

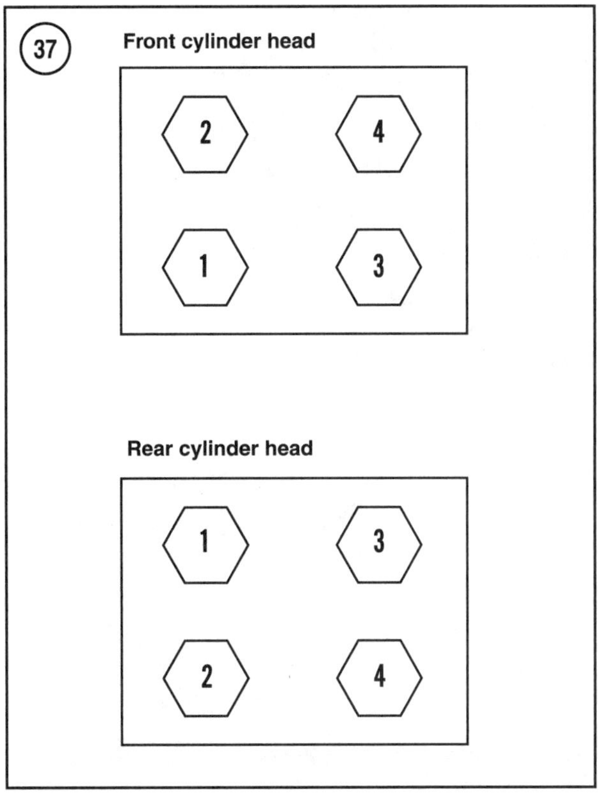

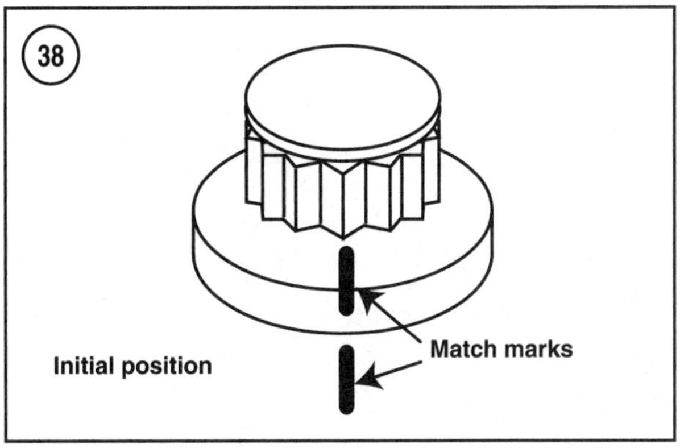

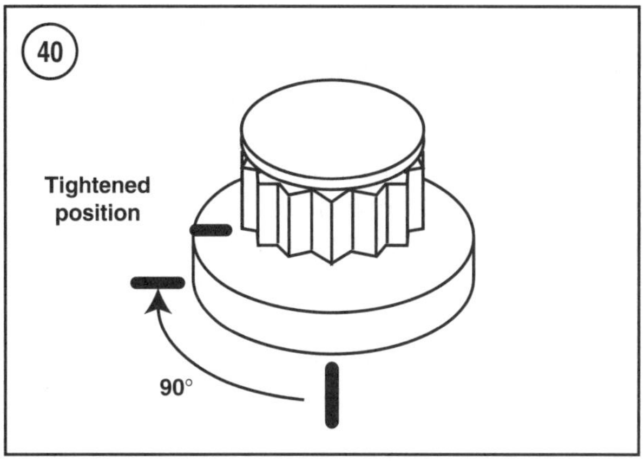

follow the manufacturer's instructions for gasket installation.

NOTE
*Identify the cylinder heads by the FRONT or REAR marks cast into the head (**Figure 27**).*

6. Install new O-rings onto the top of each pushrod cover (**Figure 36**).
7. Install the cylinder head onto the cylinder dowel pins and studs. Position the head carefully so the the head gasket is not moved out of alignment.
8. Install the cylinder head bolts and finger-tighten them. Install the long bolts in the center bolt holes; install the short bolts in the outer bolt holes (next to the spark plug hole).

CAUTION
Failure to follow the torque sequence in Step 9 may cause cylinder head distortion and gasket leaks.

9. Refer to **Figure 37** and tighten the cylinder head bolts as follows:
   a. Tighten bolt No. 1 to 96-120 in.-lb. (11-13.5 N•m). Then continue and tighten bolts, 2, 3 and 4 in order.
   b. Tighten bolt No. 1 to 13-15 ft.-lb. (18-20 N•m). Then continue and tighten bolts 2, 3 and 4 in order.
   c. Loosen all the bolts and repeat substeps a and b.
   d. Using a pen, make a vertical mark on the No. 1 bolt head and a matching mark on the cylinder head (**Figure 38**). Repeat for each bolt.

NOTE
*Use tape to place marks on black cylinder heads (**Figure 39**).*

   e. Following the torque sequence in **Figure 37**, turn each bolt head 1/4 turn (90°) clockwise (**Figure 40**), using the match marks as a guide.

f. Repeat for the remaining cylinder head.

10. Install each pushrod in its original position. Make sure each pushrod is seated in the top of its respective tappet.

11. If the pushrods are not labeled, or new pushrods are being installed, identify them as follows:

a. The exhaust pushrods (A, **Figure 41**) are marked with a purple band and are 10.800 in. (274.32 mm) long.

b. The intake pushrods (B, **Figure 41**) are marked with a single orange band and are 10.746 in. (272.94 mm) long.

12. If the front cylinder head was removed, perform the following:

a. Install the stabilizer bracket and retaining bolts onto the cylinder head.

b. Tighten the stabilizer bracket bolts to 55-65 ft.-lb. (75-88 N•m).

c. Install the stabilizer link (A, **Figure 42**).

d. Install the bolts in each end of the upper stabilizer link (B, **Figure 42**).

e. Tighten the stabilizer link bolts to 25-35 ft.-lb. (34-47 N•m).

13. Install the rocker covers as described in this chapter.

14. Install the cylinder head bracket (A, **Figure 43**) and mounting bolts. Tighten the bolts to 17-24 ft.-lb. (23-32 N•m).

15. Connect the spark plug wires (**Figure 44**) to the ignition coil.

16. Connect the spark plug wires to the spark plugs.

17. On XL1200C models, install the horn as described in Chapter Nine.

18. Install the intake manifold as described in Chapter Eight.

19. Install the carburetor as described in Chapter Eight.

20. Install the air filter assembly as described in Chapter Eight.

21. Install the exhaust system as described in Chapter Eight.

22. Install the fuel tank as described in Chapter Eight.

VALVES AND VALVE COMPONENTS

Due to the number of special tools required, it is general practice to remove the cylinder head and entrust valve service to a dealership or machine shop. The following procedures describe how to check for valve component wear and to determine what type of service is required.

Refer to **Figure 45**.

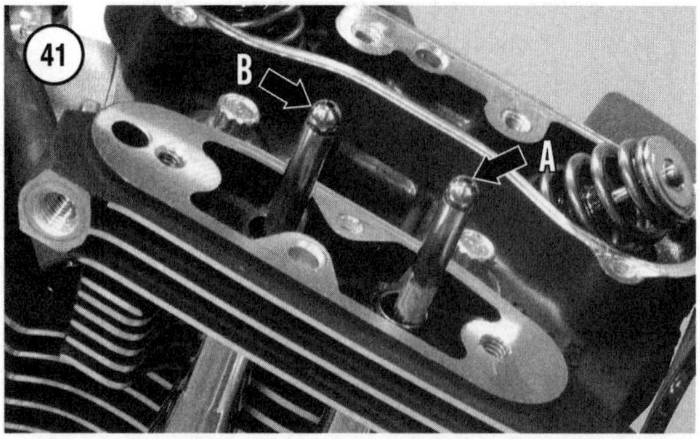

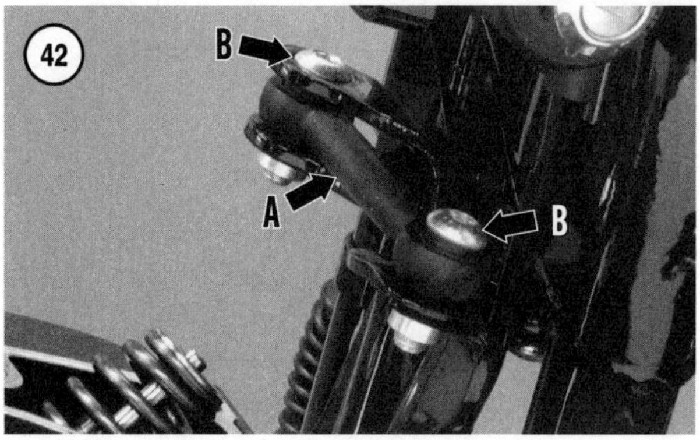

45

VALVE COMPONENTS

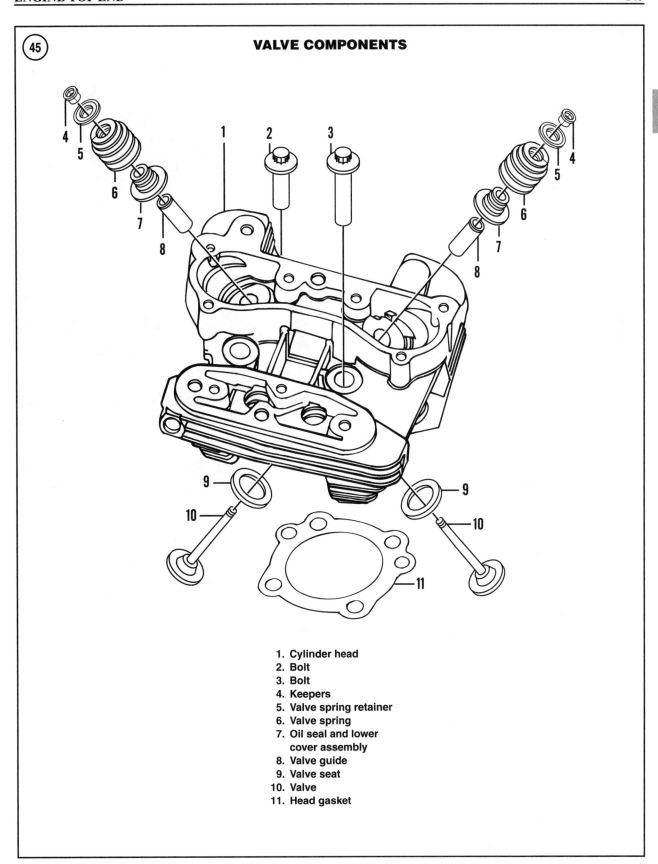

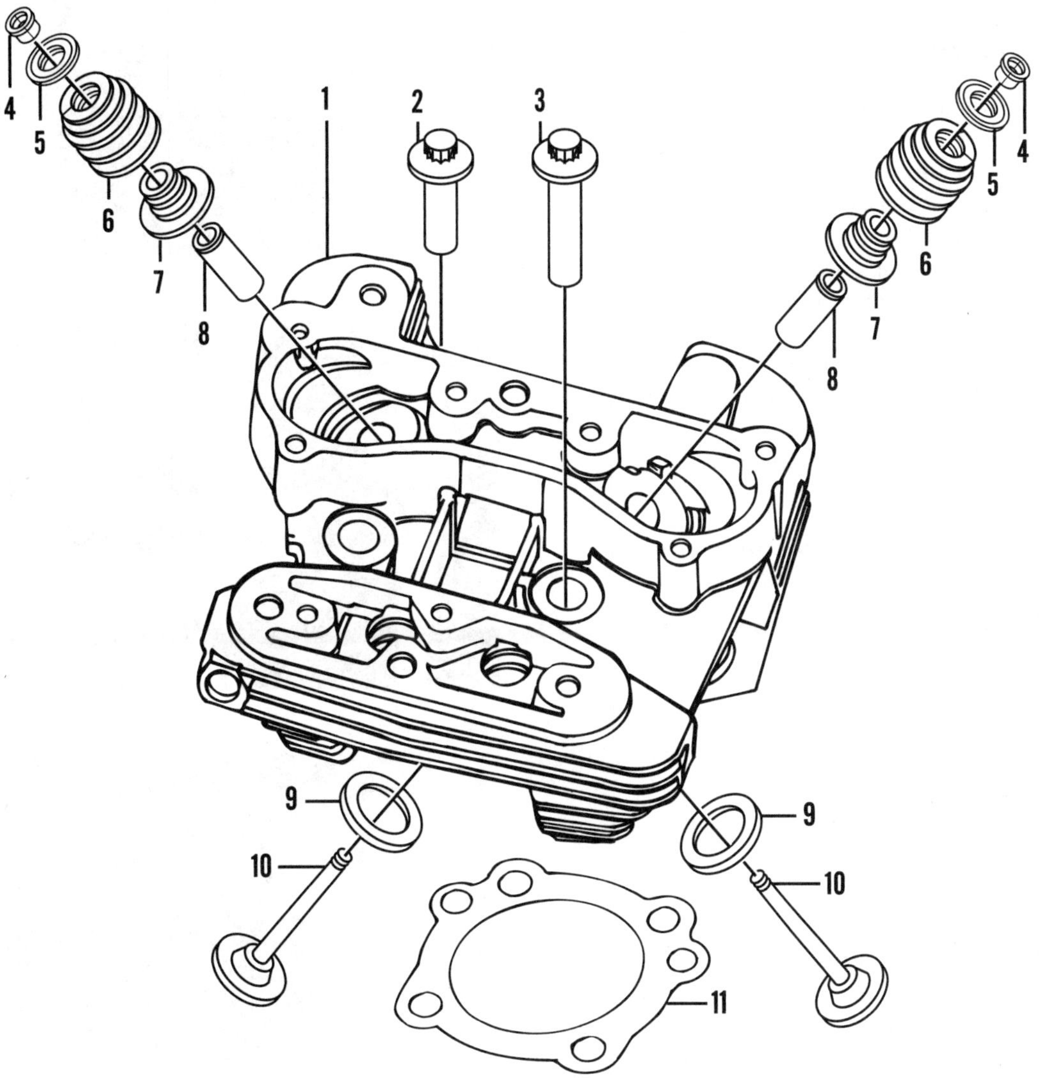

1. Cylinder head
2. Bolt
3. Bolt
4. Keepers
5. Valve spring retainer
6. Valve spring
7. Oil seal and lower cover assembly
8. Valve guide
9. Valve seat
10. Valve
11. Head gasket

Valve Removal

CAUTION
All component parts of each valve assembly must be kept together. Do not mix components or excessive wear may result.

1. Remove the cylinder head(s) as described in this chapter.
2. Install a valve spring compressor squarely over the valve retainer with the other end of the tool placed against the valve head (**Figure 46**).
3. Tighten the valve spring compressor until the valve keepers separate. Lift out the keepers using needlenose pliers (**Figure 47**).
4. Gradually loosen the valve spring compressor and remove it from the head. Lift off the valve spring retainer (A, **Figure 48**).
5. Remove the valve spring (B, **Figure 48**).

CAUTION
*Remove any burrs from the valve stem grooves (**Figure 49**) before removing the valve; otherwise, the valve guides will be damaged.*

6. Push the valve stem (A, **Figure 50**) down through the valve seal (B), then remove the valve.
7. Remove the lower valve collar and seal assembly (**Figure 51**).
8. Repeat Steps 2-7 and remove the remaining valve.

Valve Inspection

1. Clean valves with a wire brush and solvent.
2. Inspect the contact surface of each valve for burning (**Figure 52**). Minor roughness and pitting can be removed by lapping the valve as described in this section. Excessive unevenness to the contact surface means that the valve is not serviceable. The valve contact area may be surfaced on a valve grinding machine, but it is best to replace a burned or damaged valve with a new one.
3. Inspect the valve stems for wear and roughness.
4. Measure the valve stem outside diameter using a micrometer (**Figure 53**). Record the outer diameter for each valve.
5. To clean the valve guides, perform the following:
   a. Lightly hone the valve guide. Lubricate the hone with honing oil. Do not use engine oil. Drive the hone with an electric drill (500-1200 rpm).
   b. Soak the head in hot, soapy water and clean the guides using a valve guide brush.
   c. Repeat for each valve guide.

46

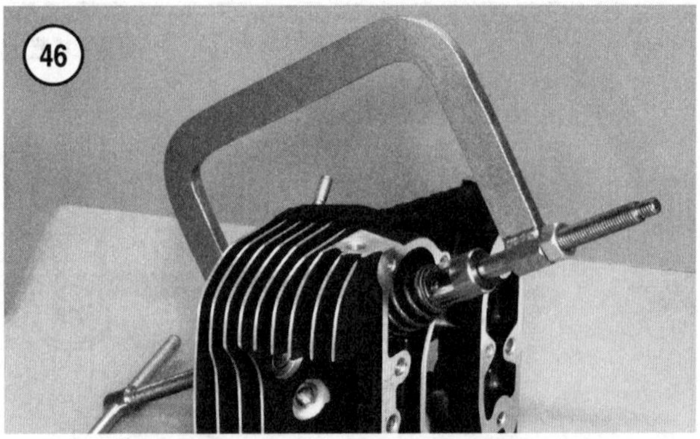

47

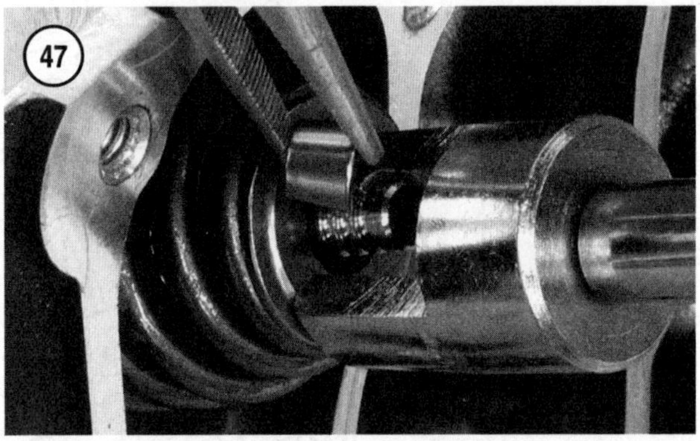

48

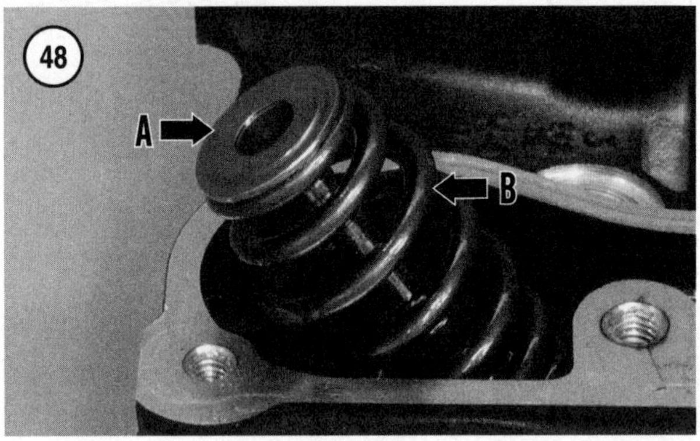

49

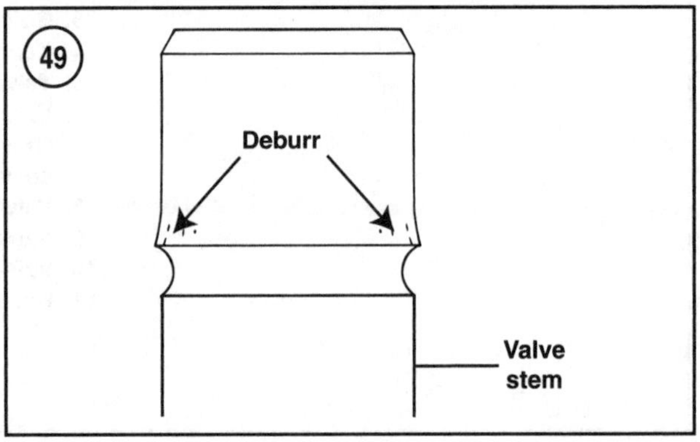

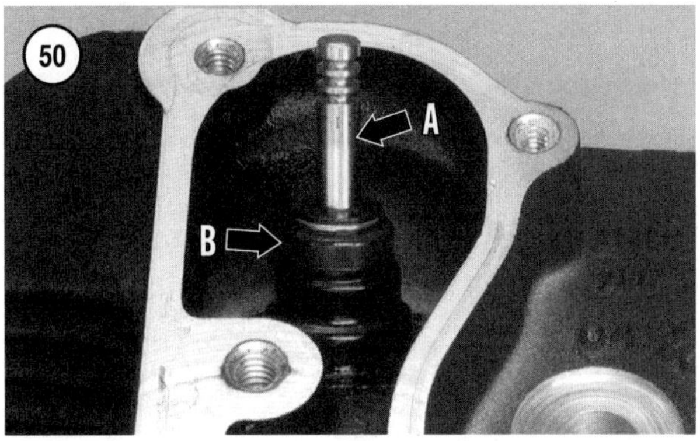

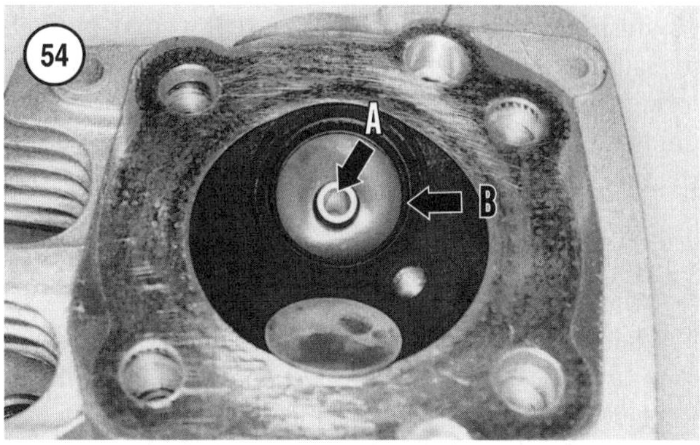

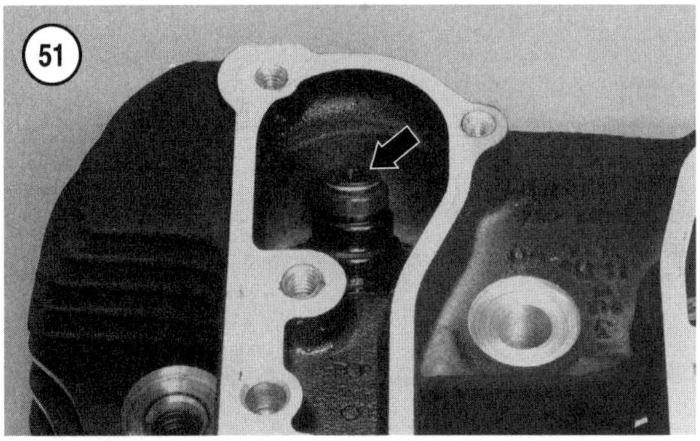

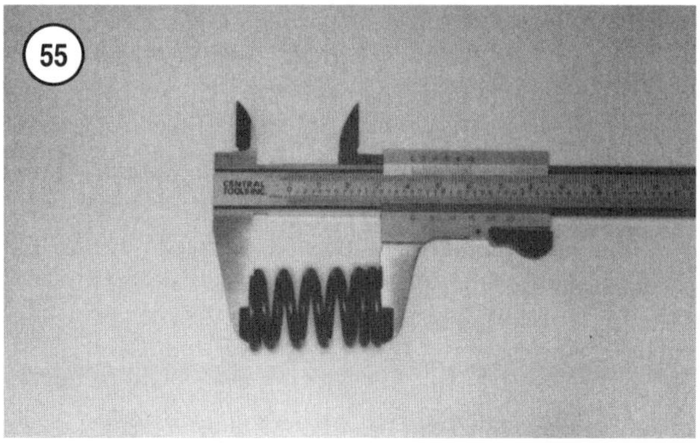

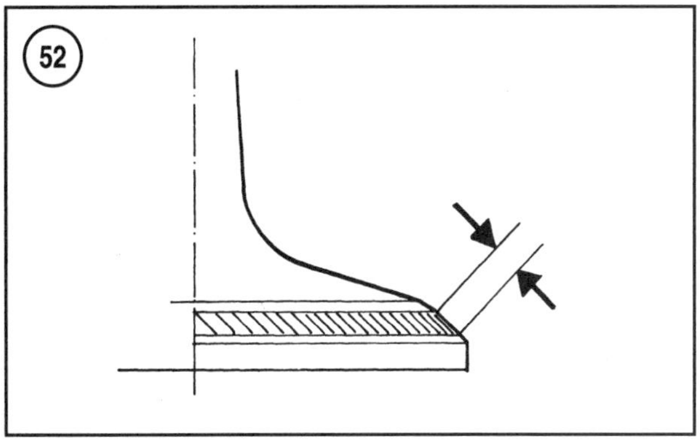

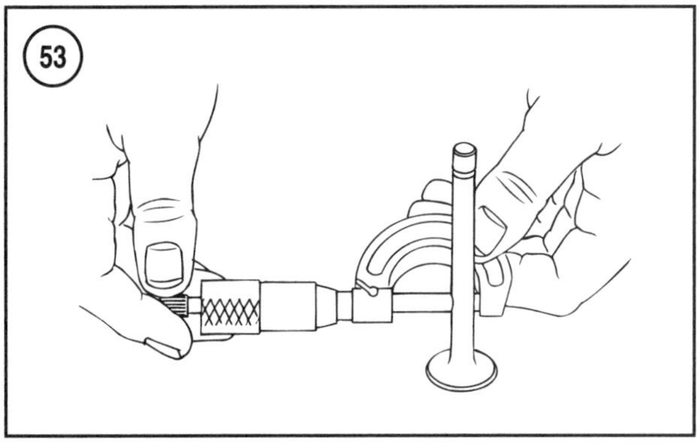

d. Rinse the head in cold water and blow dry.

6. Measure each valve guide (A, **Figure 54**) at the top, center and bottom using a small hole gauge. Record the inside diameter for each valve guide.

7. Subtract the measurement made in Step 6 from the measurement made in Step 4. The difference is the valve guide-to-valve stem clearance (**Table 2**). Replace either the guide and/or valve if the clearance is not within the specification.

NOTE
Harley-Davidson does not provide valve guide inside diameter and valve stem outside diameter measurements.

8. Measure the valve spring free length using a vernier caliper (**Figure 55**). Replace the spring if it has sagged to the service limit in **Table 2**.

9. Measure valve spring compression using a compression tool (**Figure 56**) and compare to specifications in **Table 3**. Replace weak or damaged springs.

10. If any one valve has a spring that is worn or damaged, replace the valve springs as a set.

11. Check the valve spring retainers and keepers. Replace worn or damaged parts as required.

12. Inspect valve seats (B, **Figure 54**). If worn or burned, recondition them. Have this performed by a dealership or local machine shop. Seats and valves in near-perfect condition can be reconditioned by lapping with fine carborundum paste.

Valve Guide Replacement

When guides are worn so there is excessive stem-to-guide clearance or valve tipping, replace them. Replace all the guides at the same time.

1. The following Harley-Davidson tools or their equivalents are required to replace the valve guides:
   a. Remover and installer (part No. B-45524).
   b. Valve guide reamer (part No. B-45523).
   c. Valve guide hone (part No. B-45525).
   d. Valve guide brush (part No. HD-34751).
   e. Honing oil. Only use honing oil. Do not use engine oil.
2. Place the cylinder head on a wooden surface so the combustion chamber faces down.

CAUTION
Part of H-D tool B-45524 is a sleeve that indicates when correct valve guide installation position is achieved. If this tool is not used, measuring valve guide position before removal is necessary so the new guide can be installed in the same position.

3. Shoulderless valve guides are used. Before removing the guides, note and record the shape of the guide that projects into the combustion chamber. If the H-D valve guide installation tool will not be used, measure the distance from the top of the guide to the cylinder head surface using a vernier caliper as shown in **Figure 57**. Record this distance for each valve guide so the guides can be installed to the same dimension.
4. The guides can be either driven or pressed out. Remove the valve guides as follows:

CAUTION
The correct size valve guide removal tool must be used when removing the valve guides; otherwise, the tool may mushroom the end of the guide. A mushroomed guide will widen the guide bore in the cylinder head as it passes through it.

   a. Support the cylinder head so the combustion chamber faces down. If driving out the guides, place the cylinder head on a piece of wood. If pressing the guides out, support the cylinder head in a press so the valve guide is perpendicular to the press table.

56

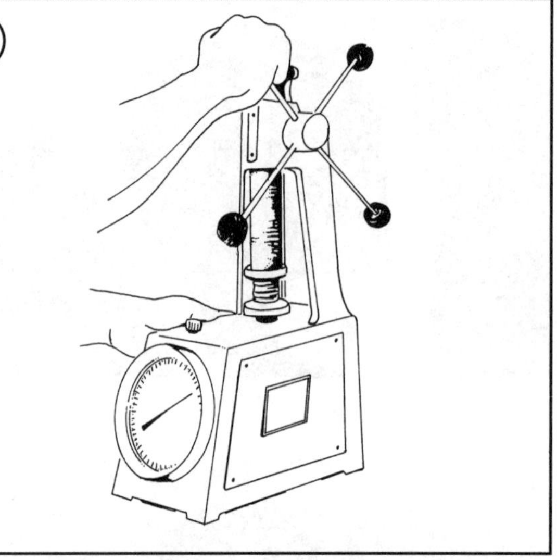

57

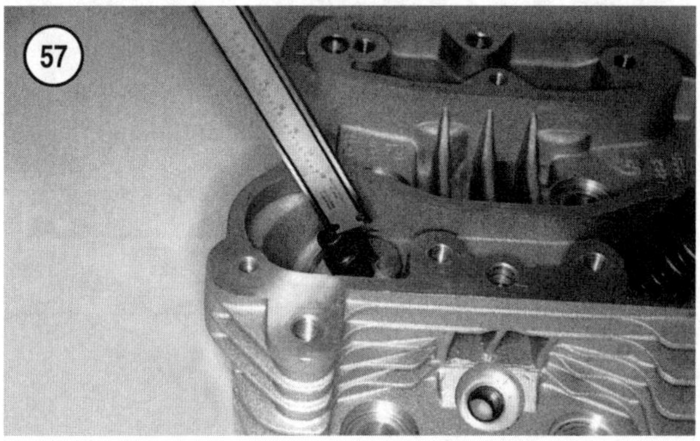

   b. Insert the driver handle and remover in the top of the valve guide.
   c. Press or drive out the valve guide through the combustion chamber.
   d. Repeat to remove the remaining valve guides.
5. Clean the valve guide bores in the cylinder head.
6. Because the valve guides are a press fit in the cylinder head, the new guide's outside diameter must be sized with the valve guide bore in the cylinder head. This is because the guide bore in the cylinder is sometimes enlarged during guide removal. Determine valve guide sizes as follows:
   a. Measure the valve guide bore diameter in the cylinder head using a small hole gauge or snap gauge. Record the bore diameter.
   b. The new valve guide outside diameter must be 0.0020-0.0033 in. (0.051-0.083 mm) larger than the guide bore in the cylinder head. When purchasing new valve guides, measure the new guide's outside diameter with a micrometer. If the new guide's out-

58

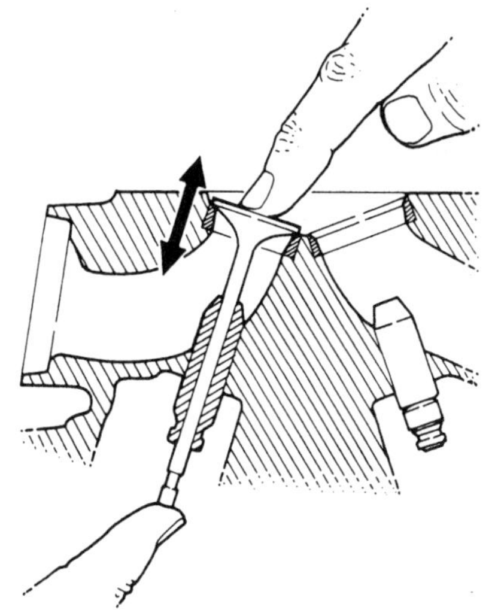

side diameter is not within these specifications, oversize valve guide(s) will be required. Contact a dealership for available sizes.

7. Apply a thin coating of molylube or white grease to the valve guide outside diameter prior to installation.

CAUTION
When installing oversize valve guides, make sure to match each guide to its respective bore in the cylinder head.

8. Install the new guide using the H-D valve guide installation tools. Press or drive the guide into the cylinder head until the valve guide installation tool bottoms on the cylinder head surface. When the tool bottoms, the valve guide has been installed to the correct height. If using aftermarket tools, install the valve to the same height recorded prior to removing the valve guide. Measure the valve guide's installed height (**Figure 57**) when installing it.

9. Because replacement valve guides are sold with their inside diameter smaller than the valve stem, each guide must be reamed to fit the valve stem. Use a valve guide reamer. Use cutting oil on the reamer when reaming the guide. Ream the guide to within 0.0001-0.0005 in. (0.013-0.025 mm) of the finished valve guide inside diameter. Refer to **Table 2** for valve stem clearances and service limits.

CAUTION
When honing the valve guides in Step 10, keep in mind the small valve stem clearance. Excessive honing may produce excessive valve stem clearance.

10. Lightly hone the valve guide using a valve guide hone. Lubricate the hone with honing oil. Drive the hone with an electric drill (500-1200 rpm). Hone the guide until the valve stem clearance specified in **Table 2** is obtained and with a crosshatch pattern of 60°.

11. Repeat for each valve guide.

12. Soak the cylinder head in a container filled with hot, soapy water. Clean the valve guides using a valve guide brush. Do not use a steel brush. Do not use cleaning solvent, kerosene or gasoline, as these chemicals will not remove all the abrasive and minute particles produced during the honing operation. Repeat this step a few times until the valve guides have been thoroughly cleaned. Rinse the cylinder head and valve guides in clear, cold water and dry with compressed air.

13. After cleaning and drying the valve guides, apply clean engine oil to the guides to prevent rust.

14. Reface the valve seats to make them concentric with the new valve guides. Refer to the *Valve Seat Reconditioning* in this section.

Valve Seat Inspection

1. Clean the valves of all carbon, then clean the valve as described in *Valve Inspection* in this section.

2. The most accurate method of checking the valve seat width and position is to use Prussian Blue or machinist's dye, available from auto parts stores. To check the valve seat with Prussian Blue or machinist's dye, perform the following:

CAUTION
Install the valves in their original locations when performing the following.

a. Thoroughly clean the valve face and valve seat with contact cleaner.
b. Spread a thin layer of Prussian Blue or machinist's dye evenly on the valve face.
c. Insert the valve into its guide.
d. Support the valve by hand and tap the valve up and down in the cylinder head (**Figure 58**). Do not rotate the valve or the reading will be false.
e. Remove the valve and examine the impression left by the Prussian Blue or machinist's dye. If the impression left in the dye (on the valve or in the cylinder head) is not even and continuous and the valve seat width (**Figure 59**) is not even and continuous within the specified tolerance in **Table 2**, recondition the cylinder head valve seat.

3. Closely examine the valve seat in the cylinder head (**Figure 59**). It should be smooth and even with a polished seating surface.
4. If the valve seat is in good condition, install the valve as described in this section.
5. If the valve seat is not correct, recondition the valve seat as described in this section.

Valve Seat Reconditioning

Valve cutters are required to properly recondition the valve seats in the cylinder head. If these tools are unavailable, have a dealership or machine shop perform this procedure.

The intake and exhaust valve seats are machined to the same angles (**Figure 60**); however, different cutter sizes are required. The valve seat cutter set (part No. HD-35758-B) can be used to cut the valve seats.

1. Clean the valve guides as described in *Valve Inspection* in this section.

CAUTION
Valve seat accuracy depends on a correctly sized and installed pilot.

2. Carefully rotate and insert the solid pilot into the valve guide. Make sure the pilot is correctly seated.

CAUTION
*Measure the valve seat contact in the cylinder head (**Figure 59**) after each cut to make sure the contact area is correct and to avoid removing too much material. Excessive cutting will sink the valve too far into the cylinder head, requiring replacement of the valve seat.*

3. Using the 46° cutter tool, descale and clean the valve seat with one or two turns.
4. If the seat is still pitted or burned, turn the 46° cutter additional turns until the surface is clean.
5. Remove the pilot from the valve guide.
6. Measure the valve seat using a vernier caliper (**Figure 59** and **Figure 60**). Record the measurement to use as a reference point when performing the following.

CAUTION
The 31° cutter removes material quickly. Work carefully and check progress often.

7. Install the 31° cutter onto the solid pilot and lightly cut the seat to remove the upper 1/4 of the existing valve seat.
8. Install the 60° cutter onto the solid pilot and lightly cut the seat to remove the lower 1/4 of the existing valve seat.

59

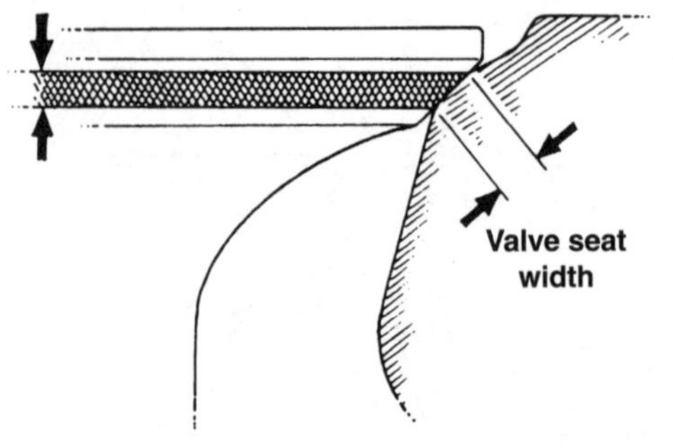

60

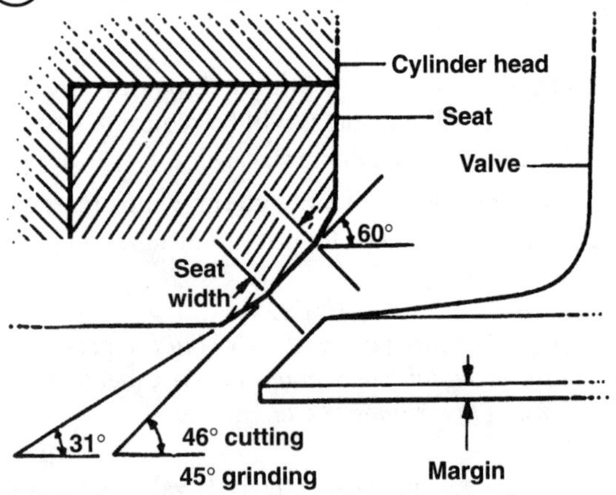

9. Measure the valve seat using a vernier caliper. Then fit the 46° cutter onto the solid pilot and cut the valve seat to the specified seat width (**Table 2**).
10. When the valve seat width is correct, check valve seating as follows.
11. Remove the solid pilot from the cylinder head.
12. Inspect the valve seat-to-valve face impression as follows:
   a. Clean the valve seat with contact cleaner.
   b. Spread a thin layer of Prussian Blue or machinist's dye evenly on the valve face.
   c. Insert the valve into its guide.
   d. Support the valve by hand and tap the valve up and down in the cylinder head (**Figure 58**). Do not rotate the valve or the reading will be false.
   e. Remove the valve and examine the impression left by the Prussian Blue or machinist's dye.

61

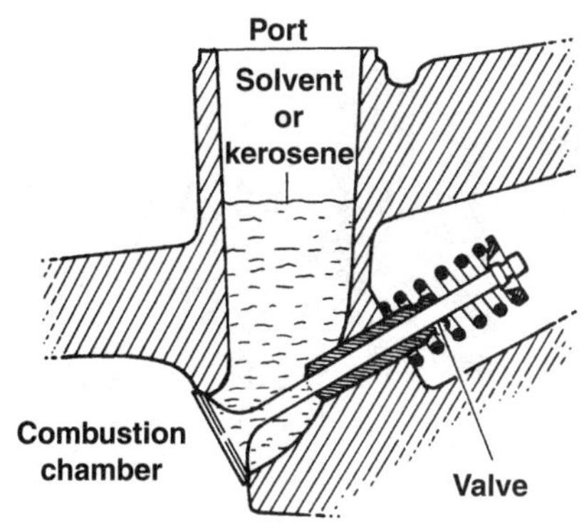

62

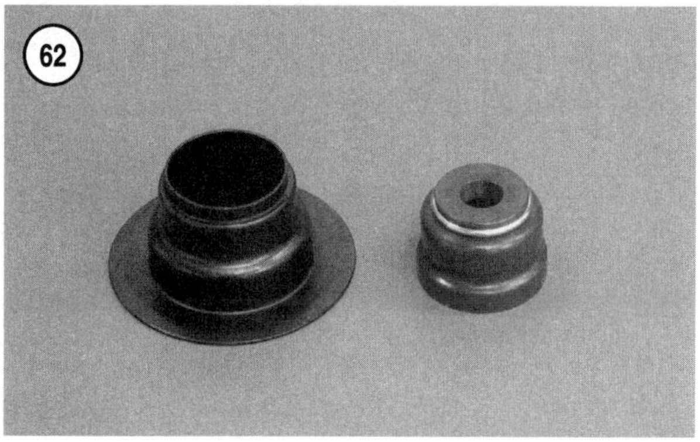

f. Measure the valve seat width (**Figure 59** and **Figure 60**).

g. The valve contact area should be approximately in the center of the valve seat area.

13. If the contact area is too high on the valve, or if it is too wide, use the 31° cutter and remove a portion of the top area of the valve seat material to lower or narrow the contact area.

14. If the contact area is too low on the valve, or if it is too wide, use the 60° cutter and remove a portion of the lower area to raise and widen the contact area.

15. After the desired valve seat position and angle is obtained, use the 46° cutter tool and very lightly clean off any burrs that may have been caused by the previous cuts.

16. Clean the valve seat and valve face. Insert the valve into the valve guide. With the valve seated in the head, use a vernier caliper to measure the valve stem protrusion (the distance from the end of the valve stem to the valve pocket in the cylinder head.) If valve stem protrusion exceeds the service limit in **Table 2**, replace the valve seat or the cylinder head.

17. Repeat Steps 1-16 for all remaining valve seats.

18. Thoroughly clean the cylinder head and all valve components in solvent, then clean with detergent and hot water and finish with a final rinsing in cold water. Dry with compressed air. Then apply a light coat of engine oil to all non-aluminum metal surfaces to prevent rust formation.

4

Valve Lapping

Valve lapping can restore the valve seal without machining if the amount of wear or distortion is not excessive.

1. Smear a light coating of fine grade valve lapping compound on the seating surface of the valve.
2. Insert the valve into the head.
3. Wet the suction cup of the lapping stick and stick it onto the head of the valve. Lap the valve to the seat by spinning the tool between your hands while lifting and moving the valve around the seat 1/4 turn at a time.
4. Wipe off the valve and seat frequently to check progress of lapping. Lap only enough to achieve a precise seating ring around the valve head.
5. Closely examine the valve seat in the cylinder head. It should be smooth and even with a smooth, polished seating ring.
6. Thoroughly clean the valves and cylinder head in solvent to remove all compound. Any compound left on the valves or the cylinder head will cause premature engine wear.
7. After completing the lapping and reinstalling the valve assemblies into the head, test the valve seal. Check the seal of each valve by pouring solvent into each of the intake and exhaust ports (**Figure 61**). There should be no leaks past the seat. If fluid leaks past any of the seats, disassemble that valve assembly and repeat the lapping procedure.

Valve Seat Replacement

Valve seat replacement requires specialized equipment. Refer this work to a dealership or machine shop.

Valve Installation

1. Coat the valve stem with engine oil and insert the valve into its valve guide in the cylinder head.
2. Place a protective cover (plastic wrap) over the end of the valve stem. The cover prevents the valve stem keeper groove from tearing the valve stem seal.
3. Assemble the two-piece seal and lower cover (**Figure 62**). Insert the seal into the lower cover so the lip on the

lower cover fits in the groove on the outside of the seal (**Figure 63**).

4. Wipe the protective cover on the valve stem with clean engine oil.
5. Slide the new valve guide seal/lower cover down around the valve stem until it seats on the cylinder head (**Figure 64**).

CAUTION
If the seal or valve is removed after installation, install a new seal as the valve stem may damage the valve seal during removal.

6. Install the valve spring (A, **Figure 65**). Then install the valve spring retainer (B).
7. Push down on the valve spring retainer with the valve spring compressor (**Figure 66**) and install the valve keepers (**Figure 67**). After releasing tension from the compressor, lightly tap the retainer with a soft-faced hammer to make sure the keepers are seated (**Figure 68**).
8. Repeat to install the remaining valve guide seals and valves.

PUSHRODS AND COVERS

Inspection and Replacement

1. Remove the inner rocker cover as described in this chapter to access the pushrods (**Figure 69**).
2. Remove the cylinder head as described in this chapter to access the pushrod covers (**Figure 70**).
3. Clean the pushrods in solvent. Blow dry with compressed air.
4. Check pushrods (**Figure 71**) for:
   a. Bending.
   b. Cracks.
   c. Cracked or excessively worn ball ends.
5. The exhaust and intake pushrods are different lengths. To identify or replace pushrods, note the following:

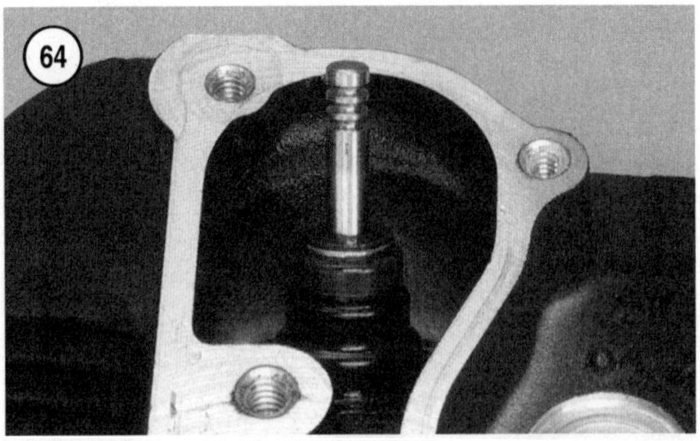

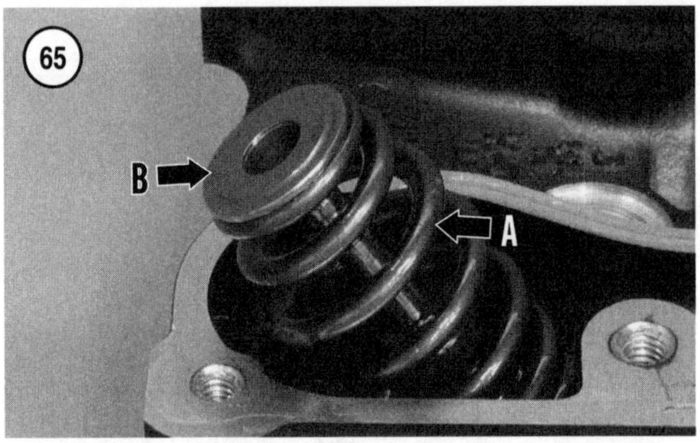

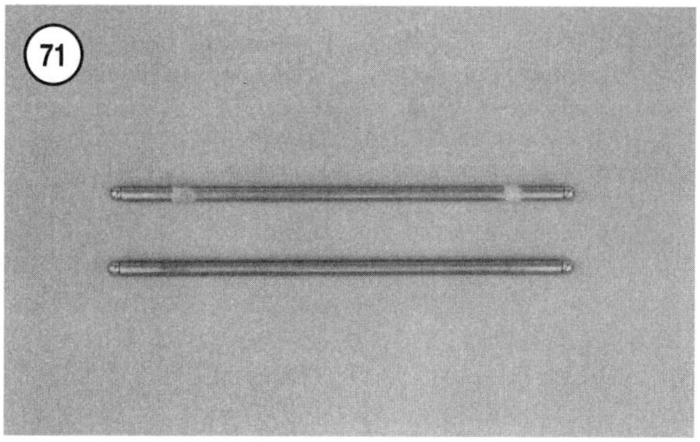

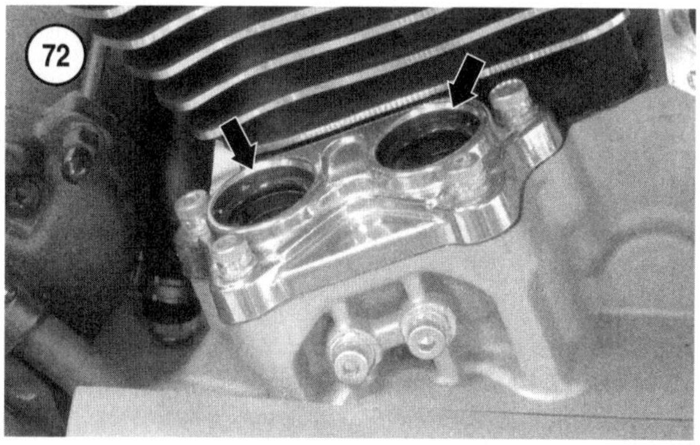

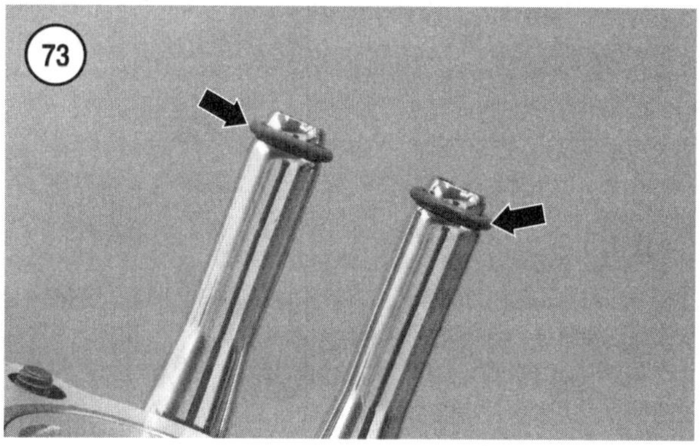

a. Front and rear exhaust pushrods are 10.800 in. (274.32 mm) long.

b. Front and rear intake pushrods are 10.746 in. (272.94 mm) long.

c. Exhaust and intake pushrods are color coded for visual identification. Exhaust pushrods have a single purple band. Intake pushrods have a single orange band.

6. The pushrod covers are sealed by an O-ring in the tappet cover (**Figure 72**) and by an O-ring at the upper end (**Figure 73**). Install new O-rings during assembly.

CYLINDER

Both cylinders can be removed with the engine in the frame.

Cylinder Removal

Refer to **Figure 74**.

1. Remove all debris from both cylinders.
2. Remove the cylinder head as described in this chapter.
3. Remove the O-rings around the dowel pins (**Figure 75**). If necessary, also remove the dowel pins.

4. Turn the engine over until the piston is at bottom dead center (BDC).
5. Loosen the cylinder by tapping around the perimeter with a soft-faced hammer.
6. Pull the cylinder straight up and off the piston and cylinder studs.

CAUTION
With the cylinder is removed, use care when working around the cylinder studs to avoid bending or damaging them. The slightest bend could cause a stud failure during engine operation.

7. Stuff clean shop rags into the crankcase opening (A, **Figure 76**) to prevent objects from falling into the crankcase.
8. Install a hose (B, **Figure 76**) around each stud to protect the piston and studs from damage.
9. Install a piston holding tool (C, **Figure 76**) to stabilize the piston. The tool may be constructed from wood as shown in **Figure 77**.
10. Remove the pistons and rings as described in this chapter.
11. Repeat Steps 1-10 for the remaining cylinder.

Cylinder Inspection

To obtain an accurate cylinder bore measurement, the cylinder must be secured between torque plates. This simulates the distortion imparted on the cylinder when it is secured between the cylinder head and crankcase. Measurements made without the torque plate can vary by 0.001 in. (0.025 mm). If torque plates are not available, refer service to a dealership.
1. Carefully remove all gasket residue from both cylinder gasket surfaces.
2. Thoroughly clean the cylinder with solvent and dry with compressed air. Lightly oil the cylinder bore to prevent rust after performing Step 3.
3. Check the top (**Figure 78**) and bottom cylinder gasket surfaces with a straightedge and feeler gauge. Replace the cylinder if the warp exceeds the service limit in **Table 2**.
4. Check the cylinder walls (**Figure 79**) for scuffing, scratches or other damage.
5. Install the torque plates onto the cylinder (**Figure 80**) following the manufacturer's instruction.
6. Measure the cylinder bore with a bore gauge or inside micrometer at the points shown in **Figure 81**. Initial measurement should be made at a distance of 0.500 in. (12.7 mm) below the top of the cylinder. The 0.500 in. (12.7 mm) depth represents the start of the ring path area; do not take readings that are out of the ring path area.

(74) PISTON AND CYLINDER

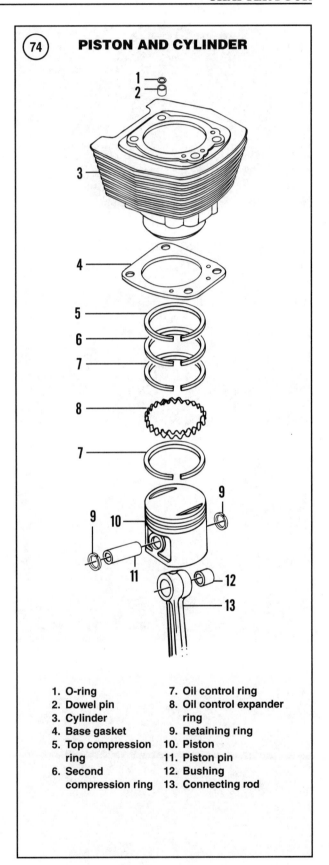

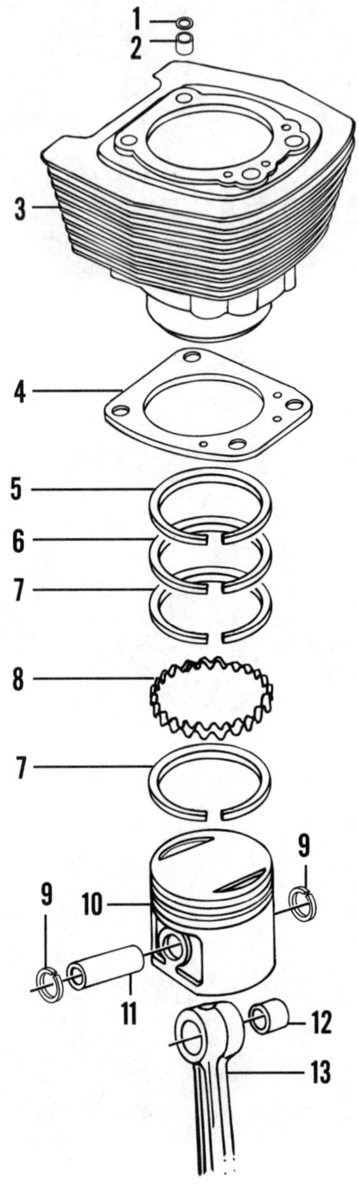

1. O-ring
2. Dowel pin
3. Cylinder
4. Base gasket
5. Top compression ring
6. Second compression ring
7. Oil control ring
8. Oil control expander ring
9. Retaining ring
10. Piston
11. Piston pin
12. Bushing
13. Connecting rod

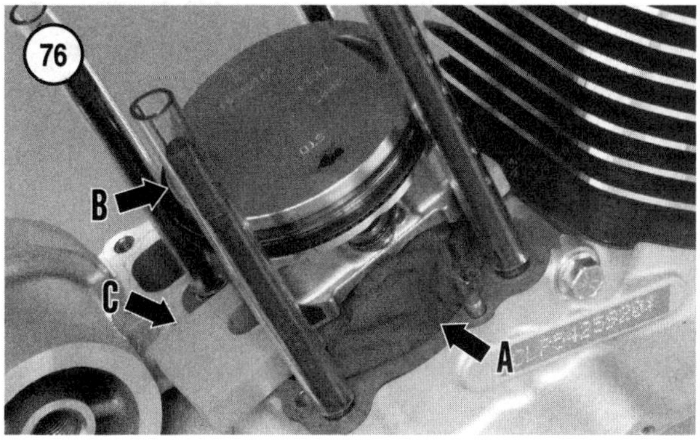

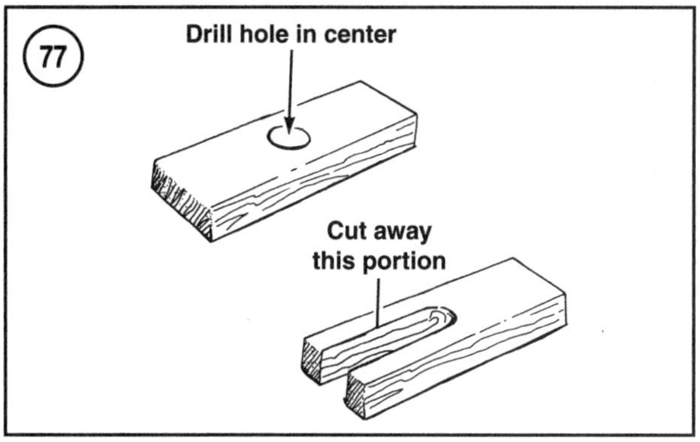

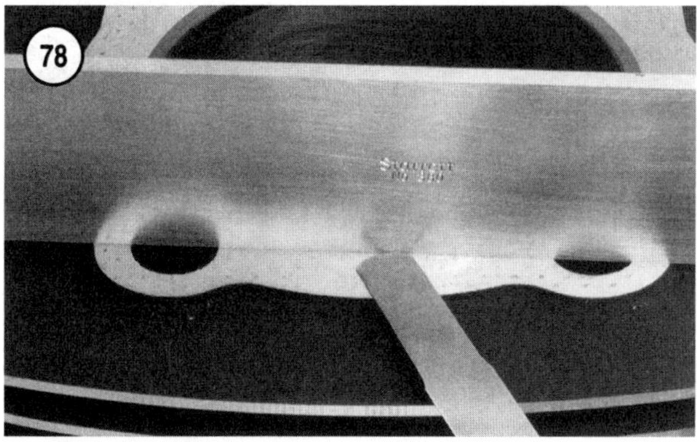

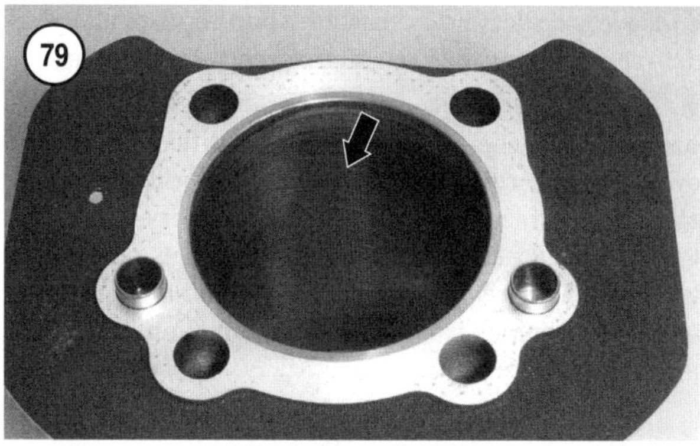

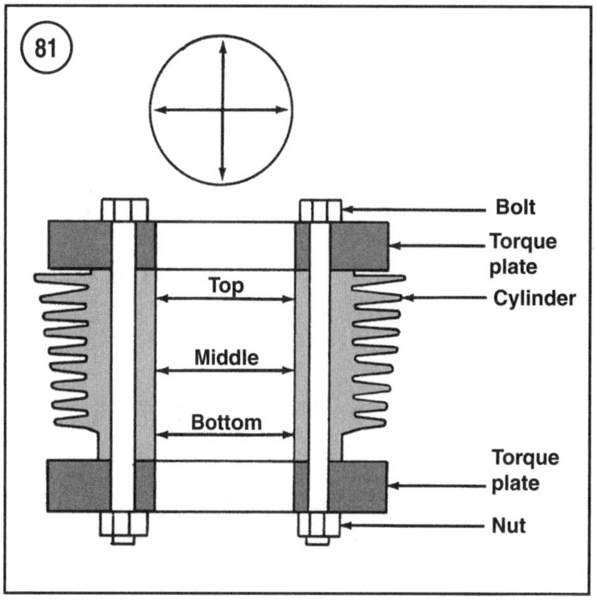

7. Measure in two axes—in line with the piston pin and at 90° to the pin. If the taper or out-of-round is greater than specifications (**Table 2**), rebore the cylinders to the next oversize and install new pistons and rings. Rebore both cylinders even though only one may be worn.

8. Have a dealership or machine shop confirm all cylinder measurements before ordering replacement parts.

9. After the cylinders have been serviced, thoroughly wash each cylinder in hot, soapy water. After washing the cylinder bore, run a clean, white cloth through it. If the cloth shows traces of grit or oil, the cylinder is not clean. Repeat until the cloth comes out clean. When the cylinder wall is clean, dry with compressed air and then lubricate with clean engine oil to prevent rust formation. Repeat for the other cylinder.

CAUTION

Hot, soapy water is the only solution that completely cleans the cylinder walls. Solvent and kerosene cannot wash fine grit out of the cylinder crevices. Residual abrasive grit in the cylinder wall causes premature engine wear.

Cylinder Stud and Cylinder Head Bolt Inspection/Cleaning

The cylinder studs and cylinder head bolts must be in good condition and properly cleaned prior to installing the cylinders and cylinder heads. Otherwise, damaged or dirty studs may cause cylinder head distortion and gasket leaks.

CAUTION

The cylinder studs, cylinder head bolts and washers are made of hardened material. If replacement is required, purchase new parts from a Harley-Davidson dealership.

1. Examine the cylinder head bolts (**Figure 82**) for head or thread damage. Replace if necessary.
2. Examine the cylinder studs (**Figure 83**) for bending, looseness or damage. Replace loose or damaged studs as described in Chapter Five. If the studs are in good condition, perform Step 3.
3. Cover the crankcase openings with shop rags to prevent debris from falling into the engine.
4. Remove all carbon residue from the cylinder studs and cylinder head bolts as follows:
    a. Apply solvent to the cylinder stud and mating cylinder head bolt threads and thread the bolt onto the stud.
    b. Hand turn the cylinder head bolt back and forth to loosen and remove carbon residue from the threads. Remove the bolt from the stud. Blow both thread sets with compressed air.
    c. Repeat until both thread sets are free of all carbon residue.

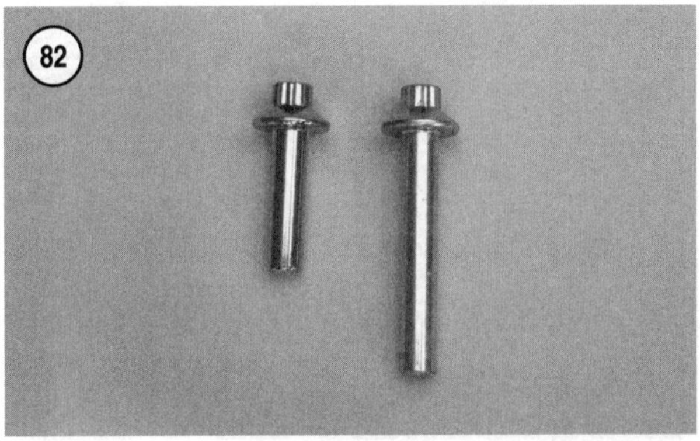

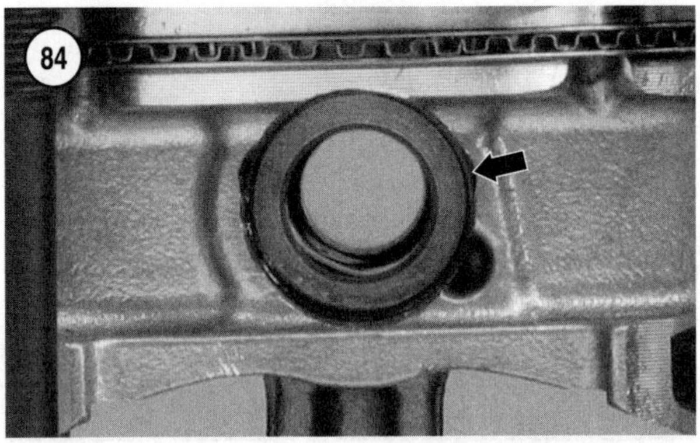

86

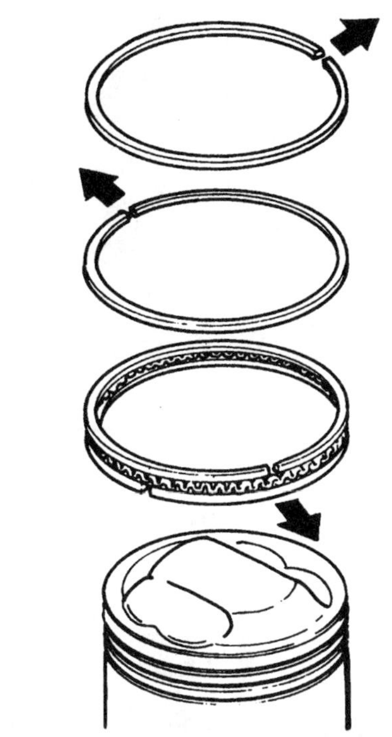

87

d. Spray the cylinder stud and cylinder head bolt with brake parts cleaner and blow dry.
e. Set the cleaned bolt aside and install it on the same stud when installing the cylinder head.

5. Repeat Step 4 for each cylinder stud and cylinder head bolt set.

Cylinder Installation

1. Install the pistons and rings as described in this chapter.
2. Check that all of the piston pin retaining rings have been properly installed (**Figure 84**).
3. Remove all gasket residue and clean the cylinders as described in this section.
4. Install the dowel pin (A, **Figure 85**) if removed.
5. Install a new cylinder base gasket (B, **Figure 85**) onto the crankcase. Make sure all holes align properly.
6. Rotate the crankshaft so the piston is at top dead center (TDC).
7. Lubricate the cylinder bore and piston liberally with clean engine oil.
8. Slide the protective hoses off the cylinder studs.
9. Position each piston ring so the end gap of adjacent rings is at least 90° apart (**Figure 86**). Ring gaps must not be within 10° of the piston's thrust face.
10. Compress the rings using a ring compressor (**Figure 87**).

CAUTION
Install the cylinders in their original positions.

11. Carefully align the cylinder with the cylinder studs and slide it down (**Figure 87**) until it is over the top of the piston. Continue sliding the cylinder down and past the rings. Once the rings are positioned in the cylinder, remove the ring compressor.
12. Continue to slide the cylinder down until it bottoms on the crankcase.
13. Repeat to install the remaining cylinder.
14. Install the cylinder heads as described in this chapter.

PISTONS AND PISTON RINGS

Refer to **Figure 74**.

Piston and Piston Rings Removal

1. Remove the cylinder head and cylinder as described in this chapter.
2. Stuff clean shop rags (A, **Figure 76**) into the crankcase opening to prevent objects from falling into the crankcase.
3. Install a hose (B, **Figure 76**) around each stud to protect the piston and studs from damage.
4. Install a piston holding tool (C, **Figure 76**) to stabilize the piston. The tool may be constructed from wood as shown in **Figure 77**.
5. Lightly mark the pistons with an F (front) or R (rear) so they can be reinstalled onto the same connecting rod.

WARNING
Wear safety glasses during piston pin retaining ring removal and installation.

6. Using a suitable tool, pry one piston pin retaining ring (A, **Figure 88**) out of the piston. Place your finger over

4

the hole to help prevent the ring from flying out during removal.

7. Support the piston and push out the piston pin (B, **Figure 88**). If the pin is difficult to remove, use a homemade tool as shown in **Figure 89**.

8. Mark the piston pin so it can be reinstalled in the same connecting rod.

CAUTION
If reusing the piston rings, identify and store the rings in a container so they can be reinstalled in their original ring grooves and on their original pistons.

9. Remove the old rings using a ring expander tool (**Figure 90**) or spread them by hand (**Figure 91**) and remove them.

10. Repeat for the other piston.

11. Inspect the pistons, piston pins and pistons rings as described in this section.

Piston Inspection

CAUTION
Do not damage the piston when removing carbon deposits. Do not use a wire brush to clean the ring grooves or piston sides. Do not remove carbon from the piston sides above the top ring groove or from the top of the cylinder bore. Carbon removal from these areas may cause increased oil consumption.

CAUTION
*A special coating is applied to the piston skirts (**Figure 92**). Do not damage the coating.*

1. Carefully clean the carbon (**Figure 93**) from the piston crown with a soft scraper. Do not remove or damage the carbon ridge around the circumference of the piston above the top ring.

2. Using a broken piston ring, remove all carbon deposits from the piston ring grooves (**Figure 94**). Do not remove aluminum from the piston ring grooves when cleaning them.

3. After cleaning the piston, examine the crown. The crown should show no signs of wear or damage. If the crown appears pecked or spongy-looking, check the spark plug, valves and combustion chamber for aluminum deposits. If aluminum deposits are found, the engine is overheating.

4. Examine each ring groove for burrs, dented edges or other damage. Pay particular attention to the top compression ring groove as it usually wears more than the others. The oil rings and grooves generally wear less than compression rings and their grooves. If the oil ring groove is worn or if the oil ring assembly is tight and difficult to remove, the piston skirt may have collapsed due to excessive heat, causing permanent deformation. Replace the piston.

5. Check the piston skirt for cracks or other damage. If a piston shows signs of partial seizure such as aluminum buildup on the piston skirt, replace the piston to reduce the possibility of engine noise and further piston seizure. If

88

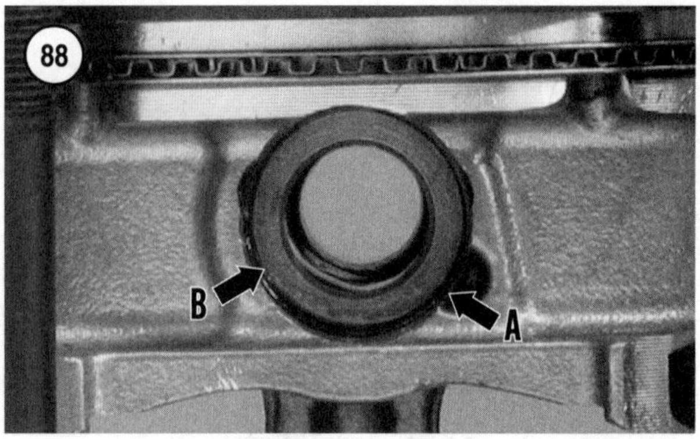

89

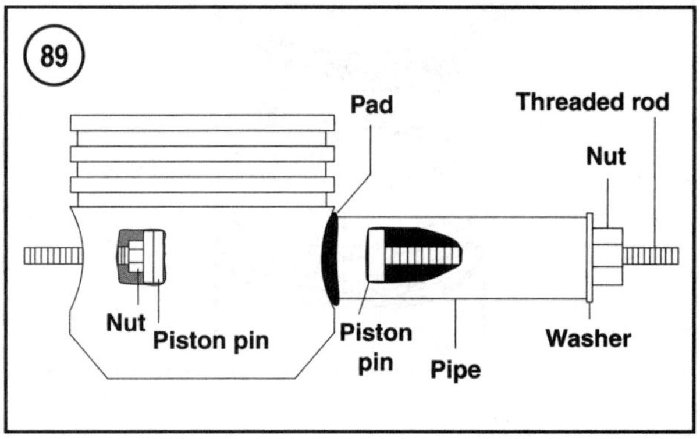

90

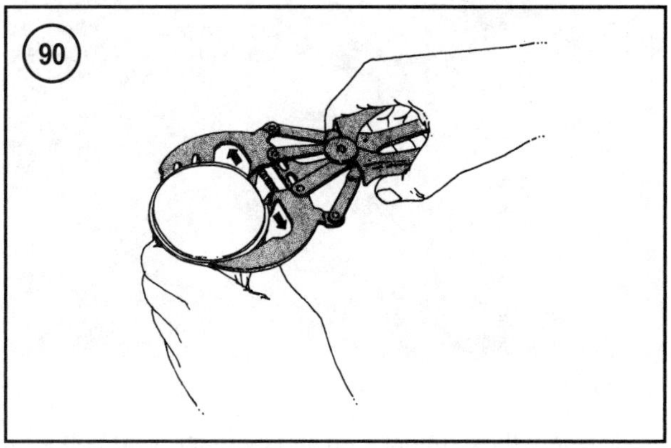

91
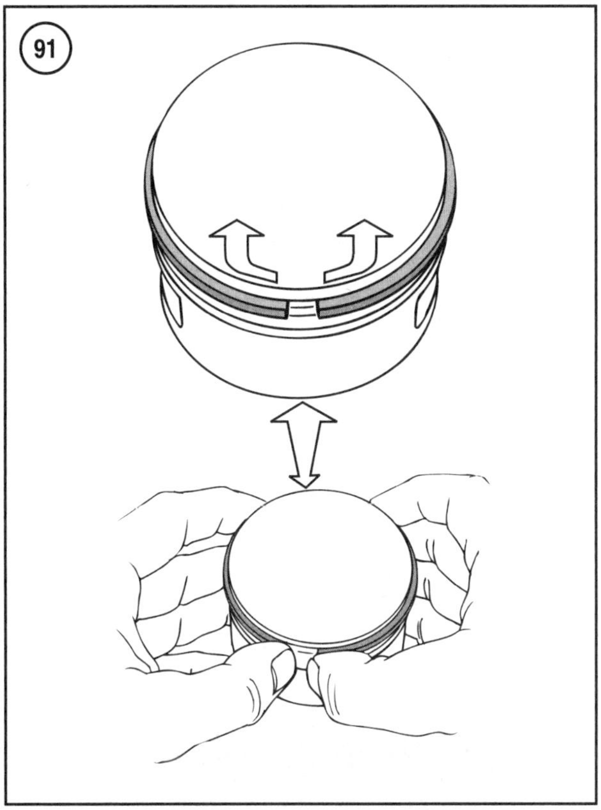

92

93
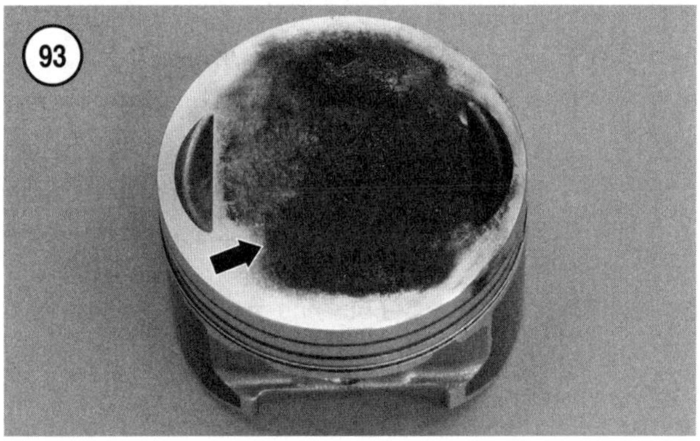

94
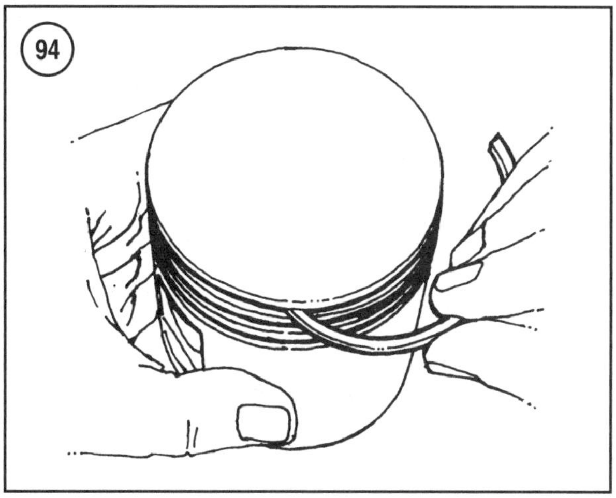

95
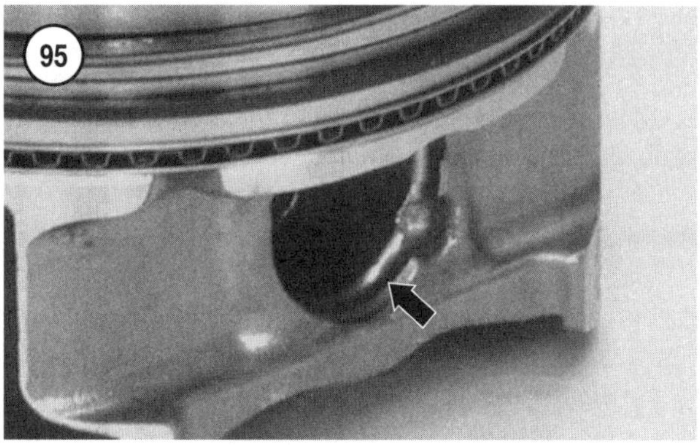

the piston skirt is worn or scuffed unevenly from side to side, the connecting rod may be bent or twisted.

6. Check the retaining ring groove (**Figure 95**) on each side for wear, cracks or other damage. If the grooves are questionable, check the retaining ring fit by installing a new retaining ring into each groove, then attempt to move the retaining ring from side to side. If the retaining ring has any side play, the groove is worn and the piston must be replaced.

7. Measure piston-to-cylinder clearance as described in this section.

8. If piston replacement is required, select a new piston as described in *Piston Clearance* in this section. If the piston, rings and cylinder are not damaged and are dimensionally correct, they can be reused.

Piston Pin Inspection

The piston pins are different. The 1200 cc piston pins are marked with a V-groove in one end and stamped with 12 in the other end of the pin (**Figure 96**). The 883 cc pins are not marked. When purchasing replacement piston pins, note the difference.

1. Clean the piston pin in solvent and dry thoroughly.
2. Replace the piston pins if cracked, pitted or scored.
3. If the piston pins are visually in good condition, check their clearance as described in the *Piston Pin Bushing Inspection* in this section.

Piston Clearance

1. Make sure the piston skirt (**Figure 93**) and cylinder bore (**Figure 79**) are clean and dry.

NOTE
The piston and cylinder must be at room temperature to obtain accurate measurements. Do not hold the piston for an extended period or piston expansion may occur.

2. Measure the cylinder bore with a bore gauge as described in *Cylinder Inspection* in this chapter.

CAUTION
*The piston skirt is coated, but a bare metal spot is located on each piston skirt (**Figure 97**). Position the micrometer so it contacts the bare metal, not the piston coating. Use a micrometer with ball ends so the micrometer only contacts the bare metal. A micrometer with flat ends may not provide an accurate measurement.*

3. Measure the piston diameter with a micrometer. Hold the micrometer at the bottom of the piston skirt at a right angle to the piston pin bore (**Figure 98**). Adjust the micrometer so the spindle and anvil just touch the bare metal spot on each skirt.
4. Subtract the piston diameter from the largest bore diameter; the difference is piston-to-cylinder clearance. If the clearance exceeds the specification in **Table 2**, replace the pistons and bore the cylinders. Purchase the new pistons first. Measure their diameter and add the specified clearance to determine the proper cylinder bore diameter.

Piston Pin Bushing Inspection

All models are equipped with a bushing (**Figure 99**) at the small end of the connecting rod. The bushing is reamed to provide correct piston pin clearance (clearance between piston pin and bushing). This clearance is critical in preventing pin knock and top end damage.

1. Inspect the piston pin bushing (**Figure 99**) for excessive wear or damage (pit marks, scoring or wear grooves). Also check the bushing for a loose fit; the bushing must be a tight fit in the connecting rod.
2. Measure the piston pin outside diameter with a micrometer where it rides in the bushing (**Figure 100**).
3. Measure the piston pin bushing inside diameter with a snap gauge or small hole gauge.
4. Subtract the pin outside diameter from the bushing inside diameter to obtain piston pin clearance.

96

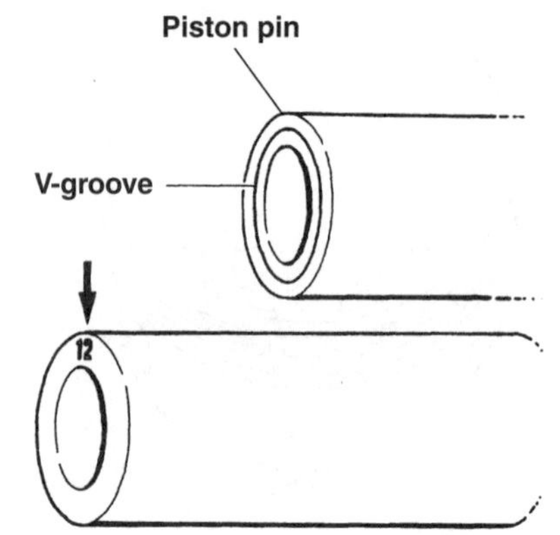

97

98

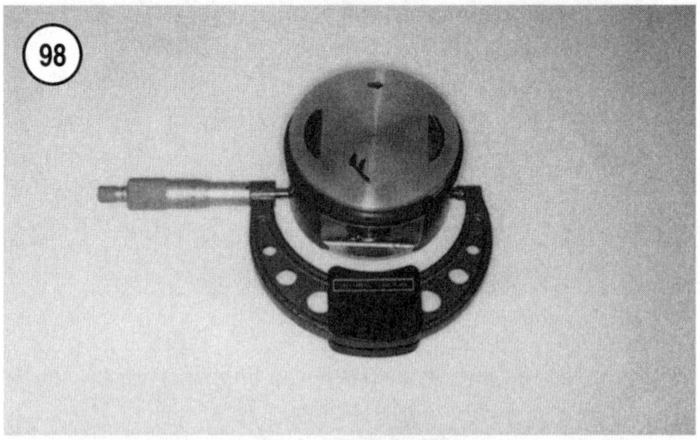

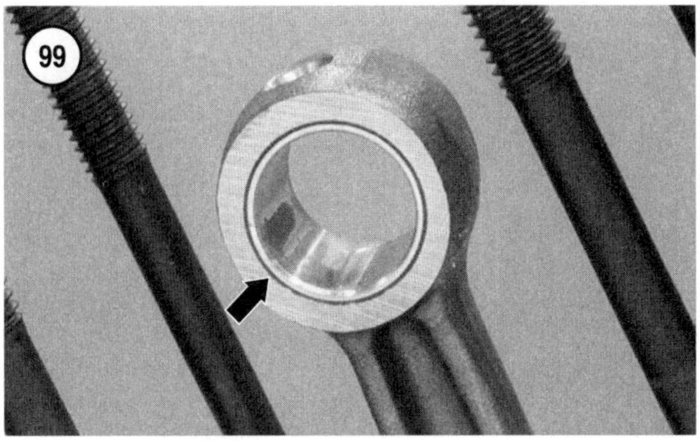
99

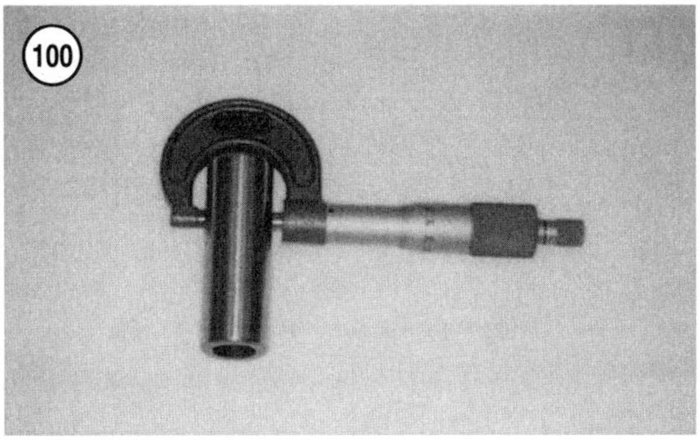
100

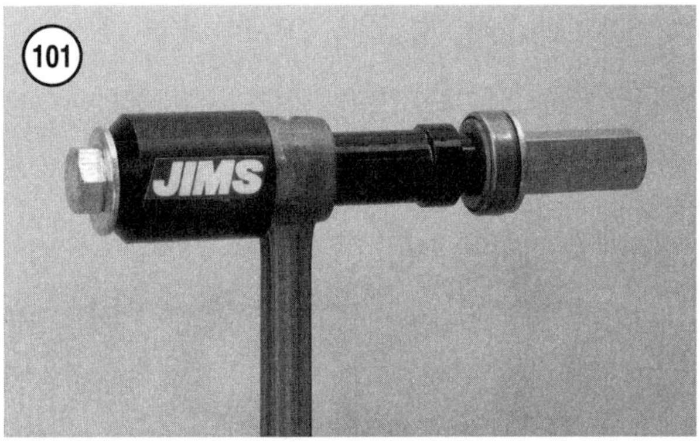

101

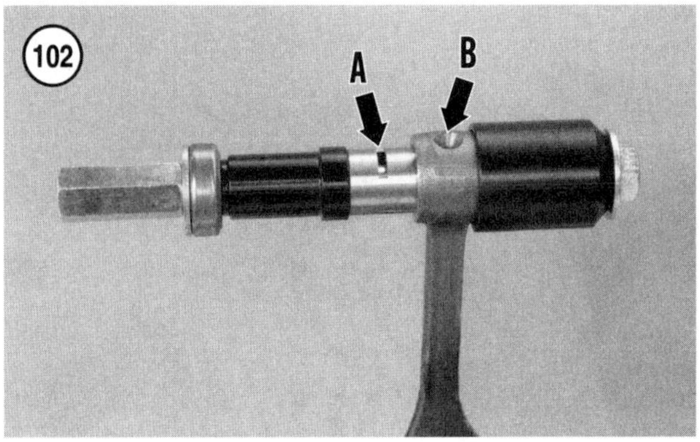

102

5. Replace the pin and bushing if the clearance meets or exceeds the connecting rod piston pin clearance service limit in **Table 2**.

Piston Pin Bushing Replacement

Special tools

The following special tools are required to replace and ream the piston pin bushings. The clamp tool is only required if the bushing is being replaced with the crankcase assembled. If these tools are not available, have a shop with the proper equipment perform the procedure.

1. Connecting rod clamp tool (JIMS part No. 1284 or HD-95952-33C).
2. Connecting rod bushing tool (JIMS part No. 95970-32C).
3. Bushing reamer tool (JIMS part No. 1726-2).
4. Connecting rod bushing hone (part No. HD-42569).

Procedure

1. Remove two of the plastic hoses protecting the cylinder studs.
2. Install the connecting rod clamping tool as follows:
   a. Install the clamp portion of the connecting rod clamping tool around the connecting rod so the slots engage the cylinder head studs. Do not scratch or bend the studs.
   b. Position the threaded cylinders with the knurled end facing up and install the cylinders onto the studs. Tighten the clamp securely.
   c. Alternately tighten the thumbscrews on the side of the connecting rod. Do not turn only one thumbscrew, as this will move the connecting rod off center and tightening the other thumbscrew will cause the connecting rod to flex or bend.
3. Cover the crankcase opening to keep bushing particles from falling into the engine.
4. Assemble the removal tool per the manufacturer's instructions (**Figure 101**) and remove the bushing.

NOTE

*When installing the new bushing, align the oil slot in the bushing (A, **Figure 102**) with the oil hole in the connecting rod (B).*

5. Press the bushing into place using the connecting rod bushing tool (**Figure 102**) following the tool manufacturer's instructions. The new bushing must be flush with both sides of the connecting rod.

6. Ream the piston pin bushing using the bushing reamer tool (**Figure 103**) following the manufacturer's instructions.

7. Hone the new bushing to obtain the connecting rod piston pin clearance specified in **Table 2**. Use honing oil, not engine oil, when honing the bushing to size.

CAUTION
If the bushing clearance is less than 0.00125 in. (0.0317 mm), the pin may seize on the rod, causing engine damage.

8. Install the piston pin through the bushing. The pin should move through the bushing smoothly. Confirm pin clearance using a micrometer and bore gauge.

9. Carefully remove the shop rags from the crankcase openings and replace them with clean rags.

Piston Ring Inspection

1. Clean the piston ring grooves of all carbon residue as described in *Piston Inspection* in this section.

2. Inspect the ring grooves for burrs, nicks, or broken or cracked lands. Replace the piston if necessary.

3. Insert one piston ring into the top of its cylinder and tap it down about 1/2 in. (12.7 mm) with the piston to square it in the bore. Measure the ring end gap with a feeler gauge (**Figure 104**) and compare with the specification in **Table 2**. Replace the piston rings as a set if any one ring end gap measurement is excessive. Repeat for each ring.

4. Roll each compression ring around its piston groove as shown in **Figure 105**. The ring should move smoothly with no binding. If a ring binds up in its groove, check the groove for damage. Replace the piston if necessary.

Piston Ring Installation

Each piston is equipped with three piston rings: two compression rings (**Figure 106**) and one oil ring assembly (**Figure 107**). The top compression ring is not marked. The second compression must be installed with its dot mark facing up.

Used piston rings must be installed on their original pistons and in their original grooves with the same sides up.

CAUTION
When installing oversize compression rings, check the number to make sure the correct rings are being installed. The ring numbers should be the same as the piston oversize number.

103

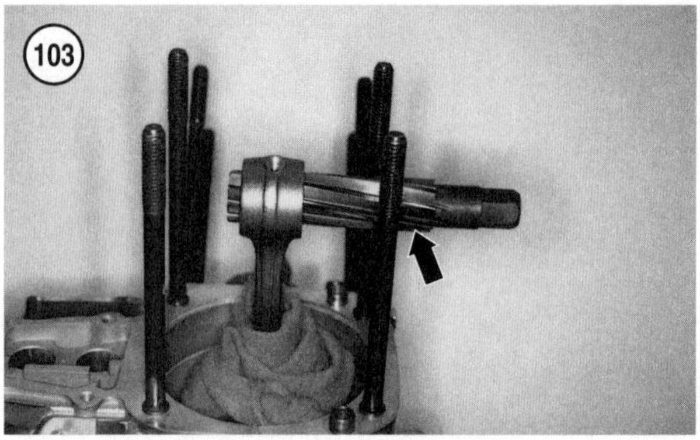

104

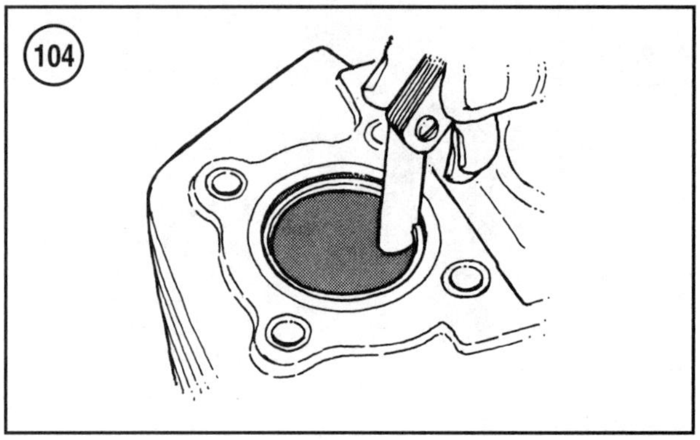

105

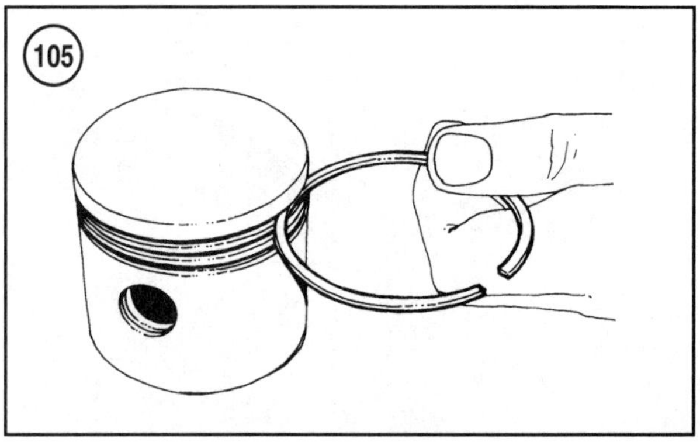

106

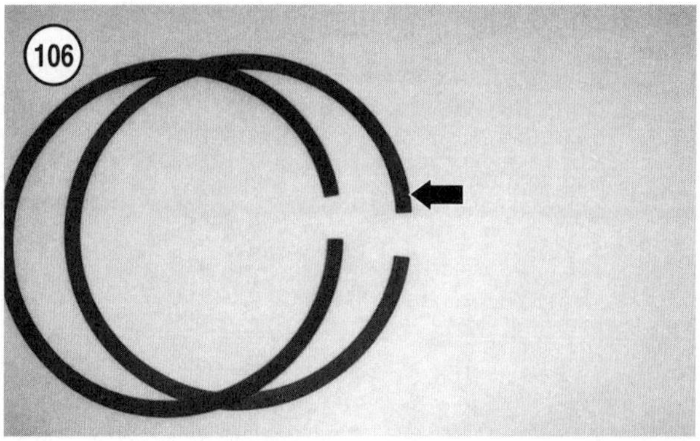

107

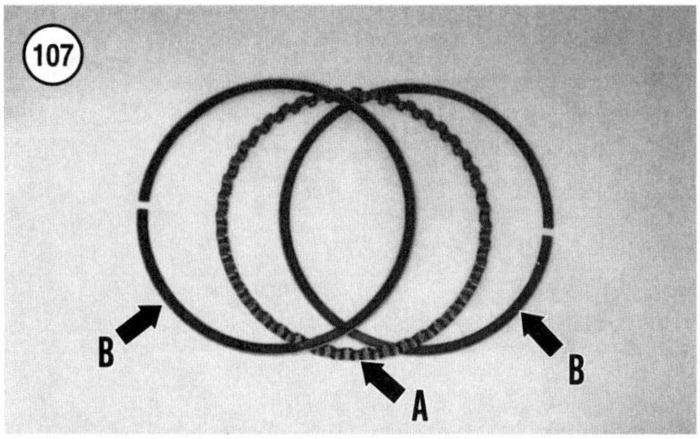

108

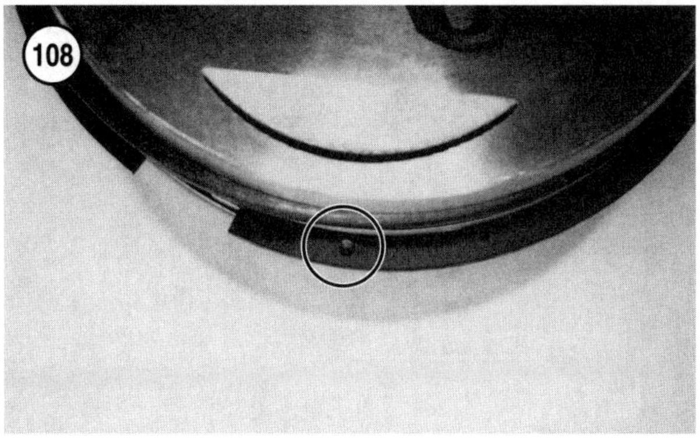

109

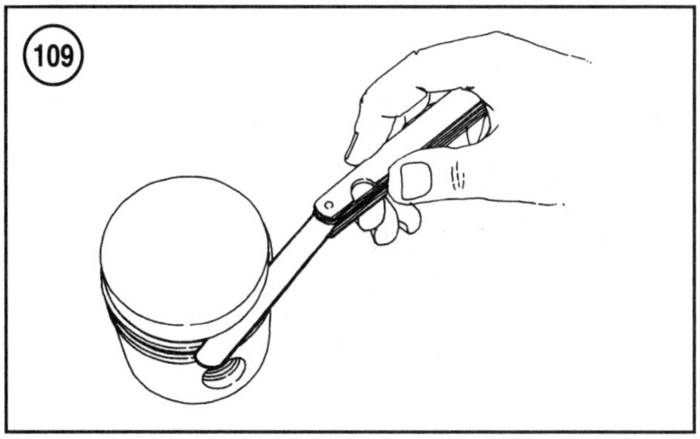

1. Wash the piston in hot, soapy water. Then rinse with cold water and blow dry. Make sure the oil control holes in the lower ring groove are clear and open.
2. Clean the piston rings carefully and dry with compressed air.
3. Install the oil ring assembly as follows:
   a. The oil ring consists of three rings: a ribbed spacer ring (A, **Figure 107**) and two steel rings (B).
   b. Install the spacer ring into the lower ring groove. Butt the spacer ring ends together. Do not overlap the ring ends.

CAUTION
Do not expand the steel rings when installing them.

   c. Insert one end of the first steel ring into the lower groove so it is below the spacer ring. Then spiral the other end over the piston crown and into the lower groove. To protect the ring end from scratching the side of the piston, place a piece of shim stock or a thin, flat feeler gauge between the ring and piston.
   d. Repeat substep c to install the other steel ring above the spacer ring.

NOTE
*When installing the compression rings, use a ring expander as shown in **Figure 90**. Do not expand the rings any more than necessary to install them.*

4. Install the second compression ring as follows:
   a. The second compression ring has a dot mark (**Figure 108**).
   b. Install the second compression ring so the dot mark faces up.
5. Install the top compression ring as follows:
   a. The top compression ring is not marked.
   b. New upper compression rings can be installed with either side facing up.
6. Check ring side clearance with a feeler gauge as shown in **Figure 109**. Check side clearance in several spots around the piston. If clearance meets or exceeds the service limit in **Table 2**, note the following:
   a. If the ring grooves were not cleaned, remove the rings and clean the grooves. Then reinstall rings and recheck clearance.
   b. If reusing the old rings to obtain measurements, replace the rings and/or the piston.
   c. If using new rings to obtain measurements, replace the piston.
7. Stagger the ring gaps around the piston as shown in **Figure 110**. Make sure the ring gaps are not within 10° of the piston's thrust face centerline.

Piston Installation

1. Cover the crankcase openings with a clean shop towel to prevent debris from entering.
2. Install a new piston pin retaining ring into one groove in the piston. Make sure the ring seats in the groove completely.
3. Coat the connecting rod bushing and piston pin with assembly oil.

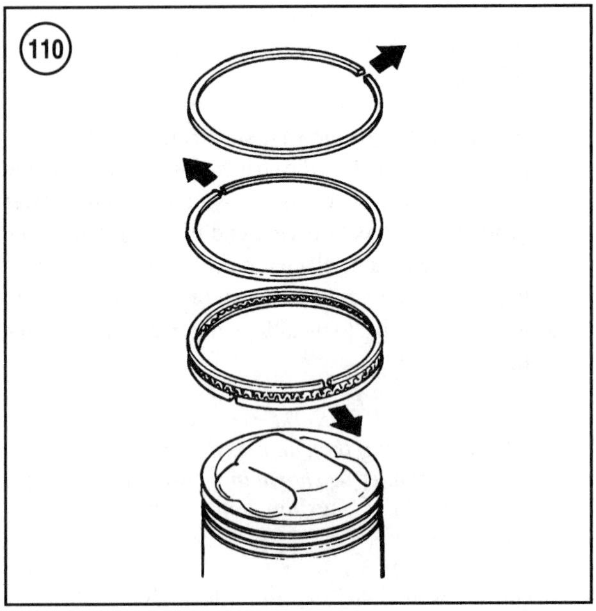

4. Place the piston onto the connecting rod with the arrow mark facing forward (**Figure 111**). Install used pistons onto their original connecting rods; refer to the marks made on the piston during removal. Oversize pistons must be installed in the cylinder (front or rear) that they were originally fitted to during the boring process.
5. Insert the piston pin through the piston. Hold the rod so the lower end does not take any shock. Push the piston pin in until it contacts the retaining ring on the opposite side.
6. Install the remaining new piston pin retaining ring (A, **Figure 112**). Make sure the ring end gap does not coincide with the notch on the side of the piston (B, **Figure 112**). Make sure the retaining ring seats in the groove completely.
7. Install the cylinders as described in this chapter.

OIL TANK AND OIL HOSE

Hose Clamps

CAUTION
Do not reuse removed clamps as removal damages them.

The oil hoses are secured by band-type hose clamps (A, **Figure 113**). Use diagonal pliers or another suitable tool to separate the clamp bands. Then remove the clamp. Use H-D hose clamp pliers (HD-97087-65B) to compress the clamp bands during installation.

NOTE
*End cutting pliers (B, **Figure 113**) may be modified to compress the band clamps.*

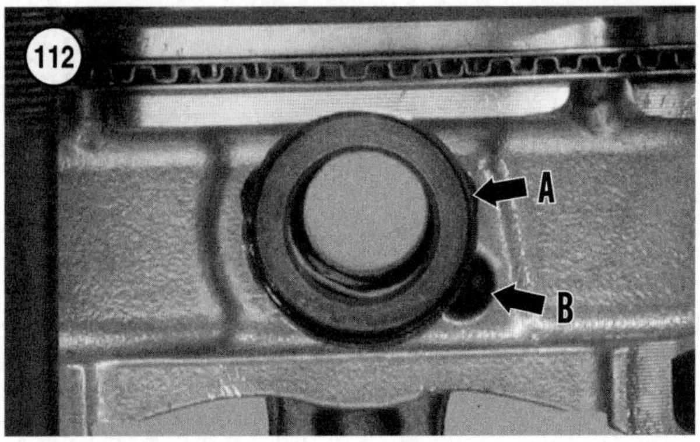

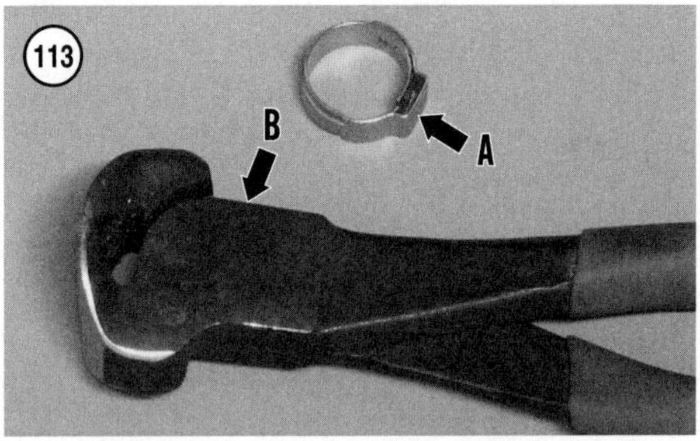

Make sure to test the performance of the tool by checking the fit and integrity of the installed clamp.

Oil Hoses

Refer to **Figure 114** and **Figure 115** for hose identification and routing. The threaded hose end fittings are not replaceable; the fittings and hose are available only as an assembly.

114

OIL HOSE ROUTING

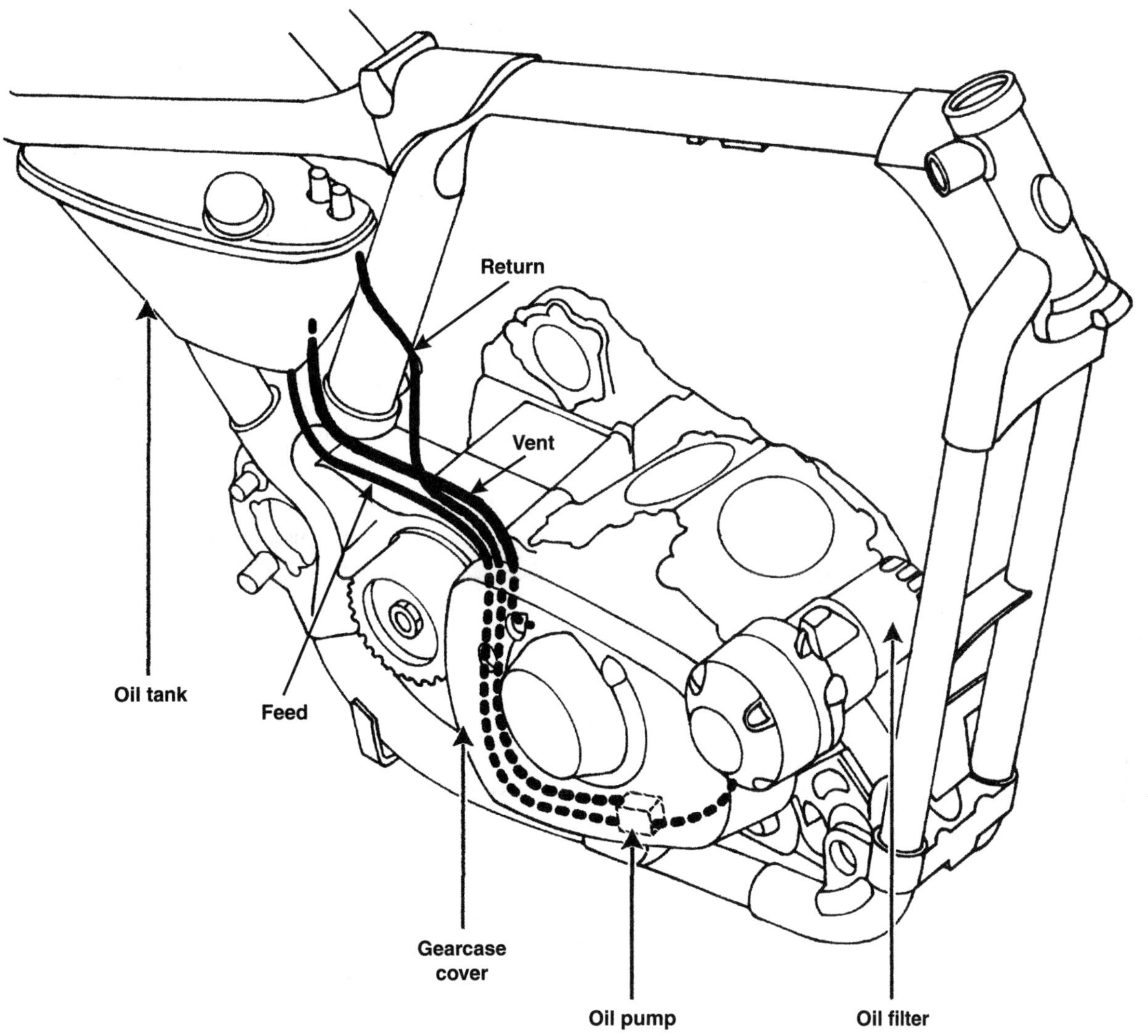

Oil Tank

Removal/installation

Refer to **Figure 114** and **Figure 115** when performing the following procedure.

1. Refer to Chapter Three and drain the oil tank as described in *Engine Oil and Filter Change* (oil filter removal is not necessary).
2. Refer to Chapter Nine and remove the battery.
3. Remove the ICM as described in Chapter Nine.
4. Remove the oil tank cap.
5. Remove the right shock absorber lower mounting bolt (**Figure 116**), washer and locknut.
6. Remove the belt guard mounting bolt (A, **Figure 117**), washer and locknut, then remove the belt guard (B).
7. Remove the rear fender (Chapter Fourteen).

(115)

OIL TANK AND HOSES

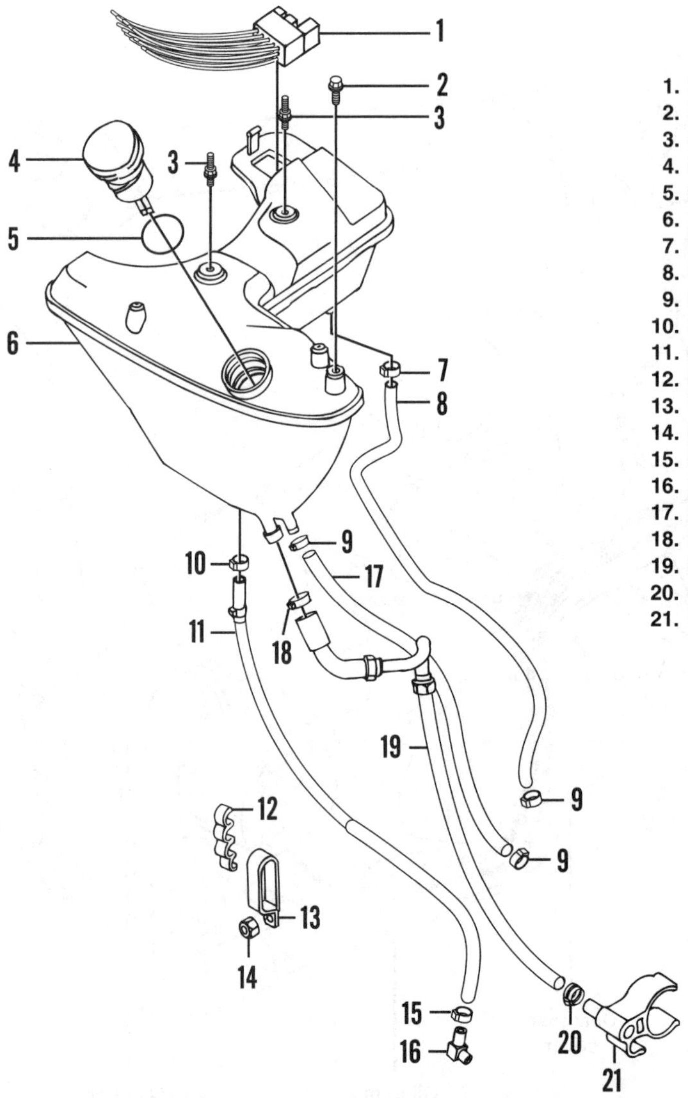

1. Fuse block
2. Bolt
3. Stud
4. Oil cap
5. O-ring
6. Oil tank
7. Clamp
8. Oil return hose
9. Clamp
10. Clamp
11. Oil vent hose
12. Hose retainer
13. Clamp
14. Locknut
15. Clamp
16. Elbow fitting
17. Oil feed hose
18. Clamp
19. Oil drain hose
20. Clamp
21. Hose clip/plug

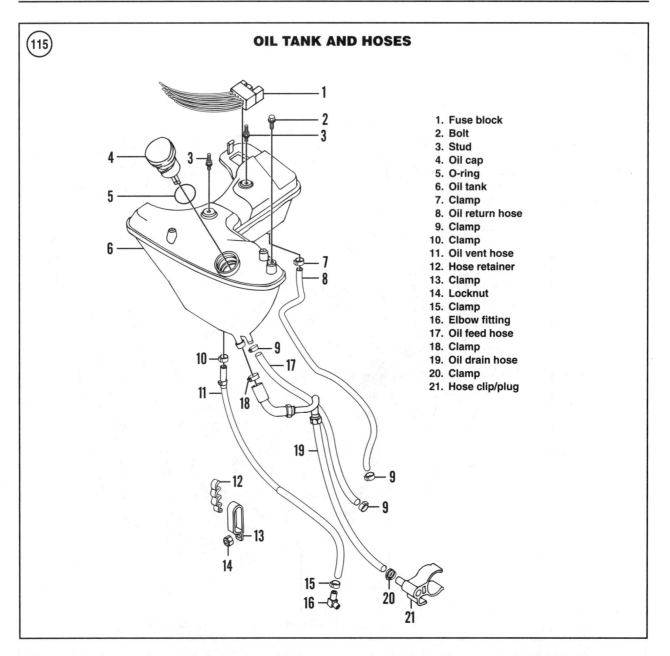

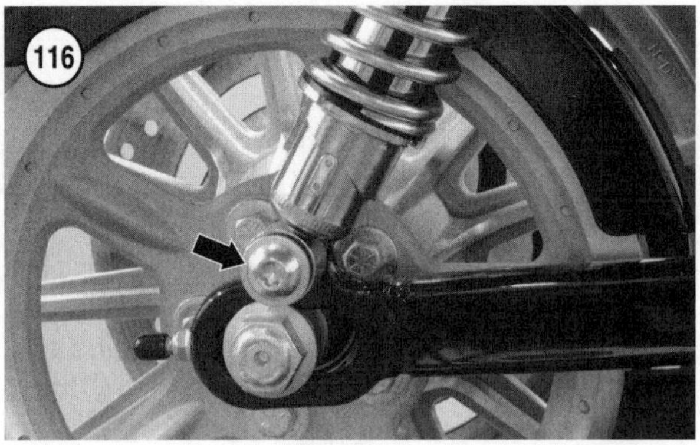

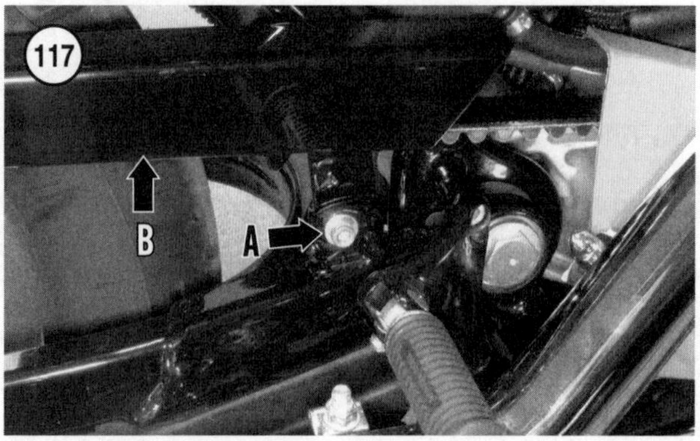

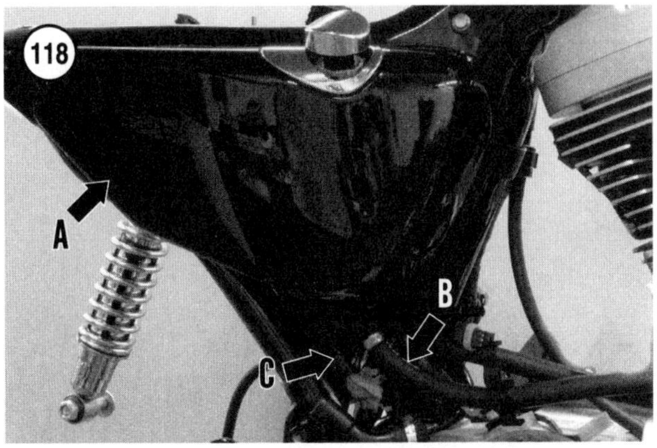

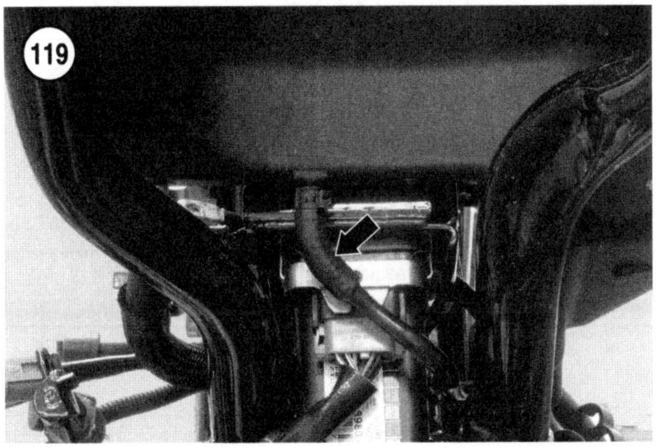

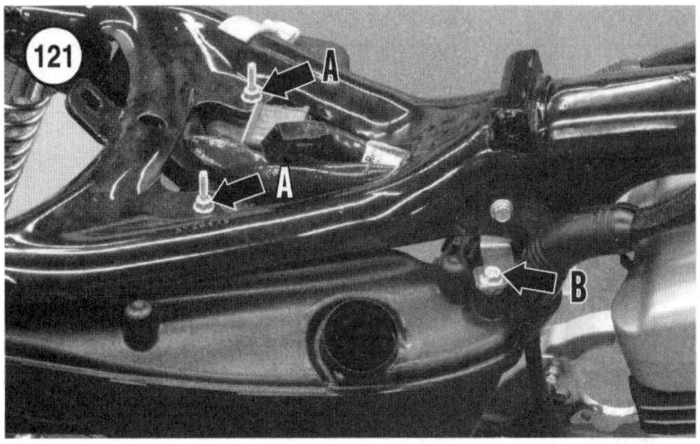

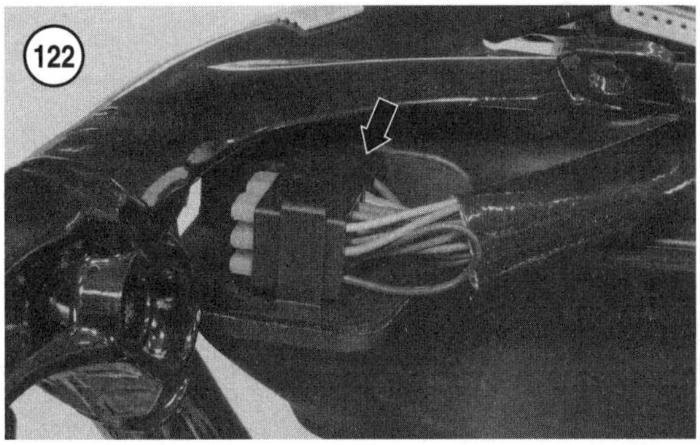

4

8. Remove the right side cover (A, **Figure 118**).
9. Disconnect the oil feed line (B, **Figure 118**) from the right side of the oil tank.
10. Disconnect the vent hose from the rear of the oil tank (**Figure 119**).
11. Disconnect the oil return hose from the left side of the oil tank (**Figure 120**).
12. Remove the studs (A, **Figure 121**) and bolt (B) securing the oil tank to the frame.
13. Remove the oil tank through the right side of the frame while unlatching the fuse block (**Figure 122**) during removal.
14. Reverse the removal steps to install the oil tank. Make sure to install new hose clamps. Check for oil leaks after refilling the oil tank and running the engine.

Table 1 GENERAL ENGINE SPECIFICATIONS

Type	45° V-twin, air-cooled
Bore and stroke	
883 cc	3.000 × 3.812 in. (76.2 × 96.8 mm)
1200 cc	3.498 × 3.812 in. (88.85 × 96.8 mm)
Displacement	
883 cc	53.9 cu. in. (883 cc)
1200 cc	73.2 cu. in. (1203 mm)
Compression ratio	
883 cc	8.9:1
1200 cc	9.7:1
Compression pressure (at sea level)	approx. 120 psi (828 kPa)
Torque	
883 cc	51 ft.-lb. (69.2 N•m) at 4300 rpm
1200 cc	79 ft.-lb. (107.2 N•m) at 3500 rpm
Oil Pressure	
At idle	7-12 psi (48-83 kPa)
At 2500 rpm	10-17 psi (70-117 kPa)

Table 2 ENGINE TOP END SPECIFICATIONS

	New in. (mm)	Service limit in. (mm)
Connecting rods		
Piston pin clearance	0.00125-0.00175 (0.0318-0.0445)	0.00200 (0.0508)
Cylinder		
Taper	–	0.002 (0.051)
Out-of-round	–	0.003 (0.076)
Gasket surface (warp limit)		
Top	–	0.006 (0.152)
Bottom	–	0.008 (0.203)
Cylinder bore diameter (883 cc)*		
Standard	3.0005 (76.213)	3.0035 (76.289)
Oversize		
0.005 in. (0.13 mm)	3.0048 (76.322)	3.0078 (76.398)
0.010 in. (0.25 mm)	3.0098 (76.449)	3.0128 (76.525)
0.020 in. (0.51 mm)	3.0198 (76.703)	3.0228 (76.779)
Cylinder bore diameter (1200 cc)*		
Standard	3.4978 (88.844)	3.5008 (88.920)
Oversize		
0.005 in. (0.13 mm)	3.502 (88.950)	3.505 (89.027)
0.010 in. (0.25 mm)	3.507 (89.078)	3.510 (89.154)
0.020 in. (0.51 mm)	3.517 (89.332)	3.520 (89.408)
Cylinder head		
Gasket surface (warp limit)	–	0.006 (0.152)
Valve guide fit in head	0.0033-0.0020 (0.084-0.050)	–
Valve seat fit in head	0.0035-0.0010 (0.089-0.025)	–
Piston (883 cc)		
Compression ring end gap	0.010-0.023 (0.254-0.584)	0.032 (0.812)
Oil control ring rail end gap	0.010-0.053 (0.254-1.346)	0.065 (1.651)
Compression ring side clearance		
Top	0.0020-0.0045 (0.051-0.114)	0.0065 (0.165)
Second	0.0020-0.0045 (0.051-0.114)	0.0065 (0.165)
Oil control ring side clearance	0.0014-0.0074 (0.036-0.188)	0.0094 (0.239)
Cylinder clearance	–	0.003 (0.076)

(continued)

Table 2 ENGINE TOP END SPECIFICATIONS (continued)

	New in. (mm)	Service limit in. (mm)
Piston (1200 cc)		
Compression ring end gap	0.007-0.020 (0.177-0.508)	0.032 (0.812)
Oil control ring rail end gap	0.009-0.052 (0.228-1.320)	0.065 (1.651)
Compression ring side clearance		
Top	0.0020-0.0045 (0.051-0.114)	0.0065 (0.165)
Second	0.0016-0.0041 (0.041-0.104)	0.0065 (0.165)
Oil control ring side clearance	0.0016-0.0076 (0.041-0.193)	0.0094 (0.239)
Cylinder clearance	–	0.003 (0.076)
Rocker arm		
Shaft clearance in bushing	0.0005-0.0020 (0.013-0.051)	0.0035 (0.089)
End clearance	0.003-0.013 (0.08-0.33)	0.025 (0.635)
Bushing clearance in rocker arm	0.004-0.002 (0.10-0.05)	–
Rocker arm shaft		
Shaft clearance in rocker arm bushing	0.0007-0.0022 (0.018-0.055)	0.0035 (0.089)
Valves		
Guide-to-valve stem clearance		
Intake	0.001-0.003 (0.025-0.076)	0.0038 (0.096)
Exhaust	0.001-0.003 (0.025-0.076)	0.0038 (0.096)
Seat width	0.040-0.062 (1.016-1.574)	0.090 (2.286)
Stem protrusion from cylinder valve pocket	2.028-2.064 (51.51-51.42)	2.082 (52.88)
Valve spring compression specifications	Refer to Table 3	
Valve spring free length	–	2.325 (59.06)

*+/-0.0002 in. (0.005 mm).

Table 3 VALVE SPRING COMPRESSION SPECIFICATIONS*

	Compression length in. (mm)	Pressure lb.	 kg
Closed	1.850 (47.0)	135	61.2
Open	1.300 (33.0)	312	141.5

*Specifications apply to both intake and exhaust valves on all models.

Table 4 ENGINE TOP END TORQUE SPECIFICATIONS

	ft.-lb.	in.-lb.	N•m
Breather valve retaining screw	–	35-55	4.0-6.2
Cylinder head bolts*			
Cylinder head bracket mounting bolts	17-24	–	23-32
Lower rocker cover bolts			
Rocker arm shaft bolts	18-22	–	25-30
Hex bolts	–	135-155	15.3-17.5
Socket head bolts	–	135-155	15.3-17.5

(continued)

Table 4 ENGINE TOP END TORQUE SPECIFICATIONS (continued)

	ft.-lb.	in.-lb.	N•m
Rocker cover retaining bolts		120-168	13.6-19.0
Upper stabilizer (front cylinder)			
Stabilizer bracket bolts	55-65	–	75-88
Stabilizer link bolts	25-35	–	34-47

*Refer to text.

NOTE: Refer to the Supplement at the end of this manual for information unique to 2007-2011 models.

CHAPTER FIVE

ENGINE LOWER END

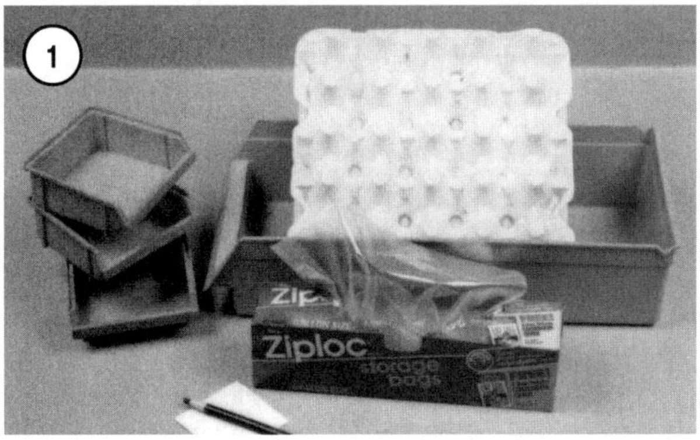

This chapter describes service procedures for lower end engine components, including engine removal and installation. Specifications are in **Table 1** and **Table 2** at the end of this chapter.

All models covered in this manual are equipped with the Evolution engine, an air-cooled, four-stroke, overhead-valve, V-twin engine.

ENGINE

Before servicing the engine, note the following:

1. Review *Basic Service Methods* and *Measuring Tools* in Chapter One. Accurate measurements are critical to a successful engine rebuild.
2. Viewed from the engine's right side, crankshaft rotation is clockwise.
3. Throughout the text there are references to the left and right side of the engine. This refers to the engine as it is mounted in the frame, not how it may sit on the workbench.

CAUTION
The engine is assembled with hardened fasteners. Do not install fasteners with a lower strength grade classification.

4. Always replace worn or damaged fasteners with those of the same size, type and torque requirements. Make sure to identify each bolt before replacing it. If a specific torque value is not in **Table 2**, refer to the general torque specifications in Chapter One.
5. Use special tools where noted. Refer to **Table 10** in Chapter One.
6. Store parts in boxes, plastic bags and containers (**Figure 1**). Use masking tape and a permanent, waterproof marking pen to label parts.
7. Use a box of assorted size and color vacuum hose identifiers, such as those shown in **Figure 2** (Lisle part No. 74600), to identify hoses and fittings during engine removal and disassembly.
8. Use a vise with protective jaws to hold parts.
9. Use a press or special tools when force is required to remove and install parts. Do not try to pry, hammer or otherwise force them on or off.

10. Replace all O-rings and oil seals during reassembly. Apply a small amount of grease to the inner lips of each new seal to prevent damage when the engine is first started.
11. Record the location, position and thickness of all shims while removing them.

Service In Frame

The following components can be serviced while the engine is mounted in the frame:
1. Rocker arm cover and rocker arms.
2. Cylinder heads.
3. Cylinders and pistons.
4. Camshafts.
5. Gearshift mechanism.
6. Clutch and primary drive assembly.
7. Carburetor.
8. Starter and gears.
9. Alternator and electrical systems.

Special Tools

Engine service requires a number of special tools. These tools and their part numbers are described in the procedures. All of the special tools mentioned in this manual, are listed in Chapter One (**Table 10**).

When purchasing special tools, make sure to specify that the tools required are for 2004-on Sportster models. Many of the tools are specific to this engine. Tools for other engine models may be slightly different.

Engine Stand

Most engine service can be performed with the engine supported in an engine stand. Attaching the engine to the engine stand using the front and rear mounting points allows for service work, except when servicing the right crankcase half.

A suitable engine stand can be fabricated using angled steel of heavy gauge and bolting it to an automotive engine stand as shown in **Figure 3**. Use large washers on each side of the mounting hole to hold the crankcase (**Figure 4**). Make sure to test the capacity of the stand before mounting an engine, and before rotating the engine on the stand.

Removal

1. Remove the seat as described in Chapter Fourteen.

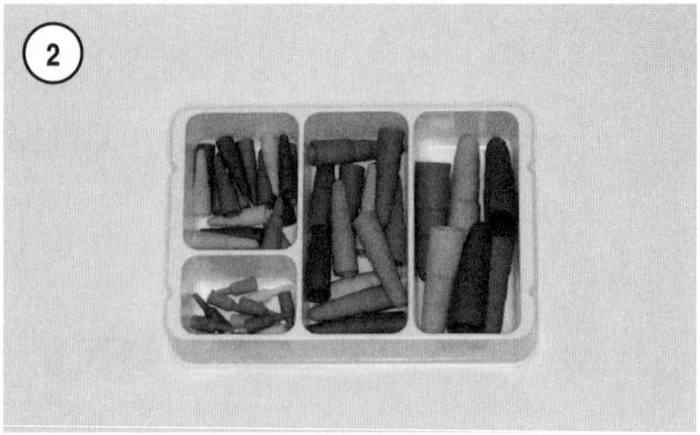

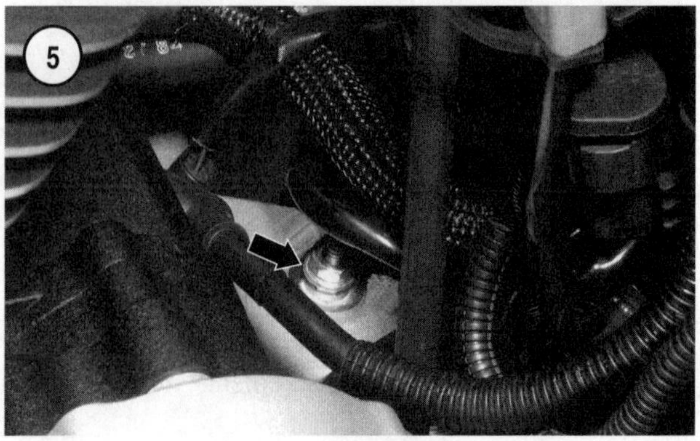

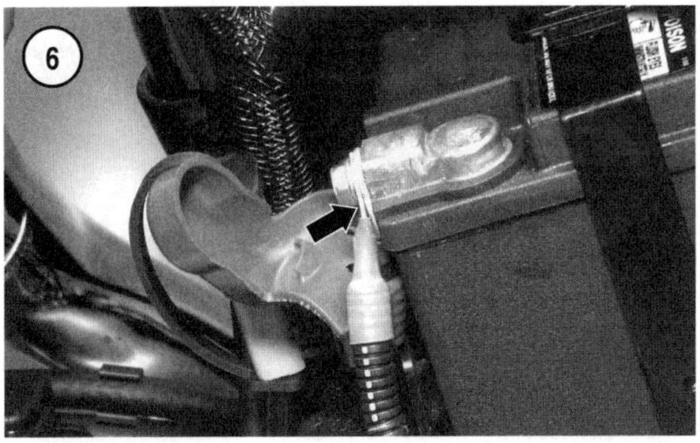

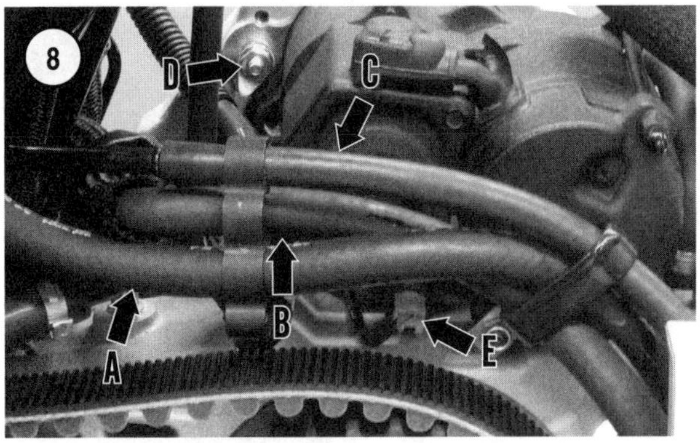

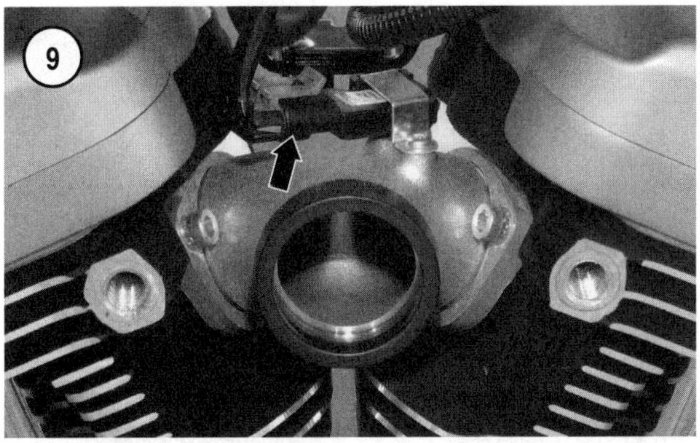

CAUTION

After disconnecting the negative battery cable end in Step 2, position the cable end so it cannot contact metal parts while disconnecting the battery.

2. Disconnect the negative battery cable end from the stud on top of the crankcase (**Figure 5**).
3. Remove the Maxi-fuse as described in Chapter Nine.
4. Remove the retaining screw and disconnect the positive battery cable and Maxi-fuse cable from the positive battery terminal (**Figure 6**).
5. Place a drain pan underneath the primary drive cover, remove the oil drain plug (**Figure 7**) and allow the transmission oil to drain out. Install the drain plug and tighten to 14-30 ft.-lb. (19-40 N•m).
6. Refer to *Engine Oil and Filter Change* in Chapter Three and drain oil from the oil tank. Do not reconnect the drain hose to the holder on the frame.
7. Remove the exhaust system, including the exhaust mounting bracket, as described in Chapter Eight.
8. Refer to Chapter Fourteen and remove the rider and passenger footrests and linkage from both sides.
9. Refer to *Clutch Cable* in Chapter Six and detach the clutch cable from the engine.
10. Disconnect the oil feed hose (A, **Figure 8**), return hose (B) and vent hose (C) from the oil tank.
11. Refer to Chapter Seven and remove the drive sprocket and drive belt.
12. Remove the fuel tank as described in Chapter Eight.
13. Remove the carburetor as described in Chapter Eight. Position the throttle cables so they are out of the way.
14. Remove the ignition coil as described in Chapter Nine.
15. Remove the crank position sensor (CKP) as described in Chapter Nine. Do not disconnect the sensor, but place it in a protected position out of the way. Plug the hole in the crankcase.
16. Disconnect the following electrical connectors:
   a. Manifold absolute pressure sensor connector (**Figure 9**).
   b. Neutral indicator switch connector (**Figure 10**).

NOTE

To improve access to the voltage regulator and oil pressure switch connectors, remove the oil filter.

   c. Voltage regulator connectors (A, **Figure 11**).
   d. Oil pressure switch connector (B, **Figure 11**).
   e. Vehicle speed sensor connector (A, **Figure 12**).
   f. Ground connectors (D, **Figure 8**).
   g. Starter cable (B, **Figure 12**).

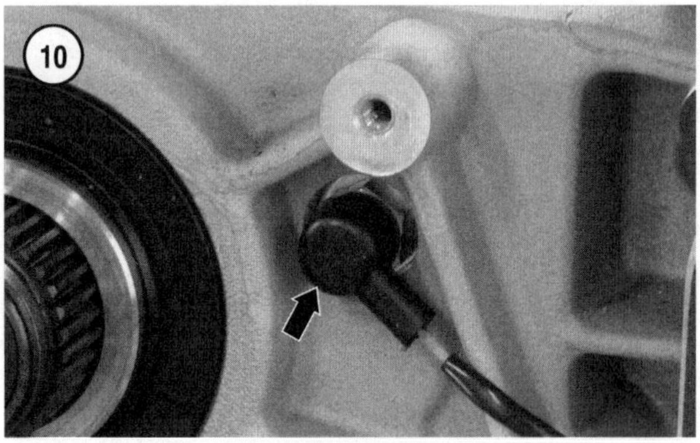

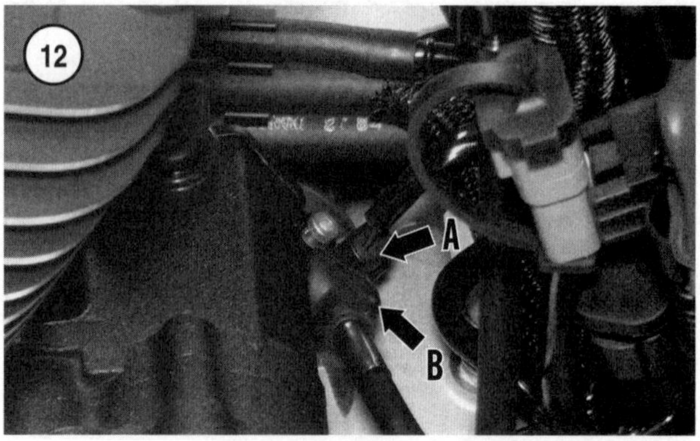

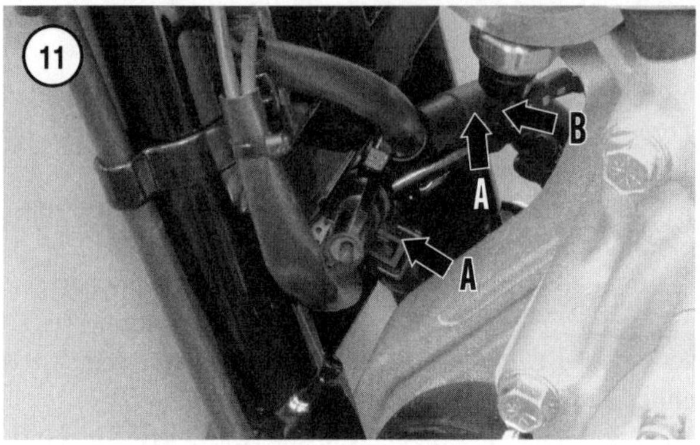

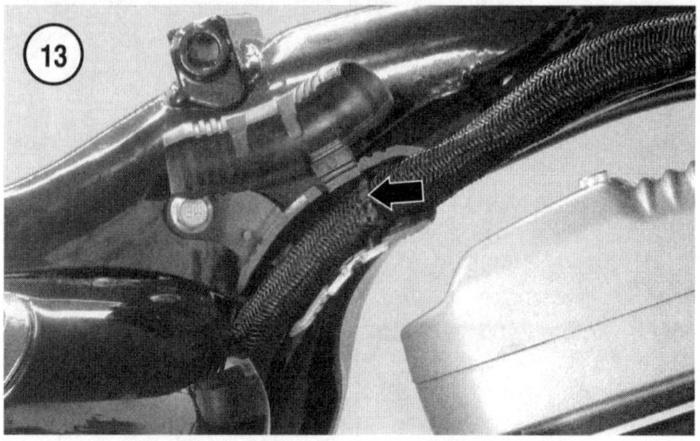

h. Starter relay connector (E, **Figure 8**).

17. On XL1200C models, remove the horn.

NOTE

The wiring harness bracket on the top frame tube must be moved to prevent interference with the cylinder head during engine removal and installation.

18. Open the wiring harness guides on each side of the frame adjacent to the rear cylinder. Cut the tie wrap around the wiring harnesses (**Figure 13**). This will provide additional harness free play.

19. Move the wiring harness bracket on the top frame tube (A, **Figure 14**) forward so it disengages from the bracket post (B).

20. On California models, remove the EVAP canister and hoses.

21. Remove the rear stabilizer link bolts (A, **Figure 15**), ground strap (B), link (C) and spacer (D).

22. Remove the bolt securing the upper stabilizer link to the engine (A, **Figure 16**).

23. Remove the stabilizer bracket mounting bolts and remove the link and bracket assembly (B, **Figure 16**). If necessary, remove the horn as described in Chapter Nine.

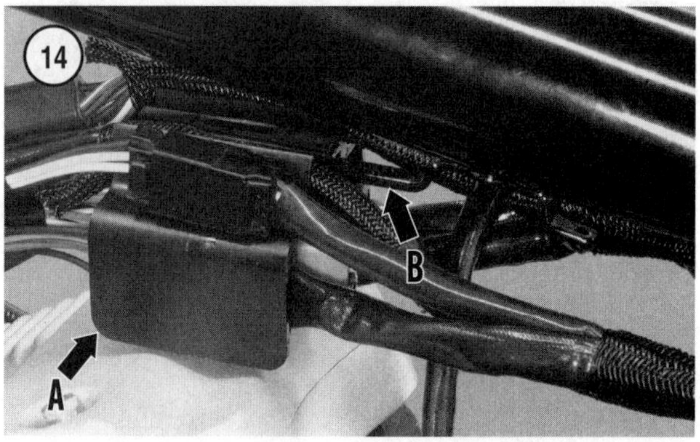

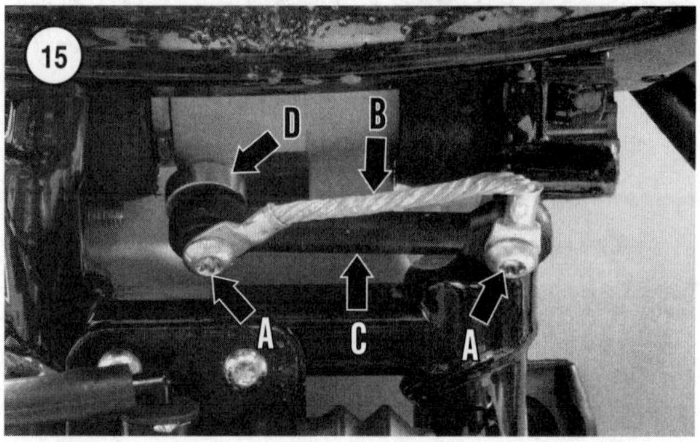

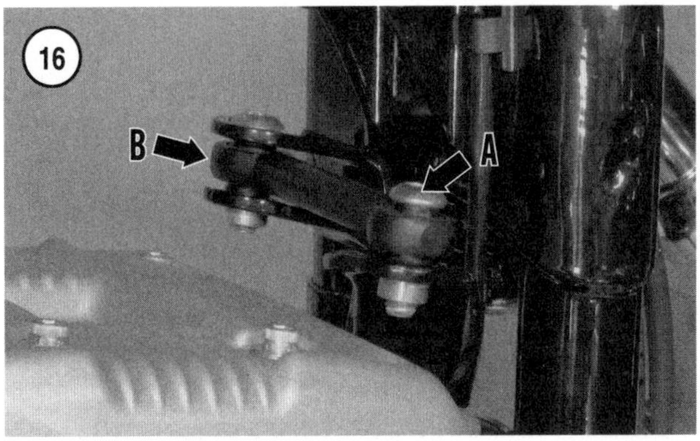

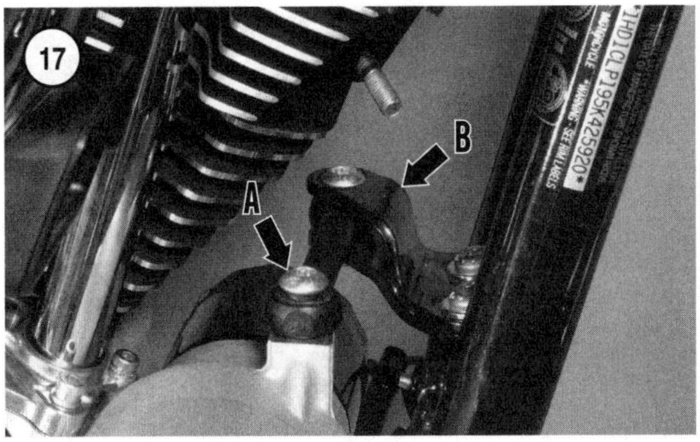

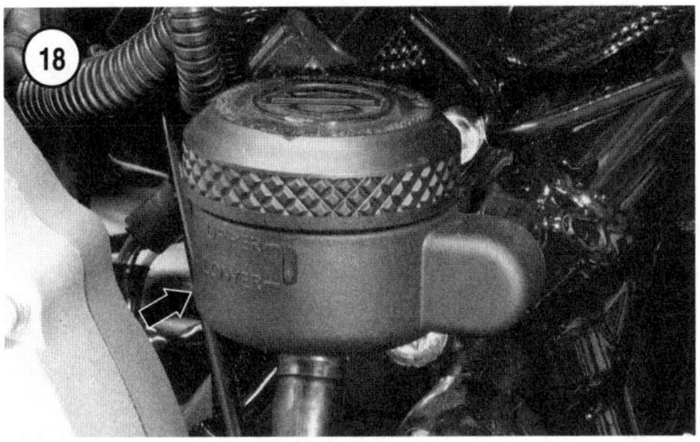

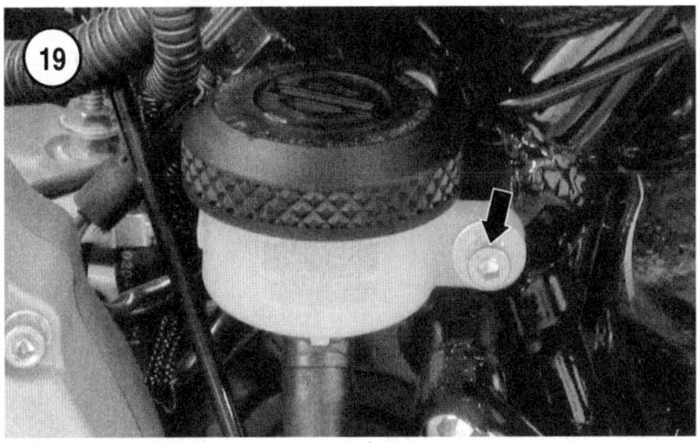

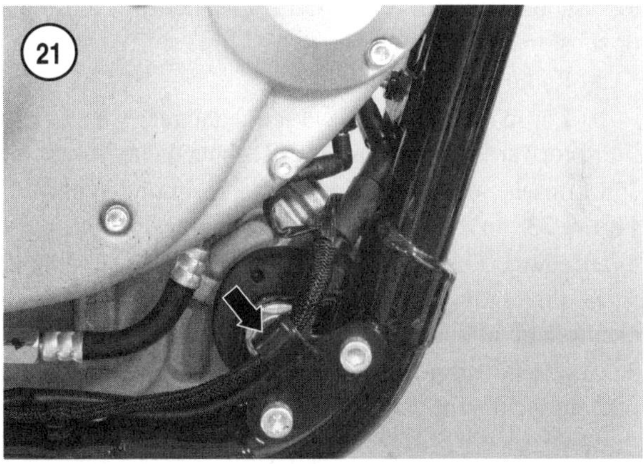

24. Remove the bolt securing the lower stabilizer link to the engine (A, **Figure 17**).

25. Remove the stabilizer bracket mounting bolts and remove the link and bracket assembly (B, **Figure 17**).

26. Remove the rear brake reservoir cover (**Figure 18**).

27. Remove the rear brake reservoir retaining bolt (**Figure 19**) and suspend the reservoir out of the way. Keep the brake reservoir upright so air does not enter the brake fluid. The brake system must be bled if air enters the system.

28. Disconnect the connectors from the rear brake light switch (A, **Figure 20**).

29. Remove the rear brake light switch mounting bolt (B, **Figure 20**), then carefully move the switch out of the way. Do not bend or damage the brake tubing.

30. On XL883, XL883L, XL883R, XL1200L and XL1200R models, remove the wire retaining clip bolts, then remove the clip (**Figure 21**).

NOTE

*The wiring harness may be retained either by clips (A, **Figure 22**) on the frame or wire retainers that fit into holes (B) in the frame.*

31. Disengage the wiring harness located on the lower frame tubes from the clips on the tubes or from the wiring retainer holes. Move the wiring harness out of the way.

NOTE
Because the rear engine mount also serves as the swing arm pivot, it is necessary to support the rear of the frame because the swing arm must disengage from the frame. Depending on the equipment available, it may be easier to remove the rear wheel from the swing arm, or leave the rear wheel installed.

32. Support the rear of the frame, then perform substep a or substep b.
   a. Remove the rear wheel.
   b. Loosen the axle nut and move the rear wheel fully forward in the swing arm. Tighten the axle nut.

33. Loosen—do not remove—the mounting bolts (A, **Figure 23**) on the front engine mount bracket.
34. Remove the swing arm bolts (**Figure 24**) on both sides, then move the swing arm rearward sufficiently to clear the pivot bosses.
35. Loosen—do not remove—the mounting bolts on the rear engine mount bracket (A, **Figure 25**).

CAUTION
Make sure the jack or lift used in Step 36 will not damage the engine crankcase due to improper support points.

36. Place a suitable jack or lift under the engine, then raise the engine sufficiently to remove engine weight from the engine mounts.
37. Remove the front engine mount bolt (B, **Figure 23**).
38. Remove the oil tank vent line.
39. Remove the rear engine mount bracket bolts (A, **Figure 25**), then remove the bracket (B).
40. Remove the front engine mount bracket bolts (A, **Figure 23**), then remove the bracket (C).
41. Make sure everything has been disconnected and there are no obstructions to engine removal.

WARNING
The following steps require the aid of a helper to safely remove the engine assembly from the frame.

CAUTION
Place tape or other protective material on the frame and engine to prevent scratches or other damage during removal and installation.

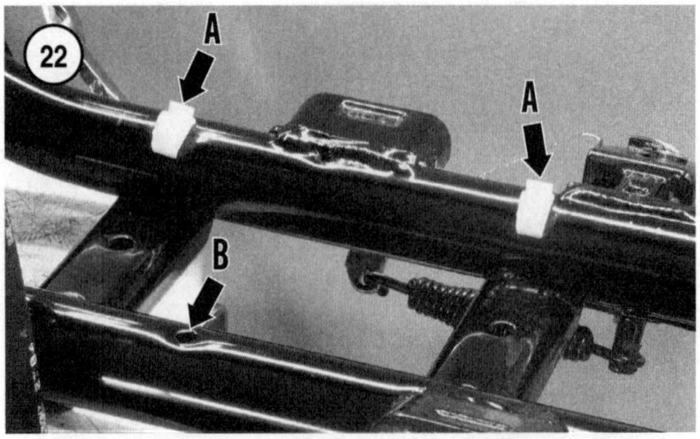

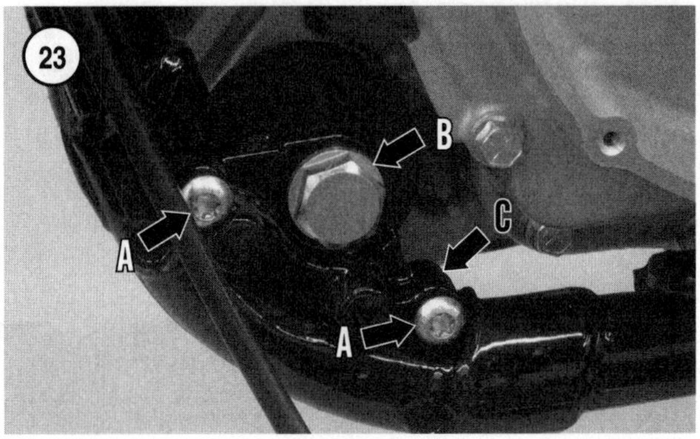

42. Lift the engine out by moving the rear of the engine out first, then separate the front of the engine from the frame.
43. Move the engine to a workbench or engine stand.

Inspection

After engine removal, perform the following.
1. Inspect the frame for cracks or other damage. If found, have the frame inspected by a Harley-Davidson dealership or frame alignment specialist.
2. Clean the frame before installing the engine.
3. If paint has been removed from the frame during engine removal or cleaning, touch it up as required.
4. Remove the oil tank and thoroughly flush. Then reinstall the oil tank and plug the oil hoses to prevent contamination.
5. Replace any worn or damaged oil hoses and clamps.
6. Check the exposed hoses and cables for chafing or other damage. Replace loose, missing or damaged hose clamps and cable ties.
7. Check all engine mounting fasteners for corrosion and thread damage. Clean each fastener in solvent to remove oil and threadlock residue. Replace worn or damaged fasteners before reassembly.

8. Inspect the wiring harness for signs of damage that may have occurred when removing the engine. Repair or replace damaged wires as required.

Installation

CAUTION
*Before engine installation, check the wiring harness clips (A, **Figure 22**) on the frame. Replace faulty clips.*

1. Make sure the engine mounts are correctly installed. Refer to *Engine Mounting System* in this chapter. The front mounts must be installed prior to engine installation. The rear mounts are installed during engine installation.

2. Place tape or other protective material on the frame and engine to prevent scratches or other damage during installation.

CAUTION
Support the engine in the frame using a suitable jack or lift so the engine can be moved as needed to align the engine mounts.

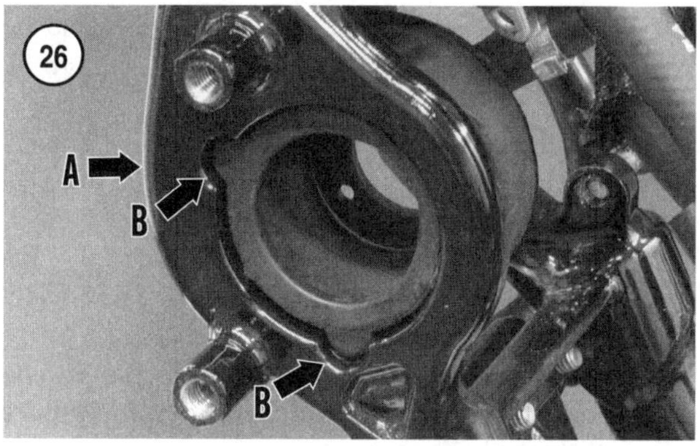

3. Install the right, rear engine mount (A, **Figure 26**) into the frame. The mount bosses must fit into the frame notches (B, **Figure 26**).
4. Install the engine into the frame. First insert the front of the engine while simultaneously guiding the swing arm pivot shaft into the right rear mount.
5. Install the left rear engine mount into the bracket so the mount bosses fit into the notches in the bracket.
6. Install the bracket (B, **Figure 25**) so the mount fits around the swing arm pivot shaft, then install the bracket retaining bolts (A). Do not tighten the bolts.
7. Install the front engine mount bracket (C, **Figure 23**) and bolts (A). Do not tighten the bolts.
8. Install the front engine mount bolt (B, **Figure 23**), but do not tighten.
9. Make sure the front engine mount fits properly, then tighten the mounting bracket bolts (A, **Figure 23**) to 25-35 ft.-lb. (34-47 N•m).
10. Make sure the rear engine mount/swing arm pivot fits properly, then tighten the mounting bracket bolts (A, **Figure 25**) to 25-35 ft.-lb. (34-47 N•m).
11. Install the oil tank vent line.
12. Move the swing arm so it aligns with the swing arm pivot shaft. Install the swing arm bolts (**Figure 24**) on both sides and tighten to 60-70 ft.-lb. (82-95 N•m).
13. Remove the nut on the front engine mount bolt and apply Loctite 243 to the threads. Tighten the front engine mount bolt (B, **Figure 23**) to 60-70 ft.-lb. (82-95 N•m).
14. Install the rear stabilizer link (C, **Figure 15**), spacer (D), ground strap (B) and bolts (A). Note that the left bolt is longer. Tighten the bolts to 25-35 ft.-lb. (34-47 N•m).
15. If removed, install the rear wheel.
16. On California models, install the EVAP canister and hoses.
17. Install the front, lower stabilizer bracket and link assembly (B, **Figure 17**). Tighten the bracket bolts to 25-35 ft.-lb. (34-47 N•m).

18. Install the bolt securing the lower stabilizer link to the engine (A, **Figure 17**). Tighten the bolts to 25-35 ft.-lb. (34-47 N•m).
19. Install the front upper stabilizer bracket and link assembly (B, **Figure 16**). Tighten the bracket bolts to 25-35 ft.-lb. (34-47 N•m).
20. Install the bolt securing the upper stabilizer link to the engine (A, **Figure 16**). Tighten the bolts to 25-35 ft.-lb. (34-47 N•m).
21. On XL883, XL883L, XL883R, XL1200L and XL1200R models, install the wire retaining clip (**Figure 21**). Tighten the bolts securely.
22. Install the wiring harness located on the lower frame tubes into the clips on the tubes or the wiring retainer holes. Make sure the harness is secure. Replace any faulty clips or retainers.
23. Install the rear brake light switch. Tighten the mounting bolt (B, **Figure 20**) to 72-120 in.-lb. (9-13 N•m).
24. Attach the connectors (A, **Figure 20**) to the rear brake light switch.
25. Move the rear brake reservoir into its original position. Tighten the retaining bolt (**Figure 19**) to 20-25 in.-lb. (2.2-2.8 N•m).
26. Install the rear brake reservoir cover (**Figure 18**).
27. Move the wiring harness bracket on the top frame tube (A, **Figure 14**) onto the bracket post (B).
28. Attach the wiring harnesses on each side of the frame to the harness guide using a tie wrap (**Figure 13**). Close the harness guide and engage the locking tabs.
29. On XL1200C models, install the horn.
30. Connect the following electrical connectors:
   a. Manifold absolute pressure sensor connector (**Figure 9**).
   b. Neutral indicator switch connector (**Figure 10**).
   c. Voltage regulator connectors (A, **Figure 11**).
   d. Oil pressure switch connector (B, **Figure 11**).
   e. Vehicle speed sensor connector (A, **Figure 12**).
   f. Ground connectors (D, **Figure 8**).
   g. Starter cable (B, **Figure 12**).
   h. Starter relay connector (E, **Figure 8**).
31. Install the crank position sensor (CKP) as described in Chapter Nine.
32. Install the ignition coil as described in Chapter Nine.
33. Install the carburetor as described in Chapter Eight.
34. Install the fuel tank as described in Chapter Eight.
35. Install the drive sprocket and drive belt as described in Chapter Seven.

CAUTION
Make sure the oil hoses are properly connected. Refer to ***Oil Tank*** *in Chapter Four.*

(27) TAPPETS AND PUSHRODS

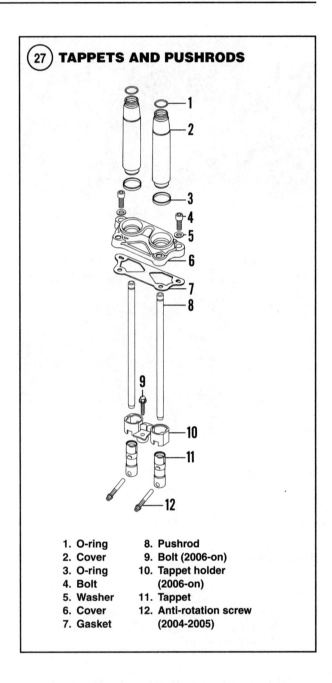

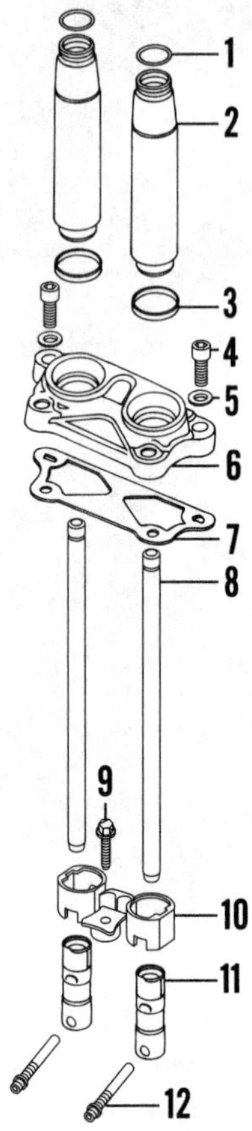

1. O-ring
2. Cover
3. O-ring
4. Bolt
5. Washer
6. Cover
7. Gasket
8. Pushrod
9. Bolt (2006-on)
10. Tappet holder (2006-on)
11. Tappet
12. Anti-rotation screw (2004-2005)

CAUTION
If the oil hose fittings were removed from the oil pump, apply Hylomar or Teflon Pipe Sealant to the fitting threads prior to installation.

36. Connect the oil tank feed hose (A, **Figure 8**), return hose (B) and vent hose (C) to the oil tank.
37. Attach the clutch cable to the engine as described in Chapter Six.
38. Install the rider and passenger footrests, and linkage as described in Chapter Fourteen.

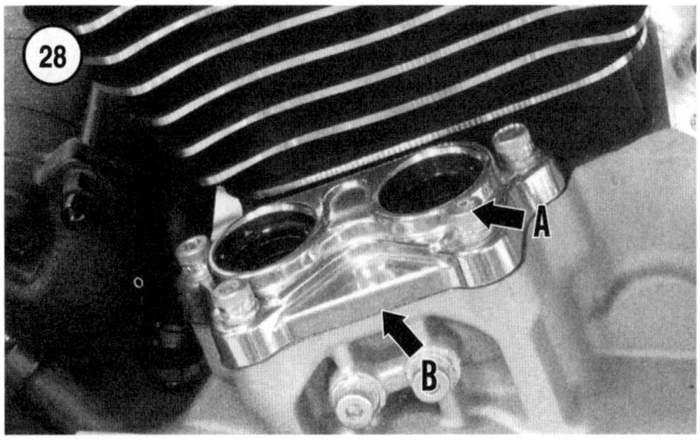

28

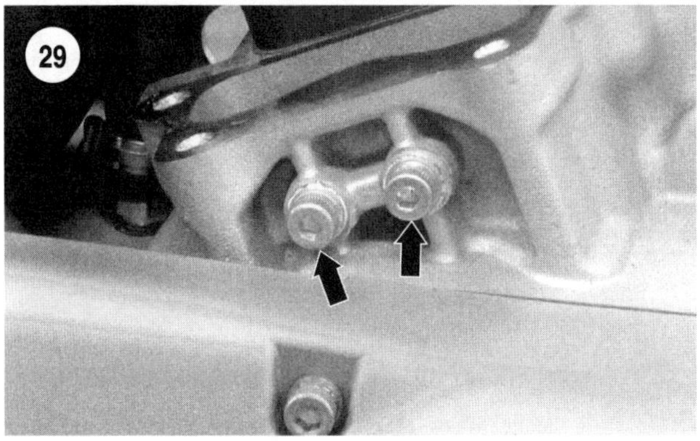

29

30

39. Install the exhaust system as described in Chapter Eight.

CAUTION
Before connecting the positive battery cable end, make sure the negative cable end is not contacting metal parts.

40. Connect the positive battery cable and Maxi-fuse cable to the positive battery terminal (**Figure 6**). Position the cable ends so the battery cable contacts the battery terminal and the Maxi-fuse cable contacts the bolt head. Tighten the bolt to 40-50 in.-lb. (4.5-5.7 N•m).
41. Install the Maxi-fuse as described in Chapter Nine.
42. Connect the negative battery cable end to the stud on top of the crankcase (**Figure 5**). Tighten the retaining nut to 55-75 in.-lb. (6.2-8.4 N•m).
43. Install the seat as described in Chapter Fourteen.
44. If removed, install a new oil filter.
45. Fill the transmission with oil as described in Chapter Three.
46. Fill the engine with oil as described in Chapter Three.
47. Start the engine and check for oil leaks.
48. Operate all controls and adjust as needed.
49. Shift the transmission into gear and check clutch and transmission operation.
50. Slowly test ride the motorcycle to ensure all systems are operating correctly.

VALVE TAPPETS

During engine operation, the tappets are pumped full of engine oil, thus taking up play in the valve train. When the engine is turned off, the tappets leak down after a period of time as some of the oil drains out. When the engine is started, the tappets click momentarily until they refill with oil. The tappets are working properly if they stop clicking after the engine runs for a few minutes. If the clicking persists, there may be a problem in the tappet(s).

On 2004-2005 models, anti-rotation pins retain the valve tappets. On 2006-on models, a holder secures the valve tappets.

Refer to **Figure 27**.

Removal

The cylinder head must be removed to access the tappets. After removal, store the tappets in order so they can be installed in their original positions.

1. Remove the pushrods and pushrod covers as described in Chapter Four.
2. Using a ball-end type Allen wrench, remove the tappet cover retaining bolts (A, **Figure 28**), then remove the cover (B).

NOTE
It may be necessary to use an L-shaped tool to withdraw the tappet in Step 3A. Push the tool tip into the groove at the inner top of the tappet.

3A. On 2004-2005 models, remove the anti-rotation screw for each tappet (**Figure 29**). Extract the valve tappet (**Figure 30**).

3B. On 2006-on models, remove the tappet holder retaining bolt (9, **Figure 27**). Lift out the tappet holder (10, **Figure 27**), then remove the tappets from the crankcase.

4. If tappet inspection is not necessary, store the tappet upright in a container of clean engine oil.

5. Remove the cover gasket, then cover the opening to prevent entry of debris.

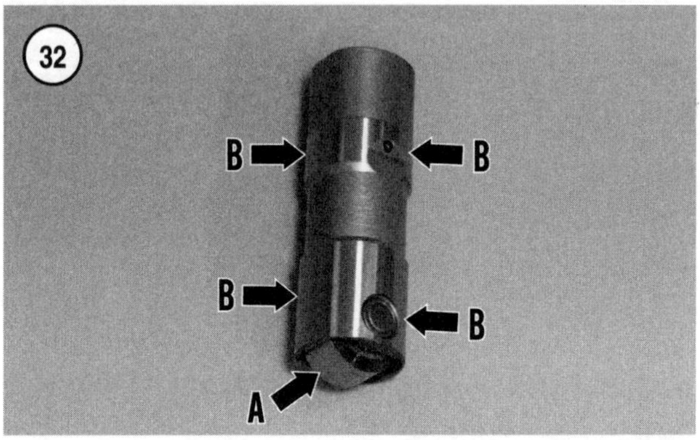

Inspection

CAUTION
Place the tappets on a clean, lint-free cloth during inspection. Place inspected tappets in a container of clean engine oil.

1. Check the pushrod socket (**Figure 31**) in the top of the tappet for wear or damage.

2. Check the tappet roller (A, **Figure 32**) for pitting, scoring, galling or excessive wear. If the roller is worn excessively, check the mating cam lobe for the same wear condition.

3. Clean the tappet roller with cleaner. Then measure the roller clearance on pin and end clearance, and compare them to the specifications in **Table 1**. Replace the tappet assembly if either part is not within specification.

4. Determine the tappet-to-crankcase bore clearance as follows:

   a. Measure the tappet bore in the crankcase and record the measurement.

   b. Measure the tappet outside diameter (B, **Figure 32**) and record the measurement.

   c. Subtract substep b from substep a to determine the tappet-to-crankcase bore clearance, then compare the measurement to the service limit in **Table 1**. Replace the tappet or crankcase if the clearance is worn to the service limit.

5. If a tappet does not show visual damage, it may be contaminated with dirt or have internal damage. If so, replace it. The tappets are not serviceable.

6. After inspecting the tappets, store them in a container filled with clean engine oil until installation.

7. If most of the oil has drained out of the tappet, refill it with a pump-type oil can through the oil hole in the side of the tappet.

8. Clean all gasket material from the mating surfaces of the crankcase and the tappet cover.

9. Inspect the tappet cover (**Figure 33**) for cracks or damage.

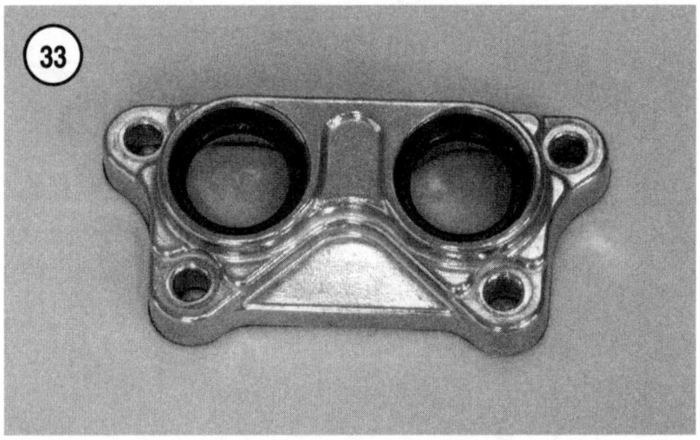

Installation

NOTE
The cam for each valve tappet must be positioned so the base circle (lowest section) will contact the tappet.

1. Remove the cover over the crankcase opening.

2. Remove two of the tappets from the oil-filled container and keep them vertical.

3A. On 2004-2005 models, proceed as follows:

   a. Install the tappets (**Figure 30**) into the crankcase receptacles with the flat surfaces facing toward the front and rear of the engine.

(34) **GEARCASE ASSEMBLY**

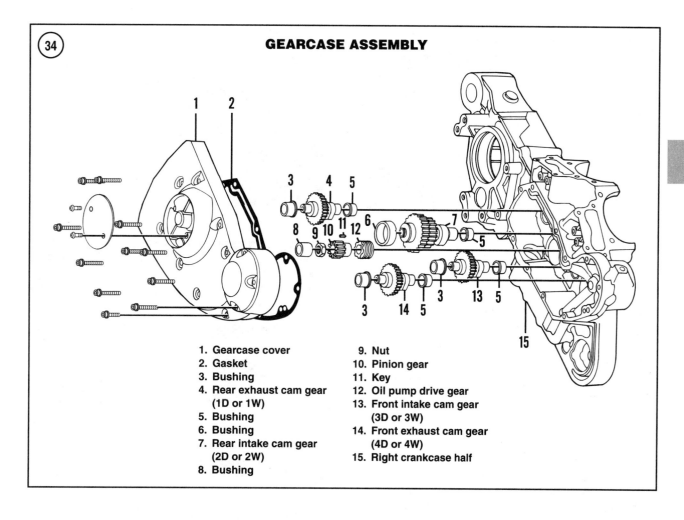

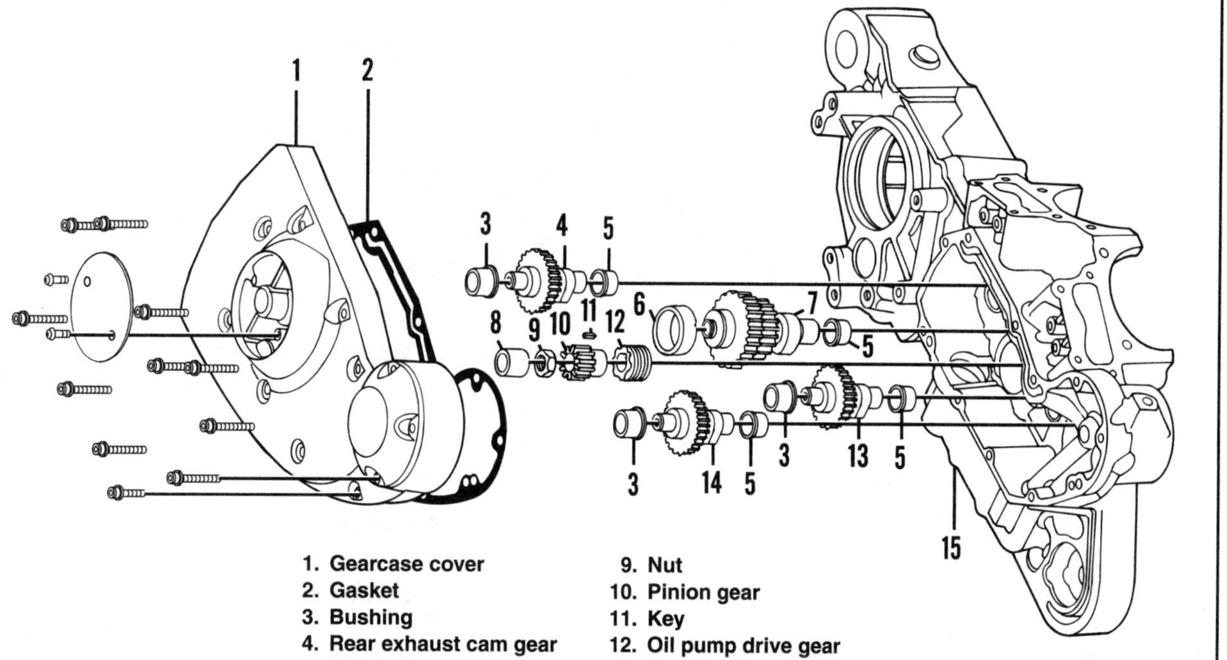

1. Gearcase cover
2. Gasket
3. Bushing
4. Rear exhaust cam gear (1D or 1W)
5. Bushing
6. Bushing
7. Rear intake cam gear (2D or 2W)
8. Bushing
9. Nut
10. Pinion gear
11. Key
12. Oil pump drive gear
13. Front intake cam gear (3D or 3W)
14. Front exhaust cam gear (4D or 4W)
15. Right crankcase half

CAUTION
Failure to install the anti-rotation pin will allow the tappet to rotate off the camshaft lobe, and cause internal engine damage.

b. Install the anti-rotation pin (**Figure 29**). Make sure it is seated correctly within the crankcase receptacle and against the flats on the tappet. Tighten the pin to 55-65 in.-lb. (6.2-7.3 N•m).

c. Rotate the engine until both tappets for the cylinder being serviced seat onto the cam's lowest position (base circle). The tappets should be an equal distance below the top surface of the crankcase.

3B. On 2006-on models, proceed as follows:

a. Install the tappets into the tappet holder (10, **Figure 27**) so the flat surfaces on the upper end of the tappets will face toward the front and rear of the engine when the holder is installed in the crankcase.

b. Install the tappet holder and tappets into the crankcase.

c. Install the tappet holder retaining bolt. Tighten the bolt to 80-110 in.-lb. (9.0-12.4 N•m).

4. Install a new tappet cover gasket.
5. Install the tappet cover (B, **Figure 28**) and tighten the cover bolts (A) to 80-110 in.-lb. (9.0-12.4 N•m).
6. Install the pushrod covers and pushrods as described in Chapter Four.

GEARCASE COVER AND TIMING GEARS

The gearcase assembly (**Figure 34**) consists of the following components:

1. Four cam gears.
2. Four cam gear bushings (installed in right crankcase half).
3. Four cam gear bushings (installed in gearcase cover).
4. Pinion gear.
5. Oil pump drive gear.
6. Oil seal (installed in gearcase cover).

The cam gears are closely matched for optimum operation and performance.

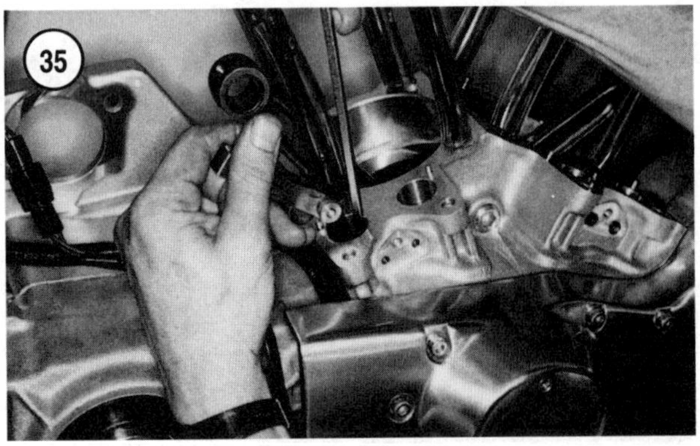

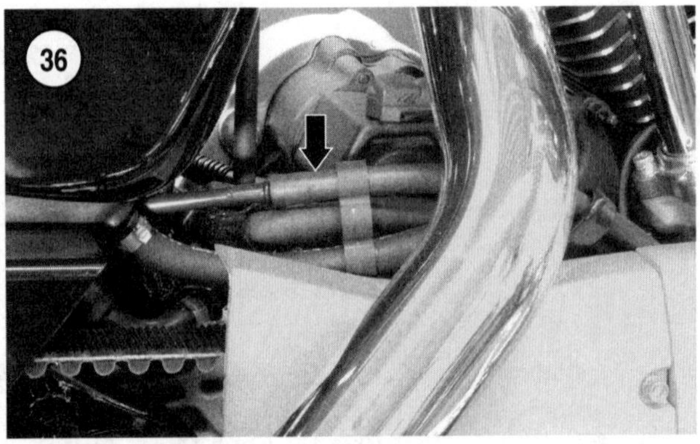

Removal

1. Remove the front exhaust system as described in Chapter Eight.
2. Remove the right footpeg assembly as described in Chapter Fourteen.
3. Refer to *Valve Tappets* in this chapter and remove the pushrods and valve tappets.
4. Before removing the gearcase cover, check cam gear end play as follows:
   a. Rotate the crankshaft counterclockwise so the cam being checked has its lobe facing up.
   b. Pry the cam gear toward the gearcase cover with a wide-blade screwdriver.
   c. Measure the gap between the cam gear shaft thrust face and the bushing in the crankcase with a feeler gauge (**Figure 35**). Record the end play measurement.
   d. Repeat for each cam gear.
   e. If the end clearance is incorrect, replace the bushing and/or cam gear as described in this section.
5. Place an empty oil pan underneath the crankcase cover.
6. Disconnect and plug the oil vent hose (**Figure 36**). Remove the oil hose from the hose clips.

NOTE

The gearcase cover is retained by different length bolts. Create a drawing on cardboard in the shape of the gearcase, then punch each screw through the cardboard at its location.

7. Remove the gearcase cover mounting bolts (**Figure 37**).
8. Remove the gearcase cover from the engine. If the cover is stuck in place, tap the cover lightly with a soft-faced hammer to free it from the gasket or sealer.
9. Remove and discard the gasket.

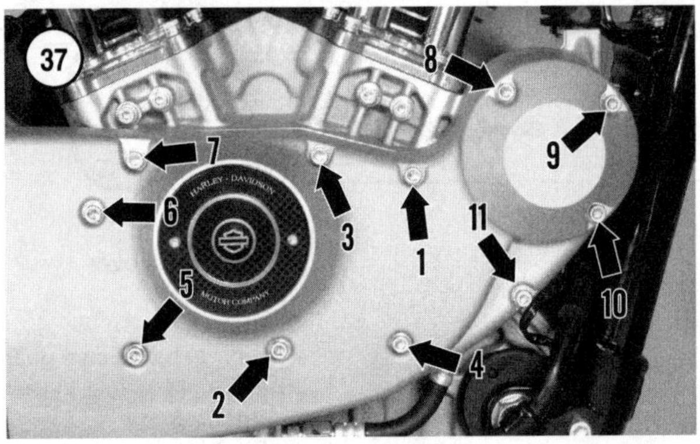

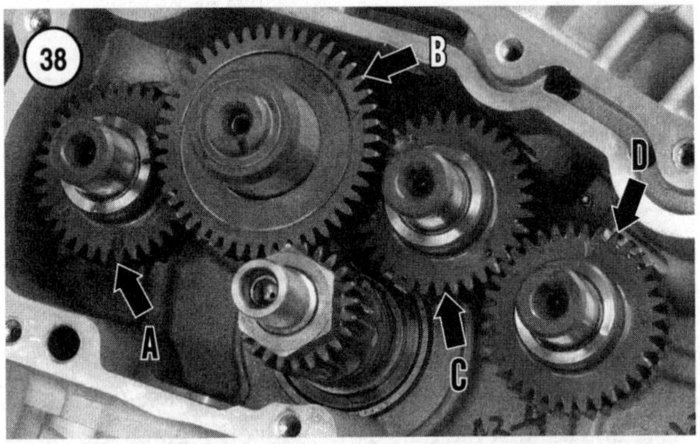

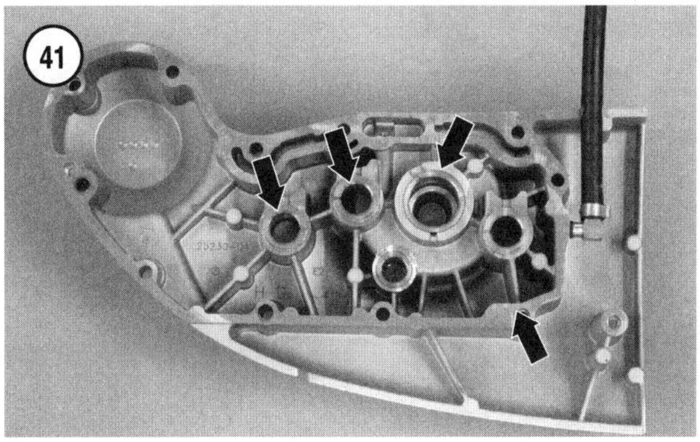

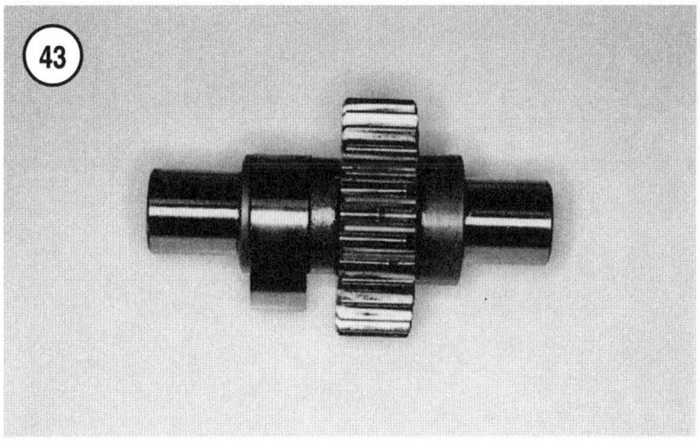

CAUTION
After removing a cam gear, label and then place it in a container in order to reinstall it in its original position.

10. Remove and identify each cam gear (**Figure 38**):
    a. Rear exhaust cam gear (A, **Figure 38**).
    b. Rear intake cam gear (B, **Figure 38**).
    c. Front intake cam gear (C, **Figure 38**).
    d. Front exhaust cam gear (D, **Figure 38**).
11. Install crankshaft locking tool JIM'S 1665 or HD-43984 (A, **Figure 39**).
12. Loosen, then remove the pinion gear nut (B, **Figure 39**). The pinion gear nut is secured with Loctite 272.
13. Slide the pinion gear (A, **Figure 40**) and oil pump drive gear (B) off the pinion shaft. Do not lose the Woodruff key in the pinion shaft.

Inspection

1. Thoroughly clean the gearcase compartment, cover and components with solvent. Blow out all oil passages with compressed air. Make sure all traces of gasket compound are removed from the gasket mating surfaces.
2. Check the pinion gear and cam gear bushings in the gearcase cover (**Figure 41**) for grooving, pitting or other damage. If the bushings appear visibly worn, replace them.
3. Inspect the cam gears (**Figure 42**) for cracks, deep scoring or excessive wear. The gears (**Figure 43**) will show signs of pattern polish , but there should be no other apparent wear or damage.

Cam Gear Identification

1. The cam gear group consists of the following:
    a. Rear exhaust cam gear (A, **Figure 38**).
    b. Rear intake cam gear (B, **Figure 38**).
    c. Front intake cam gear (C, **Figure 38**).
    d. Front exhaust cam gear (D, **Figure 38**).
    e. Pinion gear (A, **Figure 40**).
2. The cam lobes are stamped with a number (1, 2, 3 or 4) and a letter (D or W). Refer to **Figure 44**. The number identifies the cam gear function and location in the engine. The letter identifies engine application. Cam lobes stamped with the letter D are for 883 cc models. Cam lobes stamped with the letter W are for 1200 cc models.
3. The cam lobe markings are as follows:
    a. ID (or W): rear exhaust cam gear.
    b. 2D (or W): rear intake cam gear.
    c. 3D (or W): front intake cam gear.
    d. 4D (or W): front exhaust cam gear.

5

Cam Gear and Pinion Gear Bushing Inspection

Excessive cam gear and pinion gear bushing clearance can cause excessive cam gear backlash.

1. Measure the cam/pinion gear outside diameter with a micrometer. Record the outside diameter measurement.
2. Measure the corresponding bushing inside diameter with a small hole gauge. Record the inside diameter measurement.
3. Subtract the measurement made in Step 2 from the measurement made in Step 1. The difference is the cam gear- or pinion gear-to-bushing clearance. Refer to **Table 1** for the cam and pinion gear clearances. If clearance is excessive, replace the bushing as described in this section.

Bushing Removal

Gearcase cover (**Figure 41**) and crankcase (**Figure 45**) bushing replacement requires special tools. Incorrect bushing installation will cause increased gear noise and premature wear. Refer bushing service to a Harley-Davidson dealership or service shop.

Installation

1. Apply engine oil to the pinion shaft, oil pump drive gear and pinion shaft gear.
2. Clean the pinion shaft threads and the pinion shaft nut of all threadlock residue.
3. Install the oil pump drive gear Woodruff key (**Figure 46**), if removed.
4. Slide the oil pump drive gear (**Figure 47**) onto the pinion shaft.
5. Align the pinion gear timing mark (A, **Figure 48**) with the center of the pinion shaft keyway (B) and install the gear.
6. Install crankshaft locking tool JIMS 1665 or HD-43984 (A, **Figure 39**).

49

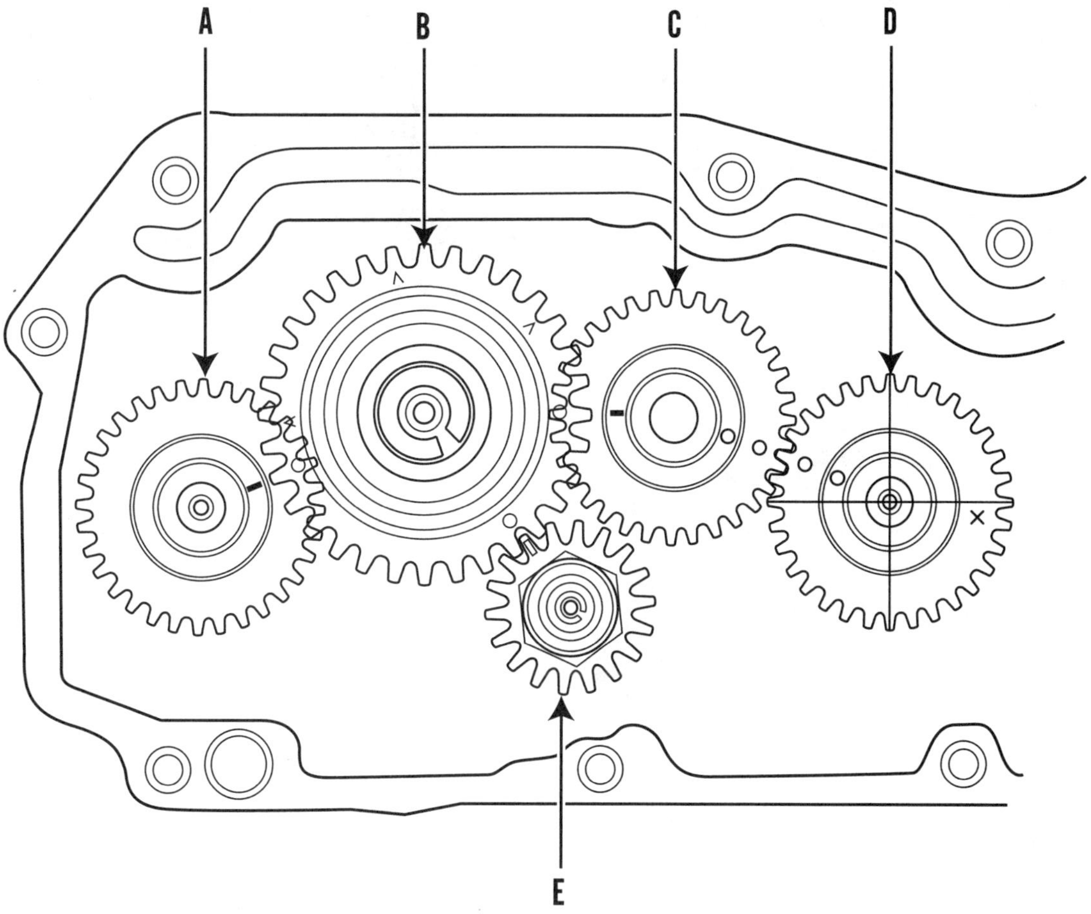

A. Rear exhaust cam gear (1D or 1W)
B. Rear intake cam gear (2D or 2W)
C. Front intake cam gear (3D or 3W)
D. Front exhaust cam gear (4D or 4W)
E. Pinion gear

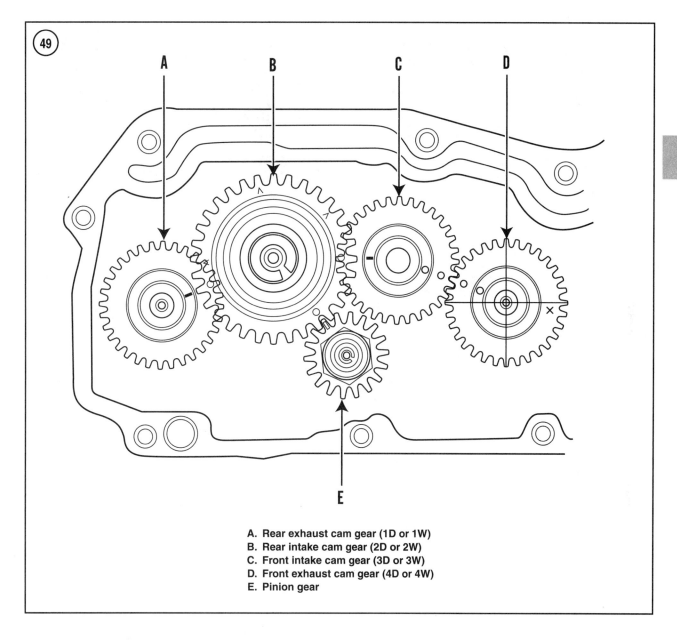

7. Apply Loctite 272 (red) to the pinion shaft nut (B, **Figure 39**) prior to installation. Install the nut and tighten to 35-45 ft. lb. (48-61 N•m).

8. Identify the cam gears as described in this section.

9. Apply engine oil to the bushings, gears and gear shafts prior to installation.

10. Aligning the cam gear timing marks as shown in **Figure 49**, install the cam gears in the following order:

a. Rear exhaust cam gear (A, **Figure 50**).

b. Front intake cam gear (B, **Figure 50**).

c. Rear intake cam gear (**Figure 51**).

d. Front exhaust cam gear (**Figure 52**).

e. Make sure the cam gear timing marks are properly aligned (**Figure 49**).

11. Install a new gearcase cover gasket.
12. Install the gearcase cover.
13. Install the gearcase cover bolts into their correct mounting positions. Tighten the bolts finger-tight at first, then tighten in the sequence shown in **Figure 37** to 80-110 in.-lb. (9.0-12.4 N•m).
14. Check the cam gear end play for each cam gear as described in *Removal*.
15. Install the valve tappets as described in this chapter.
16. Install the footpeg assembly as described in Chapter Fourteen.
17. Install the front exhaust system as described in Chapter Eight.

OIL PUMP

The oil pump (**Figure 53**) is located underneath the front of the engine and can be removed with the engine installed in the frame and without removing the gearcase cover.

The oil pump (**Figure 54**) consists of two sections: a feed pump which supplies oil under pressure to the engine components, and a scavenger pump which returns oil to the oil tank from the engine.

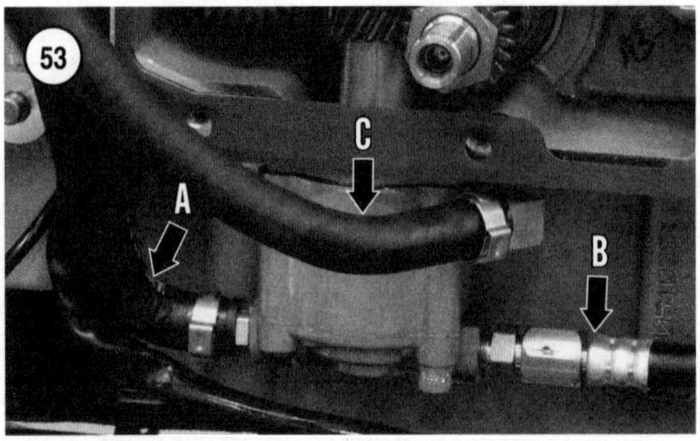

54 **OIL PUMP**

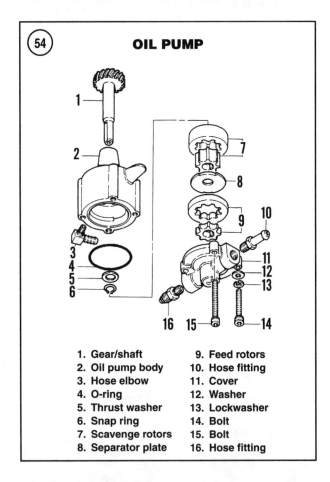

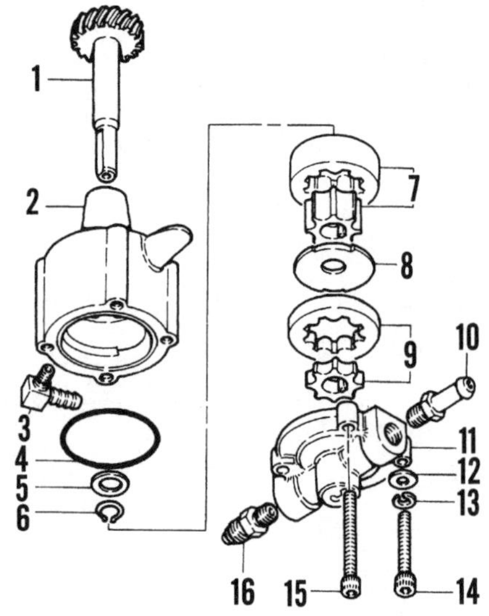

1. Gear/shaft
2. Oil pump body
3. Hose elbow
4. O-ring
5. Thrust washer
6. Snap ring
7. Scavenge rotors
8. Separator plate
9. Feed rotors
10. Hose fitting
11. Cover
12. Washer
13. Lockwasher
14. Bolt
15. Bolt
16. Hose fitting

Removal

CAUTION

Label all gears and Woodruff keys during removal so they can be installed in their original positions.

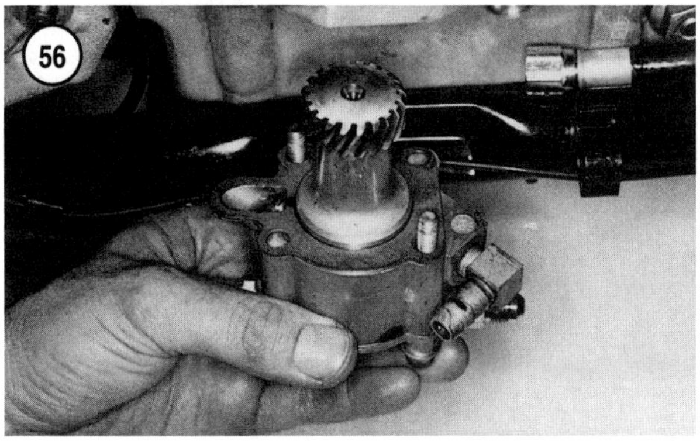

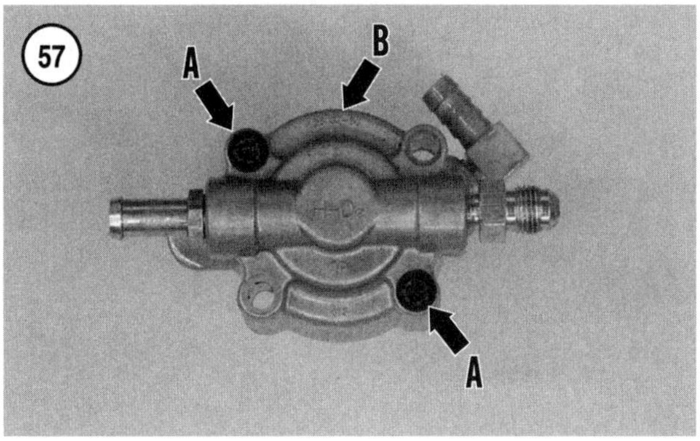

5

1. Remove the front exhaust system as described in Chapter Eight.
2. Remove the right footpeg assembly as described in Chapter Fourteen.
3. Drain the oil tank as described in Chapter Three.
4. Wipe off each oil hose and fitting at the oil pump.
5. Label each oil hose (**Figure 53**) prior to disconnecting it.
   a. Feed hose (A, **Figure 53**) from tank.
   b. Feed hose (B, **Figure 53**) to crankcase.
   c. Oil return hose (C, **Figure 53**).
6. Disconnect the oil hoses from the oil pump. Plug the open end of each line to prevent oil leaks and contamination.
7. Loosen the oil pump mounting bolts (**Figure 55**). Remove the bolts and oil pump from the engine (**Figure 56**).
8. Remove the oil pump gasket.
9. Cover the oil pump opening to keep debris from entering the engine.
10. Store the oil pump in a plastic bag until disassembly or installation.

Disassembly

1. Remove the oil pump housing screws (A, **Figure 57**), lockwashers and flat washers.
2. Remove the oil pump cover (B, **Figure 57**).
3. Remove and discard the O-ring (**Figure 58**).
4. Slide off the feed rotor assembly (**Figure 59**).
5. Remove the separator plate (**Figure 60**).
6. Slide off the scavenge rotor assembly (**Figure 61**).
7. Remove the snap ring (**Figure 62**).
8. Remove the thrust washer (**Figure 63**).
9. Remove the oil pump gear/shaft (**Figure 64**).

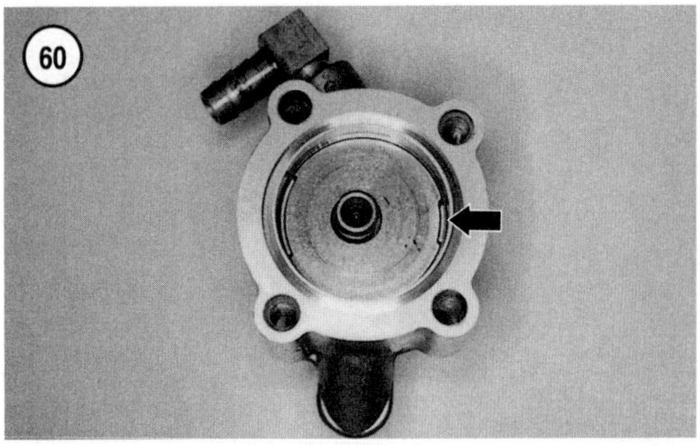
60

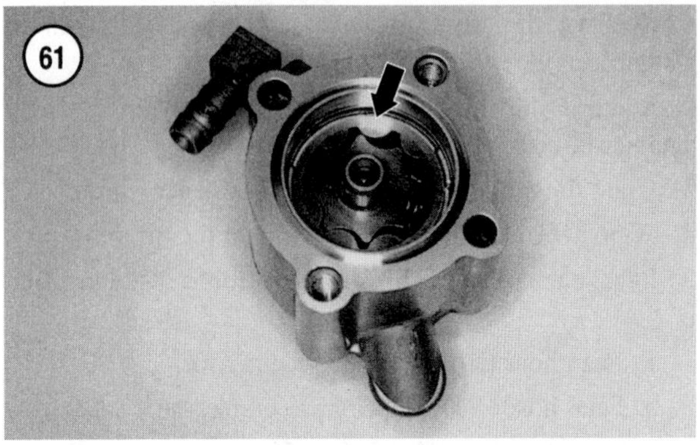
61

Inspection

1. Thoroughly clean all parts in solvent and blow dry. Blow out all oil passages with compressed air. Place cleaned parts on a clean, lint-free cloth during inspection and reassembly.

2. Inspect the cover and body (**Figure 65**) for scratches, scoring or excessive wear. Both rotor inside surfaces will show some scoring, but it should not be excessive. If these areas are heavily scored, replace the oil pump assembly.

3. Inspect the gear/shaft assembly (**Figure 66**) for wear. The gear will show signs of pattern polish, but there should be no other apparent wear or damage.

4. Check the fit of the shaft where it passes through the oil pump body (**Figure 64**). The gear should turn smoothly with no binding or excessive play.

5. Inspect the separator plate (**Figure 67**) for warp, cracks or other damage.

6. Check both rotor sets for scoring, cracks or excessive wear. Refer to **Figure 68**.

7. Measure the thickness of each feed rotor with a micrometer (**Figure 69**). Both rotors must be the same thickness. If they are not the same thickness, replace the feed rotors as a set.

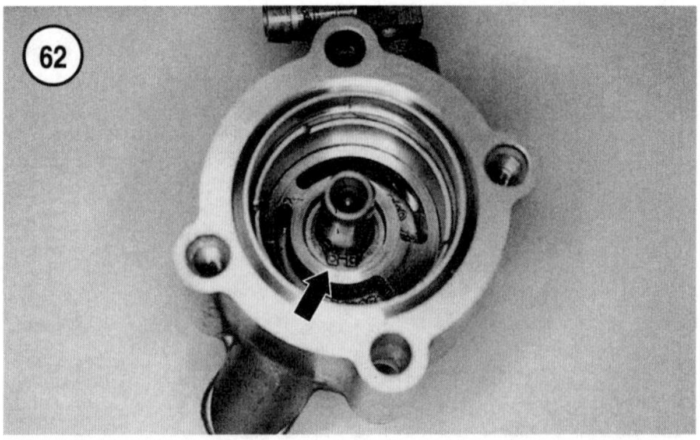
62

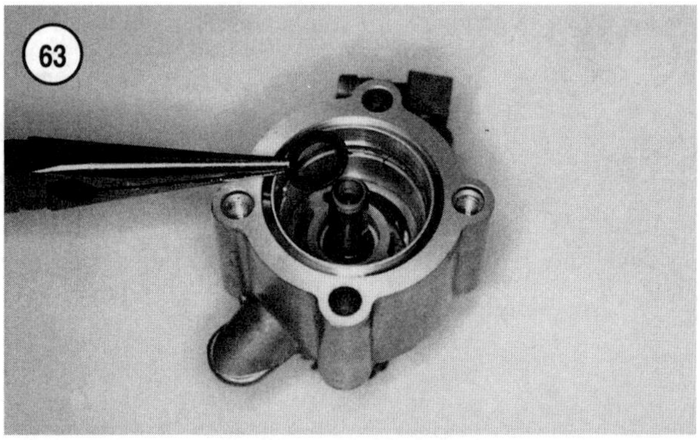
63

64

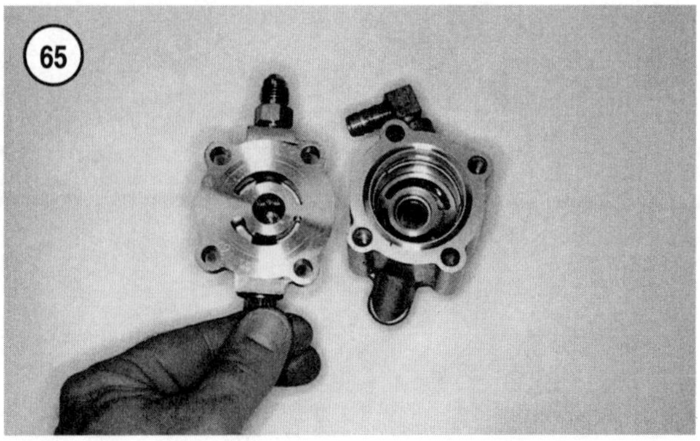
65

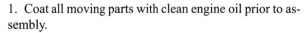

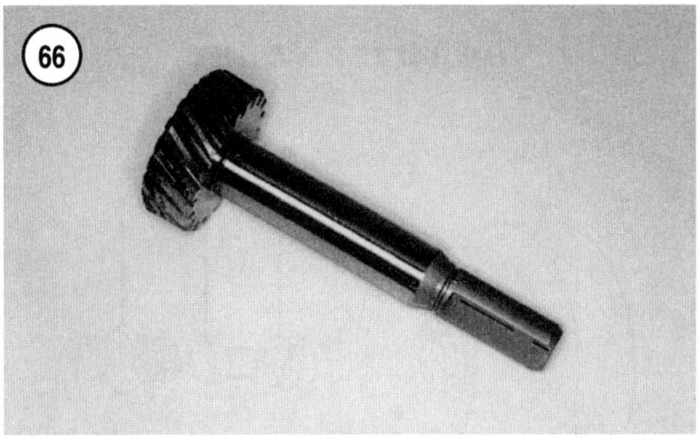

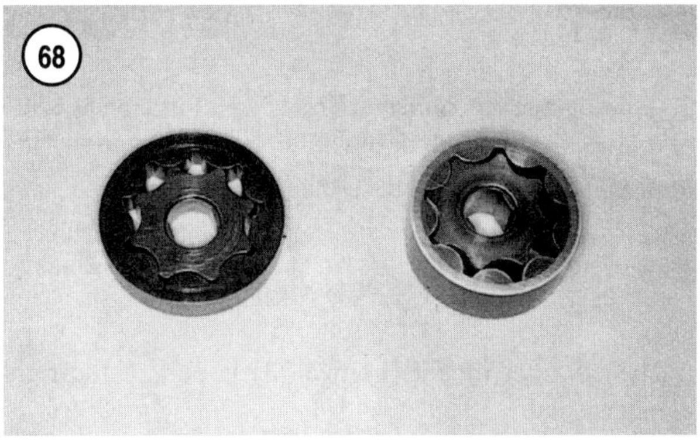

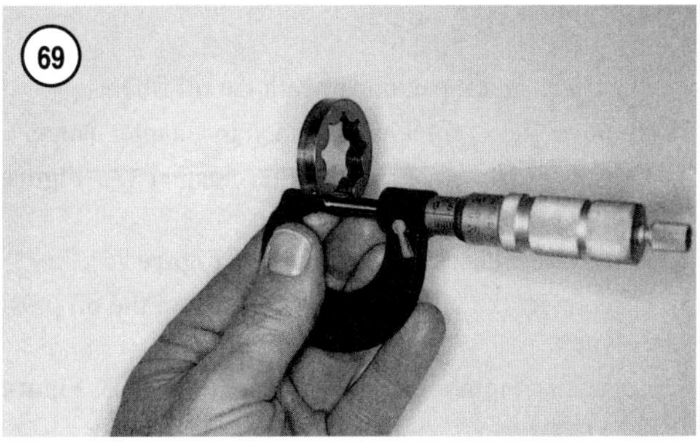

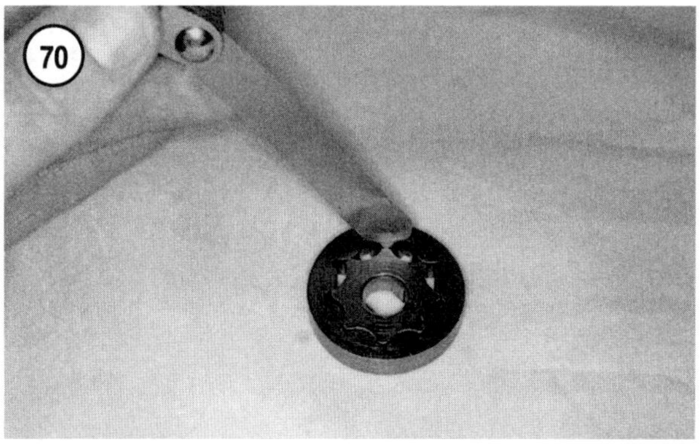

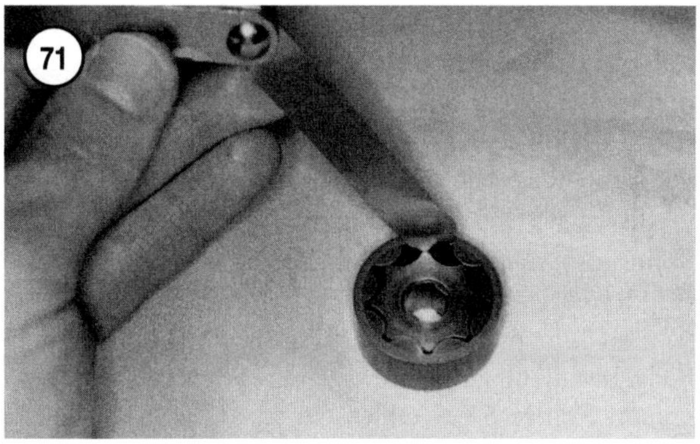

8. Assemble the feed rotors and measure the clearance between the gear teeth with a feeler gauge as shown in **Figure 70**. If the gear clearance is worn to the service limit in **Table 1**, replace the feed rotors as a set.

9. Assemble the scavenge rotors and measure the clearance between the gear teeth with a feeler gauge as shown in **Figure 71**. If the gear clearance is worn to the service limit in **Table 1**, replace the scavenge rotors as a set.

Reassembly

CAUTION
All parts must be clean prior to assembly. If necessary, reclean them.

1. Coat all moving parts with clean engine oil prior to assembly.

2. Install the gear/shaft (**Figure 64**) through the bottom of the oil pump body.

3. Install the thrust washer (**Figure 63**) onto the shaft.

4. Install a *new* snap ring into the shaft groove (**Figure 62**). Make sure the snap ring seats in the groove completely. Turn the gear by hand; it should turn smoothly with no binding or excessive play.

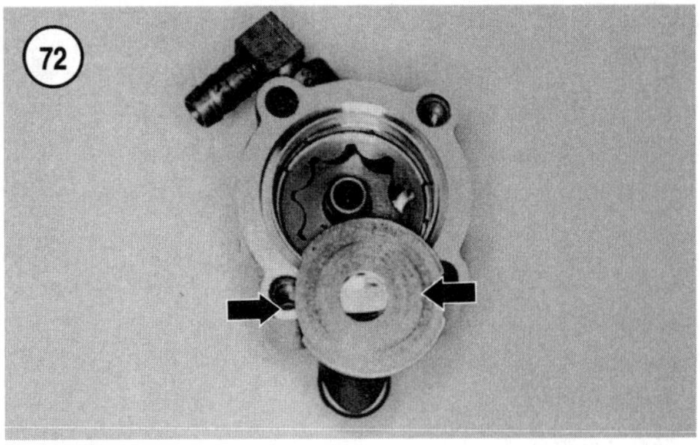

5. Install the inner, then the outer scavenge rotors. Refer to **Figure 61**.
6. Install the separator plate (**Figure 72**) into the oil pump body; align the separator plate slots with the tabs inside the pump body. See **Figure 60**.
7. Install the feed rotors (**Figure 59**) over the shaft.
8. Install a *new* O-ring into the oil pump cover groove (**Figure 58**).
9. Install the pump cover (B, **Figure 57**) onto the pump body. Install oil pump screws, lockwashers and flat washers (A, **Figure 57**). Tighten the screws to 70-80 in.-lb. (7.9-9.0 N•m).
10. Turn the gear by hand; the pump should turn smoothly.

CAUTION
If the oil hose fittings were removed from the oil pump, apply Hylomar or Teflon Pipe Sealant to the fitting threads prior to installation.

Installation

1. Thoroughly clean the oil pump and engine gasket surfaces.
2. Install a *new* oil pump gasket. Then install the oil pump (**Figure 56**) onto the crankcase. Install the oil pump mounting bolts and tighten to 125-150 in.-lb. (14.1-16.9 N•m).

CAUTION
*When installing the original equipment hose clamps, refer to **Hose Clamps** in Chapter Four. A screw-type hose clamp may be substituted.*

CAUTION
If the oil hose fittings were removed from the oil pump, apply Hylomar or Teflon Pipe Sealant to the fitting threads prior to installation.

(73) **OIL FILTER MOUNT**

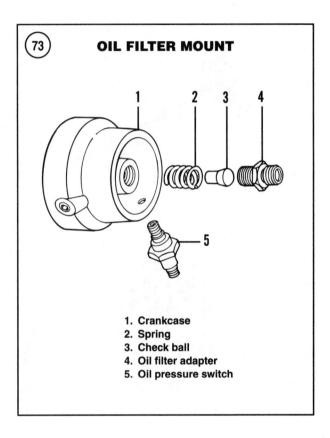

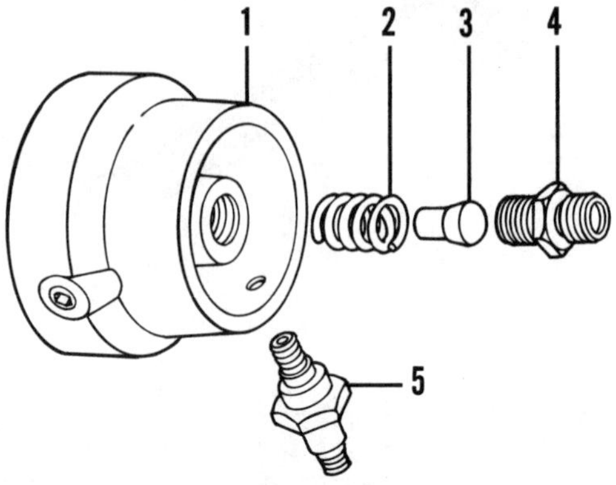

1. Crankcase
2. Spring
3. Check ball
4. Oil filter adapter
5. Oil pressure switch

3. Unplug, then reconnect the oil hoses (**Figure 53**) at the oil pump. Secure each hose with *new* hose clamps.
4. Refill the oil tank as described in Chapter Three.

OIL FILTER MOUNT

The oil filter mount (**Figure 73**) is part of the right crankcase half.

Disassembly

1. Place a clean oil pan underneath the oil filter.
2. Remove the oil filter as described in Chapter Three.
3. Loosen and remove the oil filter adapter (A, **Figure 74**) from the oil filter mount.
4. Remove the check ball and spring (**Figure 75**).
5. Disconnect the electrical connector from the oil pressure switch.
6. Loosen and remove the oil pressure switch (B, **Figure 74**).

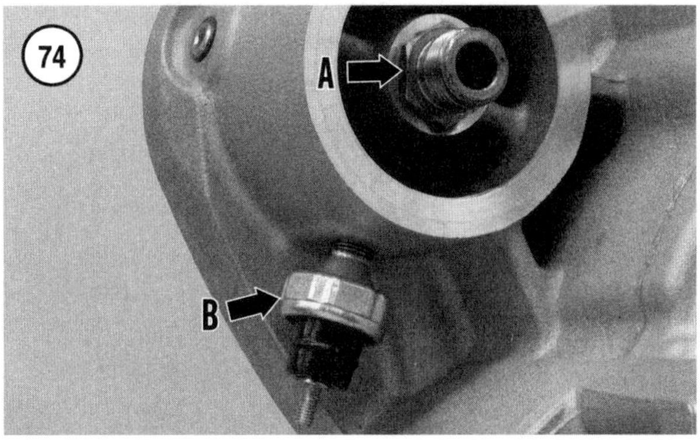

Inspection

1. Remove thread sealant residue from all threaded parts.
2. Clean the check ball, spring and oil filter adapter in solvent and dry thoroughly.

Reassembly

1. Apply Hylomar or Teflon Pipe Sealant to the oil pressure switch threads prior to installation. Install the switch and tighten to 50-70 in.-lb. (5.6-7.9 N•m).
2. Install the oil filter adapter as follows:
   a. The ends on the oil filter adapter are symmetrical; either end may be installed into the oil filter mount.
   b. Apply Loctite 243 (blue) onto the oil filter adapter threads that will be installed into the oil filter mount. Do not install thread sealant on the oil filter end.
   c. Install the spring, then the check ball into the hole in the center of the oil filter mount (**Figure 75**). Then push the oil filter adapter (Loctite end) against the check ball and thread it into the oil filter mount. Tighten the oil filter adapter to 96-144 in.-lb. (11-16 N•m).
3. Reconnect the electrical wire onto the oil pressure switch.
4. Install the oil filter as described in Chapter Three.
5. Start the engine and check for oil leaks.

CRANKCASE AND CRANKSHAFT

The crankcase (**Figure 76**) must be disassembled to service the crankshaft, connecting rod bearings, pinion shaft bearing and sprocket shaft bearing. This section describes procedures that can be performed in the home shop. Refer specialized service procedures to a Harley-Davidson dealership or other qualified shop.

CAUTION
Do not lift the crankcase assembly by grabbing the cylinder studs. Bent or damaged cylinder studs may cause oil leaks.

CAUTION
*Install hoses around the cylinder studs (**Figure 77**). Install foam insulation sleeves (**Figure 78**) around the connecting rods to protect them and the crankcase.*

Crankshaft End Play Inspection

Crankshaft end play is not adjustable. Measure crankshaft end play prior to disassembling the crankcase to obtain an indication of crankshaft component wear.

When measuring end play, the crankshaft must be moved in and out. To do this, a special tool must be fabricated. The tool can be made by welding two handles onto a spare flywheel rotor nut.

NOTE
The left crankshaft shaft is referred to as the sprocket shaft; the right shaft is referred to as the pinion shaft.

1. Remove the engine from the frame as described in this chapter.
2. Secure the crankcase to a workstand or workbench.
3. Remove the gearcase cover as described in this chapter.
4. Remove the primary chain and sprocket as described in Chapter Six.
5. Attach a dial indicator so the plunger touches against the pinion shaft end of the crankshaft as shown in **Figure 79**.
6. Install the flywheel rotor retaining nut (with handles) onto the sprocket shaft and tighten until the nut is tight.
7. Pull the sprocket shaft (**Figure 79**) in and out and note the end play reading on the dial indicator. If the total indicator reading is not within the crankshaft end play specifi-

(76)

CRANKSHAFT AND CRANKCASE

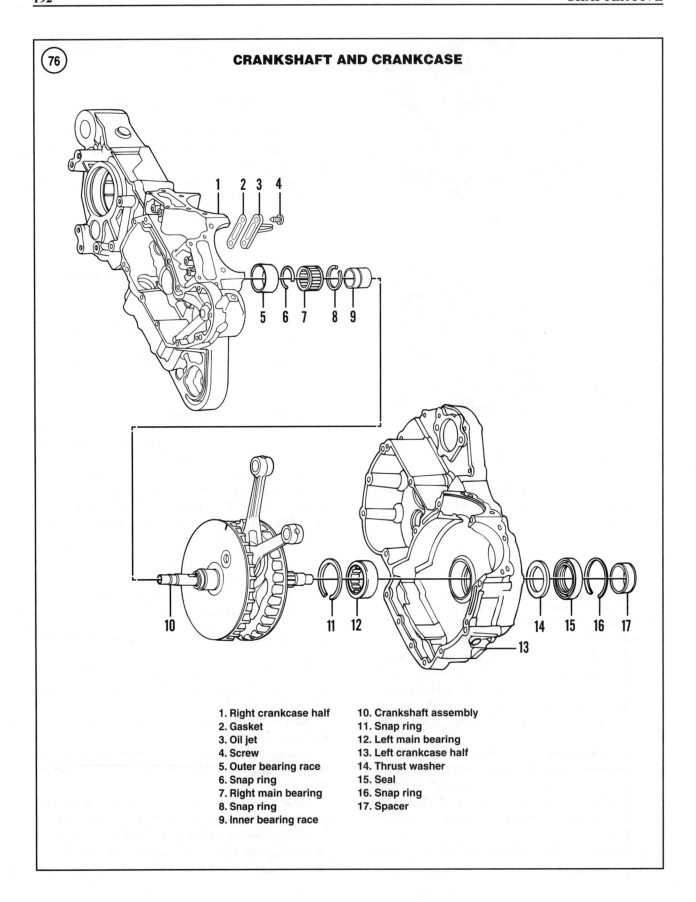

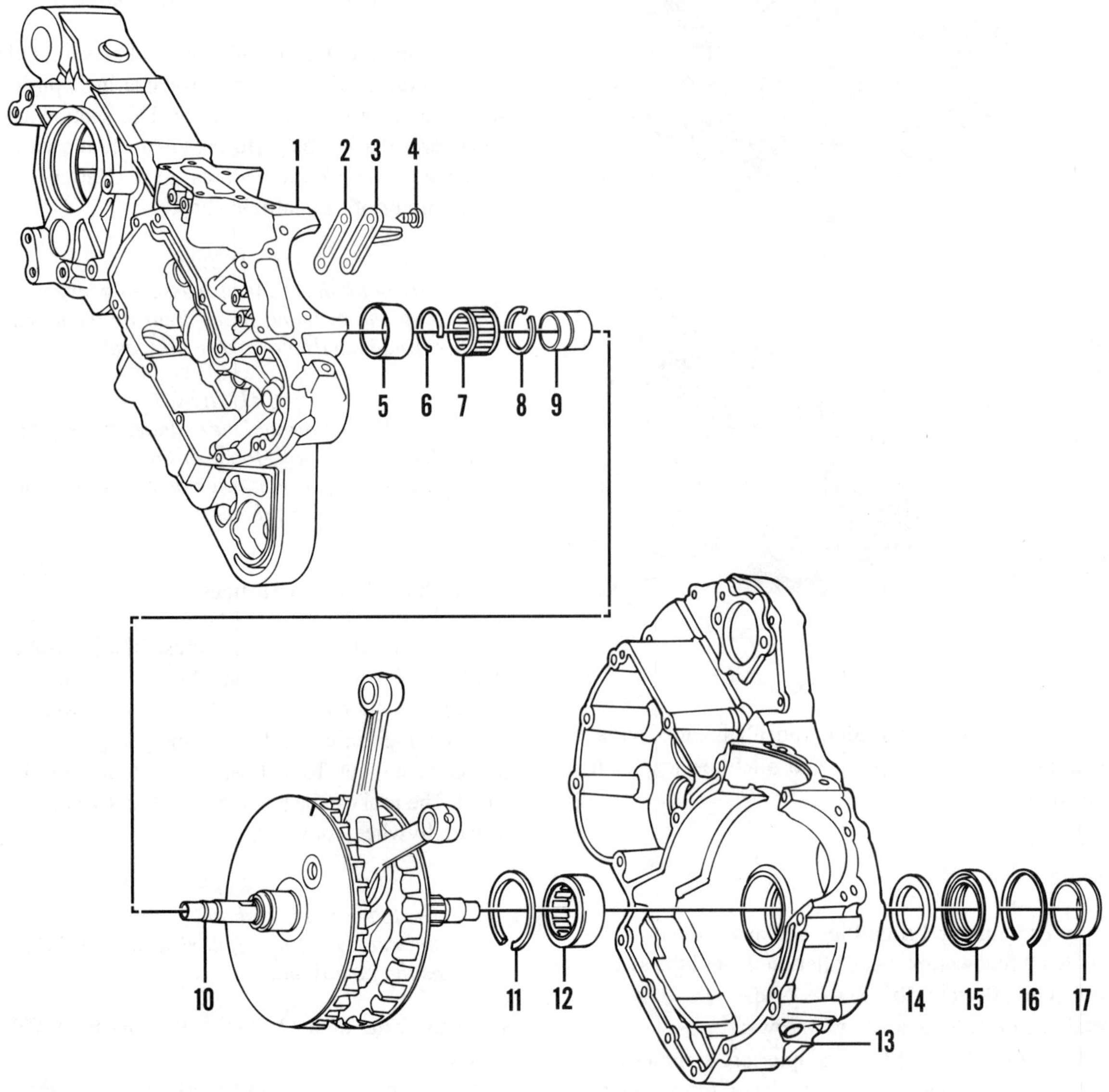

1. Right crankcase half
2. Gasket
3. Oil jet
4. Screw
5. Outer bearing race
6. Snap ring
7. Right main bearing
8. Snap ring
9. Inner bearing race
10. Crankshaft assembly
11. Snap ring
12. Left main bearing
13. Left crankcase half
14. Thrust washer
15. Seal
16. Snap ring
17. Spacer

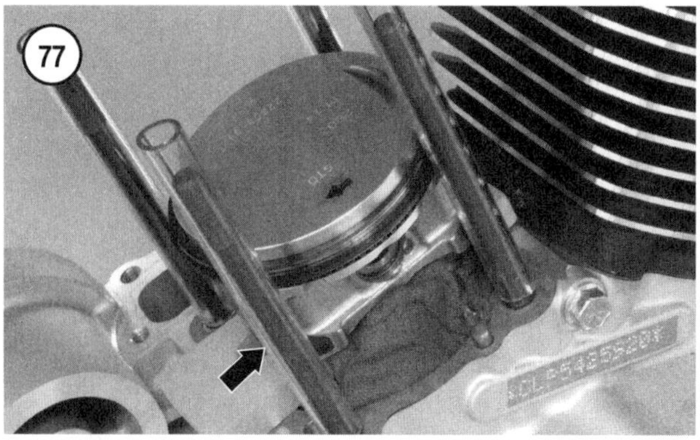

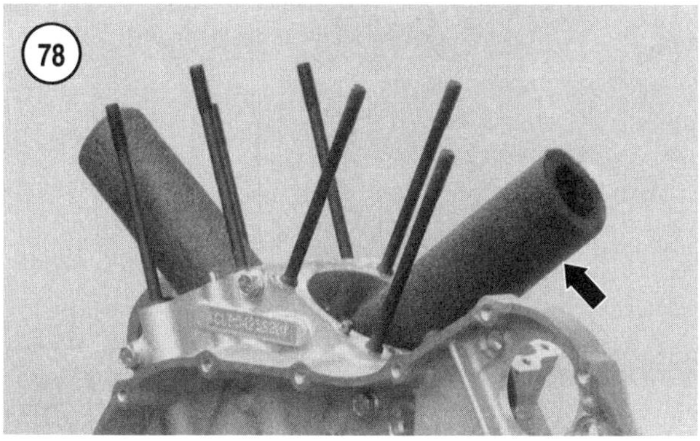

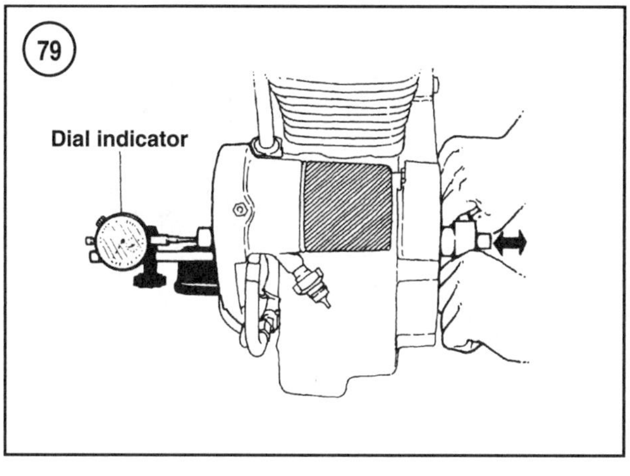

cation in **Table 1**, excessive wear is present. Inspect the crankshaft components to determine which require replacement.

8. Remove the dial indicator and flywheel rotor retaining nut (with handles).

Crankcase Disassembly

1. Remove the engine as described in this chapter.

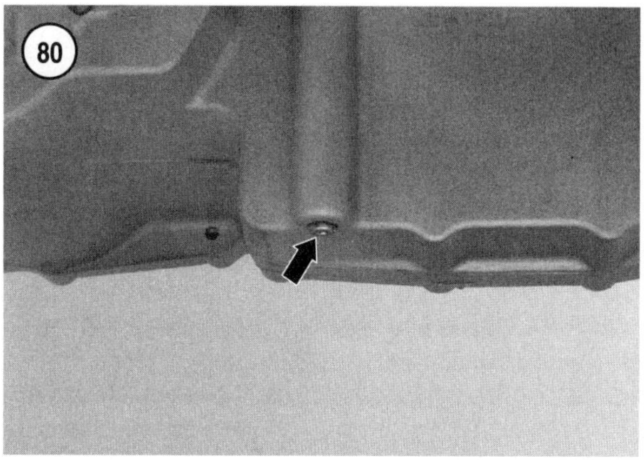

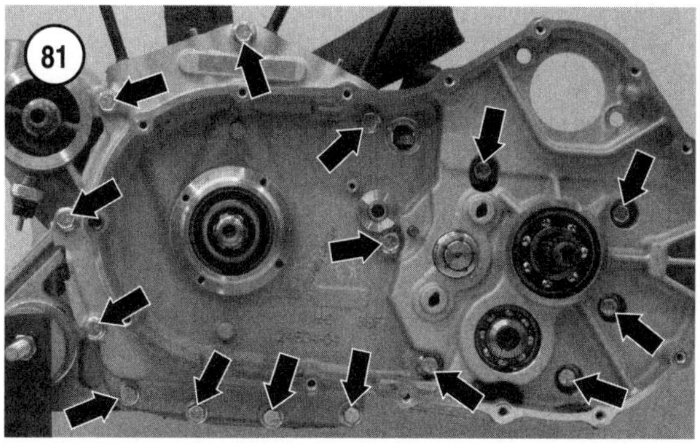

2. Secure the crankcase to a workstand or workbench.
3. Remove the plug (**Figure 80**) on the underside of the right crankcase half to drain additional oil trapped in internal passages.
4. Remove the starter as described in Chapter Nine.
5. Remove the oil pump as described in this chapter.
6. Remove the cam gears, pinion gear and oil pump drive gear as described in this chapter.
7. Remove the primary chain and sprocket as described in Chapter Six.
8. Remove the external shift components as described in Chapter Six.
9. Check the crankshaft end play as described in this section.
10. Loosen, then remove the crankcase bolts and washer (**Figure 81**).
11. Position the crankcase assembly so that the left side faces up.
12. Tap the crankcase with a plastic mallet and remove the left crankcase half.
13. Lift out the crankshaft assembly.
14. Remove the transmission as described in Chapter Seven.

5

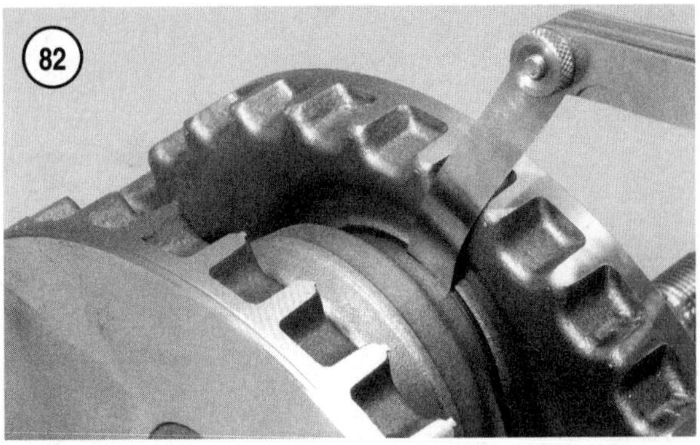

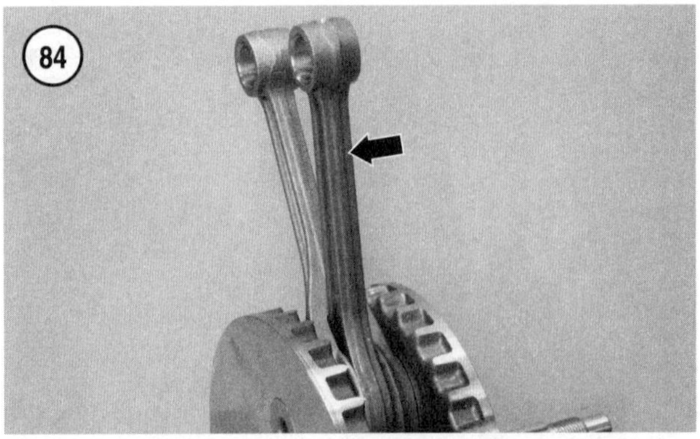

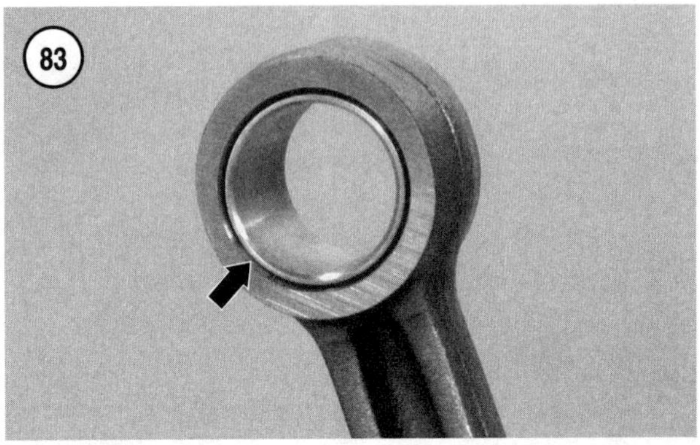

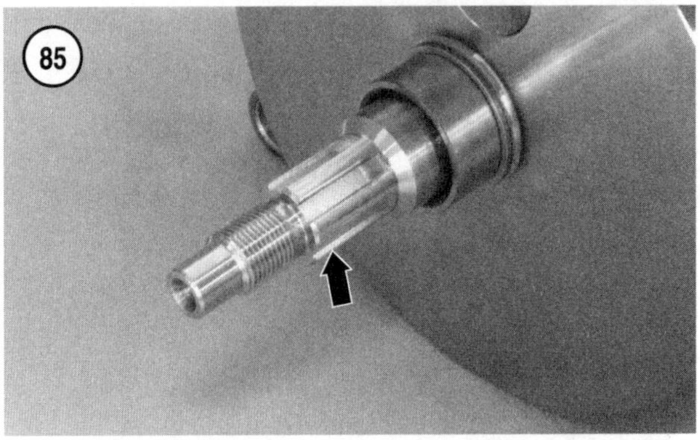

Inspection

1. Measure connecting rod side play with a feeler gauge as shown in **Figure 82**. If the side play is not within the specifications in **Table 2**, refer service to a Harley-Davidson dealership.

2. Inspect the piston pin bushings (**Figure 83**) for exessive wear or damage. Replace the bushings as described in Chapter Four.

3. Inspect the connecting rods (**Figure 84**) for damage.

4. Inspect the sprocket shaft (**Figure 85**) and pinion shaft (A, **Figure 86**) for excessive wear or damage. If there is damage, refer replacement to a Harley-Davidson dealership.

5. Inspect the right main bearing (B, **Figure 86**) for excessive wear or damage.

6. Inspect the left main bearing (A, **Figure 87**) in the left crankcase half for excessive wear or damage.

7. If either bearing is excessively worn or damaged, refer to *Left Side Main Bearing Assembly Replacement* in this section.

8. Support the crankshaft at the bearing surfaces on a truing stand and check the runout at the shaft ends (A, **Figure 88**) and the flywheel (B) with a dial indicator. If the

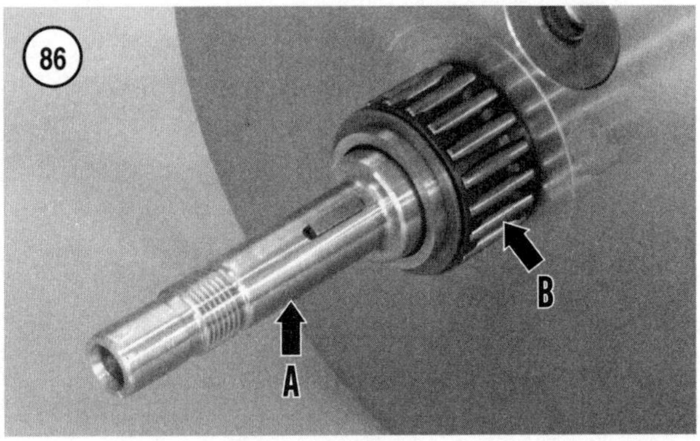

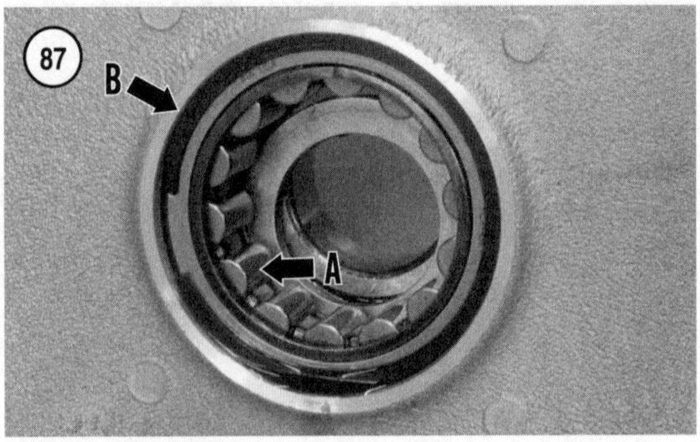

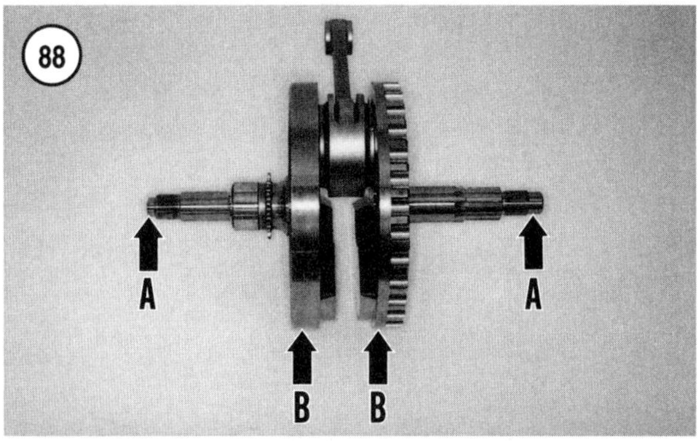

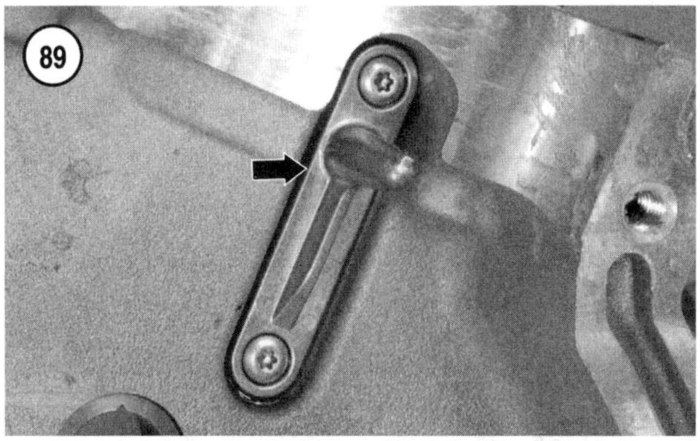

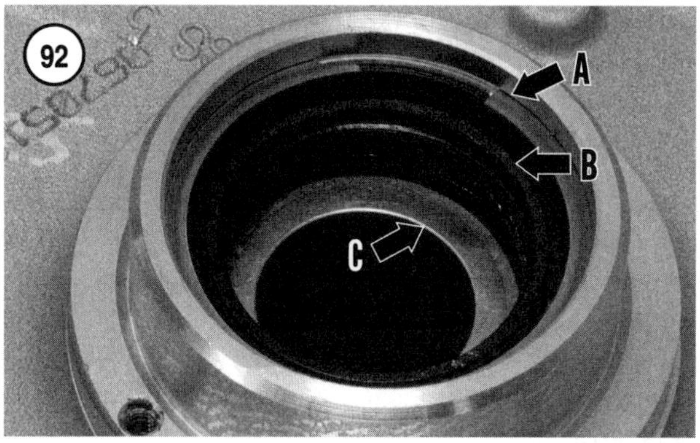

runout exceeds the service limit in **Table 1**, have the crankshaft trued or overhauled.

NOTE
The oil jet gasket is not available separately, only as an assembly with the oil jet.

9. Make sure the piston oil jets (**Figure 89**) are clear. If necessary, remove the jet retaining screws and jet. Clean the jet with compressed air. Apply Loctite 222 (purple) to the oil jet retaining screws and tighten to 25-35 in.-lb. (2.8-4.0 N•m). Make sure the oil jets point upward.

Left Side Main Bearing Assembly Replacement

Tools

The following tools or their equivalents are required to remove and install the left side main bearing (**Figure 76**):

1. Hydraulic press.
2. Crankshaft roller bearing pilot/driver (B-45655).
3. Crankshaft roller bearing support tube (HD-42720-2).
4. Adapter (HD-46663).

Bearing removal

1. Place the crankcase on the workbench with the inboard surface facing up.
2. If still in place, remove the crankshaft spacer (**Figure 90**). Inspect the spacer (**Figure 91**). Replace it if a groove exists were the oil seal lip contacts the spacer.
3. Remove the snap ring that secures the oil seal (A, **Figure 92**).
4. Remove the seal (B, **Figure 92**).
5. Remove the thrust washer (C, **Figure 92**).
6. Remove the snap ring (B, **Figure 87**) that secures the bearing (A).

7. Position the support tube (A, **Figure 93**) on the press bed.
8. Position the crankcase half with the outer side facing up and position the crankshaft's bearing bore over the support tube. Correctly align the two parts.
9. Position the adapter (B, **Figure 93**) on top of the bearing.
10. Slide the pilot/driver (C, **Figure 93**) through the adapter, crankcase bearing and into the support.
11. Center the press arm (D, **Figure 93**) directly over the pilot/driver (B) and slowly press the bearing out of the crankcase.
12. Remove the crankcase and special tools from the press bed.
13. Clean the crankcase half in solvent and dry it with compressed air.

Bearing installation

1. Apply clean engine oil, or press lube, to the bearing receptacle in the crankcase and to the outer race of the new bearing.
2. Position the support tube on the press bed.
3. Position the crankcase half with the inner side facing up and position the crankshaft's bearing bore over the support tube. Correctly align the two parts.
4. Correctly position the new bearing in the crankcase bore.
5. Slide the pilot/driver through the new bearing and the crankcase, and into the support.
6. Center the press arm directly over the pilot/driver and slowly press the bearing into the crankcase until it lightly bottoms in the crankshaft bearing bore.
7. Remove the crankcase and special tools from the press.
8. Make sure the bearing has been pressed in past the retaining ring groove. If the groove is not visible above the bearing, repeat Steps 2-6 until the groove is visible.
9. Position the crankcase on the workbench with the inner surface facing up.
10. Install the snap ring (B, **Figure 87**). Make sure the snap ring fits properly in the groove.

CAUTION

If the snap ring does not correctly seat in the crankcase groove, the bearing is not correctly seated in the crankcase bore. Repeat Steps 2-6.

11. Install the thrust washer (C, **Figure 92**).
12. Install a new seal (B, **Figure 92**).
13. Install the snap ring (A, **Figure 92**).
14. Install the crankshaft spacer (**Figure 90**).

93

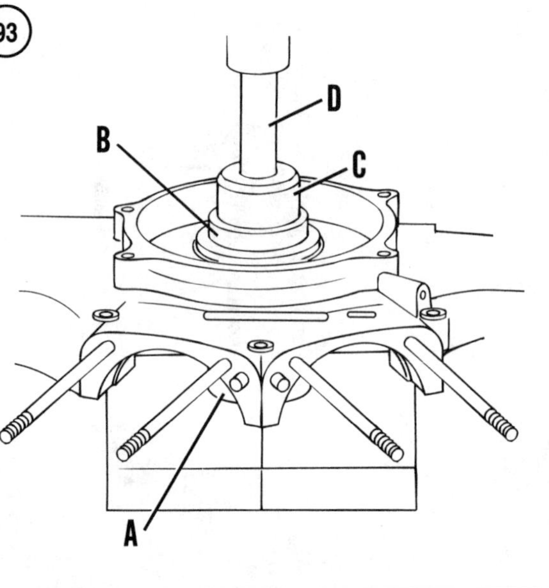

94

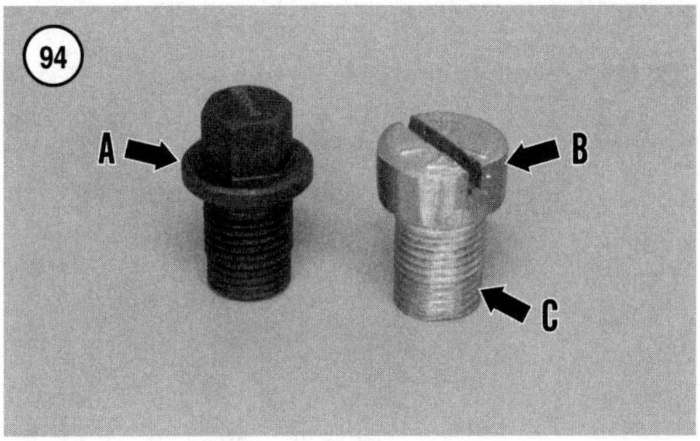

Right Side Main Bearing Assembly Replacement

The right side main bearing consists of components which must be selectively fitted and machined to precise tolerances. Refer right side main bearing replacement to a Harley-Davidson dealership.

Crankshaft Installation/Crankcase Assembly

1. If removed, install the crankcase dowel pins.
2. Install the transmission and internal shift components as described in Chapter Seven.
3. Install the pilot/driver (A, **Figure 94**) into the neutral switch hole (A, **Figure 95**) in the right crankcase half while pulling back the shift detent lever (B). Allow the le-

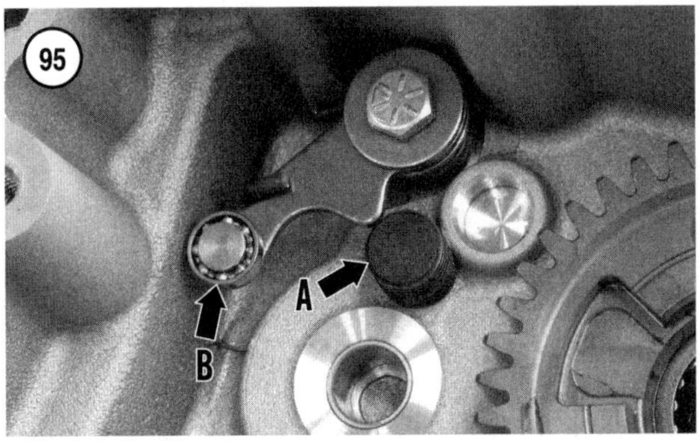

ver to rest against the tool end. A substitute tool (B, **Figure 94**) may be fabricated as follows:

a. Grind down the head of a 9/16 in. bolt so it will enter the neutral switch recess.

b. Cut a screwdriver slot in the bolt head.

c. Cut off the bolt so the length extends just far enough to support the shift detent lever as shown in **Figure 95**.

d. Grind down the threads on the end of the bolt (C, **Figure 94**) so the detent lever will slide off the bolt easily when the bolt is unscrewed from the crankcase.

4. Lubricate all parts with the appropriate oil, engine oil or transmission oil. Make sure to lubricate all seal lips.

5. Install the crankshaft assembly into the right crankcase half (**Figure 96**).

6. Make sure the crankcase mating surfaces are clean, then coat the crankcase mating surfaces with H-D Gray High Performance Sealant or equivalent.

7. Align the crankcase halves and install the left crankcase half assembly, which includes the transmission.

NOTE
The short crankcase bolts are located in positions 1, 2, 3 and 4 in ***Figure 97****.*

8. Install the crankcase bolts and tighten in the sequence shown in **Figure 97**. Tighten the bolts to 180-228 in.-lb. (20.3-25.7 N•m).
9. Remove the shift detent lever holder tool, then install the neutral indicator switch (**Figure 98**). Tighten the switch to 36-60 in.-lb. (4.1-6.7 N•m).
10. If removed, lubricate, then install the spacer (**Figure 99**) into the left side seal.

NOTE
Based on the equipment available, such as a workstand, it may be preferable to assemble the complete engine before installation in the frame. However, consider the additional weight that must be lifted.

11. Install the engine in the frame as described in this chapter.
12. Install all the engine sub-assemblies as described in this chapter.
13. If new engine components were installed, perform the *Engine Break-In* procedure in this chapter.

Cylinder Stud Replacement

Improper stud replacement can cause oil leaks. If all of the tools required to install the studs are not available, have a dealership install the studs.

CAUTION
The cylinder studs, cylinder head bolts and washers are made of hardened material. If replacement is required, purchase new parts from a Harley-Davidson dealership.

1. If the engine is assembled, stuff clean shop towels into the crankcase opening to prevent debris from falling into the engine.
2. Remove the damaged stud with a stud remover.
3. Clean the crankcase threads and the new stud with brake parts cleaner. Blow dry.

NOTE
*The cylinder studs have a shoulder on the lower end (****Figure 100****).*

4. Drop a small steel ball into a cylinder head bolt and thread the bolt onto the top of the new stud.
5. Hand-thread the new stud into the crankcase, then install it with an impact wrench until the shoulder on the stud contacts the crankcase base gasket surface.

97

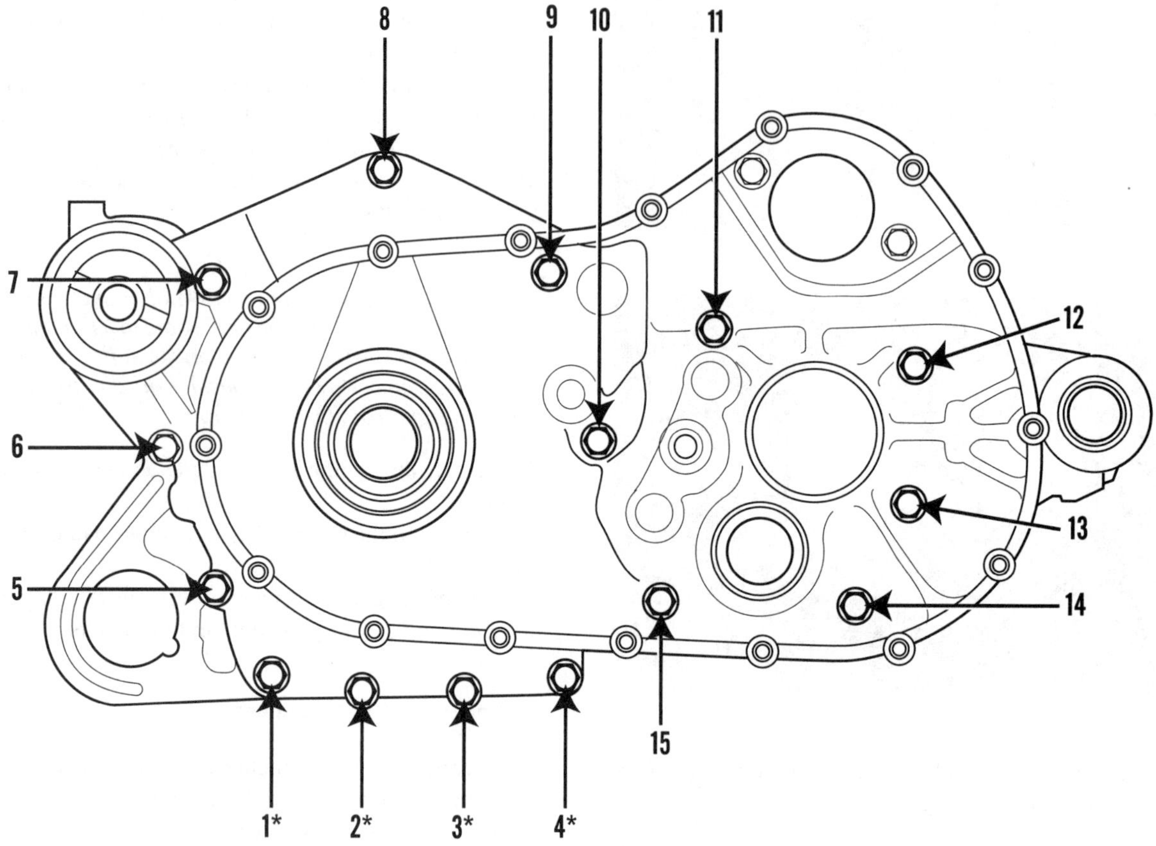

*Short bolts

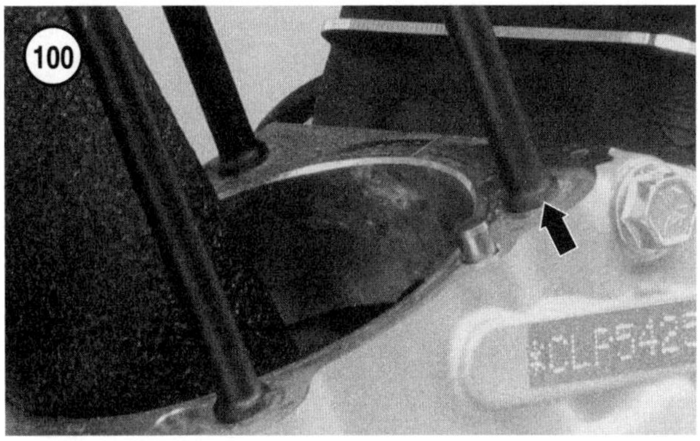

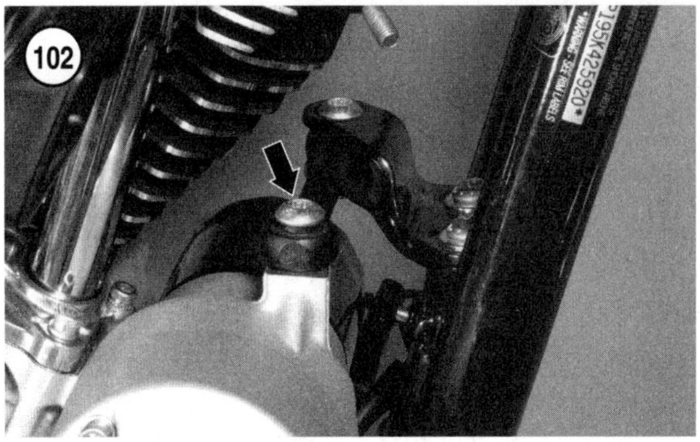

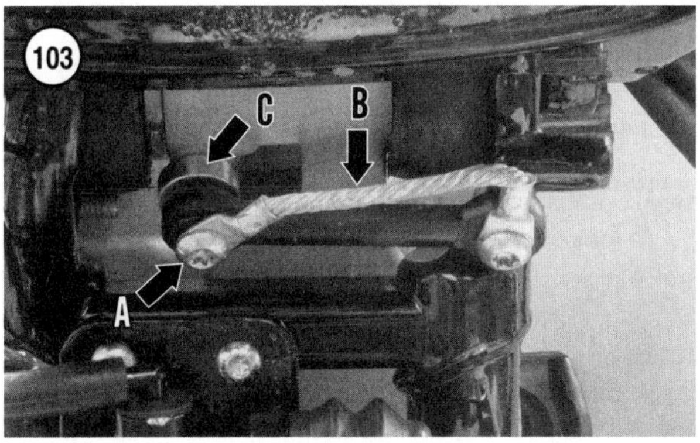

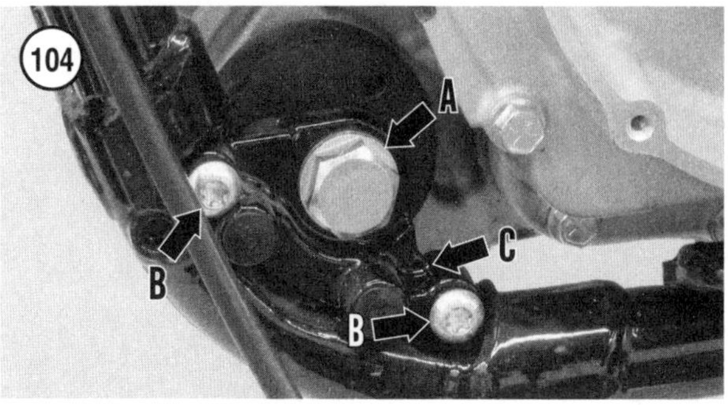

6. Tighten the stud to 120-240 in.-lb. (14-27 N•m).
7. Remove the cylinder head bolt and steel ball from the cylinder stud.
8. Place a protective hose around the stud.
9. Repeat Steps 2-8 for each stud.

ENGINE MOUNTING SYSTEM

The engine is supported in the frame by rubber isolator mounts. The rear mounts also serve as the pivot support for the swing arm.

A set of stabilizer links are used to control side-to-side engine movement. Two links are attached to the front of the engine at the cylinder head and the crankcase. A stabilizer link is also attached to the rear of the crankcase.

Front Isolator Replacement/Inspection

1. Support the motorcycle in an upright position.
2. On 883C and 1200C models, remove the foot controls on both sides.
3. Remove the bolt securing the upper stabilizer link to the bracket (**Figure 101**).
4. Remove the bolt securing the lower stabilizer link to the bracket (**Figure 102**).
5. Remove the rear stabilizer link bolt (A, **Figure 103**), ground strap end (B) and spacer (C).

CAUTION
Make sure the jack or lift used in Step 6 will not damage the engine due to improper support points.

6. Place a suitable jack or lift under the front of the engine, then raise the engine sufficiently to remove engine weight from the front engine mount.
7. Remove the front engine mount bolt (A, **Figure 104**).
8. Remove the front engine mount bracket bolts (B, **Figure 104**), then remove the bracket (C).

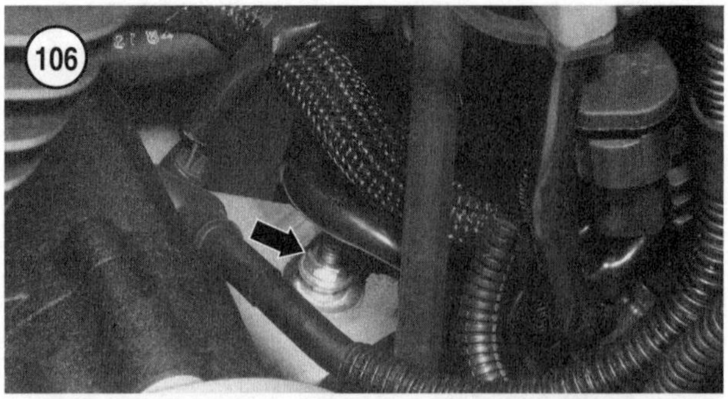

9. Remove the left isolator mount.
10. Carefully push the front of the engine to the left and remove the right isolator mount.
11. Inspect each isolator mount (**Figure 105**). Replace the mount if cracks, tears, deterioration or separation is apparent.
12. Install the mounts by reversing the removal steps while noting the following:
    a. Install each mount into the crankcase so the boss on the mount (**Figure 105**) fits into the groove in the crankcase.
    b. Install the front engine mount bracket (C, **Figure 104**) and bolts (B). Do not tighten the bolts.
    c. Install the front engine mount bolt (A, **Figure 104**), but do not tighten.
    d. Make sure the front engine mount fits properly, then tighten the mounting bracket bolts (B, **Figure 104**) to 25-35 ft.-lb. (34-47 N•m).
    e. Remove the nut on the front engine mount bolt and apply Loctite 243 to the threads. Tighten the front engine mount bolt (A, **Figure 104**) to 60-70 ft.-lb. (82-95 N•m).
    f. Tighten the rear stabilizer bolt (A, **Figure 103**) to 25-35 ft.-lb. (34-47 N•m).
    g. Tighten the lower stabilizer link bolt (**Figure 102**) to 25-35 ft.-lb. (34-47 N•m).
    h. Tighten the upper stabilizer link bolt (**Figure 101**) to 25-35 ft.-lb. (34-47 N•m).

Rear Isolator Replacement/Inspection

1. Remove the seat as described in Chapter Fourteen.

CAUTION
After disconnecting the negative battery cable end, position the cable so it cannot contact metal parts while disconnecting the battery.

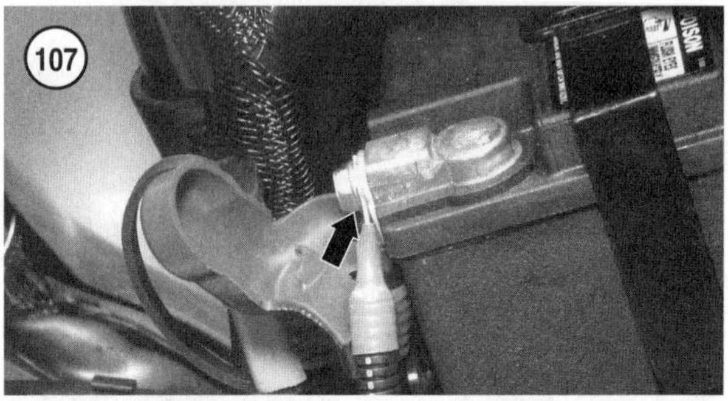

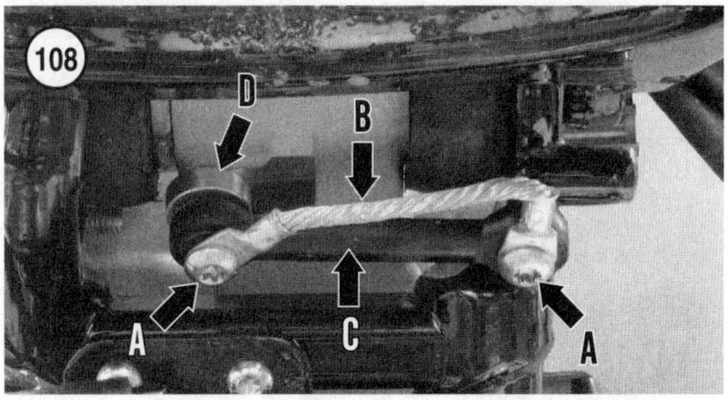

2. Disconnect the negative battery cable end from the stud on top of the crankcase (**Figure 106**).
3. Remove the Maxi-fuse as described in Chapter Nine.
4. Remove the retaining screw and disconnect the positive battery cable and Maxi-fuse cable from the battery positive terminal (**Figure 107**).
5. Remove the exhaust system, including the exhaust mounting bracket, as described in Chapter Eight.
6. Remove the rider and passenger footrests, and linkage from both sides as described in Chapter Fourteen.
7. Remove the drive sprocket and drive belt as described in Chapter Seven.
8. On California models, remove the EVAP canister and hoses.
9. Remove the rear stabilizer link bolts (A, **Figure 108**), ground strap (B), link (C) and spacer (D).

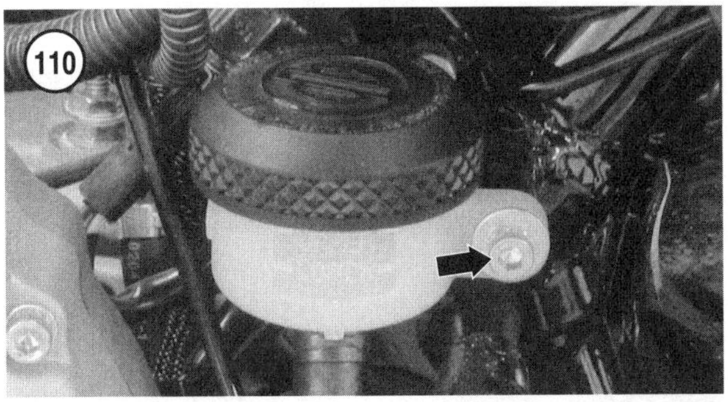

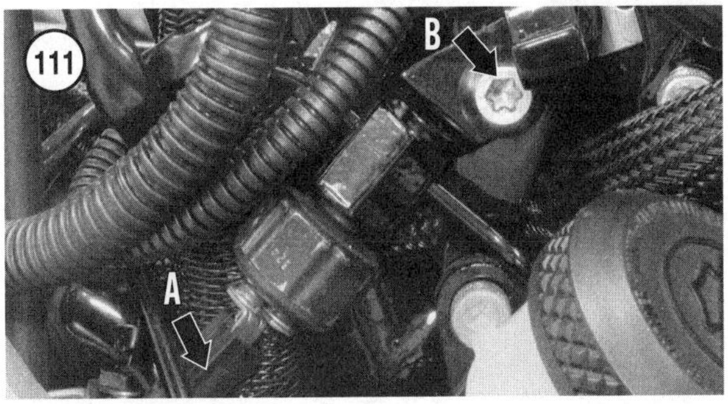

10. Remove the bolt securing the upper stabilizer link to the bracket (**Figure 101**).

11. Remove the bolt securing the lower stabilizer link to the bracket (**Figure 102**).

CAUTION

Because the rear engine mount also serves as the swing arm pivot, it is necessary to support the rear of the frame because the swing arm must disengage from the frame. Depending on the equipment available, it may be easier to remove the rear wheel from the swing arm, or leave the rear wheel installed.

12. Support the rear of the frame, then perform substep a or b.

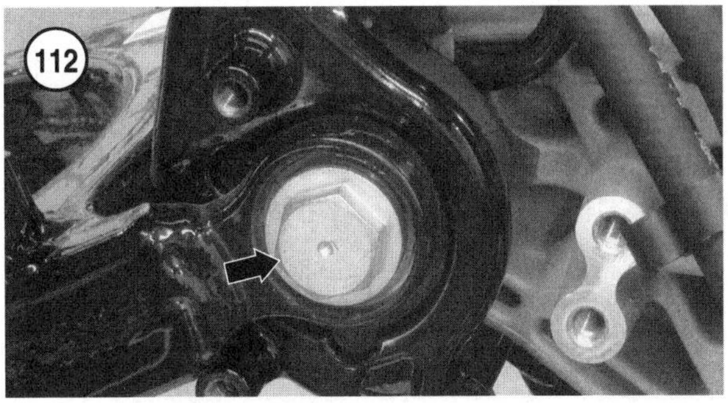

a. Remove the rear wheel.

b. Loosen the axle nut and move the rear wheel fully forward in the swing arm. Tighten the axle nut.

13. Remove the rear brake reservoir cover (**Figure 109**).

14. Remove the rear brake reservoir retaining bolt (**Figure 110**) and suspend the reservoir out of the way. Keep the brake reservoir upright so air does not enter the brake fluid. The brake system must be bled if air enters the system.

15. Disconnect the connectors from the rear brake light switch (A, **Figure 111**).

16. Remove the rear brake light switch mounting bolt (B, **Figure 111**), then carefully move the switch out of the way. Do not bend or damage the brake tubing.

17. Remove the swing arm bolts (**Figure 112**) on both sides, then move the swing arm rearward sufficiently to clear the pivot bosses.

CAUTION

Make sure the jack or lift does not damage the engine due to improper support points.

18. Place a suitable jack or lift under the rear of the engine, then raise the engine sufficiently to remove engine weight from the rear engine mount.

19. Remove the rear engine mount bracket bolts (A, **Figure 113**), then remove the bracket (B).

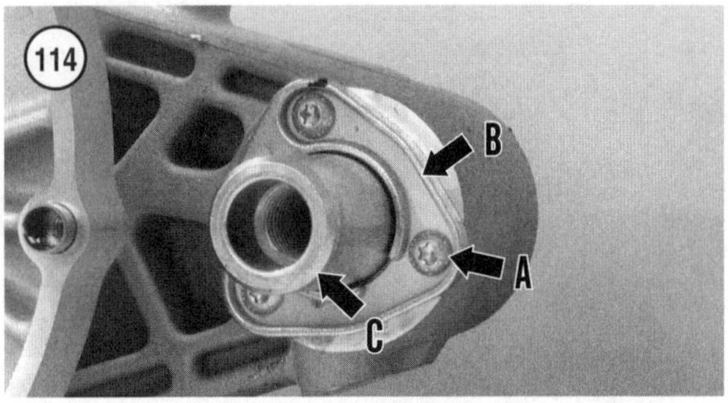

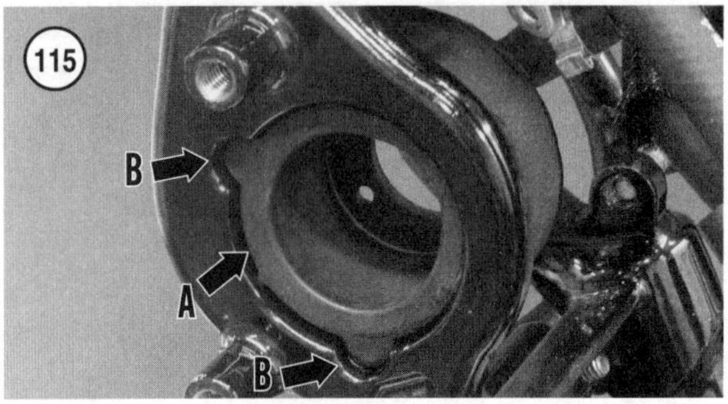

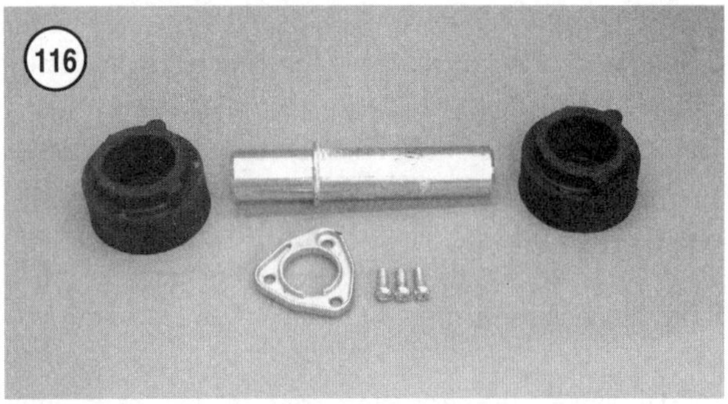

20. Remove the pivot shaft retaining bolts (A, **Figure 114**), then remove the pivot shaft lockplate (B) and pivot shaft (C).

21. Push the rear of the engine to the left and remove the right isolator mount (A, **Figure 115**) from the frame.

22. Inspect each isolator mount and the pivot shaft (**Figure 116**). Replace the mount if cracks, tears, deterioration or separation is apparent.

23. Install the mounts by reversing the removal steps while noting the following:

   a. Install each mount into the frame and mount bracket so the bosses on the mount (**Figure 117**) fit into the grooves in the frame and bracket.
   b. Install the pivot shaft in the engine so the flange cutout (A, **Figure 118**) is adjacent to the mounting bolt hole (B). Install the lockplate so the tab (C, **Figure 118**)

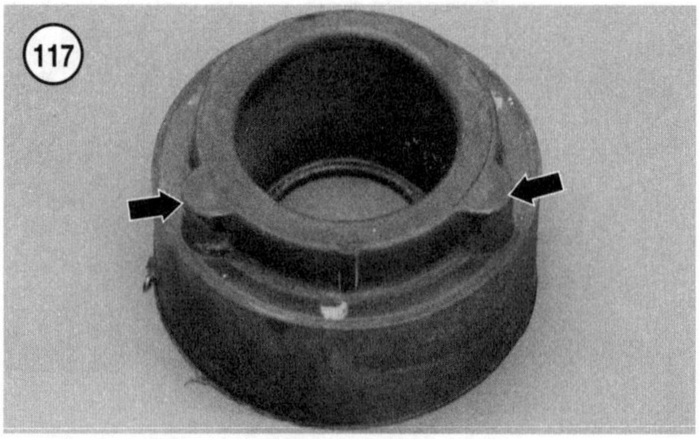

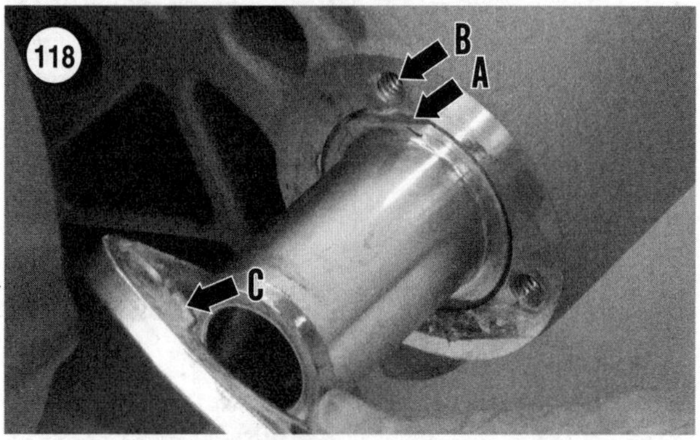

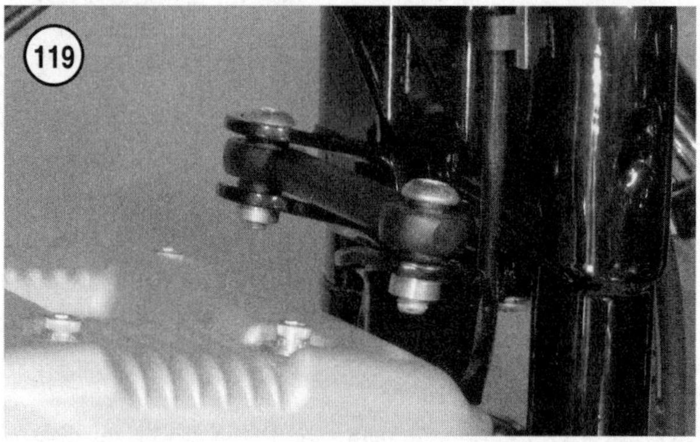

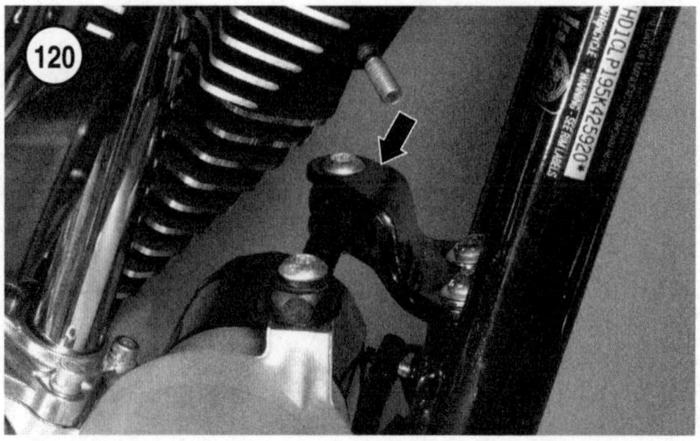

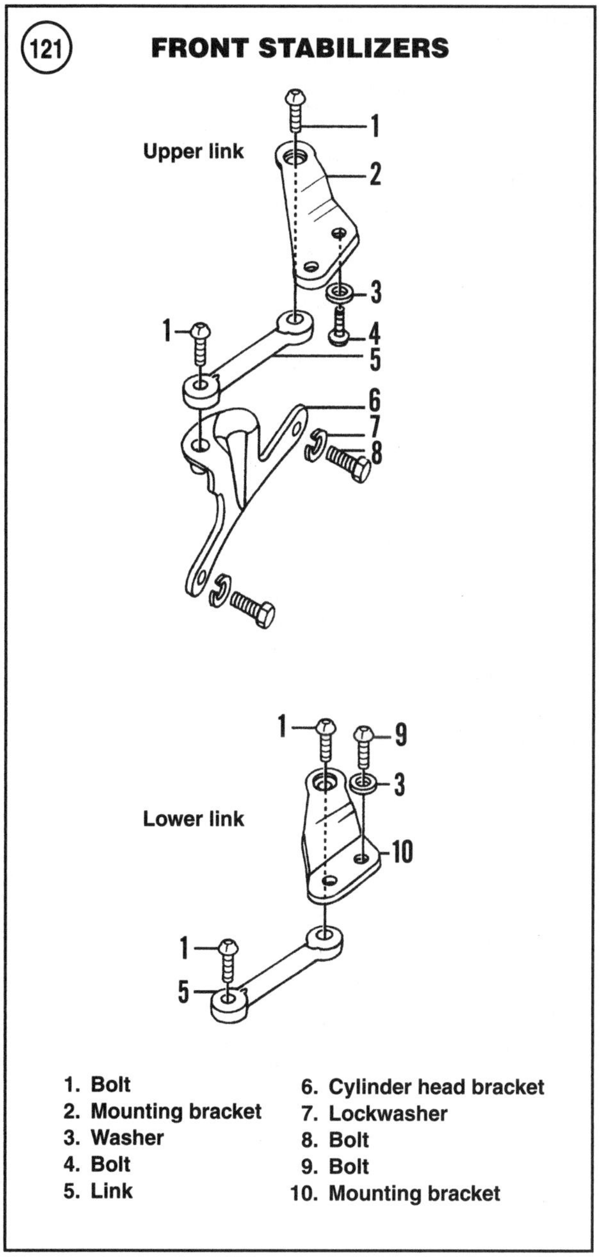

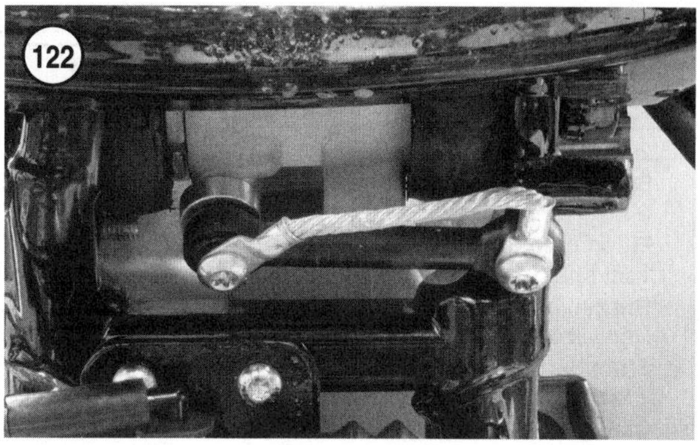

enters the flange cutout (A). Tighten the lockplate bolts to 80-120 in.-lb. (9.0-13.5 N•m).

c. Make sure the rear engine mount/swing arm pivot fits properly, then tighten the mounting bracket bolts (A, **Figure 113**) to 25-35 ft.-lb. (34-47 N•m).
d. Move the swing arm so it aligns with the swing arm pivot shaft. Install the swing arm bolts (**Figure 112**) on both sides and tighten to 60-70 ft.-lb. (82-95 N•m).
e. Install the rear stabilizer link (C, **Figure 108**), spacer (D), ground strap (B) and bolts (A). Note that the left bolt is longer. Tighten the bolts to 25-35 ft.-lb. (34-47 N•m).
f. Tighten the lower stabilizer link bolt (**Figure 102**) to 25-35 ft.-lb. (34-47 N•m).
g. Tighten the upper stabilizer link bolt (**Figure 101**) to 25-35 ft.-lb. (34-47 N•m).
h. Tighten the rear brake light switch mounting bolt (B, **Figure 111**) to 72-120 in.-lb. (9-13 N•m).
i. Tighten the rear brake reservoir retaining bolt (**Figure 110**) to 20-25 in.-lb. (2.2-2.8 N•m).
j. When connecting the positive battery cable and Maxi-fuse cable to the positive battery terminal, position the cable ends so the battery cable contacts the battery terminal and the Maxi-fuse cable contacts the bolt head. Tighten the bolt to 40-50 in.-lb. (4.5-5.7 N•m).
k. Connect the negative battery cable end to the stud on top of the crankcase (**Figure 106**). Tighten the retaining nut to 55-75 in.-lb. (6.2-8.4 N•m).

Front Stabilizer Links

Two stabilizer links are attached to the front of the engine. The upper link connects the front cylinder head to the frame (**Figure 119**). The lower link connects the engine crankcase to the frame (**Figure 120**). Refer also to **Figure 121**. Tighten the bolts to 25-35 ft.-lb. (34-47 N•m).

Rear Stabilizer Link

The rear stabilizer link is located above the rear brake master cylinder (**Figure 122**). Note the following when servicing the rear stabilizer link.

1. The left bolt is longer.
2. Install the spacer at the left end of the link.
3. Tighten the bolts to 25-35 ft.-lb. (34-47 N•m).

Table 1 ENGINE LOWER END SERVICE SPECIFICATIONS

	New in. (mm)	Service limit in. (mm)
Connecting rods		
Side play at crankshaft	0.005-0.025 (0.13-0.64)	0.030 (0.762)
Piston pin clearance	0.00125-0.00175 (0.0318-0.0445)	0.0020 (0.051)
Fit on crankpin	0.0004-0.0017 (0.010-0.043)	0.0027 (0.0686)
Crankshaft		
Runout at flywheel	0.000-0.010 (0.00-0.25)	0.010 (0.25)
Runout at shaft ends	0.000-0.002 (0.00-0.05)	0.002 (0.05)
End play	0.003-0.010 (0.076-0.254)	0.010 (0.25)
Gearcase		
Cam gear-to-bushing clearance	0.0007-0.0022 (0.018-0.056)	0.003 (0.076)
Cam gear end play (minimum)		
Rear intake cam gear	0.006-0.024 (0.15-0.61)	0.040 (1.016)
All other cam gears	0.005-0.024 (0.13-0.61)	0.025 (0.635)
Oil pump		
Shaft-to-pump clearance	0.0025 (0.064)	–
Feed/scavenge inner/outer rotor clearance	0.003 (0.08)	0.004 (0.102)
Pinion shaft bearing		
Pinion shaft journal diameter	1.2496-1.2500 (31.740-31.750)	1.2494 (31.735)
Outer race diameter in crankcase	1.5646-1.5652 (39.741-39.756)	1.5672 (39.807)
Cover bushing clearance	0.0023-0.0043 (0.058-0.109)	0.0050 (0.127)
Bearing running clearance	0.00012-0.00088 (0.0030-0.0224)	–
Sprocket shaft bearing		
Outer race clearance in crankcase (interference)	0.006 (0.152)	–
Bearing inner race clearance on crankshaft (interference)	0.006 (0.152)	–
Tappets		
Crankcase bore clearance	0.0008-0.0023 (0.020-0.058)	0.003 (0.076)
Roller clearance on pin	0.0006-0.0013 (0.015-0.033)	–
Roller end clearance	0.008-0.022 (0.203-0.559)	0.026 (0.66)

Table 2 ENGINE LOWER END TORQUE SPECIFICATIONS

	ft.-lb.	in.-lb.	N•m
Battery negative cable stud nut	–	55-75	6.2-8.4
Battery terminal bolts (2004-2006)	–	40-50	4.5-5.7
Crankcase bolts	–	180-228	20.3-25.7
Cylinder studs	–	120-240	14-27
Front engine mount bolt	60-70	–	82-95
Front engine mounting bracket bolts	25-35	–	34-47
Front stabilizer			
Lower stabilizer link bolts	25-35	–	34-47
Lower stabilizer bracket bolts	25-35	–	34-47
Upper stabilizer bracket bolts	25-35	–	34-47
Upper stabilizer link bolts	25-35	–	34-47
Gearcase cover bolts	–	80-110	9.0-12.4
Neutral indicator switch	–	36-60	4.1-6.7
Oil filter adapter	–	96-144	11-16
Oil jet retaining screws	–	25-35	2.8-4.0
Oil pressure switch	–	50-70	5.6-7.9
Oil pump cover screws	–	70-80	7.9-9.0
Oil pump mounting bolts	–	125-150	14.1-16.9
Pinion shaft nut (2004-2008)	35-45	–	48-61

(continued)

Table 2 ENGINE LOWER END TORQUE SPECIFICATIONS (continued)

	ft.-lb.	in.-lb.	N•m
Rear brake light switch mounting bolt	–	72-120	9-13
Rear brake reservoir retaining bolt	–	20-25	2.2-2.8
Rear engine mount/swing arm pivot			
Mounting bracket bolts	25-35	–	34-47
Pivot shaft lockplate bolts	–	80-120	9.0-13.5
Rear stabilizer link bolts	25-35	–	34-47
Swing arm bolts	60-70	–	82-95
Tappet anti-rotation pins (2004-2005)	–	55-65	6.2-7.3
Tappet cover bolts	–	80-110	9.0-12.4
Tappet holder bolts (2006-on)	–	80-110	9.0-12.4
Transmission/primary case drain plug	14-30	–	19-40

NOTE: Refer to the Supplement at the end of this manual for information unique to 2007-2011 models.

CHAPTER SIX

PRIMARY DRIVE, CLUTCH AND EXTERNAL SHIFT MECHANISM

This chapter contains service procedures for the following components:

1. Primary drive cover.
2. Primary drive.
3. Clutch assembly.
4. Clutch cable.
5. External shift mechanism.

Specifications are in **Table 1** and **Table 2** at the end of this chapter.

PRIMARY DRIVE COVER

Removal

Refer to **Figure 1**.

1. Disconnect the negative battery cable.
2. Remove the left side footrest assembly as described in Chapter Fourteen.
3. Place a drain pan under the primary drive cover and remove the oil drain plug (**Figure 2**). Allow the oil to drain.
4. Loosen the locknut (A, **Figure 3**) and turn the primary chain adjuster screw (B, **Figure 3**) counterclockwise to loosen the chain.
5. Slide the rubber boot (A, **Figure 4**) upwards off the clutch in-line cable adjuster.
6. Loosen the adjuster lock nut (B, **Figure 4**) and turn the adjuster (C) to provide maximum cable free play.
7. Remove the clutch inspection cover (**Figure 5**).
8. Remove the quad ring (A, **Figure 6**).
9. Remove the spring and lockplate (B, **Figure 6**).
10. Turn the clutch adjusting screw (A, **Figure 7**) clockwise and release the ramp (B) and coupling mechanism (C). Turn the clutch adjusting screw clockwise to move the ramp assembly forward. Then unscrew the nut (D, **Figure 7**) from the end of the adjusting screw and remove it.
11. Pivot the hook on the ramp to the rear of the cable end coupling. Then disconnect and remove the clutch cable from the slot in the coupling. Remove the coupling and ramp assembly.
12. Unscrew the clutch cable housing fitting (**Figure 8**) from the primary cover.
13. Remove the clamp bolt and washer (A, **Figure 9**) securing the shift lever to the shift shaft, then remove the shift lever (B).
14. Remove the primary chain cover mounting bolts, then remove the cover (**Figure 10**) and gasket.
15. Remove the dowel pins (**Figure 11**), if necessary.
16. If necessary, remove the clutch mechanism as described in this chapter.

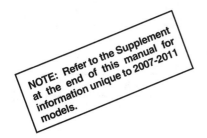

(1)

PRIMARY DRIVE COVER

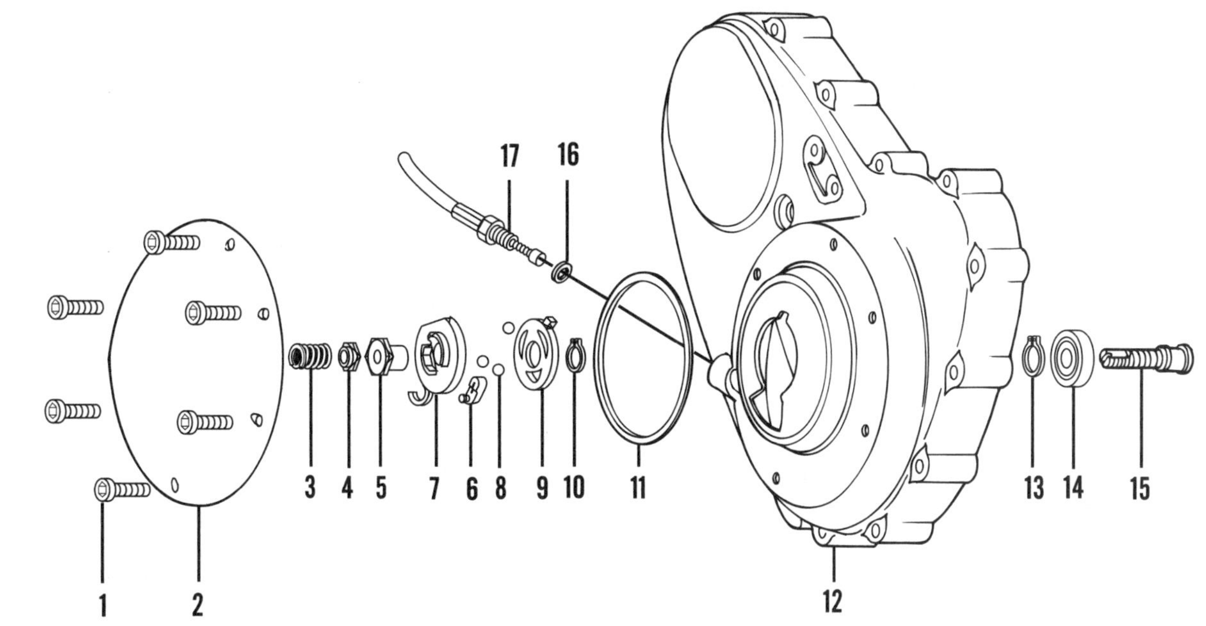

1. Torx screw and washer
2. Clutch inspection cover
3. Spring
4. Lockplate
3. Spring
4. Lockplate
5. Well nut
6. Coupling
7. Outer ramp
8. Balls (3)
9. Inner ramp
10. Snap ring
11. Quad ring
12. Cover
13. Snap ring
14. Bearing
15. Adjuster screw
16. O-ring
17. Clutch cable

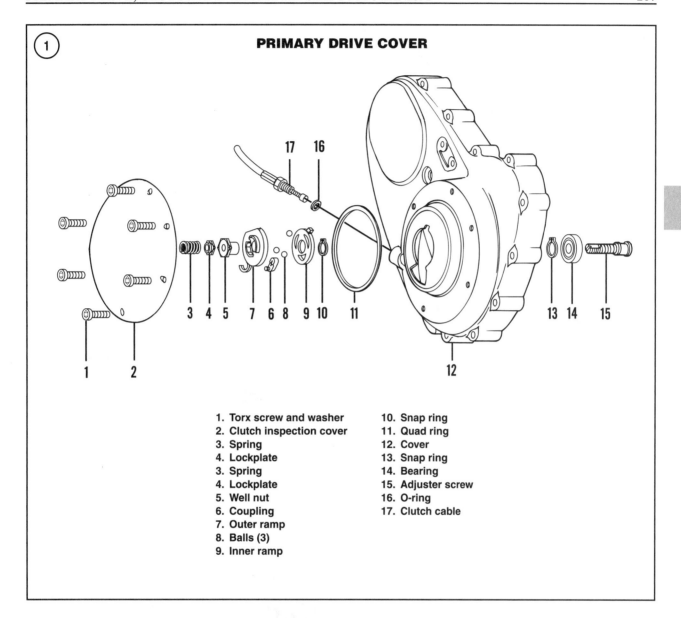

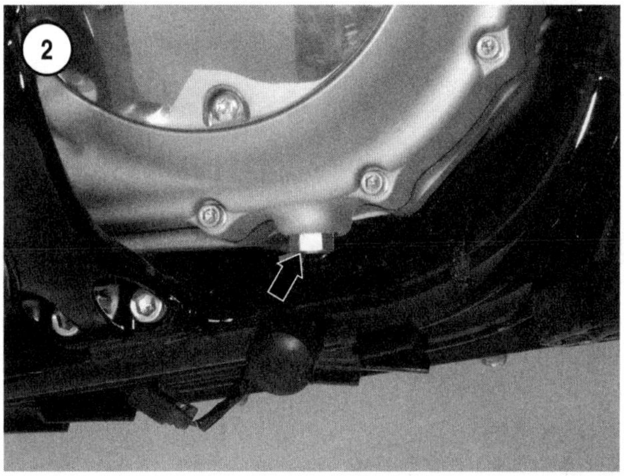

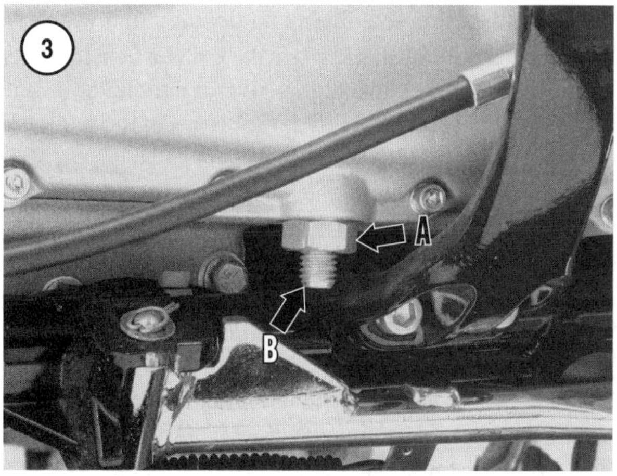

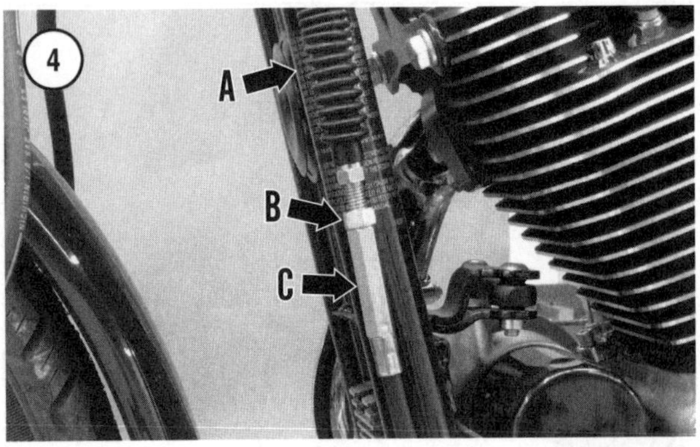

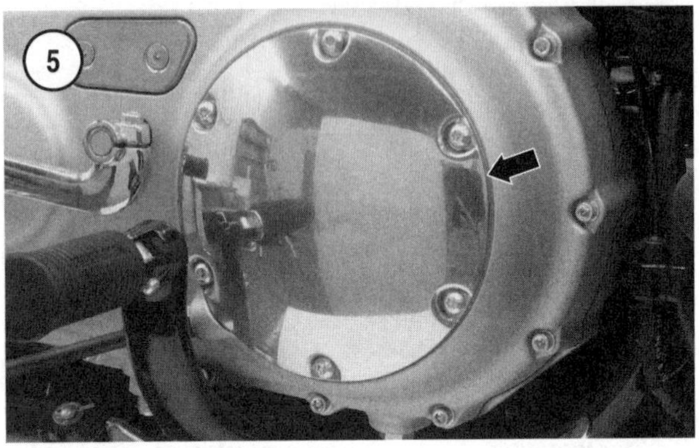

17. If necessary, service the following components as described in this chapter:
   a. Clutch release mechanism.
   b. Primary chain adjuster.
   c. Shift shaft oil seal.

Installation

1. Clean the primary drive cover and engine crankcase gasket surfaces.
2. Clean the cover in solvent and dry thoroughly.
3. Using a new gasket, install the primary chain cover onto the crankcase. Install the cover mounting bolts and tighten to 90-120 in.-lb. (10.2-13.6 N•m) in the sequence shown in **Figure 12**.
4. Inspect the O-ring on the end of the clutch cable. Replace if damaged.
5. Install the cable and tighten to 36-60 in.-lb. (4.1-6.8 N•m).
6. Install the coupling onto the cable end with the rounded side facing in and the ramp connector button facing out. With the retaining side of the ramp facing in, install the ramp hook around the coupling button. Then rotate the assembly counterclockwise until the tang on the inner ramp fits into the primary cover slot.

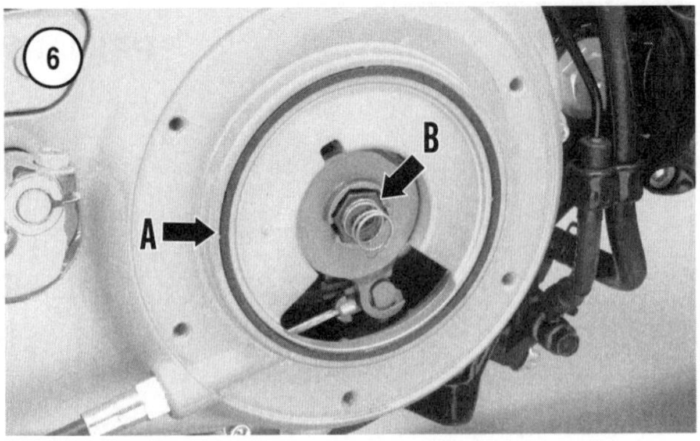

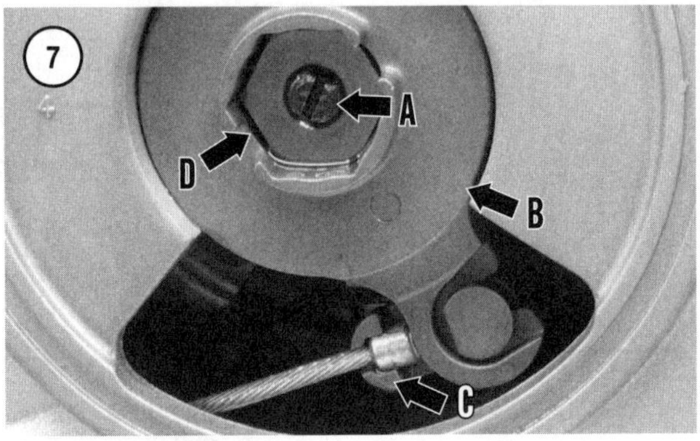

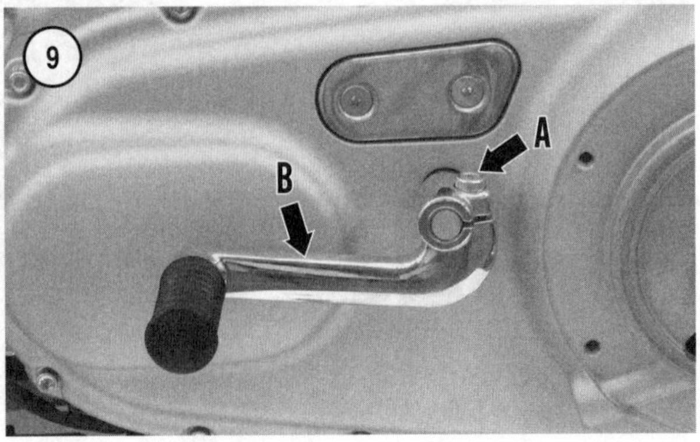

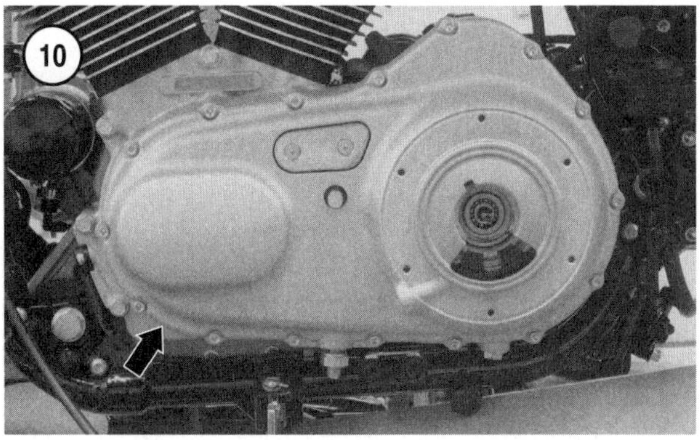

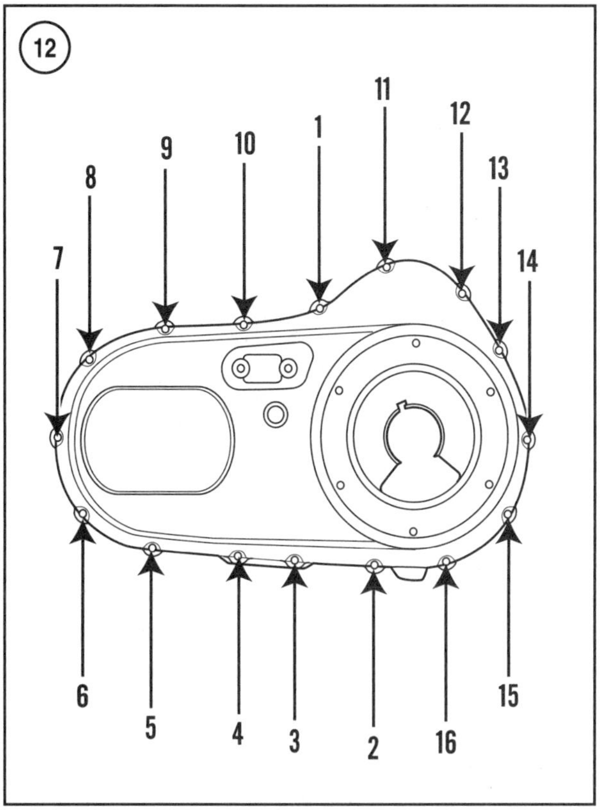

7. Thread the nut onto the clutch adjusting screw until the slot in the end of the screw is accessible with a screwdriver. Then align and install the hex portion on the nut into the outer ramp recess. Turn the clutch adjusting screw counterclockwise until resistance is felt, then back off 1/4 turn.
8. Adjust the clutch as described in Chapter Three. The spring and lockplate shown in **Figure 6** will be installed during the clutch adjustment procedure.
9. Adjust the primary chain as described in Chapter Three.
10. Clean the transmission drain plug and reinstall it into the cover. Tighten the plug to 14-30 ft.-lb. (19-40 N•m).
11. Refill the transmission oil as described in Chapter Three.
12. Install the shift lever (B, **Figure 9**) and tighten the clamp bolt to 16-20 ft.-lb. (22-27 N•m).
13. Install the left side footrest as described in Chapter Fourteen.
14. Reconnect the negative battery cable.

CLUTCH RELEASE MECHANISM

Removal

Refer to **Figure 13**.
1. Disconnect the negative battery cable.
2. Remove the left side footrest assembly as described in Chapter Fourteen.
3. Slide the rubber boot (A, **Figure 4**) upwards off the clutch in-line cable adjuster.
4. Loosen the adjuster locknut (B, **Figure 4**) and turn the adjuster (C) to provide maximum cable free play.
5. Remove the clutch inspection cover (**Figure 5**).
6. Remove the quad ring (A, **Figure 6**).
7. Remove the spring and lockplate (B, **Figure 6**).
8. Turn the clutch adjusting screw (A, **Figure 7**) clockwise and release the ramp (B) and coupling mechanism (C). Turn the clutch adjusting screw clockwise to move the ramp assembly forward. Then unscrew the nut (D, **Figure 7**) from the end of the adjusting screw and remove it.
9. Pivot the hook on the ramp to the rear of the cable end coupling. Disconnect and remove the clutch cable from the slot in the coupling. Remove the coupling and ramp assembly.
10. Remove the snap ring (**Figure 14**) securing the inner and outer ramp halves. Separate the halves and remove the ramps and balls.

Inspection

1. Wash the clutch release mechanism in solvent and dry thoroughly.
2. Check the balls and ramp sockets (**Figure 15**) for pitting, excessive wear or other damage.

13

CLUTCH RELEASE MECHANISM

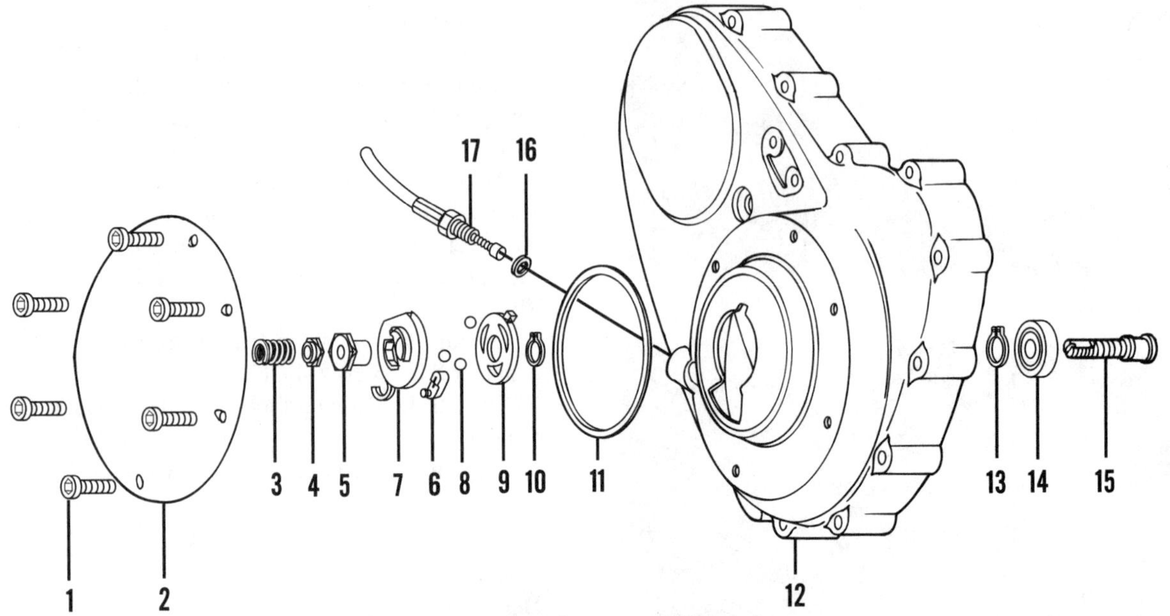

1. Torx screw and washer
2. Clutch inspection cover
3. Spring
4. Lockplate
5. Well nut
6. Coupling
7. Outer ramp
8. Balls (3)
9. Inner ramp
10. Snap ring
11. Quad ring
12. Cover
13. Snap ring
14. Bearing
15. Adjuster screw
16. O-ring
17. Clutch cable

3. Check the adjusting screw (**Figure 16**) for thread or bearing damage.
4. Replace the lockplate if the tabs are weak or broken.
5. Replace excessively worn or damaged parts as required.

Installation

1. Apply grease to the ball and ramp surfaces (**Figure 15**) and insert the balls into the outer ramp sockets.
2. Install the inner ramp on the outer ramp hook so the punch mark (A, **Figure 17**) on the inner ramp aligns with the hook of the outer ramp (B).
3. Fit the coupling over the clutch cable with the rounded side facing in and the ramp connector button facing out. With the retaining side of the ramp facing in, install the ramp hook around the coupling button. Then rotate the assembly counterclockwise until the tang on the inner ramp fits into the primary cover slot.

14

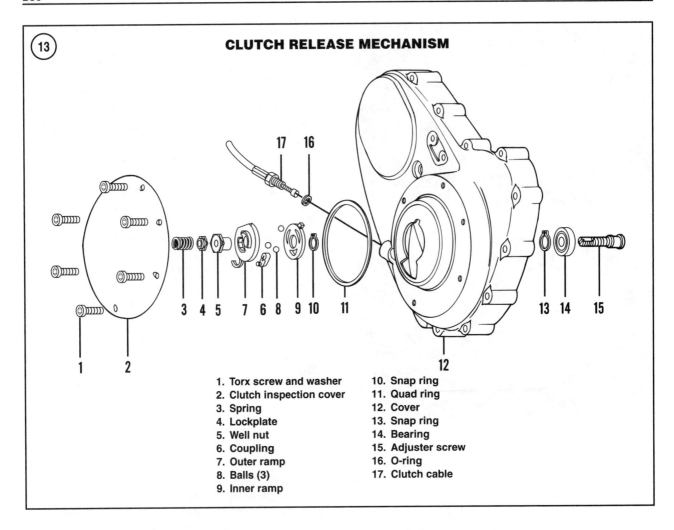

4. Thread the nut onto the clutch adjusting screw until the slot in the end of the screw is accessible with a screwdriver. Then align and install the hex portion on the nut into the outer ramp recess (**Figure 18**). Turn the clutch adjusting screw counterclockwise until resistance is felt, then back off 1/4 turn.

15
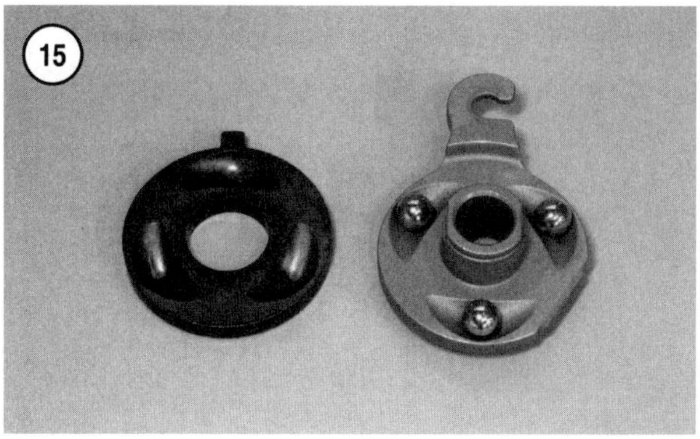

16
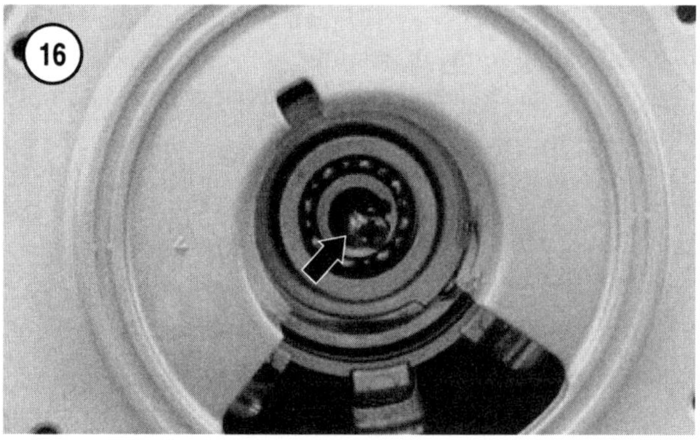

17
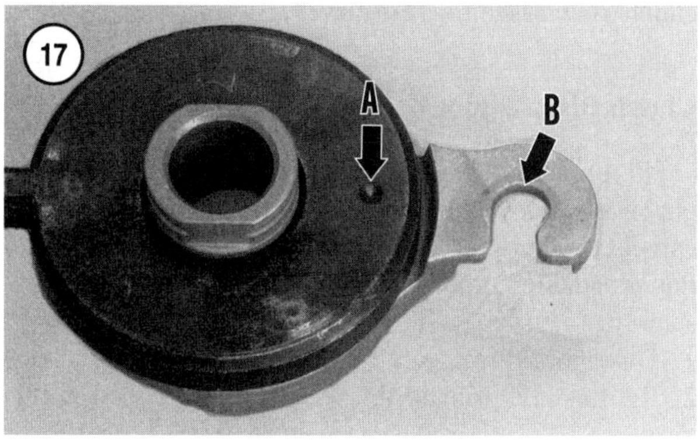

18
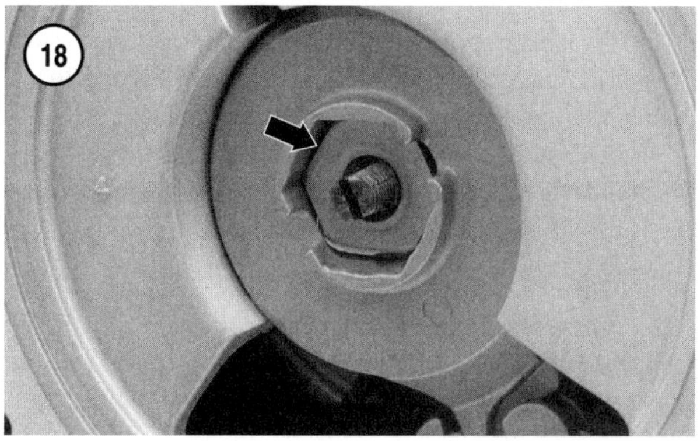

19
PRIMARY CHAIN ADJUSTER
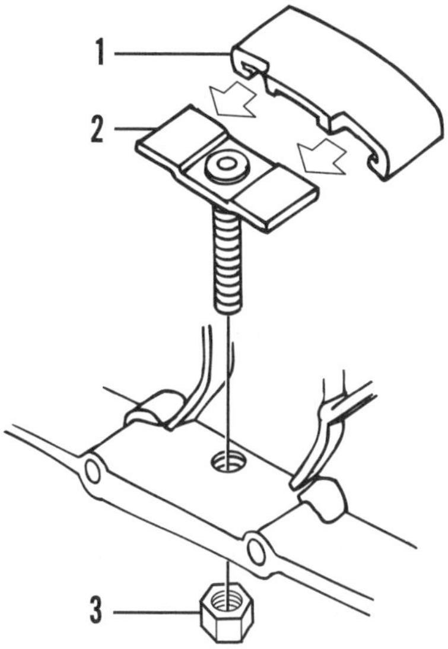

1. Adjuster shoe
2. Adjuster screw
3. Locknut

5. Adjust the clutch as described in Chapter Three. The spring and lockplate shown in **Figure 6** will be installed during the clutch adjustment procedure.

PRIMARY CHAIN ADJUSTER

The primary chain adjuster assembly (**Figure 19**) is mounted inside the primary drive cover.

Removal

Refer to **Figure 19**.

1. Remove the primary drive cover as described in this chapter.
2. Remove the adjuster screw locknut (A, **Figure 20**).
3. Turn the adjuster screw (B, **Figure 20**) to remove it from the threaded boss in the primary cover.
4. Slide the adjuster shoe (C, **Figure 20**) off the shoe plate.
5. Remove the upper locknut and shoe plate.

Inspection

1. Clean all parts in solvent and dry thoroughly.
2. Replace the adjuster shoe (C, **Figure 20**) if excessively worn or damaged.

3. Replace the locknut and adjuster screw if thread damage is apparent.

Installation

1. Install the adjuster shoe onto the top of the adjuster screw.
2. Place the adjuster assembly (C, **Figure 20**) into the primary drive cover so the closed side of the adjuster shoe faces toward the primary cover.
3. Thread the adjuster screw into the boss at the bottom of the cover.
4. Thread the lower locknut (A, **Figure 20**) onto the adjuster screw.
5. Install the cover as described in this chapter.
6. Adjust the primary chain as described in Chapter Three.

PRIMARY DRIVE/CLUTCH

Refer to **Figure 21**.

Service Precautions

Complete disassembly of the clutch requires the use of the Harley-Davidson spring compression tool (part No. HD-38515A [**Figure 22**]), or equivalent. If a compression tool is not available, remove the clutch intact from the bike and take it to a Harley-Davidson dealership or other qualified shop for disassembly and service. Do not disassemble the clutch without the special tool. The clutch diaphragm spring is under considerable pressure and will fly off, possibly causing severe injury, if the tool is not used.

Clutch/Primary Chain/Engine Sprocket Removal

This procedure describes removal of the clutch, primary chain and engine sprocket, without clutch disassembly. If necessary, refer to *Clutch Disassembly* in this section.

1. Shift the transmission into fifth gear.
2. Disconnect the negative battery cable.
3. Remove the primary drive cover as described in this chapter.
4. Install the Harley-Davidson sprocket locking link (part No. HD-38362 or HD-46283) or equivalent between the engine sprocket and clutch shell as shown in **Figure 23**.
5. Loosen and remove the engine sprocket nut (A, **Figure 24**).
6. Loosen the engine sprocket by pulling it outward (do not remove it). If the engine sprocket is tight, break it loose with a puller and two bolts installed on the sprocket face (B, **Figure 24**).

20

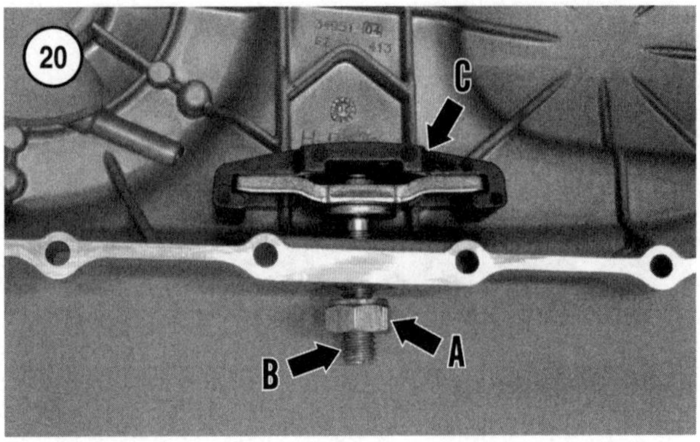

7. Remove the snap ring (**Figure 25**) holding the release plate/adjusting screw in position.
8. Remove the release plate/adjusting screw assembly (**Figure 26**).

NOTE
*The clutch nut (**Figure 27**) has left-hand threads.*

9. Turn the clutch nut (**Figure 27**) clockwise to loosen it. Then remove the clutch nut and washer (**Figure 28**).
10. Remove the locking link (**Figure 23**) installed during Step 4.
11. Remove the engine sprocket, primary chain and clutch as an assembly (**Figure 29**).

Clutch Disassembly

This procedure describes clutch plate removal while the clutch assembly is mounted on the motorcycle. Engine sprocket and primary chain removal is not required. Read this procedure completely through before starting disassembly.

1. Disconnect the negative battery cable.
2. Remove the primary drive cover as described in this chapter.
3. To remove the diaphragm spring snap ring, perform the following:
   a. Thread the spring compression tool forcing screw into the clutch adjusting screw as shown in **Figure 30**.
   b. Position the spring compression tool (**Figure 31**) against the diaphragm spring and thread the tool handle (A, **Figure 32**) onto the end of the forcing screw.

CAUTION
Turn the compression tool handle only the amount required to compress the diaphragm spring and remove the snap ring in substep c. Excessive compression of the diaphragm spring may damage the clutch pressure plate.

(21)

CLUTCH

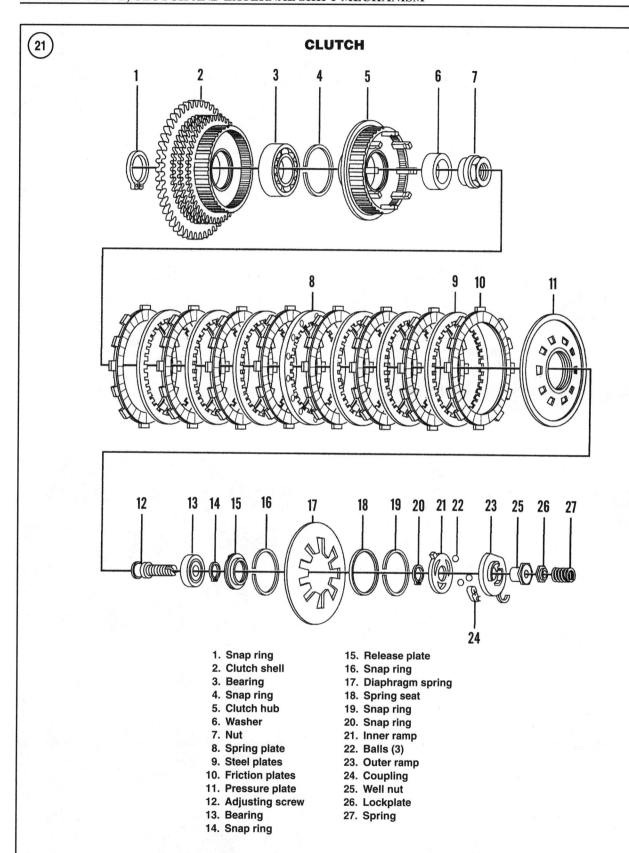

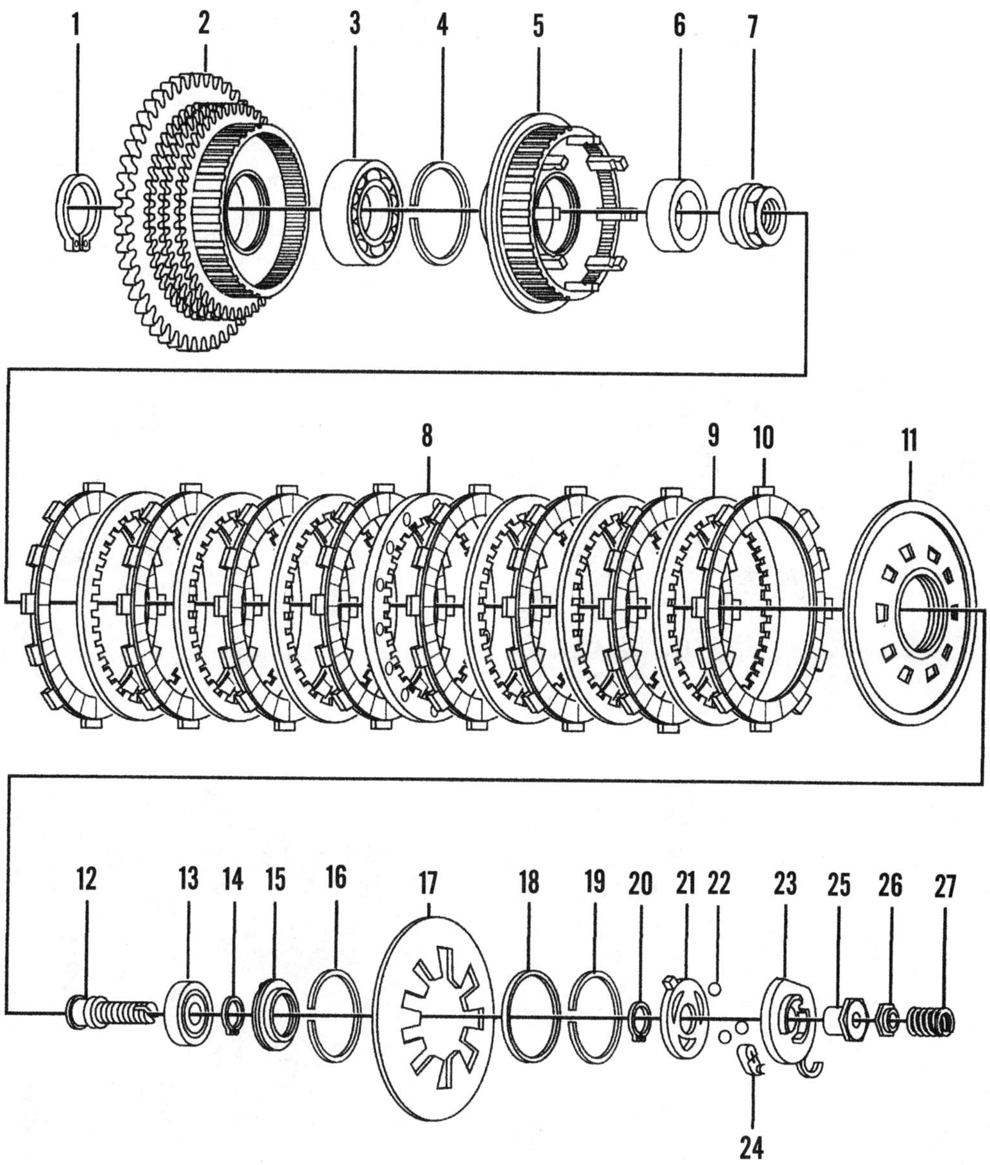

1. Snap ring
2. Clutch shell
3. Bearing
4. Snap ring
5. Clutch hub
6. Washer
7. Nut
8. Spring plate
9. Steel plates
10. Friction plates
11. Pressure plate
12. Adjusting screw
13. Bearing
14. Snap ring
15. Release plate
16. Snap ring
17. Diaphragm spring
18. Spring seat
19. Snap ring
20. Snap ring
21. Inner ramp
22. Balls (3)
23. Outer ramp
24. Coupling
25. Well nut
26. Lockplate
27. Spring

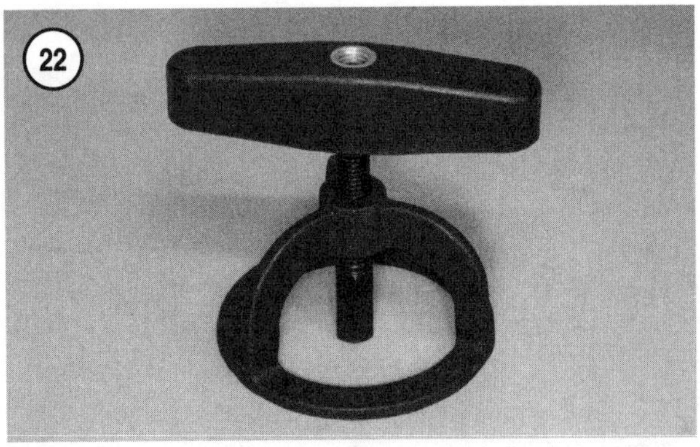

c. Hold the compression tool forcing screw with a wrench (B, **Figure 32**) and turn the tool handle clockwise to compress the diaphragm spring.
d. Remove the snap ring (**Figure 33**) and spring seat (**Figure 34**) from the groove in the clutch hub.
e. Remove the diaphragm spring, pressure plate, clutch adjusting screw and spring compressing tool as an assembly (**Figure 35**).

NOTE
Do not loosen the spring compressing tool to remove the diaphragm spring or

pressure plate unless these parts require close inspection or replacement. Loosening and removing the compressing tool will require repositioning of the diaphragm spring during reassembly. This step will not be required as long as the compressing tool is not removed from these parts.

4. Remove the friction and steel clutch plates (**Figure 36**) (and the spring plate) from the clutch assembly in order as shown in **Figure 21**. Note the spring plate in-

6

stalled between the fourth and fifth friction plates (**Figure 37**).

NOTE
Further removal steps are not required unless it is necessary to separate the clutch hub and shell assembly. If necessary, remove these parts as described in ***Clutch Hub and Shell Disassembly/Reassembly*** *in this section.*

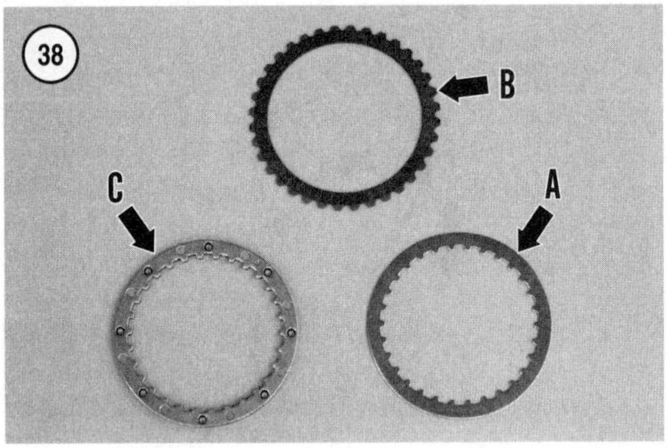

Clutch Inspection

1. Clean all parts (except friction plates and bearing) in a non-oil based solvent and thoroughly dry with compressed air. Place all cleaned parts on lintfree paper towels.
2. Check each steel plate (A, **Figure 38**) for visual damage such as cracks or wear grooves. Then place each plate on a surface plate or a piece of plate glass and check for warp with a feeler gauge. Replace the steel plates as a set if any one plate is warped more than the specification in **Table 1**.
3. Inspect the friction plates (B, **Figure 38**) for worn or grooved lining surfaces; replace the friction plates as a set if any one plate is damaged. If the friction plates do not show visual wear or damage, wipe each plate thoroughly with a lint-free cloth to remove as much oil from the plates as possible. Stack each of the eight friction plates on top of each other and measure the thickness of the assembly with a vernier caliper or micrometer. Replace the friction plates as an assembly if the combined thickness of the plate pack is less than the service limit in **Table 1**.
4. Check the spring plate (C, **Figure 38**) for cracks or damage. Check for loose or damaged rivets. Replace the spring plate if necessary.
5. Check the diaphragm spring for cracks or damage. Check also for bent or damaged tabs. Replace the diaphragm spring if necessary.
6. A ball bearing is pressed into the clutch shell and the clutch hub is pressed into the bearing. Hold the clutch hub and rotate the clutch shell by hand. The shell should turn smoothly with no sign of roughness or tightness. If the clutch shell binds or turns roughly, the bearing is damaged and must be replaced.
7. The steel clutch plate inner teeth mesh with the clutch hub splines. Check the splines for cracks or galling. They must be smooth for chatter-free clutch operation. If the clutch hub splines are damaged, replace the clutch hub.
8. The friction plates (B, **Figure 38**) have tabs that slide in the clutch shell grooves. Inspect the shell grooves for cracks or wear grooves. The grooves must be smooth for chatter-free clutch operation. If the clutch shell grooves are damaged or worn excessively, replace the clutch shell.
9. Check the primary chain sprocket and the starter ring gear on the clutch shell for cracks, deep scoring, excessive wear or heat discoloration. If either the sprocket or ring gear is excessively worn or damaged, replace the clutch shell; If the sprocket is worn, also check the primary chain and the engine sprocket as described in this section.
10. If the clutch hub, shell or bearing require replacement, refer to *Clutch Hub and Shell Disassembly/Reassembly* in this section.

39

40

41

42

Primary Chain Inspection

Replace the primary chain if excessively worn or damaged. Do not repair the chain, as engine damage will result if the chain breaks. If the primary chain is worn or damaged, check the engine sprocket and clutch shell sprocket for wear or damage. Replace parts as required.

Clutch Hub and Shell Disassembly/Reassembly

The clutch hub and shell should not be separated unless replacement of the hub, shell or bearing is required. Disassembly of the hub and shell will damage the ball bearing; bearing replacement will be required during reassembly. A press is required for this procedure.

Read this procedure completely before starting disassembly.

1. Remove the clutch plates from the clutch hub and shell assembly. Refer to *Clutch Disassembly*.
2. Remove the snap ring from the clutch hub groove using snap ring pliers (**Figure 39**).
3. Support the clutch hub and shell in a press (**Figure 40**) and press the clutch hub out of the bearing. See **Figure 41**. Remove the clutch shell from the press.
4. Locate the snap ring (**Figure 42**) securing the bearing in the clutch shell. Carefully remove the snap ring from the clutch shell groove.

CAUTION

When removing the bearing in Step 5, note that the bearing must be removed through the front side of the shell. The clutch shell is manufactured with a shoulder on the rear (primary chain) side.

5. Support the clutch shell in the press and press the bearing out of the shell. Discard the bearing.
6. Discard worn or damaged parts. Clean reusable and new parts (except bearing and snap rings) in solvent and dry thoroughly.
7. Place the clutch shell into the press. Then align the bearing with the clutch shell and press the bearing into the shell until the bearing bottoms out against the lower shoulder. When pressing the bearing into the clutch shell, press only on the outer bearing race. Installing the bearing by pressing on its inner race will damage the bearing. Refer to Chapter One for general bearing replacement.
8. Install a new bearing snap ring into the clutch shell groove (**Figure 42**). Make sure the snap ring seats in the groove completely.
9. Press the clutch hub into the clutch shell as follows:

a. Place the clutch shell in a press. Support the inner bearing race with a sleeve as shown in **Figure 43**.

CAUTION
Failure to support the inner bearing race properly will cause bearing and clutch shell damage. Make sure the inner bearing race is supported properly.

b. Align the clutch hub with the bearing and press the clutch hub into the bearing until the clutch hub shoulder seats against the bearing.

c. Using snap ring pliers, install a new clutch hub snap ring (**Figure 39**). Make sure the snap ring seats in the clutch hub groove completely.

10. After completing assembly, hold the clutch hub and rotate the clutch shell by hand. The shell should turn smoothly with no roughness or binding. If the clutch shell binds or turns roughly, the bearing may have been damaged during reassembly.

Clutch Assembly

This section describes clutch assembly. After assembly, the clutch will be installed back onto the motorcycle. If the clutch assembly was not disassembled, refer to *Clutch Installation* in this section.

1. Soak all the clutch plates in clean transmission oil for approximately 5 minutes before installing them.

NOTE
Before installing the clutch plates, count the number of each plate type. The set should include eight friction plates, six steel plates and one spring plate.

2. Align the tabs on a friction plate with the clutch shell grooves and install the plate type. Then align the inner teeth on a steel plate with the clutch hub grooves and install the plate. Repeat until all the clutch plates have been installed. Install the spring plate (**Figure 37**) between the fourth and fifth friction plates. The last plate installed must be a friction plate.

NOTE
During clutch removal, if the spring compressing tool was not removed from the diaphragm spring and pressure plate, proceed to Step 4. If the spring compressing tool was removed and the diaphragm spring was separated from the pressure plate, continue with Step 3.

3. Assemble the pressure plate and diaphragm spring as follows:

43

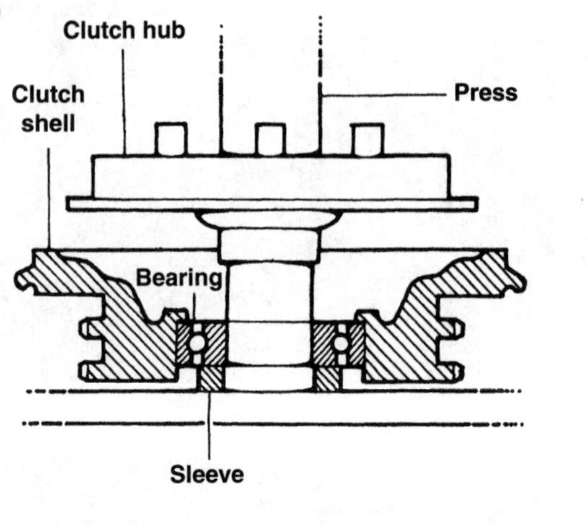

44

a. Install the adjusting screw assembly (release plate, snap ring, bearing and adjusting screw) into the pressure plate. Install the release plate by aligning its tabs with the slots in the pressure plate. Secure the release plate by installing the retaining ring into the pressure plate groove. Make sure the retaining ring seats in the groove completely.

b. The diaphragm spring is concave. Install the diaphragm spring onto the pressure plate so the concave side faces the pressure plate—the convex side must face out.

c. Install the spring seat with its flat, larger outer diameter side facing toward the diaphragm spring.

4. To install the diaphragm spring snap ring, perform the following:

a. Thread the spring compression tool forcing screw onto the clutch adjusting screw.

b. Position the spring compression tool against the diaphragm spring and thread the tool handle onto the end of the forcing screw. Do not apply pressure against the diaphragm spring at this time.

45

46

47

c. Align the square holes in the pressure plate and diaphragm spring with the prongs on the face of the clutch hub. Then place the spring seat, snap ring, diaphragm spring, pressure plate, adjusting screw assembly and compressing tool onto the clutch hub (**Figure 35**).

CAUTION
Turn the compression tool handle only the amount required to compress the diaphragm spring and install the snap ring in substep e. Excessive compression of the diaphragm spring may damage the clutch pressure plate.

d. Hold the compression tool forcing screw with a wrench and turn the tool handle clockwise to compress the diaphragm spring.
e. Install the spring seat and snap ring into the groove in the clutch hub prongs.
f. After making sure the snap ring is seated completely in the clutch hub groove, slowly turn the compressing tool handle counterclockwise while checking that the clutch spring seat lip seats inside the snap ring. After all tension has been removed from the compressing tool, remove it from the release plate.

5. Remove the release plate retaining ring. Then remove the adjusting screw assembly (release plate, retaining ring, bearing and adjusting screw).

6

Clutch Installation

1. Assemble the clutch assembly as described in this section.
2. The engine sprocket, primary chain and clutch are installed as an assembly. Assemble the engine sprocket, clutch and primary chain as shown in **Figure 44**.

CAUTION
The rotor is mounted on the engine sprocket. Carefully inspect the inside of the rotor for debris that may have been picked up by the magnets. Metal debris can cause damage to the alternator stator assembly.

3. Lift the primary drive assembly as a unit and slide the engine sprocket and clutch into the primary chaincase. See **Figure 45**.
4. Install the Harley-Davidson sprocket locking link (part No. HD-38362 or HD-46283) or equivalent between the engine sprocket and clutch shell as shown in **Figure 46**.

WARNING
Make sure to hold the sprocket securely when tightening the nut.

5. Apply 2-3 drops of Loctite 262 (red) to the engine sprocket nut threads and install the nut (**Figure 47**) onto the sprocket shaft. Tighten the engine sprocket nut to 190-210 ft.-lb. (259-285 N•m).
6. Install the clutch nut Belleville washer onto the mainshaft so OUT faces out (**Figure 48**).

CAUTION
The clutch nut has left-hand threads.

7. Apply 2-3 drops of Loctite 262 (red) to the clutch nut threads and install the nut onto the mainshaft by turning the nut *counterclockwise*. Tighten the clutch nut (**Figure 49**) to 70-80 ft.-lb. (96-108 N•m).

8. Remove the sprocket locking link (**Figure 46**).
9. Install the adjusting screw assembly (**Figure 50**) by aligning the two tabs on the release plate perimeter with the two recesses in the pressure plate.
10. Install a new snap ring (**Figure 51**).
11. Install the primary drive cover as described in this chapter.
12. Adjust the primary chain as described in Chapter Three.
13. Refill the primary chain housing with oil as described in Chapter Three.
14. Reconnect the negative battery cable.

CLUTCH CABLE

Removal/Inspection/Installation

Refer to **Figure 52** and **Figure 53**.

1. Disconnect the negative battery cable.
2. Remove the left side footrest assembly as described in Chapter Fourteen.
3. Slide the rubber boot (A, **Figure 54**) up and off the clutch in-line cable adjuster.
4. Loosen the cable adjuster lock nut (B, **Figure 54**) and turn the adjuster (C) to provide maximum free play.
5. Remove the clutch inspection cover (**Figure 55**).
6. Remove the quad ring (A, **Figure 56**).
7. Remove the spring and lockplate (B, **Figure 56**).
8. Turn the clutch adjusting screw (A, **Figure 57**) clockwise and release the ramp (B) and coupling mechanism (C). Turn the clutch adjusting screw clockwise to move the ramp assembly forward. Then unscrew the well nut (D, **Figure 57**) from the end of the adjusting screw and remove it.
9. Pivot the hook on the ramp to the rear of the cable end coupling. Then disconnect and remove the clutch cable from the slot in the coupling. Remove the coupling and ramp assembly.
10. Unscrew the clutch cable (**Figure 58**) from the primary drive cover.
11. At the clutch lever, remove the retaining clip on the lower end of the pivot pin, then remove the pivot pin (**Figure 59**).
12. Slide the clutch lever out of its bracket.
13. Disengage the cable fitting and lever from the control lever bracket.
14. Push out the cable retaining pin from the lever and separate the cable from the control lever.
15. Note the routing of the clutch cable and the position of all cable clamps, then remove the clutch cable.
16. If necessary, remove the screw and anti-rattle spring from the bottom of the clutch lever.
17. Inspect the bushing in the control lever bracket. Replace it if damaged or excessively worn. Install the bushing so the flanged end is up.

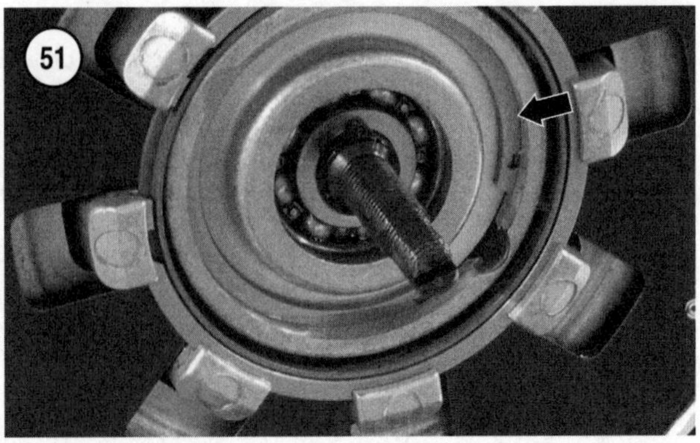

52

CLUTCH RELEASE MECHANISM

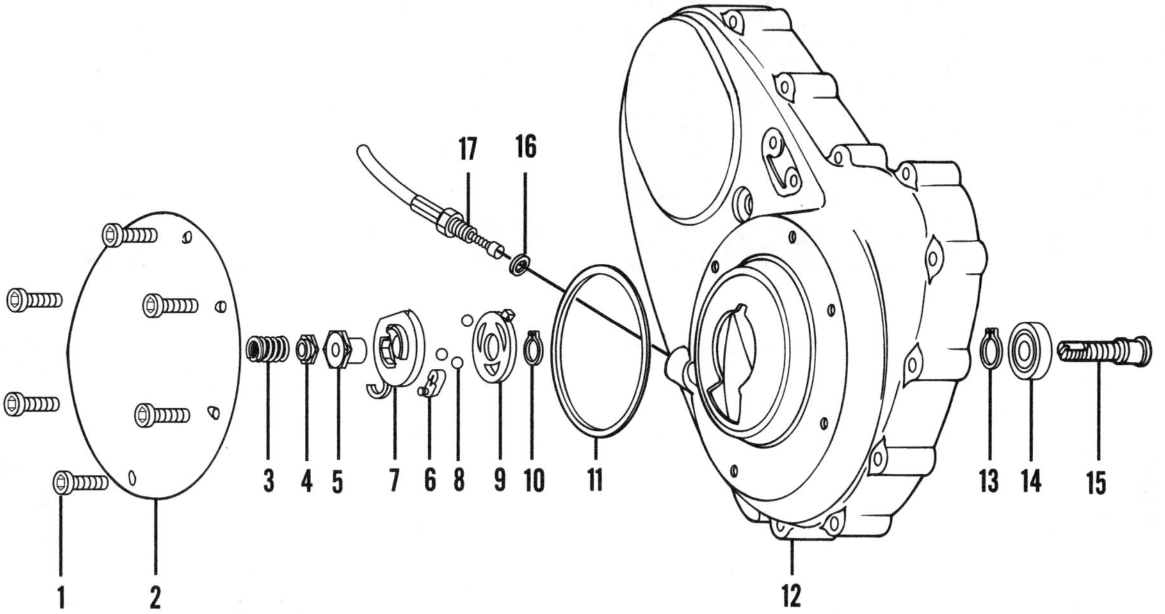

1. Torx screw and washer
2. Clutch inspection cover
3. Spring
4. Lockplate
5. Well nut
6. Coupling
7. Outer ramp
8. Balls (3)
9. Inner ramp
10. Snap ring
11. Quad ring
12. Cover
13. Snap ring
14. Bearing
15. Adjuster screw
16. Washer
17. Clutch cable

53

CLUTCH LEVER ASSEMBLY

1. Clutch cable
2. Pivot pin
3. Clutch lever bracket
4. Retaining ring
5. Clutch cable pin
6. Anti-rattle spring
7. Screw
8. Clamp
9. Washer
10. Screw
11. Bushing
12. Clutch lever

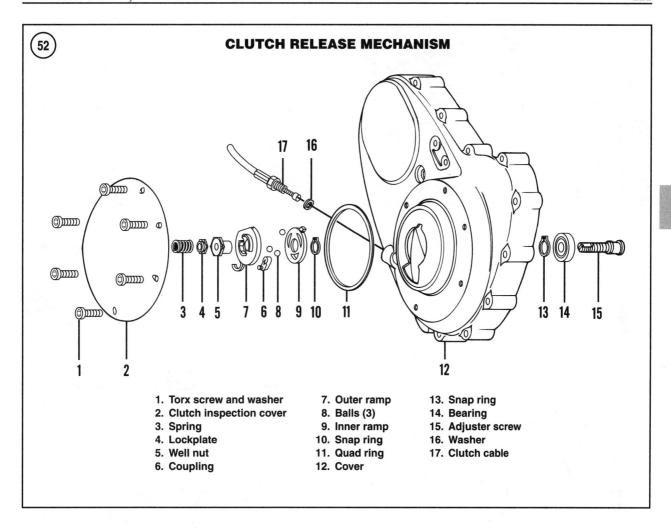

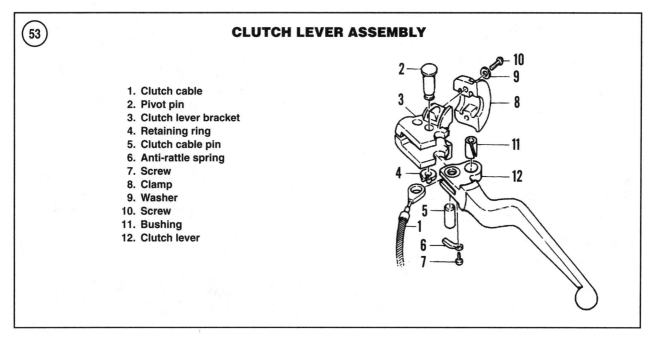

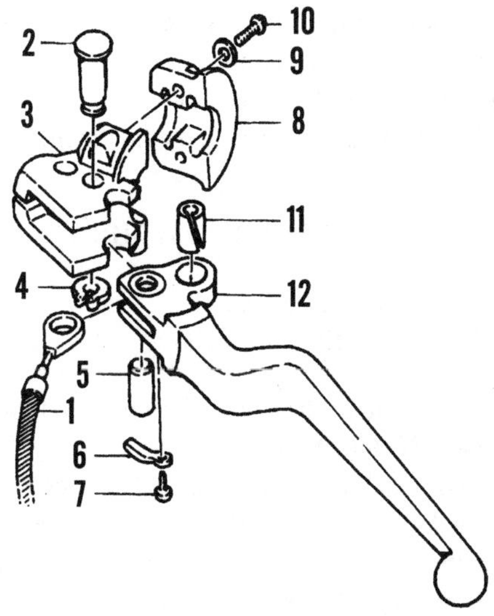

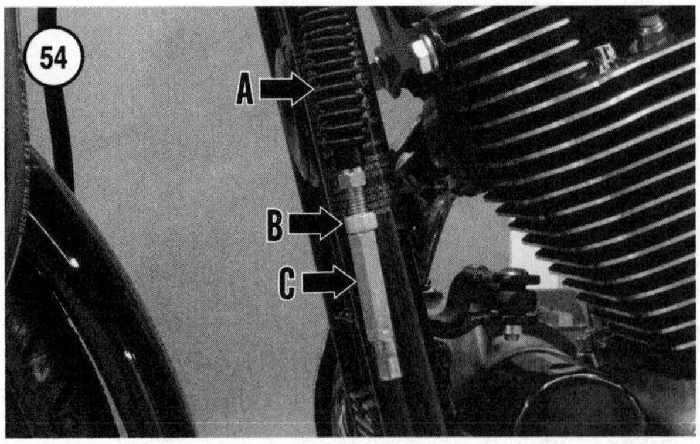

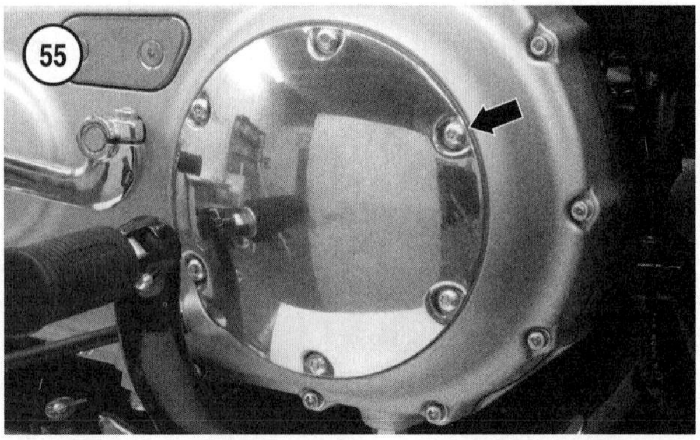

18. Inspect the pivot pin and replace if damaged or excessively worn.
19. Inspect the cable retaining pin. Replace it if damaged or excessively worn.
20. Install the clutch cable by reversing the removal steps while noting the following:
   a. Install a new O-ring on the end of the clutch cable (**Figure 60**).
   b. Install the cable into the cover and tighten to 36-60 in.-lb. (4.1-6.8 N•m).
   c. Install the coupling onto the lower cable end with the rounded side facing in and the ramp connector button facing out. With the retaining side of the ramp facing in, install the ramp hook around the coupling button. Then rotate the assembly counterclockwise until the tang on the inner ramp fits into the primary cover slot.
   d. Thread the nut onto the clutch adjusting screw until the slot in the end of the screw is accessible with a screwdriver. Then align and install the hex portion on the nut into the outer ramp recess. Turn the clutch adjusting screw counterclockwise until resistance is felt, then back off 1/4 turn.
   e. Adjust the clutch as described in Chapter Three. The spring and lockplate shown in **Figure 56** will be installed during the clutch adjustment procedure.

SHIFT LEVER ASSEMBLY

Shift Lever Height Adjustment (XL883C and XL1200C Models)

The foot-operated shift lever height is adjustable on models XL883C and XL1200C.

1. Loosen the locknuts (A, **Figure 61**) on the shift rod.
2. Remove the front rod end retaining bolt (B, **Figure 61**).
3. Rotate the rod end and shift rod as needed to adjust the position of the shift lever footpeg. The desired height angle is 45°.

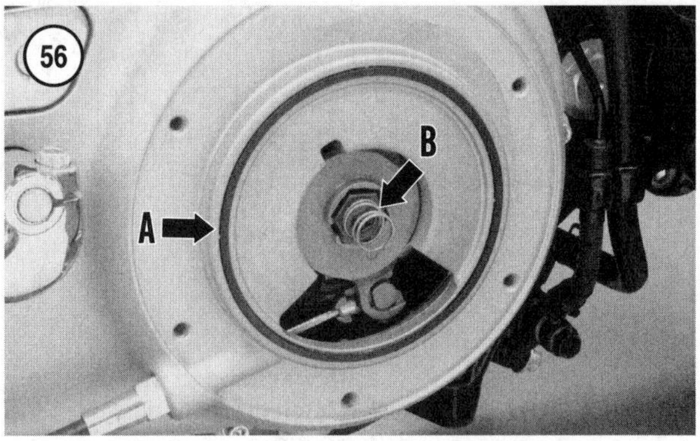

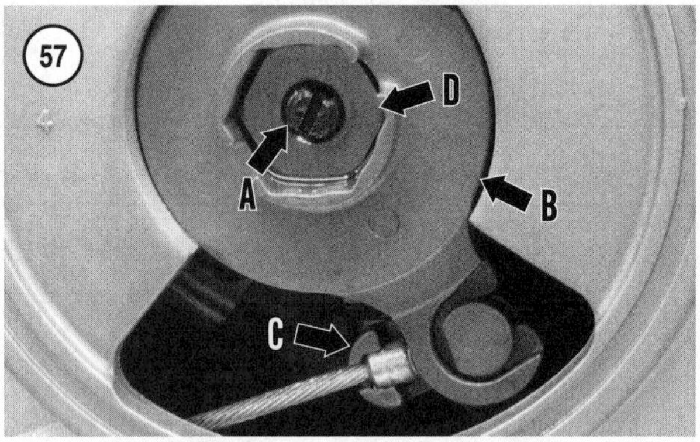

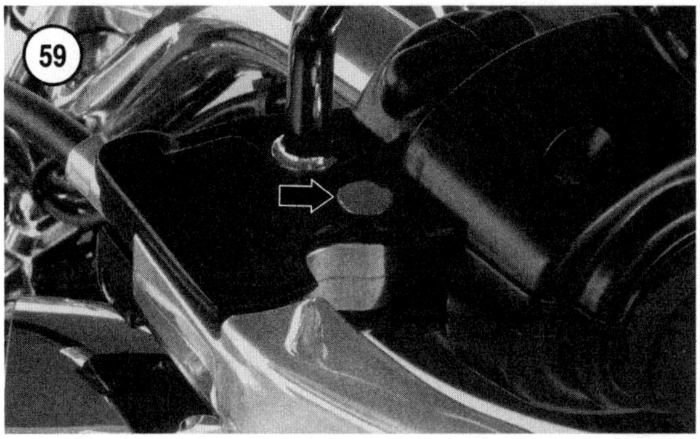

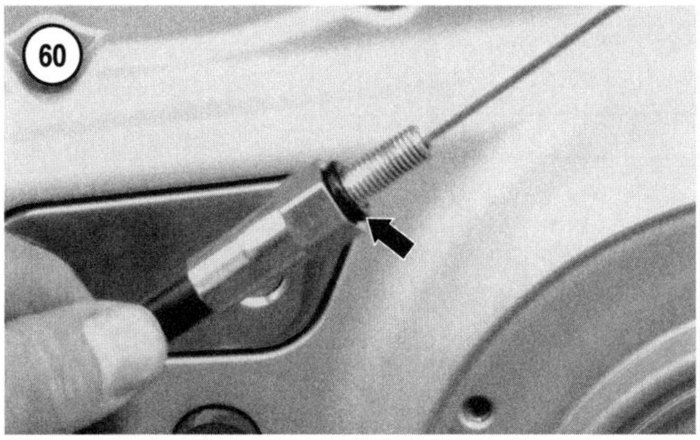

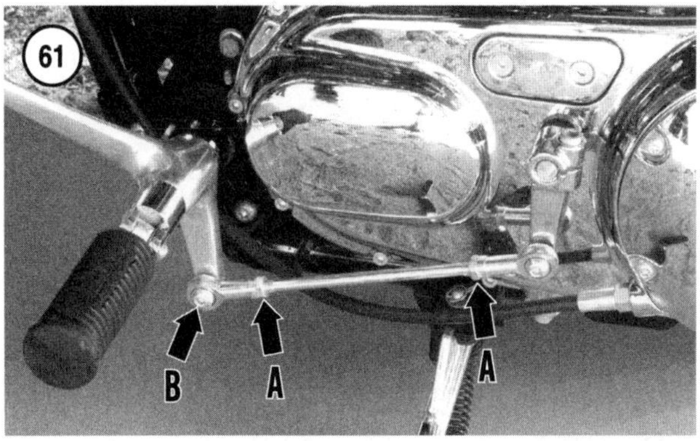

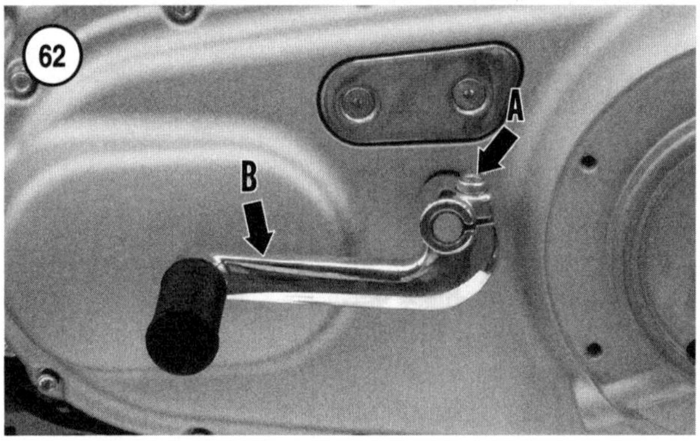

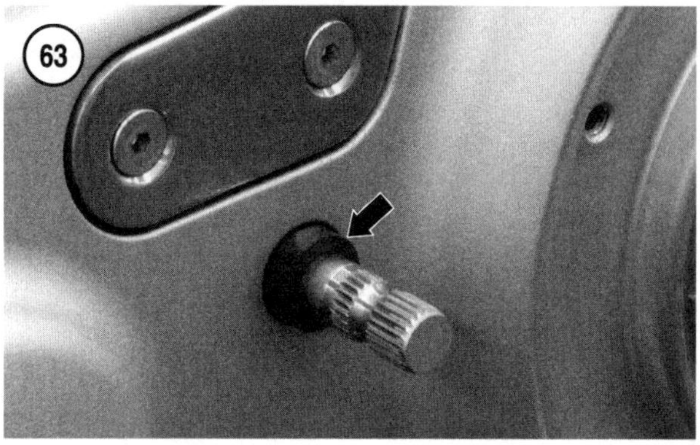

6

4. Tighten the shift rod end retaining bolt to 120-180 in.-lb. (14-20 N•m).
5. Tighten the locknuts on the shift rod.

Removal/Installation

XL883, XL883L, XL883R, XL1200L and XL1200R models

1. Remove the shift lever clamp bolt (A, **Figure 62**).
2. Pull the shift lever (B, **Figure 62**) off the shift shaft.
3. If necessary, remove the rubber washer (**Figure 63**).
4. Inspect the shift lever.
5. If necessary, unscrew the footpeg.
6. Reverse the removal steps to install the shift lever while noting the following:
   a. Engage the master splines on the shift lever and shaft.
   b. Tighten the clamp bolt (A, **Figure 62**) to 16-20 ft.-lb. (22-27 N•m).

XL883C and XL1200C models

On XL883C and XL1200C models the transmission shift lever is actuated through a shift rod by the foot-operated shift lever.

Refer to **Figure 64**.

1. Remove the shift rod end retaining bolts at each end (A, **Figure 65**), then remove the shift rod (B).
2. Remove the shift lever clamp bolt (C, **Figure 65**).
3. Pull the shift lever (D, **Figure 65**) off the shift shaft.
4. If necessary, remove the rubber washer (**Figure 63**).
5. Remove the left footrest assembly as described in Chapter Fourteen.
6. Remove the snap ring (A, **Figure 66**).
7. Remove the clevis locating bolt (B, **Figure 66**), then remove the clevis and shift lever assembly.
8. Remove the shift lever and bushing from the clevis.
9. If necessary, unscrew the footpeg from the shift lever.

64

SHIFT LEVER ASSEMBLY (XL883C AND XL1200C)

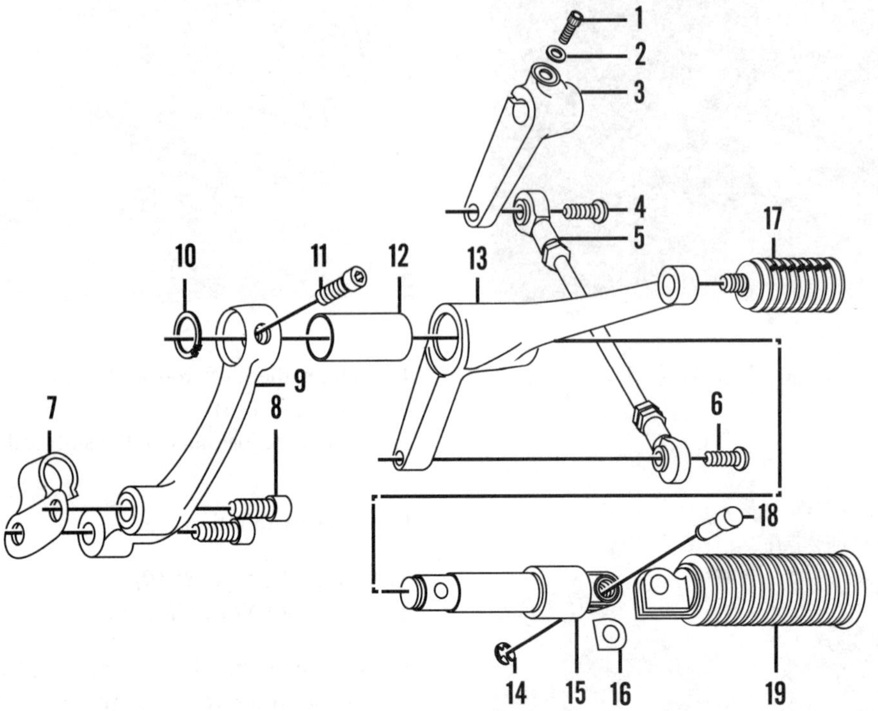

1. Bolt
2. Washer
3. Shift lever
4. Bolt
5. Shift rod
6. Bolt
7. Clip
8. Bolt
9. Support bracket
10. Snap ring
11. Locating bolt
12. Bushing
13. Shift lever
14. E-clip
15. Clevis
16. Spring washer
17. Shift peg
18. Clevis pin
19. Foot peg

10. Inspect the components for excessive wear and damage.

NOTE
The shift rod is available only as a complete assembly.

11. Reverse the removal steps to install the shift lever assembly while noting the following:

   a. Engage the master splines on the shift lever (D, **Figure 65**) and shaft.

   b. Tighten the clamp bolt (C, **Figure 65**) to 16-20 ft.-lb. (22-27 N•m).

   c. Tighten the footpeg clevis locating bolt (B, **Figure 66**) to 18-22 ft.-lb. (25-30 N•m).

   d. Tighten the shift rod end retaining bolts (A, **Figure 65**) to 120-180 in.-lb. (14-20 N•m).

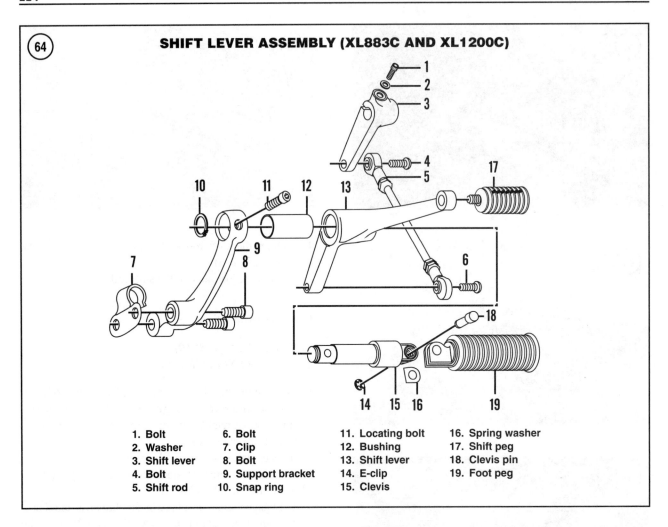

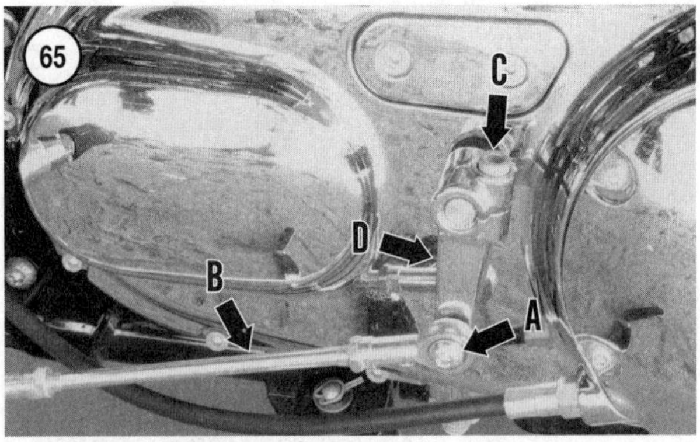

SHIFT SHAFT

Removal/Installation

Refer to **Figure 67**.

1. Remove the clutch as described in this chapter.

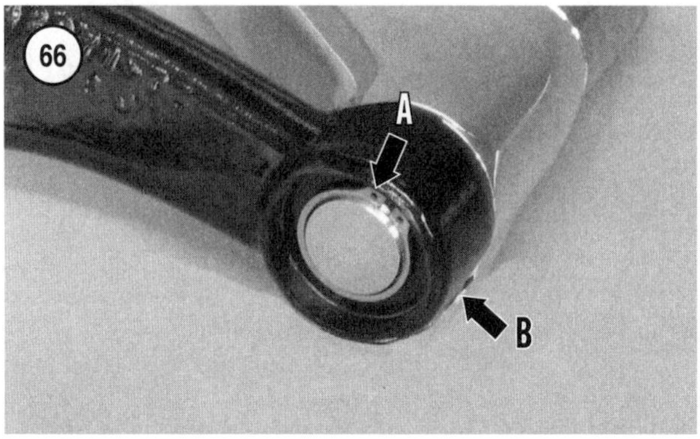

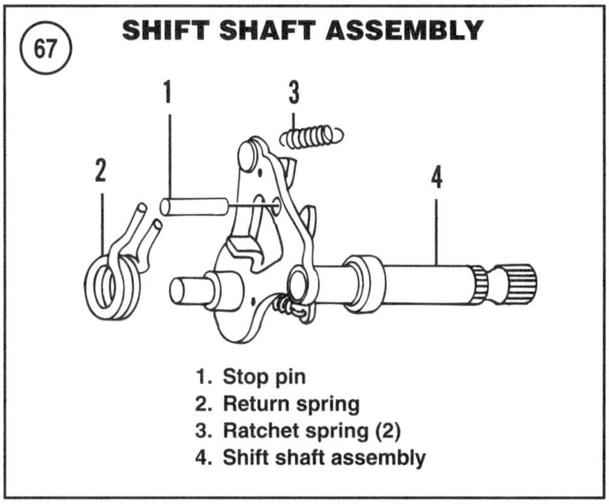

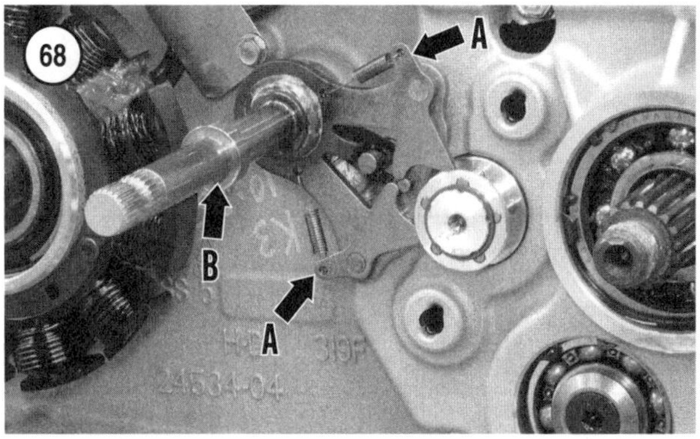

2. Push in the ratchet arms (A, **Figure 68**) so they are disengaged from the shift drum pins.

3. Remove the shift shaft assembly (B, **Figure 68**).

4. Reverse the removal steps to install the shift shaft assembly while noting the following:

   a. Make sure the return spring ends (A, **Figure 69**) fit around the shaft tab.

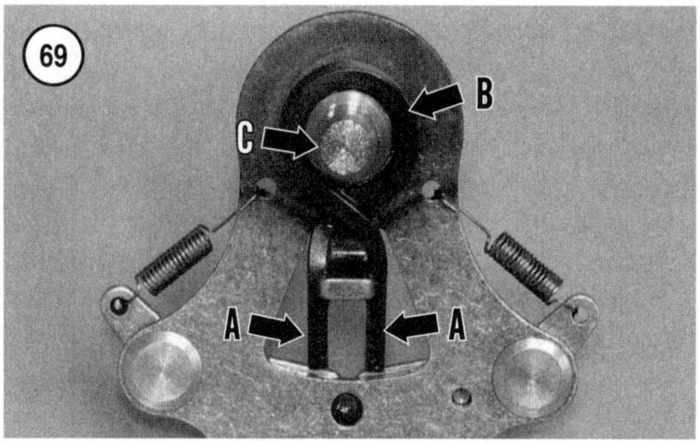

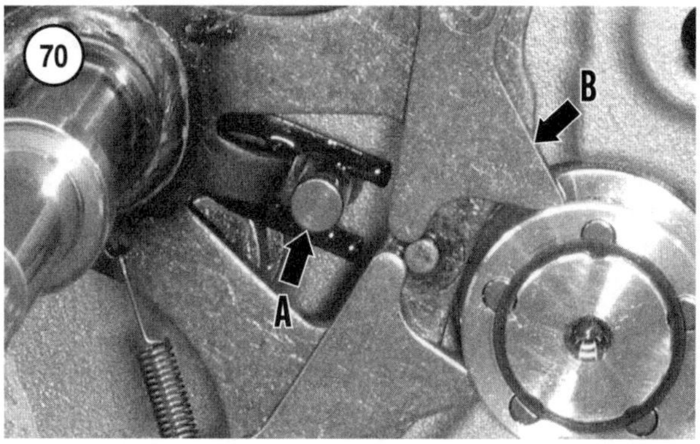

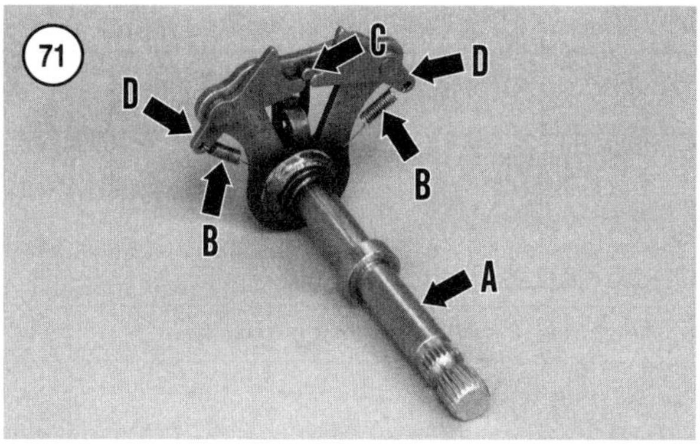

   b. Position the spring ends around the index pin (A, **Figure 70**).

   c. Make sure the ratchet arms (B, **Figure 70**) properly engage the shift drum pins.

Inspection

1. Inspect the shift shaft (A, **Figure 71**) for straightness, excessive wear and damaged splines.

2. Inspect the ratchet springs (B, **Figure 71**) and replace if deformed or damaged.

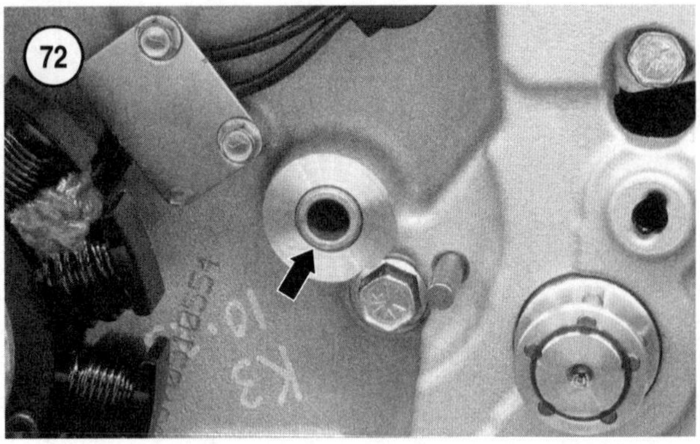
72

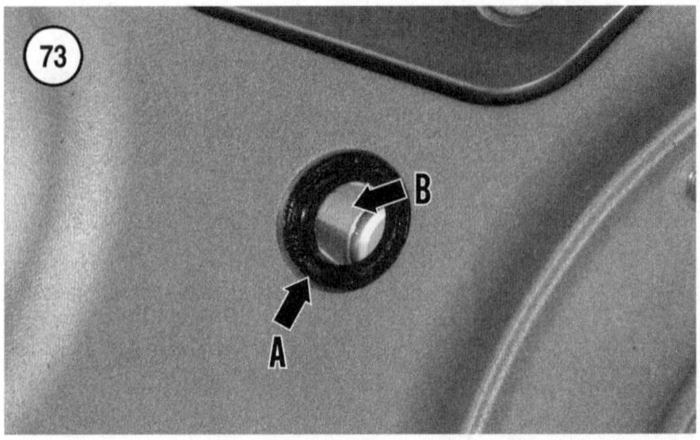

73

3. Make sure the stop pin (C, **Figure 71**) fits tightly in the shaft plate.
4. Inspect the ratchet arms (D, **Figure 71**) for wear. Excessive wear on the ratchet arms and shift drum pins will cause erratic shifting.
5. Check the movement of the ratchet arms. They should operate freely without excessive wobble.
6. Inspect the return spring (B, **Figure 69**) and replace if deformed or damaged.
7. Inspect the inner shaft (C, **Figure 69**) for excessive wear or damage.
8. Inspect the bushing in the crankcase (**Figure 72**). Replace the bushing if excessively worn or damaged using a blind bushing removal tool. Refer to Chapter One for general bearing procedures.

9. Inspect the seal in the primary drive cover (A, **Figure 73**). Replace the oil seal if it is hardened or damaged.

10. Inspect the bushing in the primary cover (B, **Figure 73**). Replace the bushing if excessively worn or damaged.

Table 1 CLUTCH SPECIFICATIONS

	New in. (mm)	Service limit in. (mm)
Friction plates		
Thickness	0.0835-0.0897 (2.121-2.278)	–
Friction plate pack*	–	0.6610 (16.79)
Steel plate thickness	0.0609-0.0649 (1.547-1.647)	–
Warp (all plates)	–	0.0059 (0.150)

*Refer to text for measurement procedure.

Table 2 CLUTCH AND PRIMARY DRIVE TORQUE SPECIFICATIONS

	ft.-lb.	in.-lb.	N•m
Clutch cable	–	36-60	4.1-6.8
Clutch inspection cover bolts	–	90-120	10.2-13.6
Clutch nut*	70-80	–	96-108
Engine sprocket nut (2004-2006)	190-210	–	259-285
Footpeg clevis locating bolt	18-22	–	25-30
Primary drive cover bolts	–	100-120	11.3-13.5
Shift lever clamp bolt	16-20	–	22-27
Shift rod end retaining bolt	–	120-180	14-20
Transmission drain plug	14-30	–	19-40

*Left-hand threads

NOTE: Refer to the Supplement at the end of this manual for information unique to 2007-2011 models.

CHAPTER SEVEN

TRANSMISSION AND INTERNAL SHIFT MECHANISM

7

This chapter covers service to the transmission and internal gearshift assemblies. Specifications are in **Table 1** and **Table 2** at the end of this chapter.

When the clutch is engaged, the mainshaft is driven by the clutch hub, which is driven by the primary chain sprocket/clutch outer housing. Power flows from the mainshaft through the selected gear combination to the countershaft, which drives the main drive gear and transmission sprocket.

To access the transmission and internal shift mechanism, it is necessary to remove the engine and disassemble the crankcase as described in Chapter Five.

INTERNAL GEARSHIFT MECHANISM (2004-2005 MODELS)

Removal/Disassembly

Refer to **Figure 1**.

1. Remove the engine as described in Chapter Five.

NOTE

*During engine disassembly, mark the end of the shift drum and crankcase with reference lines to indicate neutral position (**Figure 2**). Neutral is indicated when the neutral switch pin on the shift drum is visible in the switch hole (**Figure 3**). The neutral reference will help when checking shift mechanism operation.*

2. Separate the crankcase as described in Chapter Five.
3. To remove the shift fork shafts (**Figure 4**), insert a punch through the access slot for each shaft (**Figure 5**). Tap on each end of the shaft and remove each shift fork shaft.
4. Move the shift forks away from the shift drum.
5. Remove the shift drum (**Figure 6**).
6. Label each shift fork in order to install it in its original position.
7. Remove all three shift forks (**Figure 7**).
8. If necessary, remove the detent lever retaining bolt (A, **Figure 8**) and remove the detent lever (B) assembly.
9. Thoroughly clean all parts in solvent and dry with compressed air.

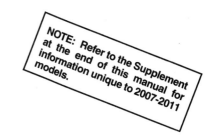

1

INTERNAL GEARSHIFT MECHANISM (2004-2005 MODELS)

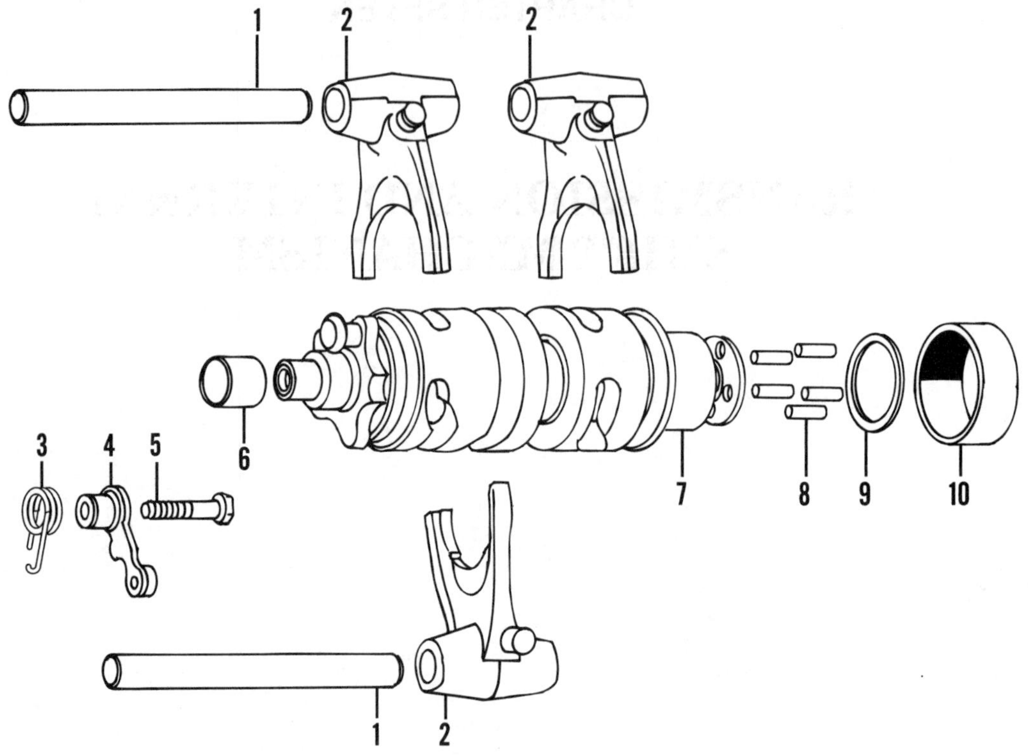

1. Shift fork shaft
2. Shift fork
3. Spring
4. Shift detent lever
5. Bolt
6. Bushing
7. Shift drum
8. Shift pins
9. Snap ring
10. Bushing

2

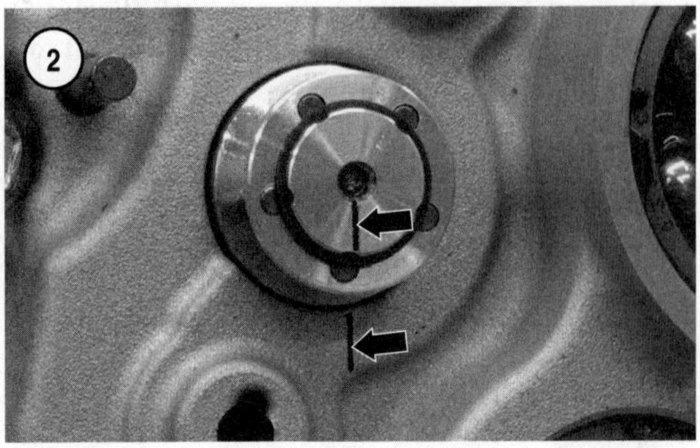

3

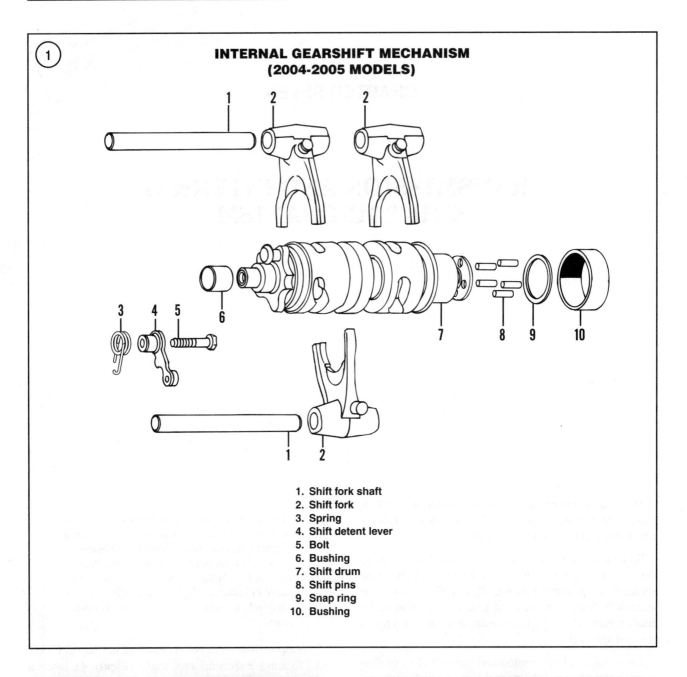

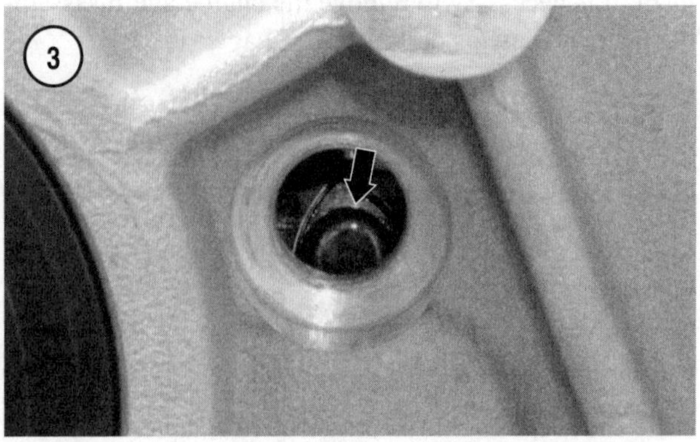

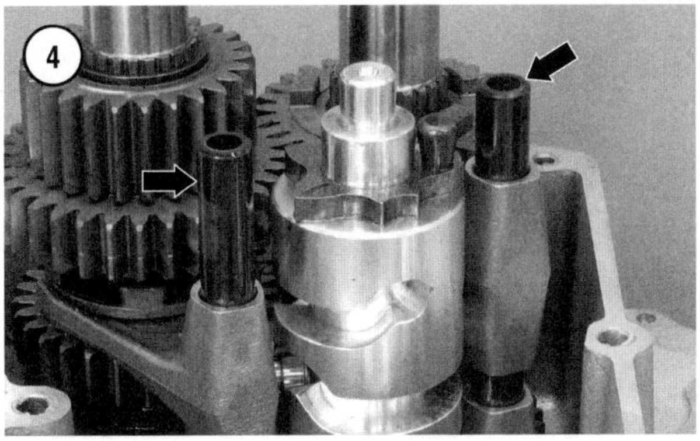

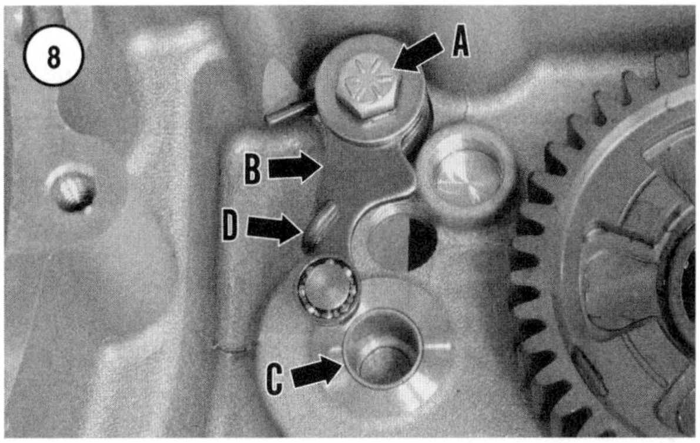

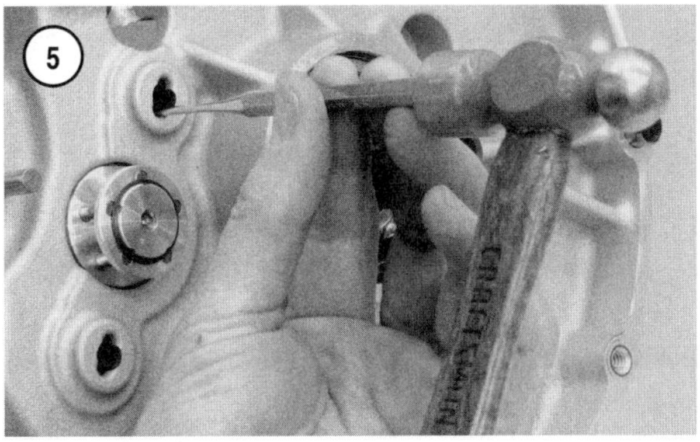

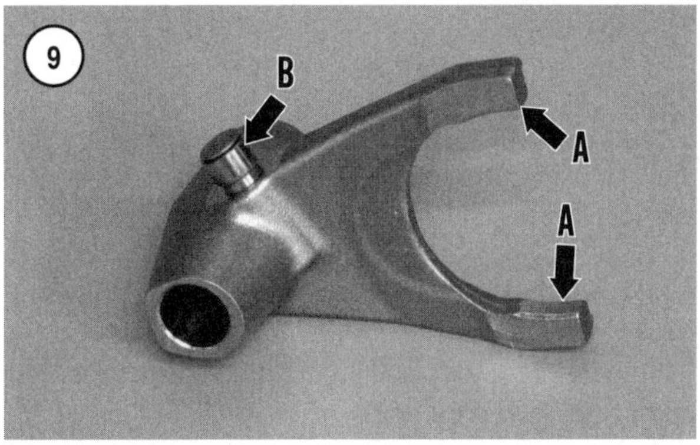

Inspection

1. Inspect each shift fork for wear or cracking. Check for any arc-shaped wear or burned marks on the fingers of the shift forks (A, **Figure 9**). This indicates that the shift fork has come in contact with the gear causing the fork fingers to become excessively worn; replace the fork.

2. Check the bore of each shift fork and the shift fork shaft for burrs, wear or pitting. Replace any worn parts.

3. Install each shift fork onto its shaft (**Figure 10**) and make sure it moves freely on the shaft with no binding.

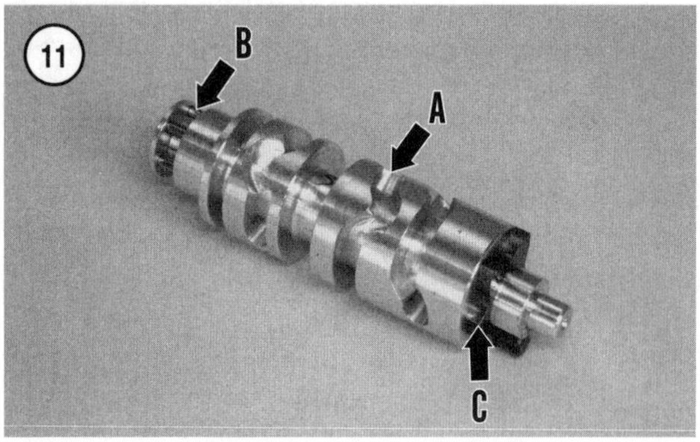

4. Check the cam follower bearing (B, **Figure 9**) on each shift fork that rides in the shift drum for wear or damage. Replace the shift fork(s) as necessary.

5. Roll the shift fork shafts on a flat surface such as a piece of plate glass and check for any bends. If a shaft is bent, replace it.

6. Check the grooves in the shift drum (A, **Figure 11**) for wear or roughness. If any of the groove profiles have excessive wear or damage, replace the shift drum.

7. Inspect the shift locating pins (B, **Figure 11**) on the end of the shift drum for wear or damage. Replace the shift drum if necessary.

8. Inspect the detent cam (C, **Figure 11**) for wear or damage. Replace the shift drum if necessary.

9. Check the shift drum bushing in the right crankcase half (C, **Figure 8**) and in the left crankcase half (A, **Figure 12**). Make sure they are not excessively worn or damaged. If the bushing is damaged, replace it while noting the following:

   a. Install the bushing in the right crankcase half (C, **Figure 8**) so it is flush with the crankcase surface.

   b. Install the bushing in the left crankcase half (A, **Figure 12**) so it bottoms in the crankcase bore.

10. Inspect the shift shaft mounting holes (B, **Figure 12**) in the crankcase halves. The shift shaft should fit snugly in the hole.

11. Check the neutral switch contact plunger and spring for wear or damage. If the spring has sagged, replace it.

Assembly/Installation

1. If removed, install the detent lever (B, **Figure 8**) and spring (D), then install the detent lever bolt (A). Make sure the spring is installed as shown in **Figure 8**. Tighten the bolt securely.

2. Apply a light coat of oil to the shift fork shafts, the inside bores of the shift forks, the shift drum bearing surfaces and to the bearings in the crankcase prior to installing any parts.

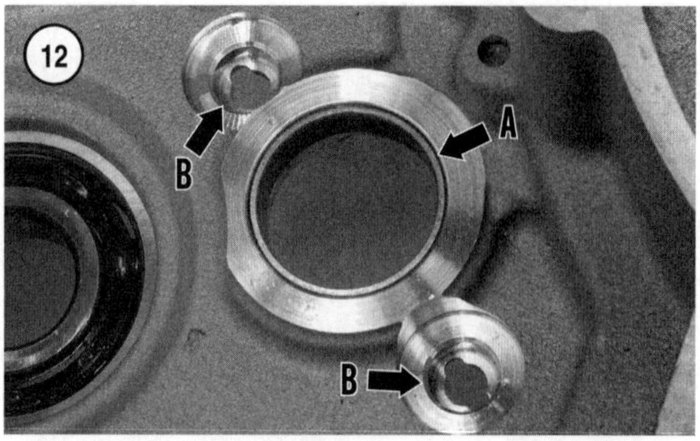

3. Install all three shift forks (**Figure 7**) into their respective gears. Refer to identification marks made during disassembly. Make sure all shift fork pins point inward as shown in **Figure 7**.

4. Move the shift forks out to allow room for the installation of the shift drum.

5. Install the shift drum (**Figure 6**) and push it down until it stops. Make sure it rotates smoothly with no binding.

NOTE

Move the gears up or down as needed to insert the shift fork pin into the shift drum groove.

6. Move the shift forks into place in the shift drum. Make sure the guide pin on each fork is indexed into its respective groove in the shift drum.

7. Install the shift shafts all the way through the shift forks (**Figure 13**). Tap each shaft down until it bottoms in the crankcase.

8. Make sure the shift fork guide pins are correctly meshed with the grooves in the shift drum.

9. Assemble the crankcase as described in Chapter Five.

10. Install the engine as described in Chapter Five.

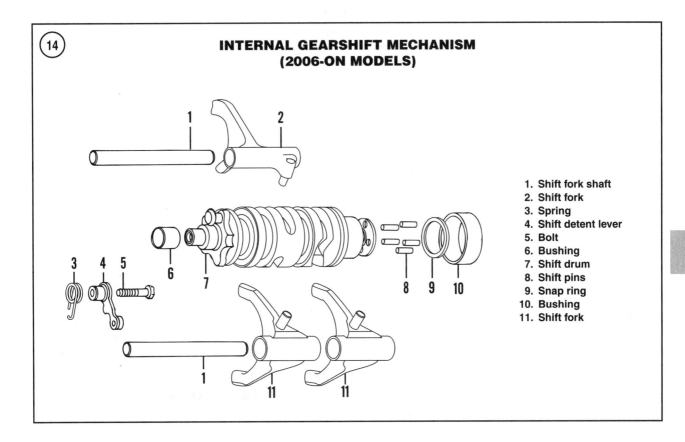

14

INTERNAL GEARSHIFT MECHANISM
(2006-ON MODELS)

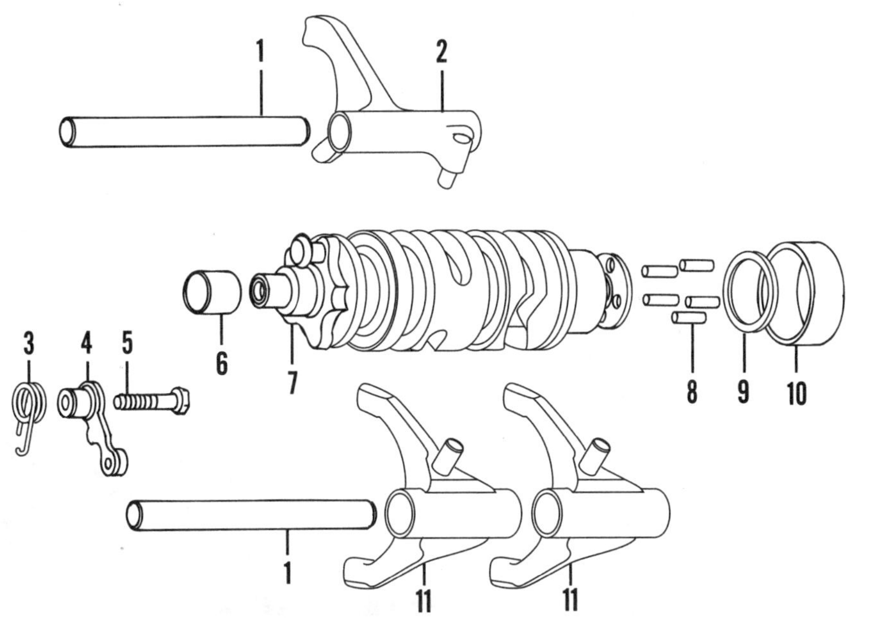

15

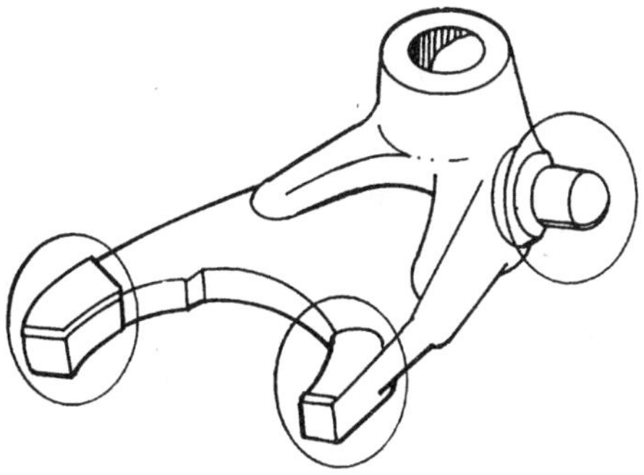

INTERNAL GEARSHIFT MECHANISM (2006-ON MODELS)

Removal/Disassembly

Refer to **Figure 14**.

1. Remove the engine as described in Chapter Five.

NOTE

*During engine disassembly, mark the end of the shift drum and crankcase with reference lines to indicate neutral position (**Figure 2**).*

*Neutral is indicated when the neutral switch pin on the shift drum is visible in the switch hole (**Figure 3**). The neutral reference will help when checking shift mechanism operation.*

2. Separate the crankcase as described in Chapter Five.
3. To remove the shift fork shafts, insert a punch through the access slot for each shaft (**Figure 5**). Tap on each side of the shaft and remove each shift fork shaft.
4. Move the shift forks away from the shift drum.
5. Remove the shift drum (7, **Figure 14**).
6. Remove all three shift forks. Label each shift fork in order to install it in its original position.
7. If necessary, remove the detent lever retaining bolt (A, **Figure 8**) and remove the detent lever (B) assembly.
8. Thoroughly clean all parts in solvent and dry with compressed air.

Inspection

1. Inspect each shift fork for wear or cracking. Check for any arc-shaped wear or burned marks on the fingers of the shift forks (**Figure 15**, typical). This indicates that the

shift fork has come in contact with the gear causing the fork fingers to become excessively worn; replace the fork.
2. Check the bore of each shift fork and the shift fork shaft for burrs, wear or pitting. Replace any worn parts.
3. Install each shift fork onto its shaft (**Figure 16**, typical) and make sure it moves freely on the shaft with no binding.
4. Check the cam follower bearing (B, **Figure 9**, typical) on each shift fork that rides in the shift drum for wear or damage. Replace the shift fork(s) as necessary.
5. Roll the shift fork shafts on a flat surface such as a piece of plate glass and check for any bends. If a shaft is bent, replace it.
6. Check the grooves in the shift drum (A, **Figure 11**, typical) for wear or roughness. If any of the groove profiles have excessive wear or damage, replace the shift drum.
7. Inspect the shift locating pins (B, **Figure 11**, typical) on the end of the shift drum for wear or damage. Replace the shift drum if necessary.
8. Inspect the detent cam (C, **Figure 11**, typical) for wear or damage. Replace the shift drum if necessary.
9. Check the shift drum bushing in the right crankcase half (C, **Figure 8**) and in the left crankcase half (A, **Figure 12**). Make sure they are not excessively worn or damaged. If the bushing is damaged, replace it while noting the following:
   a. Install the bushing in the right crankcase half (C, **Figure 8**) so it is flush with the crankcase surface.
   b. Install the bushing in the left crankcase half (A, **Figure 12**) so it bottoms in the crankcase bore.
10. Inspect the shift shaft mounting holes (B, **Figure 12**) in the crankcase halves. The shift shaft should fit snugly in the hole.
11. Check the neutral switch contact plunger and spring for wear or damage. If the spring has sagged, replace it.

Assembly/Installation

1. If removed, install the detent lever (B, **Figure 8**) and spring (D), then install the detent lever bolt (A). Make sure the spring is installed as shown in **Figure 8**. Tighten the bolt securely.
2. Apply a light coat of oil to the shift fork shafts, the inside bores of the shift forks, the shift drum bearing surfaces and to the bearings in the crankcase prior to installing any parts.
3. Install all three shift forks into their respective gears. Refer to identification marks made during disassembly. Make sure all shift fork pins point inward.
4. Move the shift forks out to allow room for the installation of the shift drum.
5. Install the shift drum and push it down until it stops. Make sure it rotates smoothly with no binding.

16

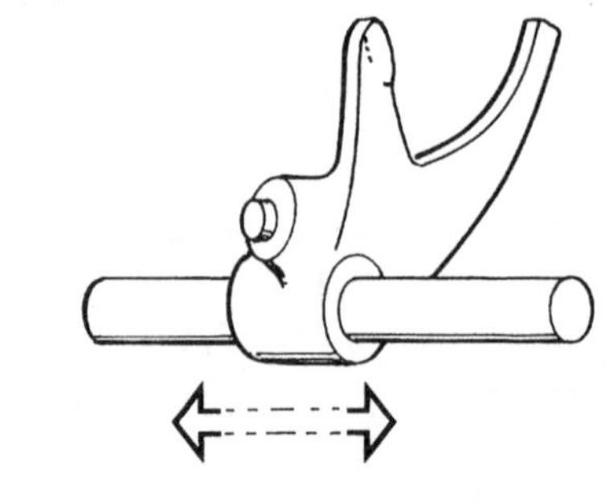

17

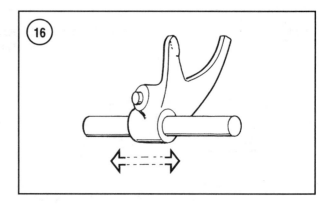

NOTE
Move the gears up or down as needed to insert the shift fork pin into the shift drum groove.

6. Move the shift forks into place in the shift drum. Make sure the guide pin on each fork is indexed into its respective groove in the shift drum.
7. Install the shift shafts all the way through the shift forks. Tap each shaft down until it bottoms in the crankcase.
8. Make sure the shift fork guide pins are correctly meshed with the grooves in the shift drum.
9. Assemble the crankcase as described in Chapter Five.
10. Install the engine as described in Chapter Five

TRANSMISSION (2004-2005 MODELS)

Transmission Service Notes

1. To assist in parts identification and location, store each part in order and in a divided container.
2. The snap rings can bend and twist during removal. Discard old snap rings and install new snap rings during assembly.

(18) **TRANSMISSION (2004-2005 MODELS)**

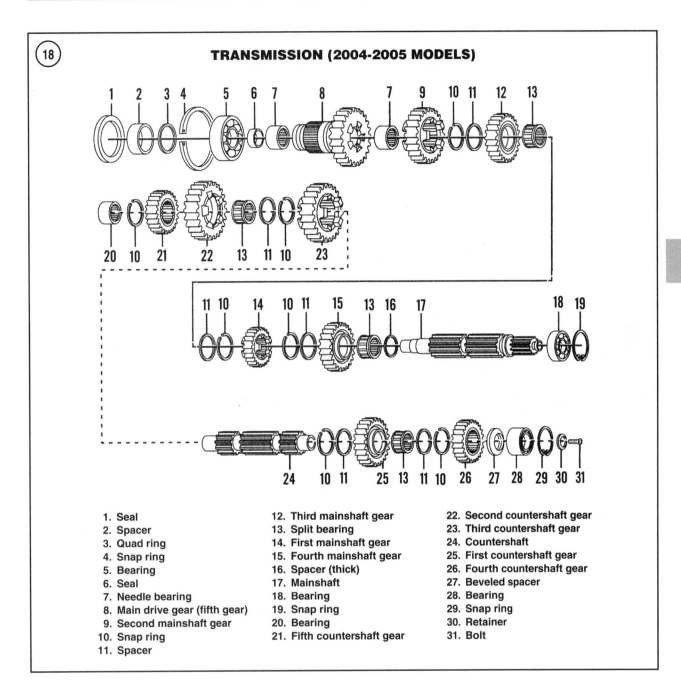

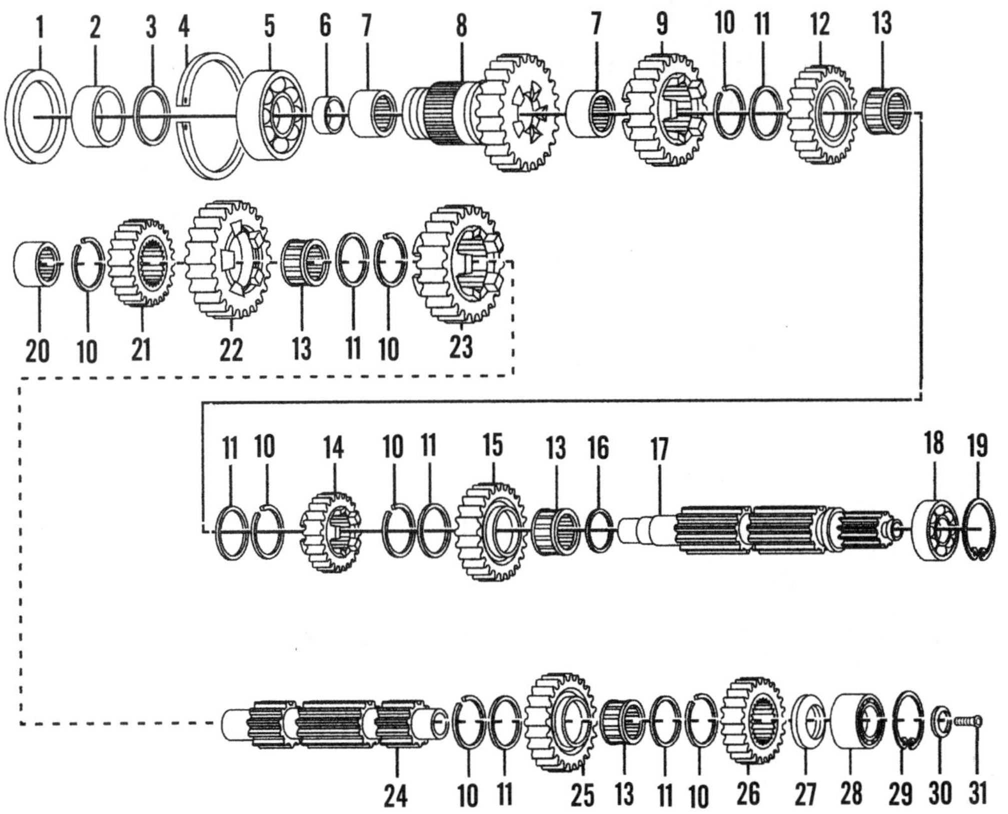

1. Seal
2. Spacer
3. Quad ring
4. Snap ring
5. Bearing
6. Seal
7. Needle bearing
8. Main drive gear (fifth gear)
9. Second mainshaft gear
10. Snap ring
11. Spacer
12. Third mainshaft gear
13. Split bearing
14. First mainshaft gear
15. Fourth mainshaft gear
16. Spacer (thick)
17. Mainshaft
18. Bearing
19. Snap ring
20. Bearing
21. Fifth countershaft gear
22. Second countershaft gear
23. Third countershaft gear
24. Countershaft
25. First countershaft gear
26. Fourth countershaft gear
27. Beveled spacer
28. Bearing
29. Snap ring
30. Retainer
31. Bolt

3. To prevent bending and twisting the new snap ring during installation, use the following installation technique: open the new snap ring using snap ring pliers while holding the back of the snap ring with pliers (**Figure 17**, typcal). Carefully slide the snap ring down the shaft and seat it into the correct shaft groove.

4. Expand a split bearing only enough to slide it over the shaft. Excessive expansion may crack the plastic bearing cage.

5. All spacers, except the mainshaft end spacer, are identical.

6. All snap rings are identical.

7. Lubricate all components during assembly with H-D Sport-Trans Fluid or equivalent.

Removal

Refer to **Figure 18**.

1. Remove the internal shift mechanism as described in this chapter.

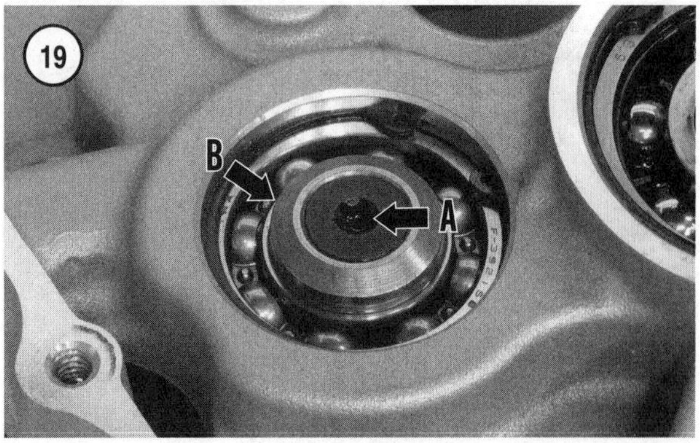

2. If not previously removed, remove the bolt in the end of the countershaft using the following procedure:

   a. Move the sliding gears on the mainshaft and countershaft so the shafts are locked and will not rotate.

   b. Unscrew and remove the bolt (A, **Figure 19**) and retainer (B).

3. Remove the mainshaft second gear (A, **Figure 20**).

4. Install the crankcase half and transmission assembly on a hydraulic press as shown in **Figure 21**. Note the following:

   a. Make sure to adequately support the crankcase.

   b. Be prepared to catch the shaft assemblies so neither is damaged.

   c. Position the press apparatus so the countershaft and mainshaft are forced evenly out of the bearings in the crankcase.

   d. Because the mainshaft is a tighter fit in its bearing, position the press arm closer to the mainshaft.

5. Press out and remove the mainshaft and countershaft assemblies.

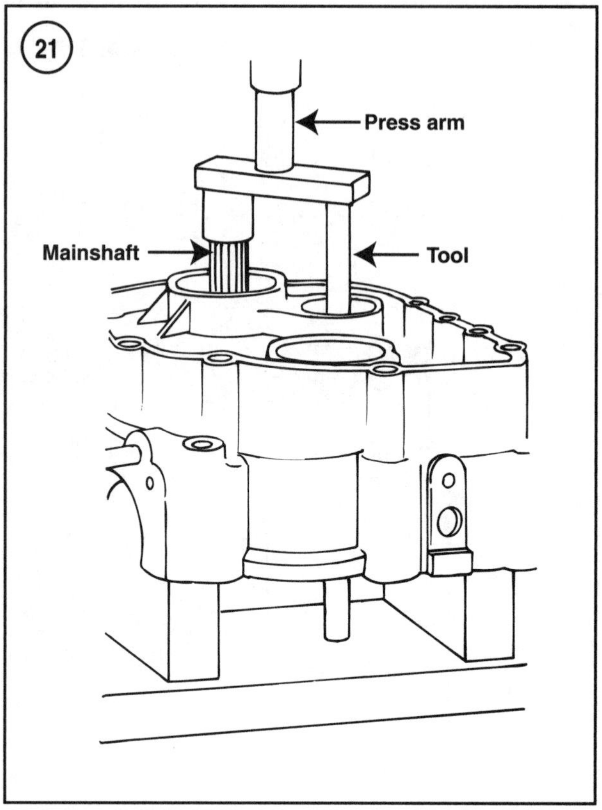

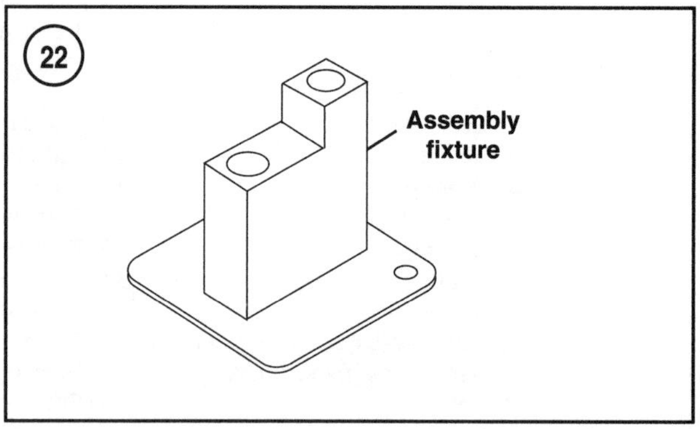

Installation

Two methods may be used to install the transmission shaft assemblies into the left crankcase half.

1. Press in assembled shafts using H-D transmission assembly fixture (**Figure 22**, HD-46285). In this procedure the shaft assemblies are simultaneously pressed into the transmission bearings in the crankcase. The assembly fixture provides proper shaft positioning while pressing in the shafts.

2. Press in the shafts, then assemble the components. In this procedure, the shafts are individually installed in the

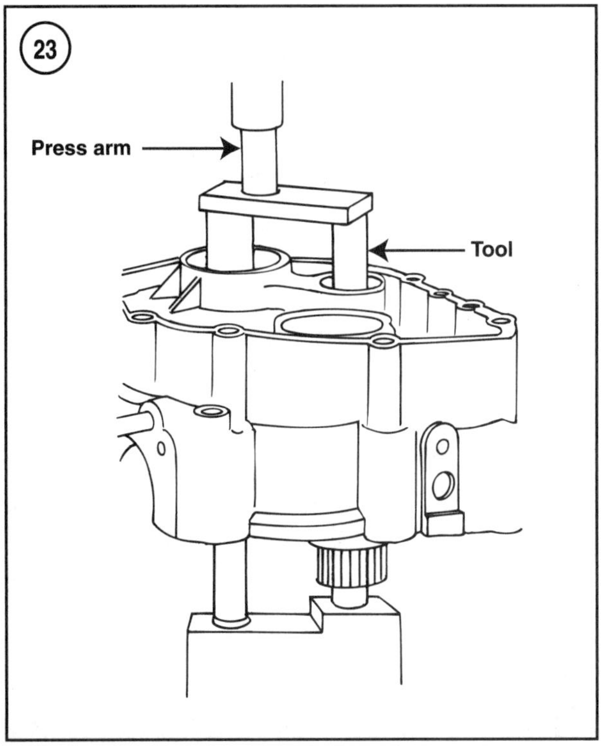

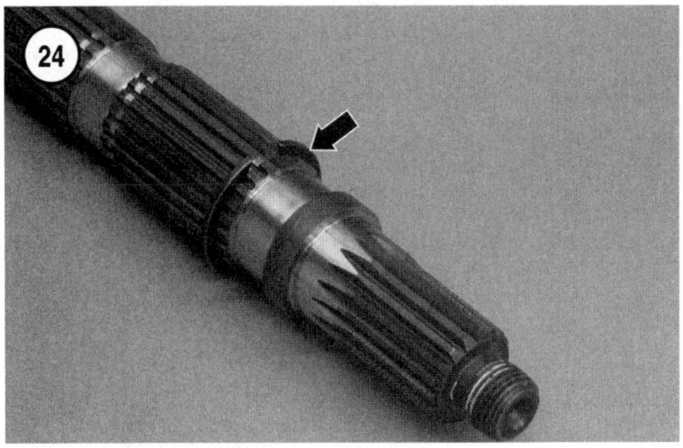

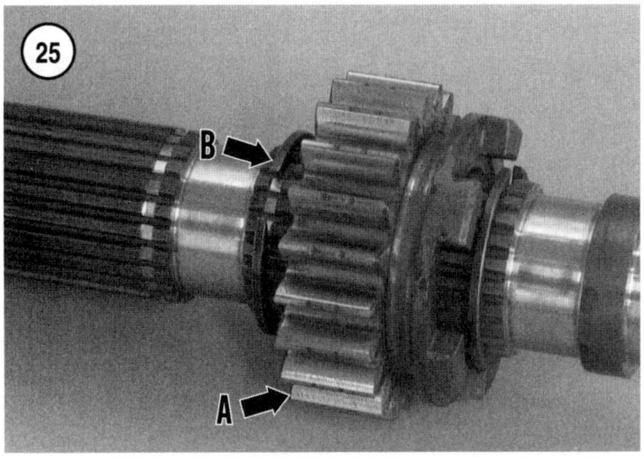

transmission bearings, then the shaft components are installed. No special tool is required.

Assembled shafts

In the following procedure the shaft assemblies are installed into the crankcase as assembled units.

1. Install the mainshaft and countershaft assemblies in the assembly fixture on the hydraulic press bed. Install tool B-43985-4 in the countershaft to help align the shaft end with the transmission bearing during installation.
2. Position the left crankcase half over the shafts (**Figure 23**). Install tool B-43985-3 or suitable equivalent press tools against the inside bearing races and the press arm.

CAUTION
Position the press apparatus so the bearings are forced evenly onto the mainshaft and crankshaft. Because the mainshaft is a tighter fit in its bearing, position the press arm closer to the mainshaft.

3. Carefully press the crankcase transmission bearings down onto the shafts until they bottom.
4. Remove the crankcase and transmission from the press.
5. Install the second mainshaft gear (A, **Figure 20**) so the shift fork groove is toward third gear (B).
6. Move the sliding gears on the mainshaft and countershaft so the shafts are locked and will not rotate.
7. Apply Loctite 243 to the threads, then install the bolt (A, **Figure 19**) and retainer (B). Tighten the bolt to 13-17 ft.-lb. (17.6-23.3 N•m).
8. Install the internal shift mechanism as described in this chapter.

Disassembled shafts

In the following procedure the shaft assemblies (**Figure 18**) are assembled in the crankcase.

1. Install the snap ring onto the mainshaft (**Figure 24**).
2. Install the first mainshaft gear (A, **Figure 25**) and snap ring (B). Install the gear so the shift groove side is toward the threaded end of the shaft.
3. Install the spacer (A, **Figure 26**).
4. Install the roller bearing (B, **Figure 26**) onto the mainshaft. Make sure the bearing ends mesh properly.
5. Install the fourth mainshaft gear (A, **Figure 27**) so the sloped side is toward the threaded mainshaft end.
6. Install the thick spacer (B, **Figure 27**).
7. The mainshaft assembly should now appear as shown in **Figure 28**.

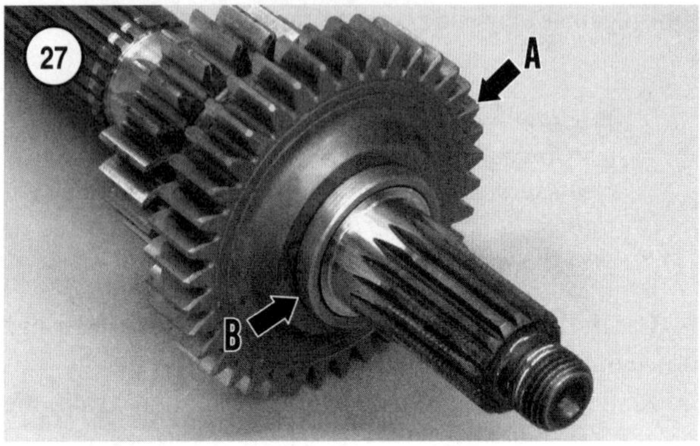

8. Press the mainshaft into the bearing in the crankcase (**Figure 29**). Force the bearing inner race onto the mainshaft until it bottoms.

9. Install the snap ring onto the countershaft (**Figure 30**).

10. Install the spacer (A, **Figure 31**) and roller bearing (B). Make sure the bearing ends mesh properly.

11. Install the first countershaft gear (A, **Figure 32**) so the sloped side is toward the shaft end.

12. Install the spacer (B, **Figure 32**).

13. Install the snap ring (**Figure 33**).

14. Install the fourth countershaft gear (A, **Figure 34**).

15. Install the beveled spacer (B, **Figure 34**) so the tapered side is toward the shaft end.

16. The assembled countershaft should appear as shown in **Figure 35**.

17. Install the countershaft into the crankcase bearing using the following procedure. This procedure reduces the possibility of shaft misalignment in the bearing.

WARNING

Wear safety glasses and protective clothing when performing this procedure to protect your eyes and exposed skin.

a. Heat the transmission inner race using a heat gun or other flameless heat source.

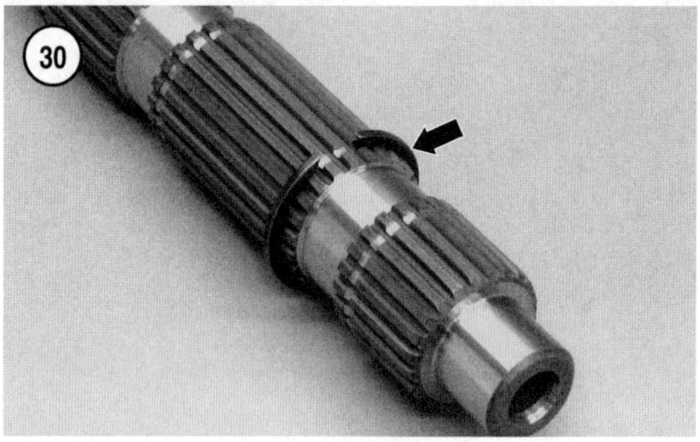

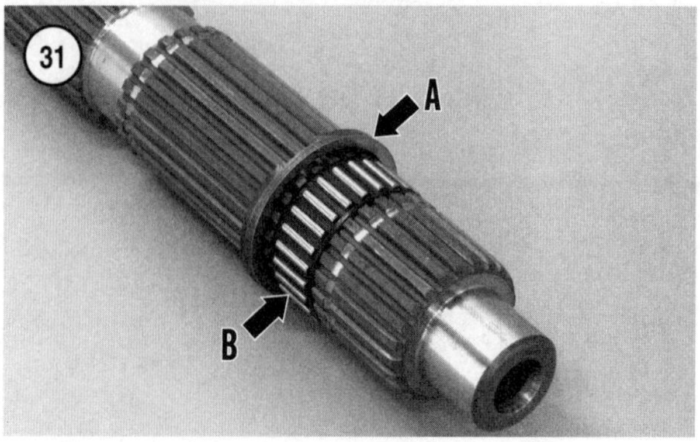

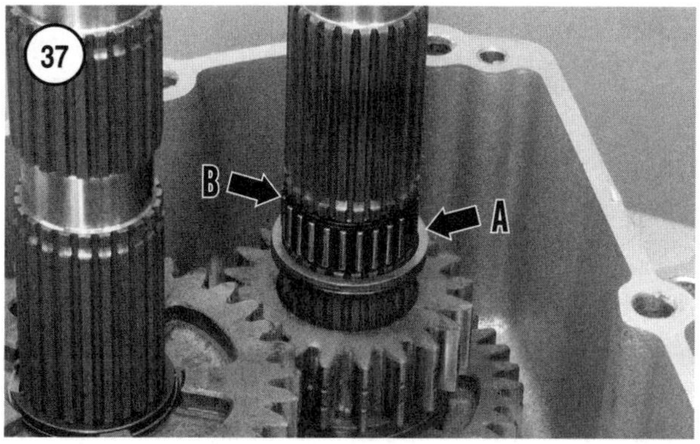

NOTE

A suitable freeze spray is expelled from an inverted dust removal aerosol can, which is available at computer stores. Apply two or three shots to chill the shaft.

b. Chill the shaft end using aerosol freeze spray, then quickly insert the shaft end into the bearing until it bottoms. If the shaft does not bottom, perform substep c.

c. If the shaft did not bottom in the bearing, install the assembly in a press and force the bearing inner race onto the countershaft until it bottoms.

18. The installed shafts should appear as shown in **Figure 36**.

19. Install the spacer (A, **Figure 37**) and bearing (B) onto the mainshaft. Make sure the bearing ends mesh properly.

20. Install the third mainshaft gear (**Figure 38**) so the shift dogs are toward the shaft end.

21. Install the spacer (A, **Figure 39**) and snap ring (B) onto the mainshaft.

22. Install the third countershaft gear (**Figure 40**) so the shift fork groove is up.

23. Install the snap ring (**Figure 41**) onto the countershaft.

24. Install the spacer (A, **Figure 42**) and bearing (B) onto the countershaft. Make sure the bearing ends mesh properly.

25. Install the second countershaft gear (**Figure 43**) so the shift dogs are down.

26. Install the fifth countershaft gear (A, **Figure 44**) and snap ring (B).

27. Install the second mainshaft gear (**Figure 45**) so the shift fork groove is down.

28. Move the sliding gears on the mainshaft and countershaft so the shafts are locked and will not rotate.

29. Apply Loctite 243 to the threads, then install the bolt (A, **Figure 19**) and retainer (B). Tighten the bolt to 13-17 ft.-lb. (17.6-23.3 N•m).

30. Install the internal shift mechanism as described in this chapter.

MAINSHAFT (2004-2005 MODELS)

The following procedures describe disassembly, inspection and assembly of a removed mainshaft assembly (**Figure 46**).

44

45

46

MAINSHAFT ASSEMBLY (2004-2005 MODELS)

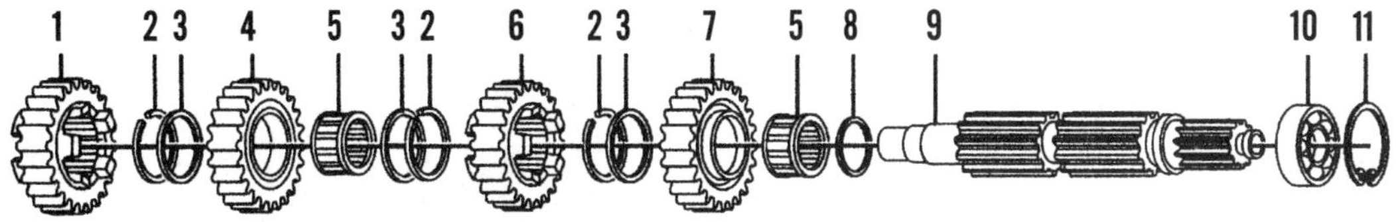

1. Second mainshaft gear
2. Snap ring
3. Spacer
4. Third mainshaft gear
5. Split bearing
6. First mainshaft gear
7. Fourth mainshaft gear
8. Spacer (thick)
9. Mainshaft
10. Bearing
11. Snap ring

47

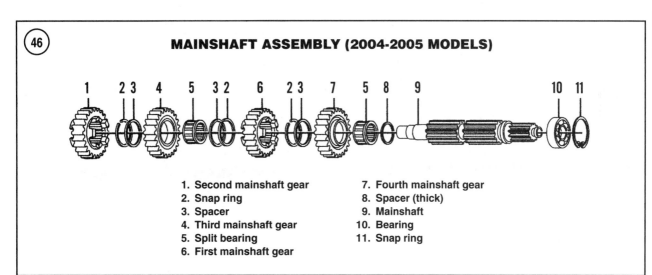

Disassembly

NOTE
*The second mainshaft gear (**Figure 20**) was removed during transmission removal.*

1. Remove the thick spacer (A, **Figure 47**) and fourth gear (B).

2. Remove the spacer, which may remain on fourth gear (B, **Figure 47**).

3. Remove the bearing (A, **Figure 48**) by separating the bearing race and sliding the bearing off the shaft.

4. Remove the snap ring (B, **Figure 48**).

5. Move the first gear (A, **Figure 49**) away from the third gear (B) for access to the snap ring (C).

6. Open the snap ring and slide it down the shaft away from the third gear (B, **Figure 49**).

7. Move the third gear toward the first gear (A, **Figure 49**) so the snap ring (A, **Figure 50**) is exposed. Remove the snap ring (A, **Figure 50**) and spacer (B).

8. Remove the third gear (**Figure 51**).

9. Remove the bearing (**Figure 52**) by separating the bearing race and sliding the bearing off the shaft.

10. Remove the previously opened snap ring (A, **Figure 53**), then remove the first gear (B).

11. Remove the snap ring (**Figure 54**).

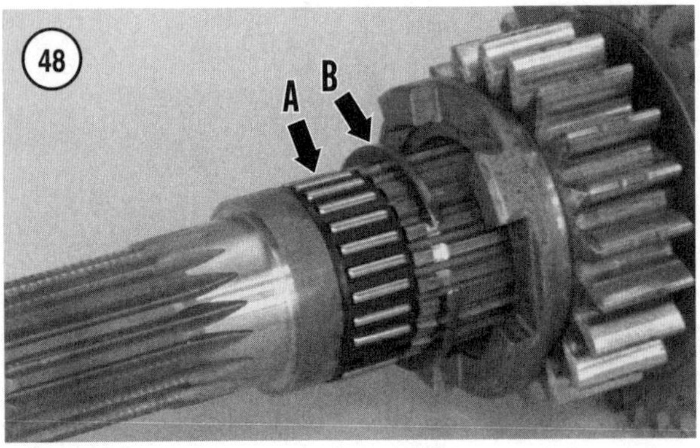

Inspection

Harley-Davidson does not provide dimensional or service specifications. Replace parts that are excessively worn or damaged.

CAUTION
Do not clean the split bearings in solvent. Removing all traces of solvent from the plastic bearing retainers is difficult. Flush the bearings clean with new transmission oil.

1. Clean and dry the shaft assembly.
2. Inspect the shaft for:
   a. Worn or damaged splines (A, **Figure 55**).
   b. Excessively worn or damaged bearing surfaces (B, **Figure 55**).
   c. Cracked or rounded-off snap ring grooves (C, **Figure 55**).
   d. Worn or damaged threads (D, **Figure 55**).
3. Check each gear for excessive wear, burrs, pitting, or chipped or missing teeth. Check the inner splines (**Figure 56**) on sliding gears.
4. Check the inner diameter of rotating gears for wear, cracks or other damage.
5. To check the sliding gears, install them in their original operating positions. The gear should slide back and forth without any binding or excessive play.
6. Check the shift fork groove (A, **Figure 57**) for wear or damage.
7. Check the dogs (B, **Figure 57**) on the gears for excessive wear, rounding, cracks or other damage. When wear is noticeable, make sure it is consistent on each gear dog. If one dog is worn more than the others, the others will be overstressed during operation and will eventually crack and fail. Check engaging gears as described in Step 9.
8. Check each gear dog slot for cracks, rounding and other damage. Check engaging gears as described in Step 9.

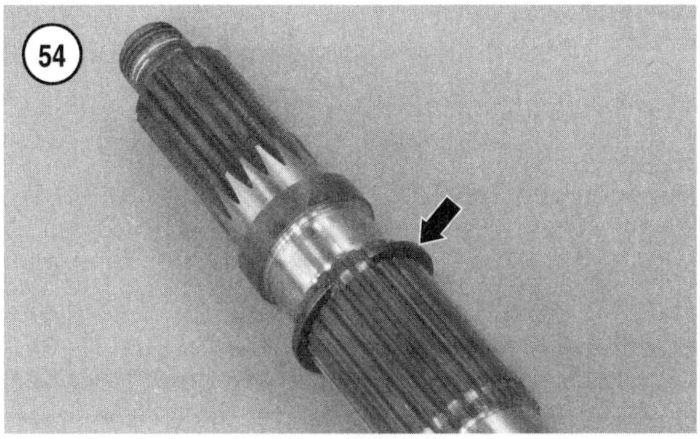

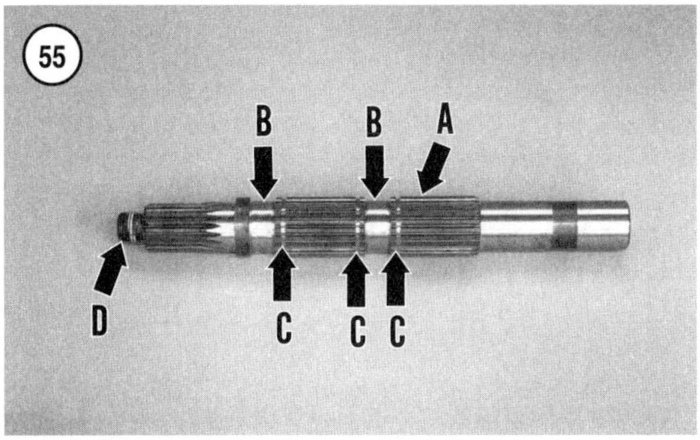

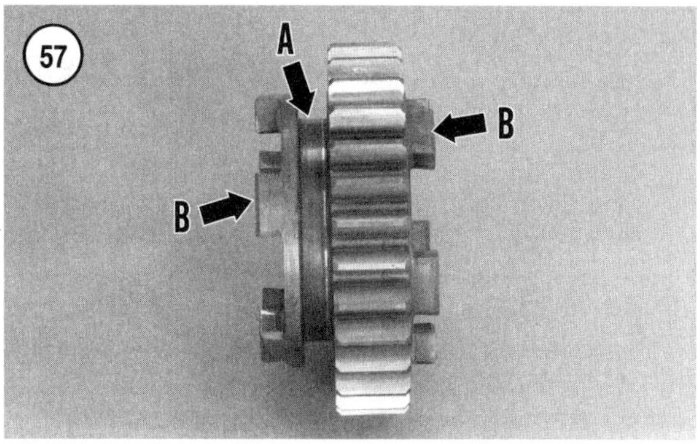

9. Check engaging gears by installing the two gears on their respective shafts and in their original operating position. Mesh the gears together. Twist one gear against the other and check the dog engagement. Then reverse the thrust load to check the other operating position. Make sure the engagement in both directions is positive and there is no slip. Make sure there is equal engagement across all the engagement dogs.

NOTE

If there is excessive or uneven wear to the gear engagement dogs, check the shift forks carefully for bends and other damage. Refer to ***Internal Gearshift Mechanism*** *in this chapter.*

NOTE

Replace defective gears and their mating gears, though the mating gears may not show as much wear or damage.

10. Inspect the spacers for wear or damage.

11. Inspect the split bearings (**Figure 58**) for excessive wear or damage.

12. Replace all snap rings during reassembly.

59

MAINSHAFT ASSEMBLY (2004-2005 MODELS)

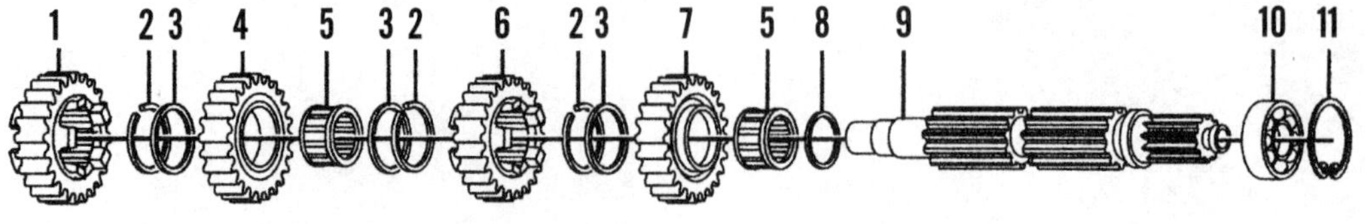

1. Second mainshaft gear
2. Snap ring
3. Spacer
4. Third mainshaft gear
5. Split bearing
6. First mainshaft gear
7. Fourth mainshaft gear
8. Spacer (thick)
9. Mainshaft
10. Bearing
11. Snap ring

Assembly

This procedure describes assembly of the mainshaft components (**Figure 59**). This procedure is applicable when installing an assembled mainshaft and an assembled countershaft together into the crankcase.

1. Install the snap ring (**Figure 60**) into the groove nearest the threaded shaft end.

2. Install first gear (A, **Figure 61**) so the shift groove is toward the threaded shaft end.

3. Install the snap ring (B, **Figure 61**).

4. Install the spacer (A, **Figure 62**), split bearing (A, **Figure 63**) and third gear (B). Position third gear so the flat side (B, **Figure 62**) faces first gear (C).

5. Install the spacer (A, **Figure 64**) and snap ring (B).

6. Install the split bearing (**Figure 65**).

7. Install the fourth gear (A, **Figure 66**) so the sloped side is toward the shaft end.

8. Install the thick spacer (B, **Figure 66**).

9. Install second gear after the mainshaft is installed in the crankcase.

60

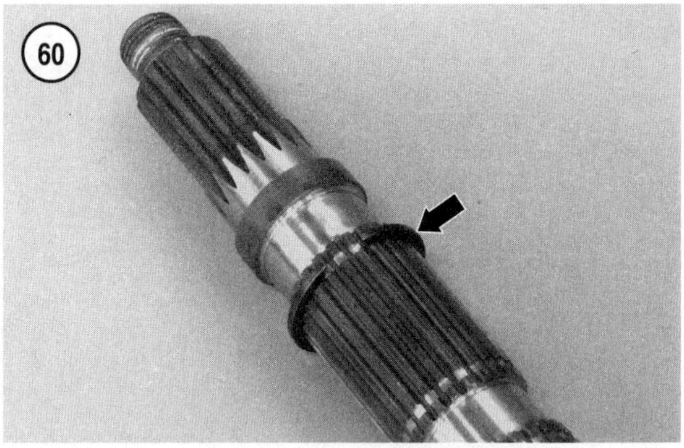

61

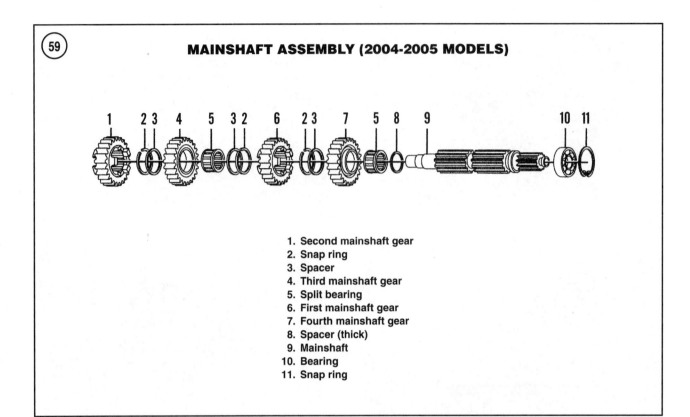

COUNTERSHAFT (2004-2005 MODELS)

The following procedures describe disassembly, inspection and assembly of a removed countershaft assembly (**Figure 67**).

Disassembly

1. Remove the tapered spacer (A, **Figure 68**).
2. Remove the fourth gear (B, **Figure 68**).
3. Remove the snap ring (A, **Figure 69**), then remove the fifth gear (B).
4. Remove the second gear (**Figure 70**).
5. Remove the split bearing (A, **Figure 71**).
6. Remove the spacer (B, **Figure 71**).
7. Remove the snap ring (**Figure 72**).
8. Remove the third gear (A, **Figure 73**).
9. Remove the snap ring (**Figure 74**).
10. Remove the spacer (**Figure 75**).
11. Remove the first gear (**Figure 76**).
12. Remove the split bearing (A, **Figure 77**).
13. Remove the spacer (B, **Figure 77**) and snap ring (C).

Inspection

Refer to *Mainshaft* in this chapter for inspection procedures.

Assembly

This procedure describes assembly of the countershaft components (**Figure 67**). This procedure is applicable when installing an assembled mainshaft and an assembled countershaft together into the crankcase.

1. Install the snap ring (C, **Figure 77**) into the second groove from the shaft end.
2. Install the spacer (B, **Figure 77**).

67

COUNTERSHAFT ASSEMBLY (2004-2005 MODELS)

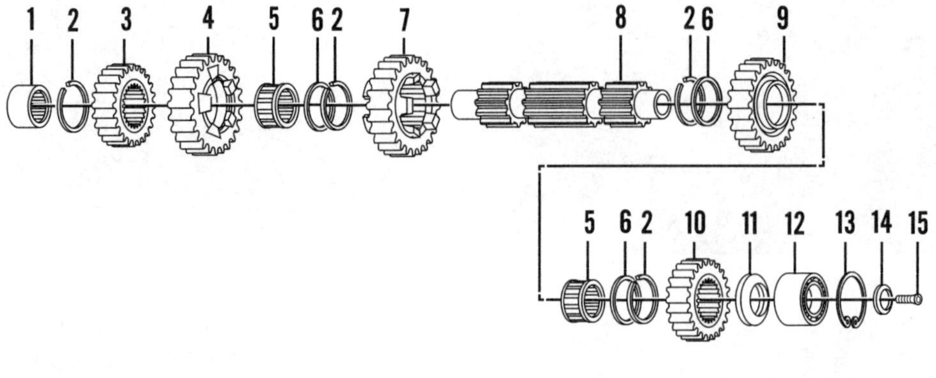

1. Bearing
2. Snap ring
3. Fifth countershaft gear
4. Second countershaft gear
5. Split bearing
6. Spacer
7. Third countershaft gear
8. Countershaft
9. First countershaft gear
10. Fourth countershaft gear
11. Beveled spacer
12. Bearing
13. Snap ring
14. Retainer
15. Bolt

68

70

69

71

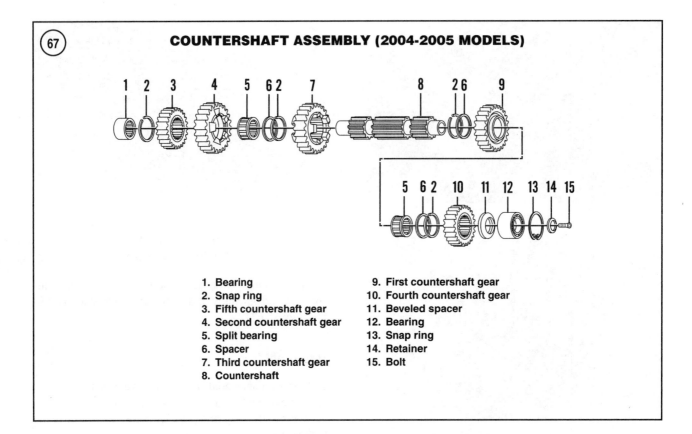

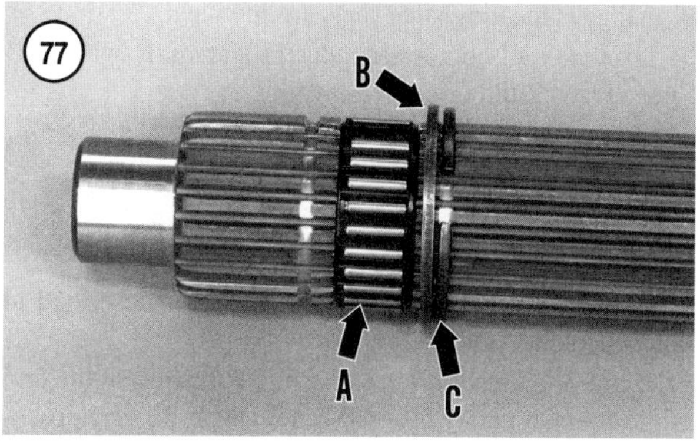

3. Install the split bearing (A, **Figure 77**).

4. Install the first gear so the tapered side faces as shown in **Figure 76**.

5. Install the spacer (**Figure 75**).

6. Install the snap ring (**Figure 74**).

7. Install the third gear (A, **Figure 73**) so the shift fork groove is away from the first gear (B).

8. Install the snap ring (**Figure 72**).

9. Install the spacer (B, **Figure 71**).

10. Install the split bearing (A, **Figure 71**).

11. Install the second gear (**Figure 70**) so the flat side is toward the shaft end.

12. Install the snap ring (A, **Figure 69**), then install the fifth gear (B).

13. Install the fourth gear (B, **Figure 68**).

14. Install the tapered spacer (A, **Figure 68**).

TRANSMISSION (2006-ON MODELS)

Transmission Service Notes

1. To assist in parts identification and location, store each part in order and in a divided container.

2. The snap rings can bend and twist during removal. Discard old snap rings and install new snap rings during assembly.
3. To prevent bending and twisting the new snap ring during installation, use the following installation technique: open the new snap ring using snap ring pliers while holding the back of the snap ring with pliers (**Figure 78**, typical). Carefully slide the snap ring down the shaft and seat it into the correct shaft groove.
4. Expand a split bearing only enough to slide it along the shaft. Too great an opening may fracture the plastic bearing cage.
5. All spacers contacting snap rings are identical.
6. All gear-locating snap rings are identical.
7. Lubricate all components during assembly with H-D Sport-Trans Fluid or equivalent.

Removal

Refer to **Figure 79**.

1. Remove the internal shift mechanism as described in this chapter.
2. If not previously removed, remove the bolt in the end of the countershaft (**Figure 80**) using the following procedure:
   a. Move the sliding gears on the mainshaft and countershaft so the shafts are locked and will not rotate.
   b. Unscrew and remove the bolt (**Figure 80**).
3. Remove the first mainshaft gear (9, **Figure 79**).
4. Install the crankcase half and transmission assembly on a press as shown in **Figure 81**. Note the following:
   a. Make sure to adequately support the crankcase half.
   b. Be prepared to catch the shaft assemblies so neither is damaged.
   c. Position the press apparatus so the countershaft and mainshaft are forced evenly out of the bearings in the crankcase.
   d. Because the mainshaft is a tighter fit in its bearing, position the press arm closer to the mainshaft.
5. Press out and remove the mainshaft and countershaft assemblies.

Installation

In the following procedure the shaft assemblies are installed into the crankcase as assembled units using H-D assembly fixture HD-46285.

1. Install the mainshaft and countershaft assemblies in the assembly fixture (**Figure 82**) on the press bed. Install

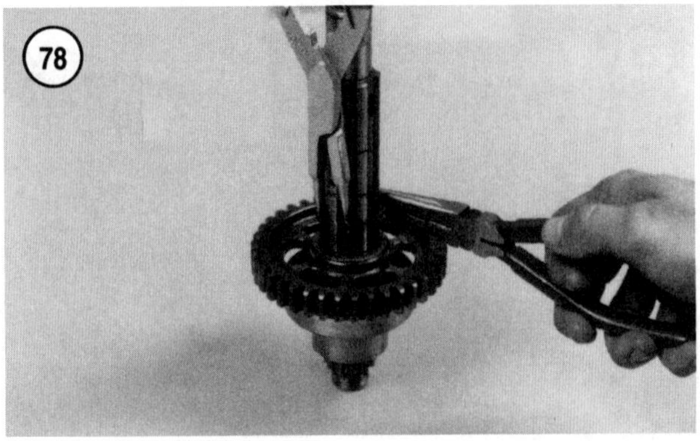

tool B-43985-4 in the countershaft to help align the shaft end with the transmission bearing during installation.
2. Position the left crankcase half over the shafts (**Figure 83**). Install tool B-43985-3 or suitable equivalent press tools against the inside bearing races and the press arm.

CAUTION
Position the press apparatus so the bearings are forced evenly onto the mainshaft and crankshaft. Because the mainshaft is a tighter fit in its bearing, position the press arm closer to the mainshaft.

3. Carefully press the crankcase transmission bearings down onto the shafts until they bottom.
4. Remove the crankcase and transmission from the press.
5. Install the first mainshaft gear (9, **Figure 79**) so the shift fork groove is toward fourth gear (12).
6. Move the sliding gears on the mainshaft and countershaft so the shafts are locked and will not rotate.
7. Apply Loctite 262 to the threads, then install the bolt (**Figure 80**). Tighten the bolt to 33-39 ft.-lb. (45-53 N•m).
8. Install the internal shift mechanism as described in this chapter.

MAINSHAFT (2006-ON MODELS)

The following procedures describe disassembly, inspection and assembly of a removed mainshaft assembly (**Figure 84**).

Disassembly

NOTE
*The first mainshaft gear (1, **Figure 84**) was removed during transmission removal.*

79

TRANSMISSION (2006-ON MODELS)

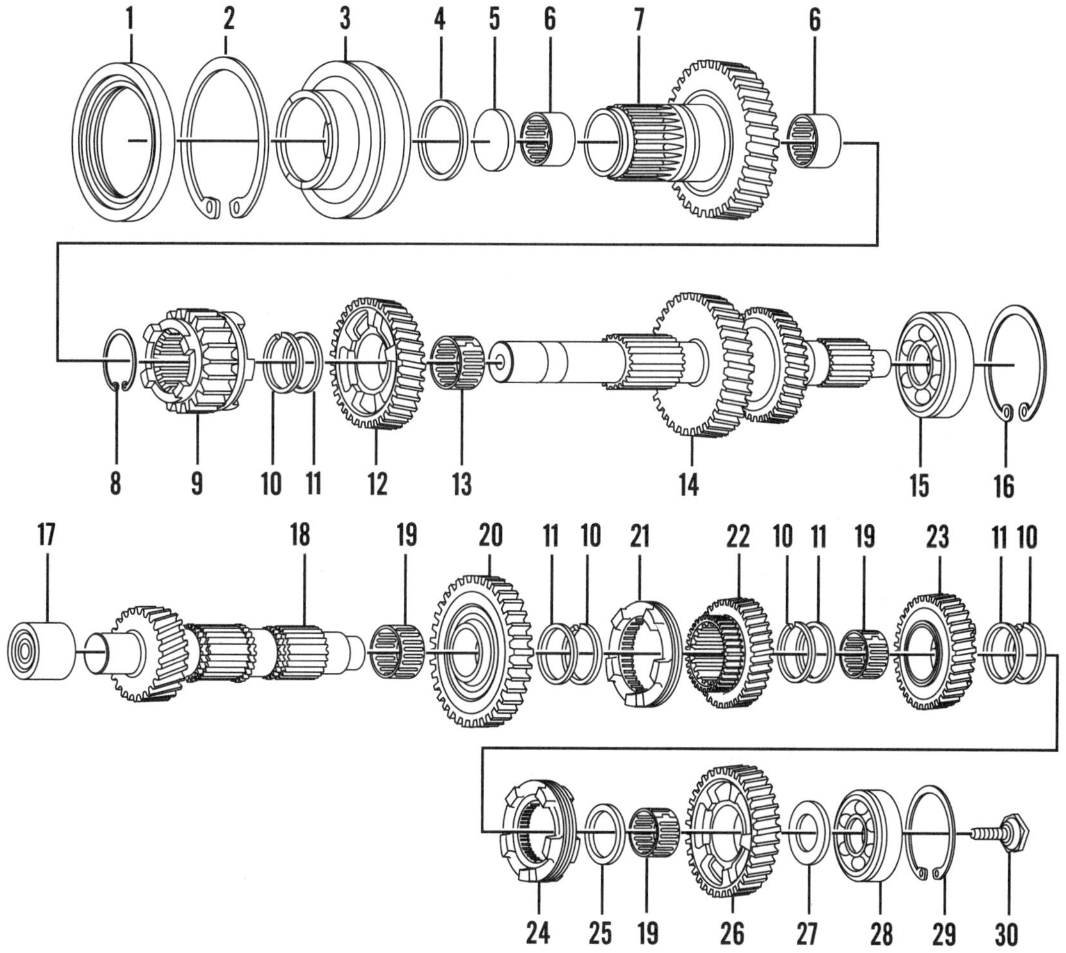

1. Seal
2. Spacer
3. Bearing
4. O-ring
5. Seal
6. Needle bearing
7. Main drive gear (fifth gear)
8. Snap ring
9. First mainshaft gear
10. Snap ring
11. Spacer
12. Fourth mainshaft gear
13. Split bearing
14. Mainshaft
15. Bearing
16. Snap ring
17. Bearing
18. Countershaft
19. Split bearing
20. First countershaft gear
21. Dog ring
22. Fourth countershaft gear
23. Third countershaft gear
24. Dog ring
25. Spacer
26. Second countershaft gear
27. Spacer
28. Bearing
29. Snap ring
30. Bolt

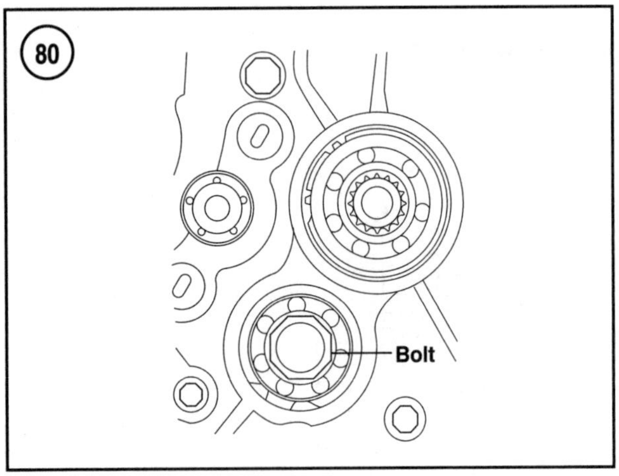

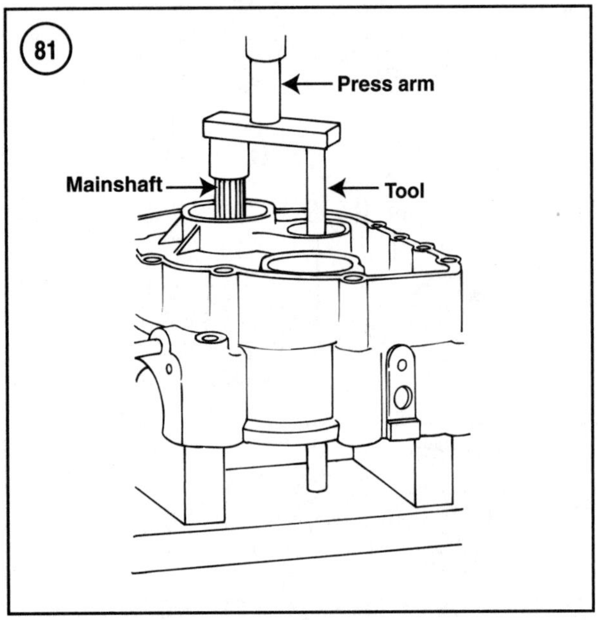

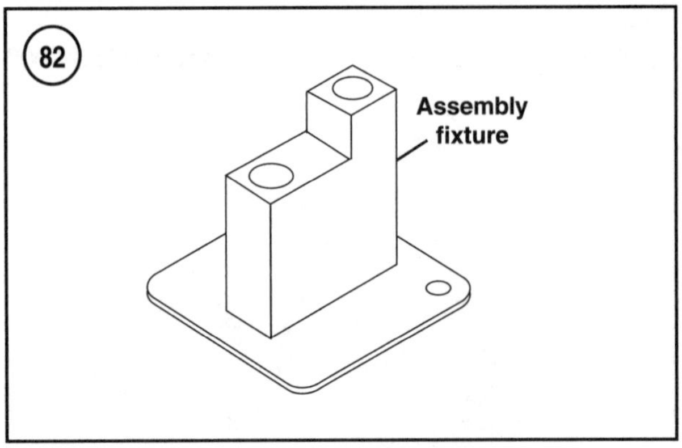

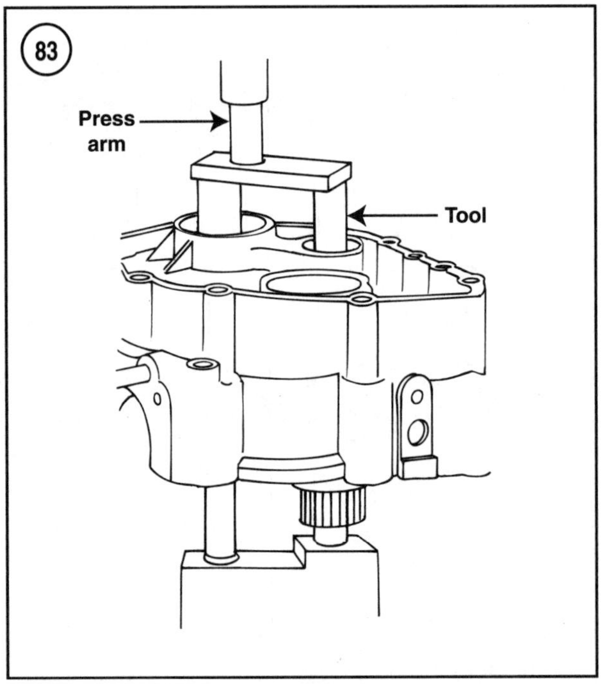

1. Remove the snap ring (2, **Figure 84**).
2. Remove the spacer (3, **Figure 84**) and fourth gear (4).
3. Remove the bearing (5, **Figure 84**) by separating the bearing race and sliding the bearing off the shaft.

NOTE
Second and third gears are part of the mainshaft.

Inspection

Harley-Davidson does not provide dimensional or service specifications. Replace parts that are excessively worn or damaged.

CAUTION
Do not clean the split bearings in solvent. Removing all traces of solvent from the plastic bearing retainers is difficult. Flush the bearings clean with new transmission oil.

1. Clean and dry the shaft assembly.
2. Inspect the shaft for:
   a. Worn or damaged splines.
   b. Excessively worn or damaged bearing surfaces.
   c. Cracked or rounded-off snap ring grooves.
3. Check each gear for excessive wear, burrs, pitting, or chipped or missing teeth. Check the inner splines on the mainshaft first gear (**Figure 85**).
4. Check the inner diameter of rotating gears for wear, cracks or other damage.

84

MAINSHAFT ASSEMBLY (2006-ON MODELS)

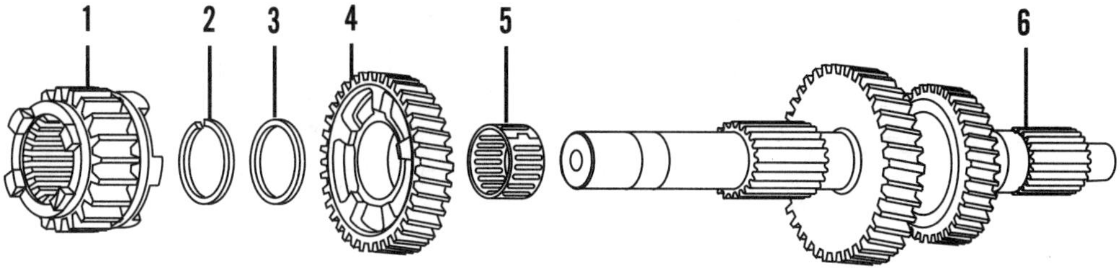

1. First mainshaft gear
2. Snap ring
3. Spacer
4. Fourth mainshaft gear
5. Split bearing
6. Mainshaft

7

85

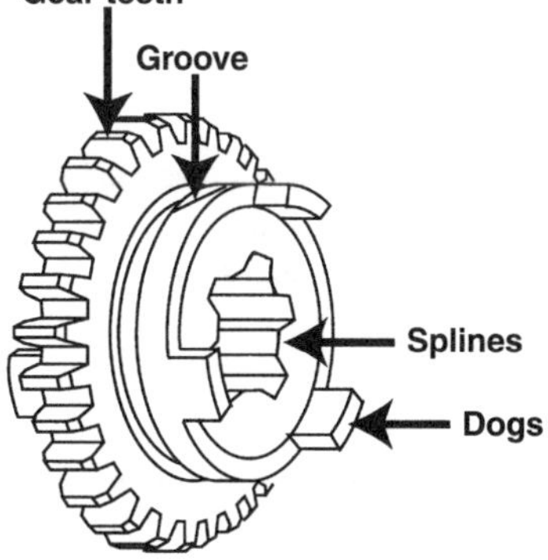

86

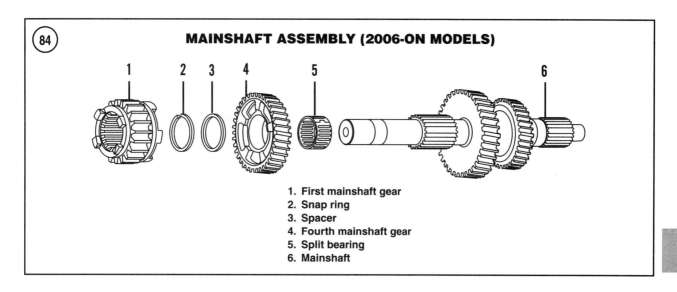

5. To check the sliding gears, install them in their original operating positions. The gear should slide back and forth without any binding or excessive play.

6. Check the shift fork groove (**Figure 85**) for wear or damage.

7. Check the dogs (**Figure 85**) on the gears for excessive wear, rounding, cracks or other damage. When wear is noticeable, make sure it is consistent on each gear dog. If one dog is worn more than the others, the others will be overstressed during operation and will eventually crack and fail. Check engaging gears as described in Step 9.

8. Check each gear dog slot for cracks, rounding and other damage. Check engaging gears as described in Step 9.

9. Check engaging gears by installing the two gears on the mainshaft and in their original operating position. Mesh the gears together. Twist one gear against the other and check the dog engagement. Then reverse the thrust load to check the other operating position. Make sure the engagement in both directions is positive and there is no slip. Make sure there is equal engagement across all the engagement dogs.

NOTE

If there is excessive or uneven wear to the gear engagement dogs, check the shift forks carefully for bends and other damage. Refer to ***Internal Gearshift Assembly*** *in this chapter.*

NOTE

Replace defective gears and their mating gears, though the mating gears may not show as much wear or damage.

10. Inspect the spacer (3, **Figure 84**) for wear or damage.

11. Inspect the split bearing (**Figure 86**) for excessive wear or damage.

12. Replace the snap ring (2, **Figure 84**) during reassembly.

(87) **COUNTERSHAFT ASSEMBLY (2006-ON MODELS)**

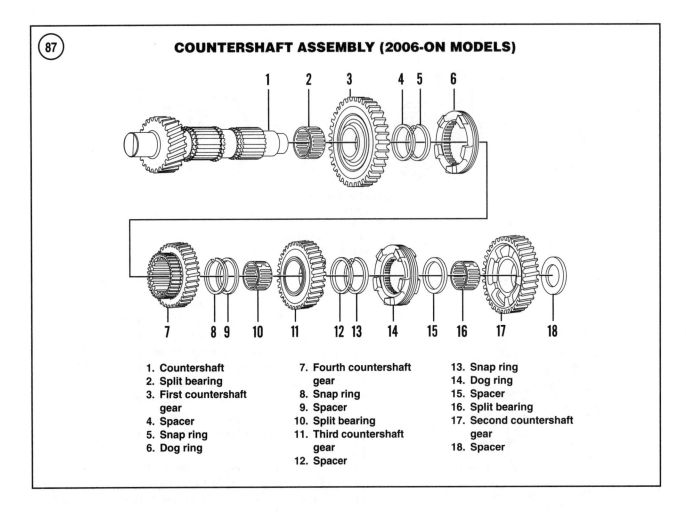

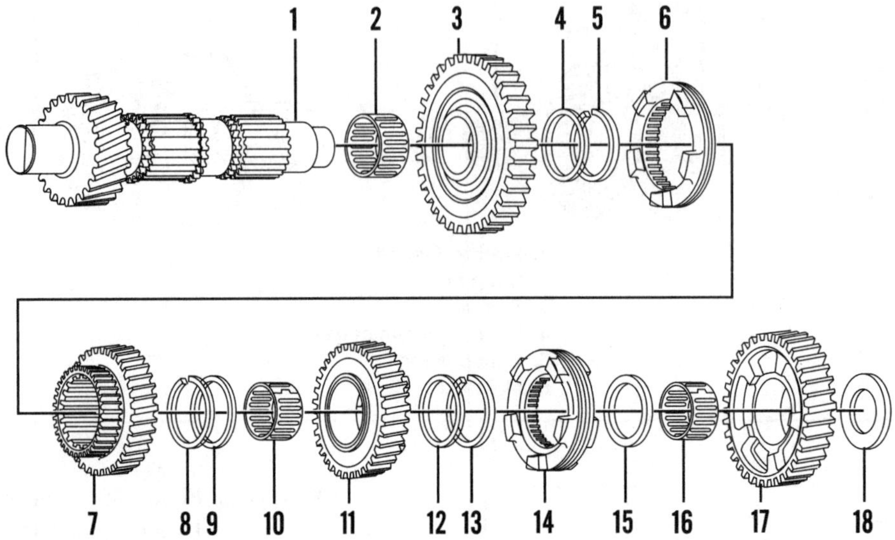

1. Countershaft
2. Split bearing
3. First countershaft gear
4. Spacer
5. Snap ring
6. Dog ring
7. Fourth countershaft gear
8. Snap ring
9. Spacer
10. Split bearing
11. Third countershaft gear
12. Spacer
13. Snap ring
14. Dog ring
15. Spacer
16. Split bearing
17. Second countershaft gear
18. Spacer

Assembly

1. Install the split bearing (5, **Figure 84**) onto the mainshaft.
2. Install the fourth gear (4, **Figure 84**) so the shift dog slots are toward the shaft end.
3. Install the spacer (3, **Figure 84**) and snap ring (2).
4. Install first gear after the mainshaft is installed in the crankcase. Install the mainshaft first gear (1, **Figure 84**) so the shift fork groove is toward fourth gear (4).

COUNTERSHAFT (2006-ON MODELS)

The following procedures describe disassembly, inspection and assembly of a removed countershaft assembly.

Disassembly

Refer to **Figure 87**.

1. Remove the large outside diameter spacer (18).
2. Remove the second gear (17).
3. Remove the split bearing (16).
4. Remove the thick spacer (15).

NOTE

Note and mark the orientation of the dog ring during removal so it can be installed in its original position.

5. Remove the dog ring (14).
6. Remove the snap ring (13).
7. Remove the spacer (12).
8. Remove the third gear (11).
9. Remove the split bearing (10).
10. Remove the spacer (9).
11. Remove the snap ring (8).
12. Remove the fourth gear (7) and dog ring (6).
13. Remove the snap ring (5).
14. Remove the spacer (4).
15. Remove the first gear (3).
16. Remove the split bearing (2).

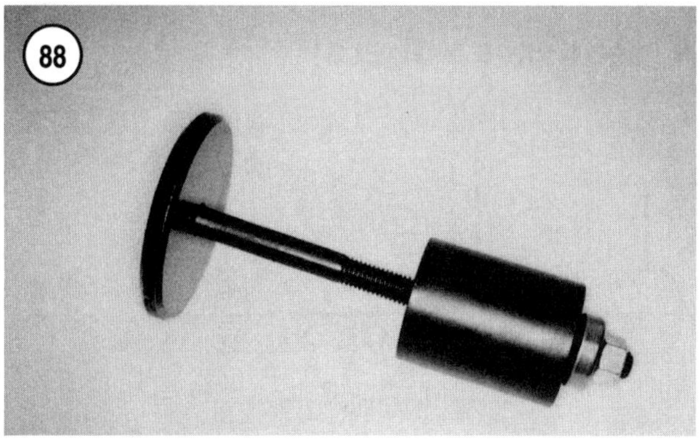

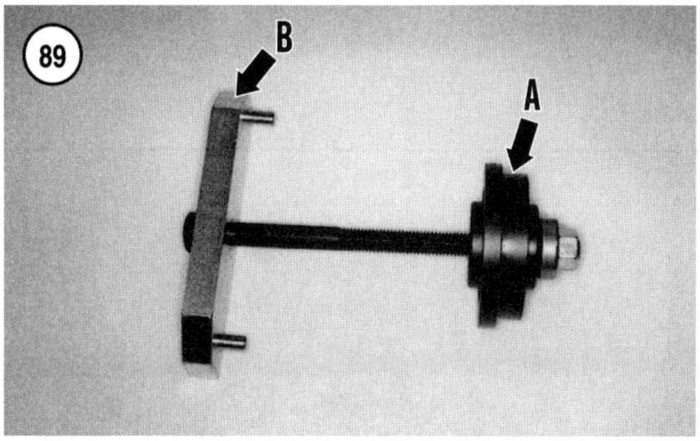

NOTE
Fifth gear is part of the mainshaft.

Inspection

Refer to *Mainshaft* in this chapter for inspection procedures.

Assembly

Refer to **Figure 87**.

1. Install the split bearing (2) onto the mainshaft.
2. Install the first gear (3) so the shift dogs are toward the shaft splines.
3. Install the spacer (4).
4. Install the snap ring (5).
5. Install the dog ring (6) onto the fourth gear (7) so the shift fork groove is toward fourth gear. Install the dog ring and gear assembly onto the mainshaft so the dog ring is toward the first gear (3).
6. Install the snap ring (8).
7. Install the spacer (9).
8. Install the split bearing (10).
9. Install the third gear (11) so the shift dogs are toward the shaft end.
10. Install the spacer (12).
11. Install the snap ring (13).
12. Install the dog ring (14) in the original orientation.
13. Install the thick spacer (15).
14. Install the split bearing (16).
15. Install the second gear (17) so the shift dog slots are toward the dog ring (14).
16. Install the spacer with the large outside diameter (18).

MAIN DRIVE GEAR (2004-2005 MODELS)

Tools

Two tools are required to remove and install the main drive gear in the right crankcase. Removing the main drive gear without these tools may cause crankcase and/or main drive gear damage. The tools include:

1. Harley-Davidson main drive gear remover and installer (part No. HD-35316-B [**Figure 88** and A, **Figure 89**]).
2. Harley-Davidson cross plate (part No. B-45847 [B, **Figure 89**]).

NOTE
*Equivalent tools are also available from JIMS, (**www.jimsusa.com**).*

Removal

Refer to **Figure 90**.

1. Remove the transmission assembly as described in this chapter.
2. Remove the spacer (**Figure 91**) from the main drive gear.
3. Remove the quad ring (**Figure 92**).
4. Tap out the seal (**Figure 93**) that is mounted in the end of the main drive gear. Use a drift inserted through the main drive gear to force out the seal. Discard the seal.
5. Assemble the Harley-Davidson or equivalent main drive gear remover and installer and the cross plate as shown in **Figure 94**. Refer to **Figure 95** and **Figure 96**.

NOTE
*Insert the two cross plate pins into the pin holes in the transmission housing. This will center the cross plate with the main drive gear. **Figure 95** shows an early version of the cross plate, which may be used if the plate is properly centered over the gear.*

6. Tighten the puller nut (**Figure 96**) to pull the main drive gear out of the main drive gear bearing. Disassemble

(90) **MAIN DRIVE GEAR ASSEMBLY (2004-2005 MODELS)**

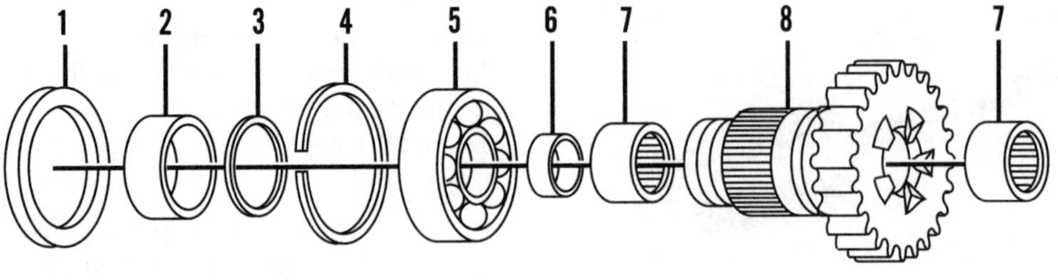

1. Seal
2. Spacer
3. Quad ring
4. Snap ring
5. Bearing
6. Seal
7. Needle bearing
8. Main drive gear (fifth gear)

the tool and remove the main drive gear (**Figure 97**) from the transmission portion of the engine crankcase.

7. Pry the main drive gear seal (**Figure 98**) out of the right crankcase.

CAUTION

Because the main drive gear inner bearing race was not supported when the main drive gear was removed, the bearing is damaged. Whenever the main drive gear is removed, replace the main drive gear bearing.

8. Replace the main drive gear bearing as described in *Crankcase Bearings* in this chapter.

Inspection

1. Clean the main drive gear in solvent and dry with compressed air.
2. Check each gear tooth (**Figure 99**) for excessive wear, burrs, galling and pitting. Check for missing gear teeth.
3. Check the gear splines for excessive wear, galling or other damage.
4. Inspect the two main drive gear needle bearings (**Figure 100**) for excessive wear or damage. Insert the mainshaft into the main drive gear to check bearing wear. If necessary, replace the bearings as described in this section.

Needle Bearing Replacement

Both main drive gear needle bearings (7, **Figure 90**) must be installed to a specific depth (**Figure 101**). Bearing installation can be performed with the Harley-Davidson or equivalent inner/outer main drive gear needle bearing installation tool HD-37842-A. If an installation tool is not available, measure the bearing position during installation.

(91)

(92)

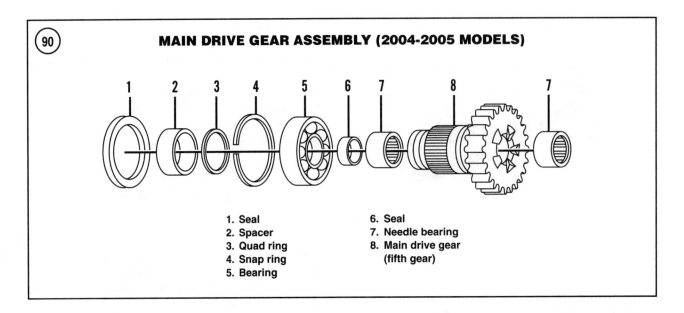

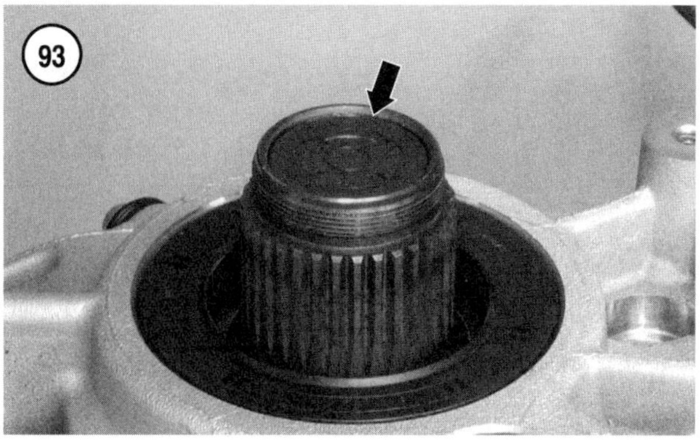
93

97

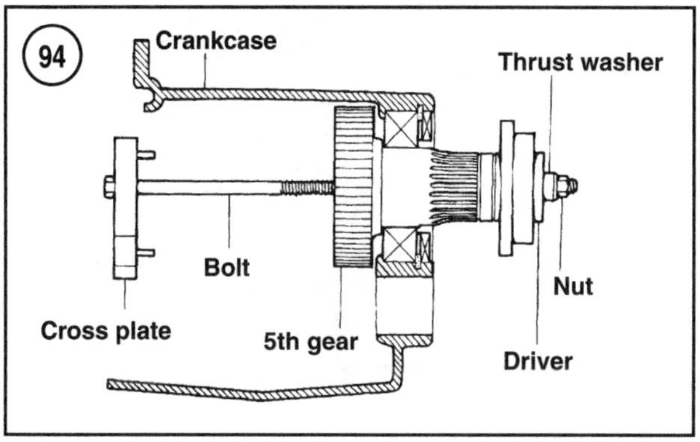
94
Crankcase
Thrust washer
Bolt
Nut
Cross plate
5th gear
Driver

98

95

99

96

100

101

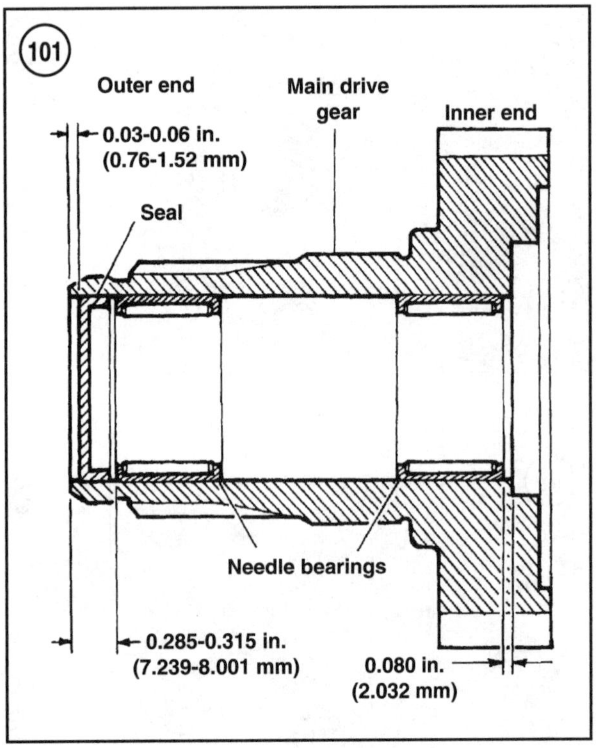

Always replace both main drive gear needle bearings at the same time.

CAUTION
Do not install a main drive gear needle bearing that has been removed. Removal damages the bearings.

1. Support the main drive gear in a press and press out both needle bearings.
2. Clean the bearing bore in solvent and dry thoroughly.

NOTE
Install both needle bearings with their manufacturer's name and size code facing out.

3A. Install the bearing *with* the special tool as follows:

a. This tool is stamped with two sets of numbers. The side stamped 0.080 is for pressing in the inner end bearing. The side stamped 0.315 is for pressing the outer end bearing (**Figure 101**).
b. Install the main drive gear in a press with the outer end facing up. Align the new bearing with the main drive gear and install the installation tool. Make sure the side stamped 0.315 is inserted into the bearing. Operate the press until the tool bottoms.
c. Turn the main drive gear over so the inner end faces up. Align the new bearing with the main drive gear

102

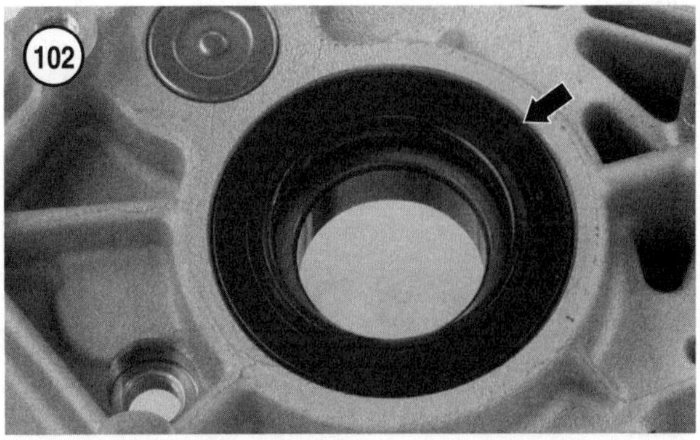

103

104

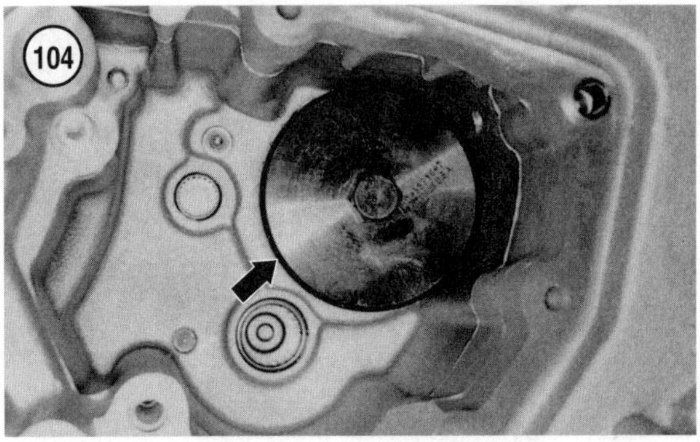

105

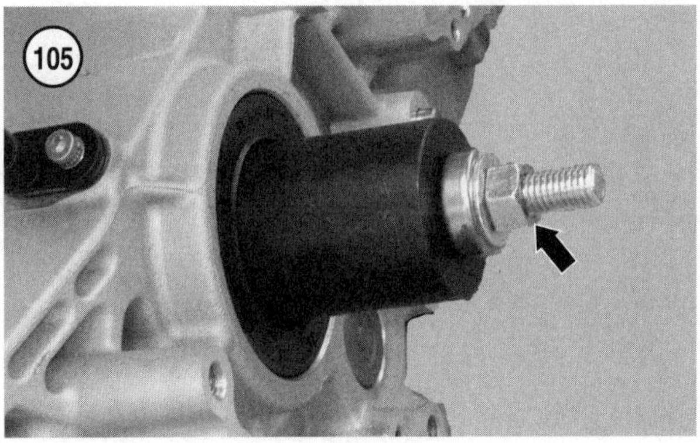

106

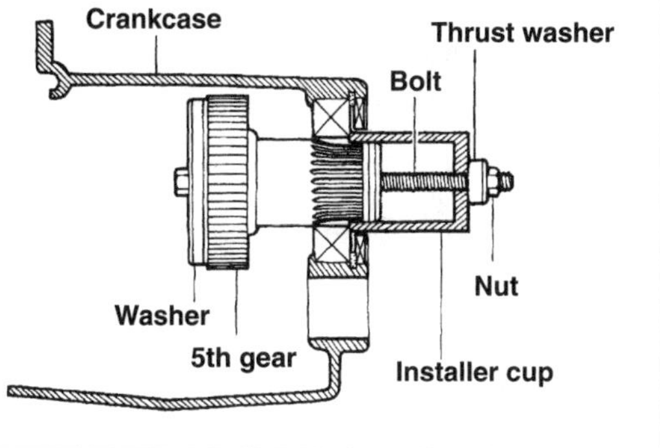

107

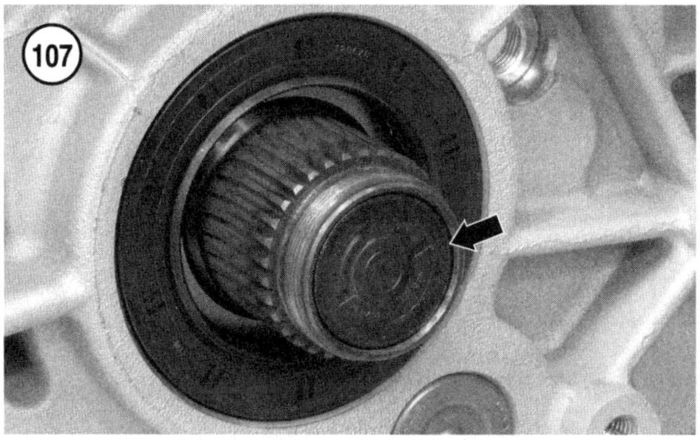

108

109

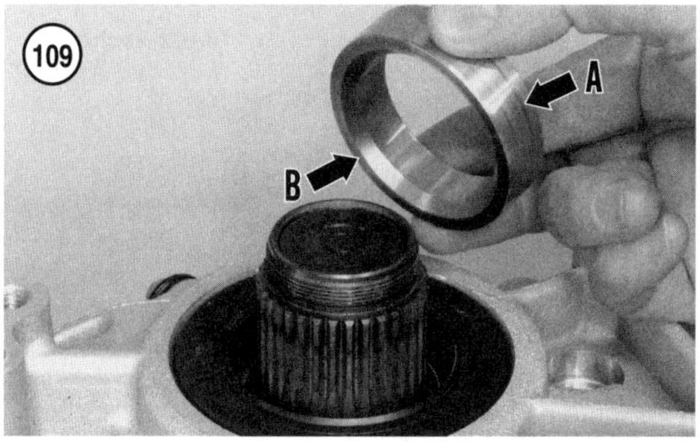

and install the installation tool with the side marked 0.080 inserted into the bearing. Operate the press until the tool bottoms.

3B. Install the bearings *without* the special tool as follows:

a. Using a suitable mandrel, press in the outer end bearing to the depth shown in **Figure 101**.

b. Using a suitable mandrel, press in the inner end bearing to the depth shown in **Figure 101**.

4. Lubricate the bearings with Harley-Davidson Special Purpose Grease or equivalent.

Installation

7

1. Replace the main drive gear bearing (5, **Figure 90**) as described in *Crankcase Bearings* in this chapter.
2. Coat the seal lips with transmission oil prior to installation.
3. Tap the seal into the crankcase until its outer surface (**Figure 102**) is flush with or slightly below (0.030 in. [0.76 mm] maximum) the bore inside surface.
4. Insert the main drive gear (**Figure 97**) into the main drive gear bearing in the transmission portion of the engine crankcase as far as it will go (**Figure 103**). Hold it in place and assemble the Harley-Davidson or equivalent main drive gear remover and installer tool as shown in **Figure 104**, typical, and **Figure 105**.

CAUTION

*Note how the installer cup (**Figure 106**) supports the main drive gear bearing inner race. If installing the main drive gear with a different tool setup, make sure the inner bearing race is supported in the same way. Otherwise, the bearing will be damaged when the main drive gear is pressed into place.*

5. Tighten the puller nut (**Figure 105**) to pull the main drive gear through the bearing. Continue until the gear's shoulder bottoms against the inner bearing race.
6. Disassemble and remove the installer tool assembly.
7. Tap a new seal (**Figure 107**) into the end of the main drive gear until its outer surface is below the bearing bore inside surface as indicated in **Figure 101**.
8. Install a new quad ring (**Figure 108**) and push it in next to the gear taper.
9. Apply oil to the end of the spacer where it contacts the seal, then slide the spacer (A, **Figure 109**), with its chamfered end (B) facing toward the quad ring, over fifth gear and seat it against the bearing.
10. Install the transmission assembly as described in this chapter.

110

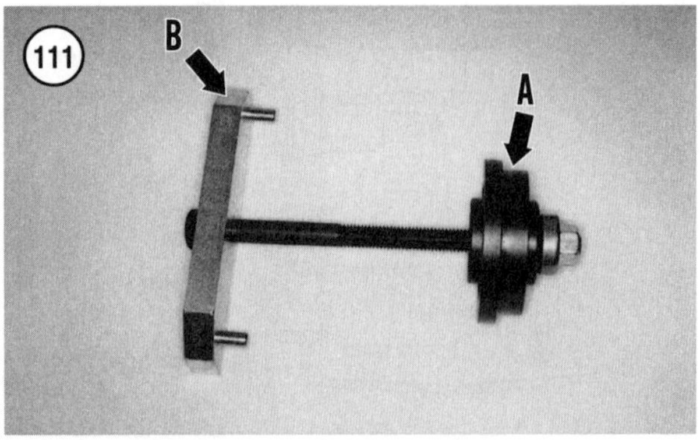
111
B
A

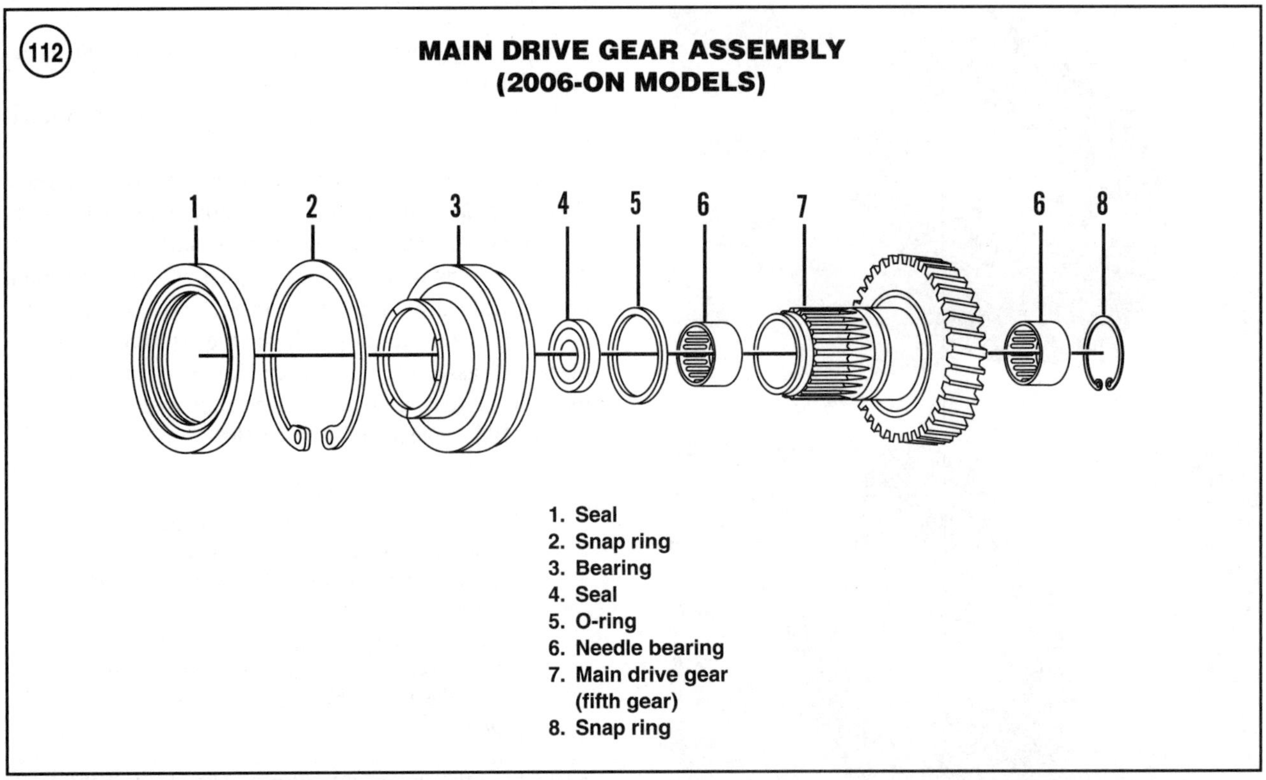
112
MAIN DRIVE GEAR ASSEMBLY
(2006-ON MODELS)
1
2
3
4
5
6
7
6
8
1. Seal
2. Snap ring
3. Bearing
4. Seal
5. O-ring
6. Needle bearing
7. Main drive gear
(fifth gear)
8. Snap ring

113

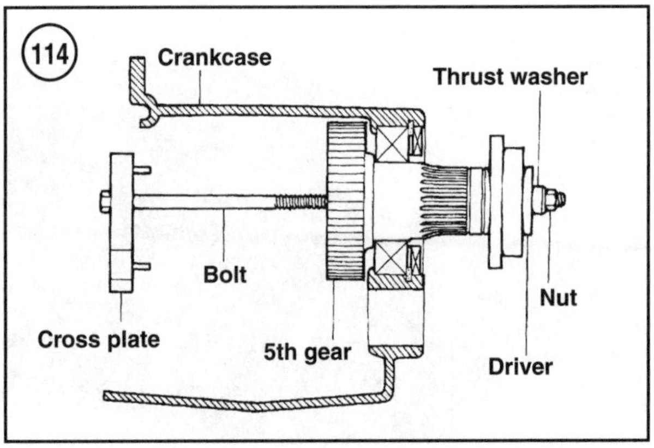
114
Crankcase
Thrust washer
Bolt
Nut
Cross plate
5th gear
Driver

MAIN DRIVE GEAR (2006-ON MODELS)

Tools

Two tools are required to remove and install the main drive gear in the right crankcase. Removing the main drive gear without these tools may cause crankcase and/or main drive gear damage. The tools include:

1. Harley-Davidson main drive gear remover and installer (HD-35316-C); similar to the tools shown in **Figure 110** and **Figure 111**.
2. Harley-Davidson cross plate (B-45847). See B, **Figure 111**.

NOTE
*Equivalent tools are also available from JIMS, (**www.jimsusa.com**).*

Removal

Refer to **Figure 112**.

1. Remove the transmission assembly as described in this chapter.

2. Tap out the seal (**Figure 113**) that is mounted in the end of the main drive gear. Use a drift inserted through the main drive gear to force out the seal. Discard the seal.
3. Assemble the Harley-Davidson or equivalent main drive gear remover and installer and the cross plate as shown in **Figure 114**. Refer to the typical examples in **Figure 115** and **Figure 116**.

NOTE
*Insert the two cross plate pins into the pin holes in the transmission housing. This will center the cross plate with the main drive gear. **Figure 115** shows an early version of the cross plate, which may be used if the plate is properly centered over the gear.*

4. Tighten the puller nut (**Figure 116**) to pull the main drive gear out of the main drive gear bearing. Disassemble the tool and remove the main drive gear from the transmission portion of the engine crankcase.
5. Pry the main drive gear oil seal (**Figure 117**) out of the right crankcase.

CAUTION
Because the main drive gear inner bearing race was not supported when the main drive gear was removed, the bearing is damaged. Whenever the main drive gear is removed, replace the main drive gear bearing.

6. Replace the main drive gear bearing as described in *Crankcase Bearings* in this chapter.
7. The bearing inner race will remain on the main drive gear after gear removal. Press the bearing inner race off the gear shaft.
8. Discard the O-ring (**Figure 118**) on the gear shaft.

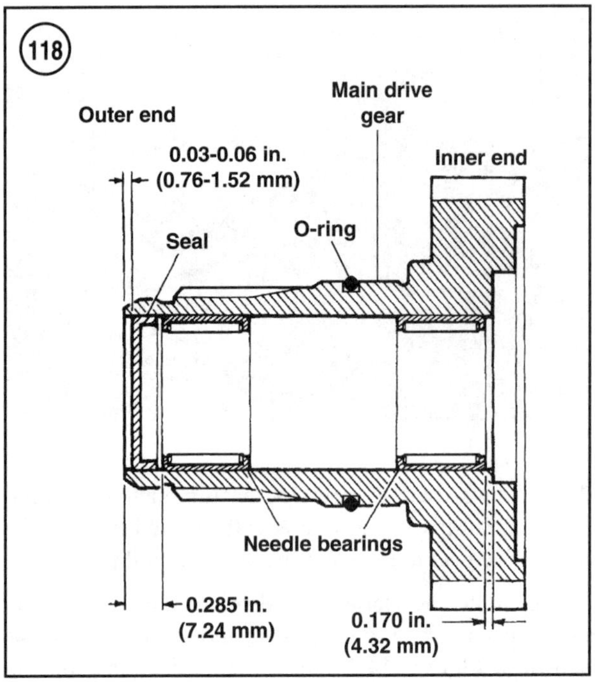

Inspection

1. Clean the main drive gear in solvent and dry with compressed air.
2. Check each gear tooth (A, **Figure 119**) for excessive wear, burrs, galling and pitting. Check for missing gear teeth.
3. Check the gear splines for excessive wear, galling or other damage.
4. Inspect the two main drive gear needle bearings (B, **Figure 119**) for excessive wear or damage. Insert the mainshaft into the main drive gear to check bearing wear. If necessary, replace the bearings as described in this section.

Needle Bearing Replacement

Both main drive gear needle bearings (6, **Figure 112**) must be installed to a specific depth (**Figure 118**). Bearing installation can be performed with the Harley-Davidson or equivalent inner/outer main drive gear needle bearing installation tool (HD-47855). If an installation tool is not available, measuring bearing position during installation is required.

Always replace both main drive gear needle bearings at the same time.

CAUTION
Do not install a main drive gear needle bearing that has been removed. Removal damages the bearings.

1. Support the main drive gear in a press and press out both needle bearings.
2. Clean the bearing bore in solvent and dry thoroughly.

NOTE
Install both needle bearings so the manufacturer's name and size code face out.

3A. Install the bearing *with* the special tool as follows:
   a. This tool is stamped on both sides. The side stamped INNER is for pressing in the inner end bearing. The side stamped OUTER is for pressing the outer end bearing (**Figure 118**).
   b. Install the main drive gear in a press with the outer end facing up. Align the new bearing with the main drive gear and install the installation tool. Make

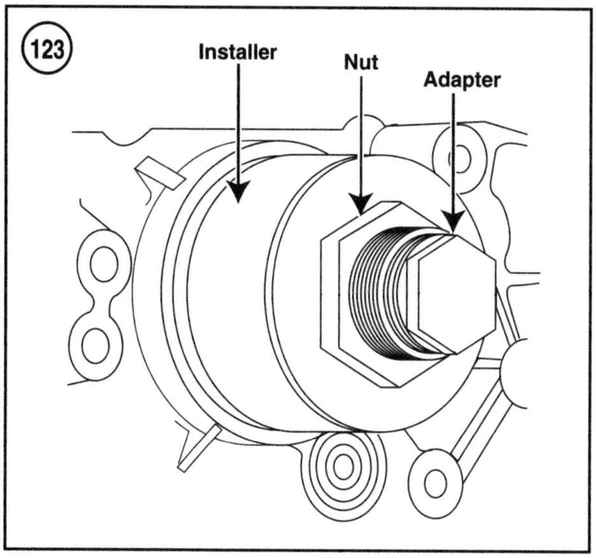

sure the side stamped OUTER is inserted into the bearing. Operate the press until the tool bottoms.

   c. Turn the main drive gear over so the inner end faces up. Align the new bearing with the main drive gear and install the installation tool with the side marked INNER inserted into the bearing. Operate the press until the tool bottoms.

3B. Install the bearings *without* the special tool as follows:

   a. Using a suitable mandrel, press in the outer end bearing to the depth shown in **Figure 118**.
   b. Using a suitable mandrel, press in the inner end bearing to the depth shown in **Figure 118**.

4. Lubricate the bearings with Harley Davidson Special Purpose Grease or equivalent.

Installation

1. Replace the main drive gear bearing (3, **Figure 112**) as described in *Crankcase Bearings* in this chapter.
2. Install a new O-ring onto the main drive gear (**Figure 118**). Lubricate the O-ring with transmission oil.
3. Insert the main drive gear (**Figure 120**) into the main drive gear bearing in the transmission portion of the engine crankcase as far as it will go. Hold it in place and assemble the Harley-Davidson or equivalent main drive gear remover and installer tool as shown in **Figure 121** and **Figure 122**.

CAUTION
*Note how the installer cup (**Figure 106**) contacts the main drive gear bearing inner race. If installing the main drive gear with a different tool setup, make sure the inner bearing race is supported in the same way. Otherwise, the bearing will be damaged.*

4. Tighten the puller nut (**Figure 122**) to pull the main drive gear through the bearing. Continue until the gear shoulder bottoms against the inner bearing race.
5. Disassemble and remove the installer tool assembly.
6. Coat the seal lips with transmission oil prior to installation. Install the seal using one of the following methods:
   a. Using a suitable seal driver, tap the seal into the crankcase until its outer surface is flush with or slightly below (0.030 in. [0.76 mm] maximum) the seal bore inside surface.
   b. Install the Harley-Davidson tool HD-47856 (**Figure 123**) and using the drive gear threads, pull the seal into position. The tool will install the seal to the proper depth.
7. Tap a new seal into the end of the main drive gear until its outer surface is below the bearing bore inside surface as indicated in **Figure 118**.
8. Install the transmission assembly as described in this chapter.

CRANKCASE BEARINGS

This section provides information for inspection and replacement of the transmission and main drive gear bearings located in the crankcase.

Refer to *Internal Gearshift Mechanism* in this chapter for the shift drum bushings.

Left Crankcase Half Bearings

The left crankcase half contains the mainshaft bearing (A, **Figure 124**) and countershaft bearing (B).

Inspection

WARNING

Do not spin the bearings with compressed air. Compressed air will spin the bearings at excess speed. This may cause the bearing to fly apart.

1. Clean both bearings in kerosene, then dry each bearing using compressed air.
2. Turn the inner bearing race slowly. The bearing should turn smoothly with no roughness, binding or excessive play. If these conditions exist, reclean and dry the bearing. If these conditions still persist, replace the bearing as described in this section.
3. If the bearing turns smoothly, check for visible damage. Check for overheating, cracked races, pitting and galling. Also check the bearing fit in the bearing bore; both bearings must be a tight fit. If the bearing is a loose fit, check the crankcase for cracks or other damage.
4. Replace the bearings, if necessary, as described in this chapter.
5. If the bearings can be reused, lubricate them thoroughly with transmission oil, then place the crankcase half in a plastic bag and seal it until transmission reassembly.

Replacement

Use this procedure to replace either bearing.

1. Remove the snap ring securing the bearing.
2. Support the crankcase half, with its inside surface facing up, in a press.
3. Using a suitable mandrel or bearing driver, press the bearing out of the crankcase half.
4. Clean the bearing bore and dry with compressed air.
5. Check the snap ring groove for excessive wear, cracks or other damage. If the groove is damaged, replace the crankcase half.
6. Support the crankcase in a press with the outside surface facing up.
7. Install the bearing so the manufacturer's name and size code face out. Place a socket or bearing driver on the outer bearing race and press the bearing into the access cover until the bearing bottoms.

127

128

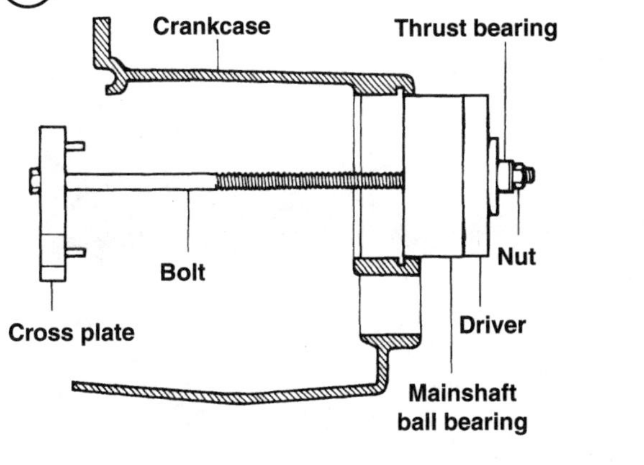

8. Install a new snap ring into the groove so its beveled side faces away from the bearing. Make sure the snap ring is fully seated in the groove.

9. Repeat for the remaining bearing.

Right Crankcase Half Bearings

The right crankcase half contains the main drive gear bearing (A, **Figure 125**) and countershaft needle bearing (**Figure 126**).

Main drive gear bearing inspection

Because the main drive gear bearing (A, **Figure 125**) is damaged when the main drive gear is removed, do not reuse the bearing. Replace the bearing as described in this section.

Countershaft needle bearing inspection

1. Clean the needle bearing (**Figure 126**) in kerosene and dry with compressed air.

2. Check the needle bearing for excessively worn, loose or damaged rollers. Check the roller cage and outer shell for damage.

3. Check each bearing for a loose fit in its bore; the bearing must be a tight fit. If the bearing is a loose fit, check the crankcase half for cracks or other damage.

4. Replace the bearing, if necessary, as described in this chapter.

5. If the bearing can be reused, lubricate them thoroughly with transmission oil.

7

Main drive gear bearing replacement

Refer to **Figure 90** or **Figure 112** when replacing the main drive gear bearing.

1. Pry the main drive gear bearing seal (**Figure 127**) out of the crankcase using a wide-blade screwdriver.

2. Remove the snap ring (B, **Figure 125**) from the crankcase groove. This snap ring is located behind the main drive gear seal.

3. Using a suitable bearing driver, drive the main drive gear bearing out of the crankcase, working from inside the transmission housing. Discard the bearing.

4. Clean the bearing bore and dry with compressed air. Check the bore for nicks or burrs. Check the snap ring groove for damage.

CAUTION

*The Harley-Davidson main drive gear remover and installer and cross plate tool are used to install the new bearing. Refer to **Main Drive Gear** in this chapter. If the H-D special tool is not available, refer to Chapter One for general bearing installation methods. Make sure the bearing is centered and force is exerted against the outer race.*

5. Install the new bearing onto the Harley-Davidson main drive gear remover and installer and cross plate tools as shown in **Figure 128**. Install it with the manufacturer's name and size code facing out.

CAUTION

In Step 6 stop applying force when the bearing bottoms. Applying excessive force may damage the crankcase.

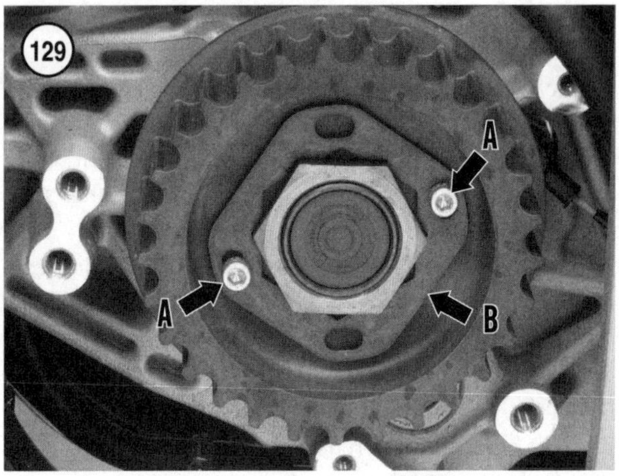

NOTE
*Insert the two cross plate pins into the pin holes (**Figure 115**) in the transmission housing. This will center the cross plate with the main drive gear bearing.*

6. Tighten the puller nut to pull the bearing into the crankcase. Continue until the bearing bottoms against the bearing bore surface.
7. Disassemble and remove the puller tool assembly.
8. Install the snap ring, with its beveled side facing out, into the crankcase groove. Make sure the snap ring is fully seated in the groove.

NOTE
*The main drive gear bearing seal is installed during the main drive gear installation procedure. Refer to the **Main Drive Gear** section in this chapter.*

9. Lubricate the bearing with transmission fluid.

Countershaft needle bearing replacement

1. Using a suitable bearing driver, drive the countershaft needle bearing (**Figure 126**) out of the crankcase working from inside the transmission housing. Discard the bearing.
2. Clean the bearing bore and dry with compressed air. Check the bearing bore for nicks or burrs.
3. Align the new bearing, with its closed side facing out, with the crankcase bearing bore.
4. Drive in the new bearing until its outer surface is flush with or 0.030 in. (0.76 mm) below the bushing bore inside surface.
5. Lubricate the bearing with transmission fluid.

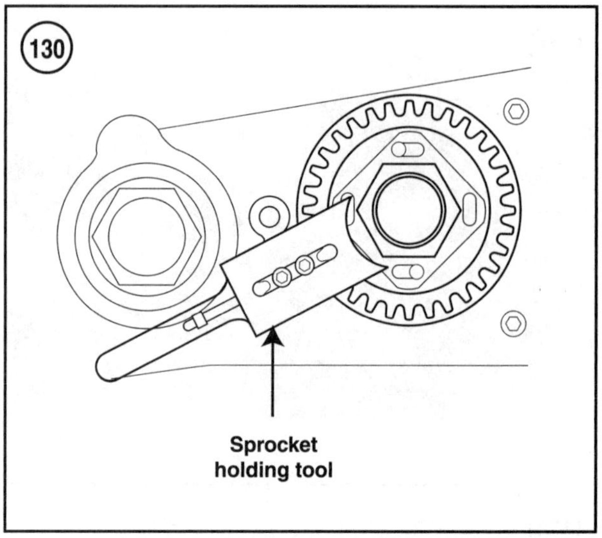

TRANSMISSION DRIVE SPROCKET

Removal/Installation

1. Remove the drive belt as described in Chapter Ten.
2. Remove the bolts (A, **Figure 129**) and lockplate (B).
3. Install the sprocket holding tool (HD-46282 or JIMS Tools equivalent) as shown in **Figure 130**.

CAUTION
The sprocket retaining nut has left-hand threads. Turn the nut clockwise to remove it.

4. Remove the sprocket retaining nut by turning it *clockwise.*
5. Remove the sprocket holding tool, then remove the drive sprocket (**Figure 131**).
6. Install the drive sprocket by reversing the removal procedure while noting the following:
   a. Use the same tool setup during installation.

b. Apply Loctite 262 (red) to the nut threads.
c. Install the nut so the shouldered side is in toward the sprocket.

CAUTION
In substep d, do not tighten the nut past an additional 45° to align the lockplate bolt holes or the nut will be damaged.

d. Tighten the nut *counterclockwise* to 50 ft.-lb. (68 N•m). Tighten the nut an additional 30° until the lockplate holes align. Do not loosen the nut to align the holes. If necessary, flip the lockplate over and recheck hole alignment.

e. Tighten the lockplate bolts to 90-110 in.-lb. (10.2-12.4 N•m).

Tables 1-2 are on the following pages.

Table 1 TRANSMISSION SPECIFICATIONS

Primary drive sprockets	
Number of gear teeth	
Engine sprocket	
883 models	34
1200 models	38
Clutch sprocket	57
Ratio	
883 models	1.676:1
1200 models	1.500:1
Final drive sprockets	
Number of sprocket teeth	
Transmission sprocket	
883 models	28
1200 models	29
Rear wheel sprocket	68
Final drive ratio	
883 models	2.429:1
1200 models	2.345:1
Secondary drive belt	
Number of teeth	
883 models	136
1200 models	137

Table 2 TRANSMISSION TORQUE SPECIFICATIONS

	ft.-lb.	in.-lb.	N•m
Countershaft bolt			
2004-2005 models	13-17	–	17.6-23.3
2006-on models	33-39	–	45-53
Drive sprocket lockplate bolts	–	90-110	10.2-12.4
Drive sprocket nut (initial)*	50	–	68

*Refer to text for tightening procedure. Nut has left-hand threads.

NOTE: Refer to the Supplement at the end of this manual for information unique to 2007-2011 models.

CHAPTER EIGHT

FUEL, EMISSION CONTROL AND EXHAUST SYSTEMS

This chapter includes service procedures for the fuel, exhaust and emission control systems. Routine air filter maintenance is described in Chapter Three. Specifications are in **Tables 1-3** at the end of this chapter.

WARNING
Gasoline is carcinogenic and extremely flammable, and must be handled carefully. Wear nitrile gloves to avoid skin contact. If gasoline does contact skin, immediately and thoroughly wash the area with soap and warm water.

AIR FILTER BACKPLATE

Removal

Refer to **Figure 1**.

1. Remove the air filter cover screws (A, **Figure 2**) and remove the cover (B).
2. Remove the air filter element screws (A, **Figure 3**) and remove the air filter element (B).
3. Remove the O-ring (A, **Figure 4**) on each hollow breather bolt.4. Unscrew and remove the hollow breather bolts (B, **Figure 4**) securing the backplate to the cylinder heads.

4A. On California models, pull the backplate (**Figure 5**) partially away from the cylinder heads and the carburetor, then disconnect the evaporation emission control clean air inlet hose and carburetor vent hose from the backplate (**Figure 6**).

4B. On all other models, except California models, pull the backplate (**Figure 5**) away from the cylinder heads and remove it.

5. Remove the carburetor gasket from the backing plate (**Figure 7**).

Inspection

1. Inspect the backplate for damage.
2. On California models, make sure the trap door swings freely (**Figure 8**, typical).
3. Make sure the breather hollow bolts (A, **Figure 9**) are clear. Clean them out if necessary.

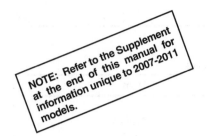

1

AIR FILTER ASSEMBLY

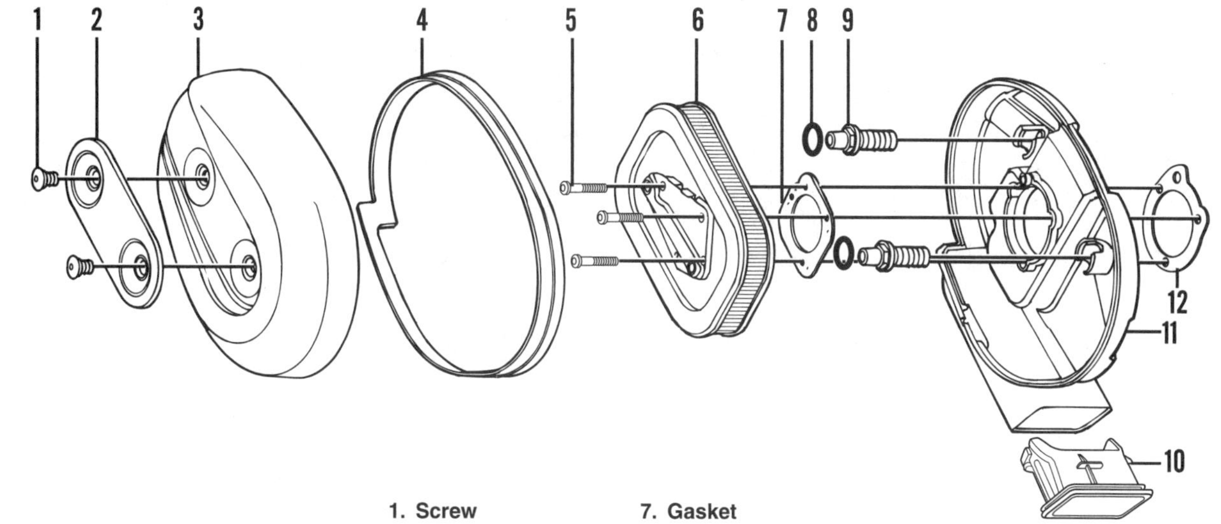

1. Screw
2. Trim panel
3. Cover
4. Seal ring
5. Torx screw
6. Air filter element
7. Gasket
8. O-ring
9. Hollow breather bolt
10. Snorkel
11. Backplate
12. Gasket

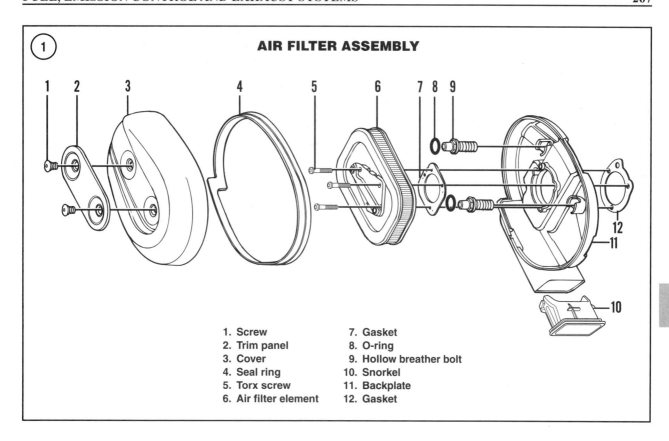

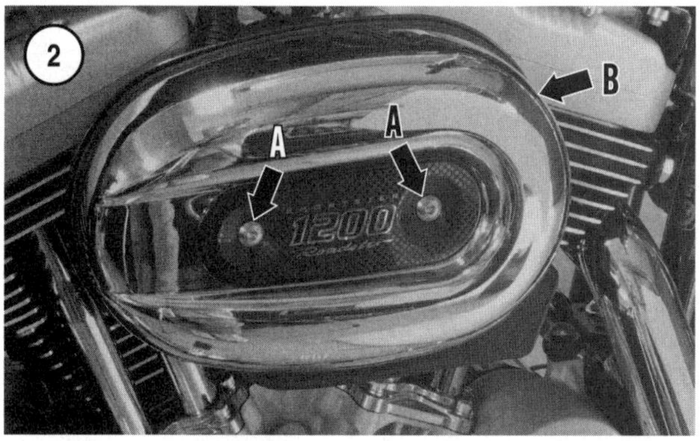

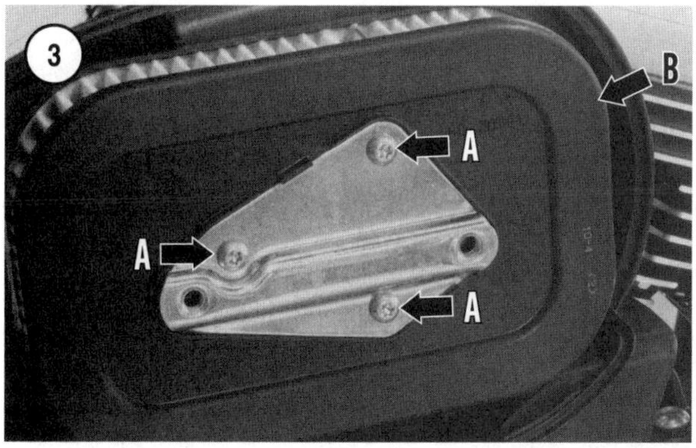

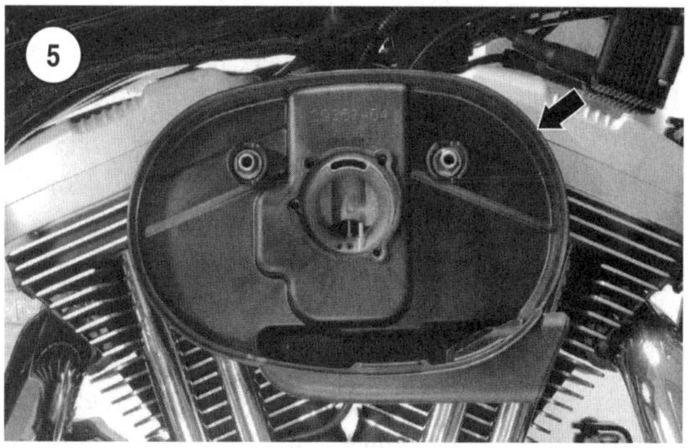

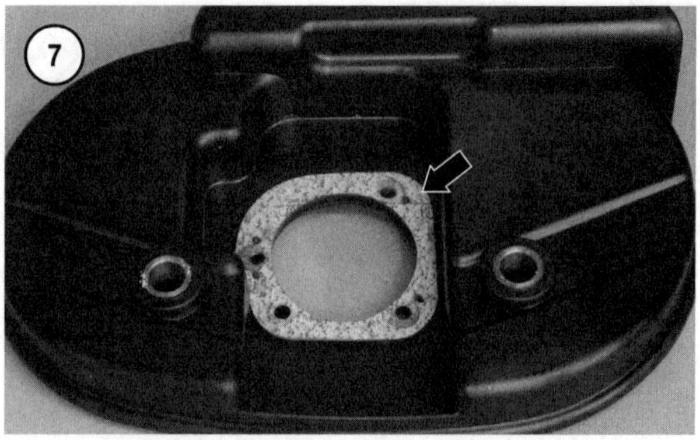

4. Inspect the O-rings (B, **Figure 9**) and replace if damaged.

Installation

1. Apply a light coat of gasket sealer to the new gasket and install it onto the backing plate (**Figure 7**).
2. Move the backplate into position.
3. On California models, move the backplate part way into position. Connect the evaporation emission control clean air inlet hose (**Figure 6**) to the port hole on the backside of the backplate. Connect the carburetor vent hose to the nipple on the backside of the backplate.
4. Position the backplate (**Figure 5**) against the carburetor and cylinder heads. Make sure the Torx bolt holes of the gasket and backplate are aligned with the carburetor. Reposition the gasket if necessary.
5. Install the breather hollow bolts (B, **Figure 4**) securing the backplate to the cylinder heads. Tighten them to 84-120 in.-lb. (9.5-13.6 N•m).
6. Install the O-rings (A, **Figure 4**). Lubricate the O-rings with engine oil before installing the O-rings and air filter element.
7. Install the gasket (**Figure 10**) onto the back of the air filter element. Make sure all holes are aligned.
8. Install the air filter element (B, **Figure 3**). Tighten the screws to 40-60 in.-lb. (4.5-6.8 N•m).
9. Inspect the seal ring (**Figure 11**) on the air filter cover for hardness or deterioration. Replace it if necessary.
10. Install the air filter cover (B, **Figure 2**) and the screws (A). Make sure the seal ring fits properly inside the backplate. Tighten the screws to 36-60 in.-lb. (4.1-6.8 N•m).

CARBURETOR

Operation

The carburetor supplies and atomizes air and fuel in the correct ratio. At the primary throttle opening (idle), a

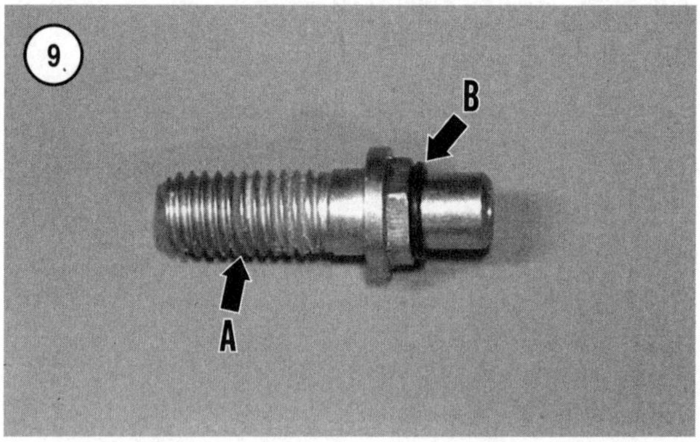

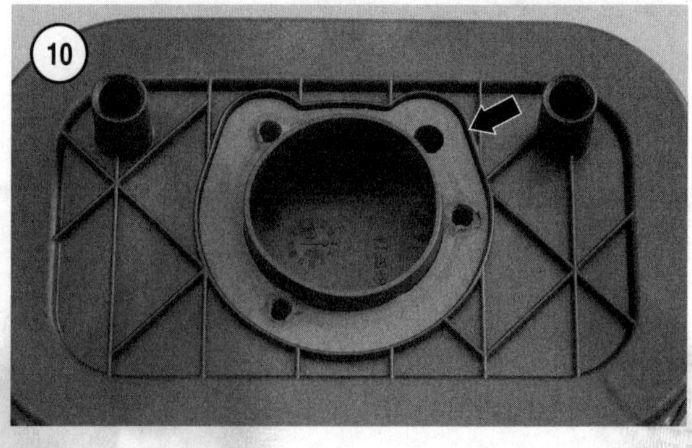

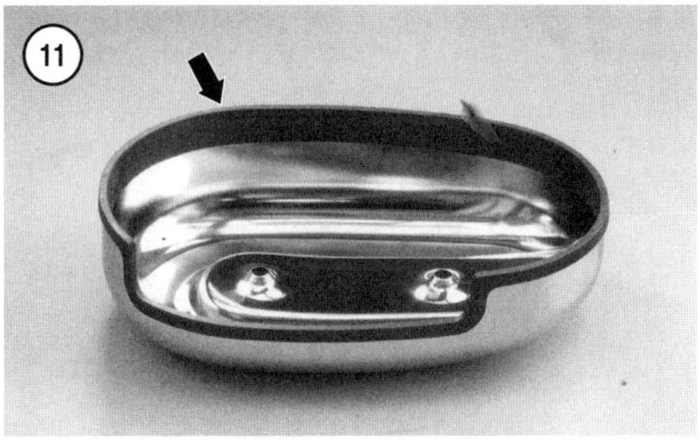

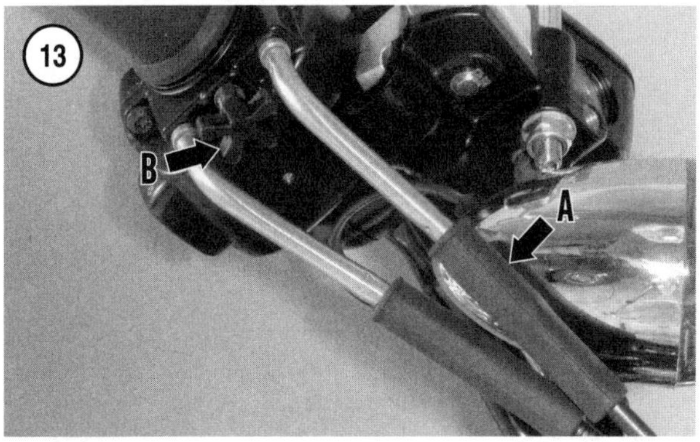

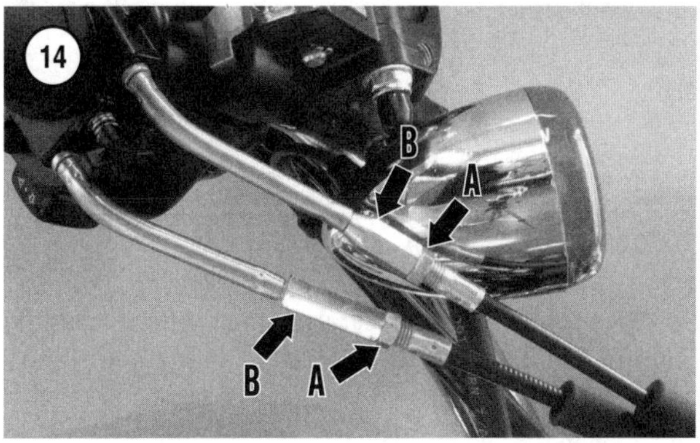

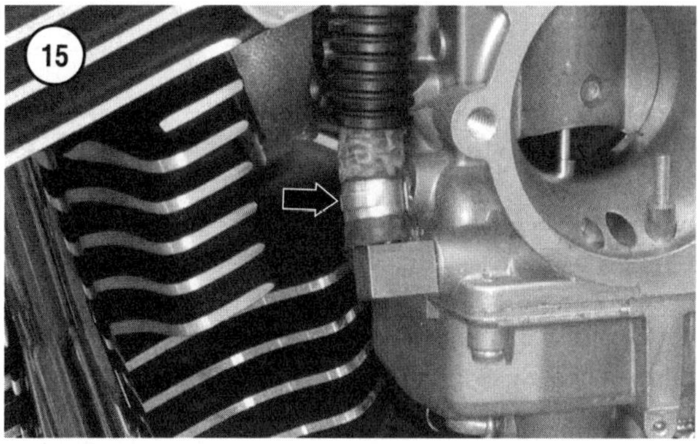

small amount of fuel is siphoned through the pilot jet by the incoming air. As the throttle is opened further, the air stream begins to siphon fuel through the main jet and needle jet. The tapered needle increases the effective flow capacity of the needle jet as it is lifted, and occupies progressively less area of the jet. At full throttle, the carburetor venturi is fully open and the needle is lifted far enough to permit the main jet to flow at full capacity.

The cold start circuit is a starting enrichment valve system. The *choke* knob under the fuel tank on the left side of the engine opens an enrichment valve, rather than closing a butterfly in the venturi area as on some carburetors. In the open position, the slow jet discharges a stream of fuel into the carburetor venturi to enrich the mixture for cold start up.

The accelerator pump circuit reduces engine hesitation by spraying fuel into the carburetor intake passage during sudden acceleration.

Removal

1. Remove the air filter and backplate as described in this chapter.
2. Remove the fuel tank as described in this chapter.
3. Loosen the hex nut (**Figure 12**) behind the mounting bracket. Disengage the starting enrichment valve cable from the mounting bracket.
4. Push the rubber boots (A, **Figure 13**) off the throttle cable adjusters.
5. Loosen the throttle friction screw (B, **Figure 13**).
6. Loosen both control cable adjuster lock nuts (A, **Figure 14**), then turn the cable adjusters (B) clockwise as far as possible to increase cable free play.
7. Refer to *Fuel Hose And Clamps* in this chapter and disconnect the fuel supply hose (**Figure 15**) from the carburetor fitting.
8. Twist and pull the carburetor off the seal ring and intake manifold.

9. Disconnect the vacuum hose (**Figure 16**) from the carburetor fitting.
10. Disconnect the overflow/drain hose (**Figure 17**) from the carburetor fitting.
11. Label the two cables at the carburetor before disconnecting them. One is the throttle control cable (A, **Figure 18**) and the other is the idle control cable (B). Disconnect the throttle control cable and the idle control cable from the carburetor cable guide and the throttle pulley.
12. Drain the gasoline from the carburetor assembly.
13. Inspect the carburetor seal ring (**Figure 19**) on the intake manifold for wear, hardness, cracks or other damage. Replace it if necessary.
14. If necessary, service the intake manifold as described in this chapter.
15. Cover the intake manifold opening.

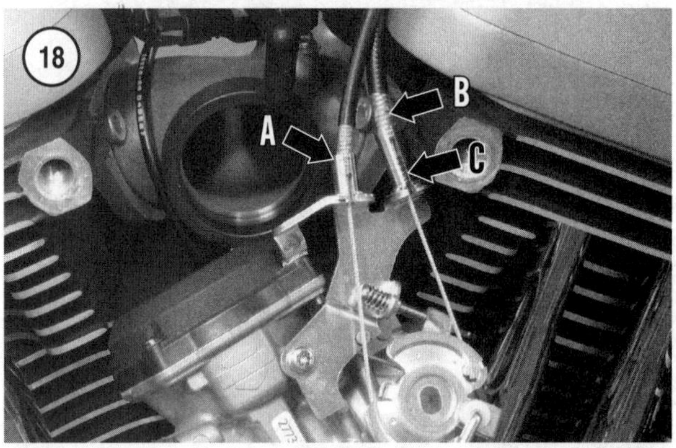

Installation

1. If removed, seat the seal ring (**Figure 19**) onto the intake manifold. Make sure it is correctly seated to avoid a vacuum leak.
2. Route the starting enrichment valve cable between the cylinders and toward its mounting bracket on the left side.
3. Connect the idle cable to the carburetor as follows:
   a. The idle cable has the small spring (C, **Figure 18**) on the end of the cable.
   b. Insert the idle cable sheath into the rear cable bracket guide on the carburetor.
   c. Attach the end of the idle cable to the throttle pulley (B, **Figure 18**).
4. Connect the throttle cable (A, **Figure 18**) to the carburetor as follows:
   a. Insert the throttle cable sheath into the front cable bracket guide on the carburetor.
   b. Attach the end of the throttle cable to the throttle pulley.
5. Operate the hand throttle a few times. Make sure the throttle pulley operates smoothly with no binding. Also make sure both cable ends are seated squarely in the cable bracket guides and in the throttle pulley.
6. Connect the vacuum hose (**Figure 16**) to the carburetor fitting. Connect the overflow/drain hose (**Figure 17**) to the carburetor fitting.

CAUTION

The carburetor must fit squarely onto the intake manifold. If it is misaligned, it may damage the intake manifold seal ring, causing a vacuum leak.

NOTE

To ease installation of the carburetor, apply a light coat of liquid dish soap to the carburetor spigot before insertion into the intake manifold seal ring.

7. Align the carburetor squarely with the intake manifold (**Figure 19**), then push it into the manifold until it bottoms. Position the carburetor so it sits square and vertical with the manifold (**Figure 20**).

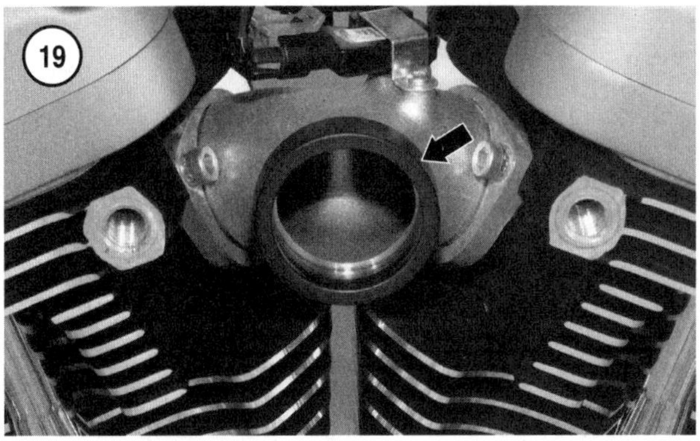

8. Slide a new hose clamp over the fuel supply hose, then connect the fuel hose to the hose fitting on the carburetor (**Figure 15**).
9. Insert the starting enrichment valve cable into the mounting bracket, then tighten the locknut (**Figure 12**) securely.
10. Before installing the fuel tank, recheck the idle and throttle cable operation. Open and release the hand throttle. Make sure the carburetor throttle valve opens and closes smoothly. Make sure both cables are routed properly. If necessary, adjust the throttle cables as described in Chapter Three.
11. Install the air filter backplate and air filter as described in this chapter.
12. Install the fuel tank as described in this chapter.
13. Start the engine and allow it to idle. Check for fuel leaks.
14. Turn the handlebar from side to side. The idle speed should remain the same. If the idle speed increases while turning the handlebars, the cables are installed incorrectly or are damaged. Remove the fuel tank and inspect the cables.

Disassembly

Refer to **Figure 21**.

1. Unscrew and remove the starting enrichment valve and cable (**Figure 22**).
2. Remove the screw and washer (A, **Figure 23**) on the side and the top screw (A, **Figure 24**) securing the throttle cable bracket to the carburetor. Remove the bracket (B, **Figure 24**).
3. Remove the collar (**Figure 25**) from the cover.
4. Remove the remaining cover screws (**Figure 26**). Remove the cover and spring (A, **Figure 27**).
5. Remove the vacuum piston (B, **Figure 27**) from the carburetor housing. Do not damage the jet needle extending out of the bottom of the vacuum piston.
6. Remove the float bowl as follows:
   a. Remove the screws (**Figure 28**) securing the float bowl to the carburetor.
   b. Slowly remove the float bowl body and withdraw the pump rod (**Figure 29**) from the boot on the bowl.
   c. Disconnect the pump rod from the lever on the carburetor (**Figure 30**).

CAUTION
*One of the float pin pedestals has an interference fit that holds the float pin in place. An arrow, (**Figure 31**) cast into the carburetor, points to this pedestal. To remove the float pin, tap it out from the interference side in the direction of the arrow. If the float pin is removed opposite of the arrow, the opposite pedestal may crack or break off.*

7. Carefully tap the float pin (**Figure 32**) out of the pedestals and remove it.
8. Remove the float and fuel valve assembly (**Figure 33**).
9. Unscrew and remove the pilot jet (**Figure 34**).
10. Unscrew and remove the main jet (**Figure 35**).
11. Unscrew and remove the needle jet holder (**Figure 36**).
12. Remove the needle jet (A, **Figure 37**) from the needle jet bore in the carburetor.

Cleaning and Inspection

CAUTION
The carburetor body is equipped with plastic parts that cannot be removed. Do not dip the carburetor body, O-rings, float assembly, fuel valve or vacuum piston in a carburetor cleaner or another harsh solution that can damage these parts. Using a caustic carburetor cleaning solvent is not recommended. Instead, clean the carburetor and related parts in a petroleum-based solvent, or Simple Green. Then rinse them in clean water.

8

(21)

CARBURETOR

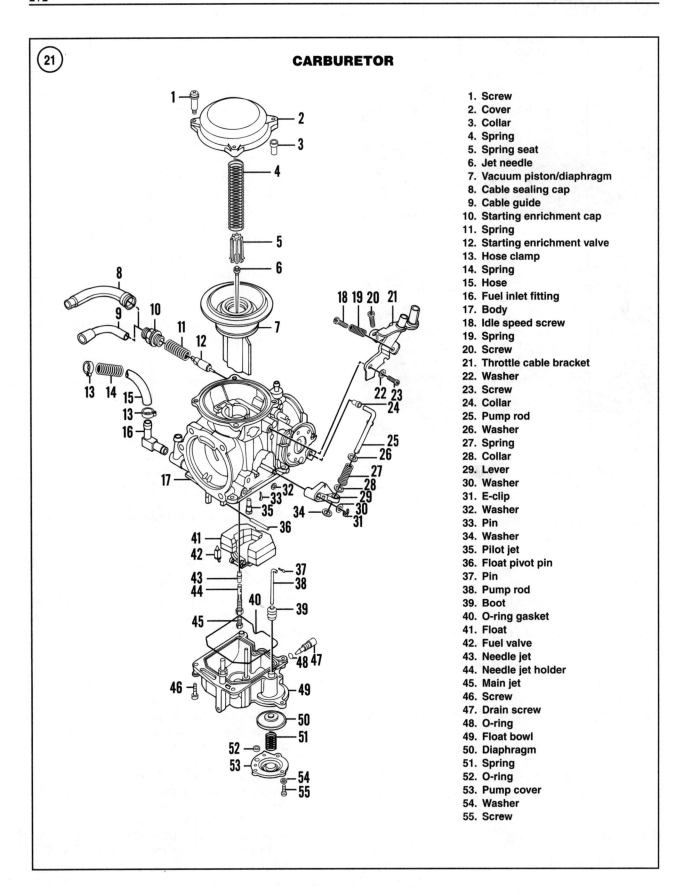

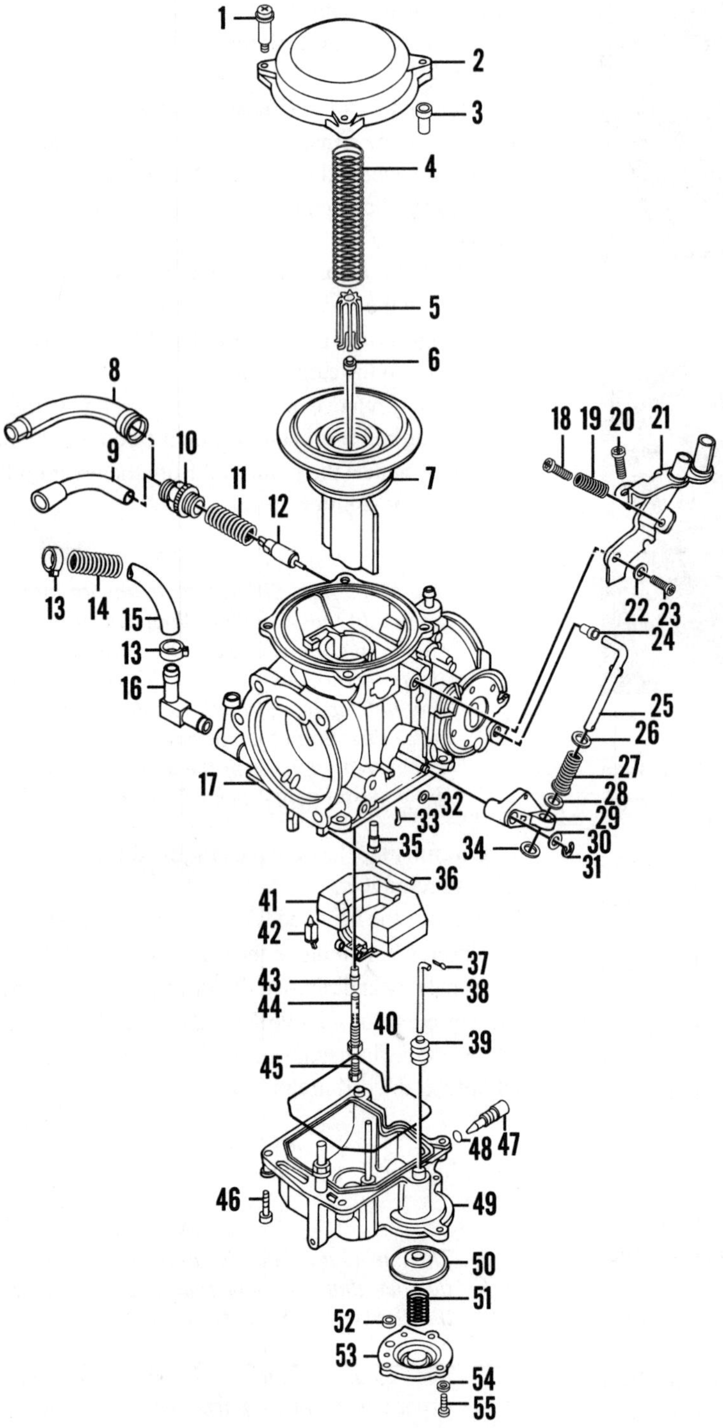

1. Screw
2. Cover
3. Collar
4. Spring
5. Spring seat
6. Jet needle
7. Vacuum piston/diaphragm
8. Cable sealing cap
9. Cable guide
10. Starting enrichment cap
11. Spring
12. Starting enrichment valve
13. Hose clamp
14. Spring
15. Hose
16. Fuel inlet fitting
17. Body
18. Idle speed screw
19. Spring
20. Screw
21. Throttle cable bracket
22. Washer
23. Screw
24. Collar
25. Pump rod
26. Washer
27. Spring
28. Collar
29. Lever
30. Washer
31. E-clip
32. Washer
33. Pin
34. Washer
35. Pilot jet
36. Float pivot pin
37. Pin
38. Pump rod
39. Boot
40. O-ring gasket
41. Float
42. Fuel valve
43. Needle jet
44. Needle jet holder
45. Main jet
46. Screw
47. Drain screw
48. O-ring
49. Float bowl
50. Diaphragm
51. Spring
52. O-ring
53. Pump cover
54. Washer
55. Screw

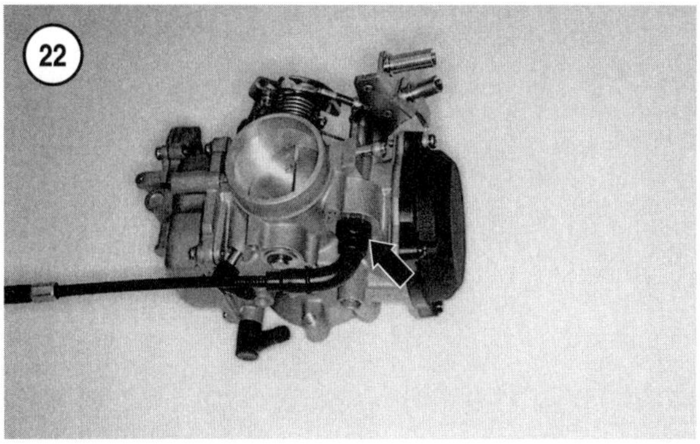
22

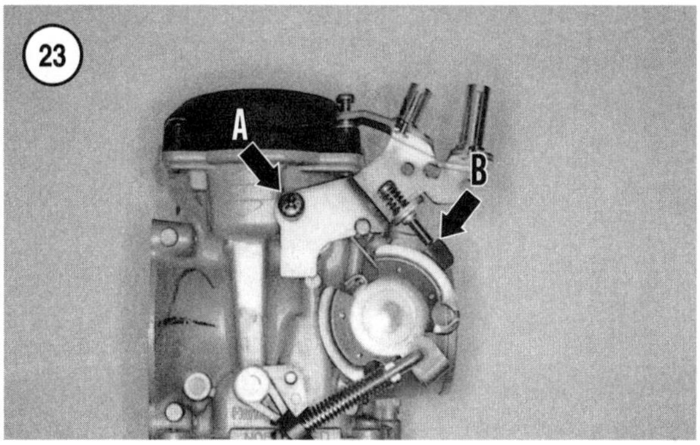
23
A
B

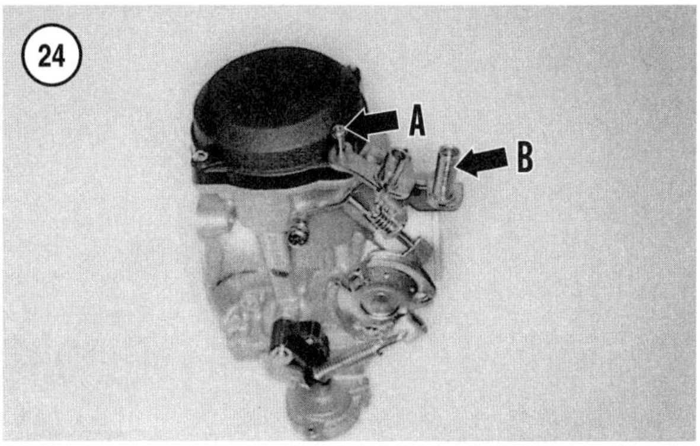
24
A
B

25

26

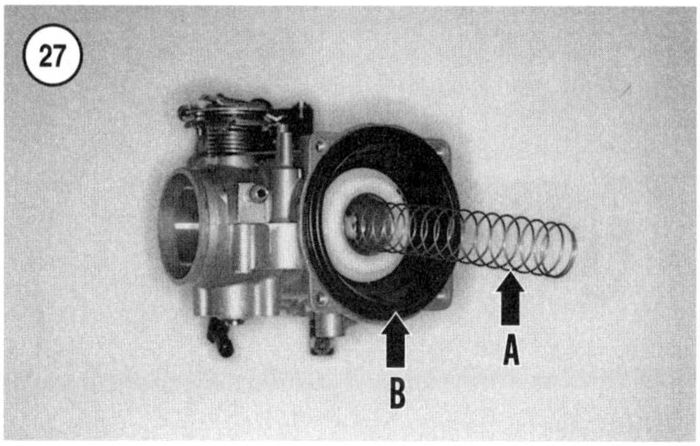
27
B
A

28

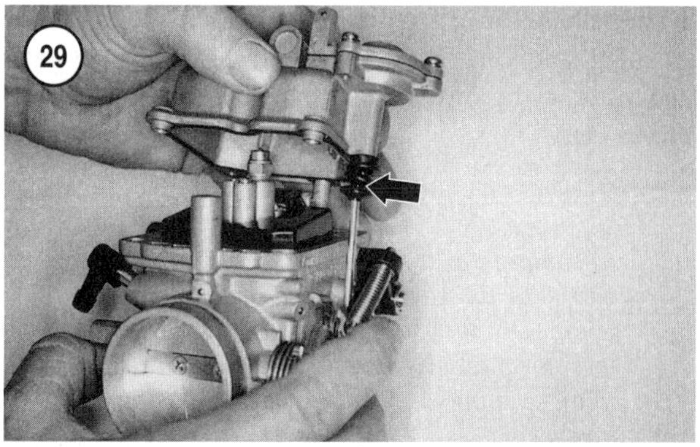
29

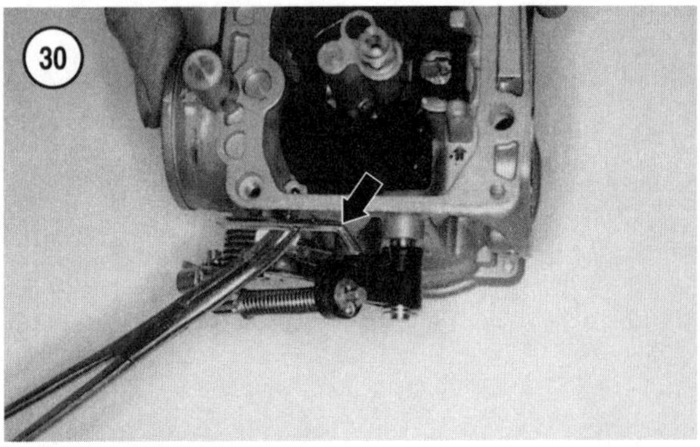

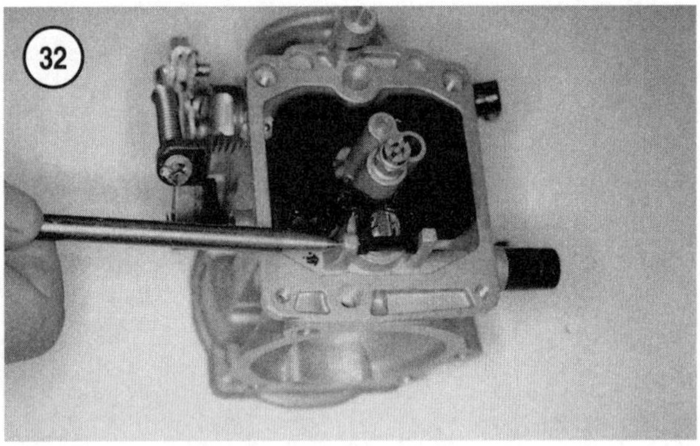

1. Initially clean all parts in a mild petroleum-based cleaning solution. Then clean them in hot, soapy water and rinse with cold water. Blow them dry with compressed air.

CAUTION

If compressed air is not available, allow the parts to air dry or use a clean, lint-free cloth. Do not use a paper towel to dry carburetor parts, as small paper particles may plug openings in the carburetor housing or jets.

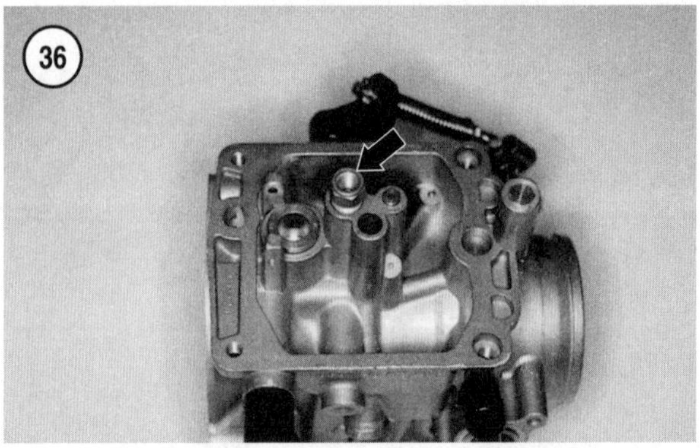

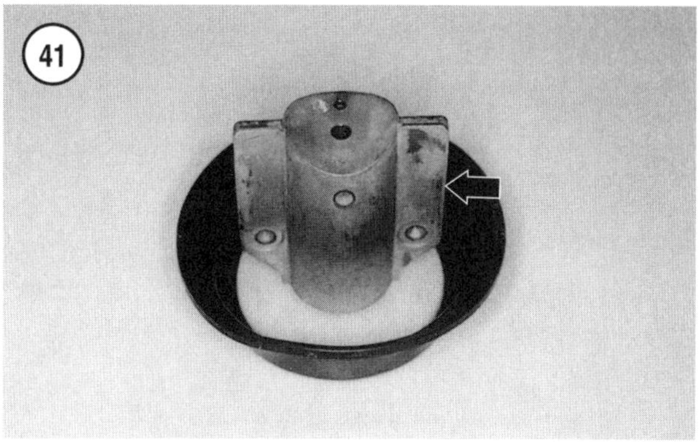

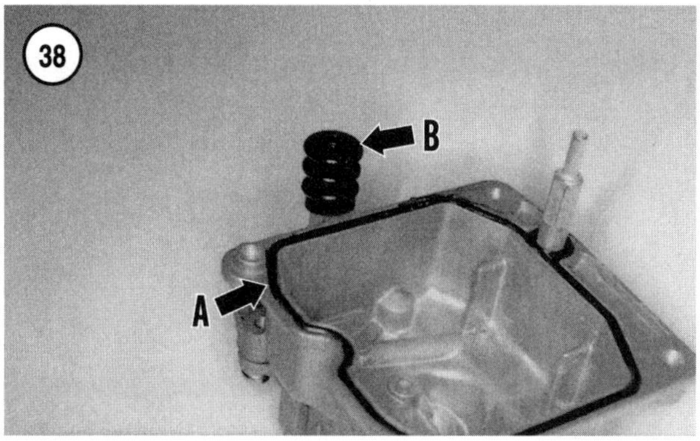

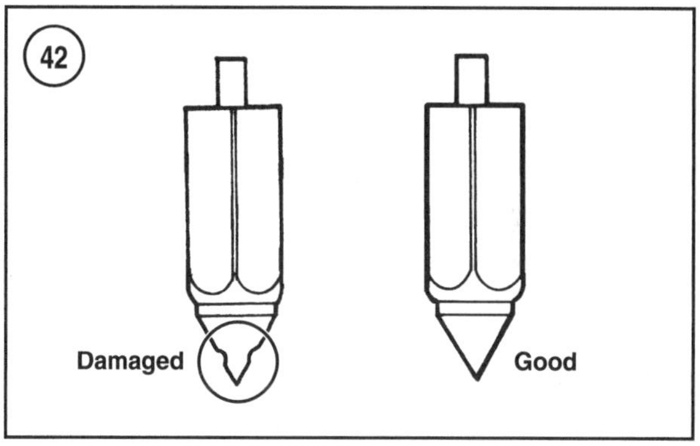

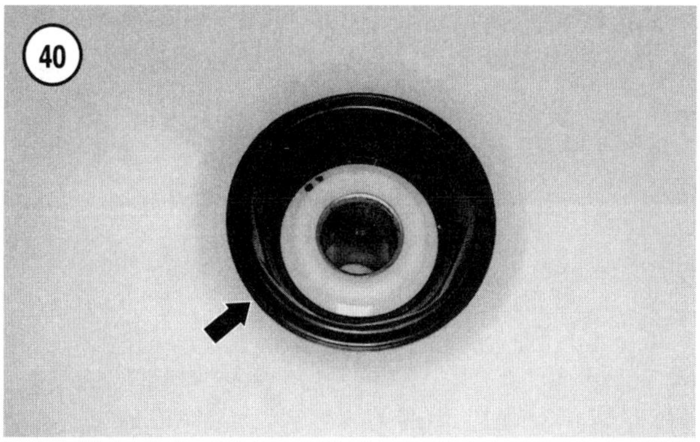

8

2. Allow the carburetor to dry thoroughly before assembly. Blow out the jets and the needle jet holder with compressed air.

CAUTION

Do not use wire or drill bits to clean jets, as minor gouges in the jet can alter the air/fuel mixture.

3. Inspect the float bowl O-ring gasket (A, **Figure 38**) for hardness or deterioration.
4. Inspect the accelerator pump boot (B, **Figure 38**) for hardness or deterioration.
5. Make sure the accelerator pump cover (**Figure 39**) screws are tight.
6. Inspect the vacuum piston diaphragm (**Figure 40**) for cracks or deterioration. Check the vacuum piston sides (**Figure 41**) for excessive wear. Install the vacuum piston into the carburetor body and move it up and down in the bore. The vacuum piston should move smoothly with no binding or excessive play. If there is excessive play, replace the vacuum piston slide and/or carburetor body.
7. Inspect the fuel valve tapered end for steps, uneven wear or other damage (**Figure 42**).
8. Inspect the fuel valve seat (B, **Figure 37**) for steps, uneven wear or other damage. Insert the fuel valve and

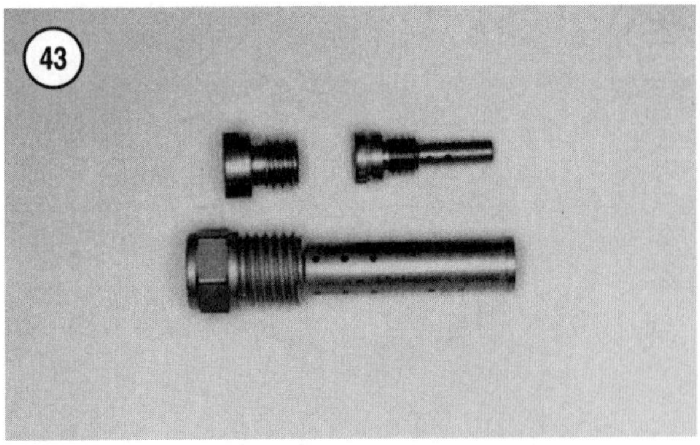

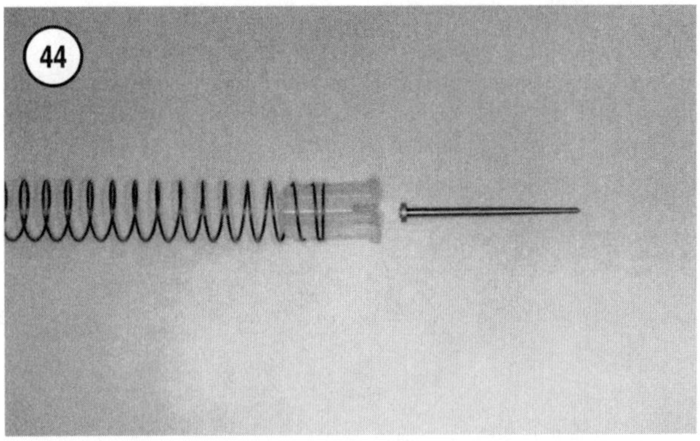

slowly move it back and forth to check for smooth operation. If either part is worn or damaged, replace both parts as a pair for maximum performance.

9. Inspect the needle jet holder, pilot jet and main jet (**Figure 43**). Make sure all holes are open and none of the parts are worn or damaged.
10. Inspect the jet needle, spring and spring seat (**Figure 44**) for deterioration or damage.
11. Inspect the jet needle tapered end for steps, uneven wear or other damage.
12. Inspect the float (**Figure 45**) for deterioration or damage. Place it in a container of water and push it down. If the float sinks or if bubbles appear, there is a leak and the float must be replaced.
13. Make sure the throttle plate screws (**Figure 46**) are tight. Tighten them if necessary.
14. Move the throttle pulley (**Figure 47**) back and forth from stop to stop and check for free movement. The throttle lever should move smoothly and return under spring tension.
15. Check the throttle wheel return spring (**Figure 48**) for free movement. Make sure it rotates the throttle wheel back to the stop position with no hesitation.
16. Make sure all openings in the carburetor housing are clear. Clean them out if they are plugged, then apply compressed air to all openings.
17. Inspect the carburetor body for internal or external damage. If there is damage, replace the carburetor assembly, as the body cannot be replaced separately.
18. Check the top cover for cracks or damage.
19. Check the starting enrichment valve and cable as follows:
    a. Check the end of the valve (**Figure 49**) for damage.
    b. Check the entire length of the cable for bends, chaffing or other damage.
    c. Check the knob, nut and lockwasher for damage. Move the knob and check for ease of movement.

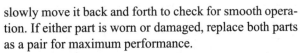

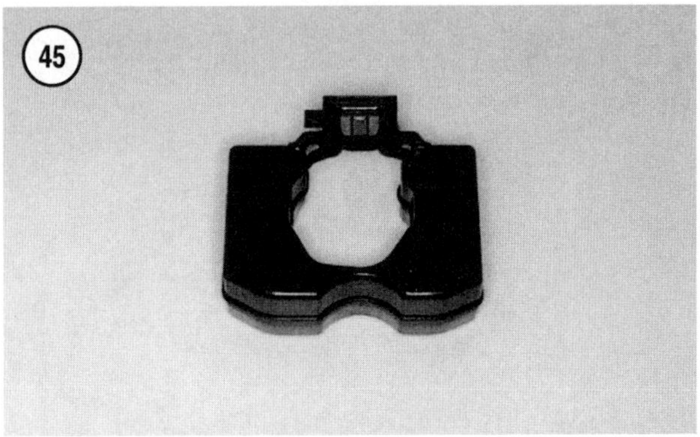

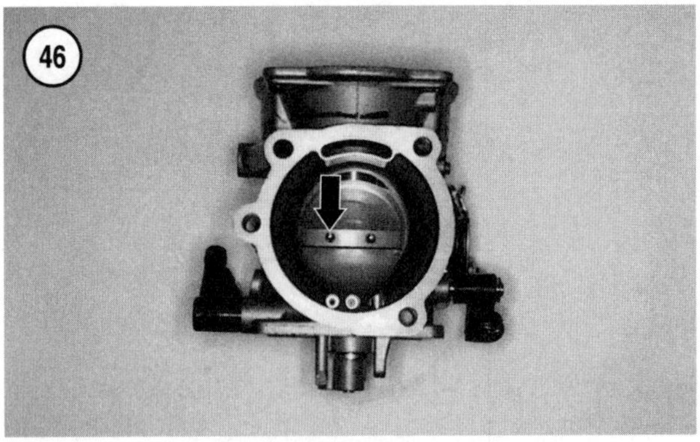

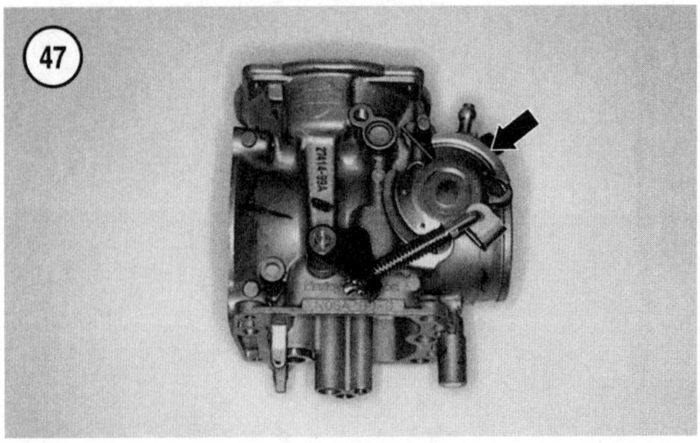

48

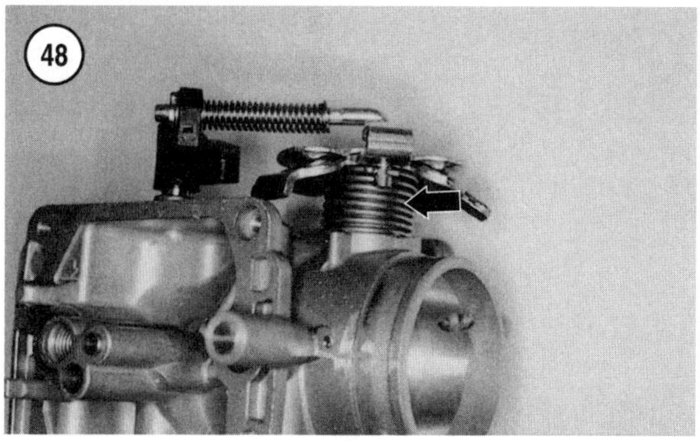

49

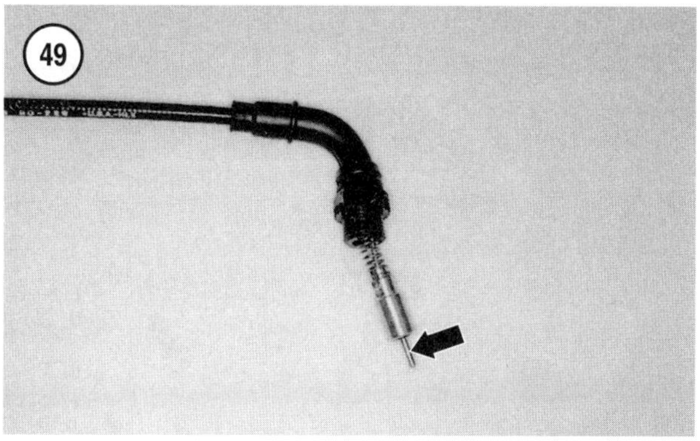

50

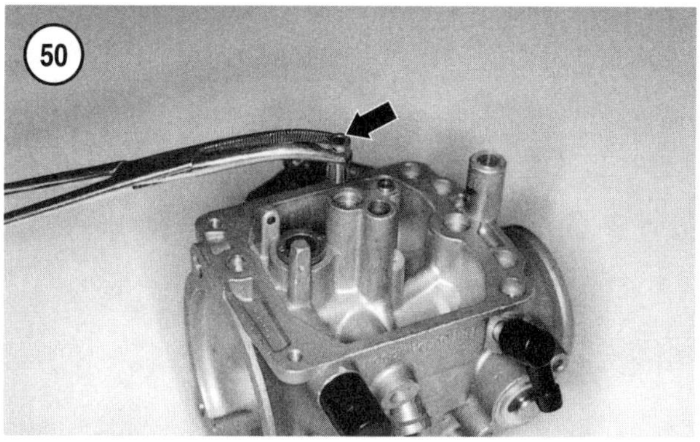

51

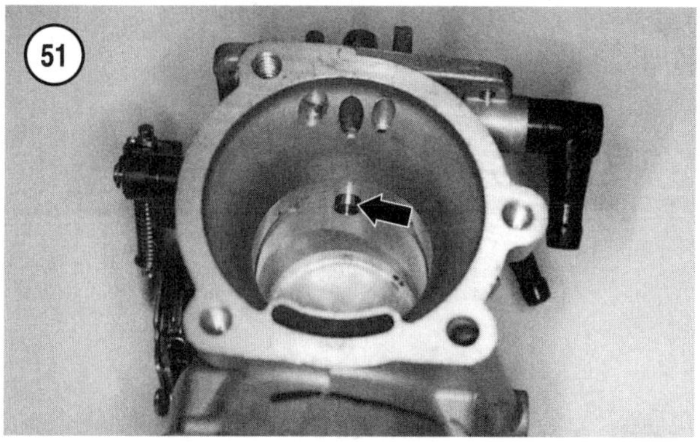

52

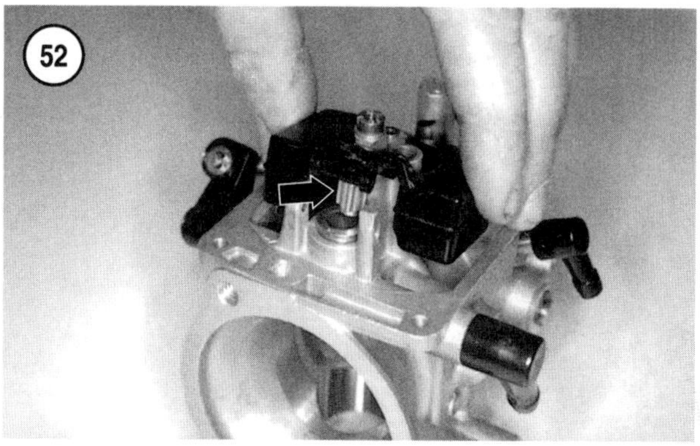

53

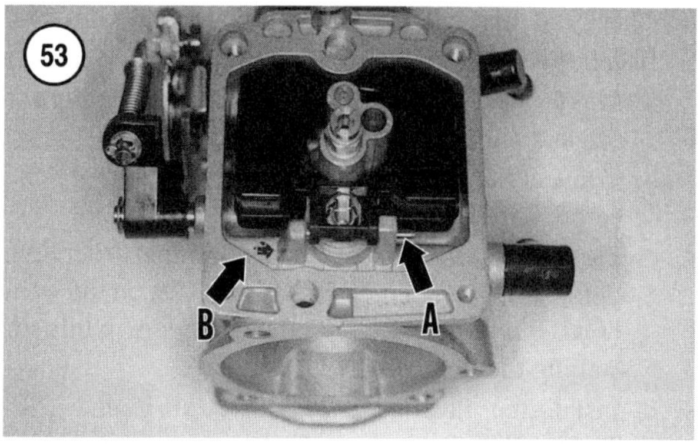

Assembly

NOTE
The needle jet has two different sides and must be installed as described in Step 1.

1. Position the needle jet with the long end going in first (**Figure 50**) and install it (A, **Figure 37**).
2. Install the needle jet holder (**Figure 36**) into the main jet passage. Make sure it passes through the opening in the venturi (**Figure 51**), then tighten it securely.
3. Install the main jet and tighten it securely (**Figure 35**).
4. Install the pilot jet and tighten it securely (**Figure 34**).
5. Install the fuel valve onto the float (**Figure 52**) and position the float onto the carburetor so the valve drops into its seat.

CAUTION
The pedestals that support the float pin are fragile. In the next step, support the pedestal on the arrow side while tapping the float pin into place.

6. Align the float pin with the two pedestals.
7. Install the float pin (A, **Figure 53**) from the side opposite the arrow (B). Support the pedestal and tap the float pin into place in the pedestal.

54
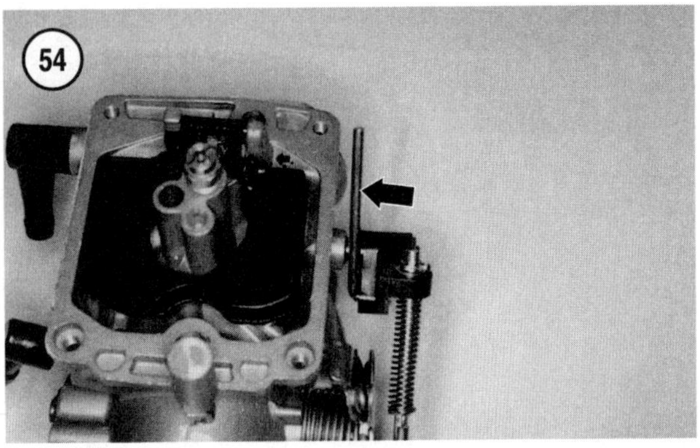

55
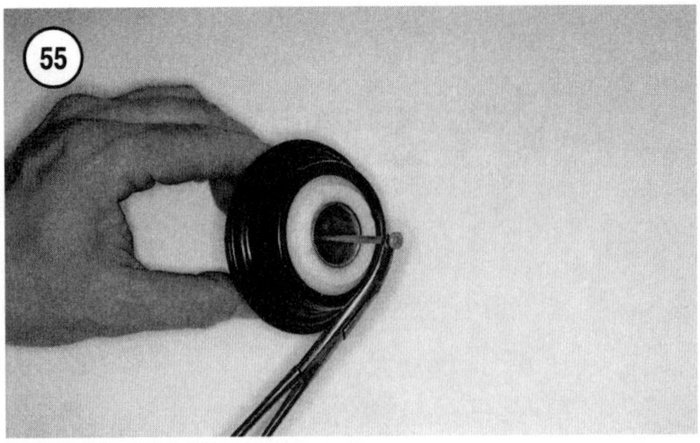

8. Check the float level as described in this section.
9. Install the float bowl as follows:
   a. Make sure the float bowl O-ring gasket (A, **Figure 38**) and pump rod boot (B) are in place.
   b. Connect the pump rod to the lever assembly on the carburetor (**Figure 54**).
   c. Slowly install the float bowl body and insert the pump rod through the boot (**Figure 29**) on the float bowl. Engage the rod with the diaphragm while installing the float bowl.
   d. Install the float bowl and screws (**Figure 28**). Tighten the screws securely in a crossing pattern.
10. Insert the jet needle (**Figure 55**) through the center hole in the vacuum piston.
11. Install the spring seat (A, **Figure 56**) and spring (B) over the top of the needle to secure it in place.
12. Align the slides (A, **Figure 57**) on the vacuum piston with the grooves (B) in the carburetor bore and install the vacuum piston. The slides on the piston are offset, so the piston can only be installed one way. When installing the vacuum piston, make sure the jet needle drops through the needle jet.
13. Seat the outer edge of the vacuum piston diaphragm into the piston chamber groove (**Figure 58**).
14. Align the free end of the spring with the carburetor top and install the top onto the carburetor.
15. Hold the carburetor top in place and lift the vacuum piston by hand (**Figure 59**). The piston should move smoothly. If the piston movement is rough or sluggish, the spring is installed incorrectly. Remove the carburetor top and reinstall the spring.
16. Install the carburetor top screws (**Figure 26**) finger-tight.
17. Install the collar (**Figure 25**) into the cover.
18. Install the throttle cable bracket (B, **Figure 24**) onto the carburetor so the end of the idle speed screw engages the top of the throttle cam stop (B, **Figure 23**). Hold the bracket in place and install the bracket's side mounting

56
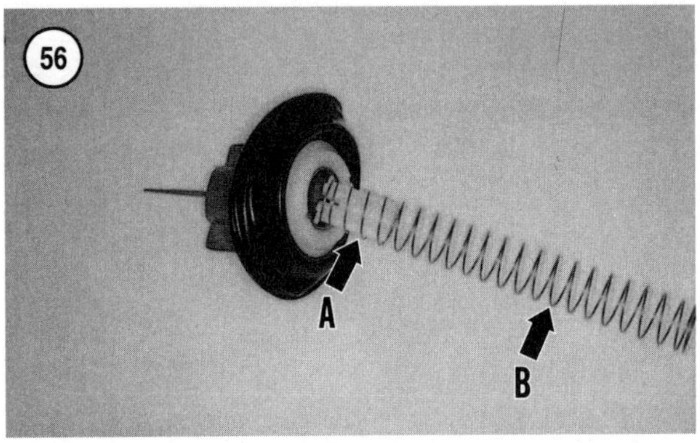

57
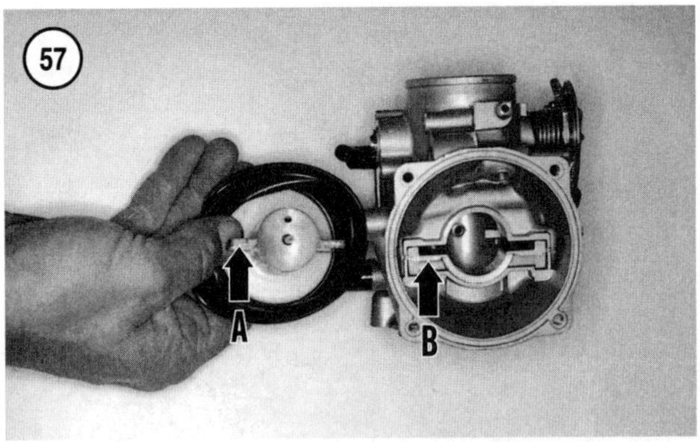

58

59

62

60
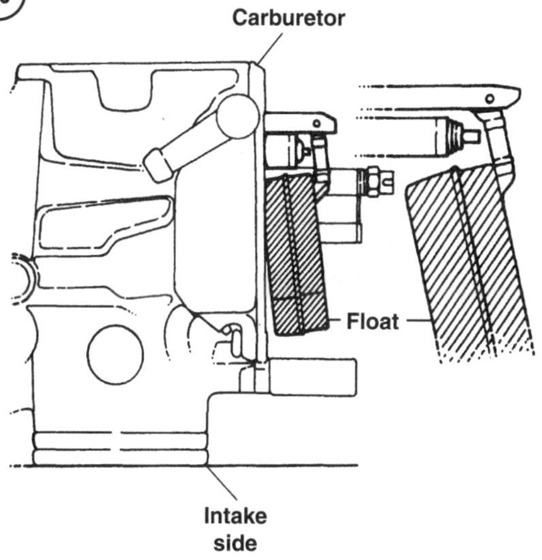

61
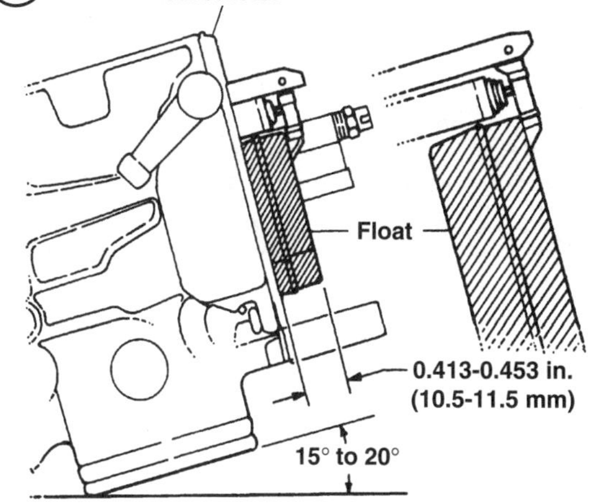

screw and washer (A, **Figure 23**). Tighten the screw securely.

19. Install the top screw (A, **Figure 24**) and tighten it securely.

20. Install the starting enrichment cable and valve into the carburetor body. Tighten the nut securely (**Figure 22**).

8

Float Adjustment

1. Remove the carburetor as described in this section.
2. Remove the float bowl as described in this chapter.
3. Place the intake manifold side of the carburetor on a clean, flat surface as shown in **Figure 60**.
4. Tilt the carburetor upward 15-20° as shown in **Figure 61**. In this position, the float will come to rest without compressing the pin return spring.

NOTE
If the carburetor is tilted less than 15° or more than 20°, the float measurement will be incorrect.

5. Measure from the carburetor flange surface to the top of the float as shown in **Figure 61**. When measuring float level, do not compress the float. Refer to **Table 1** for the float level measurement.
6. If the float level is incorrect, remove the float pin and float as described in *Disassembly* in this section.
7. Carefully bend the float tang (**Figure 62**) with a screwdriver and adjust it to the correct position.
8. Reinstall the float and the float pin as described in *Assembly* in this section. Recheck the float level.
9. Repeat steps 4-8 until the float level is correct.
10. Install the float bowl and carburetor as described in this section.

INTAKE MANIFOLD

Removal/Installation

Refer to **Figure 63**.

1. Remove the carburetor as described in this chapter.
2. Disconnect the electrical connector from the MAP sensor (A, **Figure 64**) on top of the intake manifold.
3. Remove the four Allen bolts (B, **Figure 64**) securing the intake manifold to the cylinder heads. If necessary, use a ball-end or shortened Allen wrench to access the bolts.

NOTE
*The front and rear intake manifold flanges are different. If the flanges are not marked (**Figure 65**), label them with an F and R in order to reinstall them in the correct locations.*

4. Remove the intake manifold, flanges and manifold seals.
5. Inspect the intake manifold as described in this section.
6. Install the flanges (B, **Figure 66**) and manifold seals (A) onto the intake manifold. Note that the seals (A, **Figure 67**) and flanges (B) have a tapered side. Fit the seal taper into the flange taper. Make sure the correct flange (F or R) is located at the front or rear of the manifold.

NOTE
To help align the intake manifold flanges during installation, install the left-side bolts just so they engage a couple of threads. Engage the slots of the manifold flanges with the bolts.

7. Install the intake manifold onto the cylinder head intake ports. The slotted ends (**Figure 68**) of the flanges must point to the left.
8. Make sure the front and rear seals seat squarely against the cylinder head mating surfaces.
9. Install all four Allen bolts finger-tight.
10. Temporarily install the carburetor (**Figure 69**) into the intake manifold.

CAUTION
Do not attempt to align the intake manifold after tightening the bolts. This will damage the manifold seals. If necessary, loosen the bolts, then align the manifold.

11. Make sure the intake manifold seats squarely against the cylinder heads. Then make sure the carburetor seats squarely in the intake manifold. Remove the carburetor.

NOTE
It is very difficult to get an Allen wrench and torque wrench onto the two inboard Allen bolts to tighten them to a specific torque. Tighten the outboard Allen bolts to the specified torque, then tighten the inboard Allen bolts to the same approximate tightness.

12. Tighten the intake manifold Allen bolts to 96-144 in.-lb. (11-16 N•m).
13. If the MAP sensor was removed, install a new seal in the manifold receptacle, then install the MAP sensor.

63 **INTAKE MANIFOLD**

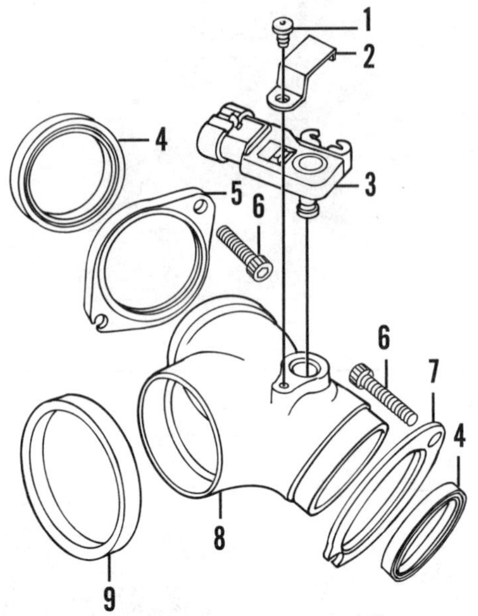

1. Screw
2. Retainer
3. MAP sensor
4. Seal
5. Flange (rear cylinder)
6. Bolt
7. Flange (front cylinder)
8. Intake manifold
9. Seal

64

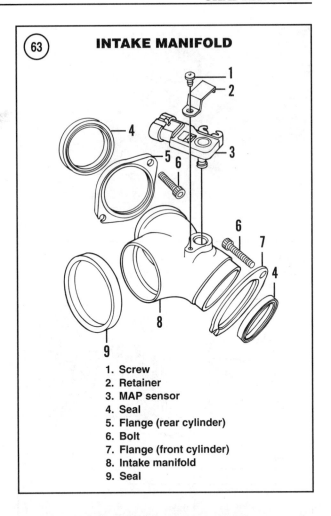

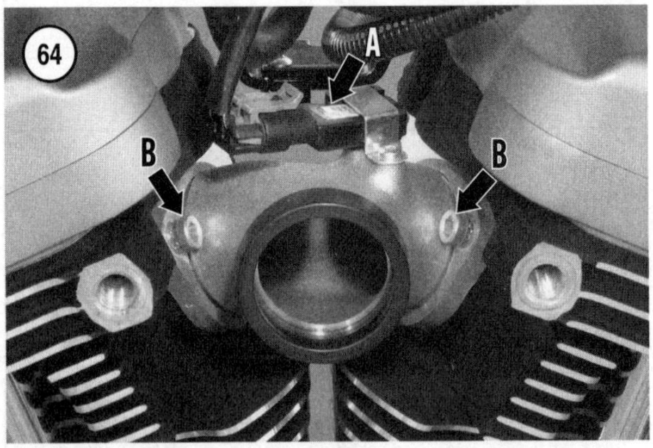

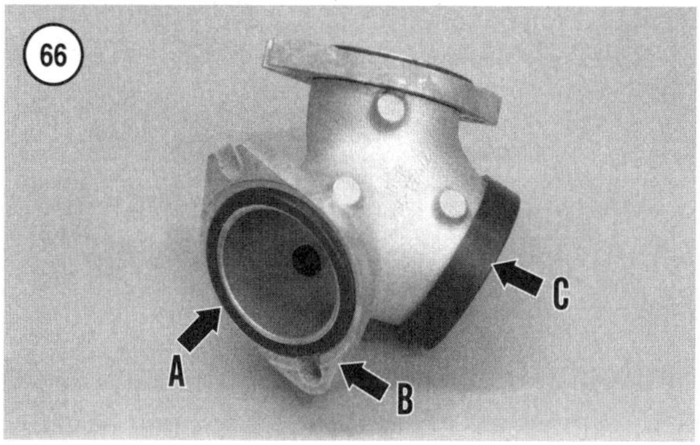

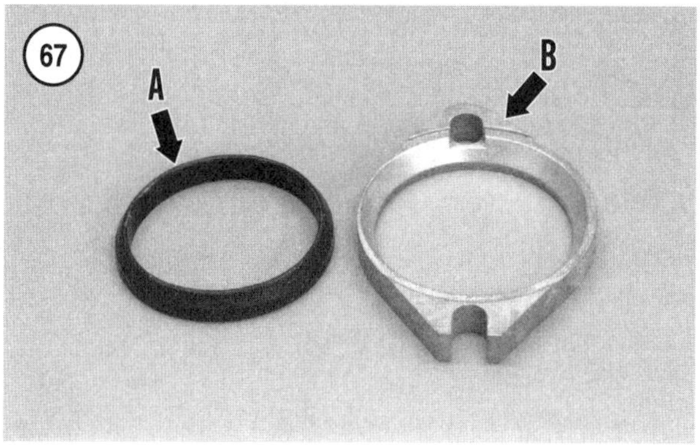

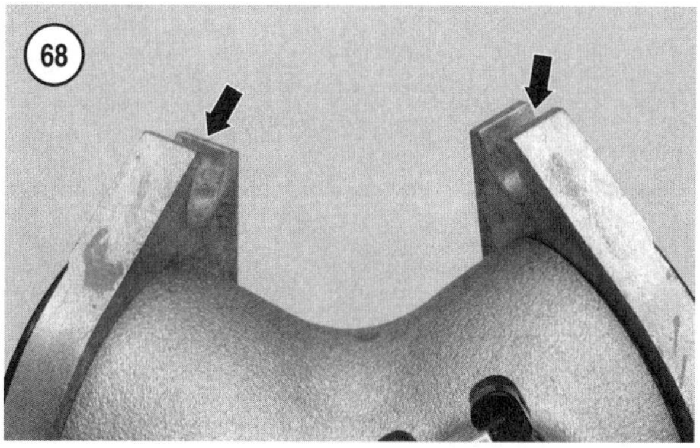

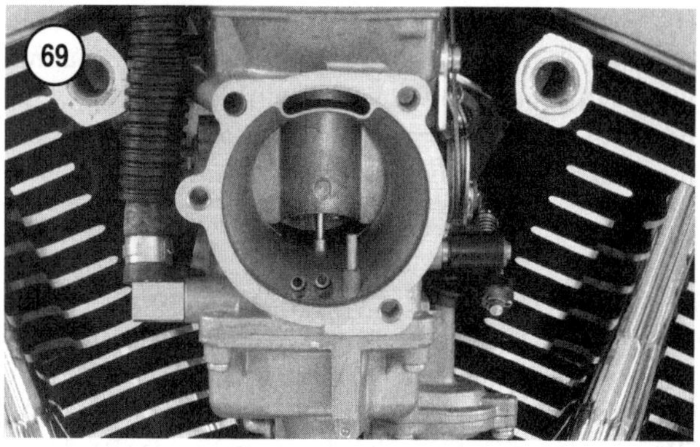

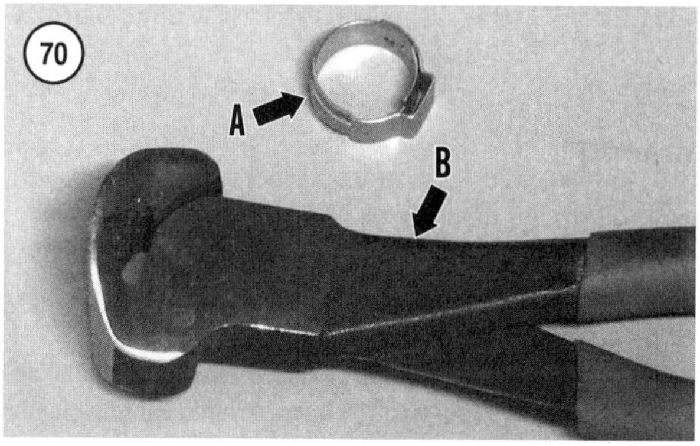

14. Connect the electrical connector to the MAP sensor (A, **Figure 64**).
15. Install the carburetor as described in this chapter.

Inspection

1. Inspect the intake manifold seals (A, **Figure 66**) for wear, deterioration or other damage. Replace the seals as a set if necessary.
2. Inspect the intake manifold seal ring (B, **Figure 66**) for cracks, flat spots or other damage. Replace it if necessary.
3. If necessary, remove the self-tapping screw and clamp, and remove the MAP sensor.

FUEL HOSE AND CLAMPS

WARNING
Do not reuse crimp-type hose clamps. They will not properly secure the fuel hose after removal.

The fuel supply hose between the fuel valve and carburetor is secured at the hose ends with non-reusable hose clamps (A, **Figure 70**). Use diagonal pliers or another suitable tool to separate the clamp bands, then remove the clamp. Use H-D hose clamp pliers HD-97087-65B to compress the clamp bands during installation. End cutting pliers (B, **Figure 70**) may be modified to compress the band clamps. Make sure to test the performance of the tool by checking the fit and integrity of the installed clamp. A screw-type hose clamp may be substituted.

THROTTLE AND IDLE CABLES

There are two different throttle cables. At the throttle grip, the front cable is the throttle control cable (A, **Figure 71**) and the rear cable is the idle control cable (B). At the carburetor, the outboard cable is the throttle control cable (A, **Figure 72**) and the inboard cable is the idle control cable (B).

Removal

1. Remove the fuel tank as described in this chapter.
2. Remove the air filter backplate as described in this chapter.
3. Note the cable routing from the carburetor through the frame to the right side handlebar.
4. At the right side handlebar, loosen both control cable adjuster locknuts (A, **Figure 73**), then turn the cable adjusters (B) clockwise as far as possible to increase cable free play.
5. Remove the screws securing the right side switch assembly (**Figure 74**).
6. Remove the ferrules from the notches on the inboard side of the throttle grip (**Figure 75**). Remove the ferrules from the cable end fittings.
7. Remove the friction shoe from the end of the tension adjust screw.
8. Remove the throttle grip from the handlebar.
9. Pull the crimped inserts at the end of the throttle and idle control cable housings from the switch lower housing. Use a rocking motion while pulling on the control cable housings. If necessary, place a drop of engine oil on the housings retaining rings to ease removal.
10. Remove the air filter and backplate as described in this chapter.
11. Twist and pull the carburetor off the seal ring and intake manifold so the throttle pulley is visible.
12. Detach the cable ends from the carburetor pulley (A, **Figure 76**).
13. Remove all clips and tie-wraps securing the throttle and idle control cables to the frame.
14. Remove the cables from the right side of the steering head.
15. Clean the throttle grip assembly and dry it thoroughly. Check the throttle slots for cracks or other damage. Replace the throttle if necessary.

71
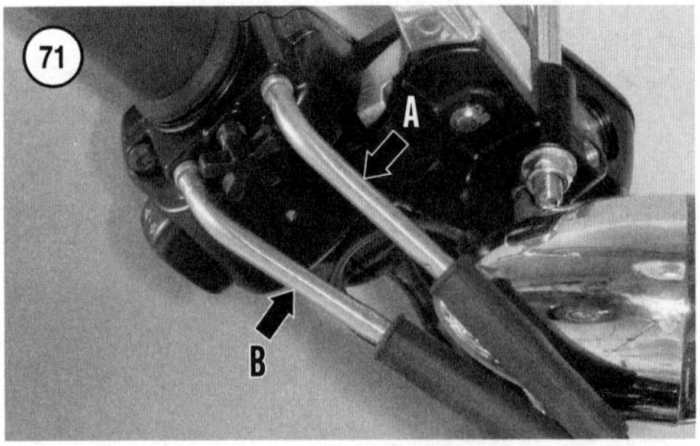

72
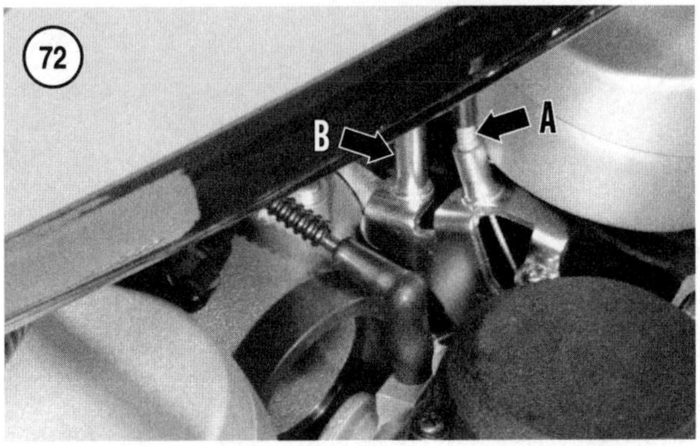

73
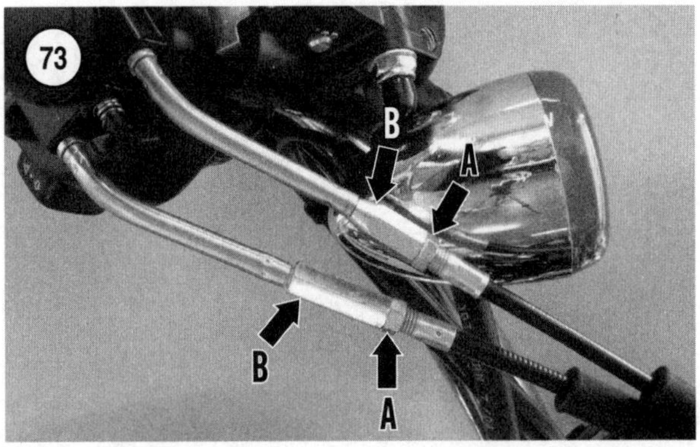

74
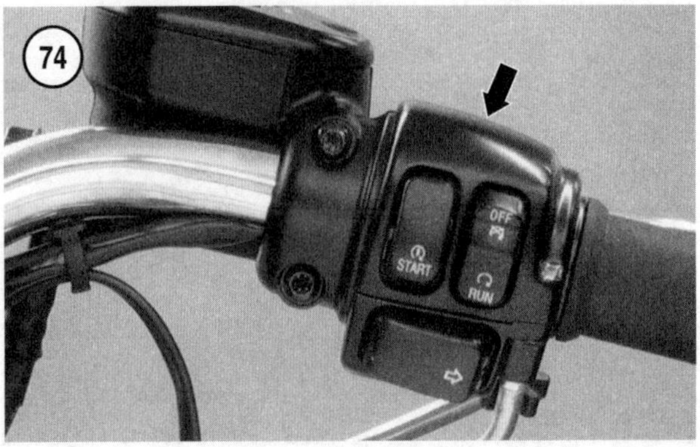

75

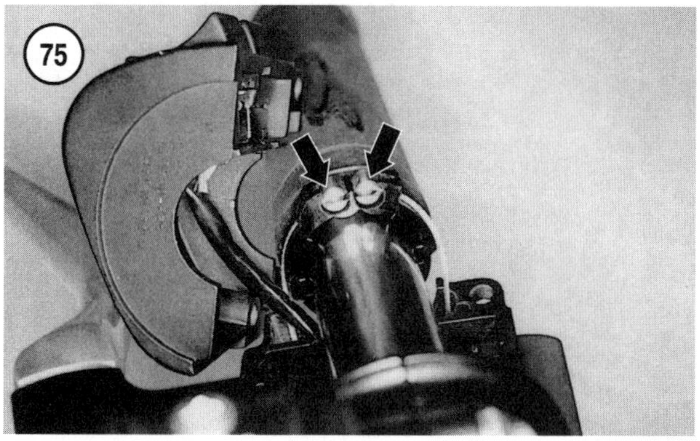

76

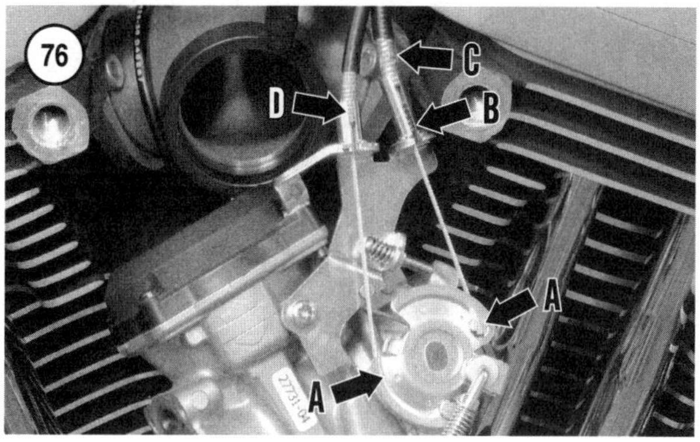

77

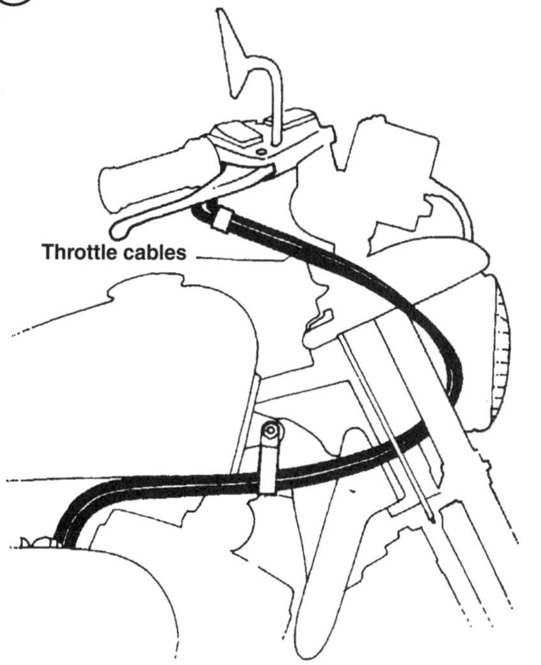

16. The friction adjust screw is secured to the lower switch housing with a circlip. If necessary, remove the friction spring, circlip, spring and friction adjust screw. Check these parts for wear or damage. Replace damaged parts and reinstall. Make sure the circlip seats in the friction screw groove completely.
17. Clean the throttle area on the handlebar with solvent.

Installation

WARNING
Do not ride the motorcycle until the throttle cables are properly adjusted. Improper cable routing and adjustment can cause the throttle to stick open.

1. Apply a light coat of graphite to the housing inside surfaces and to the handlebar.
2. On the lower switch housing, push the larger diameter silver throttle cable insert into the larger hole in front of the tension adjust screw. Push it in until it snaps into place.
3. Push the smaller diameter gold throttle cable insert into the smaller hole in the rear of the tension adjust screw. Push it in until it snaps into place.
4. Position the friction shoe with the concave side facing up and install it so the pin hole is over the point of the adjuster screw.
5. Install the throttle grip onto the handlebar. Push it on until it stops, then pull it back about 1/8 in. (3.2 mm). Rotate it until the ferrule notches are at the-top.
6. Place the lower switch housing below the throttle grip. Install the ferrules onto the cables so the end fittings seat in the ferrule recess. Seat ferrules in their respective notches on the throttle control grip. Make sure the cables are captured in the molded grooves in the grip.
7. Assemble the upper and lower switch housings (**Figure 74**) and the throttle grip. Install the lower switch housing screws and tighten them securely.
8. Operate the throttle and make sure both cables move in and out properly.
9. Correctly route the cables (**Figure 77**) from the handlebar, through the frame and to the carburetor.
10. Connect the idle cable to the carburetor as follows:
   a. The idle cable has the small spring (B, **Figure 76**) on the end of the idle cable (C).
   b. Insert the idle cable sheath into the rear cable bracket guide on the carburetor.
   c. Attach the end of the idle cable to the throttle pulley.
11. Connect the throttle cable to the carburetor as follows:
   a. Insert the throttle cable sheath (D, **Figure 76**) into the front cable bracket guide on the carburetor.
   b. Attach the end of the throttle cable to the throttle pulley.

8

12. At the throttle grip, tighten the cables to keep the cable ends from being disconnected from the throttle wheel.
13. Operate the hand throttle a few times. Make sure the throttle operates smoothly with no binding. Also make sure both cable ends are seated squarely in their cable bracket guides and in the throttle barrel.
14. Adjust the throttle and idle cables as described in Chapter Three.
15. Reinstall the carburetor as described in this chapter.
16. Install the air filter backplate and air filter as described in this chapter.
17. Install the fuel tank as described in this chapter.
18. Start the engine. Turn the handlebar from side to side. Do not operate the throttle. If the engine speed increases when turning the handlebar assembly, the throttle cables are routed incorrectly or are damaged. Recheck the cable routing and adjustment.

STARTING ENRICHMENT VALVE (CHOKE) CABLE REPLACEMENT

1. Remove the air filter and backplate as described in Chapter Three.
2. Loosen the locknut (**Figure 78**) and disconnect the starting enrichment valve cable from the mounting bracket. Move the end of the cable out of the mounting bracket.
3. Partially remove the carburetor, as described in this chapter, until the starting enrichment valve cable can be disconnected from the backside of the carburetor.
4. Unscrew and remove the starting enrichment valve and cable (**Figure 79**) from the carburetor and remove the cable from the frame.
5. Install by reversing the preceding removal steps. Note the following:
   a. Align the starting enrichment valve needle (A, **Figure 80**) with the needle passage in the carburetor (B) and install the starting enrichment valve. Tighten the valve nut securely.
   b. Position the starting enrichment valve cable into the mounting bracket, then tighten the locknut (**Figure 78**) securely.

FUEL TANK

WARNING
Some fuel may spill during this procedure. Because gasoline is flammable, perform this procedure away from all open flames, including appliance pilot lights and sparks. Do not smoke in the work area, as fire may occur. Perform the procedures in a well-ventilated area. Wipe up any spills immediately.

78

79

80

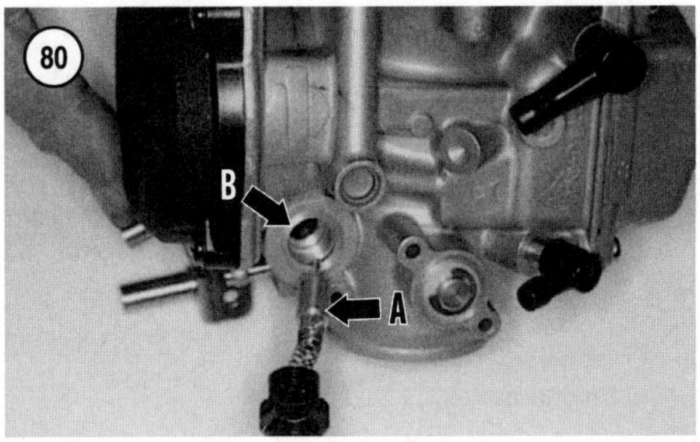

WARNING
Route the fuel tank vapor hoses so they cannot contact hot engine or exhaust components. These hoses contain flammable vapors.

Removal/Installation

NOTE
A vacuum-operated fuel valve is installed on all models. A hand-operated vacuum pump is required to drain the fuel tank.

Refer to **Figure 81**.

81

FUEL TANK

1. Cap
2. O-ring
3. Console trim
4. Bolt
5. Washer
6. Nut
7. Cap
8. Fuel tank
9. Cap
10. Trim cover
11. Trim cover
12. Bolt
13. Fuel filter
14. Gasket
15. Nut
16. Fuel valve
17. Clamp
18. Vacuum hose
19. Fuel hose
20. Insulator

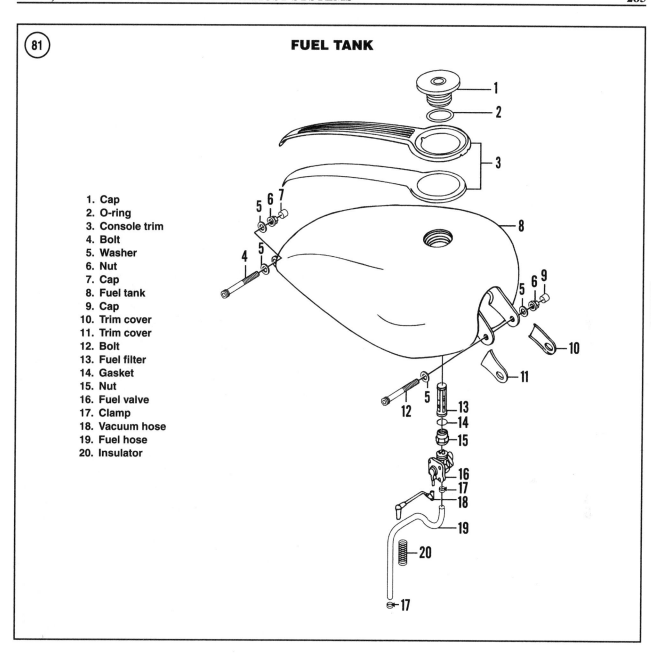

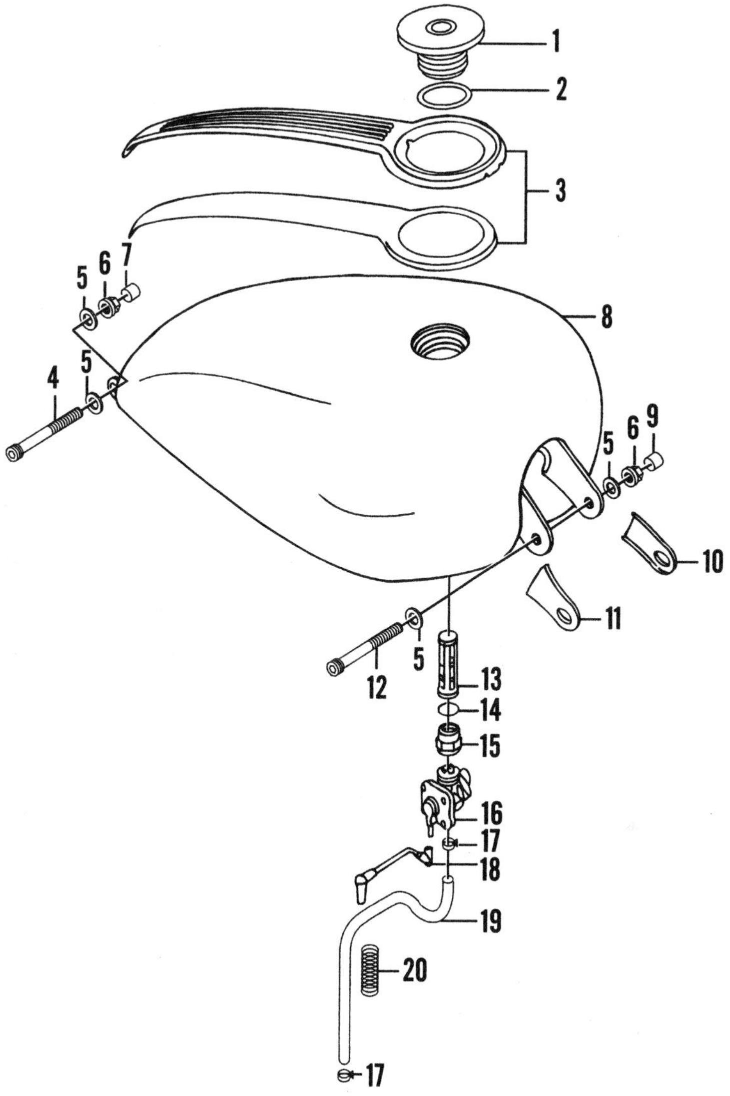

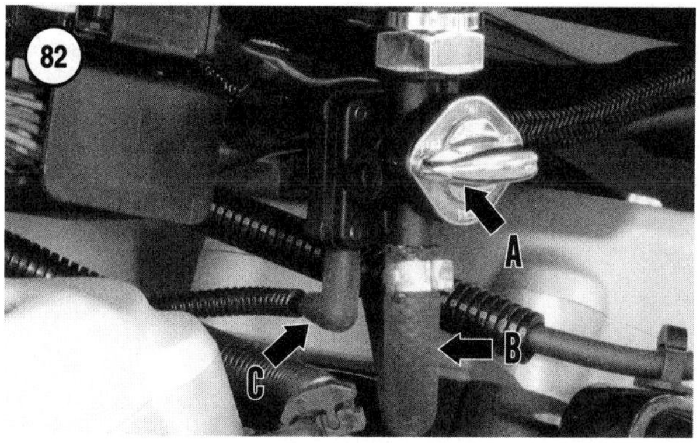

1. Remove the seat as described in Chapter Fourteen.
2. Turn the fuel valve lever (A, **Figure 82**) off.
3. Remove the hose clamp and disconnect the fuel hose (B, **Figure 82**) from the valve.
4. Drain the fuel tank as follows:
   a. Connect the drain hose to the fuel valve and secure it with a hose clamp. Insert the end of the drain hose into a gas can.
   b. Disconnect the vacuum hose (C, **Figure 82**) from the fuel valve.

c. Connect a hand-operated vacuum pump (**Figure 83**) to the fuel valve vacuum hose fitting.
d. Turn the fuel valve to reserve.

CAUTION
In the following step, do not apply more than 25 in. (635 mm) Hg of vacuum or the fuel valve diaphragm will be damaged.

e. Gently operate the vacuum pump handle and apply a vacuum. Once the vacuum is applied, the fuel will start to flow into the gas can.
f. When fuel stops flowing through the hose, turn the fuel valve off and release the vacuum. Disconnect the vacuum pump and drain hose.

5. Disconnect the vent hose from the fuel tank (**Figure 84**).
6. Remove the cap, nut and washer (**Figure 85**) on the front and rear mounting bolts.
7. Remove the rear mounting bolt and washer (**Figure 86**).
8. Remove the front mounting bolt and washer (**Figure 87**).
9. Lift and remove the fuel tank.
10. Drain any remaining fuel into a gas can.
11. Inspect the fuel tank as described in this section.
12. Installation is the reverse of the preceding steps including the following:
   a. The front mounting bolt is longer than the rear mounting bolt.
   b. Tighten the front and rear bolts and nuts to 15-20 ft.-lb. (21-27 N•m).
   c. Reconnect the fuel hose to the fuel valve and secure it with a new hose clamp as described in *Fuel Hose And Clamps* in this chapter.
   d. Refill the tank and check for leaks.

Inspection

1. Inspect the fuel hose and vent hose for cracks, deterioration or damage. Replace damaged hoses with the same type and size materials. The fuel lines must be flexible and sufficiently strong to withstand engine heat and vibration.
2. Check the fuel hose insulating sleeve for damage. Replace if necessary.
3. Check the mounting brackets (**Figure 88**) for damage.
4. Inspect the fuel tank for leaks.
5. Remove the filler cap and inspect the tank for rust or contamination. If present, thoroughly flush and clean the tank. If necessary, treat the tank with a rust inhibitor/sealer, or replace the tank.

83

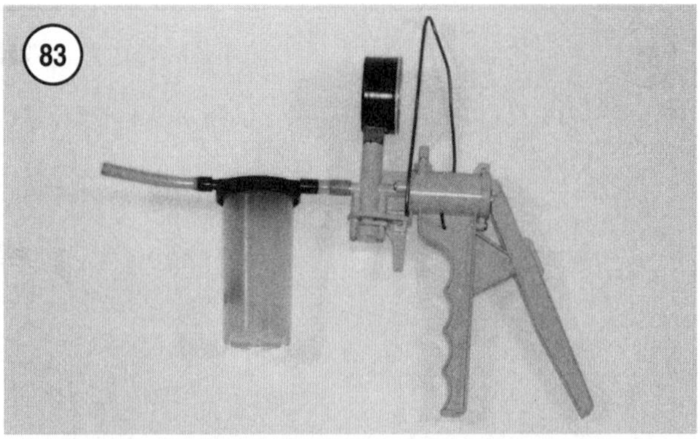

84

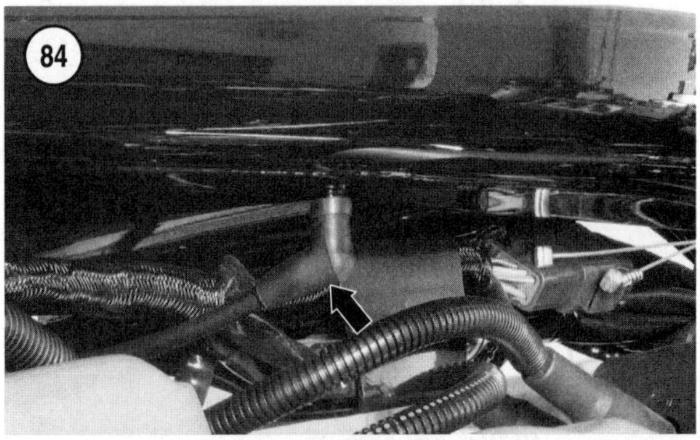

85

86

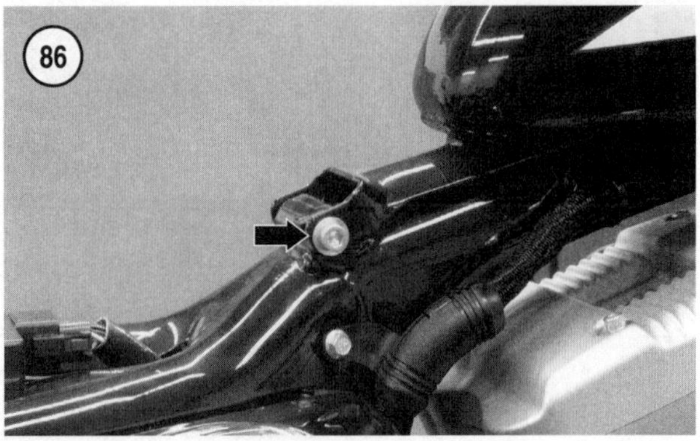

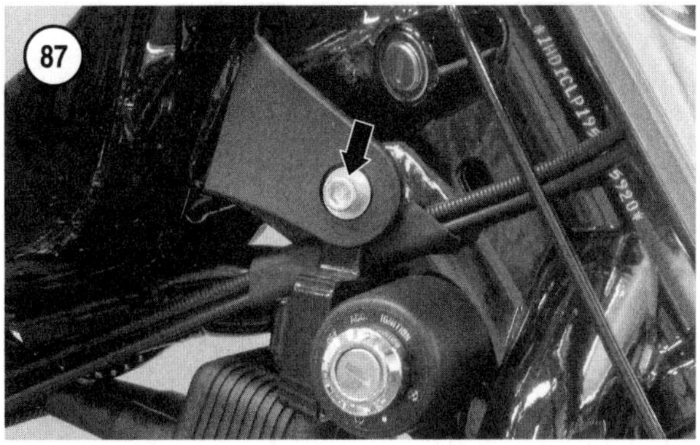

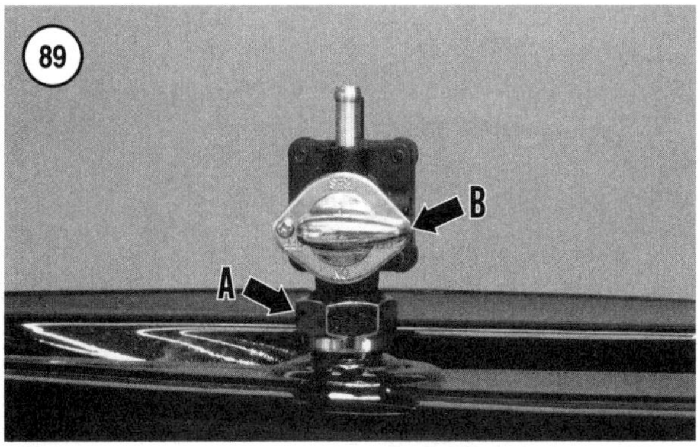

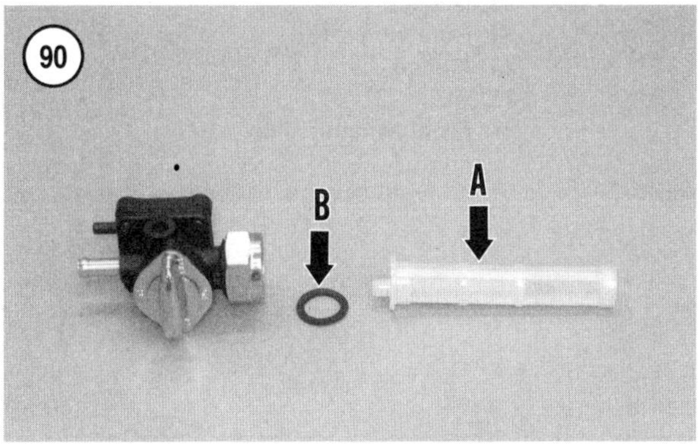

FUEL SHUTOFF VALVE

WARNING
Some fuel may spill during this procedure. Because gasoline is flammable, perform this procedure away from all open flames, including appliance pilot lights and sparks. Do not smoke in the work area, as fire may occur. Perform the procedures in a well-ventilated area. Wipe up any spills immediately.

A three-way vacuum-operated fuel shutoff valve is mounted to the left side of the fuel tank. A replaceable fuel filter is mounted at the top of the fuel shutoff valve.

Refer to *Fuel System* in Chapter Two for troubleshooting the fuel shutoff valve.

Removal

1. Disconnect the negative battery cable as described in Chapter Nine.
2. Turn the fuel shutoff valve off.
3. Drain the fuel tank as described in this chapter.

NOTE
The fuel shutoff valve can be removed with the fuel tank in place. ***Figure 89*** *shows the fuel tank removed to better illustrate the step.*

4. Loosen the fuel valve hex nut (A, **Figure 89**) and remove the fuel shutoff valve (B) from the fuel tank. Drain residual gasoline in the tank after valve removal.

Cleaning and Inspection

1. Inspect the filter (A, **Figure 90**) mounted on top of the fuel valve. Remove any contamination from the filter. Replace the filter if it is damaged.
2. Install a new filter gasket (B, **Figure 90**) before installing the filter onto the fuel valve.
3. Remove all sealant residue from the fuel tank and hex nut threads.

Installation

1. Install a new filter gasket onto the fuel shutoff valve, then install the filter.
2. Coat the fuel valve threads with Loctite Teflon pipe sealant.
3. Insert the fuel valve into the tank, then thread the hex nut onto the fuel tank two turns.

91

EXHAUST SYSTEM

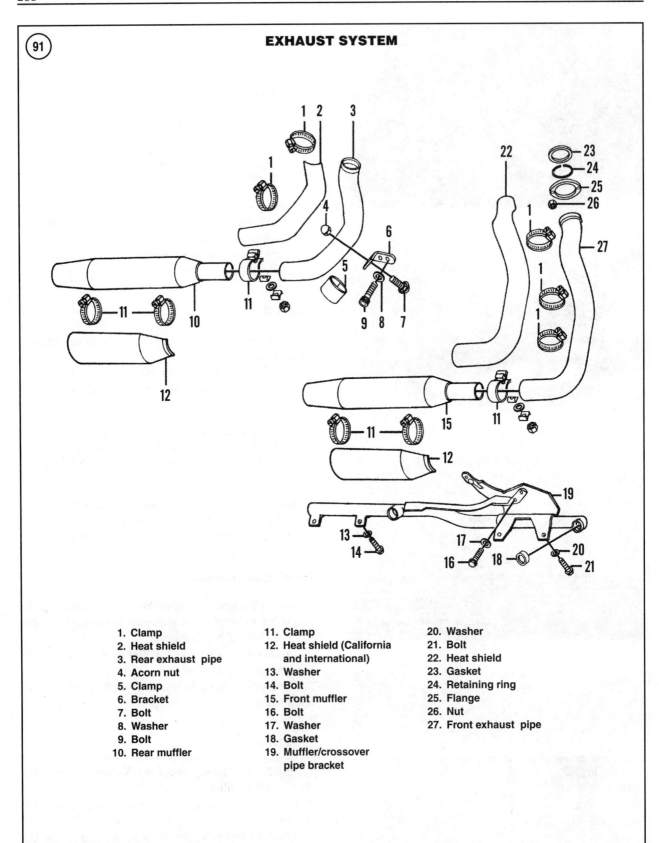

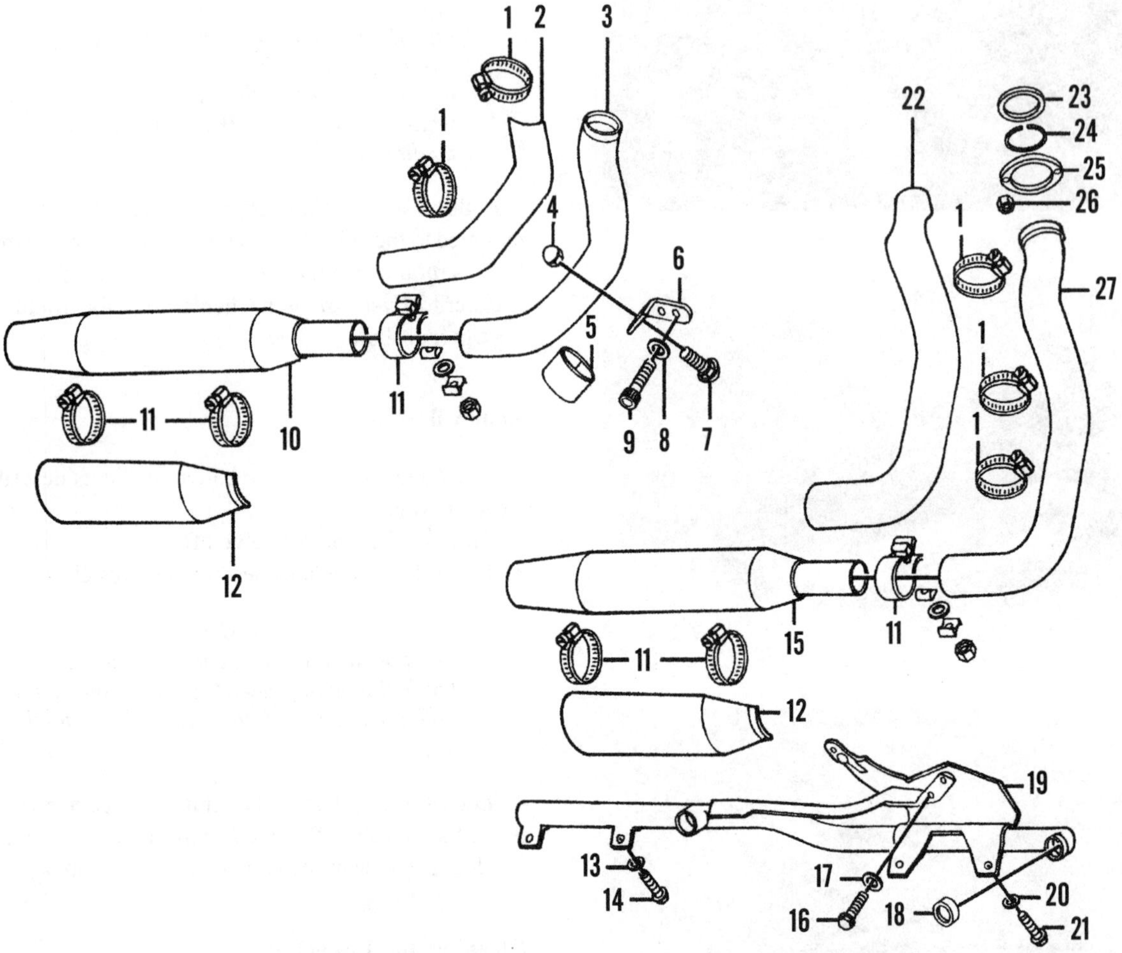

1. Clamp
2. Heat shield
3. Rear exhaust pipe
4. Acorn nut
5. Clamp
6. Bracket
7. Bolt
8. Washer
9. Bolt
10. Rear muffler
11. Clamp
12. Heat shield (California and international)
13. Washer
14. Bolt
15. Front muffler
16. Bolt
17. Washer
18. Gasket
19. Muffler/crossover pipe bracket
20. Washer
21. Bolt
22. Heat shield
23. Gasket
24. Retaining ring
25. Flange
26. Nut
27. Front exhaust pipe

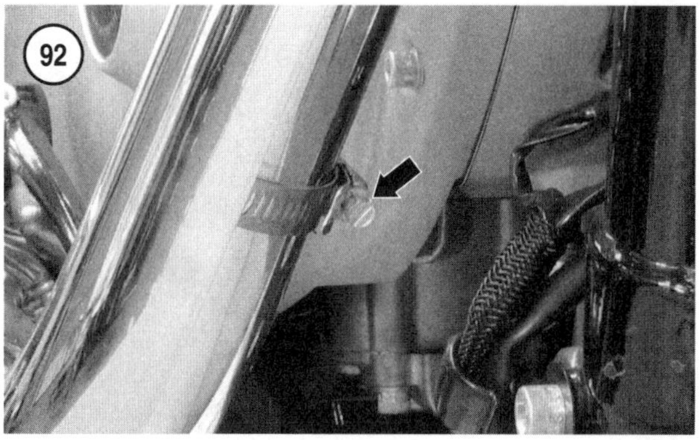

92

93

94

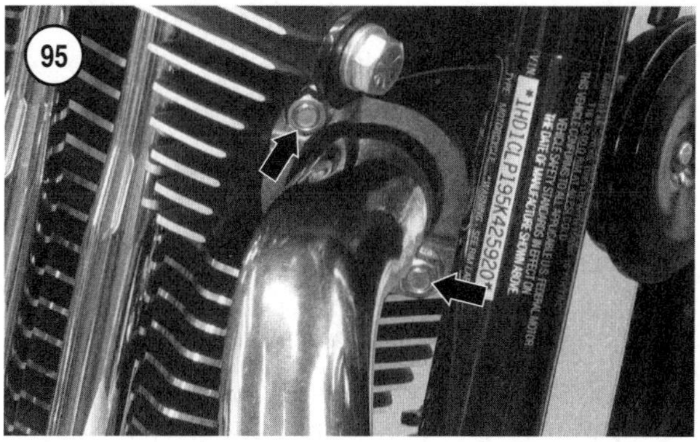

95

4. Hold the hex nut and thread the fuel valve into the fitting by turning it counterclockwise two turns.

5. Hold the fuel valve and tighten the hex nut to 15-20 ft. lb. (21-27 N•m).

WARNING
If the hex nut is turned more than two turns on the valve, it may bottom out on the valve and cause a fuel leak.

6. Reconnect the fuel hose to the fuel shutoff valve and secure it with a hose clamp. Refer to the *Fuel Hose And Clamps* in this chapter.

7. Refill the fuel tank and check for leaks.

EXHAUST SYSTEM

Removal

Refer to **Figure 91**.

CAUTION
If the system joints and/or fasteners are corroded or rusty, spray them with penetrating oil, and allow it to soak in sufficiently.

NOTE
The front or rear exhaust systems may be removed individually, and as a complete exhaust pipe/muffler unit. The following procedure describes removal of the exhaust system as a unit.

1. Support the motorcycle on a stand. Refer to *Motorcycle Stands* in Chapter Ten.

2. Loosen the clamps (**Figure 92**) and remove the heat shield.

3. Remove the bolts securing each muffler to the mounting bracket (**Figure 93**).

4. On the rear exhaust pipe, remove the clamp bolt and nut (**Figure 94**).

5. At each cylinder head, loosen and remove the two flange nuts securing the exhaust pipe to the cylinder head (**Figure 95**). Slide the exhaust pipe flange off the cylinder head studs.

6. Pull the muffler away from the crossover tube, and remove the exhaust pipe/muffler assembly.

7. To separate the muffler and exhaust pipe, loosen the Torca clamp (A, **Figure 96**) and pull apart the muffler and exhaust pipe.

8. If necessary, remove the retaining ring (A, **Figure 97**) and flange (B) from the exhaust pipe.

9. Remove the gasket in the exhaust port (**Figure 98**).

10. Remove the gasket in the muffler crossover port (B, **Figure 96**).

NOTE
The exhaust mounting bracket also supports the exhaust crossover tube.

11. If necessary, remove the mounting bracket using the following procedure:
   a. Remove the exhaust clamp bracket bolt (A, **Figure 99**).

NOTE
It may be necessary to loosen the footrest mounting bolts on models so equipped for access to the sprocket cover lower bolt.

   b. Remove the sprocket cover bolts, then remove the sprocket cover (B, **Figure 99**).
   c. Unscrew the rear brake rod end (**Figure 100**) from the rear brake bellcrank.
   d. Remove the mounting bracket retaining bolts, then remove the mounting bracket (A, **Figure 101**).

12. Inspect the exhaust system as described in this section.
13. Store the exhaust system components in a safe place until they are reinstalled.

Installation

CAUTION
To prevent exhaust leaks, do not tighten any of the fasteners until all exhaust components are in place.

1. Remove all carbon residue from the exhaust port surfaces. Then wipe the port with a rag.
2. If removed, use the following procedure to install the exhaust mounting bracket:
   a. Install the mounting bracket, bolts and washers. Tighten the bolts to 30-33 ft.-lb. (41-45 N•m).
   b. Apply Loctite 243 to the threads of the rear brake rod end and install the rod end in the bellcrank (**Figure 100**). Tighten the rod end to 120-180 in.-lb. (14-20 N•m).
   c. Install the sprocket cover (B, **Figure 99**), but do not tighten the cover screws.
   d. Install the exhaust clamp bracket and bolt. Tighten the bolt to 30-33 ft.-lb. (41-45 N•m).
   e. Tighten the sprocket cover bolts to 80-120 in.-lb. (9-14 N•m).
3. Install the clamp on the rear exhaust pipe so the square bolt hole is down.

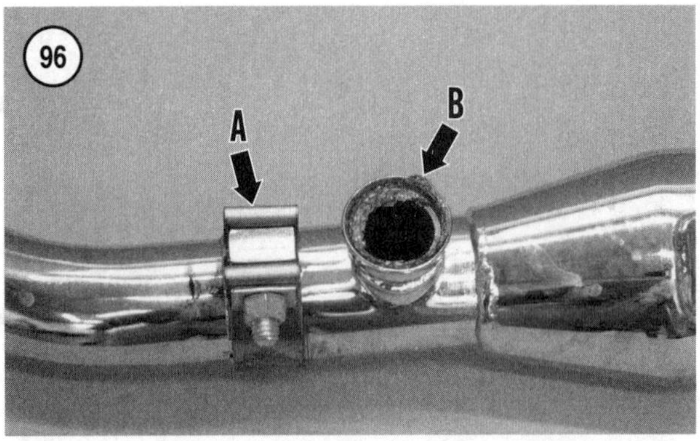

96

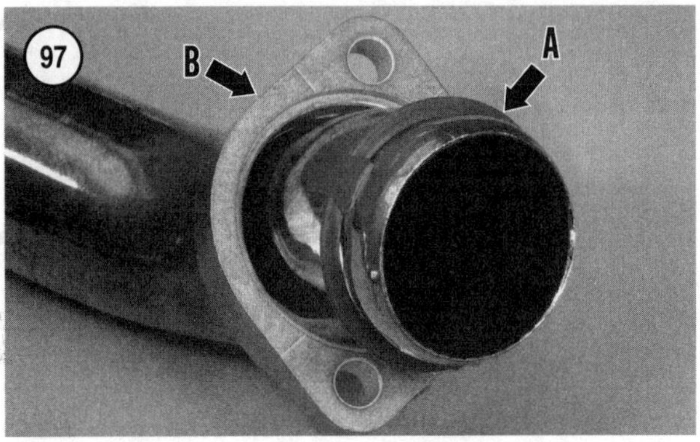

97

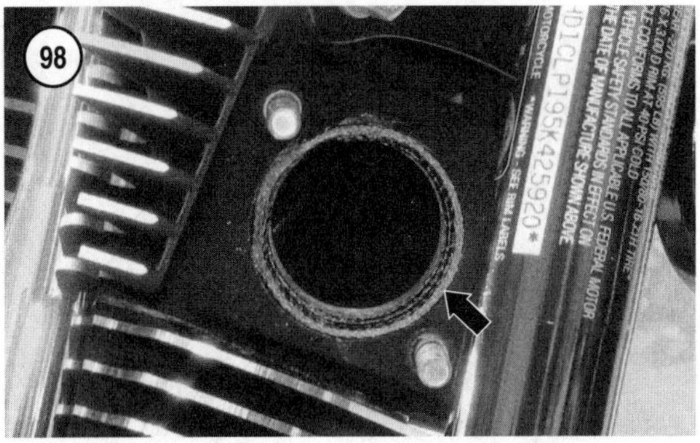
98

4. Attach the rear exhaust pipe clamp to the bracket on the sprocket cover, but do not tighten the bolt.
5. Install the flange (B, **Figure 97**) on the exhaust pipe so the stepped side faces the pipe end.
6. Install the retaining ring (A, **Figure 97**).
7. Install a new gasket in the exhaust port (**Figure 98**). The tapered side must face out.
8. Install a new gasket onto the crossover pipe port (B, **Figure 101**).
9. Install the muffler and new Torca clamp onto the exhaust pipe (A, **Figure 96**). Do not tighten the Torca clamp.

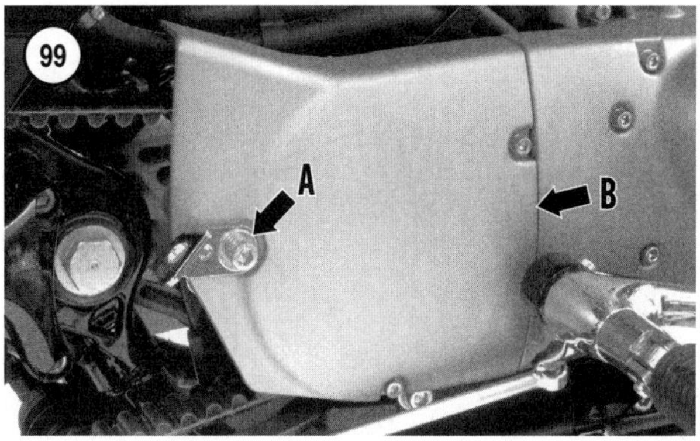

It may be possible to reuse the Torca clamps. However, to ensure a leak-free seal, replacement is recommended.

10. Install the exhaust pipes and muffler, but do not tighten the flange nuts or muffler mounting bolts.

11. Check the entire exhaust system to make sure all components are properly aligned. Adjust as needed.

12. Tighten the mounting bolts and nuts as follows:
    a. Tighten the muffler mounting bolts (**Figure 93**) to 15-19 ft.-lb. (21-26 N•m).
    b. Tighten the flange nuts at the cylinder head (**Figure 95**) to 96-120 in.-lb. (11-14 N•m).
    c. Tighten the Torca clamp bolt on each muffler to 45-65 ft.-lb. (62-88 N•m).
    d. Tighten the rear exhaust pipe clamp bolt (A, **Figure 99**) to 15-19 ft.-lb. (21-26 N•m).

13. Install the heat shields. Position the clamp so the screw is on the outboard side in the most accessible position. Tighten the clamps securely.

14. Check all heat shields to make sure none are contacting the frame. If necessary, make adjustments to prevent contact.

15. Start the engine and check for leaks.

Inspection

1. Replace rusted or damaged exhaust system components.
2. Inspect all pipes for rust or corrosion.
3. Remove all rust from exhaust pipes and muffler mating surfaces.
4. Replace the Torca clamps.
5. Replace damaged exhaust pipe retaining rings.
6. Replace damaged heat shields.

8

EVAPORATIVE EMISSION CONTROL SYSTEM (CALIFORNIA MODELS)

The evaporative emission control system (**Figure 102**) prevents fuel vapors from escaping into the atmosphere.

When the engine is not running, the system routes fuel vapors from the fuel tank through the vapor valve and into the charcoal canister. At the same time, a gravity/vacuum-operated trap door in the air filter back plate blocks the inlet port of the air filter. This prevents vapors in the intake system from escaping.

When the engine is running, fuel vapors are drawn from the canister through the purge hose and into the intake track where they are mixed with the air/fuel mixture and burned. Engine vacuum pulls the air filter back plate trap door open.

If the motorcycle should fall over, the vapor valve prevents fuel vapor from escaping from the canister.

Charcoal Canister

Inspection

Refer to **Figure 102** for hose routing. Before removing the hoses, identify the hoses and fittings with masking tape.

WARNING

Make sure the fuel tank vapor hoses are routed so they cannot contact hot engine or

102

EVAPORATIVE EMISSIONS CONTROL SYSTEM

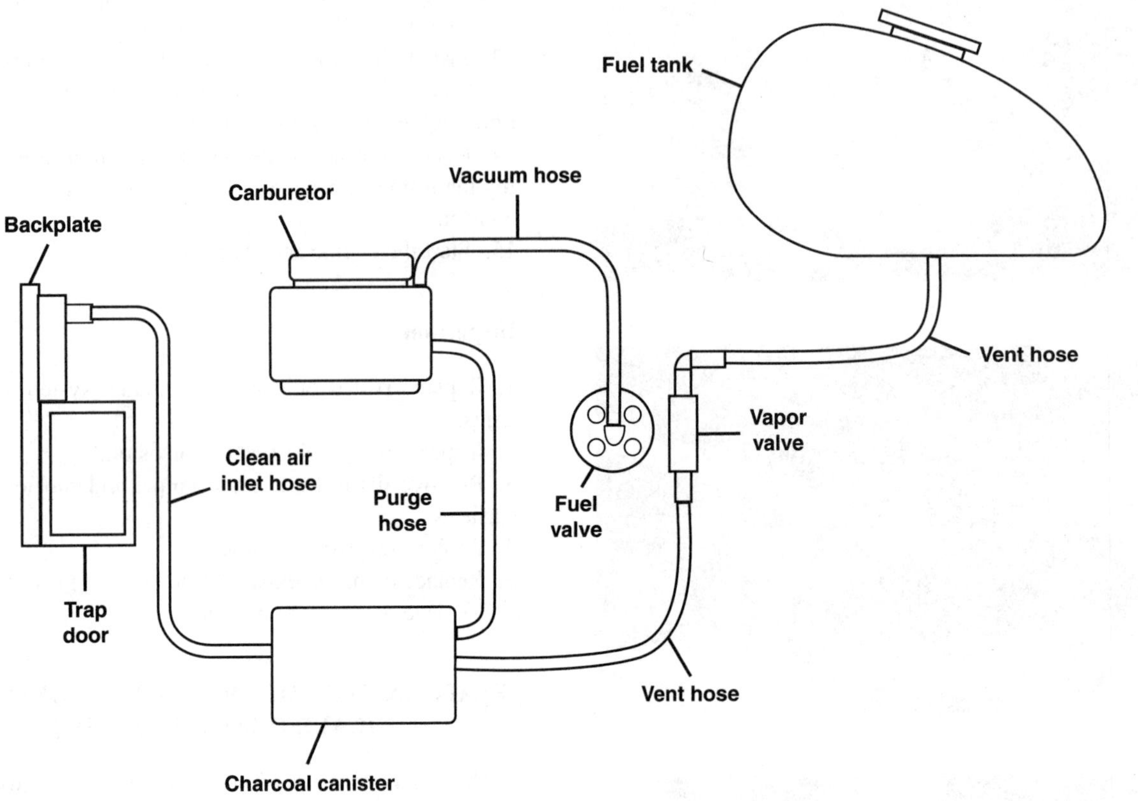

exhaust components. These hoses contain flammable vapor. If a hose melts from contact with a hot part, leaking vapor may ignite, causing excessive motorcycle damage and rider injury.

1. Check all emission control lines and hoses to make sure they are correctly routed and connected.
2. Check the physical condition of all lines and hoses in the system. Pay particular attention to hoses and lines routed near high temperature areas. These are subjected to extreme conditions, and eventually become brittle and crack. Replace damaged lines and hoses.
3. Check all components in the emission control system for damage, such as broken fittings.

Replacement

Refer to **Figure 103**.

1. Support the motorcycle on a stand with the rear wheel off the ground. Refer to *Motorcycle Stands* in Chapter Ten.
2. On the left end of the canister, remove the cover.
3. On the left end of the canister, note the CARB and TANK fittings and label the hoses prior to disconnecting them.
4. Disconnect the air filter backplate hose from the fitting on the right end of the canister.
5. Push up the locking tabs on the mounting clip, then slide the canister out toward the left side and remove it.
6. If necessary, remove the mounting clip and bracket. Remove the rear brake master cylinder reservoir and hose for access to the mounting bracket.
7. Installation is the reverse of removal. Make sure all hoses are connected to the correct fittings and are secure. Tighten the mounting bracket bolts to 17-22 ft.-lb. (24-30 N•m).

Vapor Valve

Replacement

The vapor valve is an integral part of the fuel pressure relief system. The fuel tank vapor expands as the fuel tank temperature rises. This pressure must be relieved to avoid excessive vapor buildup within the fuel tank.

(103)

CHARCOAL CANISTER

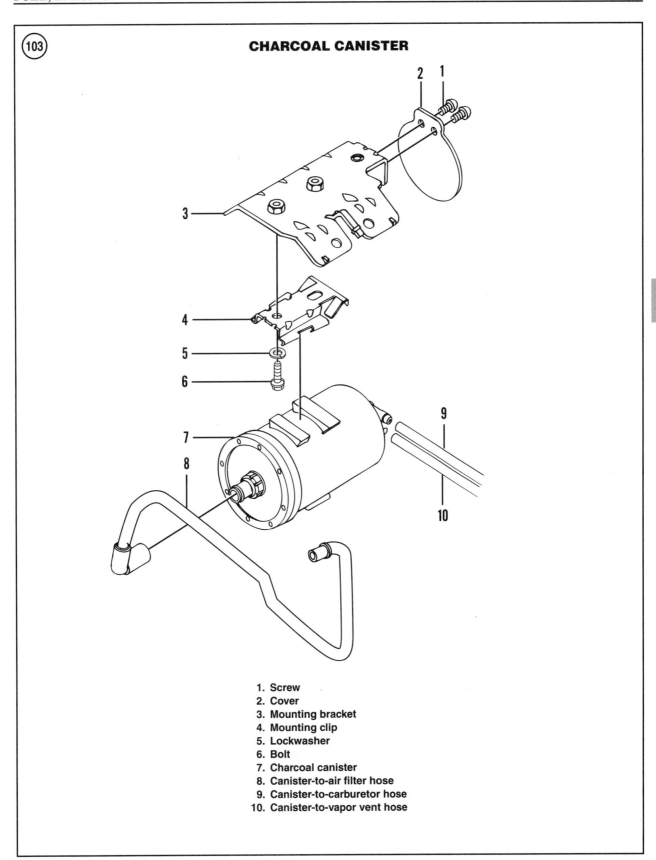

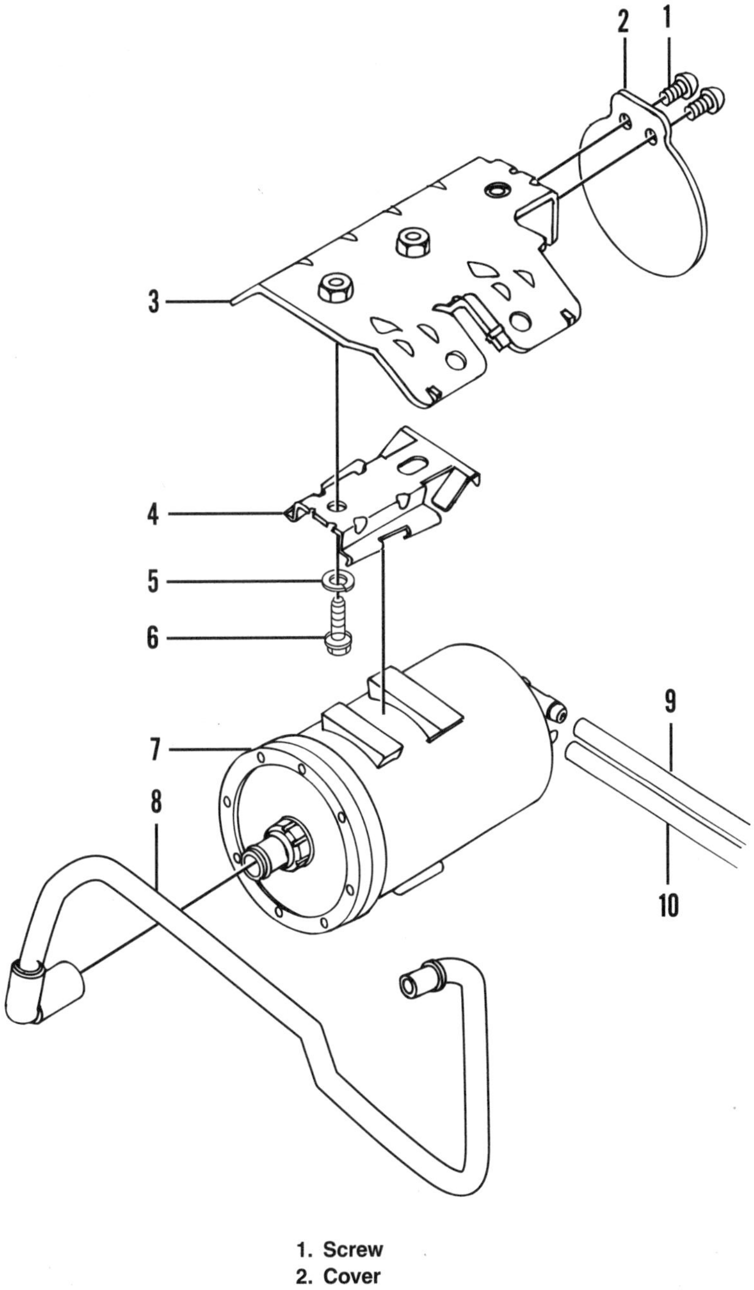

1. Screw
2. Cover
3. Mounting bracket
4. Mounting clip
5. Lockwasher
6. Bolt
7. Charcoal canister
8. Canister-to-air filter hose
9. Canister-to-carburetor hose
10. Canister-to-vapor vent hose

The lower hose is vented to the atmosphere. On California models it is connected to the charcoal canister.

WARNING
The vapor valve must be mounted in the clip in a vertical position in order to operate correctly. If installed incorrectly, excessive pressure can build up in the fuel tank and cause a fire or an explosion.

1. Label the upper hose and lower hose where they are connected to the vapor valve fittings.

2. Disconnect the hoses from the vapor valve (**Figure 104**).

3. Remove the vapor valve from the clip on the mounting bracket.

4. Correctly position the vapor valve with the long neck fitting at the top and install the vapor valve into the clip on the mounting bracket.

5. Connect the upper and lower hoses to the vapor valve.

Table 1 CARBURETOR SPECIFICATIONS

Main jet No.	
California	180
USA (except California)	175
Outside USA	170
Slow jet No.	42
Float level	0.413-0.453 in. (10.5-11.5 mm)
Idle speed	950-1050 rpm

Table 2 FUEL SYSTEM TORQUE SPECIFICATIONS

	ft.-lb.	in.-lb.	N•m
Air filter breather hollow bolts	–	84-120	9.5-13.6
Air filter element screws	–	40-60	4.5-6.8
Air filter cover screws	–	36-60	4.1-6.8
Charcoal canister mounting bracket bolts	17-22	–	24-30
Fuel tank mounting bolts	15-20	–	21-27
Fuel valve hex nut	15-20	–	21-27
Intake manifold Allen bolts	–	96-144	11-16

Table 3 EXHAUST SYSTEM TORQUE SPECIFICATIONS

	ft.-lb.	in.-lb.	N•m
Cylinder head exhaust flange nuts	–	96-120	11-14
Exhaust clamp bracket bolt	30-33	–	41-45
Exhaust/crossover pipe mounting bracket bolts	30-33	–	41-45
Muffler mounting bolts	15-19	–	21-26
Rear brake rod end	–	120-180	14-20
Rear exhaust pipe clamp bolt	15-19	–	21-26
Sprocket cover bolts	–	80-120	9-14
Torca clamp bolt	45-65	–	62-88

8

NOTE: Refer to the Supplement at the end of this manual for information unique to 2007-2011 models.

CHAPTER NINE

ELECTRICAL SYSTEM

This chapter contains service and test procedures for the electrical and ignition system components. Refer to Chapter Three for spark plug maintenance information.

The electrical system includes the following systems:

1. Charging system.
2. Ignition system.
3. Starting system.
4. Lighting system.
5. Switches and other electrical components.

Refer to **Tables 1-11** at the end of this chapter for specifications. The wiring diagram is located at the end of this manual.

NOTE

On models equipped with the TSSM security system, disarm the system before working on the motorcycle to prevent accidental activation of the warning system, including the optional siren. Refer to the system description in this chapter.

ELECTRICAL COMPONENT REPLACEMENT

Most motorcycle dealerships and parts suppliers do not accept the return of any electrical part. If the exact cause of an electrical system malfunction cannot be determined, have a Harley-Davidson dealership retest that specific system to verify the test results. This may help avert the possibilty of purchasing an expensive, unreturnable part that does not fix the problem.

Consider any test results carefully before replacing a component that tests only slightly out of specification, especially resistance. A number of variables can affect test results dramatically. These include: the testing meter's internal circuitry, ambient temperature and conditions under which the machine has been operated. All instructions and specifications have been checked for accuracy; however, successful test results depend to a great degree upon individual accuracy.

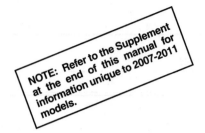

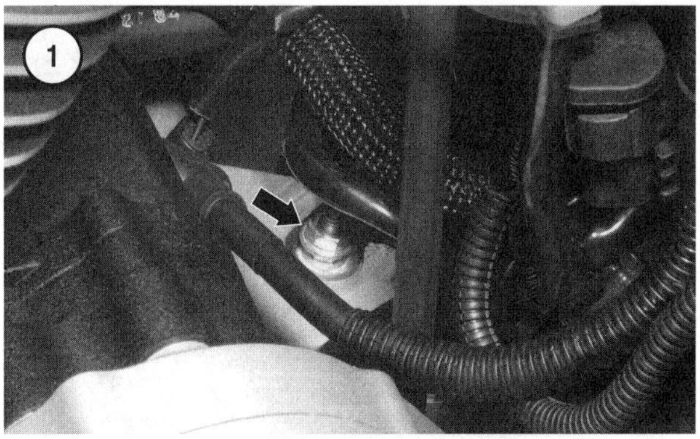

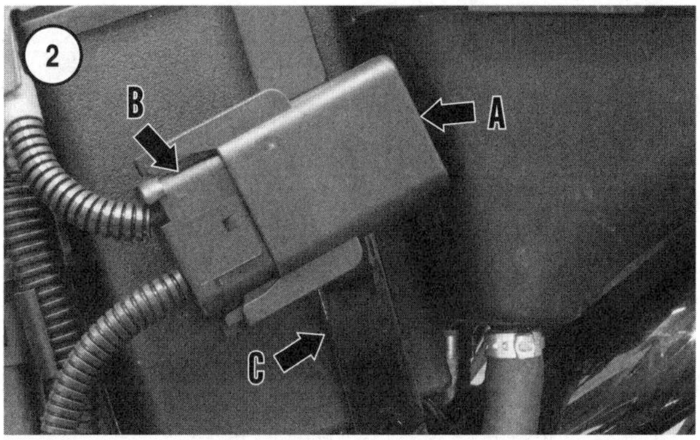

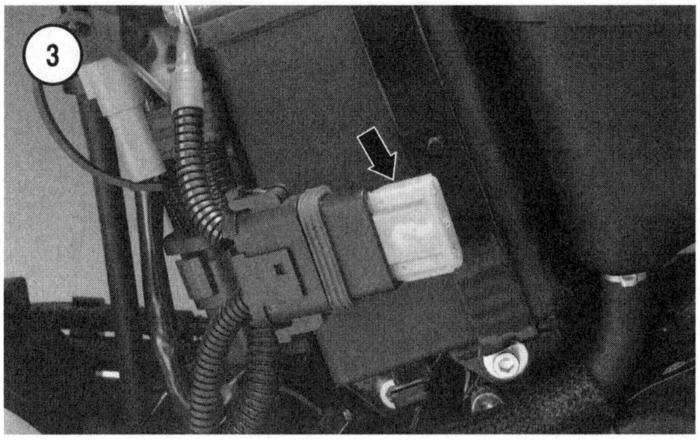

BATTERY

Many electrical system problems can be traced to the battery. Clean and inspect the battery at periodic intervals. The original equipment battery is a maintenance-free sealed battery and the electrolyte level cannot be checked.

NOTE
Always disarm the optional security system prior to disconnecting the battery or the alarm will sound.

Negative Cable

Some of the component replacement procedures and test procedures in this chapter require disconnecting the negative battery cable as a safety precaution.

1. Remove the nut (**Figure 1**) holding the negative cable to the crankcase. Secure the cable end so it cannot accidentally make contact with the frame or engine.
2. Connect the negative cable end to the ground post on the engine. Reinstall the nut and tighten to 55-75 in.-lb. (6.2-8.5 N•m).

Cable Service

To ensure good electrical contact between the battery and the electrical cables, the cables must be clean and free of corrosion.

1. If the electrical cable terminals are badly corroded, disconnect them from the motorcycle's electrical system.
2. Thoroughly clean each connector with a wire brush and a baking soda solution. Rinse thoroughly with clean water and wipe dry with a clean cloth.
3. After cleaning, apply a thin layer of dielectric grease to the battery terminals before reattaching the cables.
4. Reconnect the electrical cables to the motorcycle's electrical system if they were disconnected.
5. After connecting the electrical cables, apply a light coat of dielectric grease to the terminals to prevent corrosion of the terminals.

9

Removal/Installation

1. Remove the left side cover as described in Chapter Fourteen.
2. Remove the nut and disconnect the negative battery cable (**Figure 1**). Secure the cable end so it cannot accidentally make contact with the frame or engine.
3. Push the Maxi-fuse cover latches together. Hold the fuse cover (A, **Figure 2**) and pull the fuse holder (B) out of the cover.
4. Remove the Maxi-fuse (**Figure 3**) from the fuse holder.
5. Remove the fuse cover (A, **Figure 2**) from the battery strap (C).
6. Remove the battery strap retaining screw and washer (A, **Figure 4**).
7. Unhook the battery strap (B, **Figure 4**) from the top of the battery tray and remove the strap.
8. Move aside the rubber boot over the positive battery terminal. Remove the bolt and disconnect the positive bat-

tery cable (C, **Figure 4**) and Maxi-fuse wire from the positive battery terminal.

NOTE
The negative battery cable is attached to the battery during removal and installation.

9. Carefully slide the battery (**Figure 5**) out of the frame.
10. If necessary, disconnect the battery cable from the negative terminal (**Figure 6**).
11. Inspect the battery tray and compartment for corrosion or damage. Replace it if necessary.
12. If disconnected, reattach the negative battery cable to the battery negative terminal. The cable must hang straight down. Tighten the retaining bolt to 40-50 in.-lb. (4.5-5.6 N•m).
13. Reinstall the battery with the negative cable attached onto the battery tray in the frame. Route the cable down the right side of the frame downtube.

CAUTION
After battery installation, secure the negative cable end so it cannot accidentally make contact with the frame or engine.

14. Connect the positive battery cable (C, **Figure 4**) and Maxi-fuse wire to the positive battery terminal. Tighten the retaining bolt to 40-50 in.-lb. (4.5-5.6 N•m). Move the rubber boot over the positive battery terminal.
15. Hook the battery strap (B, **Figure 4**) to the top of the battery tray.
16. Install the battery strap retaining screw and washer (A, **Figure 4**). Tighten the retaining screw to 36-60 in.-lb. (4.1-6.8 N•m).
17. Install the fuse cover (A, **Figure 2**) onto the battery strap (C).
18. Push the Maxi-fuse (**Figure 3**) into the fuse holder.
19. Push the Maxi-fuse holder (B, **Figure 2**) into the fuse cover (A).
20. Connect the negative cable end to the ground post on the engine. Reinstall the nut and tighten to 55-75 in.-lb. (6.2-8.5 N•m).
21. Install the left side cover as described in Chapter Fourteen.

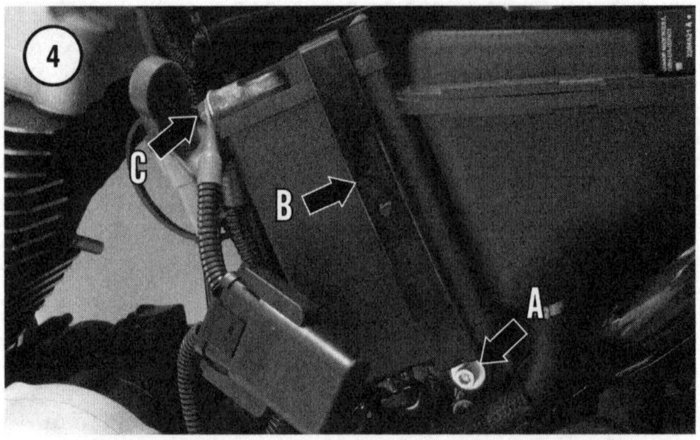

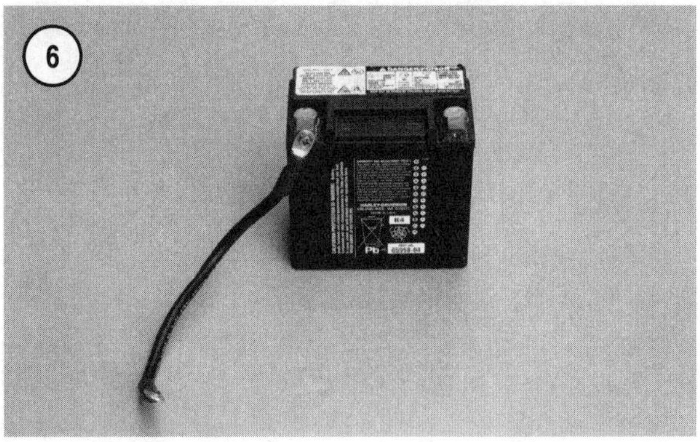

Inspection and Testing

WARNING
Electrolyte is harmful to eyes. Always wear safety glasses while working with a battery. If electrolyte gets into your eyes, call a physician immediately and force your eyes open and flood them with cool, clean water and seek medical attention.

On a maintenance-free battery, the battery electrolyte level cannot be inspected. Never remove the sealing bar cap (**Figure 7**) from the top of the battery. Refer to the charging time/rate labels (**Figure 8**, typical) on the battery, particularly if an aftermarket battery is substituted.

Even though the battery is sealed, protect eyes, skin and clothing. The battery case may be cracked and leaking electrolyte. If electrolyte is spilled or splashed on clothing or skin, immediately neutralize it with a baking soda and water solution, then flush with clean water.

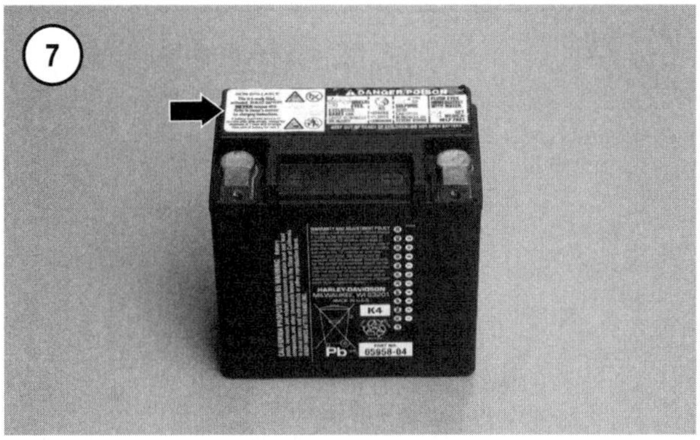

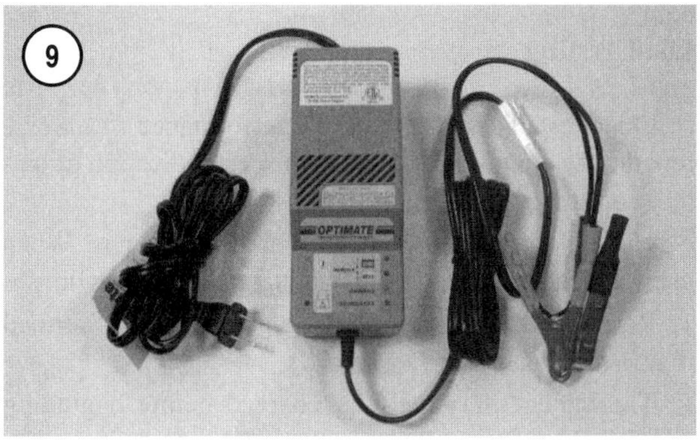

1. Remove the battery as described in this section. Do not clean the battery while it is mounted in the frame.

2. Set the battery on newspapers or shop cloths to protect the workbench surface.

3. Check the battery case for cracks or other damage. If the battery case is warped, discolored or has a raised top, the battery has been overcharged and overheated.

4. Check the battery terminal bolts, washers and nuts for corrosion or damage. Clean parts thoroughly with a baking soda and water solution. Replace corroded or damaged parts.

5. If the top of the battery is corroded, clean it with a bristle brush using the baking soda and water solution.

6. Check the battery cable ends for corrosion and damage. If corrosion is minor, clean the battery cable ends. Replace worn or damaged cables.

7. Connect a digital voltmeter between the battery negative and positive leads. Note the following:
   a. If the battery voltage is 13.0-13.2 volts (at 20° C [68° F]) the battery is fully charged.
   b. If the battery voltage is 12.0 to 12.5 volts (at 20° C [68° F]), or lower, the battery is undercharged and requires charging.

8. If the battery is undercharged, recharge it as described in this section.

9. Inspect the battery case for contamination or damage. Clean it with a baking soda and water solution.

10. Install the battery as described in this section.

Charging

WARNING

During charging, highly explosive hydrogen gas is released from the battery. Only charge the battery in a well-ventilated area away from open flames, including pilot lights on appliances. Do not smoke in the area. Never check the charge of the battery by arcing across the terminals; the resulting spark can ignite the hydrogen gas.

Refer to the *Initialization* in this section if the battery is new.

To recharge a maintenance-free battery, a digital voltmeter and a charger (**Figure 9**) specifically designed for use with maintenance-free batteries are required. If this equipment is not available, have the battery charged by a shop with the proper equipment. Excessive voltage and amperage from an unregulated charger can damage the battery and shorten service life.

The battery should only self-discharge approximately one percent of its given capacity each day. If a battery not in use, without any loads connected, loses its charge within a week after charging, the battery is defective.

If the motorcycle is not used for long periods of time, an automatic battery charger with variable voltage and amperage outputs is recommended for optimum battery service life.

CAUTION

Always disconnect the battery cables from the battery. If the cables are left connected during the charging procedure, the charger may damage the the voltage regulator/rectifier.

1. Remove the battery from the motorcycle as described in this section.
2. Set the battery on newspapers or shop cloths to protect the workbench surface.
3. Make sure the battery charger is turned off prior to attaching the charger leads to the battery.
4. Connect the positive charger lead to the positive battery terminal and the negative charger lead to the negative battery terminal.
5. Set the charger at 12 volts. If the amperage of the charger is variable, select the low setting.
6. The charging time depends on the discharged condition of the battery. Refer to the charging time/rate (**Figure 8**, typical) on the battery. Normally, a battery should be charged at 1/10 its given capacity.

CAUTION
If the battery emits an excessive amount of gas during the charging cycle, decrease the charge rate. If the battery gets hot during the charging cycle, turn the charger off and allow it to cool. Then continue with a reduced charging rate and continue to monitor the battery temperature.

7. Turn the charger on.
8. After the battery has been charged for the predetermined time, turn the charger off, disconnect the leads and measure the battery voltage. Refer to the following:
   a. If the battery voltage is 13.0-13.2 volts (at 20° C [68° F]), the battery is fully charged.
   b. If the battery voltage is 12.5 volts (at 20° C [68° F]), or lower, the battery is undercharged and requires additional charging time.
9. If the battery remains stable for one hour, the battery is charged.
10. Install the battery into the motorcycle as described in this section.

Initialization

A new battery must be fully charged before installation. To bring the battery to a full charge, give it an initial charge. Using a new battery without an initial charge will cause permanent battery damage. The battery will never be able to hold more than an 80 percent charge. Charging a new battery after it has been used will not bring its charge to 100 percent. When purchasing a new battery, verify its charge status.

NOTE
Recycle the old battery. When purchasing a new battery, turn in the old one for recycling. Most motorcycle dealerships accept the old battery in trade for a new one. Never place an old battery in the household trash since it is illegal, in most states, to place any acid or lead (heavy metal) contents in landfills.

10

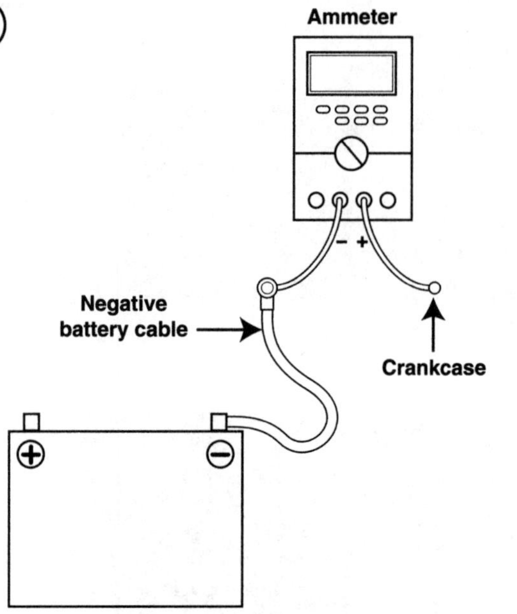

Load Testing

A load test checks the battery's performance with a current draw or load applied and is the best indication of battery condition.

A battery load tester is required for this procedure. When using a load tester, follow the manufacturer's instructions.

1. Remove the battery from the motorcycle as described in this section.
2. The battery must be fully charged before beginning this test. If necessary, charge the battery as described in this section.
3. Let the battery stand for at least one hour after charging.

WARNING
The battery load tester must be turned off prior to connecting or disconnecting the test cables to the battery. Otherwise, a spark could cause the battery to explode.

CAUTION
To prevent battery damage during load testing, do not load test a discharged battery and do not load test the battery for more than 20 seconds. Performing a load test on

(11) **STATOR**

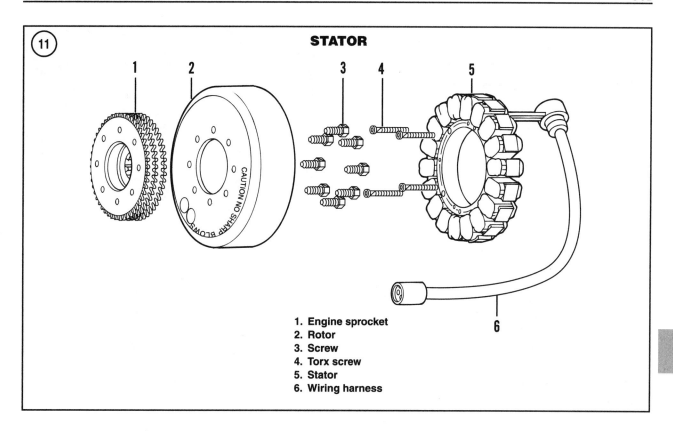

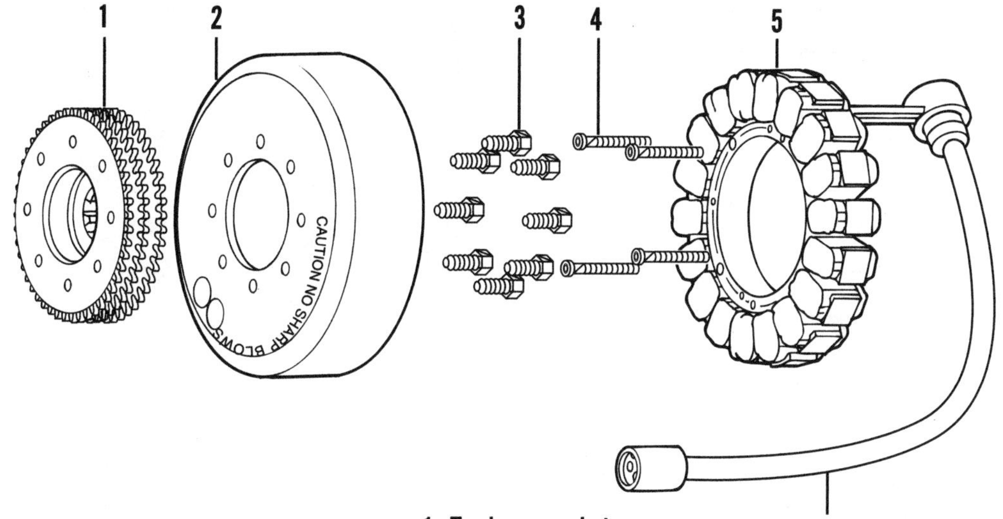

1. **Engine sprocket**
2. **Rotor**
3. **Screw**
4. **Torx screw**
5. **Stator**
6. **Wiring harness**

a discharged battery can cause permanent battery damage.

4. Load test the battery as follows:
   a. Connect the load tester cables to the battery following the manufacturer's instructions.
   b. Load the battery to 50 percent of the cold cranking amperage (CCA) for 15 seconds. Note the voltage reading and remove the load.
   c. The voltage reading with the load applied must be 9.6 volts or higher at 70° F (21 ° C).
5. If the voltage reading was 9.6 volts or higher, the battery capacity is good. If the reading was below 9.6 volts, the battery is defective.
6. With the tester off, disconnect the cables from the battery.
7. Install the battery as described in this section.

Current Draw Test

This test measures the current draw or drain on the battery when all electrical systems and accessories are off. Perform this test if the battery will not hold a charge when the motorcycle is not being used. A current draw that exceeds 3.5 mA will discharge the battery. The voltage regulator (0.5 mA), turn signal module (0.5 mA) and security system (2.5 mA) account for a 3.5 mA current draw. The battery must be fully charged to perform this test.

1. Disconnect the negative battery cable as described in this chapter.
2. Connect an ammeter between the negative battery cable end and the ground stud on the engine crankcase as shown in **Figure 10**.
3. With the ignition switch and all accessories turned off, read the ammeter. If the current draw exceeds 3.5 mA, continue with Step 4.
4. Refer to the wiring diagram at the end of this manual. Check the charging system wires and connectors for shorts or other damage.
5. Unplug each electrical connector separately and check for a reduction in the current draw. If the meter reading changes after a connector is disconnected, the source of the current draw has been found. Check the electrical connectors carefully before testing the individual component.
6. After completing the test, disconnect the ammeter and reconnect the negative battery cable.

CHARGING SYSTEM

The charging system consists of the battery, alternator and a voltage regulator/rectifier. Refer to **Figure 11**. Alternating current generated by the alternator is rectified to direct current. The voltage regulator maintains the voltage to the battery and electrical system at a constant voltage regardless of variations in engine speed and load.

Precautions

To prevent damage to the alternator and the regulator/rectifier when testing and repairing the charging system, note the following precautions:

NOTE
Always disarm the optional security system prior to disconnecting the battery or the alarm will sound.

1. Always disconnect the negative battery cable, as described in this chapter, before removing a component from the charging system.
2. Do not reverse the battery polarity. The negative cable is the ground cable.
3. Check the charging system wiring for chafing, deterioration or other damage.
4. Check the wiring for corroded or loose connections. Clean, tighten or reconnect wiring as required.

Testing

A malfunction in the charging system generally causes the battery to remain undercharged. Perform the following visual inspection to determine the cause of the problem. If the visual inspection proves satisfactory, test the charging system as described in *Alternator* in this chapter.

1. Inspect and test, and if necessary, charge the battery as described in this chapter.
2. Carefully check all connections at the alternator to make sure they are clean and tight.
3. Check the circuit wiring for corroded or loose connections. Clean, tighten or connect wiring as required. If necessary, refer to *Electrical Connectors* in this chapter.

ALTERNATOR

Rotor

Removal/installation

The rotor (A, **Figure 12**) is mounted on the engine sprocket (B).

12

13

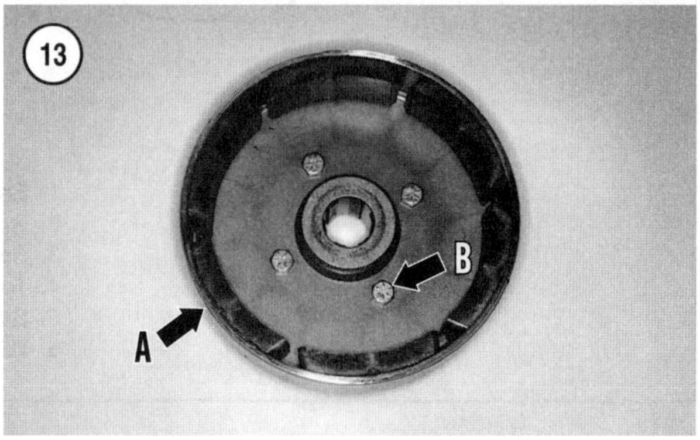

14

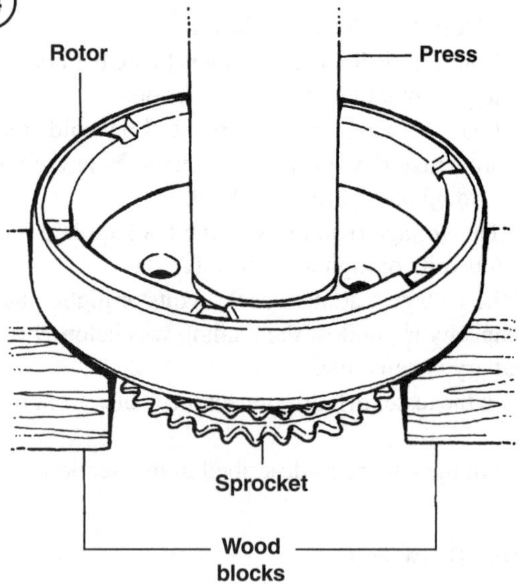

NOTE
Always disarm the optional security system prior to disconnecting the battery or the alarm will sound.

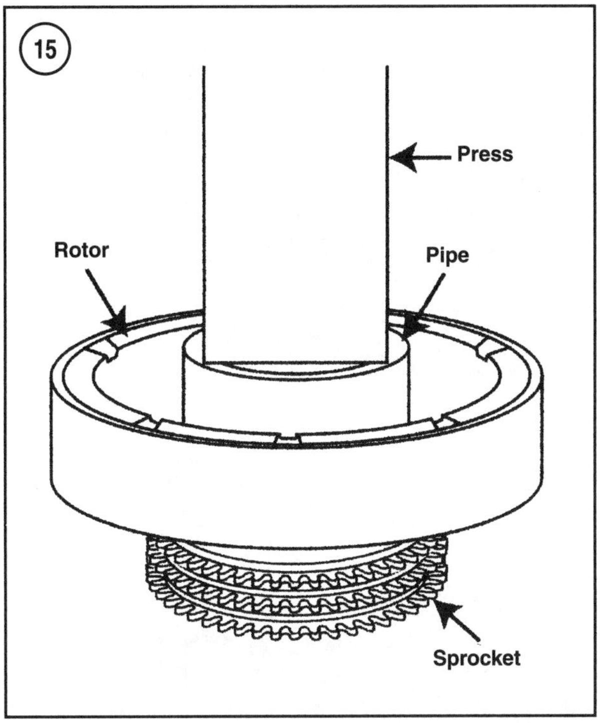

1. Disconnect the negative battery cable as described in this chapter.
2. Remove the primary chain, engine sprocket and clutch as described in Chapter Five.
3. If necessary, press the engine sprocket off the rotor as described in this chapter.
4. Install the primary chain, engine sprocket and clutch as described in Chapter Five.

CAUTION
*Carefully inspect the inside of the rotor (A, **Figure 13**) for metal debris that may have been picked up by the magnets. Metal debris can damage the alternator stator assembly.*

Disassembly/reassembly

1. Remove the rotor-to-engine sprocket mounting bolts (B, **Figure 13**).
2. Support the rotor in a press as shown in **Figure 14**. Press the engine sprocket off the rotor.
3. Clean the engine sprocket, rotor and mounting bolts in solvent and dry thoroughly. Remove any threadlock residue from the sprocket and mounting bolt threads.
4. Place the rotor on top of the sprocket, aligning the holes in the rotor with the threaded holes in the sprocket.
5. Apply Loctite 243 (blue) to the mounting bolts prior to installation. Install the bolts finger-tight.
6. Support the sprocket in a press and place a piece of pipe between the rotor and press arm. Press the rotor onto the sprocket (**Figure 15**).
7. Tighten the rotor-to-engine sprocket mounting bolts to 120-140 in.-lb. (13.6-15.8 N•m).

Inspection

WARNING
Replace a damaged rotor. It could seperate during operation, throwing metal fragments into the engine. Do not attempt to repair a damaged rotor.

1. Check the rotor (**Figure 16**) carefully for cracks or missing sections.
2. Check the rotor magnets (A, **Figure 13**) for damage or looseness.
3. Replace the rotor, if necessary, as described in this section.

Stator

Test

The stator (**Figure 17**) is mounted behind the rotor and bolted to the left crankcase.

1. With the ignition turned off, disconnect the regulator/rectifier connector (**Figure 18**) at the front of the crankcase.
2. Connect an ohmmeter between either stator connector terminal and ground. The ohmmeter should read infinity (no continuity). If the reading is incorrect, the stator is grounded and must be replaced. Repeat this test for the other stator connector terminal.
3. Connect an ohmmeter between both stator connector terminals. The ohmmeter should read 0.2-0.4 ohms. If the resistance is higher than specified, replace the stator.
4. Check stator AC output as follows:
   a. Connect an AC voltmeter between the stator connector terminals.
   b. Start the engine and slowly increase idle speed. Voltage should read 38-52 volts at 2000 rpm.
   c. If the AC voltage output reading is below the prescribed range, the trouble is probably a faulty stator or rotor. If these parts are not damaged, refer to *Charging System* in Chapter Two and test the output.
5. Reconnect the regulator/rectifier connector (**Figure 18**).

Removal/installation

The stator (**Figure 17**) is mounted behind the rotor and bolted to the left crankcase. Torx screws with a locking adhesive applied are required to secure the stator. Replace these Torx screws after removal. Failure to do so could damage the alternator assembly.

1. Remove the rotor as described in this section.
2. Make a diagram of the stator wiring harness frame routing path prior to removing the stator in the following steps.
3. Disconnect the regulator/rectifier connector (**Figure 18**) from the stator lead .
4. Remove the cable strap (A, **Figure 19**) from the stator wiring harness.
5. Remove and discard the stator plate Torx screws (**Figure 20**).
6. Remove the stator wiring grommet (B, **Figure 19**) from the crankcase.
7. Remove the stator assembly and its attached wiring harness (**Figure 21**).
8. Inspect the stator wires for fraying or damage. Check the stator connector pins for looseness or damage. Replace the stator if necessary.
9. Reverse the removal steps to install the stator and note the following:
   a. Lightly coat the stator wiring grommet (B, **Figure 19**) with engine oil. Then insert the grommet into the crankcase.
   b. Install *new* stator Torx screws (**Figure 20**) and tighten to 30-40 in.-lb. (3.4-4.5 N•m).

18

19

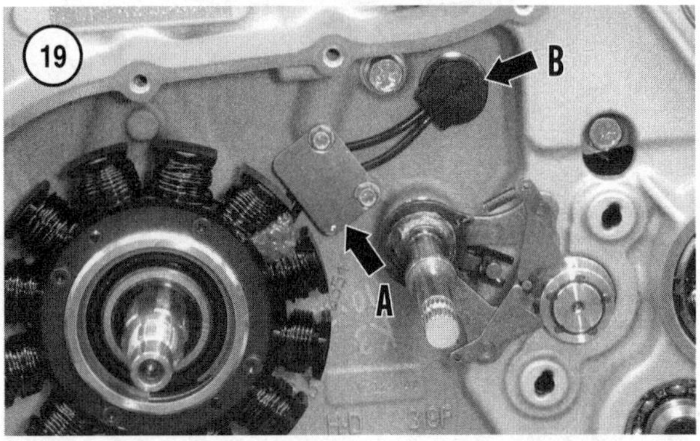

20

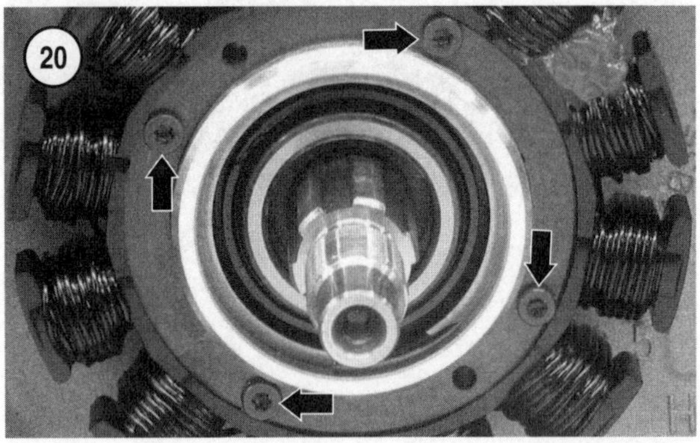

21

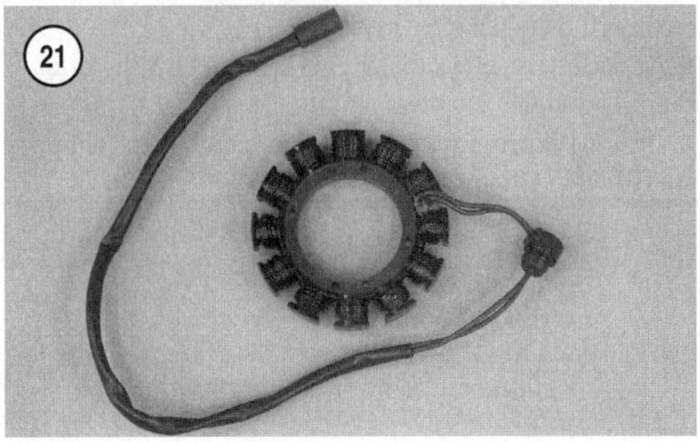

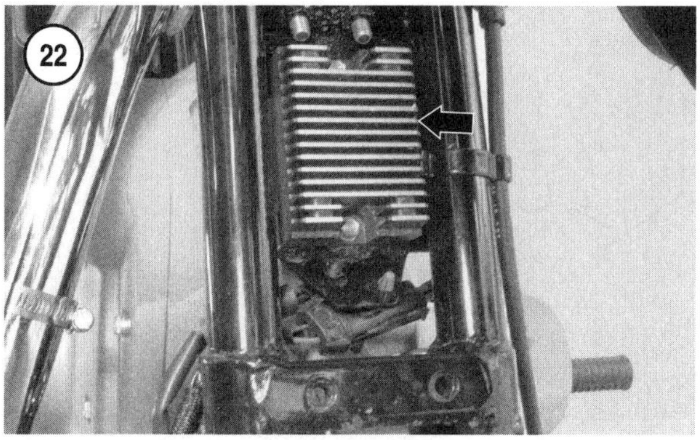

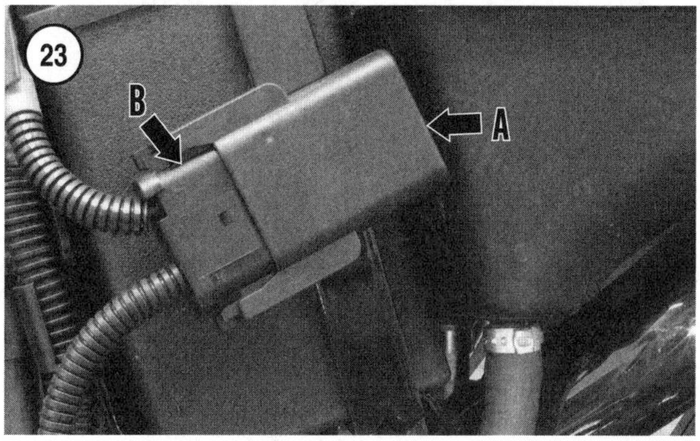

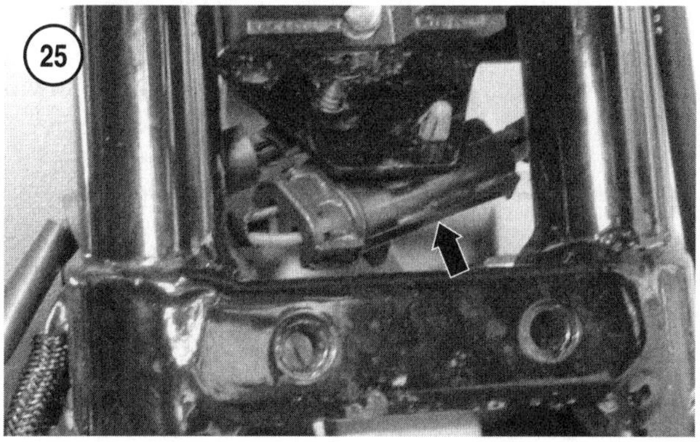

c. Correctly route the stator wiring harness along the frame. Secure the harness with the proper cable straps.

CAUTION

When bringing the wiring harness out from underneath the gearcase cover, the harness should be routed 1 1/2 in. (38 mm) forward of the rear gearcase edge. This distance is necessary to prevent the secondary drive belt or sprocket from damaging the wiring harness.

d. Install the rotor as described in this section.

Voltage Regulator

Ground test

The voltage regulator must be grounded to the mounting bracket and the frame for proper operation.

1. Connect one ohmmeter lead to a good engine or frame ground and the other ohmmeter lead to the regulator base. Read the ohmmeter scale. The correct reading is 0 ohm. Note the following:
   a. If there is low resistance (0 ohm), the voltage regulator is properly grounded.
   b. If there is high resistance, remove the voltage regulator and clean its frame mounting points.
2. Check the voltage regulator connectors and make sure they are clean and tightly connected.

Removal/installation

The voltage regulator is mounted on the front frame downtubes (**Figure 22**).

NOTE

Always disarm the optional security system prior to disconnecting the battery or the alarm will sound.

1. Remove the left side cover as described in Chapter Fourteen.
2. Push the Maxi-fuse cover latches together. Hold the fuse cover (A, **Figure 23**) and pull the fuse holder (B) out of the cover.
3. Remove the Maxi-fuse (**Figure 24**) from the fuse holder.
4. Disconnect the voltage regulator-to-stator wiring connector (**Figure 18**).
5. Disconnect the voltage regulator connector (**Figure 25**). Detach the connector from the frame bracket. Lift the latches to disengage the connectors.
6. Remove any wiring retaining straps.

9

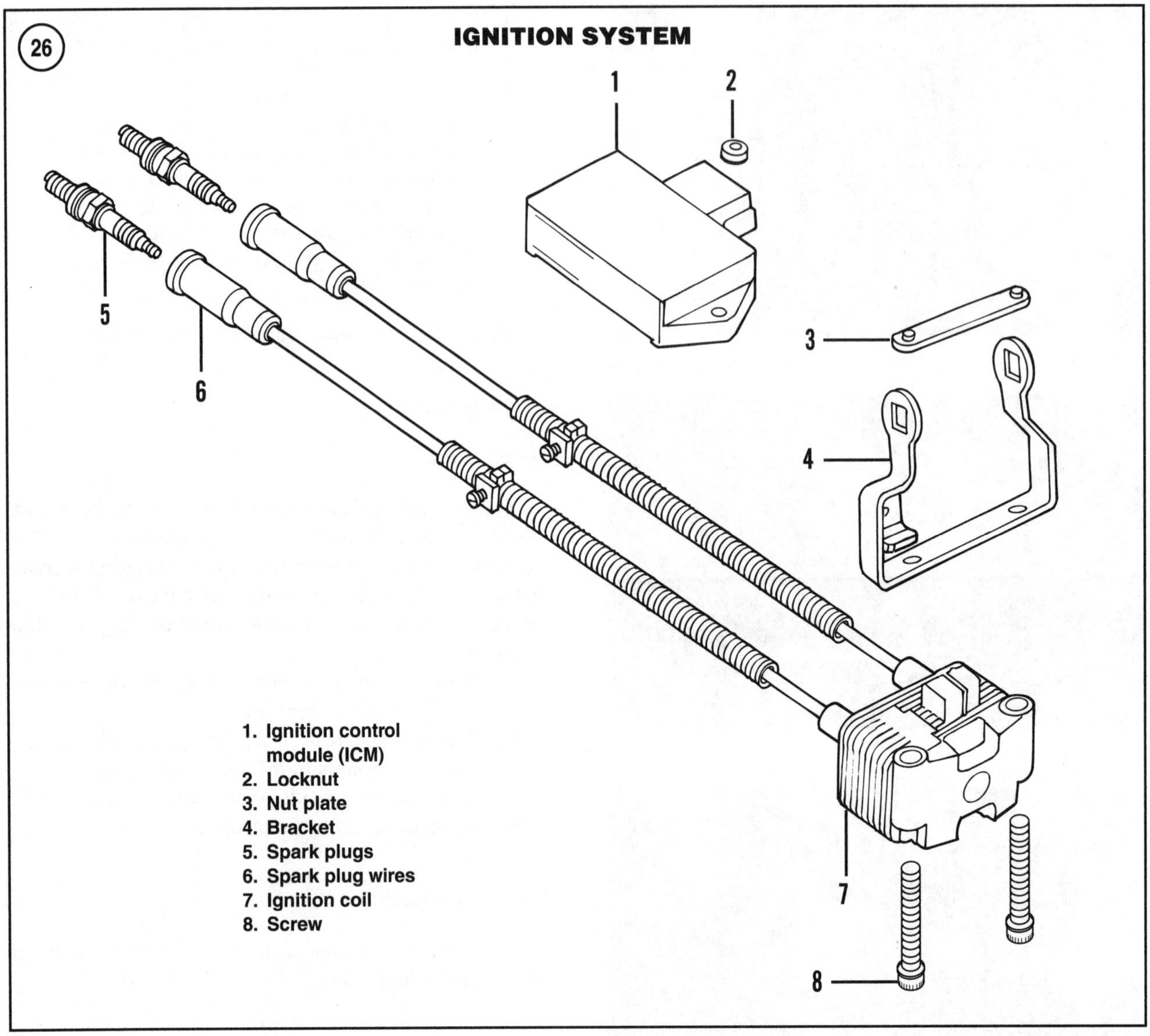

7. Remove the voltage regulator mounting screws and remove the voltage regulator.
8. Reverse the removal steps to install the voltage regulator.

IGNITION SYSTEM

The ignition system (**Figure 26**) consists of an ignition coil, two spark plugs, the ignition control module (ICM), crankshaft position sensor (CKP), manifold absolute pressure sensor (MAP), and the bank angle sensor (BAS).

The ignition module is located under the seat. It determines the spark advance for correct ignition timing based on signals from the CKP and MAP sensors. The ignition system fires the spark plugs near top dead center for starting, then varies the spark advance from 0° to 58° depending on engine speed, crankshaft position and intake manifold pressure. It also regulates the low-voltage circuits between the battery and the ignition coil. The ignition module is not repairable and must be replaced if defective.

The MAP sensor is located on top of the intake manifold. This sensor monitors the intake manifold vacuum and sends this information to the ignition module. The module adjusts the ignition timing advance curve.

The bank angle sensor is an integral part of the turn signal/turn signal security module (TSM/ TSSM), which is located underneath the battery in the battery tray. The sensor consists of a small magnetic disc that rides within a V-shaped channel. If the motorcycle is tilted at a 45° angle for more than one second, the ICM shuts off the ignition

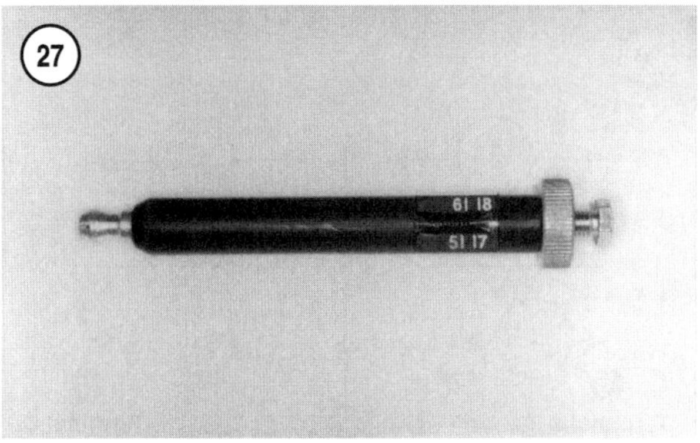

27

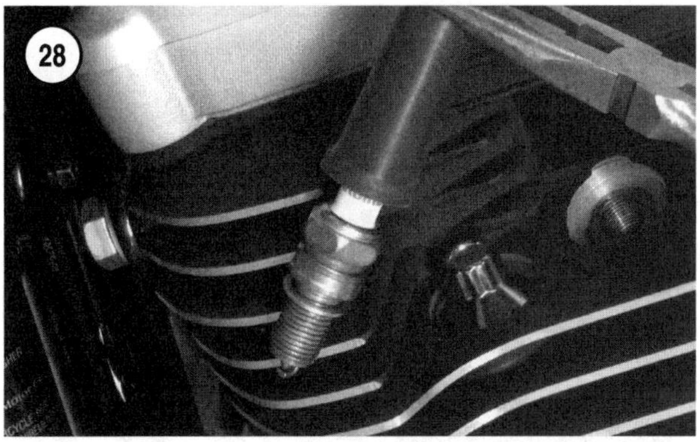

28

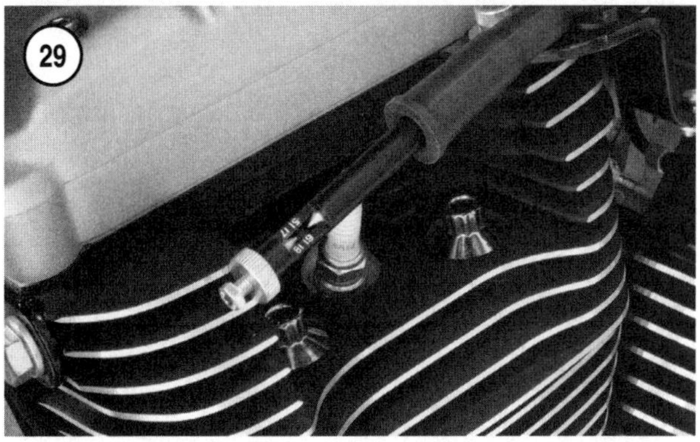

29

system. Once the sensor is activated, the motorcycle must be returned to vertical and the ignition switch turned off and on. Then, the ignition system is operational and the engine can be restarted.

Ignition Coil

Performance test

1. Disconnect the plug wire and remove one of the spark plugs as described in Chapter Three.

NOTE
A spark tester is useful for testing the ignition system spark output. ***Figure 27*** *shows the Motion Pro Ignition System Tester (part No. 08-0122). This tool is inserted in the spark plug cap and its base is grounded against the cylinder head. The tool's air gap is adjustable and it allows visual inspection of the spark while testing the intensity of the spark.*

2. Insert a clean shop cloth into the spark plug hole in the cylinder head to reduce gasoline vapors emitting from the hole.
3. Insert the spark plug (**Figure 28**), or spark tester (**Figure 29**), into its cap and touch the spark plug base against the cylinder head to ground it. Position the spark plug so the electrode is visible.

WARNING
Position the spark plug, or tester, away from the spark plug hole in the cylinder so the spark or tester cannot ignite the gasoline vapors in the cylinder. If the engine is flooded, do not perform this test. The firing of the spark plug can ignite fuel ejected through the spark plug hole.

WARNING
Do not hold the spark plug, wire or connector or a serious electrical shock could occur. If necessary, hold onto the spark plug wire with a pair of insulated pliers.

NOTE
When not using a spark tester, always use a new spark plug for this test procedure.

4. Crank the engine over with the starter. A fat blue spark should be evident across the spark plug electrode or spark tester. If there is strong sunlight on the plug, or tester, shade it so the spark is more visible. Repeat for the other cylinder.
5. If there is a fat blue spark, the ignition coil is good. If there is not, perform the following resistance test.

Resistance test

1. Remove the ignition coil as described in this section.
2. Disconnect the secondary wires from the ignition coil.
3. Use an ohmmeter and measure the primary coil resistance between terminals A and B, then terminals B and C

(**Figure 30**) at the primary connector terminals on the ignition coil. The specified resistance is in **Table 1**.

4. Use an ohmmeter and measure the secondary coil resistance between terminals B and R, then terminals B and F (**Figure 30**) at the backside of the ignition coil. The specified resistance is in **Table 1**.

5. If the resistance is less than specified, there is probably a short in the coil windings. Replace the coil.

6. If the resistance is more than specified, this may indicate corrosion or oxidation of the coil terminals. Thoroughly clean the terminals, then spray them with an aerosol electrical contact cleaner. Repeat Step 3 and Step 4. If the resistance remains high, replace the coil.

7. If the coil resistance does not meet (or come close to) either of these specifications, replace the coil. If the coil is visibly damaged, replace it as described in this section.

8. Install the ignition coil as described in this section.

Removal/installation

NOTE
Always disarm the optional security system prior to removing the Maxi-fuse or the alarm will sound.

1. Remove the left side cover as described in Chapter Fourteen.

2. Push the Maxi-fuse cover latches together. Hold the fuse cover (A, **Figure 31**) and pull the fuse holder (B) out of the cover.

3. Remove the Maxi-fuse (**Figure 32**) from the fuse holder.

NOTE
Label all wiring connectors prior to disconnecting them in the following steps.

4. Detach the rear cylinder secondary wire connector (A, **Figure 33**) from the ignition coil.

5. Detach the front cylinder secondary wire connector (B, **Figure 33**) from the ignition coil.

6. Remove the bolts and lockwashers (C, **Figure 33**) securing the ignition coil to the mounting bracket.

7. Lower the ignition coil away from the mounting bracket and disconnect the primary wire connector (**Figure 34**) from the ignition coil.

8. Remove the ignition coil.

9. Install the ignition coil by reversing the preceding steps.

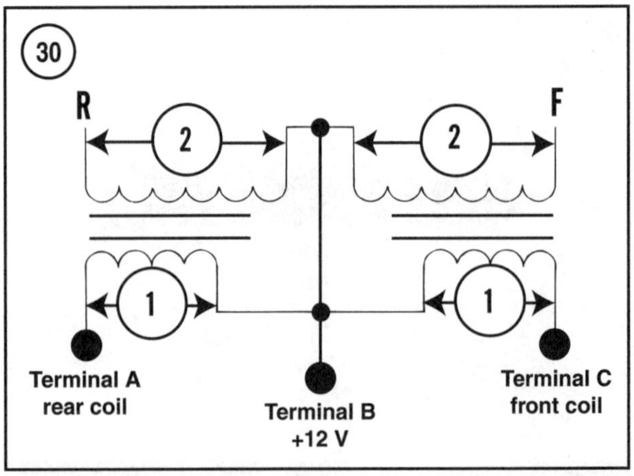

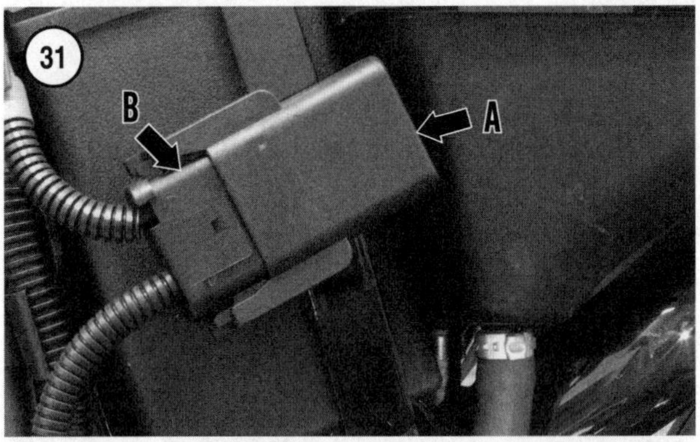

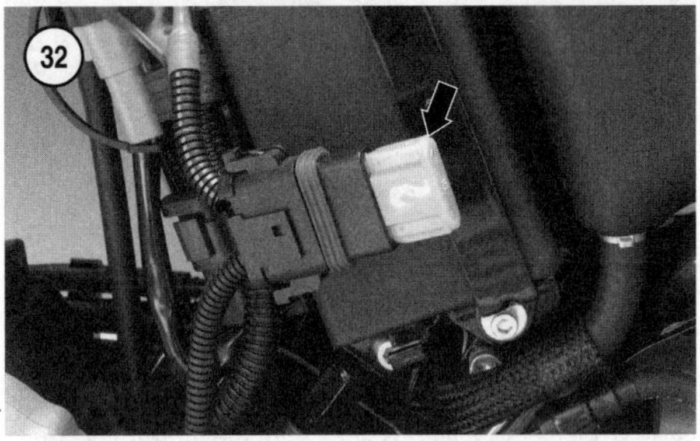

Ignition Control Module (ICM) Removal/Installation

The ignition control module (ICM) is located under the seat.

NOTE
After installing a new ICM, a dealership equipped with H-D Digital Technician must reprogram the ICM.

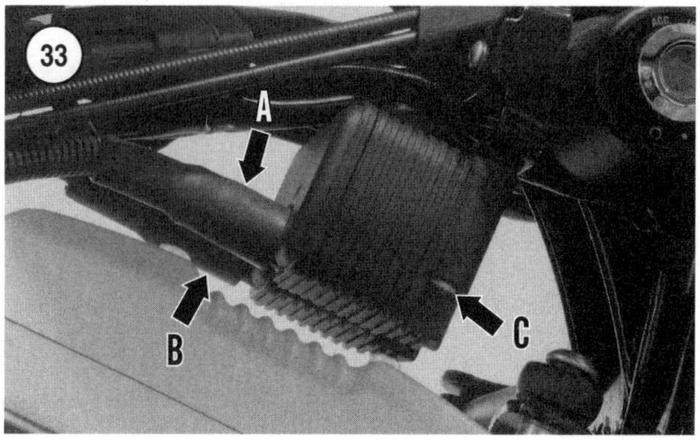

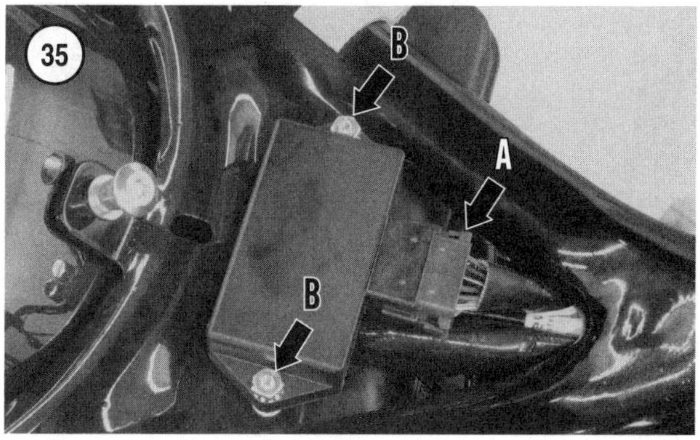

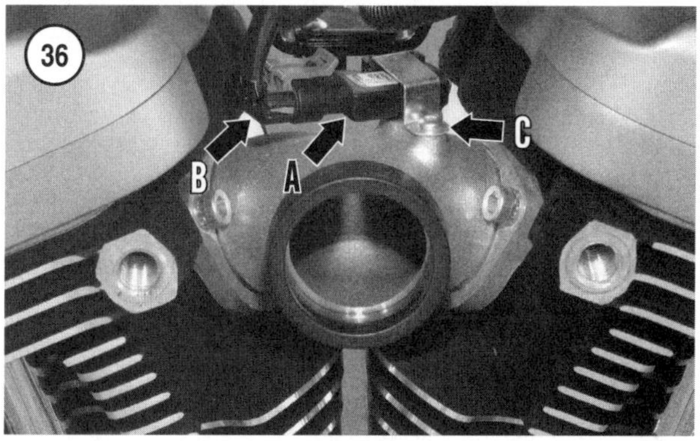

NOTE
Always disarm the optional security system prior to removing the Maxi-fuse or the alarm will sound.

1. Remove the seat as described in Chapter Fourteen.
2. Remove the left side cover as described in Chapter Fourteen.
3. Push the Maxi-fuse cover latches together. Hold the fuse cover (A, **Figure 31**) and pull the fuse holder (B) out of the cover.
4. Remove the Maxi-fuse (**Figure 32**) from the fuse holder.
5. Depress the external latches on the ICM electrical connector (A, **Figure 35**). Carefully pull and disconnect the connector from the ignition module.
6. Remove the locknuts (B, **Figure 35**) securing the ignition module to the mounting bracket.
7. Remove the ignition module from the frame.
8. Install the ignition module by reversing the preceding steps. Note the following:
   a. Apply a light coat of dielectric compound to the electrical connectors prior to installing them.
   b. Make sure the electrical connector is pushed tightly onto the ignition module.
   c. Have a dealership reprogram the ICM.

9

Manifold Absolute Pressure (MAP) Sensor Removal/Installation

The MAP sensor (A, **Figure 36**) is located on top of the intake manifold.

NOTE
Always disarm the optional security system prior to removing the Maxi- fuse or the alarm will sound.

1. Remove the left side cover as described in Chapter Fourteen.
2. Push the Maxi-fuse cover latches together, then pull the fuse cover (A, **Figure 31**) rearward to separate the cover from the fuse holder (B).
3. Remove the Maxi-fuse (**Figure 32**) from the fuse holder.
4. On XL883C and XL1200C models, remove the fuel tank as described in Chapter Eight.
5. Remove the carburetor as described in Chapter Eight, but leave the throttle cables attached (**Figure 37**) and place the carburetor out of the way.
6. Disconnect the electrical connector (B, **Figure 36**) from the MAP sensor.

7. Remove the retainer screw and retainer bracket (C, **Figure 36**).
8. Pull the MAP sensor (A, **Figure 36**) straight up out of the seal in the intake manifold.
9. Reverse the removal steps to install the MAP sensor and note the following:
   a. Apply a light coat of dielectric compound to the electrical connector prior to installing it.
   b. Make sure the electrical connector is pushed tightly onto the MAP sensor.
   c. If necessary, replace the seal in the intake manifold.

Crankshaft Position Sensor (CKP) Removal/Installation

The CKP sensor (**Figure 38**) is mounted on the front left side of the crankcase next to the oil filter.

NOTE
Always disarm the optional security system prior to removing the Maxi- fuse or the alarm will sound.

1. Remove the left side cover as described in Chapter Fourteen.
2. Push the Maxi-fuse cover latches together. Hold the fuse cover (A, **Figure 31**) and pull the fuse holder (B) out of the cover.
3. Remove the Maxi-fuse (**Figure 32**) from the fuse holder.
4. Disconnect the CKP sensor electrical connector beneath the primary cover (**Figure 39**).
5. Detach the sensor wiring harness from the frame wire retainers.
6. Remove the sensor retaining bolt and withdraw the CKP sensor and O-ring from the crankcase.
7. Reverse the removal steps to install the CKP sensor and note the following:
   a. Apply a light coat of dielectric compound to the electrical connector before installing it.
   b. The new O-ring on the CKP sensor has a blue Teflon coating and does not require lubrication prior to installation.
   c. Install the sensor and tighten the retaining bolt to 80-100 in.-lb. (9-11 N•m).

Bank Angle Sensor (BAS)

The BAS is an integral part of the turn signal module (TSM)/turn signal security module (TSSM). Refer to *Turn Signal Security Module* in this chapter.

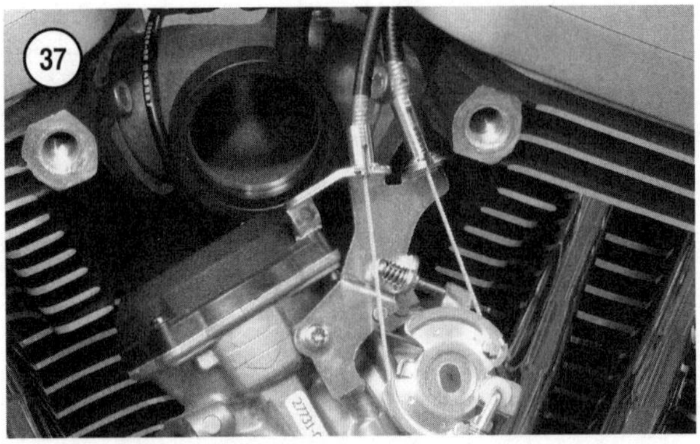

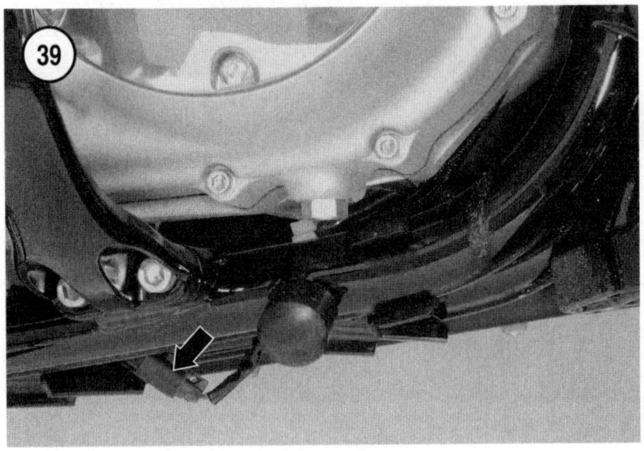

STARTER

The starting system consists of the starter, starter gears, solenoid and the starter button.

When the starter button is pressed, it engages the starter solenoid switch that completes the circuit allowing current to flow from the battery to the starter.

When servicing the starting system, refer to the wiring diagram located at the end of this manual. Troubleshooting is covered in Chapter Two.

40

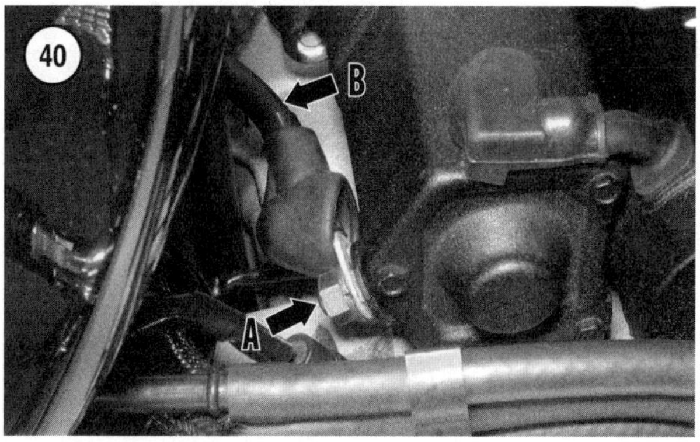

41

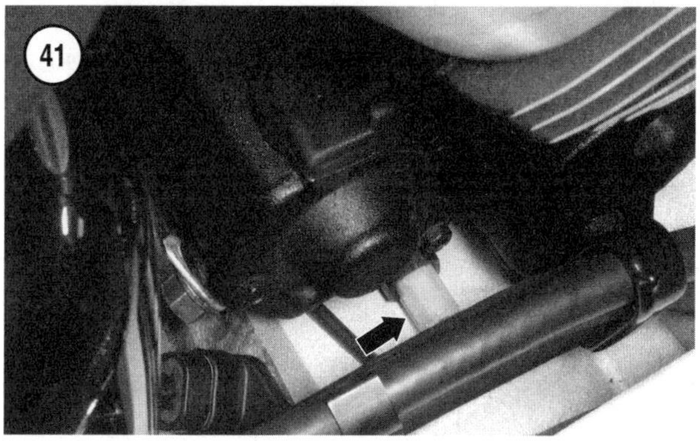

42

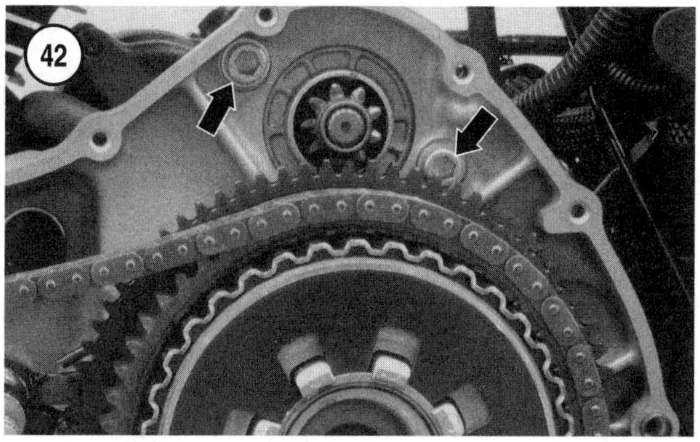

43

CAUTION
Do not operate the starter for more than five seconds at a time. Let it cool approximately ten seconds before operating it again.

Removal

1. Remove the left side cover as described in Chapter Fourteen.
2. Disconnect the negative battery cable as described in this chapter.
3. Remove the primary cover as described in Chapter Six.
4. Remove the rear exhaust pipe as described in Chapter Eight.
5. Slide back the rubber boot, then remove the nut (A, **Figure 40**) securing the positive cable end (B) to the starter terminal. Disconnect the positive cable from the starter.
6. Disconnect the solenoid electrical connector from the starter (**Figure 41**).
7. Remove the bolts and washers (**Figure 42**) that hold the starter to the left crankcase. Remove the starter and gasket from the right side.
8. Service the starter (**Figure 43**) as described in this section.

Installation

1. Install a new gasket onto the starter.
2. Install the starter and gasket into the crankcase.
3. Install the mounting bolts (**Figure 42**) and washers. Tighten the starter mounting bolts to 13-20 ft.-lb. (18-27 N•m).
4. Clean, then reconnect the electrical connectors at the starter. Tighten the positive cable retaining nut to 60-85 in.-lb. (6.8-9.6 N•m).
5. Install the primary cover as described in Chapter Six.
6. Install the rear exhaust pipe as described in Chapter Eight.
7. Reconnect the negative battery cable.

Disassembly

NOTE
*If servicing the starter solenoid, refer to the **Starter Solenoid** in this chapter.*

Refer to **Figure 44**. Refer to **Table 2** for specificatons.
1. Clean all debris from the starter.
2. Disconnect the field coil wire (**Figure 45**).
3. Loosen and remove the two starter housing throughbolts (A, **Figure 46**).

9

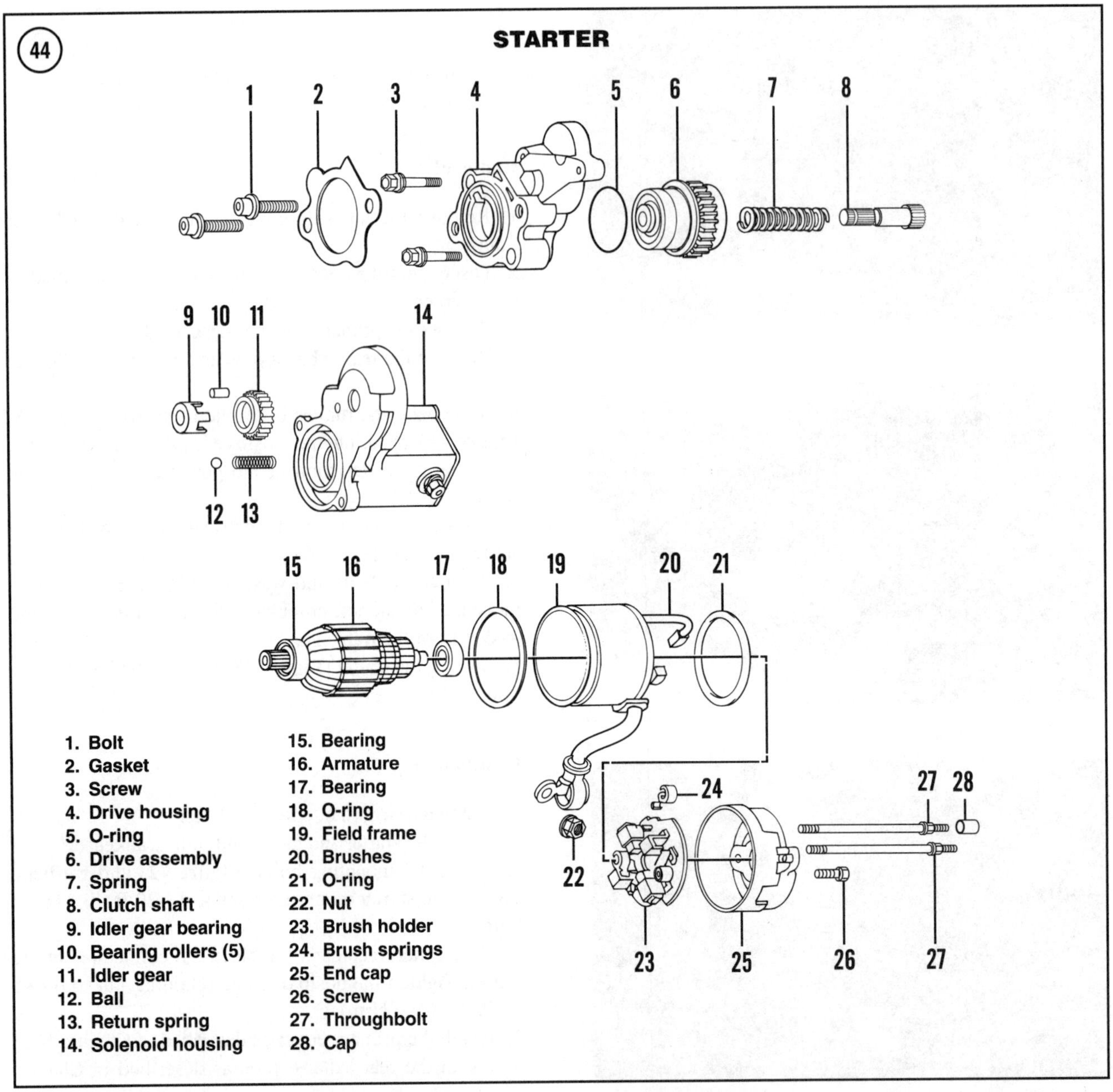

4. Separate the starter field and armature assembly (**Figure 47**) from the solenoid housing.

5. Remove the two screws (A, **Figure 48**) securing the end cap to the brush holder. Remove the end cap (B, **Figure 48**).

6. Lift the field coil brush springs out of their holders with a small hook and remove the brushes from their holders.

7. Slide the brush holder (**Figure 49**) off the commutator.

8. Separate the armature (**Figure 50**) from the field coil assembly.

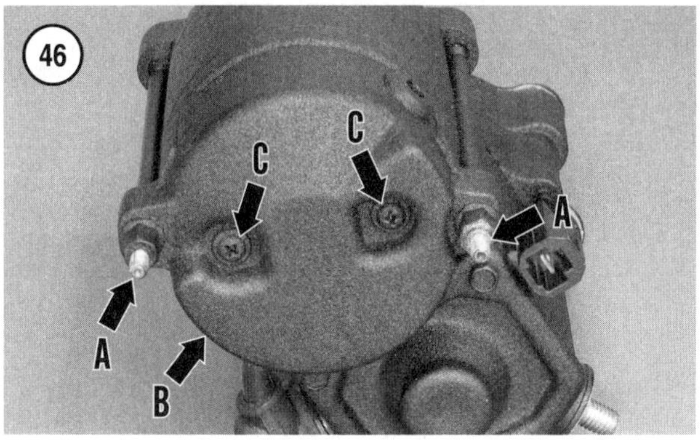

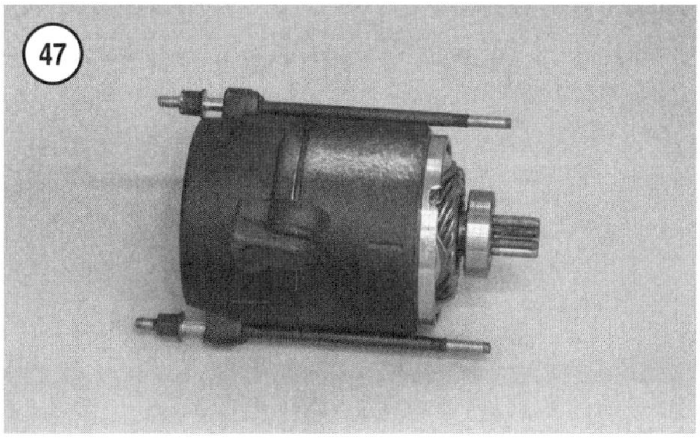

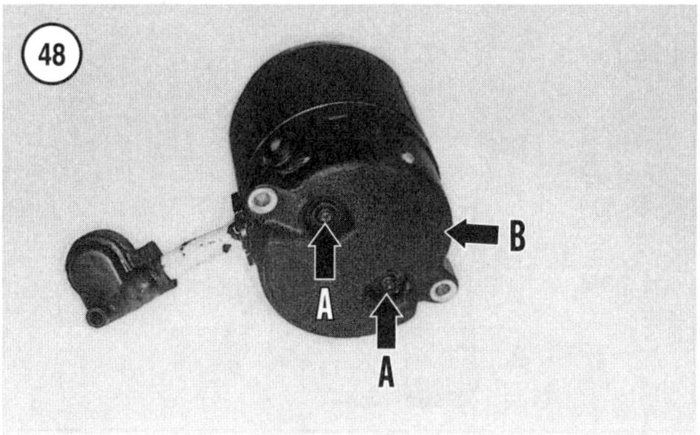

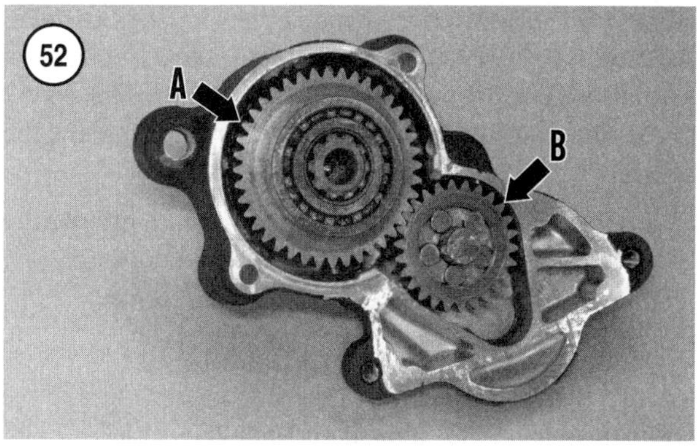

9. Remove the drive housing mounting screws (**Figure 51**).

10. Tap the drive housing and separate it from the starter (**Figure 52**).

11. Remove the ball and spring (**Figure 53**) from the solenoid housing.

12. Remove the drive assembly (A, **Figure 52**), idler gear (B) and the idler gear bearing assembly (**Figure 54**) from the drive housing.

13. Carefully pry the O-ring (**Figure 55**) out of the groove in the bottom of the drive housing.

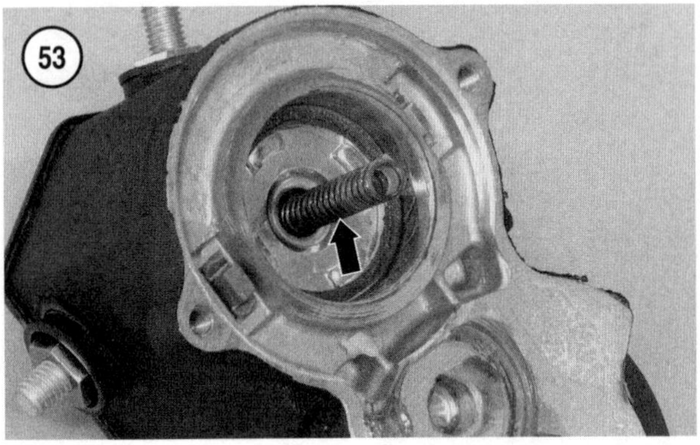

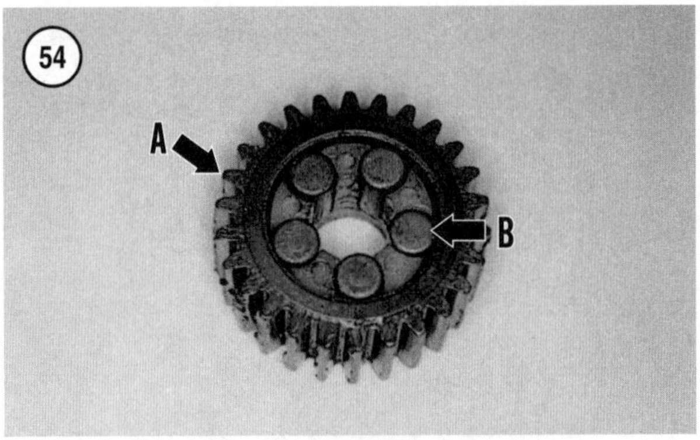

14. Inspect the starter assembly as described in this section.

Inspection

1. Clean the starter components. Do not clean the field coils or armature in any cleaning solution that could damage the insulation. Wipe these parts off with a clean rag. Likewise, do not soak the overrunning clutch in any cleaning solution as the chemicals could dissolve the lubrication within the clutch.

2. Measure the length of each brush with a vernier caliper (**Figure 56**, typical). If the length of any brush is less than the minimum length specification in **Table 2**, replace the brushes as a set of four. If necessary, refer to **Figure 57** (field coil) and **Figure 58** (brush holder), and replace the brushes as follows:

   a. The field coil brushes are in position. Unsolder the brushes soldered and remove the old brushes.

   b. Solder the new brushes in place with rosin core solder—do not use acid core solder.

3. Inspect the condition of the commutator (A, **Figure 59**). The mica in the commutator should be at least 0.008 in. (0.20 mm) undercut. If the mica undercut is less than this amount, undercut the mica with a piece of hacksaw blade to a depth of 1/32 in. (0.79 mm). This procedure can also be performed by a dealership or electrical repair shop with an undercutting machine. When undercutting mica, each groove must form a right angle. Do not cut the mica so that a thin edge is left next to the commutator segment. **Figure 60** shows the proper angle. After undercutting the mica, remove burrs by sanding the commutator lightly with crocus cloth.

4. Inspect the commutator copper bars for discoloration. If a pair of bars is discolored, grounded armature coils are indicated.

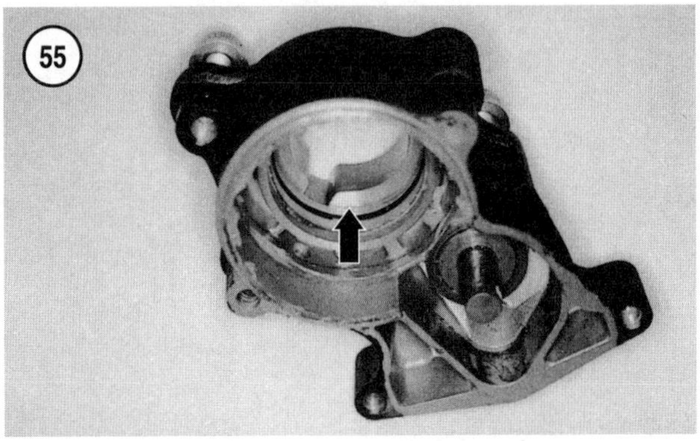

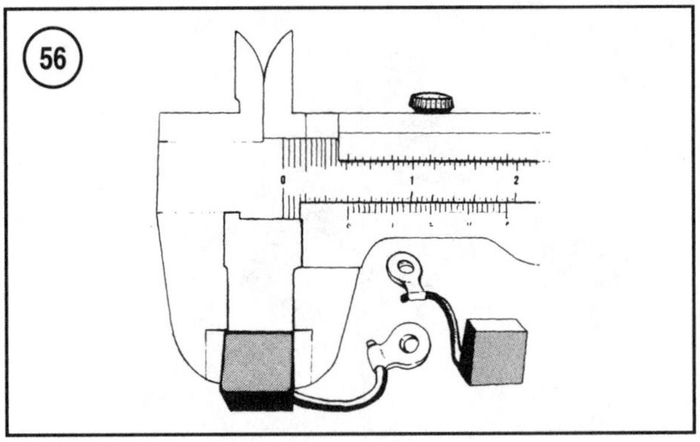

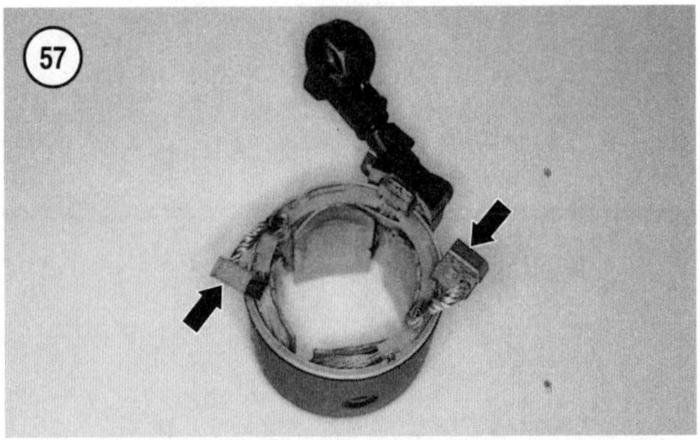

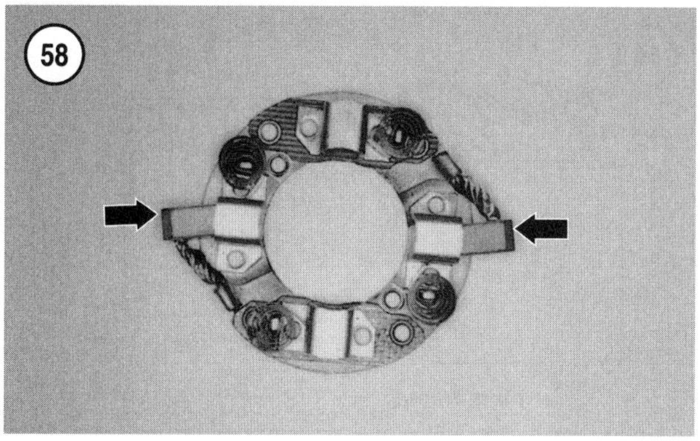

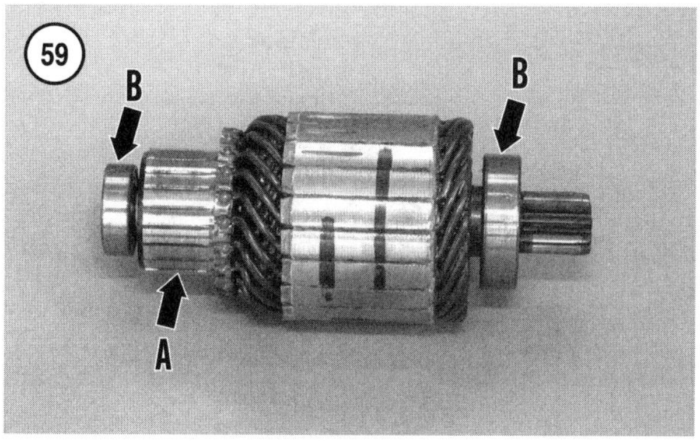

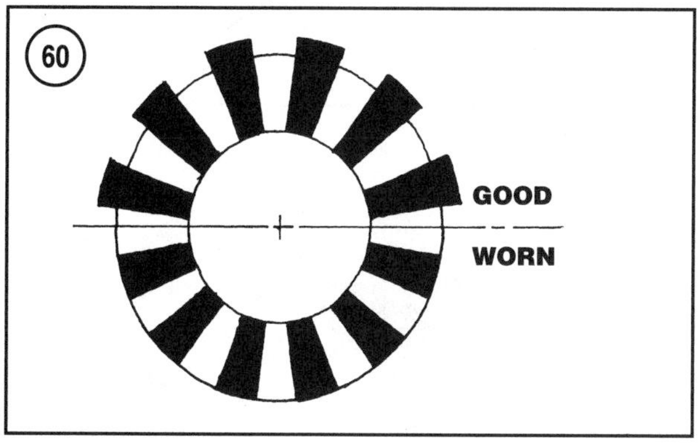

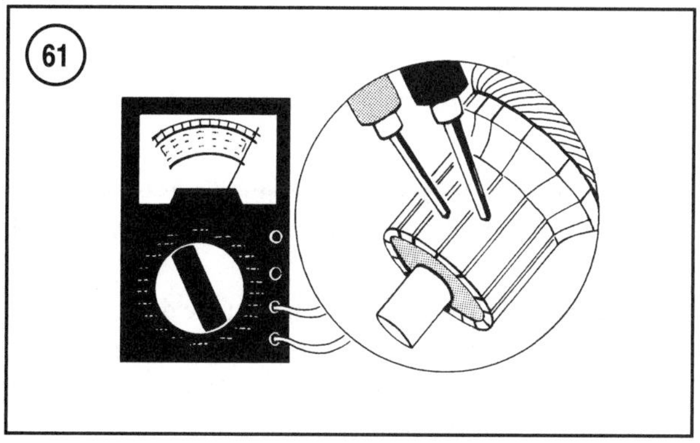

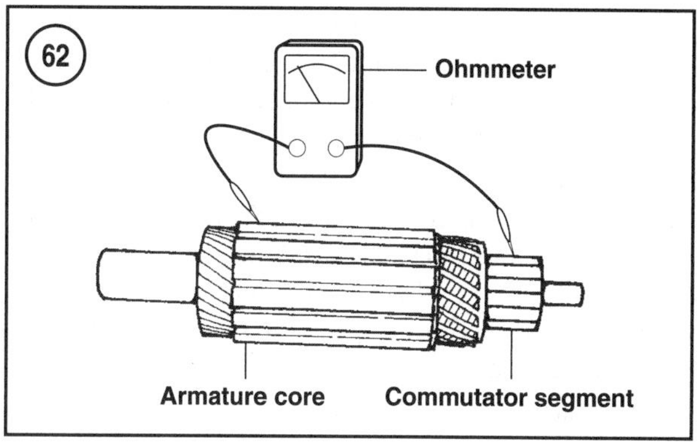

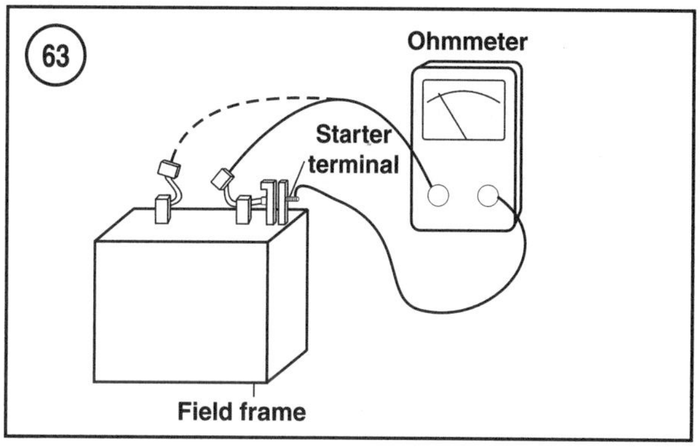

5. The armature can be checked for winding shorts using a growler. Refer this test to a dealership or electrical repair shop.

6. Place the armature in a lathe or between crankshaft centers and check commutator runout with a dial indicator. If runout exceeds the specification, true the commutator in a lathe. When truing the commutator to eliminate the out-of-round condition, make the cuts as light as possible. Replace the armature if the commutator outer diameter meets or is less than the minimum specification.

7. Use an ohmmeter and check for continuity between the commutator bars (**Figure 61**); there should be continuity between pairs of bars. If there is no continuity between pairs of bars, the armature is open. Replace the armature.

8. Connect an ohmmeter between any commutator bar and the armature core (**Figure 62**); there should be no continuity. If there is continuity, the armature is grounded. Replace the armature.

9. Connect an ohmmeter between the starter cable terminal and each field frame brush (**Figure 63**); there should be continuity. If there is no continuity at either brush, the field windings are open. Replace the field frame assembly.

10. Connect an ohmmeter between the field frame housing and each field frame brush (**Figure 64**); there should be no continuity. If there is continuity at either brush, the field windings are grounded. Replace the field frame assembly.

11. Connect an ohmmeter between the brush holder plate and each insulated brush holder (**Figure 65**); there should be no continuity. If there is continuity at either brush holder, the brush holder or plate is damaged. Replace the brush holder plate.

12. Service the armature bearings as follows:

CAUTION
Note that the bearings installed on the armature shaft have different part numbers. When replacing the bearings, identify the old bearings before removing them in relationship to their position on the armature. This information can then be used to make sure the new bearings are installed correctly.

a. Check the bearings (B, **Figure 59**) on the armature shaft. If worn or damaged, remove and install new bearings with a bearing splitter and a press.
b. Check the bearing bores in the end cap and solenoid housing. Replace the cap or housing if this area is excessively worn or cracked.

13. The drive assembly is bolted onto the end of the solenoid housing. Inspect it as follows:
a. Check the teeth on the idler gear (A, **Figure 54**) and drive assembly (A, **Figure 66**) for wear or damage.
b. Check for chipped or worn bearing rollers (B, **Figure 54**). Damaged rollers will cause the pinion to turn roughly in the overrunning direction.
c. Check the idler gear shaft in the drive housing for excessive wear or damage.
d. Replace worn or damaged parts as required.

14. Check the pinion gear teeth (B, **Figure 66**) for cracks, deep scoring or excessive wear.

15. Check the drive assembly bearings (C, **Figure 66**) for excessive wear or damage.

64

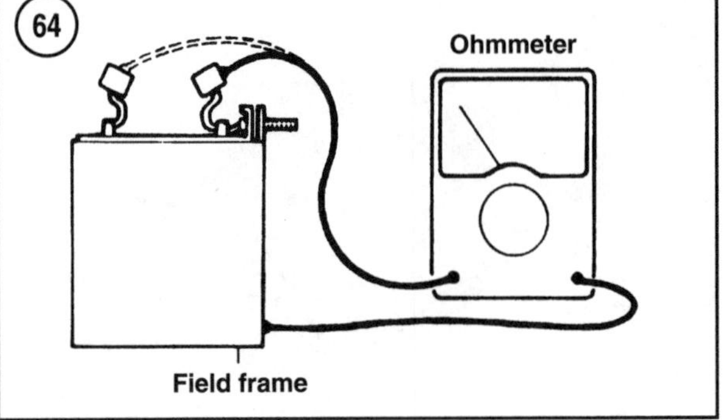

65

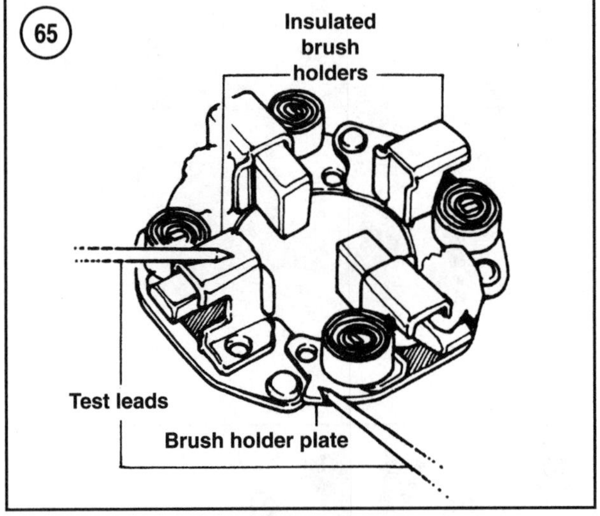

66

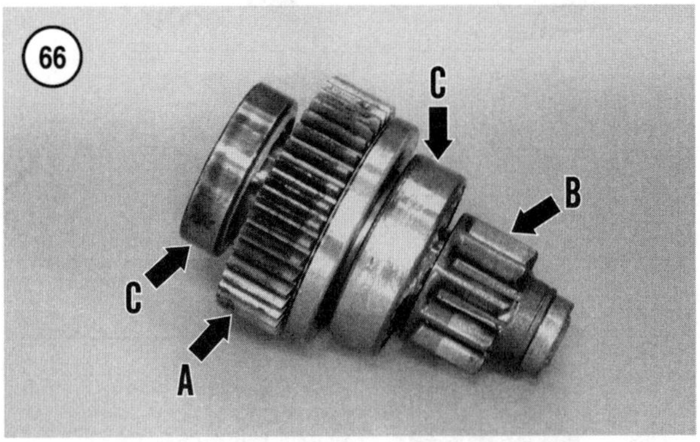

Assembly

1. Prior to assembly, perform the *Inspection* procedure to make sure all worn or defective parts have been repaired or replaced. Thoroughly clean all parts before assembly.

2. Apply a thin film of Lubriplate 110 onto the drive housing O-ring and insert the O-ring into the groove in the bottom of the housing (**Figure 55**). Make sure the O-ring seats squarely in the groove.

3. After the drive assembly components have been cleaned and dried, lubricate all components with Lubriplate 110.

4. Place the idler gear onto the shaft in the drive housing. Then place the idler bearing cage in the gear so that the open cage end faces toward the solenoid; see B, **Figure 54**. Install the bearing pins in the cage.

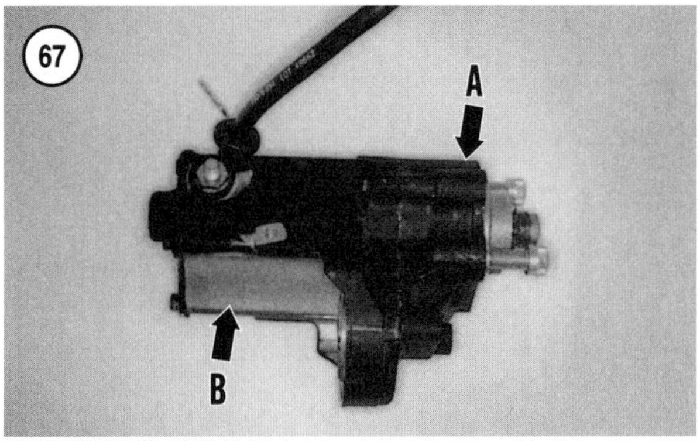

5. Insert the drive assembly (A, **Figure 52**) into the drive housing.
6. Drop the ball into the shaft and slide the spring (**Figure 53**) onto the solenoid plunger shaft.
7. Align the drive housing (A, **Figure 67**) with the solenoid housing (B) and assemble both housings. Secure the drive housing with the screws (**Figure 51**). Tighten the screws securely.
8. Pack the armature bearings with Lubriplate 110. Then install the armature (**Figure 68**) onto the solenoid housing.

NOTE
*The armature is not shown in **Figure 69** for clarity.*

9. Note the slot in the solenoid housing rim (**Figure 69**) and the boss on the field frame (**Figure 70**). Install the field frame around the armature and into the solenoid housing while inserting the boss into the slot.
10. Install the brush plate (**Figure 71**) into the end of the frame and install the four brushes so that they ride on the commutator.
11. Install the two positive brushes as follows:
   a. The positive brushes are soldered to the field coil assembly.
   b. Pull a positive brush out of its brush holder. A piece of wire bent to form a small hook on one end can be used to access the brushes.
   c. Insert the positive brush into its brush holder.
   d. Release the spring so that tension is applied against the brush.
   e. Repeat for the other positive brush.
12. Install the two negative brushes as follows:
   a. The negative brushes are mounted on the brush holder.
   b. Pull a negative brush out of its brush holder. A piece of wire bent to form a small hook on one end can be used to access the brushes.
   c. Insert the negative brush into its brush holder.

9

72

STARTER SOLENOID

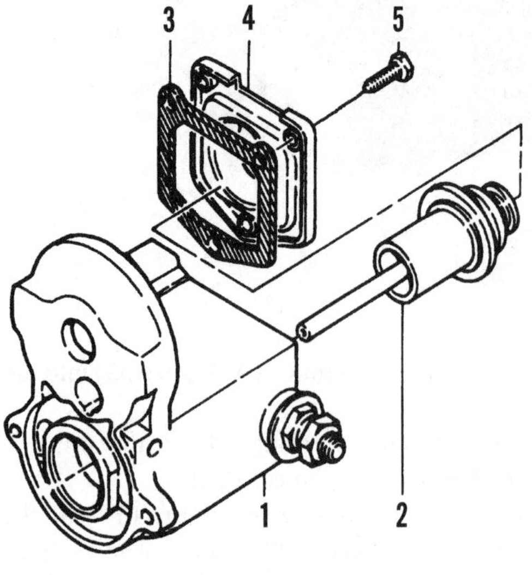

1. Solenoid housing
2. Plunger
3. Gasket
4. Cover
5. Bolt

73

d. Release the spring so that tension is applied against the brush.

e. Repeat for the other negative brush.

13. Align the slot in the end cap with the terminal in the frame and install the end cap (B, **Figure 46**). Install the throughbolts (A, **Figure 46**) through the starter assembly. Tighten the starter through- bolts to 39-65 in.-lb. (4.4-7.3 N•m).

14. Secure the brush holder to the rear cover with the two screws (C, **Figure 46**) and washers. Tighten the screws securely.

74

75

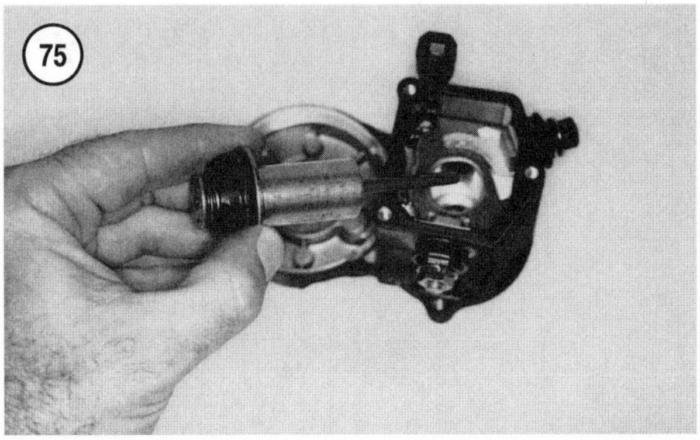

76

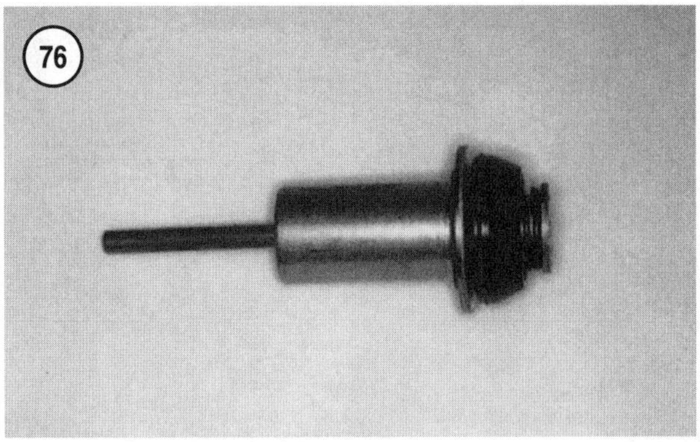

77

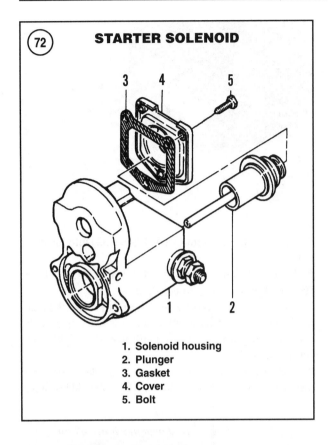

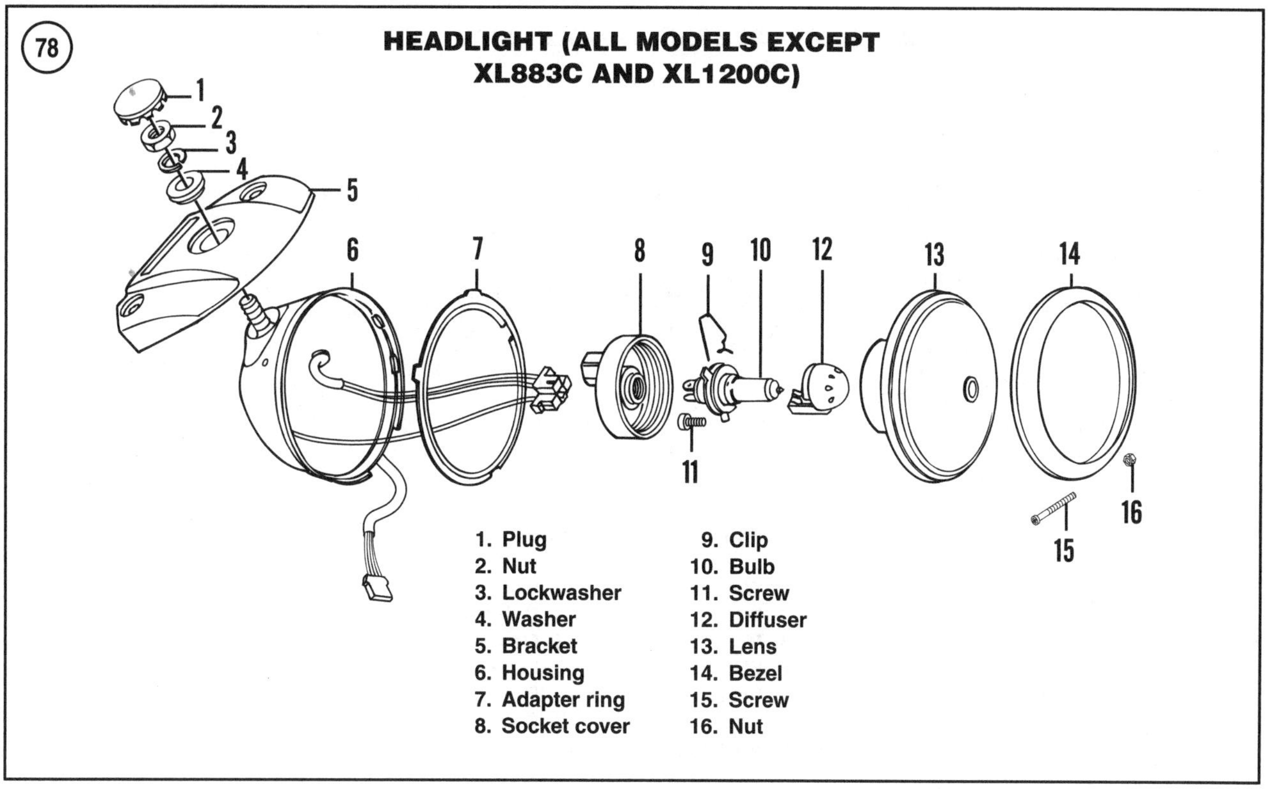

15. Reconnect the solenoid wire (**Figure 45**).

STARTER SOLENOID

Disassembly/Reassembly

Refer to **Figure 72**.

CAUTION
*Do not tighten the inner retaining nut (**Figure 73**) unless the plunger is removed. Otherwise, the internal contact may move and be damaged during operation.*

1. Remove the starter as described in this chapter.
2. Separate the solenoid (B, **Figure 67**) from the starter assembly as described in this chapter.
3. Remove the screws and washers that hold the cover to the solenoid housing. Then remove the cover and gasket (**Figure 74**).
4. Remove the solenoid plunger from the solenoid housing (**Figure 75**).
5. Inspect the plunger (**Figure 76**) for excessive wear or damage.
6. Inspect the solenoid housing (**Figure 77**) for wear, cracks or other damage. The solenoid housing is not available separately.
7. Make sure the flat surface of each internal contact is parallel to the end of the housing. Loosen the retaining nut and reposition the contact as needed.
8. Reassemble by reversing the steps and making sure the solenoid plunger shaft engages the spring in the drive assembly shaft.

LIGHTING SYSTEM

The lighting system consists of a headlight, taillight/brake light combination, turn signals, indicator lights and meter illumination lights.

Always use the correct bulb wattage. Refer to **Table 3** for bulb specifications.

Headlight

Replacement

Refer to **Figure 78** or **Figure 79**.

WARNING
If the headlight has just burned out or has just been turned off, it will be hot. Do not touch the bulb until it cools.

79

HEADLIGHT (XL888C AND XL1200C MODELS)

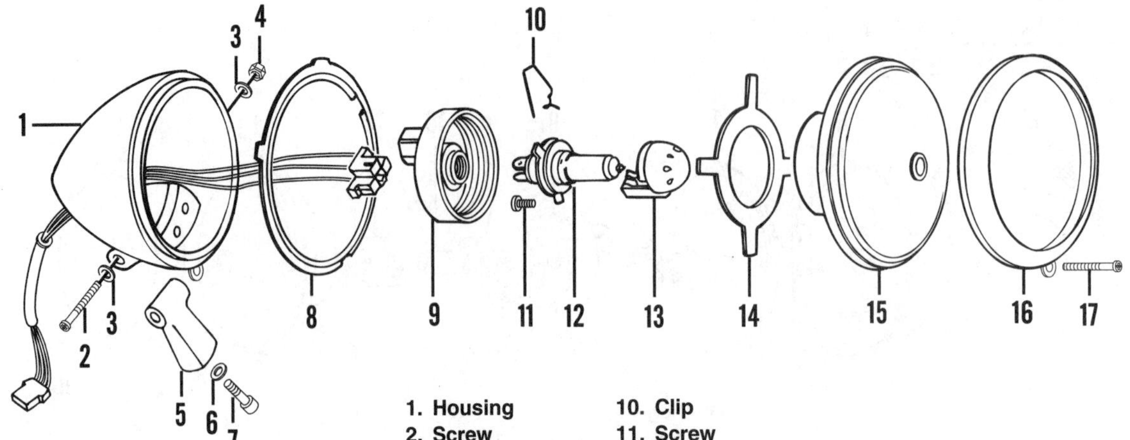

1. Housing
2. Screw
3. Washer
4. Nut
5. Mount
6. Washer
7. Screw
8. Adapter ring
9. Socket cover
10. Clip
11. Screw
12. Bulb
13. Diffuser
14. Gasket
15. Lens
16. Bezel
17. Screw

1. Remove the bezel retaining screw, then remove the trim ring (**Figure 80**).
2. Carefully pry the headlight lens assembly from the housing.
3. Depress the locking tabs on both sides of the electrical connector (**Figure 81**). Then hold the locking tabs down and pull the connector off the headlight terminals. Remove the headlight lens assembly.
4. Remove the socket cover (A, **Figure 82**) from the back of the headlight lens assembly.
5. Depress the ends of the bulb retaining clip (A, **Figure 83**) and unhook the clip from the headlight assembly slots. Pivot the retaining clip away from the bulb.

CAUTION
*When handling a quartz halogen bulb (**Figure 84**), do not touch the bulb glass. Traces of oil on the bulb drastically reduce the life of the bulb. Clean oil from the bulb glass with alcohol or lacquer thinner.*

6. Lift the bulb (B, **Figure 83**) out of the headlight lens assembly.
7. Replace the retaining clip (A, **Figure 83**) if damaged.
8. Install by reversing the preceding steps while noting the following:

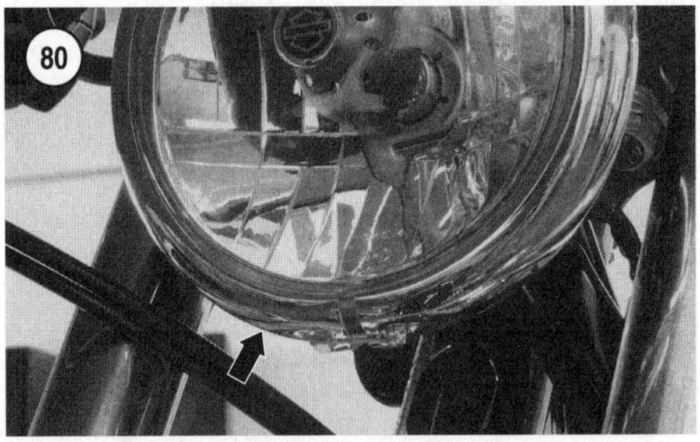
80

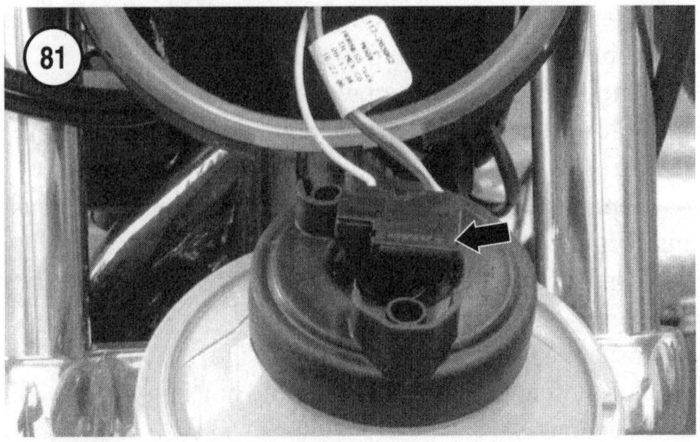
81

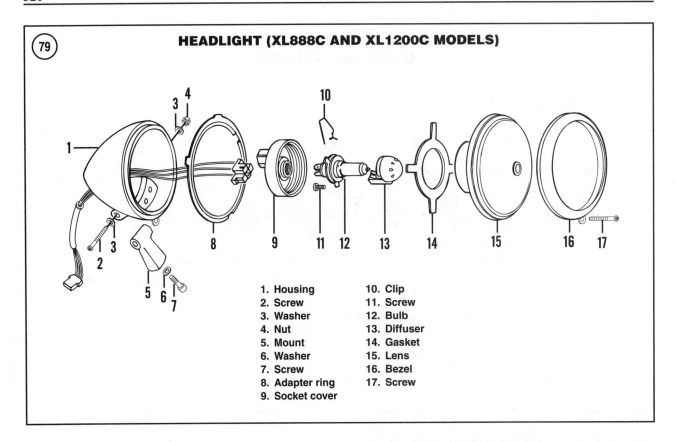

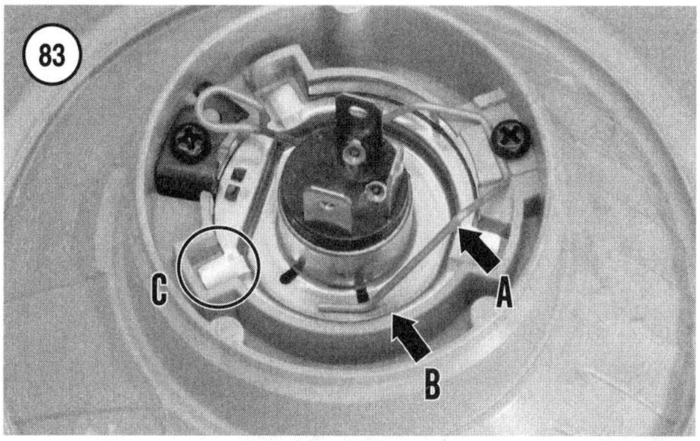

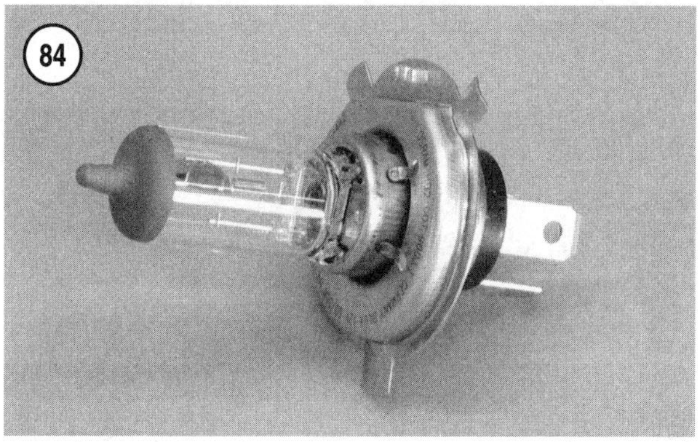

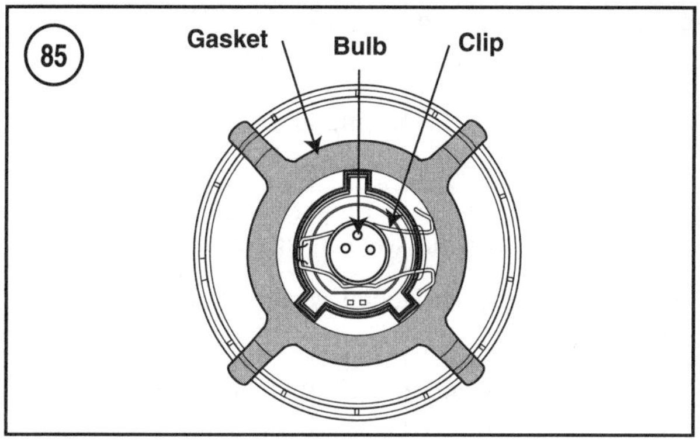

a. On XL883C and XL1200C models, reinstall the gasket (**Figure 85**), if removed, so the small notch properly fits around the bulb holder base.
b. Install the bulb and make sure the tabs on the bulb fit into the slots in the lens bulb holder; see C, **Figure 83**.
c. Position the socket cover with the TOP mark (**Figure 86**) located at the top. This ensures that the vent holes in the socket cover are positioned at the bottom. Push it on until it is completely seated.
d. Make sure the electrical connector is free of corrosion and that the wiring in the headlight housing will not be pinched when the headlight lens is installed.
e. Make sure the electrical connector is pushed on tightly.
f. Check that the headlight operates properly before riding the motorcycle.
g. Check headlight adjustment as described in this section.

9

Adjustment

Adjust the headlight horizontally and vertically as follows or according to local Department of Motor Vehicle regulations if they differ.

1. Park the motorcycle on a level surface approximately 25 ft. (7.6 m) from a wall (**Figure 87**).
2. Make sure the tires are inflated to the correct pressure when performing this adjustment.
3. Have an assistant of the same approximate weight as the primary rider sit on the seat.
4. Draw a horizontal line on a wall that is 35 in. (889 mm) above the floor.
5. Aim the headlight at the wall and turn on the headlight. Switch the headlight to high beam.
6. Check the headlight beam alignment. The broad, flat pattern of light (main beam of light) should be centered on

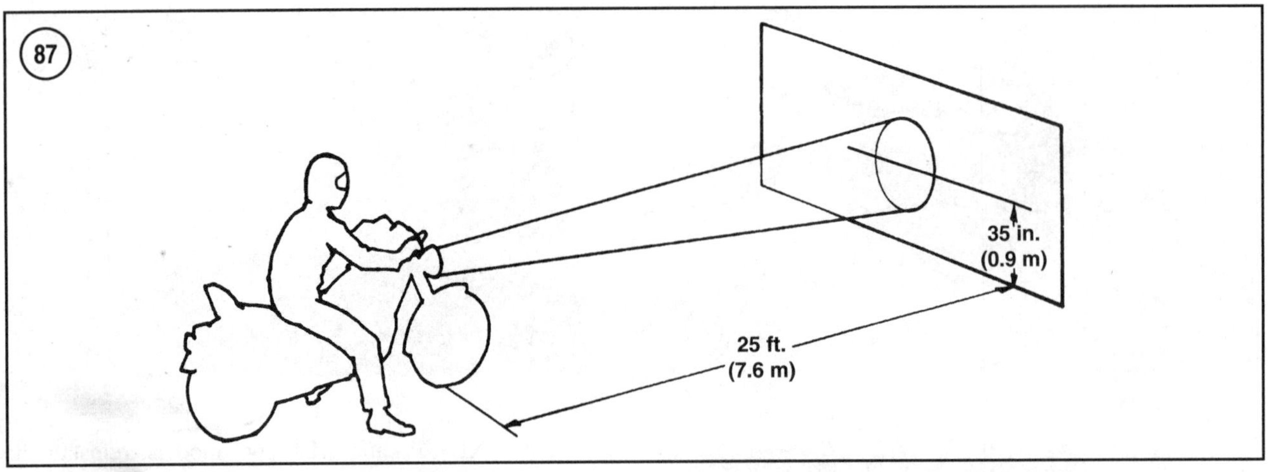

the horizontal line (equal area of light above and below line).

7. Check the headlight beam lateral alignment. With the headlight beam pointed straight ahead (centered), there should be an equal area of light to the left and right of center.

8A. On XL883, XL883L, XL883R, XL1200L and XL1200R models, if the beam is not aligned as described in Steps 6 and/or 7, adjust it by performing the following.

   a. Remove the plug on top of the headlight bracket (**Figure 88**).
   b. Loosen the mounting nut (**Figure 89**).
   c. Tilt or rotate the headlight assembly to adjust the beam position.
   d. Tighten the mounting nut to 120-240 in.-lb. (14-27 N•m).
   e. Install the plug (**Figure 88**).

8B. On XL883C and XL1200C models, if the beam is not aligned as described in Step 6 and/or Step 7, adjust it by performing the following.

   a. Loosen the vertical mounting bolt (A, **Figure 90**).

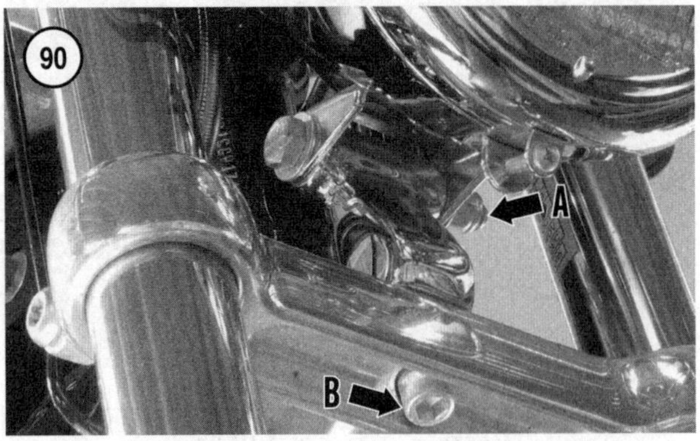

   b. By hand, tilt the headlight assembly up or down to adjust the beam vertically.
   c. When the beam is properly adjusted, tighten the mounting bolt to 30-35 ft.-lb. (41-47 N•m).
   d. Loosen the horizontal mounting bolt (B, **Figure 90**).
   e. Move the headlight left or right to adjust the beam horizontally.

91

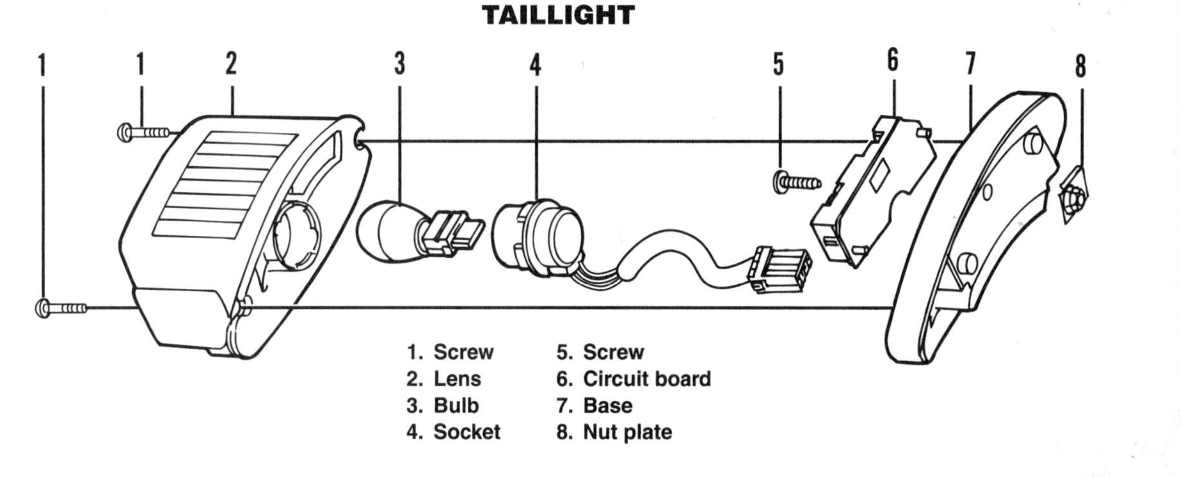
TAILLIGHT
1 1 2 3 4 5 6 7 8
1. Screw
2. Lens
3. Bulb
4. Socket
5. Screw
6. Circuit board
7. Base
8. Nut plate

92

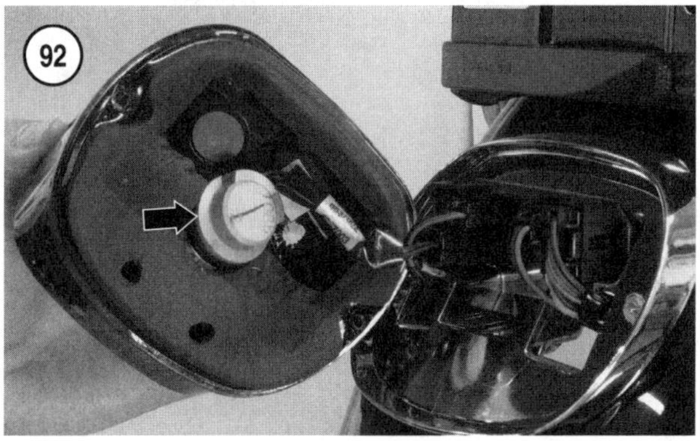

93

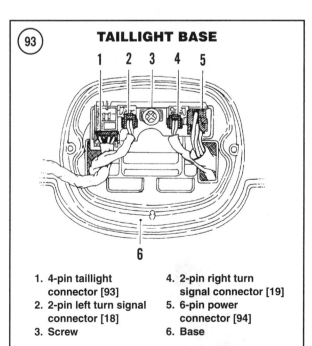

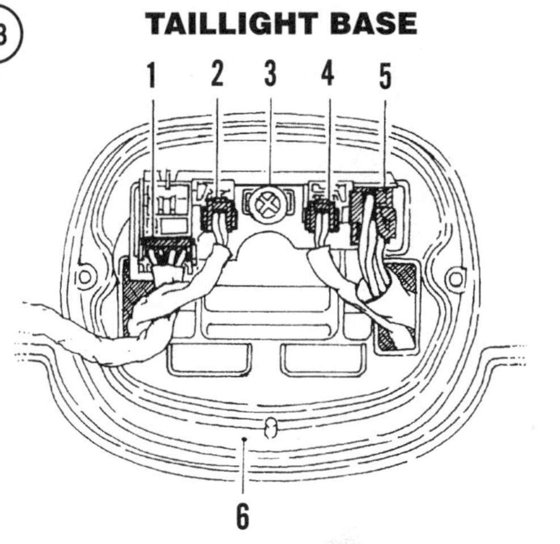
TAILLIGHT BASE
1 2 3 4 5
6
1. 4-pin taillight connector [93]
2. 2-pin left turn signal connector [18]
3. Screw
4. 2-pin right turn signal connector [19]
5. 6-pin power connector [94]
6. Base

f. When the beam is properly adjusted, tighten the mounting bolt to 30-35 ft.-lb. (41-47 N•m).

Taillight/Brake Light Replacement

WARNING
Make sure the taillight and brake light operate correctly before operating the motorcycle.

Refer to **Figure 91**.

1. Remove the two mounting screws and remove the lens assembly from the taillight base.
2. Turn the bulb socket (**Figure 92**) one-quarter counterclockwise and pull the socket from the lens.
3. Remove the bulb from the socket.
4. Apply a coat of dielectric grease to the new bulb and insert the bulb into the socket.
5. Install the bulb socket into the lens assembly.
6. Install the lens. Tighten the taillight lens mounting screws to 20-24 in.-lb. (2.3-2.7 N•m).

Taillight Base Replacement

WARNING
Make sure the taillight and brake light operate correctly before operating the motorcycle.

Refer to **Figure 93**.

1. Remove the two mounting screws and remove the lens assembly from the taillight base.
2. Depress the locking tab and remove the 4-pin taillight connector (1, **Figure 93**) from the circuit board in the base.

3. Use the terminal pick (part No. HD-39621-28) to depress the locking tab on the top of each remaining connector and remove the left- and right- turn signal connectors and the power connector from the circuit board in the base.
4. Remove the pin housing/circuit board mounting screw from the base.
5. Lift the pin housing (A, **Figure 94**) from the circuit board (B), and then remove the circuit board from the base.
6. Remove the two nuts and bolts, and then remove the base from the fender.
7. Installation is the reverse of removal. Note the following:
   a. Tighten the base mounting screws to 45-48 in.-lb. (5.1-5.4 N•m).
   b. Make sure the circuit board snaps into place in the base.

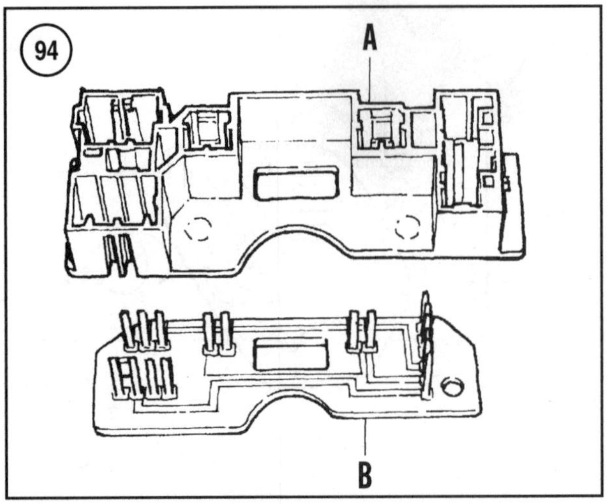

Turn Signal Bulb Replacement

WARNING
Make sure the turn signals operate correctly before operating the motorcycle.

1. Using a coin or a suitable screwdriver, twist the notch in the turn signal lens to dislodge the lens from the housing.
2. Push in the bulb, rotate it and remove it.
3. Install a new bulb.
4. Push in the lens and make sure the latches fully engage the housing.

Front Turn Signal Housing Removal/Installation

WARNING
Make sure the turn signals operate correctly before operating the motorcycle.

NOTE
Always disarm the optional security system prior to removing the Maxi- fuse or the alarm will sound.

1. Remove the left side cover as described in Chapter Fourteen.
2. Push the Maxi-fuse cover latches together. Hold the fuse cover (A, **Figure 95**) and pull the fuse holder (B) out of the cover.
3. Remove the Maxi-fuse (**Figure 96**) from the fuse holder.
4. Remove the fuel tank as described in Chapter Eight.

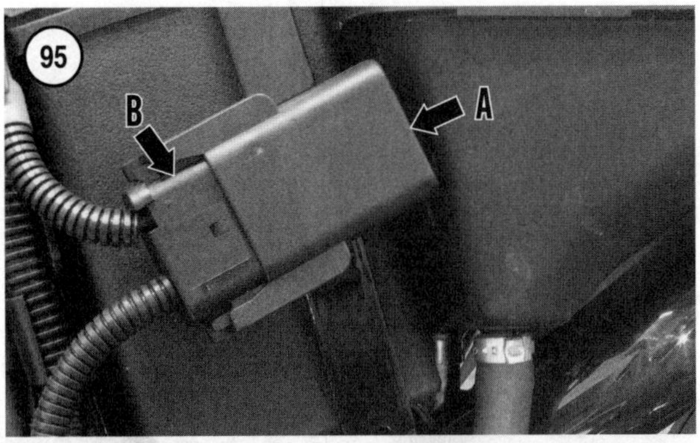

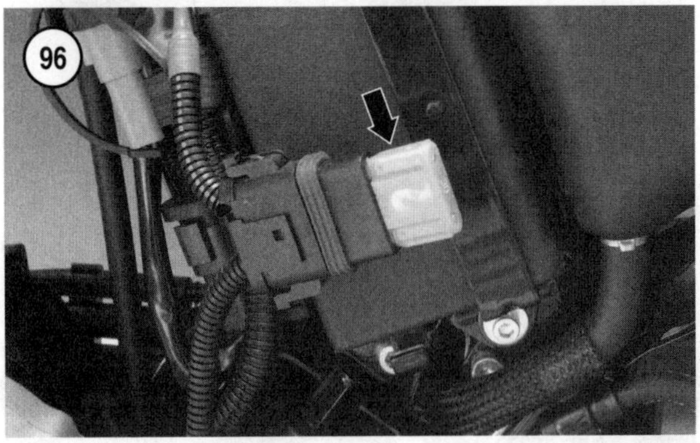

5. On XL883C and XL1200C models, remove the cover on the back of the handlebar riser.
6. Push the turn signal connector unit (**Figure 97**) forward to disengage it from the frame bracket. Disconnect the turn signal connector.
7. Refer to *Electrical Connectors* in this chapter and remove the appropriate turn signal terminals (refer to the wiring diagram at the end of this manual).

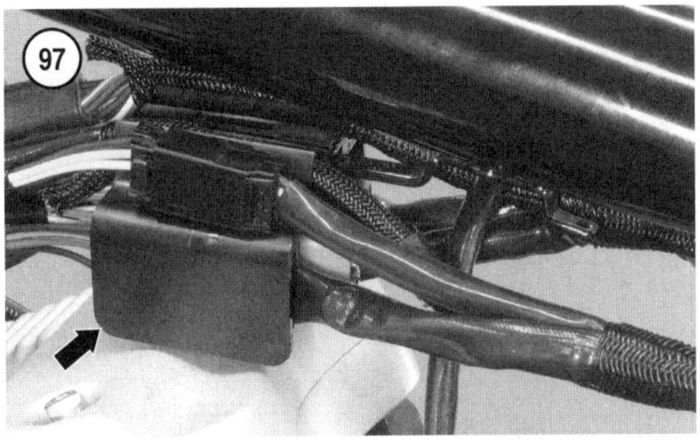

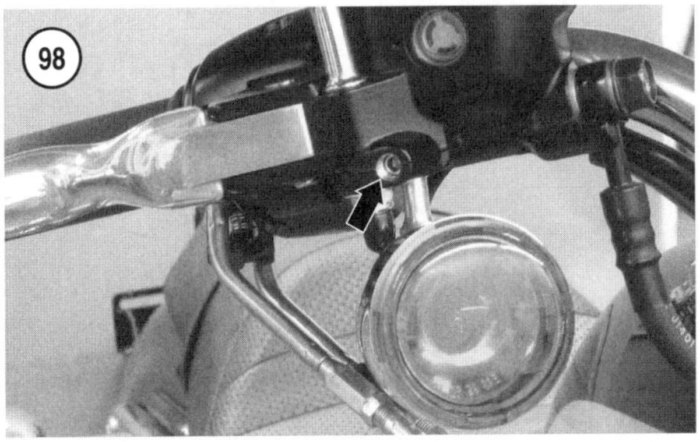

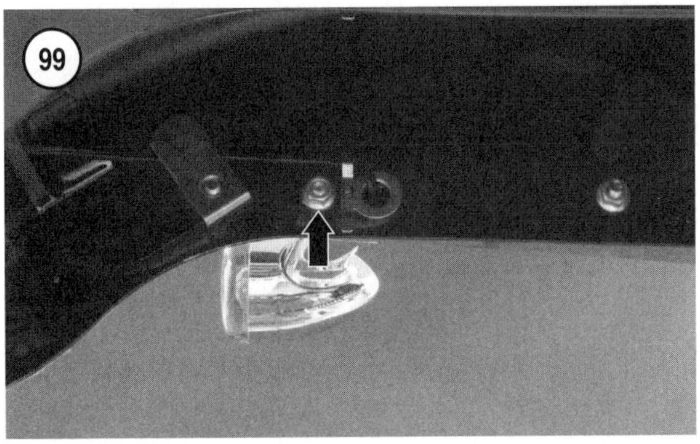

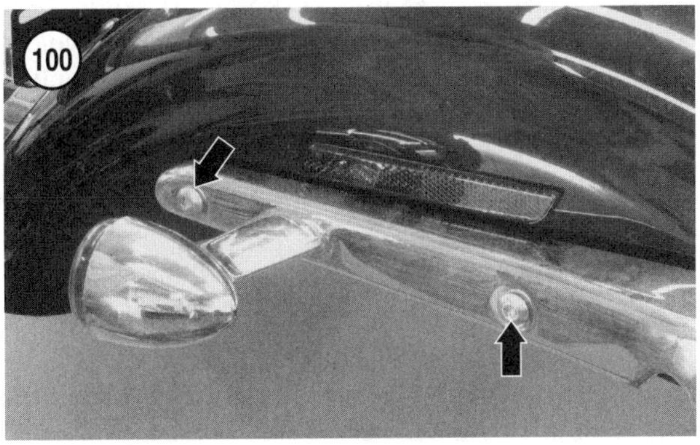

NOTE
Be prepared to catch the turn signal when loosening the screw in Step 8.

8. Loosen the Allen head screw in the handlebar lever housing (**Figure 98**) and separate the turn signal housing and ball stud from the handlebar lever housing.
9. Note the routing of the wires, then remove the turn signal.
10. If necessary, remove the ball stud from the turn signal housing.
11. Reverse the removal steps to install the turn signal housing while noting the following:
   a. Cut the wires on the new turn signal to the same length as the old turn signal wires. Refer to *Electrical Connectors* in this chapter to install new wire terminals.
   b. If removed, install the ball stud in the turn signal housing and tighten to 96-156 in.-lb. (11-17 N•m).
   c. Tighten the socket-head screw (**Figure 98**) to 96-156 in.-lb. (11-17 N•m).

9

Rear Turn Signal Housing Removal/Installation

WARNING
Be sure the turn signals operate correctly before operating the motorcycle.

NOTE
Always disarm the optional security system prior to removing the Maxi- fuse or the alarm will sound.

1. Remove the left side cover as described in Chapter Fourteen.
2. Push the Maxi-fuse cover latches together. Hold the fuse cover (A, **Figure 95**) and pull the fuse holder (B) out of the cover.
3. Remove the Maxi-fuse (**Figure 96**) from the fuse holder.
4. Remove the seat as described in Chapter Fourteen.
5. Remove the two mounting screws (1, **Figure 91**) and remove the lens assembly from the taillight base (7).
6. Depress the locking tab, and remove the 4-pin taillight connector (1, **Figure 93**) from the circuit board in the base.
7. Note the location of the turn signal connectors in **Figure 93** and unplug the appropriate connector.
8. Remove the retaining nut on the turn signal mounting stud inside the rear fender (**Figure 99**).
9. Detach the turn signal wire from the retaining clamps.
10. Remove the rear strut cover mounting bolts and washers (**Figure 100**), then remove the strut cover with the turn signal.

(101) **INDICATOR LIGHTS (XL883C AND XL1200C MODELS)**

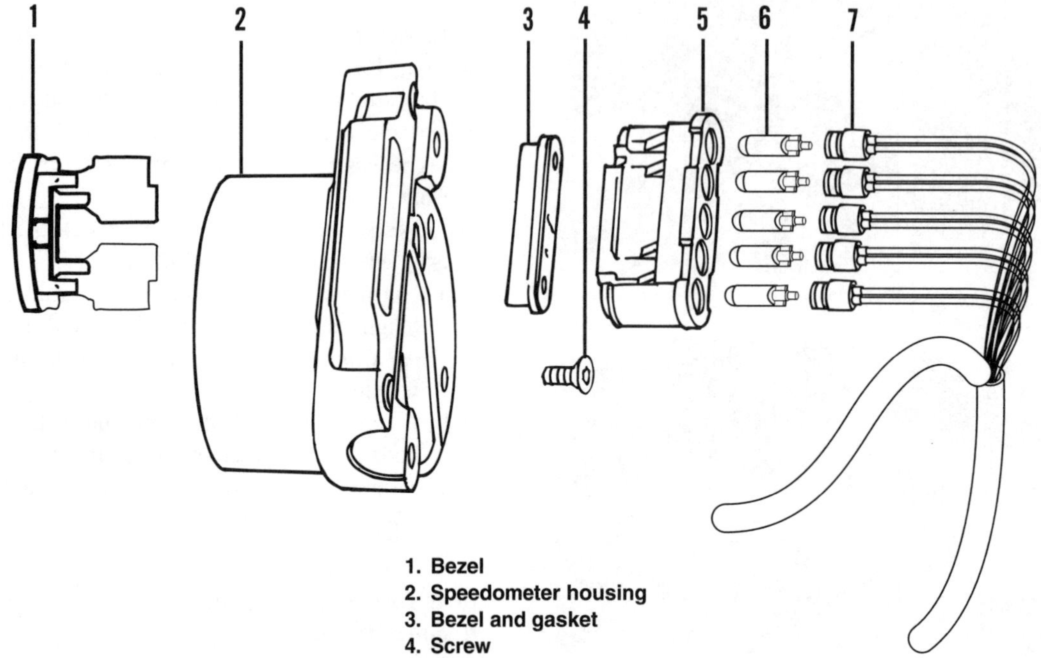

1. Bezel
2. Speedometer housing
3. Bezel and gasket
4. Screw
5. Bulb housing
6. Bulb
7. Sockets

11. Unscrew the strut, then separate the turn signal from the strut cover.

12. Reverse the removal steps to install the turn signal housing while noting the following:
   a. Cut the wires on the new turn signal to the same length as the old turn signal wires. Refer to *Electrical Connectors* in this chapter to install new wire terminals.
   b. Tighten the turn signal stud to 132-216 in.-lb. (15-24 N•m).
   c. Tighten the strut cover bolts (**Figure 100**) to 132-216 in.-lb. (15-24 N•m).
   d. Tighten the turn signal stud inner nut (**Figure 99**) to 132-216 in.-lb. (15-24 N•m).
   e. Check for proper turn signal operation before operating the motorcycle.

Indicator Lights Replacement

A panel of indicator lights adjacent to the speedometer provides information concerning the turn signals, high beam, neutral position and oil pressure.

1. Remove the Maxi-fuse as described in this chapter.
2. On XL883C and XL1200C models, remove the fuel tank as described in Chapter Eight.
3. On XL883C and XL1200C models, remove the cover on the rear of the handlebar riser.

CAUTION
Hold the speedometer assembly when performing Step 4 to prevent damage to it or adjacent parts.

4. On XL883, XL883L, XL883R, XL1200L and XL1200R models, remove the front handlebar holder bolts, which also secure the speedometer mounting bracket.
5. From the back of the bulb housing, pull out the wire lead of the bulb requiring replacement (**Figure 101** or **Figure 102**).
6. Pull out the indicator bulb, then install the new bulb.
7. Reverse the removal steps for installation while noting the following:
   a. Lubricate the socket with alcohol or glass cleaner before inserting it into the bulb housing.

102

INDICATOR LIGHTS (XL883, L, R AND XL1200L, R MODELS)

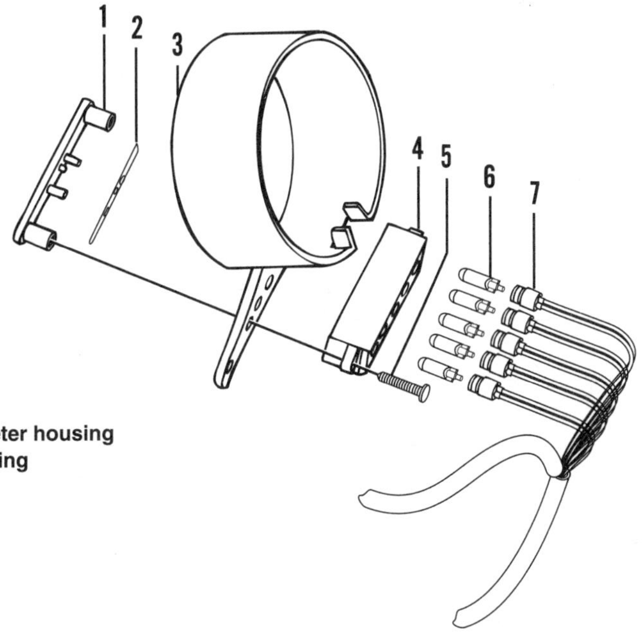

1. Bezel
2. Gasket
3. Speedometer housing
4. Bulb housing
5. Screw
6. Bulb
7. Sockets

103

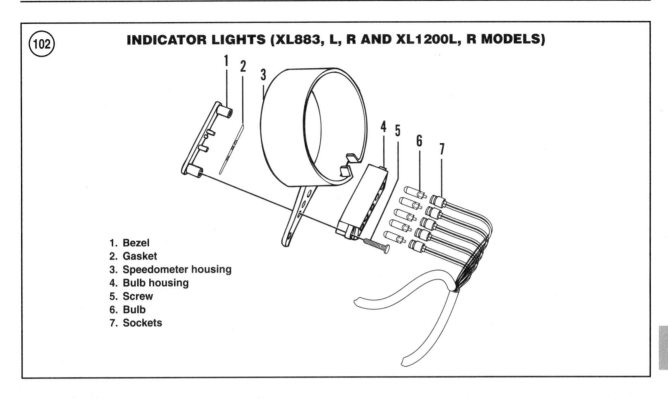

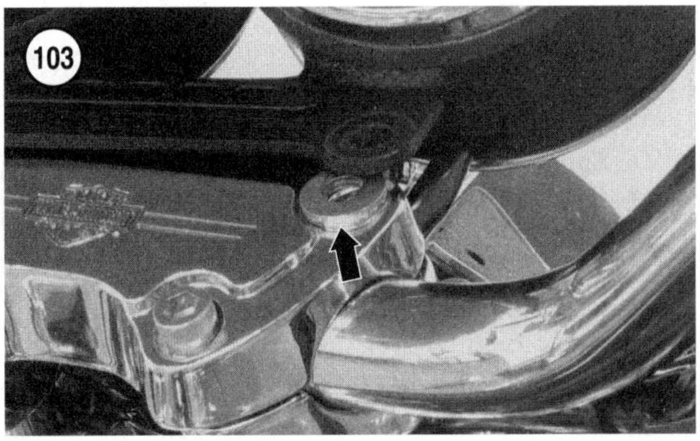

b. On XL883, XL883L, XL883R, XL1200L and XL1200R models, make sure to install the spacer between the handlebar holder and speedometer bracket (**Figure 103**) for each bolt. Tighten the bolts to 12-18 ft.-lb. (17-24 N•m).

SWITCHES

Testing

Test switches for continuity by using an ohmmeter or a self-powered test light (see Chapter One) at the switch connector plug and operating the switch in each of its operating positions. Compare the results with the switch operating diagrams included in the wiring diagram located at the end of this manual.

For example, **Figure 104** shows the continuity diagram for a typical ignition switch. It shows which terminals should show continuity when the switch is in a given position. When the ignition switch is in the *ignition* position, there should be continuity between the red/black, red and red/gray terminals. Note the line on the continuity diagram. An ohmmeter connected between these three terminals should indicate little or no resistance, or a test light should light. When the starter switch is *off*, there should be no continuity between the same terminals. Replace the switch or button if it does not perform properly.

When testing the switches, note the following:

1. Check the battery as described in this chapter. Charge or replace the battery if necessary.

2. Disconnect the negative battery cable as described in this chapter before checking the continuity of any switch.

3. Detach all connectors located between the switch and the electrical circuit.

4. When separating two connectors, pull on the connector housings and not the wires.

5. After locating a defective circuit, check the connectors to make sure they are clean and properly connected. Check all wires going into a connector housing to make sure each wire is positioned properly and the wire end is not loose.

(104) **IGNITION SWITCH (TYPICAL)**

Position \ Switch	Red/black	Red	Red/gray
Off		●	
Accessory		●	●
Ignition	●	●	●

(105) **HANDLEBAR SWITCH (LEFT SIDE)**

1. Upper housing
2. Screw
3. Switch-headlight dimmer and horn
4. Electrical connector
5. Switch-left turn signal
6. Lower housing
7. Screw

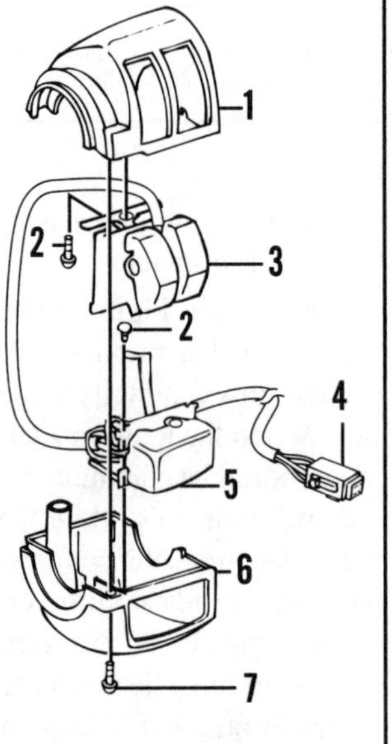

(106) **HANDLEBAR SWITCH (RIGHT SIDE)**

1. Upper housing
2. Screw
3. Switch-engine stop and engine start
4. Clip
5. Switch-stop lamp
6. Spring clip
7. Electrical connector
8. Switch-right turn signal
9. Lower housing
10. Screw

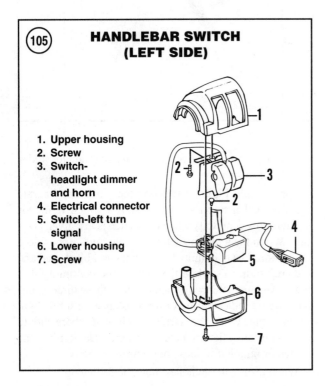

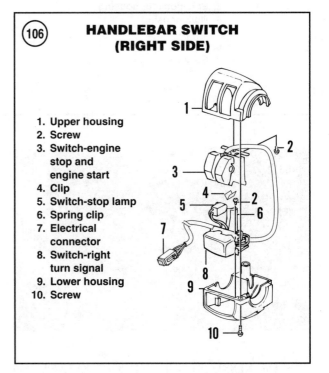

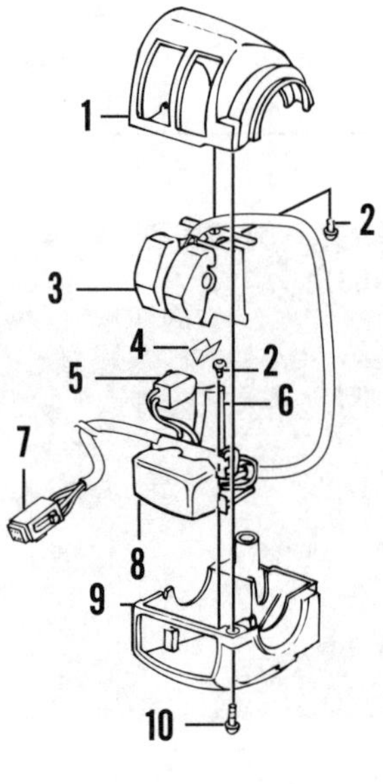

6. To reconnect connectors properly, push them together until they click or snap into place.

Handlebar Switches

WARNING
Do not ride the motorcycle until the throttle cables are properly adjusted. Also, the cables must not catch or pull when turning the handlebars. Improper cable routing and adjustment can cause the throttle to stick open.

Left handlebar switch

The left side handlebar switch housing (**Figure 105**) is equipped with the following switches:

1. Headlight dimmer.
2. Horn.
3. Left side turn signal.

Right handlebar switch

The right side handlebar switch housing (**Figure 106**) is equipped with the following switches:

107

109

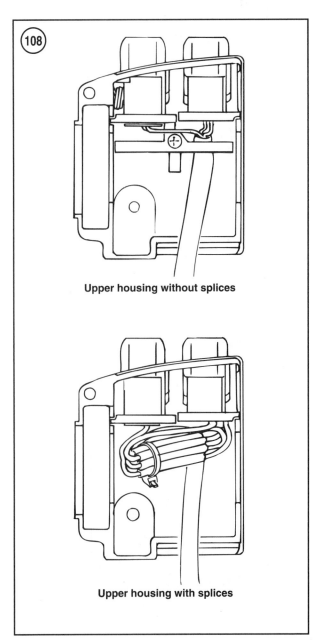

108

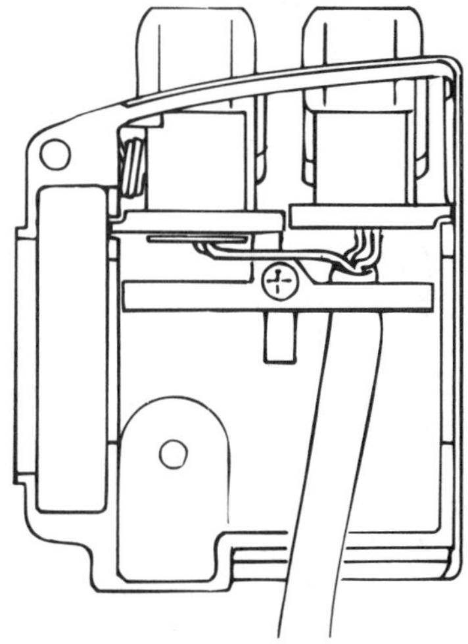

Upper housing without splices

Upper housing with splices

1. Engine stop/run.
2. Start.
3. Right side turn signal.
4. Front brake light.

Replacement

1. Remove the screws securing the left side switch housing (**Figure 107**) to the handlebar. Carefully separate the switch housing (**Figure 108**) to access the defective switch.
2. Remove the screws securing the right side switch housing (**Figure 109**) to the handlebar. Carefully separate the switch housing (**Figure 110**) to access the defective switch.
3A. On models without splices, remove the screw and bracket.
3B. On models with splices, remove the cable strap.
4. Pull the switch(es) out of the housing.
5. Cut the switch wire(s) from the defective switch(es).
6. Slip a piece of heat shrink tubing over each cut wire.
7. Solder the wire end(s) to the new switch. Shrink the tubing over the wire(s).
8. Install the switch by reversing the preceding steps. Note the following:
   a. When clamping the switch housing onto the handlebar, check the wiring harness routing position to make sure it is not pinched between the housing and handlebar.
   b. To install the right side switch housing, refer to *Throttle and Idle Cable Replacement* in Chapter Eight.

Front Brake Light Switch Replacement

WARNING
Do not ride the motorcycle until the throttle cables are properly adjusted. The cables

9

must not catch or pull when the handlebars are turned. Improper cable routing and adjustment can cause the throttle to stick open.

The front brake light switch (**Figure 111**) is mounted in the right side switch lower housing.

1. Separate the right side switch housing as described in *Handlebar Switches* in this section.
2. If the wedge between the switch and the switch housing is still in place, remove it.
3. Cut the switch wires 1.0 in. (25.4 mm) from the defective switch.
4. While depressing the switch plunger, slowly rotate the switch upward, rocking it slightly, and remove it from the switch housing.
5. Check that the plunger is square in the bore and that the boot is not compressed, collapsed or torn. Work the plunger in and out until the boot is fully extended.
6. Slip a piece of heat shrink tubing over each cut wire.
7. Solder the wire ends to the new switch. Then shrink the tubing over the wires.
8. Install the switch by reversing these steps. Note the following:
   a. When clamping the switch housing onto the handlebar, check the wiring harness routing position to make sure it is not pinched between the housing and handlebar.
   b. To install the right side switch housing, refer to *Throttle and Idle Cable Replacement* in Chapter Eight.

Ignition/Light Switch Removal/Installation

The ignition switch (A, **Figure 112**) is located on the right side adjacent to the steering head. The switch is available only as a unit assembly; it is not repairable.

1. Remove the Maxi-fuse as described in this chapter.
2. Remove the fuel tank as described in Chapter Eight.
3. Using a suitable spanner, remove the face nut (B, **Figure 112**).
4. Remove the decal (C, **Figure 112**).
5. Remove the retaining screw (D, **Figure 112**).
6. Remove the switch cover (A, **Figure 113**).
7. Cut the switch wires approximately 3 in. from the switch.
8. Splice the new ignition switch (B, **Figure 113**) to the harness. Splice similar color wires to each other and follow the *Sealed Butt Connectors* procedure under *Electrical Connectors* in this chapter.
9. Install the switch by reversing the removal procedure. Tighten the retaining screw (C, **Figure 113**) to 35-45 in.-lb. (4.0-5.0 N•m).

(110)

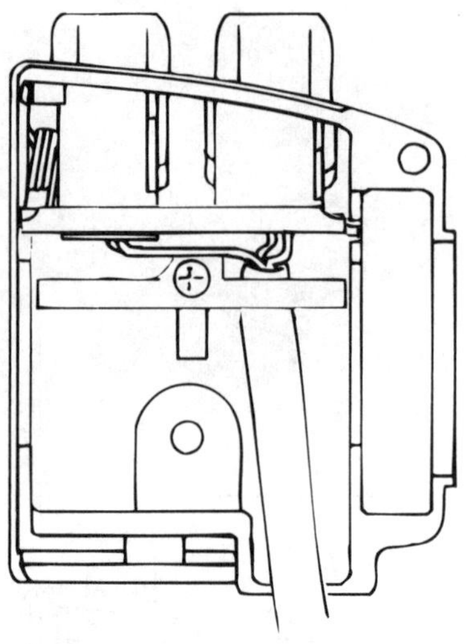

Upper housing without splices

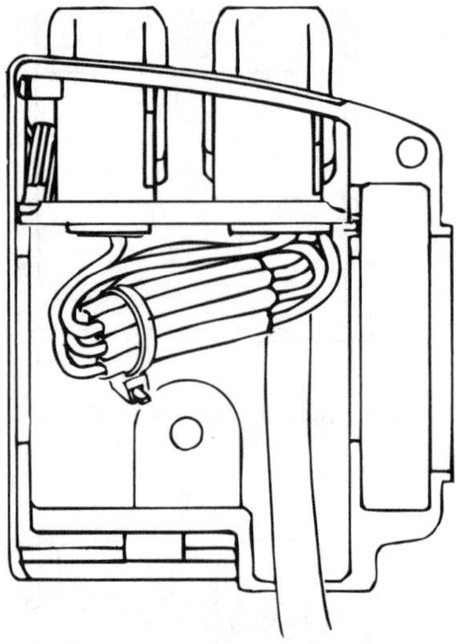

Upper housing with splices

(111)

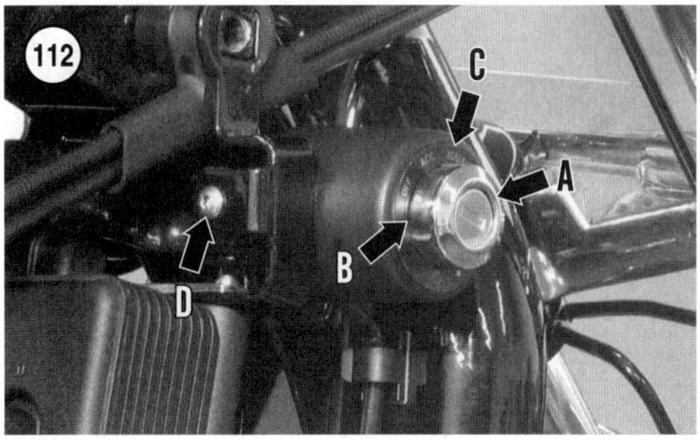

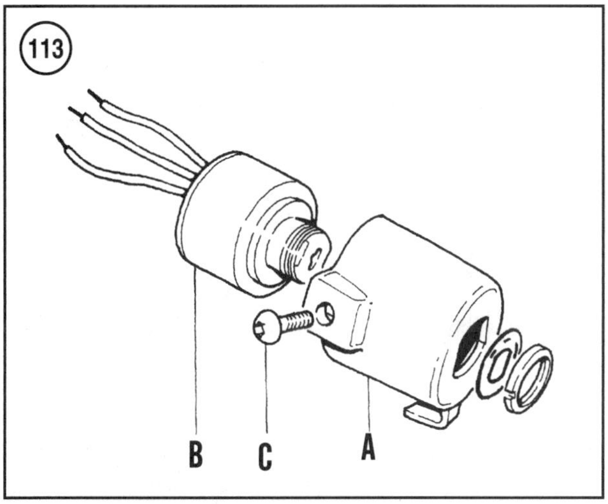

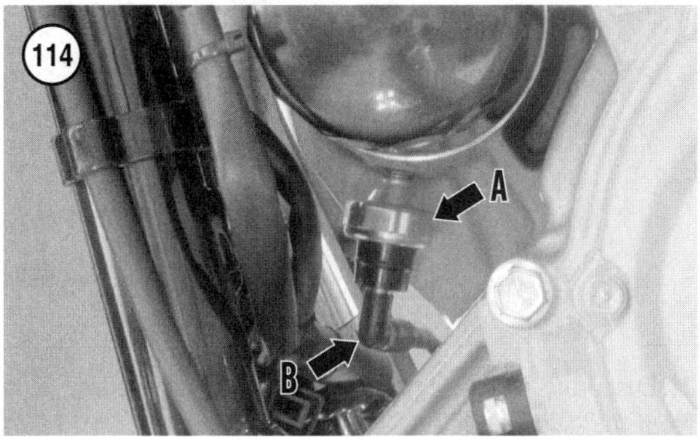

Oil Pressure Switch

Operation

The oil pressure switch (A, **Figure 114**) is located under the oil filter mounting boss on the crankcase. When the oil pressure is low or when oil is not circulating through a running engine, spring tension inside the switch holds the switch contacts closed. This completes the signal light circuit and causes the low oil pressure indicator lamp to light.

The oil pressure signal light should turn on when any of the following occurs:

1. The ignition switch is turned on prior to starting the engine.
2. The engine speed idle is below 1000 rpm.
3. The engine is operating with low oil pressure.
4. Oil is not circulating through the running engine.

NOTE
The oil pressure indicator light may not come on when the ignition switch is turned off then back on immediately. This is due to the oil pressure retained in the oil filter housing. Test the electrical part of the oil pressure switch in the following steps. If the oil pressure switch, indicator lamp and related wiring are in good condition, inspect the lubrication system as described in Chapter Two.

9

Testing/replacement

1. Disconnect the electrical connector (B, **Figure 114**) from the switch.
2. Turn the ignition switch on.
3. Ground the switch wire to the engine.
4. The low oil pressure indicator lamp on the instrument panel should light.
5. If the indicator lamp does not light, check for a defective indicator lamp, and inspect all wiring between the switch, or sender, and the indicator lamp.

6A. If the oil pressure warning light operates properly, attach the electrical connector to the pressure switch. Make sure the connection is tight and free of oil.

6B. If the warning light remains on when the engine is running above 1000 rpm, shut the engine off. Check the engine lubrication system as described in Chapter Two.

7. To replace the switch, perform the following:
   a. Unscrew the switch (A, **Figure 114**) from the engine.
   b. If reinstalling the original switch, apply Loctite Teflon pipe sealant to the switch threads prior to installation. A new switch already has sealant on the threads. Do not add any additional sealant to a new switch.
   c. Install the switch and tighten it to 50-70 in.-lb. (6-8 N•m).
   d. Test the new switch as described in Steps 1-4.

Neutral Indicator Switch Replacement

The neutral indicator switch is located on the right side of the crankcase in front of the drive sprocket. The neutral indicator light on the instrument panel should light when the ignition is turned on and the transmission is in neutral.

1. Make sure the transmission is in neutral.
2. Disconnect the electrical connector adjacent to the lower, right frame tube (adjacent to the oil pump) that leads to the neutral indicator switch (**Figure 115**).
3. Turn the ignition switch on.
4. Ground the upper end of the neutral indicator switch wire to the engine or any other suitable ground.
5. If the neutral indicator lamp lights, the neutral switch or attached wire lead is faulty. Verify the condition of the switch wire lead is good, and if so, replace the neutral indicator switch and retest.
6. If the neutral indicator lamp does not light, check for a burned out indicator lamp, faulty wiring or a loose or corroded connection. If necessary, replace the lamp as described in this chapter.

7A. If the problem was solved in Steps 3-6, reconnect the electrical connector to the neutral switch. Make sure the connection is tight and free from oil.

7B. If the problem was not solved in Steps 3-6, replace the neutral indicator switch as described in the following steps.

8. Remove the drive sprocket as described in Chapter Seven.
9. Disconnect the wire lead (A, **Figure 116**) from the switch.
10. Unscrew the switch (B, **Figure 116**) from the right crankcase.
11. Install the switch and tighten to 36-60 in.-lb. (4.1-6.8 N•m).
12. Reconnect the switch wire lead to the switch.
13. Install the drive sprocket as described in Chapter Seven.

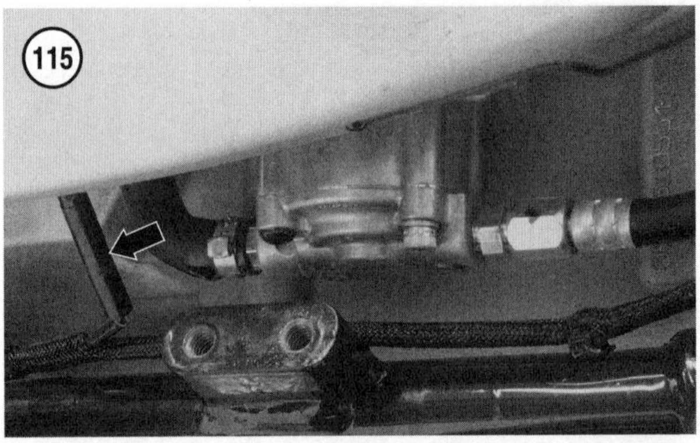

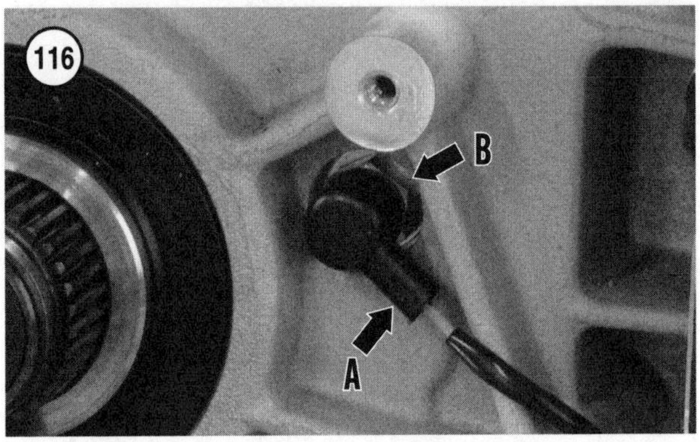

Rear Brake Light Switch Testing/Replacement

A hydraulic, normally open rear brake light switch is used on all models. The rear brake light is located behind the left side cover inline with the rear brake caliper brake hose assembly (A, **Figure 117**). When the rear brake pedal is applied, hydraulic pressure closes the switch contacts, providing a ground path so the rear brake lamp comes on. If the rear brake lamp does not come on, perform the following:

1. Remove the left side cover as described in Chapter Fourteen.
2. Disconnect the electrical connectors (B, **Figure 117**) from the switch.
3. Connect an ohmmeter between the switch terminals. Check the following:
   a. Apply the rear brake pedal. There should be continuity.
   b. Release the rear brake pedal. There should be no continuity.
   c. If the switch fails either of these tests, replace the switch.

4. If necessary, replace the brake light switch as described in the following steps.
5. Remove the rear brake master cylinder reservoir cover (**Figure 118**) from the reservoir.
6. Remove the reservoir mounting bolt (A, **Figure 119**), then move the reservoir (B) out of the way.
7. Place a drip pan under the switch, as some brake fluid will drain out when the switch is removed.

CAUTION
Make sure to hold the T-fitting with a wrench when performing Step 8.

8. Unscrew the switch from the T-fitting on the rear brake line.
9. Thread the new switch into the fitting and tighten it to 84-120 in.-lb. (9.5-13.6 N•m).
10. Reconnect the switch electrical connectors.
11. Bleed the rear brake as described in Chapter Thirteen.
12. Check the rear brake light with the ignition switch on and the rear brake applied.

HORN

Testing

1. Label, then disconnect the electrical connectors (**Figure 120**, typical) from the horn.
2. Connect a positive voltmeter test lead to the yellow/black electrical connector and the negative test lead to ground.
3. Turn the ignition switch on.
4. Press the horn button. If battery voltage is present, the horn is faulty or is not grounded properly. If there is no battery voltage, either the horn switch or the horn wiring is faulty.
5. Replace the horn or horn switch as necessary.

Replacement

XL1200C models

1. Remove the Maxi-fuse as described in this chapter.
2. Label, then disconnect the electrical connectors (**Figure 120**, typical) from the horn.
3. Remove the Acorn nut and lockwasher securing the horn assembly to the rubber mount stud.
4. Remove the horn assembly and remove the wire clip from the backside of the horn bracket.
5. Remove the locknut from the recess in the horn bracket, then remove the horn.
6. Install the horn by reversing the preceding removal steps while noting the following:
   a. Make sure the electrical connectors and horn spade terminals are free of corrosion.
   b. Apply Loctite 271 to the threads of the nut (6, **Figure 121**). Tighten the nut to 80-100 in.-lb. (9.0-11.0 N•m).
   c. Tighten the Acorn nut (12, **Figure 121**) to 60-180 in.-lb. (6.8-20.3 N•m).
   d. Make sure the horn operates correctly.

All models except XL1200C

1. Remove the Maxi-fuse as described in this chapter.

(121)

HORN (XL1200C MODELS)

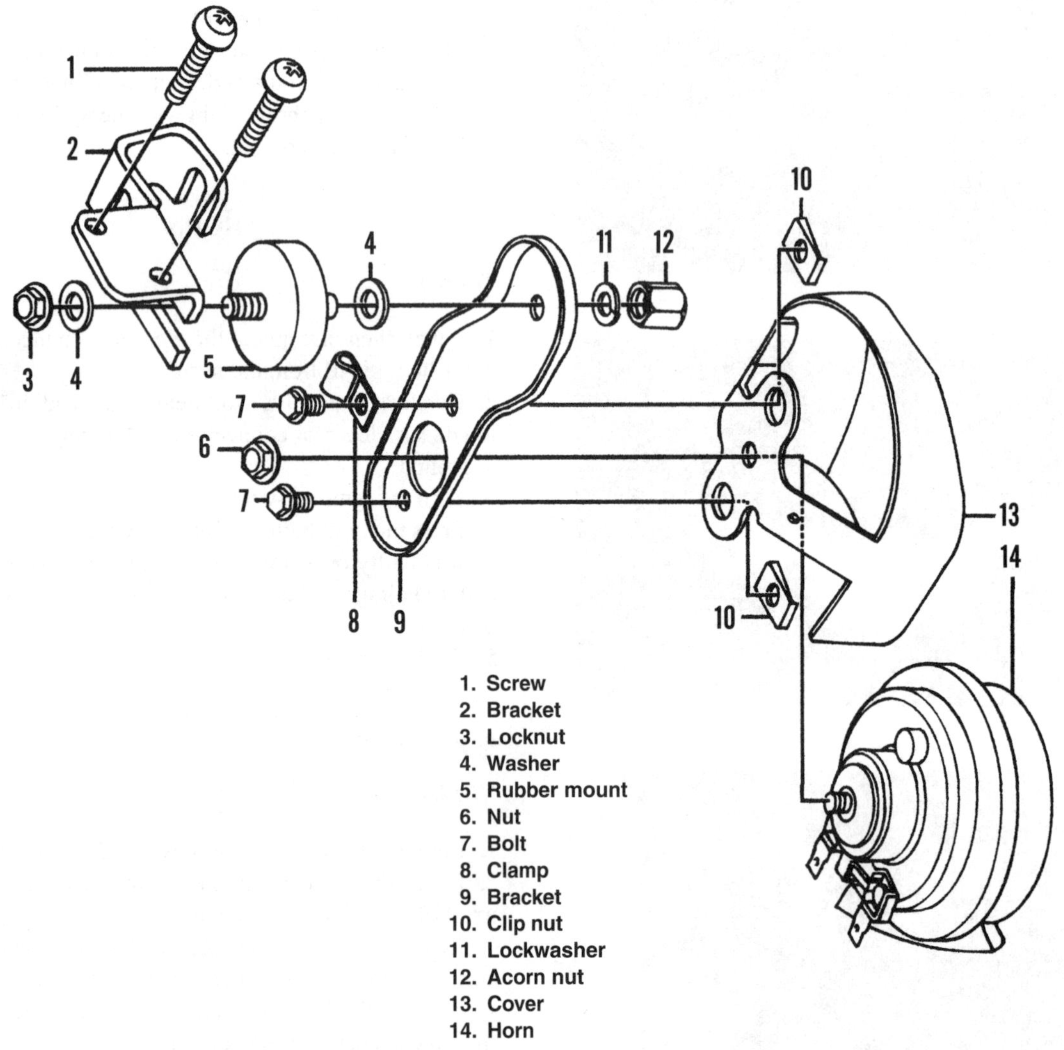

(122)

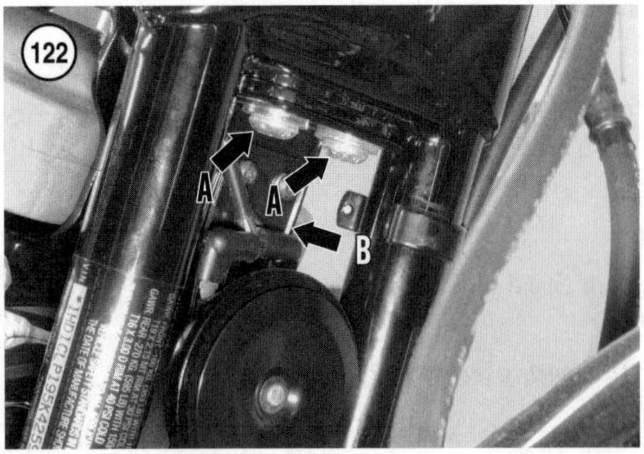

(123)

(124) **SPEEDOMETER (XL883C AND XL1200C MODELS)**

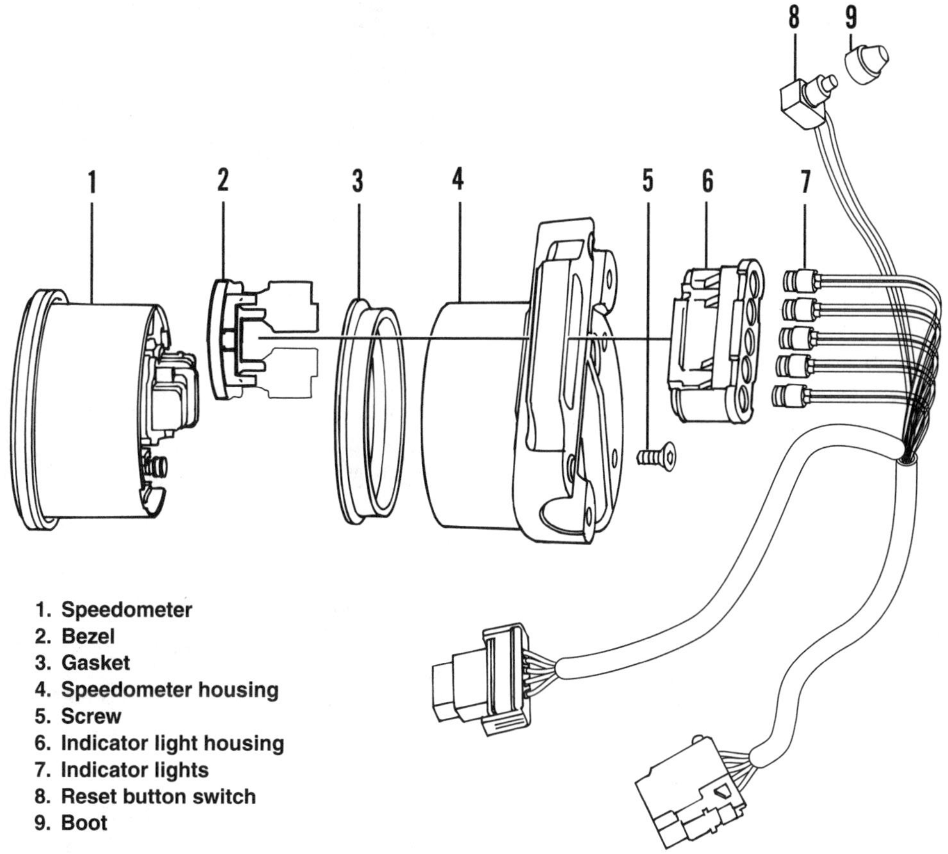

1. Speedometer
2. Bezel
3. Gasket
4. Speedometer housing
5. Screw
6. Indicator light housing
7. Indicator lights
8. Reset button switch
9. Boot

2. Label, then disconnect the electrical connectors (**Figure 120**) from the horn.

3. Remove the screws and washers (A, **Figure 122**) securing the horn assembly bracket (B) to the frame mounting bracket.

4. Remove the frame bracket screws and separate the bracket from the horn flange.

5. Install the horn by reversing the preceding removal steps while noting the following:

   a. Make sure the electrical connectors and horn spade terminals are free of corrosion.
   b. Tighten the frame bracket screws.
   c. Make sure the horn operates correctly.

STARTER RELAY SWITCH

Troubleshooting

Refer to *Starting System* in Chapter Two.

Replacement

1. Remove the Maxi-fuse as described in this chapter.
2. Unplug and remove the starter relay switch (**Figure 123**).
3. Reverse the removal steps to install the starter relay switch.

SPEEDOMETER

Troubleshooting

Refer to *Electronic Diagnostic System* in Chapter Two.

Removal/Installation

XL883C and XL1200C models

Refer to **Figure 124**.

1. Remove the Maxi-fuse as described in this chapter.

2. Remove the handlebar riser cover.
3. Remove the two screws (5, **Figure 124**) on the backside of the speedometer housing that secure the speedometer.
4. Push a suitable rod through the vent hole in the handlebar bracket to push the speedometer out of the housing.
5. Disconnect the speedometer connector and remove the speedometer housing.
6. Inspect the connector, wiring and gasket. Replace if damaged.
7. Reverse the removal steps to install the speedometer while noting the following:
   a. If necessary, lubricate the gasket with glass cleaner or alcohol to ease speedometer insertion.
   b. Tighten the riser cover screws to 8-12 in.-lb. (0.9-1.4 N•m).

XL883, XL883L, XL883R, XL1200L and XL1200R models

1. Remove the Maxi-fuse as described in this chapter.
2. Remove the reset button boot (A, **Figure 125**).
3. Remove the speedometer rear cover screws (B, **Figure 125**).
4. Disconnect the speedometer connector (**Figure 126**).
5. Push up the speedometer and remove it.
6. Inspect the connector, wiring and gasket. Replace if damaged.
7. Reverse the removal steps to install the speedometer. If necessary, lubricate the gasket with glass cleaner or alcohol to ease speedometer insertion.

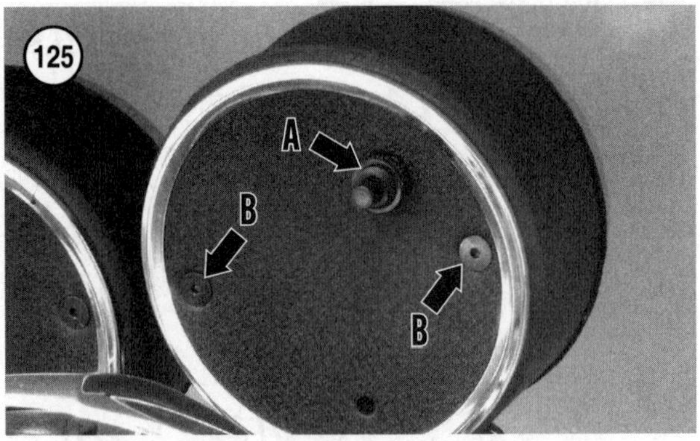

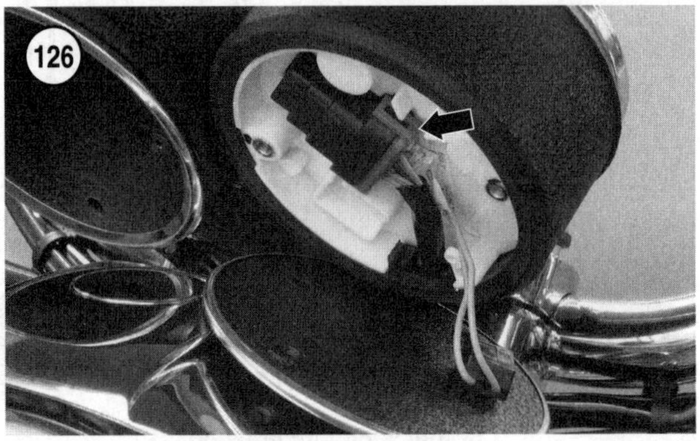

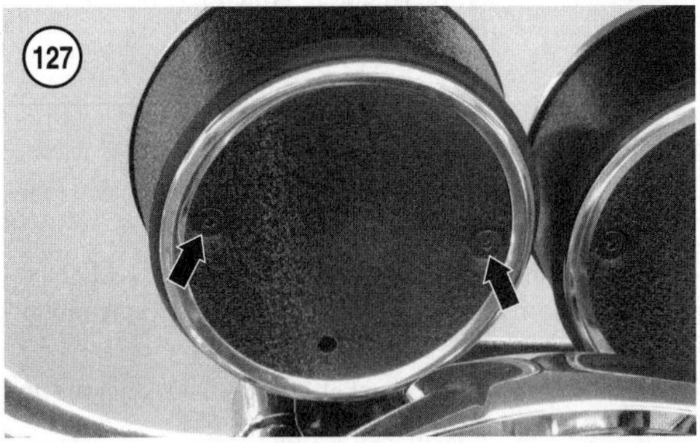

TACHOMETER

Troubleshooting

Refer to *Electronic Diagnostic System* in Chapter Two.

Removal/Installation XL1200R Models

1. Remove the Maxi-fuse as described in this chapter.
2. Remove the tachometer rear cover screws (**Figure 127**).
3. Disconnect the tachometer connector (**Figure 128**).
4. Push up the tachometer and remove it.
5. Inspect the connector, wiring and gasket. Replace if damaged.
6. Reverse the removal steps to install the tachometer. If necessary, lubricate the gasket with glass cleaner or alcohol to ease tachometer insertion.

VEHICLE SPEED SENSOR

All models are equipped with a vehicle speed sensor (VSS) mounted on the top of the crankcase behind the starter. The VSS monitors gear tooth movement on fourth gear and sends the data to the ICM.

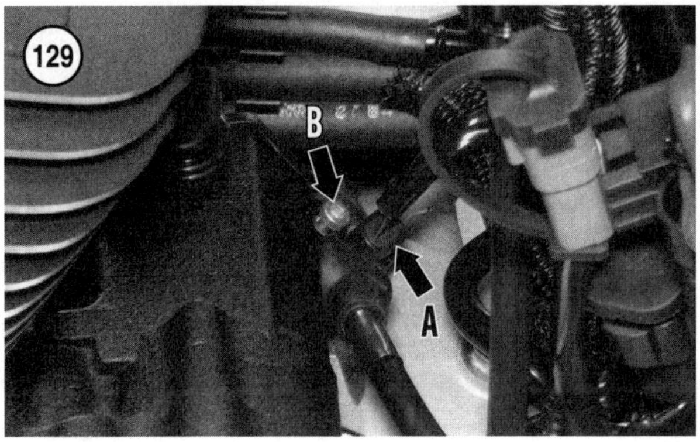

Troubleshooting

Refer to *Electronic Diagnostic System* in Chapter Two.

Removal/Installation

1. Remove the Maxi-fuse as described in this chapter.
2. Disconnect the VSS connector (A, **Figure 129**).
3. Remove the VSS retaining screw (B, **Figure 129**), then extract the VSS.
4. Reverse the removal steps to install the VSS while noting the following:
   a. New O-rings are coated with teflon and do not require additional lubrication.
   b. Tighten the retaining screw to 80-100 in.-lb. (9-11 N•m).

TURN SIGNAL MODULE (TSM) AND TURN SIGNAL SECURITY MODULE (TSSM)

The (TSM) controls the turn signals and four-way hazard flasher. The TSM receives its information from the speedometer and turn signal switches. On models equipped with a security system, the turn signal operartion is incorporated into the TSSM module. Refer to *Security System* in this chapter. TSM and TSSM modules are not interchangeable.

The TSM/TSSM is located in a compartment underneath the battery box.

When there is a problem with either system, a diagnostic fault code(s) is set (Chapter Two).

NOTE

Always disarm the optional security system prior to disconnecting the battery or the siren will sound. If the system is in auto-alarming mode, disarm the system with two clicks of the key fob, and disconnect the battery or remove the TSSM fuse before the 30 second arming period expires.

Operation

Automatic cancellation

NOTE

The TSM/TSSM will not cancel the signal before the turn is actually completed.

1. When the turn signal button is pressed and released, the system begins a 20 count. As long as the motorcycle is moving above 7 MPH (11 KPH) and the TSM does not receive any additional input, the turn signals will cancel after 20 bulb flashes.
2. If the motorcycle's speed drops to 7 MPH (11 KPH) or less, the turn signals will continue to flash. The count resumes when the motorcycle reaches 8 MPH (13 KPH) and the turn signal will cancel when the total count equals 20 bulb flashes.
3. The turn signals will cancel two seconds after a turn of 45° or more is completed.

Manual cancellation

1. After the turn signal button is pressed and released, the system begins a 20 count. To cancel the turn signal, press the turn signal button a second time.
2. If the turn direction is changed, press the opposite turn signal button. The primary signal is cancelled and the opposite turn signal will flash.

Four-Way Flashing

1. Turn the ignition key on. On models so equipped, disarm the security system. Press the right and left turn signal buttons at the same time. All four turn signals will flash at the same time.

2. On models with the TSSM, the system can be armed so all four signals flash for up to two hours. Turn the ignition key off and arm the security system. Press both the right and left turn signal buttons at the same time.
3. To cancel the four-way flashing, disarm the security system, on models so equipped, and press both the right and left turn signal buttons at the same time.

Bank angle sensor (BAS)

The BAS automatically shuts off the engine if the motorcycle tilts more than 45° for longer than one second. The shutoff will occur even at a very slow speed.

To restart the motorcycle, return the motorcycle to vertical. Turn the ignition key off then on, and then restart the engine.

TSM/TSSM Removal/Installation

The TSM/TSSM is located in a compartment underneath the battery box (**Figure 130**).

1. Remove the battery as described in this chapter.
2. Push up the TSM/TSSM from underneath so the connector (**Figure 131**) is accessible.
3. Disconnect the connector from the TSM/TSSM and remove it.
4. Reverse the removal steps to install the TSM/ TSSM. Make sure the top of the module is flush with the battery tray floor. Configure the TSSM as described in *Security System* in this chapter.

SECURITY SYSTEM

Operation

The motorcycle may be equipped with an optional security system, which is incorporated into the turn signal security module (TSSM). This system prevents motorcycle operation unless the operator uses a key fob or enters a personal code number using the turn signal switches.

If a theft attempt is detected and the system is armed, it immobilizes the starting and ignition systems. It also flashes the right and left turn signals alternately and sounds the siren, if so equipped. The following conditions activate the armed security system:

1. Small motorcycle movement—the turn signals flash three times and the optional siren chirps once. If the motorcycle is not returned to its original position, the warnings reactivate after four seconds. This cycle will repeat a maximum of 255 times.
2. Large motorcycle movement—the system activates for 30 seconds, and then turns off. If the motorcycle is not returned to its original position, the warnings will reactivate after ten seconds. This cycle may repeat a maximum of ten times.
3. Tampering of the security lamp circuit—the system activates for 30 seconds. The cycle repeats for each tampering incident.
4. A battery ground or ground disconnect has occurred while the system is armed—the siren will sound, if so equipped, but the turn signals will not flash.
5. The key security symbol on the speedometer face (**Figure 132**) indicates the status of the security system as follows:
   a. Symbol unlit—security system inactive.
   b. Symbol flashes every second—security system inactive for 10 minutes after failed attempt to enter personal code number.
   c. Symbol flashes every 2 seconds—security system armed.
   d. Symbol flashes three times per second—personal code number entry mode.
   e. Symbol constantly illuminated with ignition key off—auto-arming in progress.
   f. Symbol constantly illuminated more than 8 seconds with ignition key on—trouble code (DTC) set. Refer to Chapter Two.

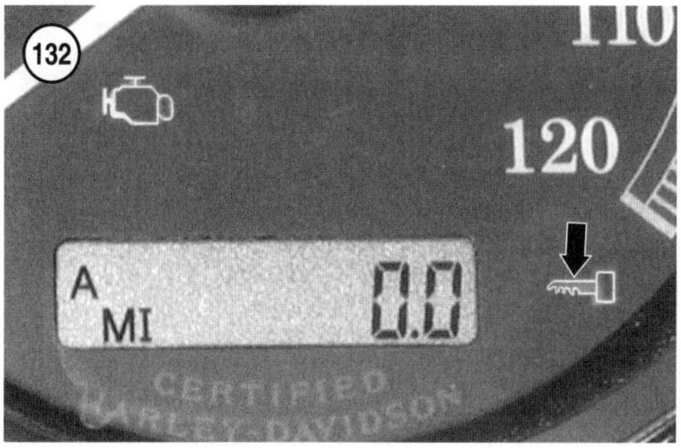

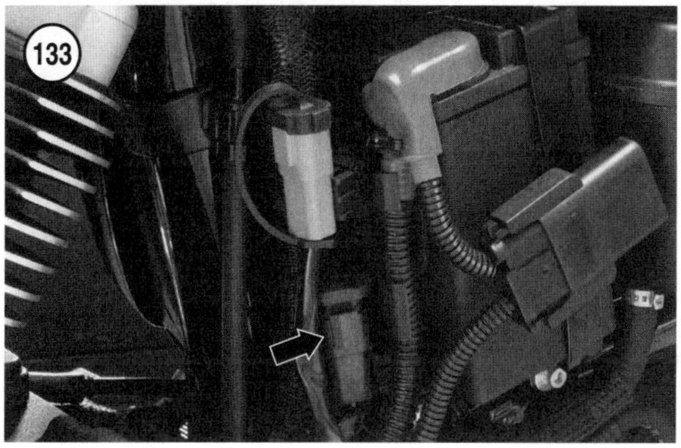

Arming

The security system may be armed either using the key fob button or automatically. The system may be armed only when the ignition is off. International models are equipped with automatic arming systems which cannot be disabled. When the system is armed, the security symbol on the speedometer (**Figure 132**) flashes every 2 seconds.

To use the remote arming method, the operator must press the key fob button until the motorcycle turn signals flash twice and, if so equipped, the siren sounds twice. The system must be configured to recognize the key fob as outlined in **Table 4**.

If auto-arming is enabled, the system arms itself automatically 30 seconds after the ignition is turned off. The security symbol will illuminate and stay on during the arming period, then the turn signals flash twice, the siren (if equipped) sounds twice, and the security symbol flashes every 2 seconds to indicate the security system is enabled. The motorcycle may be moved during the arming period (30 seconds) without triggering the alarm. Refer to **Table 7** to enable auto-arming.

Disarming

The security system may be disarmed either using the key fob button or entering a personal code number using the turn signal switches.

NOTE

*If a key fob is lost, damaged or otherwise unuseable, entering a personal code number is the only means to disarm the security system. If a personal code number has not been entered, the TSSM must be replaced to disarm the system. Refer to **Table 5** for personal code number entry instructions.*

To disarm the system using the key fob, position the key fob in front of the motorcycle and press the fob button twice quickly. The turn signals will flash once to indicate disarmament.

NOTE

If auto-alarm is enabled, the system will rearm if the ignition is not turned on within 30 seconds.

To disarm the system using the personal code number, refer to **Table 6**.

Transport and Storage Modes

The security system may be programmed for use when transporting or storing the motorcycle.

In the transport mode the motion detector is inactive which allows moving or transporting the motorcycle with the security system operating but unresponsive to movement.

The security system will enter storage mode after a set period of time whether the system is armed or not. This prevents battery discharge due to current draw from the security system. Turning the ignition key on reactivates the system. If the system was armed when the storage mode was entered, the ignition key must be turned on and off quickly or the alarm will be triggered. If desired, disarm the system as previously described.

Refer to **Table 8** or **Table 9** to program the system for transport or storage mode.

Siren

A siren may be connected to the black connector (**Figure 133**) adjacent to the battery box. The siren contains a 9-volt battery that powers the siren if the battery is disconnected.

If a siren malfunction occurs, note the following and see if a diagnostic fault code(s) was set. Refer to Chapter Two for troubleshooting information.

1. If the internal siren battery is defective the siren will sound three times rather than twice during arming.

2 The siren should sound two or three times during arming. If not, check for defective wiring, connections or a defective siren.

3. The internal siren battery will not charge fully if the motorcycle battery voltage is less than 12.5 volts.

4. If the security system is triggered while armed, and the siren is powered by its internal battery, the siren cycles on and off ten times. The siren sounds for 20-30 seconds, then stops for 5-10 seconds.

Key Fob

A new key fob must be activated before it can be used to operate the security system. Follow the steps outlined in **Table 4**.

A key fob may not trigger the security system if the button has been pressed several times out of range of the motorcycle. To synchronize the key fob with the security system, press the button for 10-15 seconds until the turn signals flash twice, indicating normal operation is resumed.

Battery replacement

Replace the key fob battery every 2 years.

1. Split the case and rear cover (similar to a watch) for access to the battery.

2. Install a Panasonic 2032 battery or equivalent so the positive side contacts the case terminal.

3. Install the rear cover being sure it seats properly.

Configuration

System configuration is required if the TSSM is replaced. System features such as alarm sensitivity, auto-alarm, transport mode and storage mode may also be activated and adjusted.

Refer to **Tables 4-10** to configure or adjust the system.

FUSES

All models are equipped with five 15 amp fuses (**Figure 134**) that protect the electrical system circuits. The Maxi-fuse protects the entire electrical system. Refer to *Maxi-fuse* in this chapter.

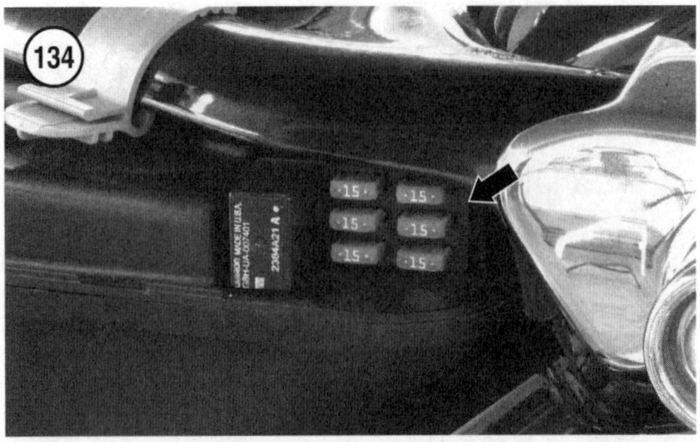

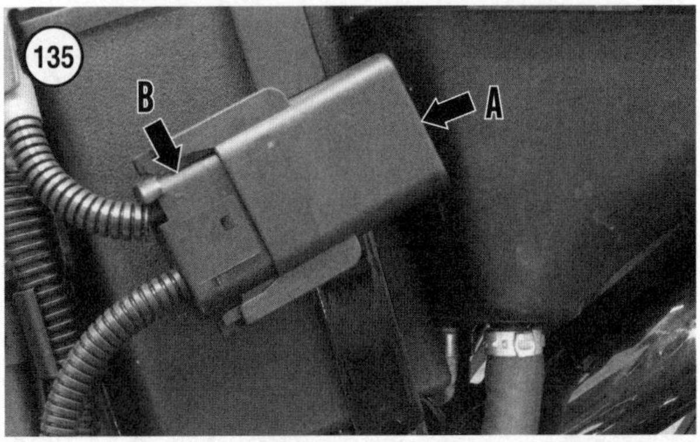

Remove the left side cover for access to the fuses. Make sure to replace a fuse with a new fuse of the same amperage.

Whenever a fuse blows, determine the cause before replacing the fuse. Usually the trouble is a short circuit in the wiring. Worn-through insulation or a short to ground from a disconnected wire may cause this.

CAUTION

If replacing a fuse, make sure the ignition switch is turned off. This lessens the chance of a short circuit.

CAUTION

Never substitute any metal object for a fuse. Never use a higher amperage fuse than specified. An overload could cause a fire and the complete loss of the motorcycle.

MAXI-FUSE

The 30-amp Maxi-fuse serves as the main fuse for the electrical system.

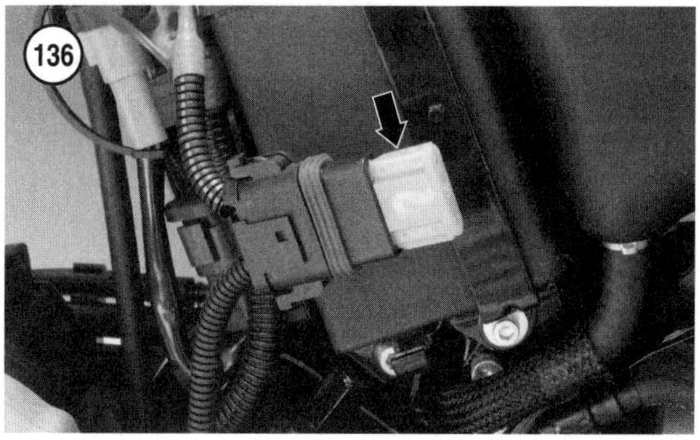

Removal/Installation

1. Remove the left side cover as described in Chapter Fourteen.
2. Push the Maxi-fuse cover latches together. Hold the fuse cover (A, **Figure 135**) and pull the fuse holder (B) out of the cover.
3. Remove the Maxi-fuse (**Figure 136**) from the fuse holder.
4. Push the Maxi-fuse (**Figure 136**) into the fuse holder.
5. Push the Maxi-fuse cover (A, **Figure 135**) onto the fuse holder (B).
6. Install the left side cover as described in Chapter Fourteen.

ELECTRICAL CONNECTORS

Many electrical problems can be traced to damaged wiring, or contaminated or loose connectors.

The electrical system uses various types of connectors. If individual wires or terminals of a particular connector require repair or replacement, refer to the procedures for disassembly of the connector.

Electrical System/Connector Inspection

Perform the following steps if there is an electrical system fault:

1 Always check the wire colors to verify the correct connector/component is being tested. Refer to the wiring diagram.
2. Inspect the wiring in the suspect circuit for damage.
3. Check the Maxi-fuse (**Figure 136**).
4. Check the individual fuse(s) for each circuit.
5. Inspect the battery as described in this chapter. Make sure it is fully charged and the battery cables are clean and securely attached to the battery terminals.
6. Clean the connectors with an aerosol electrical contact cleaner. After a thorough cleaning, pack multi-pin electrical connectors with dialectic grease to seal out moisture.
7. Disconnect electrical connectors in the suspect circuits and check for bent or damaged terminals. The male and female terminals must connect or an open circuit will result.
8. Make sure the terminals are pushed all the way into the plastic connector. If they are not, carefully push them in with a narrow-blade screwdriver.
9. After everything is checked, push the connectors together and make sure they are fully engaged and locked together.
10. Never pull on the electrical wires when disconnecting an electrical connector. Only pull on the connector plastic housing.

Deutsch Connectors Socket Terminal Removal/Installation

This procedure shows how to remove and install the socket terminals from the socket housing connector half. This procedure is shown on a 12-pin Duetsch connector and is the same for 2-, 3-, 4- and 6-pin Duetsch connectors.

Refer to **Figure 137** and **Figure 138.**

1. Disconnect the negative battery cable as described in this chapter.
2. Disconnect the connector housing.
3. Remove the secondary locking wedge (7, **Figure 138**) as follows:
   a. Locate the secondary locking wedge in **Figure 137** or **Figure 138.**
   b. Insert a wide-blade screwdriver between the socket housing and the locking wedge. Turn the screwdriver 90° to force the wedge up (**Figure 139**).
   c. Remove the secondary locking wedge (7, **Figure 138**).
4. Lightly press the terminal latches inside the socket housing and remove the socket terminal (14, **Figure 138**) through the holes in the rear wire seal.
5. Repeat Step 3 for each socket terminal.
6. If necessary, remove the wire seal (12, **Figure 138**).
7. Install the wire seal (12, **Figure 138**) into the socket housing if it was removed.
8. Hold onto the socket housing and insert the socket terminals (14, **Figure 138**) through the holes in the wire seal so they enter their correct chamber hole. Continue until the socket terminal locks into place. Then lightly tug on the wire to make sure it is locked into place.

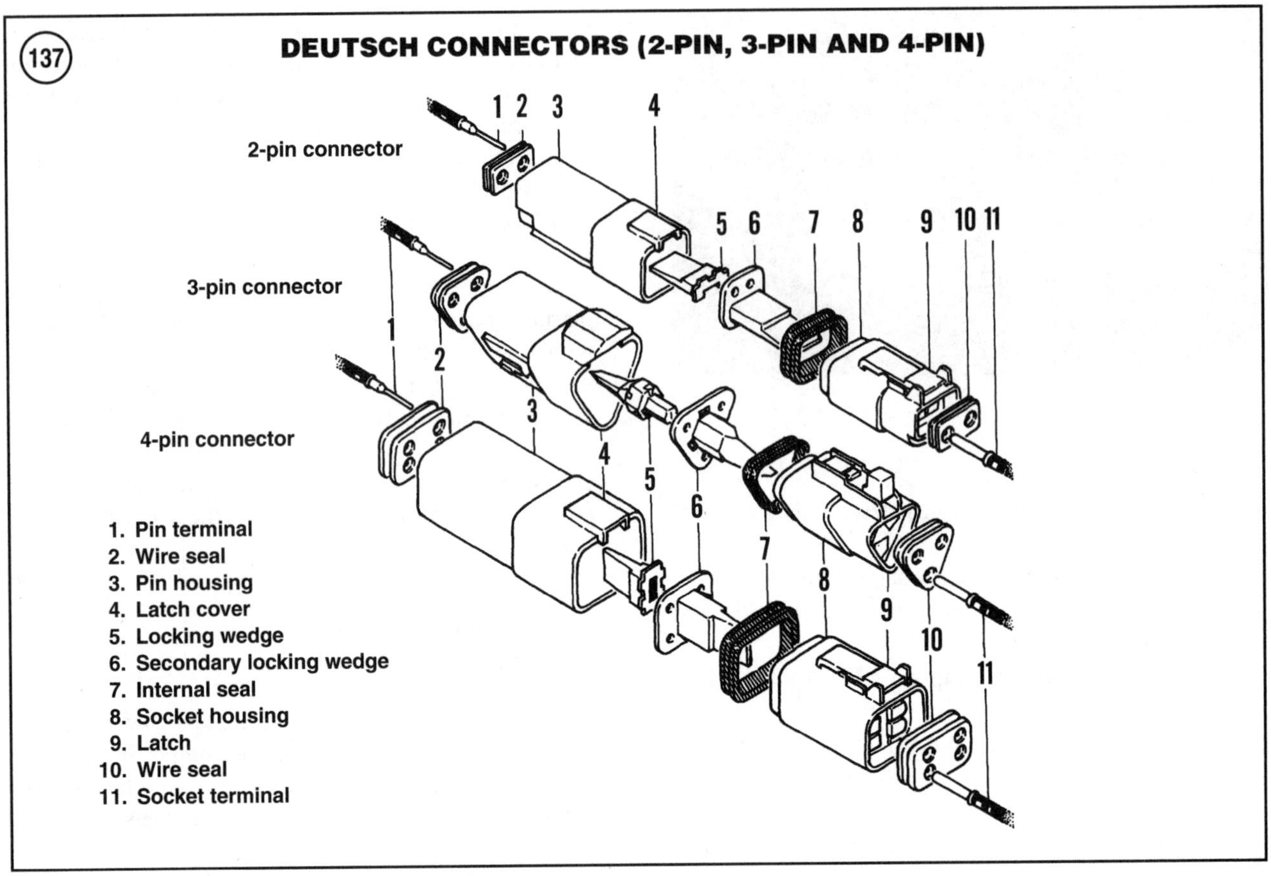
137
DEUTSCH CONNECTORS (2-PIN, 3-PIN AND 4-PIN)
2-pin connector
3-pin connector
4-pin connector
1. Pin terminal
2. Wire seal
3. Pin housing
4. Latch cover
5. Locking wedge
6. Secondary locking wedge
7. Internal seal
8. Socket housing
9. Latch
10. Wire seal
11. Socket terminal

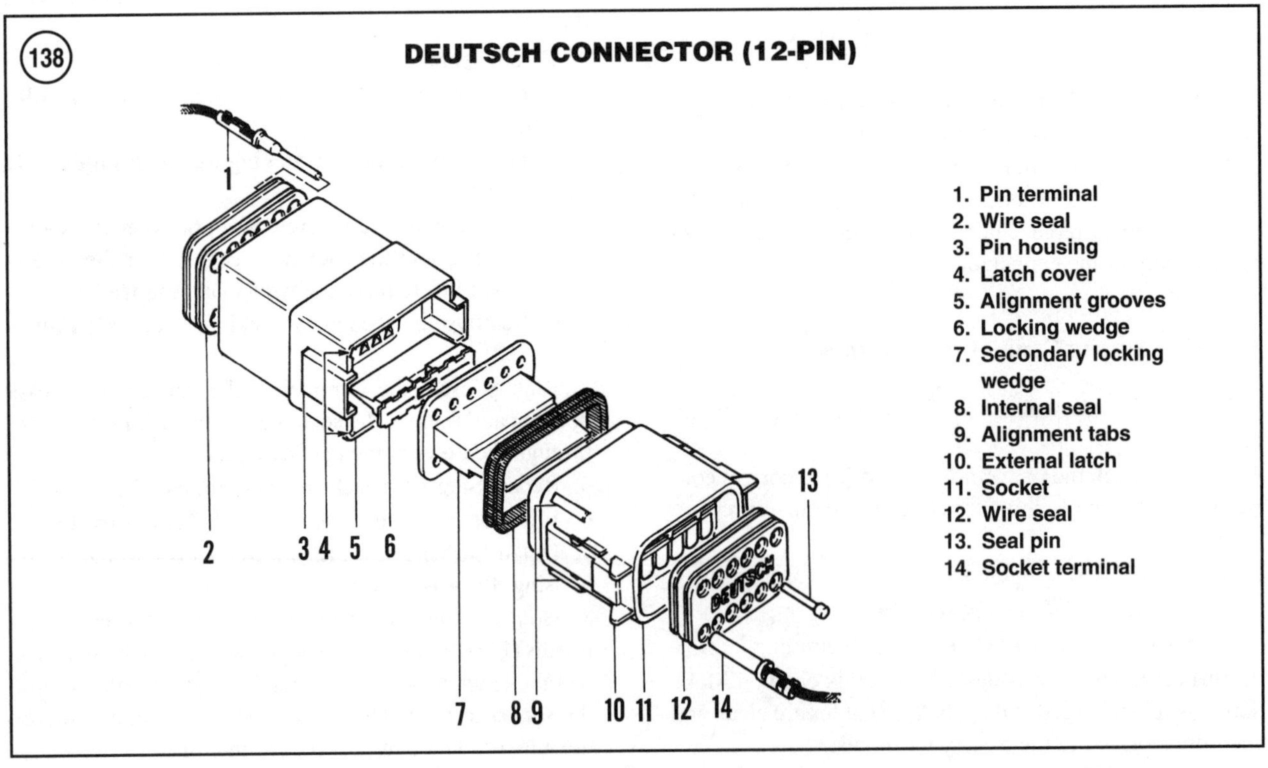
138
DEUTSCH CONNECTOR (12-PIN)
DEUTSCH
1. Pin terminal
2. Wire seal
3. Pin housing
4. Latch cover
5. Alignment grooves
6. Locking wedge
7. Secondary locking wedge
8. Internal seal
9. Alignment tabs
10. External latch
11. Socket
12. Wire seal
13. Seal pin
14. Socket terminal

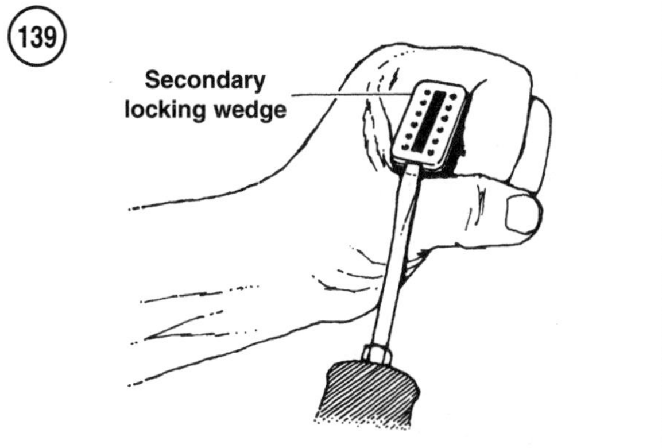

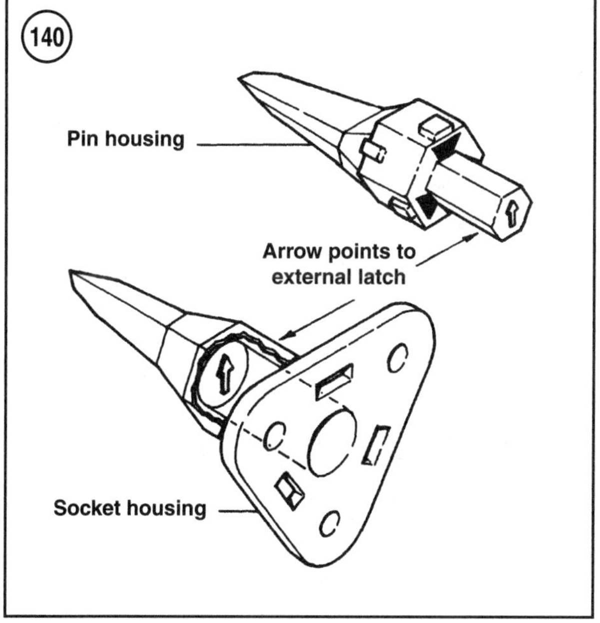

9. Set the internal seal (8, **Figure 138**) onto the socket housing if it was removed.

NOTE
*With the exception of the 3-pin Duetsch connector, all the secondary locking wedges are symmetrical. When assembling the 3-pin connector, install the connector so the arrow on the secondary locking wedge is pointing toward the external latch as shown in **Figure 140**.*

NOTE
If the secondary locking wedge does not slide into position easily, one or more of the socket terminals are not installed correctly. Correct the problem at this time.

10. Install the secondary locking wedge into the socket housing as shown in **Figure 137** or **Figure 138**. Press the secondary locking wedge down until it locks into place.

Deutsch Connectors Pin Terminal Removal/Installation

This procedure shows how to remove and install the pin terminals from the pin housing connector half. This procedure is shown on a 12-pin Duetsch connector and relates to all the Duetsch connectors (2-, 3-, 4- and 6-pin).

Refer to **Figure 137** and **Figure 138**.

1. Disconnect the negative battery cable as described in this chapter.
2. Disconnect the connector housing.
3. Use needlenose pliers to remove the locking wedge (6, **Figure 138**).
4. Lightly press the terminal latches inside the pin housing and remove the pin terminal(s) (1, **Figure 138**) through the holes in the rear wire seal.
5. Repeat Step 3 for each socket terminal.
6. If necessary, remove the wire seal (2, **Figure 138**).
7. Install the wire seal (2, **Figure 138**) into the socket housing if it was removed.
8. Hold onto the pin housing and insert the pin terminals (1, **Figure 138**) through the holes in the wire seal so they enter their correct chamber hole. Continue until the pin terminal locks into place. Then lightly tug on the wire to make sure it is locked into place.

NOTE
*With the exception of the 3-pin Duetsch connector, all of the secondary locking wedges are symmetrical. When assembling the 3-pin connector, install the connector so the arrow on the secondary locking wedge is pointing toward the external latch as shown in **Figure 140**.*

NOTE
If the locking wedge does not slide into position easily, one or more of the pin terminals are not installed correctly. Correct the problem at this time.

9. Install the locking wedge into the pin housing as shown in **Figure 137** or **Figure 138**. Press the secondary locking wedge down until it locks into place. When properly installed, the wedge will fit into the pin housing center groove.

9

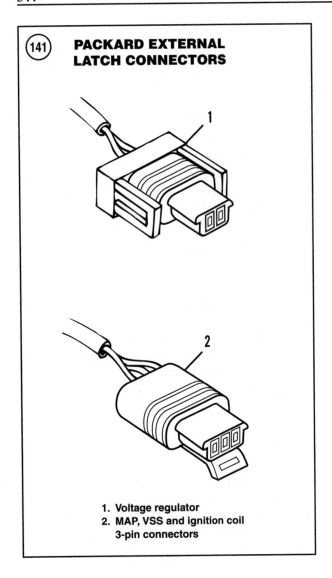

(141) **PACKARD EXTERNAL LATCH CONNECTORS**

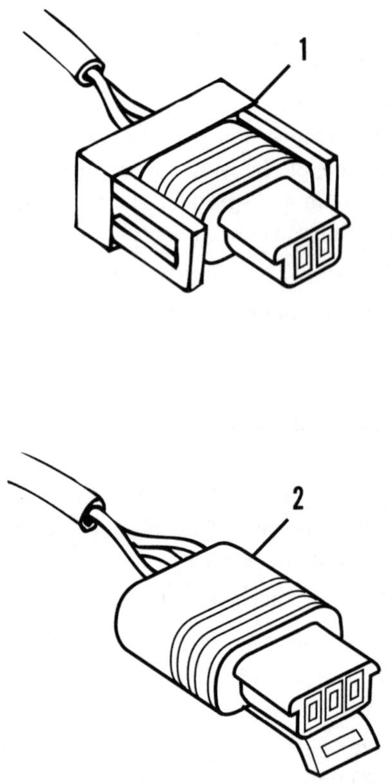

1. Voltage regulator
2. MAP, VSS and ignition coil 3-pin connectors

(142)

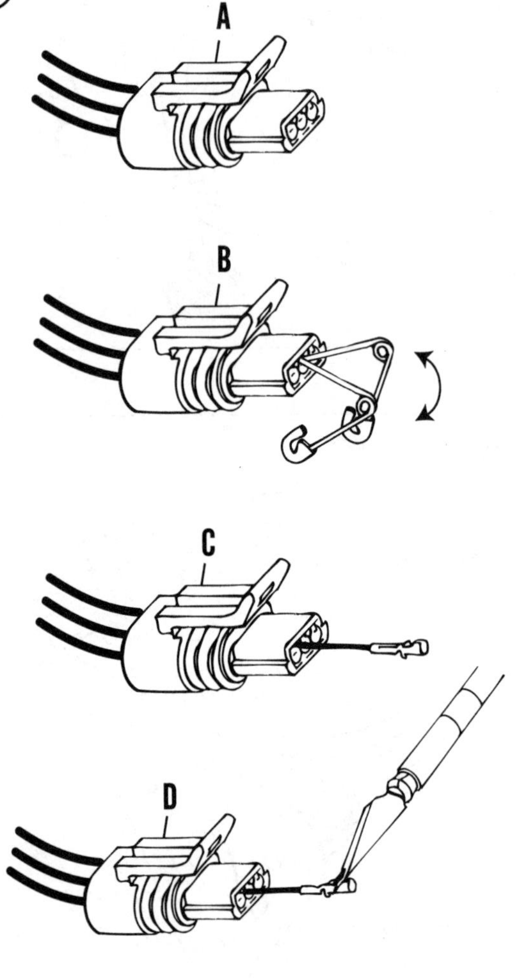

Packard External Latch Connectors Removal/Installation

This procedure shows how to remove and install the electrical terminals from the external latch connectors with pull-to-seat terminals (**Figure 141**).

1. Disconnect the negative battery cable as described in this chapter.
2. Bend back the external latch(es) slightly and separate the connector.
3. Look into the mating end of the connector and locate the locking tang (A, **Figure 142**) in the middle chamber and on the external latch side of connector. On locking ear connectors, the tang is on the side opposite the ear.
4. Insert the point of a one-in. safety pin about 1/8 in. into the middle chamber (B, **Figure 142**). Pivot the end of the safety pin up toward the terminal body until a click is heard. Repeat this step several times. The click is the tang returning to the locked position as it slips from the point of the safety pin. Continue to pick at the tang until the clicking stops and the safety pin seems to slide in at a slightly greater depth indicating the tang has been depressed.
5. Remove the safety pin, push the wire end of the lead and remove the lead from the connector (C, **Figure 142**). If additional slack is necessary, pull back on the harness conduit and remove the wire seal at the back of the connector.
6. To install the terminal and wire back into the connector, use a thin, flat blade of an X-Acto knife to carefully bend the tang away from the terminal (D, **Figure 142**).
7. Carefully pull the lead and terminal into the connector until a click is heard indicating the terminal is seated correctly within the connector. Gently push on the lead to ensure the terminal is correctly seated.

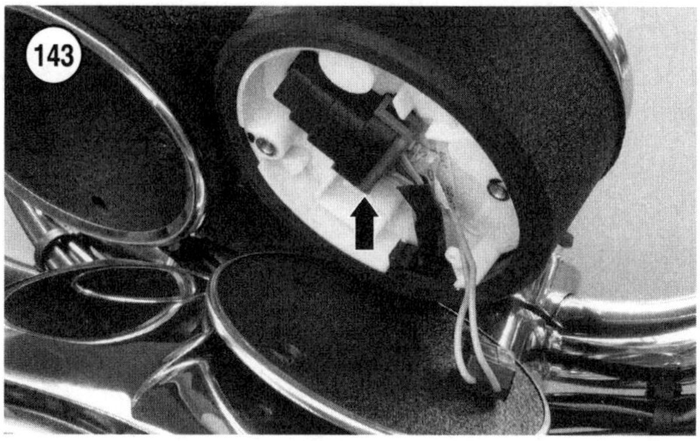

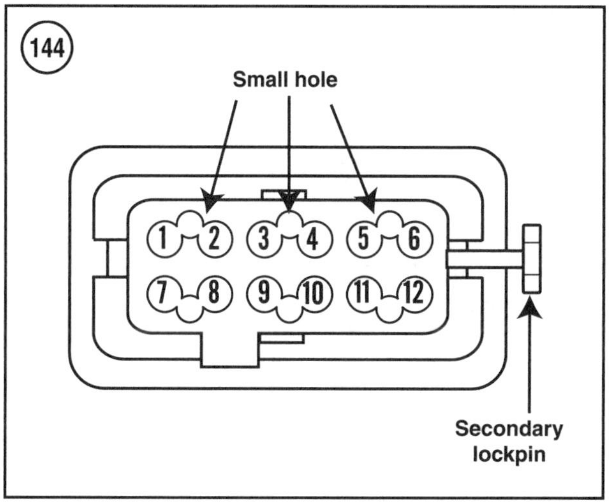

8. If necessary, install the wire seal and push the harness conduit back into position on the backside of the connector.
9. Push the socket halves together until the latch(es) are locked together.

Packard Micro 64 Connectors Removal/Installation

This procedure shows how to remove and install the electrical terminals from the speedometer and tachometer connectors (**Figure 143**).
1. Disconnect the negative battery cable as described in this chapter.
2. Bend back the external latches slightly and separate the connector.
3. Find the secondary lockpin on the side of the connector (**Figure 144**). Pry out and remove the lockpin.

NOTE
Connector terminals are numbered 1-6 in one row and 7-12 in the remaining row. The numbers 1, 6, 7 and 12 are stamped on the connector to identify the row numbers.

4. Locate the small hole adjacent to the desired terminal (**Figure 144**).
5. Push in the terminal wire requiring removal.

NOTE
The terminal removal tool contacts two terminals simultaneously.

6. Using H-D tool No. HD-45928, Packard Electric tool No. 15381651-2 or an equivalent, insert the pin end of the tool into the desired small hole between two terminals (**Figure 144**). Push in the tool until it bottoms.
7. With the tool in place, gently pull out the wire to extract the terminal. Note that both adjacent terminals may be removed.
8. To install the terminal(s), push it into the connector until it is locked in place. Gently pull on the terminal wire to verify the terminal is secured.
9. Position the lockpin so the ear points toward the mating face of the connector.
10. Push in the lockpin so the head is flush with the connector surface.
11. Push the connector halves together until the latches lock together.

Amp Connectors Socket and Pin Terminals Removal/Installation

This procedure shows how to remove and install the socket and pin terminals from the pin and socket housing connector (**Figure 145**).
1. Disconnect the negative battery cable as described in this chapter.
2. Press the button on the socket on the terminal side and pull the connector apart.
3. Slightly bend the latch back and free one side of the secondary lock. Repeat this step for the other side.

NOTE
*A 10-pin connector is shown in **Figure 146**, but the service procedures apply to all connectors.*

4. Rotate the secondary lock (A, **Figure 146**) out on the hinge to access the terminals within the connector.

NOTE
Do not pull too hard on the wire until the tang is released or the terminal will be difficult to remove.

(145)

AMP MULITLOCK CONNECTORS

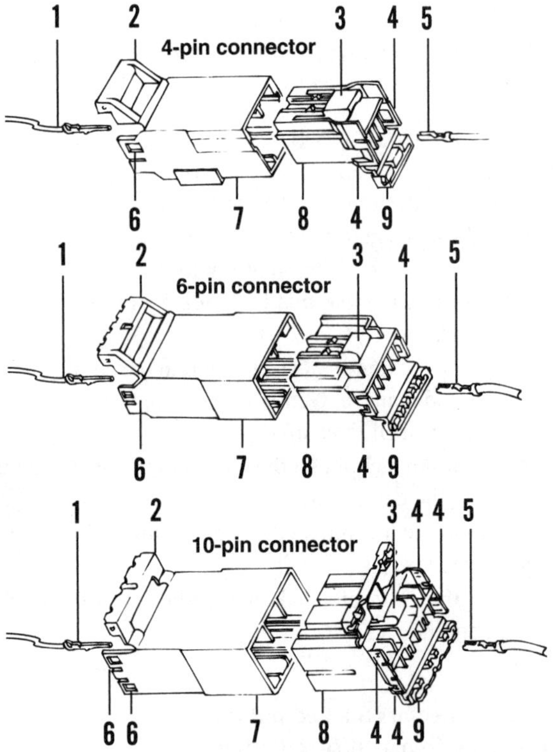

1. Pin terminal
2. Secondary lock
3. Button
4. Latch
5. Socket terminal
6. Latch
7. Pin housing
8. Socket housing
9. Secondary lock

(146)

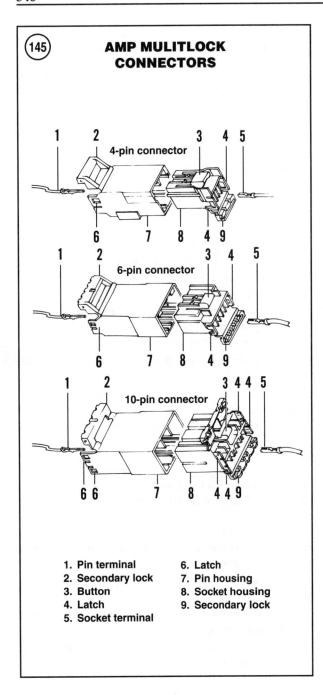

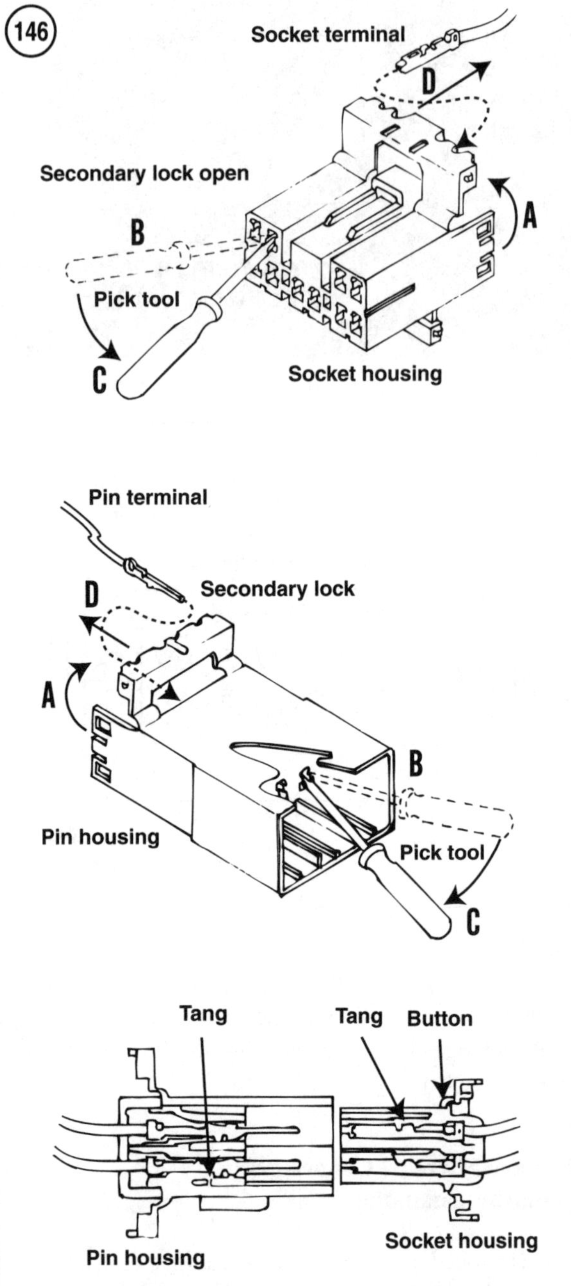

5. Insert a pick tool (B, **Figure 146**) into the flat edge of the terminal cavity until it stops. Pivot the pick tool away (C, **Figure 146**) from the terminal and gently pull on the wire to pull the terminal (D) from the terminal cavity. Note the wire location number on the connector (**Figure 147**, typical).

NOTE
The release button used to separate the connectors is at the top of the connector.

6. The tang in the chamber engages the pin terminal slot to lock the terminal into position. The tangs (**Figure 146**) are located as follows:

a. Pin housing side—the tangs are located at the bottom of each chamber. The pin terminal slot, on the side opposite the crimp tails, must face downward.

b. Socket housing side—the tangs are located at the top of each chamber. The pin terminal slot, on the same side as the crimp tails, must face upward.

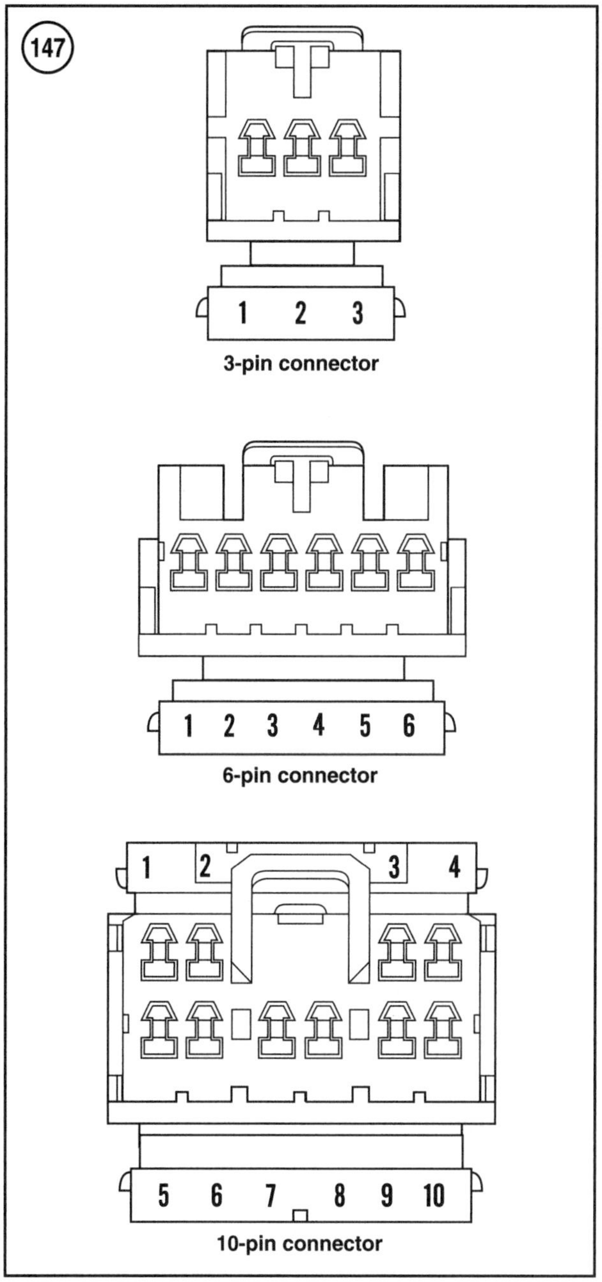

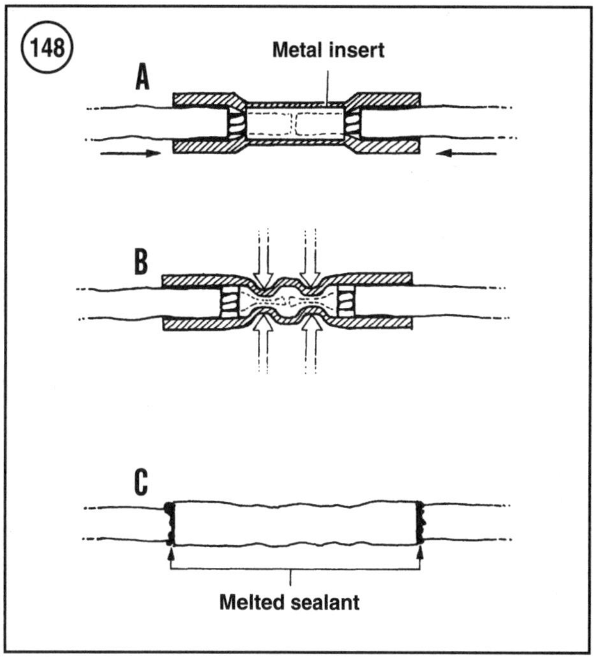

7. On the secondary lock side of the connector, push the wire and terminal into the correct location until it snaps into place. Gently pull on the lead to ensure the terminal is correctly seated.

8. Rotate the hinged secondary lock down and inward until the tabs are fully engaged with the latches on both sides of the connector. Pull upward to make sure the tabs are locked in place.

9. Insert the socket housing into the pin housing and push it in until it locks into place.

Sealed Butt Connectors

Replacing the ignition switch requires sealed butt connectors to connect the new switch wiring to the existing wiring. Stagger the position of the connectors so they are not side-by-side.

Refer to **Figure 148**.

1. Insert the stripped wire ends into the connector (A).
2. Crimp the connector/wire ends (B).
3. Heat the connector and allow it to cool (C).

WIRING DIAGRAM

A color wiring diagram for all models is located at the end of this manual.

Tables 1-11 are on the following pages.

Table 1 ELECTRICAL SPECIFICATIONS

Alternator	
Stator coil resistance	0.2-0.4 ohms
AC voltage output	19-26 V per 1000 rpm
Battery capacity	12 volt, 12 amp hr.
Ignition coil	
Primary resistance	0.5-0.7 ohms
Secondary resistance	5500-7500 ohms
Voltage regulator	
DC voltage output	14.3-14.7 V at 75° F
Amps at 3600 rpm	22 amps

Table 2 STARTER SPECIFICATIONS

Brush length (minimum)	0.443 in. (11.0 mm)
Commutator diameter (minimum)	1.141 in. (28.98 mm)
Commutator runout (maximum)	0.016 (0.41 mm)
Current draw	
Normal	160-200 amps
Maximum	250 amps
Maximum no-load current at 11.5 volts	90 amps
Minimum no-load speed at 11.5 volts	3000 rpm

Table 3 BULB SPECIFICATIONS

Item	Wattage (quantity)
Headlight-halogen (high/low beam)	60/55
Position light*	4
Front turn signal (running light)	27/7 (2)
Front turn signal*	21 (2)
Rear turn signal	27 (2)
Rear turn signal*	21 (2)
Tail/brake light	7/25

*Bulb specification for HDI models.

Table 4 KEY FOB ASSIGNMENT*

Action	Expected result	Note
RUN/OFF engine switch set to OFF.		Verify security symbol is not flashing, indicating system is disarmed.
Turn ignition key ON-OFF-ON-OFF-ON.		
Press and release left turn signal switch two times.	Turn signals flash 1-3 times.	1 flash=TSM, no security. 2 flashes=TSSM configuration (domestic). 3 flashes=TSSM configuration (linternational).
Press and release right turn signal switch one time	Turn signals flash once.	

(continued)

Table 4 KEY FOB ASSIGNMENT (continued)*

Action	Expected result	Note
Press and release left turn signal switch one time	Turn signals flash twice.	
Press and hold key fob button.	Turn signals flash twice.	10-25 seconds may elapse.
Second key fob: press and hold second key fob button.	Turn signals flash twice.	Only required for use of a second key fob.
Turn ignition key to OFF.		

*There must be no pauses between steps that exceed 10 seconds. Do not proceed to next action until expected result occurs.

Table 5 PERSONAL CODE NUMBER ENTRY*

Action	Expected result	Note
RUN/OFF engine switch set to OFF.		Verify security symbol is not flashing, indicating system is disarmed.
Turn ignition key ON-OFF-ON-OFF-ON.		
Press and release left turn signal switch two times	Turn signals flash 1-3 times.	1 flash=TSM, no security 2 flashes=TSSM configuration (domestic). 3 flashes=TSSM configuration (international).
Press and release key fob button two times	Turn signals flash once. Odometer displays five digits. If no existing code, digits are dashes. First digit blinks.	Odometer display indicates system is in personal code number entry mode. First digit may be entered or changed.
Press and release left turn switch one time.	Security symbol flashes 1-9 times if code number exists.	No flashes indicate no code umber exists.
Press and release left turn switch until the desired number appears.	Security symbol flashes according to number selected.	For example, number 6 selected; symbol flashes six times.
Press and release key fob button two times quickly.	Turn signals flash twice. Second digit in odometer panel blinks.	First digit is entered and second digit is ready for selection.
Repeat Steps 4-7 until all five digits have been selected.		Turn signals flash according to digit position. For instance, turn signals flash four times and the fourth digit blinks.
After selecting fifth digit, press and release key fob button two times quickly.	Turn signals flash once. First digit blinks.	Code number entry cycle completed.

(continued)

9

Table 5 PERSONAL CODE NUMBER ENTRY (continued)*

Action	Expected result	Note
Turn ignition key to OFF.		
Record personal code number. Arm system and use personal code number to disarm system. See Table 6.		

*No personal code number exists in system. Do not proceed to next action until expected result occurs.

Table 6 DISARM USING PERSONAL CODE NUMBER*

Action	Expected result	Note
RUN/OFF engine switch set to OFF.		
Turn ignition key to ACC. Hold in both turn signal switches until security symbol flashes quickly.	Security symbol flashes quickly.	OK to enter personal code.
Press left turn signal switch equal to first number in personal code.		
Press right turn signal switch one time.		Enters first number.
Repeat Steps 4 and 5 until all five digits in personal code number are entered.	Security symbol stops flashing.	System is disarmed.

*Do not proceed to next action until expected result occurs.

Table 7 AUTO-ARM SELECTION*

Action	Expected result	Note
RUN/OFF engine switch set to OFF.		Verify security symbol is not flashing, indicating system is disarmed.
Turn ignition key ON-OFF-ON-OFF-ON.		
Press and release left turn signal switch two times.	Turn signals flash 1-3 times.	1 flash=TSM, no security 2 flashes=TSSM configuration (domestic). 3 flashes=TSSM configuration (international).
Press and hold key fob button until turn signals flash once.	Turn signals flash once.	
Press and hold left turn signal switch until turn signals flash twice.	Turn signals flash twice.	

(continued)

Table 7 AUTO-ARM SELECTION (continued)*

Action	Expected result	Note
Press and release left turn signal switch one time.	Turn signals flash.	1 flash=auto-arm disabled. 2 flashes=auto-arm enabled.
Press and release left turn signal to change mode.	Turn signals flash when mode is selected.	
Turn ignition key to OFF.		
*Does not apply to international models. Do not proceed to next action until expected result occurs.		

Table 8 TRANSPORT MODE OPTIONS*

Action	Expected result	Note
RUN/OFF engine switch set to OFF.		Verify security symbol is not flashing, indicating system is disarmed.
Turn ignition key to ON.		
Press and hold key fob button until turn signals flash three times.	Turn signals flash three times.	
Turn ignition key to OFF.		
Press and hold key fob button until turn signals flash three times.	Turn signals flash three times.	Motorcycle movement possible without triggering alarm.
*Do not proceed to next action until expected result occurs.		

Table 9 STORAGE MODE OPTIONS*

Action	Expected result	Note
RUN/OFF engine switch set to OFF.		Verify security symbol is not flashing, indicating system is disarmed.
Turn ignition key ON-OFF-ON-OFF-ON.		
Press and release left turn signal switch two times.	Turn signals flash 1-3 times.	1 flash=TSM, no security. 2 flashes=TSSM configuration (domestic). 3 flashes=TSSM configuration (international).
Press and hold key fob button until turn signals flash once.	Turn signals flash once.	
Release and hold key fob button until turn signals flash twice.	Turn signals flash twice.	
Release and hold key fob button until turn signals flash three times.	Turn signals flash three times.	

(continued)

Table 9 STORAGE MODE OPTIONS (continued)*

Action	Expected result	Note
Press and release left turn signal switch one time.	Turn signals flash.	1 flash=10 days. 2 flashes=20 days. 3 flashes=60 days. 4 flashes=infinity.
Press and release left turn signal to select next option.	Turn signals flash for each selection.	
Turn ignition key to OFF.		

*Do not proceed to next action until expected result occurs.

Table 10 ALARM SENSITIVITY*

Action	Expected result	Note
RUN/OFF engine switch set to OFF.		Verify security symbol is not flashing, indicating system is disarmed.
Turn ignition key ON-OFF-ON-OFF-ON.		
Press and release left turn signal switch two times.	Turn signals flash 1-3 times	1 flash=TSM, no security. 2 flashes=TSSM configuration (domestic). 3 flashes=TSSM configuration (international).
Press and hold key fob button until turn signals flash once.	Turn signals flash once.	
Press and release left turn signal switch one time.	Turn signals flash.	1 flash=very low sensitivity. 2 flashes=low sensitivity. 3 flashes=medium sensitivity. 4 flashes=high sensitivity.
Press and release left turn signal to select next option.	Turn signals flash for each selection.	
Turn ignition key to OFF.		

*Do not proceed to next action until expected result occurs.

Table 11 ELECTRICAL SYSTEM TORQUE SPECIFICATIONS

	ft.-lb.	in.-lb.	N•m
Battery cable retaining bolt	–	40-50	4.5-5.6
Battery negative cable end nut	–	55-75	6.2-8.5
Battery strap retaining screw	–	36-60	4.1-6.8
CKP sensor bolt	–	80-100	9-11
Front turn signal ball stud	–	96-156	11-17
Front turn signal ball stud Allen-head screw	–	96-156	11-17

(continued)

Table 11 ELECTRICAL SYSTEM TORQUE SPECIFICATIONS (continued)

	ft.-lb.	in.-lb.	N•m
Handlebar holder bolts (XL883, XL883L, XL883R, XL1200L, XL1200R)	12-18	–	17-24
Handlebar riser cover screws	–	8-12	0.9-1.4
Headlight mounting bolts (XL883C, XL1200C)	30-35	–	41-47
Headlight mounting nut (XL883, XL883L, XL883R, XL1200L, XL1200R)	–	120-240	14-27
Horn acorn nut (XL1200C)	–	60-180	6.8-20.3
Horn stud nut (XL1200C)	–	80-100	9.0-11.0
Ignition switch retaining screw	–	35-45	4.0-5.0
Neutral indicator switch	–	36-60	4.1-6.8
Oil pressure switch	–	50-70	6-8
Rear brake light switch	–	84-120	9.5-13.6
Rear turn signal stud	–	132-216	15-24
Rear turn signal stud inner nut	–	132-216	15-24
Rotor mounting bolts	–	120-140	13.6-15.8
Starter positive cable nut	–	60-85	6.8-9.6
Starter mounting bolts	13-20	–	18-27
Starter throughbolts	–	39-65	4.4-7.3
Stator screws*	–	30-40	3.4-4.5
Strut cover bolts	–	132-216	15-24
Taillight base mounting screws	–	45-48	5.1-5.4
Taillight lens mounting screws	–	20-24	2.3-2.7
VSS retaining screw	–	80-100	9-11

*Install new fasteners.

NOTE: Refer to the Supplement at the end of this manual for information unique to 2007-2011 models.

CHAPTER TEN

WHEELS, TIRES AND DRIVE BELT

This chapter includes procedures for disassembly and repair of the front and rear wheels, wheel hubs, tire service and the drive belt. Refer to Chapter Three for routine maintenance.

Tables 1-4 are located at the end of this chapter.

MOTORCYCLE STANDS

Many procedures in this chapter require lifting the front or rear wheel off the ground. A motorcycle front end stand (**Figure 1**), swing arm stand or suitable size jack is required. Before purchasing or using a stand, check the manufacturer's instructions to make sure the stand will work with the specific model being worked on. If any adjustments or accessories are required, perform the necessary adjustments and install the correct parts before lifting the motorcycle. When using the stand, have an assistant stand by to help. Some means to tie down one end of the motorcycle may also be required. Make sure the motorcycle is properly supported on the stand.

If a motorcycle stand is not available, use a scissor jack (**Figure 2**) with adapters that securely fit onto the frame tubes (**Figure 3**, typical).

FRONT WHEEL

Removal

1. Support the motorcycle with the front wheel off the ground. Refer to *Motorcycle Stands* in this chapter.
2. Remove the front fender as described in Chapter Fourteen.
3. Remove the caliper mounting bolts and remove the caliper (A, **Figure 4**) as described in Chapter Thirteen. On XL1200R models, remove both calipers.

NOTE
Place a plastic or wooden spacer between the brake pads in place of the disc. Then, if the brake lever is inadvertently applied, the pistons will not be forced out of the caliper. If the pistons are forced out, disassemble the caliper to reseat the pistons.

4. Insert a drift or screwdriver through the front axle hole in the right end (A, **Figure 5**) to prevent axle rotation in the next step.
5. Remove the axle nut (B, **Figure 4**), lockwasher and flat washer.
6. On the right side, loosen the nut on the axle clamp bolt (B, **Figure 5**).

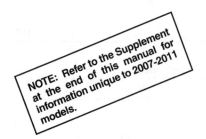

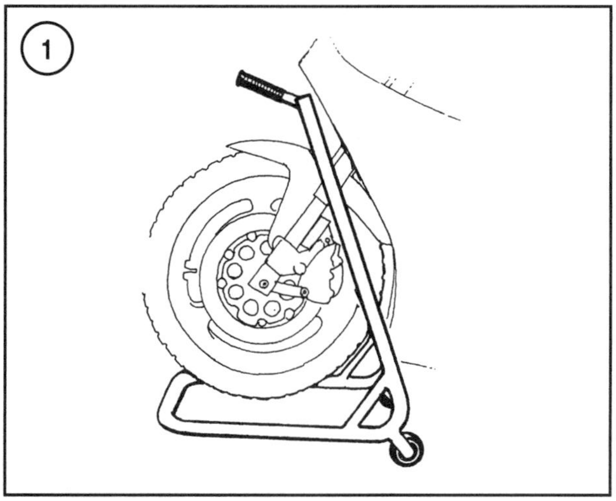

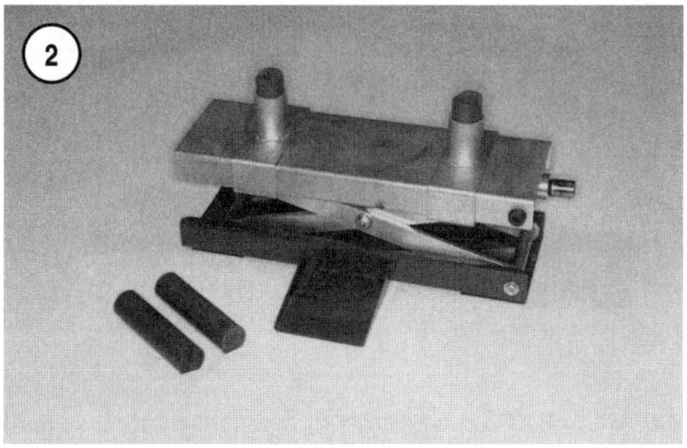

CAUTION
Identify the wheel spacers during removal so they can be returned to their original positions.

7. Prior to removing the front axle, note the location of the right side spacer and left side spacer. Make sure to reinstall the spacers on the correct sides during installation.

8. Withdraw the front axle (**Figure 6**) from the fork legs and front wheel.

9. Remove the front wheel.

10. Remove the spacers from both sides (**Figure 7**) of the wheel.

CAUTION
Do not set the wheel down on the brake disc surface, as it may be damaged.

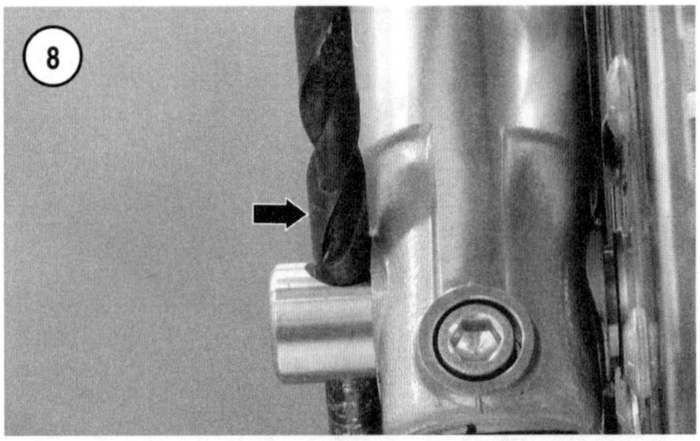

11. Inspect the front wheel assembly as described in this chapter.

Installation

1. Clean the axle in solvent and dry it thoroughly. Make sure the axle bearing surfaces on both fork sliders and the axle are free of burrs and nicks.
2. Lubricate the axle shaft prior to installation.
3. If the bearings were replaced, check front axle spacer alignment as described in *Front and Rear Hubs* in this chapter.
4. Install the wheel between the fork legs while also installing the spacers on each side (**Figure 7**). The thin spacer fits on the right side; the thick spacer fits on the left side.
5. Install the axle from the right side (**Figure 6**). Push the front axle through the right fork leg, right side spacer, hub, left side spacer and left fork leg.
6. Make sure the axle spacers are installed correctly.
7. Install the flat washer, lockwasher and axle nut (B, **Figure 4**). Tighten the nut finger-tight.
8. Insert a drift or screwdriver through the hole (A, **Figure 5**) in the right axle end to prevent axle rotation in the next step.
9. Tighten the front axle nut (B, **Figure 4**) to 50-55 ft.-lb. (68-75 N•m).
10. Make sure the front wheel is centered between the fork sliders. If it is not, check the position of the left and right axle spacers.
11. On XL1200R models, insert a 7/16-inch drill bit into the axle hole (**Figure 8**). Push the fork leg against the drill bit. This properly aligns the brake discs with the brake calipers.
12. Tighten the clamp nut (B, **Figure 5**) to 21-27 ft.-lb. (29-37 N•m).
13. Install the front brake caliper(s) as described in Chapter Thirteen.

14. With the front wheel off the ground, rotate it several times and apply the front brake to seat the brake pads against the disc(s).
15. Install the front fender.
16. Remove the stand and lower the front wheel to the ground.

Inspection

1. Turn each bearing inner race by hand (**Figure 9**, typical). The bearing should turn smoothly. Some axial play is normal, but radial play should be negligible. See **Figure 10**. If one bearing is damaged, replace both bearings as a set. Refer to *Front and Rear Hubs* in this chapter.
2. Clean the axle and axle spacers in solvent to remove all grease and dirt. Make sure the axle contact surfaces are clean.
3. Check the axle runout with a set of V-blocks and a dial indicator (**Figure 11**, typical).
4. Check the spacers for wear, burrs and damage. Replace as necessary.
5. Check the brake disc bolts (**Figure 12**) for tightness. To service the brake disc, refer to Chapter Thirteen.

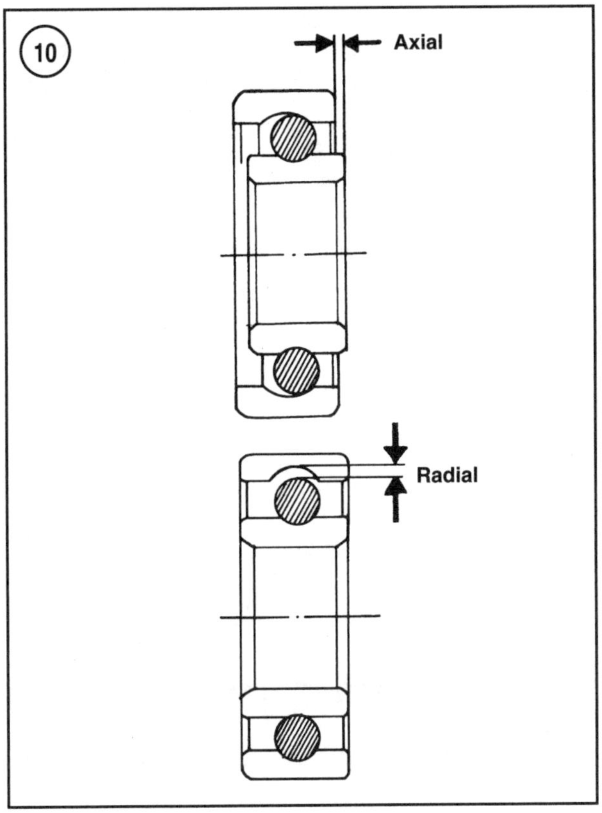

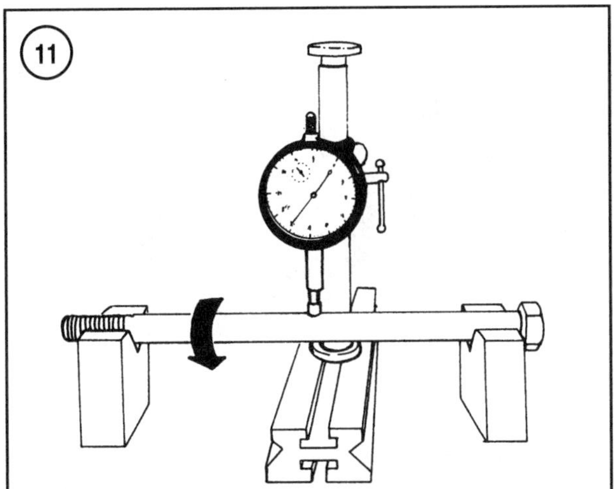

6. Check wheel runout and spoke tension (laced wheels) as described in this chapter.

REAR WHEEL

Removal

1. Refer to Chapter Eight and remove the rear muffler.

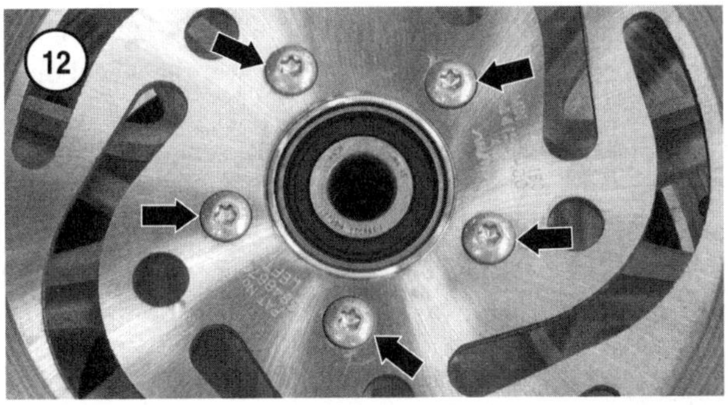

2. Support the motorcycle so the rear wheel is off the ground.

CAUTION
The rear wheel is heavy and can be difficult to remove. Check the tire-to-ground clearance before removing the rear axle. If necessary, have an assistant help or place wooden blocks under the wheel.

NOTE
The axle nut is retained by a spring clip on 2004 models or an E-clip on 2005-on models. The torque specification is also different.

3. Remove the spring clip or E-clip (A, **Figure 13**) and loosen the rear axle nut (B).

CAUTION
Identify the wheel spacers during removal so they can be returned to their original positions.

4. Remove the axle nut and washer (C, **Figure 13**).
5. On both sides, loosen the drive belt adjusting nuts (D, **Figure 13**). Move the rear wheel forward.
6. Using a soft hammer, gently tap the axle end toward the right side.

10

7. From the right side, withdraw the rear axle (**Figure 14**) while holding onto the rear wheel. Lower the wheel onto the wooden blocks or the ground.
8. Move the rear wheel forward and disengage the drive belt from the driven sprocket.
9. Raise the motorcycle sufficiently to allow the rear wheel to roll back and clear the rear fender.
10. Remove the rear wheel and lower the motorcycle to a safe level.

NOTE
Place a plastic or wooden spacer between the brake pads in place of the disc. Then, if the brake pedal is inadvertently depressed, the pistons will not be forced out of the caliper. If the pistons are forced out, disassemble the caliper to reseat the pistons.

11. If still in place, remove the wheel spacers (**Figure 15**) from the right side and the left side of the wheel.

CAUTION
Do not set the wheel down on the brake disc surface, as it may be damaged.

12. Inspect the rear wheel as described in this chapter.

Installation

CAUTION
The rear wheel spacers must be installed into the correct side of the rear wheel. If installed incorrectly, the wheel will be offset to the wrong side within the swing arm. This will result in the drive belt being out of alignment with the driven sprocket, causing rapid drive belt wear.

1. Clean the axle in solvent and dry it thoroughly. Make sure the bearing surfaces on the axle are free of burrs and nicks.
2. Lubricate the axle shaft prior to installation.
3. Make sure the adjusters (**Figure 16**) are properly oriented in the axle recesses.
4. Raise the motorcycle sufficiently to allow the rear wheel to roll forward and clear the rear fender.
5. Move the rear wheel forward so the brake disc fits between the brake pads (**Figure 17**).
6. Install the drive belt onto the driven sprocket (**Figure 18**), then move the wheel rearward.
7. Lower the motorcycle to a level where the rear axle can be installed.
8. Identify the spacers. The right side spacer (A, **Figure 19**) is wide; the left side spacer is thin (B).

14

15

16

17

18

19

20

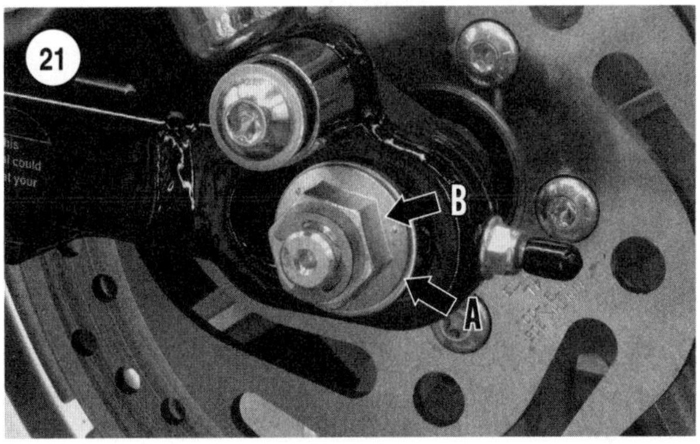

21

22

9. Install the right side spacer into the wheel and hold it in place.
10. From the right side, carefully install the rear axle (**Figure 20**) through the right side of the swing arm, axle adjuster, spacer and rear hub.
11. Install the left side spacer into the wheel and hold it in place.
12. Continue to push the rear axle through the left side spacer, axle adjuster and the swing arm.
13. Install the washer (A, **Figure 21**) and axle nut (B). Tighten the axle nut finger-tight at this time.
14. Adjust drive belt tension as described in Chapter Three.

WARNING
There are two methods and torque requirement used to retain the rear axle nut.

15. Tighten the axle nut as described in Chapter Three.
16. Install the rear muffler as described in Chapter Eight.
17. Rotate the wheel several times to make sure it rotates freely. Apply the rear brake pedal several times to seat the pads against the disc.
18. Remove the stand and lower the rear wheel to the ground.

Inspection

Replace worn or damaged parts as described in this section.

1. Turn each bearing inner race (**Figure 22**) by hand. The bearing should turn smoothly. Some axial play is normal, but radial play should be negligible. See **Figure 10**. If one bearing is damaged, replace both bearings as a set. Refer to *Front and Rear Hubs* in this chapter.
2. Clean the axle and axle spacers in solvent to remove all grease and dirt. Make sure the axle contact surfaces are free of dirt and old grease.
3. Check the axle runout with a set of V-blocks and a dial indicator (**Figure 11**, typical).

4. Check the bearing spacers for wear, burrs and damage. Replace as necessary.
5. Check the brake disc bolts (**Figure 23**) for tightness. To service the brake disc, refer to Chapter Thirteen.
6. Check the final drive sprocket bolts (**Figure 24**) for tightness. Service for the final drive sprocket is covered in Chapter Seven.
7. Check wheel runout as described in this chapter.

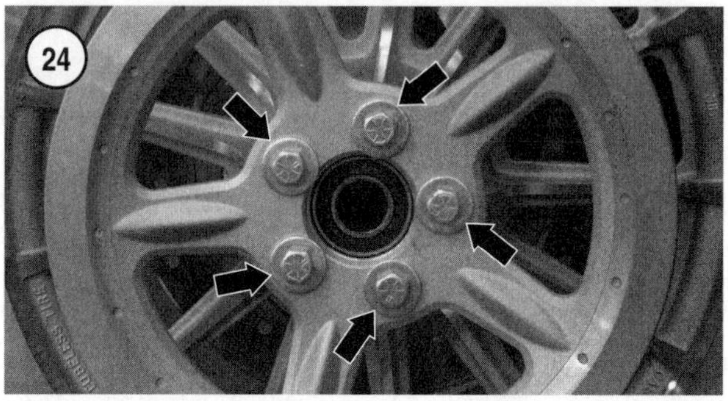

FRONT AND REAR HUBS

Sealed ball bearings are installed on each side of the hub.

CAUTION
Do not remove the wheel bearings for inspection as they will be damaged during the removal process. Remove wheel bearings only if they need replacement.

Preliminary Inspection

Check wheel bearing end play after tightening the front or rear wheel axle nut. Checking end play will indicate wheel bearing wear.

1. Make sure the axle nut is tightened to the torque specification in **Table 4**.
2. Mount a dial indicator so the plunger contacts the end of the axle (**Figure 25**).
3. Grasp the wheel and try to move it back and forth by pushing and pulling it along the axle centerline. Measure end play by watching the dial indicator.
4. Note the specified end play in **Table 1**.
5. Check the end play a second time if the observed end play is out of specification.
6. If the measured end play is incorrect, continue with Step 7.
7. Perform Steps 1-3 of *Disassembly* in this section.
8. Turn each bearing inner race (**Figure 22**) by hand . The bearings should turn smoothly.
9. Inspect the play of the inner race of each wheel bearing. Check for excessive axial play and radial play (**Figure 10**). Replace the bearing if the measured end play or bearing free play is excessive.

Disassembly

This procedure applies to both the front and rear wheel and hub assemblies. Differences between the hubs are identified. Refer to **Figure 26** and **Figure 27**.

1A. Remove the front wheel as described in this chapter.
1B. Remove the rear wheel as described in this chapter.
2. Remove the axle spacers from each side of the hub if they are still in place.

CAUTION
Make sure the brake disc(s) will not be damaged while performing the following procedure. If damage may occur, remove the brake disc(s).

3. If necessary, remove the bolts securing the brake disc(s) (**Figure 23**) and remove the disc(s).

4. Before proceeding, inspect the wheel bearings as described in this section. If they must be replaced, proceed as follows.

26

FRONT WHEEL

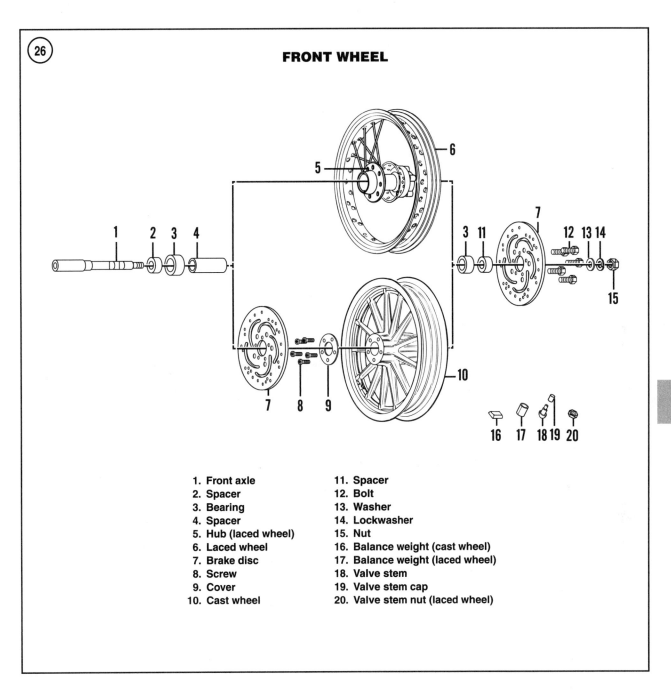

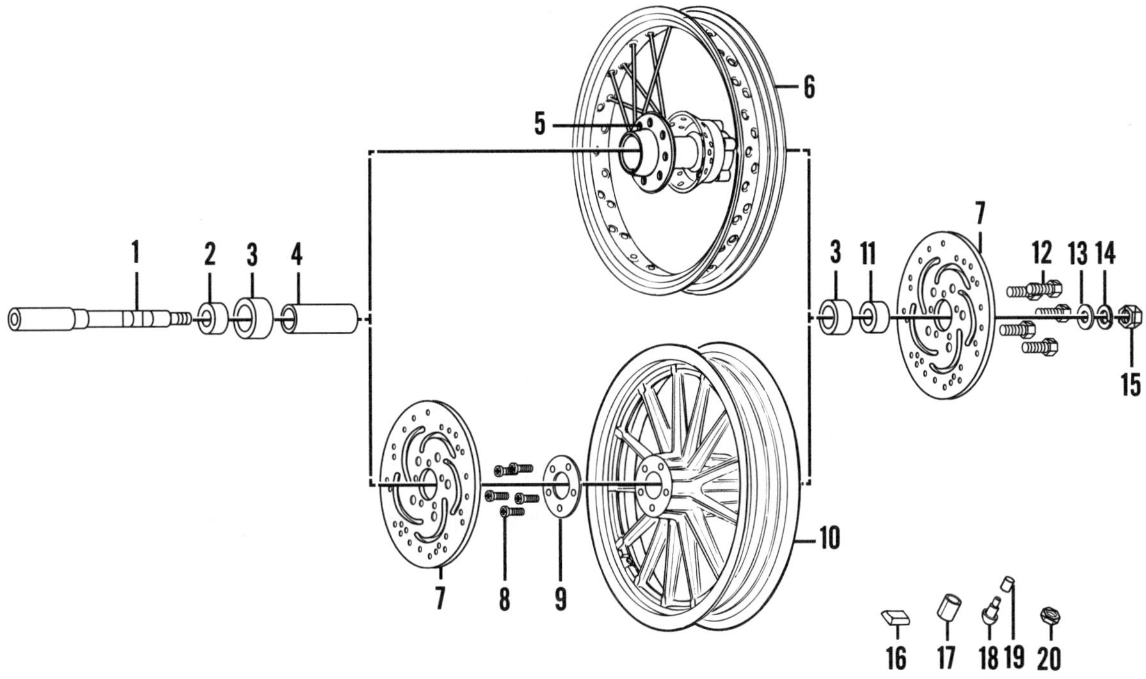

1. Front axle
2. Spacer
3. Bearing
4. Spacer
5. Hub (laced wheel)
6. Laced wheel
7. Brake disc
8. Screw
9. Cover
10. Cast wheel
11. Spacer
12. Bolt
13. Washer
14. Lockwasher
15. Nut
16. Balance weight (cast wheel)
17. Balance weight (laced wheel)
18. Valve stem
19. Valve stem cap
20. Valve stem nut (laced wheel)

WARNING
Wear safety glasses while removing the wheel bearings.

5A. If the special tools are not used, perform the following:

a. To remove the right and left bearings and spacer collar, insert a soft aluminum or brass drift into one side of the hub.

b. Push the spacer collar over to one side and place the drift on the inner race of the lower bearing.

c. Tap the bearing out of the hub with a hammer, working around the perimeter of the inner race (**Figure 28**). Remove the bearing and distance collar.

d. Repeat substep b and substep c for the bearing on the other side.

27

REAR WHEEL

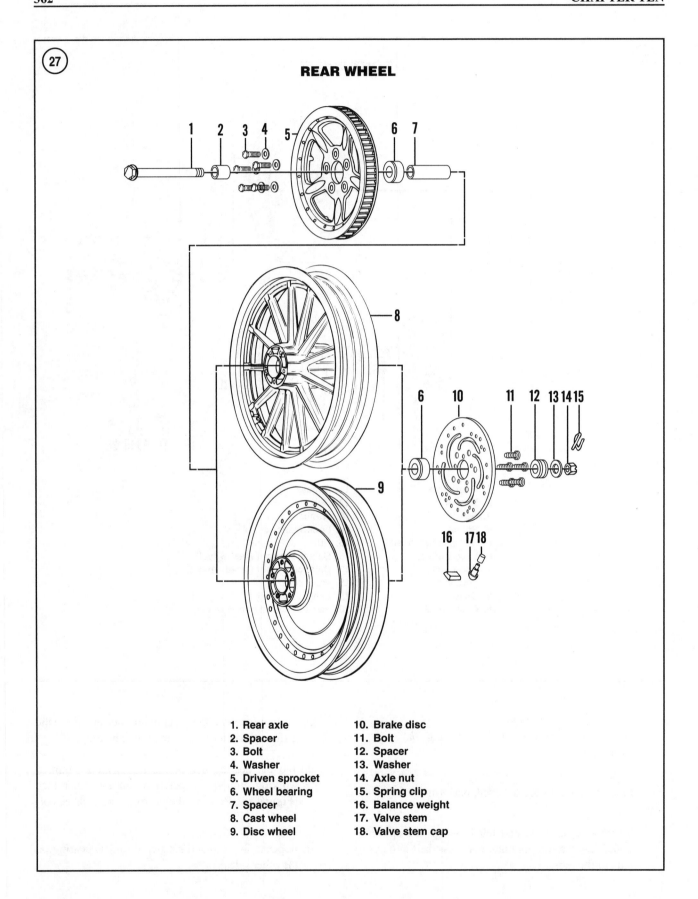

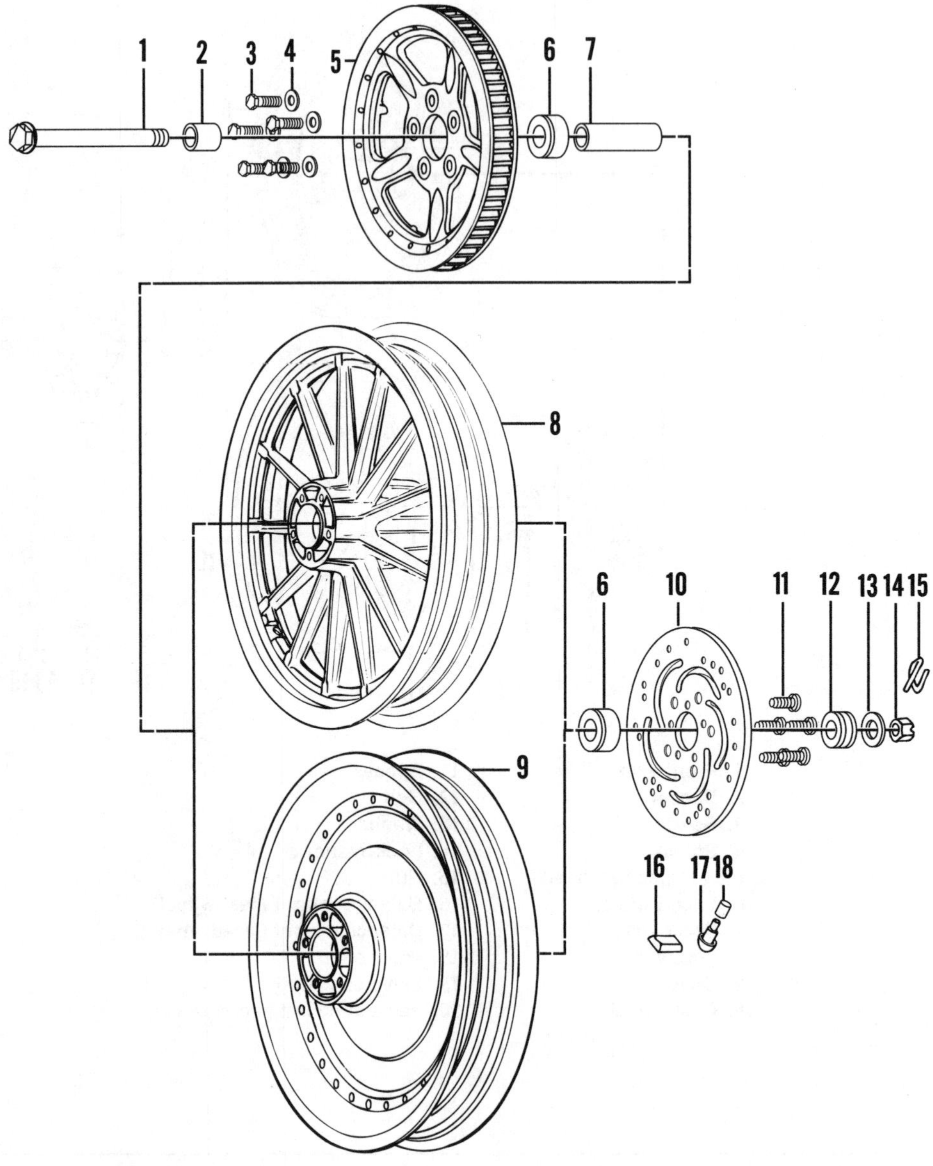

1. Rear axle
2. Spacer
3. Bolt
4. Washer
5. Driven sprocket
6. Wheel bearing
7. Spacer
8. Cast wheel
9. Disc wheel
10. Brake disc
11. Bolt
12. Spacer
13. Washer
14. Axle nut
15. Spring clip
16. Balance weight
17. Valve stem
18. Valve stem cap

(28)
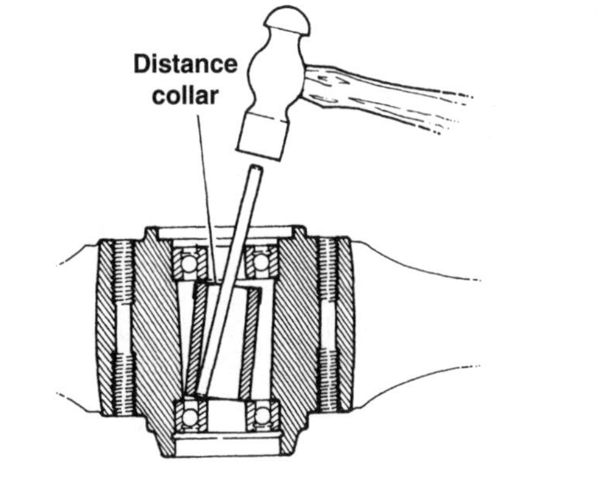

(29)
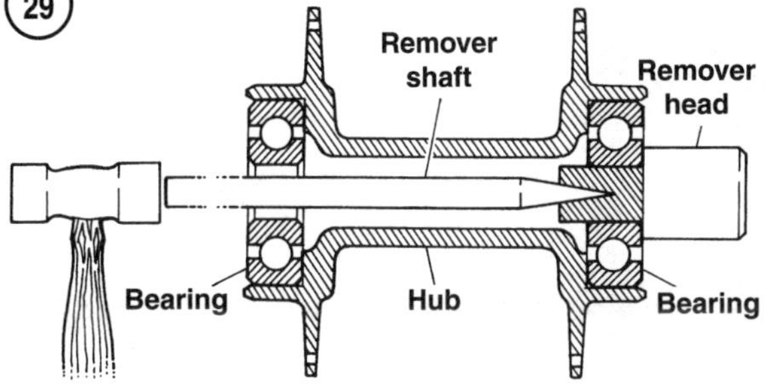

(30)
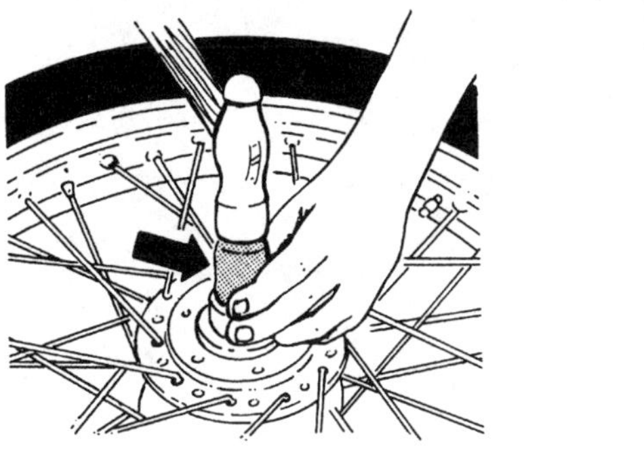

5B. To remove the bearings with a wheel bearing remover set, refer to **Figure 29** and perform the following:

a. Select the correct size remover head tool and insert it into the bearing.

b. Turn the wheel over and insert the remover shaft into the backside of the remover head. Carefully tap the shaft and force it into the slit in the remover head. This forces the remover head against the bearing inner race.

c. Continue to tap the end of the remover shaft to drive the bearing out of the hub. Remove the bearing and the distance collar.

d. Repeat substeps a-c for the bearing on the other side.

6. Clean the inside and the outside of the hub with solvent. Dry it with compressed air.

Assembly

CAUTION

The removal process will usually damage the bearings. Replace the wheel bearings in pairs. Never reinstall bearings after removing them.

1. Blow any debris out of the hub prior to installing the new bearings.
2. Apply a light coat of wheel bearing grease to the bearing seating areas of the hub. This will make bearing installation easier.
3. Select a driver, or socket (**Figure 30**), with an outside diameter slightly smaller than the bearing's outside diameter.

CAUTION

Install non-sealed bearings with the single sealed side facing out.

4. Tap on the outer race of the bearing until the bearing bottoms in the hub bore. Make sure the bearing is square in the bore and seated.
5. Turn the wheel over on the workbench and install the inner spacer.
6. Use the same tool set-up to drive in the remaining bearing.
7. If removed, install the removed brake disc(s) as described in Chapter Thirteen.

8A. Install the front wheel as described in this chapter.

8B. Install the rear wheel as described in this chapter.

DRIVEN SPROCKET ASSEMBLY

Inspection

Inspect the sprocket teeth (**Figure 31**). If the teeth are visibly worn, replace the drive belt and both sprockets.

Removal/Installation

1. Remove the rear wheel as described in this chapter.
2. Remove the bolts and washers (**Figure 24**) securing the driven sprocket to the hub, and remove the sprocket.

3. Position the driven sprocket onto the rear hub.
4. Apply a light coat of Loctite 262, or an equivalent, to the bolts prior to installation.
5. Install the bolts and washers and tighten the bolts to 55-65 ft.-lb. (75-88 N•m).

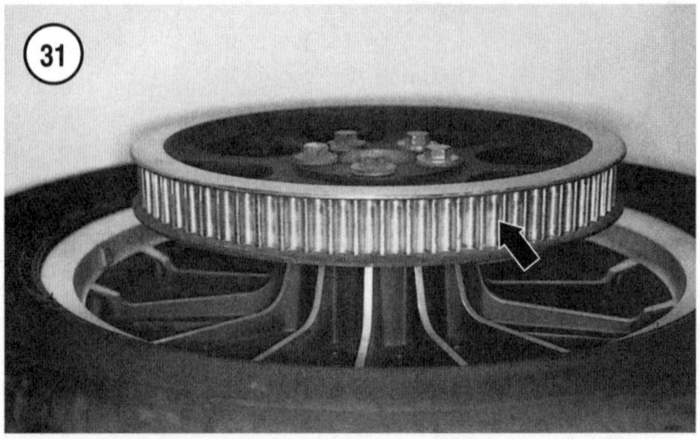

DRIVE SPROCKET

The drive sprocket is covered in Chapter Seven.

DRIVE BELT

CAUTION
When handling a new or used drive belt, never wrap the belt in a loop smaller than 5 in. (127 mm) or bend it sharply. This will weaken or break the belt fibers and cause premature belt failure.

CAUTION
If reinstalling the existing drive belt, install it so it travels in the same direction. Before removing the belt, draw an arrow on the top surface of the belt facing forward.

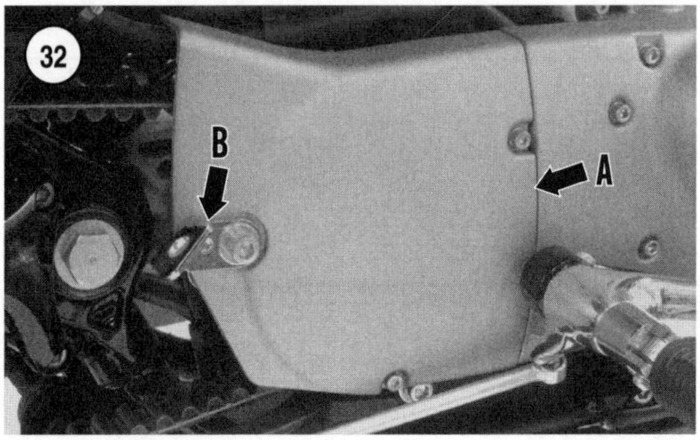

Removal

1. Remove the exhaust system as described in Chapter Eight.
2. Except on XL883C and XL1200C models, remove the right footrest and brake pedal assembly as described in Chapter Fourteen.
3. Remove the drive sprocket cover screws, then remove the sprocket cover (A, **Figure 32**).
4. Remove the spring clip or E-clip (A, **Figure 33**) and loosen the rear axle nut (B).
5. On both sides, loosen the drive belt adjusting nuts (C, **Figure 33**). Move the rear wheel forward.
6. Loosen the debris deflector retaining screws (A, **Figure 34**). The screws fit into slots in the deflector. Slide the deflector (B, **Figure 34**) forward until the screw heads pass through the large slot holes, and remove the deflector.
7. Remove the right shock absorber lower mounting bolt (**Figure 35**), washer and locknut.
8. Remove the belt guard mounting bolt (A, **Figure 36**), washer and locknut, then remove the belt guard (B).
9. Remove the drive belt (**Figure 37**).

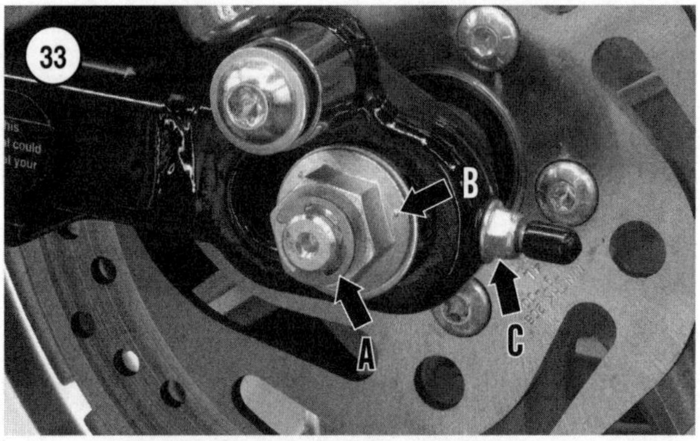

Installation

1. Install the drive belt (**Figure 37**) onto the sprockets.

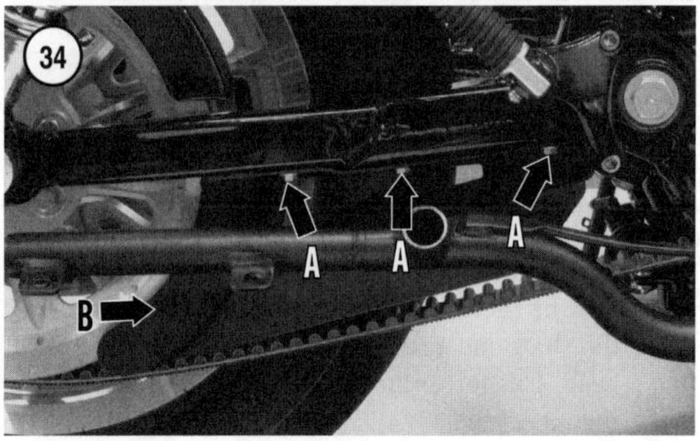

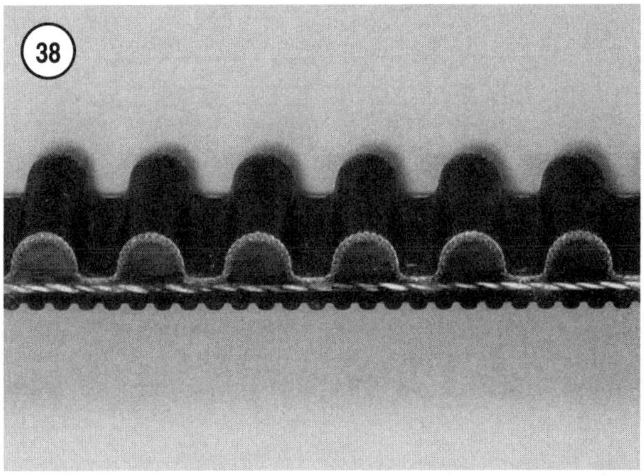

2. Install the belt guard (B, **Figure 36**) and the mounting bolt (A), washer and locknut. Tighten the locknut to 120-180 in.-lb. (14-20 N•m).
3. Install the deflector onto the retaining screws, then slide the deflector fully rearward so the screw heads fit into the narrow slots. Tighten the screws to 36-60 in.-lb. (4-7 N•m).
4. Install the right shock absorber lower mounting bolt (**Figure 35**), washer and locknut. Tighten the locknut to 45-50 ft.-lb. (61-68 N•m).
5. Install the sprocket cover (A, **Figure 32**), but do not tighten the bolts. Note the position of the exhaust bracket (B, **Figure 32**) and install it. Tighten the exhaust bracket bolt to 30-33 ft.-lb. (41-45 N•m). Tighten the sprocket cover bolts to 80-120 in.-lb. (9-14 N•m).
6. Except on XL883C and XL1200C models, install the right footrest and brake pedal assembly as described in Chapter Fourteen.
7. Install the exhaust system as described in Chapter Eight.
8. Adjust drive belt tension as described in Chapter Three.

WARNING
There are two methods and torque requirement used to retain the rear axle nut.

9. Tighten the axle nut as described in Chapter Three.

Inspection

Do not apply any type of lubricant to the drive belt. Inspect the drive belt (**Figure 38**) for excessive wear, damage or contamination.

Refer to **Figure 39** for various types of drive belt wear or damage. Replace the drive belt if it is worn or damaged.

WHEEL INSPECTION

WARNING
Do not repair damage to a disc wheel, as it will cause an unsafe riding condition.

1. Remove the front or rear wheel as described in this chapter.
2. Install the wheel in a wheel truing stand and check the wheel for excessive wobble or runout.
3. If the wheel is not running true, remove the tire from the rim as described in this chapter. Then remount the wheel into the truing stand, and measure radial and lateral runout (**Figure 40**) with a pointer or dial indicator. Compare actual runout readings with the specifications in **Table 1**. Note the following:

a. Disc or cast wheels—if the runout meets or exceeds the specification, check the wheel bearings as described in *Front and Rear Hub* in this chapter. If the wheel bearings are acceptable, replace the cast or disc wheel as it cannot be serviced. Inspect the wheel for cracks, fractures, dents or bends. Replace a damaged wheel.

b. Laced wheels—if the wheel bearings, spokes, hub and rim assembly are not damaged, the runout can be corrected by truing the wheel. Refer to *Laced Wheels* in this chapter. If the rim is dented or damaged, replace the rim and rebuild the wheel.

4. While the wheel is off, perform the following:

a. Check the brake disc mounting bolts (**Figure 41**) for tightness as described in Chapter Fourteen.

b. On the rear wheel, check the driven sprocket bolts (**Figure 42**) for tightness as described in this chapter.

LACED WHEELS

The laced or spoke wheel consists of a rim, spokes, nipples and hub containing the bearings, and spacer.

Component Condition

Wheels are subjected to a significant amount of punishment. Inspect the wheel regularly for lateral (side-to-side) and radial (up-and-down) runout, even spoke tension and visible rim damage. When a wheel has a noticeable wobble, it is out of true. This is usually caused by loose spokes, but it can be caused by an impact-damaged rim.

Truing a wheel corrects the lateral and radial runout to bring the wheel back into specification. The condition of the individual wheel components will affect the ability to successfully true the wheel. Note the following:

1. Spoke condition—Do not true a wheel with bent or damaged spokes. Doing so places an excessive amount of tension on the spoke and rim. The spoke may break and/or pull through the spoke nipple hole in the rim Inspect the spokes carefully and replace any spokes that are damaged.

2. Nipple condition—When truing the wheels, the nipples should turn freely on the spoke. It is common for the spoke threads to become corroded and make turning the nipple difficult. Spray a penetrating liquid onto the nipple and allow sufficient time for it to penetrate before trying to force the nipple loose. Work the spoke wrench in both directions and continue to apply penetrating liquid. If the spoke wrench rounds off the nipple, remove the tire from the rim and cut the spoke(s) out of the wheel.

39

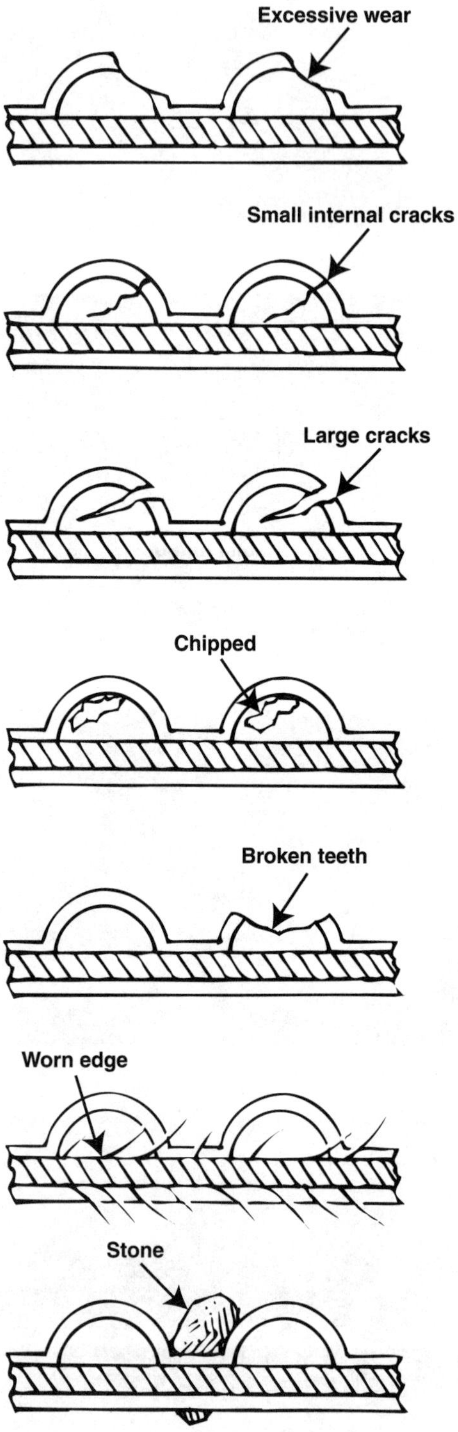

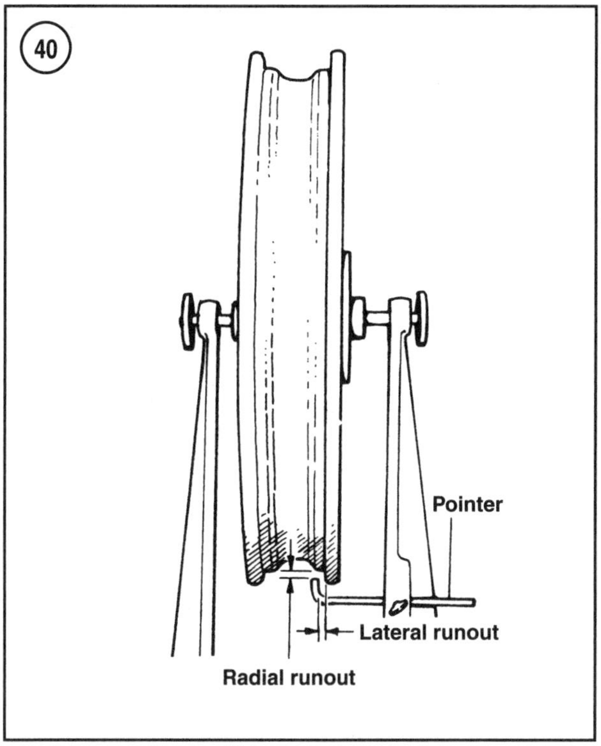

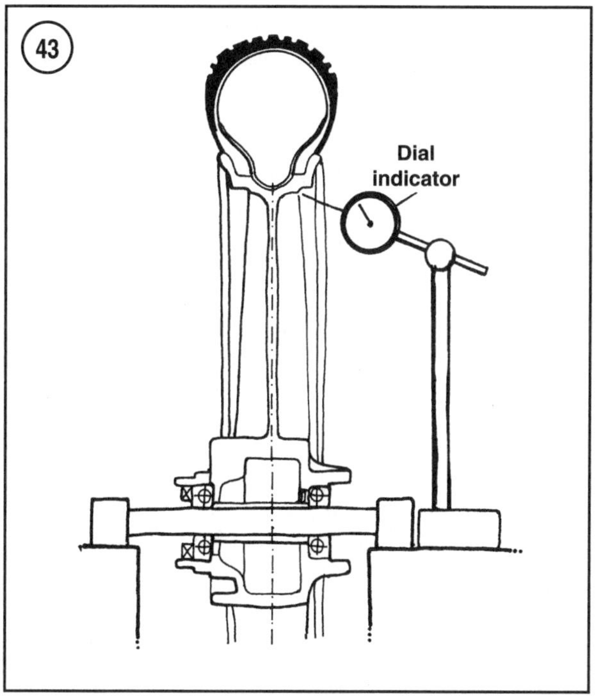

3. Rim condition—Minor rim damage can be corrected by truing the wheel; however, trying to correct excessive runout caused by impact damage causes hub and rim damage due to spoke overtightening. Inspect the rims for cracks, flat spots or dents. Check the spoke holes for cracks or enlargement. Replace rims with excessive damage.

Wheel Truing Preliminaries

Before checking runout and truing the wheel, note the following:

1. Make sure the wheel bearings are in good condition. Refer to *Front and Rear Hubs* in this chapter.

2. A small amount of wheel runout is acceptable. Do not try to true the wheel to a perfect zero reading. Doing so causes excessive spoke tension and possible rim and hub damage. Refer to **Table 1** for the maximum lateral (side-to-side) and radial (up-and-down) runout specifications.

3. The runout can be checked on the motorcycle by mounting a pointer against the fork or swing arm and slowly rotating the wheel.

4. Perform major wheel truing with the tire removed and the wheel mounted in a truing stand (**Figure 43**). If a stand is not available, mount the wheel on the motorcycle with

spacers on each side of the wheel to prevent it from sliding on the axle.

5. Use a spoke nipple wrench of the correct size. Using the wrong type of tool or one that is the incorrect size will round off the spoke nipples, making adjustment difficult. Quality spoke wrenches have openings that grip the nipple on four corners to prevent nipple damage.

6. If a torque wrench and adapter are available, tighten the spoke nipple to 40-50 in. lb. (4.5-6.7 N•m).

Wheel Truing Procedure

1. Position a pointer facing toward the rim. Spin the wheel slowly and check the lateral and radial runout. If the rim is out of adjustment, continue with Step 2.

NOTE
If there is a large number of loose spokes, make sure the hub is centered in the rim. Do this visually, as there are no hub and rim centering specifications for these models.

NOTE
The number of spokes to loosen and tighten depends on how far the runout is out of adjustment. As a minimum, always loosen two or three spokes, then tighten the opposite two or three spokes. If the runout is excessive and affects a greater area along the rim, a greater number of spokes will require adjustment.

2. If the lateral (side-to-side) runout is out of specification, adjust the wheel by using **Figure 44** as an example. To move the rim to the left, loosen and tighten the spokes as shown. Always loosen and tighten the spokes an equal number of turns.

3. If the radial (up-and-down) runout is out of specification, the hub is not centered in the rim. Draw the high point of the rim toward the centerline of the wheel by tightening the spokes in the area of the high point and on the same side as the high point, and loosening the spokes on the side opposite the high point (**Figure 45**). Tighten spokes in equal amounts to prevent distortion.

4. After truing the wheel, seat each spoke in the hub by tapping it with a flat nose punch and hammer. Then recheck the spoke tension and wheel runout. Readjust if necessary.

5. Check the ends of the spokes where they are threaded in the nipples. Grind off ends that protrude through the nipples.

44

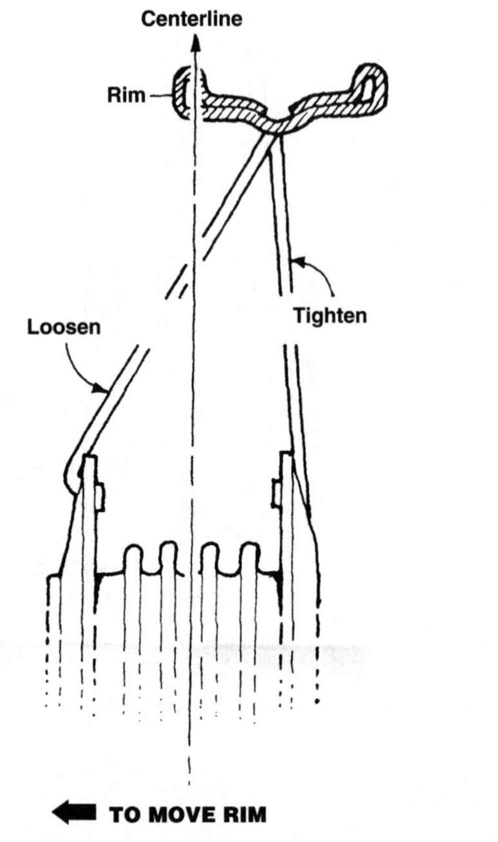

45

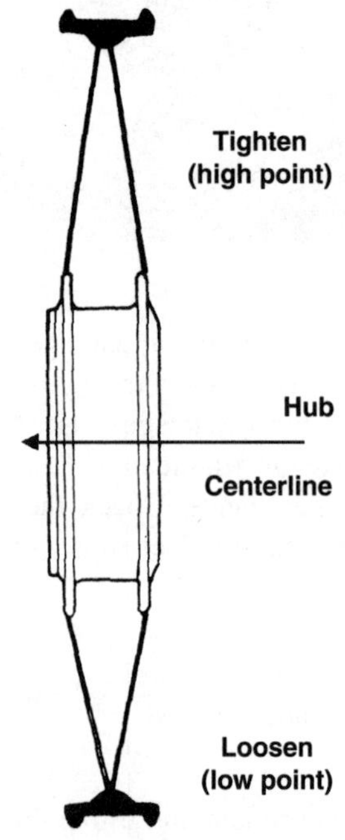

DISC AND CAST WHEELS

Disc and cast wheels consist of a single assembly equipped with bearings and a spacer sleeve.

While these wheels can not be trued, they must be checked periodically for damage. Also, check the disc wheels prior to installing new tires.

Inspection

Before checking runout, note the following:

1. Make sure the wheel bearings are in good condition. Refer to *Front and Rear Hubs* in this chapter.
2. Perform wheel runout with the tire removed and the wheel mounted in a truing stand (**Figure 43**). If a stand is not available, mount the wheel on the motorcycle with spacers on each side of the wheel to prevent it from sliding on the axle.
3. Refer to **Table 1** for the maximum lateral (side-to-side) and radial (up-and-down) runout specifications.

WARNING
Do not repair any damage to a disc or cast wheel, as it will cause an unsafe riding condition.

WHEEL BALANCE

An unbalanced wheel is unsafe. Depending on the degree of unbalance and the speed of the motorcycle, the rider may experience anything from a mild vibration to a violent shimmy that may cause loss of control.

On cast or disc wheels, weights are attached to the flat surface on the rim (**Figure 46**). On laced wheels, the weights are attached to the spoke nipples (**Figure 47**).

10

Before attempting to balance the wheel, make sure the wheel bearings are in good condition and properly lubricated. The wheel must rotate freely.

1A. Remove the front wheel as described in this chapter.

1B. Remove the rear wheel as described in this chapter.

2. Mount the wheel on a fixture (**Figure 48**) so it can rotate freely.
3. Spin the wheel and let it coast to a stop. Mark the tire at the lowest point.
4. Spin the wheel several more times. If the wheel keeps coming to rest at the same point, it is out of balance.

5A. On cast or disc wheels, tape a test weight to the upper or light side of the wheel (**Figure 46**).

5B. On laced wheels, attach a weight to the spoke (**Figure 47**) on the upper or light side of the wheel.

6. Experiment with different weights until the wheel comes to a stop at a different position each time it is spun.

WARNING
The maximum total weight installed on a wheel must not exceed 3.5 oz. (866 g). If the wheel cannot be balanced using this amount, inspect the wheel for damage.

7. On cast or disc wheels, remove the test weight and install the correct size weight.
   a. Attach the weights to the flat surface on the rim (**Figure 46**). Clean the rim of all road residue before

installing the weights; otherwise, the weights may fall off.

b. Add weights in 1/4 oz. (7 g) increments. If 1 oz. (28 g) or more must be added to one location, apply half the amount to each side of the rim.

c. To apply original equipment wheel weights, remove the paper backing from the weight and apply three drops of Loctite 420 Superbonder to the bottom of the weight. Position the weight on the rim, press it down and hold in position for 10 seconds. To allow the adhesive to cure properly, do not use the wheel for 8 hours.

8. When fitting weights on laced wheels for the final time, crimp the weights onto the spoke (**Figure 47**) with slip-joint pliers.

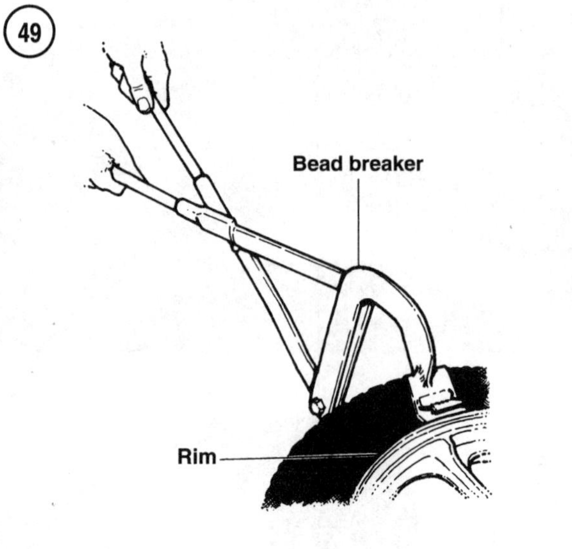

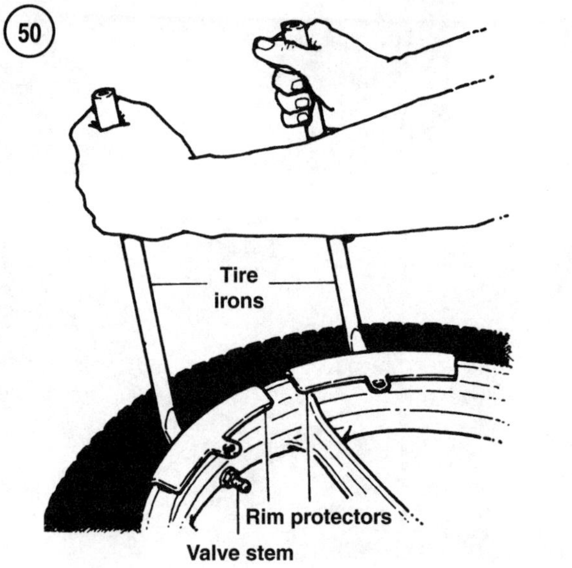

TIRES

Safety

Maintain the tire inflation pressure at the specification in **Table 3**. Tire inflation specifications are for cold tires. Do not check/adjust tire pressure after riding the motorcycle. If a different tire manufacturer used, follow their inflation recommendations.

Always allow the tires to warm up by riding before subjecting them to high cornering loads. Warm tires provide more adhesion.

New tires provide significantly less adhesion until they are broken in. Do not subject new tires to high speed or high cornering forces for at least 60 miles (100 km). Be especially careful when encountering wet conditions with new tires.

Replacement

WARNING
*Do not install an inner tube inside a tubeless tire. The tube will cause an abnormal heat buildup in the tire. Tubeless tires have **tubeless** molded into the sidewall and the rims have **suitable for tubeless tires** or an equivalent stamped or cast on them.*

Alloy (cast or disc) wheels can easily be damaged during tire removal. Take special care with tire irons when replacing a tire to avoid scratching or gouging the wheel. Insert scraps of leather between the tire iron and the rim to protect the wheel. All original equipment alloy wheels are designed for tubeless tires. All laced (spoke) wheels use a tube and tire combination.

When removing a tire, take care not to damage the tire beads, inner liner of the tire or the wheel rim flange. Use tire levers or flat handle tire irons with rounded heads.

Removal

CAUTION
To avoid damage when removing the tire, support the wheel on two wooden blocks, so the brake disc or the driven sprocket does not contact the floor.

51

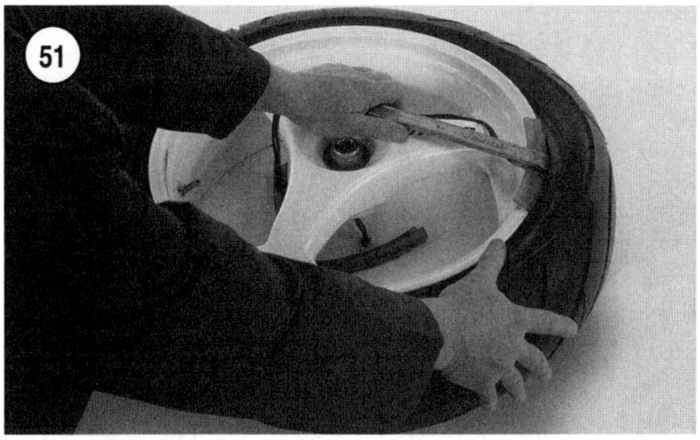

52

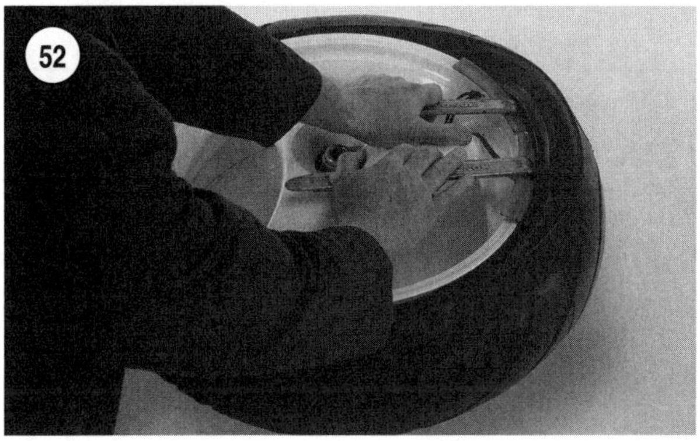

53

NOTE
To make tire removal easier, warm the new tire to make it softer and more pliable. Place the tire in the sun. If possible, place the tire in an automobile parked in the sun.

1A. Remove the front wheel as described in this chapter.

1B. Remove the rear wheel as described in this chapter.

2. If not already marked by the tire manufacturer, mark the valve stem location on the tire, so the tire can be installed in the same location for easier balancing.

3. Remove the valve cap and unscrew the core from the valve stem and deflate the tire or tube.

WARNING
The inner rim and tire bead areas are the sealing surfaces on the tubeless tire. Do not scratch the inside of the rim or damage the tire bead.

CAUTION
*Removal of tubeless tires from their rims can be difficult because of the tight tire bead-to-rim seal. Breaking the bead seal may require a special tool (**Figure 49**). If unable to break the seal loose, take the wheel to a motorcycle dealership or tire repair shop, and have them break it loose on a tire-changing machine.*

4. Press the entire bead on both sides of the tire away from the rim and into the center of the rim. If the bead it tight, use a bead breaker.
5. Lubricate both beads with soapy water.

CAUTION
*Use rim protectors (**Figure 50**) or insert scraps of leather between the tire iron and the rim to protect the rim from damage. Use tire irons without sharp edges. If necessary, file the ends of the tire irons to remove rough edges.*

6. Insert a tire iron under the top bead next to the valve stem (**Figure 51**). Force the bead on the opposite side of the tire into the center of the rim and pry the bead over the rim with the tire iron.
7. Insert a second tire iron next to the first iron to hold the bead over the rim. Then work around the tire with the first tire iron, prying the bead over the rim (**Figure 52**). On tube-type tires, be careful not to pinch the inner tube with the tools.
8. On tube-type tires, use your thumb and push the valve stem from its hole in the rim to the inside of the tire. Carefully pull the tube out of the tire and lay it aside.

NOTE
Step 9 is only necessary to remove the tire from the wheel completely, such as for tire replacement or tube repair.

9. Stand the wheel upright. Insert a tire iron between the back bead and the side of the rim that the top bead was pried over (**Figure 53**). Force the bead on the opposite side from the tire iron into the center of the rim. Work around the tire and pry the back bead off the rim. On tube-type tires, remove the rim band.

10. Inspect the valve stem seal. Because rubber deteriorates with age, replace the valve stem when replacing the tire.
11. On tubeless tires, remove the old valve stem and discard it. Inspect the valve stem hole (**Figure 54**) in the rim. Remove any dirt or corrosion from the hole and wipe it dry with a clean cloth. Install a new valve stem and make sure it is properly seated in the rim.
12. Carefully inspect the tire and wheel rim for damage as described in the following section.

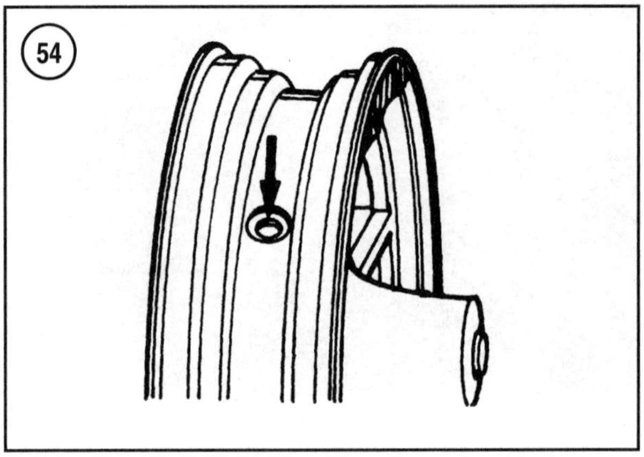

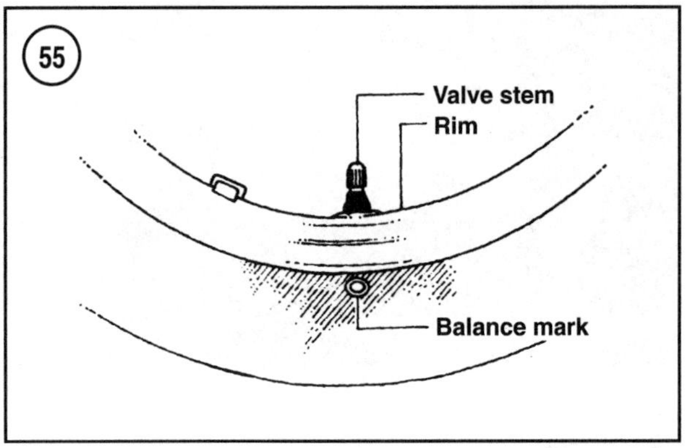

Inspection

WARNING
Carefully consider whether a tire requires replacement. If there is any doubt about tire condition, replace it with a new one. Do not risk tire failure.

WARNING
Install only original equipment tire valves and valve caps. A valve or valve/cap combination that is too long may interfere with an adjacent component when the motorcycle is under way. Damage to the valve will cause rapid tire deflation and loss of control.

1. Wipe off the inner surfaces of the wheel rim. Clean off any rubber residue or oxidation.
2. On tubeless tires, inspect the valve stem rubber grommet for deterioration. Replace if necessary.
3. If any of the following conditions are observed, replace the tire:
   a. A puncture or split whose total length or diameter exceeds 0.24 in. (6 mm).
   b. A scratch or split on the sidewall.
   c. Any type of ply separation.
   d. Tread separation or excessive abnormal wear pattern.
   e. Tread depth of less than 1/16 in. (1.6 mm) on original equipment tires. Tread depth minimum may vary on aftermarket tires.
   f. Scratches on either sealing bead.
   g. The cord is cut in any place.
   h. Flat spots in the tread from skidding.
   i. Any abnormality in the inner liner.
4. With the tire mounted on the wheel, check for excessive lateral and radial runout as follows:
   a. Position a fixed pointer next to the tire sidewall. Position the pointer tip so it is not directly in line with the molded tire logo or any other raised surface.
   b. Rotate the tire and measure lateral runout.
   c. The lateral runout should not exceed 0.080 in. (2.03 mm).
   d. Position a fixed pointer at the center bottom of the tire tread.
   e. Rotate the tire and measure the amount of radial runout.
   f. The radial runout should not exceed 0.090 in. (2.29 mm).
   g. If either runout is excessive, remove the tire from the wheel and recheck the wheel as described in this chapter. If necessary, true (laced wheel) or replace (alloy wheels) the wheel. If wheel runout is correct and the wheel bearings are in good condition, the tire runout is excessive and the tire must be replaced.

Installation

WARNING
Never exceed 40 psi (276 kPa) inflation pressure as the tire could burst, causing injury. Never stand directly over a tire while inflating it.

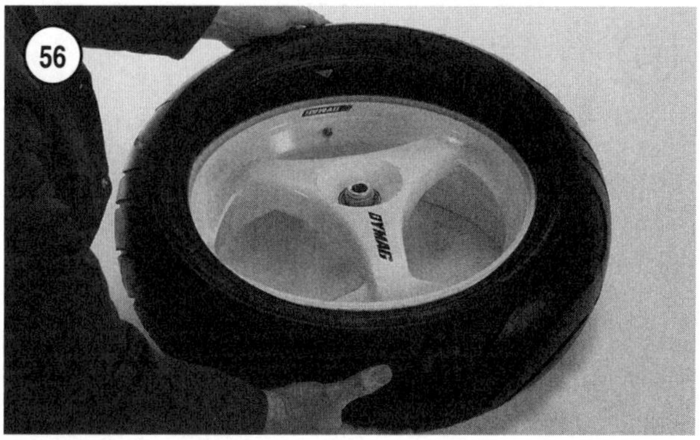

56

57

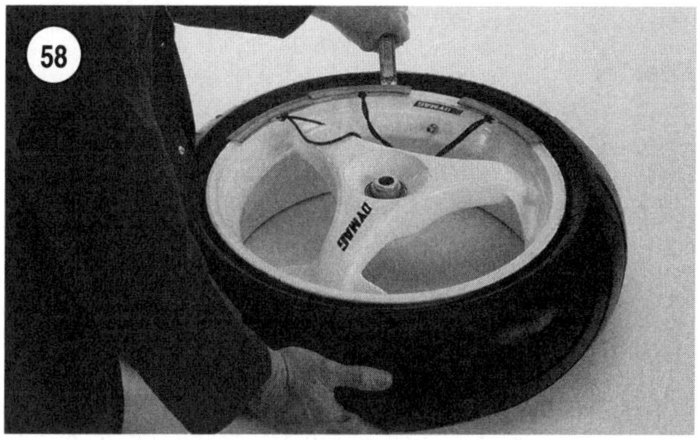

58

1. A new tire may have balancing rubbers inside. These are not patches. Do not remove them. Most tires are marked with a colored spot near the bead (**Figure 55**) that indicates a lighter point on the tire. This should be placed next to the valve stem.

2. On tube-type tires, install the rim band around the wheel and align the hole in the rim band with the hole in the rim. If installing a new rim band, make sure it is the correct diameter and width for the wheel.

3. Lubricate both beads of the tire with soapy water.

4. When installing the tire on the rim, make sure the correct tire (either front or rear) is installed on the correct wheel. Also make sure the direction arrow points in the direction of wheel rotation.

5. When remounting the old tire, align the mark made in Step 2 of *Removal* with the valve stem (**Figure 55**).

6. Place the backside of the tire onto the rim so the lower bead sits in the center of the rim while the upper bead remains outside the rim (**Figure 56**). Work around the tire in both directions and press the lower bead by hand into the center of the rim. Use a tire iron for the last few inches of bead.

7. On tube-type tires, perform the following:
   a. Dust the inner tube with talcum powder before installing it in the tire. The talcum powder will prevent the tube from sticking to the tire.
   b. Inflate the tube just enough to round it out. Too much air will make installation difficult.
   c. Place the tube on top of the tire, aligning the valve stem with the matching hole in the rim. Insert the tube into the tire.
   d. Lift the upper bead away from the rim with a hand and insert the tube's valve stem through the rim hole. Check to make sure the valve stem is straight up (90 degrees), not cocked to one side. If necessary, reposition the tube in the tire. If the valve stem wants to slide out of the hole and back into the tire, install the valve stem nut at the top of the valve; do not tighten the nut at this time.

8. Press the upper bead into the rim opposite the valve stem. Working on both sides of this initial point, pry the bead into the rim with the tire tool, and work around the rim to the valve stem (**Figure 57**). On tube-type tires, do not pinch the inner tube during the last few inches. If the tire wants to pull up on one side, either use another tire iron or one knee to hold the tire in place. The last few inches are usually the toughest to install. Continue to push the tire into the rim by hand. Re-lubricate the bead if necessary. If the tire bead pulls out from under the rim, use both knees to hold the tire in place. If necessary, use a tire iron for the last few inches (**Figure 58**).

9. On tube-type tires, check to make sure that the valve stem is straight up (90°), not cocked to one side (**Figure 59**). If necessary, slide the tire along the rim in either direction while holding the rim securely. When the valve stem is straight up, tighten the valve stem nut at the top of the valve; do not tighten it against the rim at this time. Check that the tube was not forced outward so that it rests between the tire bead and the rim. If necessary, push the tube back into the tire.

10. Bounce the wheel several times, rotating it each time. This will force the tire bead against the rim flanges. After

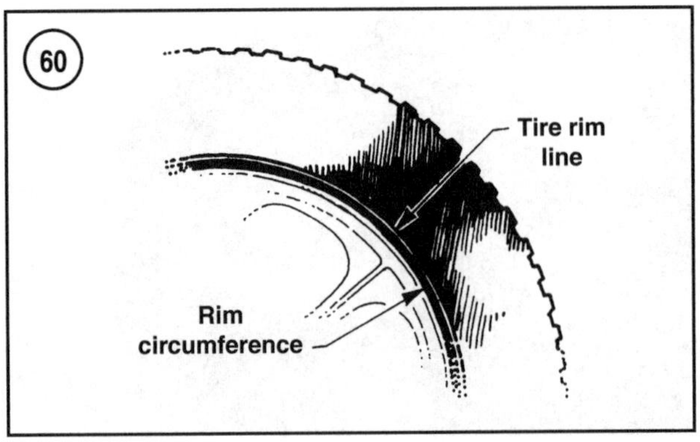

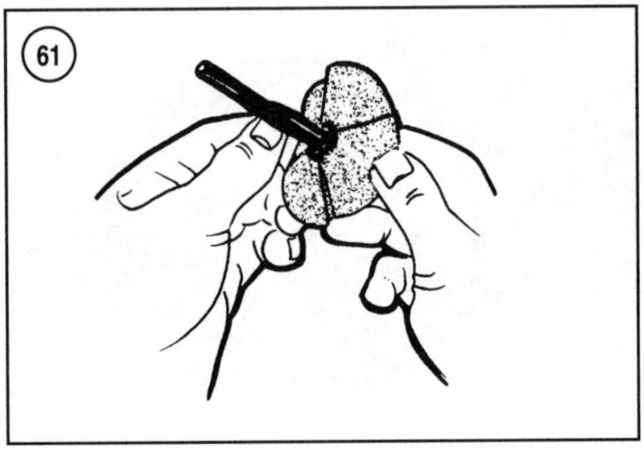

the tire beads are in contact with the rim, inflate the tire to seat the beads.

11A. On tube-type tires, perform the following:

a. Inflate the tube to it maximum tire pressure to seat the tire beads in the rim.

b. After inflating the tire, make sure the beads are fully seated and the rim lines are the same distance from the rim all the way around the tire (**Figure 60**).

c. If the tire beads do not seat properly, release the air pressure and re-lubricate the tire beads.

d. When the tire is seated correctly, remove the valve core and deflate the tire allowing the tube to straighten out within the tire.

e. Install the valve core and inflate the tire to the pressure in **Table 3**.

f. Tighten the valve stem nut securely and install the valve stem cap.

11B. On tubeless tires/perform the following:

a. Place an inflatable band around the circumference of the tire. Slowly inflate the band until the tire beads are pressed against the rim. Inflate the tire enough to make it seat, deflate the band and remove it.

b. After inflating the tire, make sure the beads are fully seated and the rim lines are the same distance from the rim all the way around the tire (**Figure 60**). If the beads will not seat, deflate the tire and lubricate the rim and beads with soapy water.

c. Re-inflate the tire to the pressure in Table 3. Install the valve stem cap.

12. Check tire runout as described in this section.

13. Balance the wheel as described in this chapter.

14A. Install the front wheel as described in this chapter.

14B. Install the rear wheel as described in this chapter.

Repairs

WARNING

*Do not install an inner tube inside a tubeless tire. The tube will cause an abnormal heat buildup in the tire. Tubeless tires have **tubeless** molded into the sidewall and the rims have **suitable for tubeless tires** or an equivalent stamped or cast on them.*

Tire repair kits are available from motorcycle dealerships and automotive parts suppliers. Make sure a considered kit is applicable for motorcycle tires/tubes.

It may be possible to use a plug applied from outside the tire and a tire sealant to inflate the tire. A combination plug/patch (**Figure 61**) applied from inside the tire is typically a safer repair.

Patch kits for tubes are available in hot and cold types. Hot patches use heat to vulcanize the patch to the tube and are typically the strongest. Cold patches use adhesive to attach the patch.

If using an internal plug/patch, external plug or patching a tube, refer to the kit manufacturer's instruction for applicability and safety precautions regarding subsequent tire/tube use.

Table 1 FRONT AND REAR WHEEL SPECIFICATIONS

	in.	mm
Alloy wheels		
Lateral	0.040	1.02
Radial	0.030	0.76
Laced wheel radial runout	0.030	0.76
Wheel bearing end play	Less than 0.002	Less than 0.05

Table 2 WHEEL SPECIFICATIONS

Alloy wheel	
16-in.	
Rim size	T16 × 3.00 D
Valve hole size	0.35 in. (8.89 mm)
19-in.	
Rim size	T19 × 2.15 MT
Valve hole size	0.45 in. (11.4 mm)
Laced wheel	
21-in.	
Rim size	T21 × 2.15 MT or TLA
19-in.	
Rim size	T19 × 2.50 TLA
16 in.	
Rim size	T16 × 3.00 D or MT

Table 3 TIRE INFLATION PRESSURE (COLD)*

	psi	kPa
Front wheel		
Rider only	30	207
Rider and passenger	30	207
Rear wheel		
Rider only	36	248
Rider and passenger	40	276

*Tire pressure for original equipment tires. Aftermarket tires may require different inflation pressure.

Table 4 WHEEL AND SUSPENSION TORQUE SPECIFICATIONS

	ft.-lb.	in.-lb.	N•m
Belt deflector screws	–	36-60	4-7
Belt guard locknut	–	120-180	14-20
Driven sprocket bolts	55-65	–	75-88
Driven sprocket cover bolts	–	80-120	9-14

(continued)

Table 4 WHEEL AND SUSPENSION TORQUE SPECIFICATIONS (continued)

	ft.-lb.	in.-lb.	N•m
Exhaust bracket bolt	30-33	–	41-45
Front axle clamp			
bolt/nut (2004-2007)	21-27	–	29-37
Front axle nut	50-55	–	68-75
Rear axle nut*			
2004	60-65	–	81-88
2005-2007	72-78	–	98-106
Shock absorber locknut	45-50	–	61-68
Spoke nipple	–	40-50	4.5-6.7

*Refer to procedure in Chapter Three.

NOTE: Refer to the Supplement at the end of this manual for information unique to 2007-2011 models.

CHAPTER ELEVEN

FRONT SUSPENSION AND STEERING

This chapter describes service procedures for the handlebar, front fork and steering components. Refer to Chapter Ten for wheel and tire service. Front suspension and steering specifications are in **Table 1** and **Table 2** at the end of this chapter.

WARNING
Replace all suspension and steering fasteners with parts of the same type. Do not substitute with a replacement type; this may affect the safety of the system.

HANDLEBAR

If replacing the original equipment handlebar with an aftermarket bar, make sure the replacement has the same outside diameter, width, height and sweep. If the replacement bar is different, make sure it has enough room to mount the controls without crowding and feels comfortable when turned from side to side. If the new bar is higher or wider than the original, move the handlebar from side to side and make sure the cables and wiring harnesses do not restrict movement.

Removal

Refer to **Figure 1** or **Figure 2**.

1. Place the motorcycle on a suitable stand.
2. Refer to Chapter Nine and remove the Maxi-fuse.
3. Remove the mirrors.
4. Make a drawing of the clutch and throttle cable routing.
5. Cut and remove any cable or wiring harness retaining straps.
6. Remove the brake master cylinder clamp (A, **Figure 3**) and suspend the master cylinder so it is out of the way. It is not necessary to disconnect the hydraulic brake line.
7. Loosen the right switch housing (B, **Figure 3**) screws (**Figure 4**, typical) so that the housing can slide off the handlebar later in this procedure. It is not necessary to separate the housing halves.
8. Remove the clutch lever clamp mounting bolts (B, **Figure 5**) and remove the clamp. Move the clutch lever so it is out of the way.
9. Remove the left switch housing (A, **Figure 5**) screws (**Figure 4**, typical) and separate the housing halves.

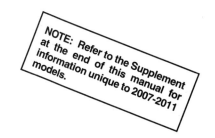

1

HANDLEBAR (ALL MODELS EXCEPT XL883C AND XL1200C)

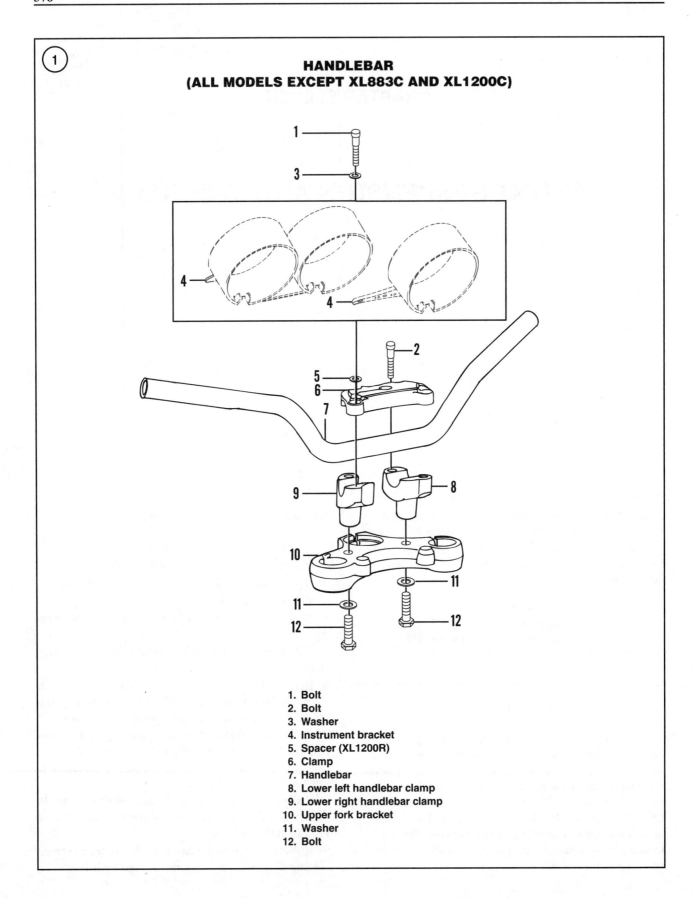

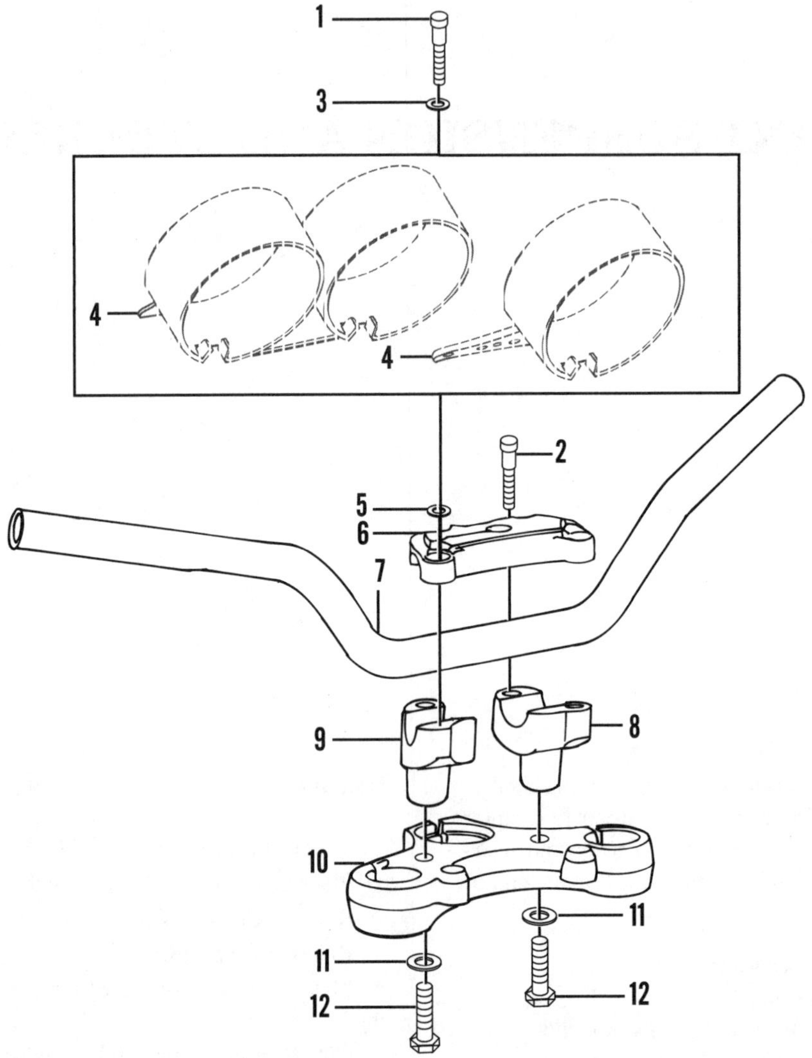

1. Bolt
2. Bolt
3. Washer
4. Instrument bracket
5. Spacer (XL1200R)
6. Clamp
7. Handlebar
8. Lower left handlebar clamp
9. Lower right handlebar clamp
10. Upper fork bracket
11. Washer
12. Bolt

(2)

HANDLEBAR
(XL883C AND XL1200C MODELS)

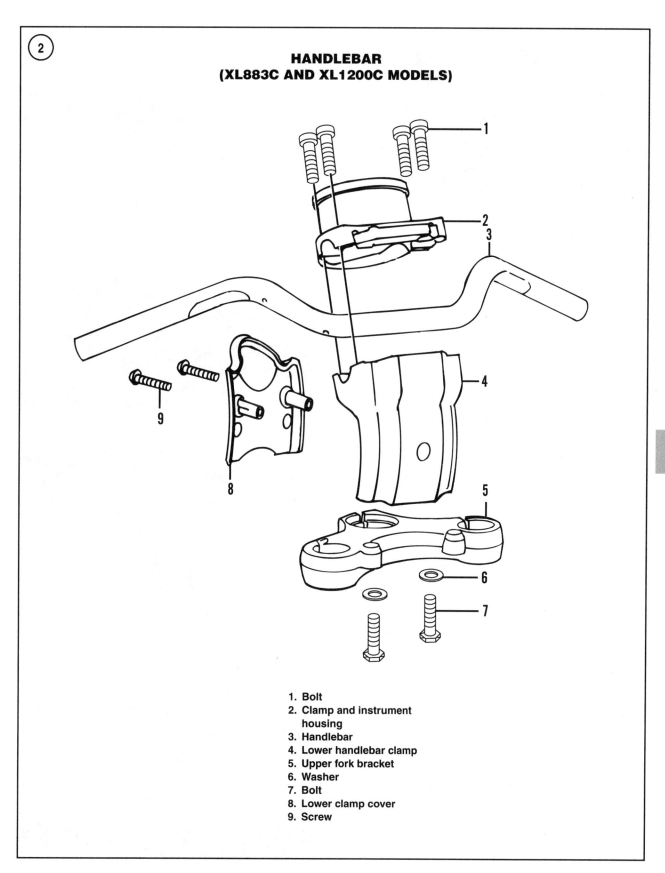

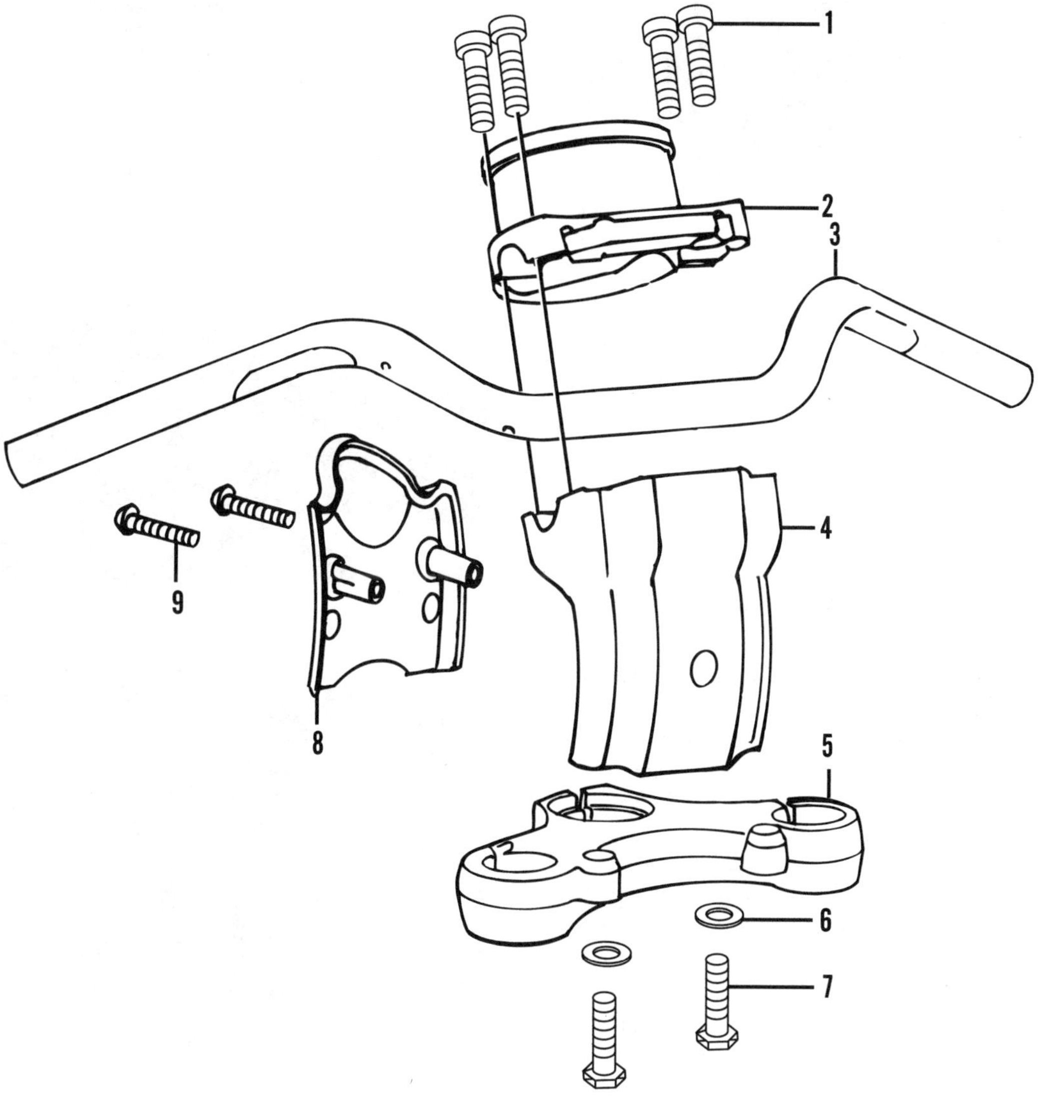

1. Bolt
2. Clamp and instrument housing
3. Handlebar
4. Lower handlebar clamp
5. Upper fork bracket
6. Washer
7. Bolt
8. Lower clamp cover
9. Screw

3
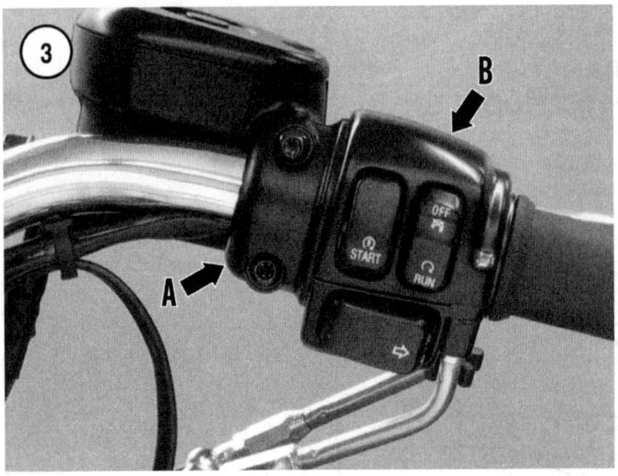

10. If lower handlebar holder removal is required, loosen the holder bolts (**Figure 6**), but do not remove the bolts.

CAUTION
Set the instrument cluster aside so it does not scratch or damage any component.

11. On XL883C and XL1200C models, remove the clamp cover (**Figure 7**).

12A. On all models except XL883C and XL1200C, loosen the rear handlebar clamp bolts (A, **Figure 8**). Remove the front handlebar clamp bolts, then remove the instrument cluster and clamp. Do not lose the washers.

NOTE
On XL883C and XL1200C models, the instrument housing and handlebar clamp are a one-piece assembly.

12B. On XL883C and XL1200C models, remove the handlebar clamp bolts (**Figure 9**). Remove the handlebar clamp and instrument housing assembly.

13. Remove the handlebar.

Inspection

1. Clean the knurled section of the handlebar with a wire brush and remove any aluminum debris in the knurling.

2. Check the handlebar for cracks, bends or other damage. Replace the handlebar if necessary. Do not attempt to repair it.

3. Clean the clamps and holders thoroughly of all residue before installing the handlebar.

4

5
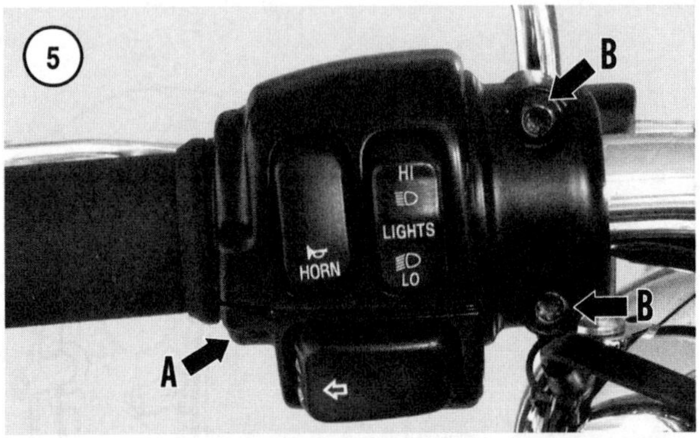

6
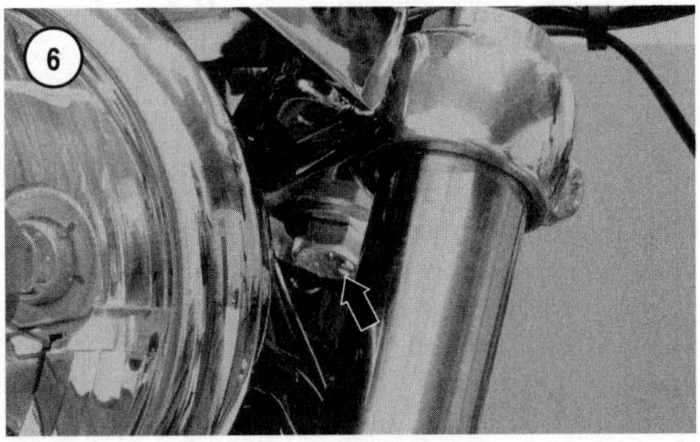

7

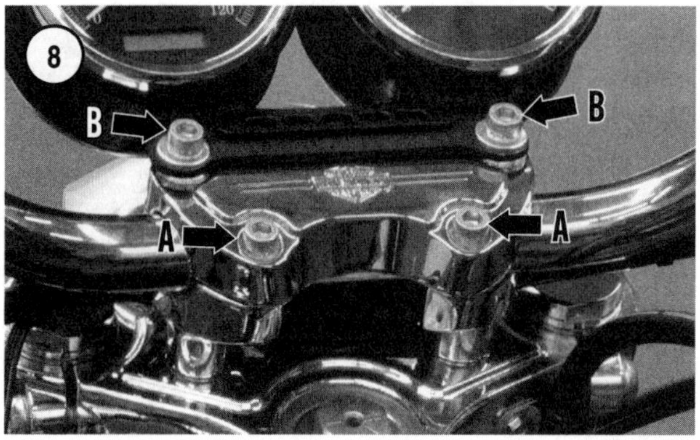

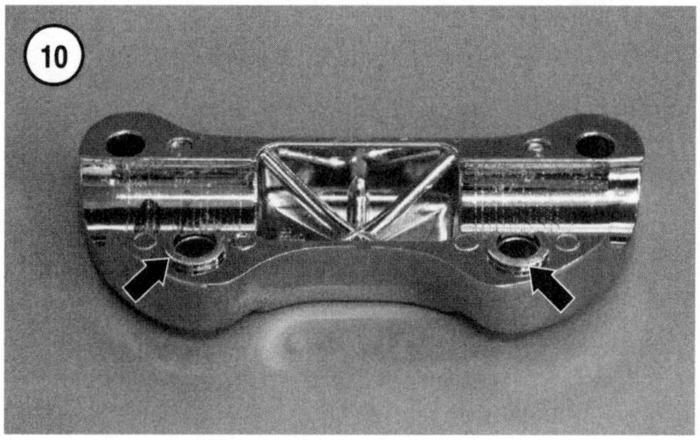

Installation

1. Install the handlebar in the lower holder(s).
2. On all models except XL883C and XL1200C, install the clamp and instrument housing as follows:
   a. Install the handlebar clamp and instrument housing.
   b. Install the handlebar clamp so the cast bolt bosses are to the rear (**Figure 10**).
   c. On XL1200R models, install the spacer washers between the clamp and the instrument housing plate on the front bolt holes (**Figure 11**).
   d. Tighten the rear clamp bolts first, then tighten the front clamp bolts. Tighten the clamp bolts to 12-18 ft.-lb. (17-24 N•m).
3. On XL883C and XL1200C models, install the clamp and instrument housing using the following procedure:
   a. Install the clamp and instrument housing.
   b. Tighten the front clamp bolts first, then tighten the rear clamp bolts. Tighten the clamp bolts to 12-18 ft.-lb. (17-24 N•m).
4. After installing the handlebar, sit on the motorcycle and check the handlebar position. Relocate the handlebar as needed.
5. Install the right switch housing. Tighten the screws to 35-45 in.-lb. (4.0-5.0 N•m).
6. Install the left switch housing. Tighten the screws to 35-45 in.-lb. (4.0-5.0 N•m).
7. Install the clutch lever. Tighten the clamp mounting bolts to 108-132 in.-lb. (13-15 N•m).
8. Position the master cylinder onto the handlebar. Align the master cylinder notch (**Figure 12**) with the locating tab on the lower portion of the right side switch.
9. Position the clamp and install the Torx bolts and washers. Tighten the upper mounting bolt, then the lower bolt. Tighten the bolts to 108-132 in.-lb (13-15 N•m).
10. Reinstall the wiring and cable retaining clamps.
11. On XL883C and XL1200C models, install the lower clamp cover.

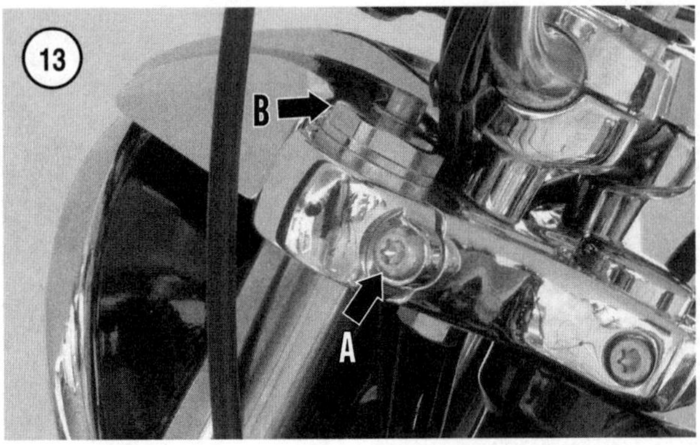

12. Refer to Chapter Nine and install the Maxi-fuse.
13. Install the mirrors.

FRONT FORK

The front suspension consists of a spring-controlled, hydraulically dampened telescopic fork.

If troubleshooting a problem, drain the fork oil and refill with the proper type and quantity as described in Chapter Three.

To simplify fork service and to prevent the mixing of parts, remove, service and install the legs individually.

Removal

1. Support the bike so the front wheel clears the ground. Double-check to make sure the bike is stable before removing the front wheel and fork.
2. Remove the front wheel as described in Chapter Ten.
3. Remove the front fender bolts and locknuts and remove the front fender.
4. Label the left and right fork tubes so they can be reinstalled in their original positions.
5. Loosen the upper fork bracket pinch bolt (A, **Figure 13**).
6. If fork tube disassembly is required, loosen but do not remove the fork cap (B, **Figure 13**).
7. Loosen the lower fork bracket pinch bolt (**Figure 14**) and slide the fork tube out of the fork brackets. If necessary, rotate the fork tube while removing it.
8. If fork service is required, refer to *Disassembly* in this section.

Installation

1. Clean off any corrosion or dirt on the upper and lower fork bracket receptacles.

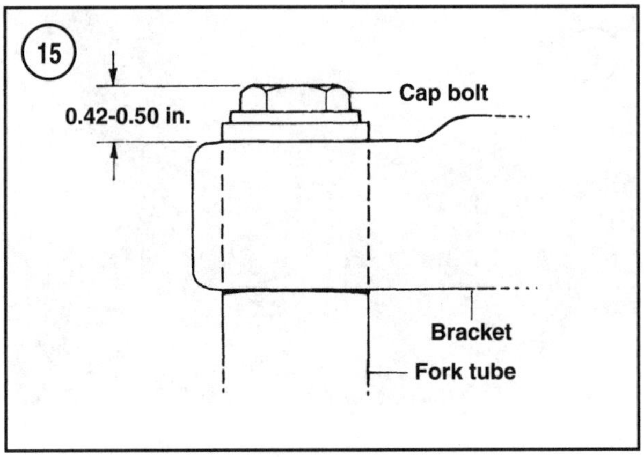

NOTE

The fork assemblies must be reinstalled on the correct side. If the fork assemblies are installed on the wrong side, the brake caliper and front fender can not be properly installed.

2. Install each fork tube so that the tube extends 0.42-0.50 in. (10.7-12.7 mm) above the upper fork bracket as shown in **Figure 15**.
3. Tighten the lower fork bracket pinch bolt (**Figure 14**) to 30-35 ft.-lb. (41-47 N•m).
4. If loose, tighten the fork cap (B, **Figure 13**) securely.
5. Tighten the upper bracket pinch bolt (A, **Figure 13**) to 30-35 ft.-lb. (41-47 N•m).
6. Install the front fender and its mounting bolts and locknuts. Tighten the front fender fasteners to 96-156 in.-lb. (11-17 N•m).
7. Install the front wheel as described in Chapter Ten.
8. Apply the front brake and pump the front fork several times to seat the fork and front wheel.

(16) **FRONT FORK**

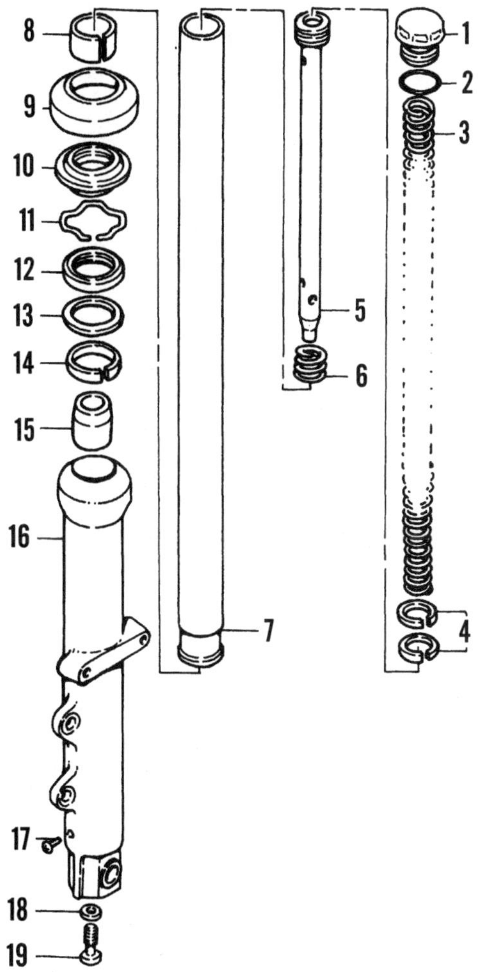

1. Fork cap
2. O-ring
3. Fork spring
4. Piston rings
5. Damper rod
6. Rebound spring
7. Fork tube
8. Fork tube bushing
9. Dust cover
10. Dust seal
11. Retaining ring
12. Oil seal
13. Seal spacer
14. Slider bushing
15. Oil lock piece
16. Slider
17. Drain screw
18. Washer
19. Allen bolt

(17)

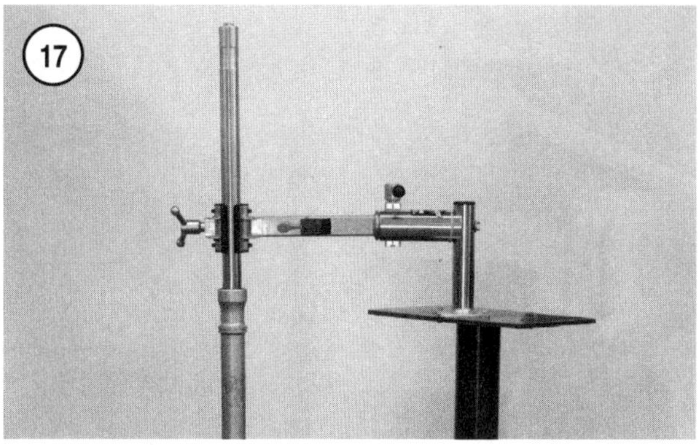

Disassembly

To simplify fork service and to prevent the mixing of parts, disassemble and assemble the fork legs individually.

Refer to **Figure 16**.

NOTE
*Work stands appropriate for holding the fork (**Figure 17, www.parktool.com**) are available. Their quick adjustability and padded clamps make them ideal for many service procedures. If a vise is used, make sure to use soft jaw inserts.*

1. Using the front axle boss at the bottom of the fork tube, clamp the slider in a holder with soft jaw inserts. Do not clamp the slider at any point above the fork axle boss.

NOTE
Loosen the bottom Allen bolt before removing the fork cap and spring. Leaving the cap on provides spring tension against the damper rod. This prevents the damper rod from spinning when attempting to loosen the Allen bolt.

2. Loosen, but do not remove, the Allen bolt (**Figure 18**) at the bottom of the slider.

WARNING
The fork cap is under spring pressure and may fly off when loosening it. In addition, make sure the fork tube is fully extended from the slider. If the fork is damaged and stuck compressed, the fork cap and spring will fly out under considerable force when the cap is removed.

3. Remove the fork cap from the top of the fork tube (**Figure 19**). Then pull the spring out of the fork tube.
4. Remove the fork tube from the holder and pour the oil into a drain pan. Pump the fork several times by hand to

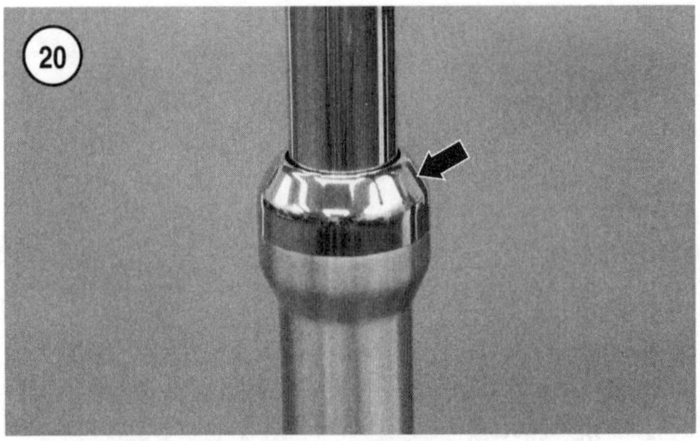

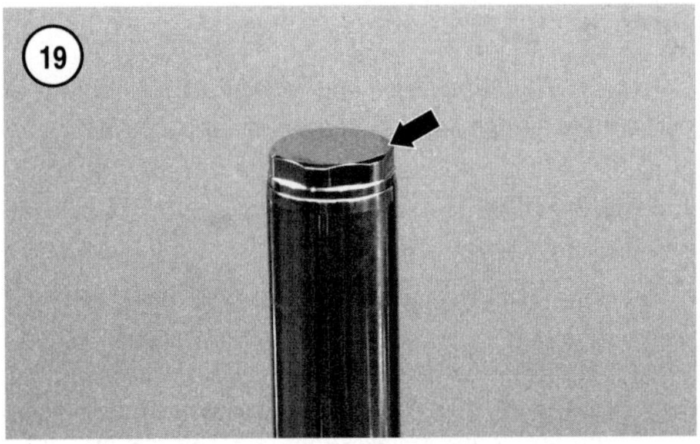

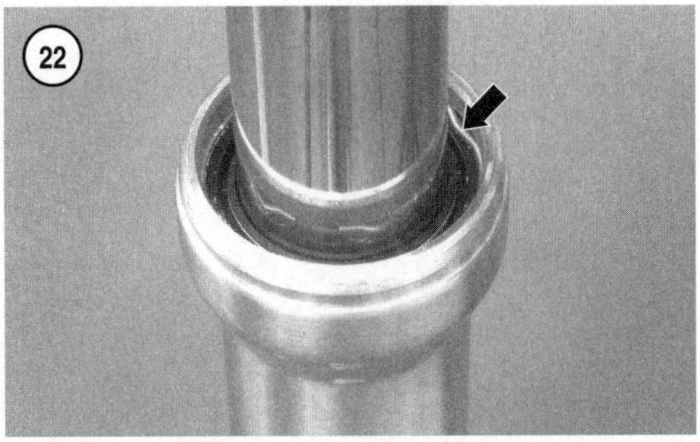

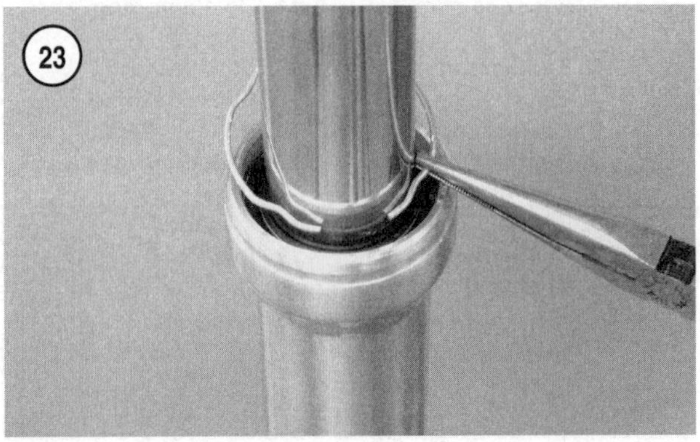

get most of the oil out. Check the oil for contamination, which indicates worn or damaged parts. Discard the oil after examining it.

5. Insert a small punch in the notch under the dust cover (**Figure 20**) and carefully drive the cover off the slider and remove it. Be careful not to damage the slider surface.

6. Insert a small flat-tipped screwdriver under the dust seal and carefully pry the seal (**Figure 21**) out of the slider and remove it. Be careful not to damage the slider surface.

7. Pry the retaining ring (**Figure 22**) out of the groove in the slider and remove it (**Figure 23**).

8. Remove the Allen bolt and washer (**Figure 24**) at the bottom of the slider.

NOTE

The slider bushing is installed with an interference fit. When separating the fork tube and slider, the slider bushing, spacer seal and oil seal will be removed at the same time.

9. Hold the fork tube in one hand then pull the slider away repeatedly, knocking the slider bushing against the fork tube bushing (**Figure 25**). As the slider bushing is knocked out of the slider, it will push the oil seal and seal spacer out

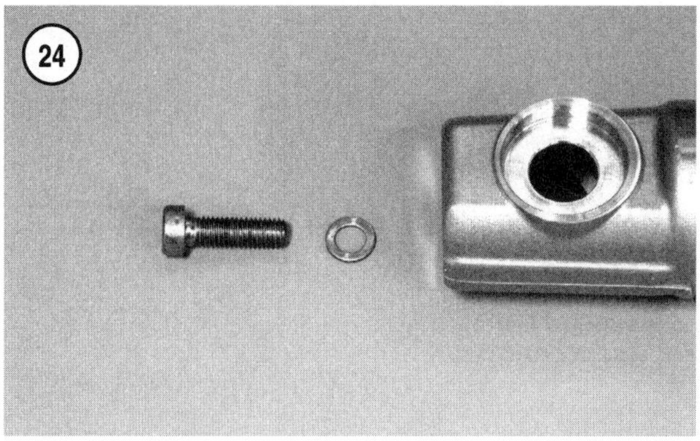

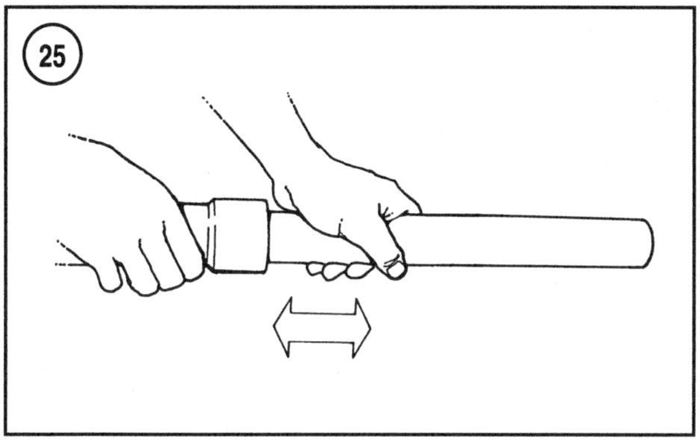

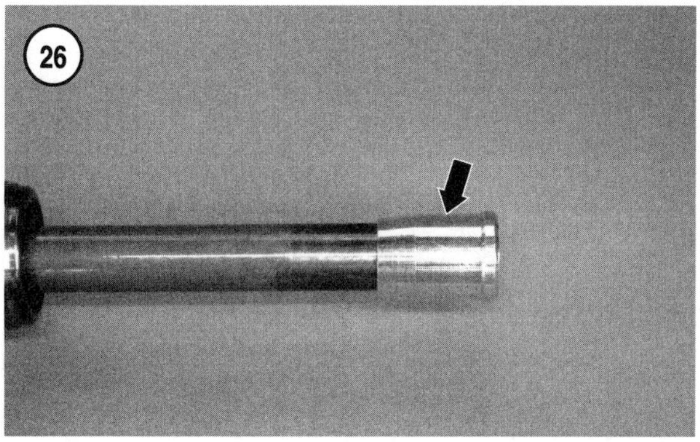

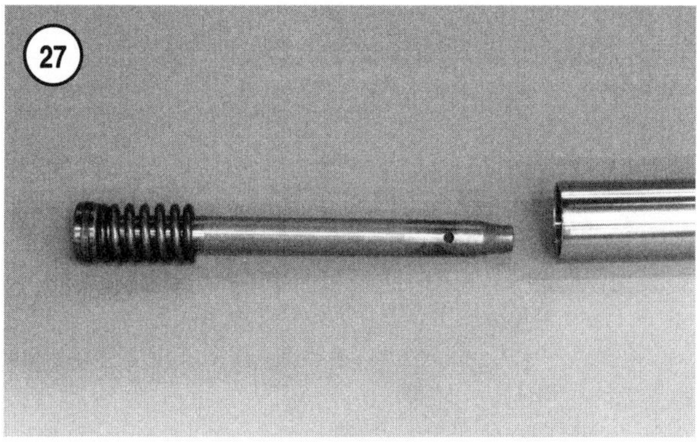

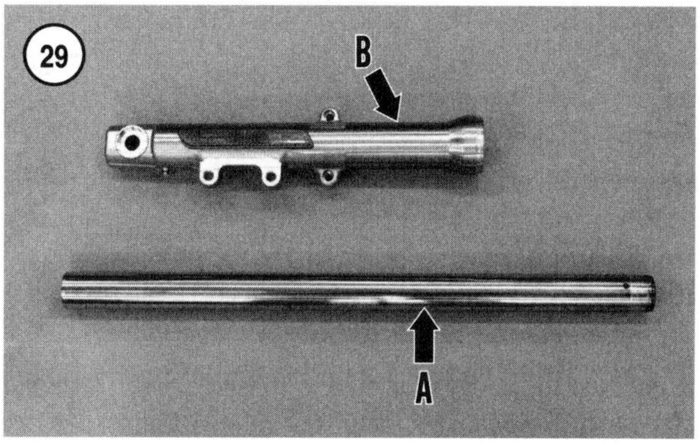

of the slider. Continue until these components are pushed out of the slider.

10. Remove the oil lock piece (**Figure 26**) from the damper rod.

11. Remove the damper rod and small spring (**Figure 27**) from the fork tube.

Inspection

CAUTION
*Handle the guide bushings (**Figure 28**) carefully when cleaning them to avoid scratching or removing any of their coating material. If there is any metal powder clinging to the guide bushings, clean them with clean fork oil and a nylon brush.*

1. Initially clean all the fork components in solvent, first making sure the solvent will not damage the rubber parts. Then clean with soap and water and rinse with clear water. Dry thoroughly.

2. Check the fork tube (A, **Figure 29**) for bending, nicks, rust or other damage. Check the fork tube for straightness with a set of V-blocks and a dial indicator. If these tools are not available, roll the fork tube on a large plate glass or

30

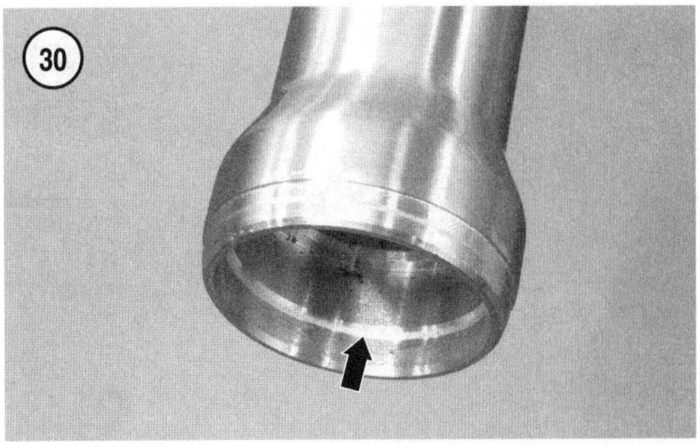

31

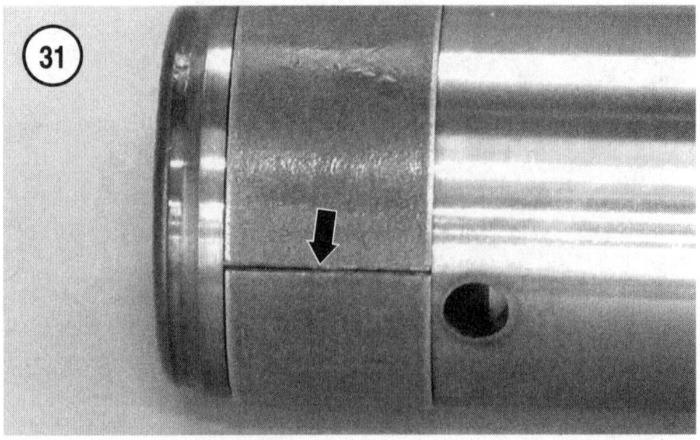

other flat surface. There are no service limit specifications for runout. If a fork tube is slightly bent, it can be straightened with a press and special blocks; see a dealership or repair shop. If a fork tube is bent, or the metal is creased or wrinkled, replace the fork tube.

3. Check the slider (B, **Figure 29**) for dents or other exterior damage. Check the retaining ring groove (**Figure 30**) in the top of the slider for cracks or other damage. Replace the slider if the groove is cracked or damaged.

4. Check the slider and fork tube bushings (**Figure 28**) for excessive wear, cracks or damage. The slider bushing was removed with the oil seal. Do not remove the fork tube bushing unless replacement is necessary. To replace the fork tube bushing, perform the following:

   a. Expand the bushing gap (**Figure 31**) with a screwdriver and slide it off the fork tube.
   b. Coat the new bushing with new fork oil.
   c. Install the new bushing by expanding the gap with a screwdriver. Expand the bushing only enough to fit it over the fork tube.
   d. Seat the new bushing (**Figure 31**) into the groove in the fork tube.

5. Replace damaged drain screw and Allen bolt washers.

6. Check the damper rod piston ring (**Figure 32**) for excessive wear, cracks or other damage. If necessary, replace the ring.

7. Check the damper rod for straightness with a set of V-blocks and a dial indicator (**Figure 33**) or by rolling it on a piece of plate glass. There are no service limit specifications for runout.

8. Make sure the oil passages in the damper rod (**Figure 34**) are open. If clogged, flush with solvent and dry with compressed air.

9. Check the threads in the bottom of the damper rod for stripping, cross-threading or sealer residue. If necessary, use a tap to true the threads or to remove any deposits.

32

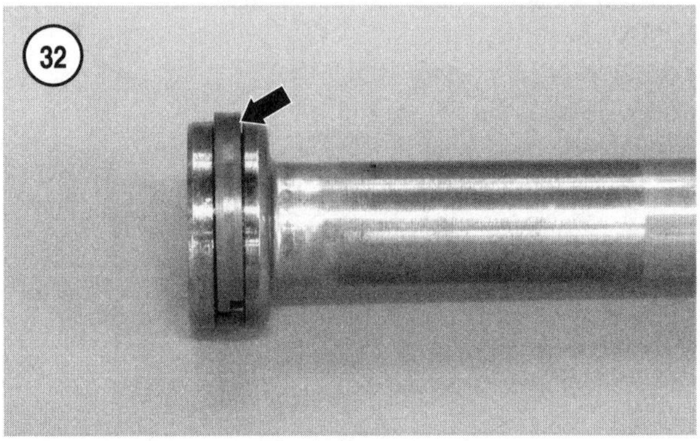

33

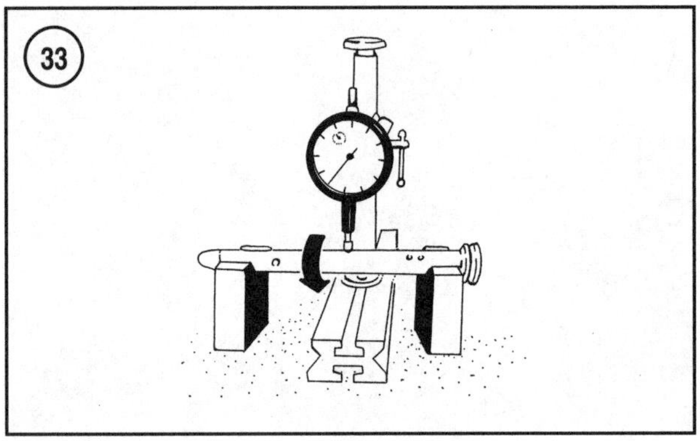

34

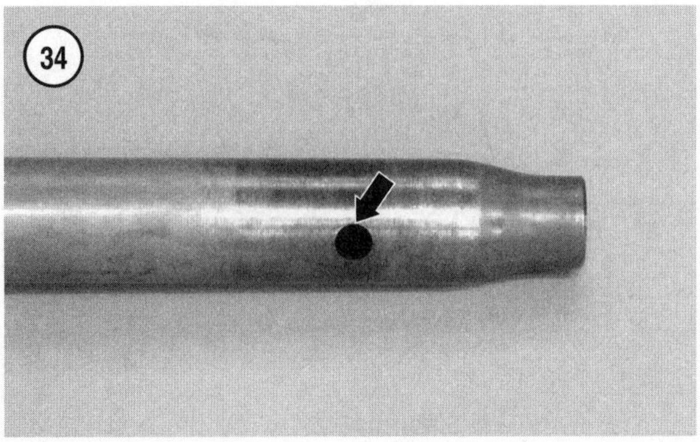

35

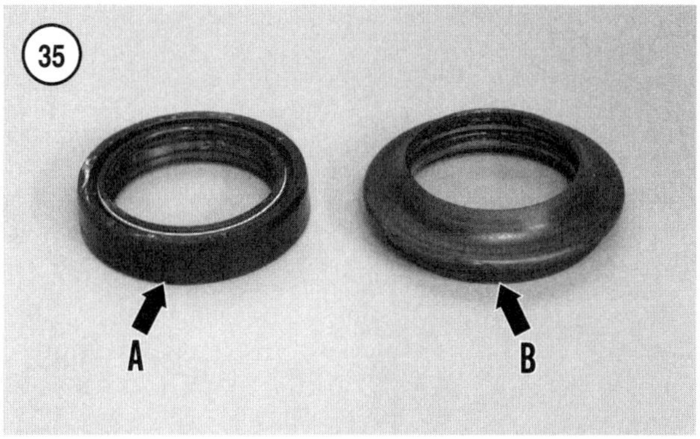

36

37

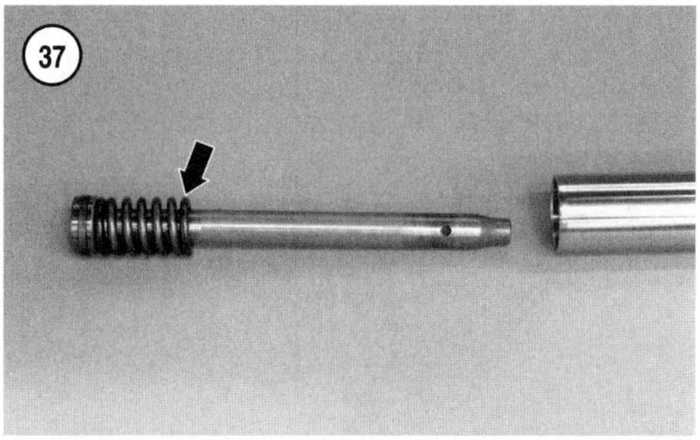

38

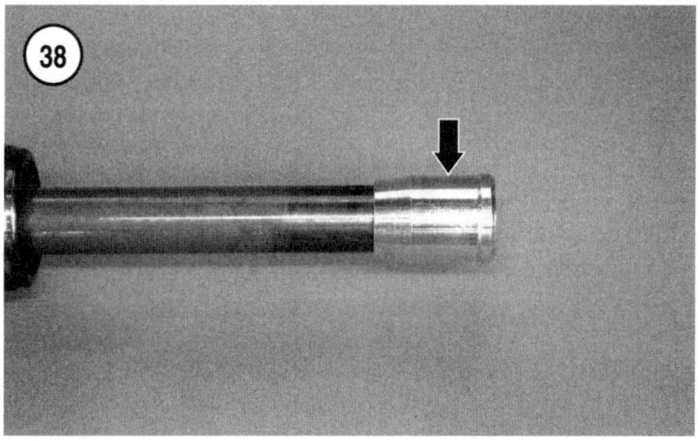

39

10. Check the damper rod rebound spring and the fork spring for wear or damage. There are no service limit specifications for spring free length.
11. The manufacturer recommends replacing oil seals (A, **Figure 35**) whenever they are removed. If installing the original oil seals, inspect them closely for wear, hardness or other damage. Always replace both oil seals as a set.
12. Inspect the outer dust seal(s) (B, **Figure 35**) for cracks, weather deterioration or other damage. Damaged dust seal(s) will allow dirt to pass through and damage the oil seal.
13. Replace the fork cap O-ring (**Figure 36**) if leaking, excessively worn or damaged.
14. Replace any parts that are worn or damaged. When replacing fork springs, replace both springs as a set; do not replace only one spring.

Assembly

1. Prior to assembly, perform the *Inspection* procedure to make sure all worn or defective parts have been repaired or replaced. Clean all parts thoroughly before assembly.
2. Coat all parts with Harley-Davidson Type E fork oil or equivalent before assembly.
3. Install the rebound spring (**Figure 37**) onto the damper rod and slide the rod into the fork tube until it protrudes from the end of the tube.
4. Install the oil lock piece (**Figure 38**) onto the end of the damper rod.
5. Insert the fork spring (**Figure 39**) into the fork tube so that the end with the closer coils enters first (toward the damper rod).
6. Install the fork cap (**Figure 40**) to compress the spring and hold the damper rod in place.
7. Install the slider over the damper rod (**Figure 41**) and onto the bottom of the fork tube until it bottoms. Make sure the oil lock piece is still mounted on the end of the damper rod.

40

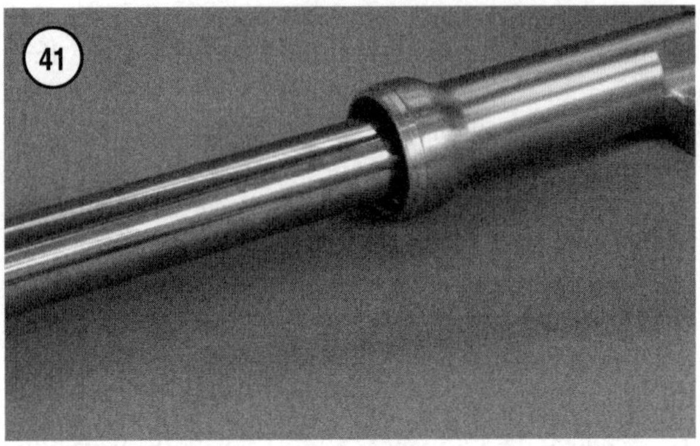
41

8. Install the washer onto the damper rod Allen bolt.
9. Insert the bolt (**Figure 42**) through the lower end of the slider and thread it into the damper rod. Tighten the bolt securely.
10. Remove the fork cap (**Figure 40**) and fork spring.

CAUTION
The slider bushing, seal spacer and oil seal are installed into the slider at the same time with a suitable driver placed over the fork tube and against the oil seal. Use a fork seal driver (part No. HD-36583) or an equivalent. A piece of pipe can also be used to drive the parts into the slider. To prevent the tool from damaging the slider, oil seal or fork tube, wrap both ends of the pipe or tool with duct tape.

11. Coat the slider bushing (A, **Figure 43**) with fork oil and slide the bushing down the fork tube and rest it against the slider bore.
12. Install the seal spacer (B, **Figure 43**) onto the fork tube (dished or concave side facing downward).

CAUTION
To protect the oil seal lips, place a thin plastic bag (A, ***Figure 44****) on top of the fork*

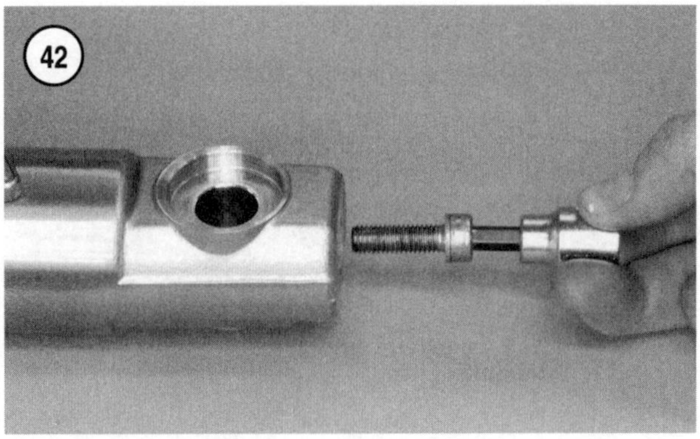
42

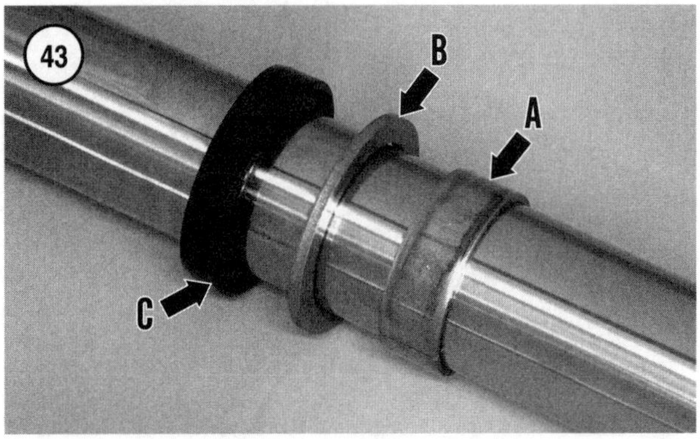

43

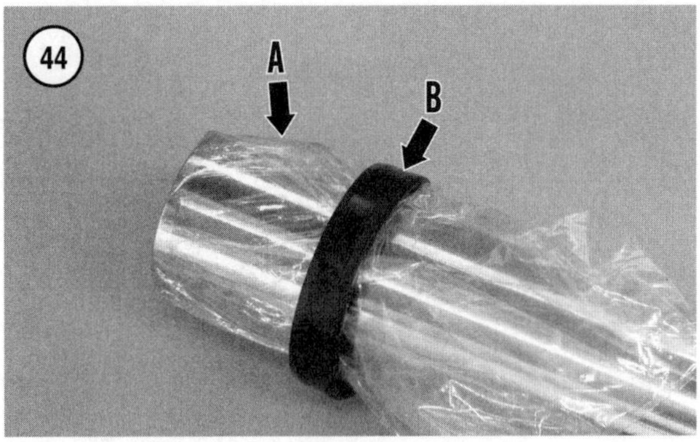

44

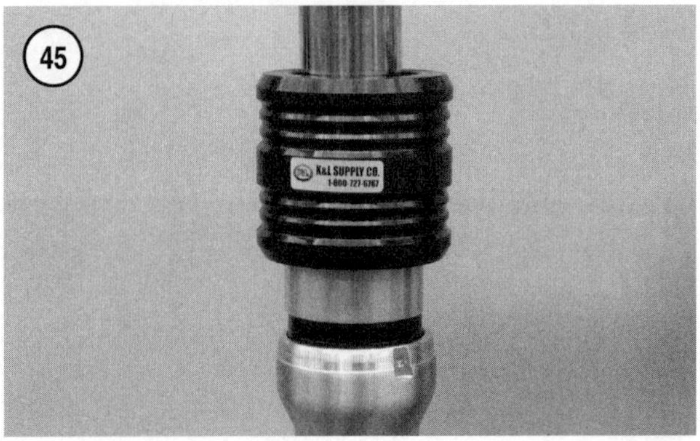
45

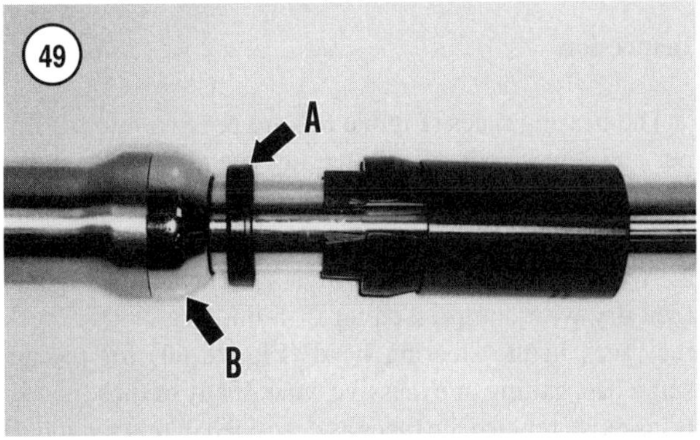

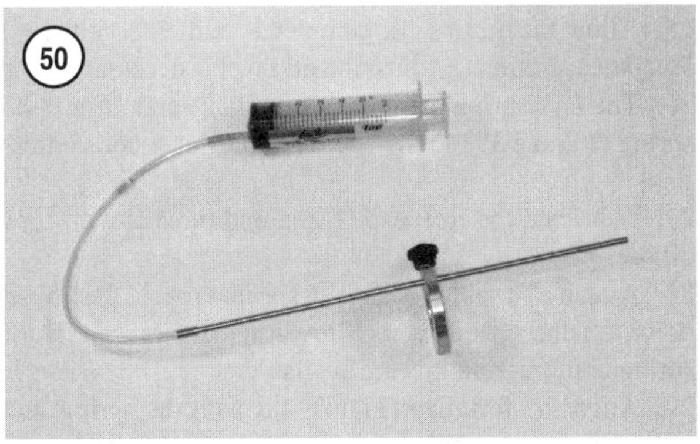

tube. Before installing the seal in the following step, lightly coat the bag and the seal lips with fork oil.

13. Slide a new oil seal (B, **Figure 44**) onto the fork tube (closed side facing up). Position the seal (C, **Figure 43**) adjacent to the seal spacer.
14. Slide the fork seal driver down the fork tube (**Figure 45**).
15. Drive the bushing, seal spacer and oil seal into the slider until the retaining ring groove (**Figure 46**) in the slider can be seen above the top surface of the oil seal.
16. Remove the fork seal driver tool.
17. Install the retaining ring (**Figure 47**) into the slider groove. Make sure the retaining ring fully seats in the groove.
18. Slide the dust seal (**Figure 48**) down the fork tube and seat it into the top of the slider.
19. Install the dust cover as follows:
   a. Slide the dust cover down the fork tube and rest it against the top of the slider.
   b. Slide one of the discarded oil seals (A, **Figure 49**) down the fork tube and rest it against the dust cover (B).
   c. Use the same fork seal driver used in Step 14 and carefully drive the dust cover onto the top of the slider as shown in **Figure 49**.
   d. Remove the driver and old seal.
20. Fill the fork tube with the correct quantity of Harley-Davidson Type E fork oil (**Table 1**).
21. Slowly raise and lower the fork tube several times to distribute the oil.
22. After the oil settles, fully compress the fork tube.
23. Hold the fork assembly as close to perfectly vertical as possible.
24. Use an accurate ruler or the Motion Pro oil level gauge part No. 08-121 (**Figure 50**), or equivalent, to achieve the correct oil level (**Table 1**). Refer to **Figure 51**.

11

25. Allow the oil to settle completely and recheck the oil level measurement. Adjust the oil level if necessary.
26. The fork spring has closer coils at one end. Install the spring (**Figure 39**) so the end with the closer coils enters first.
27. Lubricate the fork cap O-ring and threads with fork oil.
28. Attach a suitable socket to a speed wrench, then push down on the speed wrench to turn the fork cap. Fork spring compression kits are available.
29. Align the fork cap (**Figure 40**) with the spring and push down on the cap to compress the spring. Start the cap slowly. Do not cross thread it.
30. Place the slider in a holder with soft jaw inserts and tighten the fork cap to 22-58 ft.-lb. (30-78 N•m).
31. Install the fork tube as described in this chapter.

51

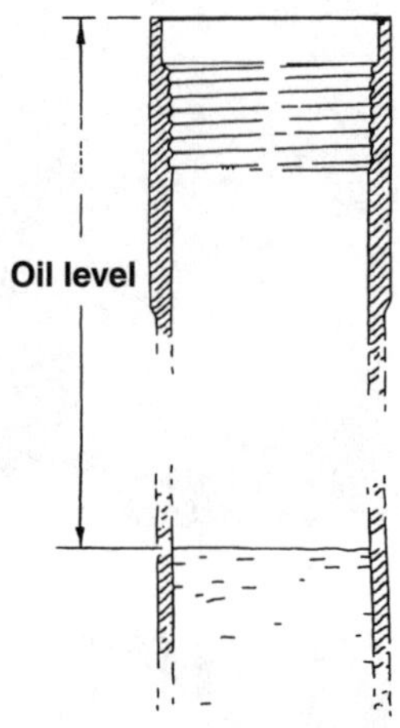

STEERING HEAD AND STEM

The lower portion of the steering stem rides on a tapered roller bearing located at the bottom of the stem. The upper end of the stem rides in a tapered roller bearing that seats in the upper portion of the steering head. Both bearings seat against races pressed into the steering head. Dust shields are used at both bearing areas to protect bearings from contamination.

Removal

Refer to **Figure 52**.

CAUTION
Although not necessary, it is advisable to remove the fuel tank as described in Chapter Eight. Otherwise, cover it with suitable material.

1. Remove the front fork as described in this chapter.
2. On XL1200R models, remove the brake line manifold retaining bolt (**Figure 53**), then separate the manifold and clamp from the bottom of the steering stem bracket.
3. On all models except XL1200R, remove the brake line clamp retaining screw on the underside of the fork stem bracket.
4. Remove the brake line clamp retaining screw on the upper fork bracket (**Figure 54**).

NOTE
If it is not necessary to remove the handlebar, the handlebar can be removed along with the upper fork bracket. If necessary, remove the handlebar as described in this chapter.

5. On XL1200R models, remove the cap (**Figure 55**) by unscrewing it from the underlying bolt head.
6. Remove the steering stem bolt (A, **Figure 56**) and washer (B).

CAUTION
Hold or secure the steering stem/ lower fork bracket to keep it from falling out when loosening the pinch bolt in Step 7.

7. Loosen the pinch bolt (C, **Figure 56**) and lift the upper fork bracket (D) off the steering stem. Carefully set the bracket aside with the cables attached.
8. Lower the stem assembly out of the steering head (**Figure 57**) and remove it.
9. Remove the upper dust shield (**Figure 58**) from the steering head.
10. Remove the bearing (**Figure 59**) from the steering head.
11. Inspect the steering stem and bearings as described in this chapter.

Inspection

The bearing races (**Figure 60**) are pressed into the upper and lower ends of the steering head. Do not remove the bearing races unless they are damaged and require replacement.
1. Wipe the bearing races with a solvent soaked rag and then dry with compressed air or a lint-free cloth. Check the races in the steering head (**Figure 60**) for pitting, scratches, galling or excessive wear. If any of these conditions exist, replace the races as described in this section. If

52

STEERING STEM

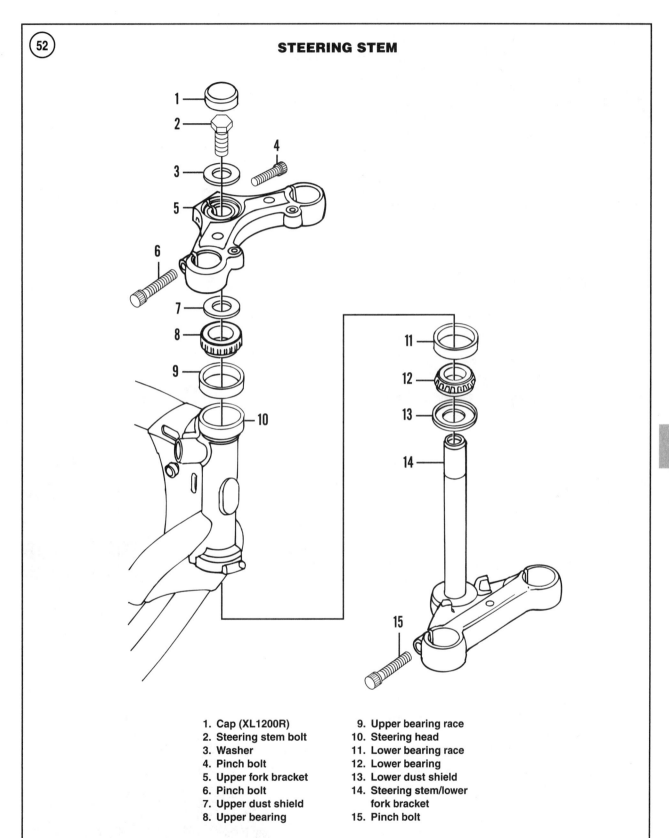

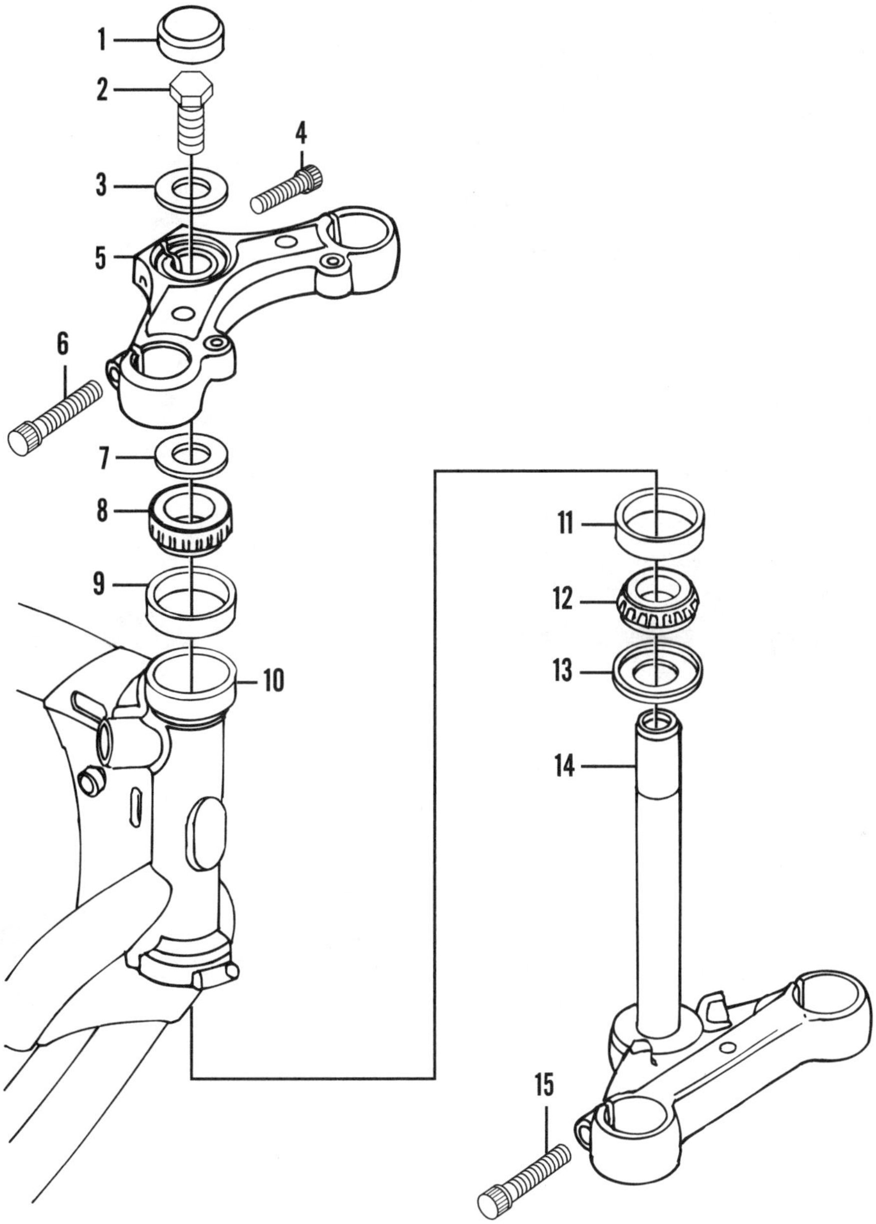

1. Cap (XL1200R)
2. Steering stem bolt
3. Washer
4. Pinch bolt
5. Upper fork bracket
6. Pinch bolt
7. Upper dust shield
8. Upper bearing
9. Upper bearing race
10. Steering head
11. Lower bearing race
12. Lower bearing
13. Lower dust shield
14. Steering stem/lower fork bracket
15. Pinch bolt

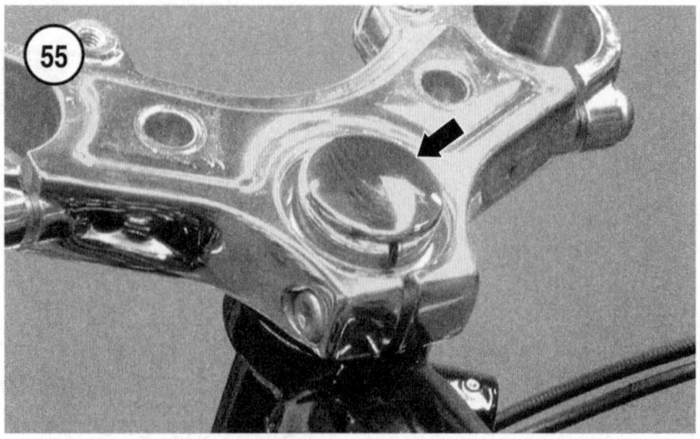

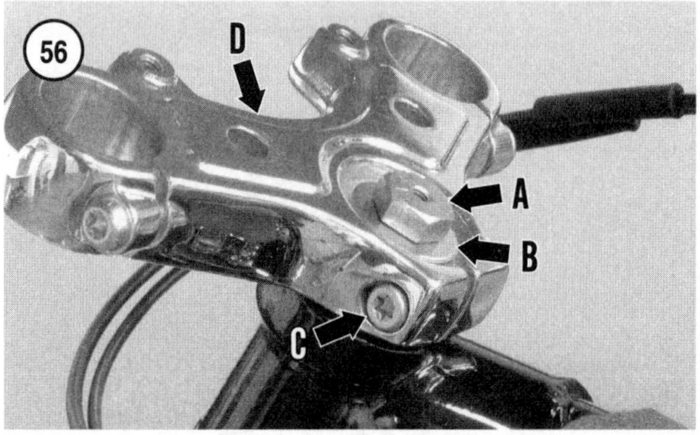

the races are in good condition, lubricate each race with grease.

2. Clean the bearings in solvent to remove all old grease. Blow the bearing dry with compressed air, making sure not to allow the air jet to spin the bearing. Do not remove the lower bearing from the fork stem unless its replacement is required; clean the bearing together with the steering stem.

3. After the bearings are dry, hold the inner race with one hand and turn the outer race with the other hand. Turn the bearing slowly, checking for roughness, looseness, trapped dirt or grit. Visually check the bearing (**Figure 59**) for pitting, scratches or visible damage. If the bearings are worn, check the dust shields for wear or damage or for improper bearing lubrication. Replace the bearing if necessary. If the bearings can be reused, pack them with grease and wrap them with wax paper or some other type of lint-free material until they can be reinstalled.

4. Inspect the steering stem (A, **Figure 61**) for cracks or damage. Check the threads for damage. Check the steering stem bolt by threading it into the steering stem; make sure the bolt threads in easily with no roughness. If necessary, clean the threads carefully with a brush and solvent or use a tap or die of the correct size.

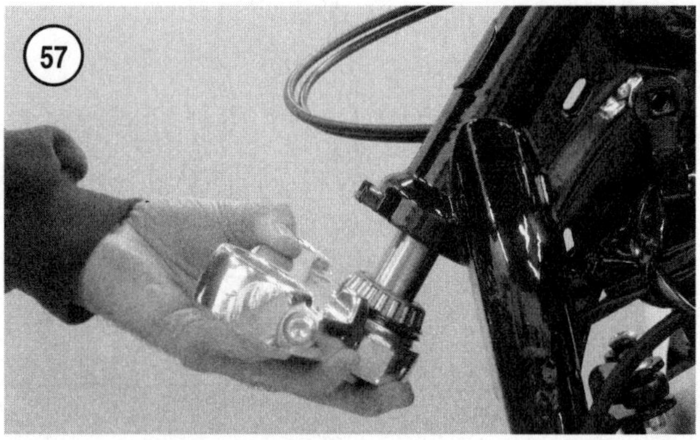

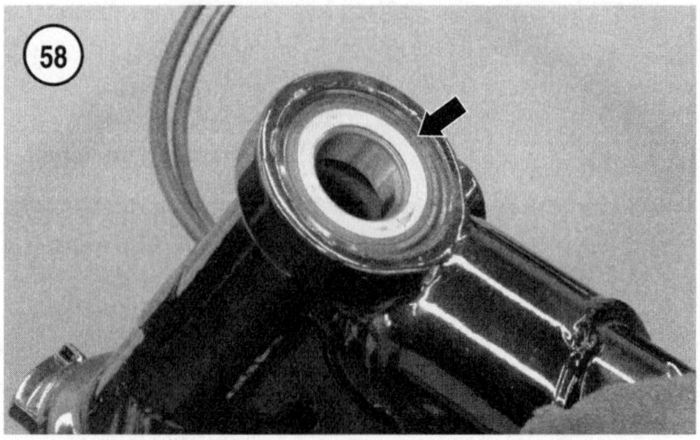

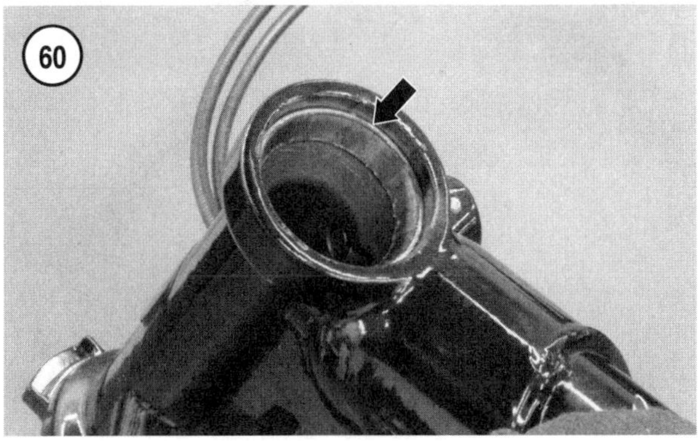

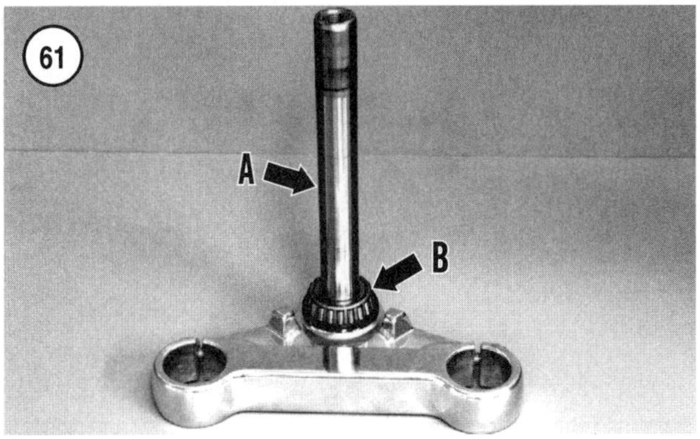

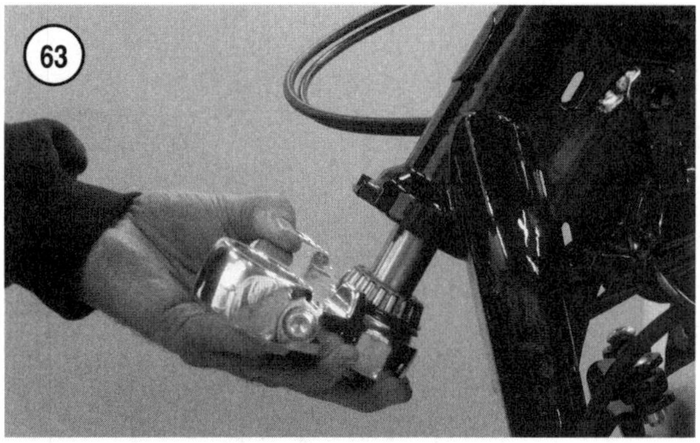

5. Replace worn or damaged parts. When discarding a bearing, replace both the upper and lower bearings and their races at the same time. Replace bearing races as described in this chapter.
6. Replace the lower steering stem bearing (B, **Figure 61**) and dust shield as described in this chapter.
7. Check for broken welds on the frame around the steering head. If there are any, have them inspected by a shop familiar with motorcycle frame repair.

Installation

1. Make sure the steering head bearing races are properly seated.
2. Wipe the bearing races with a clean lint-free cloth. Then lubricate each race with wheel bearing grease.
3. Pack the upper and lower bearings with bearing grease. The lower bearing and lower dust shield (**Figure 62**) must be installed on the steering stem prior to installing the steering stem in the steering head. If necessary, install the lower bearing as described in this chapter.
4. Insert the steering stem into the steering head (**Figure 63**) and hold it firmly in place.
5. Install the upper bearing around the fork stem and seat it into the upper race (**Figure 64**).

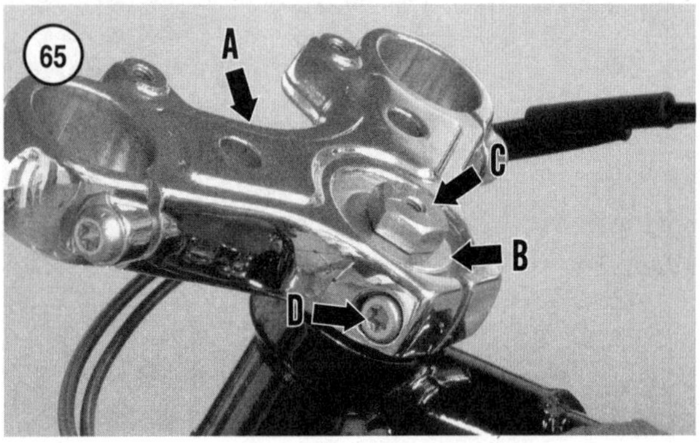

6. Install the upper dust shield so the flat, lettered side is up.
7. Install the upper fork bracket (A, **Figure 65**) onto the steering stem.
8. Install the washer (B, **Figure 65**) and the steering stem bolt (C). Tighten the bolt hand-tight only.
9. Install the front fork as described in this chapter.
10. Tighten the steering stem bolt (C, **Figure 65**) until the steering stem can be turned from side to side with no noticeable axial or lateral bearing play. When the play feels correct, tighten the steering stem pinch bolt (D, **Figure 65**) to 30-35 ft.-lb. (41-47 N•m).

CAUTION
Do not overtighten the steering stem bolt or the bearings and races may be damaged. Perform the final adjustment of the stem after installing the front wheel.

11. On XL1200R models, install the brake line manifold, clamp and retaining bolt (**Figure 66**) to the bottom of the steering stem bracket.
12. On all models except XL1200R, install the brake line clamp retaining screw on the underside of the fork stem bracket.
13. Install the brake line clamp retaining screw on the upper fork bracket (**Figure 67**).
14. Install the front wheel as described in Chapter Ten.
15. Adjust the steering play as described in this chapter.

STEERING HEAD BEARING RACE

Whenever the steering stem and bearings are removed from the steering head, cover the steering head with a cloth to protect the bearing races from accidental damage. If a race is damaged, replace the bearing and race as a set. Because the bearing races are pressed into place, do not remove them unless they are worn and require replacement.

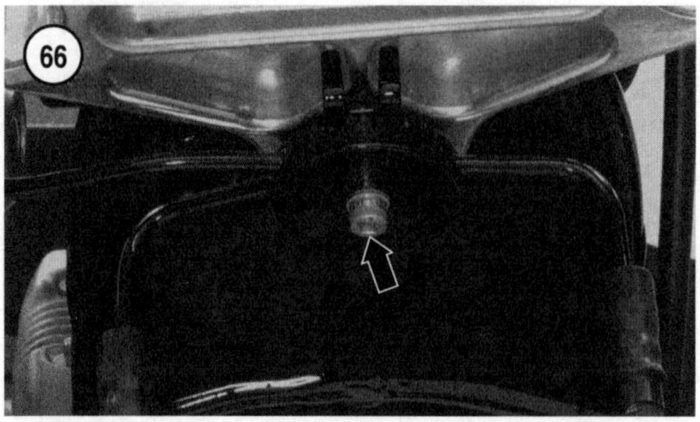

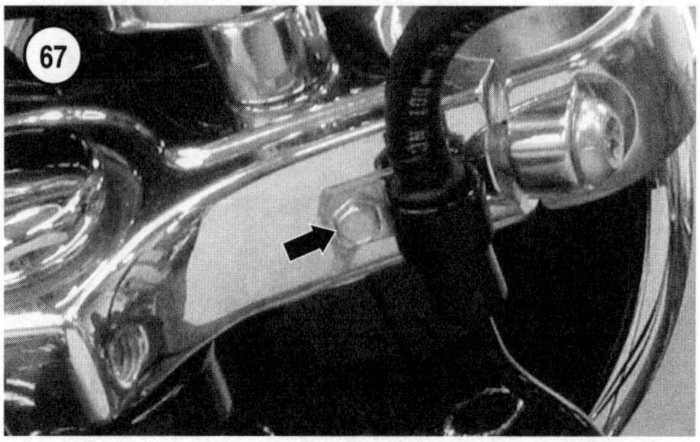

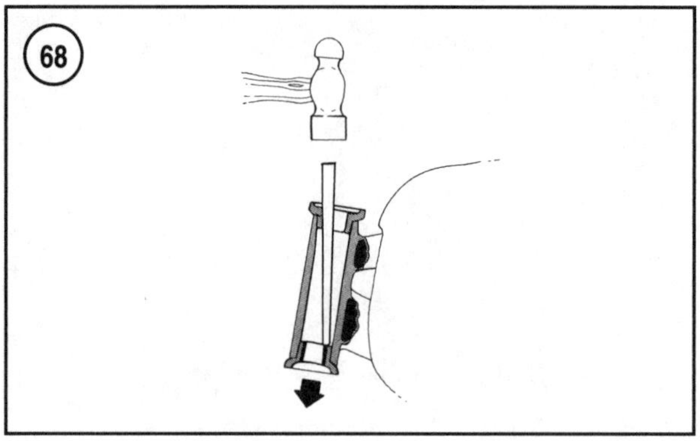

Upper and Lower Bearing Race Replacement

The upper and lower bearing races (9 and 11, **Figure 52**) are pressed into the frame steering head. Because they are easily bent, do not remove the bearing races unless they are worn and require replacement. Both races are identical (same part number) and can be purchased separately from the bearing. If bearing replacement is required, purchase the bearing and race as a set.

1. To remove a race, insert an aluminum or brass rod into the steering head and carefully tap the race out from the in-

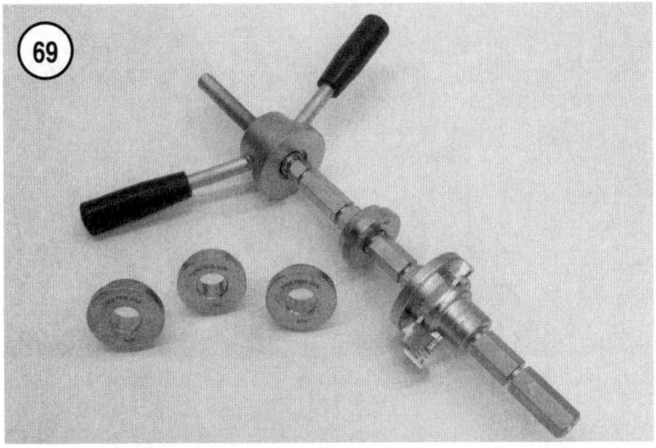

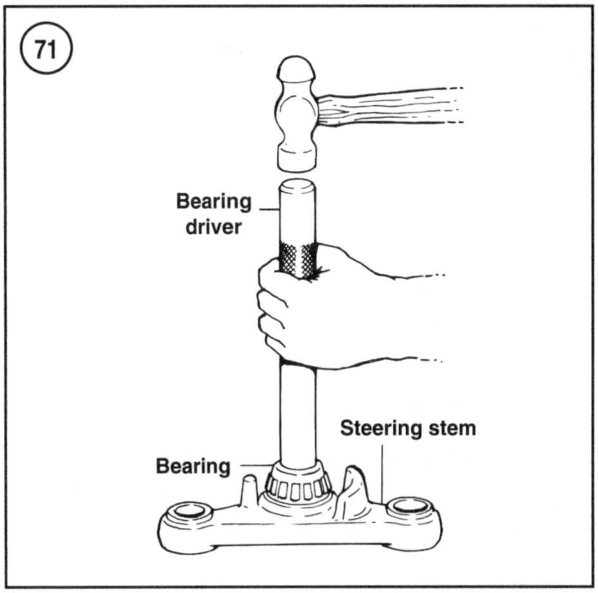

side (**Figure 68**). Tap all around the race so neither the race nor the steering head are bent.

2. Clean the steering head with solvent and dry thoroughly.

NOTE
*The bearing races can be installed using the Harley-Davidson head bearing race installation tool (part No. HD- 39302) or equivalent (**Figure 69** [www.parktool.com]). If this tool is not available, perform Step 3.*

3. Install the bearing races as follows:
   a. Clean the race thoroughly before installing it.
   b. Align the upper race with the frame steering head and tap it slowly and squarely in place with a block of wood, a suitable socket or bearing driver, making sure not to contact the bearing race tapered surface. See **Figure 69**. If an old race is available, grind its outside rim so it is a slip fit in the steering head, then use it to drive the new race into place. Drive the race into the steering head until it bottoms on the bore shoulder.
   c. Repeat to install the lower race into the steering head.

4. Lubricate the bearing races with wheel bearing grease.

Fork Stem Lower Bearing Replacement

Do not remove the fork stem lower bearing (**Figure 70**) unless it is going to be replaced with a new bearing. Do not reinstall a lower bearing that has been removed, as it is no longer true. When replacing the lower bearing, install a new lower dust shield (13, **Figure 52**).

11

WARNING
Wear safety glasses and insulated gloves during Step 1.

1. Using a chisel, break the bearing cage and rollers from the inner race. When the bearing cage and rollers are free, the inner race on the fork stem is exposed. To remove the inner race, heat the race with a torch until it expands enough to slide or drop off the fork stem. Remove and discard the dust cover after removing the bearing.
2. Clean the fork stem with solvent and dry thoroughly.
3. Pack the new bearing with grease before installing it.
4. Slide a new dust shield onto the fork stem so it bottoms on the lower bracket.
5. Align the new bearing with the fork stem and press or drive it onto the fork stem until it bottoms. When installing the bearing onto the fork stem, a bearing driver must be used against the inner bearing race (**Figure 71**). Do not install the bearing by driving against the outer bearing race.

72

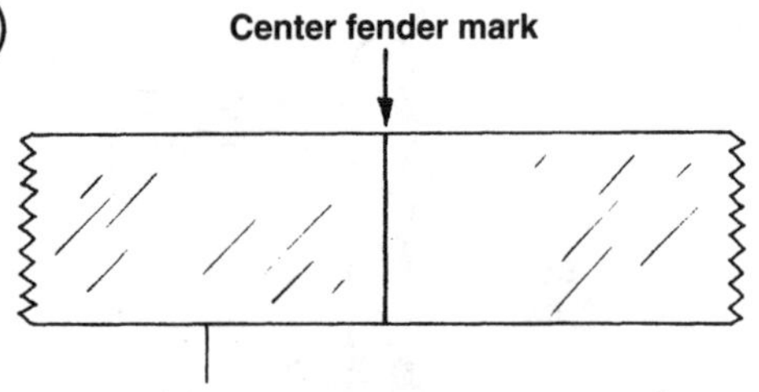

STEERING PLAY ADJUSTMENT

Check the steering play periodically or anytime the steering stem assembly has been removed and installed.

1. Support the bike so that the front wheel clears the ground.
2. Remove the windshield (if used) and all other accessory weight from the handlebar and front fork.

NOTE

If any control cable hinders handlebar movement, disconnect it.

3. Apply a strip of masking tape across the front end of the front fender. Draw a vertical line across the tape at the center of the fender (**Figure 72**). Then draw two lines on each side of the centerline, 1 in. (25.4 mm) apart from each other.
4. Turn the handlebar so the front wheel faces straight ahead.
5. Place a pointer on a stand and then center the pointer so that its tip points to the center of the fender (tape mark) when the wheel is facing straight ahead.
6. Lightly push the fender toward the right side until the front end starts to turn by itself. Mark this point on the tape.
7. Repeat Step 6 for the left side.
8. Measure the distance between the two marks on the tape. For proper bearing adjustment, the distance should be 1-2 in. (25.4-50.8 mm). If the distance is incorrect, perform Step 9.
9. Adjust steering play as follows:
   a. Loosen the lower fork bracket pinch bolts (**Figure 73**) on both sides.
   b. On XL1200R models, unscrew and remove the cap (**Figure 74**).
   c. Loosen the steering stem pinch bolt (A, **Figure 75**).

73

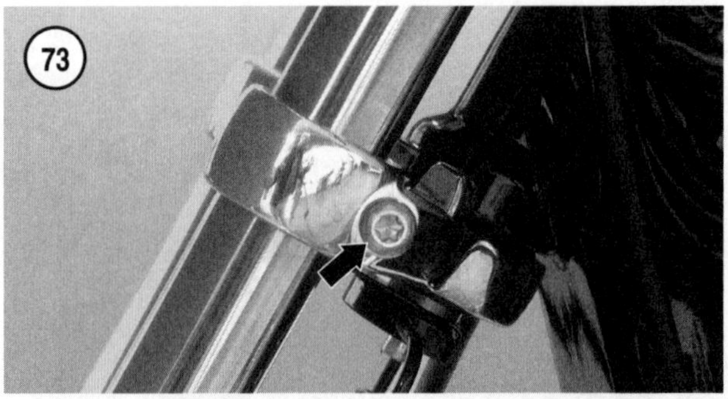

74

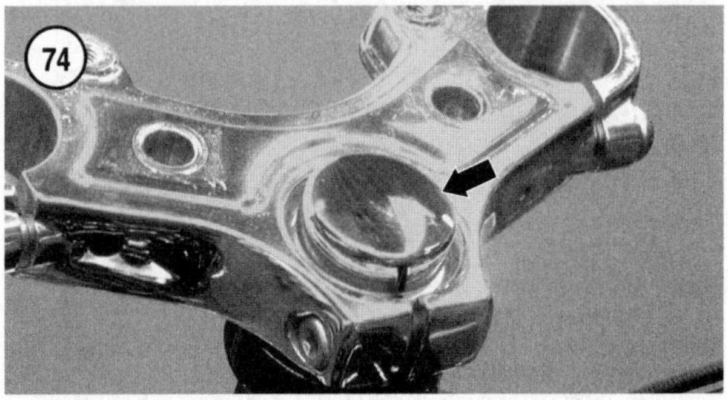

75

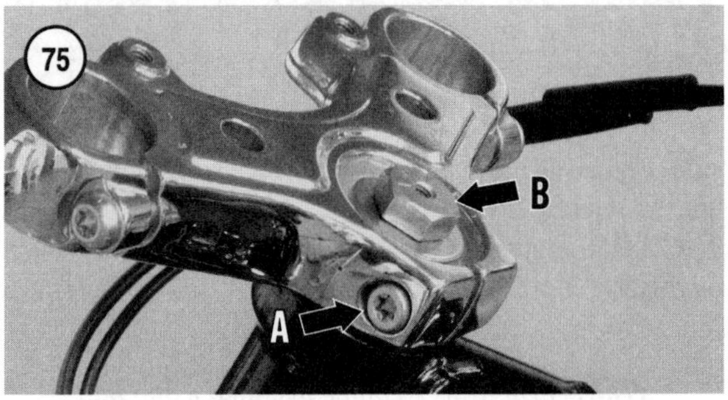

   d. Loosen or tighten the steering stem bolt (B, **Figure 75**) until the distance between the two marks is within 1-2 in. (25.4-50.8 mm).
10. When steering play adjustment is correct, perform the following:
   a. Tighten the steering stem pinch bolt (A, **Figure 75**) to 30-35 ft.-lb. (41-47 N•m).
   b. Tighten the lower fork bracket pinch bolts (**Figure 73**) to 30-35 ft.-lb. (41-47 N•m).
   c. On XL1200R models, install and tighten the cap (**Figure 74**) securely.
11. Reinstall all parts previously removed.

Table 1 FORK OIL CAPACITY AND OIL LEVEL

Model	Capacity*	Oil level
XL883L, XL1200L	12.3 oz (364 mL)	4.80 in. (122 mm)
All other models	11.6 oz (343 mL)	5.75 in. (146 mm)

*Each fork leg.

Table 2 FRONT SUSPENSION TORQUE SPECIFICATIONS

	ft.-lb.	in.-lb.	N•m
Brake hose clamp screws	–	30-40	3.4-4.5
Clutch lever clamp bolt	–	108-132	13-15
Fork bracket pinch bolts	30-35	–	41-47
Fork cap	22-58	–	30-78
Front fender fasteners	–	96-156	11-17
Handlebar lower clamp bolts	30-40	–	41-54
Handlebar upper clamp bolts	12-18	–	17-24
Master cylinder clamp bolts	–	108-132	13-15
Mirror locknut	–	96-144	11-16
Steering stem pinch bolt	30-35	–	41-47
Switch housing screws	–	35-45	4.0-5.0

CHAPTER TWELVE

REAR SUSPENSION

This chapter describes repair and replacement procedures for rear suspension components. Refer to Chapter Ten for wheel, hub, rear axle and tire service information.

Rear suspension specifications are in **Table 1** at the end of this chapter.

WARNING
Replace all suspension and steering fasteners with parts of the same type. Do not substitute with a replacement type; this may affect the safety of the system.

SHOCK ABSORBERS

The rear shocks are spring controlled and hydraulically damped. Spring preload can be adjusted on all models.

Spring Preload Adjustment

The shock absorber springs can be adjusted to suit the rider and load. Rotate the cam ring (**Figure 1**) at the base of the spring to compress the spring (heavy loads) or extend the spring (light loads). Use a spanner wrench to rotate the cam ring.

Removal/Installation

Removal and installation of the rear shocks is easier if performed separately. The remaining unit will support the rear of the motorcycle and maintain the correct relationship between the top and bottom mounts. If both shock absorbers must be removed at the same time, cut a piece of steel a few inches longer than the shock absorber and drill two holes in the steel the same distance apart as the bolt holes in the shock absorber. Install the steel support after removing one shock absorber. This allows the bike to be moved around until the shock absorbers are reinstalled or replaced.

1. Support the bike so the rear wheel clears the ground.
2. Remove the lower locknut, bolt and washer (**Figure 2**).

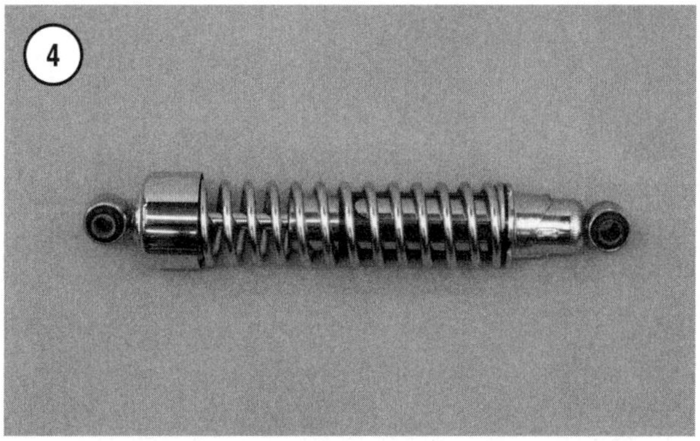

3. Remove the upper bolt, washer, stud cover and washer (**Figure 3**).
4. Remove the shock absorber (**Figure 4**).
5. Install by reversing the preceding removal steps, while noting the following:
   a. Apply Loctite 243 (blue) onto the upper shock bolt threads.
   b. Tighten the upper and lower bolt and locknut to 45-50 ft.-lb. (62-68 N•m).

Inspection

Refer to **Figure 5**.

Inspect all parts for wear or damage. Pay particular attention to the following items.

1. Replace any bushings (A, **Figure 6**) that show wear, damage or cracking.
2. Check the shock absorber for fluid leaks. Replace the shock absorber if it is leaking.

Disassembly/Reassembly

WARNING
Do not remove the shock absorber spring without a spring compressor tool.

The shock absorber body and spring are not available separately.

1. Remove the shock absorber as described in this section.
2. Adjust the cam ring to its softest setting.
3. Remove the upper spring cover (B, **Figure 6**).
4. Using a shock absorber spring compression tool, compress the shock absorber spring (**Figure 7**, typical) and remove the upper spring retainer.
5. Release spring pressure, then remove the shock absorber assembly from the tool.
6. Disassemble the shock absorber in the order shown in **Figure 5**.
7. Inspect the shock absorber as described in this section.
8. Assembly is the reverse of these steps. Lightly grease all cam parts before assembly.

SWING ARM

Removal

Refer to **Figure 8**.

1. Remove the rear wheel as described in Chapter Ten.
2. Refer to Chapter Thirteen and remove the rear brake caliper.

(5)

SHOCK ABSORBER

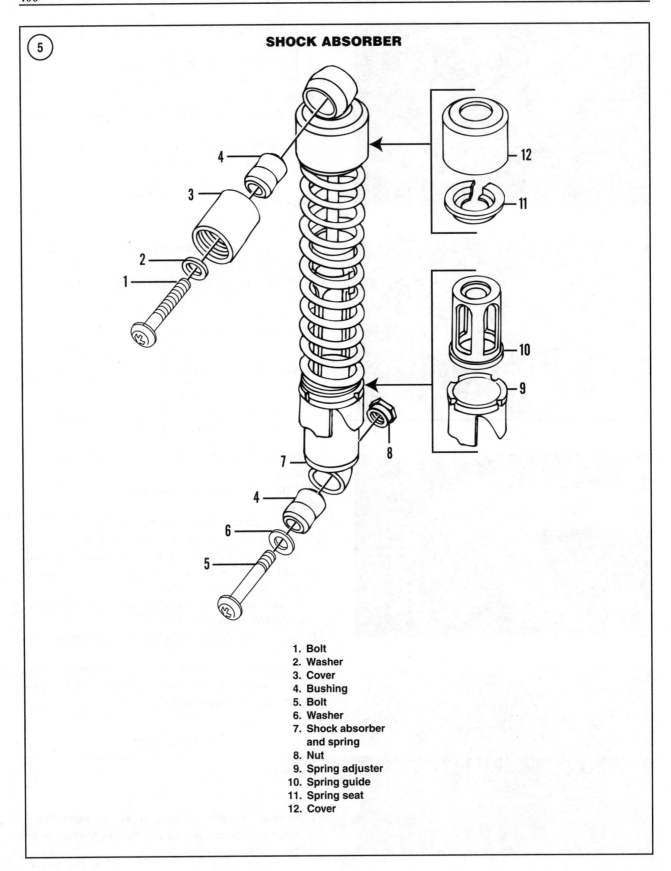

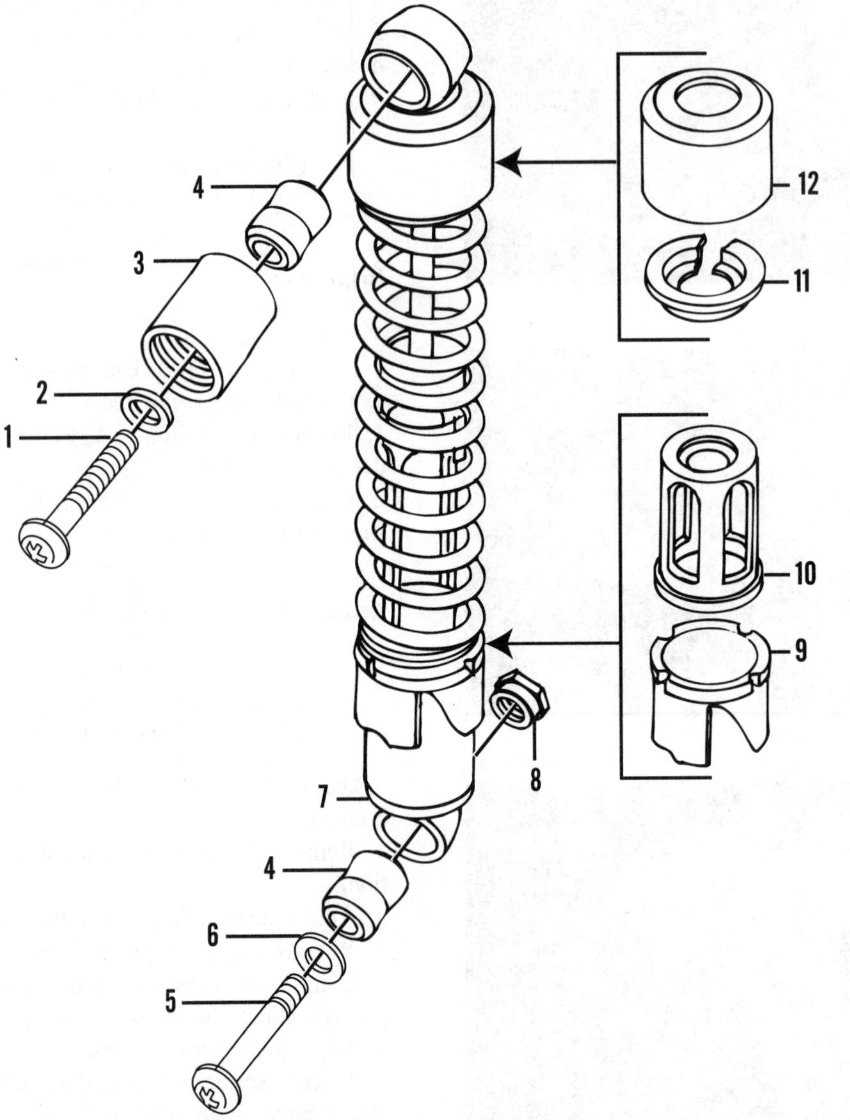

1. Bolt
2. Washer
3. Cover
4. Bushing
5. Bolt
6. Washer
7. Shock absorber and spring
8. Nut
9. Spring adjuster
10. Spring guide
11. Spring seat
12. Cover

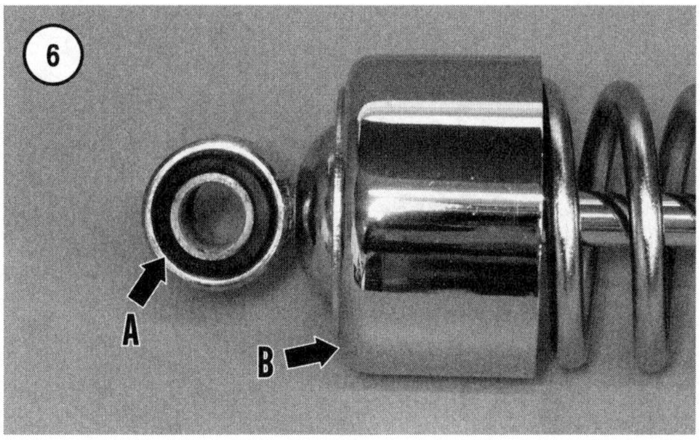

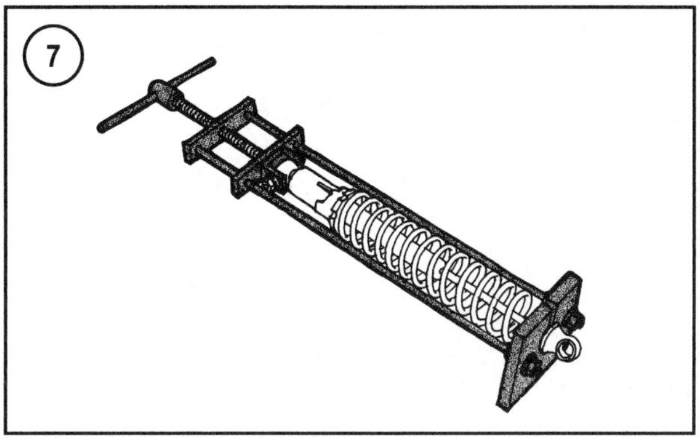

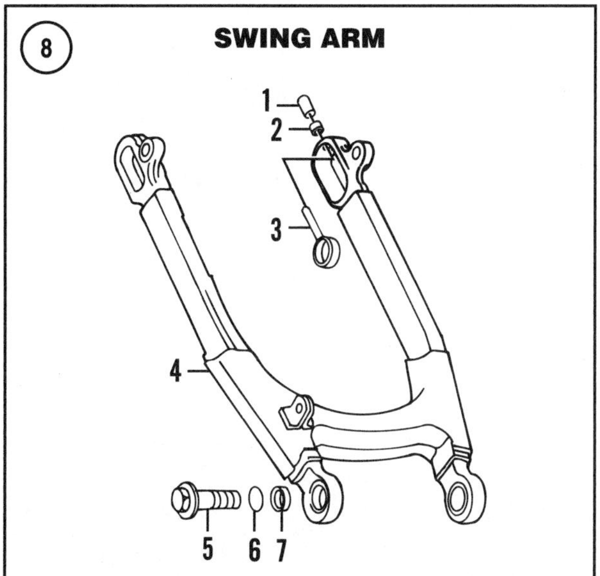

1. Cap
2. Locknut
3. Adjuster
4. Swing arm
5. Bolt
6. Retaining ring
7. Bearing

3. Remove the brake hose clamp screw and separate the clamp (**Figure 9**) from the swing arm.

4. Remove the locknut, bolt and washer (**Figure 10**) at the lower end of each shock absorber.

5. Remove the drive belt as described in Chapter Ten.

NOTE
The swing arm mounting bolts also secure the engine. The remaining engine mounting bolts will support the engine when the swing arm bolts are removed.

NOTE
Prior to swing arm mounting bolt removal, check for excessive swing arm play. Try to move the swing arm from side to side. There is no free play service limit specification. If free play is excessive, replace the swing arm bearings as described in this section.

6. Support the swing arm. Remove the swing arm mounting bolts (**Figure 11**), then remove the swing arm (**Figure 12**).

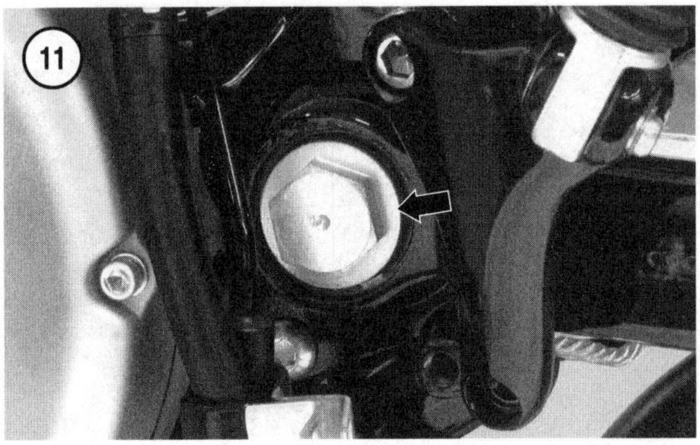

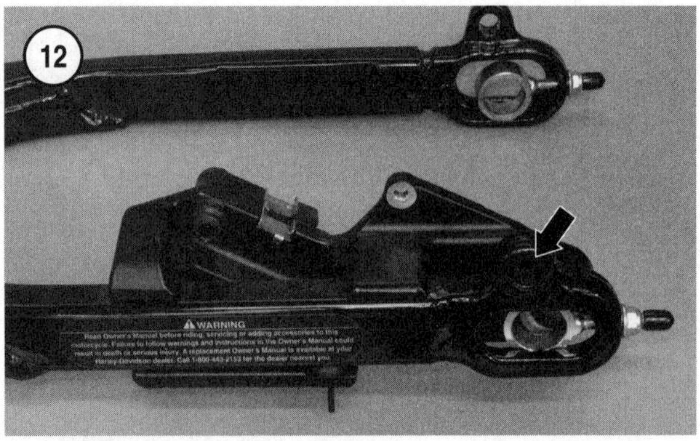

Installation

1. Install the swing arm and mounting bolts (**Figure 11**). Tighten the mounting bolts to 60-70 ft.-lb. (82-95 N•m).
2. Install the drive belt as described in Chapter Ten.
3. Install the locknut, bolt and washer (**Figure 10**) at the lower end of each shock absorber. Tighten the locknut to 45-50 ft.-lb. (62-68 N•m).
4. Install the brake hose clamp (**Figure 9**) onto the swing arm.
5. Refer to Chapter Thirteen and install the rear brake caliper.
6. Install the rear wheel as described in Chapter Ten.

Inspection

1. Check the swing arm for straightness, cracking and damage.
2. Inspect the shock absorber mounting bosses (**Figure 12**) for elongation and damage.
3. Inspect the retaining ring on each bearing (A, **Figure 13**). The retaining ring retains and positions the bearing in the swing arm and should not be bent or damaged. If necessary, replace the retaining ring.
4. Inspect the bearings (B, **Figure 13**) for damage. Make sure the bearing fits tightly in the swing arm bore. If the bearing is loose, replace the swing arm. If necessary, replace the bearings as described in the following section.
5. Inspect the swing arm mounting bolts (**Figure 14**). The bolt serves as the pivot axle for the bearing and threads into the pivot shaft (**Figure 15**). The pivot shaft also functions as the rear engine mount. Refer to *Engine Mounting System* in Chapter Five. Replace the bolt if it is galled, excessively worn or otherwise damaged.

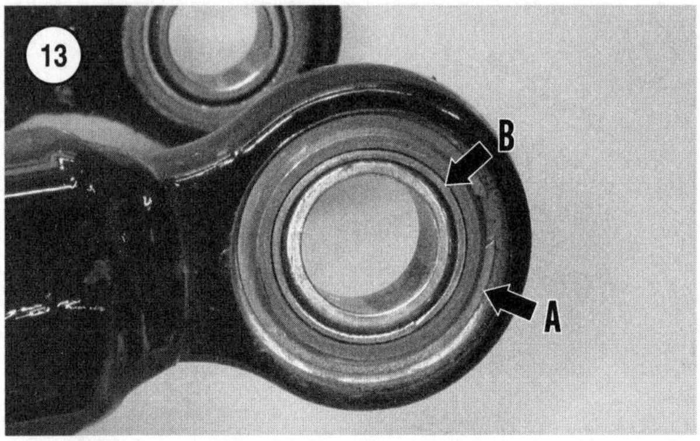

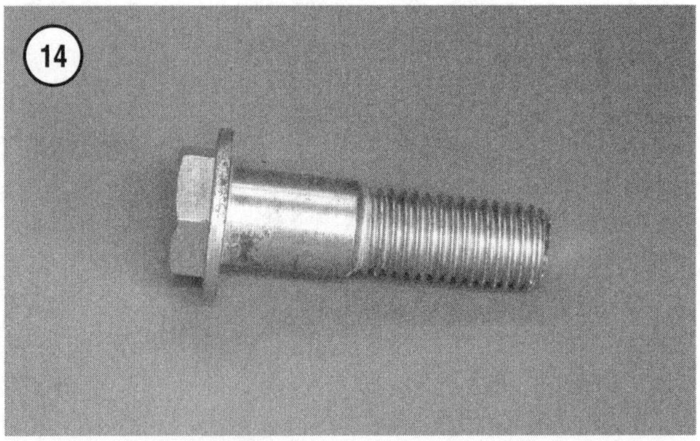

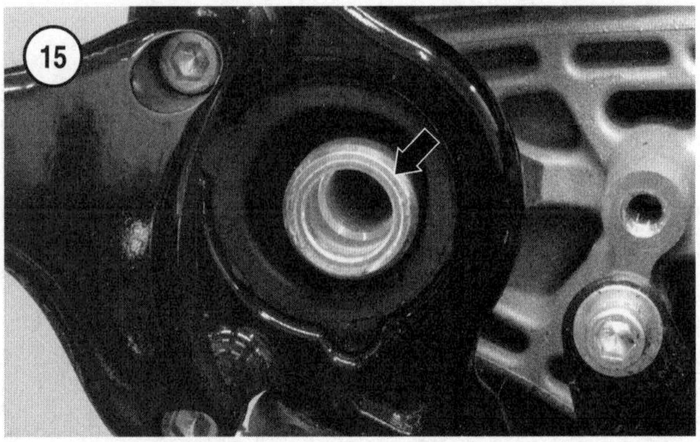

16

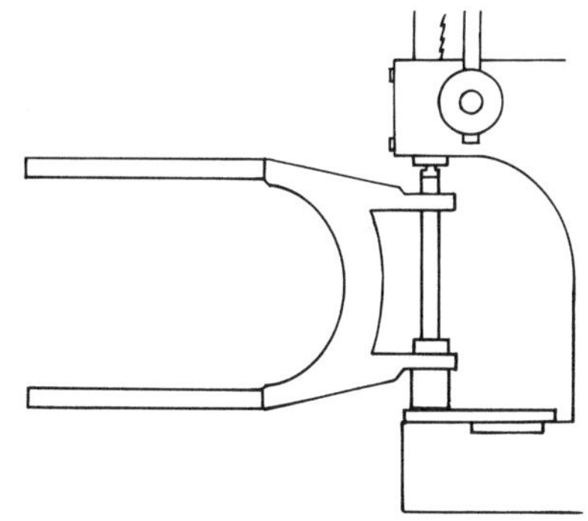

Bearing Replacement

1. Set the swing arm in a press as shown in **Figure 16** to remove the bearing. Force the bearing toward the outside of the swing arm.
2. Note the retaining ring on the bearing (A, **Figure 13**). The retaining ring serves to position the bearing during installation.
3. Set the swing arm in a press as shown in **Figure 16** to install the bearing. Apply pressure against the ring-end of the bearing. Force the bearing into the swing arm until the retaining ring seats in the recess in the swing arm.

Table 1 REAR SUSPENSION TORQUE SPECIFICATIONS

	ft.-lb.	in.-lb.	N•m
Shock absorber bolt or locknut	45-50	–	62-68
Swing arm mounting bolts	60-70	–	82-95

NOTE: Refer to the Supplement at the end of this manual for information unique to 2007-2011 models.

CHAPTER THIRTEEN

BRAKES

This chapter describes service procedures for the front and rear brakes. Refer to **Table 1** and **Table 2** at the end of this chapter for brake specifications.

BRAKE FLUID TYPE

When adding or replacing brake fluid, use DOT 5 brake fluid, which is silicone-based.

WARNING
Do not use brake fluid labeled DOT 5.1. This is a gylcol-based fluid that is not compatible with silicone-based DOT 5. DOT 5 brake fluid is purple while DOT 5.1 is amber/clear. Do not intermix these two different types of brake fluid as it can cause brake component damage and lead to brake system failure.

WARNING
Do not intermix DOT 3, DOT 4 or DOT 5.1 brake fluids as they are not silicone-based. Using non-silicone brake fluid in these models can cause brake failure.

WARNING
Never reuse brake fluid (like fluid expelled during brake bleeding). Contaminated brake fluid can cause brake failure. Dispose of used brake fluid properly.

BRAKE SERVICE

WARNING
When working on the brake system, do not inhale brake dust. It may contain asbestos, which is a known carcinogen. Do not use compressed air to blow off brake dust. Use an aerosol brake cleaner. Wear a facemask and wash thoroughly after completing the work.

The brake system transmits hydraulic pressure from the master cylinders to the brake calipers. This pressure is transmitted from the calipers to the brake pads, which grip both sides of the brake discs and slow the motorcycle. As the pads wear, the pistons move out of the caliper bores to automatically compensate for wear. As this occurs, the fluid level in the master cylinder reservoir goes down. This must be compensated for by occasionally adding fluid.

The proper operation of this system depends on a supply of clean brake fluid (DOT 5) and a clean work environment when any service is being performed. Any debris that enters the system can damage the components and cause poor brake performance.

Perform brake service procedures carefully. Do not use any sharp tools inside the master cylinders, calipers or on the pistons. Damage to these components could cause a loss of system hydraulic pressure. If there is any doubt about the ability to correctly and safely service the brake system, have a professional technician perform the task.

Consider the following when servicing the brake system:

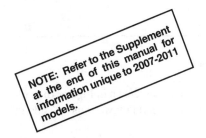

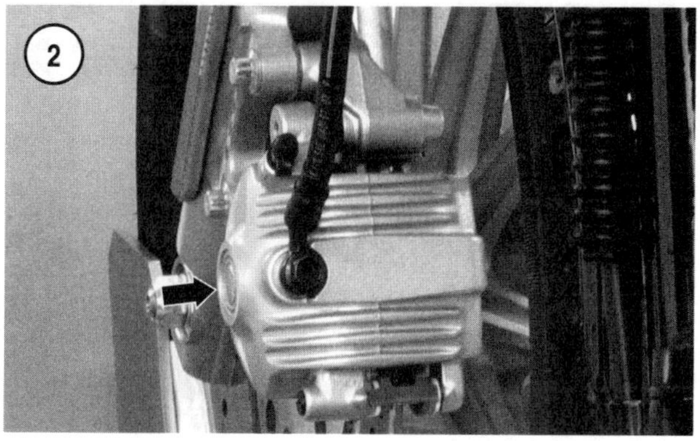

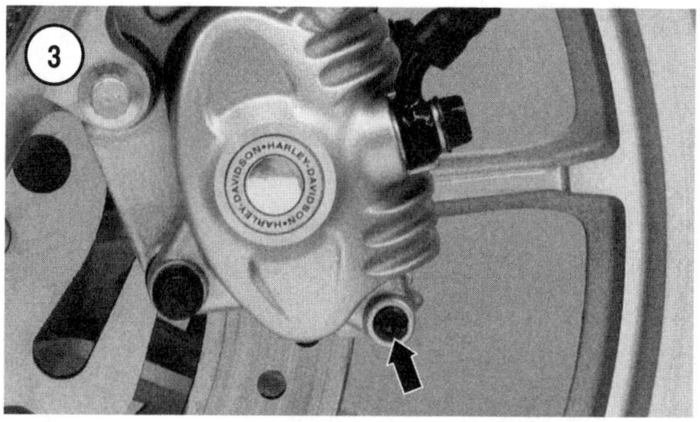

1. The hydraulic components rarely require disassembly. Make sure it is necessary.
2. Keep the reservoir covers in place to prevent the entry of moisture and debris.
3. Clean parts with an aerosol brake parts cleaner. Never use petroleum-based solvents on internal brake system components. They cause seals to swell and distort.
4. Do not allow brake fluid to contact plastic, painted or plated parts. It will damage the surface. Punch a small hole at the edge of the seal of the brake fluid containter to control the flow when adding fluid.
5. Dispose of brake fluid properly.
6. If the hydraulic system, not including the reservoir cover, has been opened, bleed the system to remove air from the system. Refer to *Brake Bleeding* in this chapter.

FRONT BRAKE PADS

There is no recommended mileage interval for replacing brake pads. Pad wear depends on riding conditions. Inspect the front brake pads for uneven wear, scoring, oil contamination or other damage. As the brake pads wear, the brake fluid level will drop.

Always replace the front brake pads in sets. Never use one new brake pad with a used brake pad in a caliper. If equipped with dual front calipers, never replace the brake pads in one brake caliper without replacing them in the other caliper. Doing so causes an unbalanced braking condition.

WARNING
Do not ride the motorcycle until the brakes are operating correctly. If necessary, bleed the brakes as described in this chapter.

Brake Pad Replacement

Refer to Chapter Three to measure brake pad wear.

1. Review *Brake Service* in this chapter.
2. Place the motorcycle on a suitable stand.
3. Place a spacer between the brake lever and the throttle grip and secure it in place. This will prevent piston expulsion from the cylinders if the brake lever is inadvertently squeezed.

WARNING
Before performing brake pad replacement, inspect the brake disc for damage and excessive wear. If evident, remove the front brake caliper and inspect the brake disc as described in this chapter.

4. Clean the top of the master cylinder of all debris.
5. Position the handlebar so the front brake master cylinder is level. Remove the screws securing the cover (**Figure 1**). Remove the cover, diaphragm plate and diaphragm.
6. Using a shop syringe or a cooking baster, draw brake fluid out of the master cylinder reservoir to prevent overflow.
7. Push against the side of the brake caliper (**Figure 2**) so the brake pad pushes in the caliper pistons. The pistons should move freely into the caliper. If they do not, remove and service the caliper as described in this chapter.
8. Remove the pad pin plug (**Figure 3**).
9. Loosen but do not remove the pad pin (**Figure 4**).

10. Withdraw the pad pin just until the inner brake pad is free, then remove the brake pad (**Figure 5**).

NOTE
Inspect the old pads and caliper during pad replacement. If the old pads exhibit uneven wear or fluid leakage is evident, refer to ***Front Brake Caliper*** *in this chapter.*

11. Install the new inner brake pad so the mounting tab (A, **Figure 6**) fits into the mounting slot in the caliper. Hold the pad so it does not fall out.
12. Fully withdraw the pad pin so the outer brake pad is free, then remove the brake pad (**Figure 7**).
13. Install the new outer brake pad so the mounting tab (A, **Figure 6**) fits into the mounting slot in the caliper. Hold the pad so it does not fall out.
14. Insert a 1/8-inch drill bit or rod so it engages the mounting hole (B, **Figure 6**) on each pad. This temporarily holds the pads in place.
15. Inspect the pad pin (**Figure 8**) for damage and excessive wear. Clean any corrosion or dirt from the pad pin surface. A dirty or damaged pad pin surface prevents the brake pads from sliding properly and causes brake drag and overheating of the brake disc. Replace the pin if worn or indented more than 0.011 in. (0.28 mm).

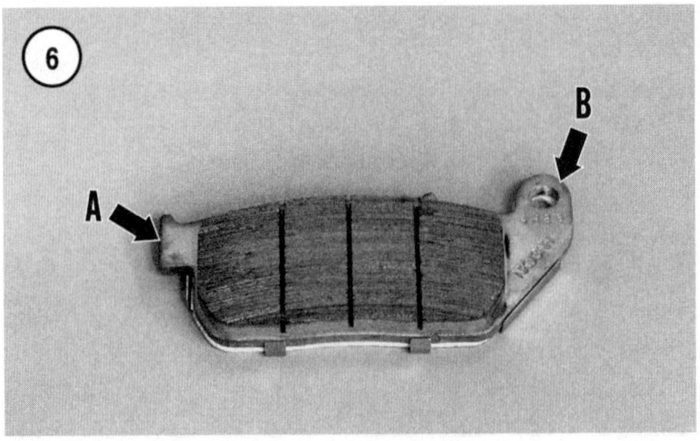

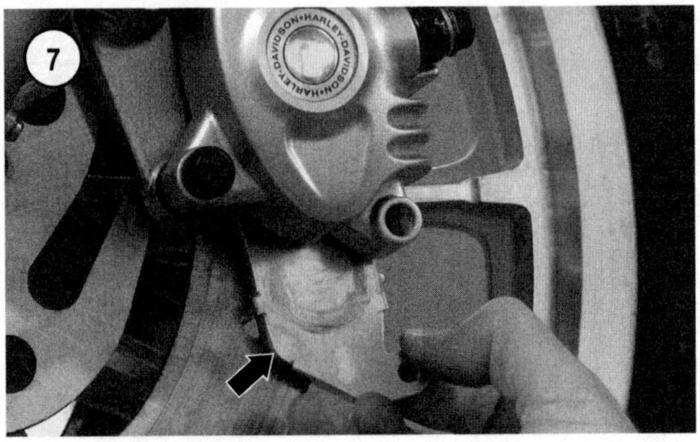

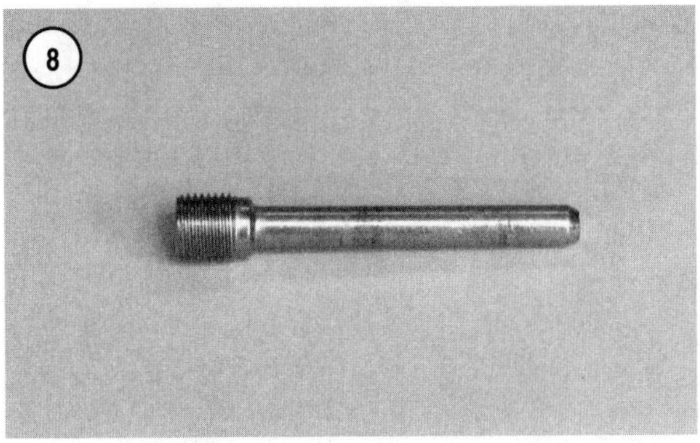

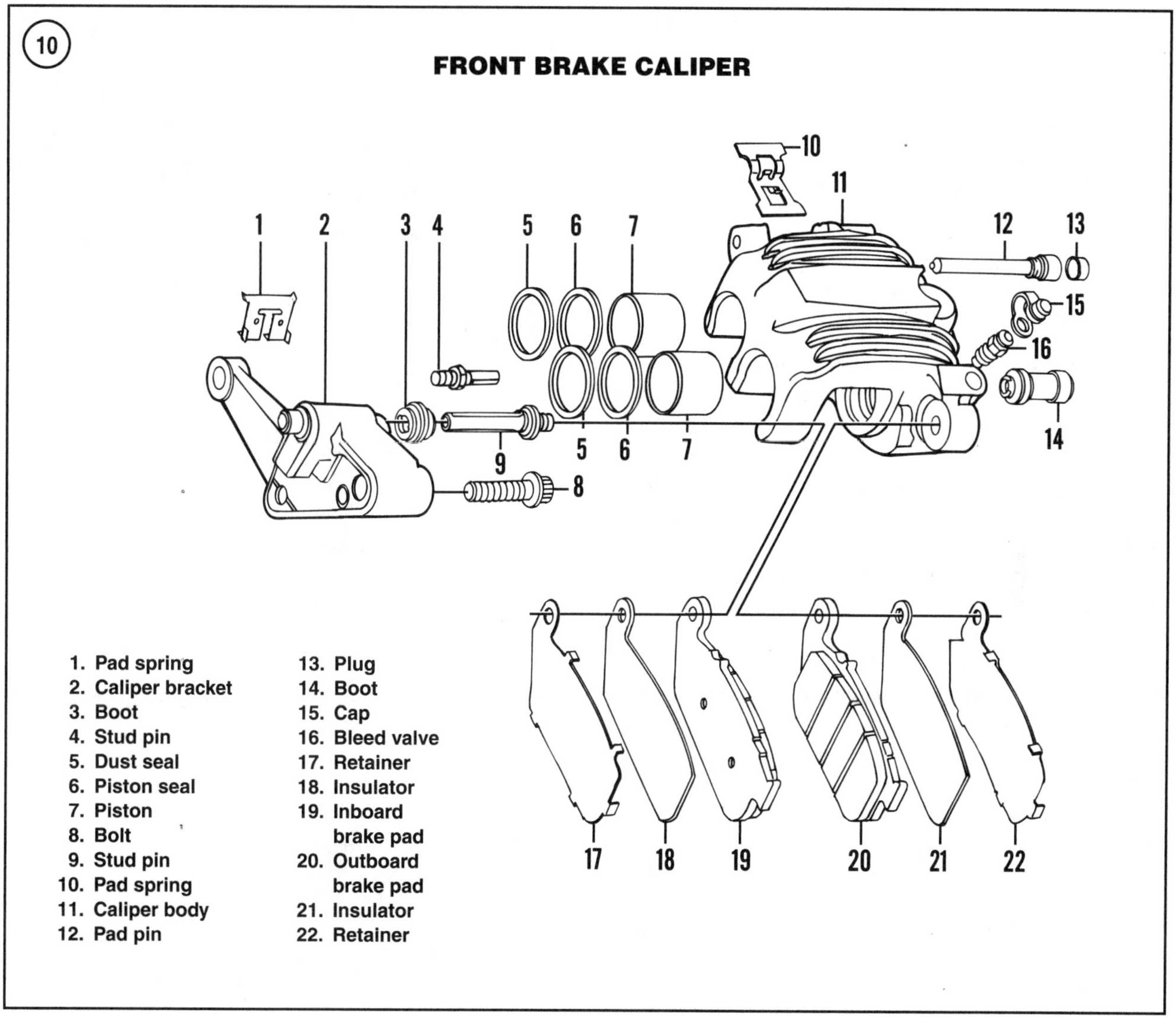

16. Make sure the pad spring (**Figure 9**) is properly positioned in the caliper before final installation of the pad pin.

17. Remove the drill bit or rod and install the pad pin (**Figure 4**). Tighten the pad pin to 131-173 in.-lb. (15-19.5 N•m).

18. Install the pad pin plug (**Figure 3**) and tighten to 18-25 in.-lb. (2.0-2.9 N•m).

19. On XL1200R models, repeat Steps 6-16 and remove the brake pads in the other caliper assembly.

20. Remove the spacer from the front brake lever.

21. Pump the front brake lever to reposition the brake pads against the brake disc. Roll the motorcycle back and forth and continue to pump the brake lever as many times as needed to fully position the brake pads against the disc.

22. Refill the master cylinder reservoir as described in Chapter Three. Install the diaphragm, diaphragm plate and cover. Tighten the cover retaining screws securely.

23. Break in the pads gradually for the first 100 miles (160 km) by using only light pressure as much as possible. Immediate hard application glazes the new pads and reduces their effectiveness.

FRONT BRAKE CALIPER

Removal/Installation

WARNING
Do not ride the motorcycle until the brakes operate correctly.

Refer to **Figure 10**.

1. If the caliper is going to be disassembled for service, perform the following:

a. Remove the brake pads as described in this chapter.

CAUTION
During the following procedure, do not allow the pistons to come in contact with the brake disc. If this happens the pistons may damage the disc during caliper removal.

NOTE
By performing substep b, compressed air may not be necessary for piston removal during caliper disassembly.

b. Slowly apply the brake lever to push the pistons part way out of the caliper assembly for ease of removal during caliper service.

2. Remove the union bolt (A, **Figure 11**) and sealing washers attaching the brake hose to the caliper assembly. There should be two sealing washers—one on each side of the union bolt.
3. Place the loose end of the brake hose in a reclosable plastic bag to prevent brake fluid from leaking onto the wheel or fork.
4. If the brake pads were not previously removed, remove the pad pin plug (**Figure 3**). Loosen but do not remove the pad pin (**Figure 4**).
5. Remove the two caliper mounting bolts (B, **Figure 11**) and lift the brake caliper off the disc.
6. If necessary, disassemble and service the caliper as described in this section.
7. Install by reversing the preceding removal steps while noting the following:

a. Carefully install the caliper onto the disc while being careful not to damage the leading edge of the brake pads.
b. Install the two caliper mounting bolts (B, **Figure 11**) and secure the brake caliper to the front fork. Tighten the caliper mounting bolts to 28-38 ft.-lb. (38.0-51.6 N•m).
c. Connect the brake hose to the caliper. Install a new sealing washer on each side of the union bolt (A, **Figure 11**). Position the union so it contacts the boss on the caliper (**Figure 12**). Tighten the union bolt to 20-25 ft.-lb. (27-34 N•m).
d. Bleed the brake as described in this chapter.

Disassembly

Refer to **Figure 10**.

1. Remove the caliper and brake pads as described in this chapter.
2. Separate the mounting bracket (**Figure 13**) from the caliper.

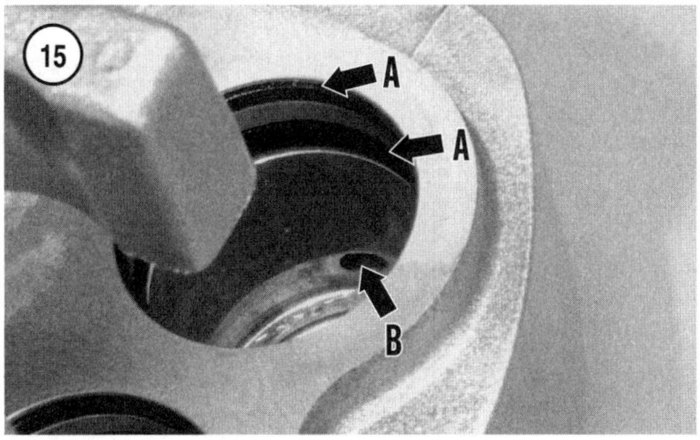

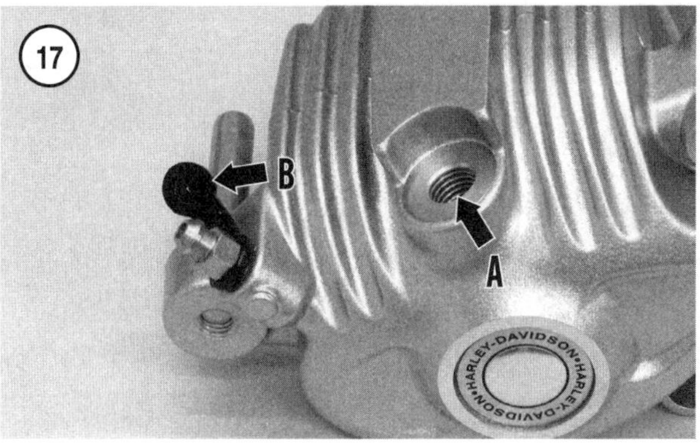

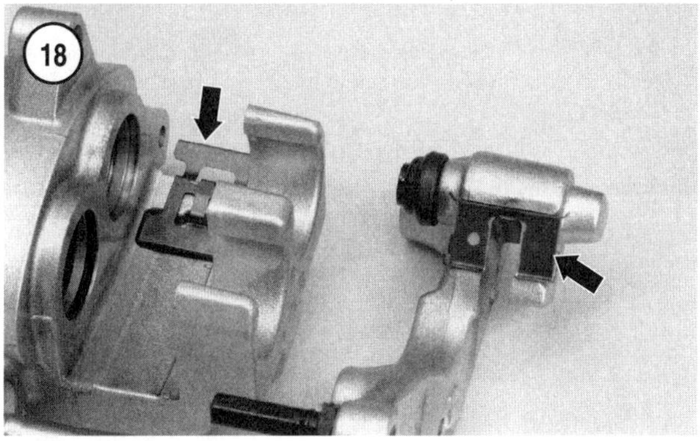

3. When removing the pistons, identify each piston so it can be reinstalled in its original cylinder.

WARNING
Be careful when using compressed air. The piston and/or debris can fly from the caliper at great speed and cause injury. Keep your fingers out of the way. Wear safety glasses and shop gloves and apply compressed air gradually. Do not use high pressure air or place the air hose nozzle directly against the hydraulic fluid passageway in the caliper. Hold the air nozzle away from the inlet allowing some of the air to escape during the procedure.

4. Place a rag or piece of wood in the path of the pistons and place the caliper on the workbench so that the pistons face down.
5. Blow the piston out with compressed air directed into the hydraulic fluid hole (**Figure 14**).
6. Remove the piston seals and dust seals.
7. Inspect the caliper body as described in this chapter.

Inspection

1. Clean the caliper and pistons with an aerosol brake cleaner. Thoroughly dry the parts with compressed air.
2. Remove the piston seals (A, **Figure 15**).
3. Make sure the fluid passageways (B, **Figure 15**) in the base of the piston bores are clear. Apply compressed air to the openings to make sure they are clear. Clean the passages if necessary.
4. Inspect the piston and dust seal grooves (**Figure 16**) in the caliper body for damage. If any groove is damaged or corroded, replace the caliper.
5. Inspect the union bolt threaded hole (A, **Figure 17**) in the caliper body. If worn or damaged, clean it out with a thread tap or replace the caliper.
6. Remove the bleed valve and dust cap (B, **Figure 17**). Inspect the bleed valve. Apply compressed air to the opening and make sure it is clear. If necessary, clean it out. Install the bleed valve, and tighten it to 35-61 in.-lb. (4.0-6.9 N•m).
7. Inspect the bleed valve threaded hole in the caliper body. If worn or damaged, clean the threads with a tap or replace the caliper.
8. Remove the pad springs (**Figure 18**) from the caliper.
9. Inspect the caliper body (A, **Figure 19**) for damage and replace the caliper body if necessary.
10. Inspect the cylinder bores (B, **Figure 19**) for scratches, scoring or other damage. Replace the caliper if the cylinder bores are damaged.

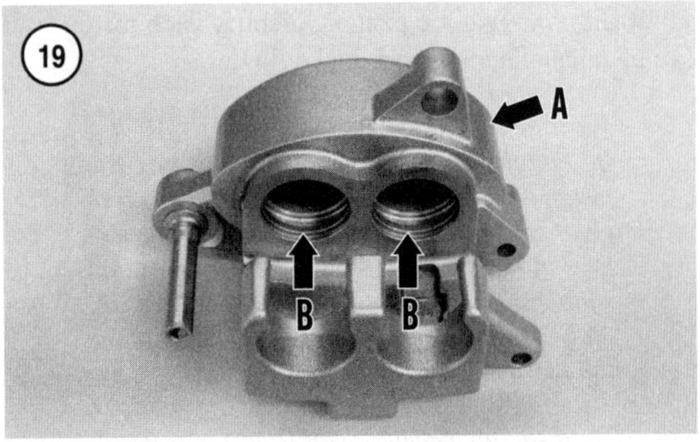

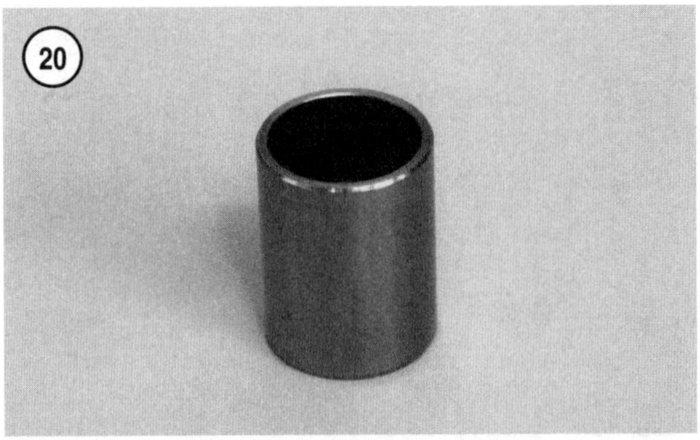

11. Inspect the pistons (**Figure 20**) for scratches, scoring or other damage. Replace damaged pistons.

12. The piston seal helps maintain correct brake pad-to-disc clearance. If the seal is worn or damaged, the brake pads will drag and cause excessive wear and increase brake fluid temperature. It is a good practice to replace the seals whenever disassembling the caliper.

13. Inspect the mounting pins on the caliper and bracket (A, **Figure 21**) for wear or damage. Replace if necessary.

14. Inspect the brake pads for uneven wear, damage or grease contamination.

CAUTION

When the brake system is operating correctly, the inboard and outboard brake pads will show approximately the same amount of wear. If there is a large difference in pad wear, the caliper is not sliding properly along the mounting pins causing one pad to drag against the disc. Worn caliper piston seals also cause uneven pad wear.

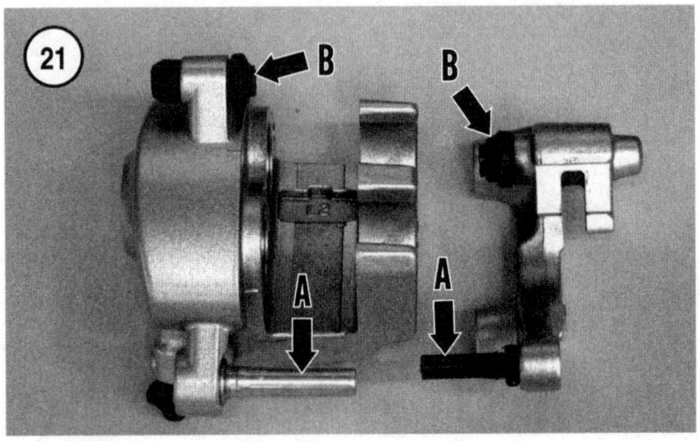

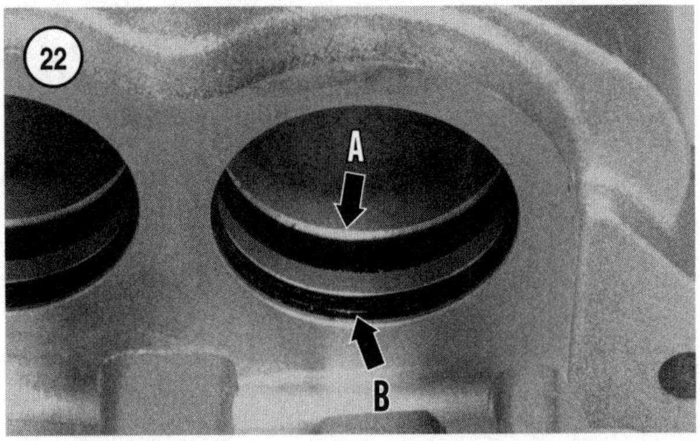

Assembly

Refer to **Figure 10**.

1. Coat the new dust seals and piston seals and piston bores with clean DOT 5 brake fluid.

2. Carefully install the new piston seals (A, **Figure 22**) into the inner grooves. Make sure the seals are properly seated in their respective grooves.

3. Carefully install the new dust seals (B, **Figure 22**) into the outer grooves. Make sure the seals are properly seated in their respective grooves.

4. Coat the pistons with clean DOT 5 brake fluid.

5. Position the pistons with the *closed end facing in* and install the pistons into the caliper cylinders. Push the pistons in until they bottom (**Figure 23**).

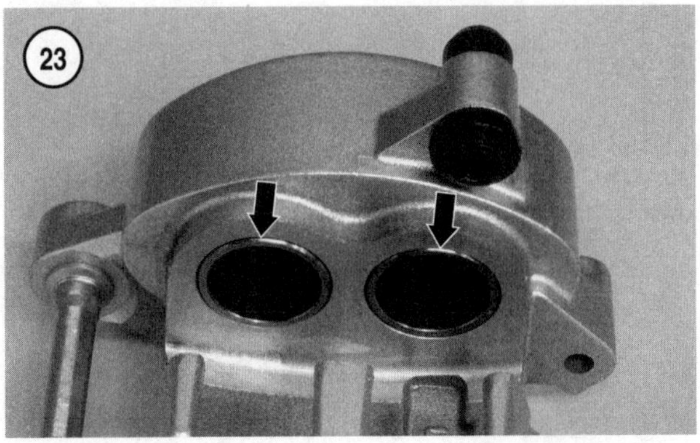

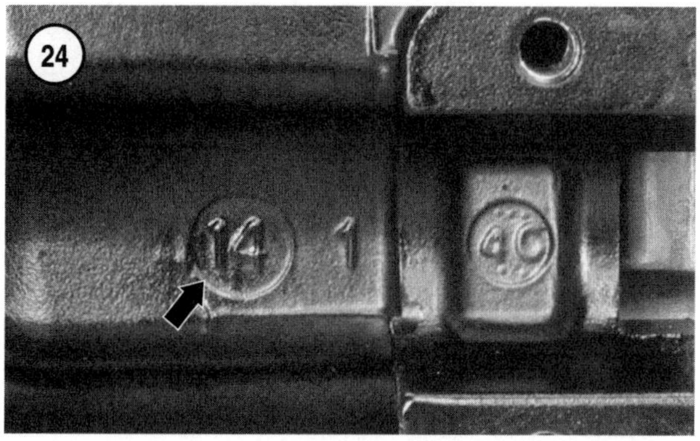

24

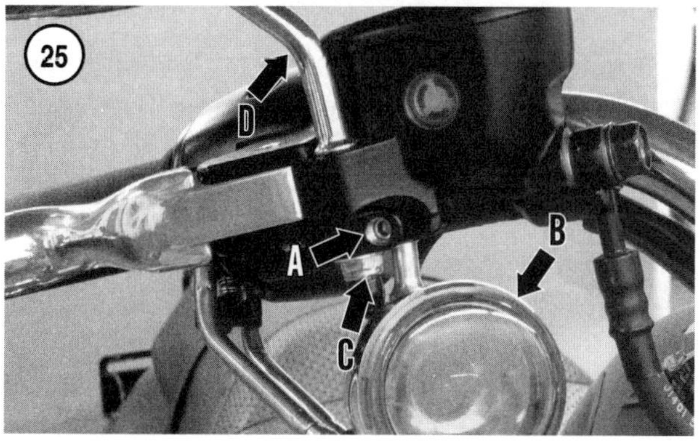

25

26

27

NOTE
*Prior to installing the caliper mounting bracket, apply silicone grease to the bracket pins and to the inside surfaces of the boots (B, **Figure 21**) on the caliper assembly. This will make installation easier and will ensure that the caliper will move easily after installation on the fork slider.*

6. Install the caliper bracket boots (B, **Figure 21**).
7. Install the brake pad anti-rattle springs (**Figure 18**) and make sure they are properly seated.
8. Carefully slide the caliper mounting bracket (**Figure 13**) onto the caliper assembly. Push the bracket on until it bottoms. Make sure the boots slide fully onto the mounting pins.
9. Install the caliper and brake pads as described in this chapter.

FRONT BRAKE MASTER CYLINDER

Identification

The master cylinder for a single brake disc has a smaller bore than the master cylinder used with dual brake discs.

The master cylinder body has a number cast into it (**Figure 24**) for identification. The number *1/2* is a master cylinder for a single-disc brake. The number *14* is a master cylinder for dual-disc brakes.

Removal/Installation

1. Loosen the turn signal clamp screw (A, **Figure 25**).
2. Unscrew the turn signal (B, **Figure 25**) from the master cylinder.
3. Remove the locknut (C, **Figure 25**) and washer, then remove the rear view mirror (D) from the master cylinder.
4. Clean the top of the master cylinder of all debris.
5. Remove the screws securing the cover (**Figure 26**). Remove the cover, diaphragm plate and diaphragm.
6. Use a shop syringe or a cooking baster to draw all the brake fluid out of the master cylinder reservoir.
7. Temporarily install the diaphragm, diaphragm plate and cover onto the reservoir. Tighten the screws finger-tight at this time.
8. Place a shop cloth under the union bolt (**Figure 27**) to catch spilled brake fluid that will leak out.
9. Unscrew the union bolt securing the brake hose to the master cylinder. Do not lose the sealing washer on each side of the hose fitting. Tie the loose end of the hose up to the handlebar and cover the end to prevent the entry of

moisture and debris. Cover the loose end with a re-closable plastic bag.

CAUTION
Failure to install the spacer in Step 10 may cause damage to the rubber boot and plunger on the front brake switch.

10. Insert a 5/32 in. (4 mm) thick spacer between the brake lever and lever bracket (**Figure 28**). Make sure the spacer stays in place during the following steps.
11. Remove the Torx bolts, washers and clamp (**Figure 29**) securing the front master cylinder to the handlebar and remove the master cylinder.

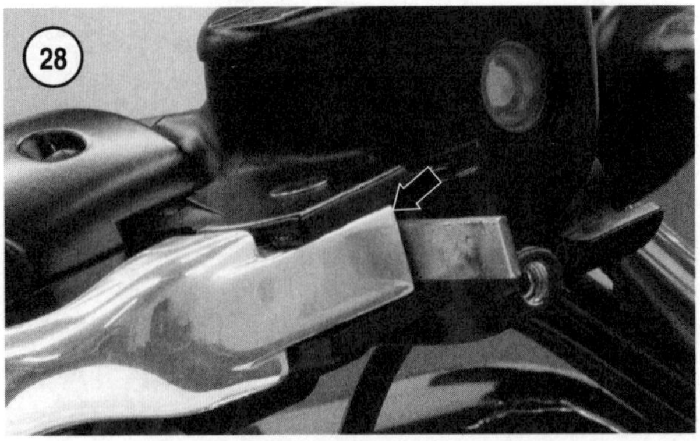

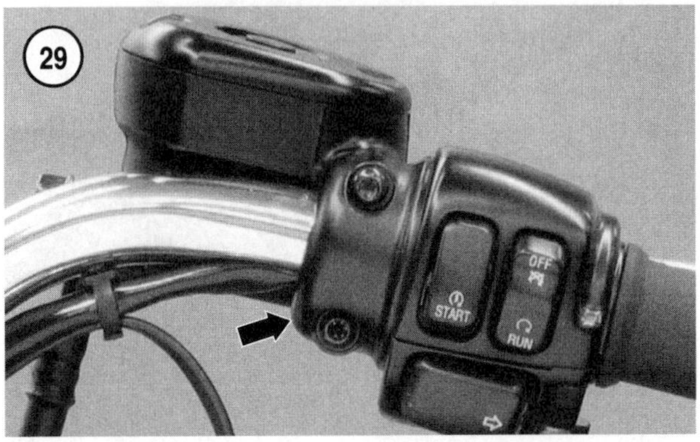

Installation

1. If not in place, insert the 5/32 in. (4 mm) thick spacer between the brake lever and lever bracket (**Figure 28**). Make sure the spacer stays in place during the following steps.

CAUTION
*Do not damage the front brake light switch and rubber boot (**Figure 30**) when installing the master cylinder.*

2. Position the front master cylinder onto the handlebar. Align the master cylinder notch (**Figure 31**) with the locating tab on the lower portion of the right side switch.
3. Position the clamp and install the Torx bolts and washers. Tighten the upper mounting bolt, then the lower bolt. Tighten the bolts to 108-132 in.-lb (13-15 N•m).
4. Install new sealing washers and the union bolt (**Figure 27**) securing the brake hose to the master cylinder. Tighten the union bolt to 20-25 ft.-lb. (27-34 N•m).
5. Remove the spacer from the brake lever.
6. Install the mirror, washer and locknut onto the master cylinder. Tighten the locknut to 96-144 in.-lb. (11-16 N•m).
7. Install the turn signal onto the master cylinder. Tighten the turn signal clamp screw (A, **Figure 25**) to 96-120 in.-lb. (11-13 N•m).
8. Refill the master cylinder reservoir and bleed the brake system as described in this chapter.

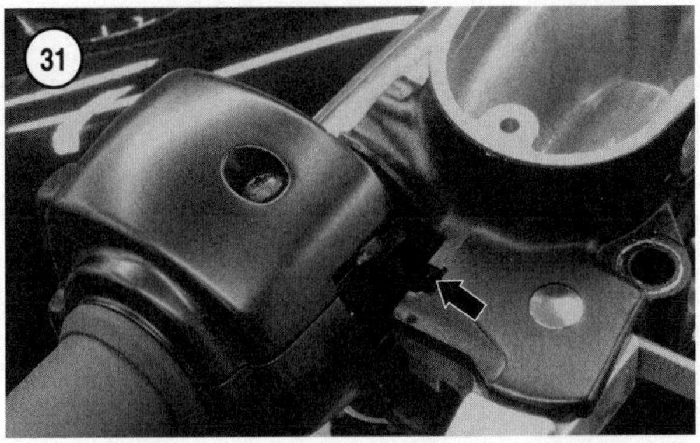

Disassembly

Refer to **Figure 32**.
1. Remove the master cylinder as described in this section.
2. If not already removed, remove the screws securing the cover and remove the cover, diaphragm plate and diaphragm; pour out any residual brake fluid and discard it. Never reuse brake fluid.

32

FRONT BRAKE MASTER CYLINDER

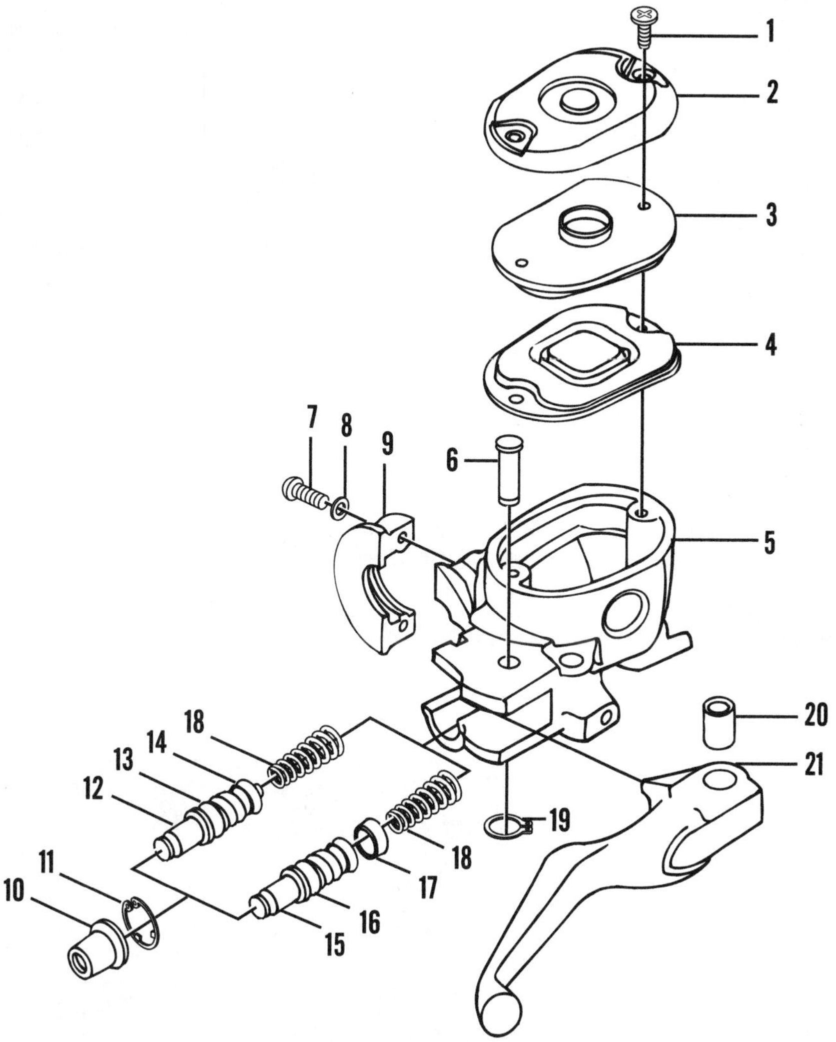

1. Screw
2. Cover
3. Diaphragm plate
4. Diaphragm
5. Housing
6. Pivot bolt
7. Screw
8. Washer
9. Clamp
10. Dust boot
11. Snap ring
12. Piston (except XL1200R)
13. Secondary cup (except XL1200R)
14. Primary cup (except XL1200R)
15. Piston (XL1200R)
16. Seondary cup (XL1200R)
17. Primary cup (XL1200R)
18. Spring
19. Snap ring
20. Bushing
21. Brake lever

33

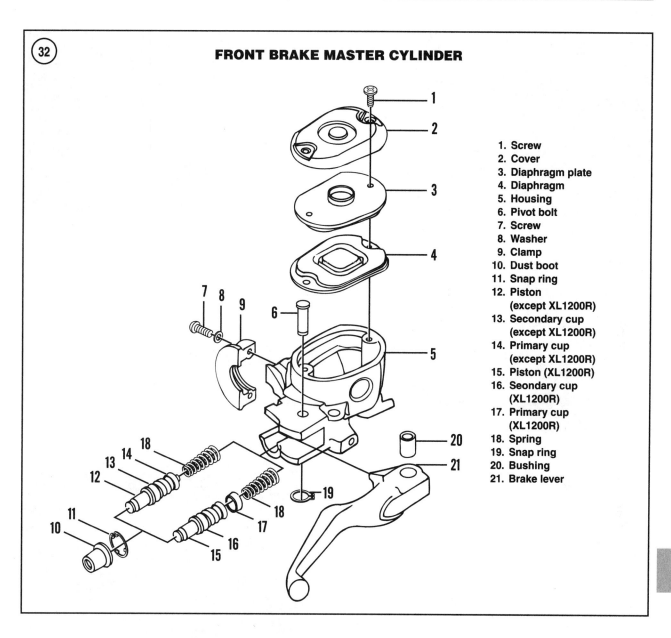

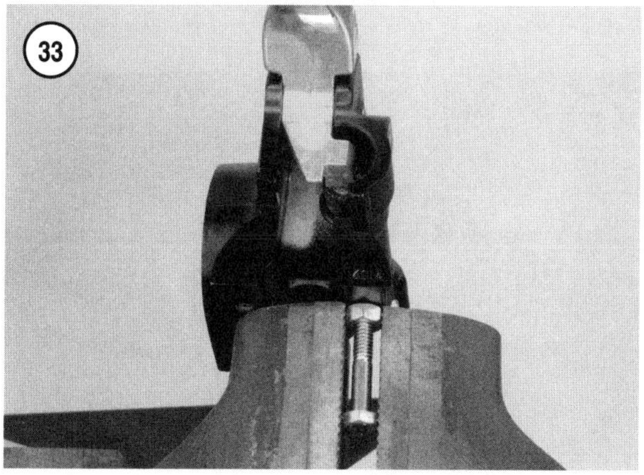

3. To hold the master cylinder, thread a bolt with a nut into the master cylinder. Tighten the nut against the master cylinder to lock the bolt in place, then clamp the bolt and nut in a vise as shown in **Figure 33**.

4. Remove the snap ring (A, **Figure 34**) securing the brake lever pin (B). Remove the pin and the brake lever.

5. Remove the dust boot (**Figure 35**) from the piston.

6. Using snap ring pliers, remove the snap ring (**Figure 36**) from the body.

NOTE

On dual-disc master cylinders, the primary cup is loose. On single-disc master cylinders, the primary cup is mounted on the piston.

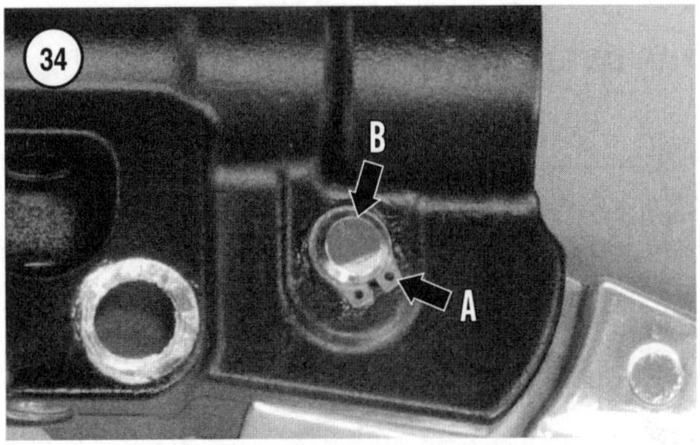

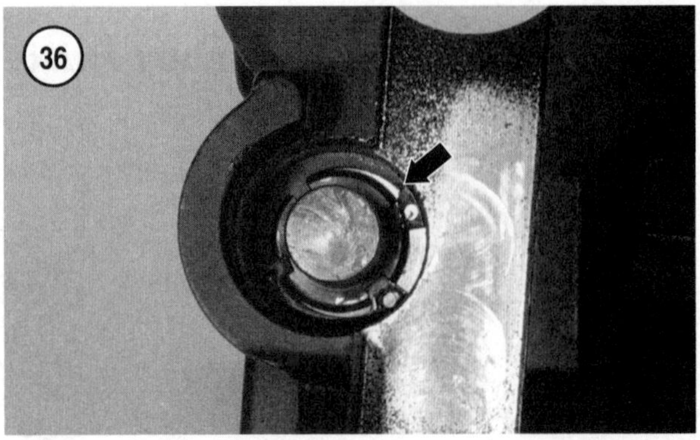

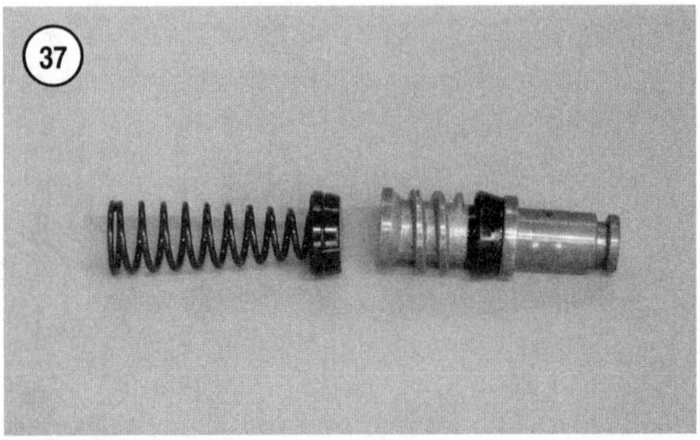

7. Remove the piston and spring assembly (**Figure 37**).

Inspection

Install a new piston kit assembly whenever the master cylinder is disassembled.

1. Clean all parts in brake fluid.
2. Inspect the cylinder bore (**Figure 38**) for wear and damage. If less than perfect, replace the master cylinder. The entire master cylinder must be replaced; the body is not available separately.
3. Make sure the passage (**Figure 39**) in the bottom of the master cylinder body is clear. Clean out if necessary.
4. Inspect the piston contact surfaces (A, **Figure 40**, typical) for wear and damage. If less than perfect, replace the piston assembly.
5. Check the end of the piston (B, **Figure 40**, typical) for wear caused by the hand lever. If worn, replace the piston assembly.

WARNING

*Refer to **Figure 41** to identify the single-disc master cylinder piston assembly (A) and dual-disc master cylinder piston assembly*

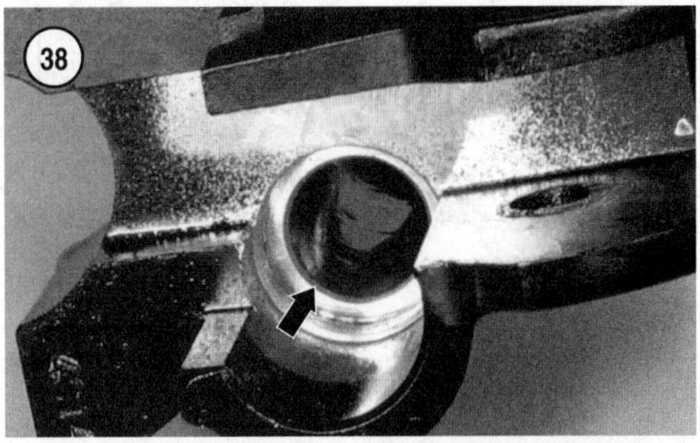

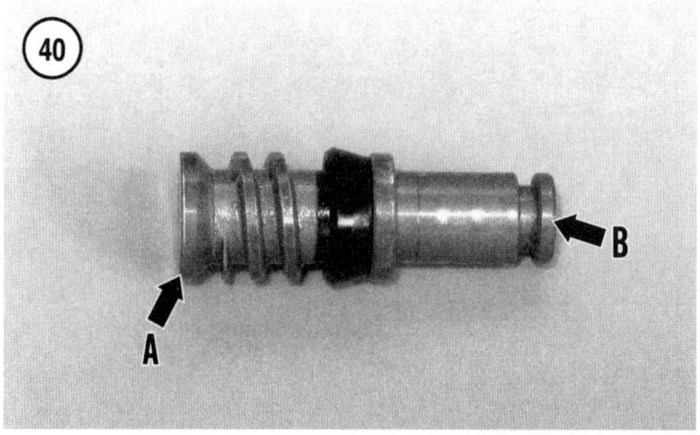

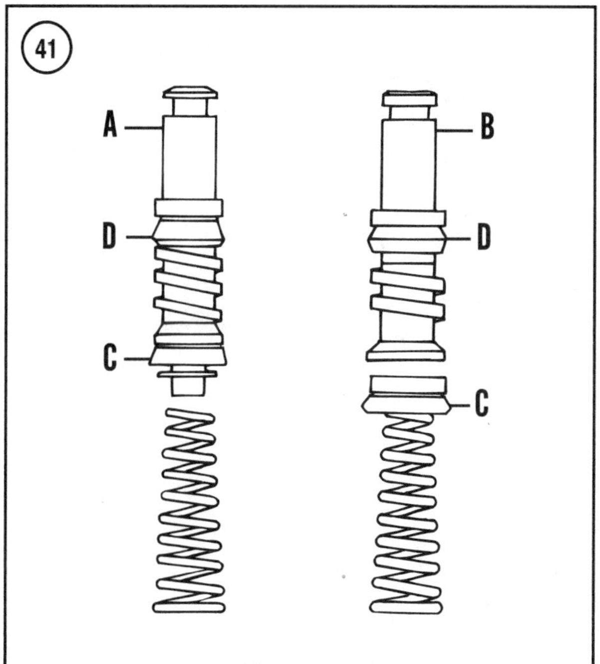

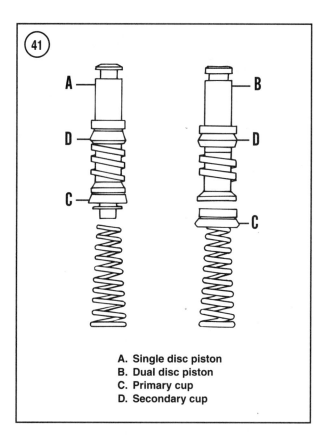

A. Single disc piston
B. Dual disc piston
C. Primary cup
D. Secondary cup

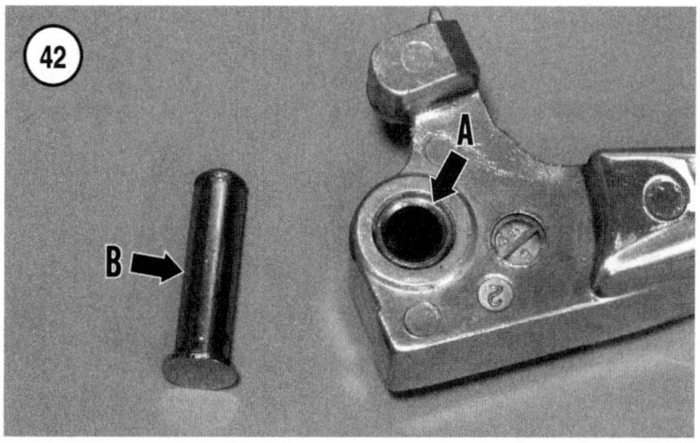

(B). Make sure to install the correct piston assembly.

6. Replace the piston assembly if either the primary (C, **Figure 41**) or secondary cups (D) require replacement. The cups cannot be replaced separately.

7. Inspect the hand lever pivot pin bushing (A, **Figure 42**) in the master cylinder body for excessive wear or damage. If damaged, replace the bushing.

8. Inspect the pivot pin (B, **Figure 42**). If worn or damaged, replace the pin.

9. Inspect the union bolt threads in the bore (**Figure 43**). If damaged, replace the master cylinder assembly.

10. Inspect the reservoir cover and diaphragm for damage and deterioration and replace as necessary.

Assembly

1. Soak the new, or existing, piston assembly in fresh DOT 5 brake fluid for at least 15 minutes to make the cups pliable. Coat the inside of the cylinder bore with fresh brake fluid prior to the assembly of parts.

CAUTION
When installing the piston assembly, do not allow the cups to turn inside out as they will be damaged.

2. Install the spring with the tapered end facing toward the primary cup on the piston (**Figure 37**), then install the spring and the piston assembly into the cylinder bore. On dual-disc master cylinders, install the primary cup so the cupped side is toward the spring.

3. Push the piston assembly into the bore and hold it in place. Install the snap ring (**Figure 36**) and make sure it seats correctly in the master cylinder body groove.

4. Install the dust boot and push it all the way down until it stops.

5. Install the brake lever onto the master cylinder body, then install the pivot pin and snap ring.
6. Install the diaphragm, diaphragm plate, cover and screws. Do not tighten the screws at this time as fluid will have to be added.
7. Install the master cylinder as described in this section.

REAR BRAKE PADS

There is no recommended mileage interval for replacing the brake pads. Pad wear depends on riding conditions. Inspect the rear brake pads for uneven wear, scoring, oil contamination or other damage. Replace the brake pads if the wear limit grooves are no longer visible. To maintain even brake pressure, replace both brake pads at the same time. Never use one new brake pad with a used brake pad in the other side.

CAUTION
Due to the amount of pad material remaining after the wear limit grooves are worn away, check the brake pads frequently. If pad wear is uneven, the backing plate may contact the disc.

Brake Pad Replacement

WARNING
Do not ride the motorcycle until the brakes are operating correctly. If necessary, bleed the brake as described in this chapter.

1. Review *Brake Service* in this chapter.
2. Place the motorcycle on a suitable stand so the bike is level.

WARNING
Before performing brake pad replacement, inspect the brake disc for damage and excessive wear. If evident, remove the rear brake caliper and inspect the brake disc as described in this chapter.

3. Clean the top of the master cylinder reservoir of all debris, then remove the reservoir cap (**Figure 44**).
4. Using a shop syringe or a cooking baster, draw brake fluid out of the master cylinder reservoir to prevent overflow.
5. Push against the side of the brake caliper (**Figure 45**) so the brake pad pushes in the caliper piston. The piston should move freely into the caliper. If it does not, remove and service the caliper as described in this chapter.
6. Remove the pad pin plug (**Figure 46**).
7. Loosen but do not remove the pad pin (**Figure 47**).

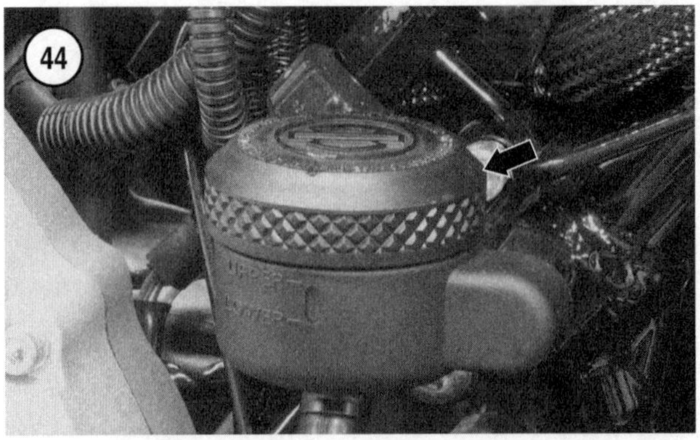

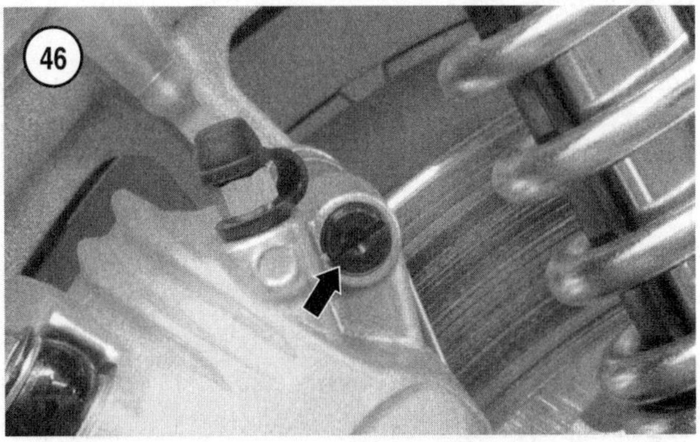

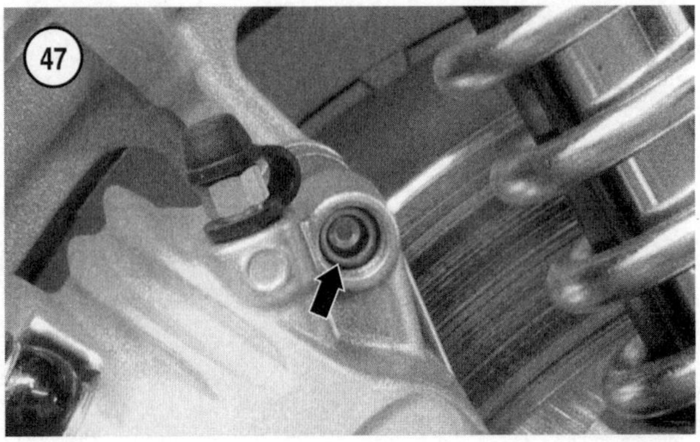

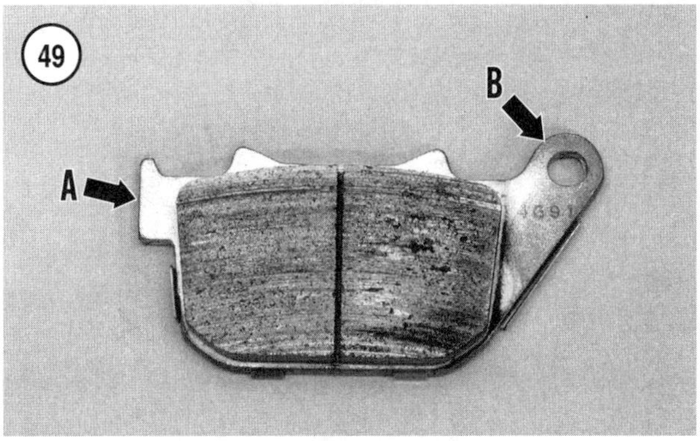

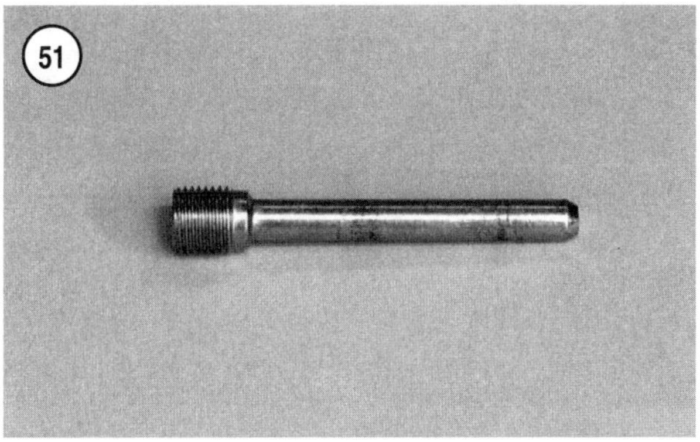

8. Withdraw the pad pin until the inner brake pad is free, then remove the brake pad (**Figure 48**).

NOTE
*Inspect the old pads and caliper during pad replacement. If the old pads exhibit uneven wear or oil contamination, refer to **Rear Brake Caliper** in this chapter.*

9. Install the new inner brake pad so the mounting tab (A, **Figure 49**) fits into the mounting slot in the caliper. Hold the pad so it does not fall out.
10. Fully withdraw the pad pin so the outer brake pad is free, then remove the brake pad (**Figure 50**).
11. Install the new outer brake pad so the mounting tab (A, **Figure 49**) fits into the mounting slot in the caliper. Hold the pad so it does not fall out.
12. Insert a 1/8 in. drill bit or rod so it engages the mounting hole (B, **Figure 49**) on each pad. This temporarily holds the pads in place.
13. Inspect the pad pin (**Figure 51**) for damage and excessive wear. Clean any corrosion or dirt from the pad pin surface. A dirty or damaged pad pin surface prevents the brake pads from sliding properly and casues brake drag and overheating of the brake disc. Replace the pin if worn or indented more than 0.011 in. (0.28 mm).
14. Make sure the pad spring (**Figure 52**) is properly positioned in the caliper before final installation of the pad pin.
15. Remove the drill bit or rod and install the pad pin (**Figure 47**). Tighten the pad pin to 131-173 in.-lb. (15-19.5 N•m).
16. Install the pad pin plug (**Figure 46**) and tighten to 18-25 in.-lb. (2.0-2.9 N•m).
17. Pump the rear brake pedal to reposition the brake pads against the brake disc. Roll the motorcycle back and forth and continue to pump the brake lever as many times as it takes to fully position the brake pads against the disc.

18. Refill the master cylinder reservoir as described in Chapter Three. Install the cap.
19. Break in the pads gradually for the first 100 miles (160 km) by using only light pressure as much as possible. Immediate hard application glazes the new pads and greatly reduces their effectiveness.

REAR BRAKE CALIPER

WARNING

Do not ride the motorcycle until the rear brake operates correctly.

Removal/Installation

1. Securely support the motorcycle.
2. Remove the brake pads as described in *Rear Brake Pads*.
3. If servicing the caliper, perform the following:
   a. Drain the brake fluid from the rear master cylinder as described in this chapter.
   b. Remove the brake hose union bolt and washers (A, **Figure 53**) from the caliper. Plug the hose, then place it in a reclosable plastic bag to prevent leakage and hose contamination.
4. Remove the caliper mounting bolt pin (B, **Figure 53**).
5. Move the caliper outward as far as possible from the brake disc.
6. Unscrew the caliper mounting stud pin (**Figure 54**) using an open-end wrench.
7. Lift the caliper off the brake disc and mounting bracket.
8. If the brake hose was not disconnected from the caliper, insert a spacer block between the caliper piston and caliper body and support the caliper with a wire hook.

NOTE

The spacer block prevents the piston from being forced out of the caliper if the rear brake pedal is accidentally depressed while the brake caliper is removed from the brake disc.

9. If necessary, service the brake caliper as described in this section.
10. Check that the brake pads were not contaminated with brake fluid. If so, replace the brake pads after caliper installation.
11. If the brake caliper was not completely removed from the motorcycle, remove the spacer block installed inside the caliper.
12. Make sure the caliper bracket is installed properly on the caliper mounting bracket (A, **Figure 55**).

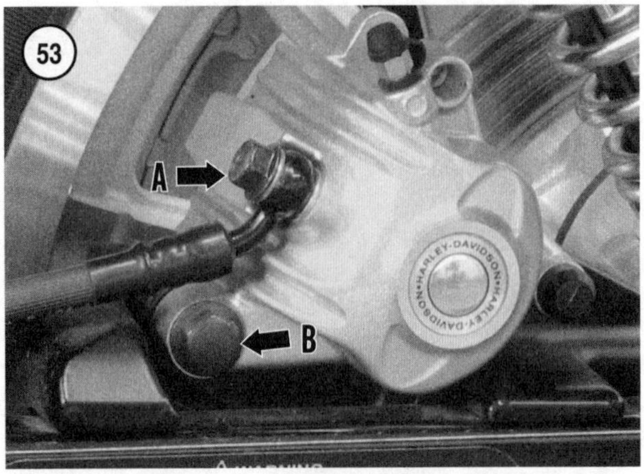

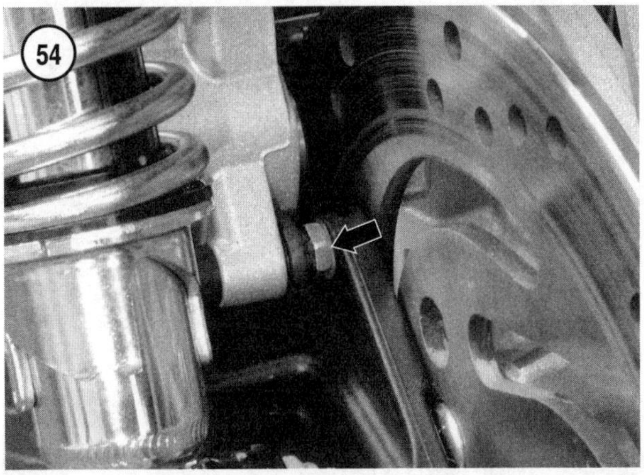

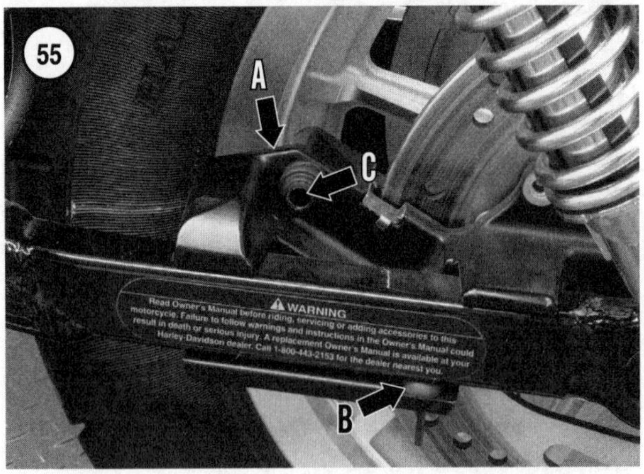

13. Make sure the damper (B, **Figure 55**) and boot are installed on the caliper retainer bracket.

NOTE

Prior to installing the caliper, apply silicone grease to the bracket pins and to the inside

surfaces of the boots on the caliper assembly. This will make installation easier and will ensure that the caliper will move easily after installation.

14. Apply Loctite 272 to the mounting stud threads (**Figure 56**).

15. Install the brake caliper over the brake disc and into position on the mounting bracket.

16. Tighten the mounting stud (**Figure 54**) to 87-130 in.-lb. (10-14 N•m).

17. Apply Loctite 272 to the threads of the caliper mounting bolt pin.

18. Insert the caliper mounting bolt pin (B, **Figure 53**) through the boot and install it. Tighten the caliper mounting bolt pin to 15-18 ft.-lb. (21-24 N•m).

CAUTION

After caliper installation make sure the boots fit over the entire exposed length of each pin.

19. If removed, place a new sealing washer on each side of the brake hose union fitting. Install the union bolt (A, **Figure 53**) into the caliper. Make sure the fitting contacts the boss on the caliper body (**Figure 57**). Tighten the union bolt to 20-25 ft.-lb. (27-34 N•m).
20. Install the brake pads as described in this chapter.
21. Refill the master cylinder with new DOT 5 brake fluid as described in Chapter Three.
22. If the brake hose was disconnected, bleed the rear brake system as described in this chapter.
23. Operate the rear brake pedal to seat the pads against the brake disc.

Disassembly

Refer to **Figure 58**.

1. Remove the pad spring (**Figure 59**).

WARNING

Cushion the piston with a shop rag. Do not try to cushion the piston with your hand or fingers as injury could result.

2. Cushion the caliper piston with a shop rag. Apply compressed air through the brake line port (**Figure 60**) and remove the piston.
3. Remove the dust and piston seals (**Figure 61**) from the piston bore.
4. Remove the bleed valve (**Figure 62**).

Inspection

1. Clean the caliper and piston with an aerosol brake cleaner. Thoroughly dry the parts with compressed air.
2. Make sure the fluid passageways (**Figure 63**) in the base of the piston bore are clear. Apply compressed air to the openings to make sure they are clear. Clean the passages if necessary.
3. Inspect the piston and dust seal grooves (**Figure 64**) in the caliper body for damage. If any groove is damaged or corroded, replace the caliper assembly.
4. Inspect the union bolt threaded hole (A, **Figure 65**) in the caliper body. If worn or damaged, clean out with a thread tap or replace the caliper assembly.
5. Inspect the bleed valve (**Figure 66**). Apply compressed air to the opening and make sure it is clear. If necessary, clean it out.
6. Inspect the bleed valve threaded hole in the caliper body (B, **Figure 65**). If worn or damaged, clean the threads with a tap or replace the caliper assembly.
7. Inspect the caliper body (A, **Figure 67**) for damage and replace the caliper body if necessary.

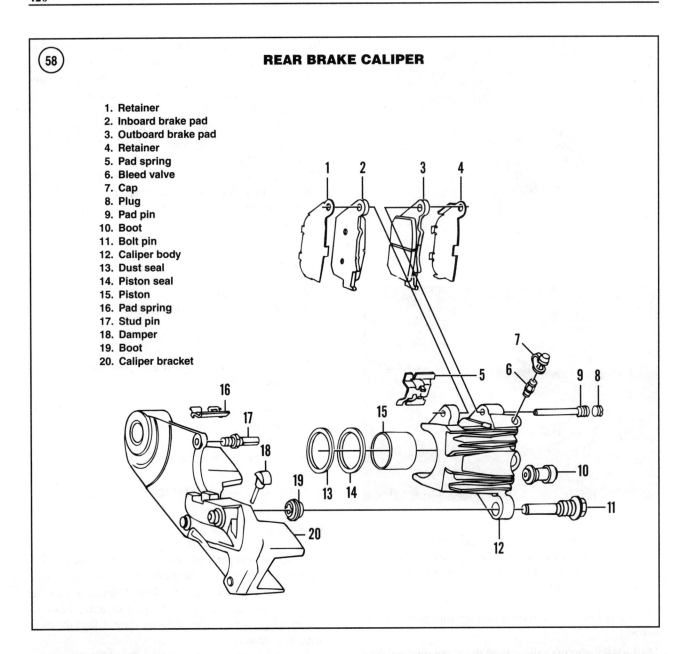

58

REAR BRAKE CALIPER

1. Retainer
2. Inboard brake pad
3. Outboard brake pad
4. Retainer
5. Pad spring
6. Bleed valve
7. Cap
8. Plug
9. Pad pin
10. Boot
11. Bolt pin
12. Caliper body
13. Dust seal
14. Piston seal
15. Piston
16. Pad spring
17. Stud pin
18. Damper
19. Boot
20. Caliper bracket

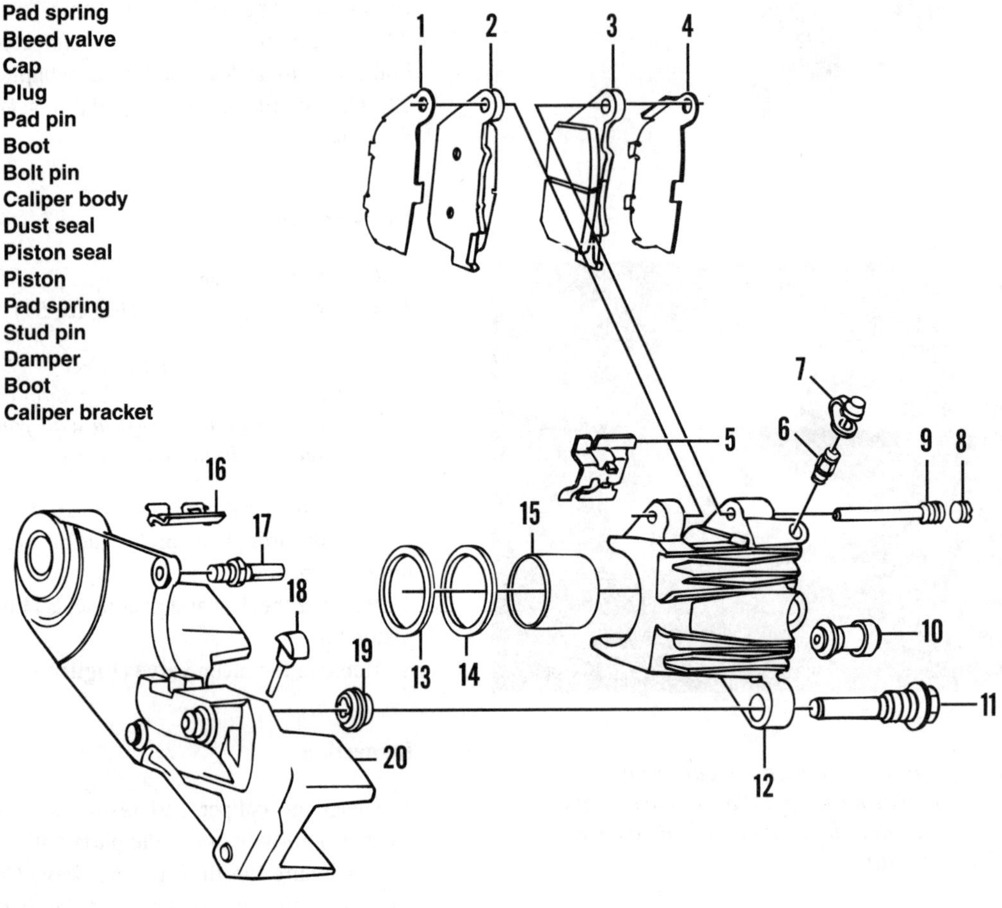

59

60

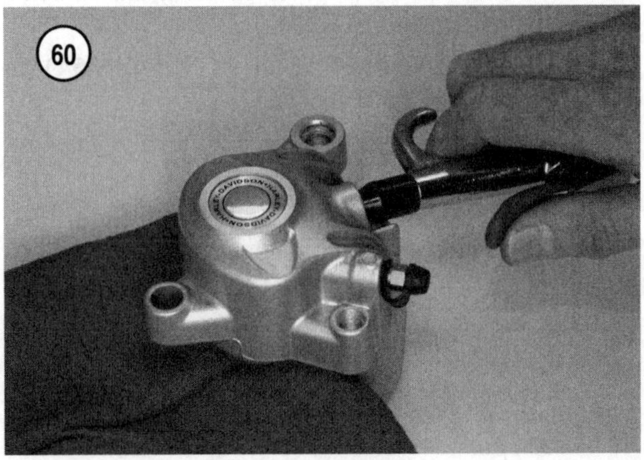

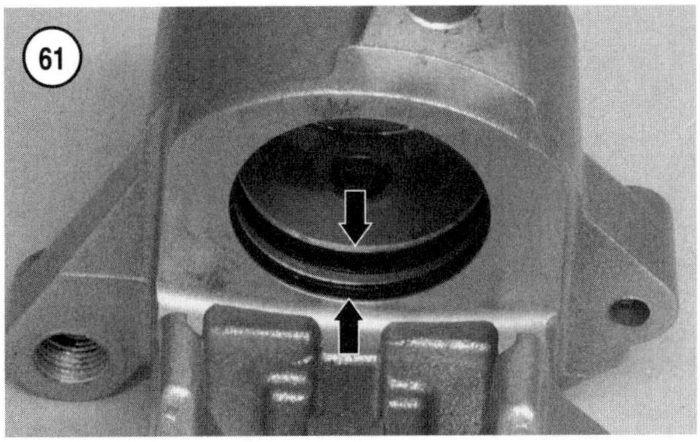

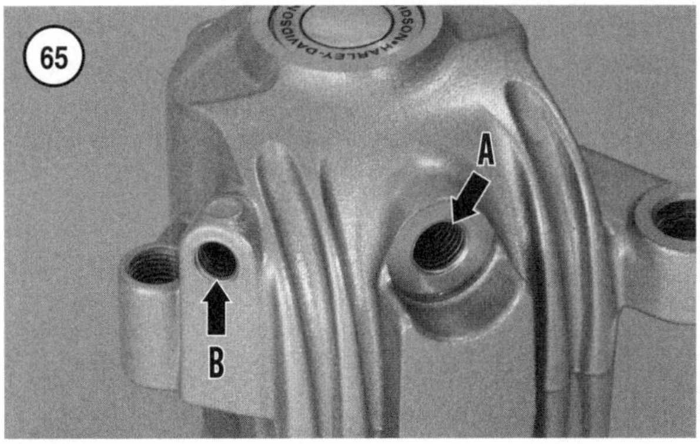

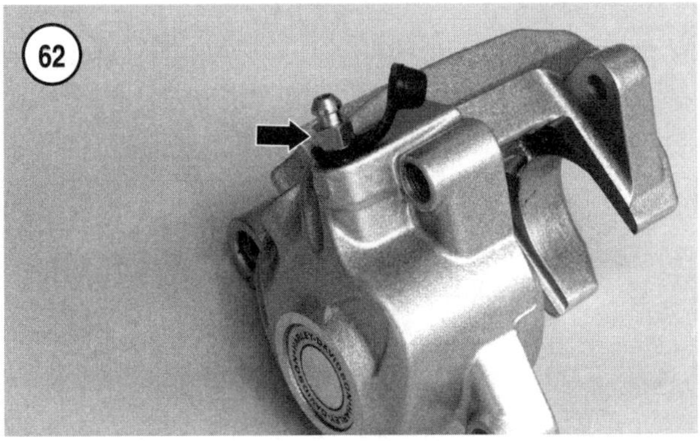

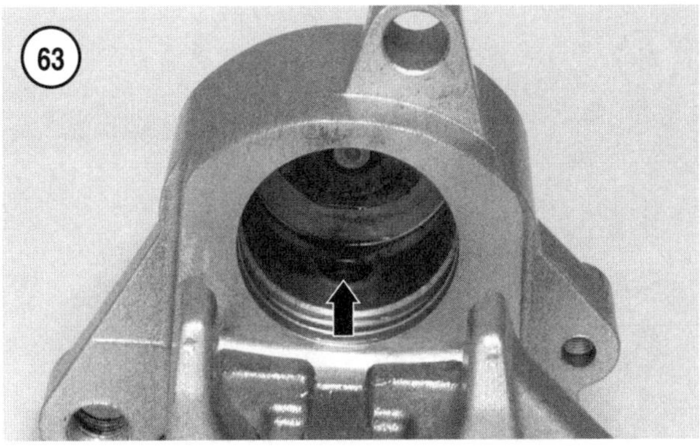

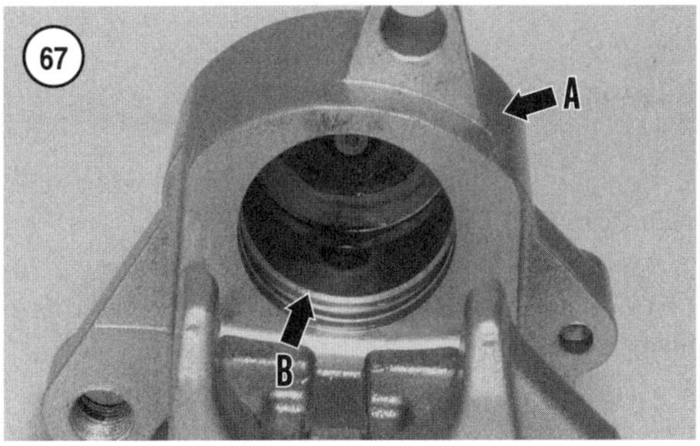

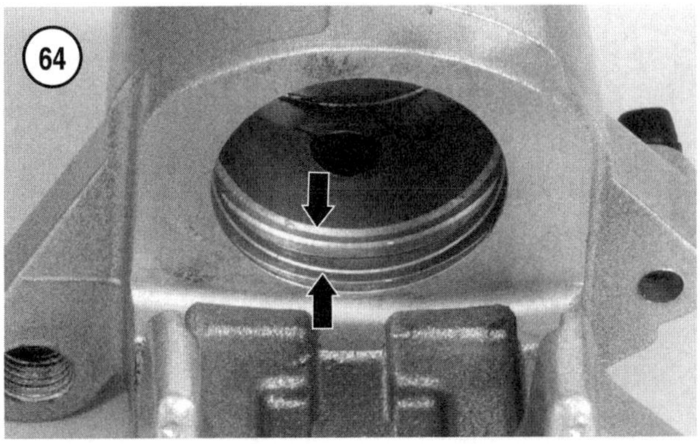

8. Inspect the caliper cylinder bore (B, **Figure 67**) for scratches, scoring or other damage. Replace the caliper if the cylinder bores are damaged.

9. Inspect the piston (**Figure 68**) for scratches, scoring or other damage. Replace a damaged piston.

10. The piston seal helps maintain correct brake pad-to-disc clearance. If the seal is worn or damaged, the brake pads will drag and cause excessive wear and increase brake fluid temperature. It is a good practice to replace the seals whenever disassembling the caliper.

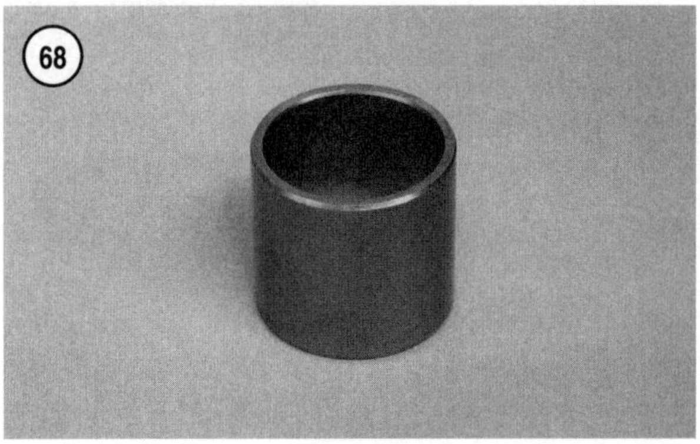

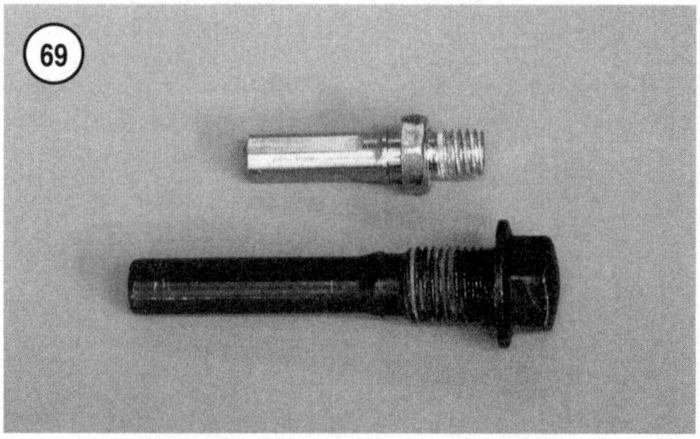

11. Inspect the stud and bolt pins (**Figure 69**) for wear or damage. Replace if necessary.

12. Inspect the brake pads for uneven wear, damage or grease contamination.

NOTE
When the brake system is operating correctly, the inboard and outboard brake pads will show approximately the same amount of wear. If there is a large difference in pad wear, the caliper is not sliding properly along the mounting pins causing one pad to drag against the disc. Worn caliper piston seals also cause uneven pad wear.

Assembly

1. Coat the new dust seals, piston seals and piston bores with clean DOT 5 brake fluid.

2. Carefully install the new piston seal (A, **Figure 70**) into the inner groove. Make sure the seal properly seats in the groove.

3. Carefully install the new dust seal (B, **Figure 70**) into the outer groove. Make sure the seal properly seats in the groove.

4. Coat the piston with clean DOT 5 brake fluid.

5. Position the piston with the *closed end facing in* and install the piston into the caliper cylinder. Push the piston in until it bottoms (**Figure 71**).

6. Install the bleed valve and tighten it to 35-61 in.-lb. (4.0-6.9 N•m).

7. Install the mounting pin boot (A, **Figure 72**).

8. Install the brake pad spring (B, **Figure 72**) and make sure it is properly seated.

9. Install the caliper and brake pads as described in this chapter.

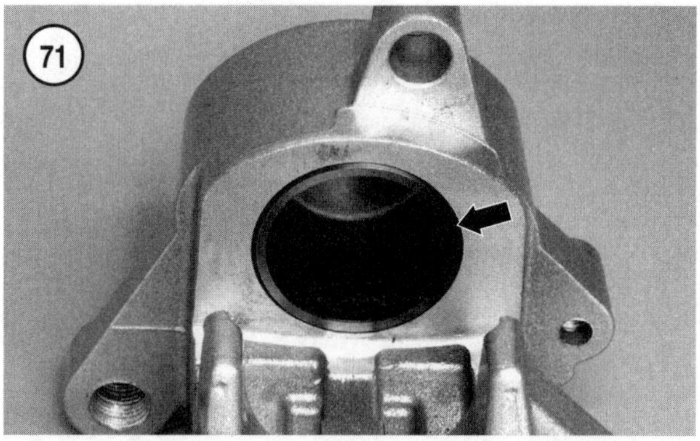

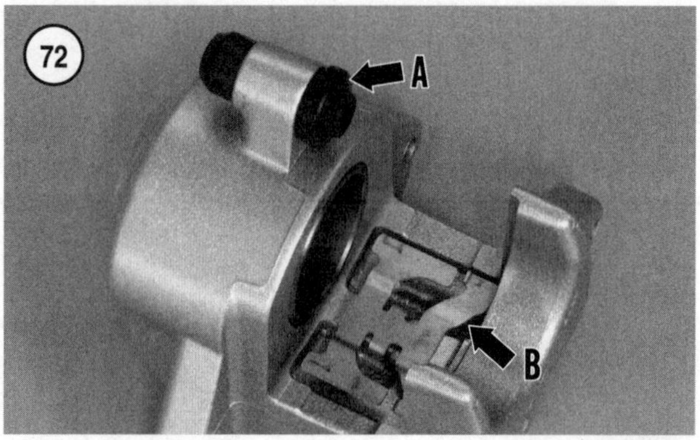

73

REAR BRAKE MASTER CYLINDER

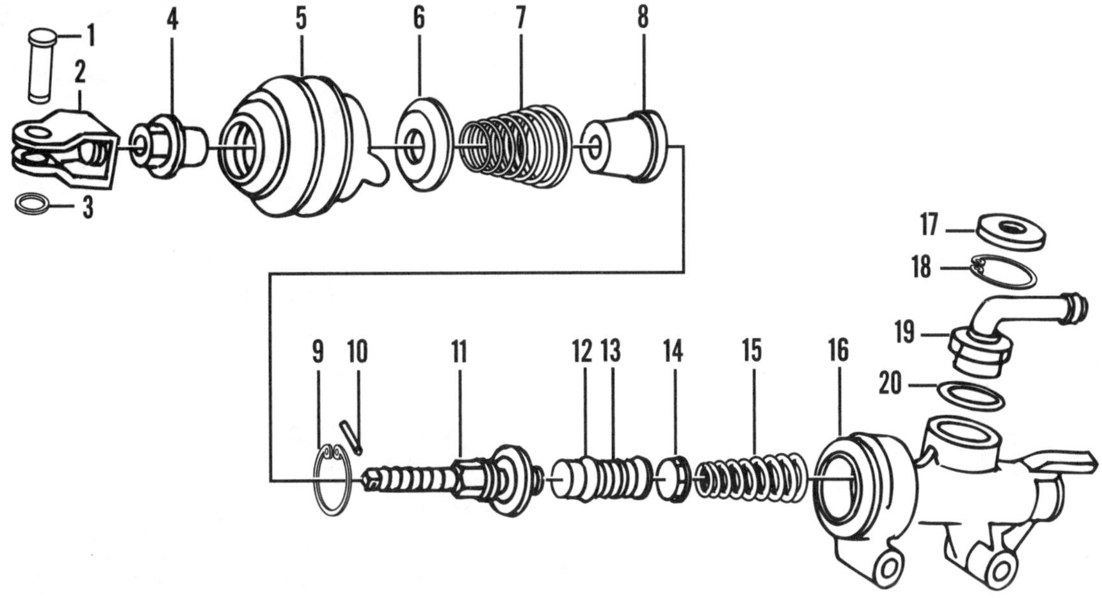

1. Clevis pin
2. Clevis
3. Retaining ring
4. Bolt
5. Boot
6. Spring retainer
7. Spring
8. Boot
9. Snap ring
10. Spring pin
11. Pushrod assembly
12. Secondary cup
13. Piston
14. Primary cup
15. Spring
16. Master cylinder
17. Dust cover
18. Snap ring
19. Hose fitting
20. O-ring

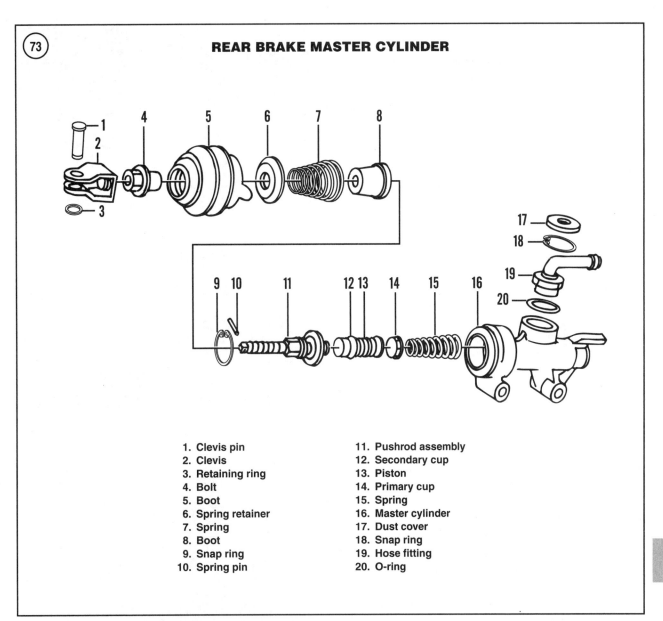

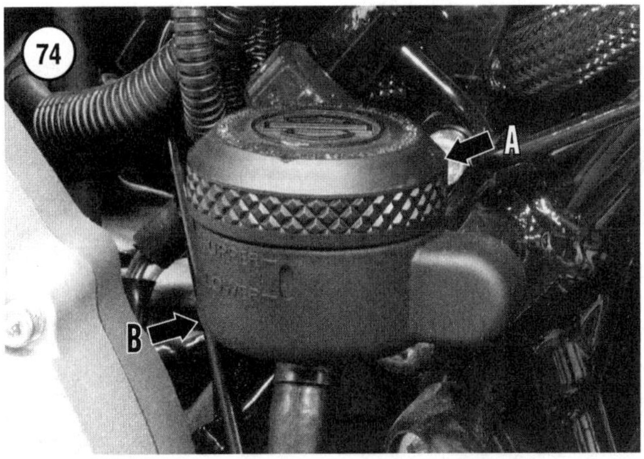

REAR MASTER CYLINDER

Removal

WARNING
Do not ride the bike until the rear brake is working properly.

Refer to **Figure 73**.

1. Support the motorcycle on a suitable stand.
2. Remove the reservoir cap (A, **Figure 74**).
3. Remove the rear brake reservoir cover (B, **Figure 74**).

NOTE

*If necessary, remove the plastic washer (A, **Figure 75**) and rubber insert (B) when draining the reservoir.*

4. Hold the reservoir and remove the reservoir mounting bolt. Tip the reservoir over and drain the brake fluid in the reservoir and hose into a container.
5. If removed, reinstall the rubber insert (B, **Figure 75**) and plastic washer (A). Install the resevoir cap (A, **Figure 74**). Then reinstall the resevoir and mounting bolt.

CAUTION

Be prepared to catch brake fluid that will flow from disconnected brake hoses in the following steps.

6. Move the clamp (A, **Figure 76**) from the end of the feed hose, then disconnect the feed hose from the rear master cylinder fitting (B).
7. Unscrew the union bolt (C, **Figure 76**) securing the brake hose to the master cylinder. Do not lose the sealing washer on each side of the hose fitting.
8. Remove the retaining ring from the pivot pin (A, **Figure 77**).
9. Disengage the clevis (B, **Figure 77**) from the bellcrank end (C).
10. Remove the master cylinder mounting bolts and washers (A, **Figure 78**), then remove the master cylinder (B).

Installation

1. Install the master cylinder onto the frame. Tighten the master cylinder mounting bolts (A, **Figure 78**) to 15-20 ft.-lb. (21-27 N•m).
2. Secure the brake hose to the master cylinder with the union bolt (C, **Figure 76**). Install a new washer on each side of the brake hose fitting. The fitting must contact the boss on the master cylinder. Tighten the union bolt to 20-25 ft.-lb. (27-34 N•m).
3. Connect the feed hose to the fitting (B, **Figure 76**) and move the clamp around the end of the hose.
4. Connect the brake bellcrank lever to the master cylinder clevis, then install the clevis pin (A, **Figure 77**) and a new retaining ring.
5. Refill the master cylinder with brake fluid and bleed the brake system as described in this chapter.

Disassembly

Refer to **Figure 73**.

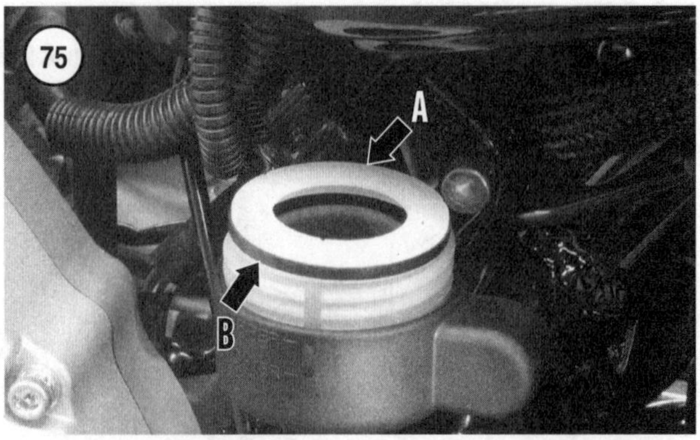

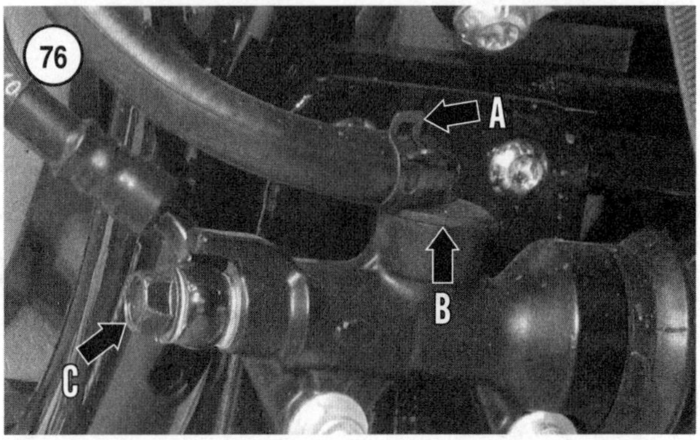

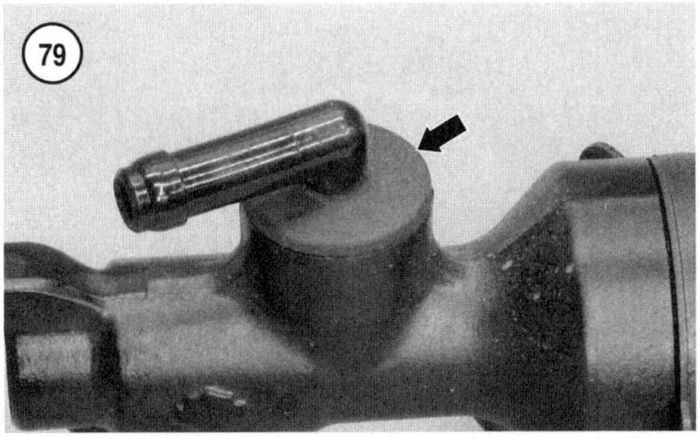

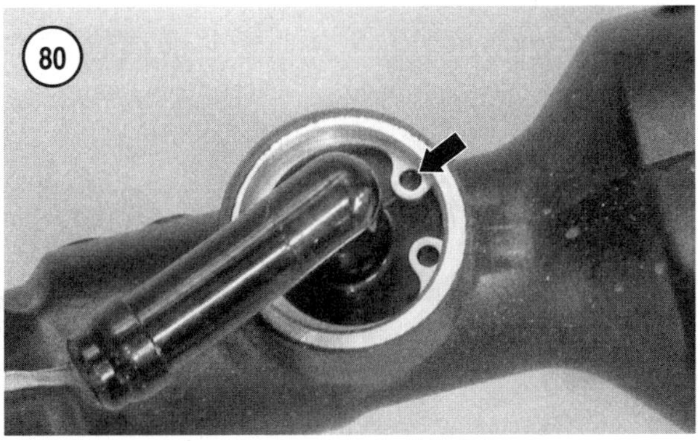

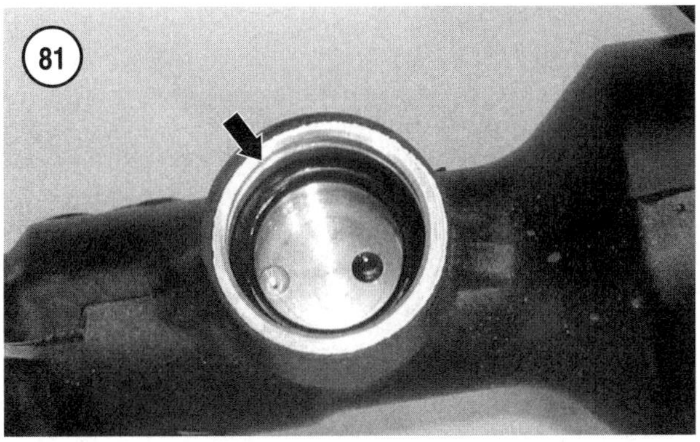

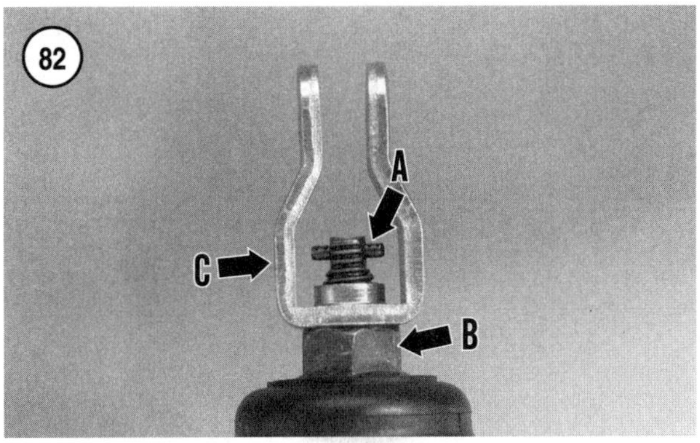

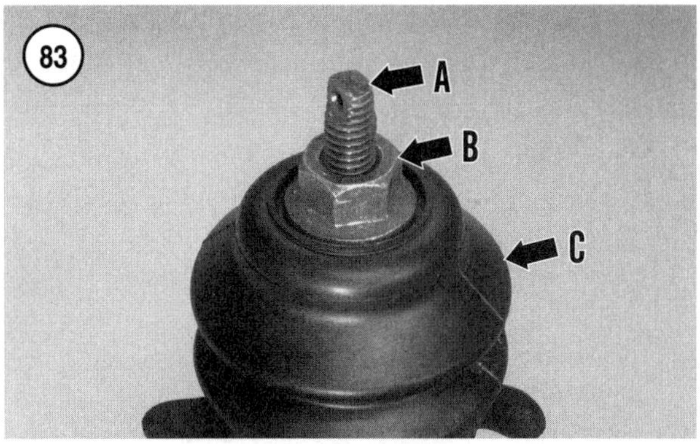

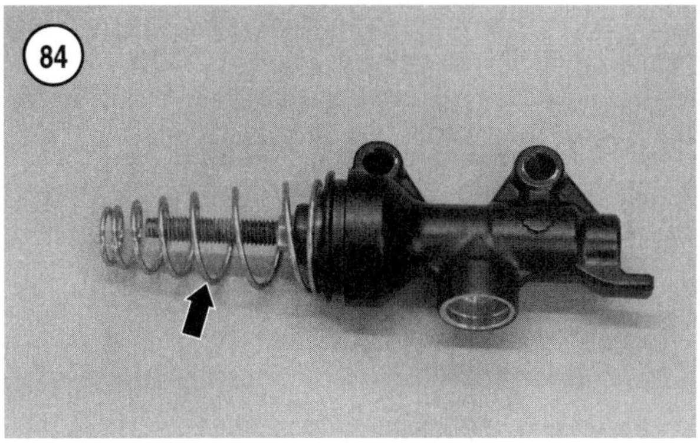

1. Remove the master cylinder as described in this section.
2. Remove the dust cover (**Figure 79**) around the hose fitting .
3. Remove the snap ring (**Figure 80**) and pull the hose fitting out of the master cylinder.
4. Remove the O-ring (**Figure 81**) from the master cylinder.
5. Drive out the spring pin (A, **Figure 82**).

CAUTION
When tightening the clevis, grasp the clevis on the edges, not the flats, which may bend the clevis.

6. Hold the nut (B, **Figure 82**), then unscrew the clevis (C).
7. Hold the pushrod flats (A, **Figure 83**), then unscrew the nut (B) and remove the boot (C).

NOTE
The spring retainer will remain inside the boot.

8. Remove the spring (**Figure 84**).
9. Remove the boot (**Figure 85**).

13

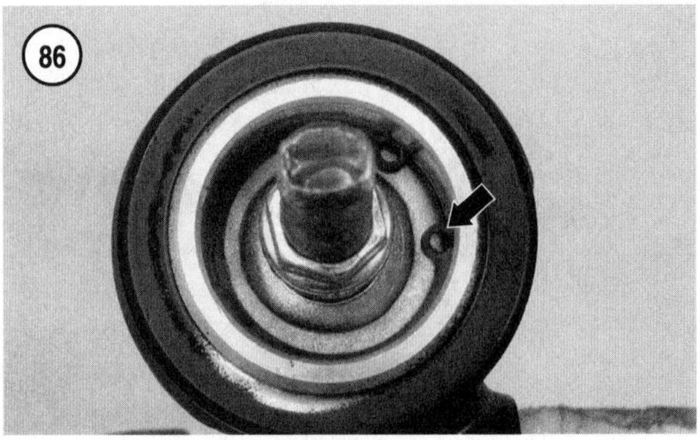

10. Compress the piston, then remove the snap ring (**Figure 86**) from the groove in the master cylinder.
11. Remove the pushrod (**Figure 87**) and piston assembly (**Figure 88**) from the master cylinder bore.

Inspection

WARNING
Do not get any oil or grease onto any of the master cylinder components. Petroleum based chemicals will cause the rubber parts in the brake system to swell, causing brake system failure.

1. Clean and dry the master cylinder housing and the other metal parts. Clean parts using denatured alcohol or new DOT 5 brake fluid and then place them on a clean lint-free cloth until reassembly.

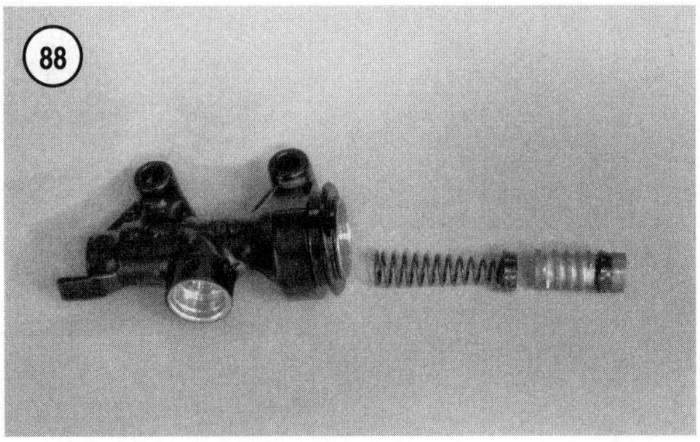

CAUTION
Do not remove the secondary cup from the piston assembly. If the cups are damaged, replace the piston assembly.

2. Check the piston assembly (**Figure 89**) for:
   a. Broken, distorted or collapsed piston return spring (A).
   b. Worn, cracked, damaged or swollen primary (B) and secondary cups (C).
   c. Scratched, scored or damaged piston (D).
   d. Excessively worn or damaged pushrod cover.
   e. If any of these parts are worn or damaged, replace the piston assembly.
3. If the master cylinder was leaking brake fluid, the pushrod (**Figure 87**) may be corroded. Carefully inspect the pushrod assembly for:
   a. Bent or damaged clevis.
   b. Damaged pushrod.
   c. Cracked or swollen boots.
   d. Corroded, bent or damaged snap ring.

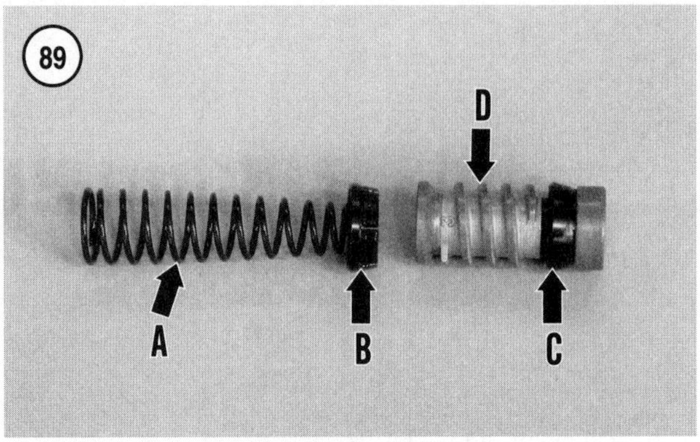

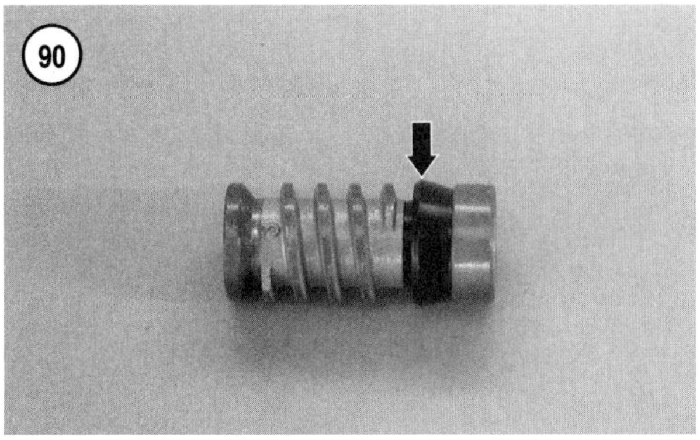
90

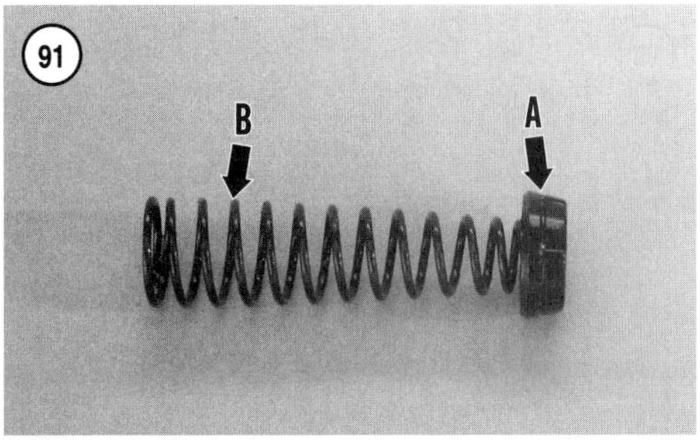

91

92

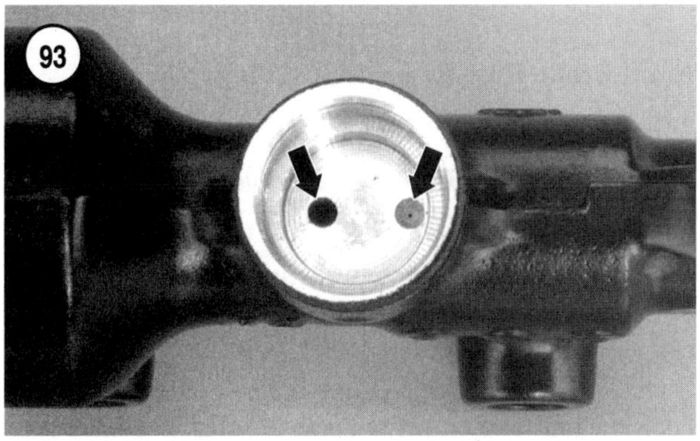
93

e. Damaged pushrod washer.

NOTE
A piston kit includes the piston, spring and both cups. The snap ring and boots are available separately.

4. To assemble a new piston assembly, perform the following:
   a. When replacing the piston, installation of the new secondary cup (**Figure 90**) onto the piston is necessary.
   b. Use the original piston assembly as a reference when installing the new cups.
   c. Before installing the new piston cups, soak them in DOT 5 brake fluid for approximately 15 minutes. This will soften them and ease installation. Clean the new piston in brake fluid.
   d. Install the secondary cup (**Figure 90**) onto the piston.
   e. Install the primary cup (A, **Figure 91**) onto the spring (B) so it seats on the tapered end of the spring.
5. Inspect the master cylinder bore (**Figure 92**). Replace the master cylinder if the bore is corroded, scored or damaged in any way. Do not hone the master cylinder bore to remove scratches or other damage.
6. Check for plugged supply and relief ports in the master cylinder (**Figure 93**). Clean with compressed air.
7. Replace the O-ring (**Figure 81**) if it is excessively worn, deteriorated or damaged.

Assembly

1. Clean all components before reassembly.
2. If installing a new piston assembly, assemble it as described in *Inspection* in this section.
3. Lubricate the piston assembly and cylinder bore with DOT 5 brake fluid.
4. If not previously installed, install the primary piston cup (A, **Figure 91**) onto the tapered end of the spring (B).

CAUTION
Do not allow the piston cups to tear or turn inside out when installing the piston into the master cylinder bore. Both cups are larger than the bore. To ease installation, lubricate the cups and piston with DOT 5 brake fluid.

5. Install the spring and primary cup into the master cylinder so the large end of the spring enters first.
6. Insert the piston assembly into the master cylinder bore so the secondary cup end enters last.

7. Compress the piston assembly and install the pushrod, washer and snap ring (**Figure 86**). Install the snap ring with the flat side facing out.

NOTE
*The snap ring must seat in the groove (**Figure 86**) completely. Push and release the pushrod a few times to make sure it moves smoothly and that the snap ring does not pop out.*

8. Slide the boot over the pushrod (**Figure 85**) and seat it against the snap ring.

9. Install the spring (A, **Figure 94**), spring retainer (B) and nut (C).

10. Install the clevis (A, **Figure 95**) onto the pushrod (B), but do not install the retaining pin.

CAUTION
When tightening the clevis, grasp the clevis on the edges, not the flats, which may bend the clevis.

11. Adjust the position of the clevis to the dimension shown in **Figure 96**. Tighten the clevis and nut securely.

12. Install the retaining pin (A, **Figure 82**).

13. If removed, lubricate and install the O-ring into the master cylinder (**Figure 81**).

14. Install the inlet fitting into the master cylinder so it points toward the brake hose end of the master cylinder.

15. Install the snap ring—flat edge facing up—into the groove in the master cylinder (**Figure 80**). Make sure the snap ring sits in the groove completely.

16. Install the dust cover (**Figure 79**) around the hose fitting.

17. Install the master cylinder as described in this section.

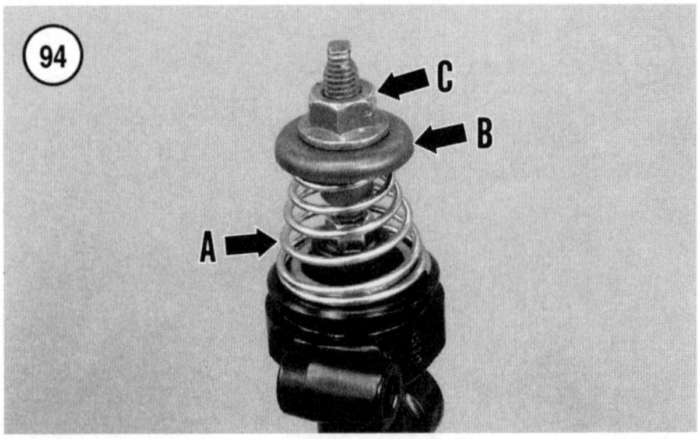

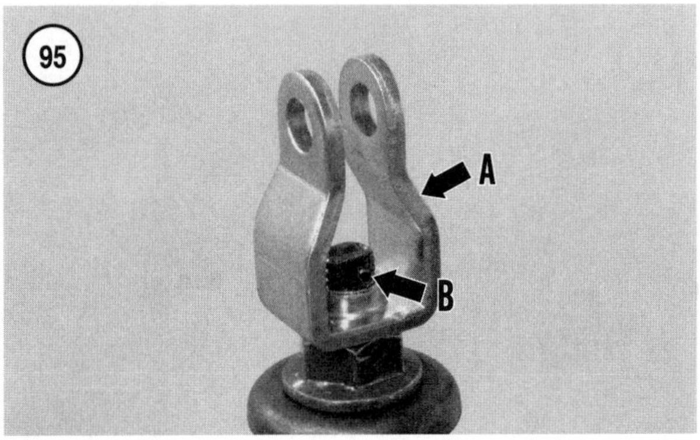

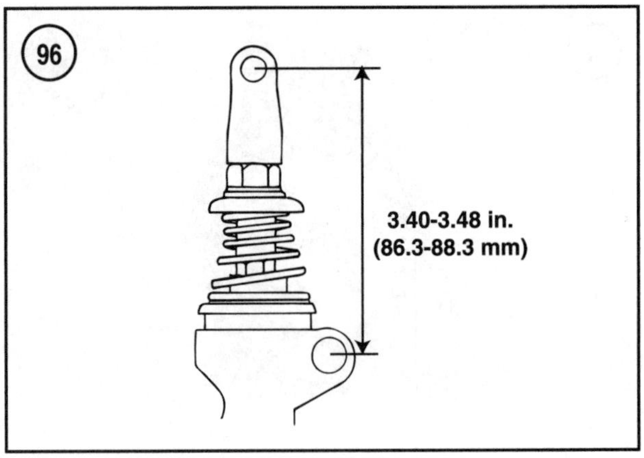

BRAKE HOSE AND LINE REPLACEMENT

A combination of steel and flexible brake lines connect the master cylinder to the brake calipers. Union fittings and bolts connect brake hoses to the master cylinder and brake calipers. Steel washers seal the union fittings.

Replace a hose if the flexible portion is swelling, cracking or damaged. Replace the brake hose if the metal portion leaks or if there are dents or cracks.

Review *Brake Fluid Type* and *Brake Service* in this chapter.

Front Brake Hose Removal/Installation

WARNING
Do not ride the motorcycle until the front brakes operate correctly.

A single combination steel/flexible brake hose (**Figure 97**) connects the front master cylinder to the front brake caliper on all models except XL1200R.

On XL1200R models (**Figure 97**) a single hose connects the master cylinder to the manifold. From the mani-

97 **FRONT BRAKE HOSE**

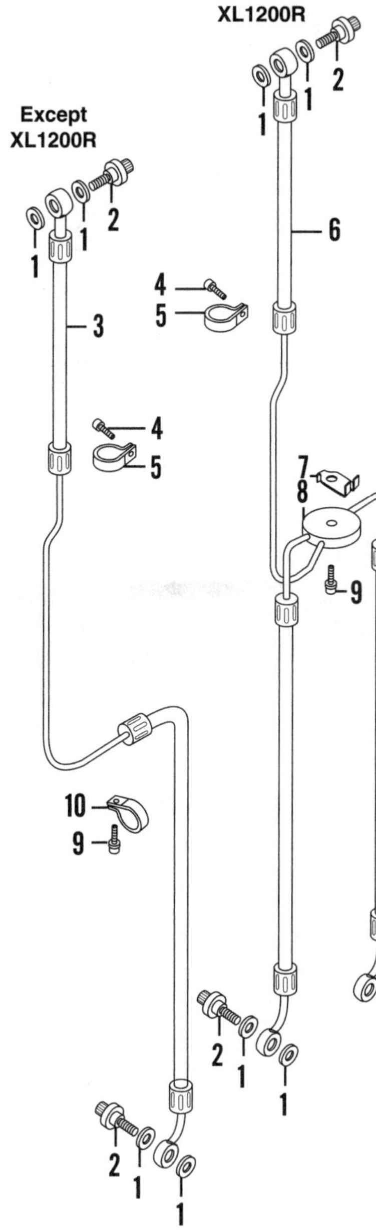

1. Washer
2. Union bolt
3. Brake hose
4. Screw
5. Clamp
6. Brake hose
7. Clamp
8. Manifold
9. Screw
10. Clamp

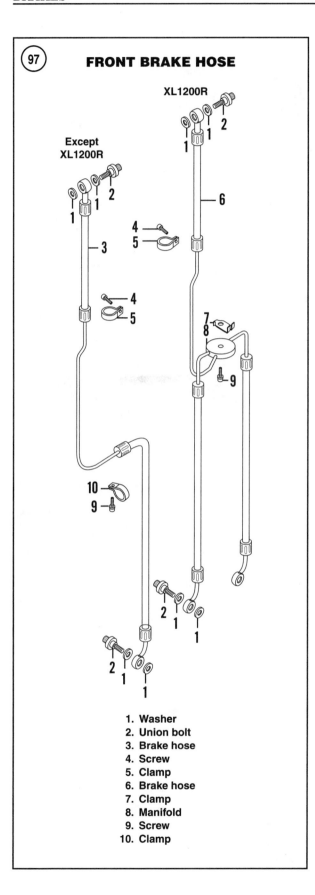

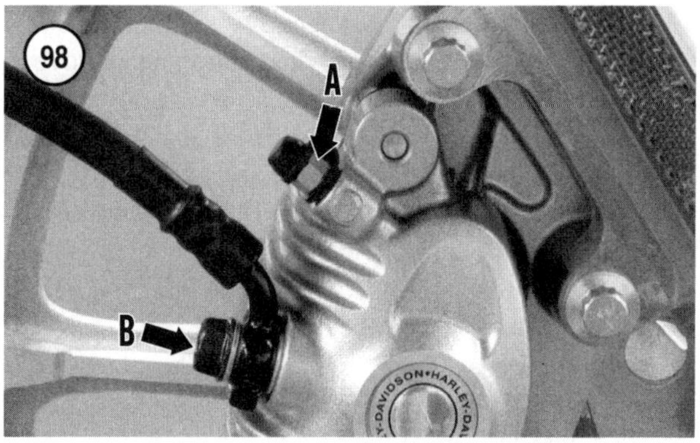

fold two brake hoses run to the brake calipers. The hoses and manifold are only available as a unit assembly.

When purchasing a new hose, compare it to the old hose to make sure the length and angle of the steel hose portion are correct. Install new union bolt washers at both ends.

1. Drain the front brake system as follows:
   a. Connect a hose to the bleed valve (A, **Figure 98**) on the brake caliper. On the Model XL1200R brake system, connect hoses to the bleed valve on each caliper.
   b. Insert the loose end of the hose into a container to catch the brake fluid.
   c. Open the bleed valve and apply the front brake lever to pump the fluid out of the master cylinder and brake line. Continue until the fluid is removed.
   d. Close the bleed valve(s) and disconnect the hose.

2. Before removing the brake line assembly, note the brake line routing from the master cylinder to the caliper. Note the number and position of metal hose clamps and/or plastic ties used to hold the brake line in place.

3. Remove any metal clamps or cut any plastic ties.

4. On XL1200R models, remove the bolt securing the brake hose manifold (**Figure 99**) to the lower steering bracket. Do not lose the clamp.

5. Remove the screw or nut securing the metal clamps around the brake line. Spread the clamp and remove it from the brake line.
6. Remove the union bolt (B, **Figure 98**) and washers securing the hose to the brake caliper.
7. Remove the union bolt (**Figure 100**) and washers securing the hose to the front master cylinder.
8. Cover the ends of the brake hose to prevent brake fluid from leaking out.
9. Remove the brake hose assembly from the motorcycle.
10. If the existing brake hose assembly is going to be reinstalled, inspect it as follows:
   a. Check the metal tubes where they enter and exit at the flexible hoses. Check the crimped clamp for looseness or damage.
   b. Check the flexible hose portions for swelling, cracks or other damage.
   c. If there is wear or damage, replace the brake hose assembly.
11. Install the brake hose, new sealing washers and union bolts (B, **Figure 98** and **Figure 100**) in the reverse order of removal. Note the following:
   a. On XL1200R models, install the brake hose manifold (A, **Figure 101**) so the prongs straddle the rib (B) on the lower steering bracket.
   b. Install new sealing washers against the side of each hose fitting.
   c. Carefully install the clips and guides to hold the brake hose in place, but do not tighten the clamp screws.
   d. Position the master cylinder and caliper hose end against the locating boss on the master cylinder or caliper (**Figure 102**). Tighten the union bolts to 20-25 ft.-lb. (27-34 N•m).
   e. Position the brake tube (A, **Figure 103**) so it is 1/4 in. (6.4 mm) from the fork clamp bolt (B). Tighten the clamp screws, and on XL1200R models, the manifold clamp bolt (**Figure 99**).
   f. Refill the front master cylinder with clean DOT 5 brake fluid. Bleed the front brake system as described in this chapter.

Rear Brake Hose Removal/Installation

WARNING
Do not ride the motorcycle until the rear brake is operating correctly.

A single combination steel and rubber brake hose (**Figure 104**) connects the rear master cylinder to the rear brake caliper. The rear brake switch is installed in the rear brake hose. When buying a new hose, compare it to the

100

101

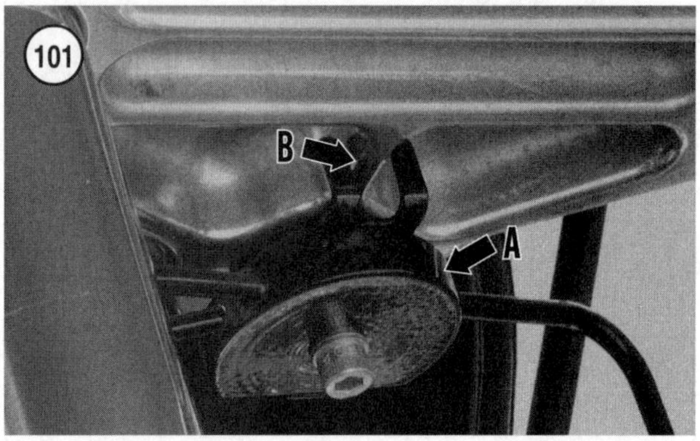

102

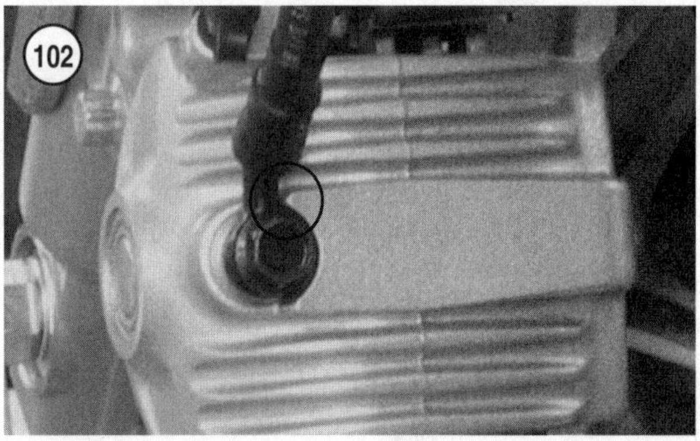

103

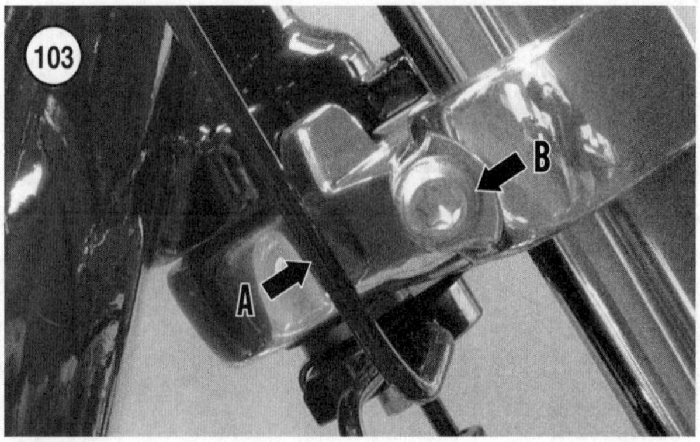

(104) **REAR BRAKE HOSE**

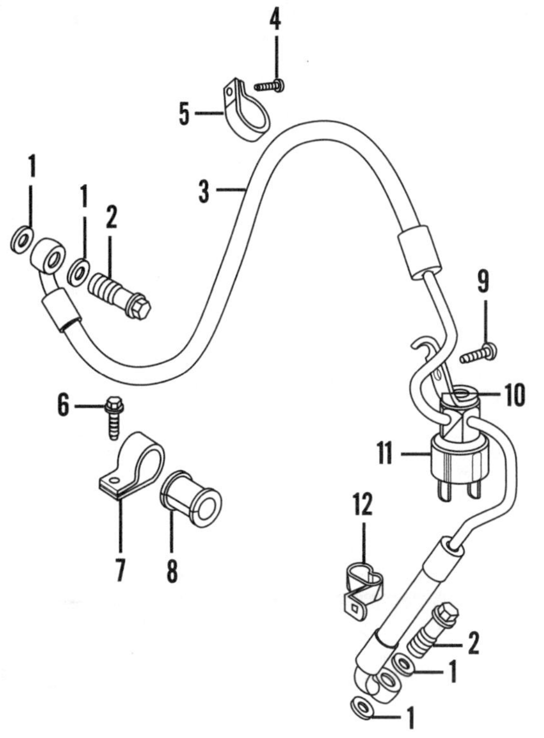

1. Washer
2. Union bolt
3. Brake hose
4. Screw
5. Clamp
6. Screw
7. Clamp
8. Bushing
9. Bolt
10. Tee
11. Brake switch
12. Clamp

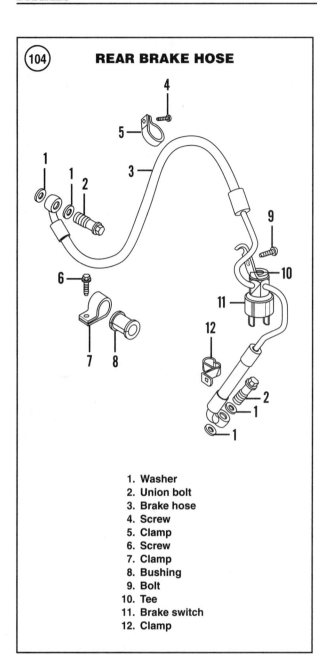

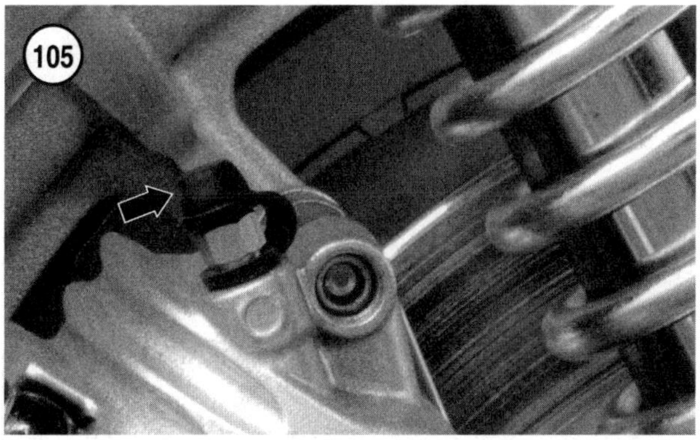

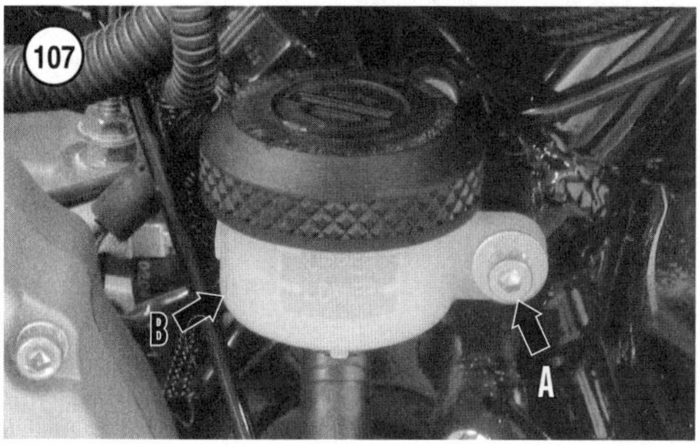

old hose. Make sure the length and angle of the steel hose portion are correct. Install new union bolt washers at both hose ends.

1. Drain the hydraulic brake fluid from the rear brake system as follows:
   a. Connect a hose to the rear caliper bleed valve (**Figure 105**).
   b. Insert the loose end of the hose in a container to catch the brake fluid.
   c. Open the caliper bleed valve and operate the rear brake pedal to pump the fluid out of the master cylinder and brake line. Continue until all the fluid is removed.
   d. Close the bleed valve and disconnect the hose.
2. Remove the left side cover as described in Chapter Fourteen.
3. Remove the rear brake master cylinder reservoir cover (**Figure 106**) from the reservoir.
4. Remove the reservoir mounting bolt (A, **Figure 107**), then move the reservoir (B) out of the way.
5. Disconnect the electrical connector from the rear brake switch (A, **Figure 108**).
6. Hold the tee nut (B, **Figure 108**) with a wrench, then unscrew and remove the switch (C).

7. Remove the brake switch bracket mounting bolt (D, **Figure 108**).
8. Before removing the brake line, note the brake line routing from the master cylinder to the caliper. Note the number and position of the clamps.
9. Remove the mounting screw and detach the clamp (A, **Figure 109**) from the swing arm.
10. Remove the mounting screw and detach the clamp (**Figure 110**) from the battery tray bracket .
11. Remove the union bolt (**Figure 111**) and washers securing the hose fitting to the brake caliper.
12. Remove the union bolt (**Figure 112**) and washers securing the hose fitting to the master cylinder.
13. Remove the rear brake hose through the lower hose clamp (**Figure 113**).
14. If the existing brake hose assembly is going to be reinstalled, inspect it as follows:
   a. Check the metal pipe where it enters and exits the flexible hose. Check the crimped clamp for looseness or damage.
   b. Check the flexible hose portion for swelling, cracks or other damage.
   c. If there is wear or damage, replace the brake hose.
15. Installation is the reverse of removal. Note the following:
   a. Install and tighten the rear brake switch to 80-123 in.-lb. (9-14 N•m).
   b. Install new sealing washers against the side of each hose fitting.
   c. Do not stretch or twist the hose. Make sure the hose and bushing (B, **Figure 109**) fit squarely in the clamp.
   d. Tighten the clamp screws to 30-40 in.-lb. (3.4-4.5 N•m).
   e. Tighten the union bolts to 20-25 ft.-lb. (27-34 N•m).
   f. Refill the master cylinder with clean DOT 5 brake fluid. Bleed the rear brake system as described in this chapter.

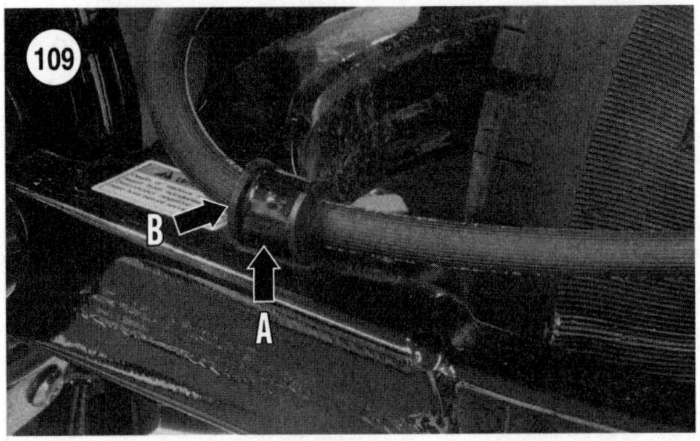

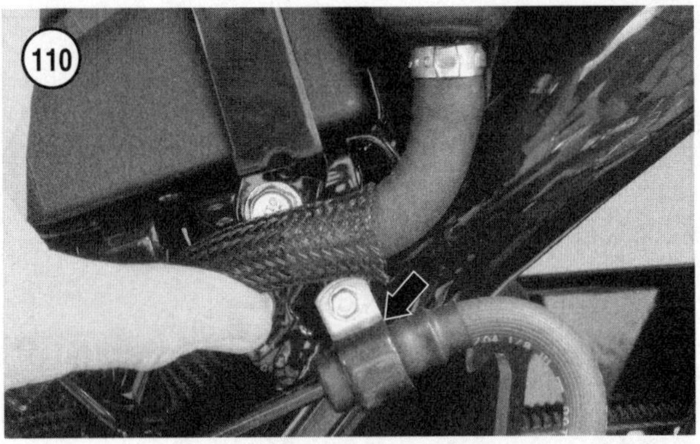

BRAKE DISC

The brake discs are separate from the wheel hubs and can be removed once the wheel is removed from the motorcycle.

Inspection

The front and rear brake discs can be inspected while installed on or removed from the motorcycle. Small marks on the disc are not important, but deep scratches or other

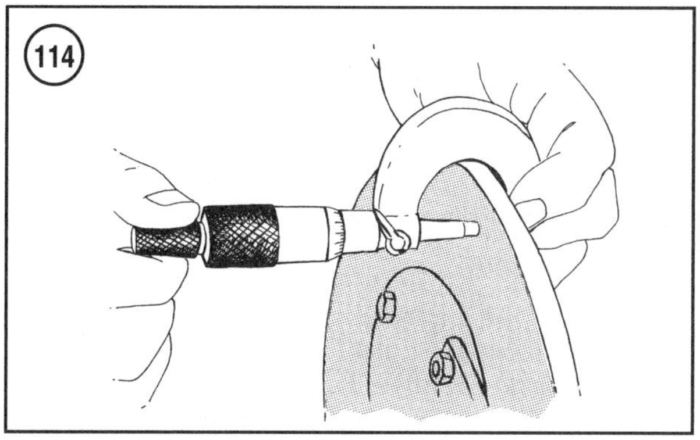

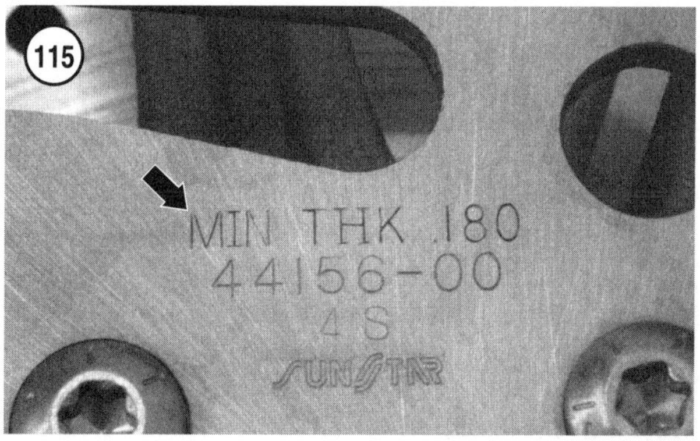

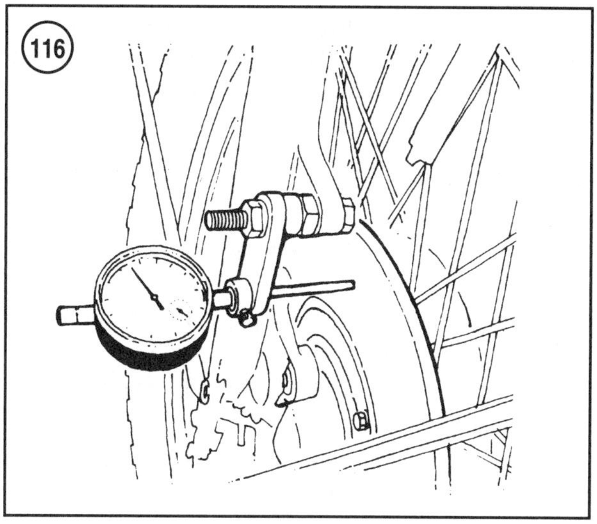

marks may reduce braking effectiveness and increase brake pad wear. If these grooves are evident and the brake pads are wearing rapidly, replace the brake disc.

The specifications for the standard and service limits are in **Table 1**. Each disc is also marked with the minimum (MIN) thickness. If the specification marked on the disc differs from the one in **Table 1**, use the specification on the disc.

When servicing the brake discs, do not have the discs surfaced to compensate for warp. The discs are thin, removing material only reduces their thickness, causing them to warp rapidly. A warped disc may be caused by dragging brake pads.

1. Measure the thickness of the disc at several locations around the disc with a vernier caliper or a micrometer (**Figure 114**). Replace the disc if the thickness in any area is less than the MIN dimension on the disc (**Figure 115**).
2. Make sure the disc mounting bolts are tight prior to performing this check. Check the disc runout with a dial indicator as shown in **Figure 116**.

NOTE
When checking the front disc, turn the handlebar all the way to one side, then to the other side.

3. Slowly rotate the wheel and watch the dial indicator. If the runout exceeds the specification in **Table 1**, replace the disc.
4. If the disc is warped, consider the following:
   a. The brake caliper piston seals are worn or damaged.
   b. The master cylinder relief port is plugged.
   c. The primary cup on the master cylinder piston is worn or damaged.

13

5. Clean the disc of any rust or corrosion and wipe it clean with brake cleaner. Never use an oil-based solvent that may leave an oil residue on the disc.

Removal/Installation

1. Remove the front or rear wheel as described in Chapter Ten.
2. Remove the Torx bolts (**Figure 117**) securing the brake disc to the hub and remove the disc.
3. Check the brake disc bolts for thread damage. Replace worn or damaged fasteners.
4. Check the threaded bolt holes for the brake disc in the wheel hub for thread damage. True them with a tap if necessary.
5. Clean the disc and the disc mounting surface thoroughly with brake cleaner. Allow the surfaces to dry before installation.
6. Install the disc onto the wheel hub.
7. Apply Loctite 243 or an equivalent to the threads of new Torx bolts prior to installation.
8. Install the bolts and tighten to 16-24 ft.-lb. (22-32 N•m).

REAR BRAKE PEDAL

Removal/Installation

WARNING
Do not ride the motorcycle until the rear brake, brake pedal and brake light operate properly.

Refer to **Figure 118** or **Figure 119**. The XL1200R model is shown in the following illustrations; other models are similar.

1. Remove the right footrest assembly as described in Chapter Fourteen.
2. Remove the retaining ring (A, **Figure 120**) at the end of the clevis.
3. Remove the retaining bolt (B, **Figure 120**).
4. Separate the clevis (A, **Figure 121**) and brake pedal (B).
5. Inspect the brake pedal bushing (C, **Figure 121**) for fractures or damage, and replace it if necessary.
6. Install the pedal by reversing the preceding removal steps. Tighten the clevis retaining bolt (B, **Figure 120**) to 96-156 in. lb. (11-17 N•m).

117

BRAKE BLEEDING

Bleeding the brakes removes air from the brake system. Air in the brake system increases brake lever or pedal travel while causing it to feel spongy and less responsive. Under extreme braking (heat) conditions, it can cause complete loss of brake action.

The brake hose systems can be filled manually or with the use of a vacuum pump. Both methods are described in this section. When the brake lines are full of brake fluid, the brakes are bled manually. Both procedures are described in this section.

When adding brake fluid during the bleeding process, use DOT 5 brake fluid. Do not reuse brake fluid drained from the system or use DOT 3, 4 or 5.1 (glycol based) brake fluid. Wipe up any spills immediately.

WARNING
Do not ride the motorcycle until the front and/or rear brake are operating correctly.

NOTE
When bleeding the brakes, check the fluid level in the front and rear master cylinders frequently to prevent them from running dry, especially when using a vacuum pump. If air enters the system it must be bled again.

General Bleeding Tips

When bleeding the brakes, note the following:

1. Review *Brake Fluid Type* and *Brake Service* in this chapter.
2. Clean the bleed valves and the area around the valves of all debris. Make sure the passageway in the end of the valve is open and clear.
3. Use a box-end wrench to open and close the bleed valves. This prevents damage to the hex-head, especially if the valve is rusted.

118

REAR BRAKE PEDAL
(XL883, L, R AND XL1200L, R MODELS)

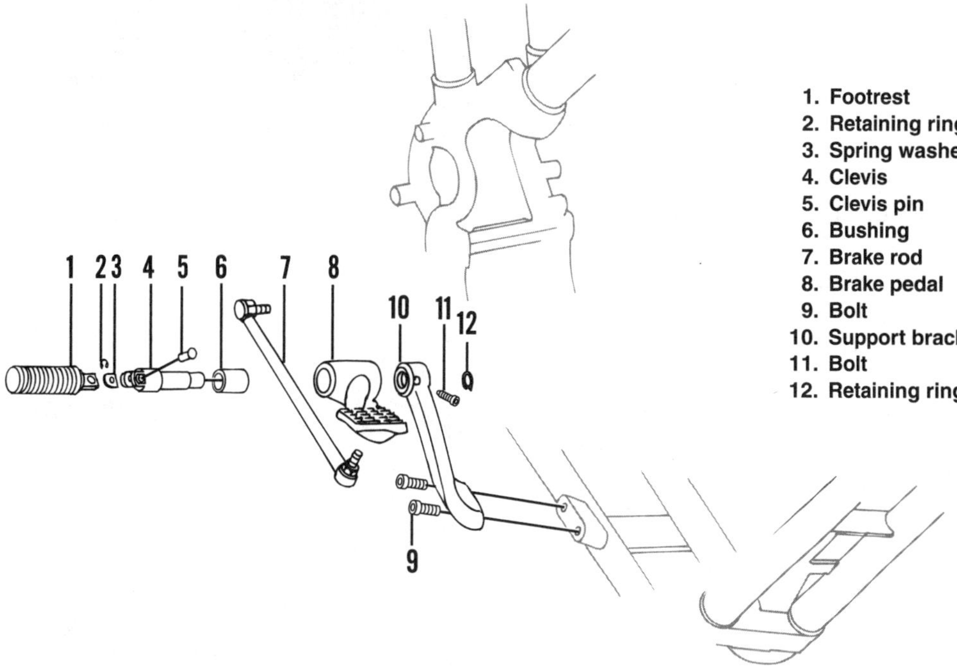

1. Footrest
2. Retaining ring
3. Spring washer
4. Clevis
5. Clevis pin
6. Bushing
7. Brake rod
8. Brake pedal
9. Bolt
10. Support bracket
11. Bolt
12. Retaining ring

119

REAR BRAKE PEDAL
(XL883C AND XL1200C MODELS)

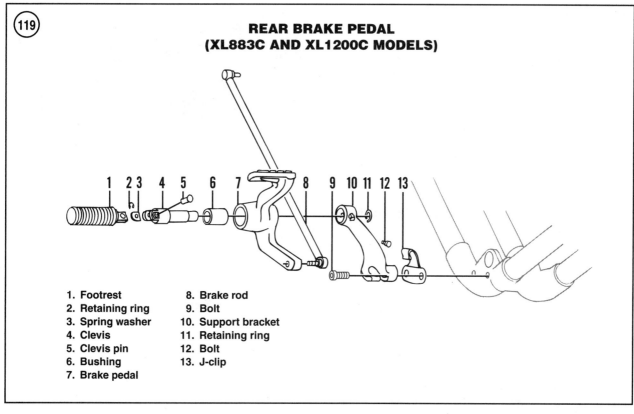

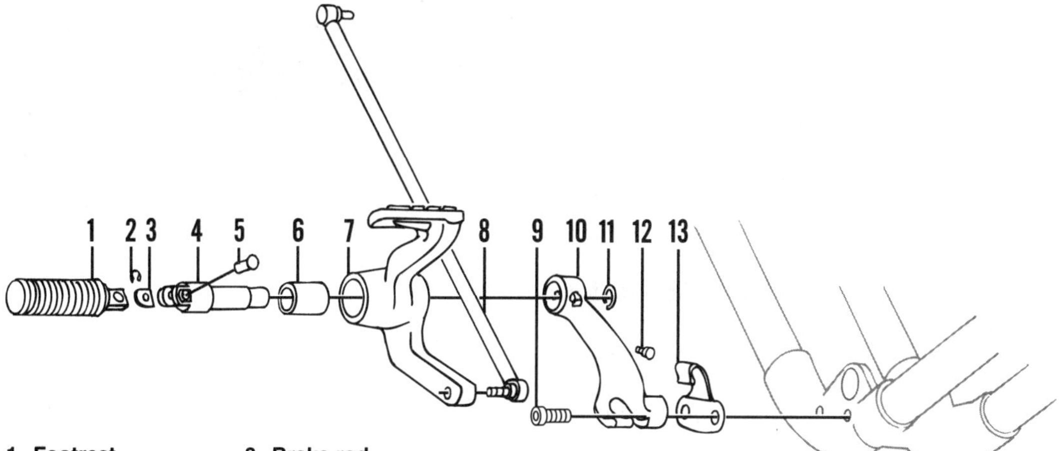

1. Footrest
2. Retaining ring
3. Spring washer
4. Clevis
5. Clevis pin
6. Bushing
7. Brake pedal
8. Brake rod
9. Bolt
10. Support bracket
11. Retaining ring
12. Bolt
13. J-clip

4. Install a box-end wrench (**Figure 122**) on the bleed valve before installing the catch hose. This allows operation of the wrench without having to disconnect the hose.

NOTE
*The catch hose (**Figure 122**) is the hose installed between the bleed valve and catch bottle.*

5. Replace damaged bleed valves. If rounded off, the valves cannot be tightened fully and are also difficult to loosen.
6. Use a clear catch hose to allow visible inspection of the brake fluid as it leaves the caliper. Air bubbles visible in the catch hose indicate that there still may be air trapped in the brake system.
7. Depending on the play of the bleed valve when it is loosened, it is possible to see air exiting through the catch hose even though there is no air in the brake system. A loose or damaged catch hose also causes air leaks. In both cases, air is being introduced at the bleed valve threads and catch hose connection, and not from within the brake system itself.
8. Open the bleed valve just enough to allow fluid to pass through the valve and into the catch bottle. The farther the bleed valve is opened, the looser the valve becomes. This allows air to be drawn into the system from around the valve threads.

WARNING
Do not apply an excessive amount of grease to the bleed valve threads. This can block the bleed valve passageway and contaminate the brake fluid.

9. If air is suspected of entering the bleed system from around the bleed valve threads, remove the bleed valve and apply silicone brake grease to the valve's threads to prevent air from passing by them. Then reinstall the bleed valve into the brake caliper.
10. If the system is difficult to bleed, tap the union bolt on the master cylinder as well as the brake caliper and connecting hoses a few times. It is not uncommon for air bubbles to become trapped in the hose connection where the brake fluid exits the master cylinder and caliper. When a number of bubbles appear in the master cylinder reservoir after tapping the union bolt, air was trapped in this area.

Brake Bleeder Procedure

This one-person procedure uses the Mityvac hydraulic brake bleeding kit (**Figure 123**). This tool and equivalents

120

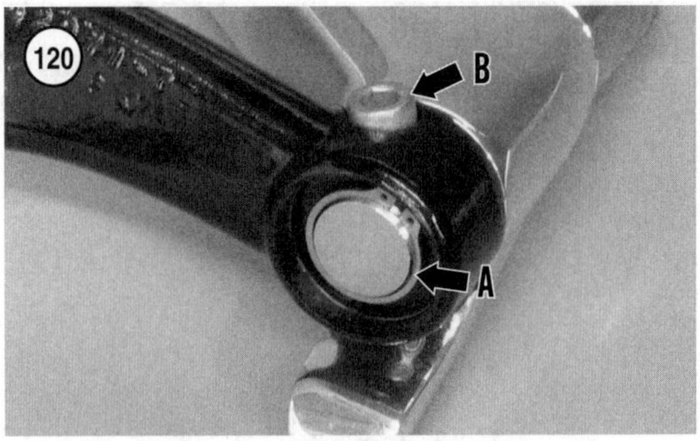

121

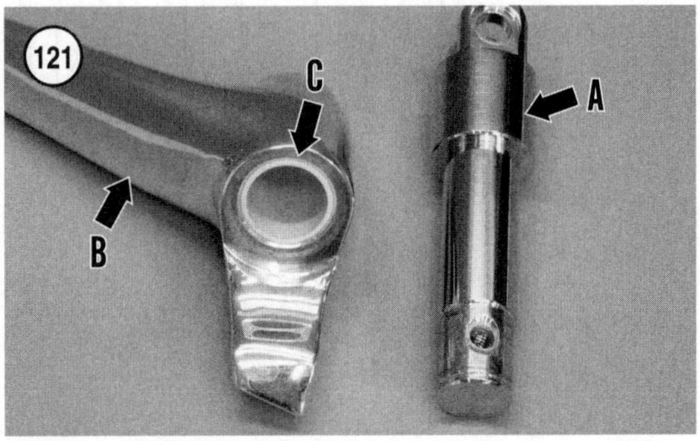

122

123

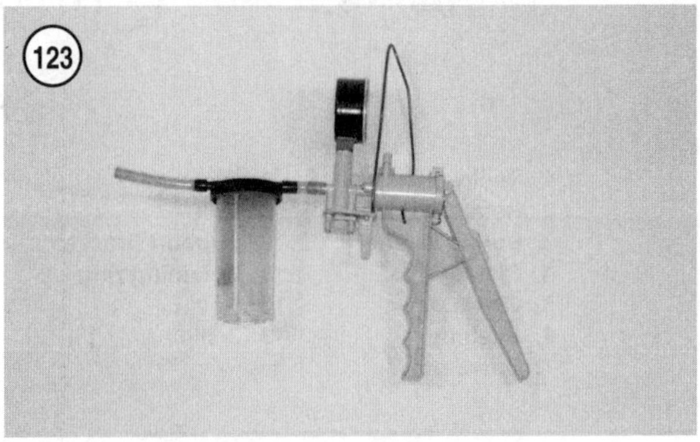

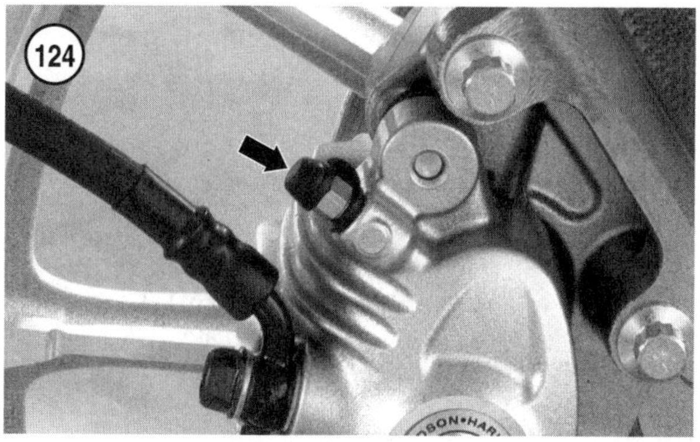
124

125

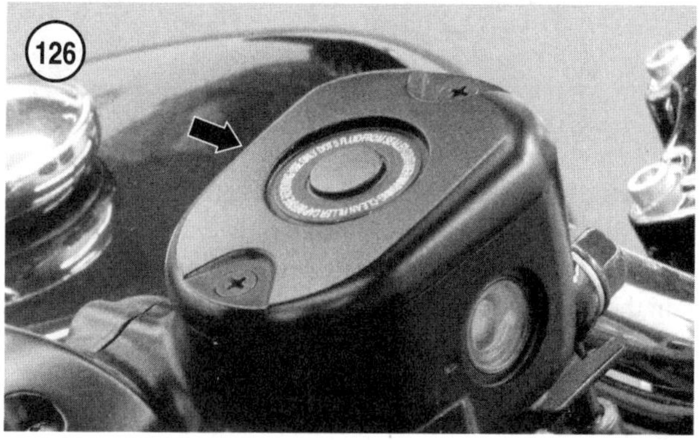
126

127

are available from automotive or motorcycle supply stores.

1. Support the motorcycle on a suitable stand.
2. Remove the dust cap (**Figure 124**) from the caliper bleed valve.
3. Place a clean shop cloth over the caliper to protect it from accidental brake fluid spills.
4. Assemble the Mityvac tool according to the manufacturer's instructions. Connect it to the caliper bleed valve (**Figure 125**).
5. Clean the top of the master cylinder reservoir of all debris.
6. Turn the handlebars to level the front master cylinder and remove the reservoir cover (**Figure 126**), diaphragm and diaphragm plate.
7. Make sure the reservoir contains DOT 5 brake fluid at the full level, which is the casting line on the inside of the reservoir (**Figure 127**). Reinstall the diaphragm, diaphragm plate and cover. Leave the cover in place during this procedure to prevent the entry of dirt.
8. Operate the pump several times to create a vacuum in the line. Open the bleed valve. Brake fluid will quickly draw from the caliper into the pump's reservoir. Tighten the caliper bleed valve before the fluid stops flowing through the hose. To prevent air from being drawn into the system through the master cylinder, add fluid to maintain its level at the top of the reservoir.

NOTE
Do not allow the master cylinder reservoir to empty during the bleeding operation or more air will enter the system. If this occurs, repeat the procedure.

9. Continue the bleeding process until the fluid drawn from the caliper is bubble free. If bubbles are withdrawn with the brake fluid, more air is trapped in the line. Repeat Step 8 while being sure to refill the master cylinder to prevent air from being drawn into the system.
10. When the brake fluid is free of bubbles, tighten the bleed valve and remove the brake bleeder assembly. Reinstall the bleed valve dust cap.
11. If necessary, add fluid to correct the level in the master cylinder reservoir as described in Chapter Three.
12. On XL1200R models, repeat Steps 1-11 for the other front brake caliper.
13. Reinstall the reservoir diaphragm, diaphragm plate and cover (**Figure 126**).
14. Test the feel of the brake lever or pedal. It must be firm and offer the same resistance each time it is operated. If it feels spongy, it is likely that there is still air in the system and it must be bled again. After bleeding the system,

check for leaks and tighten all fittings and connections as necessary.

15. Test ride the motorcycle slowly at first to make sure the brakes are operating properly.

Manual Procedure

NOTE
Before bleeding the brake, check that all brake hoses and lines are tight.

1. Support the motorcycle on a suitable stand.

NOTE
The rear brake caliper is equipped with two bleeder valves. Perform the following procedure using one bleeder valve, then repeat the procedure using the other bleeder valve.

2. Remove the dust cap (**Figure 124**) from the caliper bleed valve.
3. Place a clean shop cloth over the caliper to protect it from accidental brake fluid spills.
4. Clean the top of the master cylinder reservoir of all dirt and foreign matter.
5. Turn the handlebars to level the front master cylinder and remove the reservoir cover (**Figure 126**), diaphragm plate and diaphragm.
6. Make sure the reservoir contains DOT 5 brake fluid at the full level, which is the casting line on the inside of the reservoir (**Figure 127**). Reinstall the diaphragm, diaphragm plate and cover. Leave the cover in place during this procedure to prevent the entry of dirt.
7. Connect a length of clear tubing to the bleed valve on the caliper (**Figure 128**). Place the other end of the tube into a clean container. Fill the container with enough fresh DOT 5 brake fluid to keep the end of the tube submerged. The tube must be long enough so that a loop can be made higher than the bleeder valve to prevent air from being drawn into the caliper during bleeding.
8. Make sure the reservoir contains DOT 5 brake fluid at the full level and reinstall the diaphragm plate, diaphragm and cover. Leave the cover in place during this procedure to prevent the entry of dirt.

NOTE
During this procedure, it is important to check the fluid level in the master cylinder reservoir often. If the reservoir runs dry, air will enter the system.

9. Slowly apply the brake lever several times. Hold the lever in the applied position and open the bleed valve about a 1/2 turn. Allow the lever to travel to its limit.

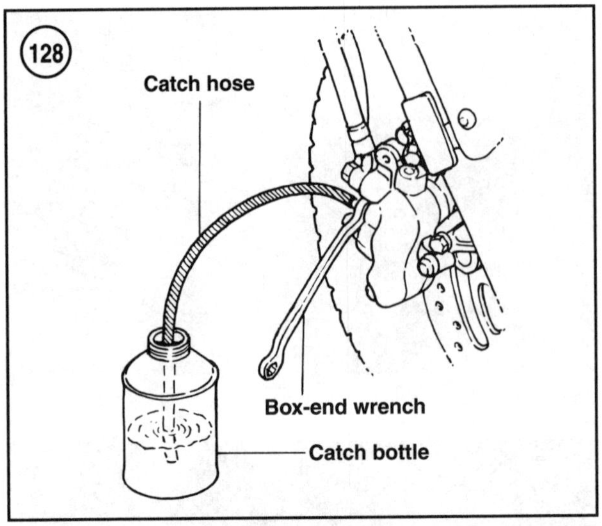

When the limit is reached, tighten the bleed valve, then release the brake lever. As the brake fluid enters the system, the level will drop in the master cylinder reservoir. Maintain the full fluid level in the reservoir to prevent air from being drawn into the system.

10. Continue the bleeding process until the fluid emerging from the hose is completely free of air bubbles. If the fluid is being replaced, continue until the fluid emerging from the hose is clean.

NOTE
If bleeding is difficult, allow the fluid to stabilize for a few hours. Repeat the bleeding procedure when the tiny bubbles in the system settle out.

11. Hold the lever in the applied position and tighten the bleed valve. Remove the bleed tube and install the bleed valve dust cap.
12. If necessary, adjust the fluid level in the master cylinder reservoir as described in Chapter Three.

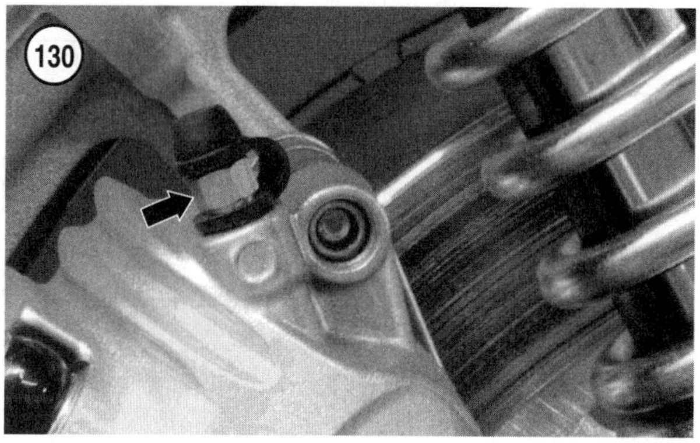

13. On XL1200R models, repeat Steps 1-12 for the other caliper.
14. Install the diaphragm, diaphragm plate and cover.
15. Test the feel of the brake lever or pedal. It must be firm and offer the same resistance each time it is operated. If it feels spongy, it is likely that there is still air in the system and it must be bled again. After bleeding the system, check for leaks and tighten all fittings and connections as necessary.
16. Test ride the motorcycle slowly at first to make sure the brakes are operating properly.

BRAKE FLUID DRAINING AND FLUSHING

Before disconnecting a brake hose from the front or rear brake, drain the brake fluid as described in this section. Doing so reduces the amount of brake fluid that can spill out when disconnecting the brake hoses and lines from the system.

When flushing the brake system, use DOT 5 brake fluid as a flushing fluid. Flushing consists of pulling new brake fluid through the system until the new fluid appears at the caliper and without of any air bubbles. To flush the brake system, follow one of the bleeding procedures described in this chapter.

Front Brake Lever Line

1. Read *Brake Bleeding* in this chapter.
2. Support the motorcycle on a suitable stand.
3. Turn the handlebars to level the front master cylinder and remove the reservoir cover (**Figure 126**), diaphragm plate and diaphragm.
4. Connect a brake bleeder to the front brake caliper bleed valve (**Figure 125**) as described in this chapter. Operate the bleeder tool to remove as much brake fluid from the system as possible.
5. Close the bleed valve and disconnect the brake bleeder tool.
6. Repeat for the other caliper.
7. Service the brake components as described in this chapter.

Rear Brake Pedal Line

1. Read *Brake Bleeding* in this chapter.
2. Support the motorcycle on a suitable stand.
3. Remove the rear brake master cylinder reservoir cap (**Figure 129**) from the reservoir.
4. Connect a brake bleeder to the rear brake caliper bleed valve (**Figure 130**) as described in this chapter. Operate the bleeder tool to remove as much brake fluid from the system as possible.
5. Disconnect the brake bleeder and remove it from the brake caliper.
6. Service the brake components as described in this chapter.

Table 1 BRAKE SYSTEM SPECIFICATIONS

Brake fluid	DOT 5 silicone base
Brake pad minimum thickness	0.04 in. (1.02 mm)
Brake disc runout (max.)	0.008 in. (0.2 mm)

Table 2 BRAKE SYSTEM TORQUE SPECIFICATIONS

	ft.-lb.	in.-lb.	N•m
Bleed valve	–	35-61	4.0-6.9
Brake disc mounting bolts	16-24	–	22-32
Brake hose clamp screws	–	30-40	3.4-4.5
Brake pedal/footrest support bracket bolts	45-50	–	62-68
Brake rod end	–	120-180	14-20
Front caliper mounting bolts	28-38	–	38.0-51.6
Front master cylinder clamp bolts	–	108-132	13-15
Mirror locknut	–	96-144	11-16
Pad pin	–	131-173	15-19.5
Pad pin plug	–	18-25	2.0-2.9
Rear brake pedal clevis retaining bolt	–	96-156	11-17
Rear caliper mounting bolt pin	15-18	–	21-24
Rear caliper mounting stud pin	–	87-130	10-14
Rear master cylinder mounting bolts	15-20	–	21-27
Rear brake switch	–	80-123	9-14
Turn signal clamp screw	–	96-120	11-13
Union bolt	20-25	–	27-34

NOTE: Refer to the Supplement at the end of this manual for information unique to 2007-2011 models.

CHAPTER FOURTEEN

BODY

SEAT

Removal/Installation

1. Remove the seat retaining bolt (**Figure 1**).

2. Push the seat forward to disengage the seat slot from the frame post.

3. Lift up the rear of the seat and remove it rearward so the seat tab disengages from the frame.

4. Reverse the removal steps to install the seat. Make sure the seat is secure before operating the motorcycle.

FRONT FENDER

Removal/Installation

1. Hold the front fender so it cannot fall after removing the mounting bolts.

2. Remove the locknuts and bolts on both sides of the fender (**Figure 2**).

3. Remove the front fender.

4. Reverse the removal steps to install the front fender. Tighten the locknuts to 96-156 in.-lb. (11-17 N•m).

REAR FENDER

Removal/Installation

Refer to **Figure 3**.

1. Remove the seat as described in this chapter.

2. Disconnect the negative battery cable from the crankcase as described in Chapter Nine.

3. Remove the ICM as described in Chapter Nine.

4. Disconnect the rear lighting connector under the ICM (**Figure 4**).

5. Remove the rear turn signals as described in Chapter Nine.

NOTE
*The rear fender mounting bolt (**Figure 5**) also serves as the seat post.*

6. Remove the rear fender mounting bolt (**Figure 5**), then remove the rear fender.

7. Reverse the removal steps to install the rear fender. Tighten the rear fender mounting bolt (**Figure 5**) to 96-156 in.-lb. (11-17 N•m).

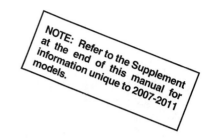

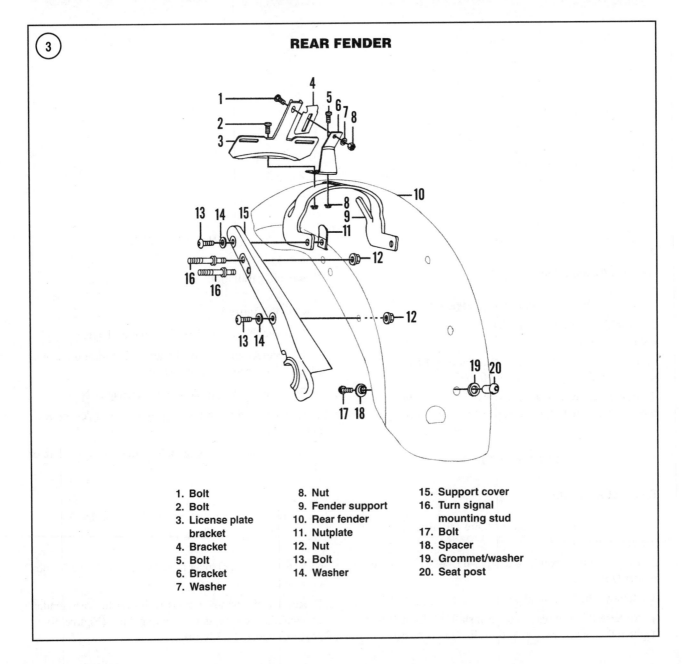

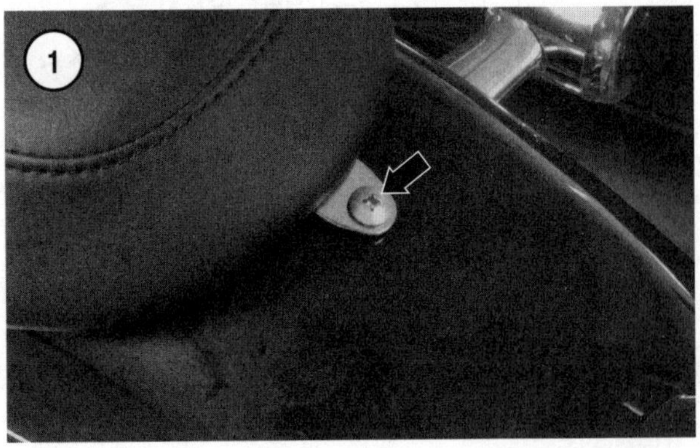

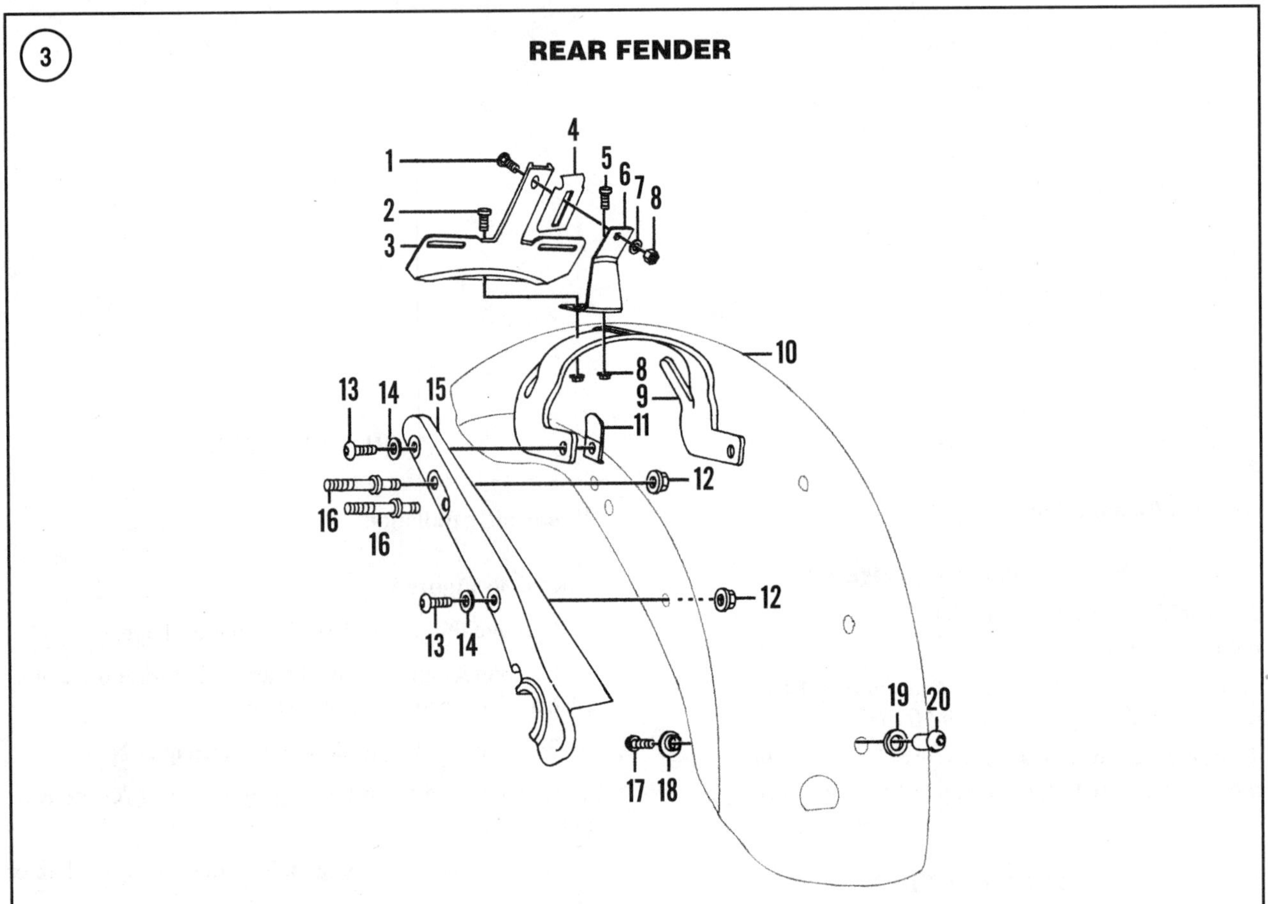

1. Bolt
2. Bolt
3. License plate bracket
4. Bracket
5. Bolt
6. Bracket
7. Washer
8. Nut
9. Fender support
10. Rear fender
11. Nutplate
12. Nut
13. Bolt
14. Washer
15. Support cover
16. Turn signal mounting stud
17. Bolt
18. Spacer
19. Grommet/washer
20. Seat post

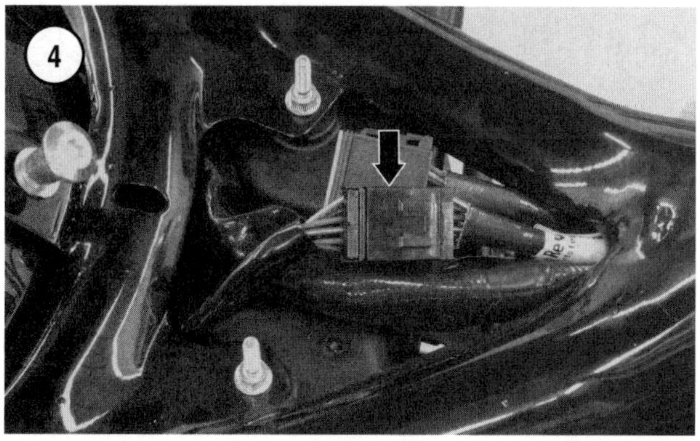

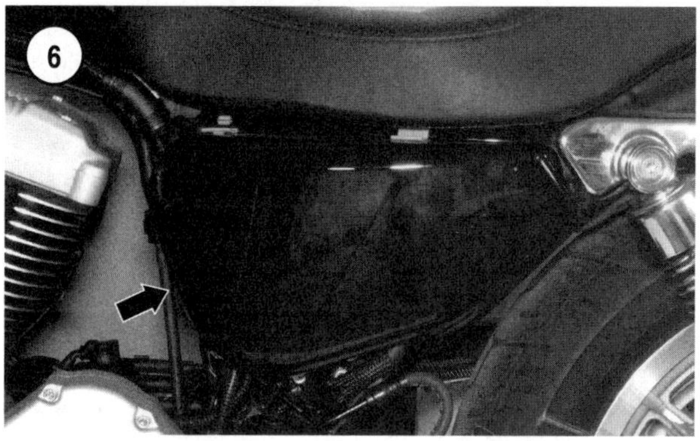

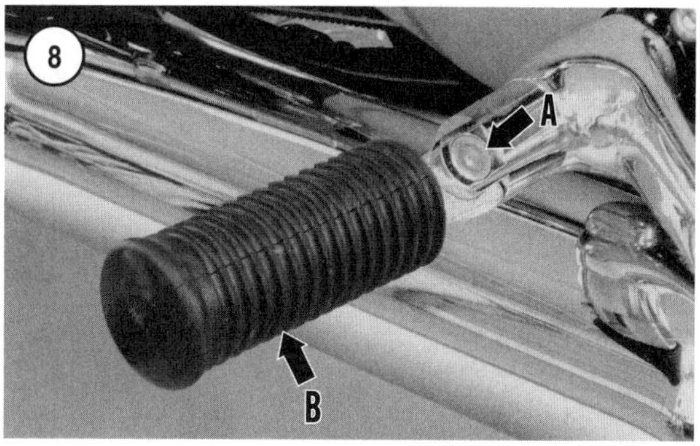

LEFT SIDE COVER

Removal/Installation

1. To remove the left side cover (**Figure 6**), grasp the cover at the upper corners and pull straight out.
2. Disengage the bottom of the side cover from the latch and remove the cover.
3. Reverse the removal steps to install the cover. Make sure the slot in the bottom of the cover fits around the frame latch.

RIGHT SIDE COVER

Removal/Installation

1. To remove the right side cover, which covers the oil tank, remove the seat.
2. Gently pry the cover off the top of the oil tank boss, and remove the cover.
3. To install the right side cover, push it onto the oil tank until it snaps over the retaining lugs on the oil tank.

FOOTRESTS

Removal/Installation

1. Remove the snap ring (A, **Figure 7**) on the underside of the footrest pivot pin.
2. Remove the pivot pin (A, **Figure 8**).

NOTE

*When removing the footrest, do not lose the spring washer (B, **Figure** 7) between the footrest and clevis.*

3. Remove the footrest (B, **Figure 8**).
4. Install the footrest by reversing the removal steps. Install the spring washer (B, **Figure 7**) so the square end is toward the inside.

FOOTREST BRACKETS

Removal/Installation

Each footrest is supported by a bracket that attaches to the frame. Each rider or passenger bracket is secured by two mounting bolts. Note that the rider bracket may also support shift or brake components, which are covered elsewhere in this manual.

NOTE
Remove the front exhaust pipe as described in Chapter Eight to access the right rider footrest bracket bolts.

1. Remove the two bolts securing the footrest mounting bracket (**Figure 9** or **Figure 10**).
2. Remove the bracket assembly.
3. Install the bracket by reversing the removal procedure. Tighten the mounting bolts to 45-50 ft.-lb. (62-68 N•m).

SIDESTAND

Removal/Installation

WARNING
The sidestand is spring-loaded. Exercise caution when working on the sidestand assembly.

1. Place the motorcycle on a suitable stand so the sidestand can be moved freely without contacting the ground.
2. Remove the rubber frame bumper (**Figure 11**) to allow greater sidestand travel.
3. Place the sidestand in the retracted position.
4. Remove the retaining clip (**Figure 12**).
5. Hold the sidestand securely, then extract the clevis pin until it disengages from the upper mounting hole.
6. Detach the spring.

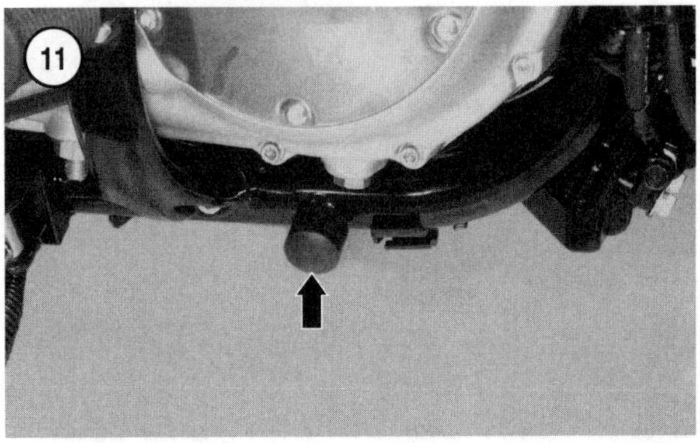

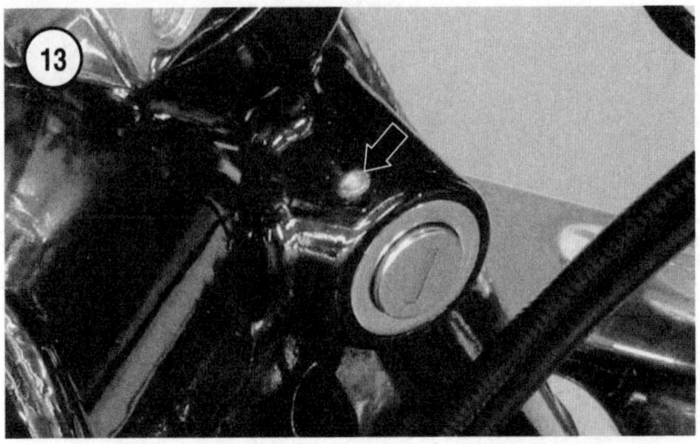

7. Remove the clevis pin and remove the sidestand.

8. Clean all components. Lubricate the clevis pin, spring mounting points and sidestand with wheel bearing grease.

9. Reverse the removal procedure to install the sidestand. Install the bushings so the shouldered side fits into the frame bracket holes.

FORK LOCK

Replacement

1. Disconnect the negative battery cable from the crankcase as described in Chapter Nine.

2. Remove the fuel tank.

NOTE

Depending on the tools used, it may be necessary to remove or move handlebar components to access the fork lock.

3. Using a 5/64-in. drill bit, drill a hole in the center of the lockpin (**Figure 13**). Make sure to drill down the center, otherwise lockpin removal will be difficult.

4. Install a screw extractor into the lockpin and pull out the lockpin.

5. Remove the lock assembly.

6. Install the new lock so the lockpin holes in the lock and frame are aligned.

7. Drive in a new lockpin so it is flush with the frame.

8. Check lockpin operation. Make sure the handlebar can be moved through a full range of motions.

Table 1 BODY TORQUE SPECIFICATIONS

	ft.-lb.	in.-lb.	N•m
Fender fasteners	–	96-156	11-17
Footrest bracket mounting bolts	45-50	–	60-67
Fuel tank mounting bolts	15-20	–	21-27
Mirror locknut	–	96-144	11-16
Taillight base mounting screw	–	45-48	5.1-5.4
Turn signal clamp screw	–	96-120	11-13

SUPPLEMENT

2007-2011 SERVICE INFORMATION

This Supplement contains all procedures and specifications unique to the 2007-2011 models. If a specification or procedure is not included, refer to the procedure in the appropriate chapter (2-14).

This Supplement is divided into sections that correspond to those in the other chapters in this manual. **Tables 1-30** are located at the end of the appropriate section.

CHAPTER ONE

GENERAL INFORMATION

Table 1 MOTORCYCLE DIMENSIONS

Overall length	
2007-2009	
XL883L, XL1200L	89.1 in. (2263 mm)
XL883, XL883R, XL1200R	90.1 in. (2289 mm)
XL883C, XL1200C	90.3 in. (2294 mm)
XL1200N	85.8 in. (2179 mm)
2010	
XL883R	90.1 in. (2289 mm)
XL883C, XL1200C	90.3 in. (2294 mm)
XL883L, XL1200L	89.1 in. (2263 mm)
XL883N, XL1200N	85.8 in. (2179 mm)

(continued)

Table 1 MOTORCYCLE DIMENSIONS (continued)

2011	
XL883R	90.1 in. (2289 mm)
XL883L	86.1 in. (2187 mm)
XL883N, XL1200N	85.8 in. (2179 mm)
XL1200L	89.1 in. (2263 mm)
XL1200C	87.1 in. (2212 mm)
XL1200X	88.6 in. (2250 mm)
Overall width	
2007-2009	
XL883, XL883R, XL883C, XL1200C	32.7 in. (831 mm)
XL883L, XL1200L	35.2 in. (894 mm)
XL1200R	36.7 in. (932 mm)
XL1200N	36.4 in. (925 mm)
2010	
XL883N	32.3 in. (821 mm)
XL883R, XL883C, XL1200C	32.7 in. (831 mm)
XL883L, XL1200L	35.2 in. (894 mm)
XL1200N	36.4 in. (925 mm)
2011	
XL883N	32.3 in. (821 mm)
XL883L	36.6 in. (929 mm)
XL883R, XL1200X	32.7 in. (831 mm)
XL1200N	36.4 in. (925 mm)
XL1200L	35.2 in. (894 mm)
XL1200C	33.1 in. (841 mm)
Overall height	
2007-2009	
XL883, XL883L, XL883C, XL1200C	45.7 in. (1161 mm)
XL883R	44.8 in. (1138 mm)
XL1200N	43.6 in. (1107 mm)
XL1200L	46.8 in. (1189 mm)
XL1200R	49.2 in. (1250 mm)
2010	
XL883R	44.8 in. (1138 mm)
XL883N, XL1200N	43.6 in. (1107 mm)
XL883L, XL883C, XL1200C	45.7 in. (1161 mm)
XL1200L	46.8 in. (1189 mm)
2011	
XL883R	44.8 in. (1138 mm)
XL883L	47.6 in. (1209 mm)
XL883N, XL1200N	43.6 in. (1107 mm)
XL1200L	46.8 in. (1189 mm)
XL1200C	44.9 in. (1140 mm)
XL1200X	42.0 in. (1067 mm)
Wheelbase	
2007-2009	
XL883, XL883R, XL883L, XL1200N, XL1200R	60.0 in. (1524 mm)
XL883C, XL1200C	60.4 in. (1534 mm)
XL1200L	59.7 in. (1516 mm)
2010	
XL883C, XL1200C	60.4 in. (1534 mm)
XL883R, XL883L, XL883N, XL1200N	60.0 in. (1524 mm)
XL1200L	59.7 in. (1516 mm)
2011	
XL883L	59.3 in. (1506 mm)
XL883R	60.0 in. (1524 mm)
XL883N, XL1200N, XL1200X	59.8 in. (1519 mm)
XL1200C	59.9 in. (1521 mm)
XL1200L	60.1 in. (1527 mm)

(continued)

Table 1 MOTORCYCLE DIMENSIONS (continued)

Seat height*	
2007-2009	
XL883R (2009), XL883	27.3 in. (693 mm)
XL883C, XL1200C	26.5 in. (673 mm)
XL883L, XL1200N	25.3 in. (643 mm)
XL1200L	26.3 in. (668 mm)
XL883R (2007), XL1200R	28.1 in. (714 mm)
2010	
XL883C, XL1200C,	26.5 in. (673 mm)
XL883L, XL883N, XL1200N	25.3 in. (643 mm)
XL1200L	26.3 in. (668 mm)
2011	
XL883R	27.3 in. (693 mm)
XL883L	25.5 in. (648 mm)
XL883N,XL1200N	25.7 in. (653 mm)
XL1200X	26.0 in. (660 mm)
XL1200L	26.3 in. (668 mm)
XL1200C	26.6 in. (676 mm)
Ground clearance	
2007-2009	
XL883, XL883R, XL1200R	5.6 in. (142 mm)
XL883C, XL1200C, XL1200L	4.4 in. (112 mm)
XL883L, XL1200N	3.9 in. (99 mm)
2010	
XL883R	5.6 in. (142 mm)
XL883L, XL883N, XL1200N	3.9 in. (99 mm)
XL883C, XL1200C, XL1200L	4.4 in. (112 mm)
2011	
XL883L	3.8 in. (97 mm)
XL883R	5.6 in. (142 mm)
XL883N, XL1200N. XL1200X	3.9 in. (99 mm)
XL1200C, XL1200L	4.4 in. (112 mm)

*With 180 lb. (82 kg) rider

Table 2 MOTORCYCLE WEIGHT

Dry Weight	
2007-2009	
XL883, XL883L	563 lb. (256 kg)
XL883R	568 lb. (258 kg)
XL883C, XL1200R	565 lb. (257 kg)
XL1200N	545 lb. (248 kg)
XL1200L	557 lb. (253 kg)
XL1200C	562 lb. (255 kg)
2010	
XL883L	563 lb. (256 kg)
XL883C	565 lb. (257 kg)
XL883R	568 lb. (258 kg)
XL883N	548 lb. (249 kg)
XL1200C	562 lb. (255 kg)
XL1200L	557 lb. (253 kg)
XL1200N	545 lb. (248 kg)
2011	
XL883L	536 lb. (243 kg)
XL883R	568 lb. (258 kg)
XL883N	548 lb. (249 kg)
XL1200C	553 lb. (251 kg)
XL1200L	557 lb. (253 kg)
XL1200N, XL1200X	545 lb. (248 kg)

CHAPTER TWO

TROUBLESHOOTING

Tables 3-8 are at the end of the section.

ENGINE STARTING

Engine Fails to Start (Spark Test)

Refer to *Engine Starting* in Chapter Two.

Engine is Difficult to Start

Refer to Chapter Two. Perform the following additional steps.

1. After attempting to start the engine, remove one of the spark plugs as described in Chapter Three and check for the presence of fuel on the plug tip. Note the following:
   a. If there is no fuel visible on the plug, remove the other spark plug. If there is no fuel on this plug, perform Step 2.
   b. If there is fuel present on the plug tip, go to Step 4.
   c. If there is an excessive amount of fuel on the plug, check for a clogged or plugged air filter, incorrect throttle valve operation (stuck open).
2. Perform the *Fuel Pressure Test* as described in this Supplement. Note the following:
   a. If the fuel pump pressure is correct, go to Step 3.
   b. If the fuel pump pressure is incorrect, replace the fuel pump and retest the fuel system.
3. Inspect the fuel injectors as described in this chapter.
4. Perform the spark test as described in Chapter Two. Note the following:
   a. If the spark is weak or if there is no spark, go to Step 5.
   b. If the spark is good, go to Step 6.
5. If the spark is weak or if there is no spark, check the following:
   a. Fouled spark plug(s).
   b. Damaged spark plug(s).
   c. Loose or damaged ignition coil wire(s).
   d. Damaged electronic control module (ECM).
   e. Damaged crankshaft position sensor.
   f. Damaged ignition coil(s).
   g. Damaged engine run/stop switch.
   h. Damaged ignition switch.
   i. Damaged clutch interlock switch.
   j. Dirty or loose-fitting terminals.
6. If the engine turns over but does not start, the engine compression is probably low. Check for the following possible malfunctions:
   a. Leaking cylinder head gasket(s).
   b. Valve clearance too tight.
   c. Bent or stuck valve(s).
   d. Incorrect valve timing. Worn cylinders and/or pistons rings.
   e. Incorrect pushrod length (intake and exhaust valve pushrods interchanged).
7. If the spark is good, try starting the engine by following normal starting procedures. If the engine starts but then stops, check for the following conditions:
   a. Leaking or damaged rubber intake boots.
   b. Contaminated fuel.
   c. Incorrect ignition timing due to a damaged ignition coil or crankshaft position sensor.

ENGINE PERFORMANCE

Refer to Chapter Two.

Engine Misfires

Refer to Chapter Two. Also test the TMAP sensor, fuel injection system and ECM as described in this Supplement.

Engine Runs Rough with Excessive Exhaust Smoke

Refer to Chapter Two. Also test the TMAP sensor, fuel injection system and ECM as described in this Supplement.

Engine Loses Power

Refer to Chapter Two. Also test the TMAP sensor, fuel injection system and ECM as described in this Supplement.

STARTING SYSTEM

Refer to Chapter Two. 2007-on models are equipped with a clutch switch that allows starting with the transmission in gear.

CHARGING SYSTEM

Refer to Chapter Two.

Charging System Output Test

Note that the regulated (DC) output current reading for 2007-on models is 24-30 amps.

Battery Current Draw Test

1. Turn the ignition switch off. Make sure all accessories are in the off position.
2. Disconnect the negative battery cable as described in Chapter Nine.

CAUTION
Before connecting the ammeter into the circuit in Step 3, set the meter to its highest amperage scale. This prevents a large current flow from damaging the meter or blowing the meter's fuse.

NOTE
*Even with the ignition in the off position, an initial current draw of up to 200 mA will occur directly after connecting the ammeter. This should drop to the values shown in **Table 3** within one minute.*

NOTE
For best result, disconnect the security siren, if so equipped. The siren battery can draw 20 mA for several hours when charging.

3. Connect an ammeter between the crankcase ground and the end of the negative battery cable. Note the meter reading after the initial one minute interval as follows:
   a. Add the regulator draw (0.5-1.0 mA) to the approximate values of the TSM/TSSM/HFSM in **Table**

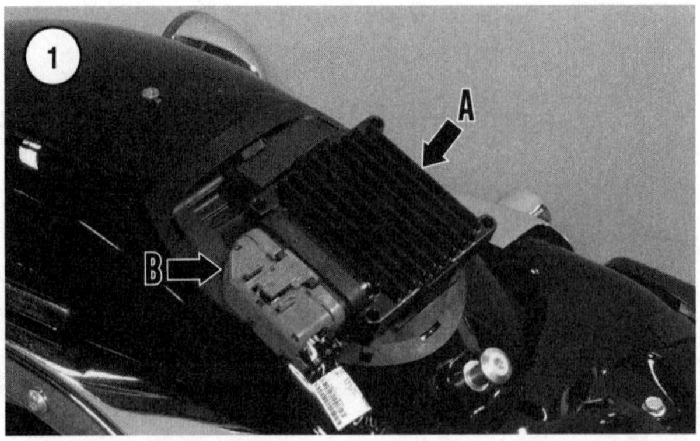

      3. If this total is less than the ammeter reading, then the current draw is within limits.
   b. If there is a higher reading, this indicates an excessive draw. Check each accessory for excessive current draw.
4. Dirt and/or electrolyte on top of the battery or a crack in the battery case can create a path for battery current to flow. If excessive current draw is noted, remove and clean the battery (Chapter Nine), then repeat the test.
5. If the current draw is still excessive, consider the following probable causes:
   a. Faulty voltage regulator.
   b. Damaged battery.
   c. Short circuit in the system.
   d. Loose, dirty or faulty electrical connectors in the charging circuit.
6. To find the short circuit, refer to the wiring diagrams at the end of this manual. Then continue to measure the current draw while disconnecting different connectors in the electrical system one by one. If the current draw returns to an acceptable level, the circuit is indicated. Test the circuit further to find the problem.
7. Disconnect the ammeter.
8. Reconnect the negative battery cable (Chapter Nine).

IGNITION SYSTEM

Precautions

Before testing the ignition system, observe the following precautions to prevent damage to the ignition system:
1. Never disconnect any of the electrical connectors while the engine is running.
2. Apply dielectric grease to all electrical connectors prior to reconnecting them. This will help seal out moisture.
3. Make sure all electrical connectors are free of corrosion and are completely coupled to each other.

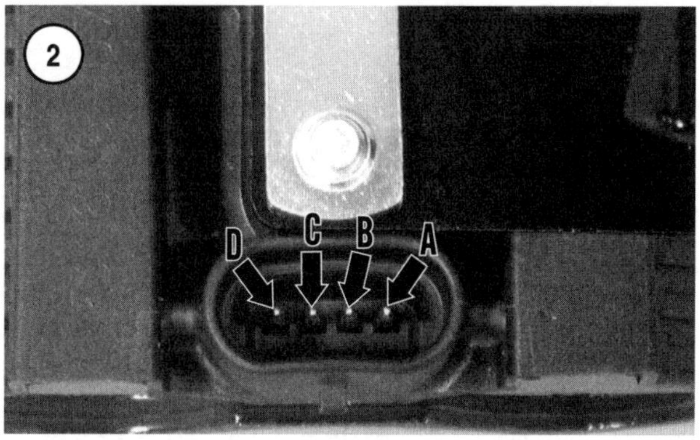

4. Make sure the ECM (A, **Figure 1**) is mounted securely.

Troubleshooting Preparation

1. Refer to the wiring diagrams at the end of this manual for the specific model.
2. Check the ignition fuse and the Maxi-fuse.
3. Check the wiring harness for visible signs of damage.
4. Make sure all connectors are properly attached to each other and locked in place.
5. Check all electrical components for a good ground.
6. Check all wiring for short circuits or open circuits.
7. Make sure the ignition circuit fuse is good (Chapter Nine).
8. Make sure the fuel tank has an adequate supply of fresh gasoline.
9. Check the spark plug cable routing and the connections at the spark plugs. If there is no spark or only a weak one, repeat the test with new spark plugs. If the condition remains the same with new spark plugs and if all external wiring connections are good, the problem is most likely in the ignition system. If a strong spark is present, the problem is probably not in the ignition system. Check the fuel system.
10. Remove the spark plugs and examine them as described in Chapter Three.

ECM Testing and Replacement

If the engine control module (ECM) is suspected of being defective, have it tested by a dealership before purchasing a replacement. The cost of the test will not exceed the cost of replacing an ECM that may not repair the problem. Most parts suppliers will not accept returns on electrical components.

Ignition Coil Testing

Use an ohmmeter to check the ignition coil secondary and primary resistance. Test the coil twice: first when it is cold (room temperature), then at normal operating temperature. If the engine will not start, heat the coil with a hair dryer, then test with the ohmmeter.

NOTE
Resistance readings may not verify that an ignition coil is good. Before purchasing a new unit check operation using a known good unit or have the coil tested at a dealership.

1. Remove the ignition coil as described in *Ignition System* in this Supplement.
2. Measure the ignition coil primary resistance between the positive terminal (A, **Figure 2**) and front cylinder primary coil terminal (B) or rear cylinder primary coil terminal (C). Compare the readings to the specification in **Table 4**. Replace the ignition coil if either reading is not within specification.
3. Check the secondary circuit of the ignition coil and refer to **Table 4.** Verify that the spark plug wires, spark plugs and ignition system components are in working order. If no spark or a weak spark exists, replace the ignition coil with a good unit and repeat the spark test.

ELECTRONIC DIAGNOSTIC SYSTEM

All models are equipped with an electronic diagnostic system that monitors the operating condition of the speedometer, electronic control module (ECM), turn signal module/turn signal security module (TSM/TSSM), hands-free security module (HFSM) and tachometer, if so equipped. A serial data bus connects the aforementioned components. If a malfunction occurs, a diagnostic trouble code (DTC) may be generated. The trouble code helps pinpoint a problem, or identifies a potential problem. To obtain a trouble code, refer to the *DTC Retrieval* in *Electronic Diagnostic System* in Chapter Two.

Not all malfunctions will cause the generation of a DTC. Refer also to *No-DTC Fault Troubleshooting* in this section.

Refer to Chapter Two for *Startup Check* and *DTC Retrieval.*

NOTE
On 2007-on models, the letters PSSPTB will appear in the odometer window. The T identifies the tachometer. The B identifies an antilock brake system, which is not used on Sportster models.

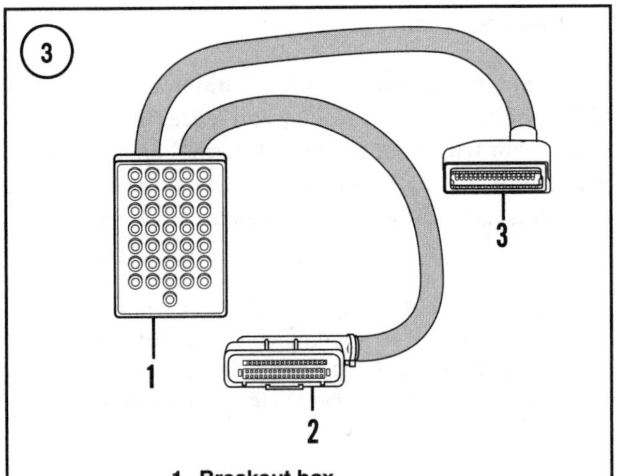

1. Breakout box
2. ECM connector
3. Wiring harness connector

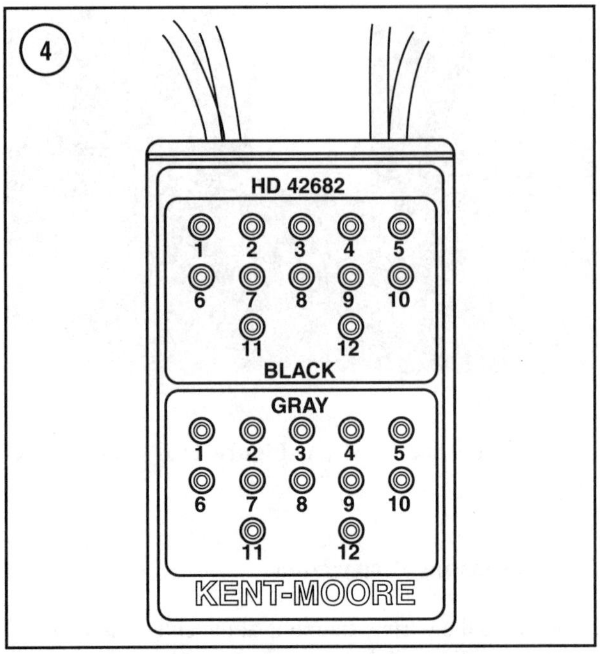

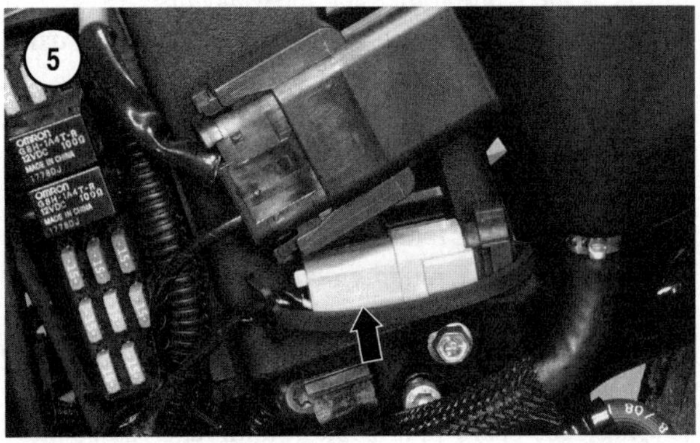

Diagnostic Tools

The troubleshooting steps in some of the flow charts in this chapter require two different H-D breakout boxes. Refer to **Figure 3** for part No. HD-43876 and **Figure 4** for part No. HD-42682.

The H-D breakout box part No. HD-42682 (**Figure 4**) is separated into two panels marked black and gray. The panel colors relate to the colors of the box connectors: one pair black; one pair gray. Refer to Chapter Two for connection of the HD-42682 breakout box to the speedometer/tachometer and TSM/TSSM/ HFSM.

Breakout box HD-43876 connects to the ECM and ECM connector. Disconnect the ECM connector (B, **Figure 1**), then connect the breakout box connectors to the ECM and its connector.

A harness connector test kit (part No. HD-41404) is available for some of the following flow charts. This test kit allows inserting the test lead probes into the various terminals without damaging them.

The H-D Digital Technician II (part No. HD-48650) must be used to obtain historic trouble codes, and to erase them. Digital Technician also displays operating values for some system components. Refer to **Table 5.** The Digital Technician is necessary to reprogram a new ECM.

Data Link Connector

The data link connector provides access to the data bus and provides a testing terminal when troubleshooting. The connector is located behind the left side cover. Remove the connector cap (**Figure 5**) for access to the connector terminals.

Troubleshooting Using DTCs

A list of DTCs is found in **Table 6** at the end of this section, which also identifies the possible problem and a troubleshooting flowchart. Refer to the applicable flowchart in **Figures 6-48.** Note the following before beginning troubleshooting:

1. Before retrieving DTCs refer to *Initial Diagnostic Check* in *Electronic Diagnostic System* Chapter Two.

2. Not all malfunctions will set a DTC. If this occurs, refer to **Figures 44-48** or to Chapter Nine to assist in troubleshooting.

3. Check for obvious causes before undertaking what may be a complicated troubleshooting procedure. Do not overlook loose or disconnected connectors, damaged wiring and bad grounds (Step 4 and Step 5 are on page 528).

6

DTC U1300, U1301, BUS ER: SERIAL DATA LOW OR SERIAL DATA OPEN/HIGH

Note the following:

1. If engine starts, then stalls and sets DTC U1300, U1301 or Bus Er, refer also to **Figure 40.**
2. The run/stop switch must be in RUN when turning the ignition key to IGNITION.

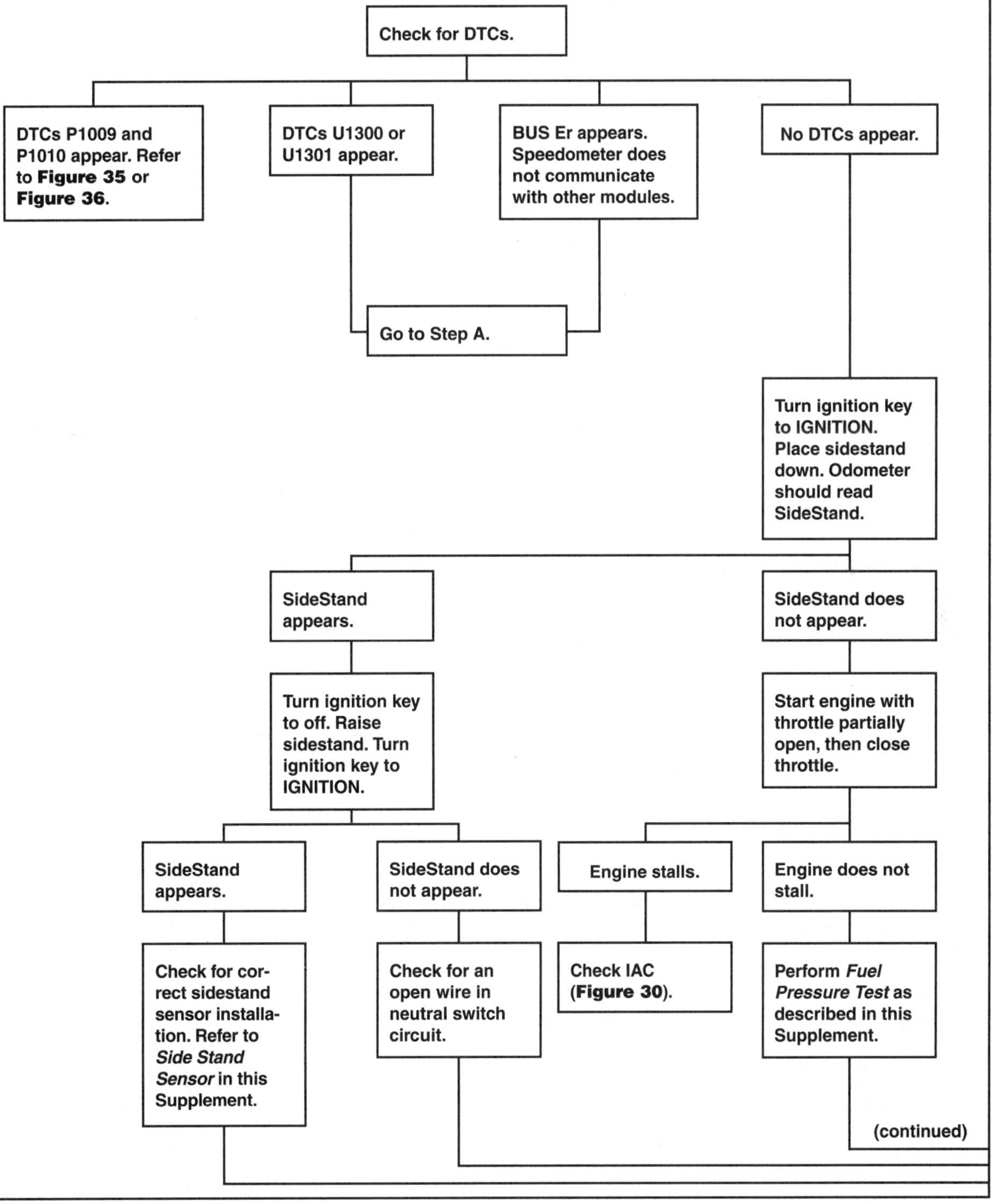
Check for DTCs.
DTCs P1009 and P1010 appear. Refer to Figure 35 or Figure 36.
DTCs U1300 or U1301 appear.
BUS Er appears. Speedometer does not communicate with other modules.
No DTCs appear.
Go to Step A.
Turn ignition key to IGNITION. Place sidestand down. Odometer should read SideStand.
SideStand appears.
SideStand does not appear.
Turn ignition key to off. Raise sidestand. Turn ignition key to IGNITION.
Start engine with throttle partially open, then close throttle.
SideStand appears.
SideStand does not appear.
Engine stalls.
Engine does not stall.
Check for correct sidestand sensor installation. Refer to Side Stand Sensor in this Supplement.
Check for an open wire in neutral switch circuit.
Check IAC (Figure 30).
Perform Fuel Pressure Test as described in this Supplement.
(continued)

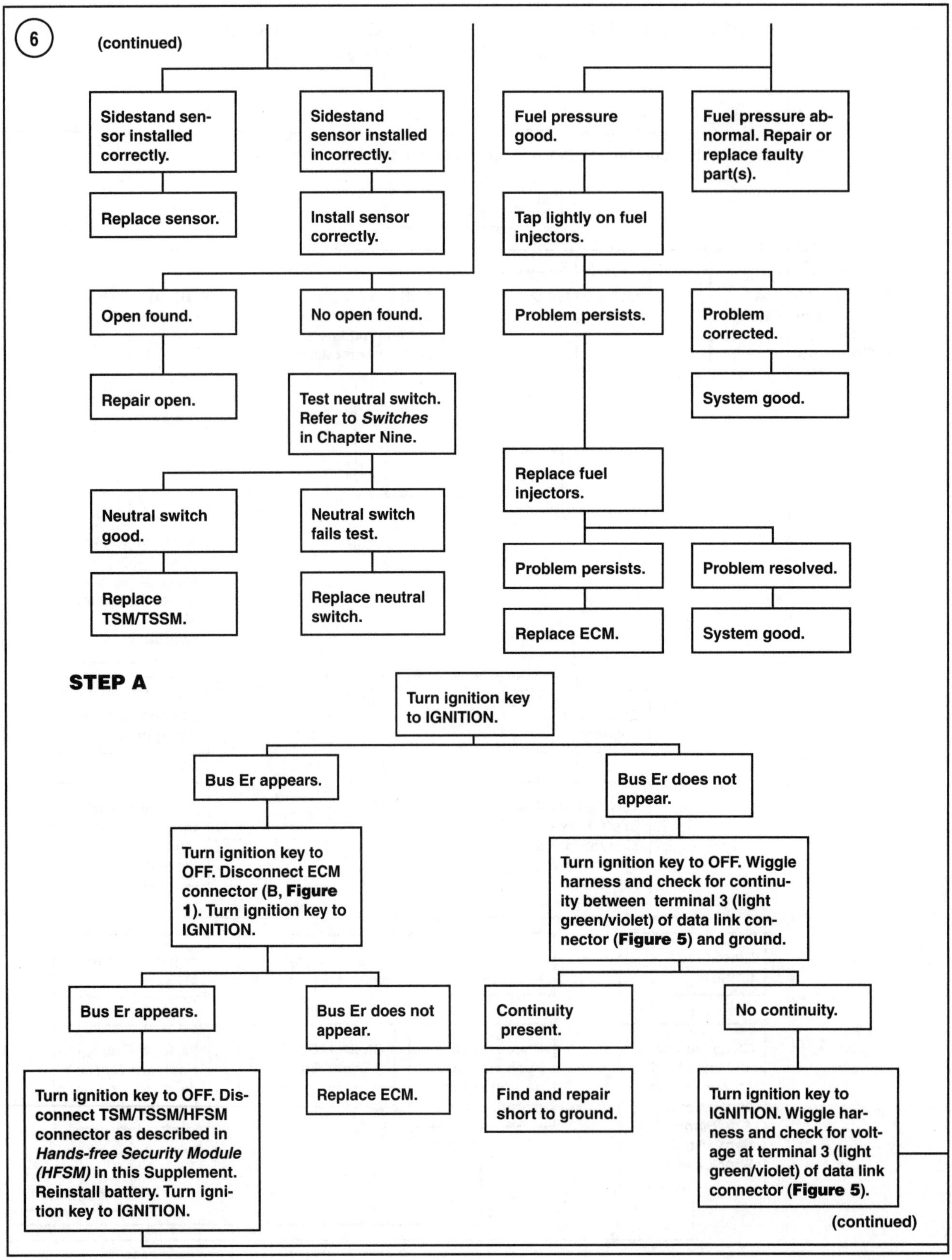
6
(continued)
Sidestand sensor installed correctly.
Replace sensor.
Sidestand sensor installed incorrectly.
Install sensor correctly.
Fuel pressure good.
Tap lightly on fuel injectors.
Fuel pressure abnormal. Repair or replace faulty part(s).
Open found.
Repair open.
No open found.
Test neutral switch. Refer to Switches in Chapter Nine.
Problem persists.
Problem corrected.
System good.
Replace fuel injectors.
Neutral switch good.
Replace TSM/TSSM.
Neutral switch fails test.
Replace neutral switch.
Problem persists.
Replace ECM.
Problem resolved.
System good.
STEP A
Turn ignition key to IGNITION.
Bus Er appears.
Turn ignition key to OFF. Disconnect ECM connector (B, Figure 1). Turn ignition key to IGNITION.
Bus Er does not appear.
Turn ignition key to OFF. Wiggle harness and check for continuity between terminal 3 (light green/violet) of data link connector (Figure 5) and ground.
Bus Er appears.
Turn ignition key to OFF. Disconnect TSM/TSSM/HFSM connector as described in Hands-free Security Module (HFSM) in this Supplement. Reinstall battery. Turn ignition key to IGNITION.
Bus Er does not appear.
Replace ECM.
Continuity present.
Find and repair short to ground.
No continuity.
Turn ignition key to IGNITION. Wiggle harness and check for voltage at terminal 3 (light green/violet) of data link connector (Figure 5).
(continued)

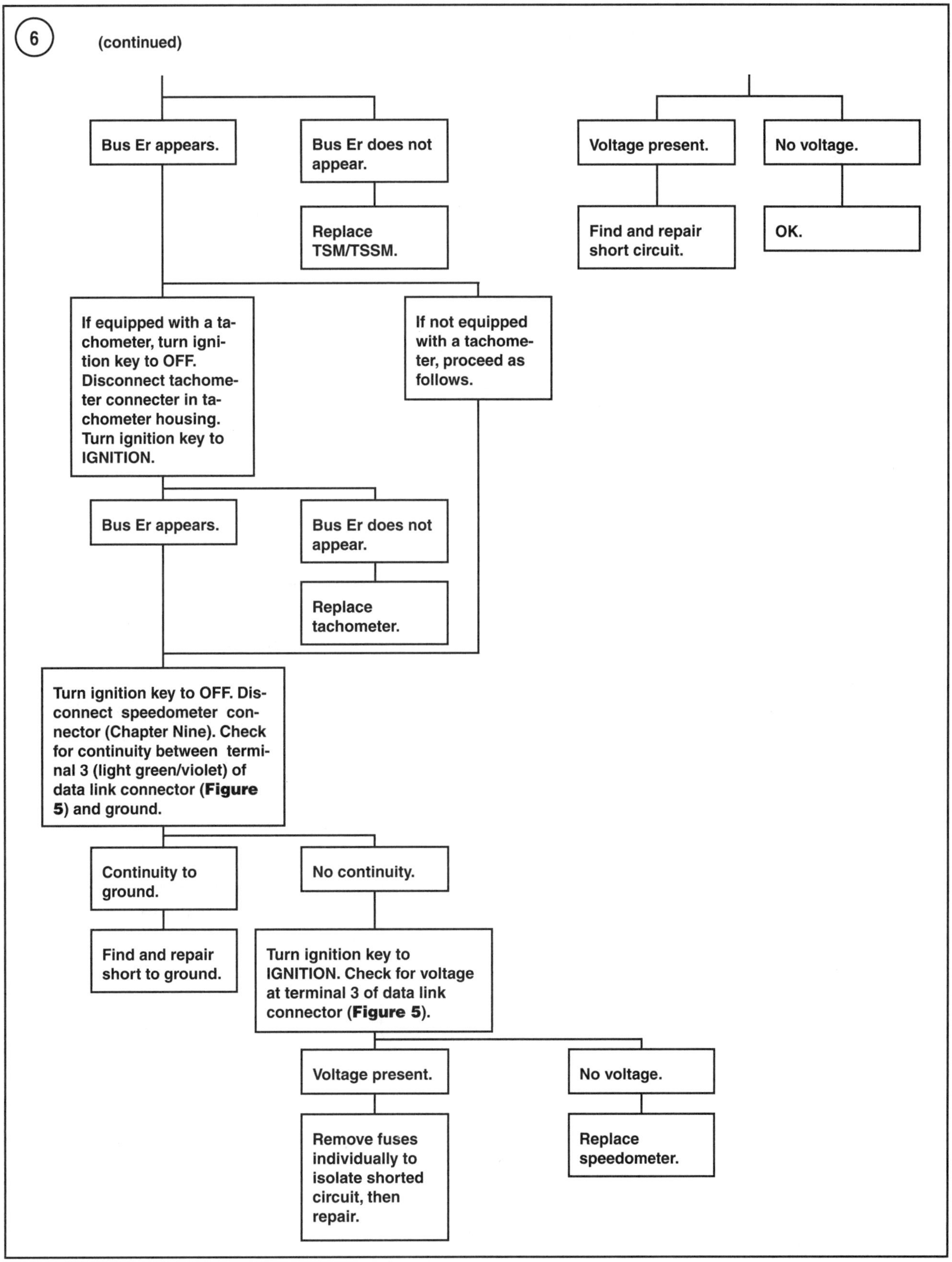
6
(continued)
Bus Er appears.
Bus Er does not appear.
Replace TSM/TSSM.
Voltage present.
No voltage.
Find and repair short circuit.
OK.
If equipped with a tachometer, turn ignition key to OFF. Disconnect tachometer connecter in tachometer housing. Turn ignition key to IGNITION.
If not equipped with a tachometer, proceed as follows.
Bus Er appears.
Bus Er does not appear.
Replace tachometer.
Turn ignition key to OFF. Disconnect speedometer connector (Chapter Nine). Check for continuity between terminal 3 (light green/violet) of data link connector (Figure 5) and ground.
Continuity to ground.
No continuity.
Find and repair short to ground.
Turn ignition key to IGNITION. Check for voltage at terminal 3 of data link connector (Figure 5).
Voltage present.
No voltage.
Remove fuses individually to isolate shorted circuit, then repair.
Replace speedometer.

7

DTC B1004: FUEL LEVEL SENDING UNIT LOW

Note:
If the fuel gauge is operating erratically, and possibly setting false DTCs, replace the fuel level resistor with a good unit and check operation.

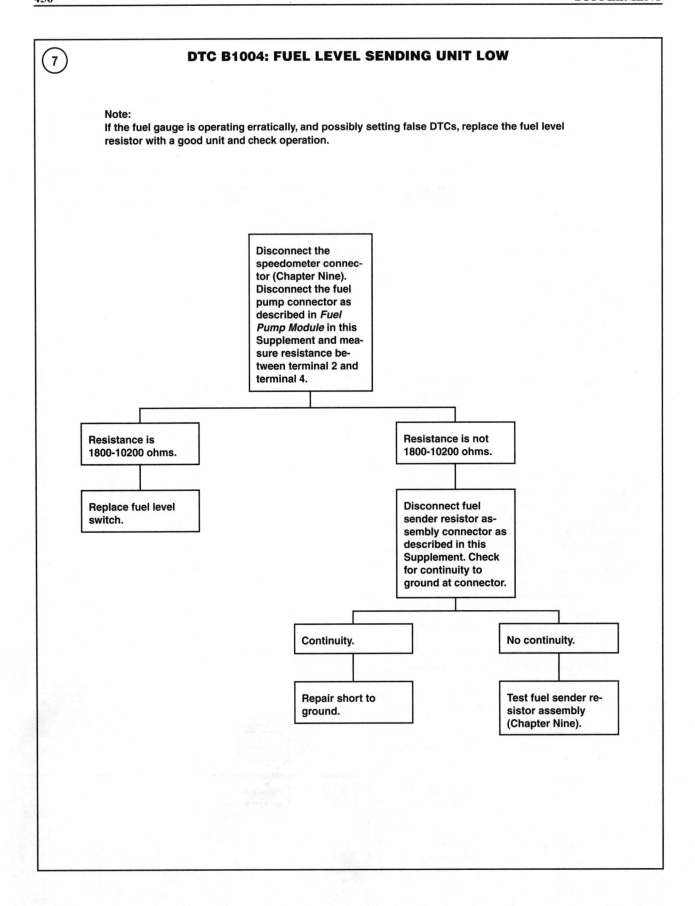

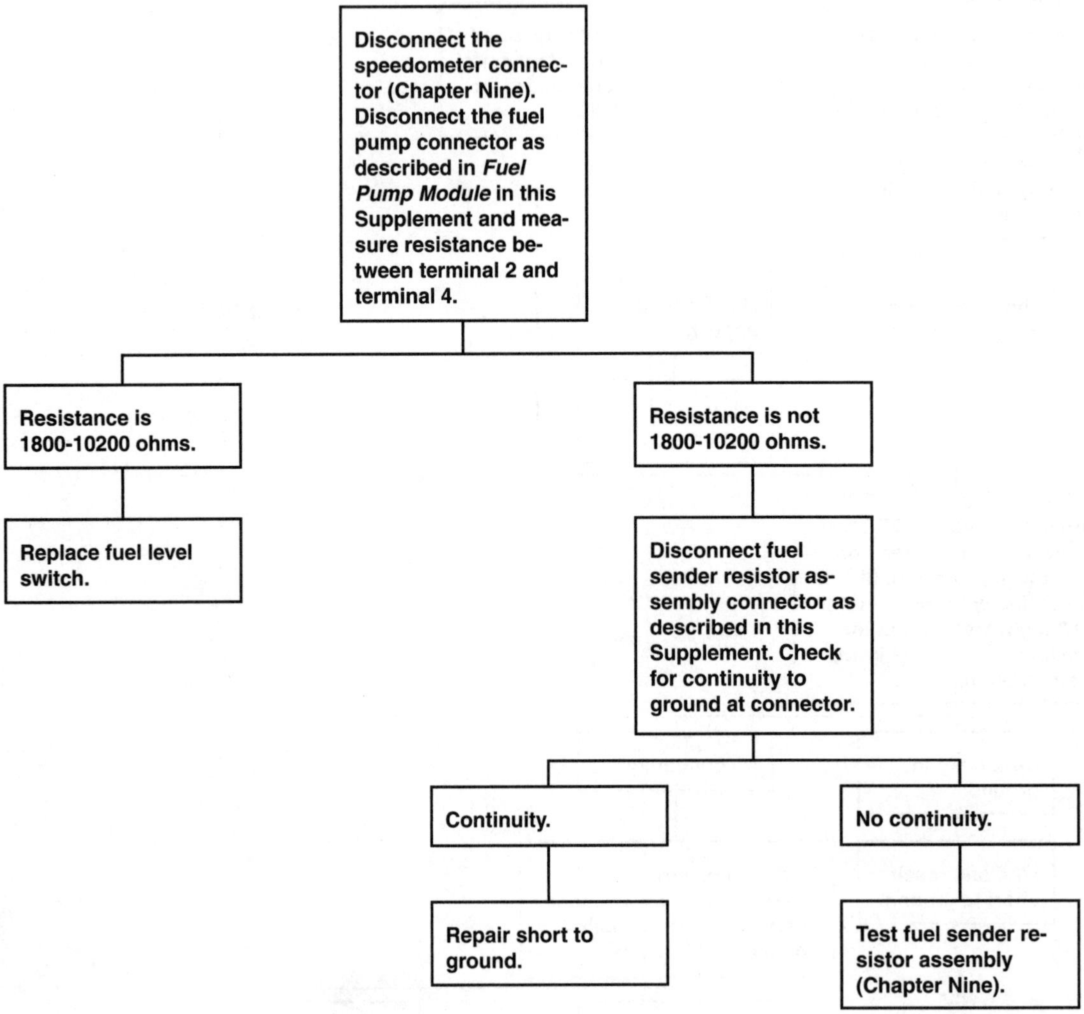
Disconnect the speedometer connector (Chapter Nine). Disconnect the fuel pump connector as described in *Fuel Pump Module* in this Supplement and measure resistance between terminal 2 and terminal 4.
Resistance is 1800-10200 ohms.
Replace fuel level switch.
Resistance is not 1800-10200 ohms.
Disconnect fuel sender resistor assembly connector as described in this Supplement. Check for continuity to ground at connector.
Continuity.
Repair short to ground.
No continuity.
Test fuel sender resistor assembly (Chapter Nine).

8

DTC B1005: FUEL LEVEL SENDING UNIT HIGH/OPEN

Note:
If the fuel gauge is operating erratically, and possibly setting false DTCs, replace the fuel level resistor with a good unit and check operation.

Disconnect speedometer connector (Chapter Nine). Disconnect fuel pump connector as described in *Fuel Pump Module* in this Supplement and measure voltage at terminal 2 (yellow/white) on the connector.

- **Voltage is zero volts.**
  - **Install breakout box HD-42682 between speedometer and wiring harness. Check continuity between terminal 2 (yellow/white) on fuel pump connector and breakout box black terminal 11.**
    - **Continuity present.**
      - **Check continuity between ground and terminal 4 (black) on the fuel pump.**
        - **Continuity present.**
          - **Test fuel sender resistor assembly as described in this Supplement.**
        - **No continuity.**
          - **Repair open.**
    - **No continuity.**
      - **Repair open.**
- **Voltage is not zero volts.**
  - **Repair short.**

9 DTC B1006, B1007: ACCESSORY OR IGNITION LINE OVERVOLTAGE

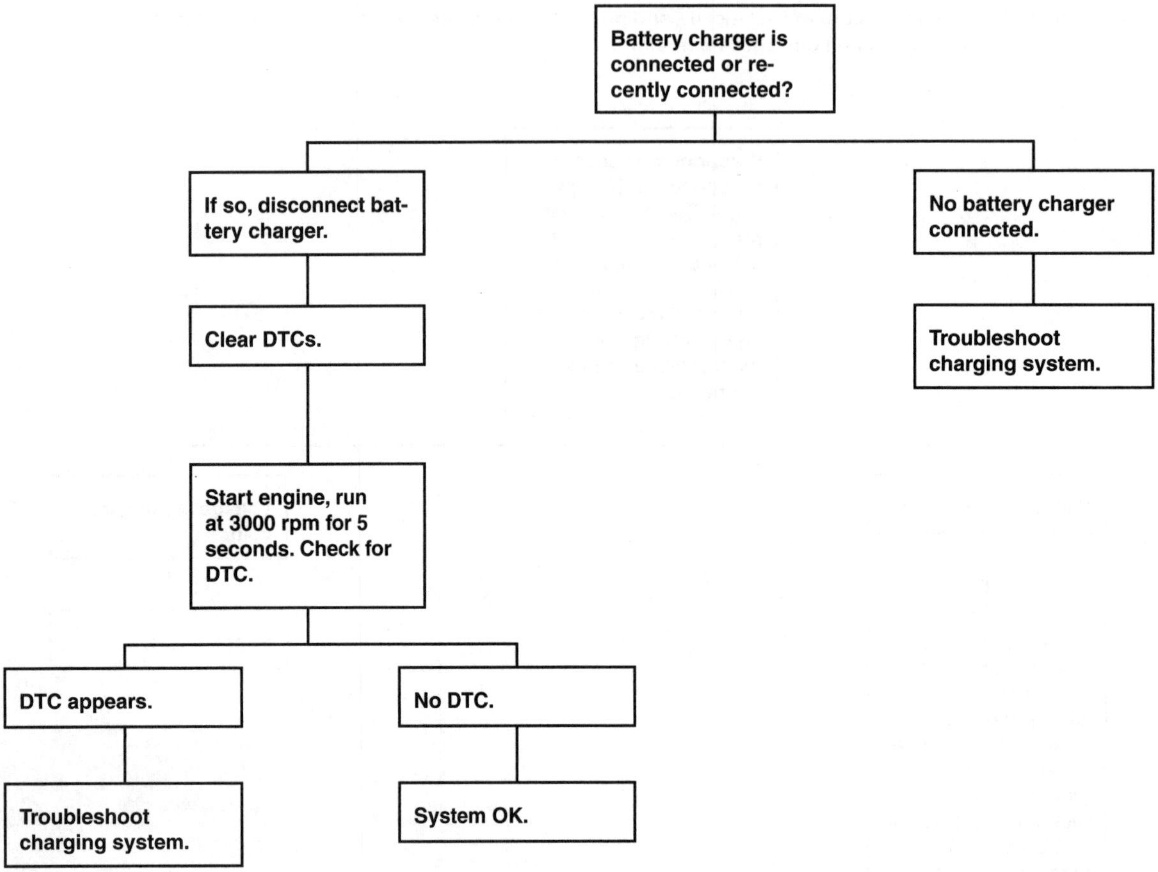

10

DTC B1008: RESET SWITCH CLOSED

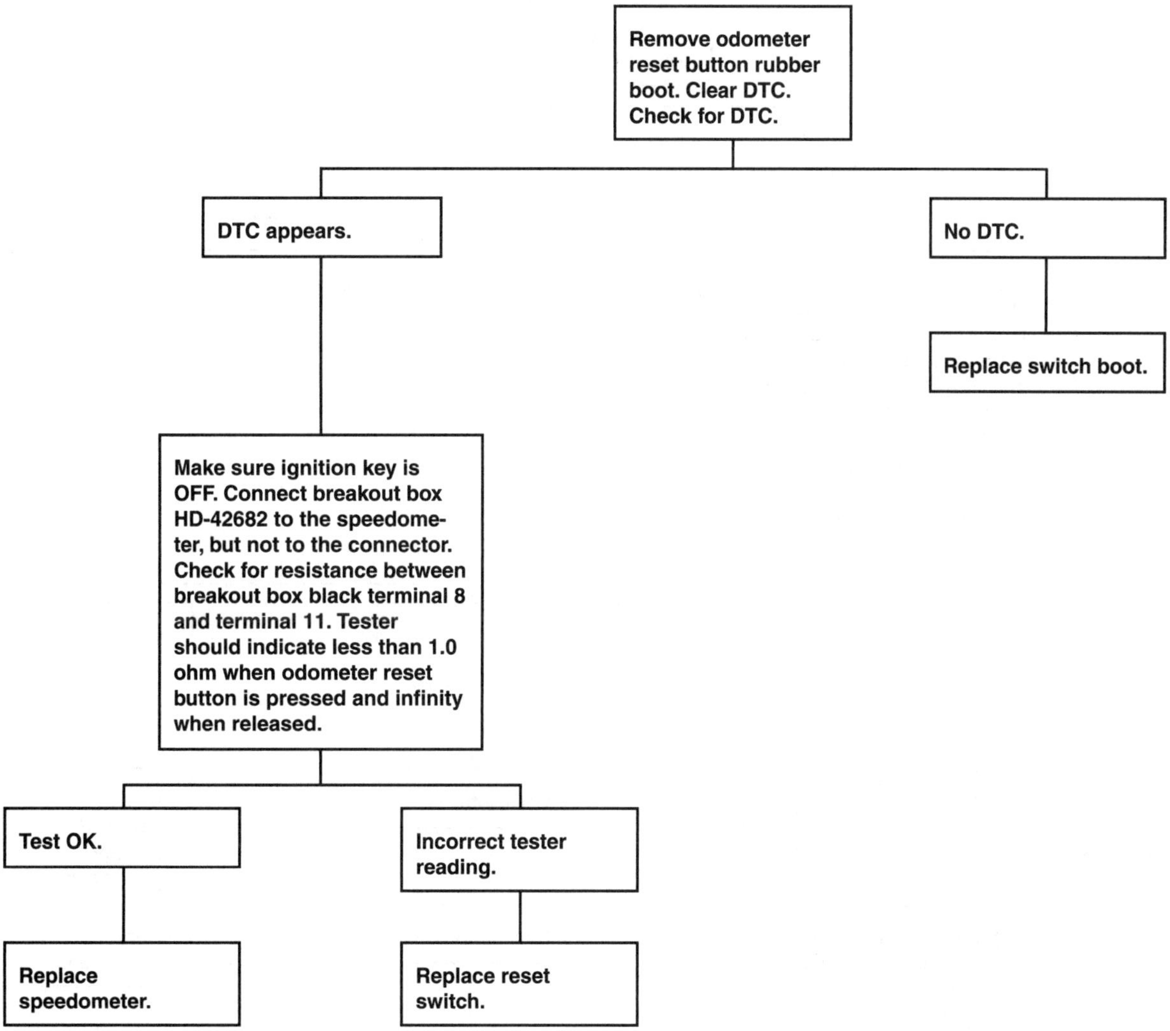
Remove odometer reset button rubber boot. Clear DTC. Check for DTC.
DTC appears.
No DTC.
Replace switch boot.
Make sure ignition key is OFF. Connect breakout box HD-42682 to the speedometer, but not to the connector. Check for resistance between breakout box black terminal 8 and terminal 11. Tester should indicate less than 1.0 ohm when odometer reset button is pressed and infinity when released.
Test OK.
Incorrect tester reading.
Replace speedometer.
Replace reset switch.

11

DTC B1121, B1122, B1141: TURN SIGNALS WILL NOT FLASH, 4-WAY FLASHERS INOPERABLE

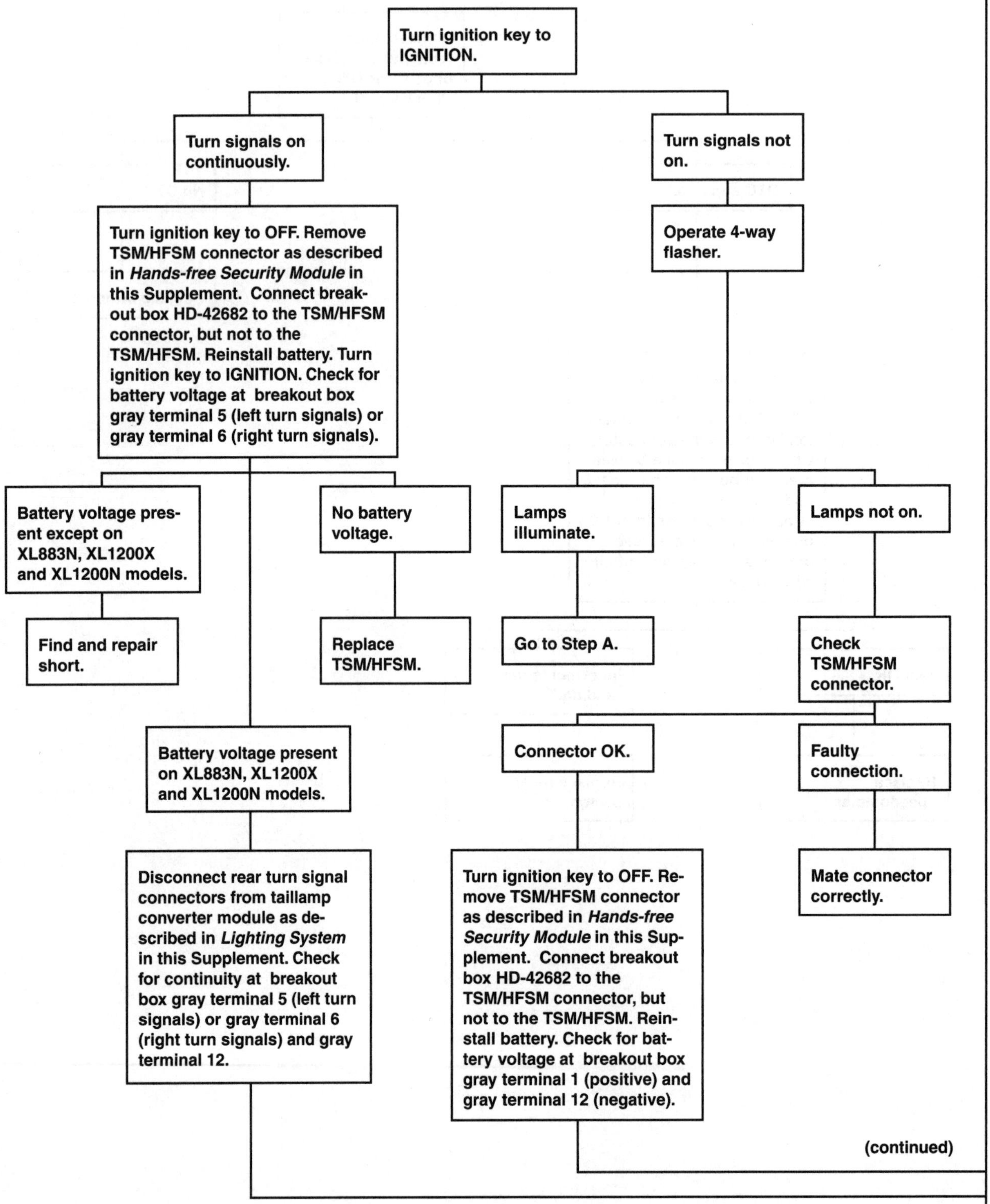
Turn ignition key to IGNITION.
Turn signals on continuously.
Turn signals not on.
Turn ignition key to OFF. Remove TSM/HFSM connector as described in *Hands-free Security Module* in this Supplement. Connect break-out box HD-42682 to the TSM/HFSM connector, but not to the TSM/HFSM. Reinstall battery. Turn ignition key to IGNITION. Check for battery voltage at breakout box gray terminal 5 (left turn signals) or gray terminal 6 (right turn signals).
Operate 4-way flasher.
Battery voltage present except on XL883N, XL1200X and XL1200N models.
No battery voltage.
Lamps illuminate.
Lamps not on.
Find and repair short.
Replace TSM/HFSM.
Go to Step A.
Check TSM/HFSM connector.
Battery voltage present on XL883N, XL1200X and XL1200N models.
Connector OK.
Faulty connection.
Disconnect rear turn signal connectors from taillamp converter module as described in *Lighting System* in this Supplement. Check for continuity at breakout box gray terminal 5 (left turn signals) or gray terminal 6 (right turn signals) and gray terminal 12.
Turn ignition key to OFF. Remove TSM/HFSM connector as described in *Hands-free Security Module* in this Supplement. Connect breakout box HD-42682 to the TSM/HFSM connector, but not to the TSM/HFSM. Reinstall battery. Check for battery voltage at breakout box gray terminal 1 (positive) and gray terminal 12 (negative).
Mate connector correctly.

(continued)

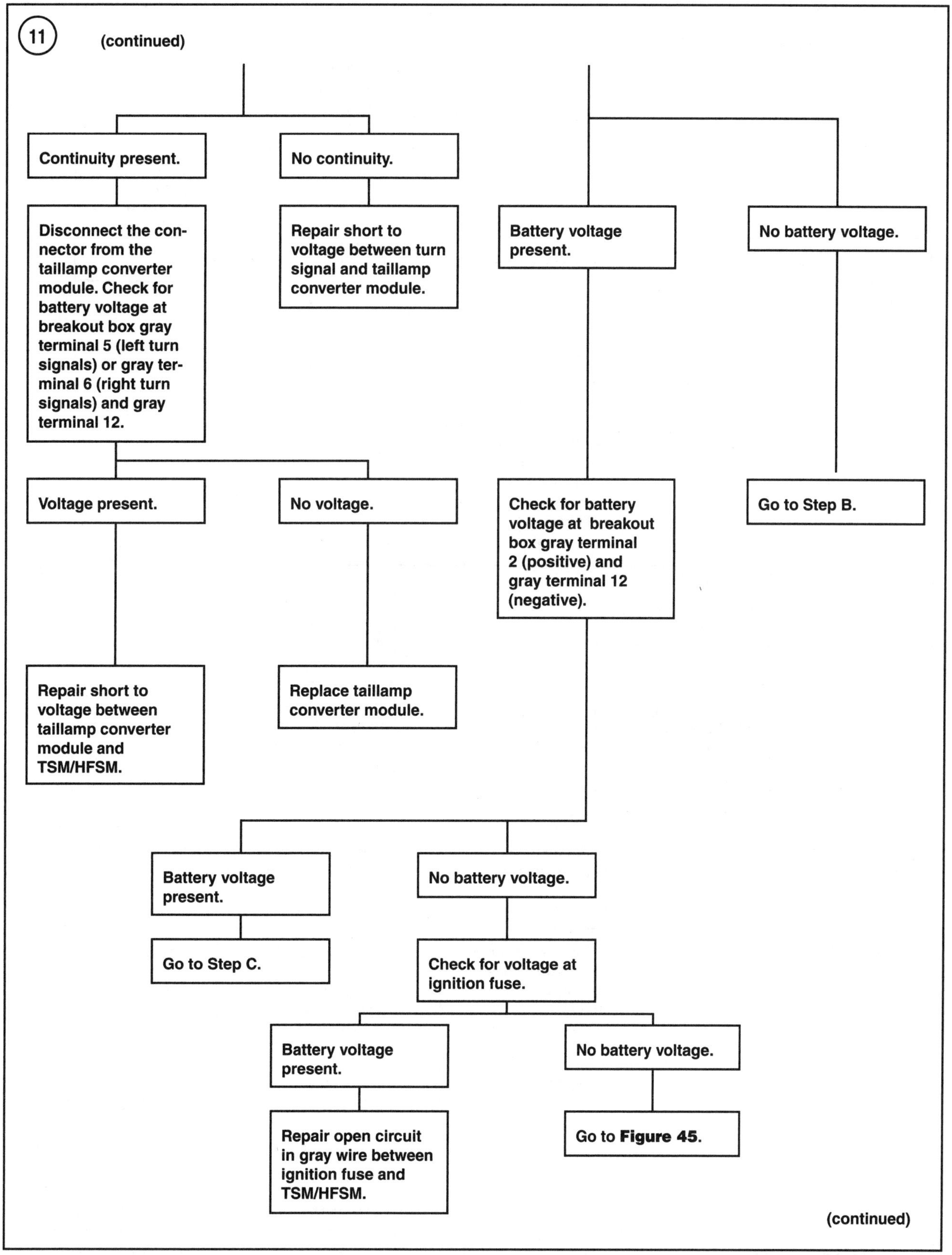
11
(continued)
Continuity present.
No continuity.
Disconnect the connector from the taillamp converter module. Check for battery voltage at breakout box gray terminal 5 (left turn signals) or gray terminal 6 (right turn signals) and gray terminal 12.
Repair short to voltage between turn signal and taillamp converter module.
Battery voltage present.
No battery voltage.
Voltage present.
No voltage.
Check for battery voltage at breakout box gray terminal 2 (positive) and gray terminal 12 (negative).
Go to Step B.
Repair short to voltage between taillamp converter module and TSM/HFSM.
Replace taillamp converter module.
Battery voltage present.
No battery voltage.
Go to Step C.
Check for voltage at ignition fuse.
Battery voltage present.
No battery voltage.
Repair open circuit in gray wire between ignition fuse and TSM/HFSM.
Go to Figure 45.
(continued)

15

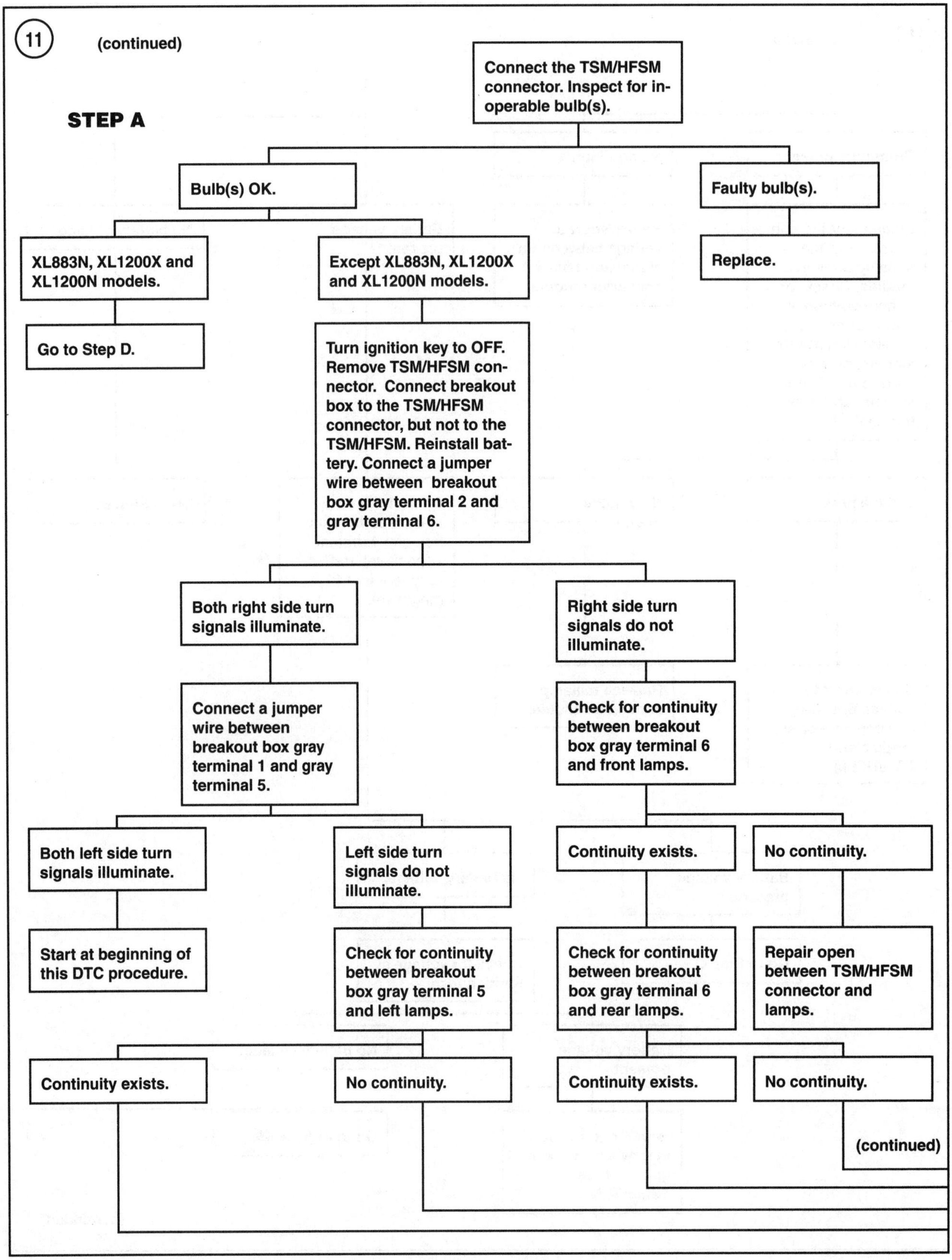
11
(continued)
STEP A
Connect the TSM/HFSM connector. Inspect for inoperable bulb(s).
Bulb(s) OK.
Faulty bulb(s).
Replace.
XL883N, XL1200X and XL1200N models.
Go to Step D.
Except XL883N, XL1200X and XL1200N models.
Turn ignition key to OFF. Remove TSM/HFSM connector. Connect breakout box to the TSM/HFSM connector, but not to the TSM/HFSM. Reinstall battery. Connect a jumper wire between breakout box gray terminal 2 and gray terminal 6.
Both right side turn signals illuminate.
Right side turn signals do not illuminate.
Connect a jumper wire between breakout box gray terminal 1 and gray terminal 5.
Check for continuity between breakout box gray terminal 6 and front lamps.
Both left side turn signals illuminate.
Left side turn signals do not illuminate.
Continuity exists.
No continuity.
Start at beginning of this DTC procedure.
Check for continuity between breakout box gray terminal 5 and left lamps.
Check for continuity between breakout box gray terminal 6 and rear lamps.
Repair open between TSM/HFSM connector and lamps.
Continuity exists.
No continuity.
Continuity exists.
No continuity.
(continued)

(11) (continued)

Check for continuity between breakout box gray terminal 5 and rear lamps.

- Continuity exists.
  - Replace TSM/HFSM.
- No continuity.
  - XL883N, XL1200X and XL1200N models.
    - Disconnect the rear turn signal connectors from the taillamp converter module as described in *Lighting System* in this Supplement. Check for continuity between breakout box gray terminal 5 and left lamp terminal 2 (violet) on the module connector. Check for continuity between the ground and right lamp terminal 2 (violet) on module connector.
  - Except XL883N, XL1200X and XL1200N models.
    - Repair open between TSM/HFSM connector and lamps.

Repair open between TSM/HFSM connector and lamps.

Replace TSM/HFSM.

- Model XL1200N.
  - Disconnect the rear turn signal connectors from the taillamp converter module as described in *Lighting System* in this Supplement. Check for continuity between breakout box gray terminal 6 and right lamp terminal 2 (violet) on the module connector. Check for continuity between the ground and right lamp terminal 2 (violet) on module connector.
    - Continuity exists.
      - Repair open between rear lamp and connector.
    - No continuity.
      - Disconnect the connector from the taillamp converter module. Check for continuity between the breakout box gray terminal 6 and terminal 2 (brown) of the main harness connector for the module. Check for continuity between ground and terminal 2 of the main harness connector for taillight module.
- Except Model XL1200N.
  - Repair open between TSM/HFSM connector and lamps.

(continued)

15

(11) (continued)

Continuity exists.

Repair open between rear lamp and connector.

No continuity.

Disconnect the connector from the taillamp converter module. Check for continuity between breakout box gray terminal 5 and terminal 6 (black) of main harness connector for the module. Check for continuity between ground and terminal 5 (violet) of the main harness connector for the module.

Continuity exists.

Replace taillamp converter module.

No continuity.

Repair open circuit.

Continuity exists.

Replace taillamp converter module.

No continuity.

Repair open circuit.

STEP B

Turn ignition key to OFF. Remove TSM/HFSM connector as described in *Hands-free Security Module (HSFM)* in this Supplement (Chapter Nine). Connect the breakout box to the TSM/HFSM connector, but not to the TSM/HFSM. Reinstall battery. Check resistance between breakout box gray terminal 12 and ground.

Resistance less than 1.0 ohm.

Resistance greater than 1.0 ohm.

(continued)

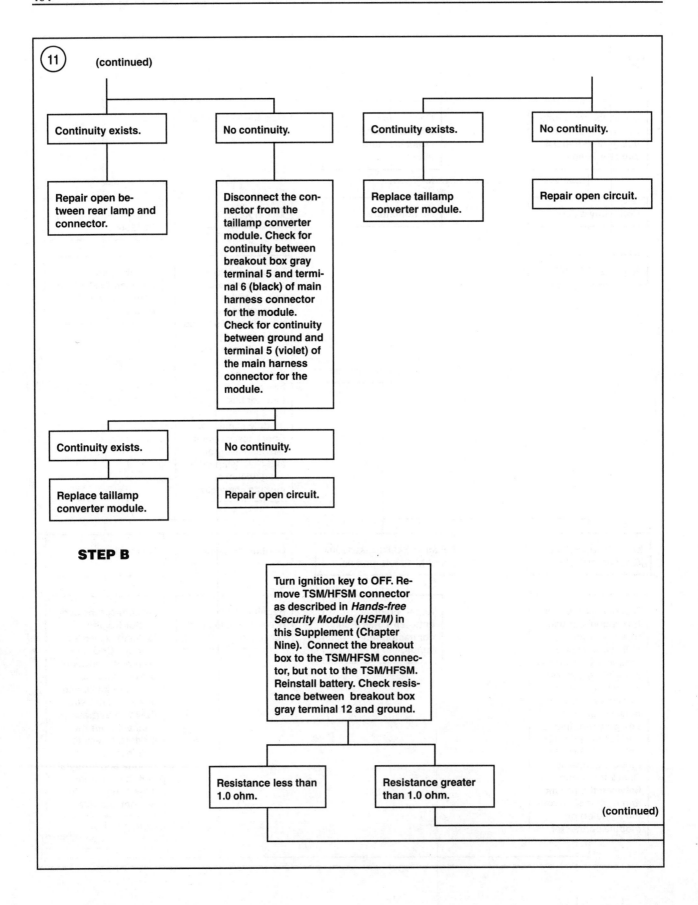

11 (continued)

Check for battery voltage at both 15 amp battery fuse terminals. Refer to *Fuses* in this Supplement.

Repair ground circuit.

Voltage present at both terminals.

Repair open in brown/gray wire between TSM/HFSM and battery fuse.

No voltage.

Voltage present at one terminal.

Replace fuse.

No voltage at either terminal.

Repair open circuit between fuse block and 30 amp Maxi-fuse.

STEP C

Turn ignition key to OFF. Remove the TSM/HFSM connector as described in *Hands-free Security Module (HFSM)* in this Supplement. Connect the breakout box to the TSM/HFSM and connector. Reinstall battery. Turn ignition key to IGNITION. Check for battery voltage at breakout box gray terminal 7 when right turn signal button is depressed. Check for battery voltage at breakout box gray terminal 8 when left turn signal button is depressed.

Battery voltage present.

Replace TSM/HFSM.

No voltage.

Turn ignition key to IGNITION. Check for battery voltage at orange/white wire terminal on switch connector at left and right handlebar switch.

(continued)

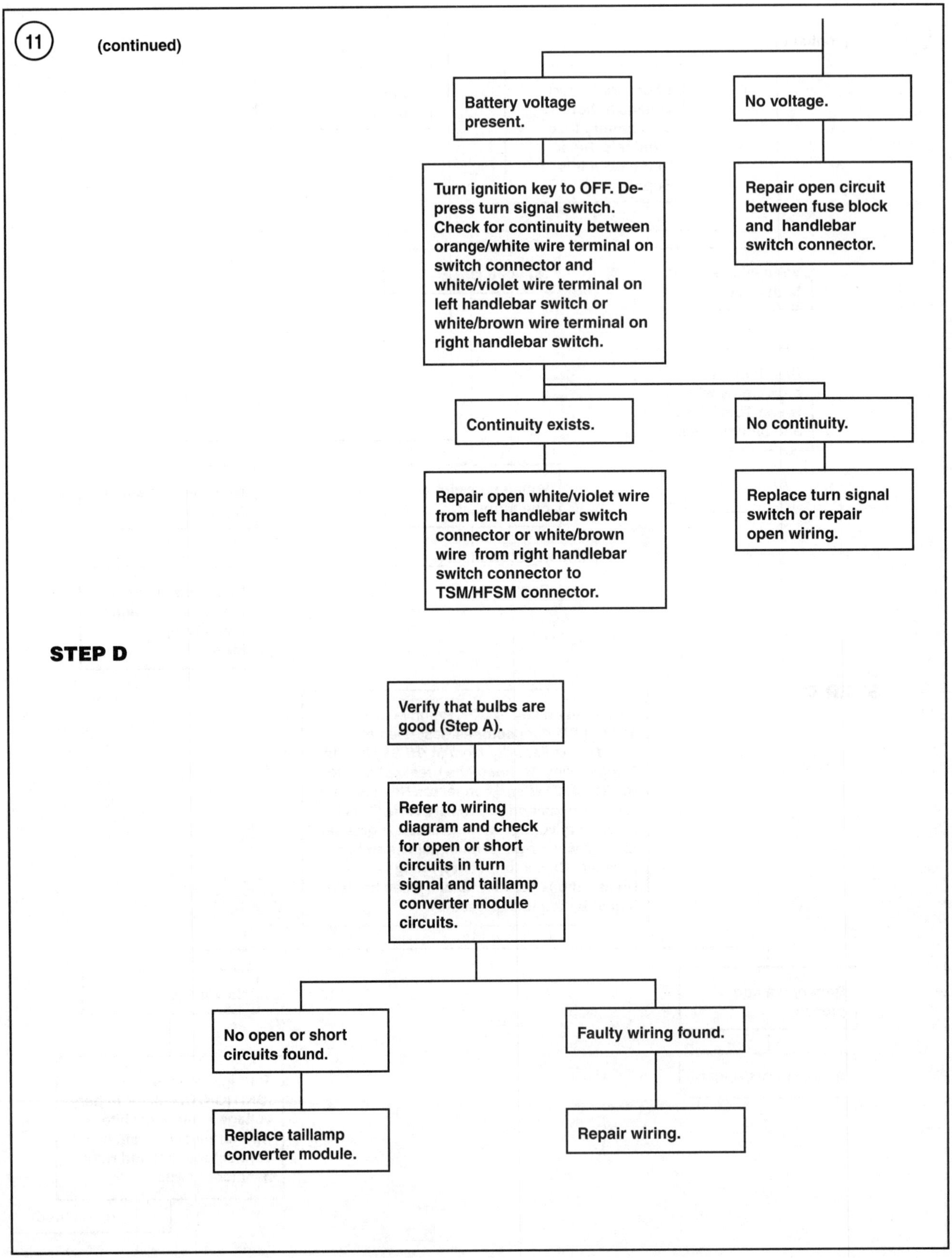
11
(continued)
Battery voltage present.
No voltage.
Turn ignition key to OFF. Depress turn signal switch. Check for continuity between orange/white wire terminal on switch connector and white/violet wire terminal on left handlebar switch or white/brown wire terminal on right handlebar switch.
Repair open circuit between fuse block and handlebar switch connector.
Continuity exists.
No continuity.
Repair open white/violet wire from left handlebar switch connector or white/brown wire from right handlebar switch connector to TSM/HFSM connector.
Replace turn signal switch or repair open wiring.
STEP D
Verify that bulbs are good (Step A).
Refer to wiring diagram and check for open or short circuits in turn signal and taillamp converter module circuits.
No open or short circuits found.
Faulty wiring found.
Replace taillamp converter module.
Repair wiring.

12

DTC B1123, B1124: TURN SIGNAL LAMP SHORT-TO-GROUND

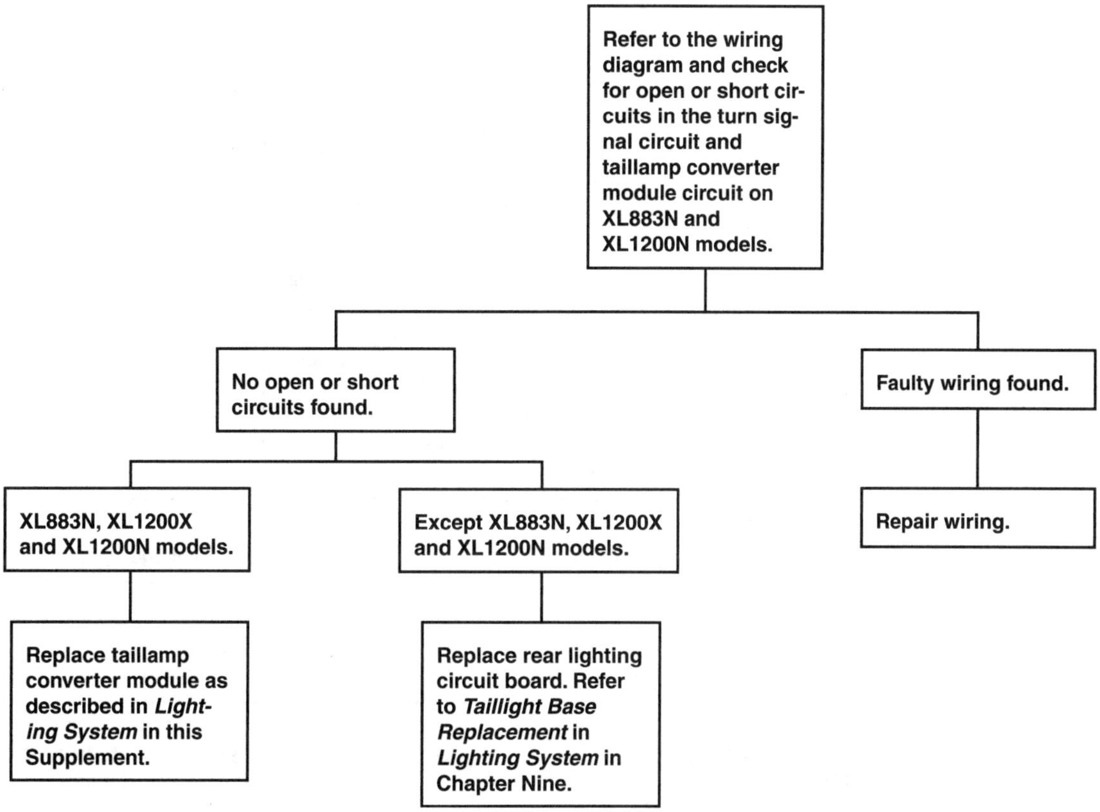
Refer to the wiring diagram and check for open or short circuits in the turn signal circuit and taillamp converter module circuit on XL883N and XL1200N models.
No open or short circuits found.
Faulty wiring found.
XL883N, XL1200X and XL1200N models.
Except XL883N, XL1200X and XL1200N models.
Repair wiring.
Replace taillamp converter module as described in *Lighting System* in this Supplement.
Replace rear lighting circuit board. Refer to *Taillight Base Replacement* in *Lighting System* in Chapter Nine.

(13)

DTC B1125, B1126: TURN SIGNAL LAMP SHORT-TO-VOLTAGE

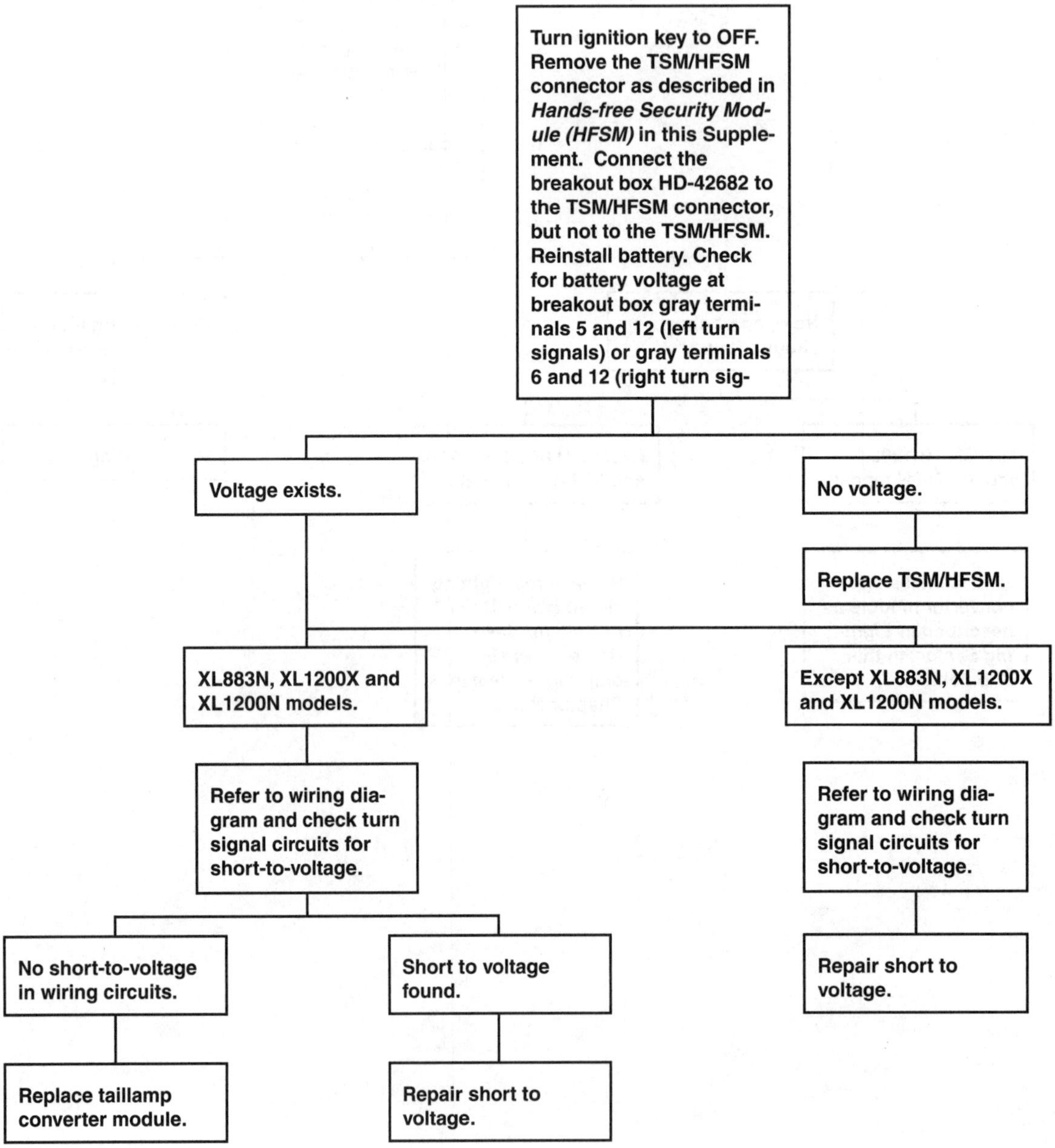

Turn ignition key to OFF. Remove the TSM/HFSM connector as described in *Hands-free Security Module (HFSM)* in this Supplement. Connect the breakout box HD-42682 to the TSM/HFSM connector, but not to the TSM/HFSM. Reinstall battery. Check for battery voltage at breakout box gray terminals 5 and 12 (left turn signals) or gray terminals 6 and 12 (right turn sig-
Voltage exists.
No voltage.
Replace TSM/HFSM.
XL883N, XL1200X and XL1200N models.
Except XL883N, XL1200X and XL1200N models.
Refer to wiring diagram and check turn signal circuits for short-to-voltage.
Refer to wiring diagram and check turn signal circuits for short-to-voltage.
No short-to-voltage in wiring circuits.
Short to voltage found.
Repair short to voltage.
Replace taillamp converter module.
Repair short to voltage.

(14)

DTC B1131, B1132: ALARM OUTPUT

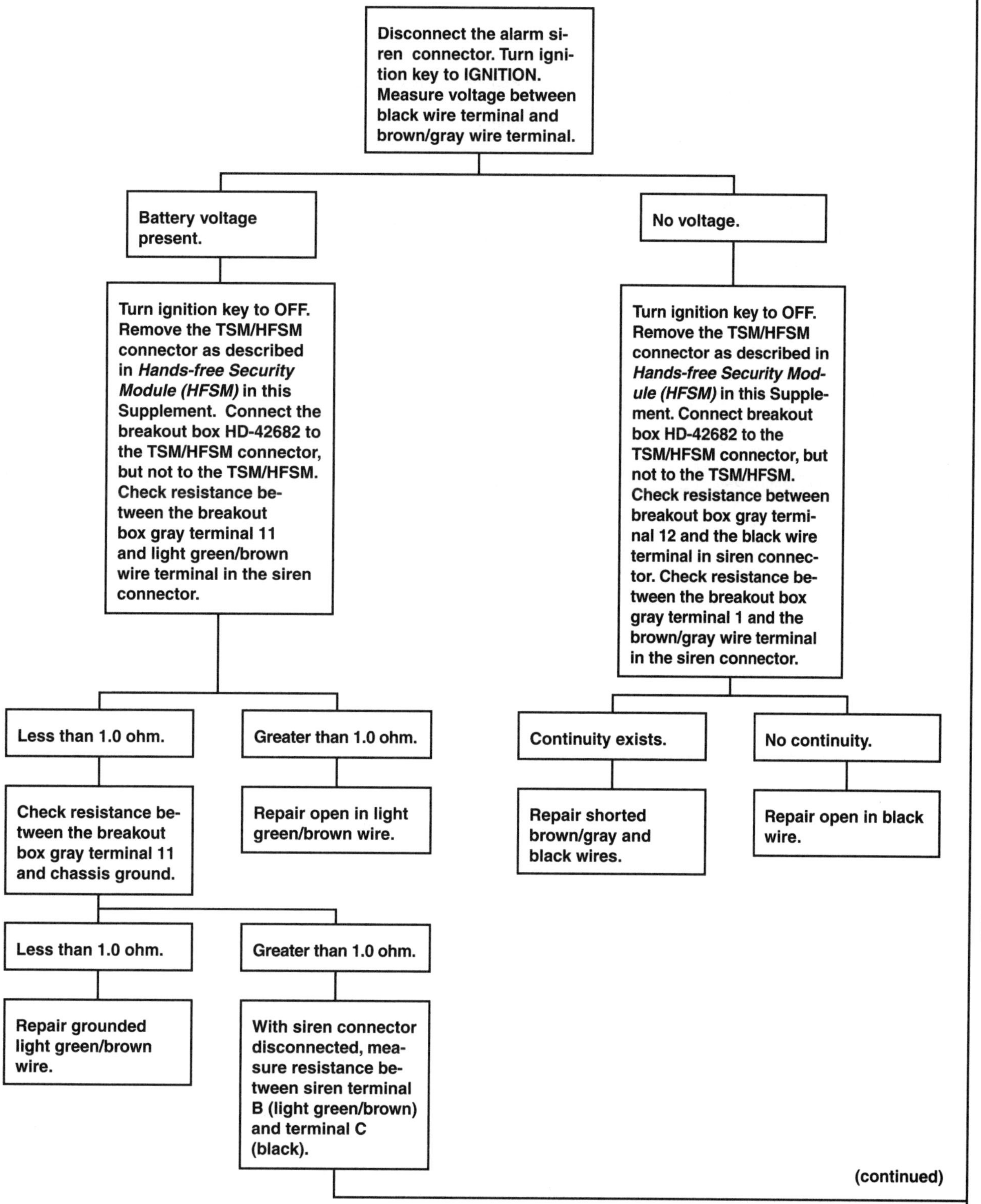

Disconnect the alarm siren connector. Turn ignition key to IGNITION. Measure voltage between black wire terminal and brown/gray wire terminal.
Battery voltage present.
No voltage.
Turn ignition key to OFF. Remove the TSM/HFSM connector as described in *Hands-free Security Module (HFSM)* in this Supplement. Connect the breakout box HD-42682 to the TSM/HFSM connector, but not to the TSM/HFSM. Check resistance between the breakout box gray terminal 11 and light green/brown wire terminal in the siren connector.
Turn ignition key to OFF. Remove the TSM/HFSM connector as described in *Hands-free Security Module (HFSM)* in this Supplement. Connect breakout box HD-42682 to the TSM/HFSM connector, but not to the TSM/HFSM. Check resistance between breakout box gray terminal 12 and the black wire terminal in siren connector. Check resistance between the breakout box gray terminal 1 and the brown/gray wire terminal in the siren connector.
Less than 1.0 ohm.
Greater than 1.0 ohm.
Continuity exists.
No continuity.
Check resistance between the breakout box gray terminal 11 and chassis ground.
Repair open in light green/brown wire.
Repair shorted brown/gray and black wires.
Repair open in black wire.
Less than 1.0 ohm.
Greater than 1.0 ohm.
Repair grounded light green/brown wire.
With siren connector disconnected, measure resistance between siren terminal B (light green/brown) and terminal C (black).

(continued)

15

14 (continued)

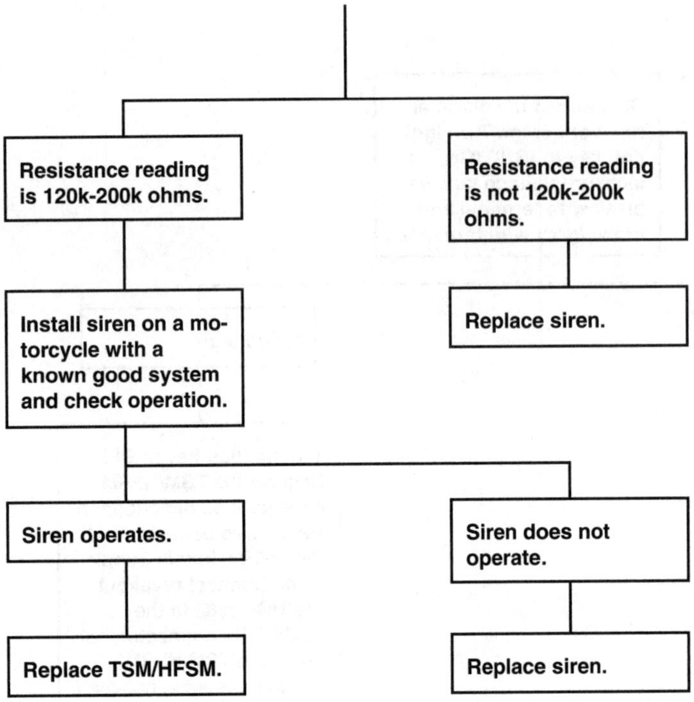
Resistance reading is 120k-200k ohms.
Resistance reading is not 120k-200k ohms.
Replace siren.
Install siren on a motorcycle with a known good system and check operation.
Siren operates.
Siren does not operate.
Replace TSM/HFSM.
Replace siren.

15

DTC B1134: STARTER OUTPUT HIGH

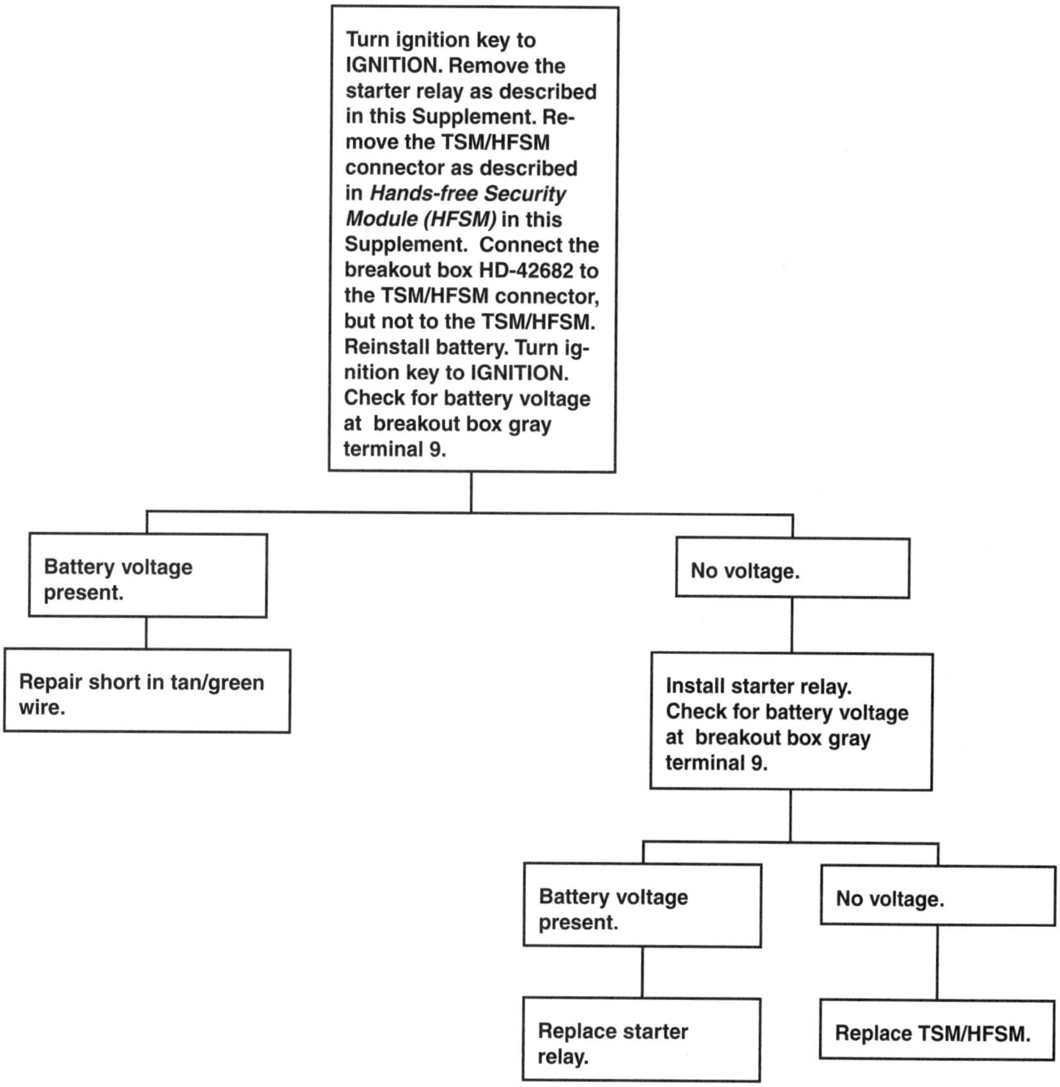
Turn ignition key to IGNITION. Remove the starter relay as described in this Supplement. Remove the TSM/HFSM connector as described in *Hands-free Security Module (HFSM)* in this Supplement. Connect the breakout box HD-42682 to the TSM/HFSM connector, but not to the TSM/HFSM. Reinstall battery. Turn ignition key to IGNITION. Check for battery voltage at breakout box gray terminal 9.
Battery voltage present.
Repair short in tan/green wire.
No voltage.
Install starter relay. Check for battery voltage at breakout box gray terminal 9.
Battery voltage present.
Replace starter relay.
No voltage.
Replace TSM/HFSM.

16

DTC B1141: IGNITION SWITCH OPEN/LOW (EQUIPPED WITH HFSM)

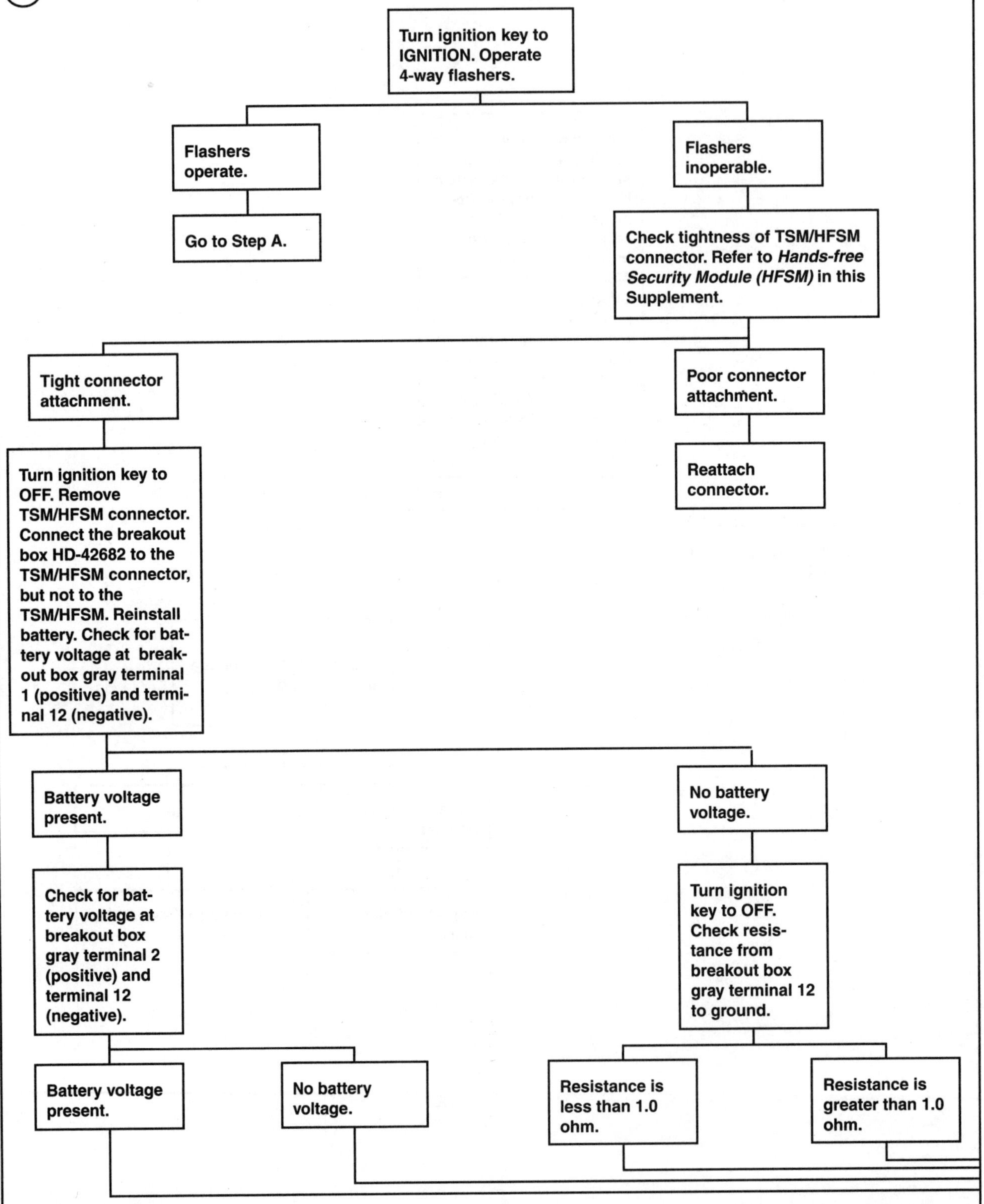
Turn ignition key to IGNITION. Operate 4-way flashers.
Flashers operate.
Go to Step A.
Flashers inoperable.
Check tightness of TSM/HFSM connector. Refer to *Hands-free Security Module (HFSM)* in this Supplement.
Tight connector attachment.
Poor connector attachment.
Reattach connector.
Turn ignition key to OFF. Remove TSM/HFSM connector. Connect the breakout box HD-42682 to the TSM/HFSM connector, but not to the TSM/HFSM. Reinstall battery. Check for battery voltage at breakout box gray terminal 1 (positive) and terminal 12 (negative).
Battery voltage present.
No battery voltage.
Check for battery voltage at breakout box gray terminal 2 (positive) and terminal 12 (negative).
Turn ignition key to OFF. Check resistance from breakout box gray terminal 12 to ground.
Battery voltage present.
No battery voltage.
Resistance is less than 1.0 ohm.
Resistance is greater than 1.0 ohm.

(continued)

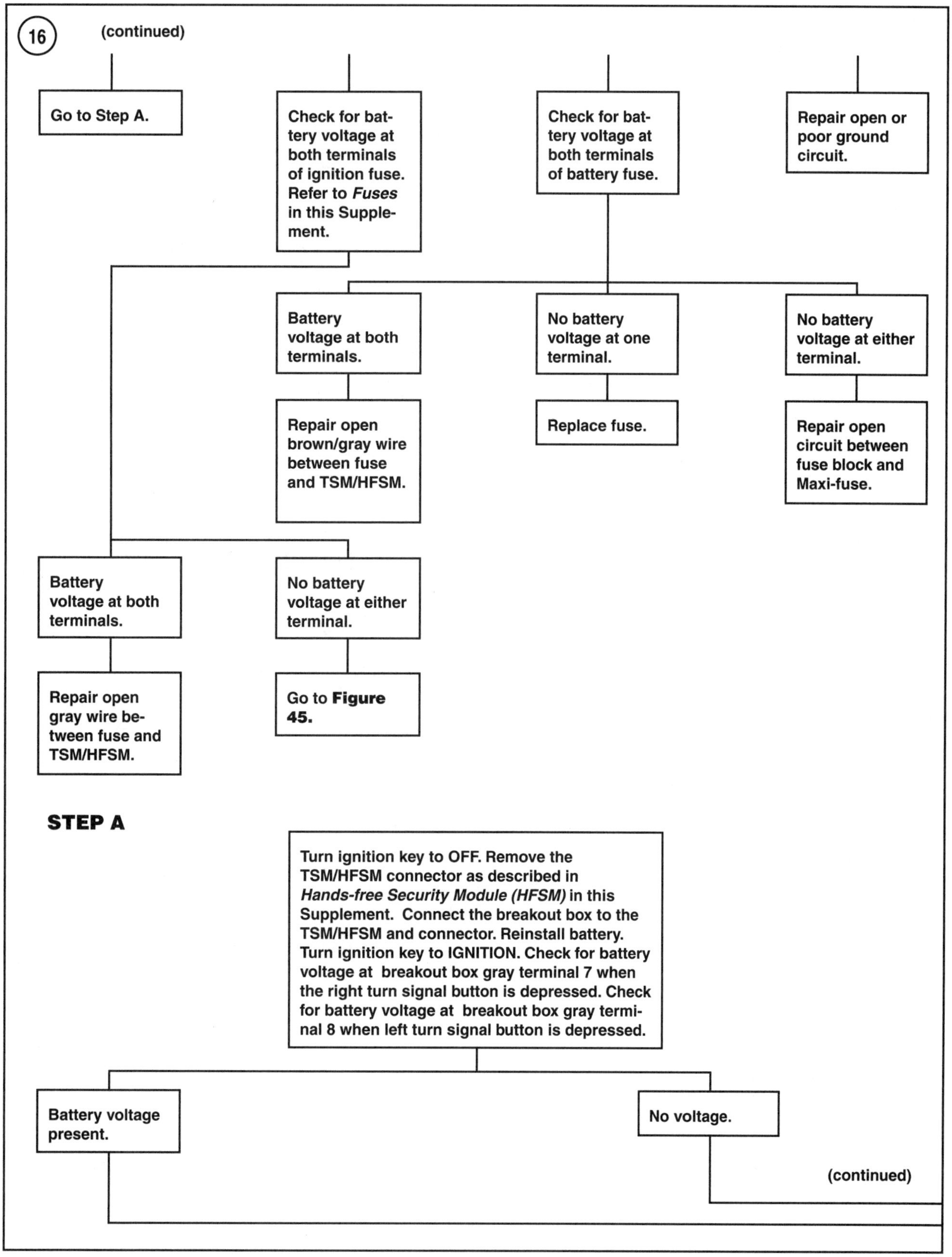
16
(continued)
Go to Step A.
Check for battery voltage at both terminals of ignition fuse. Refer to *Fuses* in this Supplement.
Check for battery voltage at both terminals of battery fuse.
Repair open or poor ground circuit.
Battery voltage at both terminals.
No battery voltage at one terminal.
No battery voltage at either terminal.
Repair open brown/gray wire between fuse and TSM/HFSM.
Replace fuse.
Repair open circuit between fuse block and Maxi-fuse.
Battery voltage at both terminals.
No battery voltage at either terminal.
Repair open gray wire between fuse and TSM/HFSM.
Go to **Figure 45.**
STEP A
Turn ignition key to OFF. Remove the TSM/HFSM connector as described in *Hands-free Security Module (HFSM)* in this Supplement. Connect the breakout box to the TSM/HFSM and connector. Reinstall battery. Turn ignition key to IGNITION. Check for battery voltage at breakout box gray terminal 7 when the right turn signal button is depressed. Check for battery voltage at breakout box gray terminal 8 when left turn signal button is depressed.
Battery voltage present.
No voltage.
(continued)

16 (continued)

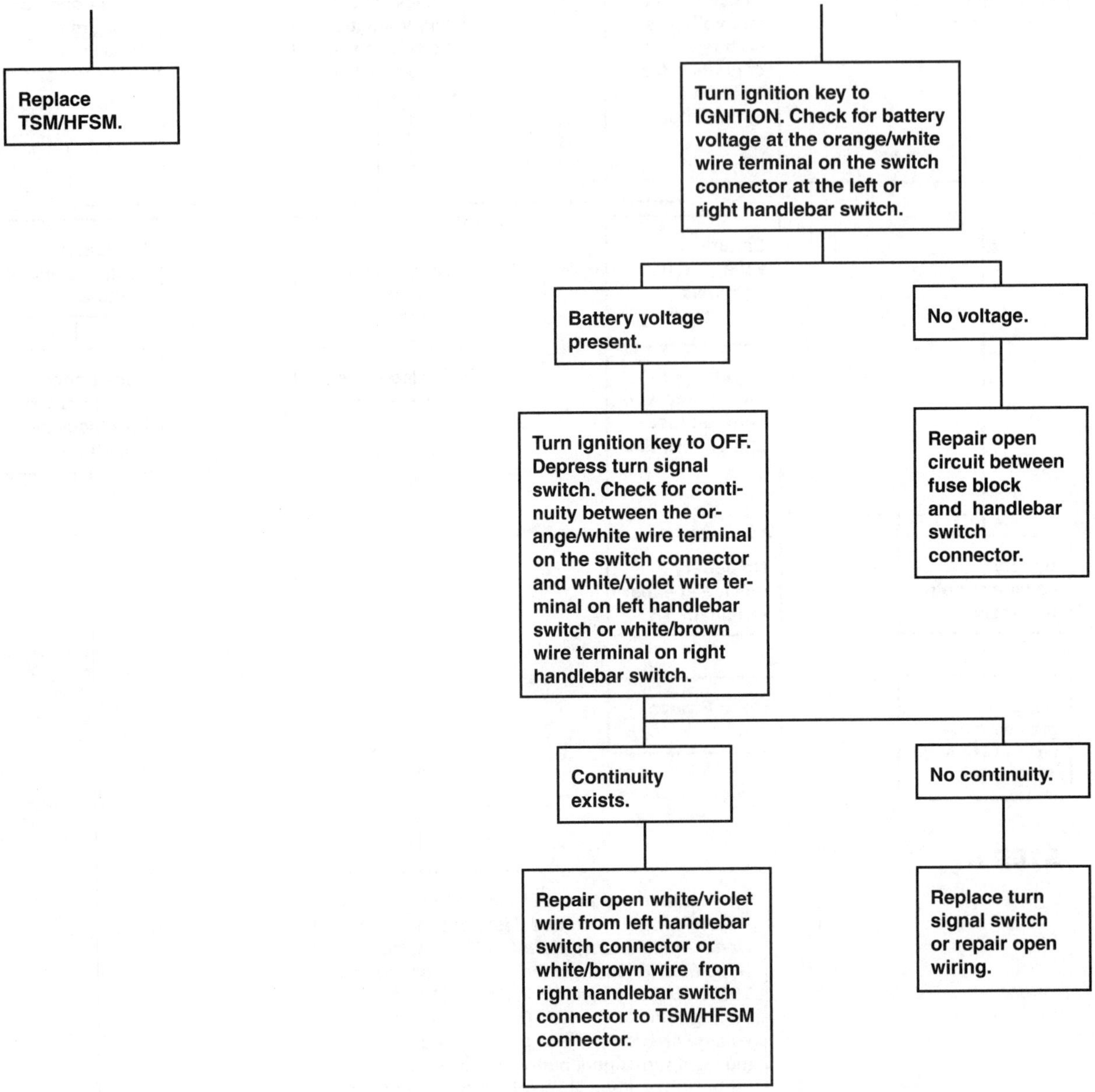
Replace TSM/HFSM.
Turn ignition key to IGNITION. Check for battery voltage at the orange/white wire terminal on the switch connector at the left or right handlebar switch.
Battery voltage present.
No voltage.
Turn ignition key to OFF. Depress turn signal switch. Check for continuity between the orange/white wire terminal on the switch connector and white/violet wire terminal on left handlebar switch or white/brown wire terminal on right handlebar switch.
Repair open circuit between fuse block and handlebar switch connector.
Continuity exists.
No continuity.
Repair open white/violet wire from left handlebar switch connector or white/brown wire from right handlebar switch connector to TSM/HFSM connector.
Replace turn signal switch or repair open wiring.

(17)

DTC B1143: SECURITY ANTENNA SHORT-TO-GROUND

NOTE: If DTC is current and returns after clearing, replace HFSM. If DTC is historic, problem may be intermittent trouble.

Detach the HFSM antenna connector from HFSM as described in this Supplement. Check for continuity between terminal 2 (orange/yellow) on the connector and ground. Check for continuity between terminal 3 (black) on the connector and ground.

- **Continuity present.**
  - **Repair short to ground.**
- **No continuity.**
  - **Replace HFSM.**

(18)

DTC B1144: SECURITY ANTENNA SHORT-TO-VOLTAGE

NOTE: If DTC is current and returns after clearing, replace HFSM. If DTC is historic, problem may be intermittent trouble.

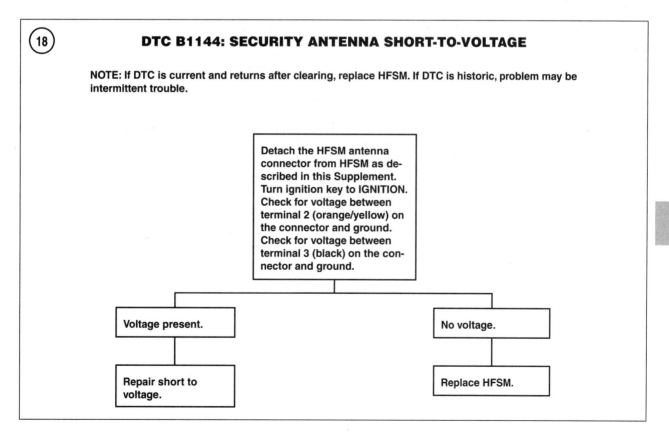

Detach the HFSM antenna connector from HFSM as described in this Supplement. Turn ignition key to IGNITION. Check for voltage between terminal 2 (orange/yellow) on the connector and ground. Check for voltage between terminal 3 (black) on the connector and ground.

- **Voltage present.**
  - **Repair short to voltage.**
- **No voltage.**
  - **Replace HFSM.**

19

DTC B1145: SECURITY ANTENNA OPEN

NOTE: If DTC is current and returns after clearing, replace HFSM. If DTC is historic, problem may be intermittent trouble.

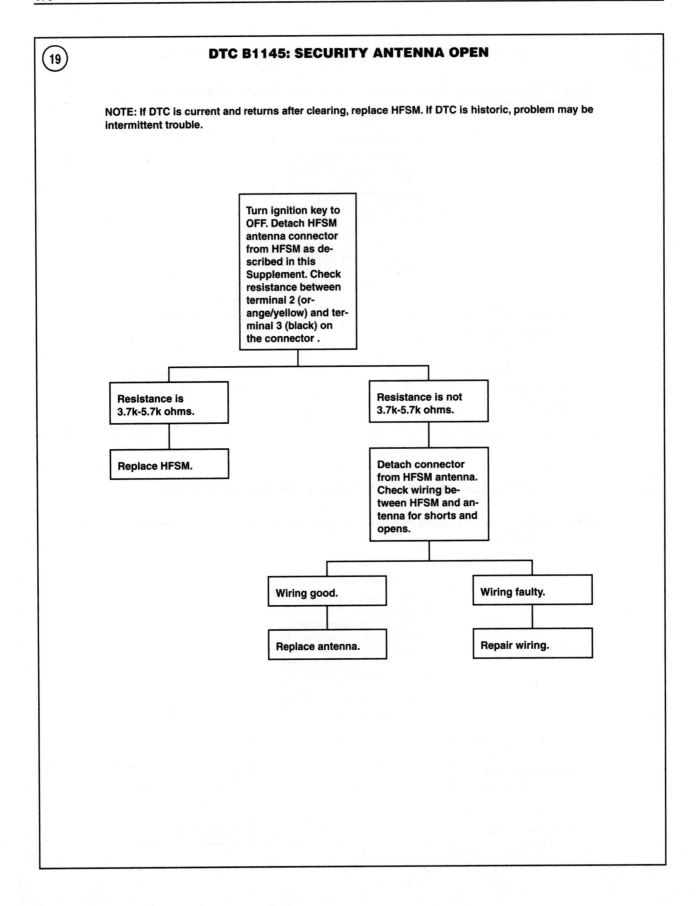

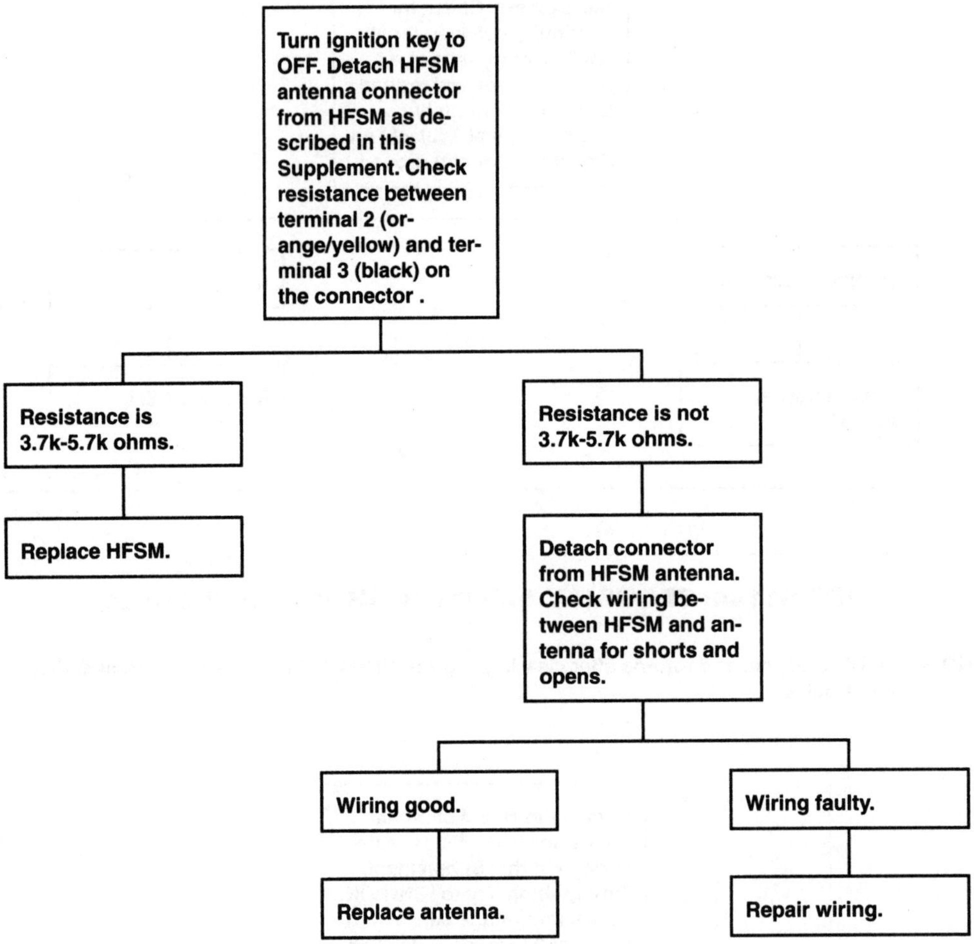

Turn ignition key to OFF. Detach HFSM antenna connector from HFSM as described in this Supplement. Check resistance between terminal 2 (orange/yellow) and terminal 3 (black) on the connector .
Resistance is 3.7k-5.7k ohms.
Replace HFSM.
Resistance is not 3.7k-5.7k ohms.
Detach connector from HFSM antenna. Check wiring between HFSM and antenna for shorts and opens.
Wiring good.
Replace antenna.
Wiring faulty.
Repair wiring.

20

DTC B1154: CLUTCH SWITCH SHORT-TO-GROUND

NOTE: This DTC may be set if the vehicle is ridden with the clutch disengaged (lever pulled in) at speeds greater than 10 mph (16.0 kg/hr) for more than 60 seconds as in riding down a mountain road.

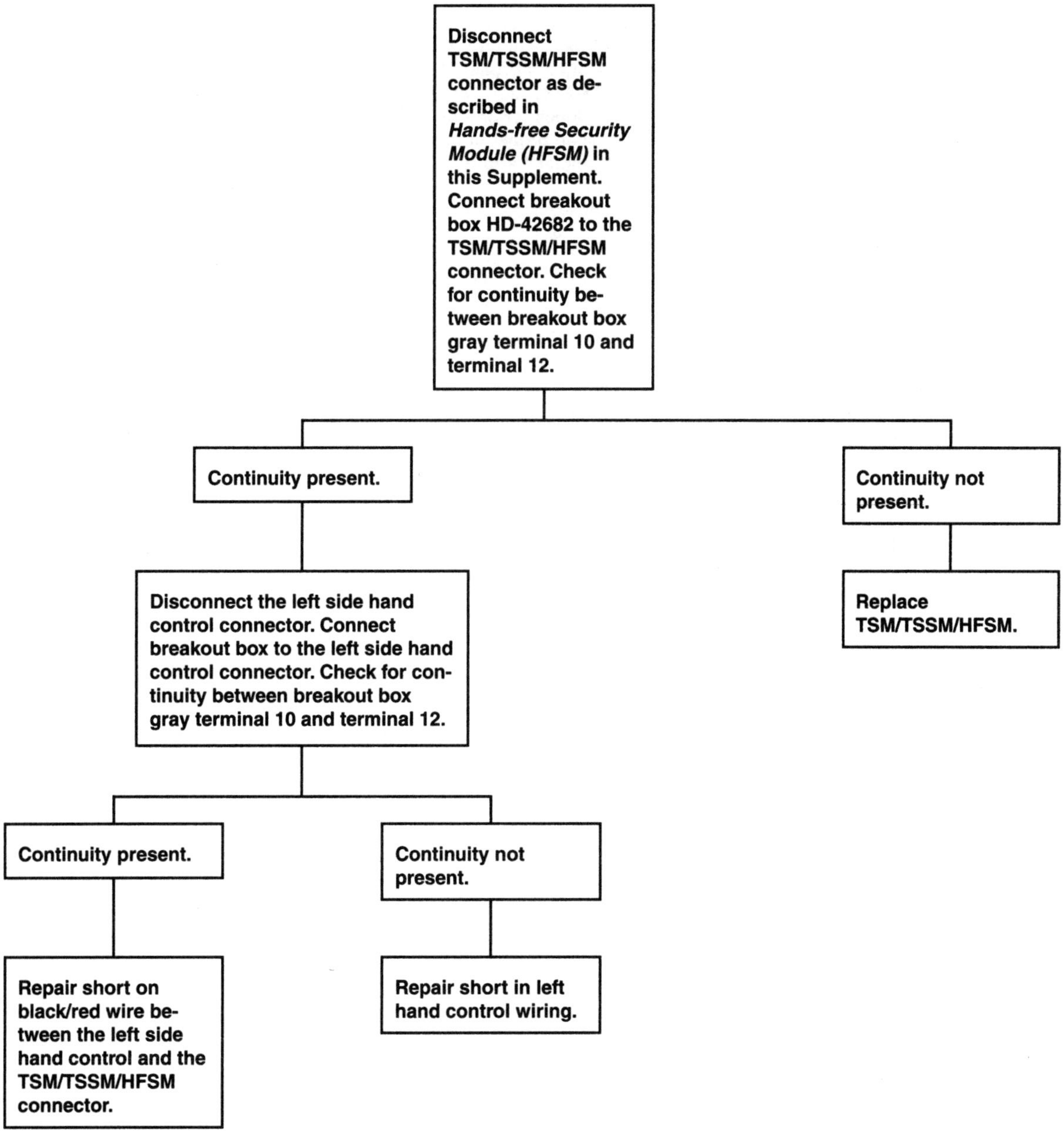
Disconnect TSM/TSSM/HFSM connector as described in *Hands-free Security Module (HFSM)* in this Supplement. Connect breakout box HD-42682 to the TSM/TSSM/HFSM connector. Check for continuity between breakout box gray terminal 10 and terminal 12.
Continuity present.
Continuity not present.
Replace TSM/TSSM/HFSM.
Disconnect the left side hand control connector. Connect breakout box to the left side hand control connector. Check for continuity between breakout box gray terminal 10 and terminal 12.
Continuity present.
Continuity not present.
Repair short on black/red wire between the left side hand control and the TSM/TSSM/HFSM connector.
Repair short in left hand control wiring.

21

DTC B1155: NEUTRAL SWITCH SHORT-TO-GROUND

Shift the transmission into 1st or 2nd gear. Disconnect the TSM/TSSM/HFSM connector as described in *Hands-free Security Module (HFSM)* in this Supplement. Connect breakout box HD-42682 to the connector. Check for continuity between breakout box gray terminal 4 and terminal 12.

Continuity present (less than 10 ohms).

Disconnect the neutral switch connector. Connect the breakout box to the connector. Check for continuity between breakout box gray terminal 4 and terminal 12.

Continuity present (less than 10 ohms).

Repair short on tan wire.

Continuity not present.

Service the neutral switch. Refer to *Switches* in Chapter Nine.

Continuity not present.

Replace TSM/TSSM/HFSM.

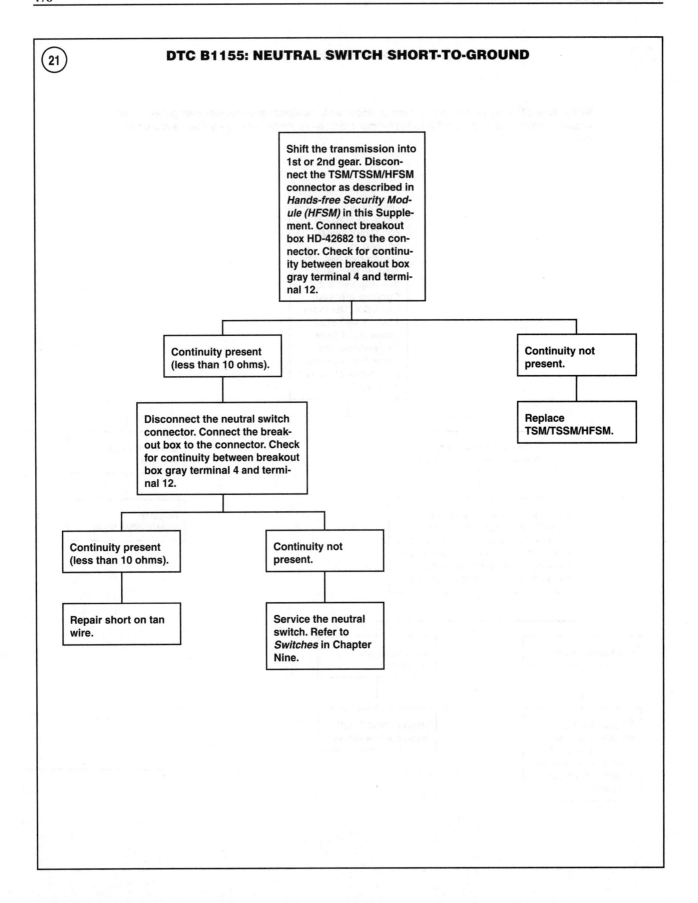

(22)

DTC P0107, P0108: MAP SENSOR

NOTE: The manifold air pressure (MAP) sensor is included in the TMAP sensor unit.

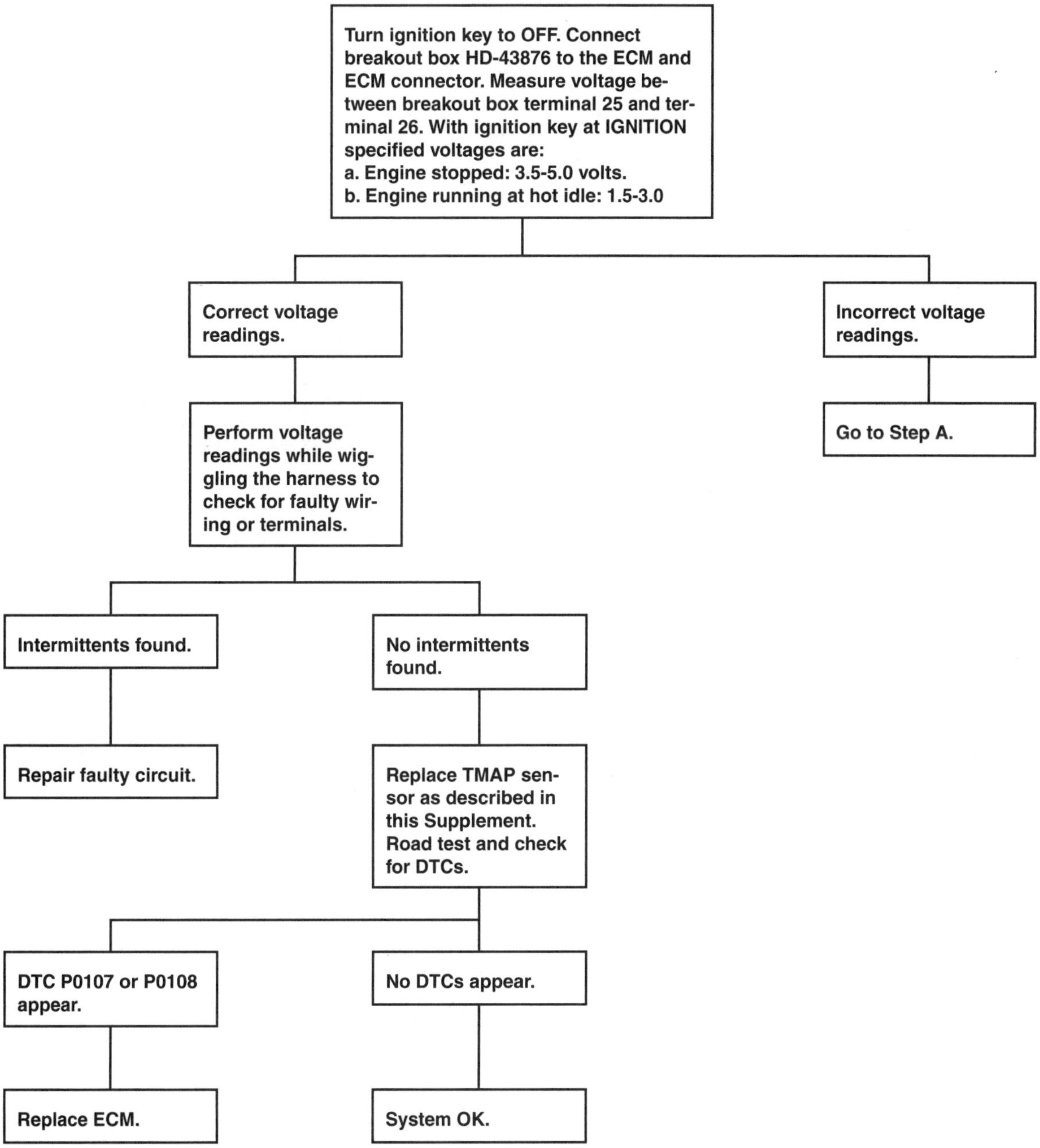
Turn ignition key to OFF. Connect breakout box HD-43876 to the ECM and ECM connector. Measure voltage between breakout box terminal 25 and terminal 26. With ignition key at IGNITION specified voltages are:
a. Engine stopped: 3.5-5.0 volts.
b. Engine running at hot idle: 1.5-3.0
Correct voltage readings.
Incorrect voltage readings.
Go to Step A.
Perform voltage readings while wiggling the harness to check for faulty wiring or terminals.
Intermittents found.
No intermittents found.
Repair faulty circuit.
Replace TMAP sensor as described in this Supplement. Road test and check for DTCs.
DTC P0107 or P0108 appear.
No DTCs appear.
Replace ECM.
System OK.

(continued)

(22) (continued)

STEP A

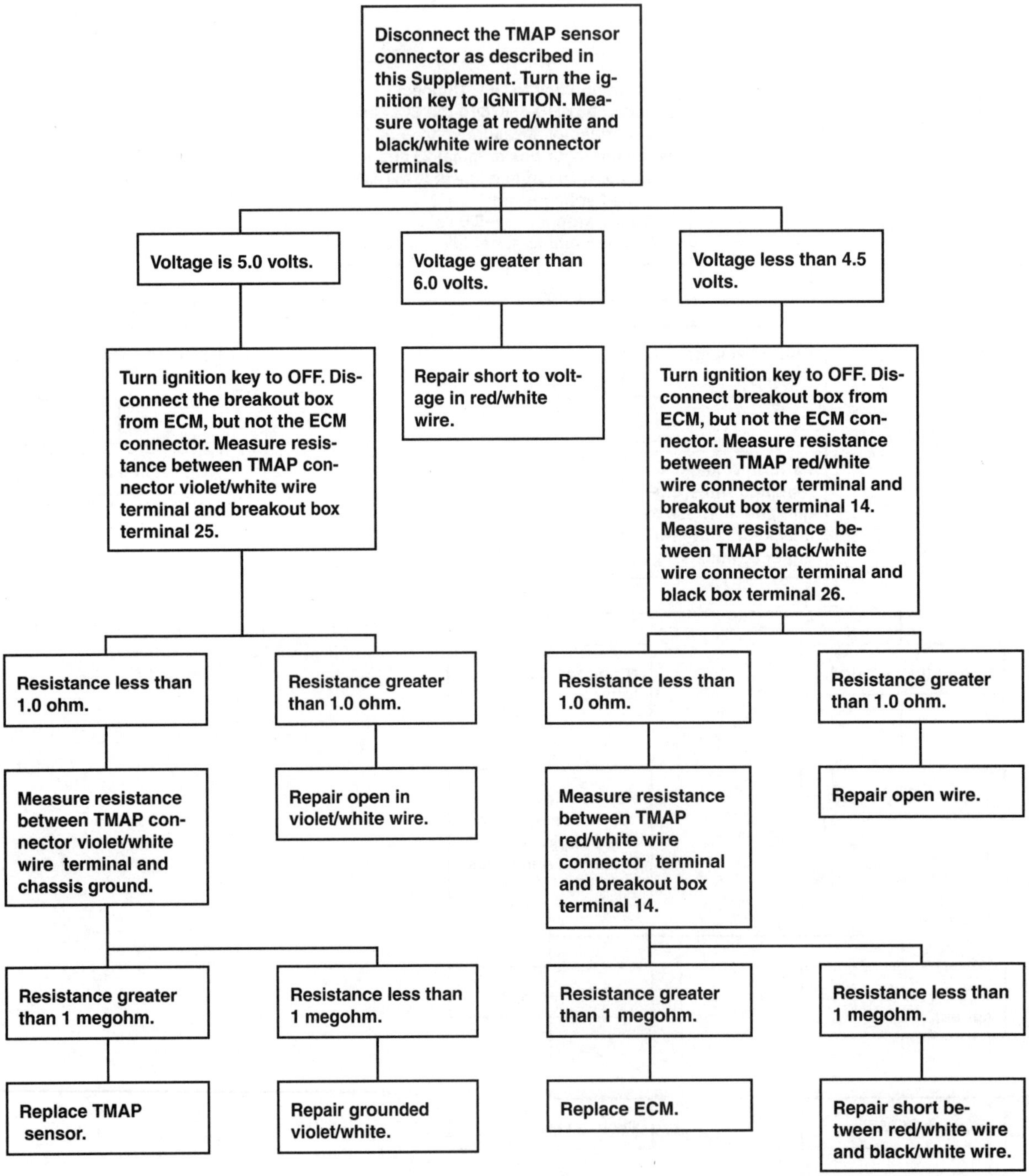
Disconnect the TMAP sensor connector as described in this Supplement. Turn the ignition key to IGNITION. Measure voltage at red/white and black/white wire connector terminals.
Voltage is 5.0 volts.
Voltage greater than 6.0 volts.
Voltage less than 4.5 volts.
Turn ignition key to OFF. Disconnect the breakout box from ECM, but not the ECM connector. Measure resistance between TMAP connector violet/white wire terminal and breakout box terminal 25.
Repair short to voltage in red/white wire.
Turn ignition key to OFF. Disconnect breakout box from ECM, but not the ECM connector. Measure resistance between TMAP red/white wire connector terminal and breakout box terminal 14. Measure resistance between TMAP black/white wire connector terminal and black box terminal 26.
Resistance less than 1.0 ohm.
Resistance greater than 1.0 ohm.
Resistance less than 1.0 ohm.
Resistance greater than 1.0 ohm.
Measure resistance between TMAP connector violet/white wire terminal and chassis ground.
Repair open in violet/white wire.
Measure resistance between TMAP red/white wire connector terminal and breakout box terminal 14.
Repair open wire.
Resistance greater than 1 megohm.
Resistance less than 1 megohm.
Resistance greater than 1 megohm.
Resistance less than 1 megohm.
Replace TMAP sensor.
Repair grounded violet/white.
Replace ECM.
Repair short between red/white wire and black/white wire.

23

DTC P0112, P0113: IAT SENSOR

NOTE: The intake air temperature (IAT) sensor is included in the TMAP sensor unit.

Turn ignition key to OFF. Detach the ECM connector and connect breakout box HD-43876 to the ECM connector, but not to the ECM. Measure resistance between breakout box terminal 7 and terminal 26 at room temperature (60° - 90° F [15.5° - 32° C]). Refer to **Table 8** for specifications related to various engine temperatures.

Resistance is 1.5k - 5.0k ohms at room temperature.

Perform resistance readings while wiggling harness to check for faulty wiring or terminals.

- **Intermittents found.**
  - Perform resistance readings in Step A while wiggling harness to check for faulty wiring or terminals.
- **No intermittents found.**
  - Disconnect the TMAP sensor connector as described in this Supplement. Turn the ignition key to IGNITION. Measure voltage at red/white and black/white wire connector terminals.

Incorrect resistance reading.

Go to Step A.

(continued)

15

23 (continued)

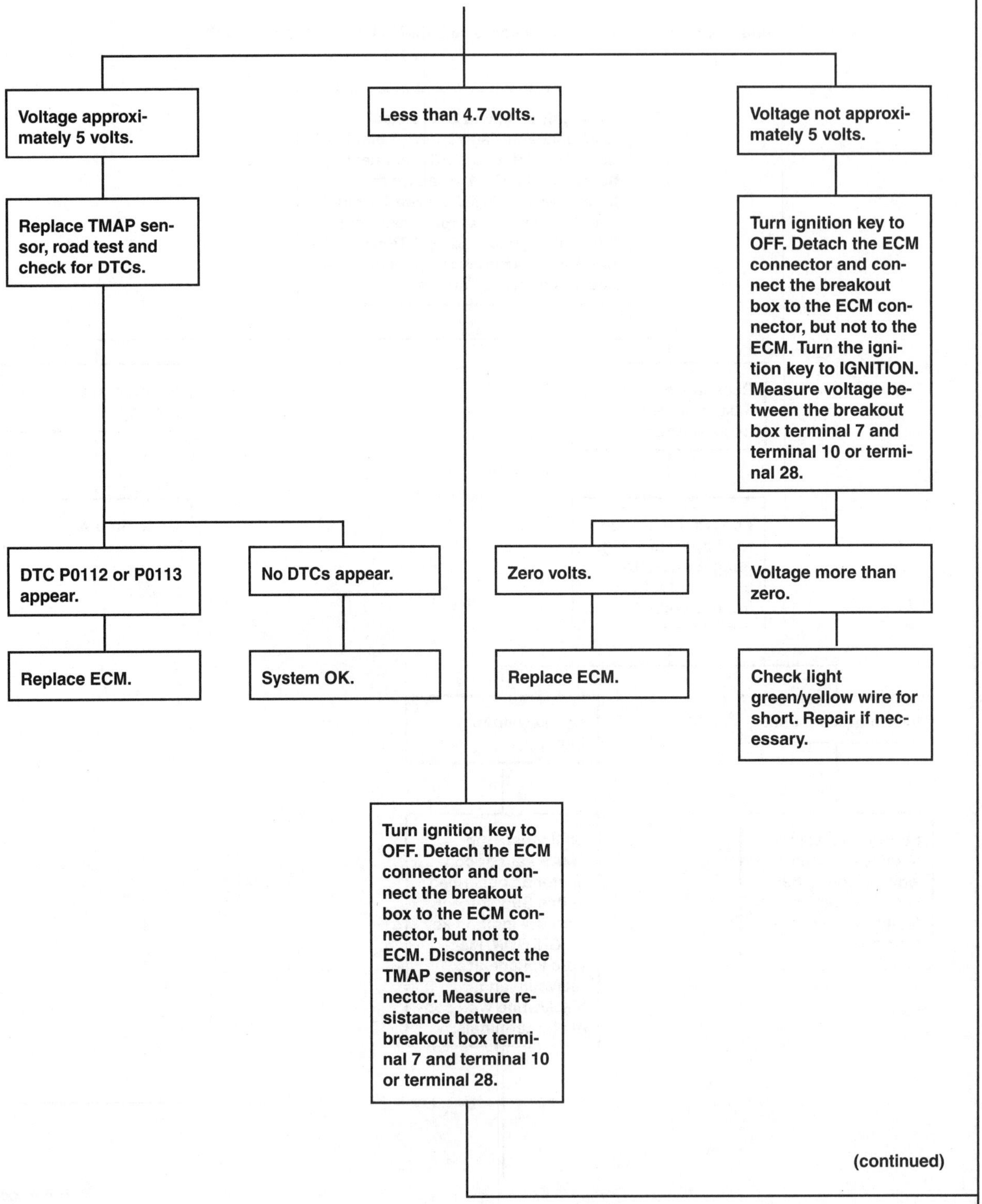
Voltage approximately 5 volts.
Less than 4.7 volts.
Voltage not approximately 5 volts.
Replace TMAP sensor, road test and check for DTCs.
Turn ignition key to OFF. Detach the ECM connector and connect the breakout box to the ECM connector, but not to the ECM. Turn the ignition key to IGNITION. Measure voltage between the breakout box terminal 7 and terminal 10 or terminal 28.
DTC P0112 or P0113 appear.
No DTCs appear.
Zero volts.
Voltage more than zero.
Replace ECM.
System OK.
Replace ECM.
Check light green/yellow wire for short. Repair if necessary.
Turn ignition key to OFF. Detach the ECM connector and connect the breakout box to the ECM connector, but not to ECM. Disconnect the TMAP sensor connector. Measure resistance between breakout box terminal 7 and terminal 10 or terminal 28.

(continued)

23 (continued)

Resistance greater than 1.0 megohm.

Replace ECM.

Resistance less than 1.0 megohm.

Check light green/yellow wire for short to ground. Repair if necessary.

STEP A

Remove TMAP as described in this Supplement. Examine unit and connector for damage.

TMAP good.

Turn ignition key to OFF. Detach the ECM connector and connect the breakout box to the ECM connector, but not to the ECM. Disconnect the TMAP sensor connector. Measure resistance between the light green/yellow wire on the TMAP connector and breakout box terminal 7.

Resistance less than 1.0 ohm.

Measure resistance between the black/white wire on the TMAP connector and breakout box terminal 26.

Resistance less than 1.0 ohm.

Check light green/yellow wire for open. Repair if necessary.

Damaged.

Repair or replace.

(continued)

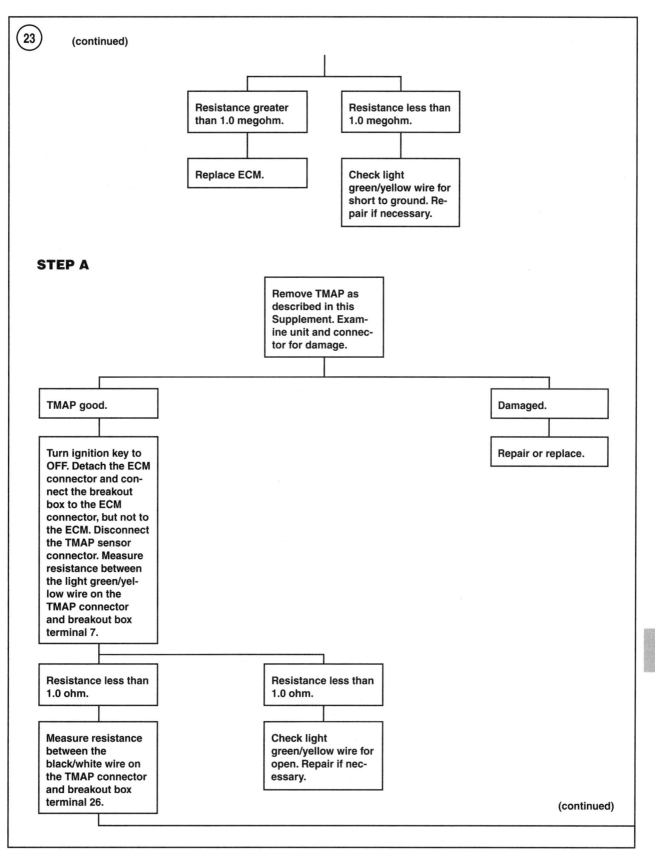

(23) (continued)

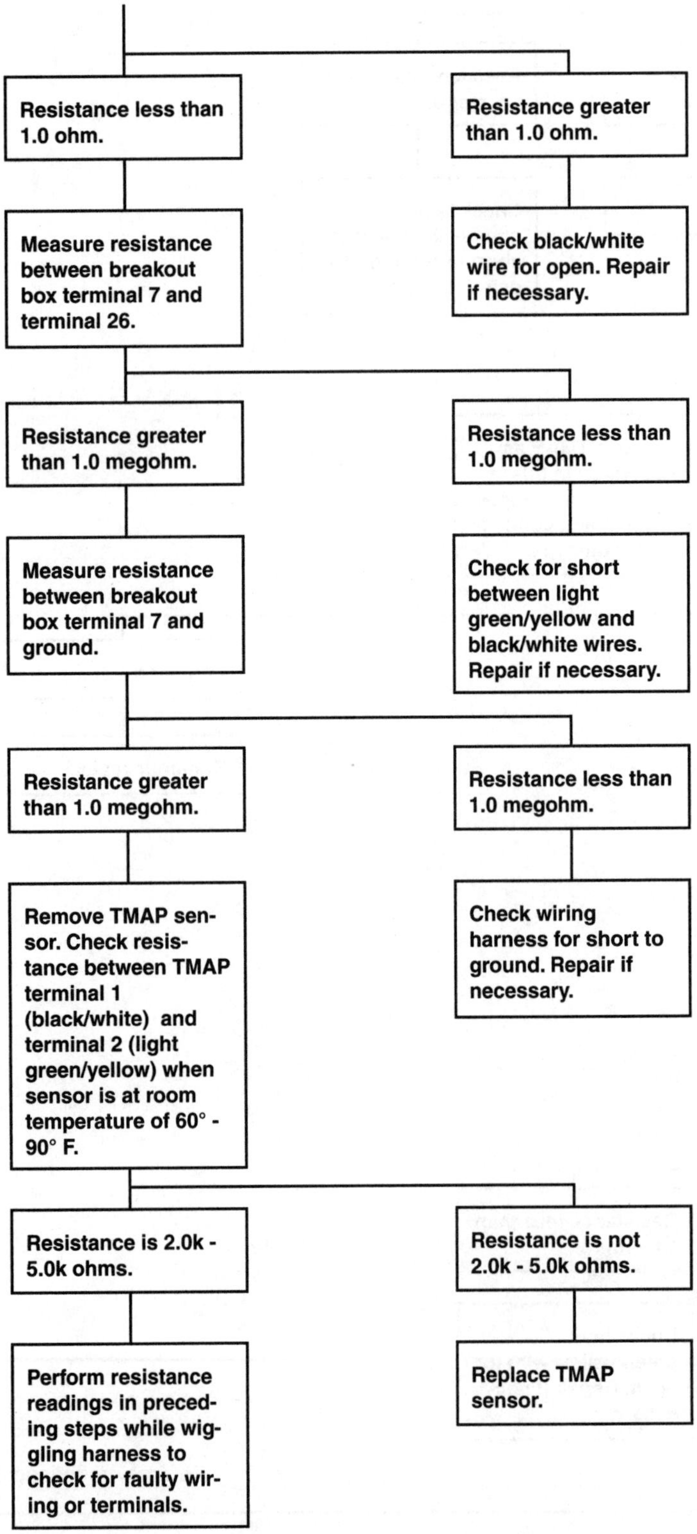
Resistance less than 1.0 ohm.
Resistance greater than 1.0 ohm.
Measure resistance between breakout box terminal 7 and terminal 26.
Check black/white wire for open. Repair if necessary.
Resistance greater than 1.0 megohm.
Resistance less than 1.0 megohm.
Measure resistance between breakout box terminal 7 and ground.
Check for short between light green/yellow and black/white wires. Repair if necessary.
Resistance greater than 1.0 megohm.
Resistance less than 1.0 megohm.
Remove TMAP sensor. Check resistance between TMAP terminal 1 (black/white) and terminal 2 (light green/yellow) when sensor is at room temperature of 60° - 90° F.
Check wiring harness for short to ground. Repair if necessary.
Resistance is 2.0k - 5.0k ohms.
Resistance is not 2.0k - 5.0k ohms.
Perform resistance readings in preceding steps while wiggling harness to check for faulty wiring or terminals.
Replace TMAP sensor.

(24)

DTC P0117, P0118: ET SENSOR

Turn ignition key to OFF. Detach the ECM connector and connect breakout box HD-43876 to the ECM connector, but not to the ECM. Measure resistance between the breakout box terminal 6 and terminal 26 at room temperature (60° - 90° F [15.5° - 32° C]). Refer to **Table 20** for specifications related to various engine temperatures.

- Resistance is 8k - 20k ohms at room temperature.
  - Perform resistance readings while wiggling harness to check for faulty wiring or terminals.
    - Intermittents found.
      - Perform resistance readings in Step A while wiggling harness to check for faulty wiring or terminals.
    - No intermittents found.
      - Disconnect the engine temperature (ET) sensor connector as described in this Supplement. Turn the ignition key to IGNITION. Measure voltage at pink\yellow and black/white wire connector terminals.
- Incorrect resistance reading.
  - Go to Step A.

(continued)

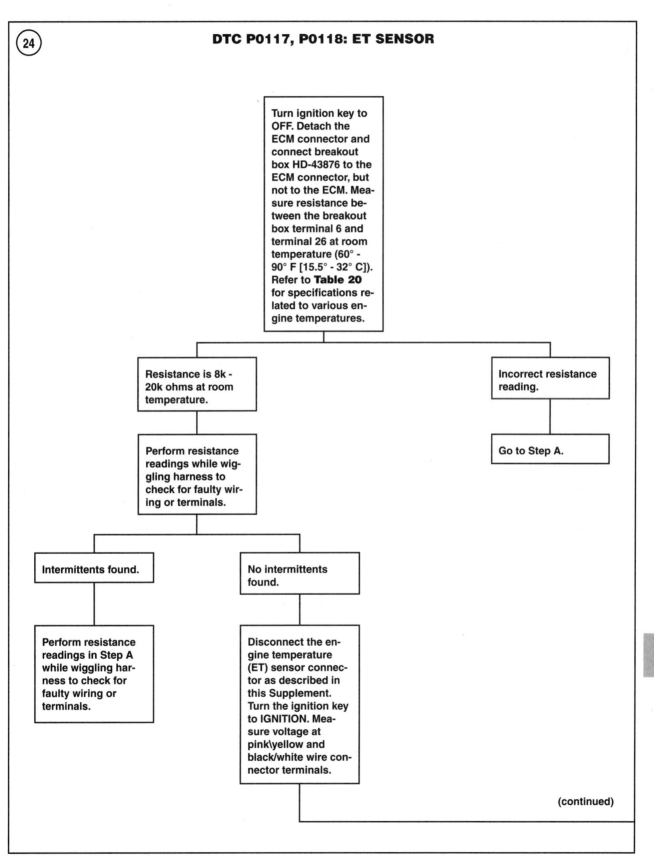

(24) (continued)

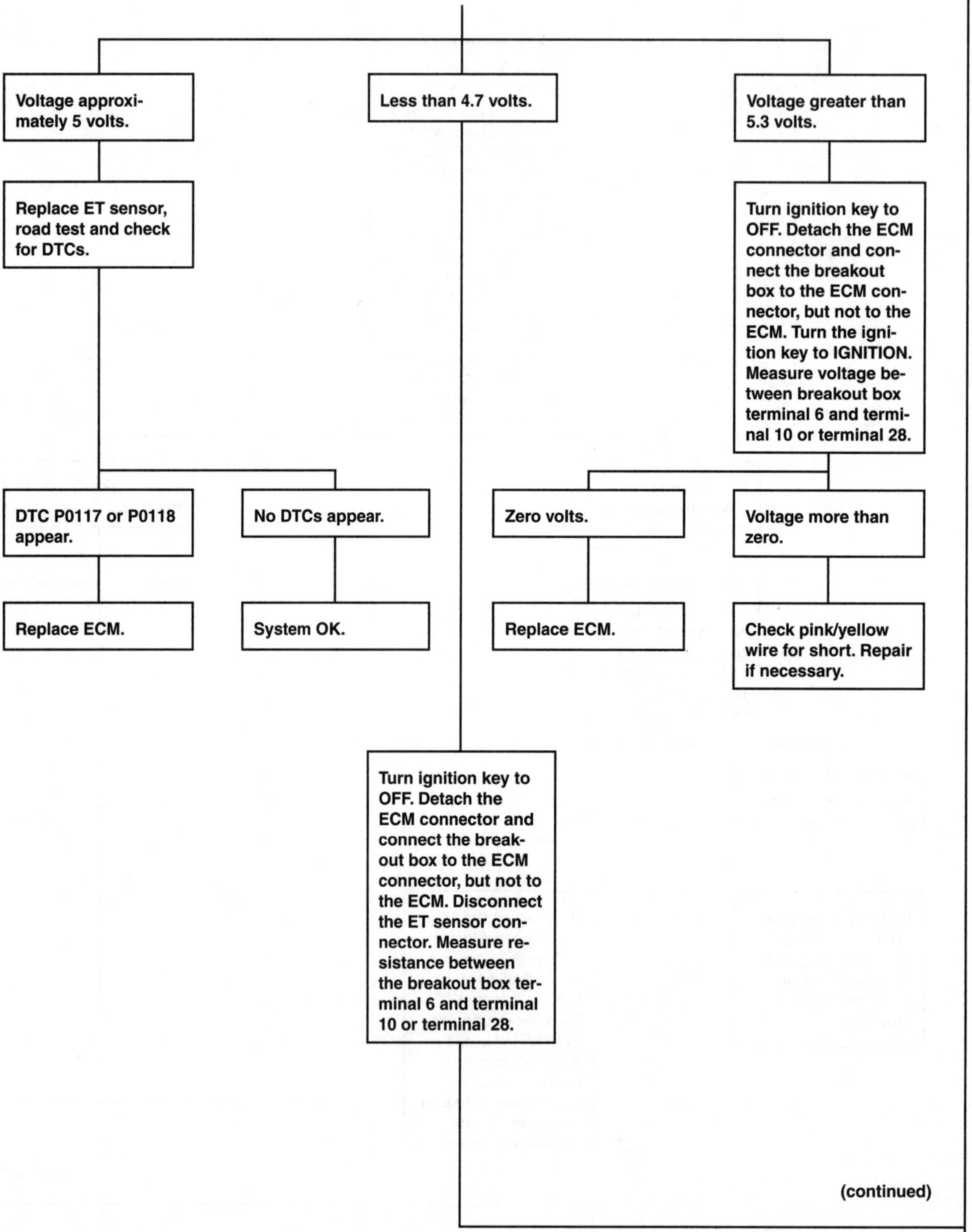
Voltage approximately 5 volts.
Less than 4.7 volts.
Voltage greater than 5.3 volts.
Replace ET sensor, road test and check for DTCs.
Turn ignition key to OFF. Detach the ECM connector and connect the breakout box to the ECM connector, but not to the ECM. Turn the ignition key to IGNITION. Measure voltage between breakout box terminal 6 and terminal 10 or terminal 28.
DTC P0117 or P0118 appear.
No DTCs appear.
Zero volts.
Voltage more than zero.
Replace ECM.
System OK.
Replace ECM.
Check pink/yellow wire for short. Repair if necessary.
Turn ignition key to OFF. Detach the ECM connector and connect the breakout box to the ECM connector, but not to the ECM. Disconnect the ET sensor connector. Measure resistance between the breakout box terminal 6 and terminal 10 or terminal 28.

(continued)

(24) (continued)

- Resistance greater than 1.0 megohm.
  - Replace ECM.
- Resistance less than 1.0 megohm.
  - Check pink\yellow wire for short to ground. Repair if necessary.

STEP A

Examine engine temperature (ET) sensor and connector for damage. Refer to *Engine Temperature Sensor (ET)* in this Supplement.

- ET sensor good.
  - Turn ignition key to OFF. Detach the ECM connector and connect the breakout box to the ECM connector, but not to the ECM. Disconnect the ET sensor connector. Measure resistance between the pink/yellow wire on the ET sensor connector and breakout box terminal 6.
    - Resistance less than 1.0 ohm.
      - Measure resistance between black/white wire on the ET sensor connector and breakout box terminal 26.
    - Resistance greater than 1.0 ohm.
      - Check pink/yellow wire for open. Repair if necessary.
- Damaged.
  - Repair or replace.

(continued)

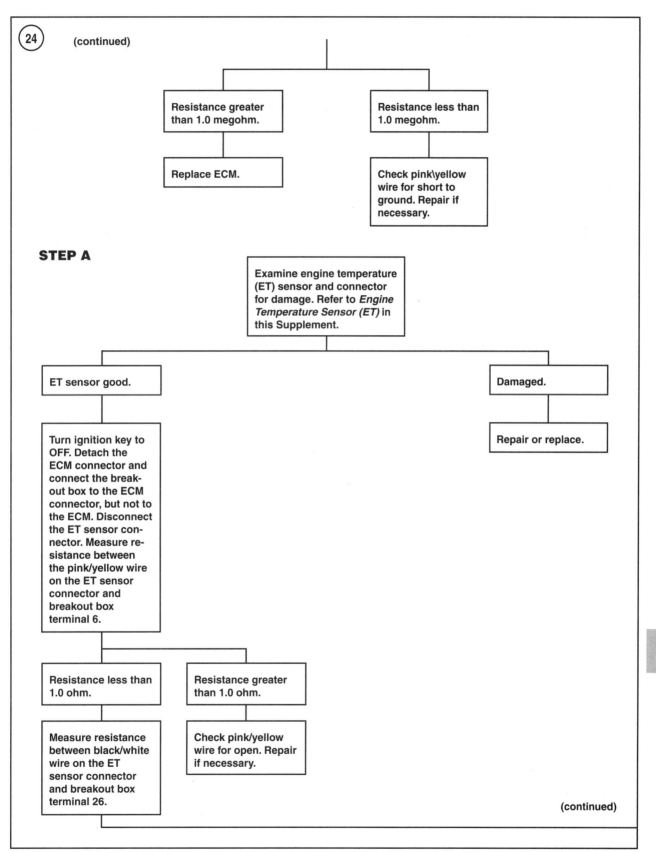

24 (continued)

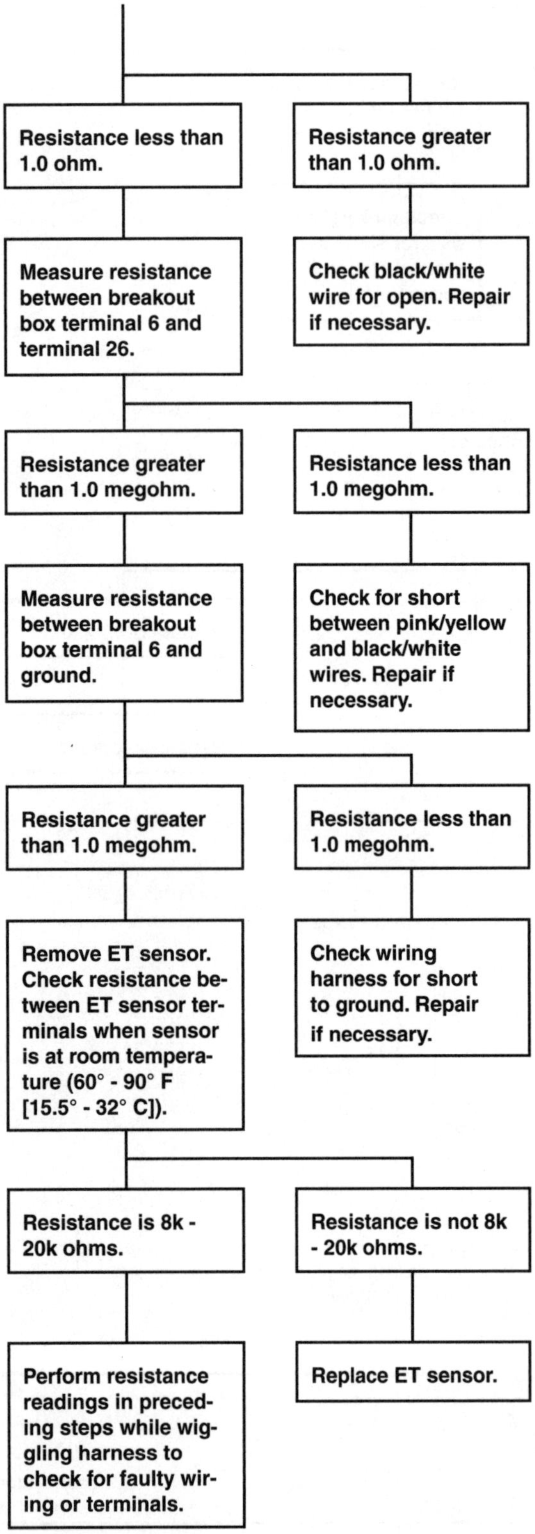

Resistance less than 1.0 ohm.
Resistance greater than 1.0 ohm.
Measure resistance between breakout box terminal 6 and terminal 26.
Check black/white wire for open. Repair if necessary.
Resistance greater than 1.0 megohm.
Resistance less than 1.0 megohm.
Measure resistance between breakout box terminal 6 and ground.
Check for short between pink/yellow and black/white wires. Repair if necessary.
Resistance greater than 1.0 megohm.
Resistance less than 1.0 megohm.
Remove ET sensor. Check resistance between ET sensor terminals when sensor is at room temperature (60° - 90° F [15.5° - 32° C]).
Check wiring harness for short to ground. Repair if necessary.
Resistance is 8k - 20k ohms.
Resistance is not 8k - 20k ohms.
Perform resistance readings in preceding steps while wiggling harness to check for faulty wiring or terminals.
Replace ET sensor.

25

DTC P0122, P0123: THROTTLE POSITION (TP) SENSOR OPEN/LOW OR HIGH

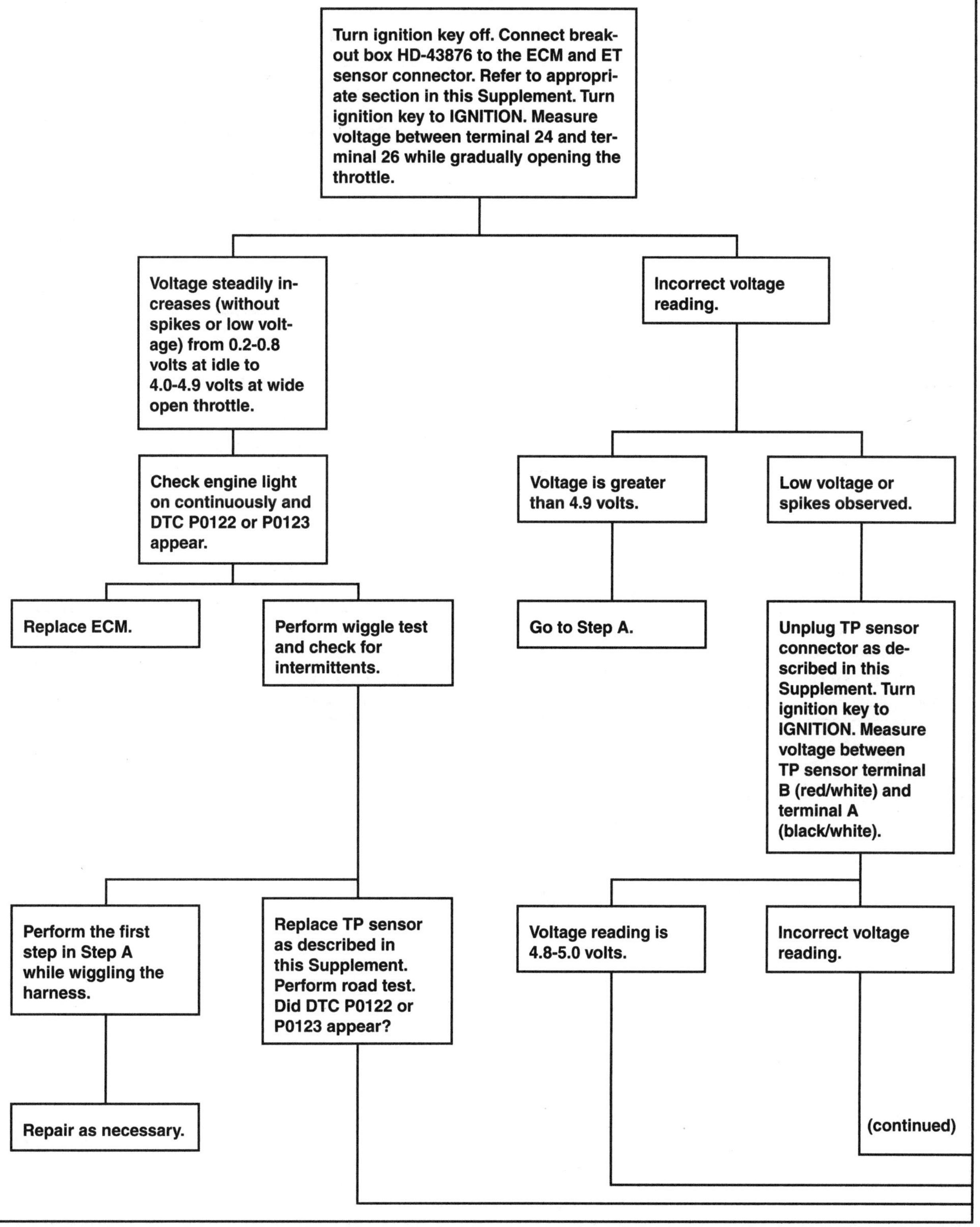

Turn ignition key off. Connect break-out box HD-43876 to the ECM and ET sensor connector. Refer to appropriate section in this Supplement. Turn ignition key to IGNITION. Measure voltage between terminal 24 and terminal 26 while gradually opening the throttle.
Voltage steadily increases (without spikes or low voltage) from 0.2-0.8 volts at idle to 4.0-4.9 volts at wide open throttle.
Incorrect voltage reading.
Check engine light on continuously and DTC P0122 or P0123 appear.
Voltage is greater than 4.9 volts.
Low voltage or spikes observed.
Replace ECM.
Perform wiggle test and check for intermittents.
Go to Step A.
Unplug TP sensor connector as described in this Supplement. Turn ignition key to IGNITION. Measure voltage between TP sensor terminal B (red/white) and terminal A (black/white).
Perform the first step in Step A while wiggling the harness.
Replace TP sensor as described in this Supplement. Perform road test. Did DTC P0122 or P0123 appear?
Voltage reading is 4.8-5.0 volts.
Incorrect voltage reading.
Repair as necessary.
(continued)

15

25 (continued)

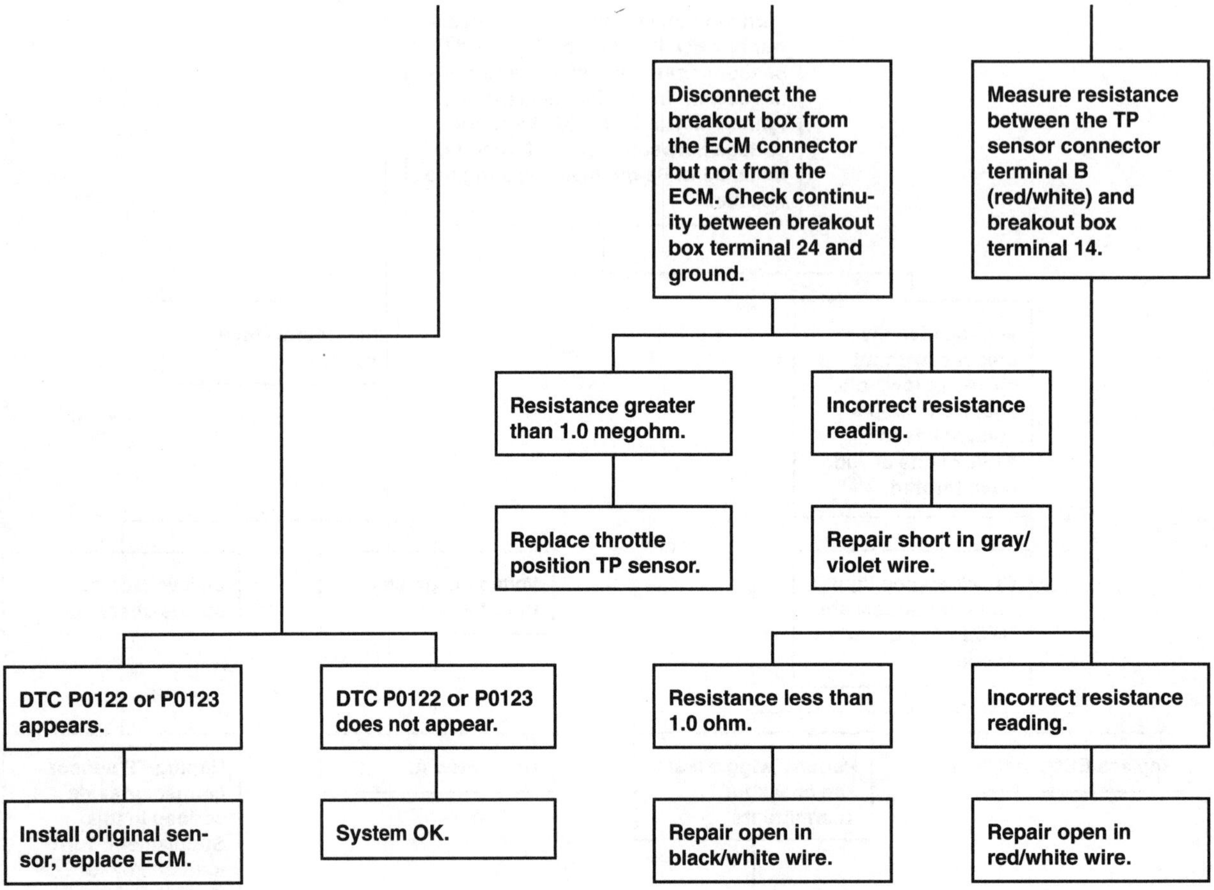
Disconnect the breakout box from the ECM connector but not from the ECM. Check continuity between breakout box terminal 24 and ground.
Measure resistance between the TP sensor connector terminal B (red/white) and breakout box terminal 14.
Resistance greater than 1.0 megohm.
Incorrect resistance reading.
Replace throttle position TP sensor.
Repair short in gray/violet wire.
DTC P0122 or P0123 appears.
DTC P0122 or P0123 does not appear.
Resistance less than 1.0 ohm.
Incorrect resistance reading.
Install original sensor, replace ECM.
System OK.
Repair open in black/white wire.
Repair open in red/white wire.

(continued)

(25) (continued)

STEP A

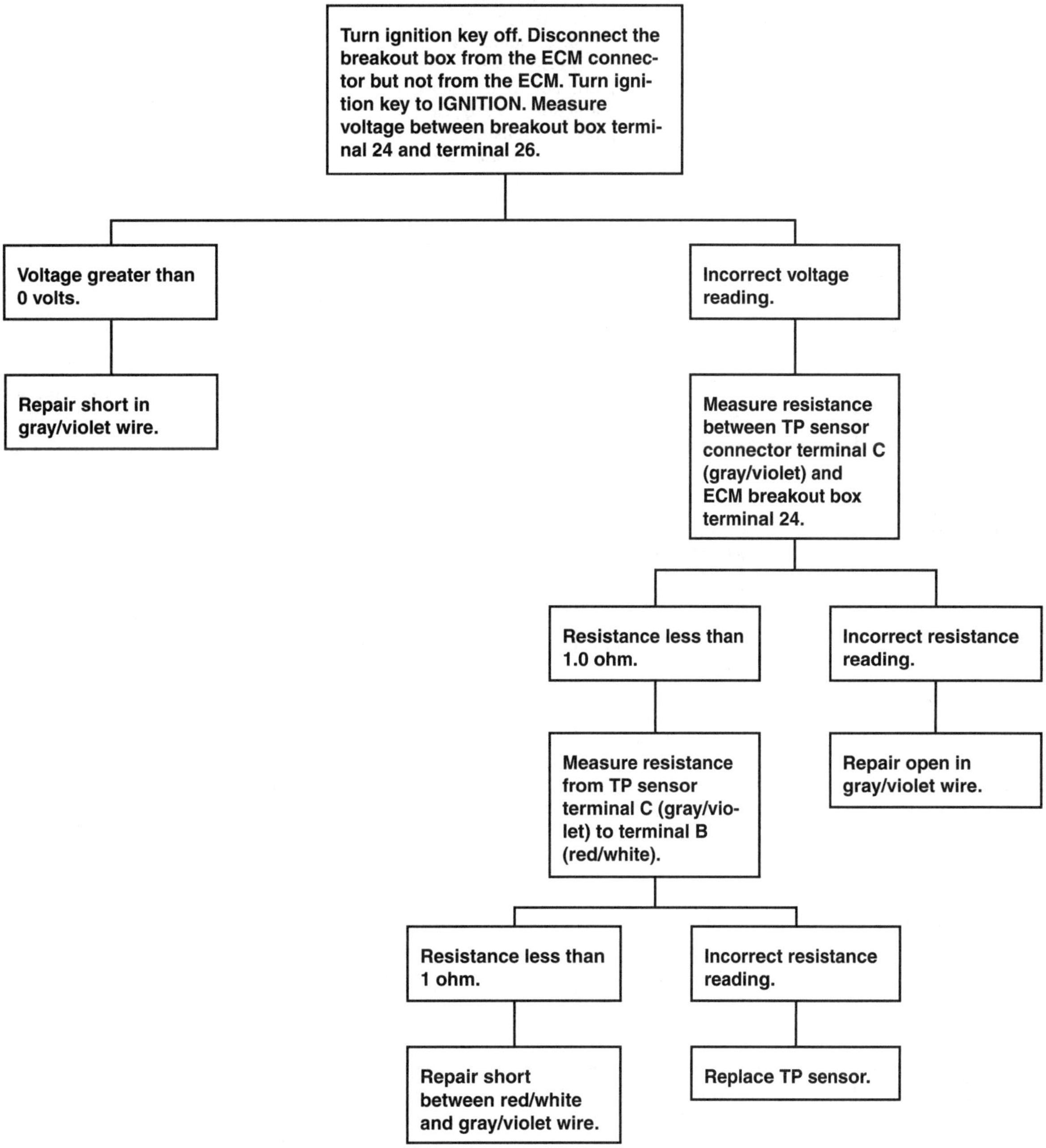

Turn ignition key off. Disconnect the breakout box from the ECM connector but not from the ECM. Turn ignition key to IGNITION. Measure voltage between breakout box terminal 24 and terminal 26.
Voltage greater than 0 volts.
Repair short in gray/violet wire.
Incorrect voltage reading.
Measure resistance between TP sensor connector terminal C (gray/violet) and ECM breakout box terminal 24.
Resistance less than 1.0 ohm.
Measure resistance from TP sensor terminal C (gray/violet) to terminal B (red/white).
Incorrect resistance reading.
Repair open in gray/violet wire.
Resistance less than 1 ohm.
Repair short between red/white and gray/violet wire.
Incorrect resistance reading.
Replace TP sensor.

(26)

DTC P0131, P0132, P0134, P0151, P0152, P0154: O2 SENSOR

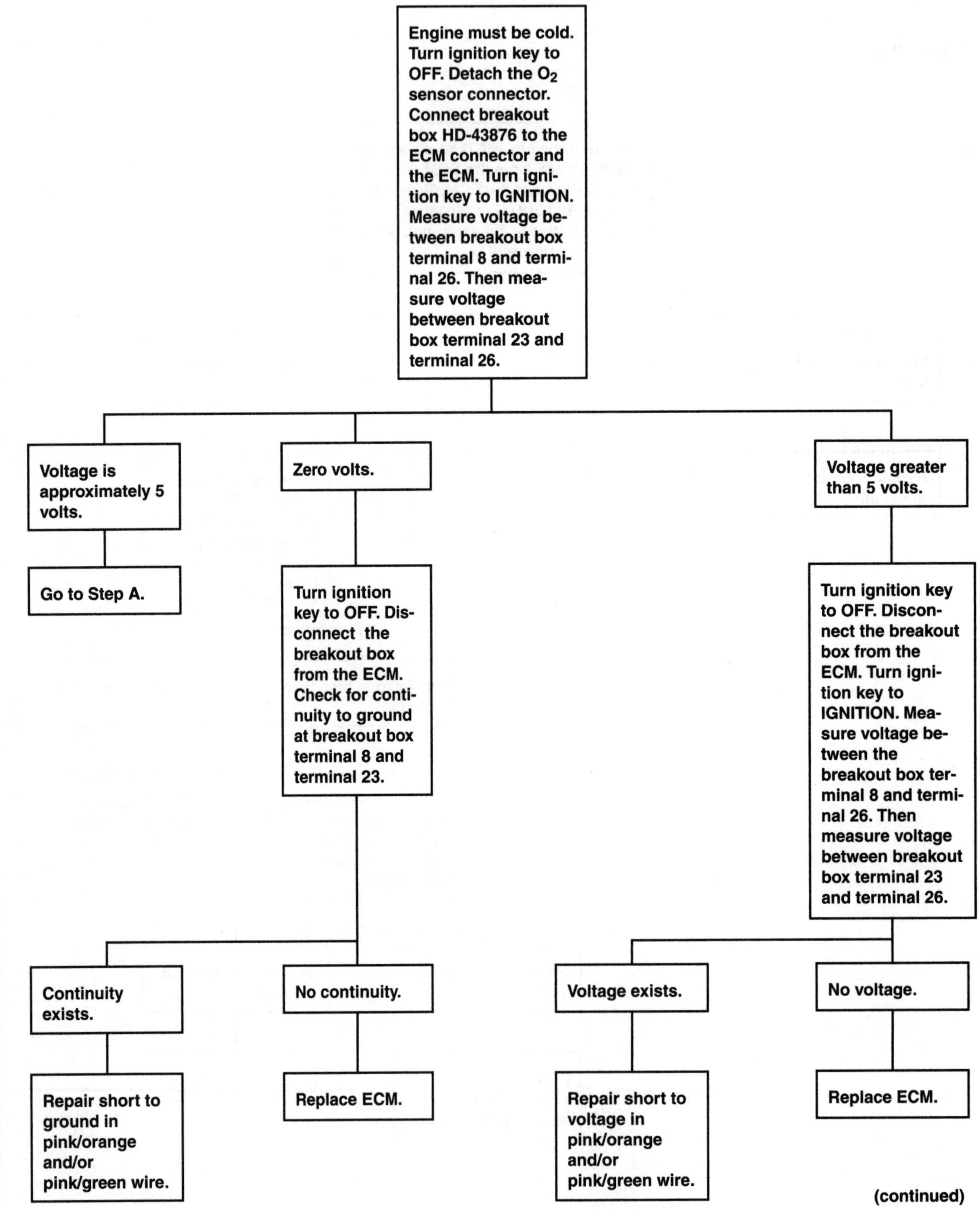
Engine must be cold. Turn ignition key to OFF. Detach the O_2 sensor connector. Connect breakout box HD-43876 to the ECM connector and the ECM. Turn ignition key to IGNITION. Measure voltage between breakout box terminal 8 and terminal 26. Then measure voltage between breakout box terminal 23 and terminal 26.
Voltage is approximately 5 volts.
Go to Step A.
Zero volts.
Turn ignition key to OFF. Disconnect the breakout box from the ECM. Check for continuity to ground at breakout box terminal 8 and terminal 23.
Continuity exists.
Repair short to ground in pink/orange and/or pink/green wire.
No continuity.
Replace ECM.
Voltage greater than 5 volts.
Turn ignition key to OFF. Disconnect the breakout box from the ECM. Turn ignition key to IGNITION. Measure voltage between the breakout box terminal 8 and terminal 26. Then measure voltage between breakout box terminal 23 and terminal 26.
Voltage exists.
Repair short to voltage in pink/orange and/or pink/green wire.
No voltage.
Replace ECM.

(continued)

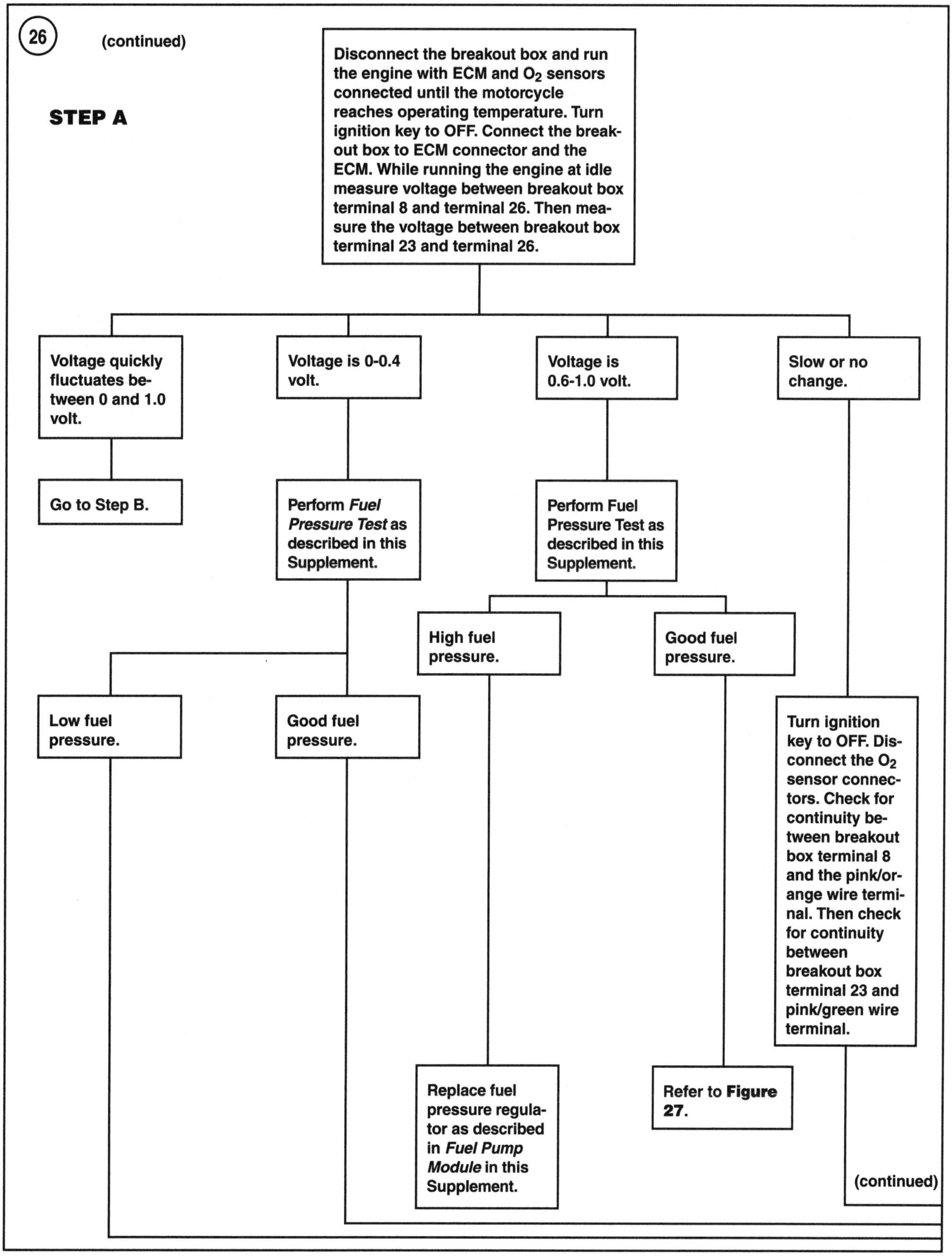
26
(continued)
STEP A
Disconnect the breakout box and run the engine with ECM and O_2 sensors connected until the motorcycle reaches operating temperature. Turn ignition key to OFF. Connect the breakout box to ECM connector and the ECM. While running the engine at idle measure voltage between breakout box terminal 8 and terminal 26. Then measure the voltage between breakout box terminal 23 and terminal 26.
Voltage quickly fluctuates between 0 and 1.0 volt.
Voltage is 0-0.4 volt.
Voltage is 0.6-1.0 volt.
Slow or no change.
Go to Step B.
Perform *Fuel Pressure Test* as described in this Supplement.
Perform Fuel Pressure Test as described in this Supplement.
High fuel pressure.
Good fuel pressure.
Low fuel pressure.
Good fuel pressure.
Turn ignition key to OFF. Disconnect the O_2 sensor connectors. Check for continuity between breakout box terminal 8 and the pink/orange wire terminal. Then check for continuity between breakout box terminal 23 and pink/green wire terminal.
Replace fuel pressure regulator as described in *Fuel Pump Module* in this Supplement.
Refer to **Figure 27**.
(continued)

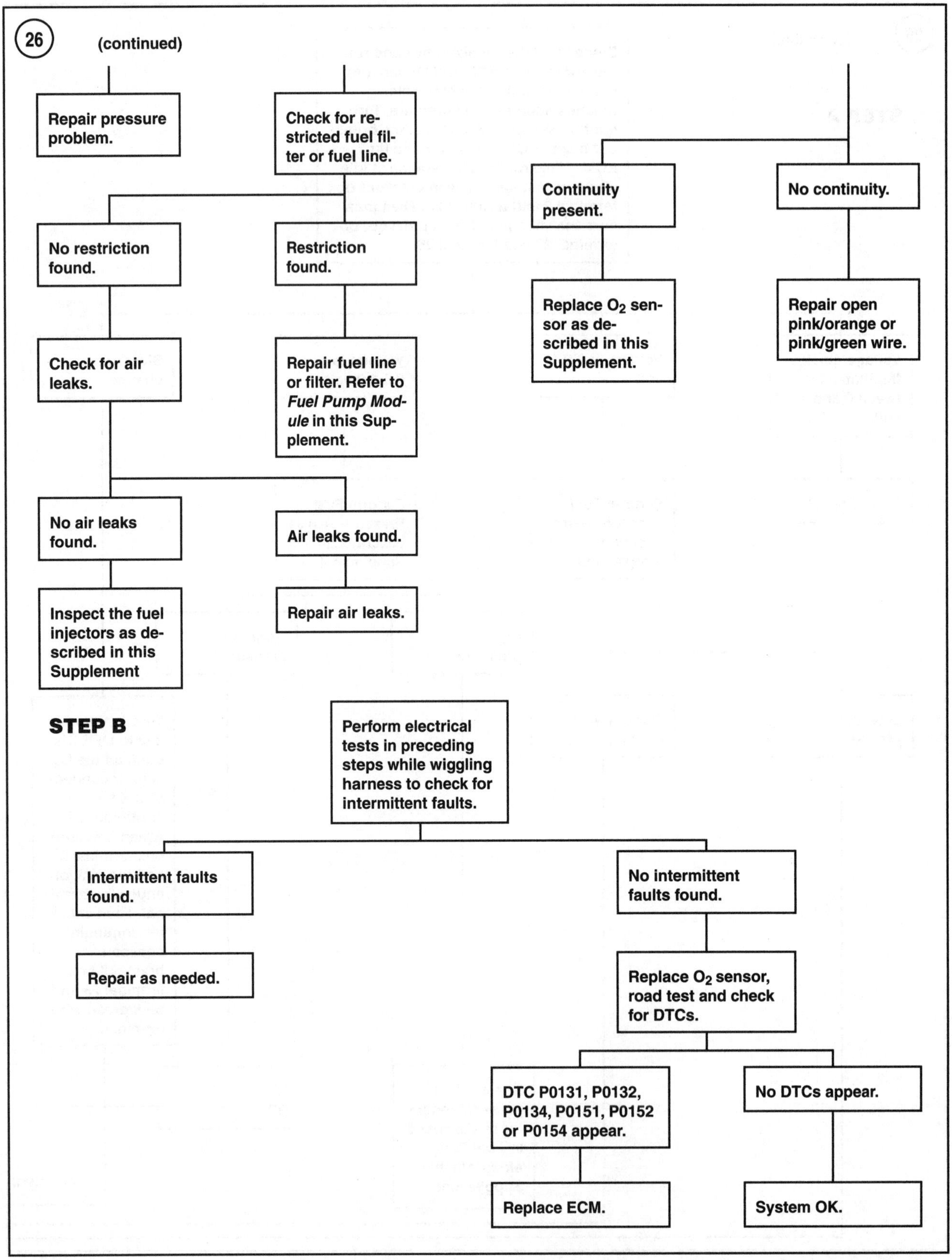
26
(continued)
Repair pressure problem.
Check for restricted fuel filter or fuel line.
No restriction found.
Restriction found.
Check for air leaks.
Repair fuel line or filter. Refer to *Fuel Pump Module* in this Supplement.
No air leaks found.
Air leaks found.
Inspect the fuel injectors as described in this Supplement
Repair air leaks.
Continuity present.
No continuity.
Replace O_2 sensor as described in this Supplement.
Repair open pink/orange or pink/green wire.
STEP B
Perform electrical tests in preceding steps while wiggling harness to check for intermittent faults.
Intermittent faults found.
No intermittent faults found.
Repair as needed.
Replace O_2 sensor, road test and check for DTCs.
DTC P0131, P0132, P0134, P0151, P0152 or P0154 appear.
No DTCs appear.
Replace ECM.
System OK.

(27) DTC P0261, P0262, P0263, P0264: FUEL INJECTORS OPEN/LOW OR HIGH

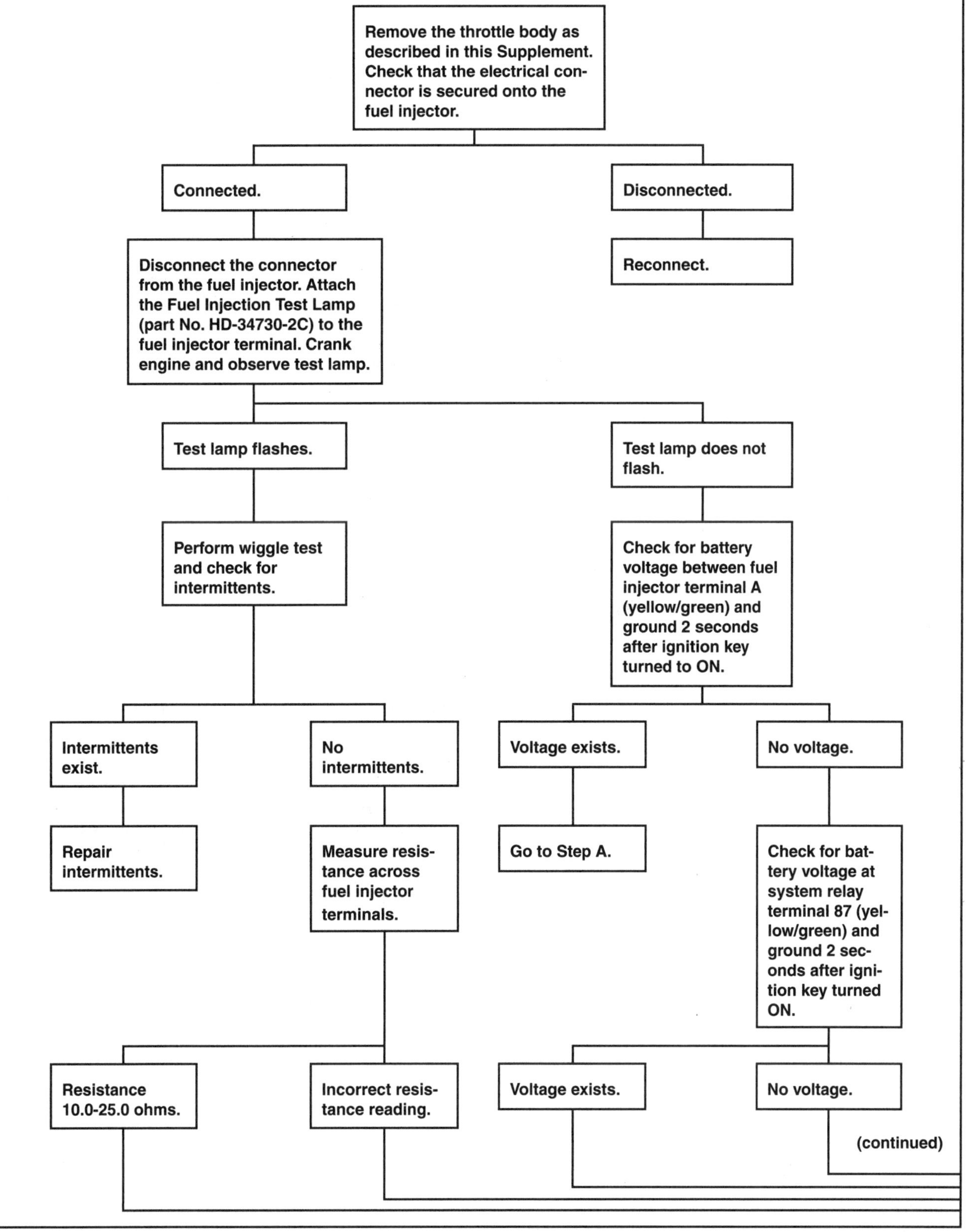
Remove the throttle body as described in this Supplement. Check that the electrical connector is secured onto the fuel injector.
Connected.
Disconnected.
Disconnect the connector from the fuel injector. Attach the Fuel Injection Test Lamp (part No. HD-34730-2C) to the fuel injector terminal. Crank engine and observe test lamp.
Reconnect.
Test lamp flashes.
Test lamp does not flash.
Perform wiggle test and check for intermittents.
Check for battery voltage between fuel injector terminal A (yellow/green) and ground 2 seconds after ignition key turned to ON.
Intermittents exist.
No intermittents.
Voltage exists.
No voltage.
Repair intermittents.
Measure resistance across fuel injector terminals.
Go to Step A.
Check for battery voltage at system relay terminal 87 (yellow/green) and ground 2 seconds after ignition key turned ON.
Resistance 10.0-25.0 ohms.
Incorrect resistance reading.
Voltage exists.
No voltage.
(continued)

(27) (continued)

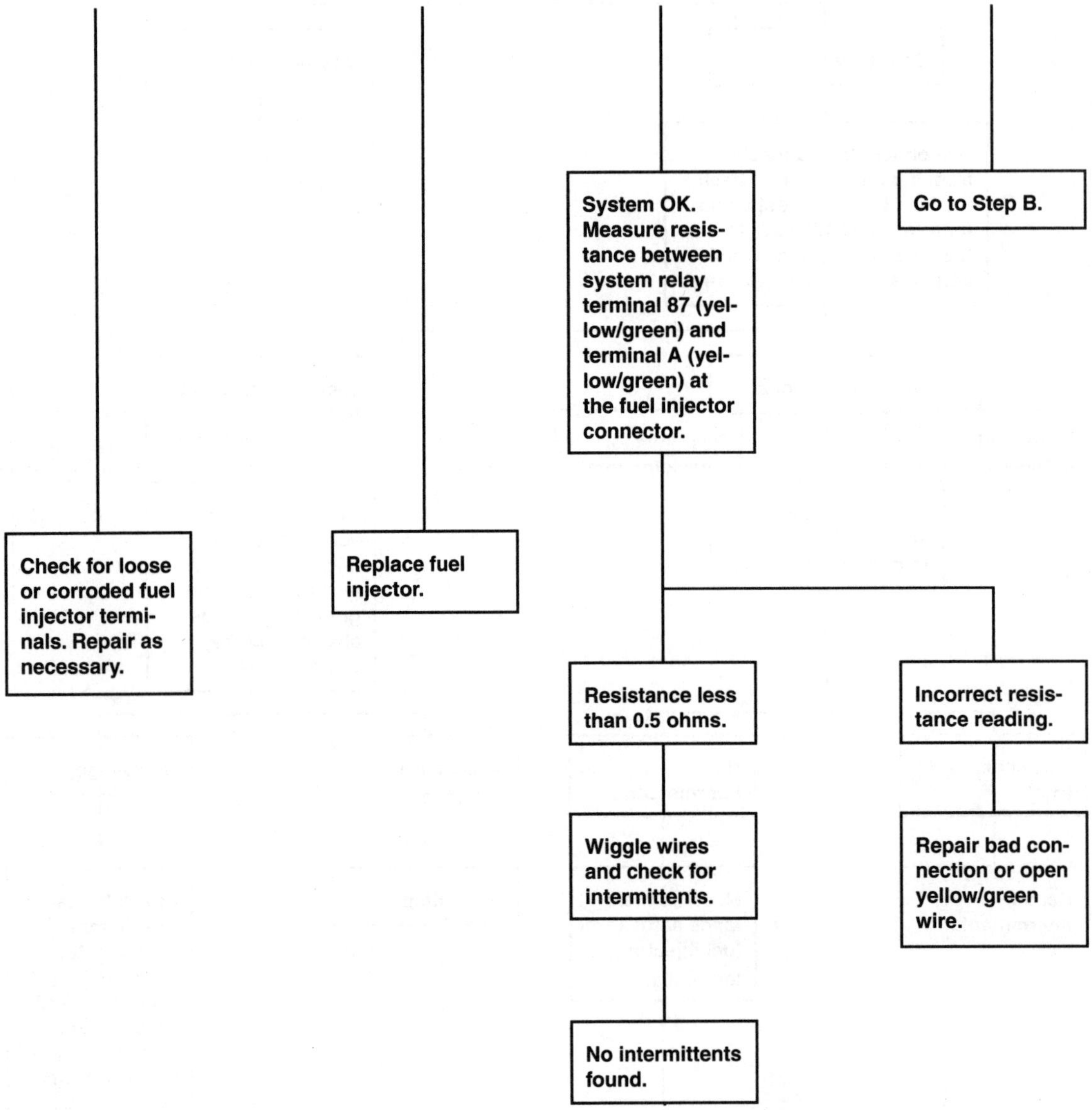
System OK. Measure resistance between system relay terminal 87 (yellow/green) and terminal A (yellow/green) at the fuel injector connector.
Go to Step B.
Check for loose or corroded fuel injector terminals. Repair as necessary.
Replace fuel injector.
Resistance less than 0.5 ohms.
Incorrect resistance reading.
Wiggle wires and check for intermittents.
Repair bad connection or open yellow/green wire.
No intermittents found.

(continued)

(27) (continued)

STEP A

Front fuel injector: DTC P0261, P0262.

Connect breakout box HD-43876 to the ECM and the ECM connector. Measure resistance between breakout box terminal 21 and terminal B (white/yellow) of the front fuel injector connector.

Rear fuel injector: DTC P0263, P0264.

Connect breakout box HD-43876 to the ECM and the ECM connector. Measure resistance between breakout box terminal 19 and terminal B (green/gray) of the rear fuel injector connector.

Resistance less than 0.5 ohm.

- Front injector: Check for continuity between breakout box terminal 10 and terminal 21.
- Rear injector: Check for continuity between breakout box terminal 10 and terminal 19.
  - Continuity exists.
    - Repair short to ground.
  - No continuity.
    - Front injector: Check for voltage between breakout box terminal 10 and terminal 21 after ignition key is turned to IGNITION for 2 seconds.
    - Rear injector: Check for voltage between breakout box terminal 10 and terminal 19 after ignition key is turned to IGNITION for 2 seconds.
      - Voltage exists.
        - Repair open in yellow/green wire.
      - No voltage.
        - Replace ECM.

Resistance greater than 0.5 ohm.

- Repair faulty connection or open in white/yellow or green/gray wire.

(continued)

15

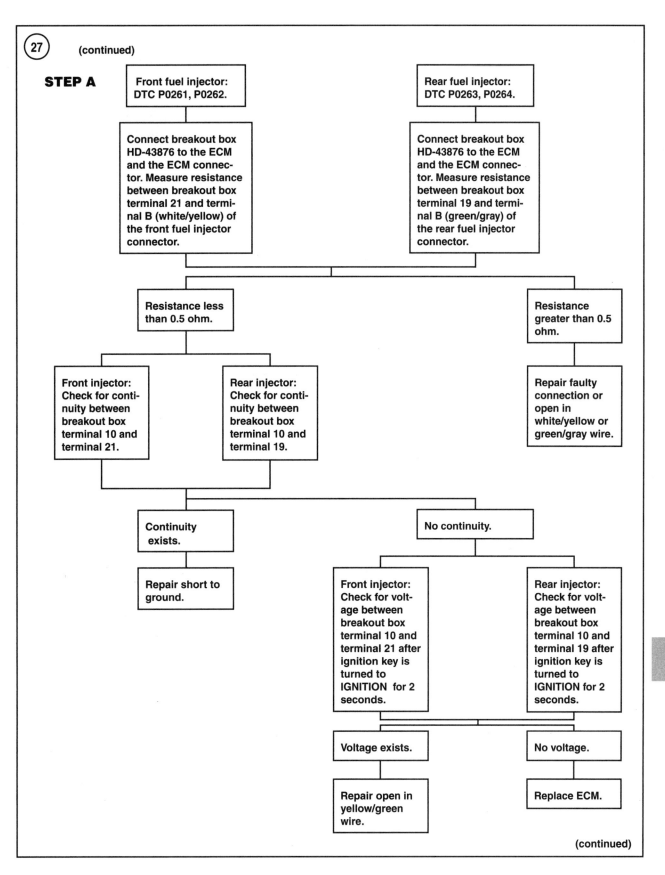

27 (continued)

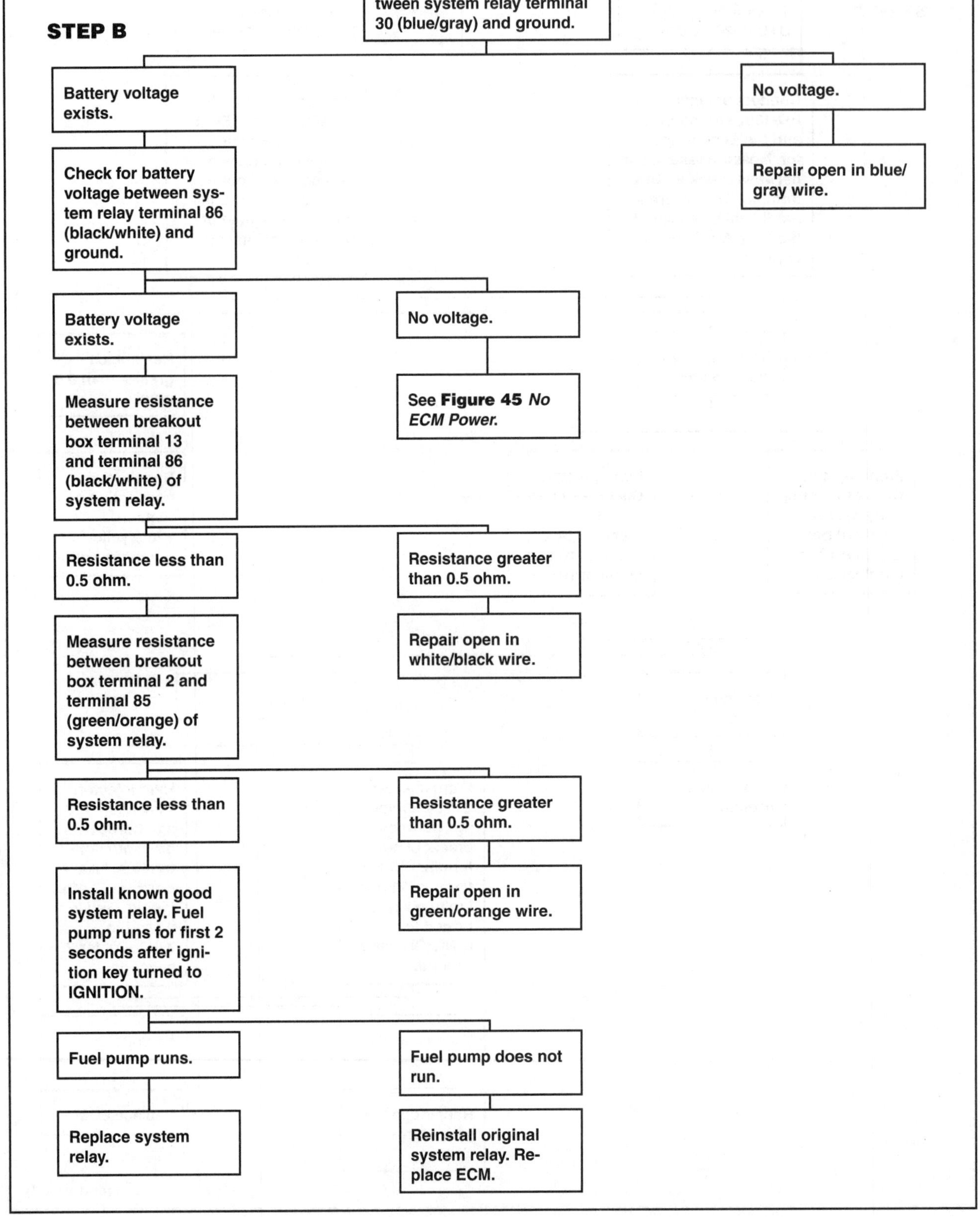
STEP B
Check for battery voltage between system relay terminal 30 (blue/gray) and ground.
Battery voltage exists.
No voltage.
Repair open in blue/gray wire.
Check for battery voltage between system relay terminal 86 (black/white) and ground.
Battery voltage exists.
No voltage.
See **Figure 45** *No ECM Power.*
Measure resistance between breakout box terminal 13 and terminal 86 (black/white) of system relay.
Resistance less than 0.5 ohm.
Resistance greater than 0.5 ohm.
Repair open in white/black wire.
Measure resistance between breakout box terminal 2 and terminal 85 (green/orange) of system relay.
Resistance less than 0.5 ohm.
Resistance greater than 0.5 ohm.
Repair open in green/orange wire.
Install known good system relay. Fuel pump runs for first 2 seconds after ignition key turned to IGNITION.
Fuel pump runs.
Fuel pump does not run.
Replace system relay.
Reinstall original system relay. Replace ECM.

28

DTC P0373, P0374: CRANK POSITION SENSOR (CKP) INTERMITTENT OR SYNCHRONIZE ERROR

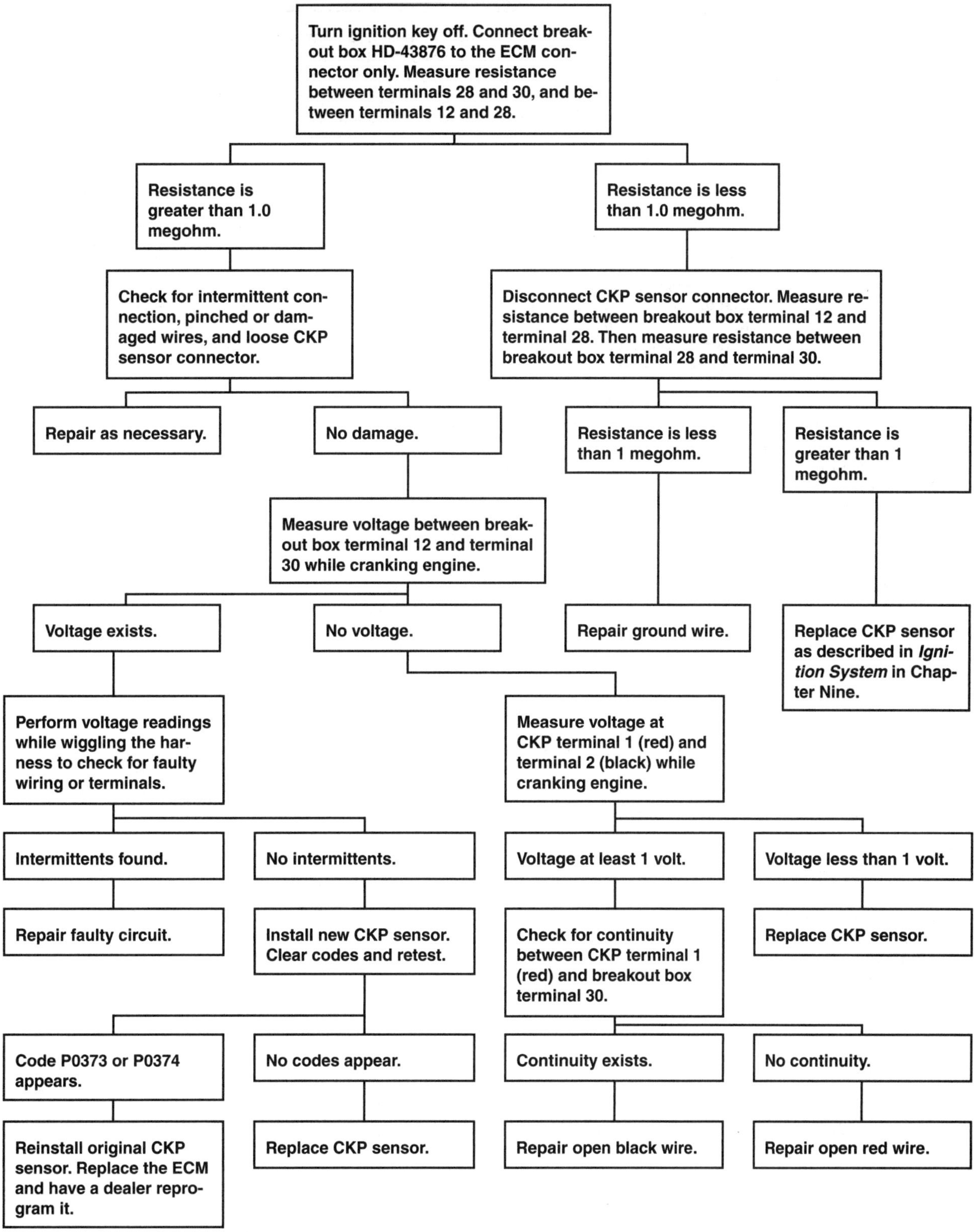
Turn ignition key off. Connect breakout box HD-43876 to the ECM connector only. Measure resistance between terminals 28 and 30, and between terminals 12 and 28.
Resistance is greater than 1.0 megohm.
Resistance is less than 1.0 megohm.
Check for intermittent connection, pinched or damaged wires, and loose CKP sensor connector.
Disconnect CKP sensor connector. Measure resistance between breakout box terminal 12 and terminal 28. Then measure resistance between breakout box terminal 28 and terminal 30.
Repair as necessary.
No damage.
Resistance is less than 1 megohm.
Resistance is greater than 1 megohm.
Measure voltage between breakout box terminal 12 and terminal 30 while cranking engine.
Voltage exists.
No voltage.
Repair ground wire.
Replace CKP sensor as described in Ignition System in Chapter Nine.
Perform voltage readings while wiggling the harness to check for faulty wiring or terminals.
Measure voltage at CKP terminal 1 (red) and terminal 2 (black) while cranking engine.
Intermittents found.
No intermittents.
Voltage at least 1 volt.
Voltage less than 1 volt.
Repair faulty circuit.
Install new CKP sensor. Clear codes and retest.
Check for continuity between CKP terminal 1 (red) and breakout box terminal 30.
Replace CKP sensor.
Code P0373 or P0374 appears.
No codes appear.
Continuity exists.
No continuity.
Reinstall original CKP sensor. Replace the ECM and have a dealer reprogram it.
Replace CKP sensor.
Repair open black wire.
Repair open red wire.

15

29

DTC PO501, PO502: VEHICLE SPEED SENSOR (VSS)

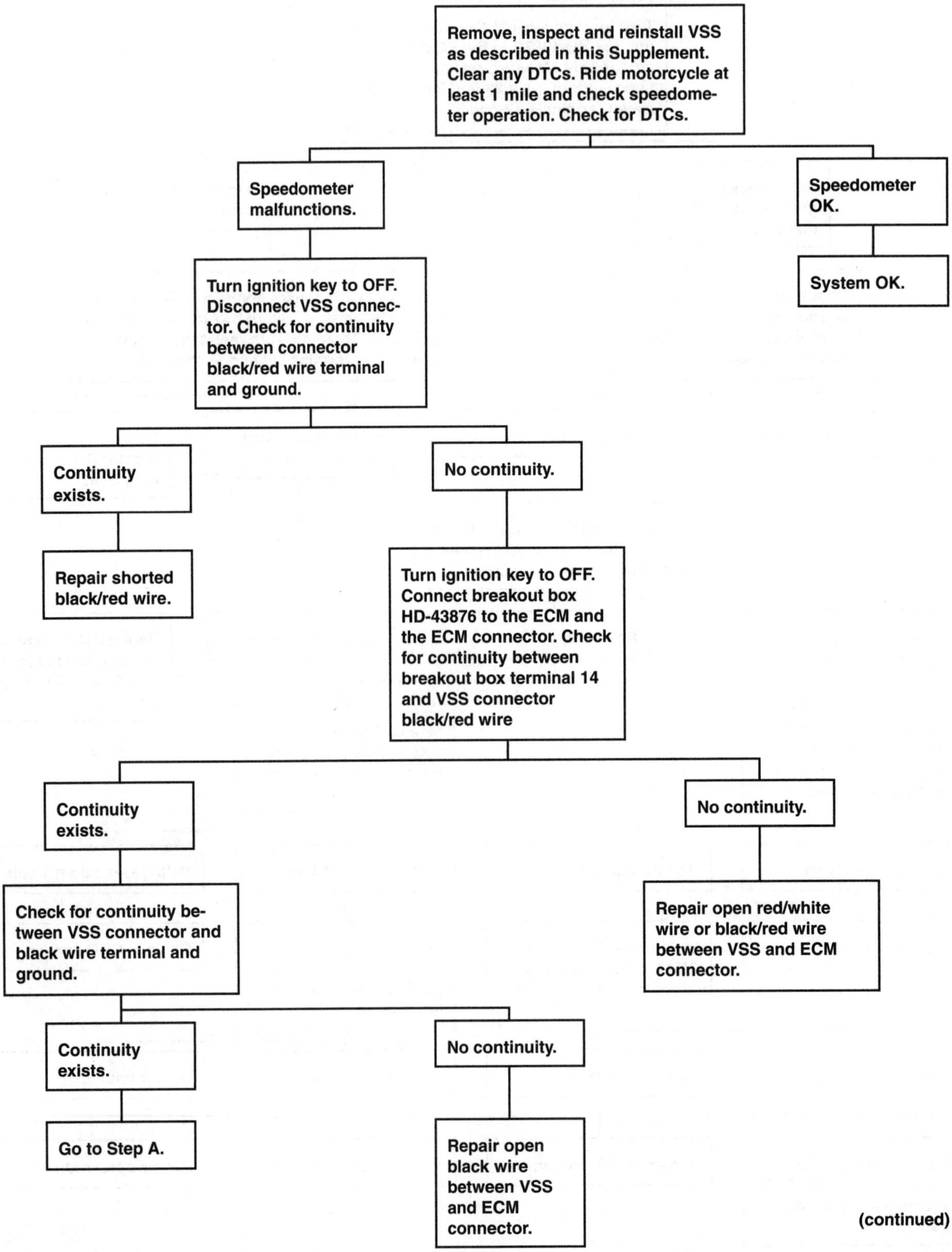
Remove, inspect and reinstall VSS as described in this Supplement. Clear any DTCs. Ride motorcycle at least 1 mile and check speedometer operation. Check for DTCs.
Speedometer malfunctions.
Speedometer OK.
System OK.
Turn ignition key to OFF. Disconnect VSS connector. Check for continuity between connector black/red wire terminal and ground.
Continuity exists.
Repair shorted black/red wire.
No continuity.
Turn ignition key to OFF. Connect breakout box HD-43876 to the ECM and the ECM connector. Check for continuity between breakout box terminal 14 and VSS connector black/red wire
Continuity exists.
Check for continuity between VSS connector and black wire terminal and ground.
Continuity exists.
Go to Step A.
No continuity.
Repair open black wire between VSS and ECM connector.
No continuity.
Repair open red/white wire or black/red wire between VSS and ECM connector.

(continued)

(29) (continued)

STEP A

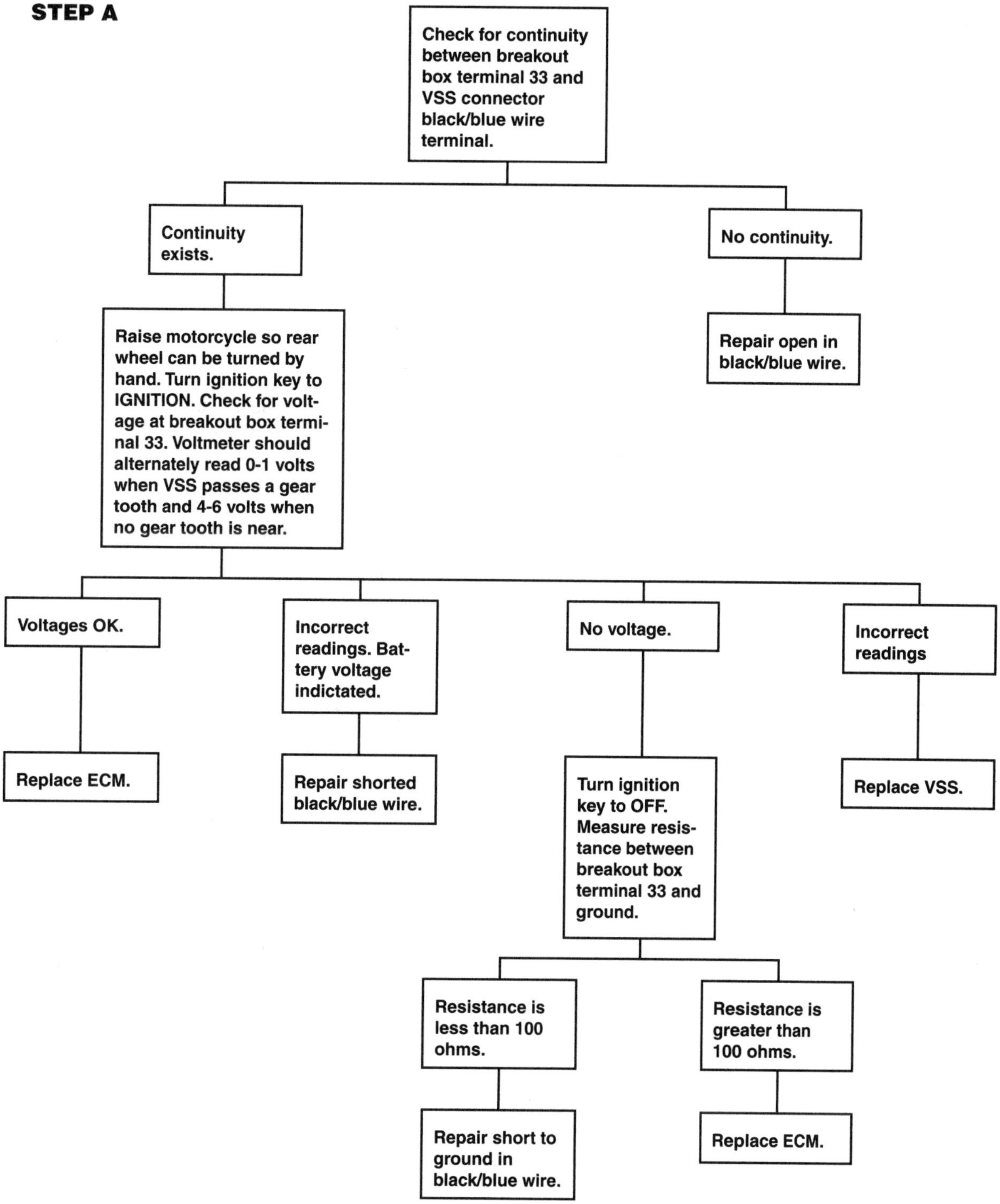

Check for continuity between breakout box terminal 33 and VSS connector black/blue wire terminal.
Continuity exists.
No continuity.
Repair open in black/blue wire.
Raise motorcycle so rear wheel can be turned by hand. Turn ignition key to IGNITION. Check for voltage at breakout box terminal 33. Voltmeter should alternately read 0-1 volts when VSS passes a gear tooth and 4-6 volts when no gear tooth is near.
Voltages OK.
Replace ECM.
Incorrect readings. Battery voltage indictated.
Repair shorted black/blue wire.
No voltage.
Turn ignition key to OFF. Measure resistance between breakout box terminal 33 and ground.
Resistance is less than 100 ohms.
Repair short to ground in black/blue wire.
Resistance is greater than 100 ohms.
Replace ECM.
Incorrect readings
Replace VSS.

30

DTC P0505: LOSS OF IDLE SPEED CONTROL

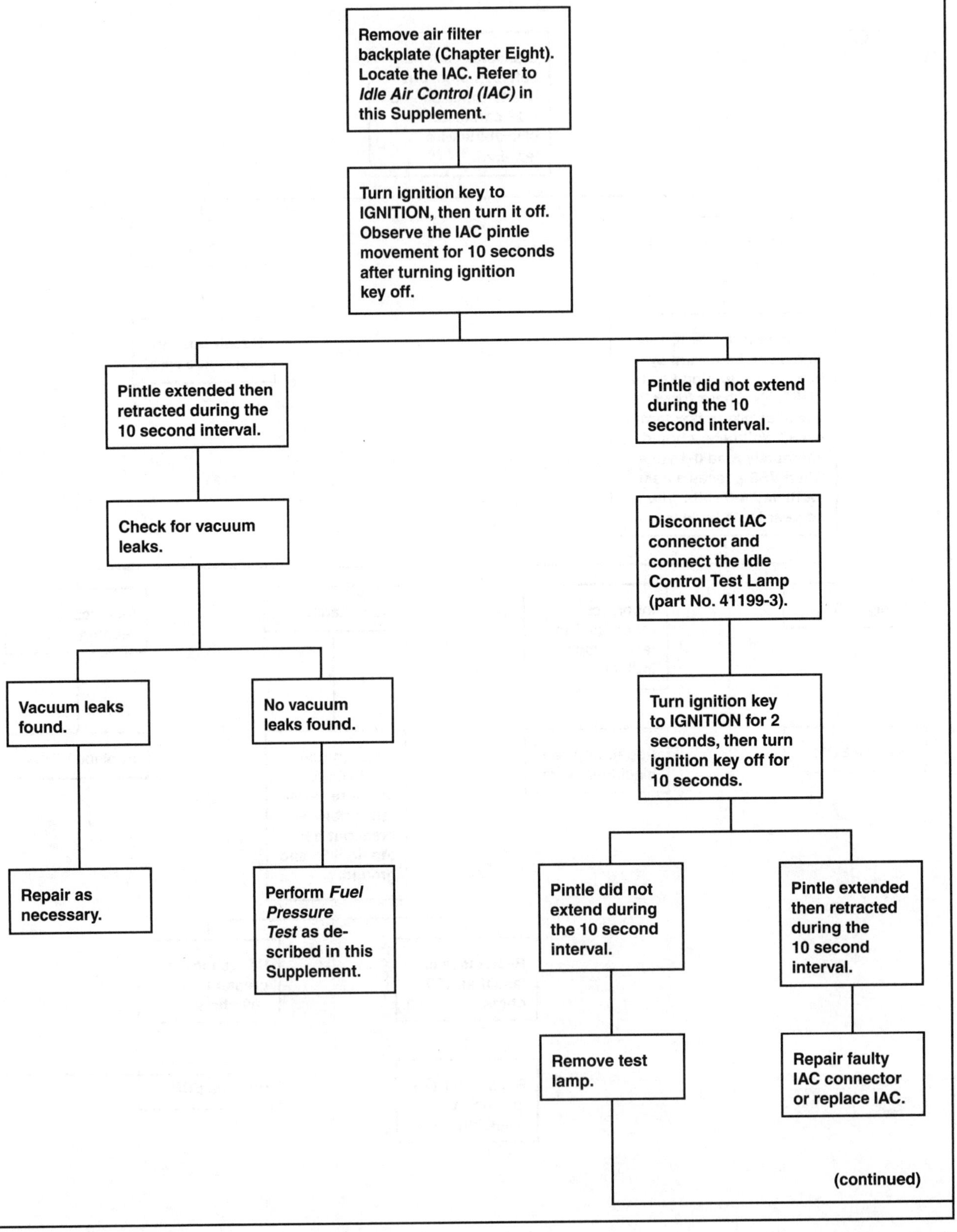
Remove air filter backplate (Chapter Eight). Locate the IAC. Refer to *Idle Air Control (IAC)* in this Supplement.
Turn ignition key to IGNITION, then turn it off. Observe the IAC pintle movement for 10 seconds after turning ignition key off.
Pintle extended then retracted during the 10 second interval.
Check for vacuum leaks.
Vacuum leaks found.
Repair as necessary.
No vacuum leaks found.
Perform *Fuel Pressure Test* as described in this Supplement.
Pintle did not extend during the 10 second interval.
Disconnect IAC connector and connect the Idle Control Test Lamp (part No. 41199-3).
Turn ignition key to IGNITION for 2 seconds, then turn ignition key off for 10 seconds.
Pintle did not extend during the 10 second interval.
Remove test lamp.
Pintle extended then retracted during the 10 second interval.
Repair faulty IAC connector or replace IAC.
(continued)

30 (continued)

Connect breakout box HD-43876 to the ECM connector. Leave the ECM disconnected. Check for battery voltage between terminal 31 and ground.

Battery voltage exists.

Check for continuity betwen IAC connector and ECM:

IAC terminal	ECM terminal
A (blue/green)	35
B (brown/red)	36
C (black/pink)	18
D (black/orange)	17

Each wire measures 0.5 ohms or less.

Turn ignition key to IGNITION. With ECM still disconnected, check for battery voltage on all four terminals at IAC connector.

Battery voltage exists.

Repair short to voltage.

No battery voltage.

Go to Step A.

Each wire measures 0.5 ohms or greater.

Repair poor connection at connectors or repair open in wire harness.

No battery voltage.

See **Figure 45** *No ECM Power.*

(continued)

15

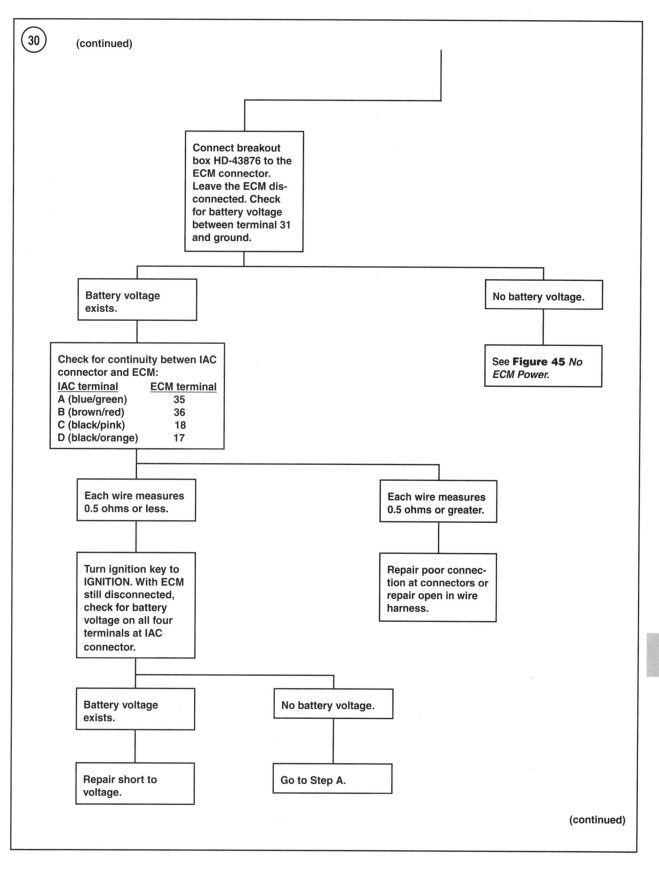

(30) (continued)

STEP A

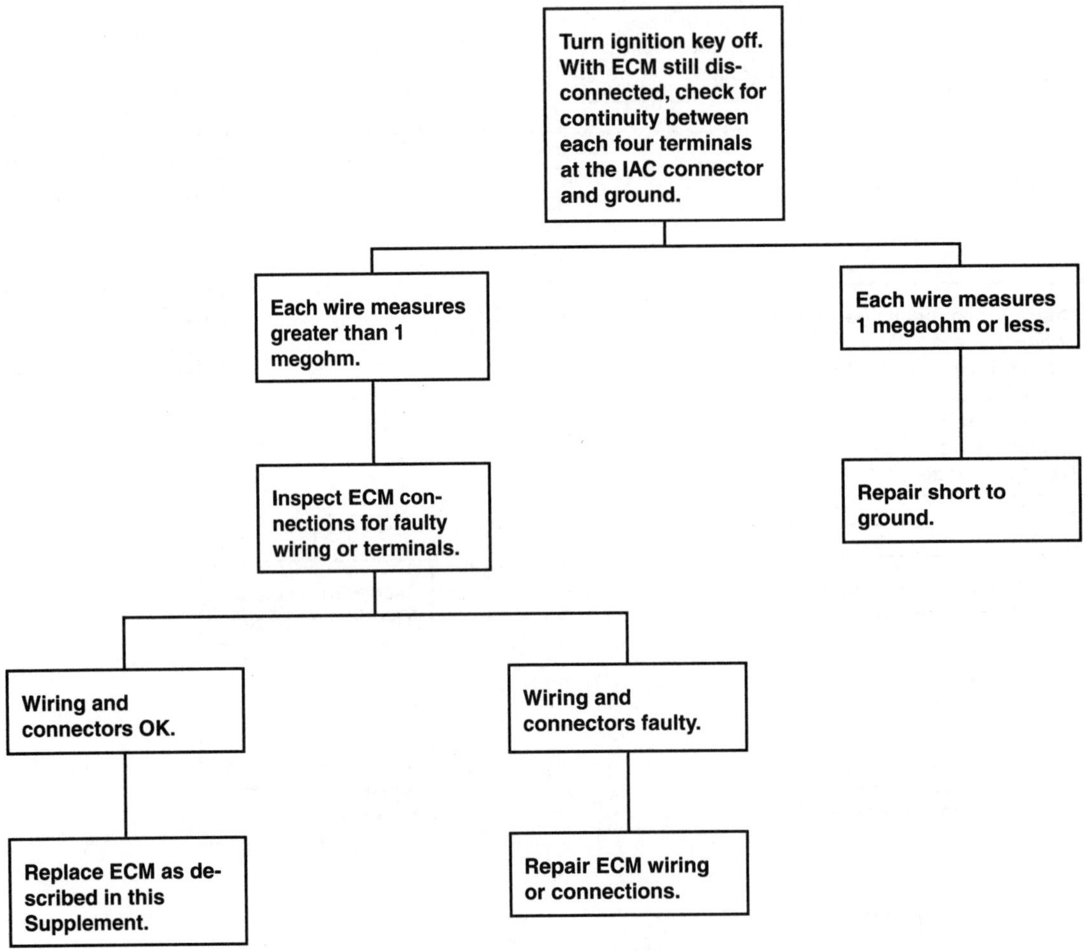
Turn ignition key off. With ECM still disconnected, check for continuity between each four terminals at the IAC connector and ground.
Each wire measures greater than 1 megohm.
Each wire measures 1 megaohm or less.
Inspect ECM connections for faulty wiring or terminals.
Repair short to ground.
Wiring and connectors OK.
Wiring and connectors faulty.
Replace ECM as described in this Supplement.
Repair ECM wiring or connections.

31

DTC P0562, P0563: BATTERY VOLTAGE

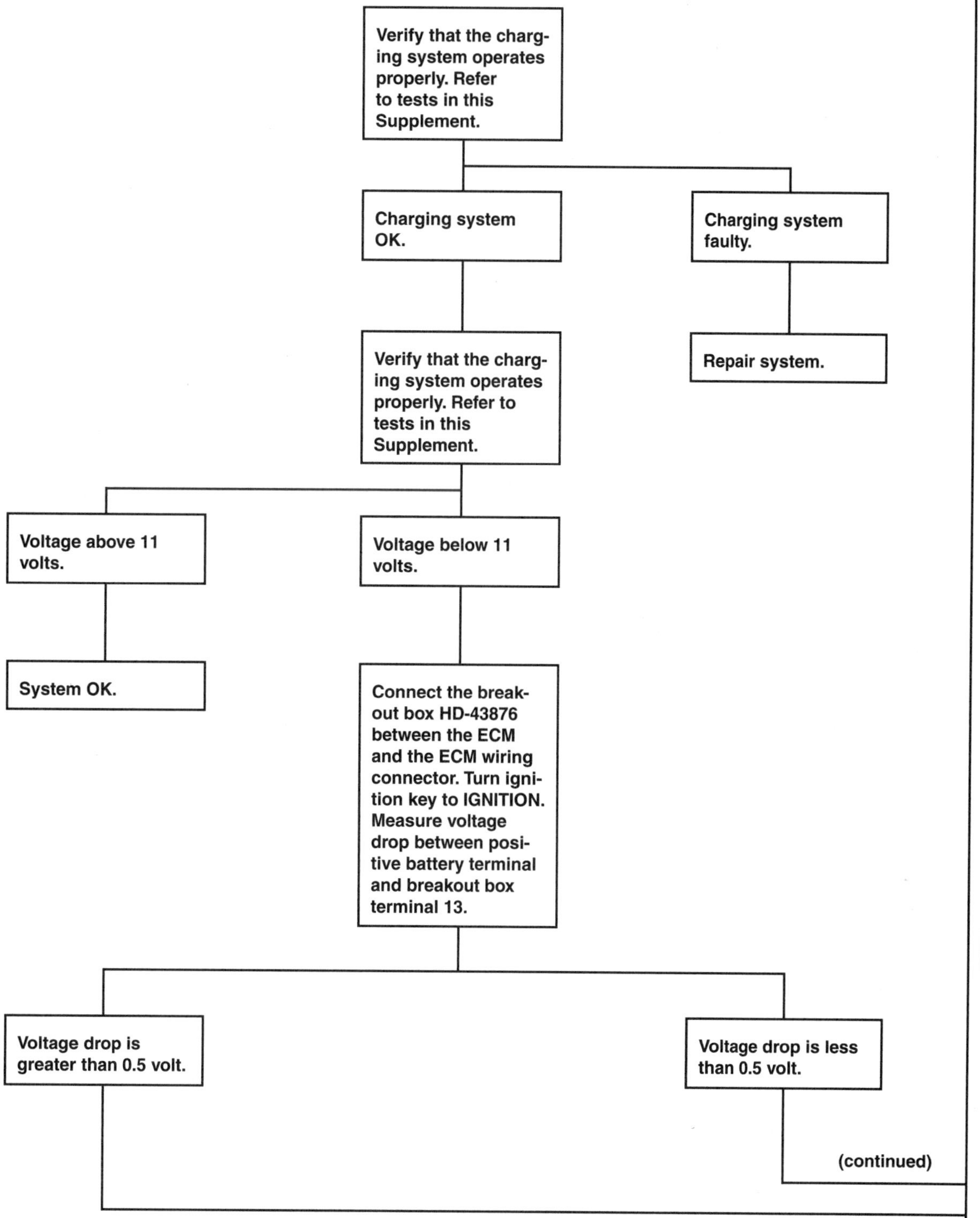
Verify that the charging system operates properly. Refer to tests in this Supplement.
Charging system OK.
Charging system faulty.
Repair system.
Verify that the charging system operates properly. Refer to tests in this Supplement.
Voltage above 11 volts.
Voltage below 11 volts.
System OK.
Connect the breakout box HD-43876 between the ECM and the ECM wiring connector. Turn ignition key to IGNITION. Measure voltage drop between positive battery terminal and breakout box terminal 13.
Voltage drop is greater than 0.5 volt.
Voltage drop is less than 0.5 volt.

(continued)

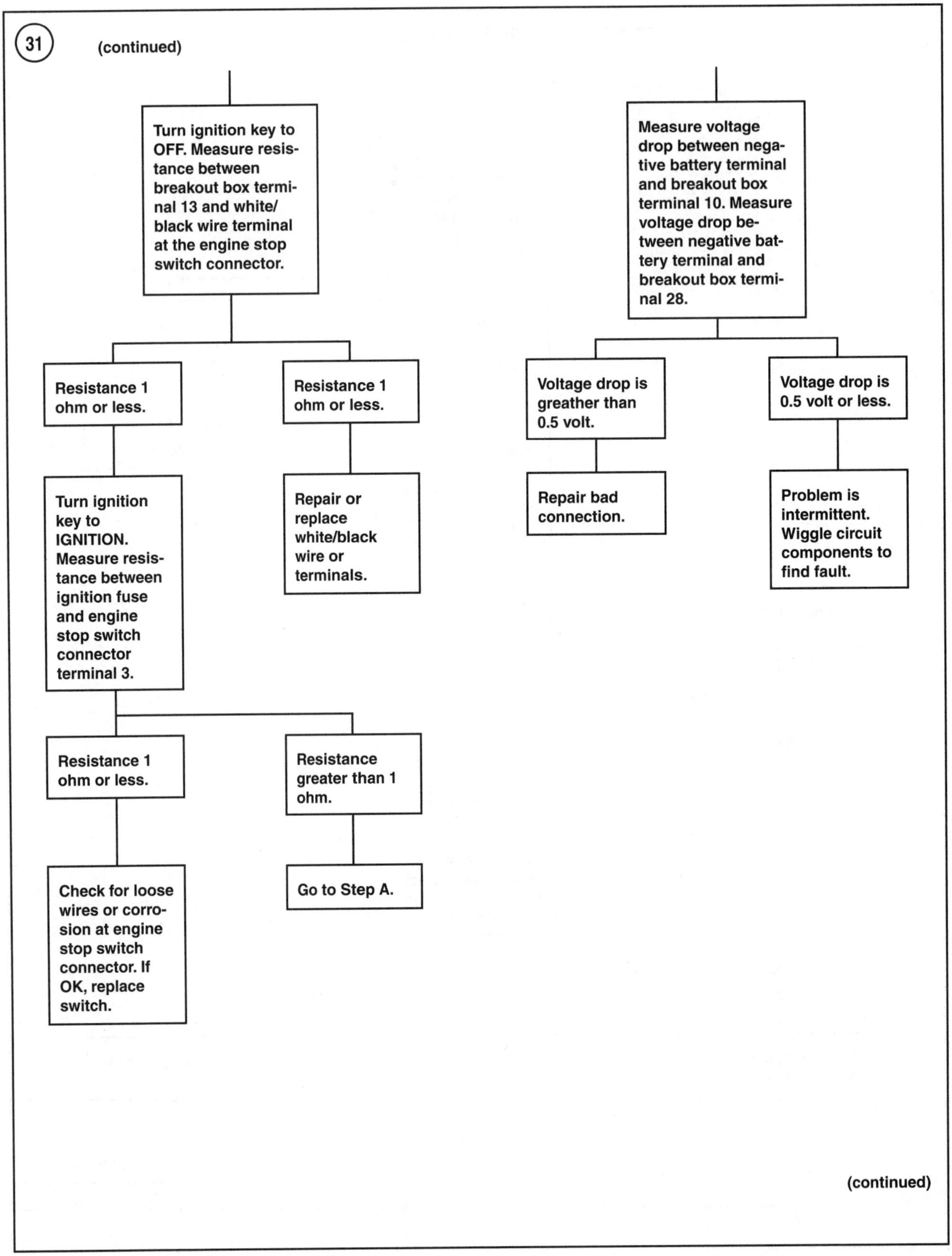
31
(continued)
Turn ignition key to OFF. Measure resistance between breakout box terminal 13 and white/black wire terminal at the engine stop switch connector.
Resistance 1 ohm or less.
Resistance 1 ohm or less.
Turn ignition key to IGNITION. Measure resistance between ignition fuse and engine stop switch connector terminal 3.
Repair or replace white/black wire or terminals.
Resistance 1 ohm or less.
Resistance greater than 1 ohm.
Check for loose wires or corrosion at engine stop switch connector. If OK, replace switch.
Go to Step A.
Measure voltage drop between negative battery terminal and breakout box terminal 10. Measure voltage drop between negative battery terminal and breakout box terminal 28.
Voltage drop is greather than 0.5 volt.
Voltage drop is 0.5 volt or less.
Repair bad connection.
Problem is intermittent. Wiggle circuit components to find fault.
(continued)

31 (continued)

STEP A

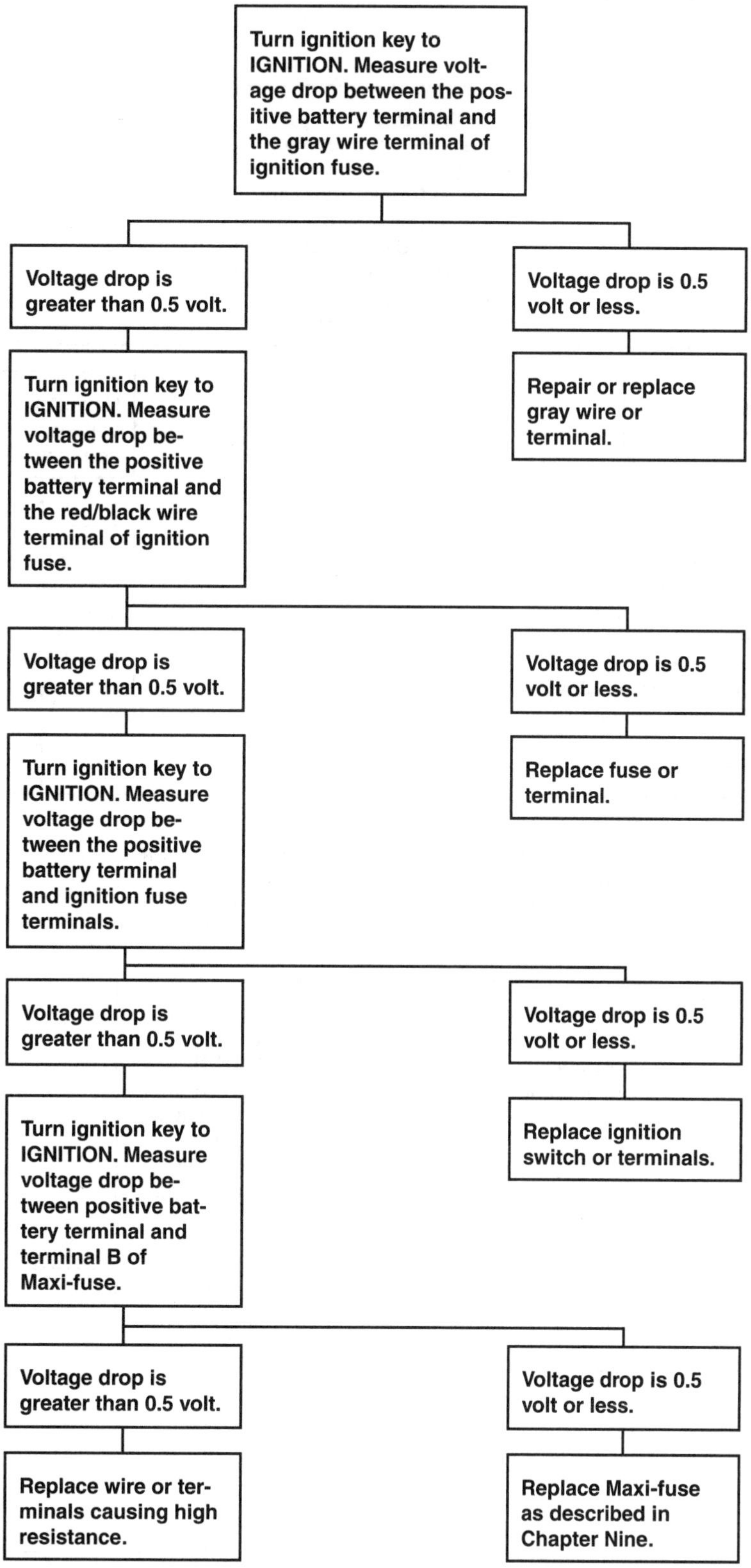
Turn ignition key to IGNITION. Measure voltage drop between the positive battery terminal and the gray wire terminal of ignition fuse.
Voltage drop is greater than 0.5 volt.
Voltage drop is 0.5 volt or less.
Repair or replace gray wire or terminal.
Turn ignition key to IGNITION. Measure voltage drop between the positive battery terminal and the red/black wire terminal of ignition fuse.
Voltage drop is greater than 0.5 volt.
Voltage drop is 0.5 volt or less.
Replace fuse or terminal.
Turn ignition key to IGNITION. Measure voltage drop between the positive battery terminal and ignition fuse terminals.
Voltage drop is greater than 0.5 volt.
Voltage drop is 0.5 volt or less.
Replace ignition switch or terminals.
Turn ignition key to IGNITION. Measure voltage drop between positive battery terminal and terminal B of Maxi-fuse.
Voltage drop is greater than 0.5 volt.
Voltage drop is 0.5 volt or less.
Replace wire or terminals causing high resistance.
Replace Maxi-fuse as described in Chapter Nine.

(continued)

(32)

DTC P1001, P1003, SYSTEM RELAY COIL OR CONTACTS OPEN

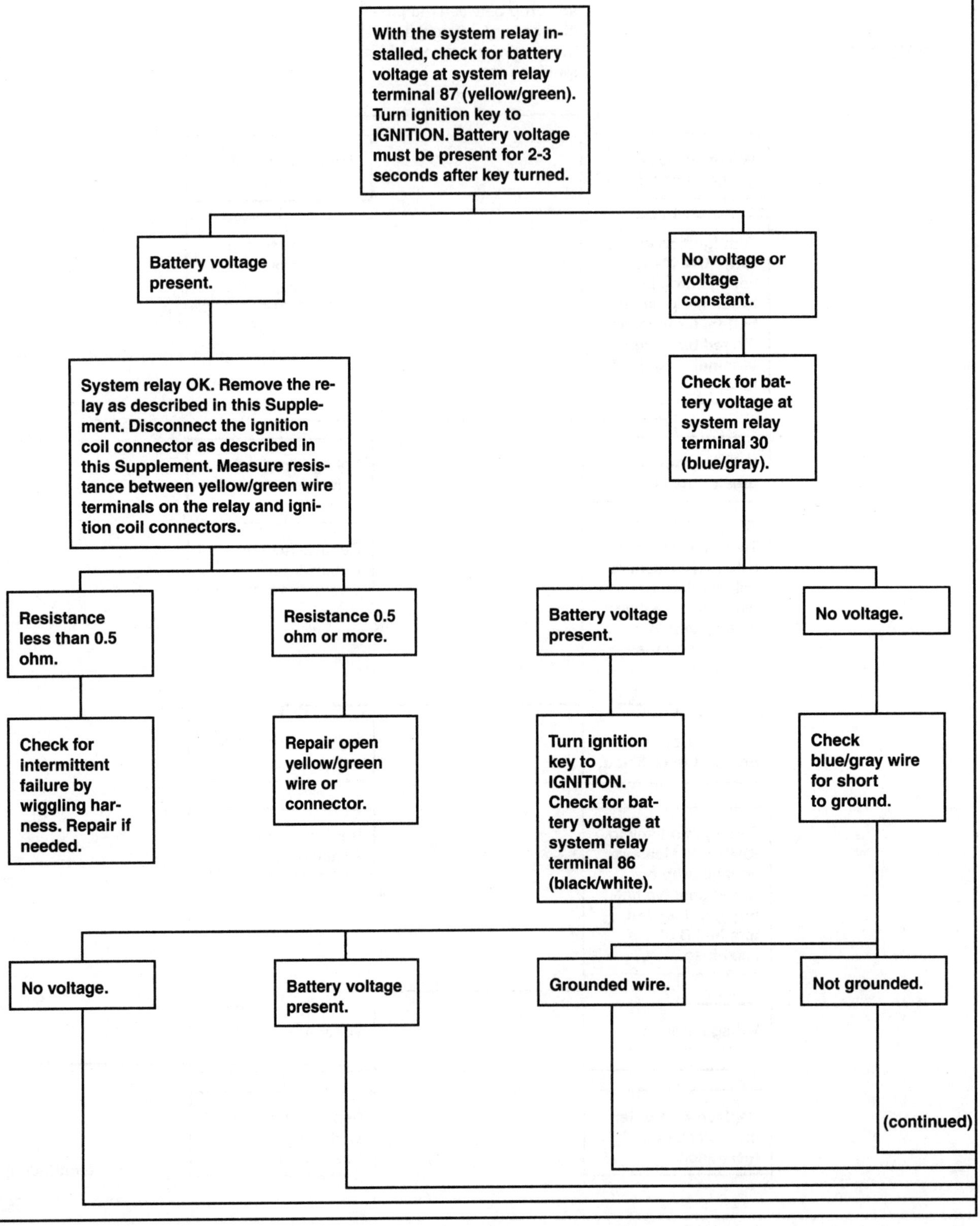

With the system relay installed, check for battery voltage at system relay terminal 87 (yellow/green). Turn ignition key to IGNITION. Battery voltage must be present for 2-3 seconds after key turned.
Battery voltage present.
No voltage or voltage constant.
System relay OK. Remove the relay as described in this Supplement. Disconnect the ignition coil connector as described in this Supplement. Measure resistance between yellow/green wire terminals on the relay and ignition coil connectors.
Check for battery voltage at system relay terminal 30 (blue/gray).
Resistance less than 0.5 ohm.
Resistance 0.5 ohm or more.
Battery voltage present.
No voltage.
Check for intermittent failure by wiggling harness. Repair if needed.
Repair open yellow/green wire or connector.
Turn ignition key to IGNITION. Check for battery voltage at system relay terminal 86 (black/white).
Check blue/gray wire for short to ground.
No voltage.
Battery voltage present.
Grounded wire.
Not grounded.
(continued)

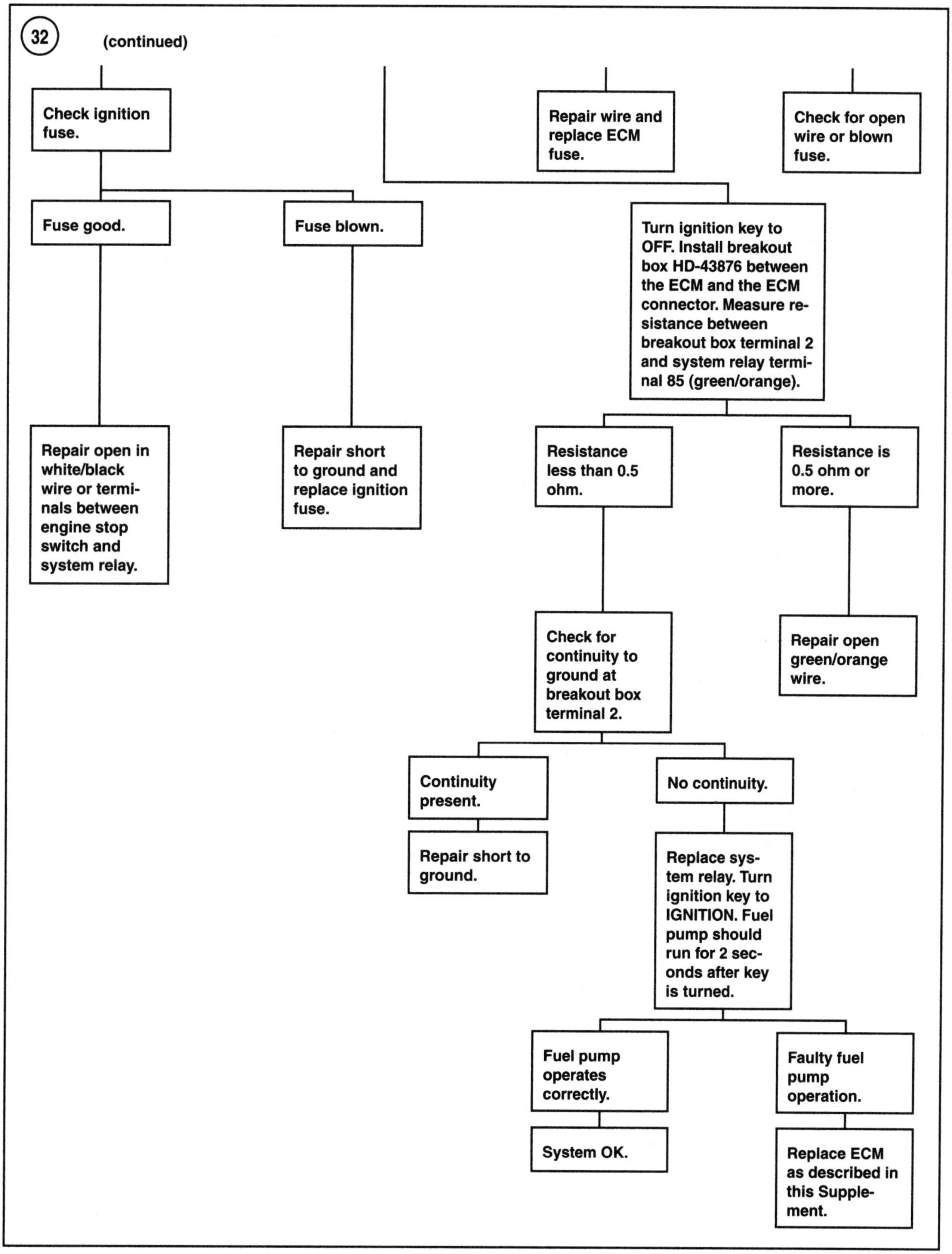
32
(continued)
Check ignition fuse.
Fuse good.
Fuse blown.
Repair open in white/black wire or terminals between engine stop switch and system relay.
Repair short to ground and replace ignition fuse.
Repair wire and replace ECM fuse.
Check for open wire or blown fuse.
Turn ignition key to OFF. Install breakout box HD-43876 between the ECM and the ECM connector. Measure resistance between breakout box terminal 2 and system relay terminal 85 (green/orange).
Resistance less than 0.5 ohm.
Resistance is 0.5 ohm or more.
Check for continuity to ground at breakout box terminal 2.
Repair open green/orange wire.
Continuity present.
No continuity.
Repair short to ground.
Replace system relay. Turn ignition key to IGNITION. Fuel pump should run for 2 seconds after key is turned.
Fuel pump operates correctly.
Faulty fuel pump operation.
System OK.
Replace ECM as described in this Supplement.

33

DTC P1002: SYSTEM RELAY COIL HIGH OR SHORTER

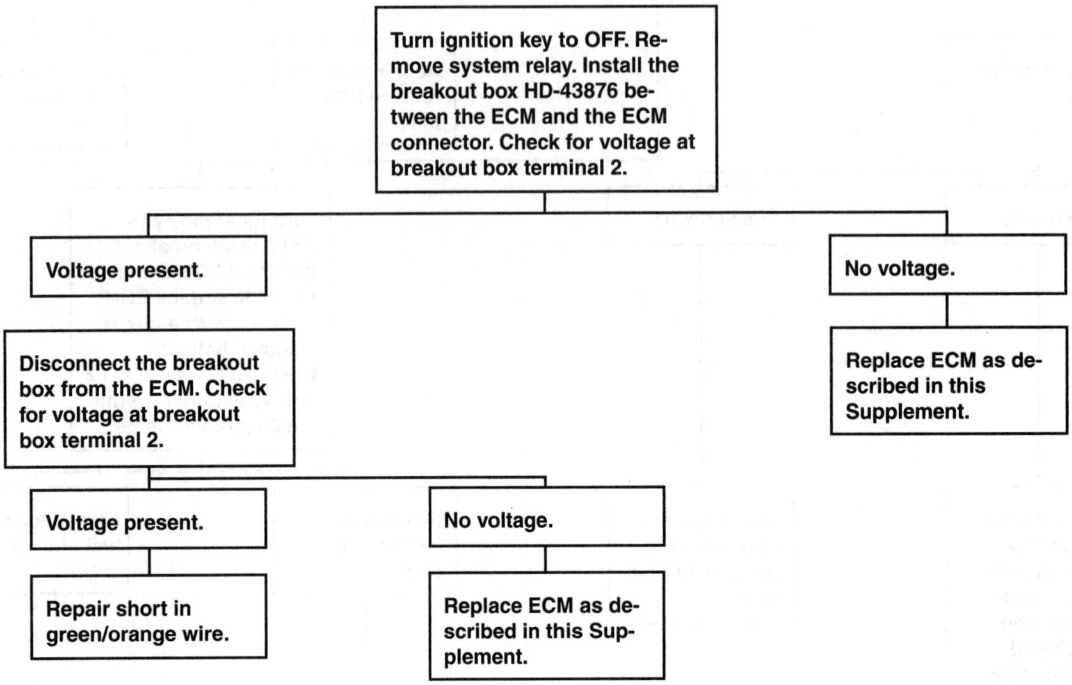
Turn ignition key to OFF. Remove system relay. Install the breakout box HD-43876 between the ECM and the ECM connector. Check for voltage at breakout box terminal 2.
Voltage present.
No voltage.
Replace ECM as described in this Supplement.
Disconnect the breakout box from the ECM. Check for voltage at breakout box terminal 2.
Voltage present.
No voltage.
Repair short in green/orange wire.
Replace ECM as described in this Supplement.

34

DTC P1004: SYSTEM RELAY CONTACTS CLOSED

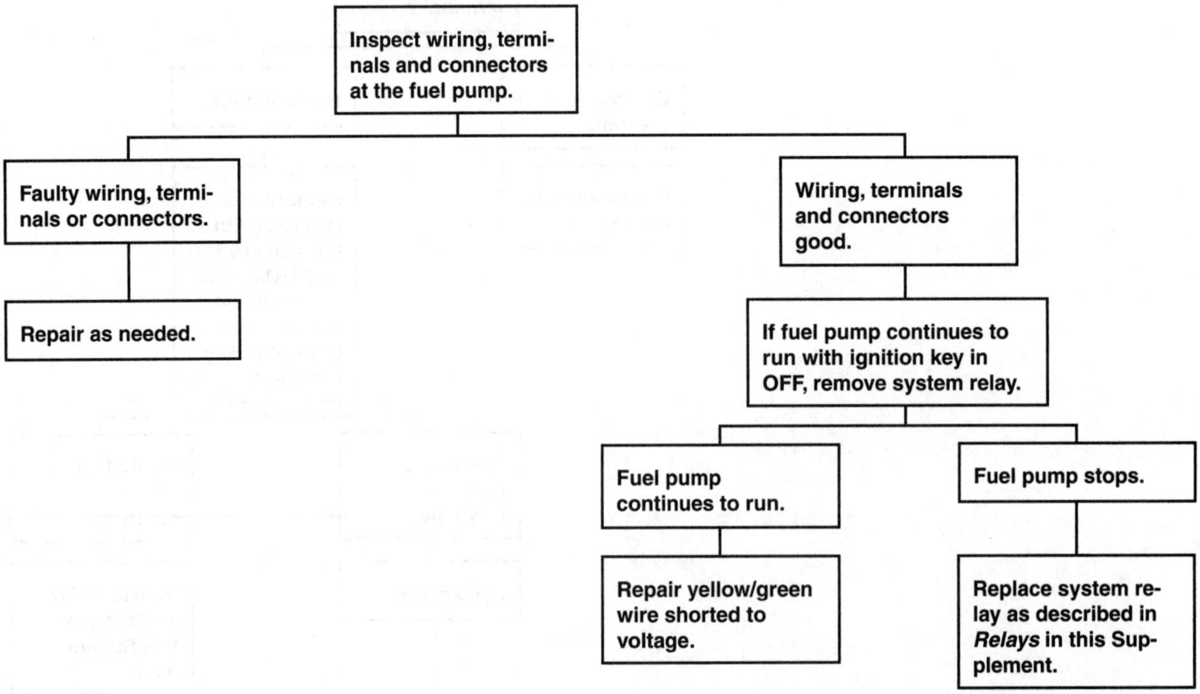
Inspect wiring, terminals and connectors at the fuel pump.
Faulty wiring, terminals or connectors.
Repair as needed.
Wiring, terminals and connectors good.
If fuel pump continues to run with ignition key in OFF, remove system relay.
Fuel pump continues to run.
Fuel pump stops.
Repair yellow/green wire shorted to voltage.
Replace system relay as described in Relays in this Supplement.

35

DTC P1009: INCORRECT PERSONAL IDENTIFICATION NUMBER (PIN)

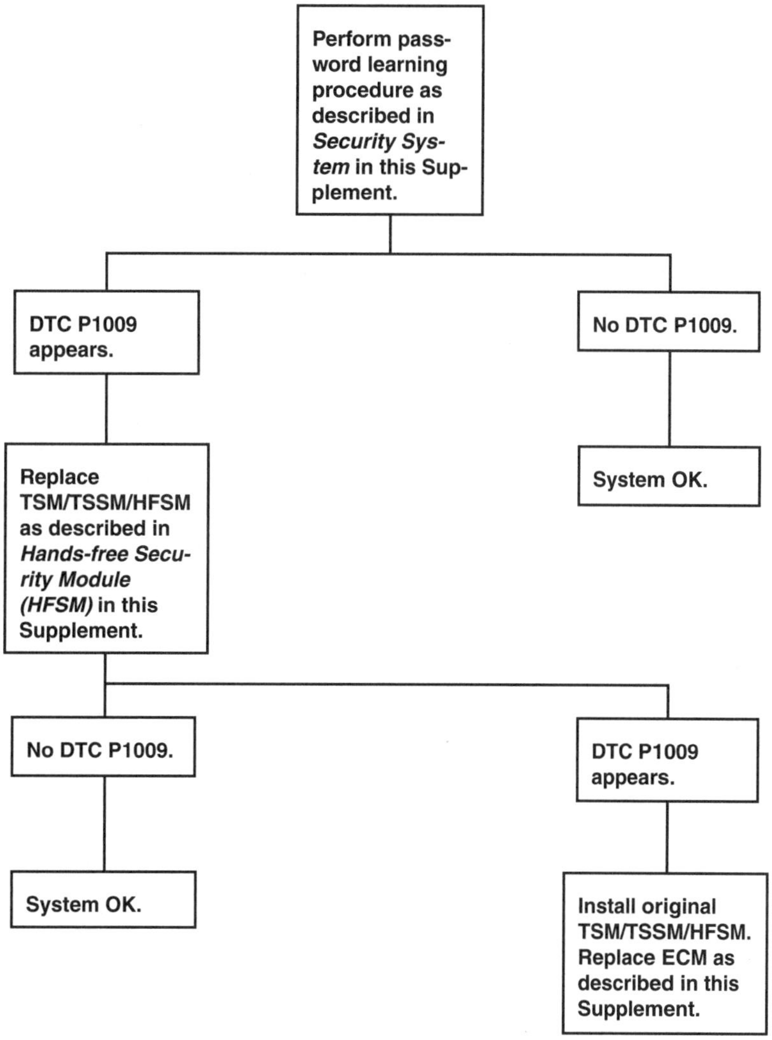

Perform password learning procedure as described in *Security System* in this Supplement.
DTC P1009 appears.
No DTC P1009.
Replace TSM/TSSM/HFSM as described in *Hands-free Security Module (HFSM)* in this Supplement.
System OK.
No DTC P1009.
DTC P1009 appears.
System OK.
Install original TSM/TSSM/HFSM. Replace ECM as described in this Supplement.

36

DTC P1010: MISSING PERSONAL IDENTIFICATION NUMBER (PIN)

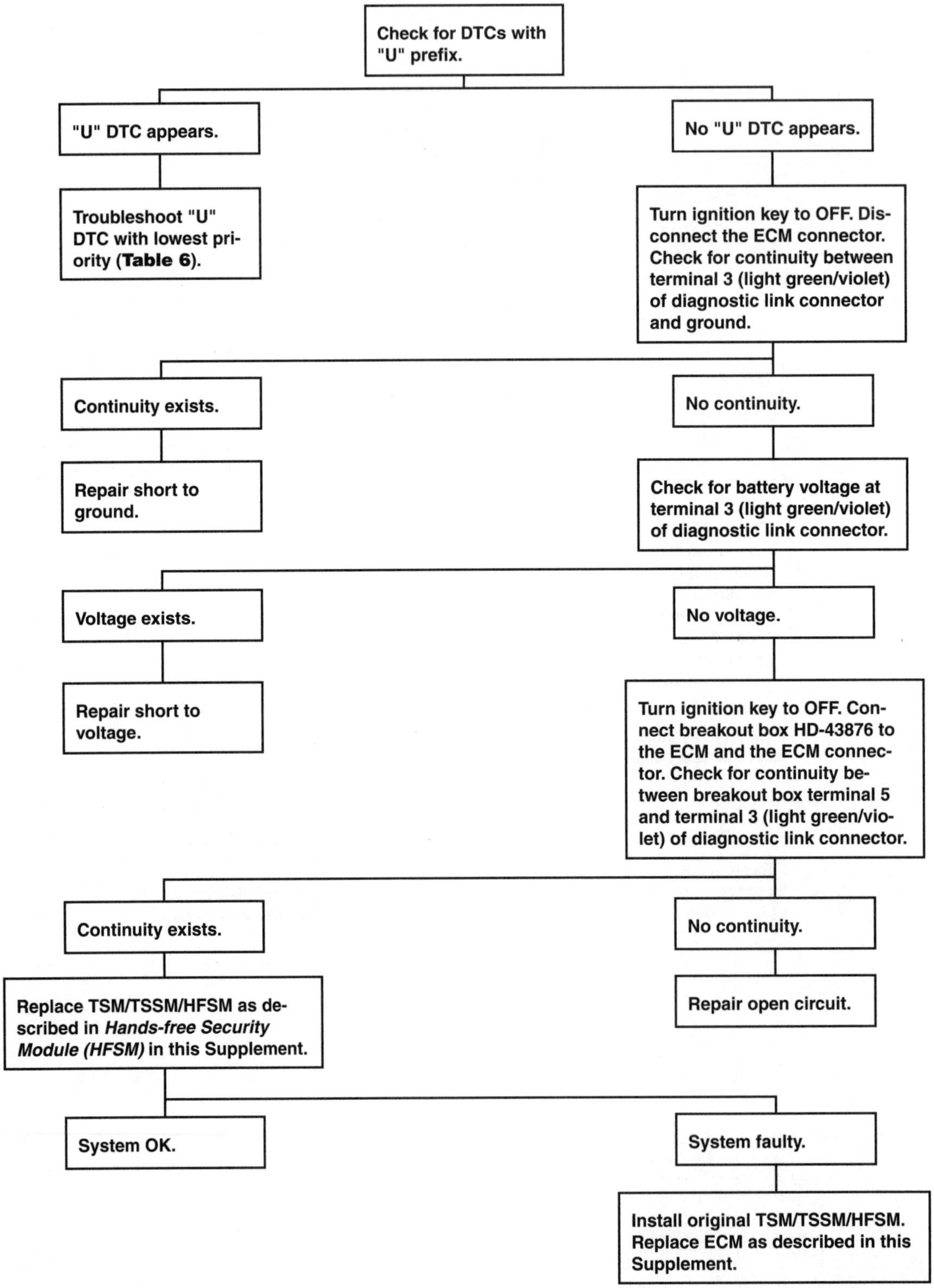
Check for DTCs with "U" prefix.
"U" DTC appears.
Troubleshoot "U" DTC with lowest priority (**Table 6**).
No "U" DTC appears.
Turn ignition key to OFF. Disconnect the ECM connector. Check for continuity between terminal 3 (light green/violet) of diagnostic link connector and ground.
Continuity exists.
Repair short to ground.
No continuity.
Check for battery voltage at terminal 3 (light green/violet) of diagnostic link connector.
Voltage exists.
Repair short to voltage.
No voltage.
Turn ignition key to OFF. Connect breakout box HD-43876 to the ECM and the ECM connector. Check for continuity between breakout box terminal 5 and terminal 3 (light green/violet) of diagnostic link connector.
Continuity exists.
Replace TSM/TSSM/HFSM as described in *Hands-free Security Module (HFSM)* in this Supplement.
No continuity.
Repair open circuit.
System OK.
System faulty.
Install original TSM/TSSM/HFSM. Replace ECM as described in this Supplement.

37

DTC P1351, P1352, P1354, P1355: IGNITION COIL

NOTE: DTC P1351, P1352, P1354 or P1355 may be set when using the test apparatus and the igniton coil is disconnected. Clear the codes and retest.

Turn ignition key to OFF. Disconnect ignition coil connector as described in *Ignition System* in this Supplement. Measure voltage at white/black wire connector terminal right handlebar switch connector 22. Be sure the engine stop switch is in RUN. Turn ignition switch to IGNITION. Voltage should equal battery voltage in first 2 seconds after ignition switch is turned to IGNITION.

- Voltage equals battery voltage.
  - Go to Step A.
- Voltage does not equal battery voltage.
  - Turn ignition key to OFF. Connect breakout box HD-43876 to the ECM and the ECM connector. Install Ignition Coil Circuit Test Adapter HD-44687 and Fuel Injector Test Lamp HD-34730-2C in breakout box terminals 13 and 29 to check front cylinder coil. To check rear cylinder coil install tester in breakout box terminals 11 and 13. Crank engine and observe test lamp.
    - Test lamp flashes.
      - Measure primary coil resistance as described in *Ignition System* in this Supplement.
        - Correct test results.
          - Go to Step A.
        - Incorrect test results.
          - Replace ignition coil.
    - Test lamp does not flash.
      - Check for battery voltage at blue/gray wire terminal on system relay for first 2 seconds after ignition key is turned to IGNITION.
        - Battery voltage present.
          - Repair open blue/gray
        - No battery voltage.
          - Check for multiple DTCs.

15

(continued)

(37) (continued)

STEP A

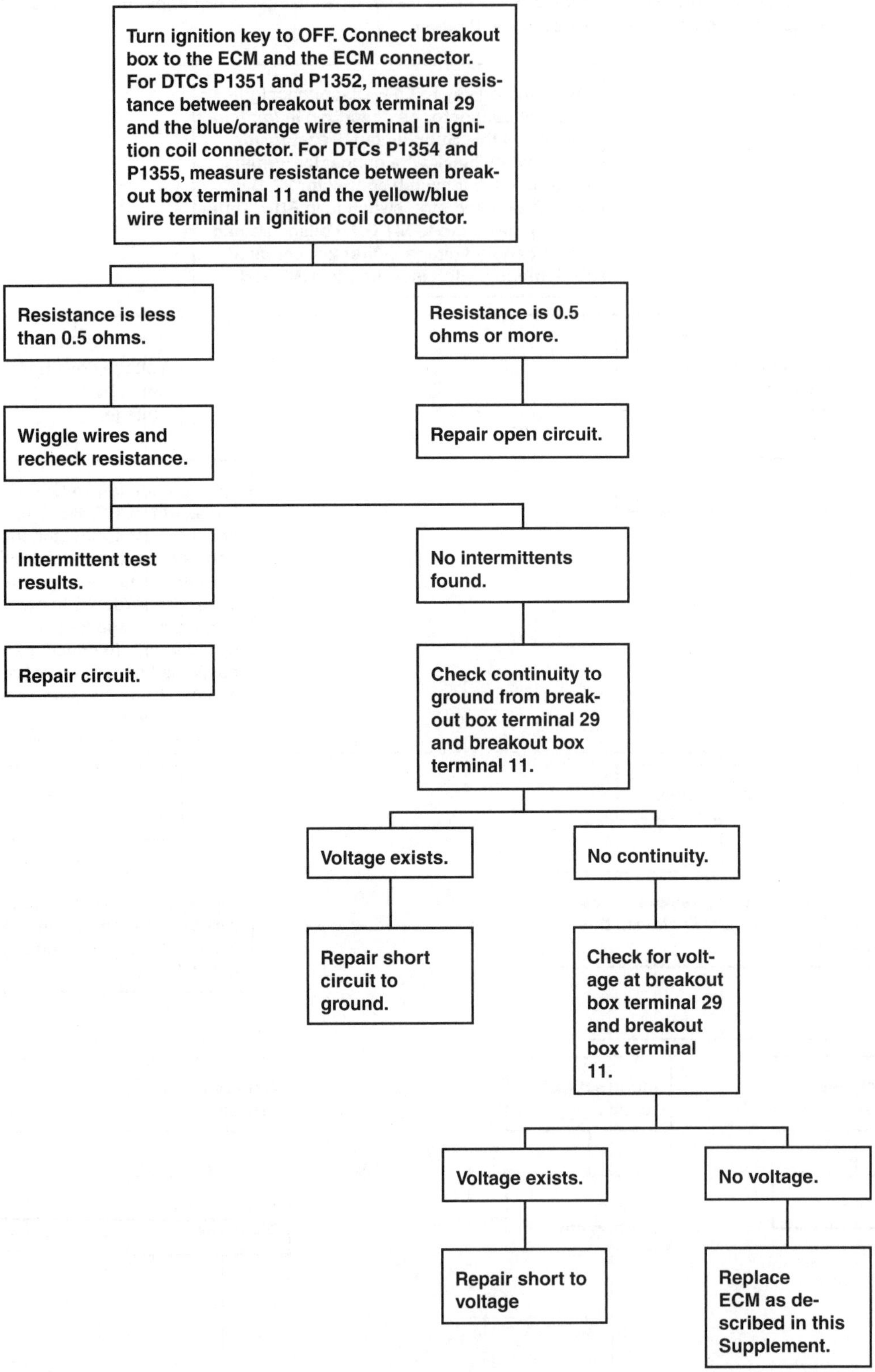

Turn ignition key to OFF. Connect breakout box to the ECM and the ECM connector. For DTCs P1351 and P1352, measure resistance between breakout box terminal 29 and the blue/orange wire terminal in ignition coil connector. For DTCs P1354 and P1355, measure resistance between breakout box terminal 11 and the yellow/blue wire terminal in ignition coil connector.
Resistance is less than 0.5 ohms.
Resistance is 0.5 ohms or more.
Wiggle wires and recheck resistance.
Repair open circuit.
Intermittent test results.
No intermittents found.
Repair circuit.
Check continuity to ground from breakout box terminal 29 and breakout box terminal 11.
Voltage exists.
No continuity.
Repair short circuit to ground.
Check for voltage at breakout box terminal 29 and breakout box terminal 11.
Voltage exists.
No voltage.
Repair short to voltage
Replace ECM as described in this Supplement.

(38)

DTC P1501: SIDE STAND SENSOR LOW

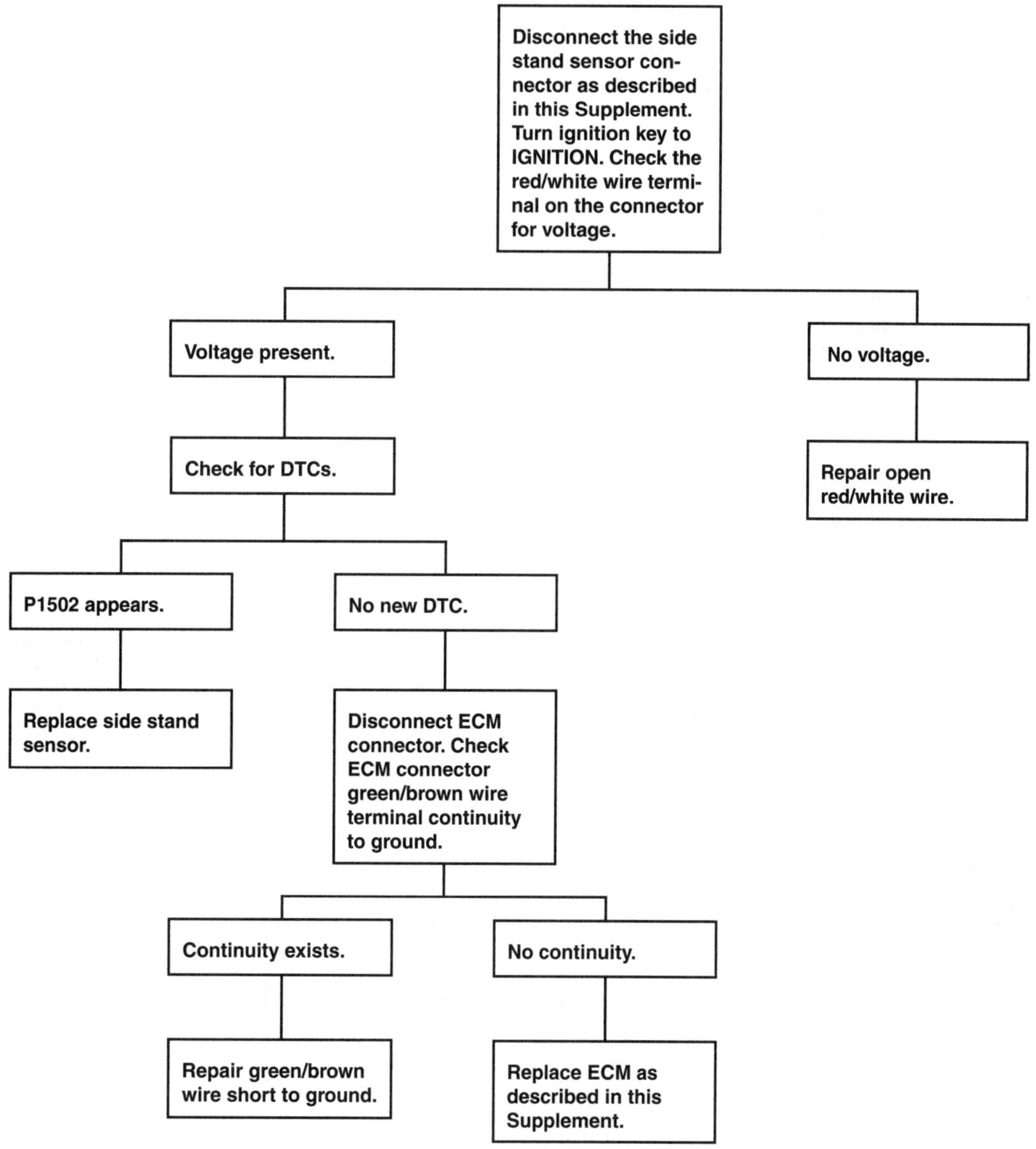
Disconnect the side stand sensor connector as described in this Supplement. Turn ignition key to IGNITION. Check the red/white wire terminal on the connector for voltage.
Voltage present.
No voltage.
Check for DTCs.
Repair open red/white wire.
P1502 appears.
No new DTC.
Replace side stand sensor.
Disconnect ECM connector. Check ECM connector green/brown wire terminal continuity to ground.
Continuity exists.
No continuity.
Repair green/brown wire short to ground.
Replace ECM as described in this Supplement.

(39)

DTC P1502: SIDE STAND SENSOR HIGH

- Disconnect side stand sensor connector as described in this Supplement. Check the black wire terminal on the connector for continuity to ground.
  - Continuity exists.
    - Turn ignition key to IGNITION. Check the right/white wire terminal on the connector for voltage.
      - Voltage present.
        - Is the voltage approximately 5 volts?
          - Yes.
            - Turn ignition key to OFF. Disconnect ECM connector. Check continuity between green/brown wire terminals on the ECM and sensor connector.
          - No.
            - Turn ignition key to OFF. Connect breakout box HD-43876 to the ECM and the ECM connector. Measure voltage at breakout box terminal 9 and ground.
      - No voltage present.
        - Turn ignition switch to OFF. Check the red/white wire terminal on the sensor connector for continuity to ground.
          - No continuity.
            - Repair red/white wire short to ground.
          - Continuity exists.
            - Disconnect the ECM connector. Check for continuity between red/white wire terminals on the sensor and the ECM connectors.
  - No continuity.
    - Locate and repair open.

(continued)

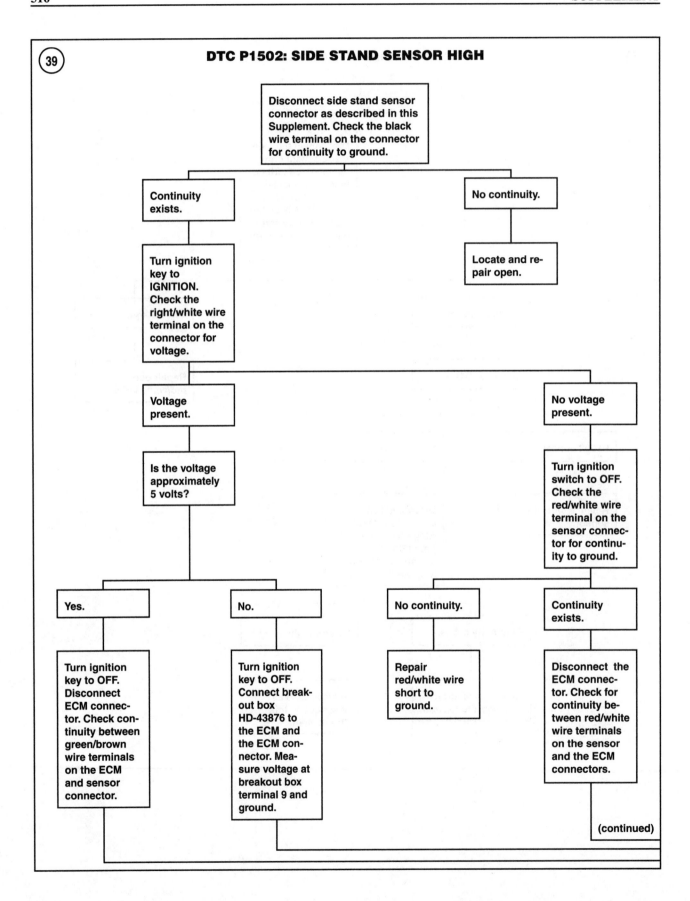

39 (continued)

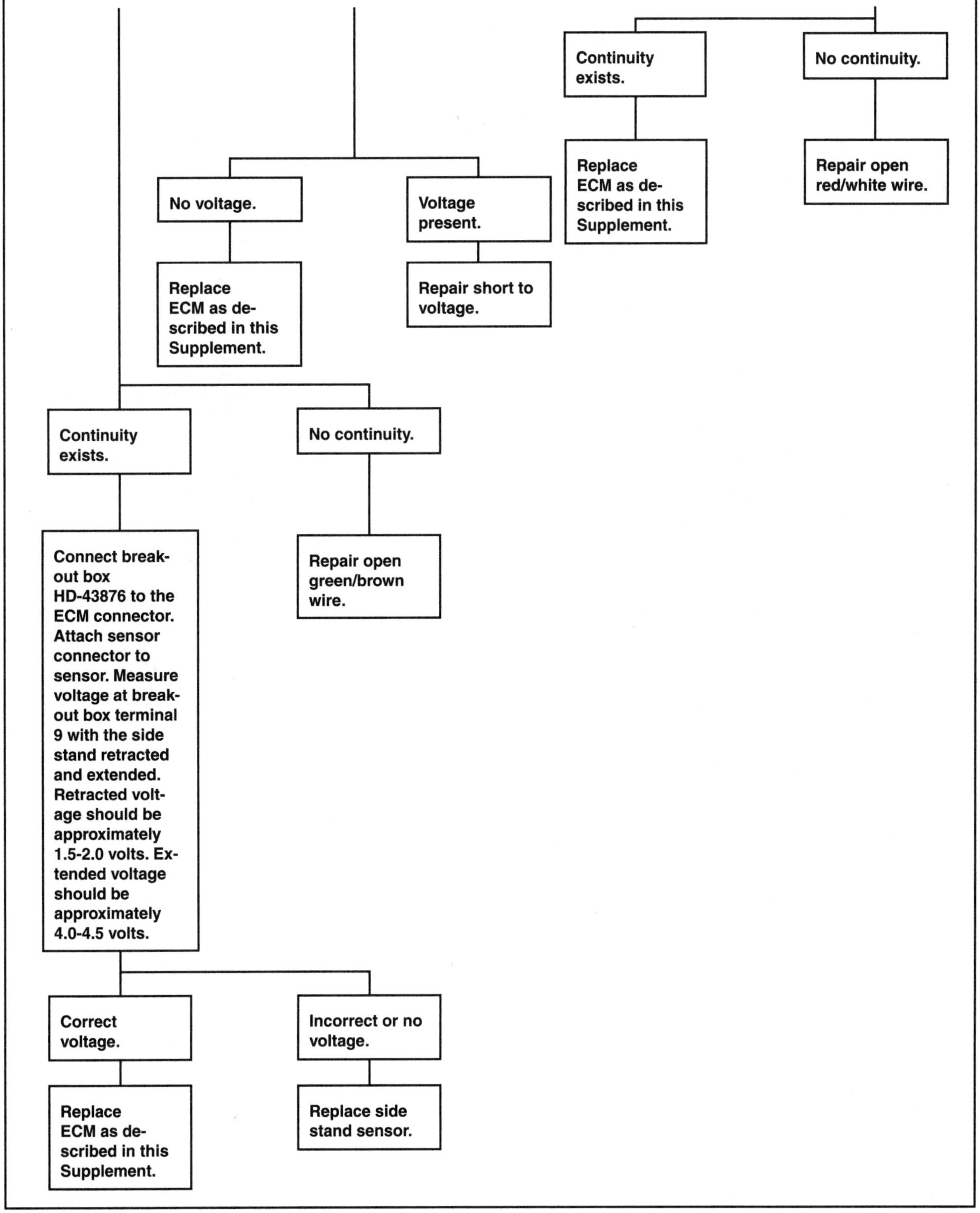
Continuity exists.
No continuity.
Replace ECM as described in this Supplement.
Repair open red/white wire.
No voltage.
Voltage present.
Replace ECM as described in this Supplement.
Repair short to voltage.
Continuity exists.
No continuity.
Connect breakout box HD-43876 to the ECM connector. Attach sensor connector to sensor. Measure voltage at breakout box terminal 9 with the side stand retracted and extended. Retracted voltage should be approximately 1.5-2.0 volts. Extended voltage should be approximately 4.0-4.5 volts.
Repair open green/brown wire.
Correct voltage.
Incorrect or no voltage.
Replace ECM as described in this Supplement.
Replace side stand sensor.

40

DTC U1016, U1255: LOSS OF ECM SERIAL DATA

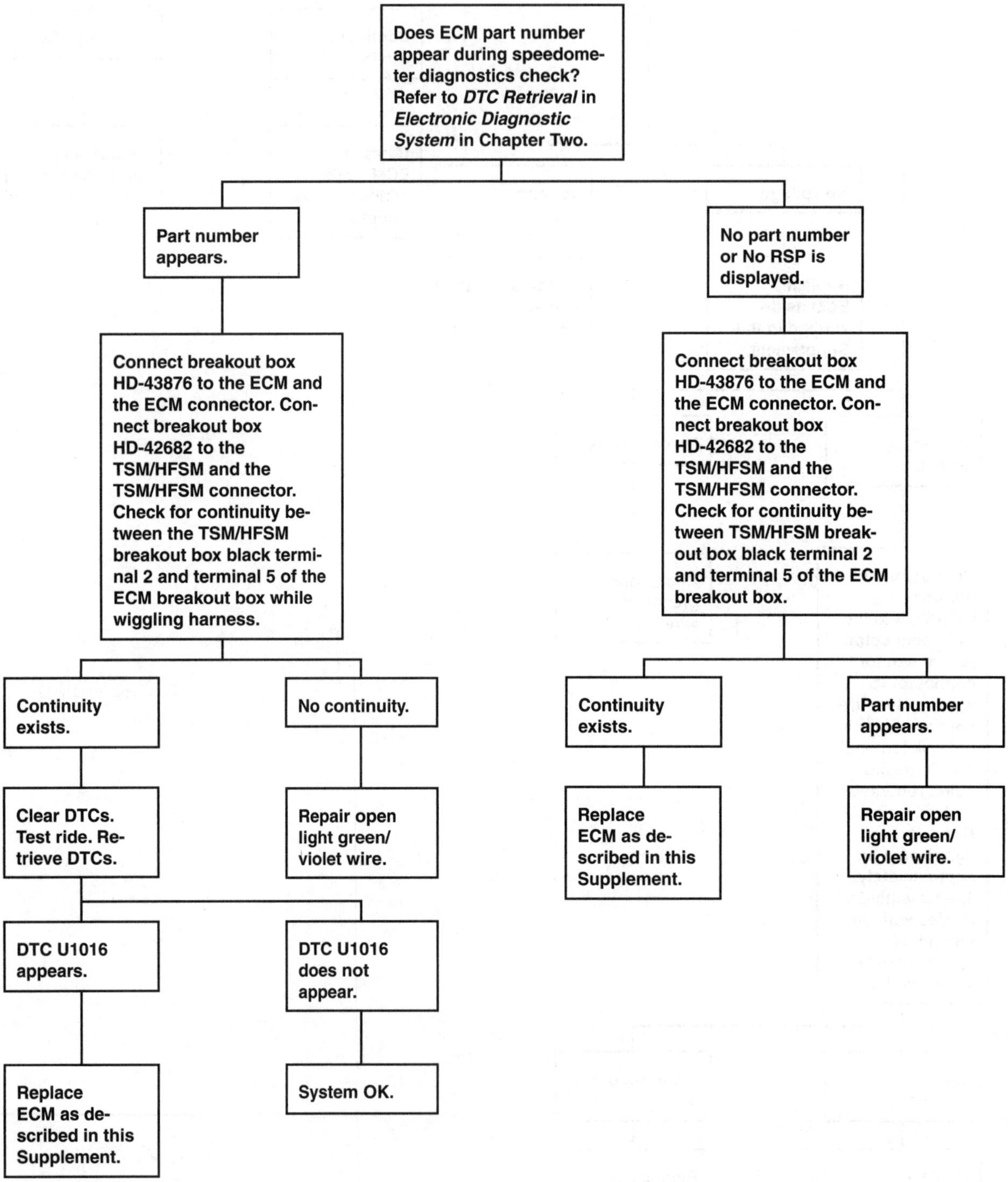

Does ECM part number appear during speedometer diagnostics check? Refer to *DTC Retrieval* in *Electronic Diagnostic System* in Chapter Two.
Part number appears.
Connect breakout box HD-43876 to the ECM and the ECM connector. Connect breakout box HD-42682 to the TSM/HFSM and the TSM/HFSM connector. Check for continuity between the TSM/HFSM breakout box black terminal 2 and terminal 5 of the ECM breakout box while wiggling harness.
Continuity exists.
Clear DTCs. Test ride. Retrieve DTCs.
DTC U1016 appears.
Replace ECM as described in this Supplement.
DTC U1016 does not appear.
System OK.
No continuity.
Repair open light green/ violet wire.
No part number or No RSP is displayed.
Connect breakout box HD-43876 to the ECM and the ECM connector. Connect breakout box HD-42682 to the TSM/HFSM and the TSM/HFSM connector. Check for continuity between TSM/HFSM breakout box black terminal 2 and terminal 5 of the ECM breakout box.
Continuity exists.
Replace ECM as described in this Supplement.
Part number appears.
Repair open light green/ violet wire.

(41)

DTC U1064, U1255: LOSS OF TSM/TSSM/HFSM SERIAL DATA

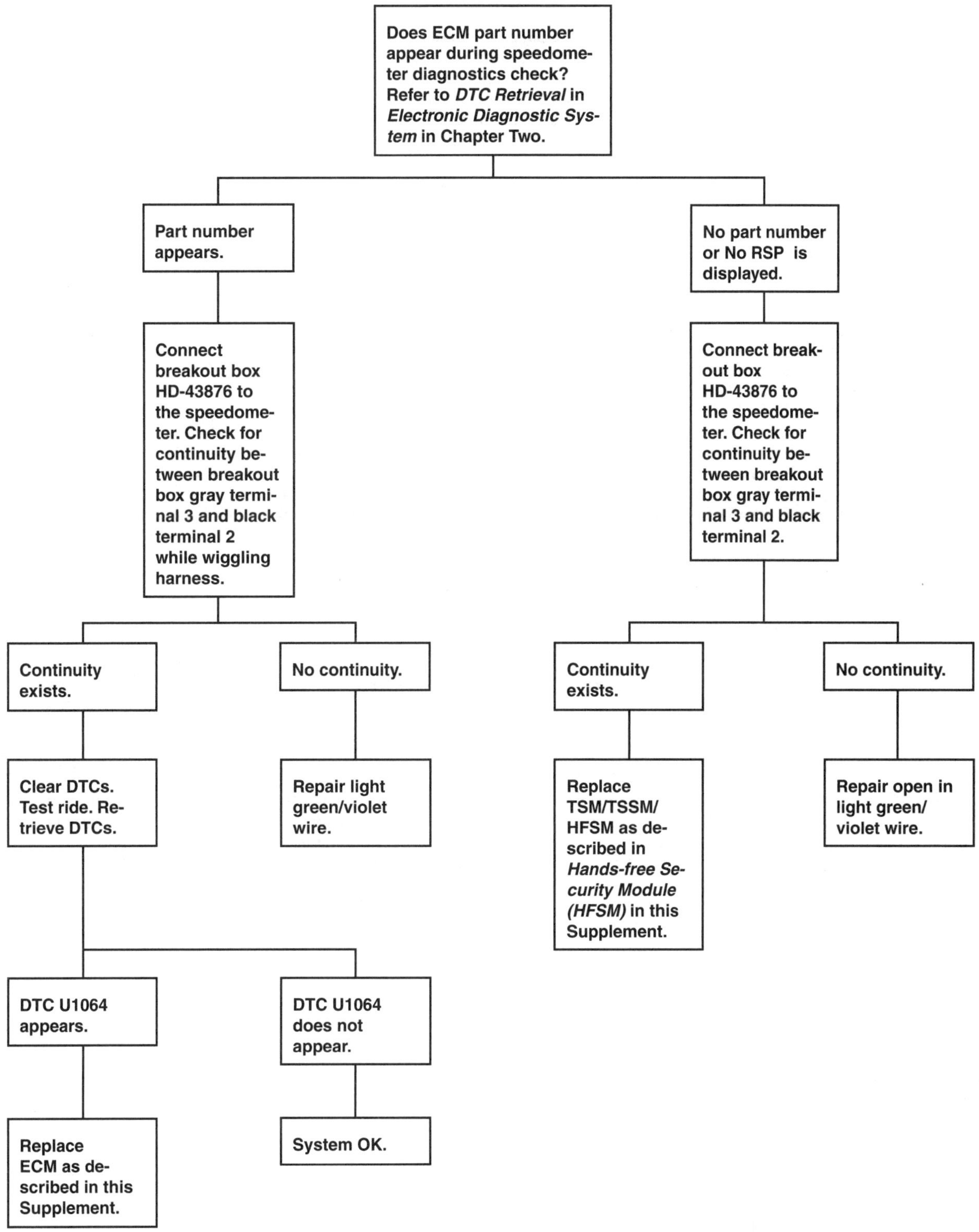

Does ECM part number appear during speedometer diagnostics check? Refer to *DTC Retrieval* in *Electronic Diagnostic System* in Chapter Two.
Part number appears.
No part number or No RSP is displayed.
Connect breakout box HD-43876 to the speedometer. Check for continuity between breakout box gray terminal 3 and black terminal 2 while wiggling harness.
Connect breakout box HD-43876 to the speedometer. Check for continuity between breakout box gray terminal 3 and black terminal 2.
Continuity exists.
No continuity.
Continuity exists.
No continuity.
Clear DTCs. Test ride. Retrieve DTCs.
Repair light green/violet wire.
Replace TSM/TSSM/HFSM as described in *Hands-free Security Module (HFSM)* in this Supplement.
Repair open in light green/violet wire.
DTC U1064 appears.
DTC U1064 does not appear.
Replace ECM as described in this Supplement.
System OK.

42

DTC U1097, U1255: LOSS OF SPEEDOMETER SERIAL DATA

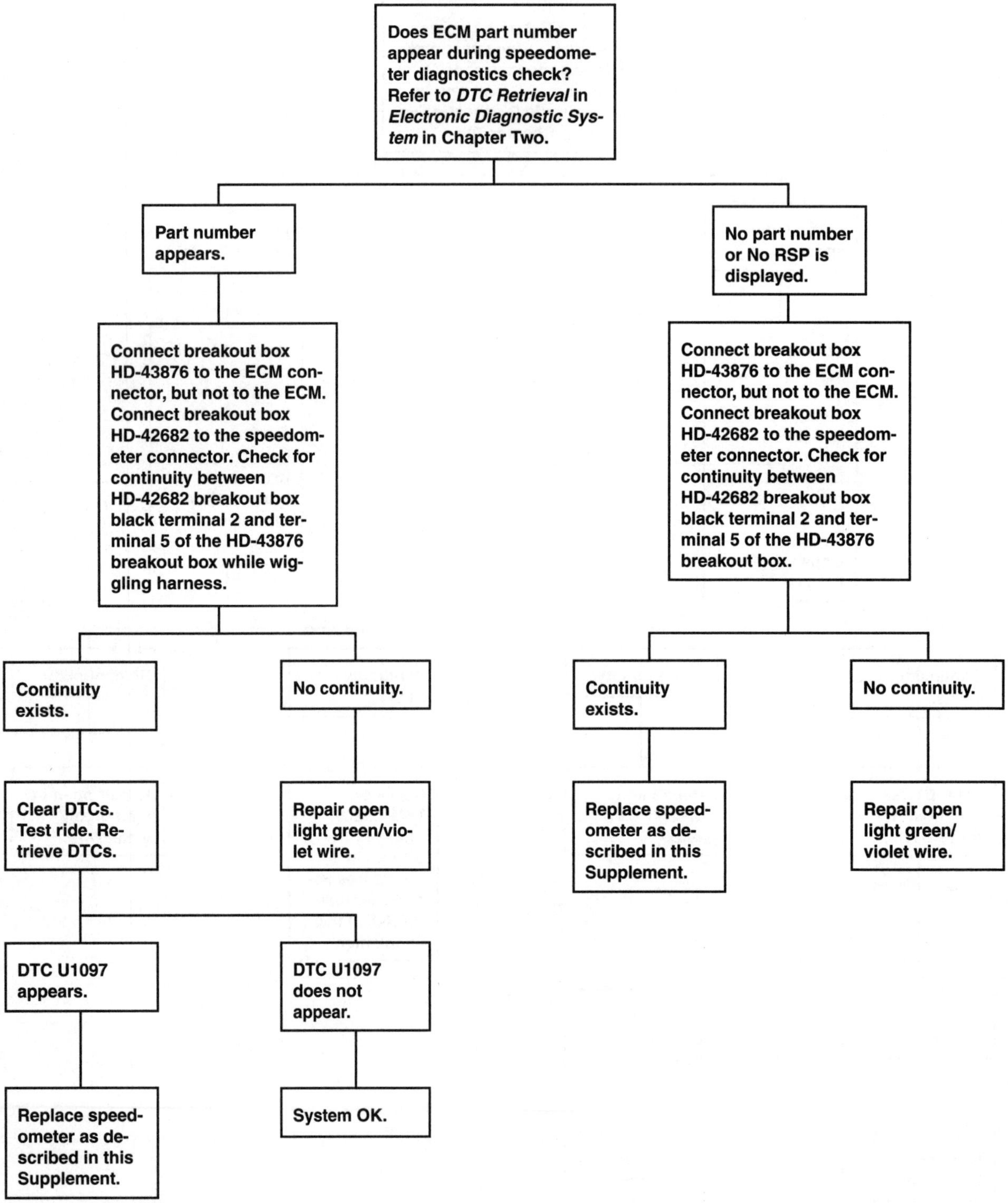

Does ECM part number appear during speedometer diagnostics check? Refer to *DTC Retrieval* in *Electronic Diagnostic System* in Chapter Two.
Part number appears.
Connect breakout box HD-43876 to the ECM connector, but not to the ECM. Connect breakout box HD-42682 to the speedometer connector. Check for continuity between HD-42682 breakout box black terminal 2 and terminal 5 of the HD-43876 breakout box while wiggling harness.
Continuity exists.
Clear DTCs. Test ride. Retrieve DTCs.
DTC U1097 appears.
Replace speedometer as described in this Supplement.
DTC U1097 does not appear.
System OK.
No continuity.
Repair open light green/violet wire.
No part number or No RSP is displayed.
Connect breakout box HD-43876 to the ECM connector, but not to the ECM. Connect breakout box HD-42682 to the speedometer connector. Check for continuity between HD-42682 breakout box black terminal 2 and terminal 5 of the HD-43876 breakout box.
Continuity exists.
Replace speedometer as described in this Supplement.
No continuity.
Repair open light green/violet wire.

43

DTC U1300, U1301, BUS ER: ENGINE STARTS THEN STALLS

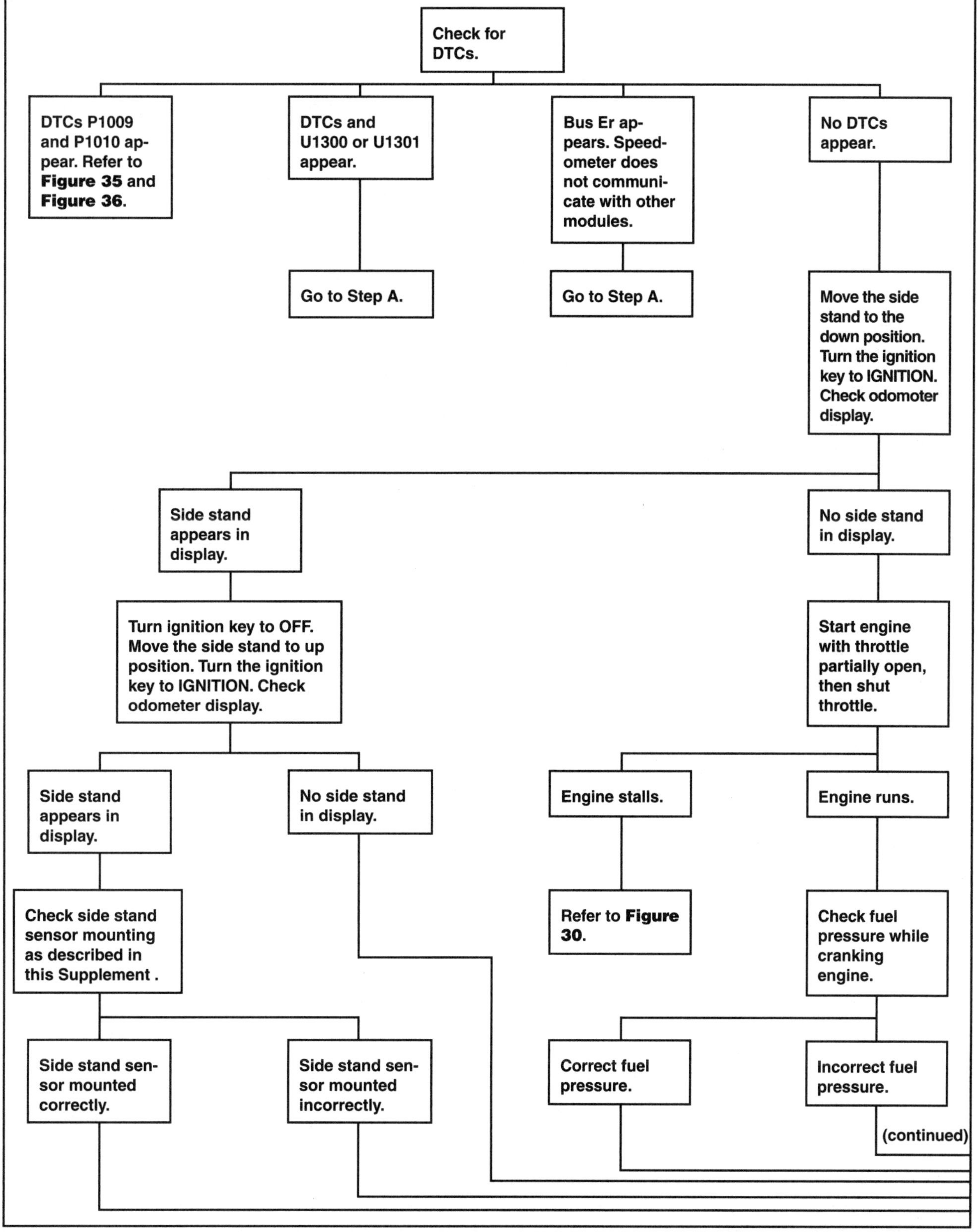
Check for DTCs.
DTCs P1009 and P1010 appear. Refer to **Figure 35** and **Figure 36**.
DTCs and U1300 or U1301 appear.
Bus Er appears. Speedometer does not communicate with other modules.
No DTCs appear.
Go to Step A.
Go to Step A.
Move the side stand to the down position. Turn the ignition key to IGNITION. Check odomoter display.
Side stand appears in display.
No side stand in display.
Turn ignition key to OFF. Move the side stand to up position. Turn the ignition key to IGNITION. Check odometer display.
Start engine with throttle partially open, then shut throttle.
Side stand appears in display.
No side stand in display.
Engine stalls.
Engine runs.
Check side stand sensor mounting as described in this Supplement .
Refer to **Figure 30**.
Check fuel pressure while cranking engine.
Side stand sensor mounted correctly.
Side stand sensor mounted incorrectly.
Correct fuel pressure.
Incorrect fuel pressure.
(continued)

15

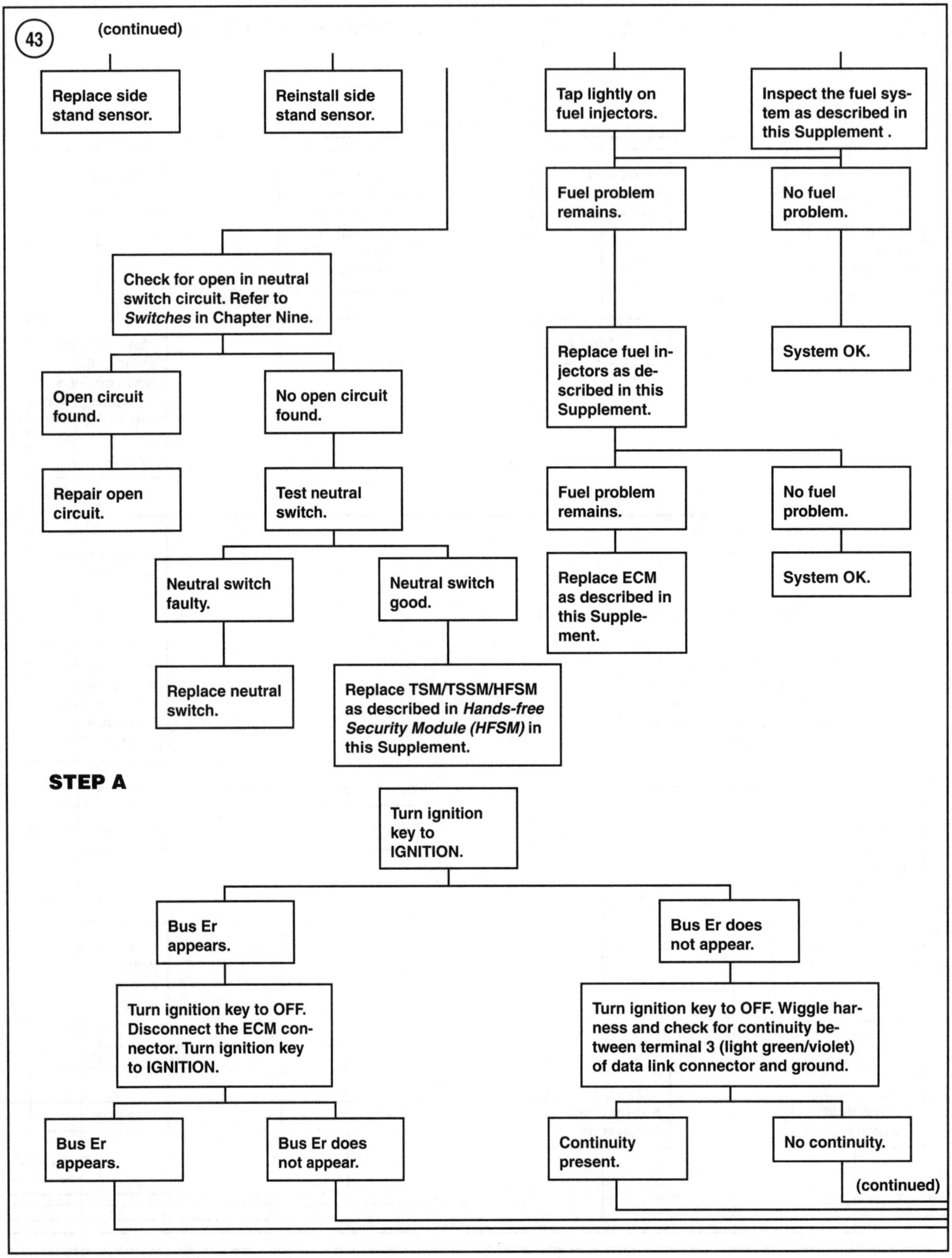
43
(continued)
Replace side stand sensor.
Reinstall side stand sensor.
Tap lightly on fuel injectors.
Inspect the fuel system as described in this Supplement .
Fuel problem remains.
No fuel problem.
Check for open in neutral switch circuit. Refer to *Switches* in Chapter Nine.
Open circuit found.
No open circuit found.
Replace fuel injectors as described in this Supplement.
System OK.
Repair open circuit.
Test neutral switch.
Fuel problem remains.
No fuel problem.
Neutral switch faulty.
Neutral switch good.
Replace ECM as described in this Supplement.
System OK.
Replace neutral switch.
Replace TSM/TSSM/HFSM as described in *Hands-free Security Module (HFSM)* in this Supplement.
STEP A
Turn ignition key to IGNITION.
Bus Er appears.
Bus Er does not appear.
Turn ignition key to OFF. Disconnect the ECM connector. Turn ignition key to IGNITION.
Turn ignition key to OFF. Wiggle harness and check for continuity between terminal 3 (light green/violet) of data link connector and ground.
Bus Er appears.
Bus Er does not appear.
Continuity present.
No continuity.
(continued)

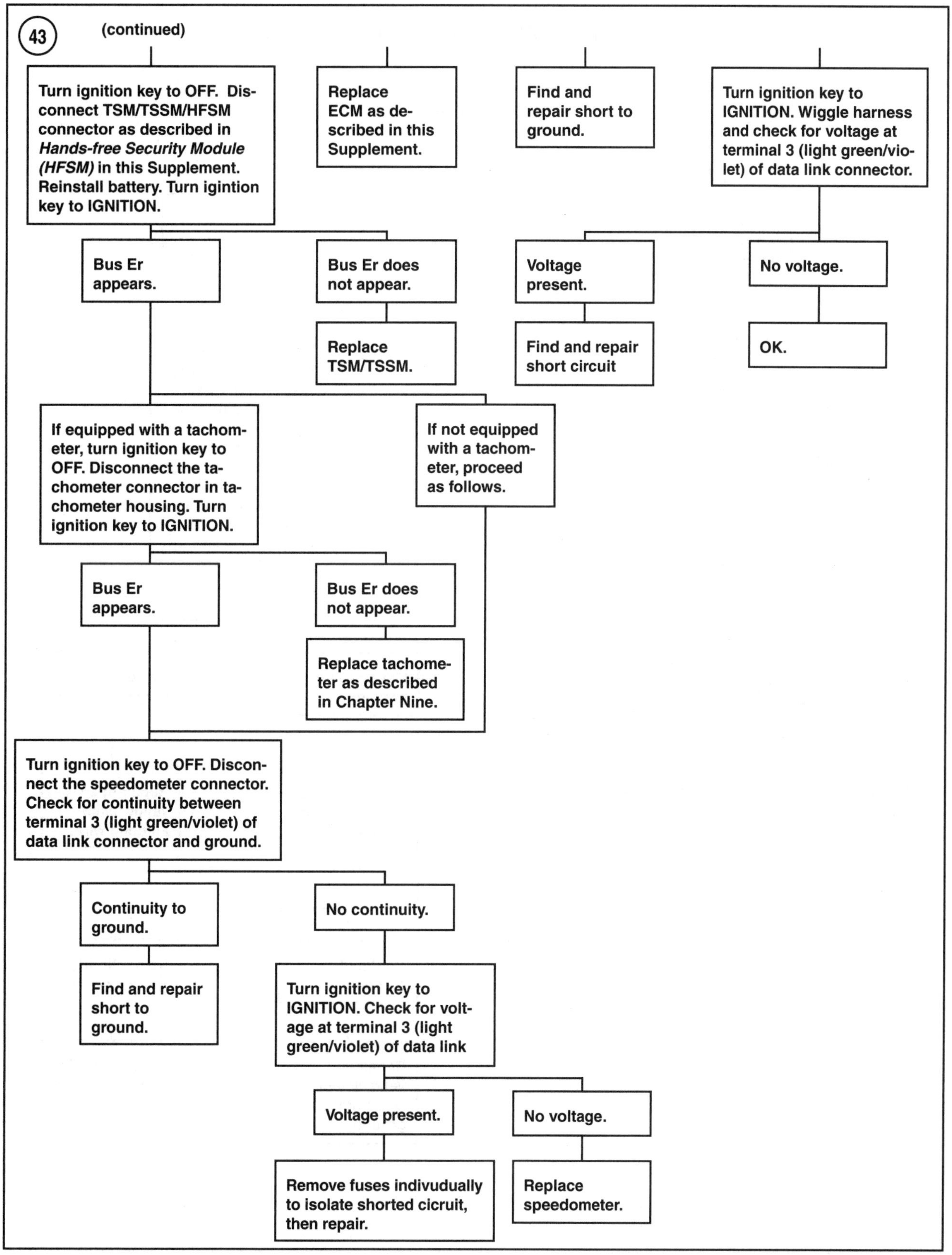
43
(continued)
Turn ignition key to OFF. Disconnect TSM/TSSM/HFSM connector as described in *Hands-free Security Module (HFSM)* in this Supplement. Reinstall battery. Turn igintion key to IGNITION.
Replace ECM as described in this Supplement.
Find and repair short to ground.
Turn ignition key to IGNITION. Wiggle harness and check for voltage at terminal 3 (light green/violet) of data link connector.
Bus Er appears.
Bus Er does not appear.
Replace TSM/TSSM.
Voltage present.
Find and repair short circuit
No voltage.
OK.
If equipped with a tachometer, turn ignition key to OFF. Disconnect the tachometer connector in tachometer housing. Turn ignition key to IGNITION.
If not equipped with a tachometer, proceed as follows.
Bus Er appears.
Bus Er does not appear.
Replace tachometer as described in Chapter Nine.
Turn ignition key to OFF. Disconnect the speedometer connector. Check for continuity between terminal 3 (light green/violet) of data link connector and ground.
Continuity to ground.
Find and repair short to ground.
No continuity.
Turn ignition key to IGNITION. Check for voltage at terminal 3 (light green/violet) of data link
Voltage present.
No voltage.
Remove fuses indivudually to isolate shorted cicruit, then repair.
Replace speedometer.

(44)

HFSM FAILS TO DISARM

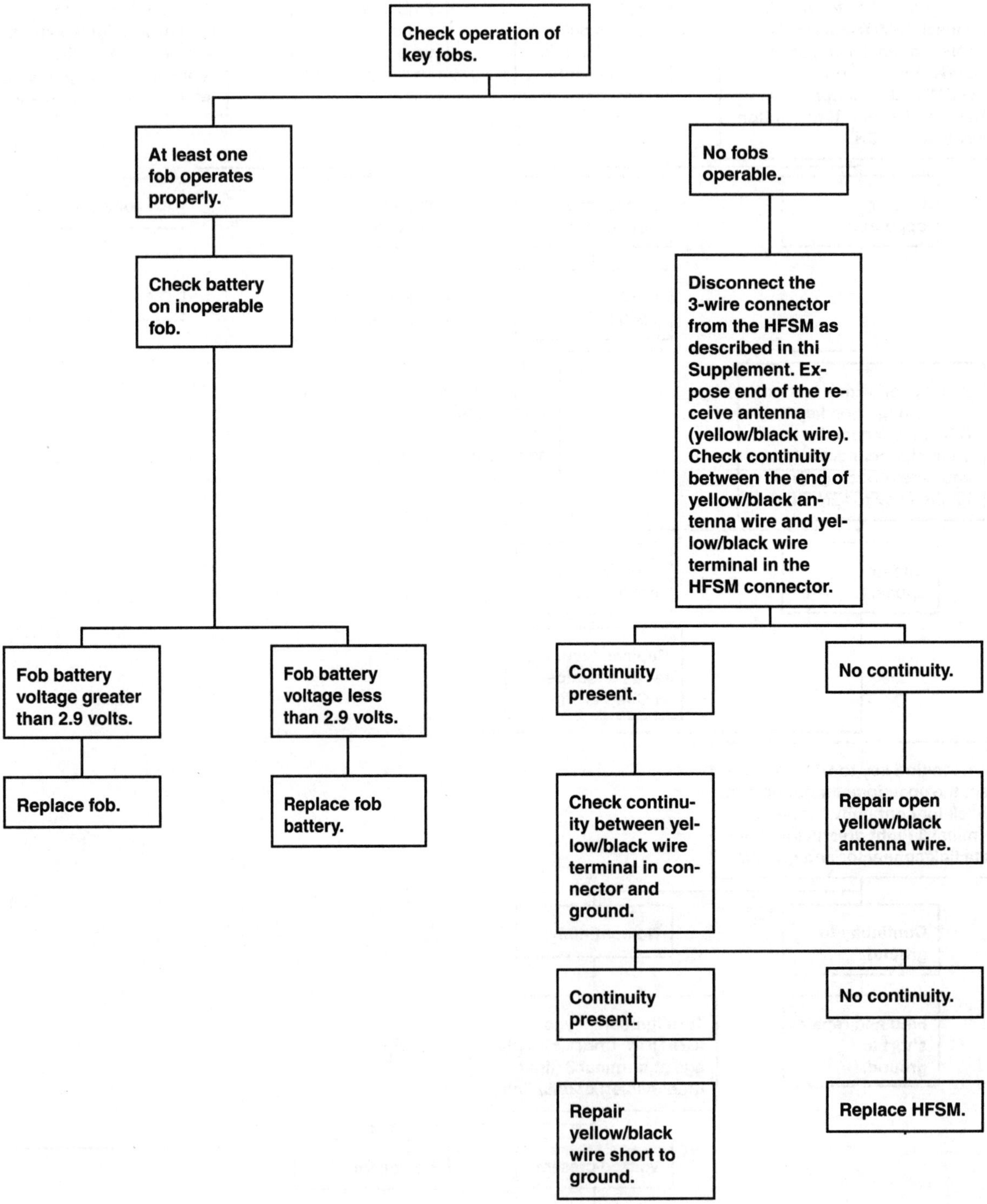
Check operation of key fobs.
At least one fob operates properly.
No fobs operable.
Check battery on inoperable fob.
Disconnect the 3-wire connector from the HFSM as described in thi Supplement. Expose end of the receive antenna (yellow/black wire). Check continuity between the end of yellow/black antenna wire and yellow/black wire terminal in the HFSM connector.
Fob battery voltage greater than 2.9 volts.
Fob battery voltage less than 2.9 volts.
Continuity present.
No continuity.
Replace fob.
Replace fob battery.
Check continuity between yellow/black wire terminal in connector and ground.
Repair open yellow/black antenna wire.
Continuity present.
No continuity.
Repair yellow/black wire short to ground.
Replace HFSM.

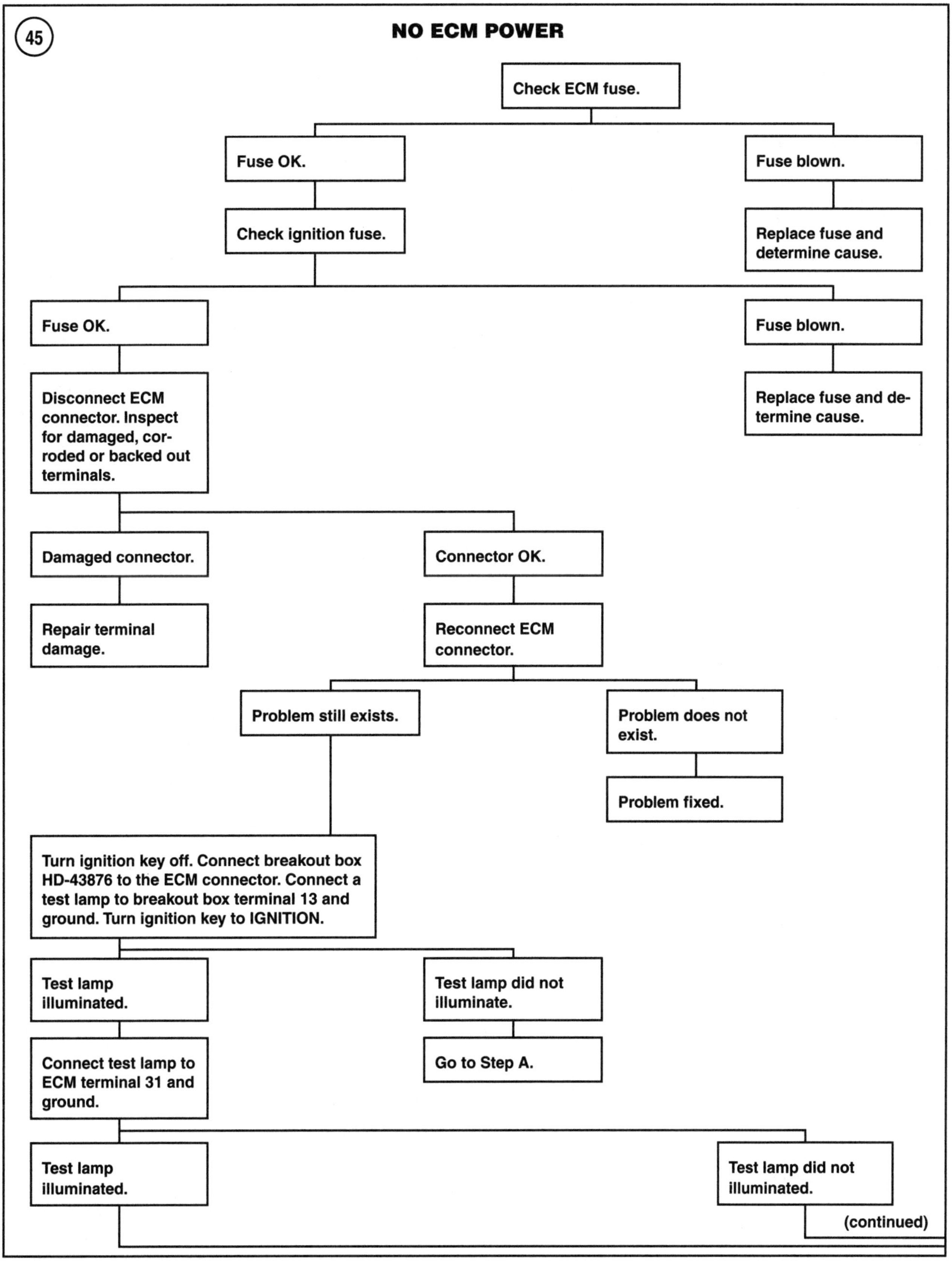
45
NO ECM POWER
Check ECM fuse.
Fuse OK.
Fuse blown.
Check ignition fuse.
Replace fuse and determine cause.
Fuse OK.
Fuse blown.
Disconnect ECM connector. Inspect for damaged, corroded or backed out terminals.
Replace fuse and determine cause.
Damaged connector.
Connector OK.
Repair terminal damage.
Reconnect ECM connector.
Problem still exists.
Problem does not exist.
Problem fixed.
Turn ignition key off. Connect breakout box HD-43876 to the ECM connector. Connect a test lamp to breakout box terminal 13 and ground. Turn ignition key to IGNITION.
Test lamp illuminated.
Test lamp did not illuminate.
Connect test lamp to ECM terminal 31 and ground.
Go to Step A.
Test lamp illuminated.
Test lamp did not illuminated.
(continued)

45 (continued)

Connect one of the test lamp leads to the battery positive terminal. Connect the other lead to the ECM terminal 10 and ground and then terminal 28 and ground.

- Test lamp illuminated.
  - Replace ECM as described in this Supplement.
- Test lamp did not illuminate.
  - Repair open in black wire.

Connect the test lamp to the ECM fuse holder red wire terminal and to ground.

- Test lamp illuminated.
  - Repair open in blue/gray wire.
- Test lamp did not illuminate.
  - Repair open in red wire.

STEP A

Turn ignition switch off. Disconnect right side handlebar switch connector (22). Turn ignition key to IGNITION. Check for battery voltage between gray wire terminal on the connector and ground.

- Voltage exists.
  - Turn ignition key to OFF. Make sure engine stop switch is in RUN position. Measure the resistance between the white/black wire terminal and the gray wire terminal on the switch connector.
    - Resistance less than 1.0 ohm.
      - Repair open white/black wire.
    - Reistance 1.0 ohm or more.
      - Repair or replace engine stop switch as described in Chapter Nine.
- No voltage.
  - Repair open in gray wire.

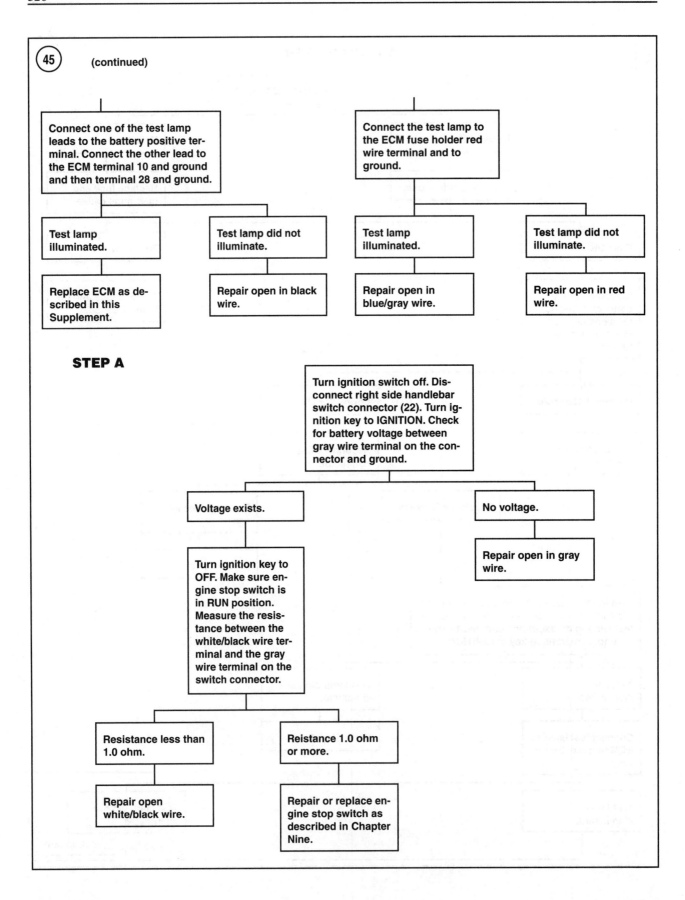

46

ODOMETER SELF-DIAGNOSTICS

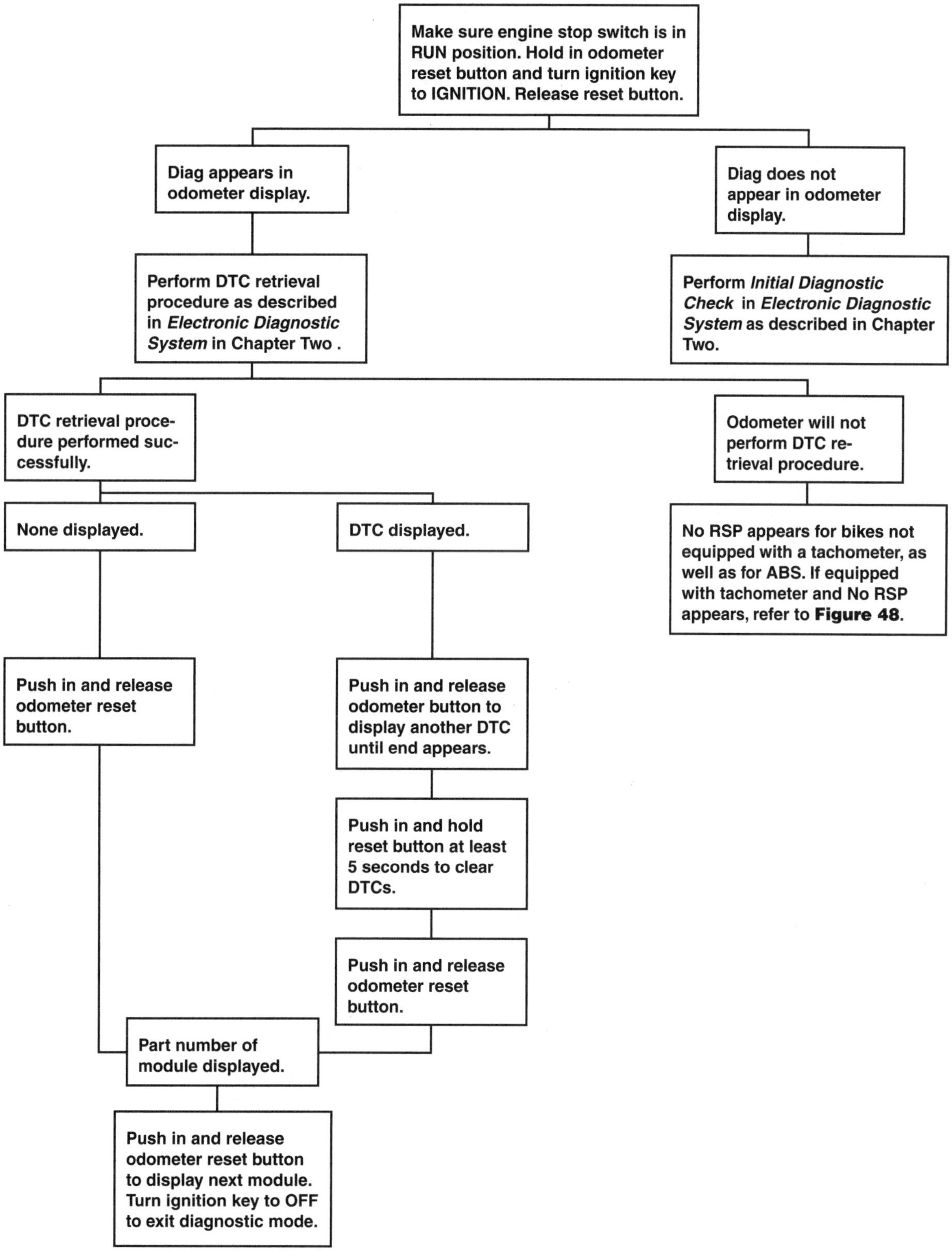

Make sure engine stop switch is in RUN position. Hold in odometer reset button and turn ignition key to IGNITION. Release reset button.
Diag appears in odometer display.
Diag does not appear in odometer display.
Perform DTC retrieval procedure as described in *Electronic Diagnostic System* in Chapter Two .
Perform *Initial Diagnostic Check* in *Electronic Diagnostic System* as described in Chapter Two.
DTC retrieval procedure performed successfully.
Odometer will not perform DTC retrieval procedure.
None displayed.
DTC displayed.
No RSP appears for bikes not equipped with a tachometer, as well as for ABS. If equipped with tachometer and No RSP appears, refer to **Figure 48**.
Push in and release odometer reset button.
Push in and release odometer button to display another DTC until end appears.
Push in and hold reset button at least 5 seconds to clear DTCs.
Push in and release odometer reset button.
Part number of module displayed.
Push in and release odometer reset button to display next module. Turn ignition key to OFF to exit diagnostic mode.

47

SIDE STAND DISPLAYED ON ODOMETER

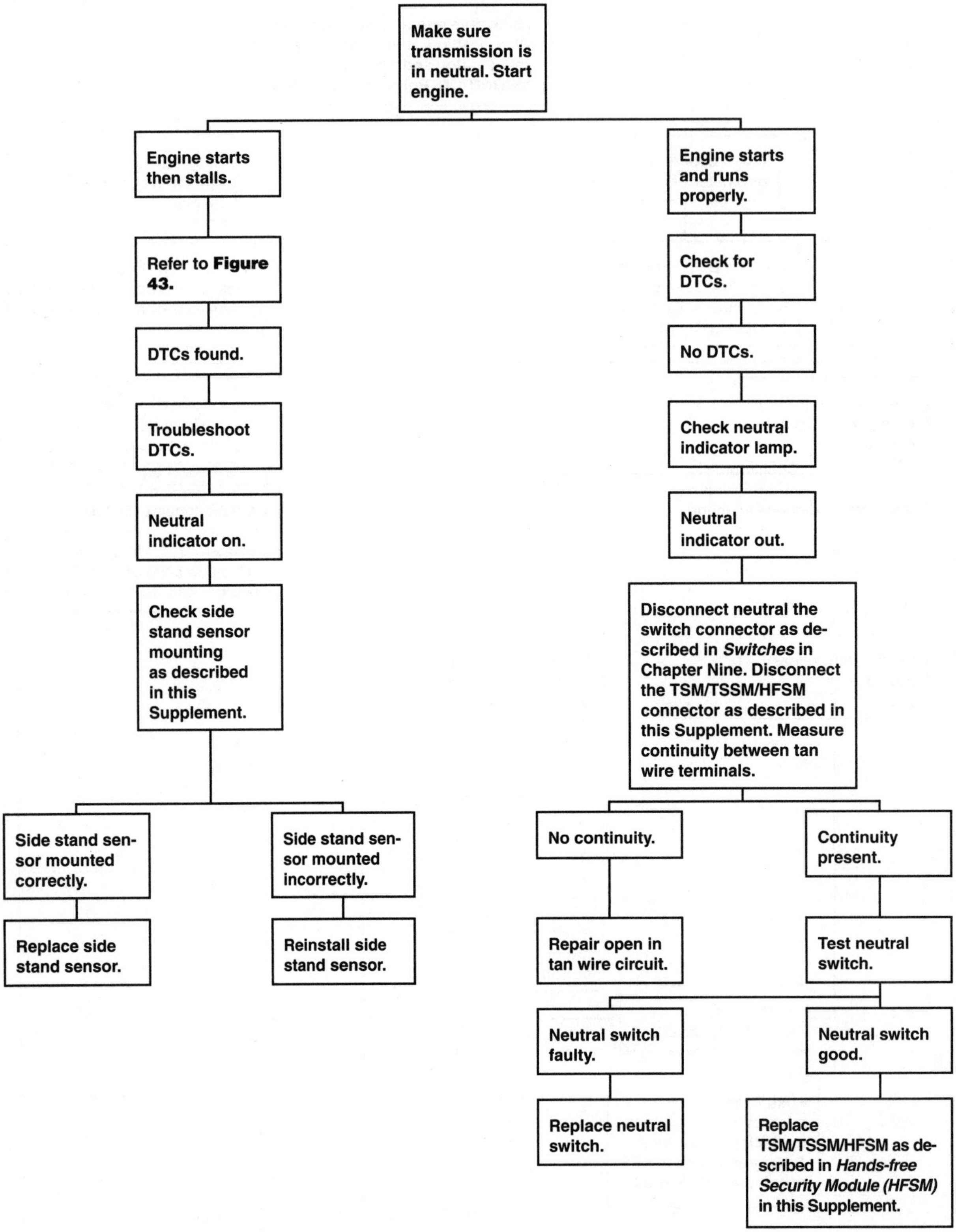
Make sure transmission is in neutral. Start engine.
Engine starts then stalls.
Refer to **Figure 43.**
DTCs found.
Troubleshoot DTCs.
Neutral indicator on.
Check side stand sensor mounting as described in this Supplement.
Side stand sensor mounted correctly.
Replace side stand sensor.
Side stand sensor mounted incorrectly.
Reinstall side stand sensor.
Engine starts and runs properly.
Check for DTCs.
No DTCs.
Check neutral indicator lamp.
Neutral indicator out.
Disconnect neutral the switch connector as described in *Switches* in Chapter Nine. Disconnect the TSM/TSSM/HFSM connector as described in this Supplement. Measure continuity between tan wire terminals.
No continuity.
Repair open in tan wire circuit.
Continuity present.
Test neutral switch.
Neutral switch faulty.
Replace neutral switch.
Neutral switch good.
Replace TSM/TSSM/HFSM as described in *Hands-free Security Module (HFSM)* in this Supplement.

48

TACHOMETER FAULTY

NOTE: The green and orange symbols in the initial test represent cruise (green) and pursuit (orange) functions on models other than Sportsters.

Perform WOW test as described in *Intitial Diagnostic Check* in *Electronic Diagnostic System* in Chapter Two. The following should occur:
a. Backlighting illuminate.
b. Needle swing to full deflection.
c. Both green and orange symbol LEDs illuminate.

- **Test OK.**
  - **Check for intermittents while wiggling harness.**
    - **Intermittents found.**
      - **Repair intermittent circuit.**
    - **No intermittents.**
      - **System OK.**
- **Faulty test.**
  - **Connect breakout box HD-42682 to the speedometer/tachometer and the speedometer/tachometer connector (20). Measure voltage at black box terminal 1.**
    - **Battery voltage present.**
      - **Turn ignition key to OFF. Check for continuity between breakout box black terminal 2 and terminal 7.**
    - **No voltage.**
      - **Check instrument fuse.**
        - **Fuse blown.**
          - **Repair cause. Replace fuse.**
        - **Fuse OK.**
          - **Repair open in orange wire circuit.**

(continued)

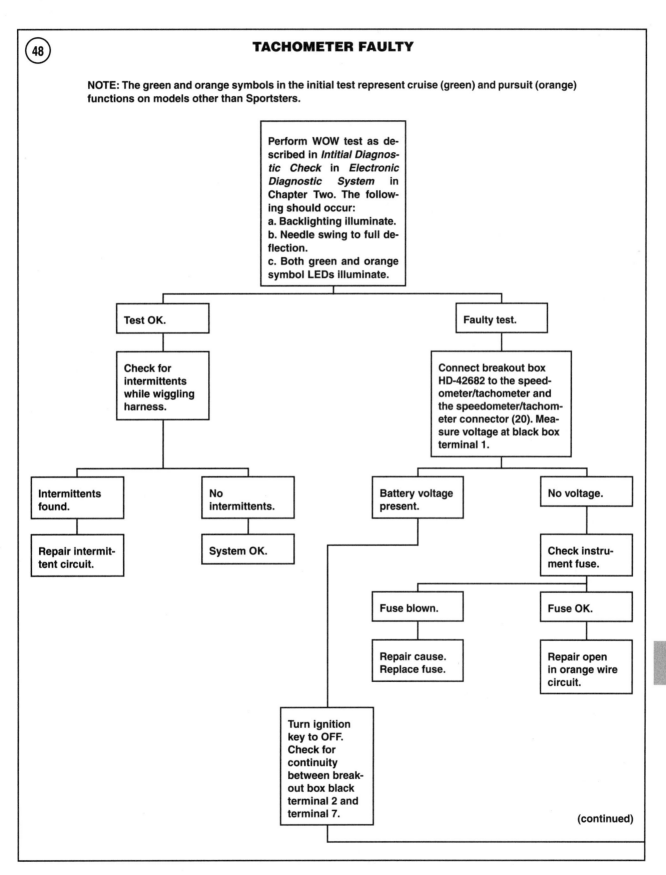

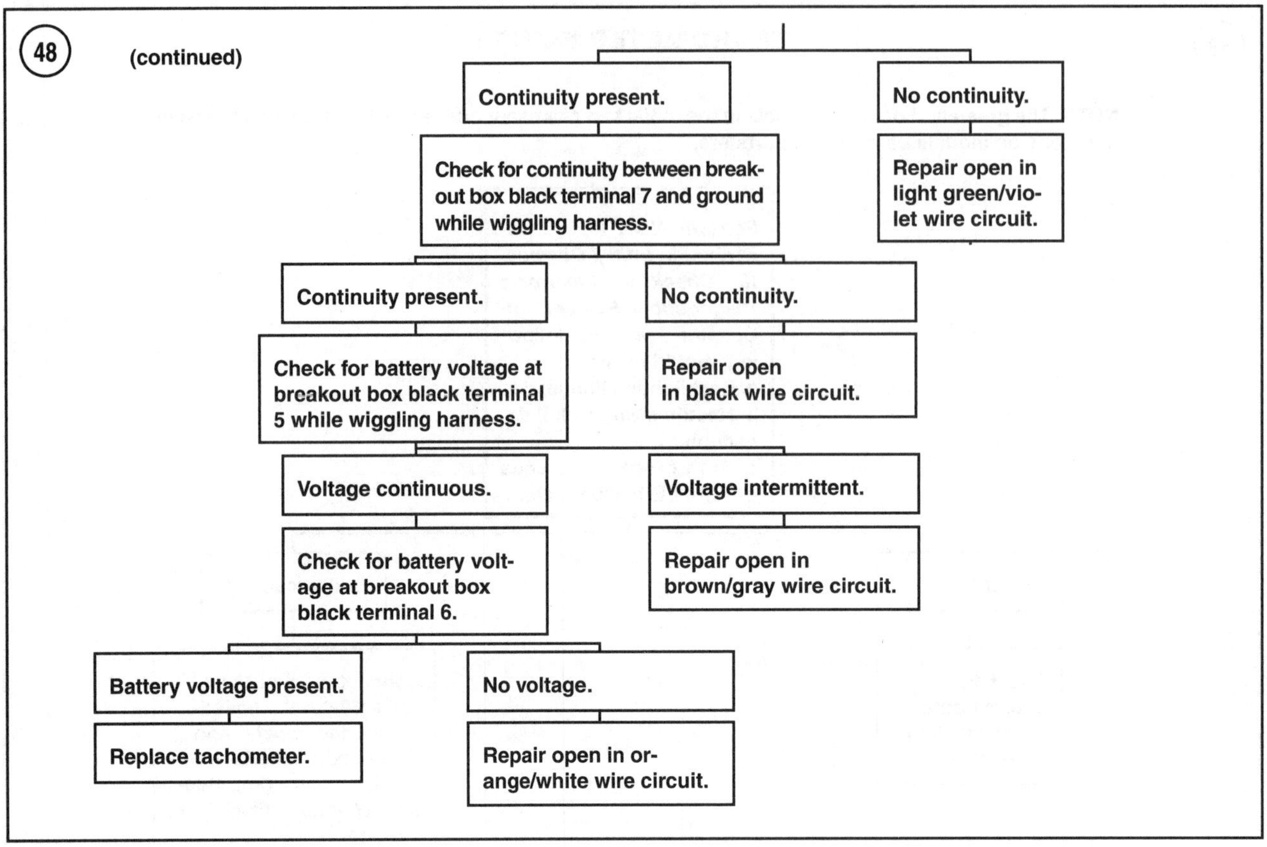

48
(continued)
Continuity present.
No continuity.
Check for continuity between break-out box black terminal 7 and ground while wiggling harness.
Repair open in light green/violet wire circuit.
Continuity present.
No continuity.
Check for battery voltage at breakout box black terminal 5 while wiggling harness.
Repair open in black wire circuit.
Voltage continuous.
Voltage intermittent.
Check for battery voltage at breakout box black terminal 6.
Repair open in brown/gray wire circuit.
Battery voltage present.
No voltage.
Replace tachometer.
Repair open in orange/white wire circuit.

4. The DTCs are prioritized according to importance. If multiple DTCs occur correct the DTC with the highest priority listed in **Table 6**. It is possible for one fault to trigger more than one DTC.
5. Refer to the wiring diagrams at the end of this manual to identify connectors. Refer to the appropriate sections in this Supplement and Chapter Nine for additional component testing.

No-DTC Fault Troubleshooting

Some malfunctions will not trigger the generation of a DTC. In those cases, the troubleshooting guidelines found in this chapter will serve to locate the problem. However, there are faults that can be diagnosed using the procedures implemented when diagnosing a DTC. The faults listed in **Table 7** may not generate a DTC, but the specified flow chart will help identify the problem.

FUEL SYSTEM

Refer to the typical symptoms listed under *Engine Performance* and *Starting The Engine* in this Supplement for conditions that may be caused by the fuel system. Refer to the appropriate sections in this Supplement and Chapter Eight for component servicing.

Because the fuel system is electronically controlled, a problem may result in the setting of a diagnostic trouble code (DTC). Refer to the *Electronic Diagnostic System* section in this Supplement.

An electrical malfunction may cause a fuel system problem. Refer to **Figure 49** to troubleshoot possible electrical faults related to fuel system operation.

BRAKES

WARNING

2007-on models use DOT 4 brake fluid. 2004-2006 models use DOT 5 brake fluid. The designated brake fluid appears on the brake master cylinder cover. Do not intermix brake fluid types. Using the incorrect brake fluid type may cause brake failure.

49

FUEL SYSTEM ELECTRICAL TEST

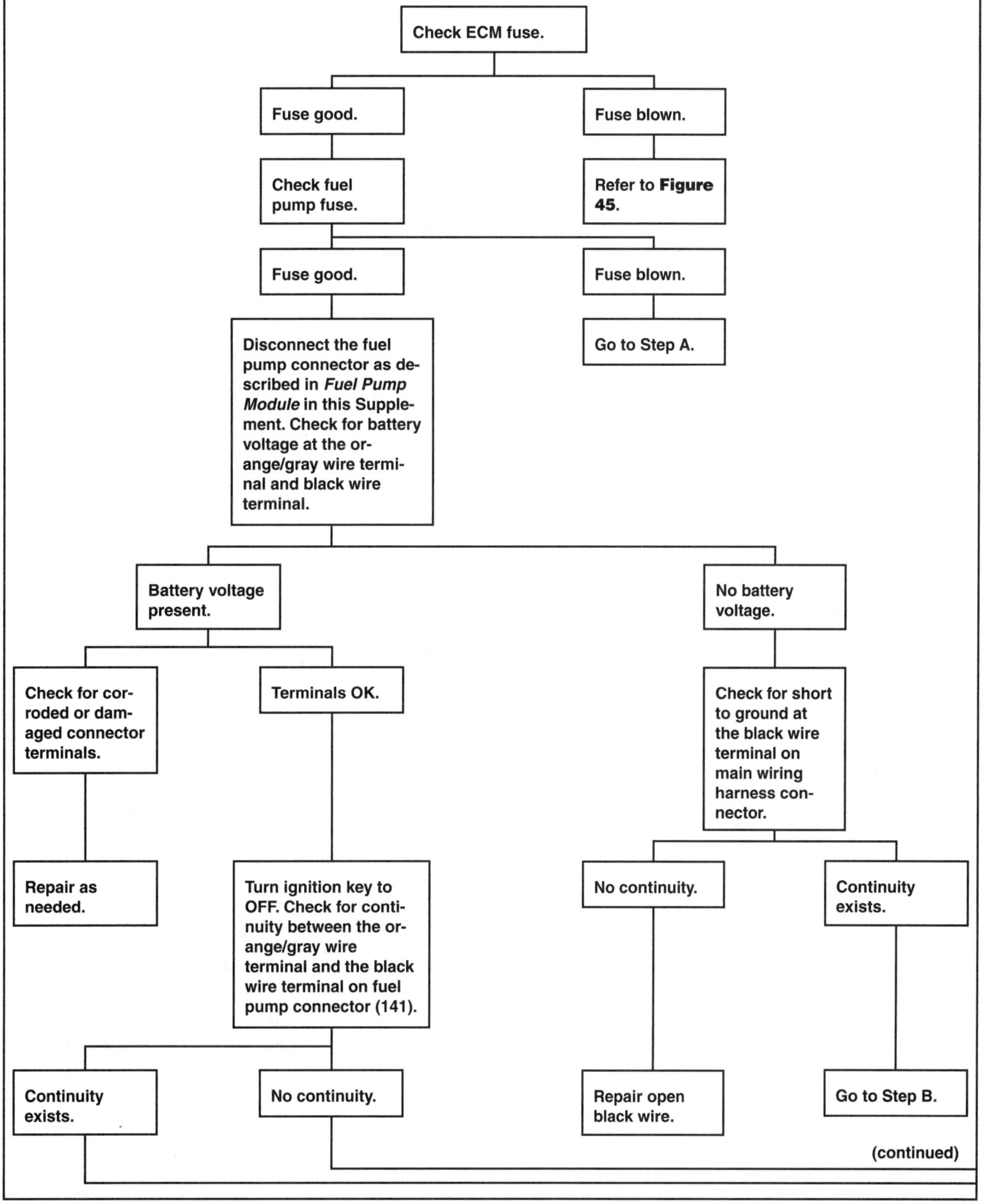
Check ECM fuse.
Fuse good.
Fuse blown.
Check fuel pump fuse.
Refer to **Figure 45**.
Fuse good.
Fuse blown.
Disconnect the fuel pump connector as described in *Fuel Pump Module* in this Supplement. Check for battery voltage at the orange/gray wire terminal and black wire terminal.
Go to Step A.
Battery voltage present.
No battery voltage.
Check for corroded or damaged connector terminals.
Terminals OK.
Check for short to ground at the black wire terminal on main wiring harness connector.
Repair as needed.
Turn ignition key to OFF. Check for continuity between the orange/gray wire terminal and the black wire terminal on fuel pump connector (141).
No continuity.
Continuity exists.
Continuity exists.
No continuity.
Repair open black wire.
Go to Step B.

(continued)

49 (continued)

Check wiring. If good, replace fuel pump.

Remove the fuel pump. Detach the connector from fuel pump. Check for continuity between motor terminals.

Continuity exists.

Check for open in wiring.

No continuity.

Replace fuel pump.

STEP A

Check for short to ground at orange/gray wire terminal on the main wiring harness connector.

Repair wiring and replace fuse.

Make sure battery is fully charged. Remove fuel pump fuse. Reattach all connectors. Install a fuel pressure gauge. Connect an ammeter to fuel pump fuse holder terminals. Turn ignition key to IGNITION and monitor ammeter and fuel pressure gauge. With fuel pressure of 55-62 psi (380-425 kPa), ammeter should read less than 4.5 amps.

(continued)

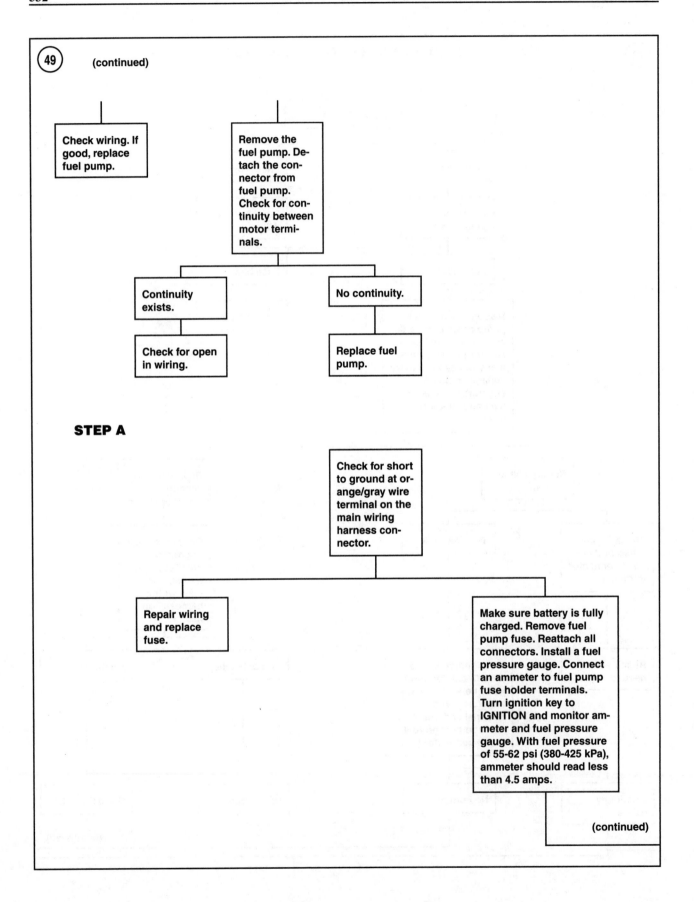

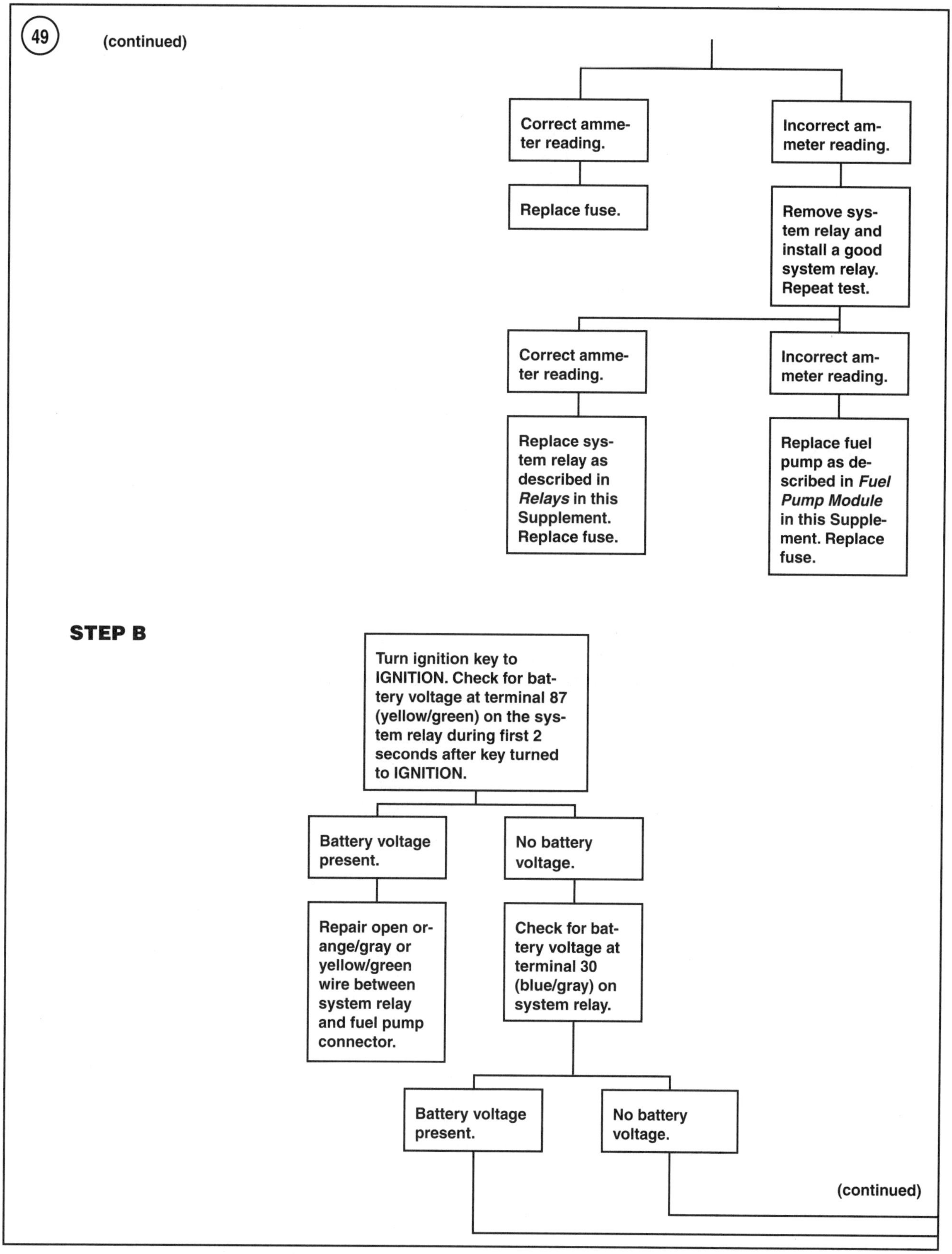
49
(continued)
Correct ammeter reading.
Replace fuse.
Incorrect ammeter reading.
Remove system relay and install a good system relay. Repeat test.
Correct ammeter reading.
Replace system relay as described in *Relays* in this Supplement. Replace fuse.
Incorrect ammeter reading.
Replace fuel pump as described in *Fuel Pump Module* in this Supplement. Replace fuse.
STEP B
Turn ignition key to IGNITION. Check for battery voltage at terminal 87 (yellow/green) on the system relay during first 2 seconds after key turned to IGNITION.
Battery voltage present.
Repair open orange/gray or yellow/green wire between system relay and fuel pump connector.
No battery voltage.
Check for battery voltage at terminal 30 (blue/gray) on system relay.
Battery voltage present.
No battery voltage.
(continued)

15

49 (continued)

Turn ignition key to IGNITION. Check for battery voltage at terminal 86 (white/black) on system relay.

Repair open blue/gray wire between system relay and ECM fuse.

- Battery voltage present.
  - Go to Step C.
- No battery voltage.
  - Repair open white/black wire.

STEP C

Insert a test probe into the green/orange wire at the system relay connector. Turn ignition key to IGNITION. Check for battery voltage during first 2 seconds after key turned to

- Battery voltage present.
  - Replace system relay.
- No battery voltage.
  - Turn ignition key to OFF. Connect breakout box HD-43876 to the ECM and the ECM connector. Connect a test light between breakout box terminal 2 and ground. Turn ignition key to IGNITION. Test light should illuminate for 2 seconds.
    - Test light illuminates.
      - Repair open green/orange wire.
    - Test light does not illuminate.
      - Replace ECM as described in this Supplement.

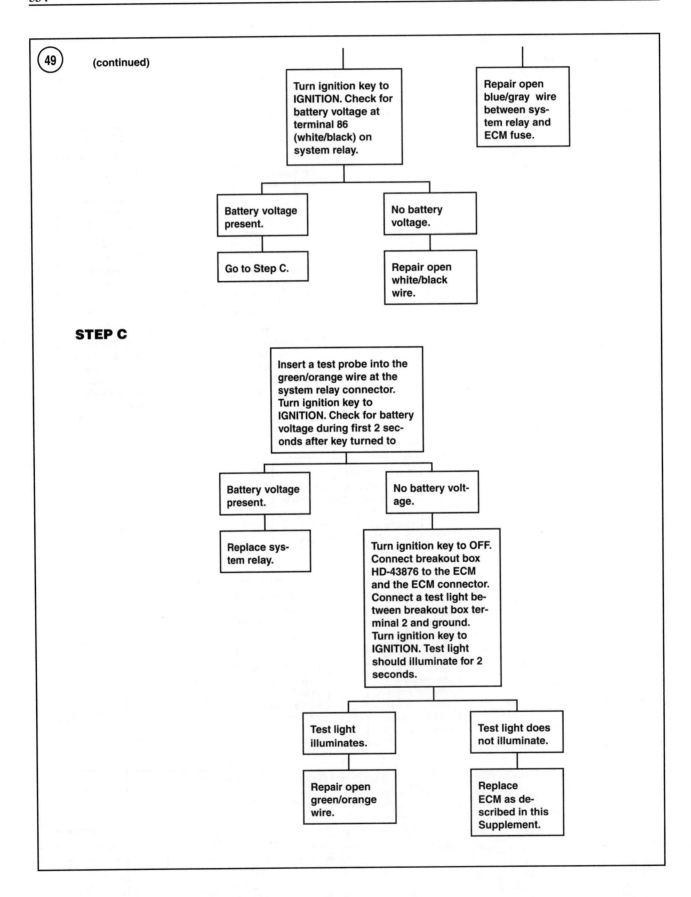

Table 3 CURRENT DRAW SPECIFICATIONS[1]

Item	Milliampere draw
HFSM	1.0
Security siren–optional	20.0[2]
Speedometer	1.0
Tachometer (if so equipped)	1.0
TSM (non security models)	1.0
TSSM/HFSM–armed	3.0
TSSM/HFSM–disarmed	3.0
TSSM/HFSM– storage mode (armed or disarmed)	1.0
Voltage regulator	1.0

1. Average readings.
2. Siren will draw for 2-24 hours from time motorcycle battery is connected and 0.05 mA once siren battery is charged. Disconnect siren during draw test. Siren will draw up to 20 mA.

Table 4 ELECTRICAL SPECIFICATIONS

Ignition coil	
Primary resistance	0.3-0.7 ohms
Secondary resistance	1500-2400 ohms
Regulated (DC) output current	24-30 amps
Voltage regulator	
Voltage output	14.3-14.7 Vdc @ 75° F
Amps @ 3600 rpm	32 amps

Table 5 ENGINE SCAN VALUES

Item	Minimum value	Maximum value	Hot idle
TMAP sensor			
MAP	10 kPa	104 kPa	35-45 kPa
	0 volt	5.1 volts	
IAT	3° F (-16° C)	248° F (120° C)	104-140° F (40-60° C)
	0.0 volt	5.0 volts	2.0-3.5 volts
TP sensor	0	100	0
	0.2 volt	4.5 volts	0.2-1.0 volt
IAC pintle	0	155	20-50 steps
RPM	800	5600	1000
ET sensor	3° F (-16° C)	464° F (240° C)	230-300° F (110-150° C)
	0.0 volt	5.0 volts	0.5-1.5 volts
Front injector			
pulse width	0	50 ms	2-4 ms
Rear injector			
pulse width	0	50 ms	2-4 ms
Advance front	0	50°	10-15°
Advance rear	0	50°	10-15°
VSS	0	120	0 MPH (km/h)
Battery voltage	10	15	13.4 volts
ENG RUN	Off	Run	Run
Idle RPM	800	1250	1000

Table 6 DIAGNOSTIC TROUBLE CODES

DTC	Problem	Priority[1]	Troubleshooting chart
Bus Er	Serial data bus fault	3	Figure 6 or 43
B0563[2]	Battery voltage high	20	
B1004	Fuel level sending unit low	9	Figure 7
B1005	Fuel level sending unit high/open	10	Figure 8

(continued)

15

Table 6 DIAGNOSTIC TROUBLE CODES (continued)

DTC	Problem	Priority[1]	Troubleshooting chart
B1006	Accessory line overvoltage	7	Figure 9
B1007	Ignition line overvoltage	6	Figure 9
B1008	Reset switch closed	8	Figure 10
B1121	Left turn output fault	11	Figure 11
B1122	Right turn output fault	12	Figure 11
B1123	Left turn lamp output short-to-ground	13	Figure 12
B1124	Right turn lamp output short-to-ground	14	Figure 12
B1125	Left turn lamp output short-to-voltage	15	Figure 13
B1126	Right turn lamp output short-to-voltage	16	Figure 13
B1131	Alarm output low	21	Figure 14
B1132	Alarm output high	22	Figure 14
B1134	Starter output high	10	Figure 15
B1135[3]	Accelerometer fault	6	
B1136[3]	Accelerometer tip-over self-test fault	7	
B1141	Ignition switch open/low (equipped with HFSM)	23	Figure 11 or 16
B1142[3]	HFSM internal fault	5	
B1143	Security antenna short-to-ground	17	Figure 17
B1144	Security antenna short-to-voltage	18	Figure 18
B1145	Security antenna open	19	Figure 19
B1151[4]			
B1152[4]			
B1153[4]			
B1154	Clutch switch input short-to-ground	8	Figure 20
B1155	Neutral switch input short-to-ground	9	Figure 21
P0107	MAP sensor failed open/low	28	Figure 22
P0108	MAP sensor failed high	29	Figure 22
P0112	IAT sensor voltage low	32	Figure 23
P0113	IAT sensor open/high	33	Figure 23
P0117	ET sensor voltage low	30	Figure 24
P0118	ET sensor open/high	31	Figure 24
P0122	TP sensor open/low	24	Figure 25
P0123	TP sensor high	25	Figure 25
P0131	Front O_2 sensor low (lean O_2)	49	Figure 26
P0132	Front O_2 sensor high (rich)	51	Figure 26
P0134	Front O_2 sensor open/not responding	53	Figure 26
P0151	Rear O_2 sensor low (lean)	50	Figure 26
P0152	Rear O_2 sensor high (rich)	52	Figure 26
P0154	Rear O_2 sensor open/not responding	54	Figure 26
P0261	Front injector open/low	38	Figure 27
P0262	Front injector high	40	Figure 27
P0263	Rear injector open/low	39	Figure 27
P0264	Rear injector high	41	Figure 27
P0373	CKP sensor intermittent	22	Figure 28
P0374	CKP not detected/cannot synchronize	23	Figure 28
P0501	VSS failed low	44	Figure 29
P0502	VSS failed high/open	45	Figure 29

(continued)

Table 6 DIAGNOSTIC TROUBLE CODES (continued)

DTC	Problem	Priority[1]	Troubleshooting chart
P0505	Loss of idle speed control	46	Figure 30
P0562	System voltage low	42	Figure 31
P0563	System voltage high	43	Figure 31
P0603[5]	EEProm memory error	2	
P0605[5]	Program memory error	1	
P1001	System relay coil open/low	18	Figure 32
P1002	System relay coil high/shorted	17	Figure 33
P1003	System relay contacts open	16	Figure 32
P1004	System relay contacts closed	19	Figure 34
P1009	Incorrect PIN	20	Figure 35
P1010	Missing PIN	21	Figure 36
P1351	Ignition coil driver front low/open	34	Figure 37
P1352	Ignition coil driver front high/shorted	36	Figure 37
P1354	Ignition coil driver rear low/open	35	Figure 37
P1355	Ignition coil driver rear high/shorted	37	Figure 37
P1501	Side stand sensor low	26	Figure 38
P1502	Side stand sensor high	27	Figure 39
P1653[6]	Tachometer low	75	
P1654[6]	Tachometer hight	76	
U1016	Loss of ECM serial data	3	Figure 40
U1064	Loss of TSM/TSSM/HFSM serial data	4	Figure 41
U1097	Loss of speedometer communication	13	Figure 42
U1255	Loss of ECM or TSM/TSSM/HFSM serial data	4	Figure 40 or 41
U1300	Serial data shorted low	1	Figure 43
U1301	Serial data shorted high	2	Figure 43

1. Priority numbers are relative. There may be more than one DTC for a specific priority number due to differing systems, such as engine management and TSM/TSSM/HFSM.
2. Follow troubleshooting procedures for the charging system in this chapter.
3. Replace the TSM/TSSM/HFSM due to an internal malfunction.
4. Not applicable to Sportster models. If DTC appears, reconfigure TSM/TSSM/HFSM.
5. Replace the ECM due to an internal malfunction.
6. This code is related to terminal three on the ECM. Inspect for aftermarket components connected to this terminal of the ECM. If no components are connected to the terminal, clear the codes and road test. Replace the ECM if codes continue to appear.

Table 7 NO-DTC FAULTS

HFSM fails to disarm–Figure 44
No ECM power–Figure 45
Odometer self-diagnostics–Figure 46
Side stand displayed on odometer–Figure 47
Tachometer faulty–Figure 48

15

Table 8 TMAP SENSOR AIR TEMPERATURE SPECIFICATIONS

°F	°C	Ohms	Volts
-4	-20	15614	4.7
14	-10	9426	4.5

(continued)

Table 8 TMAP SENSOR AIR TEMPERATURE SPECIFICATIONS (continued)

°F	°C	Ohms	Volts
32	0	5887	4.3
50	10	3791	4.0
68	20	2511	3.6
77	25	2063	3.4
86	30	1715	3.2
104	40	1200	2.7
122	50	851	2.3
140	60	612	1.9
158	70	446	1.5
176	80	329.5	1.2
194	90	246.2	1.0
212	100	186	0.8

CHAPTER THREE

LUBRICATION, MAINTENANCE AND TUNE-UP

PERIODIC MAINTENANCE

Brakes

WARNING
2007-on models use DOT 4 brake fluid. 2004-2006 models use DOT 5 brake fluid. The designated brake fluid appears on the brake master cylinder cover. Do not intermix brake fluid types. Using the incorrect brake fluid type may cause brake failure.

CAUTION
DOT 4 brake fluid will damage plastic, painted and plated surfaces. Cover exposed surfaces. Clean contaminated surfaces with soapy water and rinse thoroughly.

Final Drive Belt Deflection

2007-on models

Refer to **Table 10**.

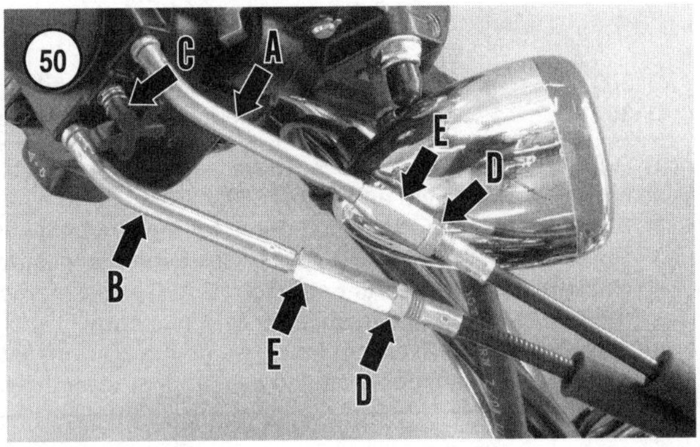

2008-on models

WARNING
Do not exceed 105 ft.-lb. (142 N•m) when tightening the rear axle nut. Overtightening the nut may cause bearing failure and possible loss of control during motorcycle operation.

Refer to Chapter Three and tighten the rear axle nut to 95-105 ft.-lb. (129-142 N•m).

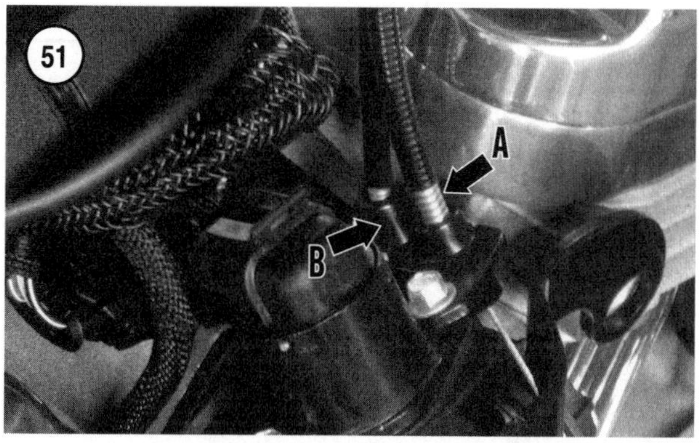

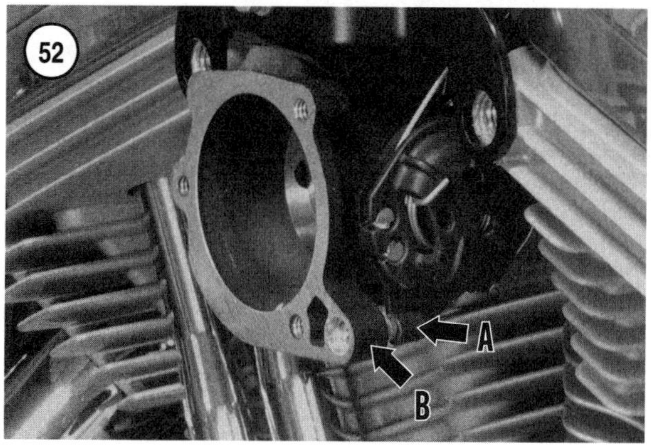

Throttle Cables

Adjustment

There are two different throttle cables. At the throttle grip, the front cable (A, **Figure 50**) is the throttle control cable and the rear cable (B) is the idle control cable.

At the throttle body, the outboard cable (A, **Figure 51**) is the idle control cable and the inboard cable (B) is the throttle control cable.

1. Remove the air filter and backplate as described in Chapter Eight.
2. Push back the rubber boots from the adjusters.
3. Loosen the throttle friction screw (C, **Figure 50**).
4. At the handlebar, loosen both control cable adjuster jam nuts (D, **Figure 50**), then turn the cable adjusters (E) clockwise as far as possible to increase cable slack.
5. Turn the handlebars so the front wheel points straight ahead. Turn the throttle grip to open the throttle completely and hold it in this position.

NOTE
*The air cleaner backplate is shown removed in **Figure 52** to better illustrate the steps.*

6. At the handlebar, turn the throttle control cable adjuster counterclockwise until the throttle cam stop (A, **Figure 52**) just touches the stop boss (B) on the throttle body. Release the throttle grip. Turn the throttle control cable adjuster counterclockwise 1/2 to 1 turn. Tighten the throttle cable adjuster jam nut.
7. Turn the front wheel all the way to the full right lock position and hold it there.
8. At the handlebar, turn the idle cable adjuster until the lower end of the idle control cable (A, **Figure 51**) just contacts the spring in the cable guide. Tighten the idle cable jam nut.
9. Install the backplate and the air filter as described in Chapter Eight.
10. Shift the transmission into neutral and start the engine.

WARNING
Do not ride the motorcycle until the throttle cables are properly adjusted. Also, the cables must not catch or pull when the handlebar is turned from side to side. Improper cable routing and adjustment can cause the throttle to stick open. This could cause loss of control and a possible crash. Recheck this adjustment before riding the motorcycle.

11. Increase engine speed several times. Release the throttle and make sure the engine speed returns to idle. If the engine speed does not return to idle, at the handlebar, loosen the idle control cable adjuster jam nut and turn the cable adjuster clockwise as required. Tighten the idle control cable adjuster jam nut.
12. Allow the engine to idle in neutral, then turn the handlebar from side to side. Do not operate the throttle. If the engine speed increases when the handlebar assembly is turned, the throttle cables are routed incorrectly or damaged. Turn off the engine. Recheck cable routing and adjustment.
13. Push the rubber boots back onto the adjusters.

PERIODIC LUBRICATION

Fork Oil Replacement

On 2011 XL883L, XL1200X and XL1200C models a fork oil drain screw is not provided at the bottom of the fork legs. The fork legs must be removed to drain and replace the fork oil. Refer to Chapter Eleven for fork leg removal, filling procedure and installation. Refer to Chapter Eleven in this Supplement for additional fork information, oil capacities and levels.

Table 9 FUEL TANK CAPACITY

Model	Capacity (including reserve)
2007, 2009, 2010	
XL883C, XL1200C, XL1200L	4.5 gal. (17.0 L)
All other models	3.3 gal. (12.5 L)
2008	
XL883C, XL1200C, XL1200L, XL1200R	4.5 gal. (17.0 L)
All other models	3.3 gal. (12.5 L)
2011	
XL883L, XL1200C, XL1200L	4.5 gal. (17.0 L)
XL1200X	2.1 gal. (7.9 L)
All other models	3.3 gal. (12.5 L)
Low fuel warning light on	
2.1 gal. tank	0.65 gal. (2.5 L)
3.3 gal. tank	0.8 gal. (3.0 L)
4.5 gal. tank	1.0 gal. (3.8 L)

Table 10 MAINTENANCE AND TUNE-UP SPECIFICATIONS AND OIL CAPACITY

Item	Specification
Drive belt deflection	
2007-2009	
XL883, XL883R, XL1200R	9/16-5/8 in. (14.3-15.9 mm)
All other models	1/4-5/16 in. (6.4-7.9 mm)
2010-2011	
XL883R	9/16-5/8 in. (14.3-15.9 mm)
All other models	1/4-5/16 in. (6.4-7.9 mm)
Engine compression	
XL883 models	
2007	125-140 psi (862-966 kPa)
2008-on	165-180 psi (1138-1242 kPa)
XL1200 models	200-225 psi (1380-1552 kPa)
Engine oil with filter replacement	
2008-2009 models	2.8 qt. (2.65 L)

Table 11 MAINTENANCE AND TUNE-UP TORQUE SPECIFICATIONS

Item	ft.-lb.	in.-lb.	N•m
Rear axle nut*			
2007 models	72-78	–	98-106
2008-on models	95-105	–	129-142

*Refer to procedure.

CHAPTER FOUR

ENGINE TOP END

CYLINDER HEAD

Removal/Installation

Removal and installation procedures are the same as described for 2004-2006 models except the induction module must be removed and installed as described in this Supplement. The induction module and fuel injection components replace the intake manifold and carburetor used on early models.

When installing a new cylinder head gasket, make sure to install the correct gasket; an overhaul gasket set may include gaskets for both 883 cc and 1200 cc engines. The gasket part number is stamped into the head gasket. Identify the gasket as follows:

a. 883 cc engines–part No. 16664-86C/D.
b. 1200 cc engines–part No. 16770-84F.

VALVES AND VALVE COMPONENTS

Valve Guide Replacement

On 2011 models, the valves guides are fitted with a snap ring at the upper end of the guide. Remove the snap ring before valve guide removal. Remove the guide by driving it toward the combustion side of the cylinder head.

OIL TANK AND OIL HOSES

For 2010-on models, the oil tank is redesigned to have the oil feed, drain and return hoses connected at the bottom of the tank. When removing hoses, mark each hose and fitting with identifying marks. When installing hoses, use care to ensure that each hose is connected to the correct fitting. Refer to **Figure 53**.

Figure 53 is located on the following page.

Table 12 ENGINE TOP END SPECIFICATIONS

Torque	
2007	
883 cc	51 ft.-lb. (69 N•m) @ 4300 rpm
1200 cc	79 ft.-lb. (107 N•m) @ 3500 rpm
2008-on	
883 cc	55 ft.-lb. (74.5 N•m) @ 3500 rpm
1200 cc	79 ft.-lb. (107 N•m) @ 4000 rpm

15

53

OIL TANK AND HOSES (2010-ON)

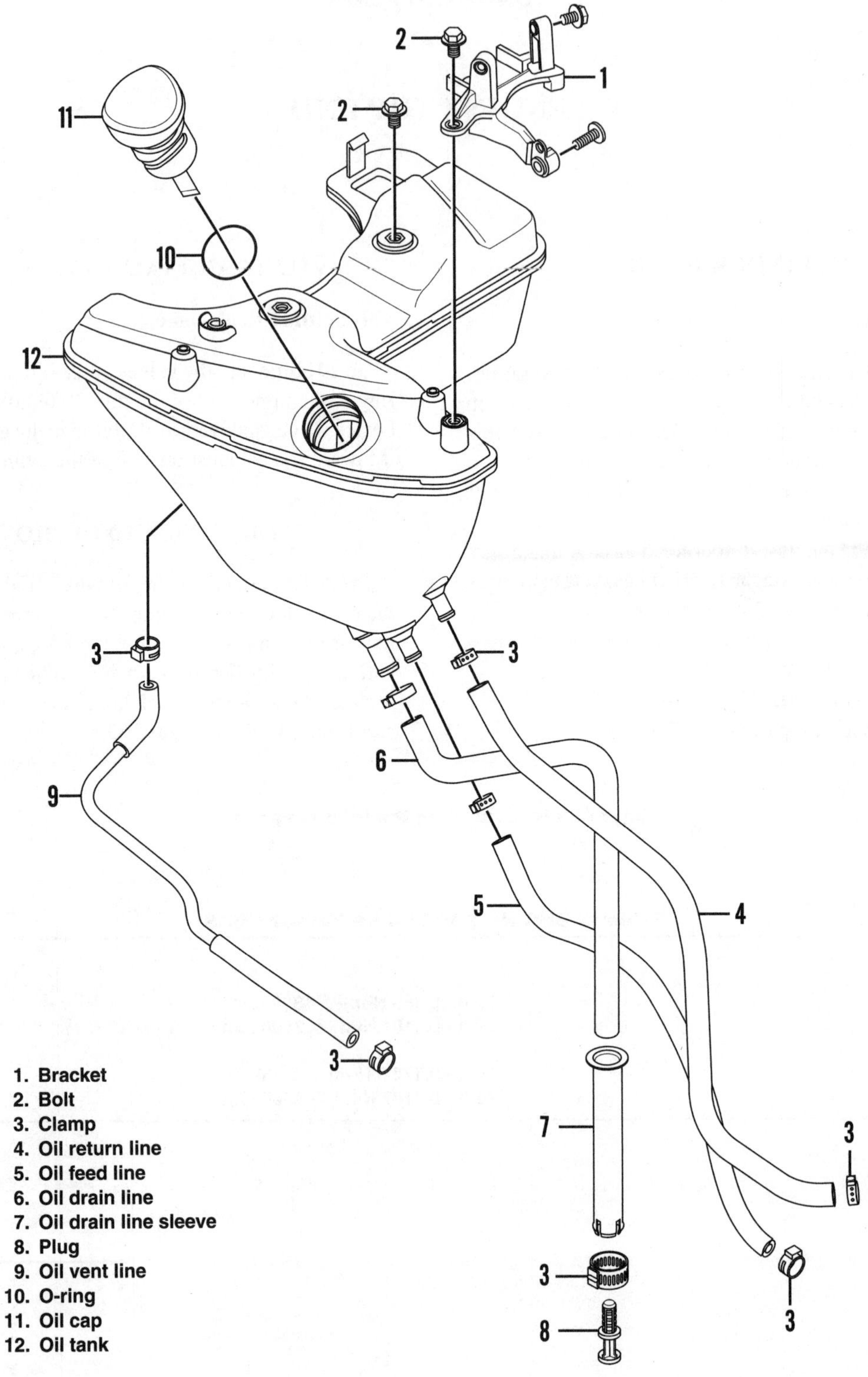

1. Bracket
2. Bolt
3. Clamp
4. Oil return line
5. Oil feed line
6. Oil drain line
7. Oil drain line sleeve
8. Plug
9. Oil vent line
10. O-ring
11. Oil cap
12. Oil tank

CHAPTER FIVE

ENGINE LOWER END

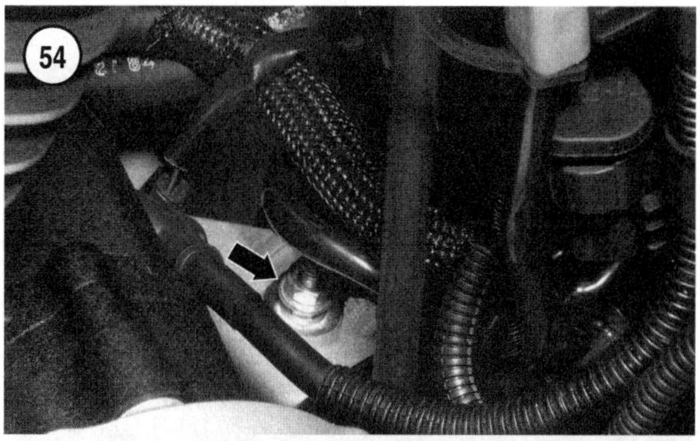
54

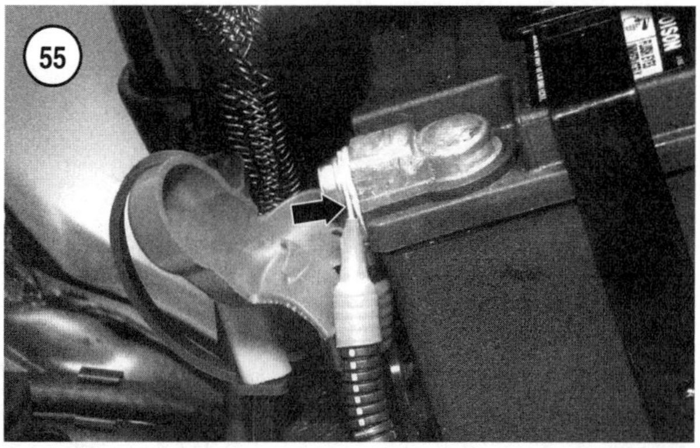
55

56

ENGINE

Removal

1. Depressurize the fuel system as described in this Supplement.
2. Remove the seat as described in Chapter Fourteen.

CAUTION
After disconnecting the negative cable end in Step 3, position the cable end so it cannot contact metal parts while disconnecting the battery.

3. Disconnect the battery negative cable end from the stud on top of the crankcase (**Figure 54**).
4. Remove the Maxi-fuse as described in Chapter Nine.
5. Remove the retaining screw and disconnect the battery positive cable and Maxi-fuse cable from the battery positive terminal (**Figure 55).**
6. Place a drain pan underneath the primary drive cover, remove the oil drain plug(**Figure 56**) and allow the transmission oil to drain out. Install the drain plug and tighten to 14-30 ft.-lb. (19-40 N•m).
7. Refer to the *Engine Oil and Filter Change* in *Periodic Lubrication* in Chapter Three and drain the oil tank. Do not reconnect the drain hose to the holder on the frame.
8. Refer to *Exhaust System* in this Supplement. Remove the exhaust system, including the exhaust mounting bracket, as described in Chapter Eight.
9. Refer to Chapter Fourteen and remove the rider and passenger footrests and linkage from both sides.
10. Refer to the *Clutch Cable* in Chapter Six and detach the clutch cable from the engine.
11. Disconnect the oil tank feed hose (A, **Figure 57**), return hose (B) and vent hose (C) from the oil tank.
12. Refer to Chapter Seven and remove the drive sprocket and drive belt.
13. Remove the fuel tank as described in this Supplement.

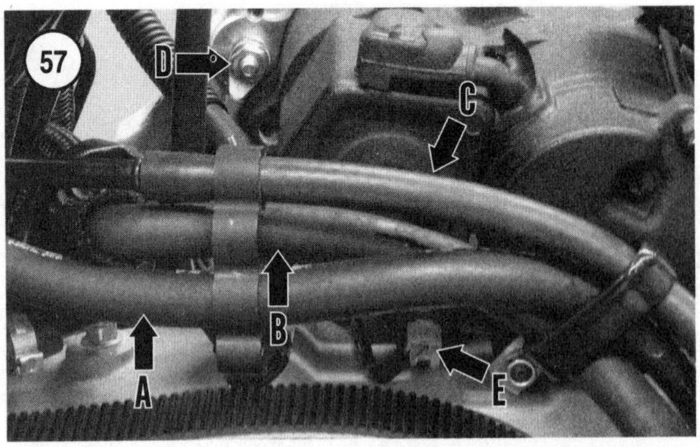

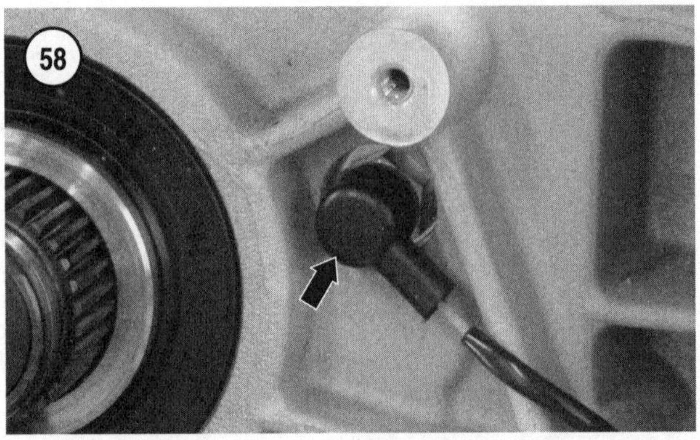

14. Remove the induction module as described in this Supplement.
15. Remove the ignition coil as described in *Ignition System* in this Supplement.
16. Remove the wiring harness caddy as described in this Supplement. Disconnect all connectors contained in the caddy.
17. Remove the crank position sensor (CKP) as described in Chapter Nine. Do not disconnect the sensor, but place it in a protected position out of the way. Plug the hole in the crankcase.
18. Disconnect the following electrical connectors:
   a. Neutral indicator switch connector (**Figure 58**).
   b. Voltage regulator connector (A, **Figure 59**).
   c. Oil pressure switch connector (B, **Figure 59).**
   d. Vehicle speed sensor connector (A, **Figure 60).**
   e. Ground connectors (D, **Figure 57).**
   f. Starter cable (B, **Figure 60).**
   g. Starter relay connector (E, **Figure 57).**
   h. Engine temperature sensor connector (A, **Figure 61**). Also detach the barbed cable retainer (B).
19. On XL1200C models, remove the horn as described in Chapter Nine.
20. On California models, remove the EVAP canister and hoses as described in this Supplement.
21. Remove the rear stabilizer link bolts (A, **Figure 62**), ground strap (B), link (C) and spacer (D).
22. Remove the bolt securing the upper stabilizer link to the engine (A, **Figure 63**).

NOTE

If tool access is not possible to perform Step 23, remove the horn as described in Chapter Nine.

23. Remove the stabilizer bracket mounting bolts and remove the link and bracket assembly (B, **Figure 63**).
24. Remove the bolt securing the lower stabilizer link to the engine (A, **Figure 64**).

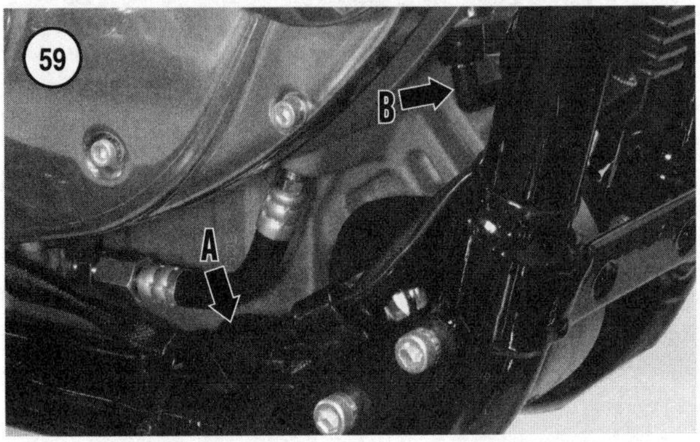

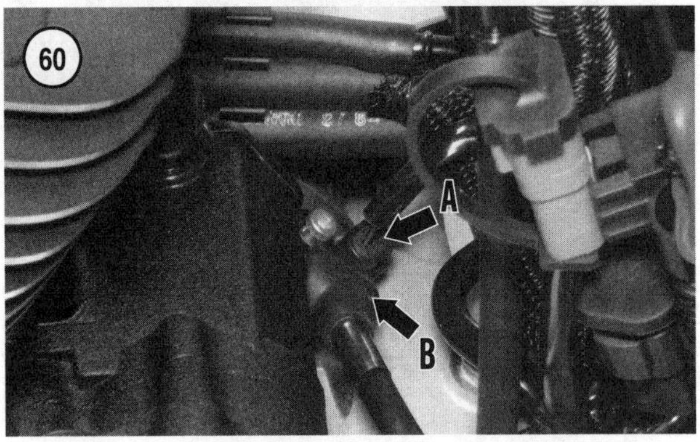

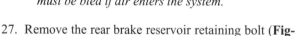

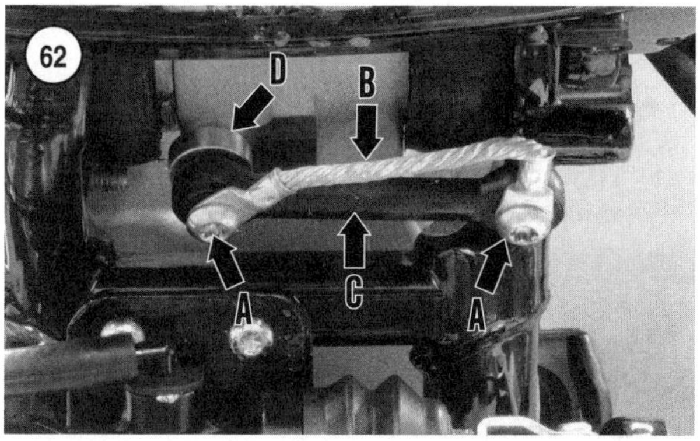

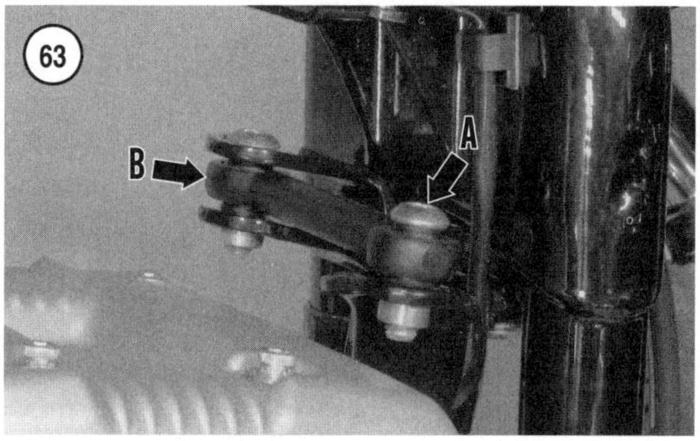

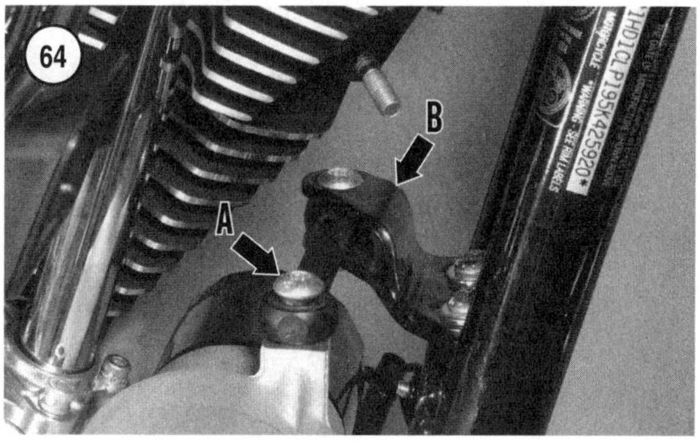

25. Remove the stabilizer bracket mounting bolts and remove the link and bracket assembly (B, **Figure 64**).

26. Remove the rear brake reservoir cover (**Figure 65**).

NOTE

Keep the brake reservoir upright so air will not enter the brake fluid. The brake system must be bled if air enters the system.

27. Remove the rear brake reservoir retaining bolt (**Figure 66**) and suspend the reservoir out of the way.

28. Disconnect the connectors from the rear brake light switch (A, **Figure 67**).

29. Remove the rear brake light switch mounting bolt (B, **Figure 67**), then move the switch out of the way. Do not bend or damage the brake tubing.

30. For models with a wire retainer clip (**Figure 68**), remove the bolts and clip.

31. Disengage any wiring harness that will interfere with engine removal and move the wiring harness out of the way.

NOTE

The rear engine mount also serves as the swing arm pivot. It is necessary to support the rear of the frame because the swing arm must disengage from the frame. Depending on the equipment available, it may be easier to remove the rear wheel from the swing arm, or leave the rear wheel installed.

32. Support the rear of the frame, then perform substep a or b.
    a. Remove the rear wheel.
    b. Loosen the axle nut and move the rear wheel fully forward in the swing arm. Tighten the axle nut.

33. Loosen–do not remove–the mounting bolts on the front engine mount bracket (A, **Figure 69**).

34. Remove the swing arm bolts (**Figure 70**) on both sides, then move the swing arm to clear the pivot bosses.

35. Loosen–do not remove–the mounting bolts on the rear engine mount bracket (A, **Figure 71**).

CAUTION
Be sure the jack or lift used in Step 36 will not damage the engine crankcase due to improper support points.

36. Place a suitable jack or lift under the engine, then raise the engine to remove engine weight from the engine mounts.

37. Remove the front engine mount bolt (B, **Figure 69**).

38. Remove the oil tank vent line.

39. Remove the rear engine mount bracket bolts (A, **Figure 71**), then remove the bracket (B).

40. Remove the front engine mount bracket bolts (A, **Figure 69**), then remove the bracket (C).

41. Inspect the engine to make sure everything has been disconnected and there are no obstructions to engine removal.

CAUTION
The following steps require the aid of a helper to safely remove the engine assembly from the frame.

NOTE
Place tape or other protective material on the frame and engine to prevent scratches or other damage during installation.

42. Lift out the engine by moving the rear of the engine out first, then separate the front of the engine from the frame.

43. Move the engine to a workbench or engine stand.

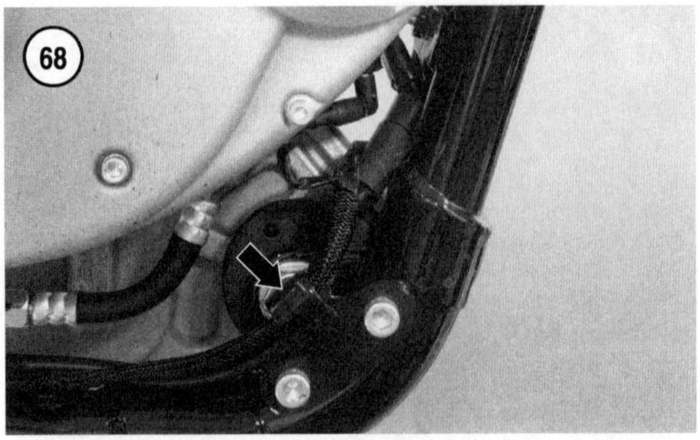

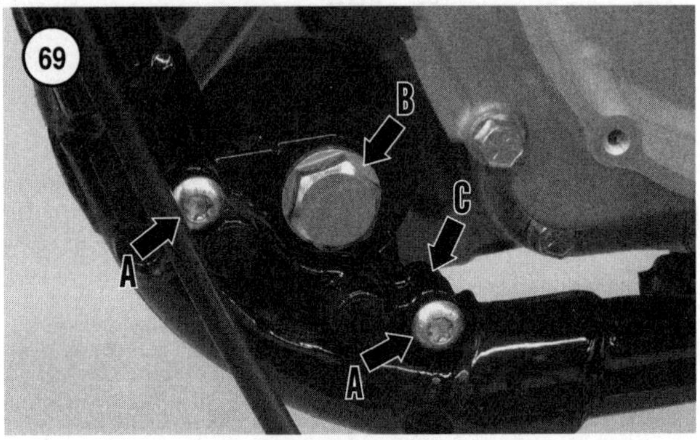

Inspection

1. Inspect the frame for cracks or other damage. If found, have the frame inspected by a dealer or frame alignment specialist.

2. Clean the frame before installing the engine.

3. If paint has been removed from the frame during engine removal or cleaning, touch up as required prior to installing the engine back in the frame.

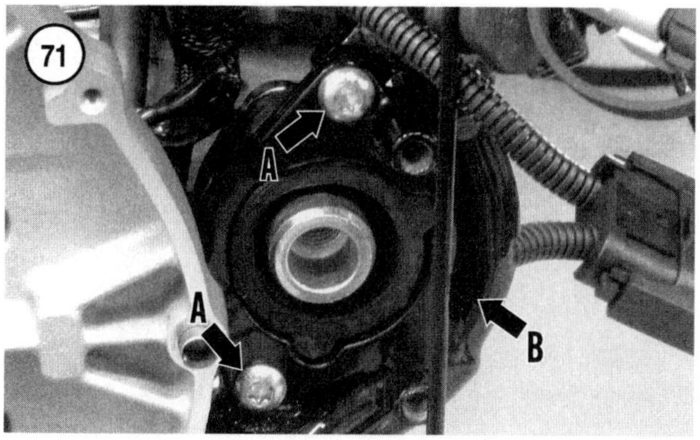

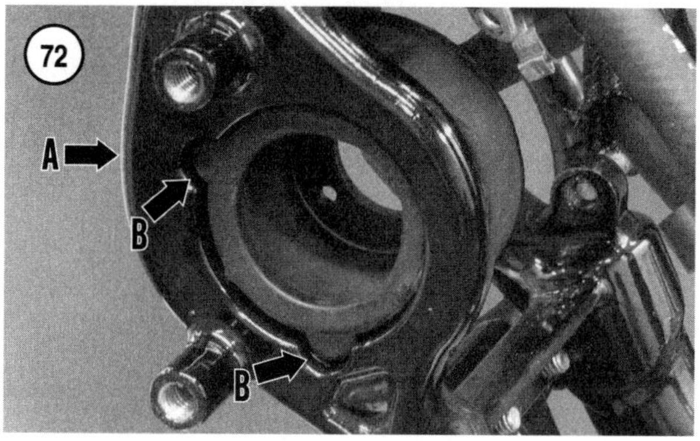

4. While the engine is removed, remove the oil tank as described in Chapter Four. Thoroughly flush the tank. Then reinstall it and plug the oil hoses to prevent contamination.

5. Replace any worn or damaged oil hoses and clamps as described in Chapter Four.

6. Check the exposed hoses and cables for chafing or other damage. Replace loose, missing or damaged hose clamps and cable ties.

7. Check all of the engine mounting fasteners for corrosion and thread damage. Clean each fastener in solvent to remove oil and threadlock residue. Replace worn or damaged fasteners before reassembly.

8. Inspect the wiring harness for signs of damage that may have occurred when removing the engine. Repair or replace damaged wires as required.

Installation

NOTE
Before engine installation check the wiring harness clips on the frame and replace as needed.

1. Make sure the engine mounts are correctly installed on the engine as described in *Engine Mounting System* in Chapter Five. The front mounts must be installed prior to engine installation. The rear mounts are installed during engine installation.
2. Place tape or other protective material on the frame and engine to prevent scratches or other damage during installation.

NOTE
Support the engine in the frame using a suitable jack or lift so the engine can be moved as needed to align the engine mounts.

3. Install the right, rear engine mount (A, **Figure 72**) into the frame. The mount bosses must fit into the frame notches (B, **Figure 72).**
4. Install the engine into the frame. Insert the front of the engine first while simultaneously guiding the swing arm pivot shaft into the right, rear mount.
5. Install the left, rear engine mount into the bracket so the mount bosses fit into the notches in the bracket.
6. Install the bracket (B, **Figure 71**) so the mount fits around the swing arm pivot shaft, then install the bracket retaining bolts (A). Do not tighten the bolts.
7. Install the front engine mount bracket (C, **Figure 69**) and bolts (A). Do not tighten the bolts.
8. Install the front engine mount bolt (B, **Figure 69**). Do not tighten.
9. Make sure the front engine mount fits properly, then tighten the mounting bracket bolts (A, **Figure 69**) to 25-35 ft.-lb. (34-47 N•m).
10. Make sure the rear engine mount/swing arm pivot fits properly, then tighten the mounting bracket bolts (A, **Figure 71**) to 25-35 ft.-lb. (34-47 N•m).
11. Install the oil tank vent line.
12. Move the swing arm so it aligns with the swing arm pivot shaft. Install the swing arm bolts (**Figure 70**) on both sides and tighten to 60-70 ft.-lb. (81-95 N•m).
13. Remove the nut on the front engine mount bolt and apply Loctite 243 to the threads. Tighten the front engine mount bolt (B, **Figure 69**) to 60-70 ft.-lb. (81-95 N•m).
14. Install the rear stabilizer link (C, **Figure 62**), spacer (D), ground strap (B) and bolts (A). Note that the left bolt is longer. Tighten the bolts to 25-35 ft.-lb. (34-47 N•m).
15. If removed, install the rear wheel as described in this Supplement.
16. On California models, install the EVAP canister and hoses as described in this Supplement.
17. Install the front, lower stabilizer bracket and link assembly (B, **Figure 64**). Tighten the bracket bolts to 25-35 ft.-lb. (34-47 N•m).

18. Install the bolt securing the lower stabilizer link to the engine (A, **Figure 64**). Tighten the bolt to 25-35 ft.-lb. (34-47 N•m).

19. Install the front, upper stabilizer bracket and link assembly (B, **Figure 63**). Tighten the bracket bolts to 25-35 ft.-lb. (34-47 N•m).

20. Install the bolt securing the upper stabilizer link to the engine (A, **Figure 63**). Tighten the bolt to 25-35 ft.-lb. (34-47 N•m).

21. For models with a wire retainer clip (**Figure 68**), install the clip and tighten the bolts securely.

22. Install the wiring harness located on the lower frame tubes into the clips on the tubes or the wiring retainer holes. Be sure the harness is secure. Replace any faulty clips or retainers.

23. Install the rear brake light switch. Tighten the mounting bolt (B, **Figure 67**) to 72-120 in.-lb. (8.1-13.6 N•m).

24. Attach the connectors to the rear brake light switch (A, **Figure 67**).

25. Move the rear brake reservoir into its original position. Tighten the retaining bolt (**Figure 66**) to 20-25 in.-lb. (2.3-2.8 N•m).

26. Install the rear brake reservoir cover (**Figure 65**).

27. Connect all connectors contained in the wiring harness caddy. Connect the caddy as described in this Supplement.

28. Install the ignition coil as described in *Ignition System* in this Supplement.

29. Install the induction module as described in this Supplement. Make sure to connect all electrical connectors.

30. On XL1200C model, install the horn as described in Chapter Nine.

31. Connect the following electrical connectors:
   a. Neutral indicator switch connector (**Figure 58**). Tighten to 36-60 in.-lb. (4.1-6.8 N•m).
   b. Voltage regulator connector (A, **Figure 59**).
   c. Oil pressure switch connector (B, **Figure 59**).
   d. Vehicle speed sensor connector (A, **Figure 60**).
   e. Ground connectors (D, **Figure 57**).
   f. Starter cable (B, **Figure 60**).
   g. Starter relay connector (E, **Figure 57**).
   h. Engine temperature sensor connector (A, **Figure 61**). Also reattach the cable retainer (B).

32. Install the crank position sensor (CKP) as described in Chapter Nine.

33. Install the fuel tank as described in this Supplement.

34. Refer to Chapter Seven and install the drive sprocket and drive belt.

CAUTION

Be sure the oil hoses are properly connected in Step 35. For 2007-2009 models, refer to ***Oil Tank and Oil Hoses*** *in Chapter Four for proper routing and connections to the oil tank. For 2010-on models, refer to Chapter Four for hose routing and* ***Figure 53*** *in this Supplement for connecting the hoses to the oil tank.*

NOTE

If the oil hose fittings were removed from the oil pump, apply Hylomar or Teflon Pipe Sealant to the fitting threads prior to installation.

35. Connect the oil tank feed hose (A, **Figure 57**), return hose (B) and vent hose (C) to the oil tank.

36. Refer to *Clutch Cable* in Chapter Six and attach the clutch cable to the engine.

37. Refer to Chapter Fourteen and install the rider and passenger footrests and linkage on both sides.

38. Refer to *Exhaust System* in this Supplement. Install the exhaust system, including the exhaust mounting bracket, as described in Chapter Eight.

CAUTION

Before connecting the positive cable end in Step 39, make sure the negative cable end is not contacting metal parts.

39. Connect the battery positive cable and Maxi-fuse cable to the battery positive terminal (**Figure 55**). Position the cable ends so the battery cable contacts the battery terminal and the Maxi-fuse cable contacts the bolt head. Tighten the bolt to 40-50 in.-lb. (4.5-5.6 N•m).

40. Install the Maxi-fuse as described in Chapter Nine.

41. Connect the battery negative cable end to the stud on top of the crankcase (**Figure 54**). Tighten the retaining nut to 55-75 in.-lb. (6.2-8.5 N•m).

42. Install the seat as described in Chapter Fourteen.

43. If removed, install a new oil filter. Refer to Chapter Three.

44. Fill the transmission with oil as described in *Transmission Oil Change* in *Periodic Lubrication* in Chapter Three.

45. Fill the engine with oil as described in *Engine Oil and Filter Change* in *Periodic Lubrication* in Chapter Three.

46. Start the engine and check for oil leaks.

47. Operate all controls and adjust as needed.

48. Shift the transmission into gear and check clutch and transmission operation.

49. Slowly test ride the motorcycle to ensure all systems are operating correctly.

GEARCASE COVER AND TIMING GEARS

Installation

On 2009 models, tighten the pinion shaft nut (A, **Figure 73**) using the following procedure:

1. Install crankshaft locking tool ([B, **Figure 73**] JIM'S 1665 or HD-43984).
2. Apply Loctite 272 (red) to the pinion shaft nut (A, **Figure 73**) prior to installation. Install the nut and tighten to 19-21 ft. lb. (26-29 N•m).
3. Tighten the nut an additional 15-19°.

CRANKCASE AND CRANKSHAFT

Crankshaft Installation/Crankcase Assembly

On some 2011 models, sixteen bolts are used on the left crankcase to secure the crankcase halves.

Table 13 ENGINE LOWER END SERVICE SPECIFICATIONS

	New in. (mm)	Service Limit in. (mm)
Crankshaft end play*	0.003-0.013 (0.076-0.33)	0.013 (0.33)

*Refer to procedure in Chapter Five.

Table 14 ENGINE LOWER END TORQUE SPECIFICATIONS

	ft.-lb.	in.-lb.	N•m
Battery negative cable stud nut	–	55-75	6.2-8.5
Battery terminal bolts	–	60-70	6.8-7.9
Front engine mount bolt	60-70	–	81-95
Front engine mounting bracket bolts	25-35	–	34-47
Front stabilizer			
Lower stabilizer link bolts	25-35	–	34-47
Lower stabilizer bracket bolts	25-35	–	34-47
Upper stabilizer bracket bolts	25-35	–	34-47
Upper stabilizer link bolts	25-35	–	34-47
Gearcase cover screws	–	80-110	9.0-12.4
Neutral indicator switch	–	36-60	4.1-6.8
Pinion shaft nut			
2007-2008	35-45	–	47-61
2009-on	Refer to text.		
Rear brake light switch mounting bolt	–	72-120	8.1-13.6
Rear brake reservoir retaining bolt	–	20-25	2.3-2.8
Rear engine mount/swing arm pivot mounting bracket bolts	25-35	–	34-47
Rear stabilizer link bolts	25-35	–	34-47
Swing arm bolts	60-70	–	81-95
Transmission/primary case drain plug	14-30	–	19-40

CHAPTER SIX

PRIMARY DRIVE, CLUTCH AND EXTERNAL SHIFT MECHANISM

SHIFT LEVER ASSEMBLY

Removal/Installation

For XL883N and XL1200N models, follow procedure described for XL883, XL883L, XL883R, XL1200L and XL1200R models.

PRIMARY DRIVE/CLUTCH

Clutch Installation

On 2007-on models, tighten the engine sprocket nut to 240-260 ft.-lb. (325-353 N•m).

Table 15 CLUTCH AND PRIMARY DRIVE TORQUE SPECIFICATIONS

	ft.-lb.	in.-lb.	N•m
Clutch nut			
2010-on models	50-60	–	68-81
Engine sprocket nut	240-260	–	325-353

Table 16 TRANSMISSION SPECIFICATIONS

Final drive sprocket	
Number of transmission sprocket teeth	
2011 883 models	50-60
Final drive ratio	
2011 883 models	2.345:1

CHAPTER EIGHT

FUEL, EMISSION CONTROL AND EXHAUST SYSTEMS

Refer to Chapter Three for routine air filter maintenance.

WARNING
Gasoline is carcinogenic and extremely flammable, and must be handled carefully. Wear nitrile gloves to avoid skin contact. If gasoline does contact skin, immediately and thoroughly wash the area with soap and warm water.

NOTE
Cover any disconnected electrical connector terminals to prevent contamination which can affect system performance.

AIR FILTER BACKPLATE

Removal/Inspection/Installation

Refer to Chapter Eight. Note that there is no vent hose attached to the backplate on 2007-on models.

ELECTRONIC FUEL INJECTION (EFI)

This section covers the electronic sequential port fuel injection system. Complete diagnostic capability on this system requires a Harley-Davidson Digital Technician, a breakout box and a number of other special tools.

However, basic troubleshooting diagnosis is no different on a fuel-injected machine than on a carbureted one. If the check engine light comes on or there is a driveability problem, read the diagnostic trouble codes described in Chapter Two. Make sure all related electrical connections are clean and secure. A high or erratic idle speed may indicate a vacuum leak. Make sure there is an adequate supply of fresh gasoline.

If a problem cannot be resolved, refer service to a dealership. Incorrectly performed diagnostic procedures can result in damage to the fuel injection system.

Electronic Control Module

The electronic control module (ECM) receives input from the engine sensors to control the fuel injection and ignition systems to provide optimum performance. The ECM triggers the fuel injectors and determines injection duration, thereby controlling fuel injection timing and the air/fuel ratio.

Refer to *Electronic Control Module* in this Supplement for service procedures.

Fuel Supply System

Refer to the appropriate section in this Supplement for service procedures.

Fuel pump and filters

The integral fuel pump and filter unit are located in the fuel tank. Refer to *Fuel Pump Module* in this Supplement.

Fuel lines

The fuel lines are attached to the bottom of the fuel tank with quick-disconnect fittings.

The fuel supply line pressure is 55-62 psi (380-425 kPa) and is controlled by the pressure regulator attached to the internal fuel filter assembly.

Fuel rail and injectors

The solenoid-actuated constant-stroke pintle-type fuel injectors consist of a solenoid plunger, needle valve and housing. The fuel injector's opening is fixed and fuel pressure is constant. The fuel injectors are mounted on the intake manifold. The fuel rail supplies fuel to the injectors and secures them to the intake manifold.

Induction module

The induction module includes the throttle body and intake manifold, which are screwed together. The TMAP sensor and fuel injectors reside on the intake manifold. The throttle body contains the throttle valve and houses the throttle position sensor and idle air control motor.

DEPRESSURIZING THE FUEL SYSTEM

The fuel system is under pressure at all times, even when the engine is not operating. The system must be depressurized before loosening any fuel lines. Gasoline will spray out unless the system is depressurized.

1. Refer to *Fuses* in this Supplement and remove the fuel pump fuse.
2. Start the engine and allow it to idle until it runs out of gasoline.
3. After the engine has stopped, operate the starter for three seconds to eliminate any residual gasoline in the fuel lines.
4. After all service procedures have been completed, install the fuel pump fuse.

INDUCTION MODULE

Removal

Refer to **Figure 74**.

1. Depressurize the fuel system as described in this Supplement.
2. Disconnect the Maxi-fuse as described in Chapter Nine.
3. Remove the air filter backplate as described in this Supplement.
4. Remove the seat as described in Chapter Fourteen.

74

INDUCTION MODULE

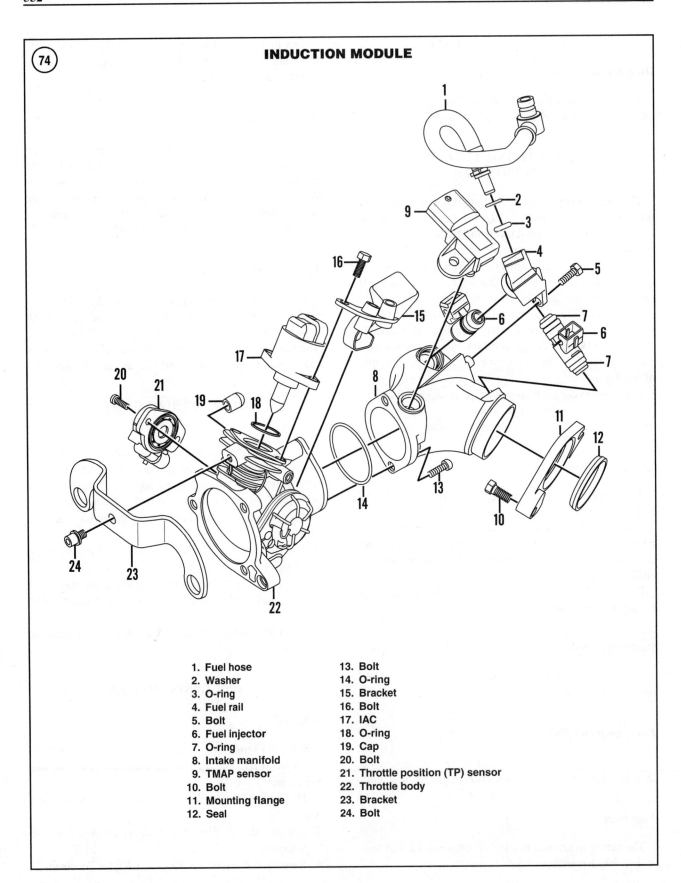

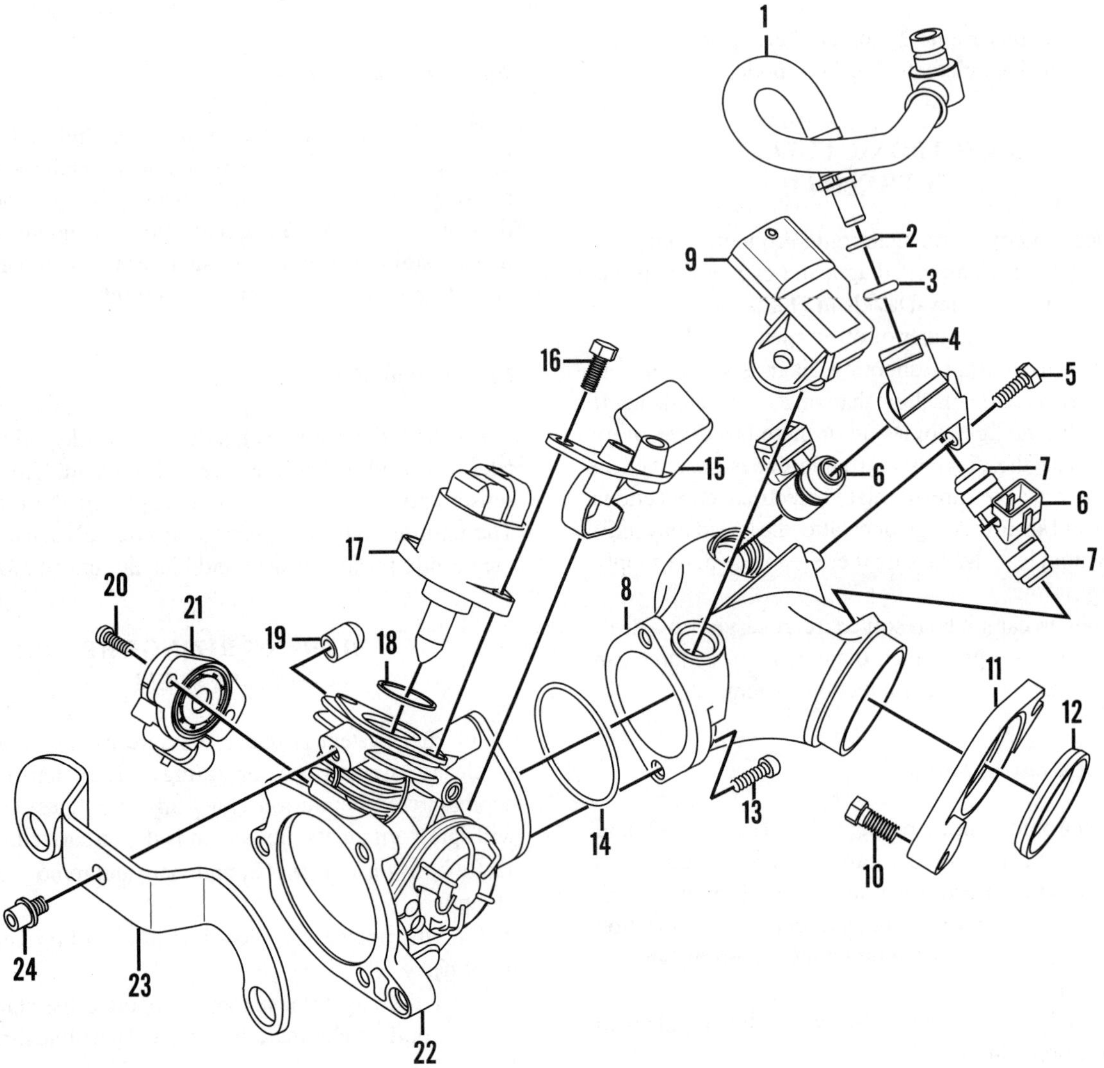

1. Fuel hose
2. Washer
3. O-ring
4. Fuel rail
5. Bolt
6. Fuel injector
7. O-ring
8. Intake manifold
9. TMAP sensor
10. Bolt
11. Mounting flange
12. Seal
13. Bolt
14. O-ring
15. Bracket
16. Bolt
17. IAC
18. O-ring
19. Cap
20. Bolt
21. Throttle position (TP) sensor
22. Throttle body
23. Bracket
24. Bolt

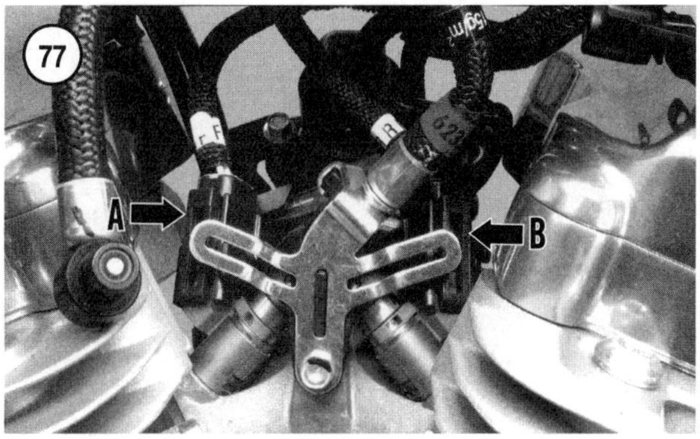

5. Refer to *Fuel Tank* in this Supplement. Loosen the front fuel tank mounting bolt. Remove the rear mounting bolts. Raise the rear of the fuel tank and support it.
6. Remove the bolt (A, **Figure 75**) securing the mounting bracket (B) and remove the bracket.
7. Detach the TMAP sensor connector (A, **Figure 76**).
8. Detach the IAC connector (B, **Figure 76**).
9. On California models, disconnect the purge hose.
10. Unplug the connectors from the front fuel injector (A, **Figure 77**) and rear fuel injector (B).
11. Detach the connector from the throttle position sensor (**Figure 78**).
12. Turn the cable slack adjusters at the handlebar end of the throttle cables to obtain maximum slack.
13. Loosen, but do not remove, the intake manifold flange bolts on both cylinders on the left side of the engine (**Figure 79**).
14. Remove the bolts securing the intake manifold flanges on the right side (**Figure 80**).
15. Lift up the mounting flanges and remove the induction module assembly from the right side of the engine.
16. There are two different throttle cables. Label the two cables at the throttle body before disconnecting them. One is the throttle control cable (A, **Figure 81**) and the other is the idle control cable (B). Disconnect the throttle control

cable and the idle control cable from the cable guide and the throttle pulley.

17. Remove the induction module.

Installation

1. Install the throttle cable (A, **Figure 81**) and the idle control cable (B). Make sure they are installed in the locations noted during removal.

2. Install the flanges (A, **Figure 82**) and manifold seals (B) onto the intake manifold. Note that the seals (A, **Figure 83**) and flanges (B) have a tapered side. Fit the seal taper into the flange taper.

NOTE

To help align the intake manifold flanges during installation, install the left-side bolts so they engage a couple of threads. Engage the slots of the manifold flanges with the bolts. Be careful not to damage the bolt threads.

3. Install the induction module onto the cylinder head intake ports. The slotted ends of the flanges must point to the left.

4. Make sure the front and rear seals seat squarely against the cylinder head mating surfaces.

5. Install all four bolts fingertight at this time.

6. Install the bracket (B, **Figure 75**) and bolt (A). Tighten the bolt finger tight.

7. Temporarily install two breather bolts (**Figure 84**) through the bracket holes to align the induction module. Tighten bracket bolt (A, **Figure 75**) to 84-108 in.-lb. (9.5-12.2 N•m).

8. Tighten the intake manifold bolts to 96-120 in.-lb. (11-13.6 N•m).

CAUTION

Do not attempt to align the intake manifold after tightening the bolts. This will damage the manifold seals. If necessary, loosen the bolts, then align the manifold.

9. Make sure the intake manifold seats squarely against the cylinder heads. Remove the breather bolts (**Figure 84**) that were temporarily installed.

10. Reconnect all electrical connectors.

11. On California models, connect the purge hose.

12. Refer to *Fuel Tank* in this Supplement and install the fuel tank.

13. Install the air filter backplate as described in this Supplement.

14. Adjust the throttle cables as described in *Periodic Maintenance* in this Supplement.

15. Connect the Maxi-fuse as described in Chapter Nine.

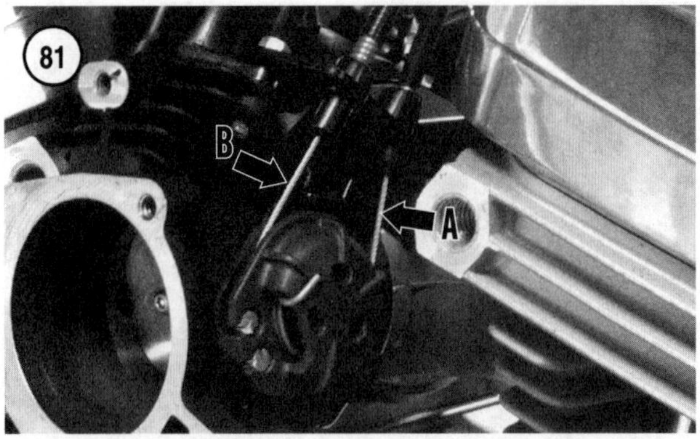

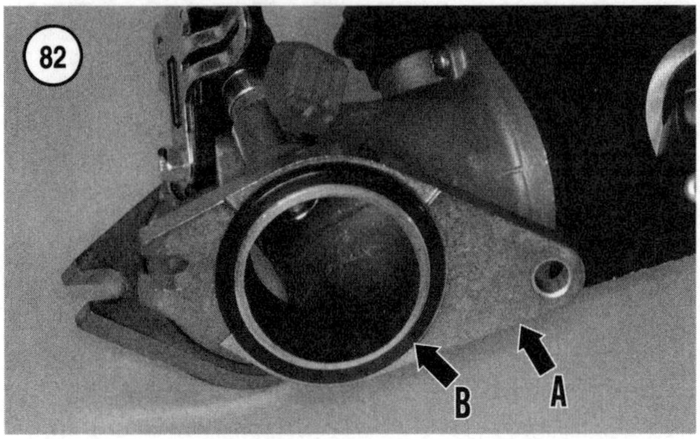

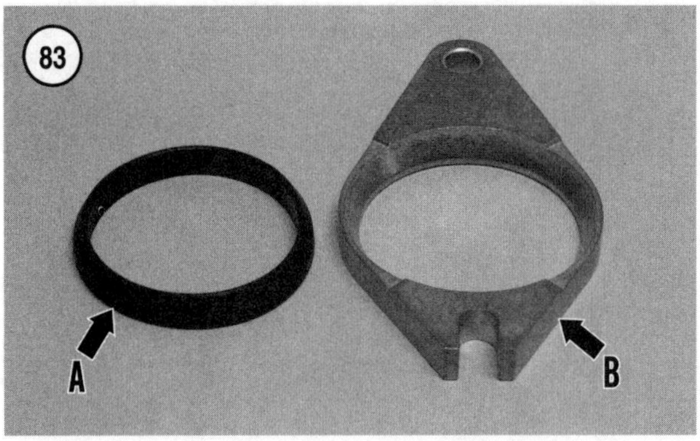

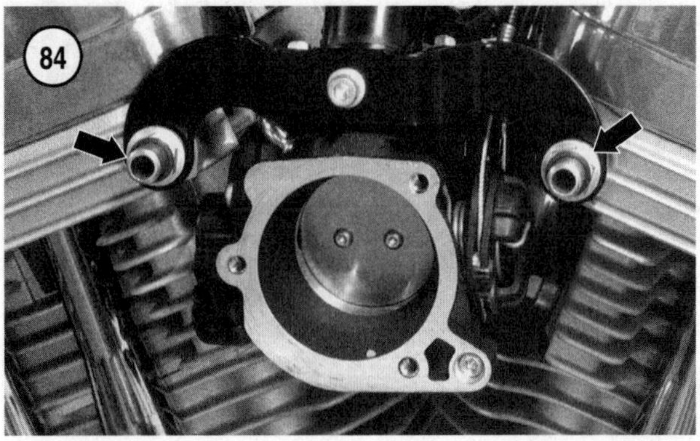

85

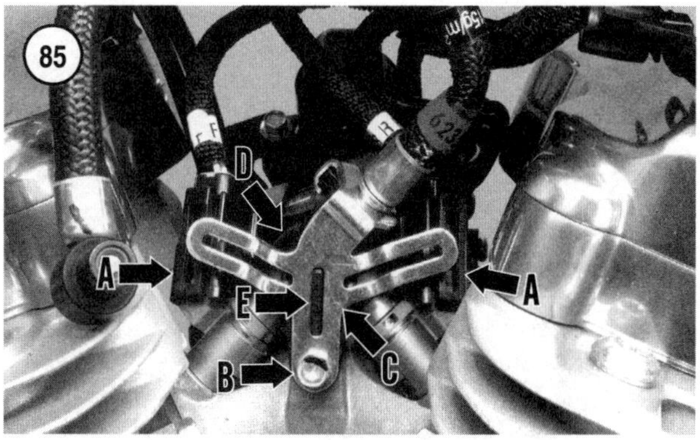

86

87

88

16. Install the fuel pump fuse as described in *Fuses* in this Supplement.
17. Install the seat as described in Chapter Fourteen.
18. Check operation and for fuel leaks.

FUEL INJECTORS

A fuel injector provides fuel for each cylinder. The fuel rail routes fuel to each fuel injector and secures the injectors in the intake manifold. The fuel injector is not serviceable, but must be replaced as a unit assembly.

Removal/Installation

1. Depressurize the fuel system as described in this Supplement.
2. Disconnect the Maxi-fuse as described in Chapter Nine.
3. Remove the seat as described in Chapter Fourteen.
4. On XL1200C, remove the horn as described in Chapter Nine.

NOTE
To increase access on models with 4.5 gallon fuel tanks, loosen the front mounting bolt and remove the rear mounting bolt. Raise and support the fuel tank.

5. Unplug the connectors from the fuel injectors (A, **Figure 85**).
6. Remove the bolt (B, **Figure 85**).
7. Lift up the bracket (C, **Figure 85**) to disengage it from the tab on the fuel rail (D). Rotate the bracket to unlock the fuel hose fitting (E, **Figure 85**).
8. Hold the fuel rail (A, **Figure 86**).Twist and pull the fuel hose (B, **Figure 86**) straight up to separate the hose from the fuel rail.
9. Hold down the fuel injectors and rock the fuel rail up and off of the fuel injectors.
10. Twist and pull out each fuel injector (A, **Figure 87**).
11. Remove the O-rings (B, **Figure 87**) from each fuel injector.
12. Apply a thin coat of engine oil and install new O-rings onto the fuel injectors.
13. Reverse the removal procedure to install the fuel injectors while noting the following:
    a. Make sure the mounting bores for the fuel injectors in the fuel rail and intake manifold are clean.
    b. Lubricate all O-rings with engine oil prior to installation.
    c. Inspect the backup washer (A, **Figure 88**) and O-ring (B) on the fuel hose end. Replace if damaged.

d. Insert the fuel hose into the fuel rail. Install the fuel rail mounting bracket while turning the hose end so the flange fits into the U slot on the mounting bracket (**Figure 89**).
e. Tighten the fuel rail bracket mounting screw to 60 in.-lb. (6.8 N•m).

Inspection

1. Visually inspect the fuel injectors for damage. Inspect the injector nozzle (**Figure 90**) for carbon buildup or damage.
2. Check for corroded or damaged fuel injector connector terminals.
3. Be sure the mounting bores for the fuel injectors in the fuel rail and intake manifold are clean.

Fuel Injector Cleaning

A fuel injector must emit a satisfactory spray pattern for optimum engine performance. A dirty or clogged fuel injector nozzle will affect the injector spray pattern. Contact a motorcycle dealership or auto service shop for referral to a company that tests and cleans fuel injectors. The nominal cost of this service is usually much less than the price of a new injector.

THROTTLE POSITION (TP) SENSOR

The throttle position (TP) sensor is mounted on the throttle body. The ECM feeds 5 volts to the TP sensor which returns a varying voltage to indicate throttle position. At idle, the voltage is approximately 0.5 volts. At full throttle, the voltage is approximately 4.5 volts. No position adjustment is available.

Removal/Installation

1. Disconnect the Maxi-fuse as described in Chapter Nine.
2. Remove the air filter backplate as described in this Supplement.
3. Detach the connector (A, **Figure 91**) from the TP sensor (B).
4. Remove the TP sensor mounting screws and remove the TP sensor.
5. Reverse the removal steps to install the TP sensor while noting the following:
   a. Make sure the throttle plate is closed.
   b. Mate the tang on the throttle shaft (A, **Figure 92**) with the slot in the TP sensor (B). After installation

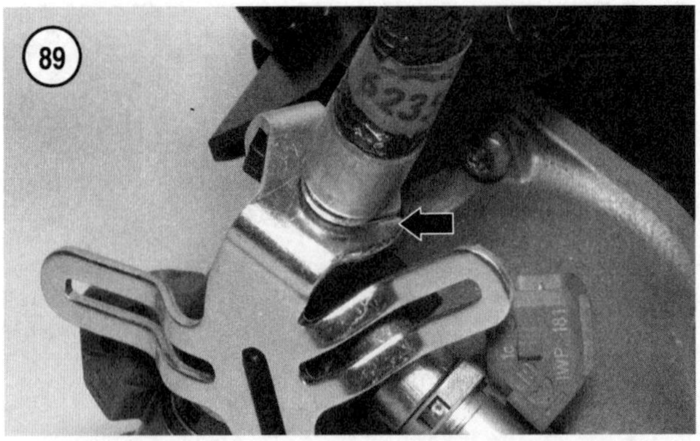

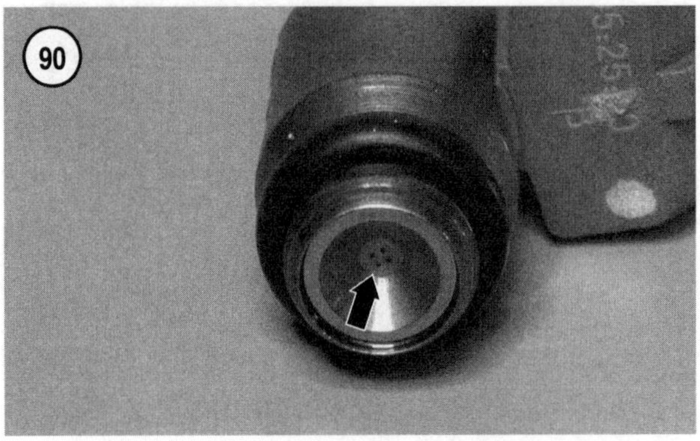

93

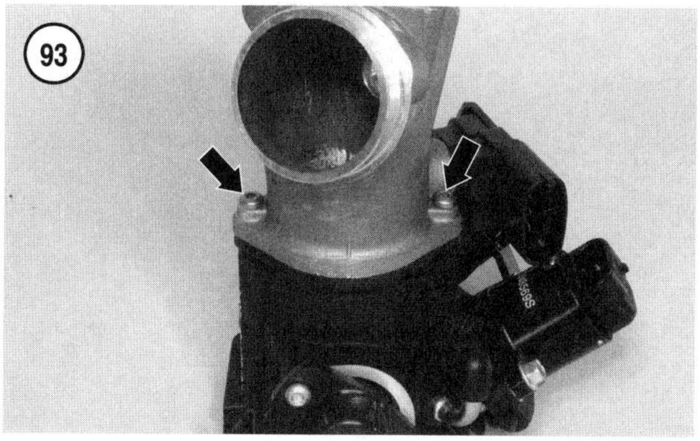

94

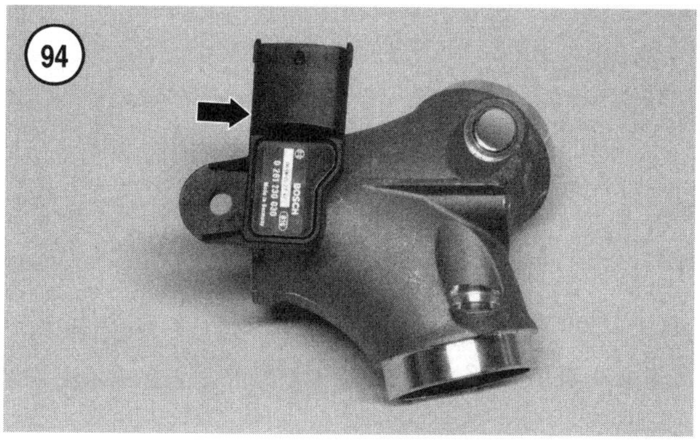

95

96

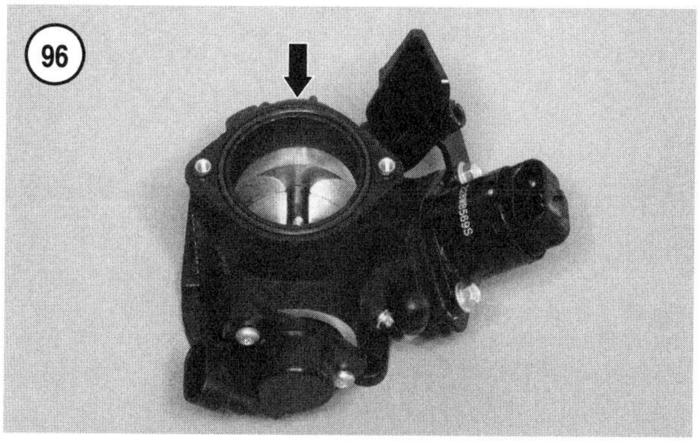

the connector terminals must be positioned as shown in **Figure 91**.

Testing

Refer to **Figure 25** in this Supplement.

TMAP SENSOR

The TMAP sensor measures intake air temperature and intake manifold absolute pressure. The TMAP sensor is connected to the ECM, which adjusts engine timing and fuel delivery to obtain best performance.

Removal/Installation

The TMAP is secured by the throttle cable bracket on the throttle body. The throttle body may be separated from the intake manifold and moved enough to disengage the TMAP sensor from the bracket.

1. Remove the induction module as described in this Supplement.
2. Remove the fuel injectors as described in this Supplement.
3. Unscrew the bolts (**Figure 93**) securing the throttle body to the intake manifold. Separate the intake manifold from the throttle body.
4. Move the throttle body to disengage the TMAP sensor and bracket.
5. Twist the TMAP sensor (**Figure 94**) and remove it from the intake manifold.
6. Reverse the removal steps for installation while noting the following:
   a. Install a new O-ring (**Figure 95**) onto the TMAP sensor, if necessary. Lubricate with engine oil.
   b. Install a new O-ring (**Figure 96**) into the groove on the throttle body, if necessary. Make sure the O-ring is properly seated in the groove.
   c. Tighten the intake manifold-to-throttle body bolts to 35 in.-lb. (4.0 N•m).

Testing

Refer to **Figure 22** and **Figure 23** in this Supplement..

IDLE AIR CONTROL (IAC)

The idle air control (IAC) is mounted on the throttle body. The IAC pintle moves in and out to regulate air entering the idle circuit. The ECM controls the IAC pintle position thereby determining engine idle speed.

Removal/Installation

1. Disconnect the Maxi-fuse as described in Chapter Nine.
2. Remove the air filter backplate as described in this Supplement.
3. Disconnect the IAC connector (A, **Figure 97**).

CAUTION
*The IAC mounting bolts (B, **Figure 97**) are secured with threadlock and must be heated prior to loosening. Use a heat gun set on low setting to soften the threadlock.*

NOTE
The IAC may be retained by Allen bolts or hex bolts. The front bolt secures the throttle cable bracket and sensor.

4. Remove the IAC mounting bolts using the following sequence:
   a. Heat the mounting bolt nearer the throttle cable bracket for two minutes, then remove the bolt.
   b. Heat the remaining bolt for one minute and remove it.
5. Rotate the IAC so the mounting ear clears the throttle cable bracket.
6. Twist the IAC and extract it from the intake manifold.
7. Clean threadlock residue from bolt threads and bolt holes.
8. Reverse the removal steps for installation while noting the following:
   a. Install a new O-ring (**Figure 98**) on the IAC sensor, if necessary. Lubricate with engine oil.
   b. Apply Loctite 243 to the bolt threads.
   c. Tighten the bolts to 60 in.-lb. (6.8 N•m).

Testing

IAC must be tested using the Digital Technician. Refer testing to a dealer.

OXYGEN (O_2) SENSOR

An oxygen (O_2) sensor is mounted on each exhaust pipe. The front cylinder O_2 sensor is shown in A, **Figure 99**. The O_2 sensor monitors the air/fuel mixture and sends a voltage signal to the ECM.

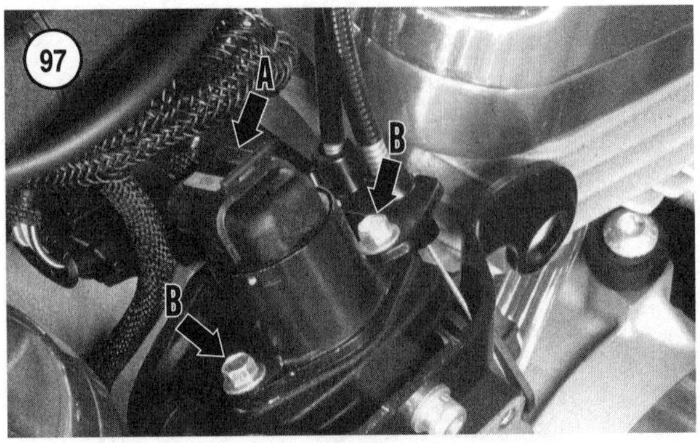

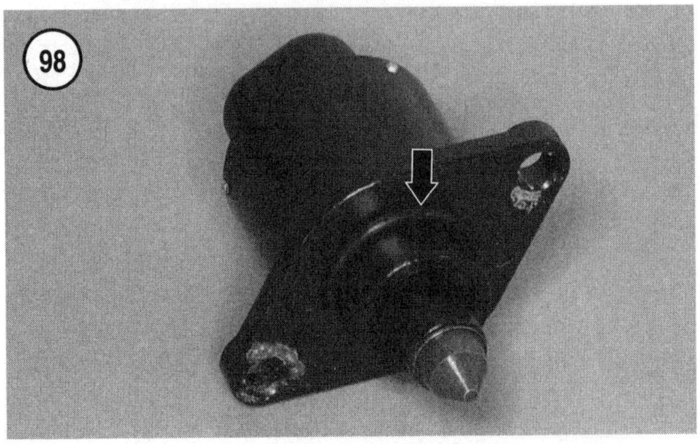

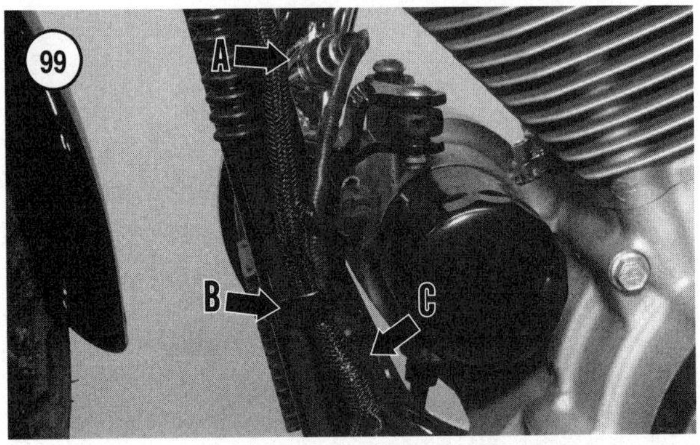

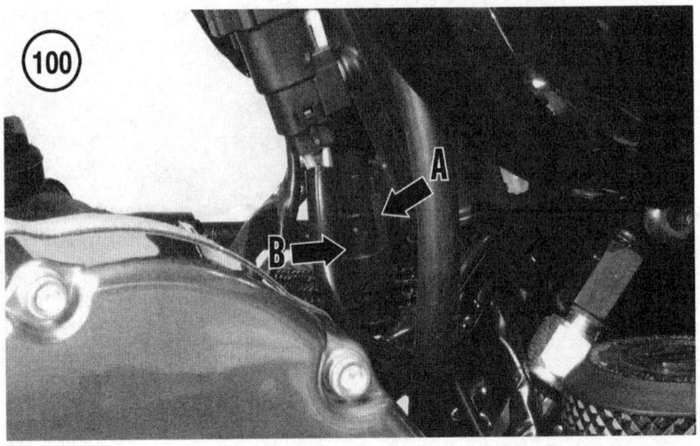

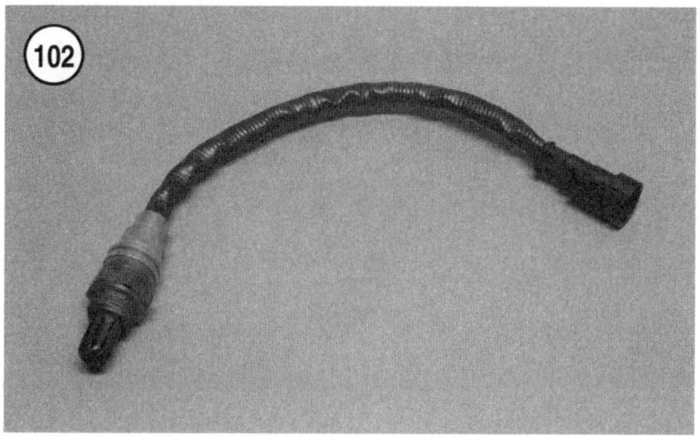

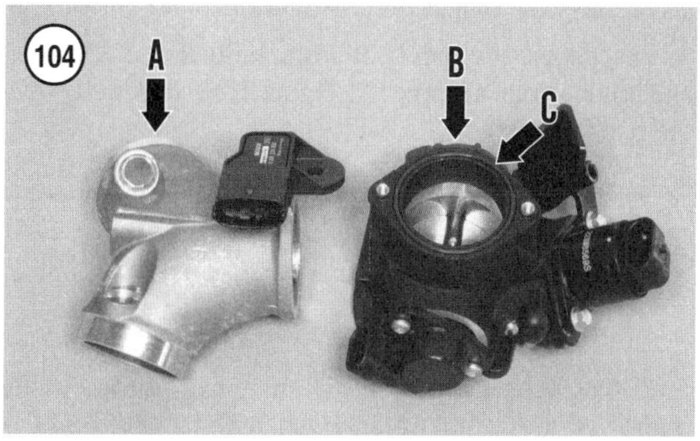

Removal/Installation

NOTE
The O_2 sensors are identical. However, reused sensors should be reinstalled in their original locations.

1A. Front O_2 sensor–Remove the wiring clip (B, **Figure 99**). Disconnect the O_2 connector (C, **Figure 99**).

1B. Rear O_2 sensor–Slide the connector off the mounting tab (A, **Figure 100**). Disconnect the connector (B).

CAUTION
Use care not to damage the O_2 sensor wiring during removal or installation.

NOTE
*The O_2 sensor threads may be corroded making the sensor difficult to unscrew. A 7/8-inch O_2 sensor removal/installation tool is recommended (**Figure 101**). The tool is a slotted socket that surrounds the wire while fully engaging the sensor nut.*

2. Using an O_2 sensor tool, remove the O_2 sensor (**Figure 102**).
3. Reverse the removal steps for installation while noting the following:
   a. Apply antiseize compound onto the sensor threads. A new sensor may be coated with antiseize compound. Do not apply dielectric grease or other compounds to the threads.
   b. Tighten the O_2 sensor to 29-44 ft.-lb. (39-60 N•m).
   c. Make sure all wiring is secure and cannot contact the exhaust system.

Testing

Refer to **Figure 26** in this Supplement.

THROTTLE BODY

15

Removal/Installation

1. Remove the induction module as described in this Supplement.
2. If not previously removed, remove the fuel rail and fuel injectors as described in this Supplement.
3. Remove the two screws (**Figure 103**) securing the intake manifold to the throttle body.
4. Separate the intake manifold (A, **Figure 104**) and throttle body (B).
5. Reverse the removal steps for installation while noting the following:

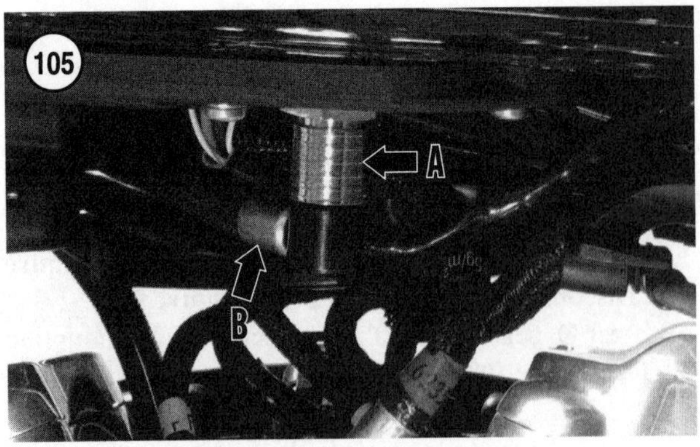

a. Install a new O-ring (C, **Figure 104**) into the groove on the throttle body, if necessary. Make sure the O-ring is properly seated in the groove.
b. Tighten the intake manifold-to-throttle body bolts (**Figure 103**) to 35 in.-lb. (4 N•m).

Disassembly/Reassembly

1. Remove the TP sensor as described in this Supplement.
2. Remove the IAC as described in this Supplement.
3. Remove the throttle cable bracket.
4. No additional disassembly is required. Remaining parts are not available separately.
5. Assembly is reversal of disassembly while noting the following:
   a. The throttle cable bracket must be installed before the IAC.
   b. Tighten the throttle cable bracket mounting screw to 60 in.-lb. (6.8 N•m).

INTAKE MANIFOLD

Removal/Installation

1. Remove the throttle body as described in this Supplement.
2. If necessary, remove the TMAP sensor as described in this Supplement.
3. Reverse the removal steps for installation.

FUEL TANK

Removal/Installation

1. Depressurize the fuel system as described in this Supplement.
2. Disconnect the Maxi-fuse as described in Chapter Nine.

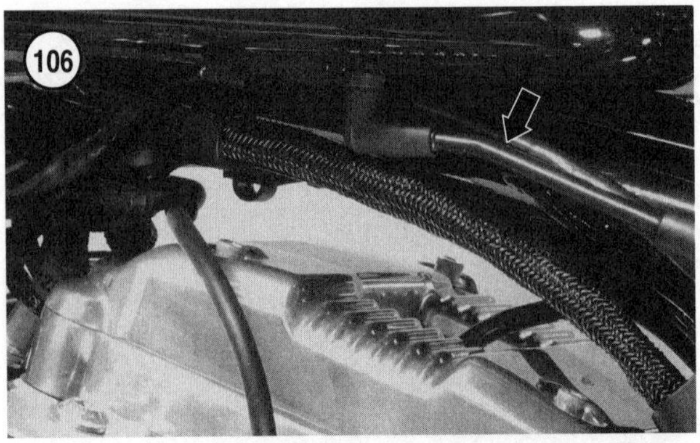

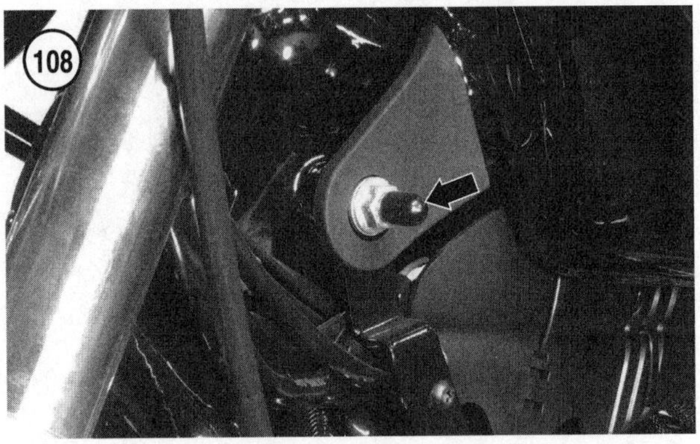

3. Remove the seat as described in Chapter Fourteen.

4. Disconnect the fuel hose from the fuel tank. Push up and hold the outer sleeve (A, **Figure 105**), then pull down the fuel hose (B).

CAUTION
Carefully insert the transfer pump intake into the fuel tank to prevent damage to the fuel injection pump.

5. If the fuel tank will be disassembled, use a transfer pump to remove fuel from the fuel tank.

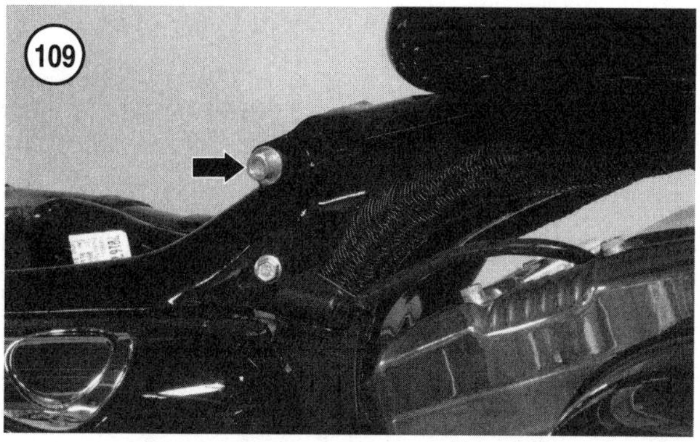

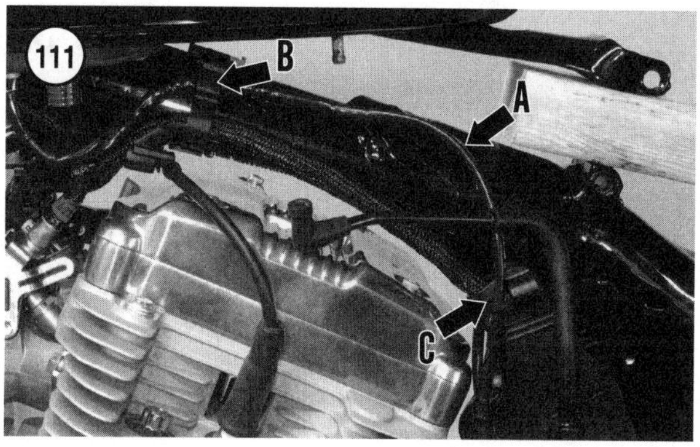

6. Detach the fuel tank vent hose (**Figure 106**) from the fuel tank fitting.

7. Detach the fuel pump wiring harness from any cable holders.

8. Disconnect the fuel pump connector (**Figure 107**).

9. Remove the cap, locknut and washer (**Figure 108**) on the front and rear mounting bolts.

10. Remove the rear mounting bolt and washer (**Figure 109**).

CAUTION
Protect the upper front of the fuel tank so it will not be damaged if it contacts the upper fork bracket.

NOTE
The rear of the fuel tank may be lifted for access to components underneath.

11. Remove the front mounting bolt and washer (**Figure 110**).

12. Detach the fuel pump wiring harness from the barbed retaining clip.

13. Lift and remove the fuel tank.

WARNING
Store the fuel tank in a safe place away from open flames or where it could be damaged.

14. Reverse the removal steps for installation while noting the following:

   a. Make sure the front fuel tank mounting legs fit outside the ignition coil bracket.
   b. Route the fuel pump wiring harness so it forms a curve (A, **Figure 111**) under the fuel tank to prevent interference between the tank and frame.
   c. The wiring harness must be secured by wiring holder (B, **Figure 111**) and clip (C). Push the clip prong into the hole in the wiring harness holder.
   d. Tighten the fuel tank mounting bolts to 15-20 ft.-lb. (20-27 N•m).
   e. Make sure the fuel hose connection is secure.

WARNING
Turn the ignition key to IGNITION and make sure the fuel pump operates. Make sure the fuel hose connection is leak-free.

FUEL PUMP MODULE

The fuel pump module includes the fuel pump, fuel pressure regulator, fuel level sensor and fuel filter. The components are mounted on a plate attached to the bottom of the fuel tank. Refer to **Figure 112**.

Removal/Installation

1. Remove the fuel tank as described in this Supplement.
2. Position the fuel tank upside down on a soft cloth.
3. Remove the fuel pump module retaining bolts (**Figure 113**).

15

112

FUEL PUMP ASSEMBLY

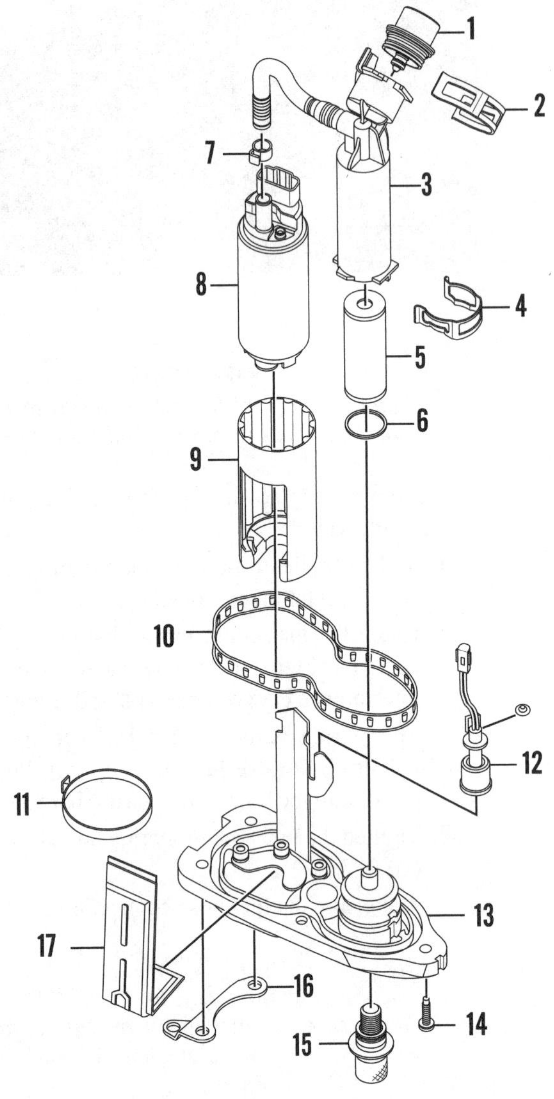

1. Fuel pressure regulator
2. Clamp
3. Fuel filter housing
4. Clamp
5. Fuel filter
6. O-ring
7. Clamp
8. Fuel pump
9. Insulator
10. Seal
11. Clamp
12. Fuel level sensor
13. Plate
14. Bolt
15. Fuel fitting
16. Bracket
17. Bracket

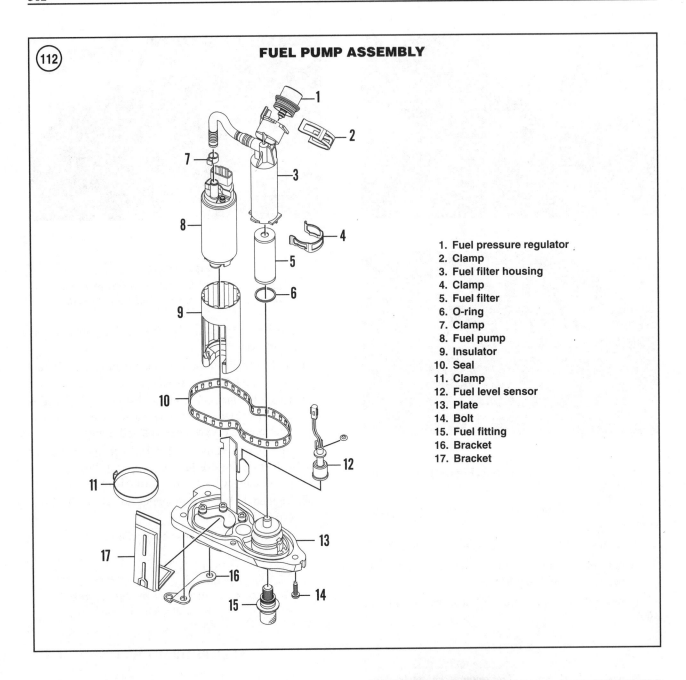

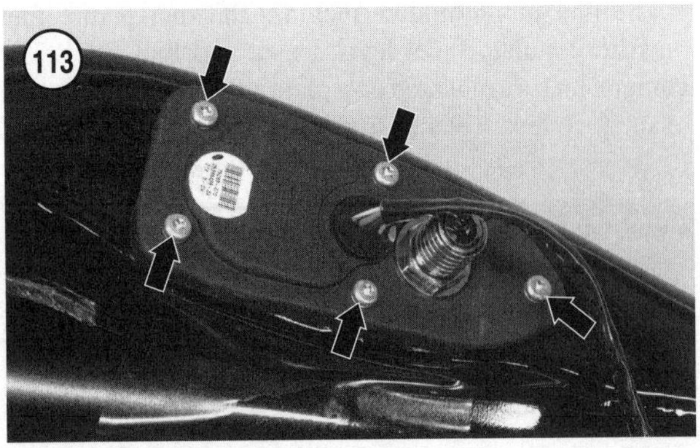

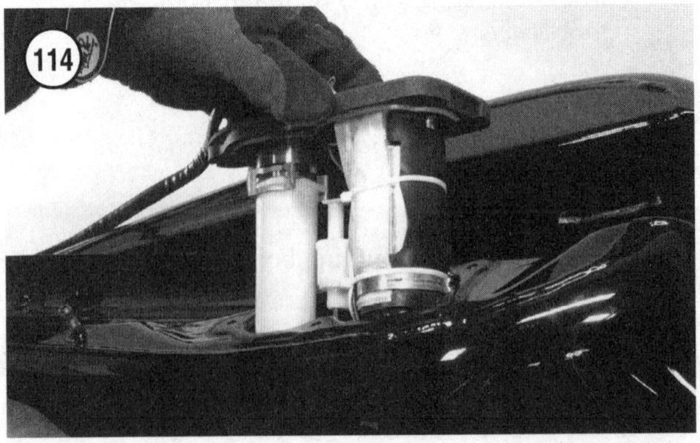

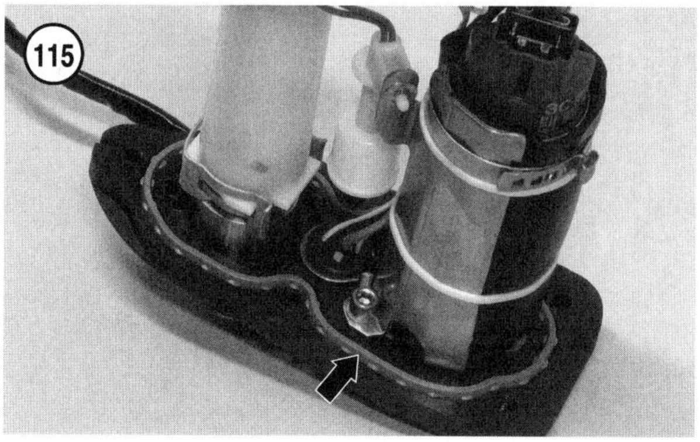

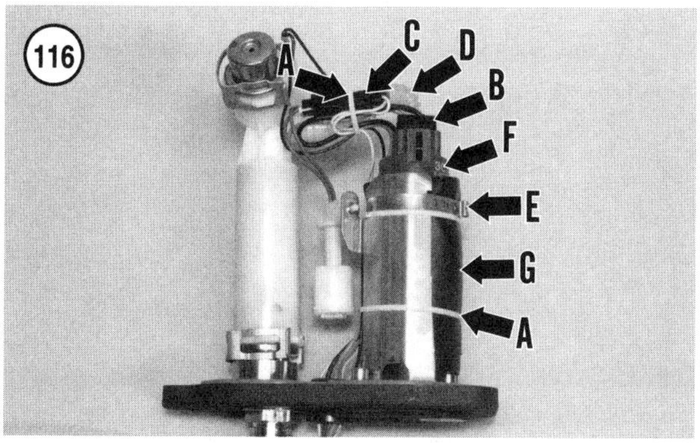

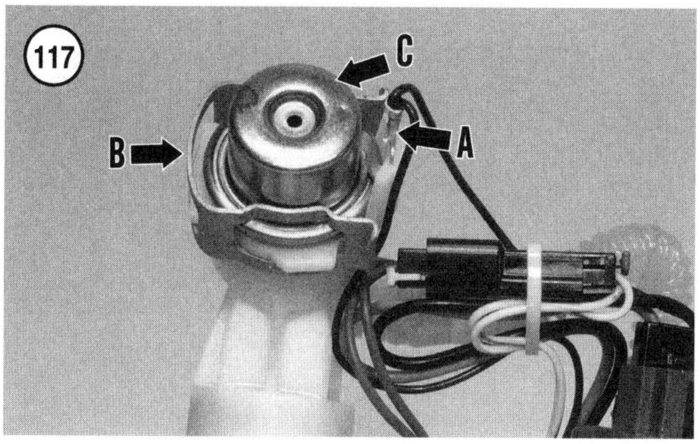

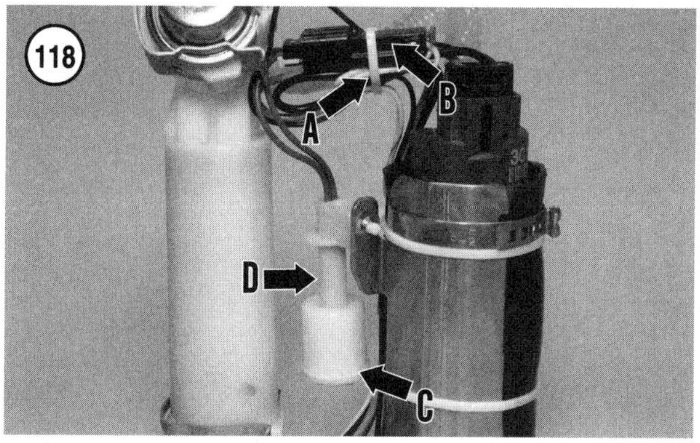

4. Remove the fuel pump module (**Figure 114**). Initially, lift the unit straight out, then tilt the unit to pass the pressure regulator through the opening.
5. Reverse the removal steps for installation while noting the following:
   a. Install a new seal (**Figure 115**) into the groove in the cover plate.
   b. Tighten the retaining bolts to 40-45 in.-lb. (4.5-5.1 N•m).

Fuel Pump

Removal/installation

1. Remove the fuel pump module as described in this section.
2. Cut the wire retaining straps (A, **Figure 116**).
3. Detach the fuel pump connector (B, **Figure 116**).
4. Detach the fuel level sensor connector (C, **Figure 116**).
5. Remove the clamp and disconnect the hose (D, **Figure 116**) from the fuel pump.
6. Remove the clamp (E, **Figure 116**).
7. Remove the fuel pump (F, **Figure 116**) and insulator (G).
8. Reverse the removal steps for installation. Install the clamp (E, **Figure 116**) so the end is toward the end of the mounting plate.

NOTE
*For information on installing the clamps refer to **Fuel Hose And Clamps** in Chapter Eight.*

Fuel Pressure Regulator

Removal/installation

1. Push in the tang on the clip, then remove the ground wire connector (A, **Figure 117**).
2. Note the position of the retaining clip (B, **Figure 117**), then remove it.
3. Remove the fuel pressure regulator (C, **Figure 117**).
4. Reverse the removal steps for installation.

Fuel Level Sensor

Removal/installation

1. Remove the cable strap (A, **Figure 118**).
2. Detach the fuel level sensor connector (B, **Figure 118**).
3. Remove the push nut (C, **Figure 118**).
4. Remove the fuel level sensor (D, **Figure 118**).
5. Reverse the removal steps for installation.

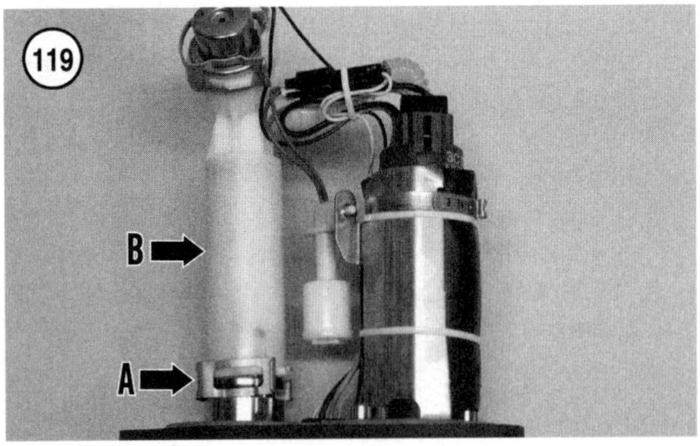

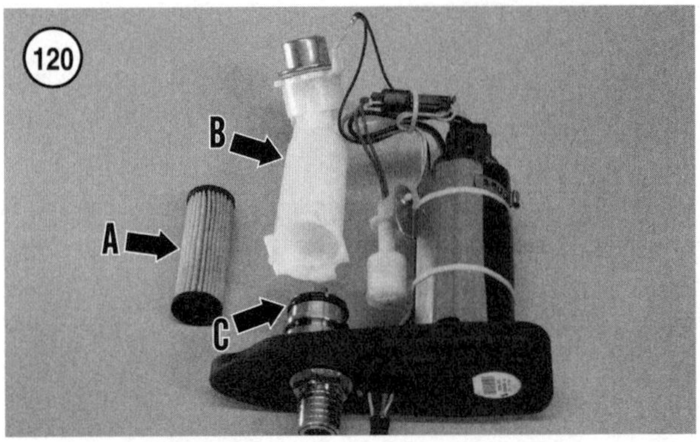

Fuel Filter

Removal/installation

1. Note the position of the retaining clip (A, **Figure 119**), then remove it.
2. Lift the filter housing (B, **Figure 119**) off the base.
3. Remove the filter (A, **Figure 120**) from the housing (B).
4. Reverse the removal steps for installation. Install a new O-ring (C, **Figure 120**).

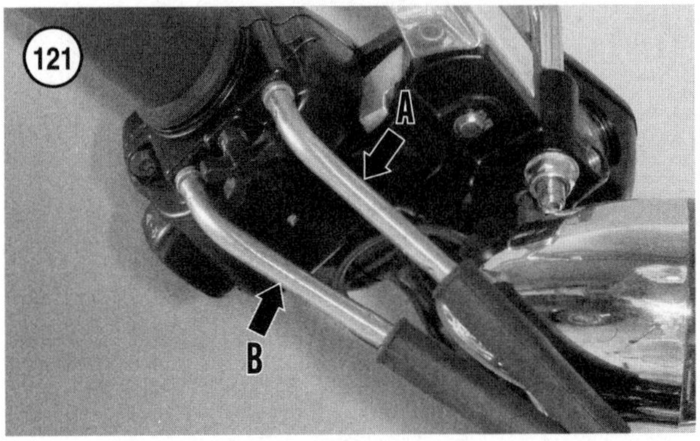

THROTTLE AND IDLE CABLES

Two cables control throttle body valve movement: a throttle cable and an idle cable. At the throttle grip, the front cable is the throttle control cable (A, **Figure 121**) and the rear cable is the idle control cable (B). At the throttle body, the outboard cable is the idle control cable (A, **Figure 122**) and the inboard cable is the throttle control cable (B).

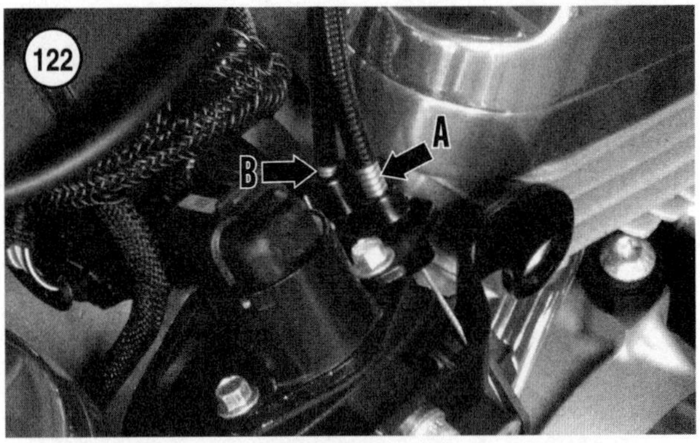

Removal

1. Remove the fuel tank as described in this Supplement.
2. Remove the air filter backplate as described in this Supplement.
3. Note the cable routing from the throttle body through the frame to the right side handlebar.
4. At the right side handlebar, loosen both control cable adjuster locknuts (A, **Figure 123**), then turn the cable adjusters (B) as far as possible to increase cable free play.
5. Remove the screws securing the right side switch assembly (**Figure 124**).
6. Remove the ferrules (**Figure 125**) from the notches on the inboard side of the throttle grip. Remove the ferrules from the cable end fittings.
7. Remove the friction shoe from the end of the tension adjust screw.

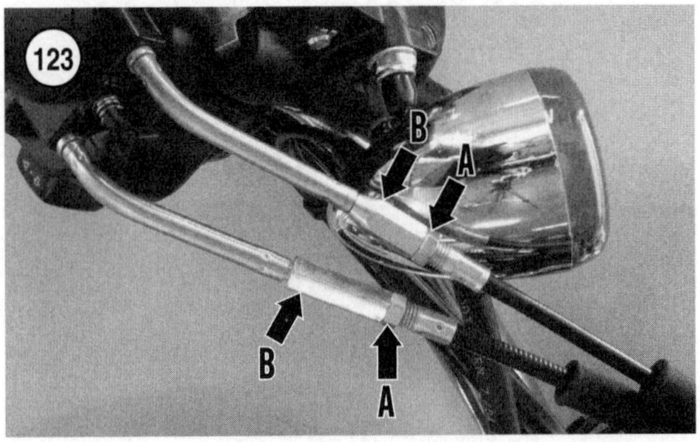

8. Remove the throttle grip from the handlebar.

9. Pull the crimped inserts at the end of the throttle and idle control cable housings from the switch lower housing. Use a rocking motion while pulling on the control cable housings. If necessary, place a drop of engine oil on the housings retaining rings to ease removal.

10. Remove the bolt (A, **Figure 126**) securing the mounting bracket (B) and remove the bracket.

11. Detach the cable ends from the throttle body pulley (**Figure 127**).

12. The throttle control cable (A, **Figure 128**) and idle control cable (B) are secured to the wire harness caddy. Proceed as follows to detach the cables:

   a. Refer to *Wire Harness Caddy* in this Supplement.

   b. Separate the wire harness caddy for access to the cable tie wraps.

   c. Cut the tie wraps to release the throttle cables.

13. Remove the cables from the right side of the steering head.

14. Clean the throttle grip assembly and dry it thoroughly. Check the throttle slots for cracks or other damage. Replace the throttle if necessary.

15. The friction adjust screw is secured to the lower switch housing with a circlip. If necessary, remove the friction spring, circlip, spring and friction adjust screw. Check these parts for wear or damage. Replace damaged parts and reinstall. Make sure the circlip seats in the friction screw groove completely.

16. Clean the throttle area on the handlebar with solvent.

Installation

WARNING

Do not ride the motorcycle until the throttle cables are properly adjusted. Improper cable routing and adjustment can cause the throttle to stick open.

1. Apply a light coat of graphite to the housing inside surfaces and to the handlebar.

NOTE

When performing Step 2, note that the idle control cable end diameter is smaller than the throttle control cable end. The cable end must fit into the corresponding hole in the switch housing.

2. On the lower switch housing, push the throttle cable ends into the holes in the housing. Push in until the cable end snaps into place.
3. Position the friction shoe with the concave side facing up and install it so the pin hole is over the point of the adjuster screw.
4. Install the throttle grip onto the handlebar. Rotate it until the ferrule notches are at the top.
5. Place the lower switch housing below the throttle grip. Install the ferrules onto the cables so the end fittings seat in the ferrule recess. Seat ferrules in their respective notches on the throttle control grip. Make sure the cables are captured in the molded grooves in the grip.
6. Assemble the switch housings (**Figure 124**) and the throttle grip. Install the switch housing screws and tighten to 35-45 in.-lb. (4.0-5.1 N•m).
7. Operate the throttle and make sure both cables move in and out properly.
8. Correctly route the cables from the handlebar, through the frame and to the throttle body (**Figure 129**).
9. Refer to **Figure 128** and note the position of the throttle cable (A) and idle cable (B) on the wire caddy groove. Secure the cables with tie wraps. Reassemble the wire caddy as described in this Supplement.
10. Connect the idle cable to the throttle body as follows:
   a. The idle cable has a small spring near the cable end (**Figure 130**).
   b. Insert the idle cable sheath into the front cable bracket guide on the throttle body.
   c. Attach the end of the idle cable to the throttle pulley.
11. Connect the throttle cable to the throttle body as follows:
   a. Insert the throttle cable sheath into the rear cable bracket guide on the throttle body.
   b. Attach the end of the throttle cable to the throttle pulley.
12. At the throttle grip, tighten the cables to keep the cable ends from being disconnected from the throttle pulley.
13. Operate the throttle a few times. Make sure the throttle operates smoothly with no binding. Also make sure both cable ends are seated squarely in their cable bracket guides and in the throttle barrel.

129

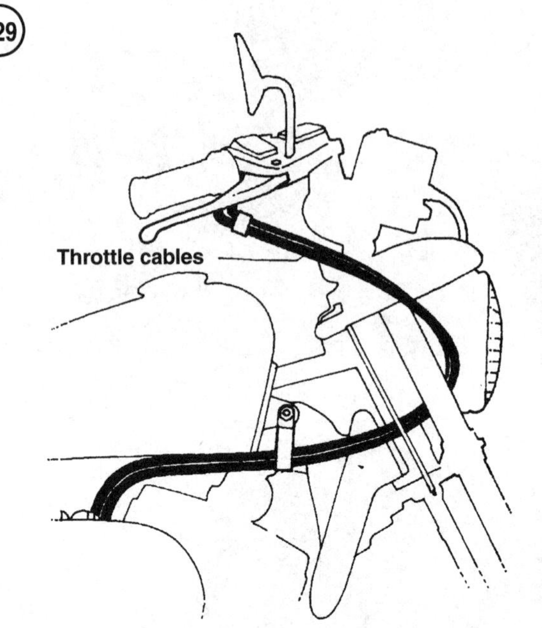

14. Adjust the throttle and idle cables as described in *Periodic Maintenance* in this Supplement.
15. Install the air filter backplate and air filter as described in this Supplement.
16. Install the fuel tank as described in this Supplement.
17. Start the engine. Turn the handlebar from side to side. Do not operate the throttle. If the engine speed increases when turning the handlebar assembly, the throttle cables are routed incorrectly or are damaged. Recheck the cable routing and adjustment.

FUEL PRESSURE TEST

WARNING

This procedure will be conducted adjacent to a hot exhaust system while handling gasoline related test equipment. Make sure to have a fire extinguished rated for gasoline fires (Class B) available.

1. The following tools are required for this test:
   a. Fuel injection pressure gauge (part No. HD-41182 or equivalent).
   b. Schrader valve adapter (part No. HD-44061).
2. Depressurize the fuel system as described in this Supplement.
3. Disconnect the fuel hose from the fuel tank.

130

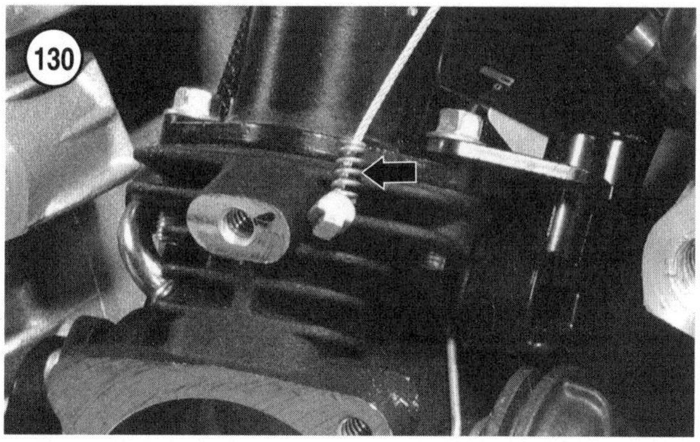

131

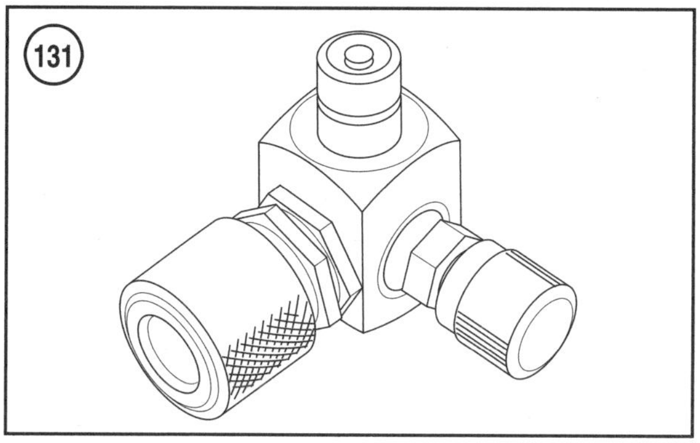

132

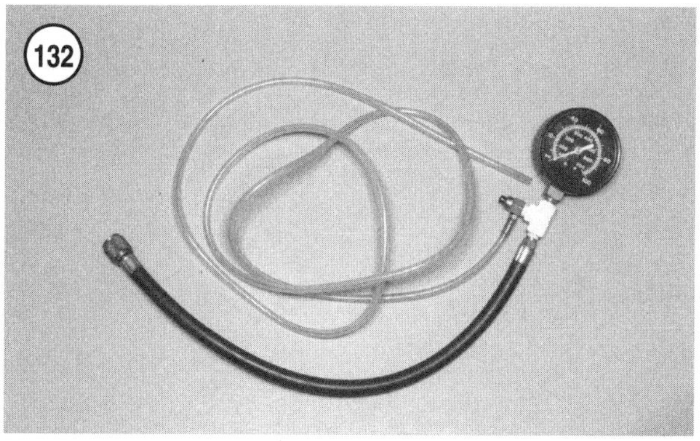

4. Install the adapter (**Figure 131**) onto the fuel tank fitting, then connect the fuel hose to the adapter.

5. Unscrew and remove the protective cap from the Schrader valve on the adapter.

6. Following manufacturer's instructions, connect the fuel injection pressure gauge (**Figure 132**) to the Schrader valve on the adapter.

7. Position the clear air bleed tube on the gauge into a suitable container

8. Start the engine to pressurize the fuel system. Allow the engine to idle.

9. Open and close the air bleed valve on the pressure gauge to purge the air from the gauge and hose. Repeat this several times until only bubble-free fuel is flowing from the bleed tube into the container. Close the bleed valve.

10. Increase engine speed above idle, then decrease engine speed several times and note the gauge readings. The fuel pressure should remain constant at all engine speeds at the specified pressure of 55-62 psi (380-425 kPa). Repeat several times.

11. Turn the engine off.

12. Open the pressure gauge bleed valve and relieve all fuel pressure and purge the pressure gauge of all fuel.

13. Place a shop cloth under the adapter and disconnect the gauge and adapter. Dispose of the shop cloth in a suitable manner.

14. Reconnect the fuel hose to the fuel tank.

EVAPORATIVE EMISSION CONTROL SYSTEM (CALIFORNIA MODELS)

The evaporative emission control system prevents gasoline vapor from escaping into the atmosphere. When the engine is not running, the system directs the fuel vapor from the fuel tank through the vapor valve and into the charcoal canister. Also, when the engine is not running, the gravity-operated trap door in the air filter backplate blocks the inlet port of the air filter. This prevents hydrocarbon vapors from the induction module escaping into the atmosphere.

When the engine is running, these vapors are drawn through a purge hose and into the induction module where they burn in the combustion chambers. The vapor valve also prevents gasoline vapor from escaping from the carbon canister if the motorcycle falls onto its side.

Also, when the engine is running, the engine vacuum pulls the air filter backplate trap door open allowing air to enter.

Charcoal Canister

Inspection

15

Refer to **Figure 133** for component placement and hose routing. Before removing the hoses from any of the parts, mark the hose and fitting with to identify them. Replace any worn or damaged components.

1. Check all emission control lines and hoses to make sure they are correctly routed and connected.

WARNING

Make sure the fuel tank vapor hoses are routed so they cannot contact hot engine or exhaust components. These hoses contain flammable vapor. If a hose melts from con-

133

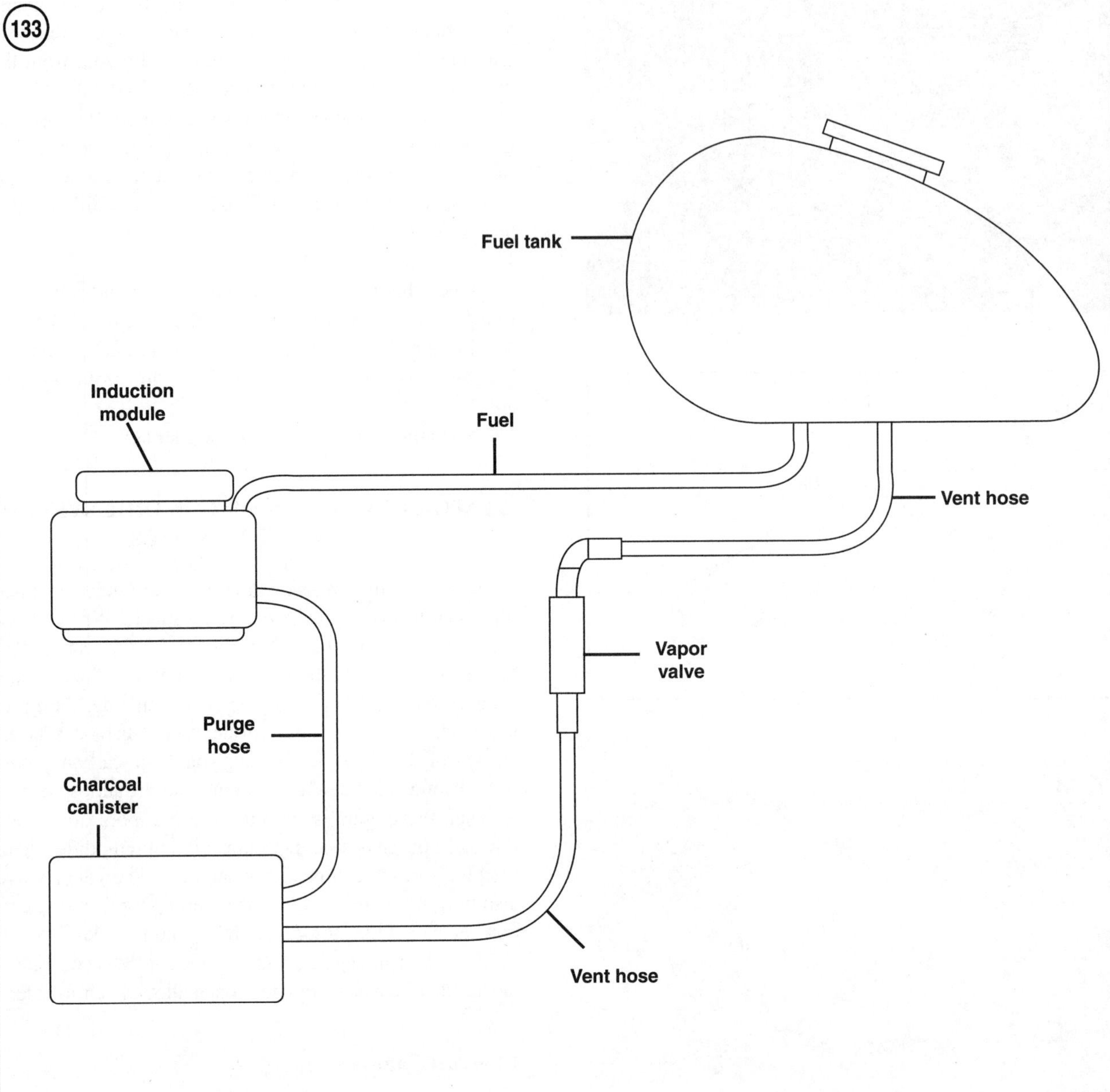

tact with a hot part, leaking vapor may ignite, causing severe motorcycle damage and rider injury.

2. Make sure there are no kinks in the lines or hoses. Also inspect the hoses and lines routed near engine hot spots for excessive wear or burning.

3. Check the physical condition of all lines, hoses and fittings in the system. Check for cuts, tears or loose connections. These lines and hoses are subjected to various temperatures and operating conditions, and eventually become brittle and crack.

Removal/installation

Refer to **Figure 134**.

1. Support the motorcycle on a work stand with the rear wheel off the ground. Refer to *Motorcycle Stands* in Chapter Ten.

2. On the left end of the canister, remove the end cover.

134

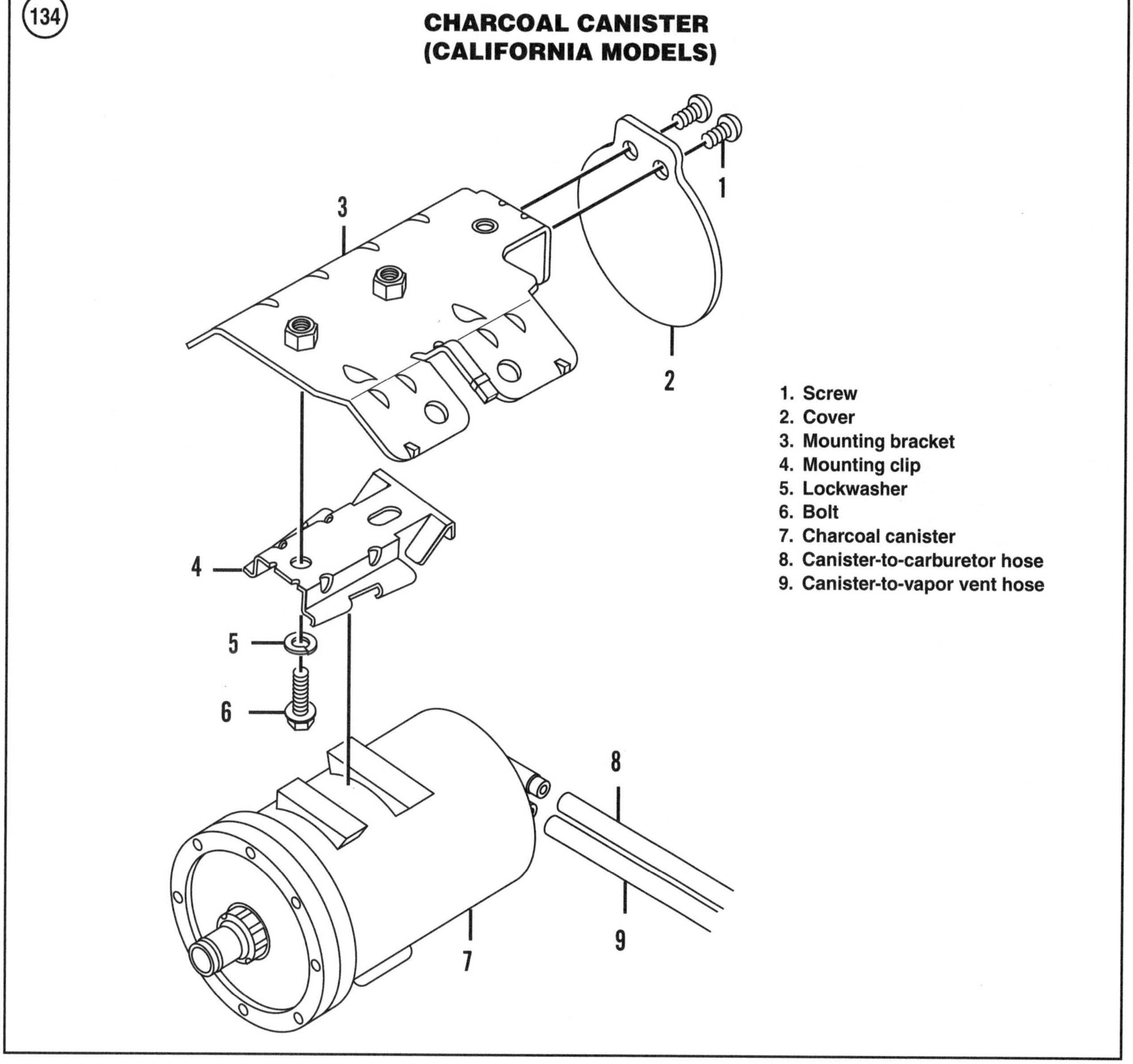

3. On the left end of the canister, mark the two hoses prior to disconnecting the hoses from the canister.

4. Push up the locking tabs on the mounting clip, then slide the canister out toward the left side and remove it.

5. If necessary, remove the mounting clip and bracket. Remove the rear brake master cylinder reservoir and hose for access to the mounting bracket.

6. Installation is the reverse of removal. Ensure that all hoses are connected to the correct fittings and are secure. Tighten the mounting bracket mounting bolts to 17-22 ft.-lb. (23-30 N•m).

Vapor Valve

Refer to *Evaporative Emission Control System (California models)* in Chapter Eight.

EXHAUST SYSTEM

2007-on models are equipped with oxygen sensors mounted on the exhaust pipes. Before servicing an exhaust pipe, disconnect, and if necessary, remove the oxygen sensor as described in this Supplement. Refer to Chapter Eight for exhaust system service information.

Table 17 FUEL SYSTEM SPECIFICATIONS

Fuel pressure	55-62 psi (380-425 kPa)

Tablle 18 FUEL SYSTEM TORQUE SPECIFICATIONS

	ft.-lb.	in.-lb.	N•m
Charcoal canister mounting bracket bolts	17-22	–	23-30
Fuel pump module retaining bolts	–	40-45	4.5-5.1
Fuel rail bracket mounting screw	–	60	6.8
Fuel tank mounting bolts	15-20	–	20-27
Handlebar switch housing screws	–	35-45	4.0-5.1
Idle air control bolts*	–	60	6.8
Induction module bracket bolt	–	84-108	9.5-12.2
Intake manifold bolts	–	96-120	11-13.6
Intake manifold-to-throttle body bolts	–	35	4
Oxygen (O_2) sensor	29-44	–	39-60
Throttle cable bracket bolts*	–	60	6.8

*One bolt secures both the idle air control and throttle cable bracket.

CHAPTER NINE

ELECTRICAL SYSTEM

Tables 19-25 are located at the end of this section.

NOTE
On models equipped with the TSSM/HFSM security system, disarm the system before working on the bike to prevent accidental activation of the warning system, including the optional siren. Always disarm the TSSM/HFSM security system prior to disconnecting the battery or the alarm will sound. Refer to the system description in this chapter.

ELECTRICAL COMPONENT REPLACEMENT

Most motorcycle dealerships and parts suppliers do not accept the return of any electrical part. If the exact cause of an electrical system malfunction cannot be determined, have a dealership retest the specific system to verify test results. This may help avert the possibility of purchasing an expensive, unreturnable part that does not fix the problem.

Consider any test results carefully before replacing a component that tests only slightly out of specification, especially resistance. A number of variables can affect test results dramatically. These include: the testing meter's internal circuitry, ambient temperature and conditions under which the motorcycle has been operated. All instructions and specifications have been check for accuracy; however, successful test results depend to a great degree upon individual accuracy.

BATTERY

Battery Cables

Tighten the battery cable terminal bolts to 60-70 in.-lb. (6.8-7.9 N•m) for both terminals.

CHARGING SYSTEM

Battery Current Draw Test

Refer to Chapter Two in manual main body.

Voltage Regulator

Removal/installation

The voltage regulator is mounted on a plate that is secured to the front frame downtubes (**Figure 135**). The mounting plate also secures the regulator DC wiring connector and neutral switch wire.

The voltage regulator cannot be rebuilt. It must be replaced as a unit.

1. Disconnect the Maxi-fuse as described in Chapter Nine.

NOTE
Each connector is secured by a latch that secures the connector halves together. Push the latch off the connector before separating the connector halves.

2. Disconnect the voltage regulator-to-stator wiring connector (**Figure 136**).
3. Detach the connector from the frame bracket. Disconnect the voltage regulator DC connector (**Figure 137**).
4. Remove any wiring retaining straps.

5. Remove the voltage regulator mounting bolts and remove the voltage regulator.
6. Reverse the removal steps to install the voltage regulator. Tighten the mounting screws to 36-60 in.-lb. (4.1-6.8 N•m).

ALTERNATOR

On 2007-on models, refer to **Table 19** when testing the stator.

IGNITION SYSTEM

The ignition system on 2007-on models is controlled by an electronic control module (ECM), which also controls the fuel injection system.

Crankshaft Position Sensor (CKP)

Removal/installation

Refer to Chapter Nine.

Ignition Coil

Removal/installation

1. Remove the fuel tank as described in this Supplement.
2. Refer to *Wire Harness Caddy* in this Supplement. Disassemble the caddy sufficiently to move the left caddy half away from the frame.

NOTE
Before removing the ignition coil and bracket, note the wiring that is retained by the bracket so it can be properly positioned during assembly.

3. Remove the ignition coil bracket mounting bolt (**Figure 138**).
4. Detach the connector (A, **Figure 139**) from the ignition coil.
5. Detach the front cylinder spark plug wire (B, **Figure 139**) from the ignition coil.
6. Detach the rear cylinder spark plug wire (C, **Figure 139**) from the ignition coil.
7. Remove the ignition coil and bracket.
8. If necessary, remove the bracket retaining bolts and separate the bracket and ignition coil.
9. Reverse the removal steps for installation. Tighten the bracket mounting bolt (**Figure 138**) to 35-45 in.-lb. (4.0-5.1 N•m).

Testing

Refer also to Chapter Two. The following test checks the primary circuit of the ignition coil. If possible, substitute a good ignition coil and check operation before replacing the original coil.

1. Remove the ignition coil as described in this section.

NOTE
Resistance readings may not verify that an ignition coil is good. Before purchasing a new unit check operation using a known

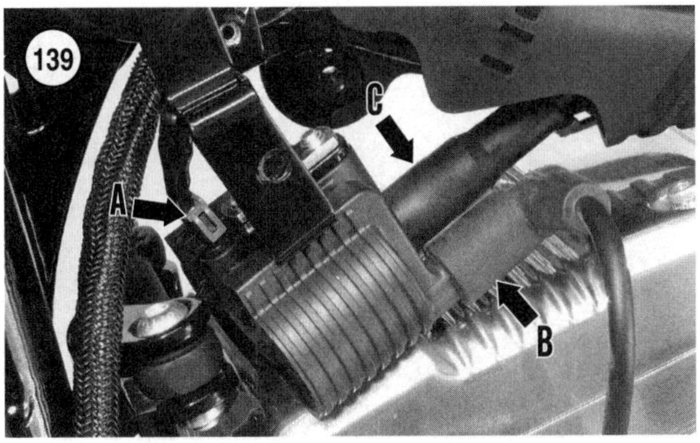

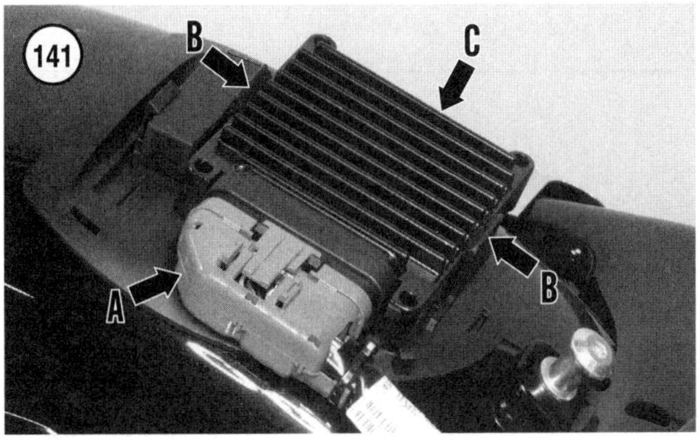

good unit or have the coil tested at a dealership.

2. Refer to **Figure 140.** Measure the ignition coil primary resistance between the positive terminal (A, **Figure 140**) and front cylinder primary coil terminal (B) or rear cylinder primary coil terminal (C). Resistance should be 0.3-0.7 ohm.
3. Check the secondary circuit of the ignition coil. Resistance should be 1500-2400 ohms.
4. Verify that the spark plug wires, spark plugs, ignition system components are in working order. If no spark or a weak spark exists, replace the ignition coil with a good unit and repeat the spark test as described in *Engine Starting* in Chapter Two.

ELECTRONIC CONTROL MODULE (ECM)

The electronic control module (ECM) contains electronic components that control the ignition and fuel injection systems.

Testing

No testing procedure is available. Refer to the appropriate sections in this Supplement for information on troubleshooting the ignition and fuel injection systems. If all other components have been tested, replace the ECM with a known good unit and recheck ignition and fuel injection system operation.

Many electrical problems are caused by faulty wiring and connections. Make sure to check all wires and connections before presuming the ECM is faulty. Because electrical components are not returnable, if possible, install a good ECM for testing purposes and check operation before purchasing a new unit.

Removal/Installation

The ECM is located under the seat.

NOTE
After installing a new ECM, a dealership equipped with the Digital Technician must reprogram the ECM.

NOTE
Always disarm the security system prior to removing the Maxi-fuse or the alarm will sound.

1. Remove the seat as described in Chapter Fourteen.
2. Remove the Maxi-fuse as described in Chapter Nine.
3. Depress the external latch on the ECM electrical connector (A, **Figure 141**). Gently pull and disconnect the connector from the ECM.
4. Push back the latches (B, **Figure 141**) and lift out the ECM (C).
5. Install the ECM by reversing the removal steps. Note the following:
   a. Apply a light coat of dielectric compound to the electrical connectors prior to installing them.
   b. Make sure the electrical connector is pushed tightly onto the ignition module.

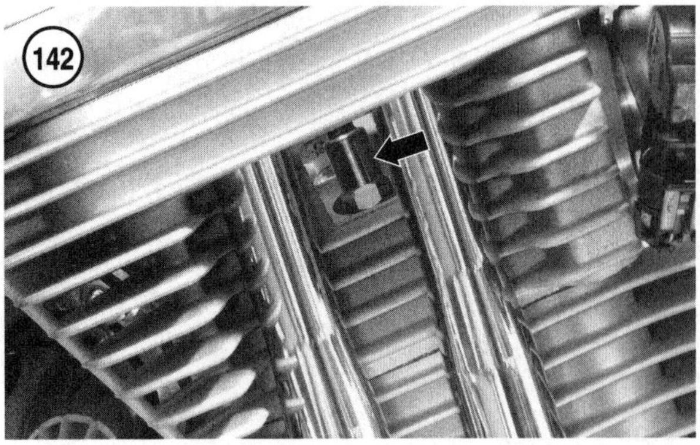

c. Reprogram the ECM using the Digital Technician.

ENGINE TEMPERATURE (ET) SENSOR

The engine temperature (ET) sensor is located on the rear cylinder head (**Figure 142**). A special tool is required for removal and installation due to the permanently attached wire lead.

Removal/Installation

CAUTION
Make sure not to damage the sensor wire lead during removal or installation.

1. Remove the fuel tank as described in this Supplement.
2. Disconnect the sensor connector (A, **Figure 143**).
3. Detach or cut the barbed cable strap (B, **Figure 143**).
4. Using the special tool (HD-48116-A [**Figure 144**] or equivalent) and remove the sensor.
5. Reverse the removal steps to install the sensor while noting the following:
   a. Tighten the sensor to 120-168 in.-lb. (13.6-19.0 N•m).
   b. Make sure there is sufficient slack in the wire lead after connection to allow for engine movement.

Testing

Refer to **Figure 24** in this Supplement for troubleshooting the ET sensor and circuit. To test the sensor, measure the resistance at the sensor connector terminals at the temperatures listed in **Table 20**.

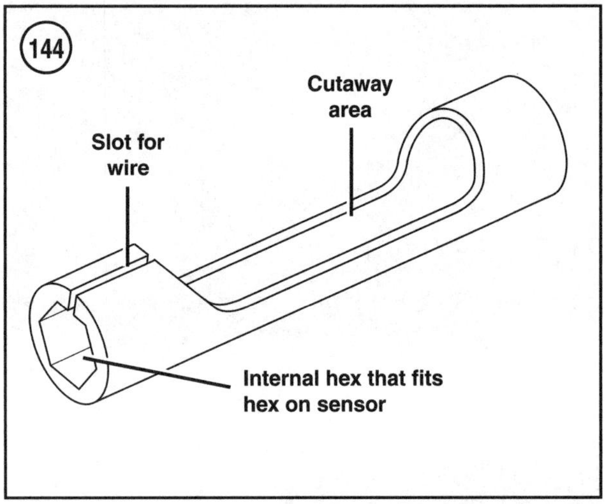

LIGHTING SYSTEM

Indicator Lights

On 2007-on models the lights located in the indicator panel are LEDs and not individual, replaceable bulbs as used on 2004-2006 models. The LED module and wiring harness must be replaced as a unit assembly.

Taillight, Brake Light and Rear Turn Signals

XL883N, XL1200X and XL1200N models

On XL883N and XL1200N models, the rear turn signals also serve as the taillight and brake lights. Each rear turn signal is equipped with a dual-filament bulb. The 7-watt filament serves as the taillight while the 27-watt filament serves as the brake light and turn signal light.

145

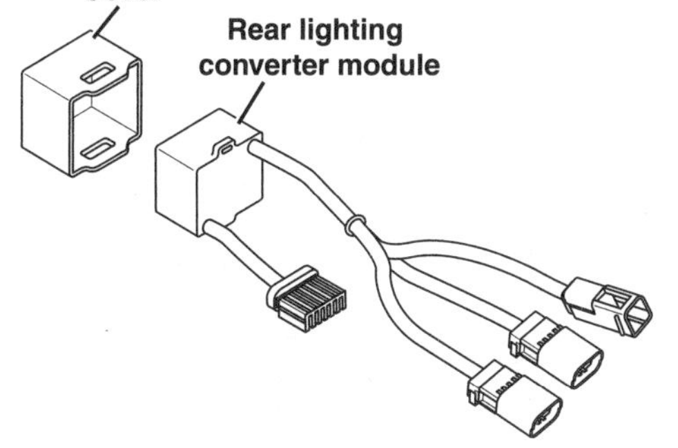

146

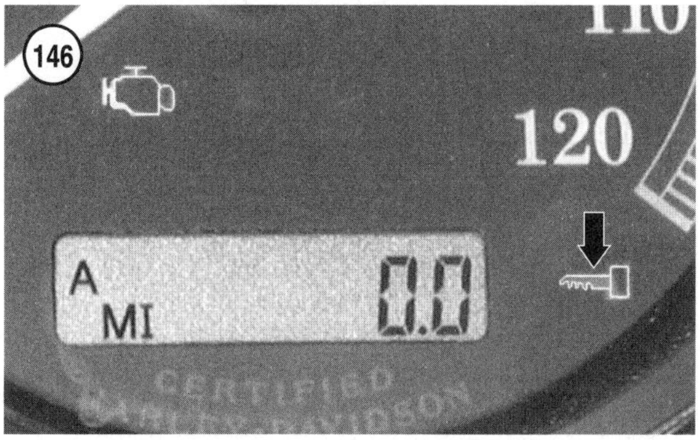

Rear Lighting Converter Module

XL883N, XL1200X and XL1200N models

A converter module (**Figure 145**) routes current to the proper bulb filaments to operate the rear turn signals, brake light and taillight.

Removal/Installation

1. Remove the seat as described in Chapter Fourteen.
2. Remove the battery as described in Chapter Nine.
3. Refer to the wiring diagram at the end of this manual and disconnect the following connectors located to the rear of the rear fuel tank bolt:
   a. Left turn signal
   b. Right turn signal
   c. License plate light
   d. Main harness
4. Push in the rubber module mounting prong on the left side of the frame below the rear fuel tank bolt.
5. Remove the module from the frame above the battery compartment.
6. Reverse the removal steps for installation.

SECURITY SYSTEM

2007-on models may be equipped with a hands-free security module (HFSM), while some international models may continue to use the turn signal security module (TSSM) used on 2004-2006 models.

The HFSM security system is similar to the TSSM described in Chapter Nine with the following differences:

1. The key fob does not have a button to activate the fob signal. The key fob constantly transmits a signal.
2. An external antenna is attached to the HFSM as opposed to the use of the left turn signal wire as the antenna.
3. A clutch switch is connected to the HFSM.
4. The neutral switch is connected to the HFSM.
5. The siren sound my be selected so the alarm will or will not chirp during arming and disarming.

NOTE
If chirpless is selected the siren will still sound if the alarm is triggered.

6. Refer to the following to configure or adjust the system:
   a. Personal code number entry: **Table 21**.
   b. Disarming using personal code number: **Table 22**.
   c. Transport mode activation: **Table 23**.
   d. Siren chirp mode: **Table 24**.

Arming

The security system arms automatically unless in the service mode. The system arms only when the ignition is off. International models are equipped with automatic arming systems which cannot be disabled. When the system is armed the security symbol on the speedometer (**Figure 146**) flashes every 2.5 seconds. The HFSM must be configured to recognize the key fob as described in **Table 21**.

The system arms itself automatically 5 seconds after the ignition is turned off. The security symbol illuminates and stays on during the arming period, then the turn signals flash twice, the siren (if equipped) sounds twice, and the security symbol flashes every 2.5 seconds to indicate the security system is enabled.

Disarming

The security system may be disarmed either using the key fob or entering a personal code number using the turn signal switches.

NOTE

*If a key fob is lost, damaged or otherwise unuseable, entering a personal code number is the only means to disarm the security system. If a personal code number has not been entered into the HFSM, the HFSM must be replaced to disarm the system. Refer to **Table 21** for personal code number entry instructions.*

To disarm the system using the key fob, turn the ignition key to IGNITION with the key fob on or near the motorcycle. The siren will sound once and the security symbol will illuminate for 4 seconds to indicate the system is disarmed.

To disarm the system using the personal code number refer to **Table 22**.

Security Symbol Indications

The security symbol on the speedometer face (**Figure 146**) indicates the status of the security system as follows:

1. Symbol unlit–security system inactive.
2. Symbol flashes every second–security system inactive for 2 minutes after failed attempt to enter personal code number.
3. Symbol flashes every 2.5 seconds–security system armed.
4. Symbol flashes four times per second–personal code number entry mode.
5. Symbol constantly illuminated with ignition key in OFF–auto-arming in progress.
6. Symbol constantly illuminated more than 4 seconds with ignition key in ON–trouble code (DTC) set. Refer to *Electronic Diagnostic System* in this Supplement.

HANDS-FREE SECURITY MODULE (HFSM)

The HFSM is similar to the TSSM used on 2004-2006 models and some international models. The HFSM is connected to an external antenna and requires the presence of a buttonless key fob to operate some alarm functions.

Removal/Installation

Refer to *Turn Signal Module (TSM) and Turn Signal Security Module (TSSM)* in Chapter Nine. On the HFSM it is necessary to disconnect and connect the 4-pin antenna connector during removal or installation.

The HFSM must be serviced as a unit assembly.

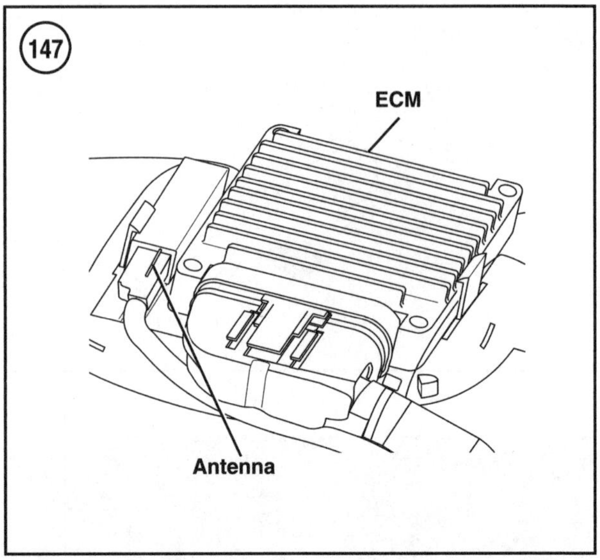

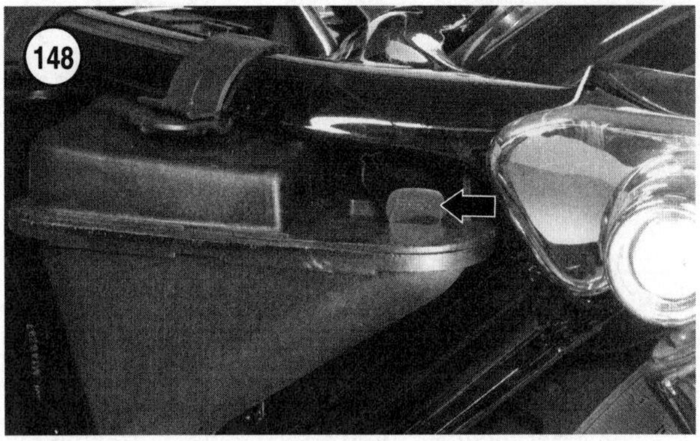

Testing

No testing procedure is available. Refer to **Figure 41** and **Figure 42** for troubleshooting procedures.

HFSM ANTENNA

The HFSM antenna enables the HFSM to detect the key fob, which is necessary for some alarm functions.

Removal/Installation

1. Remove the seat as described in Chapter Fourteen.
2. Disconnect the antenna from the retaining latch (**Figure 147**).
3. Detach the antenna from the harness connector.
4. Reverse the removal steps for installation while noting the following:

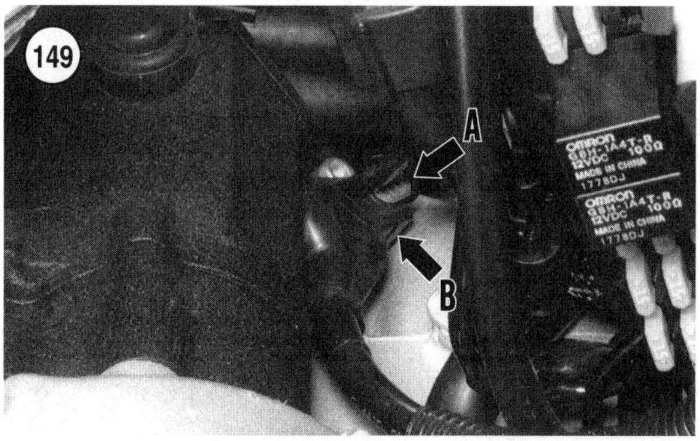

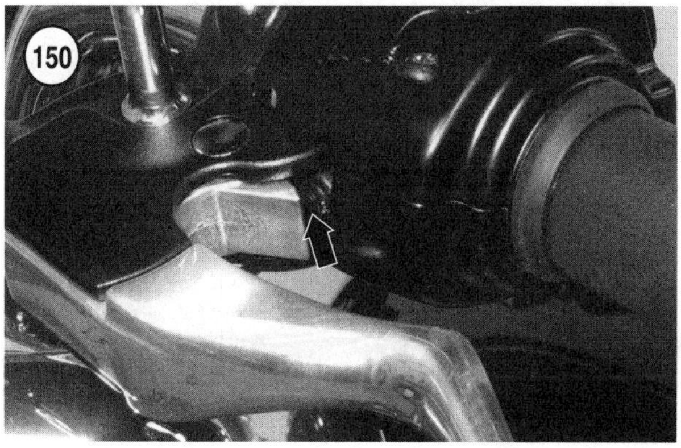

a. The antenna must be installed in its original position for optimum performance.
b. Make sure the flat side of the antenna is up.
c. Make sure the wiring is not pinched.

Testing

Refer to **Figure 41** and **Figure 42** for troubleshooting procedures.

FUEL LEVEL SENDER RESISTOR

The fuel level sender resistor (**Figure 148**) is located above the oil tank on the left side.

Removal/Installation.

1. Remove the seat as described in Chapter Fourteen.
2. Remove the left side cover as described in Chapter Fourteen.
3. Detach the connector and remove the resistor (**Figure 148**).
4. Reverse the removal steps for installation.

Testing

1. Measure resistance from the center terminal to either side terminal. The ohmmeter should read 1800-2200 ohms.
2. Repeat measurement from the center terminal to the remaining side terminal. The ohmmeter should read 1800-2200 ohms.
3. Replace the resistor if it fails either measurement.

SPEEDOMETER

For XL883N, XL1200X and XL1200N models, follow service procedures described in Chapter Nine for XL883, XL883L, XL883R, XL1200L and XL1200R models. The XL1200X speedometer does not have a back gasket.

VEHICLE SPEED SENSOR (VSS)

The VSS sends a signal to the ECM each time a gear tooth on fifth gear passes the sensor. This provides an indication of vehicle speed.

Testing

No testing procedure is available. Refer to **Figure 29** for troubleshooting procedures.

Removal/Installation

The VSS is located adjacent to the starter motor.

1. Remove the Maxi-fuse as described in Chapter Nine.
2. Disconnect the VSS connector (A, **Figure 149**).
3. Remove the mounting bolt, then remove the VSS (B, **Figure 149**).
4. Inspect the VSS for damage.
5. Reverse the removal steps for installation while noting the following:
   a. Note that a new O-ring is coated with lubricant. Do not lubricate.
   b. Lubricate a used O-ring with engine oil.
   c. Tighten the mounting bolt to 80-100 in.-lb. (9.0-11.3 N•m).

CLUTCH SWITCH

The clutch switch (**Figure 150**) is mounted in the left side switch lower housing.

Testing

The switch can be checked for continuity using an ohmmeter connected to the appropriate wire terminals in the connector. Refer to the wiring diagram at the end of this manual.

Removal/Installation

1. Separate the left side switch housing as described in *Switches* in Chapter Nine in the main manual body.
2. Remove the clutch switch from the housing (**Figure 151**).
3. Cut the switch wires 0.25 in. (6.4 mm) from the defective switch.
4. Splice the new switch leads to the main harness wiring.
5. Install the switch.
6. Assemble and install the left side handlebar switch housing.
7. Check starting system operation.

SIDE STAND SENSOR

International models may be equipped with a side stand sensor. The sensor detects the presence of the side stand leg when retracted.

The sensor prevents starting if the bike is in gear with the side stand down. The sensor also alerts the rider if the side stand extends while riding. In either instance, SidE StAnd will appear on the odometer display.

Testing

1. Extend the side stand to the down position.
2. Shift transmission into a gear.
3. Disengage the clutch.
4. Turn ignition key to IGNITION and attempt to start engine.
5. The engine should not start and SidE StAnd should appear on the odometer.
6. Retract the side stand.
7. Disengage the clutch and attempt to start the engine.
8. The engine should start and SidE StAnd should not appear.
9. If a problem occurs, refer to **Figure 38** and **Figure 39** for troubleshooting procedures.

Removal/Installation

1. Support the motorcycle so the side stand sensor is accessible.

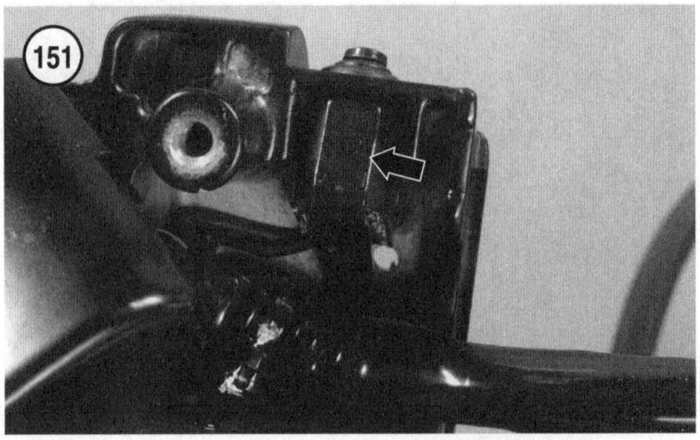

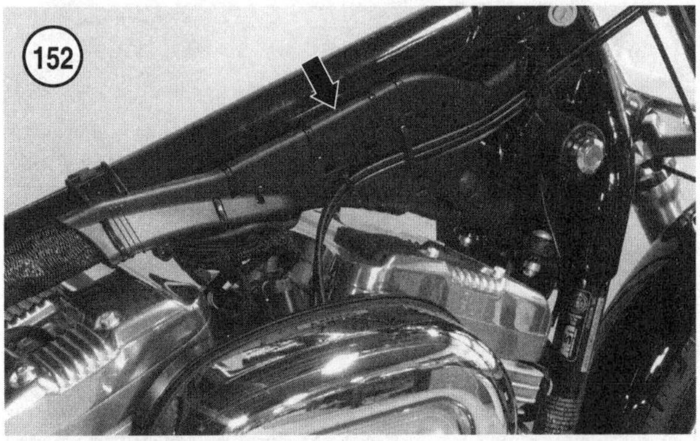

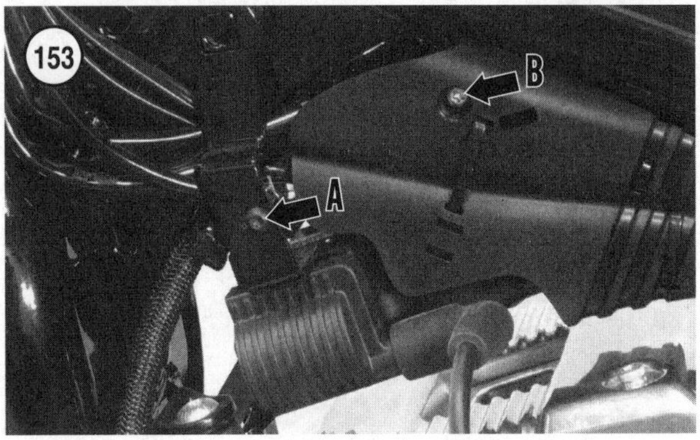

2. Disconnect the sensor connector on the left frame downtube.
3. Remove the cable straps.
4. Remove the sensor mounting bolt, then remove the sensor.
5. Reverse the removal steps for installation while noting the following:
   a. Make sure the sensor fits properly against the bracket, then install the mounting bolt.
   b. Tighten the mounting bolt to 96-120 in.-lb. (10.8-13.6 N•m).

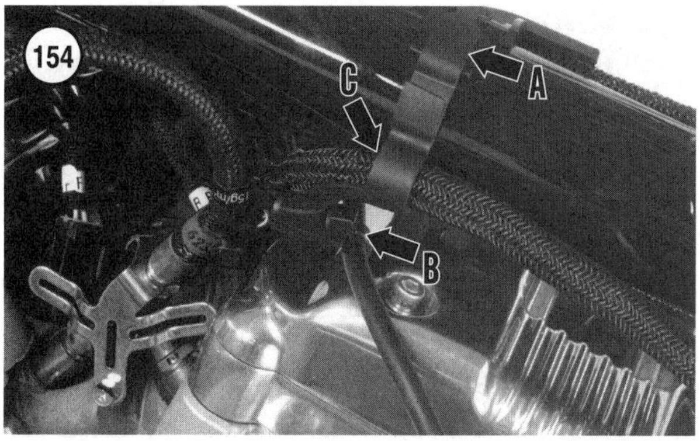

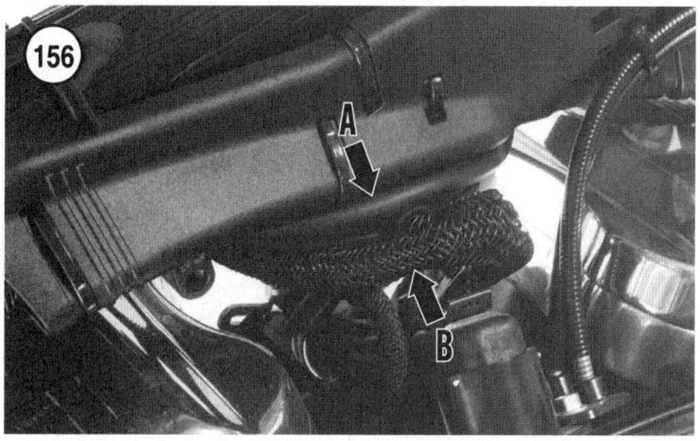

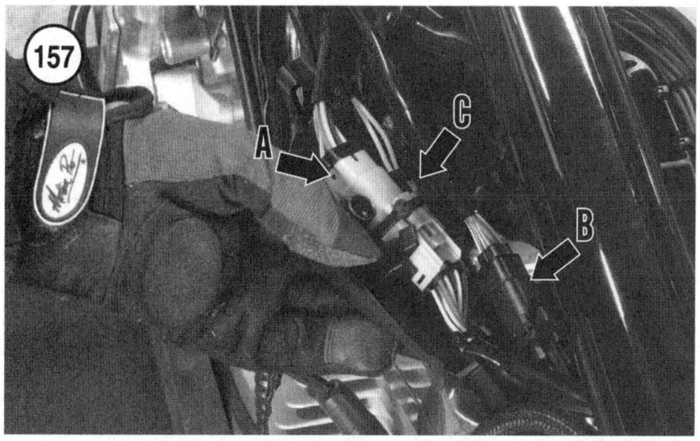

c. Make sure the sensor is no more than 0.177 in. (4.5 mm) from the tab on the side stand.

WIRE HARNESS CADDY

Wiring, connectors and the throttle cables routed along the frame backbone are housed or attached to an electrical caddy (**Figure 152**). The caddy consists of two halves that are secured together with locking tabs and a bolt.

Removal/Installation

1. Remove the fuel tank as described in this Supplement.
2. Remove the bolt (A, **Figure 153**) and detach the ignition coil mounting bracket from the mounting boss.
3. Detach the caddy latch clip (A, **Figure 154**).

NOTE
Perform Step 4 if replacing the caddy latch clip.

4. Detach the cable retainer (B, **Figure 154**) securing the rear spark plug cable to the caddy latch clip.
5. Remove the engine wire harness (C, **Figure 154**) from the caddy latch clip.
6. Remove the retaining bolt (B, **Figure 153**).
7. Detach the left caddy half from the right half.
8. If removing the right caddy half, remove the cable straps (A, **Figure 155**) securing the throttle cables to the right caddy half.
9. Separate the rear spark plug cable from the recess in the right caddy half (A, **Figure 156**).
10. Remove the cable retainer that secures the wire harness (B, **Figure 156**) to the right caddy half.
11. On California models, remove the cable strap retaining the charcoal canister purge hose to the right caddy half.
12. Remove and discard the push-in fasteners (B, **Figure 155**).
13. Detach the right caddy half from the frame bracket.
14. Move the ignition coil bracket down to allow right caddy half removal.
15. Disconnect the following connectors:
    a. Left handlebar switch connector (A, **Figure 157**).
    b. Right handlebar switch connector (B, **Figure 157**).
    c. Headlamp connector (C, **Figure 157**).
    d. Instrument connector (A, **Figure 158**).
    e. Front turn signal connector (B, **Figure 158**).
16. Note the location of all cable straps, then separate the wiring from the caddy halves.
17. Remove the caddy halves.

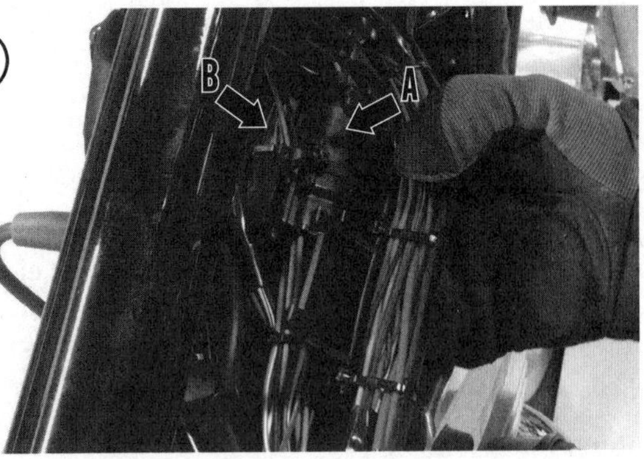

158

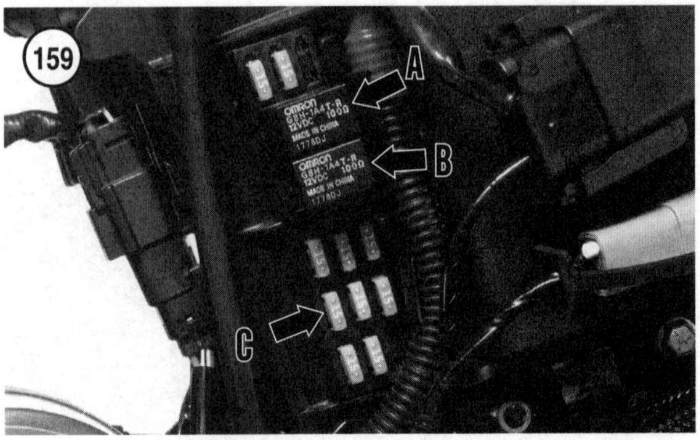

159

18. Reverse the removal steps for installation while noting the following:
   a. All wiring and cables must be routed between the ignition coil and ignition switch brackets.
   b. Tighten the ignition coil bracket bolt (A, **Figure 153**) to 35-45 in.-lb. (4.0-5.1 N•m).
   c. If removed, install the barbed cable holder on the rear spark plug cable so the holder is 7 1/8 in. (181 mm) from the cap end of the spark plug cable.

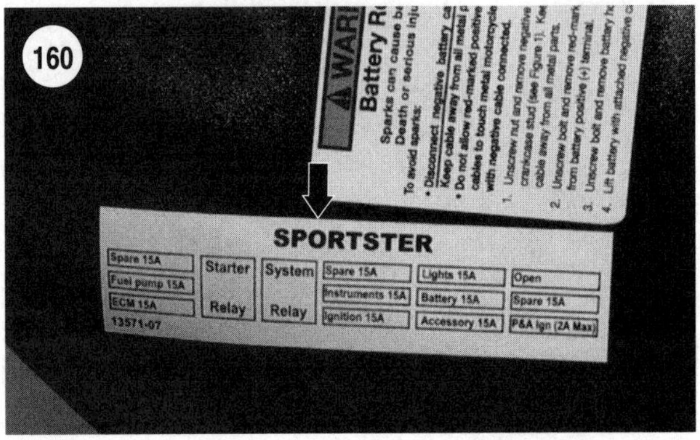

160

RELAYS

The starter relay (A, **Figure 159**) and system relay (B) are located on the fuse block. The relays are identical. Refer to Chapter Two for troubleshooting procedures for the starter relay. Use the same procedure to test the system relay.

FUSES

Fuses that protect the electrical system circuits are attached to the fuse block (C, **Figure 159**) located behind the left side cover. The Maxi-fuse protects the entire electrical system. Refer to the *Maxi-fuse* in Chapter Nine. The fuses are identified on a label (**Figure 160**) attached to the inside of the side cover.

Refer to Chapter Fourteen and remove the left side cover for access to the fuses. Be sure to replace a fuse with a new fuse of the same amperage.

Whenever a fuse blows, determine the cause before replacing the fuse. Usually, the trouble is a short circuit in the wiring. Worn-through insulation or a short to ground from a disconnected wire may cause this.

WARNING
Never substitute any metal object for a fuse. Never use a higher amperage fuse than specified. An overload could cause a fire.

161 **AMP ONE-PLACE TERMINAL**

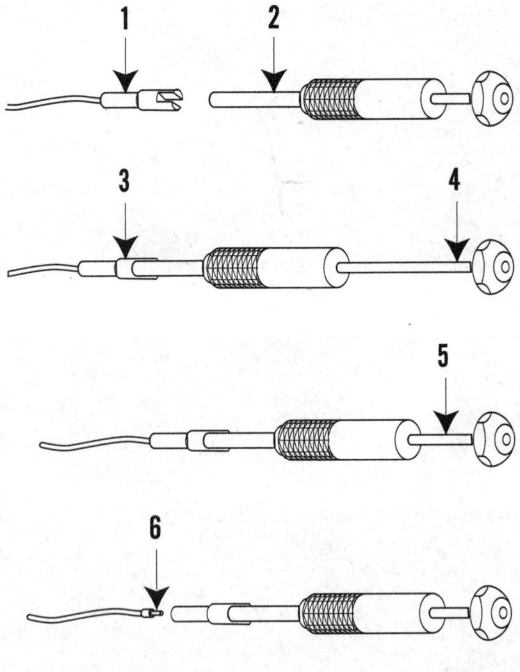

(162) **DELPHI CONNECTOR**

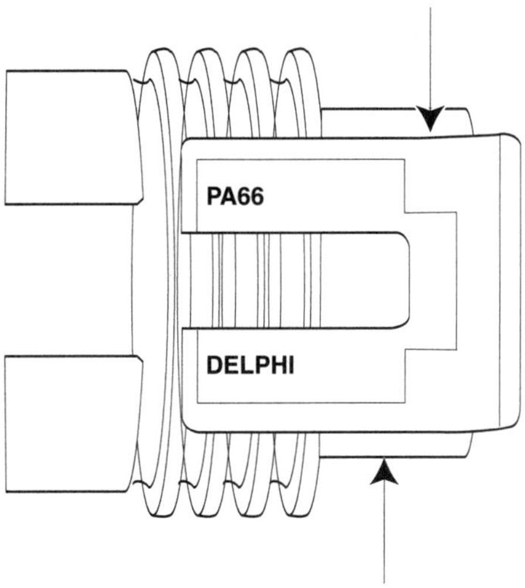

(163) **DELPHI CONNECTOR**

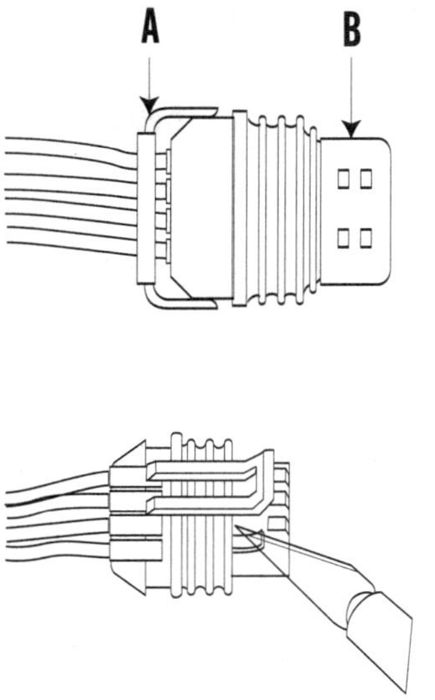

CAUTION
If replacing a fuse, make sure the ignition switch is turned to the OFF position. This lessens the chance of a short circuit.

ELECTRICAL CONNECTOR SERVICE

Refer to the following service information for electrical connectors used on 2007-on models. Refer also to Chapter Nine.

Amp Single Connector Pin Terminal Removal/Installation

1. Grasp the lead on the wire end of the pin housing and push the terminal forward toward the mating end of the connector until it stops unlocking the tang from the groove in the connector.
2. Install the barrel (1, **Figure 161**) of the socket terminal tool (part No. HD-39621-27) over the pin (2).
3. Rotate the tool and push it in until it bottoms (3, **Figure 161**) in the pin housing allowing the plunger (4) to back out of the handle.
4. Secure the pin housing and keep the tool firmly depressed.
5. Depress the plunger (5, **Figure 161**) and the pin (6) will eject out of the wire end of the connector.
6. Insert the pin into the pin housing until a click is heard. Pull on the lead to ensure the pin is correctly seated.

Delphi Connector Removal/Installation

1. Remove the Maxi-fuse as described in Chapter Nine.
2. Bend back the external latch(es) (**Figure 162**) and remove them from the socket halves.
3. Free one side of the wire lock (A, **Figure 163**) from the ear on the wire end of the socket housing. Release the wire lock on the other side.
4. Release the wire from the channels in the wire lock and remove them from the socket housing.
5. Remove the terminal lock (B, **Figure 163**) from the socket housing.
6. Use a thin blade (unsharpened end of an X-Acto knife) and gently pry the tang outward away from the terminal.
7. Pull the wire toward the back of the terminal and remove it. Do not pull on the wire until the terminal is released or it will be difficult to remove it.
8. Push the tang on the socket housing toward the chamber.
9. Position the open side of the terminal so it faces the tang and push the wire terminal into the chamber at the wire end of the socket housing. Pull on the lead to ensure the terminal is correctly seated.
10. Install the terminal lock (B, **Figure 163**) onto the socket housing.
11. Install the wire lock (A, **Figure 163**) onto each side of the socket housing. Make sure they are correctly seated.
12. Install the external latch(es) (**Figure 162**) onto the socket halves until they engage.

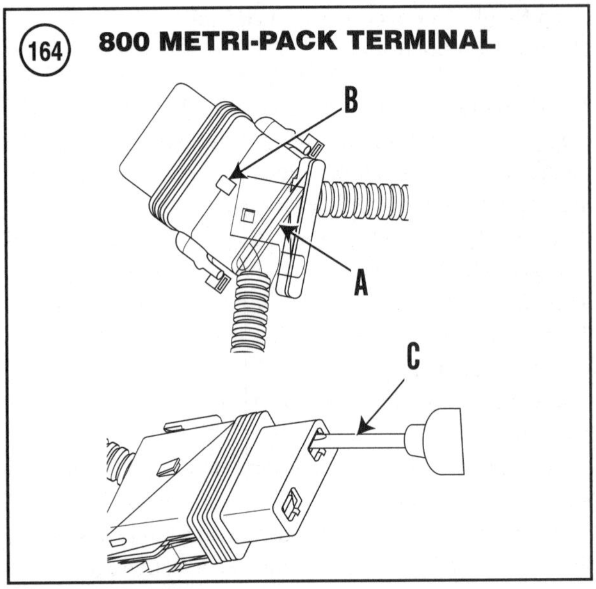

800 Metri-Pack Connectors Removal/Installation

1. Remove the Maxi-fuse as described in Chapter Nine.
2. Pull the socket housing and disengage the slots on the secondary lock (A, **Figure 164**) from the tabs (B) on the socket housing. Remove the secondary lock from the cable.
3. Insert the blade of a small screwdriver (C, **Figure 164**) into the opening until it stops. Pivot the screwdriver toward the terminal body and hold it in this position.
4. Pull the wire cable and pull the socket from the wire cable end of the housing.
5. Repeat Steps 2-4 for remaining socket terminal if necessary.
6. Use a flat blade screwdriver and bend the tang away from terminal body.
7. Insert the socket and wire lead into the wire end of the socket housing until it clicks into place. Pull on the lead to ensure the terminal is correctly seated.
8. Push the rubber seal into place on the wire end of socket terminal.
9. Repeat Steps 6-8 for remaining socket terminal if necessary.
10. Install the secondary lock (A, **Figure 164**) onto the cable and then push it onto the wire end of the socket housing until the slots engage the tabs (B) on the sides of the socket housing.

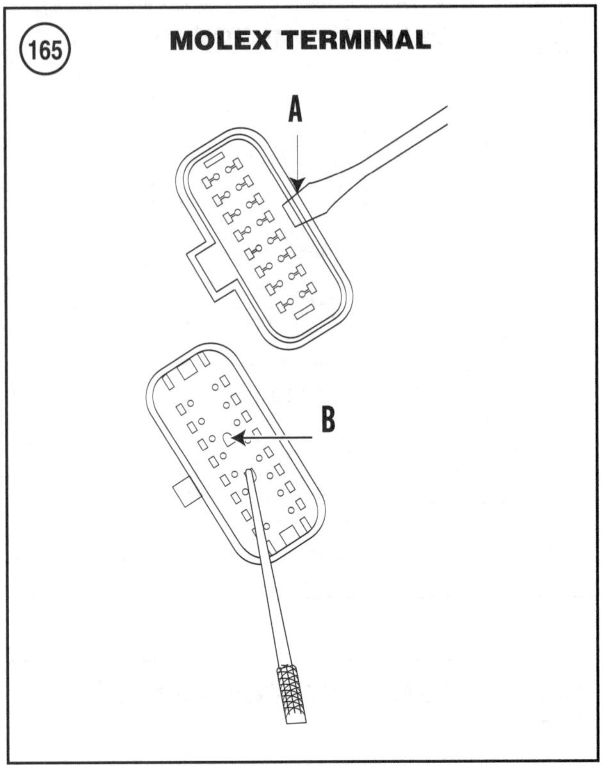

Molex Connector Removal/Installation

1. Remove the Maxi-fuse as described in Chapter Nine.
2. Insert a flat blade screwdriver into the pry slot (A, **Figure 165**) and remove the socket housing from the terminal.
3. Use a hooked pick or needle nose pliers and loosen the secondary lock (B, **Figure 165**). Do not remove the secondary lock.
4. Insert the terminal remover (part No. HD-48114) into the desired terminal pin hole until the tool bottoms.
5. Pull on the wire lead and remove it from the housing cavity.
6. Insert the wire into the correct terminal cavity.
7. Orient the terminal so the tang opposite the crimp engages the slot in the terminal cavity. Push the terminal into the cavity until it bottoms. Pull on the wire lead to ensure the terminal is correctly seated.
8. Push the secondary lock into the socket housing and lock the terminals into the housing.
9. Install the socket housing into the terminal.

Table 19 ELECTRICAL SPECIFICATIONS

Alternator	
Stator coil resistance	0.1-0.3 ohms
AC voltage output	20-28 Vac per 1000 rpm
Fuel level sender resistor resistance	1800-2200 ohms
Ignition coil	
Primary resistance	0.3-0.7 ohms
Secondary resistance	1500-2400 ohms
Side stand sensor gap (max.)	0.177 in. (4.5 mm)
Voltage regulator	
Voltage output	14.3-14.7 Vdc at 75° F
Amps at 3600 rpm	32 amps

Table 20 ENGINE TEMPERATURE SENSOR SPECIFICATIONS

°F	°C	Ohms
-4	-20	98936
14	-10	56102
32	0	32957
50	10	20000
68	20	12511
77	25	10000
86	30	8045
104	40	5304
122	50	3577
140	60	2470
158	70	1739
176	80	1246
194	90	908
212	100	671

Table 21 PERSONAL CODE NUMBER ENTRY*

Step	Action	Expected Result	Note
1.	RUN/OFF engine switch set to OFF.		Verify security symbol is not flashing, indicating system is disarmed.
2.	Turn ignition key IGNITION-OFF-IGNITION-OFF-IGNITION		
3.	Press and release left turn signal switch two times.	Turn signal flash three times	
4.	Press and release right turn signal switch once.	Odometer displays five digits. If no existing code, digits are dashes. First dash blinks.	Odometer display indicates system is in personal code number entry mode. First digit may be entered or changed.
5.	Press and release left turn switch until the desired number appears.		
6.	Press and release right turn signal switch once.	Second dash in odometer panel blinks	First digit is entered and second digit is ready for selection
7.	Repeat Steps 4-6 until all five digits have been selected.		

(continued)

15

Table 21 PERSONAL CODE NUMBER ENTRY* (continued)

Step	Action	Expected Result	Note
8.	After selecting fifth digit, press and release right turn signal switch once.	First digit blinks.	Code number entry completed
9.	Turn ignition key to OFF.		
10.	Record personal code number		

*No personal code number exists in system. Do not proceed to next step until expected result occurs. Key fob must be present.

Table 22 DISARM USING PERSONAL CODE NUMBER[1]

Step	Action	Expected Result	Note
1.	Engine stop switch set to OFF.		
2.	Turn ignition key to IGNITION		
3.	Hold in both turn signal switches until security symbol flashes quickly.[2]	Security symbol flashes quickly	OK to enter personal code.
4.	Press left turn signal switch equal to first number in personal code.		
5.	Press right turn signal switch one time.		"Enters" first number.
6.	Repeat Steps 4 and 5 until all five digits in personal code number are entered.	Security code stops flashing	System is disarmed.

1. Do not proceed to next step until expected result occurs. Key fob must be present.
2. Switch must be pushed within two seconds after key is turned to IGNITION. If system activates warning before security symbol flashes quickly, turn key to OFF. Start again after symbol flashes at 2.5-second rate.

Table 23 TRANSPORT MODE OPTIONS*

Step	Action	Expected Result	Note
1.	To enter transport mode, set engine stop switch to OFF.		Verifty security symbol is not flashing, indicating systemis disarmed.
2.	Turn ignition key to IGNITION		
3.	Turn ignition key to ACC.		
4.	Press and hold both turn signal switches.	Turn signal flash once.	The turn signal switches must be pressed within 5 seconds after turning key to ACC.
5.	Turn igntiion key to OFF.	Turn signal flashes three times.	Motorcycle movement possible without triggering alarm for one ignition cycle. Alarm sounds if engine starting is attempted.
6.	To exit transport mode, turn igntion key to IGNITION. Set engine stop switch to RUN.		

1. Do not proceed to next step until expected result occurs. Key fob must be present.

Table 24 SIREN CHIRP MODE SELECTION*

Step	Action	Expected Result	Note
1.	With alarm system disarmed and igntion key turned to IGNITION, turn key to OFF	Alarm system arms	Watch for two flashes of turn signals indicating system is armed.
2.	Turn ignition systemswitch to IGNITION.	Alarm system disarms	
3.	Turn ignition key to OFF	Alarm system arms.	
4.	Turn ignition key to IGNITION	Alarm system disarms.	System should change chirp mode.

*Rapidly perform two ignition on and off cycles to change to the alternate chirp mode. Key fob must be present.

Table 25 ELECTRICAL SYSTEM TORQUE SPECIFICATIONS

	ft.-lb.	in.-lb.	N•m
Battery cable terminal bolts	–	60-70	6.8-7.9
Engine temperature (ET) sensor	–	120-168	13.6-19.0
Ignition coil bracket mounting bolt	–	35-45	4.0-5.1
Side stand sensor mounting bolt	–	96-120	10.8-13.6
Voltage regulator mounting screws	–	36-60	4.1-6.8
VSS mounting bolt	–	80-100	9.0-11. 3

CHAPTER TEN

WHEELS, TIRES AND DRIVE BELT

Refer to *Tires and Wheels* in Chapter Three for routine maintenance procedures.

FRONT WHEEL

The front axle shape was changed in 2008 which alters the removal/installation procedure.

Removal/Installation

2007 models

Follow the procedure described in Chapter Ten.

2008-on models

Follow the procedure described in Chapter Ten. Note the following:

1. Insert the front axle until it seats against the spacer. A drill or rod is not needed to locate the axle. However, inserting a rod is neccesary to prevent axle rotation while tightening the nut.

2. Tighten the front axle nut to 60-65 ft.-lb. (81-88 N•m).

15

REAR WHEEL

For 2007 models, follow the procedures described in Chapter Three and Chapter Ten for wheel service and final belt deflection adjustment.

For 2008-on models, follow the procedure in *Periodic Maintenance* in this Supplement for final belt deflection adjustment. Follow the procedures in Chapter Ten for wheel service. Note that on 2008-on models, the rear axle nut torque specification is 95-105 ft.-lb. (129-142 N•m).

Table 26 WHEEL SPECIFICATIONS

Alloy wheel	
16-inch	
Rim size	T16 x 3.00 D or MT
17-inch	
Rim size	E17 x 5.5 M
	T17 x 4.5 M
18-inch	
Rim size	E18 x 3.5 M
	T18 x 3.5 M
19-inch	
Rim size	T19 x 2.15 D or MT

Table 27 WHEEL AND SUSPENSION TORQUE SPECIFICATIONS

	ft.-lb.	in.-lb.	N•m
Front axle nut			
2007 models	50-55	–	68-75
2008-on models	60-65	–	81-88
Rear axle nut*			
2007 models	72-78	–	98-106
2008-on models	95-105	–	129-142

*Refer to procedure.

CHAPTER ELEVEN

FRONT SUSPENSION AND STEERING

(166) **FRONT FORK**

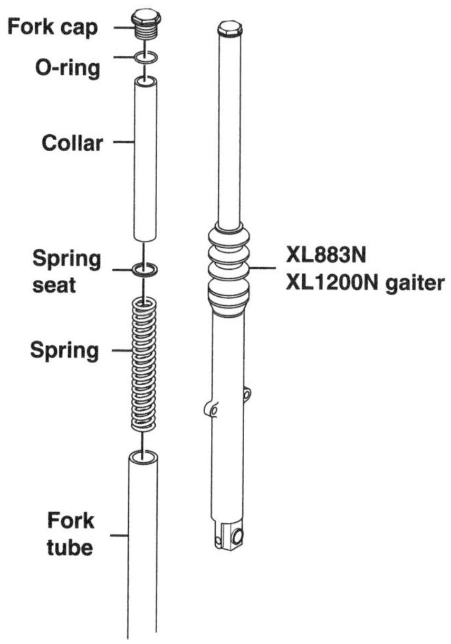

FRONT FORK

The front fork on some 2007-on models may differ slightly from the fork shown in Chapter Eleven. The differences include the appearance of the fork slider, and a collar and spring seat as shown in **Figure 166**.

On all XL883N and XL1200N models a rubber gaiter is located on each fork tube in place of the dust cover used on other models.

On models that do not have a fork oil drain screw at the bottom of the fork legs, remove the fork leg to drain and replace the fork oil. Refer to Chapter Eleven for fork leg removal, filling procedure and installation. Refer to **Table 28** in this Supplement for fork leg oil capacity and level.

Removal/Installation

Refer to Chapter Eleven. On XL883N and XL1200N models, make sure the gaiter on each fork leg is installed. After the fork leg is properly positioned, push the upper end of the gaiter up against the lower fork bracket.

Disassembly/Assembly

On models equipped with a collar and spring seat, remove the collar and spring seat prior to removing the spring during disassembly.

When assembling the fork, install and remove the collar and spring seat whenever intalling or removing the spring.

Table 28 FRONT FORK OIL CAPACITY AND OIL LEVEL

Model	Capacity*	Oil level
2007, 2008		
XL883L, XL1200L, XL1200N	12.3 oz (364 mL)	4.80 in. (122 mm)
All other models	11.6 oz (343 mL)	5.75 in. (146 mm)
2009, 2010		
XL883L, XL883N, XL1200N	13.6 oz. (402 mL)	3.11 in. (79 mm)
XL1200L	12.3 oz (364 mL)	4.80 in. (122 mm)
All other models	11.6 oz (343 mL)	5.75 in. (146 mm)

(continued)

Table 28 FRONT FORK OIL CAPACITY AND OIL LEVEL (continued)

Model	Capacity*	Oil level
2011		
XL883R	12.4 oz. (367 mL)	4.92 in. (125 mm)
XL883L, XL1200L	12.3 oz. (364 mL)	4.80 in. (122 mm)
XL883N, XL1200N	13.6 oz. (402 mL)	3.11 in. (79 mm)
XL1200C	12.4 oz. (367 mL)	4.72 in. (120 mm)
XL1200X	11.4 oz. (337 mL)	6.34 in. (161 mm)

*Each fork leg.

CHAPTER THIRTEEN

BRAKES

BRAKE FLUID

WARNING
2007-on models use DOT 4 brake fluid. 2004-2006 models use DOT 5 brake fluid. The designated brake fluid appears on the brake master cylinder cover. Do not intermix brake fluid types. Using the incorrect brake fluid type may cause brake failure.

CAUTION
DOT 4 brake fluid will damage plastic, painted and plated surfaces. Cover exposed surfaces. Clean contaminated surfaces with soapy water and rinse thoroughly.

FRONT BRAKE MASTER CYLINDER

Refer to service procedures in Chapter Thirteen. Note the following:

1. On models equipped with a single front brake caliper, a washer is located behind the snap ring that retains the piston assembly in the master cylinder (**Figure 167**).
2. When servicing the master cylinder, account for the washer (**Figure 168**).

167

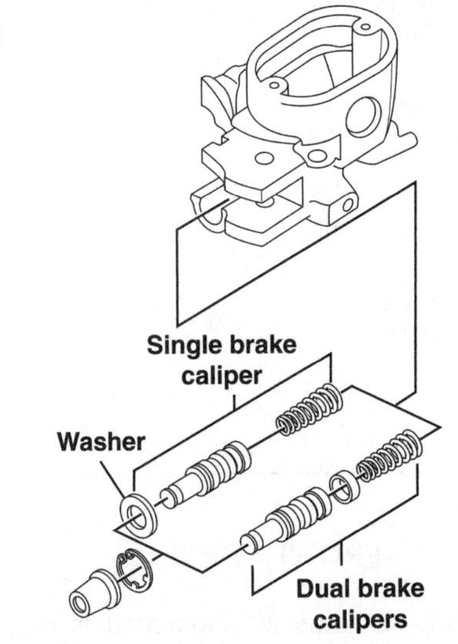

168

REAR BRAKE PEDAL

For XL883N and XL1200N models, follow service procedures described in Chapter Thirteen for XL883, XL883L, XL883R, XL1200L and XL1200R models.

For XL1200X , follow the service procedures described in Chapter Thirteen for XL883C and XL1200C models.

Table 29 BRAKE SYSTEM SPECIFICATIONS

Brake fluid (2007-on models)	DOT 4

CHAPTER FOURTEEN

BODY

REAR FENDER

Removal/Installation

All models except XL883N, XL1200X and XL1200N

The ECM and HFSM antenna, if so equipped, are mounted on the rear fender. Refer to *Rear Fender* in Chapter Fourteen while noting the following:

1. Remove but do not disconnect the HFSM antenna as described in this Supplement. Position antenna and harness out of the way.
2. Remove the ECM as described in this Supplement.
3. Remove the rear fender as described in Chapter Fourteen.
4. Reverse the removal steps for installation.

XL883N, XL1200X and XL1200N models

Refer to **Figure 169**.

1. Remove the rear wheel as described in Chapter Ten.
2. Remove the seat as described in Chapter Fourteen.
3. Remove but do not disconnect the HFSM antenna as described in this Supplement. Position antenna and harness out of the way.
4. Remove the ECM as described in this Supplement.
5. Disconnect the rear lighting connectors. Note that the harness wrapped with a brown band identifies the right side lighting harness.
6. Remove the turn signal stalk retaining nuts on the inside of the fender.
7. Remove the rear fender bracket from the underside of the fender.
8. Remove the support cover and turn signal on each side. Route the wiring harness through the fender.

NOTE

The rear fender mounting bolt also serves as the seat post.

9. Remove the rear fender mounting bolt, then remove the rear fender.
10. If necessary, remove the license plate bracket from the rear fender.
11. Reverse the removal steps to install the rear fender. Tighten the rear fender mounting bolt to 96-156 in.-lb. (10.8-11.6 N•m).

Figure 169 is located on the following page.

Table 30 BODY TORQUE SPECIFICATIONS

	ft.-lb.	in.-lb.	N•m
Rear fender mounting bolt XL883N and XL1200N models	–	96-156	10.8-11.6

(169)

REAR FENDER

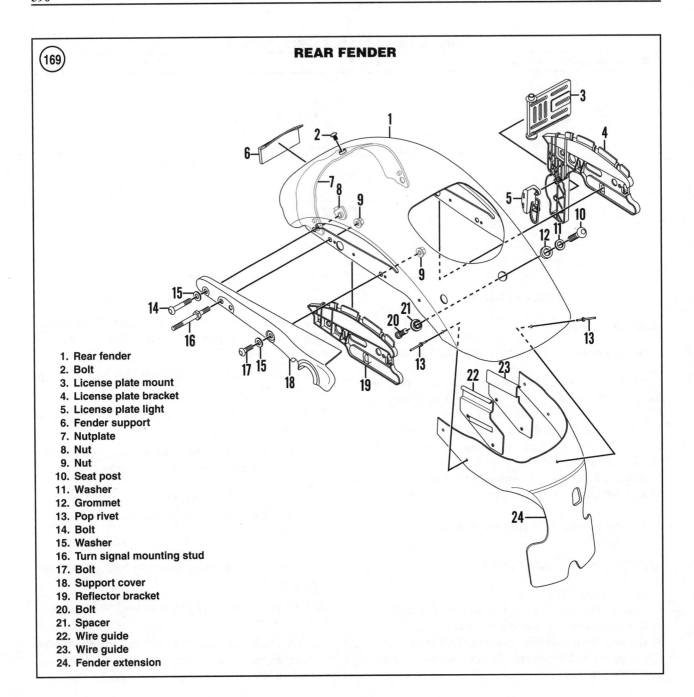

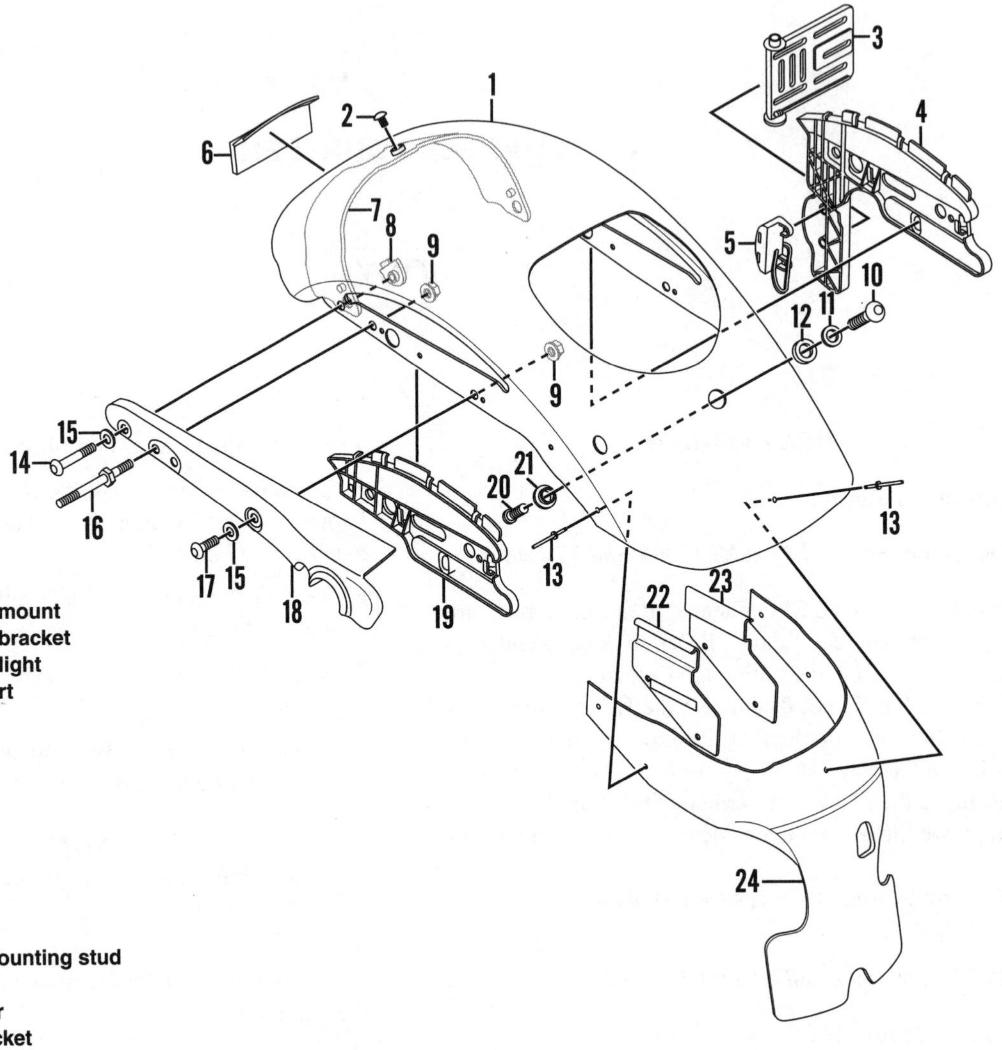

1. Rear fender
2. Bolt
3. License plate mount
4. License plate bracket
5. License plate light
6. Fender support
7. Nutplate
8. Nut
9. Nut
10. Seat post
11. Washer
12. Grommet
13. Pop rivet
14. Bolt
15. Washer
16. Turn signal mounting stud
17. Bolt
18. Support cover
19. Reflector bracket
20. Bolt
21. Spacer
22. Wire guide
23. Wire guide
24. Fender extension

INDEX

16

E

F

G

H

T

2004-2006 MODELS

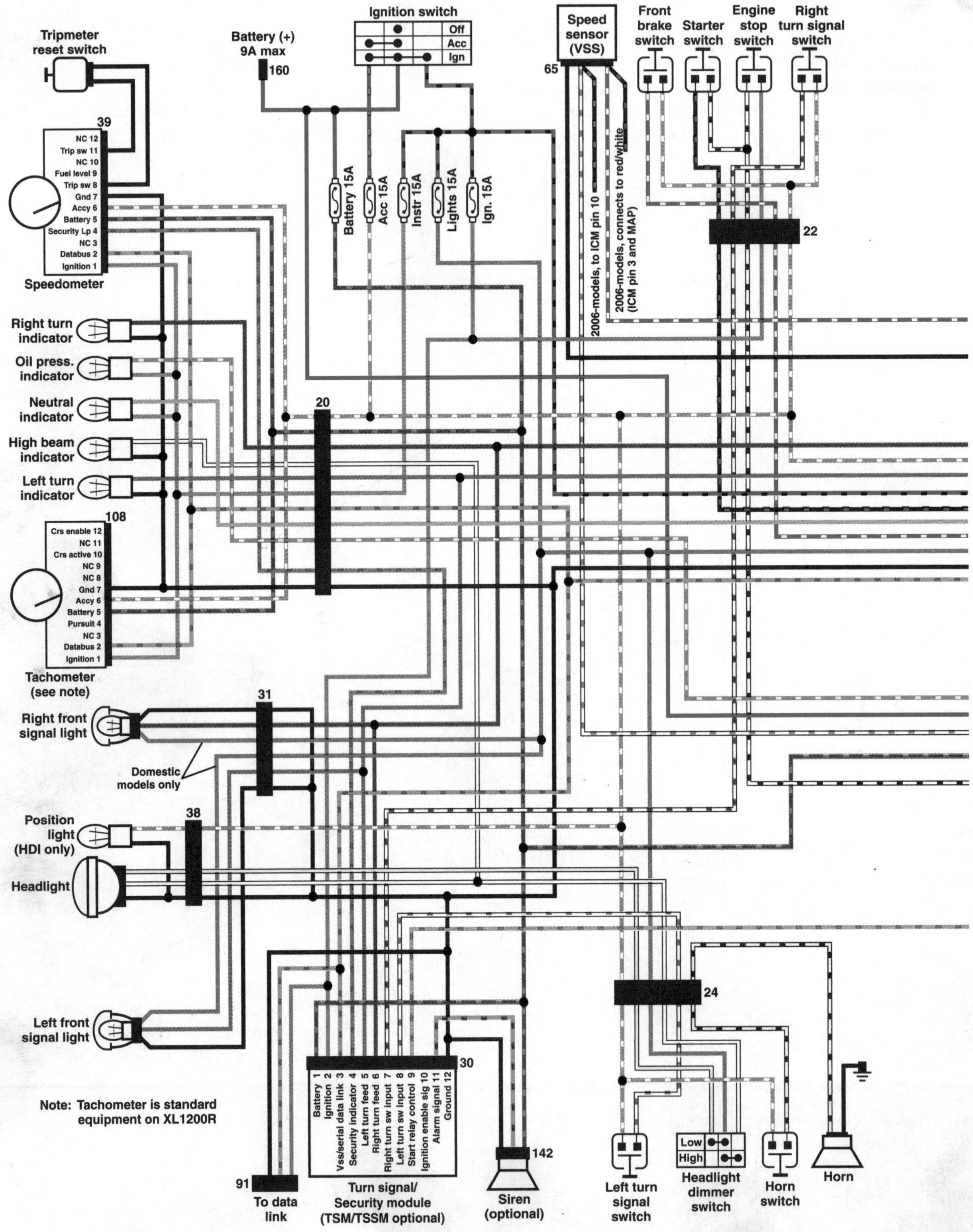

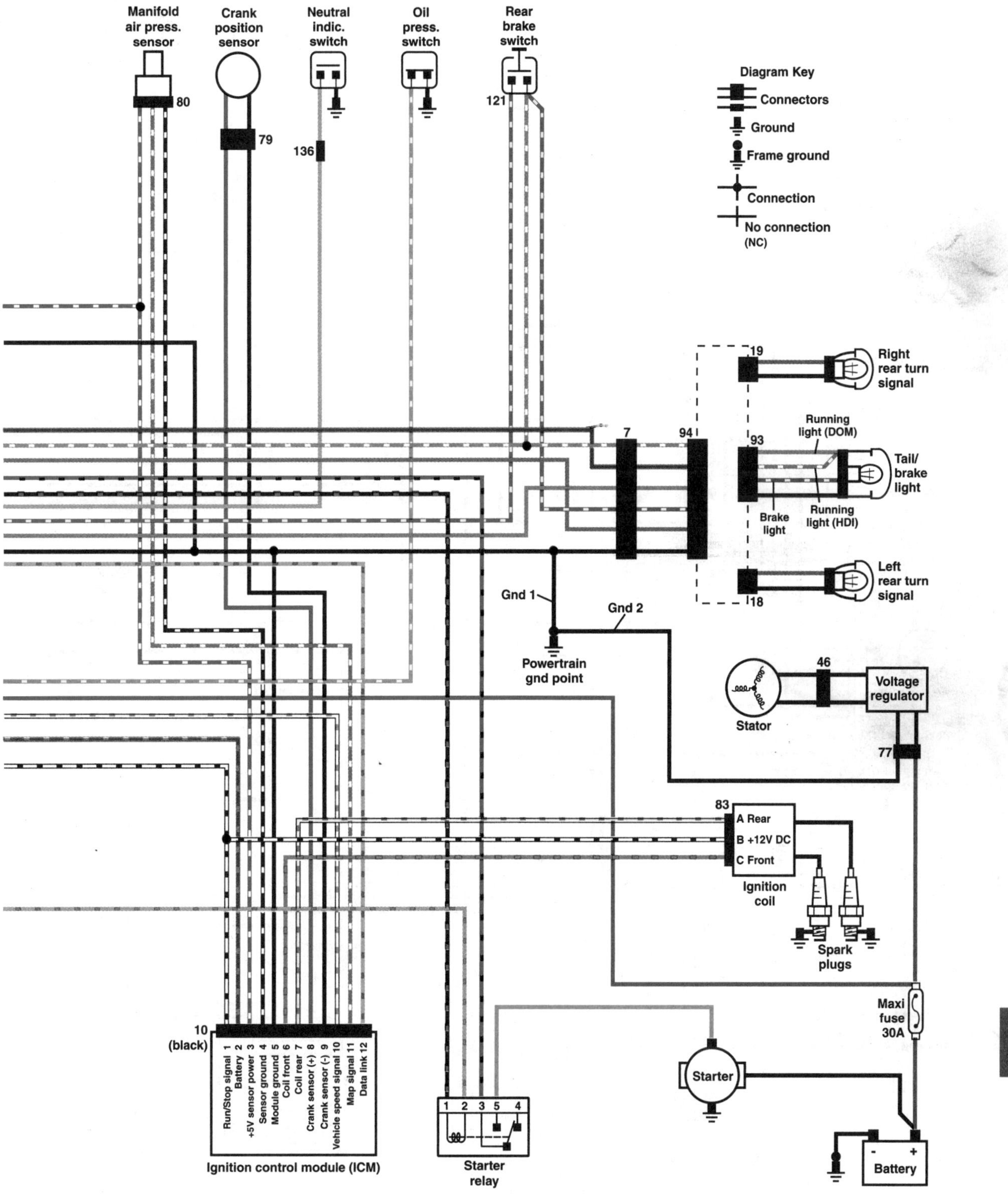

Manifold air press. sensor
Crank position sensor
Neutral indic. switch
Oil press. switch
Rear brake switch
80
79
136
121
Diagram Key
Connectors
Ground
Frame ground
Connection
No connection (NC)
19
Right rear turn signal
7
94
93
Running light (DOM)
Tail/ brake light
Brake light
Running light (HDI)
Left rear turn signal
18
Gnd 1
Gnd 2
Powertrain gnd point
46
Voltage regulator
Stator
77
83
A Rear
B +12V DC
C Front
Ignition coil
Spark plugs
Maxi fuse 30A
10 (black)
Run/Stop signal 1
Battery 2
+5V sensor power 3
Sensor ground 4
Module ground 5
Coil front 6
Coil rear 7
Crank sensor (+) 8
Crank sensor (-) 9
Vehicle speed signal 10
Map signal 11
Data link 12
Ignition control module (ICM)
1 2 3 5 4
Starter relay
Starter
Battery

17

2007-2009 MODELS

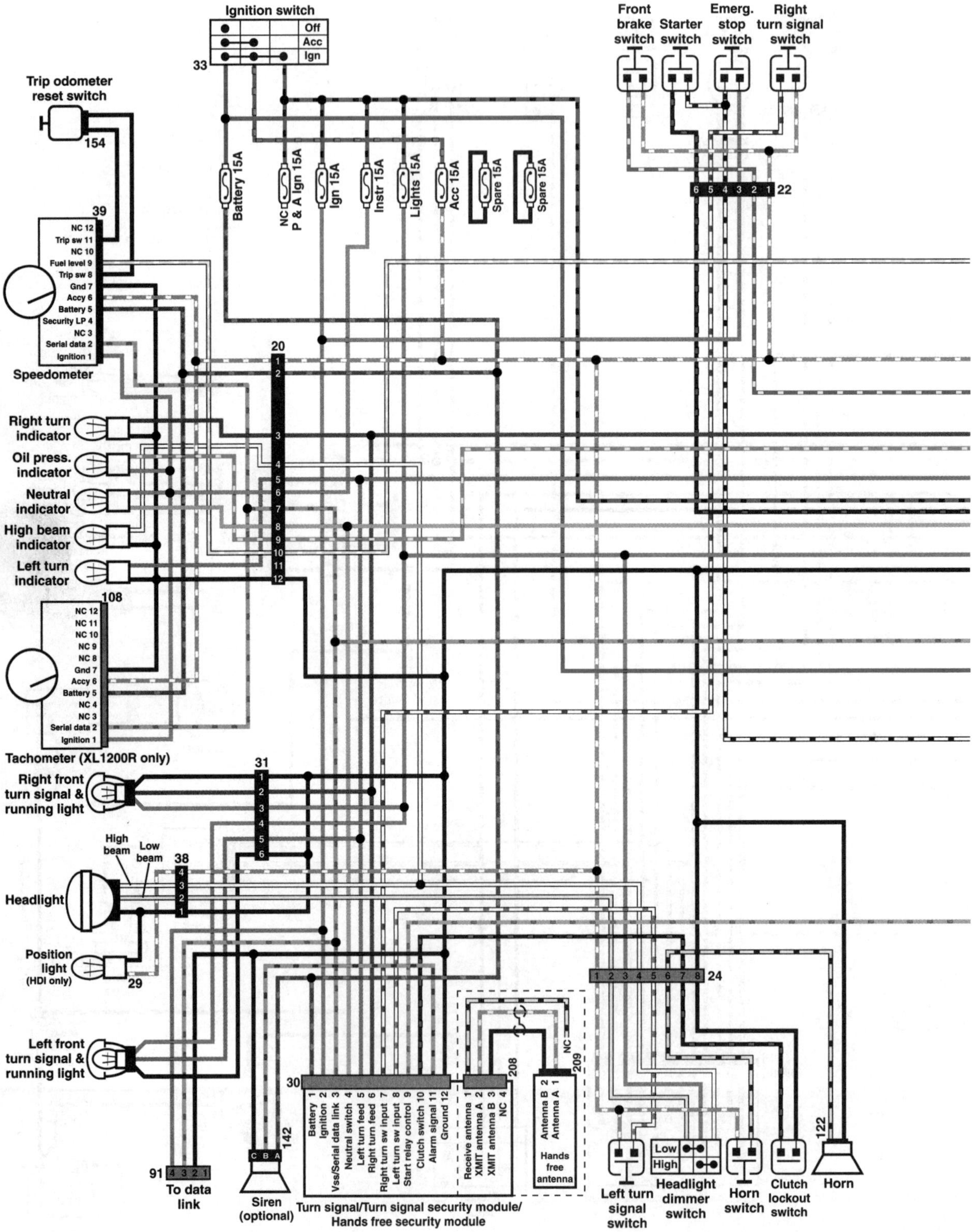

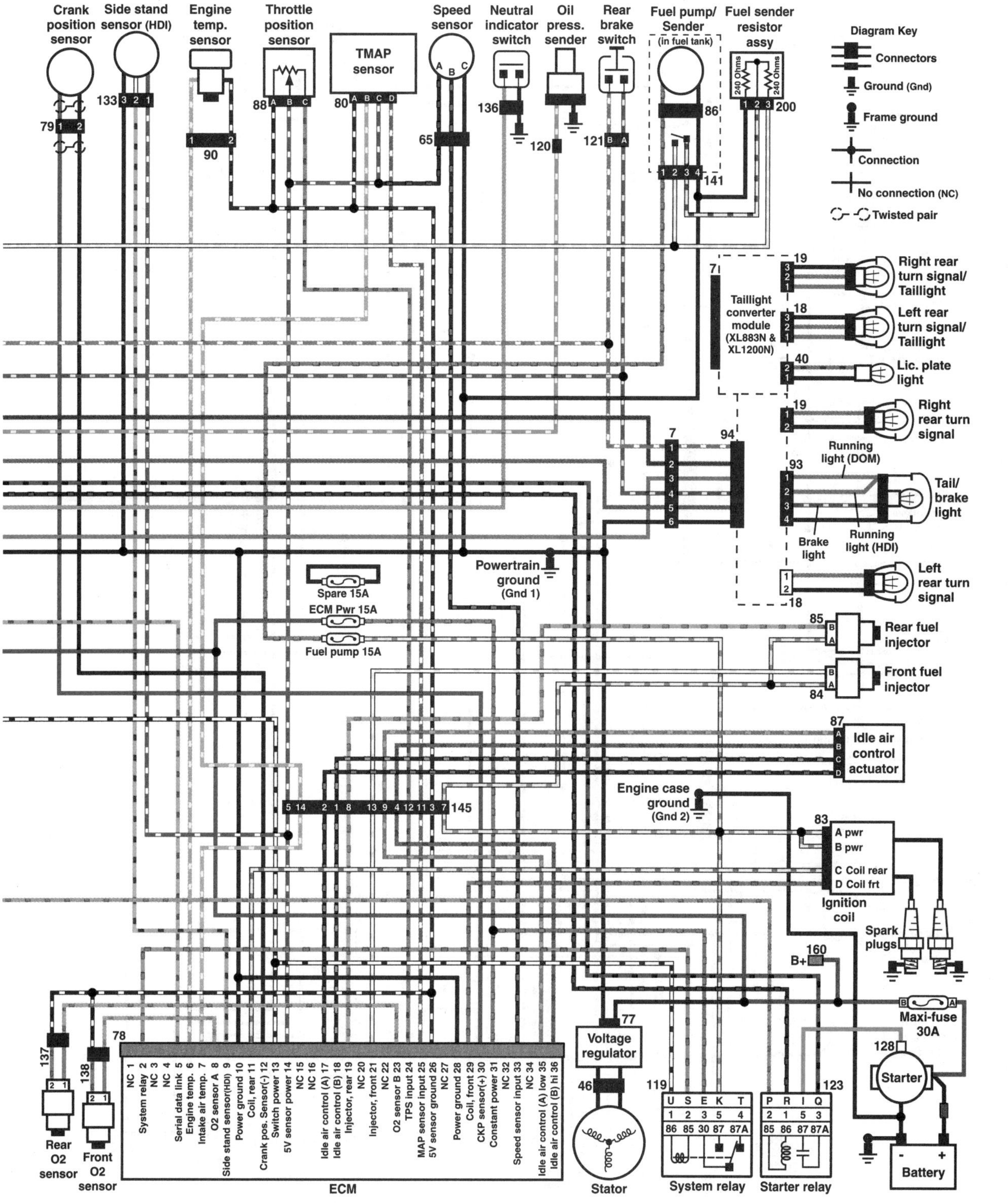
Crank position sensor
Side stand sensor (HDI)
Engine temp. sensor
Throttle position sensor
TMAP sensor
Speed sensor
Neutral indicator switch
Oil press. sender
Rear brake switch
Fuel pump/ Sender
(in fuel tank)
Fuel sender resistor assy
240 Ohms
240 Ohms
Diagram Key
Connectors
Ground (Gnd)
Frame ground
Connection
No connection (NC)
Twisted pair
Right rear turn signal/ Taillight
Taillight converter module (XL883N & XL1200N)
Left rear turn signal/ Taillight
Lic. plate light
Right rear turn signal
Running light (DOM)
Tail/ brake light
Brake light
Running light (HDI)
Left rear turn signal
Powertrain ground (Gnd 1)
Spare 15A
ECM Pwr 15A
Fuel pump 15A
Rear fuel injector
Front fuel injector
Idle air control actuator
Engine case ground (Gnd 2)
A pwr
B pwr
C Coil rear
D Coil frt
Ignition coil
Spark plugs
B+
Maxi-fuse 30A
Starter
Battery
Voltage regulator
Stator
System relay
Starter relay
Rear O2 sensor
Front O2 sensor
ECM
NC 1
System relay 2
NC 3
NC 4
Serial data link 5
Engine temp. 6
Intake air temp. 7
O2 sensor A 8
Side stand sensor(HDI) 9
Power ground 10
Coil, rear 11
Crank pos. Sensor(-) 12
Switch power 13
5V sensor power 14
NC 15
NC 16
Idle air control (A) 17
Idle air control (B) 18
Injector, rear 19
NC 20
Injector, front 21
NC 22
O2 sensor B 23
TPS input 24
MAP sensor input 25
5V sensor ground 26
NC 27
Power ground 28
Coil, front 29
CKP sensor(+) 30
Constant power 31
NC 32
Speed sensor input 33
NC 34
Idle air control (A) low 35
Idle air control (B) hi 36

17

2010-2011 MODELS

Notes:
1. Refer to *XL Speedometer and Indicator Lights* diagram for XL models.
2. Refer to *XL Rear Lighting Harness* diagram for XL models.
3. Refer to dual brake light converter module assy diagram if applicable.

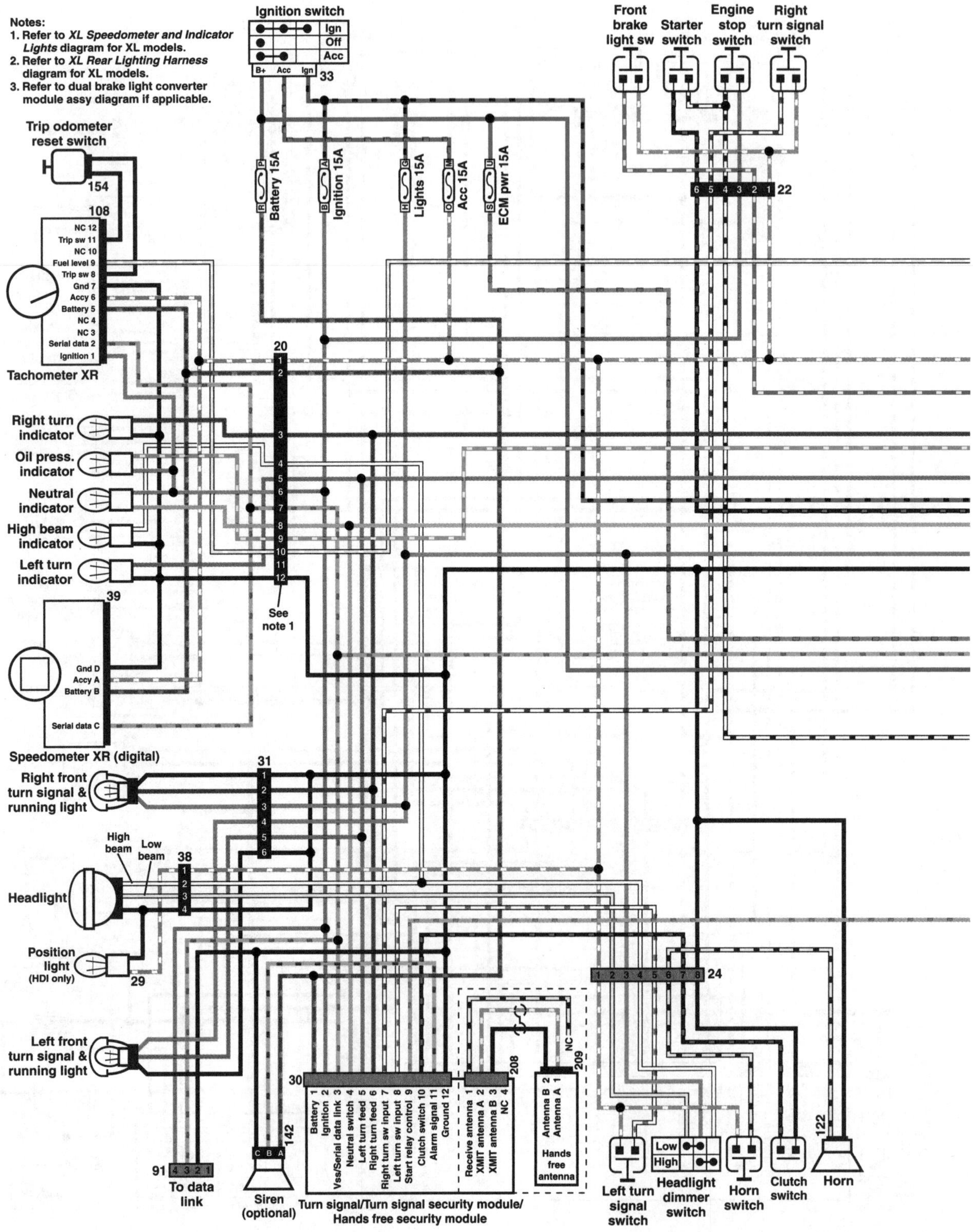

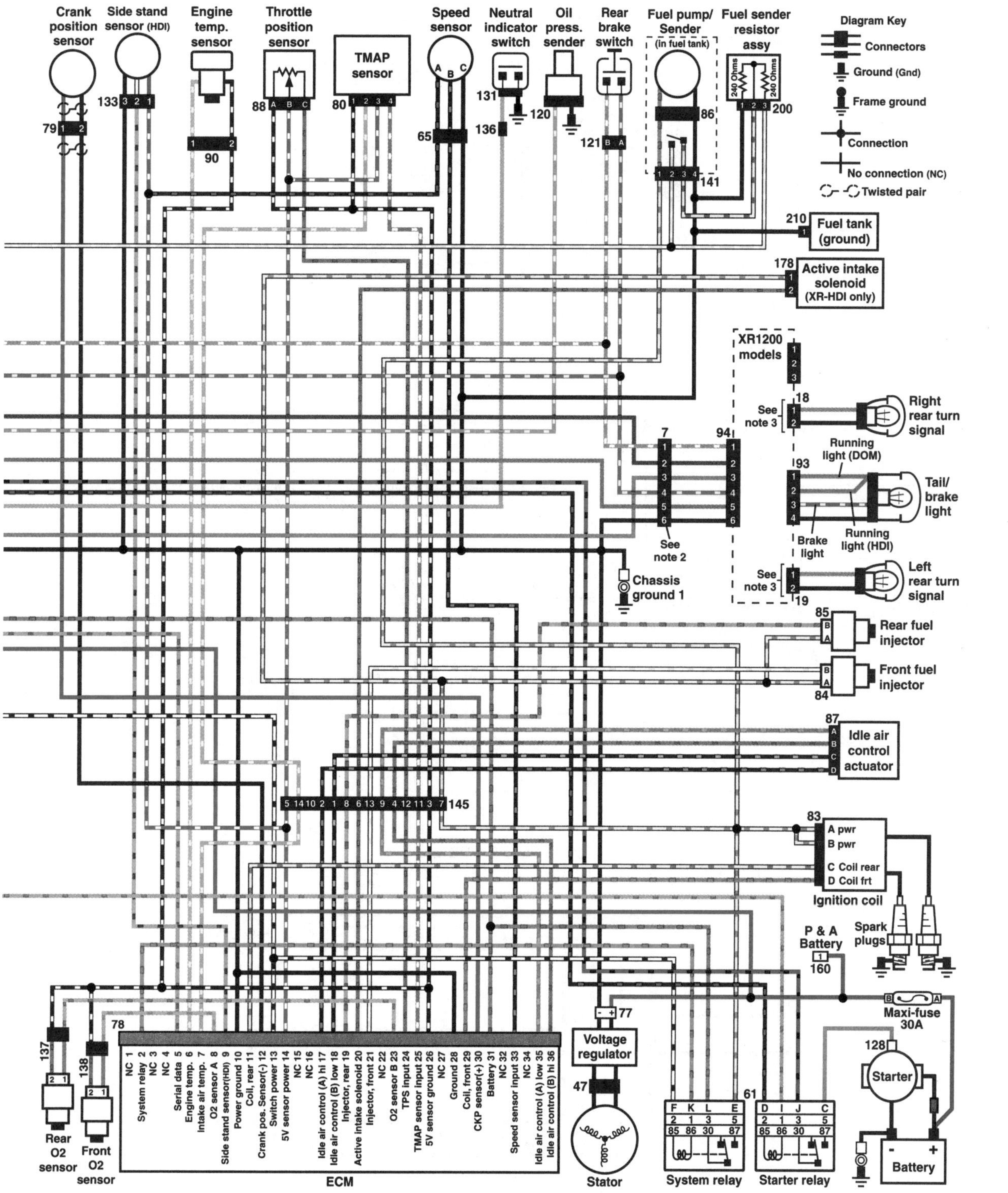

Crank position sensor
Side stand sensor (HDI)
Engine temp. sensor
Throttle position sensor
TMAP sensor
Speed sensor
Neutral indicator switch
Oil press. sender
Rear brake switch
Fuel pump/ Sender
(in fuel tank)
Fuel sender resistor assy
240 Ohms
240 Ohms
Diagram Key
Connectors
Ground (Gnd)
Frame ground
Connection
No connection (NC)
Twisted pair
Fuel tank (ground)
Active intake solenoid (XR-HDI only)
XR1200 models
See note 3
Right rear turn signal
Running light (DOM)
Tail/ brake light
Brake light
Running light (HDI)
See note 2
Chassis ground 1
Left rear turn signal
Rear fuel injector
Front fuel injector
Idle air control actuator
A pwr
B pwr
C Coil rear
D Coil frt
Ignition coil
P & A Battery
Spark plugs
Maxi-fuse 30A
Starter
Battery
Voltage regulator
Stator
System relay
Starter relay
Rear O2 sensor
Front O2 sensor
ECM
NC 1
System relay 2
NC 3
NC 4
Serial data 5
Engine temp. 6
Intake air temp. 7
O2 sensor A 8
Side stand sensor(HDI) 9
Power ground 10
Coil, rear 11
Crank pos. Sensor(-) 12
Switch power 13
5V sensor power 14
NC 15
NC 16
Idle air control (A) hi 17
Idle air control (B) low 18
Injector, rear 19
Active intake solenoid 20
Injector, front 21
NC 22
O2 sensor B 23
TPS input 24
TMAP sensor input 25
5V sensor ground 26
NC 27
Ground 28
Coil, front 29
CKP sensor(+) 30
Battery 31
NC 32
Speed sensor input 33
NC 34
Idle air control (A) low 35
Idle air control (B) hi 36

2010-2011 XL MODELS REAR LIGHTING HARNESS

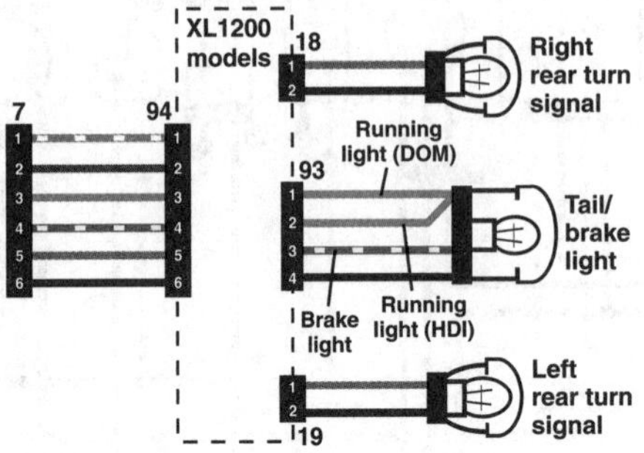

2010-2011 MODELS DUAL BRAKE LIGHTS WITH TAIL LIGHT CONVERTER MODULE ASSEMBLY (DOM)

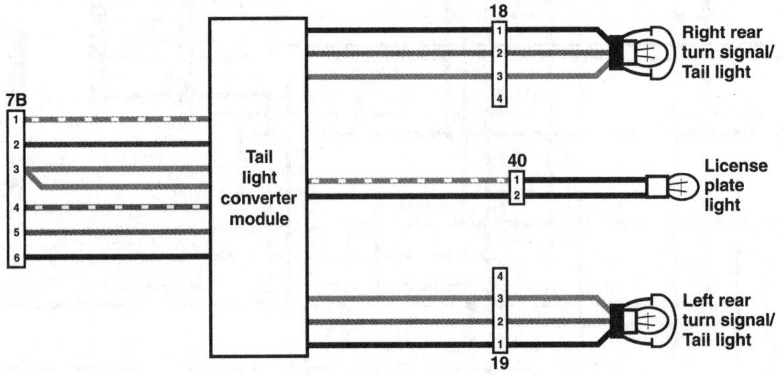

2010-2011 MODELS DUAL BRAKE LIGHTS WITHOUT TAIL LIGHT CONVERTER MODULE ASSEMBLY (HDI)

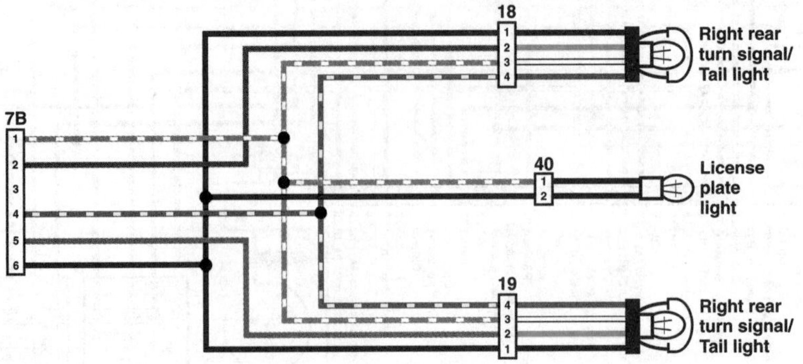

2010-2011 XL MODELS
SPEEDOMETER AND INDICATOR LIGHTS

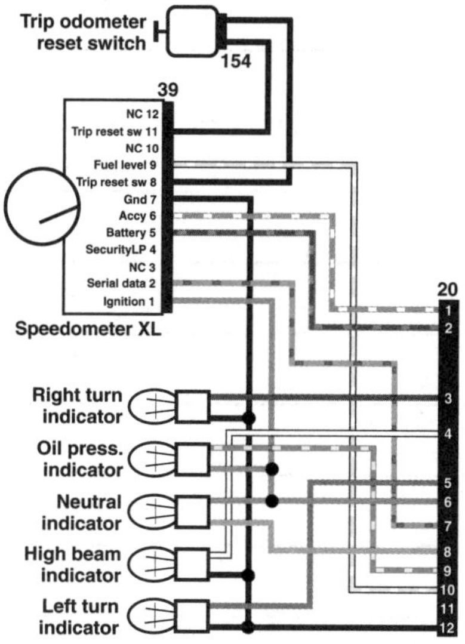

2010-2011 MODELS
HANDS FREE SECURITY MODULE

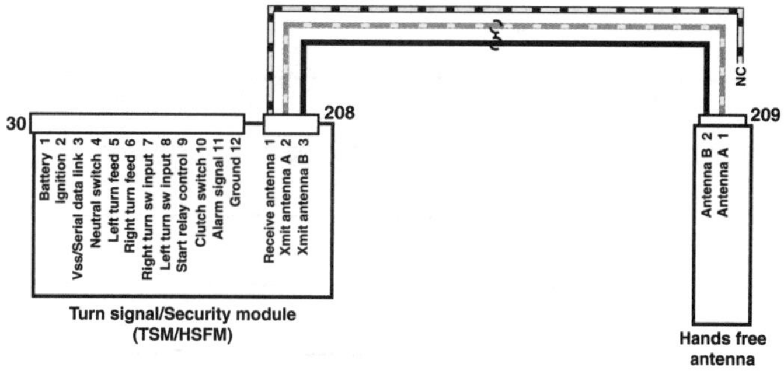

2010-2011 MODELS
SECURITY CIRCUIT WITH ANTI-THEFT TRACKING MODULE

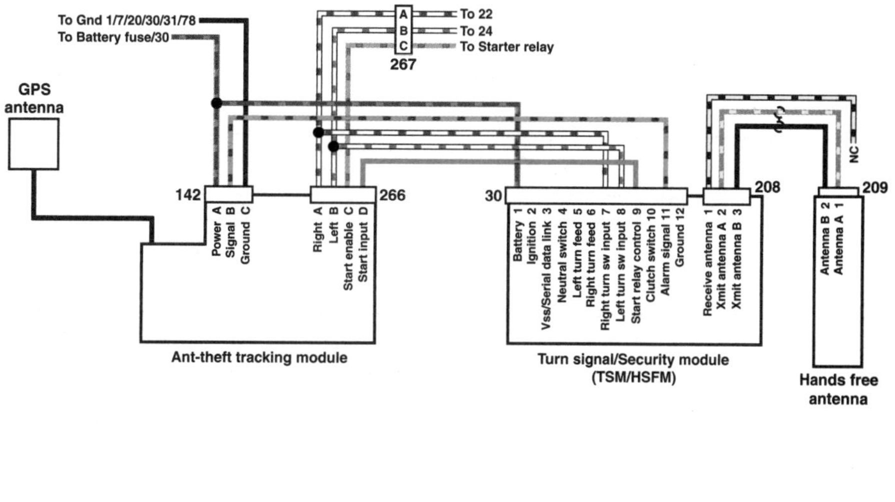

MAINTENANCE LOG

Date	Miles	Type of Service